WHO WAS WHO IN THE

AMERICAN REVOLUTION

WHO WAS WHO IN THE
AMERICAN REVOLUTION

L. Edward Purcell

Research Associate:
Sarah J. Purcell

Who Was Who in the American Revolution

Facts On File, Inc.
460 Park Avenue South
New York NY 10016
USA

Library of Congress Cataloging-in-Publication Data
Purcell, L. Edward.
  Who was who in the American revolution / L. Edward Purcell.
     p.   cm.
  Includes bibliographical references and index.
  ISBN 0-8160-2107-4 (acid-free paper)
  1. United States—History—Revolution, 1775–1783—Biography—
Dictionaries.   I. Title.
E206.P87   1993   92-19831
973.3′092′2—dc20

A British CIP catalogue record for this book is available from the British Library.

Facts On File books are available at special discounts when purchased in bulk quantities for businesses, associations, institutions or sales promotions. Please call our Special Sales Department in New York at 212/683-2244.

Jacket design by Dorothy Wachtenheim
Composition and Manufacturing by the Maple-Vail Book Manufacturing Group
Printed in the United States of America

10 9 8 7 6 5 4 3 2 1

This book is printed on acid-free paper.

CONTENTS

PREFACE

Thirty years ago, when I was an undergraduate history major, the thought occurred to me that, logically, history could be nothing more than the sum of individual biographies. This rash notion was soon swept aside by my teachers' insistence on looking at the larger picture; however, compiling the stories of the most important people of the American Revolution has rekindled the idea that our understanding of the past is limited by how well we understand individuals.

The challenging task of finding biographical information on more than 1,500 individuals was carried out to a significant degree by Sarah J. Purcell, who was research associate for the project, and who brought to bear her remarkable library skills and her boundless energy. Although she is my daughter, more than parental pride acknowledges that completion of this book would not have been remotely possible without her professional assistance.

Most of the research was done in the superb collections of the Margaret I. King Library at the University of Kentucky in Lexington. It soon came to be no surprise that the King Library had a copy of even the most seemingly obscure biography or reference book. The staff of the library, especially those in the reference department and special collections, are wonderful in both their knowledge and desire to assist their patrons. No researcher could ask for better help, and I hope that the collections and the staff may some day soon be housed in a physical setting worthy of them.

As has been the case for many, many years, nothing I do would be possible without the material, psychological and emotional support of my wife, and no expression of gratitude can be adequate.

It seems worthwhile to note that this book was written and researched in what was a western territory of Virginia during the American Revolution, and, fittingly, work began in a city named for the first battle and in a county named for the Marquis de Lafayette. It was completed in a county named after George Mason—the mid-project change of residence making it necessary to drive past the site of nearly the final battle of the war (Blue Licks) on each trip to the library.

L. Edward Purcell

Maysville, Kentucky

INTRODUCTION

The more than 1,500 biographical entries in this volume tell the personal stories of the most important people of the American Revolution. They include a broad range of historical figures from all sides of the conflict, and the profiles are based on information from a wide variety of sources. Surprisingly, no single reference work of similar scope and purpose has existed previously.

The standard of selection was direct: Whoever played an important role during the Revolution was included, so long as reliable biographical information was available. The subjects were chosen through a search of reference works and histories (specific sources are discussed in detail at the end of this volume), and the research sought diligently to make the list comprehensive, especially as to the major categories of important participants. In practice, this meant mostly white males whose lives were recorded in reasonable detail by subsequent historians and biographers.

The American Revolution encompassed a long-brewing rebellion, seven years of vicious war and the political invention of a new nation, yet the historical actors in this drama with their powdered wigs and funny clothes have often seemed dim in the popular imagination, outshone perhaps by the photographic images of the Civil War. Thus, a renewed examination of the lives of the men and women of the Revolution is refreshing—an exercise that brings quick appreciation of the momentous events of the 1770s and 1780s in human terms and the realization that beneath the antique costumes lived flesh-and-blood people much like ourselves.

Moreover, the brilliance of the Revolutionary generation has been thrown into sharper focus during the late 20th century, when the very name of George Washington is a talisman for political aspirations half the globe away from Virginia or Philadelphia.

Much history has been published about individual people of the Revolution, as well as about the great sweep of events and political ideas. The biographies in this volume draw deeply on the work of previous historians—both amateur and professional—who have long toiled to better know the period and its people.

American patriots comprise the majority of the biographies, and the most numerous among them are the soldiers of the Revolution, primarily commissioned officers. This category includes those who were members of the regular Continental Army as well as those who served as state militia (many, of course, did both). Wherever possible the service records of individuals are given in the biographical entries.

All Continental generals are included, starting with commander in chief George Washington, as well as many field-grade officers and junior officers, especially those who achieved subsequent prominence. Few private soldiers or noncommissioned officers appear, since only a tiny fraction of the tens of thousands of these lower ranks left enough on the historical record to allow substantial biographies. (One suspects that a long search of private genealogies and family histories—something vastly beyond the scope and purpose of this project— might yield an infinite number of common-man entries.)

Political leaders and officials make up a second large category of "who was who" among American patriots. For example, there are entries for all 342 men who served as delegates to the Continental and Confederation congresses between 1774 and 1789, as well as hundreds of entries for the many colonial and state officials who held public office during the Revolution. These are the men who sat in the colonial assemblies, formed the extra-legal provincial congresses and conventions, and eventually assumed places in the new state governments as executives, legislators and judges. The structures of the state governments established during the Revolution were not always tidy, especially in places like Vermont or the states where the British had control for much of the war, so official-sounding titles may reflect hopes rather than function in some cases. Also included are numerous biographies of public figures such as educators, writers, clergymen, artists and businessmen who played significant roles in Revolutionary society.

Loyalists form another large part of the entries here. Until recently, the hundreds of thousands of American loyalists of the Revolution were either ignored or dismissed as scum—the wages of being on the losing side. However, in the past two decades, scholars have taken a renewed interest in the story of the loyalists, and much has been added to our understanding of their importance. Therefore, biographies are included for a significant sample of the men and women who chose to remain loyal to the crown—and many of their stories are heartbreaking when read empathetically.

The volume also provides wide coverage of the British foes of the Revolution. All of the major military commanders of the British army and the Royal Navy whose lot it was to prosecute the war in America are included, in addition to officers who held lower rank but who played important roles. Many of the British officers in the American theater

(including the West Indies) went on to noteworthy careers during Britain's subsequent global struggles with France, but the emphasis in this volume is on their American experience. There are also dozens of entries for the most important British colonial officials, politicians, government officeholders and diplomats.

Included as well are biographies of many of the commanders of Britain's mercenary allies, the much-maligned "Hessians" from the German states, who usually fought bravely and well during the war and from whose ranks thousands left to help populate America after the Revolution.

The French allies of the American cause, without whose warships and regiments victory would have been impossible, are also represented by many biographical entries. In several cases it is instructive to trace the subsequent careers of French military officers during the tumult of the French Revolution.

The Marquis de Lafayette and the self-styled Baron von Steuben have been the best-known examples of volunteer European soldiers who fought for the American cause, but also included are biographies of the dozens more (some valuable officers, others worthless soldiers of fortune) who served in the Continental Army.

Two special categories with relatively small numbers of biographies are women and black patriots. We know there were more than a million white women and hundreds of thousands of black people (the majority slaves) living in Revolutionary America, but in contrast to the rich history of white men there is only a comparably small amount of information about them available to the compiler of a biographical directory. They were generally allowed almost no public role in 18th-century society, nor were their activities noticed and recorded. In the case of women, two recent decades of historical writing have provided a much clearer understanding of the role of women in general during the late 18th and early 19th centuries, yet still there are few biographies of individuals.

Likewise, there is a paucity of available information on individual black people of the time, although we know, for example, that hundreds, perhaps thousands, of black patriots participated in the War of Independence (Rhode Island enrolled entire military companies). Comparatively little has been published about individuals, other than notable figures such as Lemuel Haynes or Crispus

Attucks. The tens of thousands of black slaves in the southern colonies who fought and carried out the manual labor of war remain virtually unknown.

In all instances, the biographies in this volume focus on the experience of prominent people during the actual Revolution or the years immediately before and after. Some who participated in the Revolution as minor figures came to fame later, and their entries reflect this personal history. Andrew Jackson, for example, fought as a boy in the Carolina back country during the Revolution, but his great impact on American history came decades later, so his entry speaks mostly of youthful experiences.

Entries are arranged alphabetically and each begins with the name, inclusive dates (New Style whenever possible) and a brief descriptor. Variant name spellings are noted, and common usages such as "the Elder" and "the Younger" are noted in accord with the practice of the time. Titles of honor and nobility are employed as of the time of the Revolution. Alternative forms of names and titles are cross-referenced by "See" entries. The alphabetization of names follows the rules of the *Chicago Manual of Style*, so foreign names with initial articles such as "von" and "d' " are arranged under the main names—Admiral de Grasse, for example, is listed in the "G" section. Americans with foreign names such as De Peyster are alphabetized, as is the custom, by the first letter of the first name—under "D" in this case.

Whenever a person has elsewhere been the subject of an individual biography (usually a full-length book or an article in a periodical), a suggestion for further reading is appended to the person's entry, although the citations are limited to sources that readers may reasonably expect to find without recourse to highly specialized collections (few rare 18th- or 19th-century sources are listed unless they have been reprinted recently), and Ph.D. dissertations are not cited. A guide to biographical sources at the end of the volume gives information about standard sources and discusses general biographical research for the period of the American Revolution.

A

ABERCROMBY, James (d. 1775) British lieutenant colonel The youngest and least-known of three military brothers who served during the Revolution, James Abercromby was a veteran of duty in North America during the French and Indian War. He had obtained his captaincy in the 42nd Regiment of Royal Highlanders in 1756, and in 1759 he was appointed aide-de-camp to Lord Amherst. In 1760, he was gazetted major in the 78th Regiment (Fraser's Highlanders), and in September of that year he helped conduct negotiations that resulted in the French surrender of Montreal. He retired from the army on half pay in 1763 but returned to active duty seven years later with the rank of lieutenant colonel commanding the 22nd Regiment. His career was cut short at Bunker Hill, where he was mortally wounded while leading the grenadiers. He died on June 24, 1775, a week after the battle.

ABERCROMBY, James (1706–1781) British general Abercromby's career demonstrated the 18th-century British army's system of promotion based on seniority rather than merit: He achieved the highest rank despite his responsibility for one of the worst British defeats of the French and Indian War. Unrelated to the three Abercromby brothers who also were officers during the same period, he was born in Glassaugh, Scotland, entered the army as a young man, secured a seat in Parliament at age 27 and attained the rank of lieutenant colonel in the Royal Scots by the age of 40. He was a major general in 1756, when appointed second in command of British forces in North America under his close friend Lord Loudoun, and he assumed full command when Loudoun was recalled in 1758. Abercromby led an ill-considered assault on the French stronghold at Fort Ticonderoga in July 1758, commanding 6,000 regulars and 10,000 provincial troops against 4,000 French defenders, led by Montcalm. The attack was a futile, bloody failure, resulting in perhaps as many as 2,000 British casualties. Abercromby was succeeded in command by Lord Amherst and was recalled to England the following year, but due to the rules of seniority he was promoted to lieutenant general. In 1772, he became a full general. Despite his rank, the army wisely declined to employ him in the Revolution, and his main activity during the 1770s came in Parliament, where he advocated strong and repressive measures against the American colonists.

ABERCROMBY, Sir Ralph (1734–1801) British general One of the most highly regarded soldiers of his day and eventually the most famous of the three Abercromby brothers, Sir Ralph nonetheless played little role in the American war. He joined the British army in 1756 and served in Europe and Ireland before reaching the rank of lieutenant colonel in 1773. In that year, he took a seat in Parliament and vigorously opposed the government's policy of coercion against the American colonies. Consequently, he was passed over for employment during the Revolutionary War. Seniority, however, made him a major general by the outbreak of hostilities with France in the 1790s. He served with great distinction in Flanders, the West Indies, Ireland and the Netherlands in a succession of important posts, doing much to reform and rebuild the British army. In 1800, he was given command in the Mediterranean. During a campaign against Napoleon's armies in Egypt, he was struck in the thigh by a musket ball at the Battle of Aboukir and died seven days later aboard the British flagship. *Further reading:* John W. Fortescue, *Six British Soldiers* (London, 1928).

ABERCROMBY, Sir Robert (1740–1827) British general   Not quite so distinguished in reputation as his elder brother Ralph, Sir Robert came to be regarded as one of Britain's best generals, and he was the only one of the three Abercromby brothers to escape death from battle. He began his career as a volunteer in North America during the French and Indian War and, after surviving the futile assault on Fort Ticonderoga in 1758, was rewarded with an ensign's commission. He took part in the battle of Niagara and the capture of Montreal, and was promoted to captain in 1761, retiring from the army in 1763. He reentered service in 1772 as a major in the 62nd Regiment and was lieutenant colonel of the 37th a year later. He served throughout the Revolutionary War with considerable distinction at many important battles, including Brandywine, Germantown, Monmouth and the invasion of Charleston. In 1778, he led an expedition to destroy shipping on the Delaware River and commanded the light infantry that chased the American force out of Crooked Billet, Pennsylvania.

Abercromby's most daring military achievement of the Revolutionary War was at the siege of Yorktown. During the early hours of October 16, 1781 he personally led a sortie of 350 picked troops against the American and French siege lines in an attempt to disable the attackers' guns. He surprised part of the French contingent and spiked four guns before coming under attack by reinforcements and retreating. The raid was brave but ineffective: Cornwallis requested terms of surrender the following day.

Abercromby was promoted to colonel in 1782 and made aide-de-camp to the king. In 1787, he took command of the 75th Regiment, leading it to India, where his greatest achievements as a soldier came. By 1790, he was a major general as well as governor and commander in chief at Bombay. His successful campaigns won him further honors, including a knighthood, and he was appointed to succeed Lord Cornwallis as commander in chief in India in 1792. A further series of victories over native tribes and rulers followed, until deteriorating eyesight forced his retirement to Scotland in 1797. At his death in 1827, he was the oldest living British general.

ABOVILLE, François Marie, Comte d' (1730–1817)   A native of Brest, France, Aboville distinguished himself as a young artillery officer at the siege of Muenster and was colonel of artillery in Rochambeau's expeditionary force to America in 1781. Along with the American Henry Knox, he directed the effective bombardment of Lord Cornwallis' positions at Yorktown and was cited personally by Washington for his contribution to the allied victory. He was also granted a bonus for his efforts. On his return to France, he was commissioned a brigadier general, and he was commander of the French Army of the North in 1792. He served as governor of Brest in 1807. He supported the Bourbon cause and was made a peer after the restoration.

ACHARD de Bonvouloir, Julien (1749–1783) French agent   During the first year of the Revolutionary War, this shadowy figure acted as a covert, unofficial representative of France to the American colonists. At the outbreak of hostilities in 1775, worried that Britain would use the rebellion as an excuse to seize French possessions in the New World, the French foreign minister, the Comte de Vergennes, wanted information on the strength and resolve of the Americans. On the advice of the Comte de Guines, French ambassador to Britain, Vergennes authorized Achard de Bonvouloir to travel to America, but with strict orders to represent himself as a private citizen on a supposed commercial mission. Achard was instructed to report only by letters sent to Antwerp, never to mention any official connection, and even to write in disappearing ink. After a hard voyage, he reached Philadelphia in December 1775 and met with Benjamin Franklin and other members of the Secret Committee of Congress. He maintained he was speaking only as a merchant interested in privately supplying munitions, but the committee regarded him at least in part as an official spokesman for France. They issued written questions to Achard: What was the French attitude toward the colonists? Could France supply two trained engineer officers? Could the Americans get arms and supplies directly from France?

Achard was mildly encouraging to the committee but noncommittal, and he apparently had difficulty maintaining his pose. He reported favorably but inaccurately to Vergennes on the status of the American forces, but he was too timid to be effective as either a negotiator or a reporter. Vergennes ordered him home after a year, but Achard had spent all his money and was stranded until the French minister forwarded 200 louis for the return voyage. Achard entered the French army in 1779 and sailed with a French force to India in 1781. He died in Pondicherry two years later. *Further reading:* James B. Perkins, *France in the American Revolution* (reprint, New York, 1970).

ACLAND, Lady Harriet (Christian Henrietta Caroline) (1750–1815) British heroine

The daughter of the Earl of Ilchester, Lady Harriet earned sympathy on both sides of the Atlantic for her bravery in caring for her British officer husband after the second battle of Saratoga. She married John Dyke Acland in 1770 and accompanied him when he took active service in Canada in 1776. Major Acland was in command of the grenadier detachment of General John Burgoyne's invasion force in 1777, and Lady Harriet traveled with the column. She nursed her husband through illness and wounds suffered at Hubbardton on July 7, 1777. Her fame, however, was based on her actions after Saratoga. Acland had been severely wounded and captured on October 7. Most of the American army lay between Lady Harriet and her husband, but gathering a servant, a British chaplain and a safe conduct from the American commander, Horatio Gates, Lady Harriet set off down the Hudson River in a small boat on the night of October 9. She was challenged by the sentries and was made to wait on the water in the cold and dark until finally allowed to join her husband the next morning. The incident gained considerable notoriety in England after a picture of her standing in the gloom of the river was exhibited at the Royal Academy. She and her husband returned to England, and she was widowed in 1778. She died in 1815.

ACLAND, John Dyke (d. 1778) British officer, politician

An intemperate man and something of a dandy by contemporary accounts, Acland was a decent enough soldier. As a member of Parliament in 1774, he advocated pursuit of strong measures against the American colonies and even disagreed with Lord North when the prime minister considered conciliation during the following year. Acland was colonel of the Devonshire militia, but he went on active duty in 1776 after becoming major of the 20th Foot, joining Sir Guy Carleton's command in Canada (accompanied by his wife, Lady Harriet).

The following year, Acland was selected to command the grenadier detachments of General John Burgoyne's force that set out to invade the colonies from the north. Despite serious illnesses, he led his troops with distinction, suffering a wound at Hubbardton in July but returning to the field soon after. He was in the thick of the fighting at Freeman's Farm (First Saratoga) and again at Bemis Heights (Second Saratoga). During the latter battle, Acland commanded the grenadiers' key position holding a slight elevation on the British left. Despite fierce fighting, his troops were overrun, and he was wounded in both legs and taken prisoner from the field. Nursed back to health by his heroic wife, he avoided confinement with the Convention Army and made his way to New York in the care of Lieutenant Henry Brockholst Livingston, the nephew of American general Philip Schuyler, to be exchanged. Acland later reported to British general Sir Henry Clinton that Schuyler was ripe for defection, but nothing came of the scheme to pry Schuyler loose from the American cause.

After returning to Britain, Acland resumed his career in Parliament, being noted as a pugnacious legislator. He died on November 22, 1778, either from the effects of a cold he caught while fighting an inconclusive duel or, according to some sources, from complications following a stroke.

✓ADAMS, Abigail (1744–1818) Wife of John Adams; letter writer

Although she lived in an era long before "proper" women were allowed to participate fully in public matters, Abigail Adams was a tough-minded, forthright personality with a strong influence on the male members of her family, including two U.S. presidents. Moreover, she was a prolific letter writer, one of the best in American history, whose correspondence has been preserved for posterity.

She was the daughter of a Massachusetts Congregationalist parson and, while well read in her youth, lacked formal education. She married John Adams, a rising lawyer of Braintree (modern-day Quincy, Massachusetts) and Boston, in 1764, six years after the couple first met in her father's parsonage. They lived alternately in Braintree and Boston during the first eight years of marriage, and Abigail gave birth to five children, including John Quincy (eventually the sixth president of the United States).

In 1774, John Adams left for Philadelphia and the Continental Congress; he and Abigail were separated by the Revolution for the next 10 years. While her husband was away, she took over complete management of the family farm and business affairs, causing them to prosper even in the face of wartime dislocations.

During this long period Abigail kept up a constant stream of letters to John and to many others. She was an acute observer of public affairs (urging, for example, independence well in advance of the movement in Congress) and sharp in her articulation of both political and social issues. Although deeply conservative in an 18th-century way and dedicated to the preservation of what she viewed as the essential social order, including a restricted public role for women, Abigail was vocal on the issues of women's rights and slavery. In one of her most famous letters, written to husband John at the end of March 1776, she urged him to "Remember the Ladies, and be more generous and favourable to them than your ancestors. Do not put such unlimited power into the hands of the Husbands. Remember all Men would be tyrants if they could." She also attacked the evils of slavery and racial discrimination in her letters and conversation. She was outspoken whenever she perceived injustice, despite an unwillingness to overturn what she understood as the stability of the prevailing social order, and thought the political Revolution a perfect opportunity to elevate the legal status of women and to end slavery.

At the end of the Revolutionary War, she went with John to Europe, where he was American emissary in Holland, France and Great Britain. On her husband's selection as the vice president and subsequent election to the presidency, she alternated between living in Massachusetts and the successive seats of national government. She was the first president's wife to occupy the new official residence in Washington City in 1800, a few months before John's departure from the presidency. Abigail exerted a powerful influence on John during his term as president, pressing his political opponents even more harshly than he, and she was the first wife of a president to be accused by political enemies of manipulating power from behind the scenes.

From 1800 on, Abigail and John lived in Massachusetts. She continued to write a large volume of letters to friends and family, actively managed family affairs and took increasing interest in the rising career of her son. She died in Quincy, the matriarch of one of America's first political families. *Further reading:* Lynn Withey, *Dearest Friend: A Life of Abigail Adams* (New York, 1981); L. H. Butterfield, et al., eds., *The Book of Abigail and John: Selected Letters of the Adams Family, 1762–1784* (Cambridge, Massachusetts, 1975); Butterfield, *The Adams Family Correspondence* (Cambridge, Massachusetts 1963–   ).

ADAMS, Andrew (1736–1797) Delegate to Congress, militia colonel, jurist

Born in Stratford, Connecticut, Adams graduated from Yale College in 1760 and moved to Litchfield, where he practiced law and was prosecuting attorney for Litchfield County. He joined the Connecticut Committee of Safety in 1774 and in 1776 was elected to the state House of Representatives, serving until 1781, twice as speaker. He held the rank of colonel in the state militia but saw active service only briefly during the war. He was appointed as a delegate to the Continental Congress in 1777 and signed the Articles of Confederation in 1778. He then became a member of the upper house of the Connecticut General Assembly and later was appointed to the state supreme court, becoming chief justice in 1793.

ADAMS, John (1735–1826) President, statesman, diplomat

One of a handful of American patriots who truly deserve the title of Founding Father, John Adams was at the heart of the American Revolution, voicing the basic principles and devising the mechanisms that resulted in a new nation. During the later years of the Revolutionary War his duties as a diplomat were vital, even though they tended to remove him from the center of power and activity. As the second president of the United

John Adams

States, he played a central role in the early years of the new republic, although his position in the line of presidents between Washington and Jefferson and the sour difficulties of his term as chief executive, ending with his banishment from public life, have tended to obscure his contributions in the popular mind. His was one of the best-documented public lives in all of American history, and publication of his diaries and letters has raised his stock considerably in recent decades.

Adams was born in Braintree, Massachusetts (formerly called Mount Wollaston and now known as Quincy), and taught school in Worcester after graduation from Harvard in 1755. He turned to the study of law and was admitted to the bar in Boston in 1758. His active mind, impressive store of legal and historical knowledge, and facile pen buttressed his interest in public affairs, and his articles appeared often in the Boston papers. In 1764, he married Abigail Smith, forming one of the happiest and most fortuitous alliances in the annals of matrimony. They were a closely bonded couple whose mutual qualities of character and intelligence reinforced each other over more than half a century of married life.

In 1765, Adams assumed a prominent role in opposing the Stamp Act, although he was somewhat in the shadow of his cousin, Samuel Adams. He articulated the patriot cause in the public prints and formed close political ties with leaders such as James Otis. Adams' particular enemy during the prerevolutionary years was royal official Thomas Hutchinson. Adams acted as defense attorney in several key trials of patriots, including John Hancock, but he also served as defense counsel for the British soldiers accused after the Boston Massacre. In general, his position during these years decried mob violence (he was ever an opponent of democracy in the 18th-century sense), but his writings set forth the ideas that would lead to independence.

He was elected to the first Continental Congress in 1774, and he drafted a declaration of rights while sitting in Philadelphia with that body. His ideas moved more and more toward independence and the necessity for the colonies to form their own individual governments. In the second Continental Congress, he forged ties with the powerful delegates from the southern colonies and did much to defuse their suspicions of Massachusetts. He pushed for independence and was appointed to the committee to draft the Declaration in June 1776. His contributions to the language of Jefferson's draft were slight, but Adams' legislative skills were vital to the document's passage. He left Congress for an interval in late 1776 but returned in February 1777, when the body assembled in Baltimore. He departed again in November, never to return to Congress.

Adams then entered a long, difficult period of service as a diplomat in Europe. He sailed for France with his 10-year-old son, John Quincy, in February 1778 to take a place on the American commission to France. Despite French recognition of the independent colonies, the position of the American emissaries was delicate and troubled, enmeshed in the complexities of French foreign policy. Adams was by temperament impatient, a trait that sometimes damaged his effectiveness as a diplomat. Over the next few years, however, he did considerable service in securing loans for the struggling American cause, particularly from the Netherlands. He returned to Massachusetts in 1779 and wrote the constitution adopted by the state convention of Massachusetts. He was called away again to France late in the year. The following months saw a stormy relationship with the French foreign minister, Vergennes, and a delicate one with his fellow diplomat, Benjamin Franklin. Along with Franklin and John Jay, Adams negotiated the 1783 Treaty of Paris, which formally ended the Revolutionary War. Two years later, he was appointed as minister to Great Britain and wrote a *Defense of the Constitutions of Government of the United States of America,* which was well received abroad as a reasoned justification of American political ideas but offended some in America by its apparent defense of aristocracy.

When the first national government under the Constitution was selected in 1789, Adams was chosen as vice president. He was not only the first holder of the office but also the first to declare it useless and impotent, even though he cast more deciding votes in the Senate than any vice president since. On Washington's withdrawal after two terms, Adams was elected as the second president of the United States. His single term of office, however, was fraught with difficulties. The two-party system was in formation, and Adams ran afoul of the ambitions of Alexander Hamilton, ostensibly of Adams' own faction, and suffered from the machinations of several disloyal cabinet members. Even more serious was the imminent threat of war with revolutionary France, which Adams did much to avoid, although his actions cost him the last shreds of political support within the Federalist camp. He was defeated by Jefferson in the election of 1800 and withdrew to Braintree after more than a quarter century at the center of national affairs.

His later years were taken up with study, writing and observation of the rising political fortunes of John Quincy. He was reconciled eventually with Jefferson. In a great coincidence, which seems somehow pregnant with meaning, Adams died on July 4, 1826, the 50th anniversary of the Declaration of Independence, only a few hours after Jefferson. *Further reading:* Page Smith, *John Adams,* 2 vols. (Garden City, New York, 1962); Lyman H. Butterfield, et al., eds., *Diary and Autobiography of John Adams,* 4 vols. (Cambridge, Massachusetts, 1961); Robert J. Taylor, et al., eds., *The Papers of John Adams,* multivolume (Cambridge, Massachusetts 1977–   ).

ADAMS, Samuel (1722—1803) Delegate to Congress, political organizer

One of his chief enemies said accurately of Sam Adams: "I doubt whether there is a greater incendiary in the King's dominion . . ." For 10 years leading up to the break with Great Britain, Adams was the chief figure of resistance. There was scarcely any revolutionary activity in Massachusetts between 1765 and

Samuel Adams

1775 in which Adams did not figure as a master of propaganda and political organization.

Adams was born in Boston, the son of a prosperous brewer and merchant. He was educated at Harvard with little distinction and rejected prospective careers in the law or the pulpit. Instead, he tried his hand at business with consistent failure. He was rejected as an apprentice in a counting house and squandered a large financial stake advanced by his father. At his father's death in 1748, Adams received a considerable inheritance, but, characteristically, it soon disappeared in a fiscal muddle. He was a tax collector for the Town of Boston from 1756 to 1764, but he resigned when his official accounts finally showed £8,000 in arrears, a result not of graft or corruption but of simple ineptitude. From that point on, Adams supported himself and his family mainly on the gifts of friends and the income from official office.

Despite his dismal personal record, however, there was no one in the colonies to equal Adams' ability to organize and arouse popular and political passion. When the passage of the Stamp Act galvanized resistance in Boston in 1765, Adams helped organize the Sons of Liberty as a mechanism for protest. He had long been a key member of the Caucus Club, a group devoted to selecting political candidates and which formed the basis of the new, more radical organization. Adams' work throughout the Stamp Act crisis was relatively muted, but with the passage of the Townshend Acts, he came to the forefront. In 1768, Adams, by then a member of the Massachusetts House, secured passage of a Circular Letter from Massachusetts to the other American colonial legislatures, urging cooperation against the attempts of Parliament to tax the Americans in order to pay the salaries of royal officials. The letter set forth basic radical doctrines that denied Parliament's right to tax without consent. When the British government landed troops in Boston to enforce the duties, Adams led the resistance. The Townshend tariffs were repealed in 1770, and popular unrest might have settled back in Massachusetts as it did in other colonies once the economic threat lessened, but Adams was implacable. He continued to publish widely read attacks on his arch rival Lieutenant Governor Thomas Hutchinson and carried on behind-the-scenes organizing. Although he seldom overtly advocated violence, Adams kept the burning issues alive and pounded away at the constitutional questions of the rights of the colonies to be free of unwarranted taxation and abuse from the royal government. As one historian has commented: "He wrote with concentrated bitterness, in the manner of a Jeremiah denouncing the sinister aims and wicked conduct of those in high places, warning the people of the concealed conspiracy intended to deprive them of their liberty . . ." In 1772, he was instrumental in setting up a Committee of Correspondence to exchange information and ideas between towns.

A year later, the Tea Act set events in motion that culminated in open rebellion and warfare. Adams was adamant in organizing the fight against paying duties on tea. The Boston Committee of Correspondence and the Sons of Liberty hardened their position: no tea bearing the hateful new duties would be allowed to land from the ships in Boston harbor. On December 16, Adams presided at a day-long meeting, which ended with the news that Governor Hutchinson refused to send the tea back to Britain. When the meeting broke up, a group with Adams' tacit approval stole away to don Indian disguises and dump the tea. Britain's response to the Tea Party was to pass the Coercive Acts aimed at closing commerce in Boston and bringing the radicals to heel. Adams' response in turn was to advocate a meeting of colonial representatives in a congress to consider a cooperative response. In late August, wearing a splendid new suit that was the gift of the Sons of Liberty, Sam Adams joined his cousin John

Adams, Thomas Cushing and Robert Treat Paine in a carriage ride through Boston and down the road to Philadelphia, where they would represent the colony in the first Continental Congress. By the time Adams returned to Massachusetts, he was a virtual fugitive. British commander Thomas Gage dispatched his columns on the road to Lexington and Concord in April 1775 in part to capture and arrest Adams.

Despite his election to the second Congress and signing the Declaration of Independence in 1776, Sam Adams' moments in the spotlight were essentially over after the outbreak of hostilities. Those qualities that had made him effective in agitation did not serve well in the long, grinding business of conducting a war of rebellion and forming a new nation. He was adept at preserving liberties, but had little talent for building them. By all accounts he was a poor legislator and played little important part in Congress throughout the struggle with Britain after 1775. By 1781, he was back in Boston, and although he held a succession of public offices during the following years, his ambitions were frustrated for the most part by the popularity and power of John Hancock. At his rival's death in 1793, Adams became governor of the state, but he served with slight distinction. He died in Boston in 1803. *Further reading:* John C. Miller, *Sam Adams: Pioneer in Propaganda* (Boston, 1936); John R. Galvin, *Three Men of Boston* (New York, 1976).

ADAMS, Thomas (1730–1788) Delegate to Congress, legislator, businessman

Born in New Kent County, Virginia, Adams attended the local common schools and served as clerk of Henrico County before moving to England in 1762, where he was in business until the eve of the Revolution. He returned to Virginia in 1774 and became a member of the New Kent County Committee of Safety. He sat in the House of Burgesses, signing the Virginia Articles of Association in May 1774. Adams was a delegate to the Continental Congress for two years, 1778–1780, and signed the Articles of Confederation. He moved to Augusta County, Virginia, at the end of his term in Congress, and served in the state senate from 1783 until 1786.

ADDISON, Daniel Delany (or Dulany) (d. 1808) Loyalist officer

A resident of Maryland, Addison joined the Maryland loyalist militia in 1776. He was promoted to captain in 1782 and reached the rank of major by the end of the war. He was indicted for treason in Baltimore but was not convicted. Addison emigrated to Britain, receiving half pay for his military service, and died in London.

ADLUM, John (1759–1836) Revolutionary soldier, viniculturalist

Although best known as a pioneer of American grape culture and winemaking, Adlum served in the Revolutionary War as a teenage soldier and left a valuable memoir of life among the ranks. He was born in York, Pennsylvania, and joined the local militia company at age 15 in 1774. His company was called to service in New Jersey in 1776 and incorporated into the Flying Camp, a reserve mobile unit made up of Maryland, Delaware and Pennsylvania companies. Adlum observed the battles that pushed Washington out of New York, and his company, in which he served intermittently as a sergeant, was moved across the Hudson River to Fort Washington just before its capture by the British in November 1776. Adlum was taken prisoner and transported to New York City, where he became a servant to a group of paroled American officers living in a private home. His account gives a fascinating look at the life of prisoners of war in New York. He was returned to Pennsylvania under parole in January 1777, but was barred from further military service by the conditions of his parole.

Adlum turned to surveying near the end of the war, began to buy land and became wealthy by the 1790s. During the French war threat in 1798, he volunteered for military duty and was commissioned a major, but the provisional army was dissolved before he saw any actual service. He took up a serious interest in agriculture, moving to Maryland and eventually establishing an important experimental farm near Georgetown in the District of Columbia. He became the country's leading expert on grape cultivation and developed the Catawba grape in 1807. He was also the foremost expert on winemaking, publishing *Adlum on Wine* in 1826. *Further reading:* Howard H. Peckham, ed., *Memoirs of the Life of John Adlum in the Revolutionary War* (Chicago, 1968).

AFFLECK, Edmund (1723?–1788) British commodore

A career naval officer from the 1740s, Affleck commanded the 74-gun *Bedford* in 1778 as part of Admiral John Byron's North American squadron. His ship was badly damaged in a gale off New York and was forced to return to Britain, but it later sailed with Admiral Sir George Rodney in the relief of Gibraltar, where Affleck won distinction at Cape St. Vincent in January 1780. He then returned to North American waters and took part in the battle of Chesapeake Bay in March 1781 under Marriot Arbuthnot. During the following months, he was commissioner of the port of New York with the rank of commodore. He again took command of the *Bedford* and sailed with Admiral Hood in the West Indies, winning honors against the French there in 1782. On his return to Britain he was made a baronet and eventually admiral, although he was not employed on active duty. He served as a member of Parliament from 1782 until his death.

AFFLECK, Philip (1726–1799) British naval officer

The younger brother of Edmund Affleck, Philip also commanded a Royal Navy warship during the Revolution, serving during the first years of conflict with the Channel Fleet. In the spring of 1780, he sailed to the West Indies to help reinforce Admiral Sir George Rodney's fleet. His ship visited New York briefly in September. He returned to Britain in 1781, following the capture of St. Eustatius. He was later commander in chief in the West Indies and a lord of the admiralty, having attained flag rank in 1787.

AGNEW, John (c. 1727–1812) Loyalist clergyman

As Anglican rector of the Suffolk Parish in Nansemond County, Virginia, Agnew ran afoul of the local committee of safety because of his vocal support of the king and parliament. He not only condemned the rebellion, but he publicly agreed with the British government. He preached against the American position and told members of his congregation who disagreed with him to leave the church. However, it was the rector who was forced to flee with Lord Dunmore in 1776. Agnew then became chaplain of the Queen's Rangers, a loyalist corps in which his son was a captain. He later reappeared in Suffolk in the company of British troops when they raided and burned the town.

AGNEW, Stair (d. 1821) Loyalist officer

The son of Reverend John Agnew, a prominent Virginia

loyalist, Agnew served as a captain in the Queen's Rangers. He was severely wounded at the battle of Brandywine and was captured by the French while returning to Virginia. After a period of imprisonment in France, he was released and settled in New Brunswick, Canada, where he sat in the House of Assembly and as a local magistrate.

ALDEN, Ichabod (1739–1778) Continental colonel   Alden was a great-grandson of the John Alden of Pilgrim fame. Born in Duxbury, Massachusetts, he was appointed lieutenant colonel of the Plymouth militia in 1775, took part in the siege of Boston and became colonel of the 7th Massachusetts of the Continental Army in November 1776. He may have been an adequate officer under usual circumstances, but he was inexperienced in frontier warfare. Nonetheless, he was assigned the command of a small fort and garrison at Cherry Valley, about 50 miles west of Albany, New York. The outpost became the focus of a reprisal attack by a force of 800 Tories and Indians under Major Walter Butler and Joseph Brant in November 1778, following the burning of the Indian town of Unadilla by American troops. Despite advance warnings, Alden was careless in preparing for an attack. On the morning of November 11, he was caught sleeping in a house outside the fort by the first assault. He was cut down and scalped along with several other officers. Thirty people, both settlers and soldiers, were killed before the surviving Americans gathered in the fort. Butler and Brant had no artillery and could not breach the walls, so they settled for burning the settlement's houses and carrying off about 70 prisoners, most of whom were later released.

ALEXANDER, Robert (1739 or 1741–1805) Delegate to Congress, loyalist   Alexander was born near Elkton, Maryland and inherited a considerable fortune in land. He moved to Baltimore in 1762, establishing a lucrative law practice and real estate business. He was an active patriot leader in the pre-Revolutionary years, beginning with the committee of safety formed in Baltimore to protest the Stamp Act in 1766. He was also a member of several other patriot associations, was secretary of the committee of observation, served in the provincial convention (1774–77) and received a commission as lieutenant in the Baltimore militia. He was chosen as one of Maryland's delegates to the Continental Congress and attended sessions in Philadelphia until May 1776, when it became apparent that the body would soon declare independence. Despite his patriot activities to that point, Alexander could not agree to separation from Great Britain. He withdrew from Congress and moved with his wife and children to his estates in rural Maryland. As issues polarized in the state and his patriot neighbors looked on him with more and more hostility, he began to fear for his personal safety and fled to British-held Philadelphia. He accompanied the British evacuation to New York in 1778 while his wife managed affairs in Maryland. At the end of the war, Alexander went to England, leaving his family and wealth behind. He died there, having never returned to America or seen his family again. *Further reading:* Janet B. Johnson, *Robert Alexander, Maryland Loyalist* (New York, 1942; reprinted Boston, 1972).

ALEXANDER, William (Lord Stirling) (1726–1783) Continental major general   Alexander served the revolutionary army hard and well throughout all of Washington's tough campaigns of the early years of the war. He was an unexpected source of strength for the patriot cause in light of his aristocratic background, social ambitions and dissolute style of living. Born in New York, he was the son of a well-to-do Scots Jacobite emigrant from Scotland and (unusual for her day) a highly successful merchant mother. Alexander's family and social connections throughout New York and New Jersey were of the highest, and he enjoyed wealth and privilege during the first four decades of his life. In 1755, he became secretary to Massachusetts governor William Shirley, who was British commander in chief in North America, and served as commissary for Shirley's unsuccessful Oswego campaign. Alexander went with Shirley when the latter was recalled to England in 1756. Alexander lived in Great Britain until 1761, successfully pressing his claims for payments due from the campaign and living high among British political and social circles. He conceived the notion that he was a descendant of the Scottish Earl of Stirling, a title that had lapsed several generations previous, and made strenuous efforts to have his title recognized. In part this was a play to satisfy Alexander's aristocratic pretensions, but he was also interested in claiming huge sections of land in North America granted to the

William Alexander (Lord Stirling)

original earl. The British House of Lords turned down his claim, but Alexander continued to style himself as "Lord Stirling" for the rest of his life, a custom accepted by George Washington and all his eventual revolutionary colleagues.

On his return to America, Alexander thought himself too lofty to pursue business and managed to fritter away his considerable fortune in an unremitting display of pomp. He also held himself for the most part above the revolutionary fray, and most observers expected he would remain loyal to the crown in the event of war. However, in 1774, he declared himself a patriot and was expelled from his offices in New York and New Jersey by the royal governors. He was immediately appointed to command of the New Jersey militia (despite only the slimmest actual military experience), and when the New Jersey regiment was accepted into the Continental Army, Alexander became colonel. In 1776, his troops joined the army at New York, and Washington made Alexander a brigadier under John Sullivan and Israel Putnam.

During the battle of Long Island, Alexander's brigade, which included some of the army's best troops, held the American right flank and fought extremely well under his direction, repulsing a large force of British regulars. Unfortunately, British troops under General William Howe stole around the Americans' unguarded left and routed the American positions next to Alexander. Despite a fierce and valiant effort, Alexander's force was cut off, and he was captured. He was exchanged within a few months, however, and again was appointed to brigade command, although he played only a small role in the rest of the New York campaign.

He withdrew his troops to New Jersey and retreated with Washington across the state and beyond the Delaware. On December 25, 1776, Alexander's Continentals loaded onto the boats and crossed the river for the attack on Trenton, blocking the north end of the town during the ensuing fight. Afterward, Alexander moved north with Washington and fought throughout the New Jersey campaign. In February 1777, he was promoted to major general and commanded significant parts of the army under Washington at Brandywine and Germantown, although taking no important role in either battle. After a spell of sick leave, he returned and commanded the troops that anchored Washington's left at Monmouth. Following the battle, he was the president of Charles Lee's court-martial and continued to stand high in Washington's councils. From December 1778 to February 1779, Alexander was acting commander in chief of the Continental Army while Washington was away to confer with Congress. He then moved to various commands in the New York Highlands, sitting on the court that condemned the British spy Major John André in 1780. Given command at Albany, New York in 1782, his health began to decline, and he died of acute gout in January 1783. He was regarded by his contemporaries as vain and pompous, much given to the bottle and high living, with little strategic military insight, yet he was steadfast and exceptionally brave on the field of battle. *Further reading:* Paul D. Nelson, *William Alexander, Lord Stirling* (University, Ala., 1987).

ALLAN, John. Revolutionary leader The large contingent of New Englanders which settled in Nova Scotia (an area including modern-day New Brunswick) during the 1760s missed the ferment that bubbled in the 13 lower colonies, and at the outbreak of the war, most of the Nova Scotian settlers remained loyal to Britain. But a handful attempted revolt, hoping for support from Massachusetts. Allan was a patriot leader in Cumberland County, where Nova Scotia and New Brunswick meet, and along with Jonathan Eddy he launched an ill-considered and premature attack and siege against Fort Cumberland with a band of 28 Maine men and a small number of local volunteers. They were easily driven off by the British garrison. In 1801, long after the Revolutionary War, Allan was rewarded by the U.S. Congress with a land grant in the Canadian Refugee Tract in Ohio.

ALLEN, Andrew (1740–1825) Delegate to Congress, loyalist, jurist

Allen was the second son of William Allen, chief justice of the supreme court of Pennsylvania, and like the rest of his prominent family, was loyal to the crown in the end. He was born in Philadelphia, graduated from the University of Pennsylvania and studied law with Benjamin Chew and later in England at the Temple. On his return to Pennsylvania in 1765, he took up practice, becoming attorney general for the colony in 1769. In 1775 and 1776, he was both chosen a member of the Committee of Safety and elected as a delegate to the Continental Congress. He found he could not support independence, however, and fled Congress and his home city in December 1776, seeking refuge behind the British lines with Lord Howe. He thereupon renounced his congressional oath and swore allegiance to the king. Allen returned to Philadelphia with the British army in 1778 and was appointed lieutenant governor of Pennsylvania. When Philadelphia was restored to American control, he was attainted a loyalist and his property was confiscated. After the war, he was pardoned and he revisited Philadelphia but failed to regain his lost property. He then emigrated to England, receiving a pension from the government, and died there.

ALLEN, Ethan (1738–1789) Vermont leader, Continental brevet colonel, militia major general

The annals of the American Revolution contain no more colorful and controversial figure than Allen. His modern biographer calls him "a demigod to some and to others an unconscionable thug." The truth about this larger-than-life character is probably somewhere in between.

He was born in Litchfield, Connecticut, but his life was tied up with the eventual state of Vermont, known then as the New Hampshire Grants. Colonial sovereignty of this area was disputed between New Hampshire and New York, and political power, cultural differences and land ownership were all at stake.

Allen moved to the Grants with several of his brothers in the 1760s. His early education had been cut short by his father's death in 1755, and he had attempted mining, iron mongering and land speculating with indifferent success. His physical stature (the tales of his strength and endurance are legendary) and forceful personality placed Allen at the head of the Grants settlers in their constant battle with officials of New York. There was no clear jurisdiction or law in the Grants, so the settlers organized themselves: Allen formed a vigilante militia called the Green Mountain Boys with himself at the head as "colonel commandant." By 1774, he virtually ruled the Grants in concert with several powerful political allies. New York governor William Tryon put a reward of £100 on his capture.

Allen's career during the War of Independence illustrates most clearly the sometimes dual nature of the Revolution: he really was at war with New York or whoever threatened settlement or land titles in the New Hampshire Grants. When this interest ran with the interests of the emerging nation, he was a patriot; but if the two came in conflict, Allen went his own way, even to the point of treason.

At the news of Lexington and Concord, Allen and a Committee of War decided quite on their own to strike at Fort Ticonderoga, the traditional stronghold that commanded Lake Champlain and the route to Canada. The once-proud fortress had fallen into horrible disrepair and was lightly held by a small British garrison. Allen calculated that a surprise attack would win the strategic post for the new American cause, and capture of the fort would bring with it a large train of heavy artillery, a commodity completely lacking in the American arsenal. As he gathered 200 or so Green Mountain Boys and prepared to move on Ticonderoga, Allen was joined by Benedict Arnold, who had independently thought of a similar scheme and convinced the Massachusetts patriot government to authorize an expedition. Arnold had no troops or supplies, however, so Allen relegated him to a powerless post of adjunct command.

During the early morning hours of May 10, 1775, Allen and a small company of about 85 men crossed to the fort and surprised the sleeping British troops. In Allen's own account, he stormed up the stairs of the commander's quarters and demanded surrender of the king's property "in the name of the Great

Jehovah and the Continental Congress." Actually, Allen had confronted not the commander, but his lieutenant, and was reported by others to have said something more like "Come out of there you sons of British whores, or I'll smoke you out." Whatever his rhetoric, in a quick stroke Allen had captured the guns (later to play a key role in Washington's expulsion of the British from Boston) and seized control of the lower lake. His men immediately went on a drunken spree.

Allen's subsequent wartime career was less successful. He captured the British post at St. John's, Canada, but was ignominiously pushed out within a few days by a counterattack. Back at Ticonderoga, Allen's command slowly dissolved and Arnold assumed command. Allen's candle flickered even lower over the following months. After successfully petitioning Congress to absorb the Green Mountain Boys into the new Continental Army, Allen was promptly voted out of command in favor of Seth Warner.

Allen was left to attach himself to the command of General Philip Schuyler, who had been sent to direct an invasion of Canada. Sent to recruit Indian and Canadian allies, Allen decided to attempt to capture Montreal on his own, ahead of the slow-to-organize American expedition. His meager attack was easily repulsed and Allen was captured. The British authorities transported Allen to an English prison and flirted with hanging him as a traitor (the question of what constituted treason was still cloudy at that stage of the war), but decided to regard him as a prisoner of war and returned him to Halifax and eventually parole in New York. He was exchanged in May 1778, and he received a commission as brevet colonel in the Continental Army before returning to the Grants region, which now styled itself the independent Republic of Vermont. Over the following two years, Allen reestablished his local influence, accepted a commission as major general of militia, and turned all his efforts toward gaining recognition for Vermont. Congress, however, was loath to offend New York and fended off Vermont's claims (the region was left in limbo until 1791).

Rebuffed by Congress, Allen and his friends turned to the British. Modern research has revealed incontestable evidence that Allen negotiated throughout 1780 and 1781 with General Frederick Haldimand, the British governor of Canada, with the full intention of establishing Vermont as an independent province under the British crown. With Allen's connivance, a British force under Barry St. Leger was poised to invade Vermont and official proclamations were drawn and ready for declamation when Cornwallis' defeat put an end to the plot. Since Allen was still a colonel in the Continental Army at the time, treason is the only label for his behavior.

Allen's influence came to an end in 1783, and the remainder of his life was devoted to business and writing. His *Reason the Only Oracle of Man . . .* is a remarkable treatise on religion. He died of an apparent stroke in early 1789. No known likeness of Ethan Allen exists, and even the location of his grave has been lost. *Further reading:* Charles A. Jellison, *Ethan Allen: Frontier Rebel* (Syracuse, N.Y., 1969).

ALLEN, Ira (1751–1814) Militia officer The younger brother of Ethan Allen, Ira had moved with his siblings from Massachusetts to the Hampshire Grants in the 1760s. He supported his brother's political and military ambitions in the disputed area, serving as an officer in the militia known as the Green Mountain Boys. Ira also held several offices in the extralegal Vermont government set up between 1776 and 1790, including membership on the Vermont Governor's Council and as Vermont treasurer. Vermont, of course, did not exist officially as a separate political entity at the time, but this did not dissuade the Allen brothers from unceasing attempts to establish its independence from New Hampshire and New York, both of which claimed parts of the area. Ira was involved in Ethan's plot during 1780–81 to welcome an invading British column from Canada, a scheme that failed only with the news that Cornwallis had surrendered in Virginia. Ira continued to be mixed up in shady political and military schemes following the Revolution. In 1795, after Vermont had become a state, he went to England to buy arms for the Vermont militia and was arrested on the high seas by the British during his return voyage. He was finally released in 1801 but was thrown in prison in Vermont when he came home. He fled to Philadelphia after the Vermont legislature released him.

ALLEN, Isaac (d. 1806) Loyalist officer, lawyer Before the Revolution, Allen was an attorney in

Trenton, New Jersey. He volunteered for service with the crown, fought in South Carolina and by 1782 was a lieutenant colonel in the loyalist New Jersey Volunteers. His property in Pennsylvania was seized by the patriot government. After the war, he settled in New Brunswick, Canada, rising to a seat on the provincial council and eventually to the post of judge of the supreme court.

ALLEN, James (d. 1777) Loyalist   The fourth son of Chief Justice William Allen of Pennsylvania, James played no active role in the Revolution, although he presumably held loyalist sympathies similar to the rest of his family. He was in declining health by 1776 and died at his home in Philadelphia in 1777. Allen's wife was a cousin of Margaret Shippen Arnold, the duplicitous spouse of Benedict Arnold.

ALLEN, John (d. 1778) Loyalist officer   Third son of Chief Justice William Allen of Pennsylvania, John was a loyalist from the beginning and joined Lord Howe's army in 1776 to serve as an officer. He was charged with treason by the patriot government of Pennsylvania, but he died in February 1778 before the accusations were tried.

ALLEN, William (the Elder) (c. 1704–1780) Loyalist merchant and jurist   The patriarch of a loyalist clan and one of the most prominent men in prerevolutionary Philadelphia, the senior William Allen was born in America and educated to the law in England. He took up his father's mercantile business on the latter's death in 1725, growing wealthy over the ensuing decades. He meanwhile took an active part in legal and political life in Pennsylvania, succeeding his father-in-law as recorder of Philadelphia and serving on the Philadelphia Council. He became chief justice of the Pennsylvania Supreme Court in 1750, sitting on the bench until the eve of the Revolution. He was also prominent in civic and cultural affairs as a close associate of Benjamin Franklin and a patron of artist Benjamin West. He founded the town of Northampton, which was later named Allentown in his honor.

Even though he joined the protests against the Stamp Act in the mid-1760s, he favored compromise with Britain rather than rebellion. As difficulties mounted, Allen tried valiantly to persuade his fellow Pennsylvanians to resist the movement toward independence, and in 1774 he published his argu-

ments in *The American Crisis*. Giving up hope, at the end of the same year he resigned his offices and moved to England where he died, leaving two of his four sons to fight on the British side.

ALLEN, William (the Younger). Loyalist officer   The eldest son of Chief Justice William Allen of Pennsylvania, the younger William Allen maintained a role as a patriot longer than his siblings or father, and he may have actually served in the American army for a short time. Eventually, however, he changed sides and raised a body of loyalist Pennsylvania troops in 1777 or 1778 after accepting a commission from the British.

ALLISON, Patrick. Patriot clergyman   When the Continental Congress decamped from Philadelphia to Baltimore in December 1776, Allison was appointed chaplain. He was first minister of the Presbyterian Church of Baltimore and an organizer of the local Sons of Liberty.

ALMY, Mary Gould (1735–1808) Diarist   Almy was a lifelong resident of Newport, Rhode Island and the daughter of a Quaker school teacher. She married Benjamin Almy in 1762. Several members of her family were loyalists, and she herself opposed the war, although more from pacifist conviction than love for the crown. Her husband was a relatively prominent local figure, sitting in the legislature. The couple took over the house of an expelled loyalist after the beginning of the war and rented rooms to lodgers. During the American-French attempt to take Newport from British hands in August 1778, Almy kept a diary that was preserved and provides insight to the effect of the war on civilians. When George Washington visited Newport in 1790, he spent the night in one of Almy's rental rooms. *Further reading:* Elizabeth Evans, *Weathering the Storm: Women of the American Revolution* (New York, 1975).

ALSOP, John (1724–1794) Delegate to Congress, merchant   Alsop was born in rural New York and moved as a young man to New York City, where he entered business with his brother. The partnership was dissolved in 1757, and Alsop flourished on his own, becoming one of the biggest importers in the colonies and amassing a large fortune. He actively resisted the British economic mea-

Lord Jeffrey Amherst

sures leading up to the Revolution out of both personal and commercial motivations, and he was elected as a delegate to the first Continental Congress from New York, serving during September and October 1774. He was reelected to the second Congress in May 1775. He withdrew from political life late in 1775 and sat out the Revolution in Middletown, Connecticut. After the British evacuated New York City, Alsop returned and took a central role in commercial life, serving as president of the chamber of commerce.

AMBOISE, Chevalier d'. French agent Amboise acted as a confidential agent of the French government in America during the early days of the Revolution. He observed parts of the battle of Lexington and Concord in 1775 and reported to the French embassy in London on the condition of American military forces.

AMHERST, Jeffrey, Lord (1717–1797) British general During the Revolution, Amherst served as military adviser to the king, but his great fame and popularity with the British public were based on his military achievements against the French in North America from 1758 to 1760. He was born in Kent, became an ensign in the Guards in 1731 and caught the notice of two powerful military patrons, Lord Ligonier and the Duke of Cumberland, during the European wars of the mid-18th century. He was selected from among many rivals by William Pitt in 1758 to carry out the great minister's plan for defeat of the French in North America. Placed in command of an expedition to Canada, Amherst succeeded brilliantly, due in large measure to his subordinate, James Wolfe. In the space of three years, the British seized Louisbourg, Quebec and Montreal, ousting the French from the continent for good. Amherst proved less adept at postwar command. He failed to come to grips with the Indian uprising led by Pontiac, gaining lasting infamy by his suggestion that the Indians be infected with smallpox and hunted down with dogs. He was recalled to Britain in 1763. Despite his failures, he was rewarded with several sinecures, including the absentee governorship of Virginia. He was immensely popular with the British public as the hero of the Seven Years' War, and he skillfully played his political power on the side of the king during the American Revolution. Although he turned down the king's request to assume command in North America, Amherst was elevated to the peerage in 1776 and was awarded additional rank and positions. After the defeat of Burgoyne, Amherst urged the king to abandon the colonial struggle in favor of concentrating on warring against the French. Perhaps his greatest service was in suppressing the Gordon Riots in 1780. Forced out of office after the change of government in 1782, he became titular commander in chief of all British forces. He clung to his post despite ineptitude and advancing age and is blamed for many of the growing maladies of the British army during the latter decades of the century. Amherst was finally persuaded to resign in 1795 and was made a field marshal the following year. *Further reading:* Louis Des Cognets, *Amherst and Canada* (Princeton, 1962).

AMHERST, Jeffrey (d. 1815) British officer Although bearing the same name, he is unrelated to the British general of the period. This Amherst joined the 60th Regiment of Foot as a junior officer in 1771. During the Revolution he served as aide-de-camp to General James Robertson and held the local rank of major. By the end of the century, he reached major general's rank.

ANBUREY, Thomas. British officer Anburey was a lieutenant attached to General John Burgoyne's invasion force in 1777, serving under General Simon

Fraser at the capture of Fort Ticonderoga and, after Burgoyne's defeat, moving south with the Convention Army. Although he himself figured little in the campaign, Anburey gained considerable notice by publication in 1789 of two volumes of letters purportedly written during his tour of duty in America. Modern research has shown that Anburey plagiarized from other writers and stitched together the letters to appear to be his own on-the-spot writing. The account is nonetheless valuable and contains much of interest. For example, this comment on the difficulties of Burgoyne's progress across northern New York: "The nature of the country is peculiarly unfavorable in respect to military operations, it being difficult to reconnoitre the enemy, and to obtain any intelligence to be relied on; the roads, the situation of the enemy, the grounds for procuring forage, of which the army is of great want . . . are often attended with the utmost danger . . ." *Further reading:* Thomas Anburey, *Travels Through the Interior Parts of America . . .* , 2 vols. (Boston, 1923).

ANDERSON, Enoch (1753–1824) Continental officer

As an officer in the Delaware regiments, Anderson led some of the best and most reliable troops of the Continental Line and saw action in nearly all of Washington's major engagements during the first two years of the Revolutionary War. Anderson was a lieutenant in the first Delaware regiment, raised in 1776, and when 16 additional regiments were authorized by Congress, he was appointed a captain in the new Delaware unit in January 1777. He raised his own company, no little feat in loyalist-prone Delaware, and was ordered to Philadelphia. He was at the battle of Brandywine and was hotly engaged at Germantown as the captain of the Delaware light infantry company. He resigned in June 1777 and retired to his home state. In later years, he wrote a memoir of his service. *Further reading: Personal Recollections of Captain Enoch Anderson* (reprint, New York, 1971).

ANDRÉ, John (1751–1780) British officer, spy

André was a romantic and ultimately tragic figure, admired and mourned by both sides when he met his ignominious end, which seemed to belong better to someone else. He was the son of an emigrant merchant, whose Huguenot family had fled France, first to Geneva and then to England. After education in Switzerland, André joined his father's busi-

John André

ness at age 17, but an unhappy love affair inclined him to take up the military career he favored over the counting house. In 1771, he purchased a second lieutenant's commission in the Royal Welch Fusiliers, but he soon transferred to the 7th Foot as a first lieutenant. Perhaps because of his facility with languages (he spoke fluent German and French and a bit of Dutch), he was sent to Germany for advanced military training. He arrived in America in 1774, traveling via Philadelphia, Boston and up Lake Champlain to Montreal and Quebec. After the Americans took Fort Ticonderoga, André was sent to help garrison St. John's, Canada, and was captured there on November 1775, when the British commander surrendered to Montgomery. André spent the following year in captivity in Lancaster and then Carlisle, Pennsylvania.

After his exchange, André became aide-de-camp to General Charles Grey, accompanying the British force that occupied Philadelphia. He was present at Brandywine and Germantown, but he took little active part in the battles. André did fight with Grey's force at the British victory at Paoli, New York in 1777. Most of André's efforts during the Philadelphia occupation, however, were social. He was a handsome young man, well-liked among his fellow British officers and the loyalists of Philadelphia, especially the ladies. He formed a friendship with, among others, Peggy Shippen, who was soon to marry the American hero Benedict Arnold. André was a talented artist and amateur thespian as well as a charmer and a competent soldier. He organized the infamous extravagant party, known as the Mischanzia, given in Philadelphia in 1778 in honor of General William Howe on the commander's departure. After the British withdrawal to New York, General Grey left for Britain, and André transferred to the 26th regiment and became aide-de-camp to the new British commander in chief, Sir Henry Clinton. He became Clinton's indispensable man at headquarters, handling correspondence, reports and the British intelligence service. In early 1780, Clinton named André as deputy adjutant general to the army and breveted the young officer as a major (a promotion that Lord Amherst in England refused to confirm), and André served well during Clinton's successful expedition against Charleston.

In the spring of 1780, after returning from the south and being promoted to adjutant general, André learned of the treasonous correspondence opened between American major general Benedict Arnold and British headquarters. Arnold, disaffected by presumed slights and the attacks of critics, offered to sell out to the British and deliver into their hands a considerable body of troops. André took over the main responsibility of dealing with Arnold through a series of intermediaries, devising codes, secret inks and all the paraphernalia of espionage. A meeting planned with Arnold at Dobbs Ferry, New York fell through in September, but André kept in close touch with the American traitor, urging him to finagle a significant command that he could betray. When Arnold managed to be named commander of the fortress at West Point, Clinton and André began to press for action, despite their reluctance to meet Arnold's stiff price. A second meeting between Arnold and André was arranged.

Clinton ordered his adjutant specifically not to cross the American lines, to remain in uniform and to carry no incriminating documents. Unfortunately for André, the theatrical romance of a secret meeting on a dark riverbank apparently overcame his better judgment.

He sailed up the Hudson River on the armed British sloop *Vulture* in the company of loyalist Beverly Robinson. Arnold could not secure a boat and sent Joshua Hett Smith in his stead with signed passes and a message for André to join him. André rowed ashore, landing on the American-held side of the river, and parleyed with Arnold. Dawn found André still ashore, unable to return to his ship.

The capture of John André. Documents were hidden in his boots.

Smith bundled the British officer off to his house to await nightfall. To André's dismay, the *Vulture* came under fire from a shore battery, and her timid captain sailed off downstream, leaving André stranded. At Arnold's urging, André decided to return to the British lines overland, and he accepted documents in Arnold's handwriting that detailed the weaknesses of the fortifications at West Point and listed Arnold's spies. After changing into civilian clothes, André hid the papers in his stocking, mounted a horse and set off with Smith. They crossed the river and spent the following night in a farmhouse. When they neared British territory, Smith turned back. As André approached Tarrytown, New York, he was stopped by three scruffy American militiamen, whom he mistook for British partisans. He revealed that he was British and then, understanding his mistake, tried to use a pass (issued by Arnold) in the name of John Anderson. The trio searched him for booty and found the incriminating documents. They turned their prisoner over to an officer, who conveyed André and the documents to Lieutenant Colonel John Jameson. Somewhat confused by the passes and letters signed by Arnold, Jameson sent the documents to General Washington, who was traveling in the area, but ordered the prisoner to West Point with a letter telling Arnold of his capture. At the last minute, the order to transfer the prisoner was countermanded and the party turned back. The letter to Arnold, however, reached the general at his breakfast. He immediately left his house, rode to the river and made his way by barge to the *Vulture,* barely escaping Washington's arrival.

André's true identity was soon revealed. He had been captured behind American lines in disguise, using an assumed name, with incriminating documents hidden on his person. All the rules called for his summary execution as a spy, but Washington decided to convene a board of general officers to review the evidence. Clinton and André's friends were beside themselves, but their appeals that André was only acting under orders were of no avail, and Clinton could not accept the only offer of the Americans, to exchange André for Arnold. The board reached the inevitable conclusion: André must die by hanging.

The nobility and forebearance with which the handsome young officer approached his doom won the respect and even affection of his captors. Resigned to death, he petitioned Washington to allow him to be shot like a soldier, but the commander in chief refused. André was hung at Tappan, New York, on October 2, 1780. In 1821, his remains were removed to England, where they were reinterred at Westminster Abbey. *Further reading:* Robert McC. Hatch, *Major John André: A Gallant in Spy's Clothing* (Boston, 1986).

ANDREWS, John (1746–1813) Loyalist clergyman, educator

Andrews was a quiet loyalist, who took little part in the Revolution and who managed to avoid damage from his beliefs, eventually emerging as a prominent churchman, classicist and educator. Born in Cecil County, Maryland, and schooled in Pennsylvania, he went to England for ordination in the Anglican Church (America had no bishops), but he returned in 1767 to a mission parish in the Delaware seacoast town of Lewes, later a hotbed of loyalist sentiment. In 1770, he took a post in York, Pennsylvania, but he moved to Queen Anne's County, Maryland, where he lived with his family during the early months of the mounting rebellion. Andrews disagreed with the independence movement and with the war, but he kept his opinions out of his pulpit and his public utterances. To avoid conflict, he withdrew again to York during the war and began a classical school. In March 1776, he played host briefly to British Major John André who was in American custody after capture at St. John's, Canada, the year before. After the war effectively ended, Andrews returned

to Baltimore and was a leading member of the convention that organized the Protestant Episcopal Church in Maryland. In 1785, he became head of the Protestant Episcopal Academy in Philadelphia, which was absorbed six years later into the University of Pennsylvania. Andrews went on to serve as vice provost and then provost of the university.

ANGELL, Israel (1740–1832) Continental officer

Angell was born in Providence, Rhode Island, a descendant of one of Roger Williams' original band of settlers. A cooper by trade, he was commissioned a major in the first Rhode Island regiment raised in 1775 to help lay siege to Boston. When the 2nd Rhode Island regiment was formed, Angell was elected lieutenant colonel, and he took command of the regiment in January 1777 when the unit's colonel died. Leading his troops at several important engagements, including Brandywine and Monmouth, Angell won particular notice for his regiment's skillful fighting at Red Bank, New Jersey, in October 1777 and again at Springfield, New Jersey, in June 1780, in the latter case holding off an attack by a British force under the German general von Knyphausen. Angell retired from the army in January 1781 when the two Rhode Island regiments were consolidated under one colonel. He settled in Johnston, Rhode Island, resumed his cooperage business, and later became an innkeeper. He married three times, sired 17 children, and was reportedly courting a fourth wife when he died in his 92nd year. His wartime diary was preserved by his family and published late in the 19th century. *Further reading: Diary of Colonel Israel Angell . . . 1778–1781,* Edward Field, ed. (Providence, 1899; reprinted New York, 1971).

ARBUTHNOT, Marriot (1711–1794) British admiral

The period of the American Revolution coincided with a dip in leadership for the Royal Navy, a circumstance contributing mightily to the final success of the American cause. Between admirals Hawke and Nelson came admirals such as Arbuthnot. He was born of unknown parentage and came slowly to rank in the navy, reaching captain in 1747. He commanded a warship at the battle of Quiberon Bay in 1759 and was on hand for the capture of Havana in 1762. He developed an unimaginative, pompous personality with a prickly regard for his own dignity and position. In 1775, Arbuthnot was

Marriot Arbuthnot

appointed commissioner at Halifax, where he served until his recall to Britain and advancement to flag rank in 1778. The following spring, he was named to replace James Gambier as commander of the American station. Effective cooperation between Arbuthnot and Sir Henry Clinton, the commander of land forces, might have led to British success, but Arbuthnot was tactless as well as slow witted, and the two commanders were soon reduced to castigating each other through an intermediary. The admiral demanded independence of command but punctuated strategic somnolence with only infrequent bursts of misdirected and uncoordinated activity.

In late 1779, the French admiral d'Estaing threatened the British occupation of Rhode Island, yet Arbuthnot could not decide on a course of action. Luckily for the British, d'Estaing dithered and sailed away without damage. In May of the following year, Clinton laid siege to Charleston and, despite poor support from Arbuthnot, managed to capture the city. Matters went less well when the Chevalier de Ternay's fleet landed the French expedition under Rochambeau at Newport, despite advance warnings to the British high command from Benedict Arnold. The possibility of combined British operations broke down almost entirely as Arbuthnot virtually ignored Clinton's suggestions and requests for stopping the French before they could fortify. The nadir came in March 1781. A large British force under turncoat Arnold was loose in Virginia, hoping to divert American attention from Lord Cornwallis' troops to the south. Supply and communications with Arnold's army depended on British control of the sea approaches, and when a

powerful French squadron from the West Indies under Destouches arrived off the Virginia Capes, Arbuthnot was forced to battle. The resulting engagement found the British in a superior tactical position. Nonetheless, Arbuthnot's strict adherence to overly rigid fighting instructions and his muddled signaling to his ships nullified their advantages of speed and position. The confusion resulted in considerable French-inflicted damage to the British squadron, and Arbuthnot withdrew to Lynnhaven Roads after the inconclusive fight. Following the battle, he was recalled to London and replaced with the equally hapless Graves. Despite advancement in rank following his American assignment, Arbuthnot was never again employed by the Admiralty. *Further reading:* William B. Willcox, "Arbuthnot, Gambier, and Graves: 'Old Women' of the Navy," in George A. Billias, *George Washington's Opponents* (New York, 1969).

ARCHER, John (1741–1810) Officer, official, physician

A native Marylander, Archer received one of the first medical degrees awarded from a school in the colonies in 1768 when he graduated from the Philadelphia College of Medicine. He was also a graduate of Princeton. During the Revolution, he served in the Continental Army as a major and sat in 1776 in the Maryland convention called to write a state constitution. After the war, he combined medical and political careers: Archer was a founding member of a medical school in Maryland in 1799 and served in three Congresses as a U.S. representative from Maryland.

ARMAND, Charles Tuffin, Marquis de la Rouerie (1750–1793) French volunteer officer

Serving in America under the democratic name of Armand, the Marquis de la Rouerie was one of the more effective French volunteer aristocrats. He entered the French military service at an early age and served 10 years before his dismissal over a duel, after which he joined a Trappist community for a short time. In 1777, he arrived in America, narrowly avoiding capture by a British warship in Chesapeake Bay, and offered his talents to the American cause. Washington authorized him to raise a body of volunteers, but Armand was unable to do so and fell back on purchasing command of a corps raised previously by a Swiss major. He received a commission from Congress as a colonel in May 1777, attaching his troops to the Pulaski Legion, under Casimir Pulaski. The unit fought well in many engagements, including Red Bank, Brandywine and Whitemarsh. For a time, Armand served as the Marquis de Lafayette's second in command in New Jersey. The legion survived the winter quarters at Valley Forge and eventually moved to the southern theater. At Savannah in October 1779, Casimir Pulaski was killed, and Armand took his place at the head of the corps, which became known as Armand's Legion thereafter. Although Armand was a tough fighter, it was his ill fate to be part of the new command of Horatio Gates. In October 1780, Gates brought battle at Camden, South Carolina, with disastrous results. Armand's men held the left flank of the American dispositions, but were overrun by the British regulars and nearly destroyed as a unit. In 1781, Armand returned to France, dissatisfied by lack of promotion, but he continued to support the American cause by raising supplies, which he escorted across the sea in time to join the combined French and American army at Yorktown. He had no organized unit, but he took part as an individual officer in the famous assault by the Marquis de Deux-Ponts on British Redoubt Number 9. At the conclusion of peace, Armand was promoted to brigadier general. He returned to his native land, where within a few years he became embroiled in the French Revolution. He led a secret royalist organization in the Vendée and later tried to stage a revolt in Brittany. He contracted a fever (some accounts say brought on by news of the king's execution) and died on January 30, 1793. *Further reading:* "Letters of Col. Armand (Marquis de la Rouerie), 1777–1791," *New-York Historical Society Collections* 51 (1878), 287–396.

ARMSTRONG, James (1748–1828) Medical officer

The eldest son of John Armstrong Sr. and the brother of John Armstrong Jr., James was born in Carlisle, Pennsylvania and attended the Academy of Philadelphia. He pursued his interest in medicine at the School of Medicine at the College of Philadelphia (later the University of Pennsylvania), becoming one of its first graduates in 1769. During the Revolution, he served as a medical officer. After the war he practiced medicine and took an active interest in public affairs. He was elected to Congress in 1793 and served until 1795. Following his one term, he returned to medical practice in Cumberland County, Pennsylvania.

ARMSTRONG, John (1755–1816) American officer, frontiersman

Often confused with John Armstrong Jr., but unrelated, this Armstrong was also a native of Pennsylvania and fought with Pennsylvania troops during the Revolution. He was also, again like the other Armstrong, involved as a state officer in the dispute, immediately following the Revolutionary War, between Pennsylvania and Connecticut settlers in the Wyoming Valley on the Susquehanna River (sometimes called the Pennamite War). Later, he was commissioned into the regular army and served on the western frontier during the late 1780s and early 1790s, eventually settling in Ohio.

ARMSTRONG, John, Sr. (1717–1795) Continental and militia general, delegate to Congress

Armstrong was born in Ireland of Scots parents and emigrated to America with his wife about 1746, settling on the western side of the Susquehanna River in Pennsylvania. He was by training a surveyor and found steady employment in the western frontier region of the colony, working often for the Penn family in the area that was to form Cumberland County. He was elected to the provincial assembly in 1749. At the outbreak of the French and Indian War he became colonel of militia, and in September 1756 he led a highly successful raid against the Delaware Indians at Kittanning, a feat that provided him fame and reputation for the rest of his life. He was also with the force that retook Fort Duquesne in 1758, making friends with fellow officer George Washington.

At the beginning of the Revolution, Armstrong was commissioned a brigadier general in the Continental Army and sent to a command at Charleston, South Carolina. He actually took little part in the defense of Charleston, however, and returned north to recruit support in Pennsylvania. By 1777 he had resigned his Continental commission and was recommissioned as a major general in the Pennsylvania militia. Most of his subsequent wartime contributions were political rather than military. He was present at Brandywine, but had no significant action. At Germantown, he commanded a division of Pennsylvanians, which failed in support of Washington's regulars and added to the causes of defeat.

John Armstrong, Jr.

He was a delegate to Congress in 1779–80 and again in 1787–88.

ARMSTRONG, John, Jr. (1758–1843) Continental officer, delegate to Congress, statesman

A fascinating character, whose role in early national history has often been overlooked, Armstrong had a long and interesting career in public life and a deserved reputation as an accomplished writer and polemicist. As the son of John Armstrong Sr., a hero of the French and Indian War, he benefited from his father's influence during the Revolution. The outbreak of the war found him a student at the College of New Jersey (later Princeton), and he left his studies to volunteer in a Pennsylvania militia unit. His father rescued him from obscurity and obtained an appointment as aide-de-camp to General Hugh Mercer. Even though a very young man, Armstrong was never far thereafter from influential posts during the Revolution. He was with Mercer at the battles of Trenton and Princeton, suffering a wound at the latter engagement, in which Mercer was killed. Armstrong's father found another place for his son on the staff of Horatio Gates, forming a relationship that lasted for many years. Armstrong shared Gates's glory from the victory over General John Burgoyne and went as his deputy adjutant general when Gates took command in the south in 1780. An attack of malaria put Armstrong in the hospital before the debacle at Camden, however.

Armstrong was part of Gates's military family at the encampment of the Continental Army at New-burgh, New York in 1782. The war was effectively over, and Congress was faced with the problem of disbanding the army and gracefully sending the officers and troops home. Earlier in the war, the officers had been promised retirement on half pay for life and payment of back accounts; however, Congress was broke and, under the Articles of Confederation, had no means for raising money. A genuine threat arose that the army would enter the political arena in order to obtain its due reward for service. Politicians such as Alexander Hamilton and Robert Morris, who favored a stronger central authority, hoped to use the Continental officers' disaffection, coupled with a mild threat of mutiny, to force a change toward a more powerful government. Officers meeting at Gates's quarters on March 9, 1783 decided to issue an anonymous statement to the army, hoping to rally support for putting more pressure on Congress. Armstrong wrote the subsequent "Address," which was circulated the next day in the camp. Although the statement was denounced by Washington, whom they had hoped to co-opt, the group then issued a second, even stronger document, also written by Armstrong. The entire affair collapsed when Washington made an affecting speech against the so-called Newburgh Addresses, but many of Armstrong's political relationships for decades were haunted by his involvement.

When the army was disbanded peacefully, Armstrong returned to Pennsylvania, where he became secretary to the Supreme Executive Council of the state, and he commanded state troops in settling a dispute with Connecticut settlers in the Wyoming Valley in Pennsylvania. He was elected to Congress in 1787. His fortunes shot upward in 1789, when he married into the powerful Livingston family of New York. He moved to Dutchess County and thereafter was well connected with both the Livingstons and the Clintons. He served several times as U.S. senator from New York between 1800 and 1804, filling vacancies by appointment. In 1804 he was appointed as U.S. minister to France, and he spent six hard years in dealing with Napoleon. With the coming of the War of 1812, he was first commissioned a brigadier general and then made secretary of war by President James Madison. He was a strong cabinet member, but he took much of the blame for the British capture of the city of Washington and he resigned in 1814. He retired to his

Dutchess County estate and filled his later years with writing. *Further reading:* Carl E. Skeen, *John Armstrong, Jr. 1758–1843* (Syracuse, 1981).

ARNOLD, Benedict (1741–1801) Continental general, traitor

He was both one of America's finest combat generals and its greatest traitor. His career was complex, and his character complicated. Were it not for his ultimate act of betrayal, he would be known as a great hero; instead, his very name means treason and treachery.

Arnold was born in Connecticut. As a teenager he was apprenticed to a druggist, but he ran away in 1758 to join a New York militia company in the French and Indian War. He apparently deserted, reenlisted a year later, deserted again, and finally returned home to finish his apprenticeship. At his parents' death, he moved to New Haven and set himself up as a druggist and bookseller. He soon branched into mercantile trade and eventually established a prosperous business, sailing his own fleet of ships to the West Indies and Canada. In 1767, he married Margaret Mansfield, who gave birth to three sons in rapid succession. Arnold was a captain of the Connecticut militia and a somewhat restless merchant (and probably a smuggler as well) at the outbreak of the Revolution.

With the news of Lexington and Concord, Arnold marched his company to Cambridge, where he soon convinced revolutionary Massachusetts authorities to give him command of an expedition to capture Fort Ticonderoga. He set off by himself for the stronghold on Lake Champlain but discovered that Ethan Allen and the Green Mountain Boys of the New Hampshire Grants (present-day Vermont) were already ahead of him in the race to assault Ticonderoga. With no troops at his disposal, Arnold could only watch Allen's triumph while playing second fiddle. Soon, however, Arnold came to the forefront with an attack on the British post at St. John's, and he wrested control away from Allen. Typically, he soon came into conflict again over who was to command, and he withdrew to Massachusetts to face charges of financial mismanagement. This initial wartime experience was a paradigm of Arnold's career: skillful, even brilliant, battlefield leadership followed by quarrels over rank and suspect accounting. He repeated the pattern over and over.

Benedict Arnold

In September 1775, the new American commander in chief, George Washington, directed Lieutenant Colonel Arnold to lead an expedition against Quebec as part of a two-pronged attack on the British control of Canada. The plan was ill-informed and ill-conceived, however. Gathering a force of more than a thousand men, Arnold set off with inadequate supplies to cross hundreds of miles of Maine wilderness. The result was a legendary journey plagued by bad weather, lack of food and severe hardship. It is a testament to Arnold's abilities that any of the force survived to reach Quebec, yet he failed in an attack on December 31, during which he was severely wounded in the leg. Appointed a brigadier general by Congress, he eventually withdrew from Canada with the rest of the Americans. By October, Arnold was in charge on Lake Champlain, where he drew on his seafaring experience to piece together a ragtag navy in order to contest a British advance toward the colonies. In a scrambling engagement at Valcour Island, Arnold lost his ships but inflicted enough damage on the British flotilla to turn back the invasion.

He also fell into another quarrel with fellow soldiers, principally Jacobus Wynkoop, Moses Hazen and John Brown, which resulted in a series of charges, countercharges and inquiries. Assigned to a post in Rhode Island by Washington, Arnold was sent into a fury in February 1777 when he learned that Congress had promoted five officers junior to him to the rank of major general. Congress persisted over Washington's protests, on the grounds that Connecticut already had too many major generals. After he led a daring repulse of a British raid on Danbury, Arnold finally received his major generalship, but he was lower on the seniority list than the infamous five, a fact that rankled him for years. His old adversary Brown also brought new charges, and Congress began to inquire about Arnold's spending during the Quebec operations. In July 1777 he submitted his resignation but was persuaded by Washington to take a post with the army to the north, which was preparing to face General John Burgoyne.

The command of the Northern Department had passed from Philip Schuyler to Horatio Gates, and Arnold began to squabble with the new commander almost immediately. Nonetheless, when Burgoyne's army finally approached close enough to Gates's stationary position to bring on the battle of Freeman's Farm (First Saratoga), Arnold played a crucial role in stopping and nearly defeating the British force that day—as it was, darkness ended the fight before a conclusion. Over the following weeks, the internecine struggle worsened, and Gates relieved Arnold of all command. Arnold stayed with the army, however, and on October 7 when the second battle at Saratoga (Bemis Heights) began, he mounted a horse and dashed onto the field. It was his finest day. He was everywhere on the field, despite having no formal authority, and directed and rallied American troops to the right spots. Late in the day, he pressed home the final attacks that smashed Burgoyne's army, before falling himself with a new wound in the same damaged leg.

The wound kept Arnold from further battle, but by 1778 he was placed in military command of Philadelphia after the British withdrawal. He ran afoul of the civilian authorities almost at once, and there followed long and acrimonious feuding over his war profiteering, which eventually resulted in a formal reprimand from Washington. While in Philadelphia, Arnold, whose first wife had died while he was in Canada, courted and married the 18-year-old Margaret (Peggy) Shippen, the daughter of the loyalist former chief justice of Pennsylvania and a close acquaintance of British Major John André.

In May 1779, Arnold took the first fatal steps. With his wife's approval and connivance, he began his first communications with British headquarters in New York, offering to divulge military information and even to sell out a command. Working through intermediaries, Arnold carried on the treasonous correspondence for nearly a year and a half before the affair reached a climax. He never made his motivations clear (he refused in later life to speak to anyone of his treason), but it seems likely he not only failed to reconcile his constant bickering with American authority (he continued to feel mistreated and unappreciated) but he had also lost faith that independence was the proper course. And, he was doubtless moved by simple greed: he demanded £10,000 no matter what happened and double the amount if he could deliver a substantial body of troops and a key American post. He dealt with Major André, who passed on Sir Henry Clinton's messages. In September 1780, Arnold demanded a meeting with André. They eventually rendezvoused on the banks of the Hudson, near West Point, the command of which Arnold had recently assumed. A series of mischances prevented André's return to his ship, and the hapless British major was captured as he tried to return overland to British lines. He carried with him incriminating documents in Arnold's own hand, which a confused colonel sent to Washington, who was traveling to West Point at the time. However, the officer also sent a letter to Arnold detailing André's capture. In a series of events worthy of cheap fiction, the letter reached Arnold as he took breakfast at his house, where he was waiting for Washington to arrive later in the day. Pausing only to give Peggy the bad news, Arnold slipped out the door, found his barge and rowed to safety aboard a British sloop. Peggy threw a hysterical fit, hoping to divert suspicion from herself. Washington, with fears mounting by the hour, arrived just too late to catch Arnold. When the commander in chief received a letter from Arnold admitting the treason, the game was up: Arnold was secure behind British lines in New York; André was hung as a spy.

Arnold's subsequent career was—fittingly—anticlimactic and unsatisfactory. Although the British received him with formal honor and gave him a commission as brigadier, they never fully trusted him or treated him with the respect he felt was his, due. He led a force into Virginia, burning valuable tobacco and nearly capturing Governor Thomas Jefferson, and later he led a raid against New London, Connecticut that resulted in the rape and burning of the town. He was rewarded with a lump sum of more than £6,000, and Peggy, who joined him later, received a pension of £500 a year. They moved to England, but Arnold faced both public and private disdain. He turned to privateering and then business, locating for a time in Canada, but he was never able to repair his fortunes. He died deeply in debt in London. *Further reading:* Carl Van Doren, *The Secret History of the American Revolution* (New York, 1941); Willard M. Wallace, *Traitorous Hero* (New York, 1954); James T. Flexner, *The Traitor and the Spy* (New York, 1953); Wallace S. Randall, *Benedict Arnold: Patriot and Traitor* (1990).

ARNOLD, Jonathan (1741–1793) Legislator, delegate to Congress, surgeon

A native of Rhode Island, Arnold was a charter member of the Providence Grenadiers in 1774, although there is no record of military service during the Revolutionary War. He was more prominent as a member of the colonial assembly, where in 1776 he was one of the authors and supporters of a key statute that repealed the oath of allegiance to Great Britain. He was by profession and training a surgeon. During the war, Arnold organized a "revolutionary" hospital in Providence and served on the staff from 1776 until 1781. He was selected as a delegate to Congress from Rhode Island in 1782 and spearheaded Rhode Island's obstruction of the passage of a national impost under the Articles of Confederation, a move that frustrated efforts of the nationalists to stabilize the new country's public finances. He was also a strong supporter of the claims of renegade Vermont against New Hampshire and New York, with the result being a grant of land in Vermont from the governor. Arnold moved to the region, served as a county judge and a councillor, and died in St. Johnsbury, Vermont.

ARNOLD, Margaret (Peggy) Shippen (1760–1804) Wife of Benedict Arnold

For generations, most historians believed that Peggy Shippen Arnold was a more or less innocent bystander to her husband's treason. In this century, however, newly available evidence has shown she was privy to his secret negotiations with the British from the beginning and probably supported or even abetted his betrayal of his country. She was a lovely young girl of 18 when she married Arnold, whose first wife had died four years previously while he was fighting in Canada. Peggy, a belle of Philadelphia society, was the daughter of the former chief justice

of Pennsylvania, who was deposed because of his "neutralist" position (the authorities considered him a loyalist). During the British occupation of Philadelphia, Peggy had gotten much social attention from British officers, particularly Captain John André. She was more ardent than her father in her loyalism and was socially ambitious in addition, a combination that probably contributed to Arnold's decision to sell out to the British. On the fateful day that Arnold received advance warning of André's capture and his own immediate peril, Peggy went into a hysterical fit after her husband had stolen away just ahead of capture. She screamed, yelled and fainted, giving the impression of grief over his departure. It was probably all a fake to draw suspicion away from her complicity. Given the choice after André's execution, she went to her husband in British-held New York rather than return to her family in Philadelphia, and eventually, the Arnolds decamped for Great Britain.

Whatever her shortcomings from the American point of view, the dignity and strength of character she demonstrated during very difficult times in England provided much to admire. Her husband was spurned by the British, although she herself was popular among society. Peggy was granted a pension and Arnold received large sums for his act of betrayal, but there never seemed to be enough money to satisfy Arnold's tastes and he could not find employment in either the army or the East India Company. He finally turned to privateering, but only went deeper in debt. In 1785, he left Peggy and their children behind and set himself up as a merchant in New Brunswick, Canada. Before he sent for them, he fathered an illegitimate son there. While living in St. John, New Brunswick, Peggy was able to travel freely to Philadelphia and visit her family. Arnold's Canadian venture was a failure, however, and the family returned to England in 1792. Arnold's fortunes slipped even lower. He fought an inconclusive duel; ventured to the West Indies, where he was captured by the French but escaped; and took up privateering again. His health declined, and he died in 1801, leaving Peggy saddled with huge debts and a large family. She bravely faced up to her responsibilities and provided well for all of her own children as well as for Arnold's sons by his first marriage and for his maiden sister. By stringent economies she managed to settle all of Arnold's debts before her own painful death from cancer at age 44. *Further reading:* Milton Lomask, *Beauty and the Traitor* (New York, 1967).

ARNOLD, Peleg (1751–1820) Delegate to Congress, jurist

Closely associated throughout his life with his native town of Smithfield, Rhode Island, Arnold attended the College of Rhode Island (later to become Brown University) and became an attorney. During the Revolution he served in the Rhode Island legislature, but he rose to his greatest public prominence after the war. He served as a delegate to the Confederation Congress during the final terms of that body between 1787 and 1789. A tavern keeper on the side, Arnold was chief justice of Rhode Island from 1795 to 1809 and again from 1810 to 1812.

ASGILL, Charles (1762 or 1763–1823) British officer

Although Asgill later came to prominence in the British army, his place in the American war was as the near-victim of an unpleasant international episode. He was the son of a wealthy banker and baronet and had joined the army as an ensign in 1778. He was not ordered to America until early in 1781, when he joined Lord Cornwallis. At the defeat at Yorktown, Asgill was part of the surrender, and he was confined afterward under the same terms as the other British officers. His fate, however, became entwined with the bitter, lawless escapades of the Associated Loyalists of New York and New Jersey.

The Associated Loyalists had been organized by William Franklin, Benjamin Franklin's illegitimate, loyalist son and former royal governor, to give some official cloak to the actions and interests of Tories in and around New York, a region infested throughout the war with the most ruthless brigandage and murder. In April 1782, a band of Associated Loyalists asked for and got custody of a captured American partisan, Captain Joshua Huddy, ostensibly to exchange him for one of their own. Instead, they hung Huddy without trial and affixed a placard to his body proclaiming his death as vengeance.

When he learned of the murder, George Washington was outraged and demanded that the British commander, Sir Henry Clinton, turn over the officer responsible. Clinton declined but, unhappy himself with the affair, had the officer court-martialed. When the offender was freed by the court-martial, Washington directed that an officer be selected from among the British prisoners and executed in retaliation. Unfortunately, the job was bungled. Asgill was chosen, but he was covered under the terms of Cornwallis' surrender. His death would have contravened the accord and been seen as a completely dishonorable act—something Washington was particularly sensitive to. Yet, Washington was caught. He had referred the matter to Congress, which insisted on the young man's execution. In desperation, Lady Asgill, the young officer's mother, appealed to the French minister Vergennes, on the grounds that the French had also signed the surrender documents. Louis XVI and Queen Marie Antoinette learned of the affair and interceded on Asgill's behalf with Washington. The commander in chief was then able to gracefully release Asgill, who spent the rest of his life in military service in Europe and Ireland. He eventually rose to the rank of full general. *Further reading:* Katherine Mayo, *General Washington's Dilemma* (New York, 1938).

ASHE, John (1720–1781) Militia officer

As commander of North Carolina militia, Ashe directed a miserably incompetent battle at Briar Creek, Georgia in 1779 that resulted in his court-martial. He was born in North Carolina and was prominent in colonial politics before the Revolution, having served as speaker of the colonial assembly from 1762 to 1765. He was active in the patriot cause during the mid-1770s as a member of the North Carolina Committee of Safety and the Provincial Congress. At the outbreak of hostilities, he took a commission as colonel of the state militia and was a brigadier general by early 1779. In mid-February of that year, at the direction of General Benjamin Lincoln, Ashe marched 1,400 North Carolina militiamen across the Savannah River into Georgia and encamped in a swampy area near Briar Creek. The British commander at Savannah, General Augustine Prevost, dispatched two columns to attack the Americans. Ashe learned of the approach of the opposition well ahead of time, but he took almost no precautions and allowed his entire force to be pinned against the swamp. A demolished bridge over the creek would have provided a safety valve, but Ashe had delayed repairs. The British struck the North Carolinians hard, and most of the militiamen fled the scene. Many of them drowned in the creek while trying to escape. The victory secured British control over Georgia, and Ashe was called to face a court-martial, which found him guilty of failing to prepare adequately.

ASHE, John Baptista (1748–1802) Delegate to Congress, militia officer, state official

The son of Samuel Ashe, the nephew of General John Ashe, and the grandson of a previous John Baptista Ashe, this Ashe carried on the family tradition of prominence in the affairs of 18th-century North Carolina. He was born at Rocky Point and was educated at home, becoming a planter. He rallied to the patriot cause in North Carolina in 1776 as a captain of state troops. By 1781, he was a colonel (or lieutenant colonel; accounts vary) serving under Thomas Sumter, as an officer of militia. He fought at the battle of Eutaw Springs, and he probably was part of the North Carolina militia that at first performed nobly during the engagement but then broke during the latter stages of the fight and gave the British yet another victory over Nathanael Greene. Following the war, Ashe became one of his state's most active politicians and officeholders. He sat in the house of commons from 1784 to 1786, acting as speaker during the latter year. He was sent as a delegate to the Confederation Congress in 1787, but he served only a short while before resigning in November. Ashe was chairman of the North Carolina convention on the new federal constitution and a state senator in 1789. He was then elected as a representative to the first two U.S. Congresses, serving from 1790 to 1793. He took a seat in the state senate again in 1795. He was elected governor of North Carolina in 1802 but died in November before his inauguration.

ASHE, Samuel (1725–1813) State official, jurist

The son of the first John Baptista Ashe (a colonial official), the brother of General John Ashe, and the father of the second John Baptista Ashe, Samuel was himself a central figure in North Carolina government. He was born at Rocky Point, but after his mother's death he was taken to the Cape Fear region and raised by an uncle. He became an attorney and was one of the more respectable members of his profession to be warmly anti-British from the early days of agitation against the royal government in the colony. Ashe was instrumental in forming the North Carolina Council of Safety in 1774 and served as chairman in 1776. He helped devise the first state constitution and served as first speaker of the new state senate. He was elected as presiding judge of the patriot North Carolina Supreme Court in late 1776 and served in that office for nearly 20 years, until 1795. Ashe was then elected governor of the state and was chief executive until 1798.

ASPINWALL, William (1743–1823) Physician

Born in Brookline, Massachusetts, Aspinwall graduated from Harvard in 1764 and was an established physician by the time of the Revolution. He was reputed to have been among the minutemen who fought the battle of Lexington in 1775, and thereafter joined the Continental Army around Boston as a brigade surgeon. He became deputy director of an army hospital at Jamaica Plain, Massachusetts, in 1776 and continued at that post until 1781. After the Revolutionary War, he set up his practice again in Brookline, where he founded a hospital for smallpox inoculation, and he remained there the rest of his long life. Aspinwall also served in the Massachusetts General Court and on the Governor's Council.

ATHERTON, Joshua (1737–1809) Loyalist attorney

Atherton was born in Worcester County, Massachusetts and graduated from Harvard in 1762. He began his legal career in Worcester, but he moved in 1765 after his marriage to southern New Hampshire, where his practice prospered, and he was appointed register of probate for Hillsborough County. He was a conservative and objected to the idea of separation from Great Britain, but his was an unpopular belief in the intensely patriotic region. He refused to join the revolutionary cause and was jailed by the Sons of Liberty in 1777. Two years later, he relented and took an oath of allegiance to the new state of New Hampshire. His loyalism did him little harm after the war, and he came to be an important public figure, serving in two New Hampshire constitutional conventions and maintaining a large and prosperous legal practice. He was an early antislavery advocate and argued strongly against the slave trade during the state convention to ratify the federal constitution. He later served in the state senate and as state attorney general.

ATKINS, Josiah (1755?–1781) Continental soldier

Atkins was a private soldier, a native of Waterbury, Connecticut, who left a diary of his service in the 5th Connecticut Regiment, which he joined in April 1781. He traveled south with his unit to

Virginia as part of the army that was to attack Lord Cornwallis, and his diary makes it clear that he detested military life, both the physical hardships and the spiritual erosion of war. In the fall of 1781, however, he became a surgeon's assistant and developed considerable devotion to his duties as a healer. Unfortunately, he fell ill, perhaps of a fever caught in the course of dealing with the sick and wounded, and he died in October at a hospital in Hanover, Virginia. *Further reading: The Diary of Josiah Atkins*, Steven E. Kagel, ed. (reprint, New York, 1975).

ATKINSON, Theodore (1697–1779) Loyalist jurist Born in New Castle, New Hampshire, Atkinson was educated at Harvard and became a prominent jurist and officeholder in his native colony long before the Revolution. He was named secretary of New Hampshire in 1741 and chief justice in 1754. In the latter year, he led the New Hampshire delegation to the Albany Congress, which had been convened to deal with Indian problems and resulted in the presentation of a plan of union for the British-American colonies. Atkinson's diary provides one of the principal accounts of the Congress. Although he was an old man and remained relatively passive during the War for Independence, Atkinson's loyalties remained with the crown. He refused in 1775 to give the revolutionary Provincial Congress the records of his office as secretary. *Further reading:* B. McAnear, ed., ''Personal Accounts of the Albany Congress,'' *Missouri Valley Historical Review* 39 (March 1953), 727–46.

ATLEE, Samuel 1739–1786 Continental officer, delegate to Congress Although born in New Jersey, Atlee lived most of his life in Pennsylvania—he moved to Lancaster with his mother at age six. He abandoned law studies to join the army during the French and Indian War and saw extensive action, rising to captain. Thus, he was a seasoned and experienced officer when commissioned as colonel of the Pennsylvania Line at the outbreak of the Revolution. He commanded a musket battalion at the battle of Long Island in August 1776, and his troops were placed in a detached position on the left of Lord Stirling's force. Despite having never been in battle and facing veteran British regulars, Atlee's battalion gave an extremely good account of itself. Unfortunately, the bulk of the British army

had slipped around the American positions and fell on Atlee from behind. The battalion was smashed and Atlee captured. He spent more than a year as a prisoner in New York until he was exchanged in October 1777. He was elected to Congress as a delegate from Pennsylvania and served from 1778 until 1782. He also served in the state assembly and was elected as supreme executive councillor for Lancaster County in 1783. He died in Philadelphia.

ATTUCKS, Crispus (c. 1723–1770) Patriot Nothing in life so brought fame to Attucks as his death as a martyr of the Boston Massacre. A very large man for his day and age, topping six feet and heavily built, Attucks was apparently born near Framingham, Massachusetts, likely of mixed African and Indian parentage, and ran away from slavery about 1750 to the life of a free sailor. On March 5, 1770 he was living in Boston under the name Michael Johnson and took leadership of a mob that confronted a small detachment of British soldiers at the Custom House. By contemporary accounts he wielded a cordwood club and stood at the head of the assembly, berating the redcoats. He grabbed a bayonet, turned it aside and struck at a soldier. The frightened troops opened fire, and Attucks was killed instantly by two musket balls in the chest. Anti-British Bostonians staged an elaborate funeral for Attucks and the other three Bostonians killed in the Massacre. During the trial of the British soldiers, defense lawyer John Adams focused on the role of Attucks in provoking the attack, just as the prosecution made him out to be a hero. Attucks' name has since come to be a symbol of courage in the face of oppression, especially among black Americans, and a monument to him stands on Boston Common. *Further reading:* Hiller B. Zobel, *The Boston Massacre* (New York, 1970).

AUCHMUTHY, Robert (d. 1788) Loyalist official, lawyer A resident of Roxbury, Massachusetts, Auchmuthy was one of the most prominent attorneys of Boston during the tumultuous years preceding the Revolution. He held office beginning in 1767 as a judge of the infamous Vice-Admiralty Court (a royal court beyond local influence or contest) and was unwavering in his support of the royal cause in Massachusetts. Along with John Adams, he defended Captain Thomas Preston in the trial after the Boston Massacre in 1770. Adams

AMERICANS!
BEAR IN REMEMBRANCE
The HORRID MASSACRE!
Perpetrated in King-ſtreet, Boston,
New-England,
On the Evening of March the Fifth, 1770.
When FIVE of your fellow countrymen,
GRAY, MAVERICK, CALDWELL, ATTUCKS,
and CARR,
Lay wallowing in their Gore!
Being baſely, and moſt inhumanly
MURDERED!
And SIX others badly WOUNDED!
By a Party of the XXIXth Regiment,
Under the command of Capt. Tho. Preſton.
REMEMBER!
That Two of the Murderers
Were convicted of MANSLAUGHTER!
By a Jury, of whom I ſhall ſay
NOTHING,
Branded in the hand!
And diſmiſſed,
The others were ACQUITTED,
And their Captain PENSIONED!
Alſo,
BEAR IN REMEMBRANCE
That on the 22d Day of February, 1770
The infamous
EBENEZER RICHARDSON, Informer,
And tool to Miniſterial hirelings,
Moſt barbarouſly
MURDERED
CHRISTOPHER SEIDER,
An innocent youth!
Of which crime he was found guilty
By his Country
On Friday April 20th, 1770;
But remained Unſentenced
On Saturday the 22d Day of February, 1772.
When the GRAND INQUEST
For Suffolk county,
Were informed, at requeſt,
By the Judges of the Superior Court,
That EBENEZER RICHARDSON'S Caſe
Then lay before his MAJESTY.
Therefore ſaid Richardſon
This day, MARCH FIFTH! 1772,
Remains UNHANGED!!!
Let THESE things be told to Poſterity!
And handed down
From Generation to Generation,
'Till Time ſhall be no more!
Forever may AMERICA be preſerved,
From weak and wicked monarchs,
Tyrannical Miniſters,
Abandoned Governors,
Their Underlings and Hirelings!
And may the
Machinations of artful, deſigning wretches,
Who would ENSLAVE THIS People,
Come to an end,
Let their NAMES and MEMORIES
Be buried in eternal oblivion,
And the PRESS,
For a SCOURGE to Tyrannical Rulers,
Remain FREE.

A broadside reporting the Boston Massacre. The list of victims includes the name of Crispus Attucks.

had a low opinion of Auchmuthy's legal arguments, however, calling them "fluent reiterations and reiterating fluency." Auchmuthy's letters to friends in England were included among the documents sent to Massachusetts for publication by Benjamin Franklin in 1773 (along with the more famous letters of Thomas Hutchinson), and their contents damned Auchmuthy even further in the eyes of the patriots. He quartered British troops in his Roxbury house in 1775. With the British evacuation of the city the following year, Auchmuthy emigrated to England, where the government continued his vice-admiralty salary until the end of the war and awarded him a pension thereafter.

AUCHMUTY, Samuel (c. 1758–1822) American loyalist, British general   Auchmuty was a soldier of outstanding ability, who managed to rise in the British army despite beginnings as an obscure and impoverished colonial. He was born in New York, the son of the Reverend Samuel A. Auchmuty, rector of a New York City Episcopal church. At the coming of the Revolution, the entire family declared at once for the crown, and subsequently, they were dispossessed of property and place. As a form of compensation, the British government granted young Samuel a commission as ensign and then lieutenant in the 45th Regiment without purchase. He served during the American War and moved to England at the conclusion of hostilities. Still impecunious and lacking prospects in British society, Auchmuty took a military post in India, where his abilities won him higher rank and the support of powerful patrons such as Lord Cornwallis. He then embarked on a series of military adventures around the globe during Britain's imperial wars, and his exploits in Egypt and South America made him a popular hero. He capped his career in 1811 by taking Mauritius from the Dutch. When he died from injuries suffered in a riding accident in Dublin in 1822, he was a lieutenant general and a Knight of the Bath.

AUCKLAND, Lord. See EDEN, William.

AUSTIN, Jonathan Loring (1748–1826) Soldier, official   Austin was born in Boston and graduated from Harvard 10 years before the beginning of the Revolution. He was a major in the New Hampshire volunteer militia regiment that was formed four days after the battles at Lexington and Concord and was taken into the Continental Army as the 1st New Hampshire in June 1775. He apparently served only a few months. Austin became secretary to the Massachusetts Board of War before the end of the year, and his role in the Revolution thereafter was as a civilian. In 1777, he was dispatched to Paris with the news of General John Burgoyne's surrender, and he remained there as one of Benjamin Franklin's private secretaries until 1779. After the war, he was elected to the state senate and the house of representatives. He also served terms as secretary and treasurer of Massachusetts after the turn of the century.

B

BACHE, Richard (1737–1811) Postmaster general, businessman Born the youngest of 18 children in the West Riding of England, Bache followed his elder brother, Theophylact, to New York in 1765. The brothers formed a mercantile partnership that flourished in the West Indian and Newfoundland trade. Richard, however, moved to Philadelphia and made a fortunate liaison when he married Benjamin Franklin's daughter, Sarah, in 1767. Not only did his business interests make him a rich man, particularly through his issuance of private insurance policies, but Franklin's favor, combined with revolutionary inclinations, gave Bache several important offices. He was appointed by his father-in-law successively as secretary, comptroller and register of Pennsylvania. At the outbreak of the Revolutionary War, Bache was chairman of the Republican Society of Philadelphia, had been a member of the Committee on Non-Importation, and was named to the Board of War. In late 1776, he succeeded Franklin as postmaster general, holding the position until 1782. Following the Revolution, he returned to business until his retirement in 1793.

BACKUS, Isaac (1724–1806) Clergyman, historian An itinerant preacher and advocate of religious freedom in America, Backus was born in Connecticut, but he was most closely associated with the Baptists of Massachusetts. He was originally ordained as a member of one of the New Light factions of the Congregationalists in Middleborough, Massachusetts, but he converted to the Baptist sect in 1756 in a dispute with the New Lights over the proper form of baptism. Making his base in Middleborough, Backus traveled widely in the northern colonies, preaching and starting new congregations all over New England. He was a strong proponent of religious freedom and resisted the movement to name the Congregationalists as the established church in Massachusetts. In 1774, he addressed the first Continental Congress on behalf of religious liberty. After the Revolution, Backus helped organize new Baptist congregations in Virginia. He was also active with the pen and wrote a three-volume *History of New England with Particular Reference to the Denomination called Baptists*, publishing the first volume during the war in 1777 and the final one in 1796.

BACON, John (1738–1820) State official, clergyman A native of Connecticut and graduate of Princeton, Bacon was pastor of the Old South Church in Boston during the four years immediately preceding the Revolution. During the war, he was a member of the Massachusetts Committee of Correspondence, Inspection, and Safety, and he sat in the state constitutional convention in 1779 and 1780. He was also a long-time delegate to the state assembly, serving six terms between 1780 and 1793. In alternate years, he sat in the state senate. In 1801, Bacon was elected to the U.S. House of Representatives from Massachusetts, and he eventually became chief justice of the state supreme court.

BADGE, Thomas. American soldier, British spy

By vocation a soap maker and chandler, Badge was a resident of Philadelphia and a patriot during the first months of the Revolution, serving in the American army as a private soldier. In 1777, however, he was converted to the British side because he thought, in his words, "Britain would conquer." Using his cover as a tradesman, he gathered intelligence for the British and helped guide General Howe's army from the Head of Elk to Brandywine, during its advance on Philadelphia.

BAILEY, Anna Warner (1758–1851) Patriot heroine

Orphaned in childhood, Bailey lived with her uncle, Edward Mills, in Groton, Connecticut. In September 1781, the traitor Benedict Arnold led a British raid on New London and Groton. While most of the patriot forces put up only a feeble resistance, the defenders of Fort Griswold at Groton Heights, Edward Mills among them, fought hard. The British and loyalists under Arnold subdued the fort only after a vicious battle. Many of the American defenders were bayoneted after surrender. Bailey went to the scene of the battle and carried home her mortally wounded uncle, a feat that passed into local legend and earned her the nickname "Mother Bailey."

BAILEY, Francis (c. 1735–1815) Printer, journalist, soldier

Although trained in youth as a carpenter, Bailey became a printer in his native Lancaster County, Pennsylvania. By the early 1770s, he was publisher of a series of almanacs, and he naturally moved into printing documents of the Revolution, including the fourth edition of Tom Paine's *Common Sense.* He also published periodicals in German for the German-speaking population of Pennsylvania. He was an ardent patriot and served at Valley Forge in 1776 with the Pennsylvania troops. In 1778, Bailey became joint publisher of the *United States Magazine* in Philadelphia and began to solicit the custom of Congress. He prepared a large edition of the constitutions of the states, including also the Declaration of Independence and texts of the French treaties, in 1780. He eventually became the official printer for Congress and the state of Pennsylvania. In 1781, he published several volumes of his own

writing as well as the poetry of Philip Freneau. Bailey is credited with first giving George Washington the name "The Father of His Country" in a caption to a portrait published in a German-language almanac in 1779.

BALCARRES, Alexander Lindsay, Earl of (1752–1825)

The Earl of Balcarres was a tough, aristocratic British officer who probably deserved better than he got during the Revolution. He had entered service with the purchase of an ensignship in the 53rd Regiment of Foot at age 15 and had bought his way to a majority by 1776, when he was ordered to Canada. He was given command of the light infantry wing of General John Burgoyne's army with 10 companies drawn from several regiments. Because the light infantry was a key part of the force, Balcarres and his troops saw much action during the invasion campaign of 1777. He was wounded slightly at the assault on Fort Ticonderoga and again at Hubbardton. The steadfast fighting of his light infantry did much to stave off total disaster at the battle of Freeman's Farm (First Saratoga), and at the subsequent battle at Bemis Heights (Second Saratoga) he commanded the most crucial point in Burgoyne's entrenchments, withstanding Arnold's furious assaults and withdrawing only after Arnold managed to flank the position. Following Burgoyne's surrender, Balcarres was excluded from the Convention and was supposed to have been exchanged in New York, but the arrangements misfired, and he was not freed until two years had passed. His later career was filled with sinecures and promotions. He reached the rank of major general by 1793, and after commanding the forces on Jersey, was appointed governor of Jamaica. He was made a full general in 1803. *Further reading:* Alexander Crawford, *Lives of the Lindsays . . .* (London, 1849).

BALDWIN, Abraham (1754–1807) Statesman, army chaplain, educator

An outstanding legislator and man of many parts during his career, Baldwin was born the son of a blacksmith in North Guilford, Connecticut. Despite the cares of many children from two marriages, the elder Baldwin saw to it that his male children received a good education (Abraham's half-brother, Henry, became a congressman and associate justice of the U.S. Supreme Court), and moved to New Haven in 1768 so that

Abraham could attend Yale. For several years after his graduation, Baldwin flirted with the profession of preaching. He was engaged as a tutor by Yale, which was primarily a school to produce clergy, and was licensed to preach in 1775. He was still tutoring when the British raided New Haven in 1777 and chased Yale students and teachers to Glastonbury.

During the next year, Baldwin accepted an appointment from Congress as chaplain to the Continental Army and was attached to the 2nd Connecticut Brigade as part of Washington's main force. He traveled with the troops in Connecticut, New York and New Jersey and was stationed at winter quarters in Morristown in 1779–80. The chaplain's appointment carried with it the pay of a colonel, but no military rank. His chief duties were to preach, visit the sick and wounded, officiate at weddings and funerals, keep up morale and recruit. Baldwin was asked to prepare but failed to deliver a sermon at the execution of the British spy Major John André, and he performed his most prominent service in a patriotic harangue to mutinous troops of the Connecticut Line in May 1782. Toward the end of his chaplaincy, he found time to study law and was licensed to practice in 1783.

Following the War for Independence, Baldwin made a decisive and drastic change in his life. He spurned several offers to teach at Yale and left New England for the southernmost state, Georgia, where he soon became a major figure in politics and public life. He was elected to the Georgia Assembly in 1784 and almost immediately was chosen as one of the state's representatives to the Confederation Congress. While still a member of the state legislature, Baldwin wrote the charter for the University of Georgia (of which he is known as the founder) and helped secure its passage. The university was endowed with public lands by the Assembly but failed to become a reality until the turn of the 19th century. Baldwin was named the first president, but since the school existed only on paper, it was a relatively empty honor.

More substantial was Baldwin's place as a national legislator. He was one of the four Georgia delegates to the Constitutional Convention of 1787, made significant contributions to the proceedings, and signed the Constitution on behalf of his adopted state. He served continuously in Congress from 1785 until his death in 1807 and was in his day an extremely prominent figure in national affairs. He often presided over the new federal Congress and was especially regarded for his careful work in committee. In 1799, Baldwin was appointed to the U.S. Senate, and he was elected president pro tem in 1801. On his death at age 52 he was given a state funeral in Washington, D.C. *Further reading:* E. Merton Coulter, *Abraham Baldwin: Patriot, Educator, and Founding Father* (Arlington, Va., 1987).

BALDWIN, Jeduthan (1732–1788) Continental officer Possibly related to Loammi Baldwin, Jeduthan was a native of Woburn, Massachusetts and was a skilled practical engineer. He commanded a company of troops during the French and Indian War and served in the Massachusetts Provincial Congress in 1774. He put his engineering abilities to work during the siege of Boston, keeping a valuable journal as well, and was appointed as a captain assistant engineer to the Continental Army in March 1776. Later promoted to colonel, he assisted in fortifying New York City. In 1777 he labored with Tadeusz Kosciuszko on the works at Fort Ticonderoga, and in 1779 he helped construct fortifications for West Point. He resigned from the army in April 1782. *Further reading: Revolutionary Journal,* Thomas J. Baldwin, ed. (Bangor, Me., 1906).

BALDWIN, Loammi (1740–1807) Continental officer, engineer Baldwin was born in Woburn, Massachusetts and trained as an apprentice cabinetmaker. He turned, however, to surveying and eventually became a civil engineer. During his youth, he walked the considerable distance to Harvard on a regular basis to attend lectures in mathematics and physics. He was an established civil engineer as well as a major of militia when his company rallied to meet the British expedition advancing on Concord in April 1774. The following month, Baldwin was commissioned lieutenant colonel in the 38th Regiment, and he took over command as colonel during the summer when the former commander was ousted. The 38th was among the force that occupied Boston after the British evacuation. When the Continental Army was reorganized in early 1776, Baldwin's unit was increased to 10 companies and redesignated the 26th. Baldwin commanded the regiment throughout the New York campaign and the retreat across New Jersey and at the battle of Trenton. Within a week of helping to destroy the German mercenaries, Baldwin was forced to resign for reasons of ill health. He then returned to Massachusetts and the practice of engineering. He held several public offices, serving as high sheriff of Middlesex County and in the Massachusetts General Court. As a businessman, he was one of the chief promoters and builders of the 10-year Middlesex Canal project to connect the Charles and Merrimac rivers. For all his other accomplishments, he is best remembered for stumbling onto a seedling apple tree while surveying for the canal. He liked the fruit, took cuttings for grafting to his own stock, and gave the world the Baldwin apple.

BALFOUR, Nisbet (1743–1832) British officer

Born in Scotland, Balfour was the tail end of a noble Scots family. He entered the army in 1761 and was a captain by the outbreak of the American War. At Bunker Hill he was severely wounded during the British assault, but he recovered and served in the campaigns at Long Island and Brooklyn. In August 1776, he was sent home with dispatches and rewarded with a brevet promotion to major. On returning to America, he accompanied the force that occupied Philadelphia, became a close friend of both Lord Cornwallis and Lord Rawdon, and was promoted to lieutenant colonel in the 23rd Regiment. In 1778, he was with Cornwallis in the expedition against Charleston and was subsequently named commander at the British post at Ninety-Six, South Carolina, where he helped raise loyalist troops to support Cornwallis' southern campaign. In the following year, Balfour was given command of the captured city of Charleston and acquired an evil reputation among patriots for his harsh measures, including the execution of American colonel Isaac Hayne without trial. Following the American War, he received numerous honors, including advance in rank and appointment as an aide-de-camp to the king. He also served as one of the commissioners to award compensation to American loyalists. He was reemployed by the army during the Anglo-French wars of the 1790s with the rank of major general in command of a brigade. As was typical of British officers of his experience, he continued to receive sinecures and rank, and when he died he was a full general, the sixth ranking on the British army list.

BANCROFT, Edward (1744–1820) British spy, scientist, writer

Bancroft was one of the most successful penetration agents ever to worm his way into the center of American diplomacy, although the dimensions of his perfidy were not finally established until nearly 150 years after the fact. He was born in Westfield, Massachusetts, and after indifferent education as a youth ran away to the sea. He washed up in Guiana, South America, where he apprenticed himself to a physician and began independent study of native plants, especially the natural dyes and poisons used by the Indians. He moved to England and began to write on both botany and politics. In 1769, he published an *Essay on the Natural History of Guiana* and *Remarks on the Review of the Controversy between Great Britain and Her Colonies*. His antireligious novel, *Charles Wentworth*, appeared the following year.

While a London resident, Bancroft met and cultivated Benjamin Franklin. When the Continental Congress dispatched Silas Deane to France as the first American diplomat abroad, Franklin brought Bancroft and Deane together. Posing as a trusted American ally and aide, Bancroft was in reality deeply in the pay of William Eden, the British under secretary of state who ran a diplomatic espionage bureau throughout the war.

Eventually, Bancroft became the principal secretary to the American commissioners in France. There is strong evidence that he suborned Deane through financial peculations, and Franklin apparently had only faint suspicions of Bancroft's true role, having earlier paid Bancroft to supposedly act as an American spy. Only the naturally contrary Arthur Lee, the Virginia congressman, seems to have had a clear and long-lasting hostility toward Bancroft. The spy drew a salary from the Americans and as their secretary had access to all correspondence and papers and much conversation. All of this he passed almost immediately to the British. From 1776 onward he received large sums for his spying efforts, including a lifetime pension of £500 a year for past service plus an additional £500 for current activities. In addition, Bancroft used his inside knowledge of events in America to play the British stock market, and he realized large sums on his own. No sooner had the commissioners prepared dispatches and reports than Bancroft spirited them across the Channel to his British masters, where they often reached the British Cabinet before arriving in the hands of Congress. Bancroft later boasted that he had provided the British with the full terms of the two

Franco-American alliance treaties of 1778 within 48 hours. In 1781, Bancroft intercepted letters from Deane, which the British then published (pretending they had been captured), finally destroying Deane's character and standing. One historian has suggested that Bancroft had controlled and manipulated Deane from the beginning and may even, using his knowledge of rare poisons, have been responsible for Deane's suspicious death. Bancroft continued undetected as a spy in Paris throughout the negotiations for the peace. The extent of his activities was finally revealed in a British document that came to light in the 19th century.

Following the conclusion of the war, Bancroft returned to Britain and became successful in business as a result of his scientific experiments when he patented a process for deriving a commercial dye from bark. He became a fellow of the Royal Society and a member of the Royal College of Physicians, and he never returned to America, ending his days as a respected member of the British scientific community. *Further reading:* Julian Boyd, "Silas Deane: Death by a Kindly Teacher of Treason," *William and Mary Quarterly* 16 (April, July, October, 1959); Samuel F. Bemis, "The British Secret Service and the Franco-American Alliance," *American Historical Review* 29 (April 1924).

BANISTER, John (1734–1788) Militia officer, delegate to Congress

Banister was born in Virginia and studied in England, first at a private school in Wakefield and then law at the Temple in London. Returning to America, he set up a law practice in Petersburg, Virginia and participated actively in revolutionary politics. He was a member of the Virginia Assembly, the conventions in 1775 and 1776, and the house of delegates. In 1778, he was sent as a delegate to the Continental Congress and helped write the Articles of Confederation. He then took up duty as a lieutenant colonel in the Virginia militia, fighting the British during their invasion of the state in 1781.

BANKS, John. Continental soldier

Banks was one of the few black soldiers allowed to serve in the cavalry. He was a free black resident of Goochland County, Virginia and joined Colonel Theodoric Bland's 1st Regiment of Continental Light Dragoons, a unit organized by the Virginia state government in 1776 and which served as part of the Continental cavalry corps under Casimir Pulaski. Most of the understrength unit was comprised of "gentlemen volunteers."

BANKSON, Jacob. American spy

Like many of the incidental spies used by the American high command during the war in the middle states (New York, New Jersey, Pennsylvania, Maryland and Delaware), Bankson remains a relatively shadowy figure. He is reputed to have been a former marine officer who gathered military intelligence in Philadelphia during its occupation by the British in 1778. George Washington is said to have received his reports directly.

BARBE-MARBOIS, François, Marquis de (1745–1837) French diplomat

Although his career has not received much notice by American historians, Barbe-Marbois played an important role in Franco-American relations for a half century. His own career was a remarkable narrative of longevity in the face of the most severe disruptions imaginable: he served as a French diplomat and government official from the reign of Louis XV until after the seizure of power by Louis Philippe, a span during which France moved from the ancien régime through revolution and empire and into the modern era.

Barbe-Marbois was born in Metz and trained in local Jesuit schools until he left for Paris and education in the law. In 1768, he became a junior diplomat, serving most notably in Saxony and Bavaria. In 1775, he was named secretary to Anne-César de la Luzerne, who had just been appointed as the second French minister to America. Barbe-Marbois traveled to the New World with Luzerne and toured Boston before settling into business at Philadelphia. He worked closely with the minister, often taking charge when Luzerne traveled to other states. Barbe-Marbois was much taken with America and Americans and formed many close relationships with the leading political figures of the day. Like many Frenchmen, he was much smitten with George Washington. Barbe-Marbois was named consul in 1781 and two years later was promoted to consul general. When Luzerne returned to France in 1784, Barbe-Marbois was appointed French chargé d'affaires in America. He cemented his American connections in the same year by marrying Elizabeth Moore, the daughter of William Moore, who had served as president of the Executive Council of Pennsylvania.

Barbe-Marbois's subsequent career showed extraordinary footwork. He left America in 1791 to become indendant in St. Dominique, but he was chased out by rebellious planters in 1798 and returned to revolutionary France. He survived the Terror to become mayor of Metz and then a member of the national legislature. He ran afoul of the Directory and was deported to Guiana for two years, but he returned to serve Bonaparte. He reentered American history in 1803 when he conducted negotiations on the French side for the sale of the Louisiana Purchase. At Napoleon's fall, Barbe-Marbois assisted in the restoration of the Bourbon monarchy and was rewarded with elevation to a peerage. He continued in public office until 1834 through several more major changes of government. He was also a prolific writer and produced several books during his lifetime, including a highly imaginative account of Benedict Arnold's treason. *Further reading:* Elijah W. Lyon, *The Man Who Sold Louisiana* (Norman, Okla., 1942).

BARBER, Francis (1751–1783) Continental officer

Barber survived many of the important battles of the Revolution, only to die in an accident after the fighting was over. He was born in Princeton, New Jersey and was the head of an academy in Elizabethtown after his graduation from Princeton College in 1767. In 1776, he was commissioned as a major in the original 3rd New Jersey Regiment of the Continental Line. He fought at Princeton in 1777 and subsequently at the battles of Germantown and Brandywine. During the winter of 1777, he acted as an assistant to von Steuben at Valley Forge. Barber was wounded at the battle of Monmouth the following summer. He transferred as a lieutenant colonel to the 1st New Jersey in 1781 and helped deal with the mutiny of that regiment. Later in the year, he took command of the third battalion of the light infantry division organized under Lafayette to fight in Virginia, and he commanded the unit at the battle of Green Spring and at the siege of Yorktown. During 1783, in the waning months of the Revolution, Barber was promoted to colonel and placed in command of the 2nd New Jersey, but a month after taking up his new post at Newburgh, New York he was killed by a falling tree.

BARCLAY, Thomas (1753–1830) Loyalist officer, British diplomat

The son of the rector of Trinity Church, Barclay was born in New York City, was educated at King's College (now Columbia) and studied law in the office of John Jay. He was the firmest of loyalists, never wavering in his allegiance to Great Britain. His property was confiscated in one of the earliest such acts against loyalists in New York. He joined the Loyal American regiment as a captain, helped capture Forts Clinton and Montgomery and finished the war as a major. He moved with his family (he was married to one of the New York De Lanceys) to Nova Scotia when the hostilities ended, and there he returned to prominence as a member of assembly and as adjutant general of the militia. From 1796 until shortly before his death, he was employed by the British government in a series of important diplomatic posts in North America. He was one of the British commissioners under the terms of Jay's Treaty of 1794, which settled lingering problems left over from the Treaty of Paris, and was consul general for the eastern and northern states, the latter post bringing him back to his previous home in New York in the course of duty.

Joshua Barney

BARNEY, Joshua (1759–1818) American naval officer, privateer

Although born on a farm near Baltimore, Barney felt the tug of the sea early and spent most of his life adventuring in ships. He sailed aboard a bay schooner at age 11 and to England on a merchant brig two years later. Barney was a 15-year-old first mate of a merchantman when the captain (his brother-in-law) died in mid-Atlantic. Barney took over command of the ship and eventually brought a cargo home to the owners in October 1775. Hearing the news of the Revolution, he shipped as a mate aboard the sloop *Hornet*, one of the vessels of Esek Hopkins' flotilla commissioned by Congress. After Hopkins' expedition to the Bahamas, Barney's ship was damaged in a storm, and he transferred to the *Wasp*. In 1776, he was appointed a lieutenant in the U.S. Navy. During a voyage to St. Eustatius aboard the *Andrea Doria*, Barney was detached as prizemaster for a captured brig. He was himself captured by a British ship, although he was soon exchanged. As first lieutenant of the frigate *Virginia*, he was again captured by the British and for a time was confined to a prison hulk in New York Harbor. After another exchange, he took command of a merchant ship, and he was again captured and released. He spent three years in the service of a French privateer before returning to America in 1781 as lieutenant of the *Saratoga*. His luck ran true, and he was once more captured while sailing a prize and lodged in the Old Mill Prison at Plymouth, England. He managed a daring escape and after more adventures returned home to find the only berth available was with the Pennsylvania state navy as commander of a converted merchantman, the *Hyder Ally*. He sailed down the Delaware in convoy with eight merchant vessels to be greeted by two British warships and three privateers near Cape May. By skill, luck and subterfuge, Barney managed to close with and capture the strongest British ship, the *General Monk*.

In 1794, Barney turned down a captain's com-

Louis, Comte de Barras

mission in the reinstituted U.S. Navy in a dispute over rank and moved to France, where he served six years in the French Navy. During the War of 1812, he was highly successful as a privateer. Accepting a U.S. Navy commission in 1814, he tried to defend Chesapeake Bay with an inferior force and was badly wounded at the land battle at Baldensburg. *Further reading:* Ralph D. Paine, *Joshua Barney: A Forgotten Hero of the Blue Water* (New York, 1924).

BARNWELL, Robert (1761–1814) Delegate to Congress, officer, legislator   Born in Beaufort, South Carolina, Barnwell volunteered for duty in the Revolution at age 16, probably in a militia unit. He fought during the siege of Charleston in 1780 as a lieutenant and was captured with the fall of the city in May. Barnwell was held for a year aboard a British prison ship but was exchanged in 1781. He was a delegate from South Carolina to the final Confederation Congress in 1788–89 and was a representative to the new U.S. Congress from 1791 to 1793. During the following years, Barnwell sat in the state legislature, acting as speaker of the house in 1795 and president of the senate in 1805.

BARRAS, Louis, Comte de (died c. 1800) French admiral   Barras began his naval career in 1734 as a garde. By 1778 he was a squadron leader, and he was promoted to the rank of naval lieutenant general in 1782. He assumed command of part of the French fleet in American waters under d'Estaing, following the death of Admiral Ternay. In 1781, he was in command at Newport when he was requested by Washington and Rochambeau to cooperate in the rapid movement of troops and supplies south to bottle up Lord Cornwallis' troops in Virginia. Barras was contrary, however, and wanted instead an independent expedition to move on Newfoundland with the troops from Newport. He was persuaded otherwise, and in September he sailed to meet the fleet of Admiral de Grasse, which was to arrive in the Chesapeake with reinforcements from the West Indies. Barras carried with him the vital artillery that was to form the siege train at Yorktown. He was reluctant to serve under de Grasse, who was technically his junior, but the two managed to paper over differences and present a united command that dissuaded the British fleet off the Chesapeake Capes on September 5, 1781. He sailed into the harbor at Yorktown five days later. After the conclusion of the Virginia campaign, Barras sailed south with de Grasse to engage the British. In 1782 he captured Montserrat, and he retired the following year due to ill health.

BARRÉ, Isaac (1726–1802) British officer, Parliamentary orator

One of the fiercest voices of political opposition in Britain and an oratorical friend of the Americans, Barré was the son of a French Huguenot émigré to Dublin. After receiving a degree from Trinity College, Barré joined the army as an ensign in 1746. During the French and Indian War he served on General Wolfe's staff, and he was at the general's side when he fell at Quebec. Barré also attracted the favor of Lord Shelburne, whose political protégé he remained for two decades. In the 1760s, Barré ran up against the opposition of William Pitt and was frustrated in moving farther up the ranks of the army. Deprived of his rank and income, Barré took a seat in Parliament as part of the opposition and acquired a reputation as a vociferous and terrifying orator, second only to John Wilkes in his ability to paralyze the House of Commons with unrestrained invective. In 1764, he hotly protested the Stamp Act, naming those who resisted in the American colonies as "Sons of Liberty," a name they widely adopted. He became a hero to Americans, who named the town of Wilkes-Barre, Pennsylvania after him and his fellow radical orator. Continuing to thunder against the North ministry throughout the war, Barré served in several offices when the government changed after 1782. Blindness, probably brought on by a wound suffered during his military career, ended his public life shortly thereafter.

Isaac Barré

BARRINGTON, Samuel (1729–1800) British admiral

He did not fight in the North American theater, but Barrington's command in the West Indies had significant effects on what happened to the north. When he sailed as commander in chief to Barbados in 1778, Barrington was a veteran naval officer, having first signed aboard a warship as an 11-year-old ensign. He received command of his first ship in 1747 and moved from assignment to assignment throughout the wars with France. He hoisted his flag as rear admiral only five months before arriving in the West Indies. With only a precarious balance of seapower in the region, he could do nothing to prevent the French capture of Dominica over the summer, and he was pinned down by orders to await a land force from New York which was to attack the French islands. The promised campaign force never arrived, but a naval squadron did. Acting in early December, Barrington and General James Grant made an amphibious landing and seized St. Lucia. A large French force under d'Estaing was only a day behind them, however. The subsequent naval and land attack by d'Estaing was beaten off, and the British position in the Indies was secured. Barrington was superseded by Admiral Byron the following month and eventually returned to England. In 1780, he was forced to strike his flag after refusing command of the Channel fleet in the midst of extreme political confusion. He returned to employment briefly under Lord Howe after the fall of the North ministry in 1782, and he retired again the following year.

BARRINGTON, William Wildman (1717–1793) British official

Barrington was a long-time member of Parliament and officeholder, serving almost continuously from 1740 until 1778. He was the elder brother of Admiral Samuel Barrington and was himself often associated with the civilian administration of military affairs: he was one of the lords commissioners of the Admiralty in the 1740s, secretary at war during the Seven Years' War, and then chancellor of the exchequer and treasurer of the navy. He returned to the post of secretary at war in 1765 and held that position during the first years of the Revolution. In the scheme of British government at the time, his was a mostly administrative post. He was not a member of the cabinet and he refused to consider it his duty to make or comment on policy, which was the prerogative of the secretary of state, Lord George Germain. Barrington's role was to carry out the management of the details of moving and supplying ships and troops, although this was immensely complicated by the fragmented structure of the government. He faced a nearly impossible set of tasks that grew even more complex as the British armies in America failed to secure their own food and fodder and as the conflict widened. When the French entered the war on the side of the Americans, Barrington left office.

BARRON, James (1740–1787) Virginia naval officer

Against the might of the British navy, individual American states attempted at various points during the Revolutionary War to float navies of their own. The principal figure in the Virginia Navy was Barron, whose wartime career, like that of most state naval officers, was a matter of harassing the smallest of British ships. Barron was born in Mill Creek, Virginia, and his entire male family were seafarers. He entered the naval service of Virginia as a captain in late 1775 when the Virginia Convention decreed a navy for the Commonwealth and dispensed commissions. By the following year, Virginia boasted armed row galleys on the Potomac and a few ships, such as the 100-ton *American Congress*. Barron's first command was the armed brig *Liberty*, in which he managed to recapture the *Oxford*, which had been taken as a prize by U.S. Captain Nicolas Biddle off Newfoundland but had escaped during a storm. Apparently, Barron's usual tactic was to stand by on shore until he received word of a likely target. He would then quickly gather a crew from the sailors on hand and swoop out of his anchorage. In just such a maneuver in 1779 he captured the 10-gun *Fortunatus* off Hampton Roads. In 1780, Barron was named commodore of the Virginia Navy, a post he held until his death. *Further reading:* Robert A. Stewart, *A History of Virginia's Navy of the Revolution* (Richmond, Va., 1934).

John Barry

BARRY, John (1745–1803) Continental Navy captain

American captains such as Barry faced difficult odds. The British Royal Navy was the most powerful in the world, although to be sure only a portion of it ever sailed at one time in American waters during the Revolutionary War. The few warships that the American Congress could put afloat were usually outgunned and outmanned, unless able to find equal odds against isolated British ships. Mostly the Continental Navy (which was always something of a stepchild of Congress) was successful in raiding shipping. Nonetheless, a few skippers like Barry, known as "The Father of the American Navy," were able to make a mark.

Barry was an Irishman who had immigrated to Philadelphia about 1760 and established himself as a shipmaster and owner. In 1776, he was commissioned by Congress as captain of the *Lexington*, a 16-gun brig. When he took the British tender *Edward* off Cape Charles, Virginia in April, he claimed the honor of making the first capture of a British warship by a regularly commissioned U.S. vessel. In part as reward, he was given the seventh place on the list of captains and placed in command of the 32-gun *Effingham* in October 1776. Unfortunately, the British kept him completely bottled up in harbor. Barry spent the winter of 1776–77 on land as commander of a unit of Pennsylvania militia volunteers. When General William Howe moved on Philadelphia, Barry was forced to abandon the *Effingham* to British torches, but he successfully harassed British shipping on the Delaware throughout the winter by cleverly deploying eight armed barges from a protected anchorage at Port Penn.

In September 1778, Barry took command of the frigate *Raleigh,* sailing from Boston. While on patrol, he was surprised by two British ships and was forced to run his frigate aground after a long running battle. In his next ship, the *Alliance,* Barry managed to capture several prizes after a storm in mid-Atlantic scattered a British convoy. He then ferried the Marquis de Lafayette back to France, and he fought one of the final sea battles of the Revolution in an indecisive engagement against the *Sybille* in January 1783.

When Congress raised a new navy in 1794 to resist the pirates of Algiers, Barry was named senior captain and given commission of the *United States,* which he commanded during the naval hostilities with France from 1798 to 1801. *Further reading:* William B. Clark, *Gallant John Barry* (New York, 1938).

BARTLETT, Josiah (1729–1795) Government official, physician, jurist

Bartlett was born in Amesbury, Massachusetts, the last of seven children of a shoemaker. There was no money for education beyond the local common school, but Bartlett was intellectually ambitious and apprenticed himself to a relative and physician, Dr. Nehemiah Ordway. In 1750, Bartlett moved to Kingston, New Hampshire and set up a medical practice of his own. He was apparently skilled in the use of natural remedies, including quinine (known then as Peruvian bark), and he gained a good local reputation. In 1754 he married his cousin, Mary Bartlett, who proved to be a strong supporter in his political career (her letters are preserved), and she bore him 12 children. Bartlett also dabbled in real estate and farming.

He was elected to local office in 1757 and soon moved on to wider prominence. Within 10 years he was a justice of the peace, lieutenant colonel in the colonial militia, and Kingston's representative to the New Hampshire General Court, in which he served continuously until its dissolution in 1775. He was a staunch patriot and took a seat in the revolutionary Provincial Congresses of 1774 and 1775. He was selected to represent New Hampshire in the first Continental Congress in 1774 but could not serve. He did, however, take his place in Congress the following year and was active on more than the usual number of committees, although taking little

William Barton

part in debate. He was the second delegate, after president John Hancock, to sign the Declaration of Independence, and Bartlett was on the committee to draft the Articles of Confederation. Serving throughout 1776, he returned to Congress briefly in 1778.

Meanwhile, he focused his attention on public life in New Hampshire. He was elected to the new Executive Council in 1776 and was appointed a justice of the court of common pleas. He continued as a jurist for several decades, despite a lack of formal legal study. He traveled widely in New Hampshire on behalf of the government, hearing pleas, attending conferences and settling disputes. In 1777, he attended the wounded at the battle of Bennington.

Following the war, Bartlett was named to the Superior Court (the state's highest), and he was appointed chief justice in 1790. In the same year, he was elected as president of the state, and after a change in the constitution, he became the first constitutional governor of New Hampshire. He also chartered and served as president of the New Hampshire Medical Society. *Further reading: The Papers of Josiah Bartlett,* Frank C. Mevers, ed. (Hanover, N.H., 1979).

BARTON, William (1748–1831) Militia and Continental officer

A hatter by occupation, Barton was a native of Rhode Island who became a major with the state regiment, joining as an adjutant immediately after Bunker Hill. In 1777, he won notoriety for the capture of Major General Richard Prescott, commander of British forces at Newport. Hoping to bag Prescott as bait for an exchange for captured American general Charles Lee, Barton rowed with 40 specially selected men to the western shore of Rhode Island, quietly surrounded Prescott's house, silenced the guards and spirited the British commander away. Barton was rewarded with the thanks of Congress, a ceremonial sword and promotion. He ended the Revolutionary War with the rank of colonel in the Continental Army. Later, he supported the federal Constitution and was a member of the Rhode Island ratifying convention. Unfortunately, his life took a somewhat bizarre turn when he refused to pay a judgment on land he owned in Vermont. He was taken into custody and held a virtual prisoner for years in Danville, Vermont. Barton was eventually freed in 1825 through the good offices of Lafayette, who was then on a grand tour of America, and returned to Rhode Island.

BASSETT, Richard (1745–1815) Official, jurist
Born in Cecil County, Maryland, Bassett moved to Delaware sometime before the 1760s. He served on the Governor's Council in his adopted colony before the Revolution but was a patriot and a member of the Delaware Council of Safety in 1776. During the War for Independence, he served in a militia company of dragoons and sat in the constitutional convention of 1776. After the Revolution, he held a series of increasingly responsible positions, starting with the state house of representatives and senate in the 1780s. He was a delegate to the U.S. Constitutional Convention and was appointed as U.S. senator from Delaware in 1789 after the new national government was established. He then became chief justice of the Delaware Court of Common Pleas, and in 1798 he became governor of the state. After leaving state office in 1801, he was appointed to the U.S. Circuit Court.

BATES, Ann. British spy   Although little is known of her personal history, Bates was one of the most successful undercover agents serving the British after their evacuation of Philadelphia. She was an American schoolteacher of that city, who had married an armorer in General Clinton's artillery force. In 1779, she disguised herself as an itinerant peddler and set out from Clinton's headquarters in New York City to Washington's encampment at White Plains, New York. She carried her stock of trade goods from brigade to brigade, noting the American strength and the number and quality of artillery. On her way back to British headquarters she was stopped and searched, but since she carried no papers, she was released. On a second mission, she even penetrated Washington's headquarters and claimed to have gained information from a loose-tongued aide-de-camp. Stopped and questioned again during her return, she barely escaped detection. During the next year, she twice met with an unidentified female confederate of Benedict Arnold and passed messages from the traitor to the British spy Major John André.

BATES, Walter (1760–1842) Loyalist, writer
A native of Stamford, Connecticut, Bates was arrested by patriots in 1775 and thrown into jail; however, he was released and fled to the British on Long Island. Bates evacuated to New Brunswick, Canada in the spring of 1783 and later served as sheriff of King's County, Nova Scotia. His fictional account, *Kingston and the Loyalists of the "Spring Fleet" of 1783*, was not published until nearly 50 years after his death.

BATH, Marquis of. See WEYMOUTH, Viscount.

BATHURST, Henry, Earl of (1714–1794) British minister   Bathurst was one of the "least able" members of the British Cabinet during the American Revolution. He was the eldest son of the first Earl of Bathurst and progressed through the usual stages of Georgian politics and officeholding early in his career, sitting for a family seat in Parliament and holding a succession of minor offices through patronage. He was trained as a lawyer and served mostly in judicial posts such as solicitor general and judge of the common pleas. His appointment as lord chancellor by Lord North in 1771 somewhat surprised his political colleagues. He assumed the title of Earl of Bathurst on his father's death in 1775. Throughout his time as lord chancellor he had a reputation as being both ineffective and lazy, often missing key meetings and seldom taking the initiative on any matter of import. He was replaced as lord chancellor in 1778 and given the post of lord president of the council, which he held until the North ministry went out of office in 1782 after the defeat of Cornwallis. Bathurst retired from office and politics thereafter and lived the rest of his life at his country estate.

BAUM, Friedrich (d. 1777) German mercenary officer

Baum commanded the dragoon regiment of the mercenary forces hired by the British from the Duke of Brunswick to flesh out their armies in North America. Baum's heavy cavalry numbered 336 men on departure from their home in February 1776, but they sailed to America without their horses. They nonetheless retained their elaborate and cumbersome gear, including high riding boots, leather breeches and heavy cavalry sabers. Baum spoke no English but apparently was an experienced soldier. Serving under the command of Friedrich von Riedesel, the Brunswickers were assigned as part of General John Burgoyne's army in 1777 and marched with that force as it attempted an invasion of upstate New York from Canada. On August 9, Burgoyne gave Baum command of an 800-man contingent consisting of the Brunswick dragoons, some light infantry, Canadian irregulars and Indians, along with two pieces of field artillery, and directed the mercenary colonel to march toward Bennington, Vermont. Baum was to bring back horses to mount the cavalry as well as cattle to feed the army. He was also instructed to recruit among the supposed loyalists of the region, although without a common language this task would have been difficult. As Baum and his slow-moving troops advanced toward Bennington, a large American force of New Hampshire and Vermont men gathered under the command of prickly General John Stark. Baum suspected he was badly outnumbered, but he reported to Burgoyne (while asking also for reinforcements) that the Americans would likely not make a stand. On August 16, Baum found himself in a difficult position, defending hilltops but unable to concentrate his disciplined regulars against twice the number of Americans, who split forces and launched an enveloping attack. Despite a fierce resistance, the Germans were badly defeated, and Baum himself was struck mortally as he tried to carve his way out after being surrounded. He died two days later.

BAUMAN, Sebastian (1739–1803) Continental officer, cartographer

One of the principal artillery officers of the Continental Army, Bauman was German by birth and a graduate of the university at Heidelberg. He arrived in New York some time before the Seven Years' War, during which he was in the colonial militia. His first Revolutionary War service was as a captain in a New York City militia company known as the German Fusiliers. Bauman became captain in March 1776 of a New York artillery company that was absorbed in January 1777 into the new Continental Corps of Artillery as part of the original 2nd Battalion of Continental Artillery. This unit, drawn from New York, Connecticut, Rhode Island and New Hampshire, remained intact throughout the Revolutionary War, and Bauman eventually became its commander after his promotion to major in the fall of 1778. Bauman was stationed during 1779 at West Point, and with the movement south to trap Lord Cornwallis' forces in 1781, he assumed an important role as one of the chief artillerists directing the siege bombardment of Yorktown. Immediately after the battle, he began a study of the ground and subsequently prepared a map of the Yorktown battlefield, which he published in Philadelphia in 1782. He continued as a Continental officer, and when Colonel John Crane resigned in November 1783, Bauman assumed command of the remnant of the Corps of Artillery (reduced by that stage to only two companies, one of which remained in service after the Revolution). He was discharged along with almost all the rest of the remaining Continental officers in June 1784. He later served as the federal postmaster of New York City.

BAURMEISTER, Carl Leopold (1734–1803) German mercenary officer

An important staff officer, Baurmeister kept an informative wartime journal during the Revolution. He was born in Hanover and took service in an Anhalt regiment in 1756, rising to lieutenant and adjutant to the Prince of Anhalt within two years. During the mid-1760s, he became a soldier in the service of Landgrave Frederick II of Hesse-Cassel, and in 1776, when the landgrave sold the services of his troops to the British for duty in North America, Baurmeister was named captain in the Regiment von Mirbach. He sailed with his unit later the same year, arriving on Staten Island just as British general William Howe began the campaign in New York against Washington. Baurmeister was a senior staff officer for almost the entire time he was in America and commanded troops in the field only once for a brief period during the fighting around Philadelphia in 1778. He was adjutant to all three of the German commanders in chief (von Heister, von Knyphausen, and von Lossberg) and for a time was aide-de-camp to the British commander, Sir Henry Clinton. At the end of the war, he personally negotiated with Congress for the return of German prisoners and deserters. His position at army headquarters afforded Baurmeister a good vantage to observe and record events. His journals (and letters) commented on almost all facets of the Revolution as seen from the British and German perspectives. He was particularly acute in his discussion of politics and social affairs. On his return to Europe, Baurmeister resumed his military career, becoming a major general in 1793. He ended his service to Hesse-Cassel in the diplomatic corps as resident minister in London, where he died. *Further reading:* Carl Leopold Baurmeister, *The Revolution in America: Confidential Letters and Journals, 1776–1784 . . .* , Bernhard Uhlendorf, trans. (Westport, Conn., 1973).

BAYARD, John B. (1738–1807) Militia officer, delegate to Congress

Bayard, born in Maryland, came from one of America's oldest families (he was descended from a French Huguenot who was married to Peter Stuyvesant's sister). He moved in 1756 to Philadelphia, where he became a wealthy merchant. He took a close interest in the British attempts during the 1760s to regulate the colonial American economy, and in 1766 he was one of the earliest Sons of Liberty and supporters of the policy of nonimportation. Bayard sat in the initial Pennsylvania provincial convention in 1774 and later moved into a seat in the state legislature, serving from 1776 to 1779, simultaneous with holding several other offices and pursuing his military career. He was one of the officers of the Philadelphia Associators, a fine militia unit drawn from the upper economic classes of the city. Bayard fought with the Associators as a major at Brandywine, Germantown and Princeton. In 1777, he became a colonel, but the Associators saw little further action. His civilian duties during the war included service on the Pennsylvania Council of Safety and the Supreme Executive Council. He was elected to the Congress in 1785 from Pennsylvania. Following his congressional term, he moved to New Brunswick, New Jersey, where he became mayor and justice of the local court of common pleas.

BAYLEY, Richard (1745–1801) Loyalist physician

Born in Connecticut, Bayley first studied medicine in New York City but went to Britain for further training in 1769. After attending lectures in London, he returned to New York in 1772, where he set up a practice. He devised a new course of treatment for the disease known then as the "croup" (probably tuberculosis) and is reputed to have significantly lowered the mortality rate from the illness in New York. With the outbreak of the Revolutionary War, he attached himself to the British army in New York, serving as a surgeon during 1776. He apparently withdrew from active participation in the war, however, in 1777. After the Revolution, he resumed his practice, eventually becoming an eminent doctor and teacher at Columbia College, where he held the chairs of anatomy and surgery.

BAYLOR, George (1752–1784) Continental officer

Baylor served as an aide-de-camp to George Washington during the first year of the war and then took a field command. He was born in the Shenandoah Valley of Virginia, and his father was a friend of Washington, which explains Baylor's appointment in August 1775 as one of Washington's first aides after the new commander in chief took over the Continental Army. Baylor fought with distinction at Trenton in December 1776 and was deputized by Washington to carry the news of the great victory (along with a captured flag) to Congress. As was not unusual, the bearer of glad tidings was rewarded: congressional president John Hancock asked Washington to promote Baylor to colonel and give him a new horse. Washington approved the elevation in rank (and the gift horse), and Baylor left his post as aide-de-camp to recruit a new unit that became the 3rd Continental Dragoons (part of the new Corps of Continental Light Dragoons under Casimir Pulaski) with Baylor in regimental command. Most of the dragoons in Baylor's regiment were drawn from Virginia, with a few Pennsylvanians included. The regiment was assigned in the early fall of 1778 to a post at Old Tappan, New York, one of several small bodies of troops given the task of harassing a large movement by generals Cornwallis and von Knyphausen up the Hudson. Baylor and his men camped in barns and may have been careless in posting guards. A British force under General James "No Flint" Grey (the victor in a similar action at Paoli, New York, a year earlier) approached the camp under cover of darkness and surprised the Americans with a silent and vicious bayonet attack. The dragoons were nearly wiped out: 30 were killed and 50 captured, with only a few escaping. Baylor was severely wounded through the lungs and taken prisoner. Although he was exchanged, Baylor never really recovered from his wounds. He was given nominal command of the 1st Dragoons when the 3rd was absorbed into that unit, but he was physically unable to lead his men, and the dragoons fought in the Virginia campaign under field command of Colonel William Washington. At the end of hostilities, Baylor went to Barbados to recover his health, but he died of the long-term effects of his wounds in 1784.

BEACH, John (died c. 1776) Loyalist clergy

Beach was an Episcopal priest, serving a parish in Newtown, Connecticut. He steadfastly supported the crown as the revolutionary movement gained momentum in his community and congregation, and along with several other Anglican priests in the region, he came under intense public pressure to cease praying for the king and to close his church. Beach continued to conduct services and refused to alter the proscribed prayers, so in June 1776 he was seized by a rebel mob that dragged him from his church and threatened to cut out his tongue. He still refused to cave in, saying (according to a loyalist account): ". . . I am firm in my resolution while I pray at all to conform with the unmutilated liturgy of the church and pray for the King and all in authority under him." Beach was thrown in jail by the patriots and died about six months later.

BEATTY, John (1749–1826) Delegate to Congress, officer

Beatty was born in Neshaminy, Pennsylvania, the son of a parson. He graduated from the college at Princeton in 1769 and then studied medicine, opening a practice in Hartsville, Pennsylvania in 1772. He was commissioned as a captain in the Pennsylvania Battalion of 1776, a unit raised as part of the Continental Army and mustered in during February. The battalion was reorganized late in the year, and Beatty moved as a major to the 6th Pennsylvania Regiment. Despite his service with Pennsylvania troops, by the end of the war Beatty was a resident of New Jersey and a member of the state legislature. He was sent as a delegate to Congress from New Jersey in 1784 and

1785 and subsequently was elected a representative to the U.S. House for a term in the third Congress from 1793 to 1795. After returning to New Jersey, he was elected secretary of the state. In later life he was a banker and president of a bridge company.

BEAUMARCHAIS, Pierre Augustin Caron de (1732–1799) French businessman, writer

One of the most fascinating characters of the Revolution, Beaumarchais was among the foremost French playwrights of the age, and in his business guise, he organized massive material support for the American Revolution during its early years. He came from relatively humble origins (he added the name "de Beaumarchais" to the plebeian "Caron") and followed his father's trade of clockmaking. By the eve of the American Revolution, he had risen to be a favorite at the French court as well as a successful playwright, a daring businessman and a sometime secret agent for the government. He was flamboyant, energetic and brilliant in more than one area of life, and—despite his attachment to the court and royal government—he was a man of revolutionary sympathies. His two most famous plays were *The Barber of Seville* and *The Marriage of Figaro* (a play of mildly revolutionary bent that was often banned by crowned heads in Europe).

His involvement with the American Revolution probably sprang from a combination of genuine interest in its success and what he saw as a chance to make a fortune. The story of how he aided the Revolution is complex. In 1776, Beaumarchais petitioned King Louis XVI to come to the aid of the Americans against France's ancient enemy, Britain. With the support of the Comte de Vergennes, the foreign minister, Beaumarchais worked out a plan to provide war supplies to the American rebels while keeping the official hands of the French government clean of involvement. (France was still at peace with Great Britain and under intense diplomatic pressure to remain neutral.) Beaumarchais struck a deal with Silas Deane, the American envoy to France, whereby Beaumarchais would buy and ship large amounts of supplies directly to the Americans. In return, Congress would agree to pay for the supplies in shipments of rice or tobacco (or money, if any was available). Moreover, the French government secretly was to be the actual supplier of military stores in the form of cannon, uniforms, gunpowder, muskets and anything else at hand the

Americans needed. Beaumarchais, however, was to act entirely as a private commercial merchant as far as public appearances went. He set up a fictitious firm called Roderique Hortalez et Cie and conducted all the business of buying and shipping through the private company.

Operating from a grand building in Paris, Beaumarchais received 2 million livres in secret subsidies from the French and Spanish governments and supplied a million more on his own. He drew on the stocks of military matériel of the French government, which he was supposed to either replace or pay for. In spite of the best efforts of the British to quash the enterprise (Beaumarchais revealed himself to British agents while pausing at Le Havre to rehearse a performance of *The Barber of Seville*), within a few months Hortalez et Cie had ships laden with supplies on the way to America. At one stage the firm had more than 40 vessels, which usually delivered cargoes to Portsmouth, New Hampshire. The flood of arms and equipment was crucial to putting the Continental Army in the field and keeping it there during the first two years of the war. Without Beaumarchais's effort, the American cause would have been lost before 1778.

Unfortunately for Beaumarchais, he was less successful in receiving payment than in organizing the flow of supplies. He found himself in the midst of a bitter struggle between Silas Deane and his arch rival Arthur Lee. This conflict colored several aspects of the Revolution during 1777 and 1778, but Beaumarchais may have suffered most. Because of the vicious fight between Deane and Lee, Congress failed to make any payments in kind or transfer any funds in return for the huge volume of supplies shipped by Hortalez et Cie. When France entered the war in 1778 and began open shipments to America, Beaumarchais was still empty-handed. His business acumen rescued him from disaster, however, and he found a way to turn a slight profit on the entire venture by sending even more ships and supplies but making certain they paused in the West Indies for rich cargoes of sugar before returning to France. During the French Revolution, Beaumarchais was forced into exile in England, but he returned to his home shortly before his death. The American Congress continued to renege on the debts owed Beaumarchais until decades after his demise—the final bill was not settled with his heirs until 1835. *Further reading:* Arnold Whitridge,

"Beaumarchais and the American Revolution," *History Today* (February 1967), 98–105; Georges Lemaître, *Beaumarchais* (New York, 1949).

BEAUREPAIRE, Quesnay de. See QUESNAY de Beaurepaire.

BECKLEY, John (1757–1807) Government official   Beckley was born in England and moved to Virginia at age 11. Although still a teenager, he was appointed as clerk of the Henrico County Committee of Safety in November 1774 and again in 1775. He subsequently became the assistant clerk of the Virginia Committee of Safety, assistant clerk to the Council of State and clerk of the House of Delegates. During his work in Virginia he became a political protégé of Thomas Jefferson, and through Jefferson's influence, Beckley was named the first clerk of the federal U.S. House of Representatives in 1789. Beckley worked as a political operative for Jefferson, gathering information on rivals and planning strategy, and he managed the 1796 campaign for the Republicans in Pennsylvania. The Federalist victory that year turned Beckley out of his post with the Congress, but he was returned as clerk when Jefferson was elected as president in 1800. He also served as Librarian of Congress from 1800 until his death. *Further reading:* Noble E. Cunningham, Jr., "John Beckley: An Early American Party Manager," *William and Mary Quarterly* (January 1956), 40–52.

BECKWITH, George (1753–1823) British officer   The son of a British major general, Beckwith purchased a commission as an ensign in the 37th Regiment in 1771, shortly before the unit moved to America as part of the Boston garrison. By 1777, he was a captain and had served in the New Jersey campaign of the previous year. He became an aide-de-camp to von Knyphausen when the German commander was placed in charge of the British forces in New York in 1779 while Sir Henry Clinton sailed south to Charleston. Beckwith inherited the intelligence duties of the British spy Major John André in 1780 and worked with loyalist Oliver De Lancey to reorganize the British secret service in New York. After the war, Beckwith remained on the army list and served for several years as the crown's agent to report on conditions in America. He was appointed governor of Bermuda in 1795 and was promoted to major general a year later. He subsequently served as governor of St. Vincent and Barbados and seized Martinique from the French in 1809. He retired with the rank of full general.

BEDFORD, Gunning (1742–1797) Continental officer, government official

Bedford is often confused with his slightly younger cousin of the same name, since both were from Delaware and had similar careers. This Gunning Bedford (sometimes called "Colonel" or "Senior" to make the distinction) was born in Philadelphia and moved to Delaware as a child. He was commissioned as a major in the famous Delaware regiment of John Haslet in 1776 and was wounded at the battle of White Plains. He became deputy quartermaster general and eventually lieutenant colonel of his regiment late in 1776. Bedford held important state offices after the Revolution, becoming a member of the Delaware general assembly in 1784 and governor in 1796. He was elected to the Confederation Congress in 1786 but declined to serve and resigned before taking his seat.

BEDFORD, Gunning, Jr. (1747–1812) Delegate to Congress, government official

Bedford used the name "Junior" to distinguish himself from his cousin of the same name. He was born in Philadelphia and graduated from the college at Princeton in 1771. Although his daughter claimed he was an aide to George Washington, there is no corroborating evidence of his service in the military during the Revolution. He was a lawyer and practiced in Dover, Delaware, and in Wilmington. In 1783–85, he served as a delegate to the Congress and was appointed state attorney general in the middle of his term. As a delegate to the federal Constitutional Convention in 1787, Bedford was a strong advocate of the rights of the small states and spoke vociferously on the topic before the assembly. He subsequently was named a U.S. district judge for Delaware.

BEDINGER, George M. (1756–1843) Soldier, state official

Bedinger was born in York County, Pennsylvania but settled as a youngster with his family near Shepardstown in what is now West Virginia. He served several short enlistments in what were probably militia units during the first years of the Revolution, but in 1779 he began a series of trips to the Boonesborough region of Kentucky, alternating residence between there and Shepardstown. In May 1779, Bedinger was adjutant of a frontier expedition against Indian villages near Chillicothe, Ohio. He may have returned east in 1780 and enlisted again in the Virginia militia. In 1782, he was back on the frontier and an officer in the Kentucky militia force that was ambushed and defeated near Blue Licks, Kentucky, in one of the last fights of the Revolutionary War. In the following years, he served with several military expeditions against the Indians of the Old Northwest. He was elected to the legislature when Kentucky became a state and was sent to the U.S. Congress in 1803, serving two terms. *Further reading:* Danske Bedinger Dandridge, *George Michael Bedinger: A Kentucky Pioneer* (Charlottesville, Va., 1909).

BEE, Thomas (1725–1812) Delegate to Congress, government official

Born in Charleston, South Carolina, Bee went to England for his education, returning with a degree from Oxford to study law in his native city. A planter as well as a practicing attorney, Bee sat in the colonial assembly from 1762 to the eve of the Revolution. He was a member of the first South Carolina Provincial Congresses in 1775 and 1776 and was elected to the new patriot House of Representatives in 1776, serving as speaker from 1777 to 1779. He was also simultaneously a judge and member of the State Council. In 1779, he was selected as lieutenant governor of the state, holding that formal position during the British invasion. He served a term in the Congress from 1780 to 1782. After the Revolution, Bee was appointed as a judge of the U.S. District Court for South Carolina.

BELKNAP, Jeremy (1744–1798) Clergyman, historian

Born in Boston, Belknap was the son of a leather dresser and furrier. He taught school in New Hampshire after graduating from Harvard in 1762. He moved to Dover, New Hampshire in 1766 and became the pastor of the Congregational church there. He was appointed as chaplain to the New Hampshire troops at Cambridge, Massachusetts in 1775, but he declined to serve for reasons of health. In 1787, he moved to Boston and became pastor of the Federal Street Church, where he remained the rest of his life. He was a prolific writer, and his best-known work was an excellent three-volume history of New Hampshire, published between 1784 and 1792. He also produced allegories, two volumes of biography and many religious works. *Further reading:* Sidney Kaplan, "Jeremy Belknap as Literary Craftsman," *William and Mary Quarterly* (January 1964), 18–39.

BENNETT, Caleb P. (1758–1836) Soldier, official

Although born in Chester County, Pennsylvania, Bennett lived most of his life in Delaware. Unusual for someone who later served in high state office, Bennett was a private soldier for at least the first part of the Revolutionary War. He enlisted in the Continental Army in 1775 at the beginning of the conflict. He was promoted to sergeant in 1777 and served at winter quarters at Valley Forge. He was commissioned a lieutenant the following year and was later promoted to first lieutenant. He was an officer in the Delaware militia in the decades after the Revolution, and by the War of 1812, Bennett was a major in the local artillery company in New Castle and was placed in command of the defenses of the port. He also had a long career as a public official, serving 26 years as treasurer of New Castle County. In 1833, at the advanced age of 75, he was elected governor of Delaware.

BENSON, Egbert (1746–1833) Delegate to Congress, government official

Benson was born in New York and graduated from King's College (now Columbia University) in 1765, reading afterward for the law and taking up practice in Dutchess County, New York in 1772. He was an active local patriot, serving in the 1776 Provincial Congress and the Council of Safety from 1777 to 1778. He was attorney general of the state government in New York for 10 years, beginning in 1777, and simultaneously a member of the state assembly, where he drafted much of the body's legislation. He was elected as a delegate to Congress in 1781 and served until 1784, during which time he also was a member of a state commission to supervise the evacuation of loyalists from New York City. He later served two terms as U.S. congressman from New York, strongly supporting Alexander Hamilton's financial proposals and a powerful central government. In 1794, Benson became a justice of the New York Supreme Court. He was also founder and first president of the New-York Historical Society.

BERESFORD, Richard (1755–1803) Delegate to Congress, officer, state official

A native of Charleston, South Carolina, Beresford benefited from the study of law at the Middle Temple in London and returned to practice in Charleston in 1773. He served as an officer under Isaac Huger in the 1st South Carolina Regiment in 1778, and in May 1780 he was captured with the fall of Charleston. Beresford was shipped by the British to St. Augustine and held as a prisoner until 1781. He was elected to the state legislature after his release and then was chosen as lieutenant governor, but he resigned after only a brief time in office. In 1783, he represented South Carolina in the Confederation Congress.

BERKELEY, Norbonne. See BOTETOURT, Baron de.

BERKENHOUT, John (c. 1730–1801) British agent, writer

Berkenhout was attached to the British Carlisle Peace Commission in 1778 and made crude attempts to bribe American leaders. He was born in Leeds and was sent by his Dutch immigrant father to Germany for his education, presumably headed for a career in commerce. However, Berkenhout was attracted by the military life and joined the Prussian infantry as an officer. With the coming of the Seven Years' War, he transferred to the British army, but he left his regiment in 1760 to study medicine at Edinburgh, where he was the classmate and friend of American Arthur Lee. He also studied at the University of Leyden in Holland and published several works on natural history and medicine. In 1778, he became an agent of the British government, charged with helping to bring the Americans back into the British orbit before the treaty with France could be signed. The principal duties fell to the official members of the Earl of Carlisle's commission, who arrived in Philadelphia in June. Berkenhout came later, first to New York, and then, finagling a pass from American general William Maxwell, to Philadelphia in late August. He attempted to ingratiate himself with Richard Lee, treading on his old acquaintance with Arthur, Richard's brother, and Berkenhout then offered bribe money to several congressmen if they would support reconciliation with Great Britain. The Council of Pennsylvania arrested him and clapped him in jail for a few days. After cooling his heels, he was allowed to return to New York. Despite his failure,

Berkenhout received a pension in reward for his services when he arrived home in England.

BERNARD, Francis (1712–1779) British royal governor

Royal Governor Bernard was the object of prerevolutionary patriot wrath in Massachusetts during the 1760s and was hounded from office. He was the son of an English country family; educated at Oxford, he was a lawyer and a political protégé of Lord Barrington, to whom he was related by marriage. After filling minor offices in England, Bernard was appointed royal governor of New Jersey in 1758. His tenure there was uneventful, and in 1760 he was transferred to Massachusetts. His misfortune was to be the chief royal official during a tumultuous time: he was in office when the Sugar Act and the Stamp Act were passed by Parliament. Bernard was a reasonably competent administrator, but he failed to establish a base of political power in Massachusetts and his influence and ability to control events went steadily downhill as protests grew over the parliamentary acts. He came to be virtually ignored by the colonial dissidents, other than to make himself very unpopular. The final blow came in 1769 when several of his private letters written to Lord Hillsborough fell into the hands of the patriots and were published in the *Boston Gazette*. A storm of invective resulted, and the colonial assembly brought charges against him and voted for his recall. The government in Britain obliged, calling Bernard home and putting Lieutenant Governor Thomas Hutchinson in charge of the royal government in Massachusetts. Bernard retired from public life with the consolation of a baronetage. *Further reading:* Francis G. Wallett, "Governor Bernard's Undoing: An Earlier Hutchinson Letters Affair," *New England Quarterly* (June 1965), 217–26.

BERTHIER, Louis Alexandre (1753–1815) French officer

Later a marshal of France and one of Napoleon's closest associates, Berthier served with the French army in America as an aide to General Rochambeau. He was born at Versailles and was trained as an engineer, although he served primarily in the French service in the dragoons and infantry before the American Revolution. He was also a trained cartographer and was engaged in mapping the king's forests when the French expedition was formed in 1780. He did not immediately win a place with Rochambeau and sailed independently of the main French squadron, landing on his own in Newport a few weeks after Admiral Ternay's ships. His main duties were as an aide to the French commander, although his mapping talents were called on also, and he headed the movement of French artillery south to Virginia. With the end of the fighting after Yorktown, Berthier returned to France and began a career that took him to the heights of rank and military status. He managed to avoid the pitfalls of politics during the early years of the French Revolution and was chief of staff of the Army of Italy when Napoleon Bonaparte was named as its commander in 1795. Thereafter he served Napoleon continuously until 1814, primarily as chief of staff in charge of logistics. While capable as a staff officer, Berthier was a disaster as a field commander on the one occasion he was given charge of an army, in 1809. Napoleon made Berthier a marshal (and prince of Neuchâtel and Wagram), but with the emperor's defeat in 1814, Berthier defected to the restored Bourbons. During the Hundred Days, when Bonaparte returned to seize temporary power, Berthier was in Bamberg and apparently committed suicide by jumping from a window. *Further reading:* Howard C. Rice, Jr., and Anne F. Brown, eds., *The American Campaigns of Rochambeau's Army . . .* (Princeton and Providence, 1972).

BETTYS, Joseph (d. 1782) Turncoat officer

A notorious figure among patriots, Bettys was a native of Ballston, New York, who served in the American army during the first months of the war, principally with Benedict Arnold on Lake Champlain in 1776. He was captured by the British, however, and taken to Canada, where he was persuaded to change allegiance. Bettys was commissioned as an ensign in the British army and served as both a messenger and a spy. The Americans captured him but spared his life, and he escaped to the British. He took up a terrorist campaign in New York, earning a foul reputation. He was captured again by the Americans in 1782 and was executed at Albany, New York.

BIDDLE, Edward (1738–1779) Delegate to Congress, state official

The elder brother of Nicholas Biddle, Edward was a lawyer and legislator in Pennsylvania. He was born to a Quaker family in Philadelphia but apparently had no qualms about military service, since he was an officer in the co-

Nicholas Biddle

lonial forces throughout the Seven Years War. He practiced law in Reading, Pennsylvania and was a member of the assembly from 1765 to 1775, acting as speaker in 1774. Biddle took a role in patriotic activity in Pennsylvania as a member of the 1775 provincial assembly and of a committee of correspondence. He was selected as a delegate to the Continental Congress in 1774 and again in 1775.

BIDDLE, Nicholas (1750–1778) Naval officer

Biddle was one of the early naval heroes of the Revolution whose career was cut short by his death in action. He was born to a Quaker family in New Jersey and was the brother of Edward Biddle. He went to sea at age 15. After serving aboard merchantmen for several years, he went to England and obtained a commission as midshipman in the Royal Navy on the *Portland* in 1772. He put aside his commission the following year to volunteer as a member of the crew of the expedition to the North Pole sponsored by the Royal Geographical Society (an adventure he shared with Horatio Nelson). The voyage—filled with the usual hardships of such expeditions—took him as far as 81 degrees north. On his return, Biddle resigned his commission, sailed to America and offered his services to the Revolution. His first command was an armed galley on the Delaware River in August 1775, and in December he received one of the captain's commissions in the new Continental Navy and took charge of the 14-gun *Andrea Doria*. After sailing with Esek Hopkins' squadron, Biddle began independent operations against British shipping along the Atlantic coast, successfully taking many prizes among the British supply ships and defeating superior forces several times. He then took command of the new 32-gun *Randolph* and raided successfully in the West Indies. In February 1778, he sailed out of Charleston with a tiny squadron of ships outfitted by the new state of South Carolina. He encountered the vastly superior 64-gun British ship of the line, *Yarmouth*, on March 7. A brief struggle at close range wounded Biddle and disabled his ship. He was directing return fire from a chair on his quarterdeck when the *Randolph* blew up, killing Biddle and 311 of his crew of 315. *Further reading:* William B. Clark, *Captain Dauntless: The Story of Nicholas Biddle of the Continental Navy* (Baton Rouge, La., 1949).

BIGELOW, Timothy (1739–1790) Militia and Continental officer

Born in Worcester, Massachusetts, Bigelow was a blacksmith before the Revolution. He was involved in prewar patriot agitation as a member of his local committees of safety and correspondence, and in April 1775 he hastened to Cambridge with his militia company after the battle of Lexington and Concord. He held the rank of major in the Massachusetts militia when he volunteered for duty with Benedict Arnold's expedition to Quebec. Bigelow was captured in the unsuccessful American attack in December and was held by the British for a year before being exchanged. On his return to Massachusetts, he was commissioned as colonel in the Continental Army, and he was given command of the 15th Massachusetts Regiment when it was created in January 1777. Bigelow served as head of the 15th, fighting at Saratoga and Monmouth, until the unit was broken up in January 1781. Following the Revolution, Bigelow moved to the Vermont area and was one of the founders of the city of Montpelier.

BILLOPP, Christopher (1737–1827) Loyalist

Billopp was born on Staten Island under the family name of Farmer, but he adopted his wife's last name when she inherited a large tract of land. He served as an officer of loyalist troops in the New York region during the war but was captured by the patriots and imprisoned at Burlington, New Jersey. After being exchanged, Billopp served as a superintendent of police for the British on Staten Island. With the British defeat, he moved to New Brunswick, Canada.

BINGHAM, William (1752–1804) Businessman, Congressional agent, delegate to Congress

Bingham ended the Revolution as one of the richest men in the new nation while having provided good service to his country during wartime. He was a native of Philadelphia and his family had a long history of social and commercial prominence. He served as the British consul on Martinique from 1770 to 1776 and assumed the same role for the Congress with the declaration of American independence. The French authorities on the island cooperated, and Bingham used his wide commercial connections to build a thriving trade in supplies for the Revolution through the port. He formed a partnership with Pennsylvania financier Robert Morris to buy supplies on commission and ship them north to the colonies. He also established an informal admiralty court on Martinique, which allowed American privateers to bring prizes there for convenient sale. Bingham turned over all captured British dispatches to Congress and cooperated with other American agents in the Caribbean. He also made a huge personal fortune out of the trade, and he and Morris especially benefited from outfitting their own small fleet of privateers. He returned to Philadelphia in 1780 and further strengthened his connections by marriage to Anne Willig, joining her father in the banking business. In 1781, the enterprise was chartered by Congress as the Bank of North America. Bingham went to Europe for two years after the end of the war, but he returned to America to sit in Congress from 1784 to 1786 and thereafter in the Pennsylvania legislature. He served a single term as U.S. senator from 1795 to 1801. Over the years he invested wisely in land purchases throughout Pennsylvania, New York and New England and was a major owner of several trading companies. In 1801, he moved to Bath, England, and he lived with his daughter there until his death. The city of Binghamton, New York, which he founded, is named in his honor. *Further reading:* Robert C. Alberts, *The Golden Voyage: The Life and Times of William Bingham, 1752–1804* (Boston, 1969).

BIRD, Henry. British partisan officer

Nothing is known of Bird's personal background, but he commanded one of the most successful British raids of the war in the West. Between April and June of 1780, Bird led a large raiding force (eventually about 1,200 Indians and loyalists) south from Detroit into the Kentucky territory. He hauled six cannon with him, which gave his force immediate superiority over the frontier American settlements. After traveling down the Maumee and Greater Miami rivers, Bird struck settlements in central Kentucky, taking both Ruddle's and Martin's stations. Bird returned to Detroit with 350 prisoners and booty.

BIRON, Duc de. See LAUZUN, Duc de.

BISSELL, Israel. Dispatch rider

Bissell was one of the experienced couriers used by the Massachusetts patriots to spread information. On the morning of April 19, 1775, he was handed a scribbled letter by Colonel Joseph Palmer of the Braintree Committee of Safety and ordered to alert patriots "quite to Connecticut" (as the letter said). The message told "all friends of American Liberty" of the clash of arms at Lexington and Concord. Bissell exceeded his brief considerably and pounded all the way to New York City by April 23. He then rode across New Jersey to Philadelphia and carried the news of the first battle of the Revolutionary War to eager patriots there on April 25—a remarkable ride.

BLAIR, John (1732–1800) Jurist

Born in Williamsburg, Virginia, Blair was educated at the College of William and Mary and studied law in England at the Middle Temple. In 1766, he was elected to represent the college in the Virginia House of Burgesses, sitting until 1770 when he became clerk of the House. He was an early patriot, signing the nonimportation agreements in 1770. After the ouster of the royal government from Virginia, Blair attended the state constitutional convention in May 1776 and helped draw up the plan for the new government. The subsequent assembly elected him a judge of the general court, and he simultaneously served on the state Council. In 1780, he was selected as a justice of the chancery court. He was a Virginia delegate to the federal Constitutional Convention in 1787, and his support of a strong central government was rewarded by President George Washington in 1789, when Blair was named to the U.S. Supreme Court. He resigned his seat on the high bench and retired in 1796.

BLANCHARD, Claude (1742–1802) French commissary

Blanchard was the primary commissary to the French in America. He began work on the civilian side of the French army in 1762, and by the time General Rochambeau's force was directed to sail to Rhode Island in 1780, Blanchard held the post of "principal commissary of war." He kept a journal during his time in America that offers interesting comments on the French experience. His main duties were to keep the French forces supplied with food and clothing, to run hospitals for the sick and wounded and to take care of the French war chest. Blanchard returned to France after the American War but was forced to flee his official position during the French Revolution. *Further reading: The Journal of Claude Blanchard . . .* , William Duane, trans. (Albany, N.Y., 1876).

BLANCHARD, Jonathan (1738–1788) Delegate to Congress, state official

Born in Dunstable, New Hampshire, Blanchard was active in 1775 as a member of the fifth provincial congress and was selected the following year to sit in the first New Hampshire House of Representatives. In 1777, he became attorney general of the state and sat on the state committee of safety. Blanchard was sent as a delegate to the Congress in 1783 and returned to the same post again in 1784 and 1787.

BLAND, Richard (1710–1776) Delegate to Congress, colonial legislator

Bland was a long-time legislator in Virginia's House of Burgesses before the Revolution and author of one of the first published protests against British prewar taxation. He was born in the colony and educated at the College of William and Mary. His family were prosperous planters, and he apparently had the leisure during his life to devote himself to government. He first went to the Burgesses as representative of Prince Georges County in 1742, serving continuously until the change to a revolutionary government in 1775. While not a good public speaker, he was excellent with the pen. Throughout his legislative career he wrote for publication on public topics, and his private study of legal and historical precedents won him the status of an expert within the Burgesses. Bland was an anticleric in the controversy of the 1760s in Virginia over the salary of the clergy, opposing increases in the income of Church of England priests. His most important writing was *An Inquiry into the Rights of the British Colonies* (1766), in which he stated firmly the antitaxation position of the colonies. The *Inquiry* was first pub-

lished in Williamsburg and reprinted in London. Bland hoped to avoid the need for colonial independence, but he was closely involved in resisting the crown and defending the colonies. He signed the nonimportation agreements in 1769, was active in the Virginia Committee of Correspondence and was a member of the state committee of safety. After taking part in the revolutionary provincial meetings of 1775 and 1776 and attending the convention to draw up a state constitution, Bland took a seat in the first patriot state legislature. He was elected from Virginia to the first Continental Congress, serving the entire session in 1775. He was reelected to the second Congress, but he attended only a few days and declined to serve when selected as a delegate a third time. *Further reading:* Clinton L. Rossiter, "Richard Bland: The Whig in America," *William and Mary Quarterly* 10 (January 1953), 33–79; Richard Bland, *An Inquiry into the Rights of the British Colonies . . .* (reprint, Richmond, Va., 1922).

BLAND, Theodorick (1742–1790) Continental officer, physician delegate to Congress

Bland, the nephew of Richard Bland, was born in Prince Georges County, Virginia to a family of well-to-do planters. He went to England for his education at age 11, attending Wakefield and then the University of Edinburgh, where he received a medical degree in 1763. He returned to Virginia and practiced medicine until ill health forced him to retire to his plantation in 1771. He joined the prerevolutionary agitation in Virginia in 1775 when he helped seize the arms arsenal at the governor's palace in Williamsburg. In June 1776, he was appointed captain of a troop of the Virginia Cavalry, a militia unit recruited from "gentlemen volunteers." Bland eventually became major of his cavalry unit, and in January 1777, when it was absorbed into the new Corps of Continental Cavalry as the 1st Regiment of Continental Light Dragoons, Bland became commanding colonel with a Continental commission. Bland's 1st Regiment was one of the few cavalry units attached to Washington's main army during the New Jersey and Philadelphia campaigns of 1777, but it did not play a distinguished role. Bland was blamed for failing to provide information to Washington about key British movements at the battle of Brandywine in September. Although nominally in command of the dragoons until December 1779, Bland was on detached duty during late 1778 and most of 1779. In November 1778, he commanded the guard detail that moved the British Convention Army (General John Burgoyne's defeated troops) from Connecticut to Virginia, and then he was placed in charge of the American post at Charlottesville, Virginia in May 1779. Bland retired from active service in November 1779 and returned to his plantation. He was elected to the Continental Congress in 1781 and served until 1783. He later ran unsuccessfully for governor of Virginia but did win election to the House of Burgesses and as representative from Virginia to the U.S. Congress, where he served from 1788 until his death.

BLISS, Daniel (1740–1806) Loyalist Born in Concord, Massachusetts, Bliss graduated from Harvard and practiced law before the Revolution. He was proscribed as a loyalist by the state government in 1778 and served with the British as a commissary for the army during the war. He emigrated to New Brunswick after the Revolution and became a member of the provincial council and chief justice of the Court of Common Pleas.

BLOODWORTH, Timothy (1736–1814) Delegate to Congress Bloodworth was born in New Hanover County, North Carolina and served on his local committee of safety in 1775 during the period when resistance grew against royal governor Josiah Martin. During the Revolution, Bloodworth was a member of the state legislature, although it ceased to function for the most part after the British invasion of 1780. In 1784, he was selected as a delegate to the Confederation Congress, serving until 1787. In 1795, he was chosen as U.S. senator from North Carolina, and later he became collector of customs for the port of Wilmington.

BLOOMFIELD, Joseph (1753–1823) Continental officer, government official Born in Woodbridge, New Jersey, Bloomfield studied law before the Revolution in the office of Cortlandt Skinner and was admitted to the bar just before the outbreak of the war. He was commissioned as a captain in Elias Dayton's New Jersey Regiment, which was taken into the Continental service in 1776 (and reorganized a year later) as the 3rd New Jersey Regiment. Bloomfield began the march north to Quebec in 1775, but he failed to get farther than upper New York, where he became a staff officer for Philip

Schuyler. He eventually was promoted to major and became judge advocate of the northern army. He later fought—apparently once again as part of the 3rd New Jersey—at Brandywine and Monmouth. He resigned his commission in 1778. After the Revolution, Bloomfield settled in Burlington, New Jersey and entered a career in political office, serving as attorney general of the state, clerk of the assembly and register of the Court of Admiralty. He achieved most prominence after the turn of the century, sitting as governor of New Jersey almost continuously from 1801 to 1812. He organized the state militia during the War of 1812 and received a commission as brigadier general in the U.S. Army. In 1816, he was elected to the U.S. House of Representatives, serving until 1821.

BLOUNT, Thomas (1759–1812) Soldier, legislator Brother of William Blount, Thomas Blount was born in North Carolina, and in 1776, at age 16, he enlisted as a private soldier in the 5th North Carolina Regiment, which was organized in April to defend the state. His service was brief, however, since he was captured by the British and sent to England as a prisoner of war, remaining there for the duration of the conflict. When finally released, Blount returned to Tarboro, North Carolina and opened a mercantile business with his other brother, John. They prospered in the West Indies trade after the Revolution, and Blount became a prominent political figure, serving first in the state legislature and then as U.S. representative from North Carolina to the new federal Congress in 1793. He subsequently served five terms as a congressman (he was also defeated twice for election) between the early 1790s and 1812, when he died in office in Washington, D.C.

BLOUNT, William (1749–1800) Land speculator, delegate to Congress, government official Blount was an ambitious speculator in western lands who used political office to further his business fortunes. He was born in Bertie County, North Carolina and fought as a young militiaman against the Regulators in 1771. During the Revolution, Blount was paymaster of the 3rd North Carolina Regiment and a commissary for General Horatio Gates during the latter's brief time in command of the Southern Department. Late in the war, Blount began a long career in public office, which he combined with land speculation on a grand scale. He served in the North Carolina legislature from 1780 to 1784 and sat as a delegate to Congress four times between 1782 and 1787. He also attended the federal constitutional convention. George Washington appointed him governor of the Southwest Territory in 1790; Blount was already deeply involved in buying lands in the Tennessee region where he and John Sevier claimed hundreds of thousands of acres (he also was a partner in land schemes with Robert Morris). He was selected as one of Tennessee's first U.S. senators in 1796, but his primary interest was in firming up his land claims. He was involved in a plot with the British to seize New Orleans from the government of revolutionary France and a similar scheme with the Creek Indians to take the Floridas—plans known collectively as the Blount Conspiracy. The plots were revealed by a subordinate, and Blount was expelled from the U.S. Senate in 1797. He returned to Tennessee and was elected to the state senate. *Further reading:* W. H. Masterson, *William Blount* (Baton Rouge, 1954; reprint 1969).

BLOWERS, Sampson Salter (1742–1842) Loyalist official

Born in Boston, Blowers graduated from Harvard and studied law with Thomas Hutchinson. He first came to public notice in 1770 as one of the defense attorneys (along with John Adams) for the British soldiers in the trial resulting from the Boston Massacre. After the soldiers were acquitted, Blowers came more and more to be identified with the supporters of the crown. He went to England in 1774 and lived quietly among the loyalist community that formed there. He returned to Boston in 1778 and was promptly arrested and thrown in jail. After his release, Blowers went to Halifax, Nova Scotia and managed to secure an appointment as judge of the Court of Vice-Admiralty in Newport, Rhode Island, which was then in British hands. When the British evacuated Newport in 1779, Blowers went again to England and successfully sought a new appointment. He was sent to New York City as solicitor general, an office he filled until the final British withdrawal in 1783. He then moved to Nova Scotia, serving as attorney general of the province, speaker of the house, chief justice of the Supreme Court and president of the provincial council. He died a few months after his hundredth birthday.

BOARDMAN, Elijah (1760–1823) Soldier, government official

Boardman, a native of New Milford, Connecticut, served as a teenager in the Connecticut Regiment of Colonel Charles Webb, a part of the Continental Line from 1775 to 1777. By 1781, Boardman had withdrawn from military service in favor of commerce. As a successful merchant, he moved into politics and sat in the state legislatures of both Connecticut and New York. He was U.S. senator from Connecticut from 1821 until 1823. He died in Ohio.

BOERUM, Simon (1724–1775) Delegate to Congress

Boerum was born to a family of Dutch ancestry on Long Island, New York. He was a farmer and miller by occupation and a local official—county clerk and clerk of the board of supervisors from 1750 until his death. He sat in the colonial assembly from 1761 onward and was a member of the patriot provincial convention in 1775. He was selected as a delegate to the first Continental Congress in 1774 and again shortly before his death in 1775.

BOISBERTRAND, René Étienne Henri de Vic Gayault de (b. 1746) French agent and volunteer

Boisbertrand was a French officer from a noble family who entered the king's service in 1763. He inherited a family sinecure in 1768 and left active service, but he apparently continued to be listed on the army rolls and was promoted to lieutenant colonel in 1772. He carried secret dispatches from France to America sometime during 1775 or 1776 and then volunteered for service with the American army. The details of his commission and assignments are missing, but he apparently was an aide to General Charles Lee and was seriously wounded and captured with Lee at Basking Ridge in December 1776. Boisbertrand remained a captive of the British under harsh treatment for two years, but he escaped in 1778 and returned to France. He failed to regain either his health or his place on active duty, and he retired in 1791.

BOLLAN, William (1710–1782) Loyalist, colonial agent

Bollan was born in England, but he emigrated to the colony of Massachusetts sometime before the 1730s. In Boston, he studied law under the senior Robert Auchmuthy and set up a practice. He became an officeholder in 1743 with his appointment as advocate general of the colony. In 1745, he returned to Britain as the agent of Massachusetts, eventually becoming the agent for the Massachusetts Council. He continued to represent the interests of Massachusetts up until the Revolution, trying to play the role of conciliator through 1775. He never returned to America, dying before the Revolution officially ended.

BONVOULOIR, Julien, Achard de. See ACHARD de Bonvouloir, Julien.

BOONE, Daniel (1734–1820) Frontiersman, militia officer   Although his very name evokes the myth of the American frontier and historians have had difficulty separating biographical legend from fact, Boone was a flesh-and-blood frontiersman and Indian fighter who did much to encourage white settlement in Kentucky during the Revolutionary era. He was born to a Quaker family near Reading, Pennsylvania and moved to the Yadkin River region of North Carolina as a teenager. He was a teamster for the British during the Seven Years War, narrowly escaping with his life from General Braddock's defeat in 1755. His subsequent explorations west, over the Appalachian barrier by way of the Cumberland Gap, and his work of establishing the Wilderness Road route helped make possible a flow of settlers from the eastern piedmont to the interior of the Kentucky region. In 1775, as an agent of Richard Henderson's Transylvania Company, Boone founded a settlement on the Kentucky River called Fort Boonesborough and brought in families to establish a frontier station. He became an officer of the Virginia militia when the Kentucky area was formally designated as a western county in 1776. Throughout most of the Revolutionary War, Boone fought on the frontier against the western Indian tribes—he was captured and held for four months by the Shawnee in 1778—and tried to establish the basis for his and Henderson's land titles. In this he was disappointed: Henderson's grandiose scheme came to nothing, and Boone's own land claims proved to be defective. He lost all his land titles in Kentucky following the war, and in 1788 he moved to what is now West Virginia. In 1799, he moved farther west, to Spanish territory that eventually became Missouri. After the sale of Missouri to the United States under the Louisiana Purchase, Boone again lost all his land titles, although his claims were restored by Congress in 1814. He died in Missouri, although remains alleged to be

Daniel Boone

his were later returned to Kentucky and interred at Frankfort. *Further reading:* Michael Lofaro, *The Life and Adventures of Daniel Boone* (Lexington, Ky., 1978).

BORRE, Preudhomme de. See PRUEDHOMME de BORRE.

BOSE, Carl Ernst Johann von. German mercenary general   Bose was one of the more experienced German officers of the Hesse-Cassel contingent of mercenaries sent in 1776 to fight for the British. He was colonel of the Fusilier Regiment von Ditfurth that landed in New York as part of the German force under Leopold von Heister and took part in the New York campaign. He fell ill, however, and was not on duty during the fall of the year; his absence was partly responsible for the elevation of Johann Rall to command of a brigade at Trenton in December. In 1777, Bose was promoted to either lieutenant general or major general (the accounts vary) and given command of the Musketeer Regiment Landgraf. The following year, he took command of a reorganized regiment, known thereafter as the Regiment von Bose. He and his men—about a thousand—were sent south with Sir Henry Clinton's army in 1780 and formed one of the few German units to fight in the southern theater. Bose's regiment was engaged at most of the major southern battles during 1780 and 1781, notably at Guilford Courthouse and Eutaw Springs. The colonel was captured along with his remaining men at the surrender at Yorktown.

BOTETOURT, Norbonne Berkeley, Baron de (c. 1718–1770) Royal governor

A distant relative of 17th-century Virginia governor William Berkely, Botetourt had served as a member of Parliament before his appointment as royal governor of Virginia in 1768. His most recent predecessors in office had failed to set foot on Virginia soil, but Botetourt traveled in person to Williamsburg, taking with him a fancy carriage, horses and a love of public pomp. He dissolved the House of Burgesses in 1769 over the resolutions passed at Raleigh Tavern condemning taxation, but he also was sympathetic in some degree to the complaints of the colonists. He warned the British cabinet that the colonies would not accept taxation in the form desired by the government in London, but he was ignored. He resigned in 1770 and died soon after, to be remembered with relative fondness by the patriots of Virginia.

BOUCHER, Jonathan (1738–1804) Loyalist clergyman

Boucher was a conspicuous southern loyalist Episcopal priest. Born in England, he arrived in Virginia in 1759 but went back to England three years later to be ordained a priest in the Anglican Church. He returned to Virginia to become rector of Hanover Parish in King George County and then of St. Mary's in Caroline County. During the 1760s, Boucher generally supported the growing unrest in Virginia over British colonial policy, opposing the Stamp Act and the Townshend Duties, for example. In 1770, Boucher moved to Annapolis, Maryland as rector of St. Anne's, and he became chaplain to the lower house of the Maryland legislature. He was appointed as rector of Queen Anne's parish in Prince Georges County the following year by royal governor Robert Eden. His close association with the government inclined Boucher's politics toward the crown. By 1774, he came to believe the patriots wrong, and he decided to publicly support the loyal cause. He preached against resistance to the British government and held that it was a religious obligation to obey the crown. Under growing pressure from local patriots, Boucher and his family left Maryland for England in 1775. He later received a living in Surrey, and in 1797, Boucher published a collection of sermons he had preached in America during the crisis, *A View of Causes and Consequences of the American Revolution. Further reading:* Anne Y. Zimmer and Alfred H. Keely, "Jonathan Boucher: Constitutional Conservative," *Journal of American History* 63 (1971), 897–922.

BOUDINOT, Elias (1740–1821) Government official, delegate to Congress

Although as a child he lived next door to Benjamin Franklin in Philadelphia, Boudinot spent his adult life as a prominent resident of New Jersey. His Huguenot family had moved to America in the late 17th century, and he was the fourth in line to bear the same name. Following academy schooling, Boudinot read for the law with Richard Stockton (a signer of the Declaration) and married Stockton's sister, Hannah, in 1762. Practicing first in Elizabethtown and then in Princeton, Boudinot became a leading member of the New Jersey bar in the decade before the Revolutionary War. He strongly represented the interests of property, but he was also a staunch early patriot and a persistent foe of New Jersey's royal governor, William Franklin. In 1774, Boudinot was a member of the New Jersey Committee of Correspondence and supported the New Jersey Assembly in approval of the Continental Congress, and he was a delegate to the New Jersey Provincial Congress in 1775. He is credited with sending much-needed gunpowder to Washington's army at Boston in August of that year. He eventually became a close associate of Washington and in 1777 was appointed as commissary of prisoners with the equivalent rank of colonel. It was a taxing job that required him both to look after British prisoners in American hands and to monitor the welfare of Americans held by the British. He worked hard at his responsibilities, advancing at least $30,000 of his own money for aid to prisoners.

He was elected to Congress from New Jersey in late 1777 but took his seat reluctantly and probably only to lobby for reimbursement of claims against the government. Nonetheless, he continued to serve in Congress for several years. He represented the interests of the middle states in the disputes over western land claims, a position that often brought him into conflict with James Madison and others who wanted a free hand in the West.

In 1782, he was elected to a one-year term as president of the Congress, which, under the Articles of Confederation, also made him the chief executive officer of the nation. During his time in office he also served as secretary of foreign affairs and signed the preliminary peace terms with Great

Britain. The chronic shortage of national funds brought on a crisis in the midst of his presidential term, however, when dissident soldiers threatened Congress over pay issues. The members precipitously adjourned to Princeton after Pennsylvania authorities refused to guarantee their safety, and Boudinot presided over the rest of a rump Congressional session in his home town. When his presidential term expired, Boudinot declined reelection.

He returned to his law practice and was heavily involved in western land speculations in the years immediately after the Revolution. He was elected again to Congress after the adoption of the Constitution, which he strongly supported, and in 1795 he was appointed to a stormy term as superintendent of the national mint. He retired from public service in 1805 and devoted the remainder of his life to writing and to the American Bible Society, of which he was founder and first president. *Further reading: Journal; or Historical Recollections of American Events During the Revolutionary War* (Philadelphia, 1894); Donald Whisenhunt, *Elias Boudinot* (Trenton, N.J., 1975).

BOUGAINVILLE, Louis Antoine de (1729–1811) French naval officer, explorer

Bougainville was already famous for his around-the-world voyage when he fought as a naval officer during the American Revolution. He was born in Paris and won scientific honors early in life for his work as a mathematician. He combined throughout his life an interest in science, the natural world and military affairs. He served during the Seven Years' War as an aide to Montcalm in Canada and in the campaigns in Germany. After the war in Europe ended in 1763, Bougainville entered a period of world voyaging and exploration, founding a French colony in the Falkland Islands between 1763 and 1765. His most famous expedition was a two-year sea journey between 1767 and 1769, during which he circumnavigated the globe, discovering Tahiti and a large group of islands in the Solomons along the way, and becoming the first Frenchman to sail entirely around the world. On his return, Bougainville transferred from the army to the French navy and commanded a frigate in the West Indies fleet under d'Estaing in 1779. He took part in the capture of Granada and in the unsuccessful Franco-American attempt to take Savannah in October 1779. In 1781, he commanded the *Auguste* as part of Admiral de Grasse's fleet that fought the British to a standstill off the Chesapeake Bay and allowed the final allied victory at Yorktown. The following April, he was with de Grasse when the French fleet met disaster at the hands of Admiral Sir George Rodney at the battle of the Saints, but Bougainville himself emerged with his squadron and honor intact. He quarreled with de Grasse, however, and he left active service in the navy. He continued his scientific work but was nearly put to death during the dislocations of the French Revolution. *Further reading: Bougainville's Voyage*, Davis Hammond, ed. (Minneapolis, 1970); Michael Ross, *Bougainville* (1978).

BOUILLE, François Claude Amour, Marquis de (1739–1800) French officer

Although he neither commanded troops nor conducted campaigns in North America during the American Revolution, Bouille's energetic activities in the West Indies diverted British ships and men from the war in the north. He was born in the Auvergne and entered the French army at age 15, fighting with distinction during the Seven Years' War and rising to colonel. In 1768, he was appointed governor of Guadeloupe, where he served until 1771. He returned to the West Indies in 1777 as governor general of the Windward Islands. He received little cooperation during the American war from his naval counterparts, but he nonetheless managed to capture several islands from the British with a cobbled-together force of ships and men, seizing Tobago and Saint Christopher and retaking St. Eustatius in 1781. He returned to France in 1783 and was responsible for putting down a mutiny at Nancy in 1790. He supported the king during the French Revolution and subsequently fled France for England, where he died.

BOWDOIN, James (1726–1790) Official, propagandist

Bowdoin was a prerevolutionary patriot leader and propagandist in Massachusetts, although his role receded during the actual Revolution. He was born to one of the wealthiest families in New England and during his political career protected wealth and social status while strenuously opposing what he considered to be the incursions and innovations of British policy toward American economic and political well-being. His grandfather, a French Huguenot, had moved to Maine and then Boston, where he and the second generation built a commercial and financial empire, which the young Bowdoin inherited. Bowdoin was also well related by marriage to other powerful Bostonian families. He was a man of considerable learning and intellectual curiosity—a graduate of Harvard and a lifelong amateur scientist whose correspondence with Benjamin Franklin and own writings on electricity, astronomy and other physical phenomena were published in England. He took a seat in the Massachusetts lower house in 1753 but soon moved to a place on the Council, where he served until the eve of the Revolution. As the conflict with Great Britain heated in Boston during the 1760s, Bowdoin came to be a leader of the patriot faction of the Council especially opposing royal governor Francis Bernard. In 1769, Bowdoin wrote a widely-distributed pamphlet in response to letters from Bernard that had been made public. A year later, after the Boston Massacre, Bowdoin anonymously wrote *A Short Narrative of the Horrid Massacre . . .* and followed with *Additional Observations on a Short Narrative . . .* , both of which helped fan radical flames in New England. He also provided radical articles to the newspapers. Bowdoin was removed from the Council by British military governor Thomas Gage in 1774. He was then elected to be one of Massachusetts' first representatives to the first Continental Congress, but he declined to serve due to ill health and was replaced by John Hancock. He had recovered sufficiently to take a place on the executive council appointed in the summer of 1775 by the patriot Massachusetts Provincial Congress and served on what was essentially the governing body of the colony until 1777. Two years later, still plagued by poor health, Bowdoin was elected to the convention that wrote a new state constitution, serving as the meeting's president. Some patriots distrusted Bowdoin during the Revolution because of his connection with his son-in-law John Temple, who was a loyalist official of the British government. Bowdoin's most prominent political role emerged after the Revolution. He was selected as governor of the state of Massachusetts in 1785 and was the driving force that put down Shays' Rebellion. He left office in 1787 but sat in the 1788 state convention that ratified the new federal constitution. Bowdoin College, chartered after his death, was named in his honor. *Further reading:* Francis G. Wallett, "James Bowdoin: Patriot Propagandist," *New England Quarterly* (September 1950), 320–38.

BOWLER, Metcalf (1726–1789) British informer, businessman, state official Bowler was another of the secret informers for the British whose perfidy was not discovered until a century and a half later when the full documentation of the Revolution was examined. He appeared to his contemporaries at the time of the War for Independence to be a firm patriot, but in fact acted as a paid informer for British commander Sir Henry Clinton. Bowler, born in England, was a very wealthy merchant in Newport, Rhode Island before the war and was active in patriot affairs. He sat in the Rhode Island assembly from 1767 to 1776, during part of that time as speaker. He opposed the Stamp Act and was a Rhode Island delegate to the Stamp Act Congress in 1765. He served on a patriot committee of correspondence in 1773 and signed the Rhode Island declaration of independence. Bowler was also an elected judge of the Supreme Court and became chief justice in 1776. However, when the British seized Newport late in the same year, Bowler wrote almost immediately to Clinton and offered his services as a paid informer. He was motivated not by principle or belief but by the simple desire to save his property from depredation by the British (he complained of the ravages of the Hessian garrison in Newport). Bowler continued his secret correspondence with Clinton for several years, receiving payoffs and moving to Providence at the British commander's behest. Bowler produced little information of value, however, and Clinton eventually cut off the secret payments. Rather fittingly, Bowler's prosperity was destroyed by the war, and he was reduced to the status of small merchant after the Revolution. He was thought to have been a genuine patriot until Clinton's official letters were examined by American historians in the 20th century.

BOWLES, William (1763–1805) Loyalist Called by one biographer "a bold and wicked man," Bowles was a native of Maryland and joined the Maryland Loyalist Corps as a teenager in 1778. He got into trouble with his commanders and was dismissed but reinstated in 1781. He fought in the defense of Pensacola, Florida against Bernardo de Galvez in 1783 and was granted half pay at the end of the war. His subsequent career was among the Indian tribes of the south, primarily the Creek. Bowles was employed by Lord Dunmore and John Miller, two former royal governors, to run a trading company among the Creeks, and he established himself as a man of some influence in Florida and lower Georgia. He spoke three Indian languages and took both Creek and Cherokee wives. East Florida had passed to the custody of Spain after the Revolution, and Bowles consistently worked to undermine Spanish influence. He was captured by the Spanish in 1792 and transported first to Spain and then to the Philippines. He escaped from the Spanish and, after a brief stay in England, returned to Florida and tried to establish an independent Indian nation made up of Creeks, Cherokees and Seminoles under British protection. An army of mixed tribes and runaway black slaves under his command captured the Spanish post at San Marco in 1800. However, he was handed over to the Spanish by his former Indian allies in 1802 and died as a captive in Havana.

BOYD, Thomas (d. 1779) Continental officer
Boyd served as a sergeant in Thompson's Pennsylvania Rifles in 1775 and was part of the American expedition to Quebec. He was captured during the futile American assault on New Year's Eve and was not exchanged until November 1777. He subsequently received a commission in the 1st Pennsylvania Regiment and was part of General John Sullivan's campaign against the Iroquois in 1779. On September 13, he was captured with a companion while leading an advance party, taken to an Indian village and tortured to death. His remains were later disinterred and reburied with considerable ceremony. *Further reading: Notices of Sullivan's Campaign . . . Connected with the Funeral Honors to Those Who Fell with the Gallant Boyd . . .* (reprint, Port Washington, N.Y., 1970).

BRACKENRIDGE, Hugh Henry (1748–1816) Writer, clergyman, jurist
Brackenridge emigrated from Scotland at age five to a backwoods section of York County, Pennsylvania. His parents were poor farmers, but Brackenridge managed a rudimentary education on the frontier and in 1768 entered Princeton, where his intellectual gifts bloomed. He was a friend of fellow students James Madison, Philip Freneau and William Bradford, forming with them a patriot student debating society. Freneau and Brackenridge together wrote a commencement poem in the classical mode called "The Rising Glory of America." After leaving

Princeton, Brackenridge moved to Maryland and became a schoolmaster while studying divinity. He served as a chaplain to the Continental Army during the first years of the war (he wintered with the troops at Valley Forge in 1777) and wrote two plays in classical blank verse, *The Battle of Bunker Hill* and *The Death of General Montgomery,* supporting the American cause and boosting American heroism on the battlefield. He also preached fiery wartime sermons, which were later published. In 1779, Brackenridge left the pulpit, moved to Philadelphia and became editor of the *United States Magazine.* He returned to Maryland two years later to study law in Annapolis and then moved to Pittsburgh. He continued to write but also began a political career as a member of the Pennsylvania legislature. In 1792, he published his most famous work, *Modern Chivalry,* a novel satirizing frontier bumptiousness. He was appointed to the Supreme Court of Pennsylvania in 1799 and moved to Carlisle, where he lived the remainder of his life. *Further reading:* Joseph Ellis, "Hugh Henry Brackenridge: The Novelist as Reluctant Democrat," in *After the Revolution* (New York, 1979); Daniel Marder, *Hugh Henry Brackenridge* (1967).

BRADFORD, Thomas (1745–1838) Soldier, publisher
Bradford was a partner with his father, William Bradford (the Elder), in publishing the *Pennsylvania Journal.* He was an active patriot before the Revolution and served in both the Pennsylvania militia and the Continental Army. The family newspaper was suspended during the British occupation of Philadelphia. Later in life, he founded a business newspaper called the *Merchant's Daily Advertiser.*

BRADFORD, William (the Elder) (1722–1791) Printer, publisher, soldier
Probably the most important printer and publisher of the Revolution, at least in the middle colonies, Bradford was part of a family that brought printing to America in the 17th century. He was born in New York City, the grandson of the first colonial printer, also named William Bradford, who had come to the colonies along with William Penn in 1683. The latter-day William Bradford learned printing in Philadelphia from his uncle, a man who had founded the first newspaper in the middle colonies. In 1741, William Bradford went to England to learn more of the trade and to bring back to Philadelphia a stock of printing

supplies. The following year, he began the *Weekly Advertiser, or Pennsylvania Journal,* which for many decades was the premier newspaper in the colony, usually outstripping the rival *Pennsylvania Gazette* published by Benjamin Franklin. Bradford also published *The American Magazine,* set up the "London Coffee House" book store and began a successful insurance company with partner John Kidd. Not surprisingly, Bradford was a vocal opponent of the Stamp Act, publishing a since-famous skull-and-crossbones masthead when the act took effect. He also supported other patriot measures, such as the nonimportation agreements, and worked for the convening of a continental congress. In 1775, he invented the patriot symbol of the thirteen-segment snake, bearing the slogan "Unite or Die," which he used in his paper. Before the war, Bradford was a member of the Philadelphia militia company of Associators, and despite having long since reached middle age, he took up arms in 1776 as a major of militia on active duty, eventually reaching the rank of colonel. He fought at Trenton and was badly wounded at the battle of Princeton. His injuries and age forced his retirement from the militia in 1777, but he continued as an administrator, heading the Pennsylvania state navy board. He was compelled to suspend publication of his newspaper during the British occupation of Philadelphia—by this stage he was in business with his son, Thomas—but served later as the official printer to the Congress.

BRADFORD, William (the Younger) (1755–1795) Soldier, jurist

The younger son of the printer Bradford of Philadelphia, William became a lawyer rather than a publisher. He graduated from Princeton in 1775, and after a year reading the law with Edward Shippen, Bradford enlisted as a private in the Continental Army. He was soon commissioned, however, and eventually was promoted to the rank of captain. In 1777, he received a direct commission from Congress as deputy muster-master general with the equivalent rank of colonel. He resigned in 1779, citing ill health. Later in 1779, he passed the bar and moved to Yorktown, Pennsylvania to practice law. He was appointed attorney general of Pennsylvania in the same year, serving for more than a decade in that post. In 1791, he became chief justice of Pennsylvania, and in 1794, President George Washington named Bradford as the second attorney general of the United States.

Married to the daughter of Elias Boudinot and friend of political figures such as Washington and James Madison, Bradford was in a position of influence and power. His early death from a fever cut short a promising career.

BRADLEY, Stephen (1754–1830) Soldier, jurist, official

A native of Connecticut, Bradley graduated from Yale in 1775 just as the Revolution began. He served as a captain of volunteers in the Continental Army, eventually rising to colonel. He moved to Vermont after his military service and progressed through a succession of judgeships and offices, becoming speaker of the Vermont House and an associate justice of the Superior Court. He was a U.S. representative from Vermont and then senator, serving as president pro tem of the Senate for three terms.

BRANT, Joseph (c. 1742–1807) Indian leader

Brant was an intelligent, well-educated Mohawk chieftain and an able soldier who supported the British during the Revolution. He was probably the most important Indian leader of the war. Born in Ohio and named Thayendanegea, he lived as a child with his parents at Canajoharie Castle in the Mohawk Valley of New York. Following his father's death, Brant assumed his Anglicized name when his mother married Mohawk chief Nikus Brant. During his childhood, Brant spent time in the household of William Johnson, the powerful British trader and land speculator, playing with Johnson's son, John, and a nephew, Guy Johnson. Brant also attended an Anglican mission school. In 1754 at the beginning of the Seven Years' War, the Mohawk sided with the British and William Johnson. As a 13-year-old warrior, Brant fought under Johnson at the battle of Lake George. Johnson subsequently was knighted and became superintendent of Indian affairs for the British. Brant, whose sister Molly married Sir William in a Mohawk ceremony, enrolled in Eleazar Wheelock's Indian school at Lebanon, Connecticut and learned English.

In 1763, Brant served as a missionary's interpreter and also joined the Iroquois fighting with the British to suppress Pontiac's Rebellion. In 1765, he married the daughter of an Oneida chief and converted to Anglicanism. In 1774, he became personal secretary and interpreter to Guy Johnson, who had succeeded Sir William as superintendent. Brant

Joseph Brant

worked hard at persuading members of the Six Nations to support the British when the Revolution began, and in 1775, he was commissioned a captain and went to England, where he was presented at court. Benjamin West depicted him in a double portrait with Guy Johnson. Returned to America, Brant fought at the battle of Long Island in 1776. Slipping through American lines to his home in upper New York, Brant helped organize the Mohawk, Senecas, Onondagas and Cayugas for the British cause.

In the summer of 1777, Brant led the Indian troops of Barry St. Leger's force that ambushed Nicholas Herkimer at Oriskany. The battle was technically a victory for the British and their Indian allies, but was a costly one from the Indian viewpoint. Thereafter, Brant was reluctant to follow the command of British officers too far, preferring his own tactics and plans. His greatest successes were in raiding American settlements on the New York and Pennsylvania frontier, usually in conjunction with white troops commanded by John Johnson or Walter Butler—a series of conflicts during 1778 and 1779 known collectively as the Border Wars. The most notable Indian-British victory was probably at Cherry Valley, New York in November 1778. A large force under Brant and Butler caught the settlers and garrison of the American fort there unprepared and captured or killed many. Without artillery, the Indians and British could not take the fort itself, but carried off several dozen captives. Brant's reputation as a civilized and humane soldier gained considerably from the restraint he imposed on his warriors during and after the raid.

Brant and his allies continued their periodic raiding until the summer of 1779, when the expeditions under Sullivan crushed the power of the Iroquois confederation by destroying almost all the villages and crops in upper New York. Brant, by then a "colonel of Indians" under British commission, resisted peace, but he had few military options left after other Iroquois leaders surrendered. In 1784, he led many of the remaining Mohawks to Canada, where they settled on a land grant in Ontario. Henceforth, Brant's activities were peaceful, including his work to translate the Episcopal Book of Common Prayer and the Gospel of Mark into the Mohawk language. *Further reading:* Isabel T. Kelsay, *Joseph Brant: Man of Two Worlds* (Syracuse, N.Y., 1984); Harvey Chalmers and Ethel Brant Monture, *Joseph Brant: Mohawk* (East Lansing, Mich., 1955).

BRANT, Molly (c. 1735–1796) Indian leader

The sister of Mohawk chief Joseph Brant, Molly wielded considerable influence as the wife and then widow of Sir William Johnson, the British superintendent of Indian Affairs before the war. She married Johnson in the mid-1750s in a Mohawk ceremony (many biographers refer to her only as Johnson's "mistress") and served as hostess at Johnson Hall, his estate in upper New York. After Sir William's death in 1774, Molly continued to serve the British cause by supplying intelligence, particularly warnings about American troop movements before the battle of Oriskany in 1777. After the battle, she fled attacks by the Oneida, who supported the Americans, by escaping to Fort Niagara. She subsequently moved to the Mohawk postwar settlements in Ontario and became the "matron" of loyalists in the region. She received a yearly pension of £100 from the British government for her services to the royal cause. *Further reading:* Mary Archibald, *Molly Brant* (1977).

BRAXTON, Carter (1736–1797) Delegate to Congress, state official   Braxton was a wealthy Virginia planter who was probably the least committed to independence of all the signers of the Declaration. He was born in rural Virginia at his father's plantation and inherited large tracts of productive land. He attended the College of William and Mary, graduating in 1755, and then went to England in 1757 after the death of his young wife, not returning to the colonies until 1760. He became a delegate to the House of Burgesses in 1761 and served almost continuously until 1775. He sup-

ported the patriot position in the prerevolutionary conflict with Great Britain: signing the Virginia Resolves in 1769, joining the Virginia Association, sitting in the provincial conventions during 1774–1775, and serving on the governing Virginia Committee of Safety in 1775. However, he was opposed to independence and hoped to find a resolution with the mother country short of open breech. He mediated the potentially explosive dispute between patriots and Governor Dunmore in 1775 over the arsenal at Williamsburg, for example. In the fall of 1775, Braxton was appointed as a delegate to Congress to fill the vacancy left by Peyton Randolph's death. He spoke and wrote against independence and espoused a moderate form of compromise government, but he was persuaded to sign the Declaration of Independence. He was not reappointed to Congress but returned to Virginia and took a seat in the legislature, where he continued to serve for the rest of his career. He was ruined financially during the war. *Further reading:* Alonzo T. Dill, *Carter Braxton, Virginia Signer: A Conservative in Revolt* (Lanham, Md., 1983).

BREARLEY, David (1745–1790) Soldier, jurist

Brearley was born in New Jersey and was an attorney before the Revolution. He served as lieutenant colonel of the 4th New Jersey Regiment in 1776 and later was an officer in the 1st New Jersey. He left the army in 1779 to become chief justice of the state supreme court. In 1787, he was a New Jersey delegate to the Constitutional Convention, and after the new nation was founded, he became a federal district judge.

BREWSTER, Caleb. American secret agent

Brewster, about whom little biographical detail is known, was a Connecticut boatman recruited by Continental Army spymaster Benjamin Tallmadge as a courier for the famous Culper spy network in New York. Brewster was one of two principal messengers for the pseudonymous Culper Sr. and Culper Jr. (Abraham Woodhull and Robert Townsend), who reported on British activities in occupied New York City. Brewster sailed across Long Island Sound to deliver coded letters from the Culpers to Tallmadge.

BREYMANN, Heinrich Christoph (d. 1777) German mercenary officer

Breymann was a lieutenant colonel in command of the grenadier battalion of the Brunswicker contingent that fought with the British as paid troops during the Revolutionary War. He commanded between 550 and 600 men under Baron Friedrich von Riedesel. It was his misfortune to be assigned to the Burgoyne expedition in 1777. He and his grenadiers slogged with the other members of the army across upper New York state, and Breymann was dispatched—tardily—by General John Burgoyne to rescue Colonel Friedrich Baum at Bennington, but he arrived too late to prevent the disaster to the Germans inflicted by the Vermonters. At the final battle of the campaign, Breymann and his men held a key position, known as Breymann's Redoubt on the field at Bemis Heights. They fought hard and well but were overrun under a ferocious attack led by Benedict Arnold. Breymann was shot dead during the fight.

BRODHEAD, Daniel (1736–1809) Continental officer, state official

Born in Albany, New York, Brodhead moved as an infant with his family to the frontier region of Bucks County, Pennsylvania, where he grew up. In 1773, he moved to Reading and became deputy surveyor general of the colony. He attended the early patriot conventions in Philadelphia and raised a company of riflemen in 1775, which eventually became part of Miles's Pennsylvania Rifle Battalion with Brodhead in command as a lieutenant colonel. After fighting in the battles on Long Island in the summer of 1776, Brodhead transferred to the 4th Pennsylvania and then to the 8th Pennsylvania regiment as colonel in command. Following the winter at Valley Forge in 1777, he was assigned to the post at Pittsburgh and became commander of the Western Department in the spring of 1779, undertaking a successful expedition against the Indians along the Allegheny River as a corollary to General John Sullivan's campaign against the Iroquois. He was not, apparently, an easy man to get along with, and he fell into a serious dispute with his officers and several residents of Pittsburgh, which resulted in his recall. He received a brevet as brigadier general at the time of his retirement from the army, and he assumed the office of surveyor general for Pennsylvania after the war.

BROOKE, Francis Taliaferro (1763–1851) Soldier, jurist, legislator

Brooke was a native of Virginia and enlisted in the army at age 16. He won a commission and served as a lieutenant in Christian Febiger's regiment during the southern campaigns of 1781. Following the war, he became an attorney and filled a series of public posts, including membership in the Virginia house and senate. He was also a prominent judge.

BROOKS, David (1756–1838) Soldier, official

A native Philadelphian, Brooks studied law before the Revolutionary War but had not yet been admitted to practice at the bar when he received a commission in the Pennsylvania battalion of the hastily-organized Flying Camp of 1776. The troops recruited for the supposedly mobile striking force were little-trained, and most fared poorly in the battles with the British in New York. Brooks was captured at the surrender of Fort Washington and held captive for the ensuing four years. On his release, he was appointed assistant clothier general. His postwar career was mostly as an officeholder and a lawyer. He was a member of the New York Assembly, served as U.S. representative from New York, was judge and clerk of Dutchess County, and eventually became a U.S. customs officer.

BROOKS, John (1752–1825) Continental officer, physician, government official

Brooks was born in Medford, Massachusetts and studied medicine with a local doctor before setting up his own practice in Reading. He was a minuteman and rallied with his colleagues in April 1775 to the fighting at Concord and the subsequent harassment of the British on the road to Boston. His militia unit joined the siege of the British and fought at the battle of Bunker Hill. Brooks was commissioned as a major in the Continental Army in January 1776 and served with the 8th Massachusetts during the New York campaign and against General John Burgoyne the following year. In March 1778, he became an aide to von Steuben as part of the inspector general's staff. Brooks transferred to the 7th Massachusetts Regiment in November 1778 as a lieutenant colonel and served with this unit until the end of the Revolution. He was closely involved in the near uprising of Continental officers at Newburgh, New York in 1783 and was one of the three officers sent to address Congress. His exact role in the affair is unclear, but he drew the ire of John Armstrong Jr. (the main conspirator) after returning empty-handed from Philadelphia. After his discharge in June 1783,

Brooks returned to Medford and took up medical practice again. However, his public career had only begun. He sat in the Massachusetts legislature and served as a militia general during Shays' Rebellion during the late 1780s, and in 1791, President George Washington appointed Brooks to the post of federal marshal for Massachusetts. The following year, he was commissioned as a brigadier general in the revived U.S. Army, serving until 1796. He was adjutant general of Massachusetts from 1812 to 1816, when he was first elected as governor of the state. He eventually served seven terms as governor.

BROUGHTON, Nicholson. Naval officer, soldier

Broughton was a captain in John Glover's Marblehead regiment in the fall of 1775 and apparently a seafarer from one of the coastal towns of Massachusetts. When George Washington decided to do something about the unimpeded flow of supplies to the British garrison at Boston, the new commander in chief asked Glover to outfit a ship to capture or interdict British shipping. Glover chose Broughton to command the *Hannah*, a commercial schooner that was soon converted to a makeshift warship by the addition of four-pounder cannon and space for a larger-than-usual crew. Broughton was told by Washington to attack only ships in the service of the British army and to stay away from fights with armed vessels. The captain and the crew of the *Hannah* were to receive one-third of the value of any cargos and ships seized. Broughton was ready to sail by early September. His first two attempts to leave port at Beverly, Massachusetts were frustrated by the appearance of British patrols, but on September 7, he slipped out to sea and returned with a prize, the *Unity*, laden with naval stores, timber, fish and provisions. Unfortunately, the prize turned out to be the property of a New Hampshire patriot, and Washington returned the cargo and ship to its owner. Broughton's crew mutinied when they learned that their prize money was gone, and he had to find a new crew. On October 10, Broughton ran out from his anchorage and discovered an armed British sloop, the *Nautilus*, waiting. The British captain chased Broughton back toward the harbor and the Americans had to abandon ship when they ran aground on the flats. After pounding the *Hannah* with gunfire, the British captain ran aground himself and nearly lost his ship to bombardment from patriots ashore. Broughton seemed to have trouble with excess zeal. He left the command of the *Hannah* and sailed with Captain John Selman to the small Nova Scotian village of Charlottetown, where he seized several local citizens and brought them back to Washington's headquarters at Cambridge. Washington freed the captives and allowed Broughton's commission to expire in December.

BROWN, Benjamin (1756–1831) Naval physician, official

Born in Swansea, Massachusetts, Brown practiced medicine during the prewar period in the part of upper Massachusetts that eventually became Maine. He served as ship's doctor first aboard the frigate *Boston* and later aboard the *Thorne*. When the latter ship was taken by the British at the mouth of the St. Lawrence, Brown was captured and imprisoned on Prince Edward Island. He escaped, however, and made his way to Boston. Following the Revolutionary War, he served in the Massachusetts legislature and one term as U.S. representative.

BROWN, John (1736–1803) Merchant, delegate to Congress

Perhaps the most vigorous patriot among the merchant Brown brothers of Providence, Rhode Island, John withdrew from the family firm headed by Nicholas in 1770 and set up his own manufacturing and mercantile company. In 1772, he was the instigator of the *Gaspée* affair, organizing the mob of men who seized and burned the British revenue cutter after it had run aground in Narragansett Bay. The British authorities arrested Brown but failed to prove the case that he was responsible for the outrage (the British reactions to the *Gaspée* incident increased patriot sentiment throughout the colonies), and he was released after pressure on the British from his brother Moses. During the War for Independence, Brown supplied the Continental Army with food, clothing and munitions and generally put his fleet of trading ships at the service of the American cause, although not failing to take large profits for himself. He was elected to Congress in 1784 but did not take his seat. He continued to prosper after the Revolution, especially when one of his ships established a direct trade with East India and China in 1787. He was elected to the U.S. House in 1799 and served one term. Along with his brothers, he helped establish Rhode Island College in Providence, a school that became known as Brown University.

BROWN, John (1744–1780) Continental officer, attorney

Born in Massachusetts, Brown graduated from Yale in 1771, studied law in Providence, Rhode Island and was admitted to the bar in New York. He moved to Pittsfield, Massachusetts in 1773. He became a member of the local committee of correspondence in mid-1774 and represented Pittsfield in the Massachusetts Provincial Congress later in the year. In February 1775, Brown volunteered for a mission to Canada on behalf of the Boston Committee of Correspondence: he was to assess pro-American sentiment in Canada and establish communications with Canadian dissidents. His trip produced few results, but a stop at Fort Ticonderoga convinced him the place could be taken easily, a fact he reported to Massachusetts patriots. He was with Benedict Arnold and Ethan Allen when they took the fort in May 1775. He remained in the area as a major in Easton's regiment, and in July and August went again into Canada to reconnoiter. He reported to Philip Schuyler and Richard Montgomery and then collaborated with Ethan Allen in the precipitous and ill-considered attack on Montreal, narrowly escaping capture by the British. Brown and Easton operated against the British and loyalist forces in the region with minor success, but Brown embroiled himself in a dispute with Benedict Arnold over promotion and disposition of supplies—one of several such recurring disputes for Arnold. Brown and Moses Hazen accused Arnold of dealing in plunder, and Arnold responded with similar countercharges against Hazen and Brown. The dispute dragged on for months, with Brown eventually taking his case unsuccessfully to Congress. He resigned his commission in February 1777 and returned to the practice of law in Pittsfield. When General John Burgoyne invaded from the north later in the year, Brown returned to the field as an officer of the militia. He went back to his law books until 1780, when he took the field as an officer in the Massachusetts contingent that marched against Sir John Johnson and Joseph Brant in the Mohawk Valley in New York. Brown was killed at Fort Keyser in October when he led an attack against the loyalist-Indian force that outnumbered his American militiamen by ten to one.

BROWN, Joseph (1733–1785) Merchant

The second of the Brown brothers of Providence, Rhode Island, Joseph had the least public career. He entered the family mercantile and trading business at an early age and devoted most of his life to commerce. He was of a technical bent and ran the family iron works at Hope Furnace, which provided cannon to the American cause during the Revolution. He also sat in the Rhode Island assembly.

BROWN, Montforte. British official, army officer

Brown was royal governor of New Providence (now called Nassau) in the Bahamas and was captured in March 1776 by the first (and only) organized naval expedition of the Continental Navy, when Esek Hopkins' squadron assaulted the British island base. Brown was eventually exchanged along with Cortlandt Skinner for Lord Stirling. In early 1777, Brown raised the Prince of Wales American Regiment made up of Connecticut loyalists, and he was named as commanding brigadier general. While the regiment served in Rhode Island, the West Indies and the Carolinas, Brown himself seldom took the field.

BROWN, Moses (1738–1836) Businessman, legislator

The youngest and longest-lived of the Providence Brown brothers, Moses joined the family business of Nicholas Brown & Company in 1763. He worked in the firm for only 10 years, however, and retired from active participation before the Revolution. He sat in the Rhode Island General Assembly from 1764 until 1771 and had considerable political influence, which he used to help his brother John escape punishment over the *Gaspée* incident. Moses was the central figure in promoting the move of Rhode Island College from Warren to Providence and was the moving spirit behind the Brown family support of the college that came to bear their name. He founded the Rhode Island Abolition Society in 1774 and promoted other good works during his long lifetime.

BROWN, Nicholas (1729–1791) Merchant

One of the Brown family of Rhode Island merchants, Nicholas was born in Providence and joined his brothers and uncle as a partner in the family business. The company became known as Nicholas Brown & Company on the death of his uncle in 1762. The firm had one of the most extensive trades in all of the colonies in the years before the Revolution, dealing with the West Indies and most of the major trading nations of Europe. Brown also owned manufacturing interests in Rhode Island, including a candle-making factory that was part of a monopolistic combine that controlled the manufacture of candles from sperm-whale oil. He also owned a major iron-making facility at Hope Furnace. Brown supported the patriot cause and secretly imported goods at the behest of Congress. Along with his brothers, he helped establish what is now Brown University in Providence.

BROWN, Reuben. Minuteman

Brown, a saddler who operated a harness shop in Concord, Massachusetts, was a minuteman of the local militia company—one of those designated to respond instantly on warning of danger. On April 19, 1775, he assembled with his company after Dr. Samuel Prescott brought word to Concord that a British column was on the march. Brown was dispatched to ride to Lexington and confirm the news. He returned with a report that he had seen firing on Lexington Green. During the ensuing brief British occupation of Concord, the redcoats burned Brown's shop.

BROWN, Robert (1744–1823) Soldier, legislator

Brown was born in Weaversville, Pennsylvania and was an apprentice blacksmith in his youth. When the Flying Camp strategic reserve was formed in 1776, he received a commission as a lieutenant in the Pennsylvania unit. Like many of his comrades in the ill-fated organization, Brown was captured with the fall of Fort Washington and taken prisoner to New York City. He was first held on one of the infamous prison ships in the harbor but was later transferred to the jail at the old City Hall. He was paroled in 1777 but apparently was not exchanged and remained in British custody. After the war, he served in the Pennsylvania state senate, and he was elected to Congress in 1798, sitting in the House of Representatives for the following 17 years.

BROWN, Thomas. See BROWNE, Thomas.

BROWN, William (1752–1792) Army physician

A member of a medical family (his grandfather, father, brother and son were all doctors), Brown was born in Scotland and after early education in Maryland returned to the University of Edinburgh for medical training, graduating in 1770. He set up practice in Alexandria, Virginia, meeting Washington, Jefferson and Madison in the course of affairs in the busy Potomac port city. With the beginning of the war, he served as surgeon in the 2nd Virginia Regiment. In 1778, perhaps through his connection with Washington, Brown was appointed to the politically sensitive post of surgeon general to the Middle Department, succeeding Philadelphian Benjamin Rush. Brown resigned in 1780 and returned to private practice in Alexandria. While on duty as an army surgeon, Brown compiled and published one of the first American pharmacology manuals, aimed specifically at the conditions encountered in practicing military medicine.

BROWNE, Thomas (d. 1825) Loyalist officer

Perhaps a native of South Carolina where he owned lands, Browne was one of the most feared and despised southern Tory leaders for his exploits in Georgia. He was living in Augusta, Georgia in 1775 when he came in conflict with the local patriotic movement. He tried to flee from the local committee of safety but was captured and tarred and feathered. Despite the torture and public humiliation, he refused to concede his stand against rebellion. His military career began on a small scale in 1776 with raids against rebel strongholds. Throughout his activities, he and his American foes demonstrated the viciousness of the civil war in the South between loyalist and patriot. By 1778, he was a colonel and commanded a considerable body of loyalist troops, called the King's Rangers, augmented by Indian levies. His main base was Augusta, where he built up strong fortifications, and he used the town as a position from which to raid. In September 1780, a force of patriot militia under Colonel Elijah Clarke launched an attack on Browne's stronghold. The Americans drove in Browne's outlying Indians, but the main loyalist force holed up inside the fortifications and resisted all efforts to dislodge them. The patriots had artillery but their only qualified gunner was killed early in the fighting. Browne and his men had no source of water and Browne himself had taken a severe wound in the legs, but he refused to surrender. After four days, a British relief column showed up and the Americans withdrew, leaving 28 wounded behind. Browne hung the wounded men from a staircase in the fortified house. In the following spring, the Americans tried again. Militia under Clarke and regulars under Light Horse Harry Lee attacked Augusta, where Browne com-

manded 350 loyalists and 300 Indians. After holding out for nearly two weeks in the face of overwhelming odds, Browne finally surrendered and was marched off to Ninety-Six, South Carolina. He was treated as a prisoner of war, despite pleas for his death from relatives of his victims. He was ultimately exchanged and emigrated to the West Indies.

BROWNE, William (1737–1802) Loyalist official

A native of Salem, Massachusetts, Browne inherited considerable wealth from his merchant father, which he increased through his own business efforts. He served the crown as collector of the port at Salem, and he sat in the Massachusetts assembly during the 1760s. His sympathies toward revolution were mixed, and in fact he was dismissed from his job as collector because he was too lenient in enforcing the hated provisions of the Sugar Act. As conflict between Massachusetts patriots and the royal government increased, however, his attitude stiffened. He was appointed judge of the court of common pleas in Essex county in 1770 and colonel of the county militia in 1774, but he was already branded a royalist in the eyes of his neighbors, and all the officers in the militia company resigned rather than serve under him. Browne refused a request from a patriot committee to give up his offices, and in the fall of 1775, he left Salem for Boston. He evacuated to England the following year, first living in London and then settling in Wales, where he sought peace and quiet. He was soon bored, however, "without employment, without entertainment, without books, and without conversation— banished from everything that has life and motion," as he wrote about his new existence. In 1780, he was appointed governor of Bermuda and took on the task with alacrity. He served in the West Indies until 1788, when he returned to London.

BROWNSON, Nathan (1742–1796) Delegate to Congress, state official

Brownson was born in Woodbury, Connecticut and graduated from Yale in 1761. He studied medicine and briefly practiced in Woodbury before moving to rural Liberty County, Georgia in 1764 and becoming a planter. He attended the first Georgia Provincial Congress in 1775 and took a leading role in patriot affairs in the colony. He was selected as one of Georgia's delegates to the Continental Congress in 1776 (the colony had failed to send representatives to the first Congress) and served there until 1778. He may have been an army surgeon during the war. He was elected to the Georgia House of Representatives in 1781 and served there until 1788, often as speaker. During 1781, he also acted as governor of Georgia.

BRYAN, George (1731–1791) Official, merchant

Bryan was born in Ireland and moved to Pennsylvania in 1752, becoming a merchant in Philadelphia. He was named harbor commissioner in 1762 and won a seat in the Pennsylvania assembly two years later. He was also a judge of the Orphans' Court and the Court of Common Pleas. He attended the Stamp Act Congress in 1765. During the Revolution, Bryan served as an official of the Pennsylvania state navy and on the Supreme Executive Council. He was acting president of the state from 1777 to 1779. After the war, he became a judge on the Pennsylvania Supreme Court.

BUCHANAN, Thomas (1744–1815) Merchant

Buchanan was a native Scot and a graduate of the University of Glasgow. He came to New York City in 1763 and formed a highly successful mercantile and shipping partnership with Walter Buchanan (a relative). Before and during the Revolution, he was a political fence-sitter. He supported the nonimportation agreements before the war and served on patriotic committees through 1775, but—perhaps wanting to remain in business—he signed an oath of loyalty in 1776 when the British occupied New York. He was elected president of the New York City Chamber of Commerce in 1783 but declined to serve. After the Revolution, he resumed his business activities unmolested.

BUELL, Abel (1742–1822) Engraver, machine builder

Born in Killingsworth, Connecticut, Buell was a skilled engraver and devised several machines useful in the technology-poor early United States. His first venture, however, was as a counterfeiter in 1762. Buell was discovered altering Connecticut notes, and he was branded and jailed. He recovered quickly from the misadventure, however, and in 1769 built one of the first type foundries in America in Hartford, aided by a grant from the Connecticut Assembly. He was one of the first engravers to produce a map of the new United States in 1783. He also built machines to polish gemstones and make coins. In later life, Buell worked as a silversmith in Hartford.

BUFORD, Abraham (1749–1833) Continental officer

Buford was born in Culpeper County, Virginia. He raised a local militia company in 1775, and after the expulsion of Lord Dunmore, he was commissioned into the Continental Army and fought in the northern theater as a major of the 14th Virginia Regiment during 1776. He was promoted to lieutenant colonel the following year. Buford advanced to colonel in 1778 and in September took over command of the new 11th Virginia Regiment, a reorganized unit comprised of men from the former 15th Virginia. In early 1780, the 11th Virginia was in disarray, with Buford separated from his command. His men were captured when Sir Henry Clinton took Charleston, but Buford himself was outside the city in charge of a mixed force of about 350 Continentals—mostly new recruits or recalled veterans. Under orders from General Isaac Huger, Buford began a withdrawal toward Hillsborough, pursued by 2,500 British under Lord Cornwallis. The British commander detached Lieutenant Colonel Banastre Tarleton, then a little-known cavalry officer, to chase Buford's motley command. Tarleton caught up at Waxhaws, South Carolina on May 29 and completely defeated the poorly-prepared Continentals in a furious engagement. Buford's artillery was out of position; he ordered his men to wait until too late to fire their first volley; and the Americans were overwhelmed and cut down with saber and bayonet—the high casualty rate (113 killed, 203 captured and wounded) giving rise to the ironic term "Tarleton's Quarter" and the nickname "Bloody" Tarleton. Buford himself escaped on horseback. In January of the following year, Buford was appointed as commander of the 3rd Virginia Regiment, but the unit existed only on paper: all of the men and officers were prisoners of the British in Charleston. After the Revolution, Buford used land warrants granted for his wartime service to settle in Central Kentucky near Georgetown.

BULL, John (1740–1802) Delegate to Congress, legislator

Despite his name, which modern readers know as a national nickname for Britons, Bull was a native of South Carolina, born in Prince William's Parish. He was a local justice of the peace before the Revolution and a member of the colonial legislature. In 1775 and 1776, he attended the patriot provincial congresses and was chosen as a member of the first General Assembly of South Carolina. He served during almost the entire Revolution in the South Carolina legislature, and following the war he was sent as a delegate to the Confederation Congress for two terms. His long career as a legislator ended with a seat in the state senate in 1798.

BULL, William, II (1710–1791) Royal official

Bull was the son of the royal lieutenant governor of South Carolina. He received a medical degree from the University of Leyden; however, he did not practice medicine on his return to America but took up life as a planter and politician. He sat in the legislature, served on the Governor's Council and was involved in negotiations with the western Indian tribes. In 1759, he became lieutenant governor of the colony. Because the royal governors were frequently absent, Bull was acting governor five times during the period from 1760 to 1775, the crucial years of prerevolutionary activity in the colony. In effect, he was the chief royal official in South Carolina when it mattered. Bull was seldom a strident force against the rising patriot tide, showing considerable sympathy for the position of his fellow colonials: he soft-pedaled implementation of both the Stamp Act and the sale of East India tea, for example. However, he remained loyal in the end and was in effect deposed by the Provincial Congress that took over administration of the state in 1774. He stayed in South Carolina and was nominally governor during the British return in 1780, although in fact, the Royal Army controlled the administration of government in Charleston during its three-year occupation. Bull evacuated to England in 1782, although his property had not been seized by the patriot government, apparently in deference to his popularity. He settled in Bristol, England.

BULLOCH, Archibald (c. 1730–1777) State official, delegate to Congress

Bulloch was born in Charleston, South Carolina and studied there for the law. He practiced in his native state for several years and was a lieutenant in the colonial South Carolina militia before moving to Georgia about 1760 or 1762. He was one of the leaders of the revolutionary movement in Georgia, a colony that hung back during the first days of revolt and moved rather cautiously into the mainstream of the Revo-

lution. While speaker of the Georgia colonial assembly, Bulloch was appointed to correspond with northern patriots, chiefly Franklin, and to keep his fellow Georgians apprised of developments in New England. With the call for the first Georgia Provincial Congress in 1775, Bulloch was elected president, and he was reelected to the second congress the following year. He was chosen as Georgia's delegate to the Continental Congress when the colony finally felt confident enough to send a representative in 1776. The Provincial Congress took over the administration of the colony from royal governor James Wright in May 1776, and Bulloch was appointed as president and commander in chief of the state, a post he held until the new state constitution came into effect in 1777. He died the same year. Bulloch was the great-great-grandfather of U.S. president Theodore Roosevelt.

BULLOCK, Stephen (1735–1816) Soldier, legislator

Bullock was a schoolteacher before the Revolutionary War in his native Massachusetts. He served as a captain in one of the volunteer Massachusetts regiments during the conflict. He was elected to the Massachusetts constitutional convention in 1780 and to a seat in the state assembly in 1783. At the end of the century, he represented Massachusetts in the U.S. House of Representatives.

BURGES, Dempsey (1751–1800) Soldier, legislator.

Burges was born in North Carolina and served in the patriot Provincial Congress there in 1775 and 1776. He was a member of a local militia unit early in the war but was eventually commissioned as a lieutenant colonel in the Continental Army. In the 1790s, he was elected to the U.S. House of Representatives and served two terms.

BURGOYNE, John (1722–1792) British general, politician

Pompous, prolix "Gentleman Johnny" Burgoyne was a moderately competent soldier who suffered the worst defeat of British arms during the Revolution. He was ostensibly the son of a dissolute and impecunious army captain, but evidence strongly suggests he was actually fathered by Lord Bingley, who had formed a warm attachment to Burgoyne's mother. The young Burgoyne was educated at the fashionable Westminster school, there becoming the friend of Lord Strange, the eldest son of the Earl of Derby. He entered the army

John Burgoyne

as a cornet in 1740 and purchased a commission as a lieutenant the following year. He often visited the home of Lord Strange, and in 1743, he eloped with Strange's sister, Lady Charlotte Stanley. The bride's father was unhappy with the marriage, but eventually Burgoyne reconciled with his father-in-law, and he relied on Derby's influence and charity thereafter, especially following the premature death of Lord Strange. Burgoyne's early career came to a halt after only three years, however, when debts forced him to sell his commission and retire to France.

He returned to England in 1756 and regained a commission as a captain, eventually transferring to the elite Coldstream Guards. After a creditable performance as a field commander during an ill-conceived raid on the French coast in 1758 and 1759, Burgoyne won his greatest military honors as a commander of part of the British contingent serving as the backbone of the Portuguese army against the Spanish on the Iberian Peninsula.

Thus, at the end of the Seven Years' War, Burgoyne was a well-known and admired soldier enjoying the favor of the king, who endowed the officer with several lucrative posts and eventually raised him to the rank of major general. He also was a member of Parliament and supported the government throughout most of the period leading up to the eve of the American Revolution, a fact that played no small part in his preferment. A political ally with even a mild military reputation was a commodity much prized by the court and ministry. Burgoyne was a flamboyant if not terribly effective speaker, launching flights of oratory characterized by high-blown orotundity and profuse classical allusions—a style of speech and writing he cultivated during most of his public life.

Burgoyne was dispatched to Boston in April 1775 along with fellow major generals William Howe and Henry Clinton aboard the *Cerebus*. His main contribution to the defense of Boston was to write a pretentious and silly proclamation to the rebels, which drew more derision than response. He kept up a constant stream of criticism of his commander in chief, General Thomas Gage, in letters back home while simultaneously lobbying for a real command. In May 1776, he was appointed as Sir Guy Carleton's second in command in Canada and led the successful British expeditions that pushed out the remnants of the American attempt to invade Canada.

He returned to England for the winter, during which he put forward a scheme to split the northern colonies by moving down Lake Champlain and upper New York to seize Albany. Another force was to march up the Hudson River from New York City to meet Burgoyne and cut in twain rebel lines of supply and communication in the upper colonies. The plan's administration was muddled in the office of Lord George Germain, who failed to make clear the essential elements to General William Howe, now the commander in chief in New York. Communications between London and the two commanders in North America (never easy or simple) faltered, and Howe set on foot his own expedition against Philadelphia with little concern for Burgoyne's advance from Canada.

Burgoyne's command, made up of British regulars, a large contingent of German mercenaries under Baron Friedrich von Riedesel, some volunteer Canadian irregulars and a group of Indians, numbered about 10,000. He proposed to move by water down the river and lake route, recapture Fort Ticonderoga, and then strike toward Albany through the forests and hills. This plan was not unreasonable, especially considering the advice of loyalist Peter Skene, a wealthy New York landowner, who tried to convince Burgoyne that loyal Americans would support the advancing army and that rebel militia would similarly flee in the face of an organized force. The weaknesses were the very long line of supply required and the difficult terrain between Fort Ticonderoga and Albany. A better commander than Burgoyne might have insisted on a more efficient transportation system and a more streamlined organization. As it was, the army carried with it at least a thousand noncombatants, including wives, servants and camp followers, and was in general ill-equipped for slogging through dense woodlands. The plan also relied on a second column under Barry St. Leger to penetrate successfully down the St. Lawrence and along the Mohawk River as a diversion. Finally, if much went amiss with the main column, only a strong force from the British garrison at New York City could provide help, and Howe had left too few troops and unclear instructions with the commander there, General Clinton.

Departing in June, Burgoyne managed the first part of the invasion reasonably well. He easily captured Ticonderoga and began the cross-country march with enthusiasm and confidence. Soon, however, the going proved treacherous. American rebels under General Philip Schuyler felled trees and flooded swamps in a successful attempt to slow the British advance. None of the promised loyalist support turned up and the sparsely populated region provided little for Burgoyne's troops to feed on. The pace of the advance slowed to a crawl, and despite a mild victory at Hubbardstown in July, Burgoyne faced increasing difficulties in both movement and supply as the summer wore on. The column under St. Leger was stopped by battles at Fort Stanwix and at Oriskany, which made Burgoyne's position increasingly isolated. Meanwhile, the American forces grew in strength as troops detached from Pennsylvania reached the north and militia from nearby states began to gather. Eventually, the new American commander, Horatio Gates, could count close to 11,000 men under his nominal control, while Burgoyne's numbers slipped daily from death and desertion. A disastrous raid on Bennington in August by the Brunswickers further depleted Burgoyne's strength.

Even though his supporting officers counseled a change of plan, Burgoyne feared that even a strategic withdrawal or rerouting of his march would be ill-construed, so he determined to press on, betraying his relative lack of actual campaign experience. In early September, he crossed the army

General John Burgoyne meeting with Indian allies at Saratoga

to the other side of the Hudson and began to approach the main American defensive positions near Saratoga.

Two fierce battles ensued, the first near Freeman's Farm on September 19 and a second at Bemis Heights on October 7. While the British fought extremely well on both occasions, they could not win a decisive victory. Burgoyne's command was ravaged, cut off with little in the way of supply, its back to the river and an overwhelming American army in front. After much hemming and hawing, Burgoyne realized he had little choice but to surrender to Gates. Even at this dark moment, his political instincts came into play, and Burgoyne maneuvered Gates into signing terms of a "convention" rather than a capitulation. The British army was to surrender and withdraw from North America, but not be taken prisoner. Gates's foolish agreement to this plan caused no end of problem, as the Congress eventually abrogated the convention and Burgoyne's army passed a miserable existence in custody during the remainder of the war.

Burgoyne himself was released and sailed home to England. He was met with a storm of disapproval, which he spent much of the next few years attempting to fend off. He formed a political alliance with the opposition, defended himself both in Parliament and in public, and unsuccessfully demanded a court-martial to vindicate his conduct of the campaign. The king, outraged at the loss of the army and of Burgoyne's defection to the hated opposing politicians, stripped the officer of all his offices save his general's rank. There was even an abortive attempt to force Burgoyne to return to American custody. When the government fell in 1782, the new ministry rewarded Burgoyne with the post of commander in chief of Ireland, but this was short-lived since the new government dissolved with the death of Rockingham only months after taking office.

This marked the end of Burgoyne's military career, and he turned to his auxiliary interest, which he had pursued for several years: writing plays. His greatest success was *The Heiress,* which garnered considerable acclaim and a run in London in 1786. Burgoyne lived out the last years of his life with his mistress, the opera singer Susan Caulfield, who bore him several children (Lady Charlotte had died in 1776 while Burgoyne was in Canada). He died with no preliminary illness in 1792. *Further reading:* Richard J. Hargrove, Jr., *General John Burgoyne* (Newark, Del., 1983); Gerald Howson, *Burgoyne of Saratoga* (New York, 1979).

BURKE, Edmund (1729–1797) British writer, politician

Perhaps the greatest British political writer and orator of the second half of the 18th century, Burke achieved after his death a place in the firmament of political thinkers that exceeded his reputation during his life. He is particularly known for the subtlety of his conservative political philosophy that could support the American colonists yet produce a classic condemnation of the subsequent French Revolution, and Burke has long been the darling of 20th-century political conservatives who rejoice in quoting his eloquent prose. He was born in Dublin and had an unhappy early life, filled with quarrels with his father. After taking a degree at Trinity College, Burke went to England and read law at the Middle Temple but never practiced. He supported himself the rest of his life in 18th-century fashion by attachment to political mentors who offered places and employment. Burke's principal patron was the Marquis of Rockingham, for whom Burke served as private secretary from 1765 until Rockingham's death in 1782. During almost all this period, Rockingham was the leader of the most important Whig opposition faction and was out of office, a condition congenial to Burke's predilection toward speaking and writing against an opponent or a set of differing ideas. Burke himself sat in Parliament but had few practical political skills. While a strong advocate of the weak in society—especially

Edmund Burke

groups, such as the Irish and the masses of India, that he perceived as unable to help themselves— Burke nonetheless profoundly believed in rule by the aristocracy. He first came to notice in the 1750s with publication of *A Vindication of Natural Society* and *A Philosophical Inquiry into the Origin of Our Ideas of the Sublime and Beautiful.* He had a long-time interest in the American colonies, first evidenced in his *Account of the European Settlement in America,* published in 1757. The following year, Burke began the *Annual Register,* which he continued to write and edit until his death nearly 40 years later. The pages of the *Register* were filled with information and opinions about the American colonies and the Revolution, and the early American historians of the Revolution shamelessly plagiarized from Burke's work—an instrument of Burke's hidden influence on American thought and opinion that was long overlooked. Burke saw the split between mother country and America as the tragic rupture of a family. The British policies of the 1760s and early 1770s were to him a set of unwise movements to coerce children who were unjustly allowed little or no say in their destinies. He argued against the tea taxes in 1774 in *A Speech on American Taxation* and in 1775 proposed conciliation. When the North government fell in 1782 and Rockingham came to power, Burke was given a place as paymaster of the armed forces, but Rockingham's abrupt death ended Burke's short time in office. Burke subsequently teetered toward mental breakdown, which may have been responsible for his vociferous and damaging persecution of Warren Hastings in Parliament, although Burke genuinely saw Hastings as an oppressor of helpless India. Burke's greatest fame resulted from his clear-eyed and magnificently written criticism of the French Revolution as embodied in *Reflections on the Revolution in France,* an eminently quotable attack on the notion that violent political change could redress the fundamental deficiencies of human nature. *Further reading:* Stanley Ayling, *Edmund Burke: His Life and Opinions* (New York, 1988); Carl B. Cone, *Burke and the Nature of Politics: The Age of the American Revolution* (Lexington, Ky., 1957).

BURKE, Thomas (c. 1747–1783) Delegate to Congress, state official

Possessed of strong ideological views, Burke played important roles both in the national Congress and in his adopted state of North Carolina. He was one of the most intractable proponents of state sovereignty but also a committed patriot, and his stubbornness bordered on perversity. He was born in Ireland and emigrated after a family quarrel to the Eastern Shore of Virginia around 1759. He taught himself medicine but failed to establish a successful practice and turned to law, moving to Norfolk, Virginia in 1769. Three years later, Burke moved again, this time to Hillsborough, North Carolina, where he bought land and practiced as an attorney. He was chosen for the second and third provincial congresses in North Carolina, and he made a mark almost immediately with his energy and willingness to deal with the hard issues of establishing a new political order. Burke championed a strict sovereignty for the people against government structures, although he was no democrat. He was responsible for much of the new state constitution of North Carolina that emerged from the provincial meetings in 1776, and he was selected as a delegate to the Continental Congress in December of that year.

His service in Congress was stormy. He was suspicious of many of the provisions of the proposed Articles of Confederation, and Burke personally pushed through an amendment to reserve to the states all powers not specifically granted to the central government—the basis for the subsequent states' rights doctrine that so preoccupied the American political system until the Civil War. Burke was especially sensitive to what he saw as the illegitimate claims of the military on civil government, which led to his most famous display of stubborn behavior in April 1778. Exasperated with a long debate over how Congress should reply to what he thought was a preemptive letter from George Washington, Burke walked out of a late evening session, robbing the assembly of a quorum. Moreover, he refused to return when summoned, demonstrating the power of one delegate to paralyze the Congress, and the next day Burke protested an attempt to punish him by declaring he was beholden only to his state.

Burke returned to North Carolina and was confirmed in his view by reelection as a congressional delegate. He continued to serve in Congress until 1780, when he returned to Hillsborough and became governor of North Carolina. He again demonstrated his perversity by refusing to aid Johann de Kalb and General Horatio Gates with desperately needed supplies for their campaign against Lord Cornwallis, declaring the requests of the military to be an infringement of civil authority (the southern Continentals came near to starving and their ill-fed condition contributed to the disastrous defeat at Camden). On September 12, 1781, a British raiding party under loyalist David Fanning captured Burke near Hillsborough and carried him (and the members of the North Carolina Council) off to Wilmington. Burke was eventually moved to the Charleston area and imprisoned on James Island, from which he escaped in January 1782. He resumed his duties as governor after reaching safety with Nathanael Greene's army. He refused reelection and died the following year. *Further reading:* John S. Watterson, "Thomas Burke, A Paradoxical Patriot," *The Historian* (August 1979), 664–81; Elisha Douglass, "Thomas Burke, Disillusioned Democrat," *North Carolina Historical Review* 26 (April 1949), 385–98; Jennings B. Sanders, "Thomas Burke in the Continental Congress," *North Carolina Historical Review* 9 (January 1932), 22–37.

BURNET, William (1730–1791) Delegate to Congress, physician, jurist

Burnet was born near Newark, New Jersey and was associated with the city for most of his life. He was a member of the second graduating class of the College of New Jersey (later Princeton) and after studying medicine in New York set up a practice in Newark. He was a strong early patriot and a local leader against the loyalists. Burnet was chairman of the Newark and

Essex County committees of safety established in 1775, and he ordered the arrest of loyalist governor William Franklin when the latter tried to reconvene a royal legislature in New Jersey. When he became presiding judge of the Essex County courts, Burnet ruthlessly prosecuted loyalists in the area, helping to set the tone for the intense conflicts in that part of the state between civilian patriots and loyalists. He set up a military hospital in Newark in 1775 with the help of his son, also a physician. He was elected as a delegate to Congress in 1776 and returned for a second term four years later. He also carried the title of physician and surgeon general of the Eastern District during the war, but in fact spent most of his time as a local judge and running his hospital in Newark. He returned to civilian medical practice after the Revolution and continued to sit on the local bench of common pleas.

BURR, Aaron (1756–1836) Continental officer, vice president, traitor

Burr is second only to Benedict Arnold in the pantheon of American villains, but his perfidy came long after his steady service as a young officer during the Revolutionary War. He came from a notable family, the son of a president of Princeton and the grandson of the famous divine Jonathan Edwards.

Born in Newark, New Jersey and orphaned in early childhood, Burr was brought up in the household of his maternal uncle, Timothy Edwards. He was a bright and precocious student, graduating from Princeton at age 16. After a brief pass at studying for ordination in the family tradition, Burr turned to reading law in 1774.

At the outbreak of armed hostilities with the British, Burr volunteered his service to the new army forming around Boston. He was slight of build and sharp of tongue with no military training or experience, but he proved to be a doughty soldier. Refused a commission at first (despite a letter of recommendation from John Hancock), Burr attached himself to the Quebec expedition of Benedict Arnold as an aide without regular rank or assignment to a unit. Although the march through the wilderness broke many of Arnold's men, Burr was a source of strength and showed remarkable endurance. At the futile battle at the gates of Quebec on the last day of 1775, Burr attempted personally to carry General Richard Montgomery's lifeless body from the field.

By the following spring, Burr was a major and for a while acted as one of George Washington's aides. The assignment was short-lived, however, as the commander in chief and the young officer rapidly came to detest each other. By June, Burr moved on to become an aide-de-camp to General Israel Putnam, who commanded part of the American forces during the summer's battles on Long Island and Manhattan. Burr performed well in the disastrous campaign, particularly in September when he guided several of Putnam's militia detachments to safety from a British advance. Burr's most important assignment came as major of Malcolm's Regiment, a unit created in the spring of 1777. Burr was second in command but exercised virtual control over the regiment while it was assigned to duty in Orange County, New York. He wintered at Valley Forge with the Continental Army in 1777–78 and fought at Monmouth, perversely supporting Charles Lee in the controversies afterward over the conduct of the battle.

In 1779, Burr resigned his commission for reasons of health—his physical frailty finally came into play—and turned to the practice of law in Albany. His career thereafter put him in the forefront of national developments in the new republic but scarred his name forever. He moved to New York City in 1794 and entered the political arena, defeating Philip Schuyler in 1791 in the contest for the U.S. Senate. During the course of his political maneuverings Burr came into intense conflict with Alexander Hamilton (Schuyler's son-in-law), a breech which widened over the next few years. Burr allied himself loosely with the Jeffersonian opposition to the Federalists, although he was seldom completely trusted by other leaders in the developing party. He was nominated for the vice presidency behind Jefferson in 1800, and a flaw in the new U.S. Constitution (which made no distinction between candidates for president and vice president—the second highest vote getter became vice president) resulted in a tie vote when the electors cast their ballots for both Jefferson and Burr. The contest was thrown into the House of Representatives, and Jefferson was elected president only after 35 ballots. Even though he became vice president, Burr's career with the Jeffersonians was finished.

At the end of his term, Burr was called out by Alexander Hamilton, who felt their political and personal conflict had reached an unsupportable pitch.

On July 11, 1804, Burr killed Hamilton in a duel at Weehawken, New Jersey. Escaping prosecution for murder, Burr turned to a complex, nefarious scheme—still little understood—to set up a western empire by seizing Spanish territory west of the Mississippi and prying loose portions of the new United States. His conspiracy included such unsavory characters as James Wilkinson, who ultimately betrayed Burr's grand schemes. Burr was arrested while leading a band of "colonists" down the Mississippi, on the verge of declaring an independent state. He was brought to trial for treason in the U.S. Circuit Court in Virginia. The instructions to the jury by presiding judge John Marshall (also U.S. chief justice at the time) resulted in Burr's acquittal. Burr spent the next few years in Europe, flirting again with conspiracy, but he ultimately returned to New York City and resumed his law practice. His later years were bleak and impoverished. *Further reading:* Milton Lomask, *Aaron Burr*, 2 vols. (New York, 1979–82); Herbert S. Parmet and Marie B. Hecht, *Aaron Burr: Portrait of an Ambitious Man* (New York, 1967).

BURTON, Robert (1747–1825) Delegate to Congress   Burton was born near Chase City, Virginia and moved to North Carolina, where he was a planter at the time of the Revolution. He served as a quartermaster during the war. Burton took a seat on the Virginia Governor's Council in 1783 and was appointed as a delegate to Congress in 1787 and 1788. His only other public service was in 1801 as a boundary commissioner.

BUSH, Solomon. Continental officer   Bush was a member of one of the several Jewish merchant families of Philadelphia, the son of Mathias Bush who lived on Chestnut Hill. Bush was a major in an unspecified unit in 1777 and was severely wounded—his thigh was broken, in many cases a mortal injury in those days—during a skirmish with British troops advancing to take Philadelphia. He was invalided in his father's house during the time the British held Philadelphia. In 1779, he was promoted to lieutenant colonel, making him one of the highest-ranking Jewish officers in the Continental Army.

BUSHNELL, David (1742–1824) Inventor, engineer, Continental officer, physician   Bushnell invented a remarkable submarine that incorporated all the features of later underwater war craft, although it failed in actual combat during the Revolution. He was born in Saybrook, Connecticut and lived with his father on a farm nearby until his late twenties. On his father's death, Bushnell sold his inheritance and went to New Haven, where he entered Yale. While a student, he demonstrated that gunpowder would explode underwater, and after graduation in 1775 he returned to Saybrook and began construction of a small submarine. He invented and designed all the complex parts needed to make a submarine practical: a system of lead ballast to keep the craft upright; tanks and pumps to admit and blow out water so the submarine's submersion could be controlled; a rudimentary compass and depth gauge lit by phosphorus; a double system of screws to give forward motion and control of ascent and descent; and—most importantly—a clockwork torpedo that was designed to attach to the hull of an enemy ship below the waterline. The ship was built of oak timbers in the shape of two curved, oval half shells, joined to form a craft resembling two tortoise shells put together—hence the name *Turtle*. The strange contraption had a glass-windowed conning tower and a watertight hull that held enough air for a half-hour's underwater voyage. Bushnell completed his prototype in the spring of 1775 and demonstrated its capabilities with the help of his brother Ezra in a series of trials in the Connecticut River. Patriot officials Silas Deane, Jonathan Trumbull and Israel Putnam were impressed and convinced. In the spring of 1776, the *Turtle* was moved to New York and prepared for an underwater attack on the British fleet in the harbor. Sergeant Ezra Lee was trained as the operator (Bushnell himself was too frail to operate the craft) when Ezra Bushnell fell ill, and on September 6, 1776 the intrepid sergeant assaulted the British 64-gun frigate *Eagle*. Everything went right except the key point of affixing the explosive charge to the *Eagle*'s hull. The screw mechanism could not penetrate the warship's copper-clad bottom, and Lee was forced to back away after setting the clockwork mechanism. The following explosion startled the British but did no damage. A second attempt against the British frigate *Cerberus* had little more success, although an adjacent schooner was damaged in the torpedo's blast. Giving up for the time being, Bushnell had the *Turtle* loaded onto a sloop and dispatched back toward Connecticut. Unfortunately, the sloop and the *Turtle* were discovered and sunk by a British warship off the coast of Long Island. Bushnell continued to experiment with underwater demolition, and in 1778 he built floating mines from barrels and launched them on the Delaware River against the British fleet holding the key waterway. Mistiming frustrated the attack, and Bushnell apparently gave up his efforts. He was captured and held briefly by the British in May 1779 and on his release took a commission as a captain in a new company of Continental sappers and engineers. He served the rest of the war as an engineer, having command of the corps of engineers at West Point in 1783. He dropped from sight following his mustering out, although circumstantial evidence suggests he went to France and studied medicine while trying to revive the idea of the submarine. He returned to America by 1795 and taught at an academy in Warrenton, Georgia under the assumed name of Dr. Bush. He was apparently sponsored by Abraham Baldwin, a fellow Connecticuter and Yale alumnus, who was president of Franklin College in Warrenton. Following Baldwin's death, Bushnell set up a medical practice and lived the rest of his life incognito. His identity was discovered only after his death. *Further reading:* Henry L. Abbot, *Beginning of Modern Submarine Warfare under Captain David Bushnell . . .* (1881; reprint, Hamden, Conn., 1966).

BUTE, John Stuart, Earl of (1713–1792) British official   Although he served briefly as what would later be known as prime minister, Bute was known chiefly for his close relationship with George III, to whom he was tutor and chief adviser during the king's youth. Bute was an impoverished Scots aristocrat, which counted for less than nothing in the political and social world of London at mid-18th century. He served in Parliament from 1737 to 1741 but was turned out of office when he quarreled with his political sponsor; he retired to a threadbare life on the island of Bute. He returned to London in 1746 and, through fortuitous circumstance, insinuated himself into the household of the Prince of Wales, the future George III. Bute was both the boy's tutor and almost his only friend, and the Scot came to exert a powerful influence on the development of the prince. Bute was hated by nearly all the English politicians of the day—they viewed him

with extreme suspicion and fear—and he suffered from a multitude of unjust accusations (the most persistent that he was the secret lover of George's mother). Throughout his teenage years, George relied on Bute for opinions, education and moral support. When George ascended the throne in 1760, Bute found himself in a powerful position, although he did not take formal office until 1762 when he became secretary of state and the leader of the government. He was a foe of the powerful Whig political alliances, and he did much to form George's lifelong distaste for the Whig opposition. Bute, however, was a poor politician, and he resigned abruptly in 1763, although he continued to influence George for several years more. He finally fell from favor as the king learned the political ropes for himself. The victim of intense public invective, Bute was a minor player on the political scene after the mid-1760s. *Further reading:* James L. McKelvey, *George III and Lord Bute* (Durham, N.C., 1973).

BUTLER, Edward (1763–1803) Continental officer   The youngest of the five Butler brothers of Pennsylvania who served as officers in the Revolution, Edward was only 12 at the beginning of the war and delayed service until 1778, when he joined his elder brother Richard's 9th Pennsylvania Regiment as an ensign. At the end of the War for Independence, he was a lieutenant. He continued in the military and served with his brothers Richard and Thomas during the Indian War of 1791. In the aftermath of St. Clair's defeat in Ohio, Edward found both of his siblings wounded on the field but could rescue only one. He had to abandon Richard (who was mortally wounded) in order to save Thomas. When the regular army was reestablished after the turn of the century, Butler was commissioned as a major, but he died soon after.

BUTLER, James (d. 1781) Officer   Born in Prince William County, Virginia, Butler moved with his family to the region of Ninety-Six, South Carolina, in 1772. He was an officer in the militia and fought in skirmishes and patriot-loyalist clashes during the first five years of the war. He was captured at the fall of Charleston in 1780 and imprisoned at Ninety-Six when he refused to take the oath of allegiance to the crown. Butler was later returned to Charleston and lodged as a prisoner on one of the prison ships in the harbor. He was probably exchanged in the spring of 1781. Later in the same year he was killed by loyalist forces under "Bloody Bill" Cunningham at Cloud's Creek, South Carolina.

BUTLER, John (1728—1796) Loyalist officer

Butler was among the more effective loyalist military leaders of the Revolution: he recruited and led loyalist troops in the upper New York region in raids and campaigns that sapped energy and resources from the American cause. He was born in New London, Connecticut and moved to the Mohawk Valley of New York in 1742. He served with considerable distinction as a captain during the Seven Years' War, participating in several major battles and campaigns, including Crown Point, Ticonderoga and Fort Frontenac. In 1759, Butler commanded the Indian auxiliaries attached to the British army that took Montreal. He was closely associated with Sir William Johnson, the chief British Indian official on the frontier, and frequently served as an envoy to the tribes of the Six Nations of the Iroquois during the 1760s. With the coming of the Revolution, Butler fled with his son Walter to the loyalist haven in Canada. He was appointed as deputy superintendent of Indian affairs by the British under Guy Johnson (Sir William's nephew) and began to organize raids and partisan warfare in the upper New York valleys. In 1777, Butler commanded a mixed force of Indians and loyalists as part of the expedition of Barry St. Leger that was to link with General John Burgoyne; however, the march was derailed at the battle of Oriskany, despite a successful initial ambush of the Americans by Butler's Indians. Butler returned to Canada and recruited a regiment of frontier troops, known as Butler's Rangers, from among loyalist refugees. The unit served continuously until the end of the war, growing to 10 companies with field pieces by 1781. The most notorious campaign of Butler and his rangers was a march into Pennsylvania's Wyoming Valley (an isolated area with a strong loyalist presence) in July 1778. The rangers were accompanied by around 500 Indians and several loyalist volunteers—making a total force of more than 1,000. Butler attacked the American defenders, who were commanded by Colonel Zebulon Butler (no relation), near Forty Fort, killing all but 60 who sought shelter in the fortification. The survivors were soon captured, and the resulting killing and torture by Butler's Indian allies came to be known among patriots as the Wyoming

Valley Massacre: few Americans escaped death. One consequence of Butler's victory was the expedition sent forth under John Sullivan to wreck the Iroquois villages in 1779. The major battle of the Sullivan campaign was between Sullivan and Butler at Newtown, New York on August 29, when Butler's badly outnumbered loyalists and Indians tried to lure Sullivan into a trap, but failed. Butler was soundly defeated and unable to prevent Sullivan's destructive march through the Genesee Valley. Despite his failure against Sullivan, Butler was promoted to lieutenant colonel in 1780 and continued to raid sporadically. After the war, he withdrew to the loyalist settlement at Niagara (his New York lands had been seized by the rebel government) and acted as British Indian agent. *Further reading:* Howard Swiggett, *War Out of Niagara* (New York, 1933; reprint 1963).

BUTLER, Percival (1760—1821) Continental officer

The fourth of the Pennsylvania Butler brothers, Percival joined the 3rd Pennsylvania as a lieutenant in 1777. He served with the units of his elder brother Richard for most of the war, including duty in Morgan's rifle corps and with Anthony Wayne in Virginia. At the end of the war, Percival was a captain in the 2nd Pennsylvania. He moved to Kentucky after the Revolution and returned to service as an adjutant general during the War of 1812.

BUTLER, Pierce (1744—1822) Delegate to Congress, state official

Butler was born in Ireland, the son of a baronet, and served during the 1760s as an officer in the British army. He resigned his commission in 1771 and moved to Charleston, South Carolina, where he married and became a planter. He was active as a patriot, representing the back-country political interests, although himself living the life of a colonial aristocrat. He was appointed adjutant general of the state in 1779, but most of Butler's service was in legislative bodies. He was a member of the state lower house in 1778–1779 and again after the war from 1784 until 1789. He simultaneously was a delegate to the Confederation Congress in 1787. He continued as a legislator after the ratification of the new federal constitution, taking a seat in the U.S. Senate in 1789 and serving until he resigned in 1796. Butler was noticeable as a delegate to the convention that ratified the constitution, and he introduced a fugitive slave clause at the Philadelphia meeting. In 1802, Butler was appointed to serve an unexpired term in the U.S. Senate, but he resigned before the end of his appointment in 1804. *Further reading:* Francis Coglan, "Pierce Butler, 1744–1822: Senator from South Carolina," *South Carolina Historical Magazine* (April 1977), 104–19.

BUTLER, Richard (1743–1791) Continental officer

The eldest of the Pennsylvania Butler brothers and the most exalted in rank, Richard was born in Ireland and came to Pennsylvania in the company of his brother William, with whom he established a frontier trading post near Pittsburgh in the late 1760s. Richard's first military experience was as an ensign in Pontiac's War in 1764, and he led a company of Pennsylvania militia in disputes with competing Virginia militia in 1775. He was commissioned as a captain of the 2nd Pennsylvania Battalion in early 1776 and became major and then lieutenant colonel of the 8th Pennsylvania during 1776 and 1777. Butler was part of Morgan's rifle corps during the fighting against General John Burgoyne in 1777, although he was nominally the commander of the 9th Pennsylvania from 1777 until 1781. In fact, he served in several different units during the period, most impressively under Anthony Wayne at Stony Brook as leader of the 2nd Regiment of the light infantry. He was one of the few officers that the mutineers of the Pennsylvania Line agreed to negotiate with in January 1781, and afterward he took command of the reorganized 5th Pennsylvania as part of Wayne's force that subsequently campaigned in Virginia. Butler led his men at several southern battles, including Green Spring and the siege at Yorktown. At the end of the war when the Continental Army was dissolved, Butler was brevetted to the rank of brigadier general. He was not, however, a skillful soldier, despite his rank and frequency of command. After the war, Butler was named as an Indian agent and eventually became superintendent of Indian affairs for the Northern Department. He was commissioned as a major general for the Indian War of 1791 and was appointed as second in command to Arthur St. Clair. He incompetently fought as commander of the right wing at the defeat of St. Clair's army by the Miami in November 1791 and was mortally wounded. In an act of considerable nobility, however, he ordered his younger brother Edward to save his other brother

Thomas, who also was wounded in the defeat, and forfeited his own life.

BUTLER, Thomas (1754–1805) Continental officer

Thomas was born in Pennsylvania, one of five brothers who served in the same or adjoining regiments during the Revolution. He was a law student at the outbreak of the war and left his books to become lieutenant in the 2nd Pennsylvania in January 1776. He served with considerable distinction in most of the northern battles in Pennsylvania, and he received special notice from George Washington for his actions at Brandywine. During the battle of Monmouth, he successfully covered the retreat of his brother Richard's regiment. After the war, Thomas became a farmer, but he returned to duty in the Indian War in 1791 with Richard and their youngest brother, Edward, as part of Arthur St. Clair's army. He was severely wounded in the battle with Little Turtle's Miami Indians in November and was rescued from the field by Edward. He recovered and continued in military service, achieving the rank of colonel during the army reorganization of 1802.

BUTLER, Walter (c. 1752–1781) Loyalist officer

Walter was the right-hand man to his father, John Butler, in organizing and commanding loyalist and Indian troops in the upper New York region. He was born in the Mohawk Valley and was a law student when the Revolution began and he had to flee with his father to Canada. He led a mixed Indian-loyalist contingent at the fight at Montreal in September 1775 and then fought at the Cedars. He was with his father's rangers at the battle of Oriskany in 1777 and soon after went on a recruiting mission to the loyalists of the Mohawk Valley. He was captured by American militiamen, however, and sentenced to death. He was reprieved through the intercession of former friends and confined in Albany. Butler escaped from the house where he was held (his hosts may have been crypto-loyalists) and he returned to Quebec to assume a command with the rangers. In November 1778, he and Joseph Brant led a large party of Indians and rangers into the Cherry Valley of New York. On November 11, they surprised a poorly-prepared contingent of American defenders outside the walls of the fort, killed almost all the officers and men, and proceeded to butcher about 30 of the settlers, including women and children. They were unable to dislodge the remaining settlers from the fort, and Butler and Brant withdrew the next day, leaving behind the story of the Cherry Valley Massacre as a rallying point for American patriots. Butler continued to lead raids over the following years, although the Sullivan Expedition of 1779 depleted British power in upper New York. In October 1781, he was part of a raid by Major John Ross near Jerseyfield, New York. Butler, commanding the rear guard at the creek crossing, was wounded and left behind: Oneida fighting with the Americans scalped and toma-hawked him where he lay. *Further reading:* Howard Swiggett, *War Out of Niagara* (New York, 1933; reprint 1963).

BUTLER, William (d. 1789) Continental officer Although his precise birth year is unknown, William was one of the two eldest of the Pennsylvania Butler brothers, probably about the same age as Richard and like him born in Ireland. He worked with Richard as an Indian trader before the Revolution. William became a captain of the 2nd Pennsylvania in January 1776 and had advanced to lieutenant colonel of the 4th Pennsylvania Regiment by September of the same year. He became aide-de-camp to Lord Stirling in 1778 but left that post later in the year to command a significant raid against the Indians of upper New York state around Unadilla. Butler was nearly killed by an enlisted man during the mutiny of the Pennsylvania Line regiments in January 1781, but he escaped to become commander of one of the new regiments organized after the mutiny was settled.

BUTLER, William (1759–1821) Militia officer, government official The son of James Butler, William was born in Virginia and moved with his family to South Carolina in 1772. He served in various militia units as a captain during the Revolution. He sat in the South Carolina house after the war and was a steady opponent of granting leniency to loyalists (both his father and brother had been killed by loyalist partisans in 1781). During the 1790s, he was a general in the state militia. He was elected to the U.S. House of Representatives in 1800 and served there until 1813.

BUTLER, Zebulon (1731–1795) Continental officer Born in Ipswich, Connecticut, Butler moved

with his family to Lyme when he was five years old. He was a merchant seaman, trading in the West Indies as a young man, and he served as an officer in the Seven Years War, rising to the rank of captain. In 1769, Butler led a group of settlers into the Wyoming Valley, an isolated but fertile region along the Susquehanna River that was disputed between Connecticut and Pennsylvania. Control of the area was hotly contested and the dispute eventually led to open warfare between rival adherents of the two colonies. Butler commanded the Connecticut forces in the so-called Pennamite Wars that began in the early 1770s and continued through the beginning of the Revolution. Only the threat from the British and their Indian allies brought an uneasy truce to the Wyoming Valley, which harbored many loyalists. Butler began the war as a colonel of the Connecticut militia and was commissioned by Congress in late 1776 as lieutenant colonel of the 3rd Connecticut Regiment. By 1778, he was colonel of the 2nd Connecticut and home in the Wyoming Valley on leave when called on to defend the area against an invasion by John Butler (no relation) and a large force of loyalist rangers and Indians. Zebulon Butler gathered a handful of Continentals and about 300 local militiamen to make a stand near Forty Fort on July 3, 1778, but the small band was crushed by a disciplined assault from the rangers and Indians. Butler fled the scene. Most of his men who survived the initial battle were killed in what came to be known among American patriots as the Wyoming Massacre. Butler returned to the valley after the British withdrawal and resumed command of its armed forces. He was removed in 1780 and eventually was assigned to West Point.

BUTTRICK, John (1715–1791) Minuteman Buttrick was a major and the second in command of the minutemen who gathered in Concord on April 19, 1775 to repulse the British. He was at the head of the group of militia who advanced on the British light infantry companies that held the bridge at Concord and probably gave the order to return fire.

BYLES, Mather (c. 1706–1788) Loyalist clergyman, writer Byles was the grandson of Increase Mather and was raised by his uncle, Cotton Mather. He attended Boston Latin School and graduated from Harvard in 1725, later taking a master's degree from the same school. He was ordained into the Congregational ministry in 1732 and served the Hollis Street Church in Boston until the end of the Revolution. Byles was a well-known poet and theological writer in his day, publishing several volumes during the 1740s and 1750s. He was also a lifelong friend of Benjamin Franklin. However, his political sympathies were with the crown. He kept his beliefs out of his pulpit during the Revolution, but he demonstrated his affinity with the royal cause clearly while the British still occupied Boston. He remained at his post throughout the war, but when the conflict ended, Byles's congregation took vengeance and turned him out of his church. *Further reading:* Arthur Eaton, *The Famous Mather Byles* (reprint 1971).

BYRD, William, III (1728–1777) Loyalist   Byrd inherited the great Virginia landed estates and fortune developed by his father and grandfather but was himself a lesser man. Described as a spendthrift given to the aristocratic dissipations of gambling and horse racing, Byrd was nonetheless a member of the Virginia House of Burgesses and held a seat on the Council. He fought under Lord Loudoun during the Seven Years' War and eventually became commander of Virginia militia forces. His inattention and ineptitude seriously depleted his wealth by the eve of the Revolution. He apparently grew despondent over the war and his own failures: he shot himself on New Year's Day, 1777. *Further reading:* M. Tinling, ed., *The Correspondence of Three William Byrds, 1684–1776* (Charlottesville, Va., 1977).

BYRON, John (1723–1786) British admiral   The second son of a British nobleman, Byron carried the nickname "Foul-Weather Jack" during his later career. He entered the Royal Navy in 1731 and in 1740 sailed as a midshipman aboard the *Wager* as part of George Anson's expedition to the Pacific. Byron was shipwrecked on the coast of Chile and returned to England six years later only after a long series of hardships. He subsequently published a narrative of his adventures that was a popular book in its day and parts of which inspired his grandson, the poet Lord Byron. In 1769, he was appointed governor of Newfoundland, a mostly maritime post. By the time of the American war, Byron was an admiral, and when the French entered the conflict and threatened naval attacks both against the British Isles and against the squadrons in the West Indies, he was given command of a hastily assembled fleet and was sent to intercept d'Estaing's fleet sailing from Toulon in June 1778. A combination of poor management and bad weather delayed Byron's arrival in New York until October, and the British missed the French fleet, which had meanwhile taken station in the West Indies. Byron reassembled his forces that had been scattered by storms and sailed to find d'Estaing. The opposing fleets met off Grenada in July 1779. Byron was outnumbered but game, and he ordered his captains to attack. The result was inconclusive, and the French—typically—broke off the engagement. Byron returned to England in October, claiming ill health. Despite advancement in rank (due him by the simple workings of seniority), he was not again employed on active duty by the Admiralty.

C

CABELL, William (1730–1798) State official
Cabell was born and reared on the Virginia frontier, where his physician father had established a settlement and a rudimentary hospital. The younger Cabell may have attended the College of William and Mary (accounts disagree about his education). He was a frontier surveyor and involved in local government as a sheriff, coroner and magistrate. He was also a member of the House of Burgesses and generally supported early revolutionary activities. Cabell was a member of the provincial congresses in 1775 and 1776 and also held a seat on the Virginia Committee of Safety that took over administration of the colony with the ouster of Lord Dunmore. Cabell served in the new state legislature of Virginia from its inception until the mid-1780s. He was also part owner of the Hardware River Iron Company and one of the projectors of a plan for a James River canal.

CADWALADER, John (1742–1786) Militia general   Born in Philadelphia, Cadwalader was a successful merchant in business with his brother Lambert before the war (they were cousins of John and Philemon Dickinson). He was a member of a local city militia known as the "Silk-Stocking Company," drawn from the wealthy merchant class of Philadelphia and the infantry counterpart of the City Troop of Light Horse. He was appointed as brigadier general of Pennsylvania militia in 1776. Unusual for a militia officer, he was given a key assignment by George Washington for the surprise assault on Trenton in December 1776 as commander of one of the three columns that were to cross the Delaware. Cadwalader's task was to ferry his men and guns across the river and strike at Bordentown as a diversion. Unfortunately, he failed to complete the movement when ice on the river made it impossible to move his artillery. He recalled the few militiamen who had made it to the Delaware shore and dropped out of the dramatic events of the day.

Despite this crucial failure, Cadwalader retained the confidence of the commander in chief throughout the war. He was awarded a brigadier's commission in the Continental Army by Congress in February 1777, but he declined in order to retain his militia command. He helped organize militia in Maryland during early 1777 and fought as a volunteer at Brandywine and Germantown. During the so-called Conway Cabal, Cadwalader quarreled with Thomas Conway and received a challenge from the Irishman. In the ensuing duel on July 4, 1778, Cadwalader severely wounded Conway. After the Revolution, Cadwalader moved to Maryland and served in the legislature.

CADWALADER, Lambert (1743–1823) Delegate to Congress, Continental officer, official
Born in Trenton, New Jersey, Lambert was the brother of John Cadwalader. After graduating from the College of Philadelphia (which eventually became part of the University of Pennsylvania), Cad-

walader entered business with his brother in Philadelphia. They were both patriots in the conflict with Britain during the 1760s and early 1770s, and Lambert was a member of both the Philadelphia Committee of Correspondence and the Pennsylvania Provincial Convention of 1775. Also like his brother, Lambert was an officer in the Philadelphia militia formed by the upper crust of the merchant class of the city. In September 1776, he was commissioned as lieutenant colonel of the 3rd Pennsylvania Battalion, a unit formed earlier in the year as part of the Continental Army. When the Pennsylvania regiments were reorganized during November, Cadwalader became colonel in command of the new 4th Pennsylvania.

Unfortunately for him, Cadwalader was assigned to the defense of Fort Washington, New York. He and 800 men were posted outside the fort at the old defenses at Harlem Heights. His position was enveloped by greatly superior forces early in the British assault on November 16, 1776, but he handled his troops well, inflicting heavy damages on the British, and managed to withdraw a good part of his unit inside the fort, only to suffer surrender when the main attack soon took the American post. He was taken prisoner, and after his release, he resigned from the army, taking no further role in the war. After the Revolution, Cadwalader moved into public office, as a delegate to the Confederation Congress in 1785, 1786 and 1787. When the new federal government was formed, he was elected to the first U.S. Congress in 1789 and returned for a term in the third Congress.

CALDWELL, James (1734–1781) Clergyman

Although born in Virginia, Caldwell attended Princeton and spent his professional life in New Jersey. He served the First Presbyterian Church in Elizabethtown from 1761 until shortly before his death. Known as the "soldier parson," he was an active patriot during the war, serving as a chaplain in a New Jersey brigade. He also volunteered his church as a hospital until it was burned down by a loyalist in 1780. Caldwell was killed in an argument by an American sentry in 1781.

CAMBRAY-DIGNY, Louis Antoine Jean-Baptiste, Chevalier de (1751–1822) French volunteer

Born in Italy, Cambray was an unsuccessful aspirant for a commission in the French Army (he served four years as a volunteer in the artillery, but there was no vacancy for officers), so in 1778 he came to America and offered his services to Congress. He was apparently trained as an engineer, and Congress commissioned him as a lieutenant colonel in Duportail's engineering corps. In the fall of 1778, Cambray acted as the chief engineer to Lachlan McIntosh. He was then assigned to the southern theater and served under Benjamin Lincoln, helping to devise the defenses of Charleston. He was captured when the British took the city along with Lincoln's entire force in 1780. Exchanged after a period of captivity, Cambray took a leave in October 1782 and returned to France. He was discharged as a brevet colonel at the dissolution of the Continental Army in the fall of 1783, although he apparently had never returned to North America.

CAMM, John (1718–1778) Loyalist educator, clergyman

An ardent Virginia loyalist, Camm was at the center of a significant prerevolutionary controversy. He was born in Yorkshire, England, educated at Trinity College, Cambridge, and emigrated to Virginia to become pastor of a rural parish. In 1749, Camm was appointed professor of divinity at the College of William and Mary as well as minister of the nearby parish of York-Hampton. In 1755, the Virginia colonial legislature passed a law known as the Two-Penny Act, which allowed debts to be paid in money instead of in tobacco at the conversion rate of two pence a pound. One effect was to reduce the income of the state-supported Episcopal clergy, and the act was passed without the usual clause allowing the king's veto. Camm and two of his colleagues on the faculty of the college challenged the law in what came to be a long, drawn-out case (one that brought Patrick Henry to prominence in Virginia politics) involving the issues of colonial rights and the position of the established church. In the end, Camm lost the case, but it focused much attention on the growing conflict between Virginians and the crown.

Camm himself had been removed from his teaching post during the controversy but was reinstated by the Privy Council. In 1771, he was appointed president of William and Mary, named as the chief Episcopal Church official in Virginia and given a seat on the colonial governor's council. These offices were rendered powerless in 1776 when the royal government collapsed and the rebels took control of the state. Camm was removed as president of the college in 1777 and died the following year.

CAMPBELL, Archibald (1739–1791) British officer

An important British commander in the south, Campbell was a native of Scotland who had entered British military service as a captain during the Seven Years' War, serving in Quebec. His regiment was disbanded following the war with France, and he transferred to the Black Watch (42nd Regiment of Foot). Campbell had attained the rank of lieutenant colonel when he joined the new Fraser Highlander regiment (71st) raised in 1775 and sailed for America. Unfortunately for him, the captain of his transport ship entered Boston harbor in March 1776 blissfully unaware that the British garrison had left. Campbell was captured and thrown in prison, receiving harsh treatment during his two-year incarceration. He was exchanged in 1778 for Ethan Allen. At the end of the year, he was sent by Sir Henry Clinton as commander of a force to subdue Georgia. Not waiting for reinforcements from Florida, Campbell assaulted and easily took Savannah and followed up with the capture of Augusta in January 1777. Soon thereafter, Campbell fell into a quarrel with his superiors and returned to England, where he was promoted to colonel in recognition of his exploits in Georgia. In 1782, he was appointed governor of Jamaica, which he successfully defended from the French. After receiving a knighthood in 1785, Campbell went to India as governor of Madras, retiring to England four years later.

CAMPBELL, Arthur (1743–1811) Militia officer

Campbell was born on the western edge of settlement in Virginia, where his parents had moved from Pennsylvania to become farmers. In 1758, he was captured by Wyandotte Indians and taken to the Great Lakes region (what is now Michigan), where he remained among the tribe for three years until his escape and return to Virginia. He was a local official and an officer in the militia during the early 1770s. He commanded various frontier militia units during the Revolution—he may have been at the battle of King's Mountain—and in 1781 led an expedition into Tennessee against the Indians. Following the war, he began to accumulate land in Kentucky and encouraged settlement there, hoping at one stage to separate his lands from Virginia and join John Sevier in the proposed state of Franklin.

Six years before his death, Campbell moved to Kentucky near the modern-day city of Middlesboro. *Further reading:* Robert L. Kincaid, "Colonel Arthur Campbell: Frontier Leader and Patriot," *Publications of the Historical Society of Washington County, Virginia* (Fall 1965).

CAMPBELL, John (1753–1784) British officer

Not to be confused with the Scots general of the same name who also served in the American War, this Campbell was born to aristocratic parents near Dumbarton in Scotland. He was the nephew of Lord Bute, the former royal favorite. Campbell entered the British army in 1771, and 1774 found him as a lieutenant of the 7th Fusilier regiment in Canada. He was captured by the Americans during 1775, probably at Chambly, but was held only briefly before exchange. He then transferred to the new Fraser 71st Highlander regiment. He returned to England in 1780, changed regiments several times more and was promoted to lieutenant colonel. He won a place in British history for his defense of the fortress at Mangalore in India during the war against Hyder Ali, even though he was forced to surrender and died soon after from the strain of the siege.

CAMPBELL, John (d. 1806) British general

A British army veteran of the Jacobite rebellion and several European campaigns during the Seven Years' War, Campbell also fought in North America against the French in 1758. At the outbreak of the Revolutionary War, he was lieutenant colonel of the 37th Foot and sailed with the regiment when it was sent to New York. He was awarded the local rank of brigadier and commanded the troops on Staten Island in 1777 and 1778 when the main army was off in Pennsylvania. In an attempt to divert American strength, Campbell raided into New Jersey while General William Howe fought Washington in the battles around Philadelphia. In November 1778, he was sent south to take command of West Florida, but he was given few troops to oppose the Spanish and their vigorous general, Bernardo de Galvez. In May 1781, Galvez attacked Pensacola with a considerable naval force and 8,000 to 10,000 troops. Campbell had no more than 900 men to defend the fortress but held resolutely until a lucky Spanish shot exploded the British magazine and allowed the attackers to overwhelm the handful of remaining defenders. Campbell was allowed to withdraw, and he returned to New York City and an on-the-spot promotion to lieutenant general. The rank was confirmed after the war, and he eventually reached full general before his death.

CAMPBELL, Lord William (d. 1778) British royal governor

The fourth son of the Duke of Argyll, Campbell attained captain's rank in the Royal Navy during the Seven Years' War, sat in Parliament, and enjoyed considerable influence in the government. He visited South Carolina in 1763, meeting and marrying the wealthy planter Ralph Izard's daughter, Sarah. In 1766, Campbell became governor of Nova Scotia, where he held office for seven relatively uneventful years. At his own request he was transferred to his wife's home colony of South Carolina in May 1775, and there he encountered an already well developed rebellion that his predecessor, Lieutenant Governor William Bull, had been unable to quash. Campbell was virtually powerless from the moment he arrived in Charleston, but he tried to rally support from back-country loyalists during the summer through a secret correspondence, which was betrayed to the patriots by an agent. In September, Campbell was forced to flee to the safety of a British warship in the harbor. He rescued his loyalist wife and sailed to Jamaica. Campbell returned to South Carolina with Sir Henry Clinton's military expedition against Charleston in June 1776, serving as a volunteer commander of a gundeck on the British warship *Bristol*. He was wounded in the side during the futile British assault and died from the long-term effects of the injury in 1778 after returning to England.

CAMPBELL, William (1745–1781) Militia officer

Campbell was one of the more important frontier militia leaders, whose contributions to the Revolution have been slightly in the shadow of men like John Sevier and Isaac Shelby—perversely, since their greater publicity came from attempts to separate themselves and their land speculations from Virginia, whereas Campbell's abiding concern was with the safety of his home colony. Campbell was born to a well-to-do frontier family in the Holston River valley near Aspenvale, Virginia. His family was not among the great planter magnates of the Virginia tidewater, but it was prosperous and held considerable land on the frontiers of the colony. Campbell received a good education at Augusta

Academy, a school that eventually evolved into Washington and Lee College. He was physically impressive—exceptionally tall and strong for the time—and moved easily into a leader's role among his neighbors. Marriage to Patrick Henry's sister, Elizabeth, solidified his influence in Virginia politics. Campbell commanded a company of militia in Lord Dunmore's War in 1774 and soon thereafter moved into the thick of Virginia's revolution as captain of the 1st Virginia Regiment organized by his brother-in-law in June 1775. This made Campbell a Continental officer when the unit was accepted by Congress in February 1776, but he resigned his commission in October to return to the frontier and command militia as a colonel. He also served as a delegate to the Virginia legislature and as a local justice of the peace. Campbell's brightest moments in the revolutionary spotlight came in the autumn of 1780, when he led a group of 400 Virginia riflemen to the rendezvous of "over mountain men" at Sycamore Shoals, where a frontier army was forming to resist a loyalist force under British officer Patrick Ferguson. The frontier militia's leaders included Sevier, Shelby, Arthur Campbell, Charles and Joseph McDowell, Benjamin Cleveland, and others, but William Campbell was selected as the officer in overall command of the American frontiersmen. On October 7, the Americans attacked Ferguson at King's Mountain and through a combination of good luck and good tactics utterly defeated the loyalists, killing Ferguson in the bargain. Much of the credit for the victory must go to Campbell, who led his Virginians up the slope in a vicious attack, reportedly yelling: "Here they are boys . . . shout like hell and fight like devils." The triumph was tarnished to some degree by the killing of loyalists who were attempting to surrender and the subsequent hanging of captives, but the battle of King's Mountain was—aside from Bunker Hill—the greatest militia victory of the Revolutionary War. By the end of the year, Campbell received an appointment as a brigadier general of Virginia militia. He seldom again led large numbers of troops, but he was at Guilford Courthouse with a company of riflemen and later fought under Lafayette. He died two months before the final American victory at Yorktown. *Further reading:* Agnes Riley, "Brigadier General William Campbell, 1745–1781," *Publications of the Historical Society of Washington County, Virginia* (May 1985).

CARDEN, John. (d. 1783) Loyalist officer Carden was a major in the Prince of Wales's Loyal American Volunteers, one of the infantry units of Lieutenant Colonel Banastre Tarleton's British Legion. His most famous (or infamous) engagement was at Hanging Rock, South Carolina, in August 1780. He commanded part of the garrison at the British outpost, along with two other loyalist officers. American partisan forces under Thomas Sumter attacked Hanging Rock on the morning of August 6, driving in the outlying detachments and attacking Carden's infantry from three sides. Carden nearly won the day with the deft maneuver of moving his troops from the right of the line to the left and striking Sumter's flank, but the Americans held. The resulting firefight killed many of Carden's men, and he apparently lost his nerve, resigning on the spot and handing command to his subordinate. Soon, however, Sumter's ill-disciplined men abandoned the fight in order to plunder and rob the loyalist camp. Carden regained his equilibrium, reorganized his remaining troops into a hollow square, and stood off all further attacks from the disarranged American irregulars. Sumter was forced to withdraw.

CAREW, Benjamin. See HALLOWELL, Benjamin.

CARLETON, Christopher (d. 1787) British officer Both the nephew and brother-in-law of Sir Guy Carleton (they were married to daughters of the Earl of Effingham), Christopher Carleton was an effective partisan raider in the north during the Revolution. He was the second son of Sir Guy's elder brother and entered the British army as a lieutenant in the 31st Regiment of Foot in 1763. By the time of the Revolution, he was serving in Canada (probably as his uncle's aide-de-camp) and was on the army rolls as a captain. He was promoted to major of the 29th Foot in 1777, but he spent most of the war in independent operations. He personally scouted American settlements in the Mohawk Valley in the spring of 1778, traveling the region just ahead of American attempts to capture him. In October, on the orders of the new governor general of Canada, Frederick Haldiman (who had taken over from Sir Guy in June), Carleton led a raiding party of 350 British troops and 100 Indian auxiliaries in a water-borne expedition against the American settlements along Lake Champlain. He returned

with 39 prisoners and claimed to have destroyed four months' worth of provisions for the Continental Army. Two years later, Carleton raided Ballston, New York, only a few miles from Albany. He was promoted to lieutenant colonel at the end of the war and remained in Canada, where he died.

CARLETON, Sir Guy (1724–1808) British general, governor of Canada Carleton was one of the most important and able British administrators in North America, although his military leadership was at times suspect. Without his efforts, however, the crown might well have lost Canada as well as the 13 colonies to the south. Born in Ireland to a land-owning English Protestant family, Carleton joined the army in 1742. He entered the 1st Foot Guards in 1751 and was made lieutenant colonel of the regiment in 1757. He enjoyed the support of several powerful patrons, including the Marquis of Rockingham, William Pitt the Elder and especially James Wolfe, and he served as a military tutor for the Duke of Richmond, remaining for most of his career a favorite with the royal family.

Carleton's service during the Seven Years' War was distinguished: in 1758, he served at Louisbourg and then was made colonel and quartermaster general for James Wolfe; he fought and was wounded with Wolfe at Quebec in September 1759; as an acting brigadier general he participated in the siege of Belle Isle in 1761 and served at Port Andro, where he was again wounded; and having been promoted to full colonel in 1762, he was wounded once again during the siege of Havana.

He became lieutenant governor of Canada on April 2, 1766, and succeeded to the governorship the next year. Carleton played a crucial role as the chief civil and military authority in Canada, where a thin layer of British government was superimposed on a large French Catholic population. Although autocratic in manner and inclination, Carleton moved cautiously to impose British law and government, and he succeeded in winning considerable support from the French upper classes and the Roman church. He returned in 1770 to England, where he helped devise the Quebec Act that granted major political and economic rights to French-Canadian Catholics (and sent shivers through the Protestants of the American colonies) in 1774. He returned to Canada at the end of the year and in January 1775 was appointed governor of Quebec.

Sir Guy Carleton

The major focus now shifted to the threat of rebellion and invasion from the south, and Carleton was named independent commander of the British forces in Canada, splitting authority with Thomas Gage in Boston. Carleton's attempts to organize a defense of Canada were frustrated by the failure of the French Canadians to rally to the cause of the crown. The French preferred for the most part to sit out the conflict, and Carleton had only a few regular troops to stave off an expedition by the Americans. He steadfastly refused to sanction the large-scale use of Indian forces, although he was forced to accept Indian auxiliaries and to countenance raiding along the border.

Part of Carleton's difficulty sprang from his intense personal feud with Lord George Germain, who became secretary of state for the colonies in 1775. Carleton and Germain hated one another cordially—perhaps because of Germain's court-martial and cashiering after the battle of Minden—and the conflict affected British policy and actions at several crucial points. When the Americans launched a slow-motion invasion under first Philip Schuyler and then Richard Montgomery, Carleton gathered his small forces and managed to fend off defeat, although he lost key posts on the water approaches and Montreal itself fell. (Carleton personally escaped in a small boat, leaving behind mounds of supplies to American capture.) The arrival of Benedict Arnold's column late in the fall allowed the Americans to lay siege to Quebec, although Carleton's garrison outnumbered the attackers. Carleton's defense against the desperation attack by Montgomery and Arnold on the last day of the year in 1775 effectively ended the threat of an American victory, although Carleton remained penned in Quebec until reinforcements arrived in the spring. He subsequently pursued Arnold back into New York, defeating him at the lake battle of Valcour Island but allowing many Americans to escape. After advancing to Crown Point, Carleton considered the folly of marching across the difficult terrain of upper New York and withdrew back to Canada.

He was knighted in reward for his campaign, but the deepening conflict with Germain reduced Carleton's role over the next few years of the war. He was shunted aside by Germain in favor of John Burgoyne and Burgoyne's grand plan to split the northern American colonies by an invasion from Canada. Even though he had asked to be recalled to England, Carleton gave Burgoyne good support in planning and equipping the invasion in 1777, but he could not prevent Burgoyne's failure. Carleton returned to England and was made lieutenant general and awarded a lucrative sinecure as governor of Charlemont, Ireland, but a series of violently critical letters to Germain written while Carleton was still in Canada made it impossible for him to again be employed by the North government. When the defeat at Yorktown resulted in the fall of Germain and North in early 1782, Carleton again came into the limelight when the Rockingham ministry chose him as the new commander in chief in North America and commissioned him to attempt yet another peace negotiation. On arriving in New York, Carleton discovered that no chance for negotiation existed, and he turned his efforts to organizing the evacuation of the remaining British armies and the thousands of loyalists who wished to leave before the peace was concluded. He evacuated New York City in November 1783 and returned to England.

Three years later, Carleton once more became the chief civil official of Canada, although he was denied the full powers of a governor general (he was also elevated to the peerage as Lord Dorchester). He served in this post until July 1796, except for a two-year hiatus in 1791–93, and despite a number of political conflicts he managed to help establish a new system of government in a revived British empire. Shipwrecked during his return journey to England, Carleton reached Portsmouth on

September 19, 1796. The remainder of his life was spent in retirement. *Further reading:* Paul H. Smith, "Sir Guy Carleton: Soldier-Statesman," in George Billias, *Washington's Opponents*, 103–41; Arthur G. Bradley, *Lord Dorchester* (1907, 3rd ed. Toronto, 1966); A. L. Burt, *Guy Carleton, Lord Dorchester, 1724–1808* (Ottawa, 1964).

CARLETON, Thomas (1735–1817) British officer

The younger brother of Sir Guy Carleton, Thomas Carleton was born in Ireland, where he lived until 1753 when he joined the army as a volunteer in the 20th Regiment of Foot. He saw much service during the Seven Years' War and reached the rank of captain by 1763 at the end of hostilities. He was posted to Gibraltar but appealed to his political patron, Lord Shelburne, for a change from the dull assignment and went on detached duty while traveling Europe for the next decade. In 1775, Sir Guy, as commander of British forces in Canada, appointed him as quartermaster general to the army in Canada. Carleton led British and Indian forces on Lake Champlain in 1776 as lieutenant colonel of the 19th Regiment and was wounded in the battle against Benedict Arnold's flotilla at Valcour Island. Promoted to colonel of the 19th Regiment in 1782, Carleton left Canada after a quarrel with the new governor general, Frederick Haldiman, and sought a post in New York with Sir Guy, who was by then commander in chief of British forces during the waning days of the Revolution. Nothing turned up, however, and Carleton returned to England. After the changes in the British government during 1783, he received the appointment as the first governor of New Brunswick, a new Canadian province created from parts of Nova Scotia and populated by many American loyalists. He served there for 19 years. He was promoted to major general in 1793 and full general in 1803.

CARLISLE, Frederick Howard, Earl of (1748–1825) British official

Carlisle, a close friend of Charles Fox, the chief opponent of the British government during much of the Revolution, was himself a mild supporter of conciliation with the colonies. He was a member of the rich and powerful Howard family, inheriting the title as fifth earl of Carlisle. He took his seat in the House of Lords in 1769 and associated himself with Fox's party as well as the high life of gambling and fashion in London.

In 1778, the government of Lord North, needing desperately to keep the French from entering the war, decided to send a peace commission to parley with the Continental Congress. Carlisle was chosen to head the commission in the hope that his association with Fox would carry weight with the Americans. The commission was a complete disaster from the beginning, however. Carlisle was a man of no great ability, and his fellow commissioners were for the most part British secret intelligence officers bent more on bribery and cynical subterfuge than genuine negotiations. Carlisle sailed to America aboard the *Trident* in April 1778 in the company of a menagerie consisting of commissioner William Eden, Eden's pregnant wife, commissioner George Johnstone, commissioner Anthony Storer, the Scots philosopher Adam Ferguson (secretary to the commission) and Lord Cornwallis. Carlisle arrived in New York City to discover that the Congress had already resolved to discuss nothing without a full recognition of American independence as the starting point, and he was refused a meeting.

His mission was effectively ended before it began. While Carlisle waited in New York, Johnstone and two agents tried to bribe key members of Congress. The clumsy attempts to suborn the congressional delegates were revealed, and the entire enterprise collapsed. Stung by the commission's public utterances against France, the Marquis de Lafayette challenged Carlisle to a duel, but the British emissary declined. Carlisle tried a direct appeal (and an offer of personal pardons) to the American people, but without response. He returned to England in November. Carlisle subsequently served as lord lieutenant of Ireland and became a noted patron of the literary arts (Lord Byron was his nephew).

CARMICHAEL, William (d. 1795) Delegate to Congress, diplomat

Carmichael was born in Maryland to a rich planter family. He studied law in England and returned to practice in Centerville, Maryland. He was in London when the War for Independence broke out and was given dispatches for America by Arthur Lee, but he got no farther than Paris. With the arrival in Paris of the American representatives seeking an alliance with France, Carmichael acted as an assistant to Silas Deane and was offered the post of secretary to the commission. He was sent in October 1777 to the court in Berlin to represent American interests. He returned to America in May 1778 with messages for the Congress, becoming himself a delegate for Maryland during 1778 and 1779. In September of the latter year, he was sent again to Europe as secretary to John Jay, the new minister to Spain. For the next several years, Carmichael and Jay tried unsuccessfully to get Spain to sign a treaty with the United States. When Jay left for Paris in June 1782, Carmichael remained in Madrid as American chargé d'affaires, a post he held until 1794. He formed a close relationship with many Spanish officials, but since the interests of the two countries ran contrary for most of the period, he actually accomplished little. He was superseded by a colleague in June 1794, but he died before he could sail for home.

CARRINGTON, Edward (1749–1810) Continental officer, delegate to Congress, official

Carrington's military career was confusing because he alternated between service as a quartermaster and as an artillery officer, but he was an important officer in both roles. He was born in Goochland County, Virginia (the brother of Paul Carrington) and served as a delegate to his county revolutionary committees in 1775 and 1776. He received a commission as lieutenant colonel of the 1st Continental Artillery Regiment in November 1776 under the command of Colonel Charles Harrison, an officer with whom Carrington had a continuing quarrel during the war. Carrington fought well as an artillery officer at the battle of Monmouth and was part of the commission to the British command at New York that dealt with the exchange of prisoners in 1780. Later in the same year, he went south with Johann de Kalb as commander of three artillery batteries.

Soon after Carrington arrived in North Carolina, Horatio Gates took command of the department, and Carrington was assigned to scout the complex river system of the theater with an eye to establishing possible routes of march and supply. He missed the disastrous defeat at Camden and was still exploring the rivers—especially the Dan—when Nathanael Greene assumed command in the south. Greene asked Carrington to take over as head of the quartermaster department, a vital but decidedly unglamorous role. Carrington resisted the assignment but eventually acceded a few days before the

battle at Guilford Courthouse. Over the following months, he served ably as quartermaster for Greene, whose pressing problem was to keep his army mobile and supplied while racing back and forth in the Carolinas from battle to battle.

In July 1781, Carrington sloughed off his quartermaster duties and returned to the main army in the north as commander of the 4th Artillery Regiment, but without an advancement in rank. He was apparently one of the principal assistants to Knox in directing the artillery at the siege of Yorktown. After the British surrender, Carrington once again joined Greene as quartermaster and served until the end of the Revolution.

In 1785, he was elected as a delegate to Congress from Virginia and began a significant political career, first as a close friend and ally of James Madison and Thomas Jefferson and then as a strong Federalist. During the decades after the Revolution, Carrington became a wealthy and successful banker in Richmond and his political positions shifted to correspond to his interest in a sound national banking system. He was foreman of the jury that tried Aaron Burr for treason in 1807.

CARRINGTON, Paul (1733–1818) Jurist

Paul, the brother of Edward Carrington, was born in Virginia and probably attended the College of William and Mary before studying law and taking up practice in the region eventually organized as Charlotte County. He was a local king's attorney and an officer in the militia, and he sat as a delegate in the colonial assembly before the Revolution. In 1774 and 1775, Carrington attended the provincial congresses that ousted the royal government, and he was a member of the Virginia Committee of Safety that took over control with the departure of Lord Dunmore. He was appointed to the general court created by the new state government in 1779 and became chief justice in 1780. He moved to the bench of the Virginia Court of Appeals in 1789 and served there until his retirement in 1807.

CARROLL, Charles ("Barrister") (1723–1783) Delegate to Congress, state official

Known as "Barrister" to distinguish him from his cousin, Charles Carroll of Carrollton, Carroll was born in Annapolis, Maryland to a family of immense wealth. Carroll's father and uncle, immigrants from Ireland, had amassed huge land holdings in Maryland and could afford to send their sons abroad for the best education. Carroll studied first at English House in Lisbon and then went to England for study at Eton, Cambridge and the Middle Temple. He returned to Annapolis in 1746 and began the practice of law. In 1755, he filled the vacancy in the Maryland lower house created by the death of his father. Carroll was an important figure in the Revolution in Maryland, sitting in all the patriot conventions and writing or helping to write crucial revolutionary documents in the state. He was a member of the 1775 Council of Safety and drafted the "Declaration of Rights" adopted by a patriot convention the following year. He was elected as a delegate to Congress in November 1776. In 1777, he was elected to the first state senate, serving until his death.

CARROLL, Charles (of Carrollton) (1737–1832) Delegate to Congress, state official, businessman
Carroll was among the most prominent patriots of the day and the only Roman Catholic to sign the Declaration of Independence. He was a clear-minded man, possessed of immense wealth, who put his hard-won influence at the service of the Revolution at considerable risk to himself and his property. He was born in Annapolis, Maryland (cousin to Daniel Carroll, John Carroll and Charles Carroll the Barrister) to a Roman Catholic family that had sought religious refuge in Lord Baltimore's colony and prospered greatly. However, by Charles's day, Roman Catholics were barred from public life and office, and the Anglican church was the official religion in Maryland. He was educated locally by Jesuits until the age of 11, when he was sent to Europe to attend French Catholic schools in Flanders, Reims, Paris and Bourges. In 1759, he went to England for study of the law at the Middle Temple. When he returned to Maryland in 1765, he settled on a 10,000-acre estate given him by his father but was forced to sit on the political and professional sidelines by the anti-Catholic laws. He began to sign his name Charles Carroll of Carrollton about this time.

He was one of the first in Maryland to understand the full implications of resisting the royal authority, and he clearly foresaw independence and war as the consequences. In 1770, the colonial assembly passed laws decreasing the income of officials and the clergy, and during the subsequent public debate, Carroll wrote a series of cogent and effective newspaper letters under the pen name "First Citizen" that attacked the royal officers' prerogatives. The opposing side was taken by Daniel Dulany, writing as "Antilon." Carroll emerged from the literary debate with great credit among his fellow Marylanders, and from then on his influence grew. With the passage of the Intolerable Acts in 1774 the revolutionary currents began to stir too strongly to be denied in Maryland, and Carroll moved to the forefront, casting aside the former disability of his religion. He was appointed to the Maryland Committee of Correspondence and served in the patriot congress. He turned down appointment to the first Continental Congress, preferring to work in the colony to gather support for the movement toward independence.

In 1776, he was appointed by Congress (along with his cousin, John) as part of a mission to convince French Canadians to join the revolt against Britain. Even though the cousins were coreligionists with the French and fluent in their language, the mission failed. Carroll returned to Philadelphia as the movement in Congress for declaring independence gathered steam during the early summer. He and delegate Samuel Chase discovered that Maryland still opposed signing, so they left for Annapolis and helped conduct a rapid campaign to convince the patriot convention to support the Declaration, which was about to come to a vote. They were successful (with the aid of William Paca), and the convention gave instructions to sign. Maryland's delegates voted for independence on July 1, and Carroll himself became a delegate on July 4. He signed the Declaration on August 2, probably the wealthiest delegate to do so and the only Roman Catholic.

Carroll was elected to the new state senate in Maryland and held that office simultaneously with other duties until 1804. He also served on the board of war and helped draft the Maryland state constitution. In 1789, he became one of the first two U.S. senators from Maryland under the federal constitution. He retired from public life after the turn of the century, devoting himself to managing his estates—80,000 acres stretching over three states—and promoting canal and rail companies. His longevity made him the last surviving signer of the

Declaration at his death at age 95. *Further reading:* Thomas O. Hanley, *Charles Carroll of Carrollton: The Making of a Revolutionary Gentleman* (Chicago, 1982).

CARROLL, Daniel (1730–1796) Delegate to Congress

The cousin of Charles Carroll of Carrollton and Charles Carroll the Barrister, and the brother of John Carroll, Daniel Carroll was largely overshadowed by his relatives. Like them, he was a Roman Catholic of great wealth who supported the Revolution, although his role was less spectacular. He was born in Maryland and educated by the same Jesuits and at the same university in Flanders as John and Charles of Carrollton. He remained in the background until 1781, when he was chosen as a delegate to the Congress from Maryland. While a delegate he signed the Articles of Confederation and exerted considerable influence among his fellow legislators. He was a member of the first state senate of Maryland and continued to sit in the body until his death. He also was a delegate to the federal constitutional convention in 1787. George Washington appointed him as one of the commissioners to select a site for the new federal capital—Washington, D.C. is situated on what was one of his farms. *Further reading:* M. Virginia Geiger, *Daniel Carroll II: One Man and His Descendants* (Baltimore, 1978).

CARROLL, John (1735–1815) Clergyman, educator

The brother of Daniel Carroll and the cousin of Charles Carroll of Carrollton and Charles Carroll the Barrister, John Carroll was the most prominent Roman Catholic American of his day and the first Catholic bishop in the new United States. He was born in Maryland and educated in the family tradition at the University of St. Omer in Flanders. Rather than return to the colonies to tend the family fortunes as his relatives had done, John studied for holy orders and was ordained a Catholic priest in 1769, taking vows as a Jesuit two year later. He went to England in 1773 and returned to his home in Maryland in 1774. His most important role in the American Revolution was as one of the commissioners sent to Canada by Congress in 1776 to try to convince the French inhabitants to join the rebellious colonies to the south. Along with his cousin Charles Carroll of Carrollton, Benjamin Franklin and Samuel Chase, Carroll traveled north, but even though a Catholic priest and fluent in French, he failed to convert the French Canadians to the patriot cause. Following the war, Carroll worked to establish a Roman Catholic presence in the new nation. In 1784 he was named by the pope as head of missions in America, and in 1789 he became the first bishop of Baltimore (before his death he was elevated to archbishop). He was also a vigorous founder of educational institutions in the Jesuit tradition, and he was responsible for beginning the school that became Georgetown University as well as St. Mary's College and St. Joseph's College in Maryland.

CARTER, John (1737–1781) Frontiersman, land speculator

The grandson of Robert "King" Carter, one of colonial Virginia's wealthiest landowners, John Carter moved to the western frontier region of North Carolina about 1770 and began a settlement along the Watauga River in what is now Tennessee. He was chairman of the Watauga Association, a group of settlers who tried to set up their own government in the west. He was selected by inhabitants of the Washington district in modern-day northeastern Tennessee as a representative to the North Carolina Provincial Congress of 1776. He was appointed a colonel of militia and became the focal point for defense against the Indians of the frontier during the war while intermittently serving in the North Carolina senate. He was also a land speculator in business with John Sevier and Richard Henderson and personally held title to great tracts of land on the western side of the Alleghenies.

CARTER, John (1745–1814) Publisher

Born in Philadelphia, Carter as a young man was an apprentice to Benjamin Franklin. In 1768, he became editor and publisher of the Providence, Rhode Island *Gazette,* and he strongly supported, even influenced, the Revolution in his adopted state. He remained at the helm of the paper for 45 years. He also served during the Revolution as a member of the Providence Committee of Correspondence. Carter was also—like his mentor—interested in postal affairs and was postmaster of Providence from 1772 to 1792.

CARY, Archibald (1721–1787) Businessman, patriot

Cary inherited great wealth and lands in Virginia from his father, advancing his fortune during the years before the Revolution by his own business acumen. He was educated at the College of William and Mary and in 1742 took up residence in Henrico County on a 12,000-acre estate. He also was active in manufacturing iron and running a large flour mill (he supplied flour to the Congress during the Revolution). He sat in the Virginia legislature and supported the revolutionary protests of the early 1770s as a member of a committee of correspondence and of the Virginia provincial congresses. His flour mill was destroyed by Benedict Arnold during the British invasion of Virginia in 1781. Following the war, Cary supported the establishment of an American branch of the Episcopal Church.

CASWELL, Richard (1729–1789) Militia officer, delegate to Congress, state official

Caswell was closely involved in the Revolution in the south, commanding troops at two key engagements as well as serving as governor of North Carolina during the first years of the war. He was born in Maryland and moved to Raleigh, North Carolina at age 17, becoming a surveyor. He held a succession of local offices and served a long stint in the North Carolina legislature, and he commanded troops under Governor Tryon during the Regulator disturbances in 1771.

When the revolutionary movement reached the crucial stages in 1774, Caswell was at the center of activities in North Carolina, serving in patriot conventions and as a delegate to the first Continental Congress. He was also a colonel in the militia, commanding a considerable body of troops raised in the back country. In February 1776, Caswell led 800 of his Partisan Rangers to form part of the patriot force that opposed the Highlander loyalists under Donald McDonald at Moore's Creek Bridge. The patriots utterly smashed the Highlanders, who seemed to have learned little from their sorry history of trying to fight modern battles with broadswords, and the loyalist threat in the south was quashed for years to come.

Caswell was then named the first governor of the newly declared state of North Carolina by the Provincial Congress. He served until 1780, when he took a commission as major general of the state militia. His second effort at field command was less happy than the first, however. He commanded a well-fed and well-supplied body of militia and was persuaded to join the starving army of Horatio Gates only after much pleading. Caswell's troops finally added their numbers to the American army a few days before Gates and British commander Cornwallis maneuvered for a battle near Camden, South Carolina. Caswell and the North Carolina militia were placed at the center of the American line, and at the first British attack, they panicked and ran from the field, leaving the sturdy Continentals from Delaware and Maryland to be slaughtered. Caswell himself fled the battle as a pursued fugitive. His popularity among his fellow North Carolinians suffered little from the debacle, however, and he was reelected governor after the war. He died while serving as speaker of the state assembly.

CATHCART, William Schaw (1755–1843) British officer

The officer who originally raised the unit that became Tarleton's British Legion, Cathcart was the scion of a noble Scots family. He attended Eton but spent part of his youth in Russia, where his father was British ambassador. He originally studied law but in 1776 purchased a commission and became a soldier. On detached duty with the 16th Light Dragoons, Cathcart came to America and won rapid promotion through his military abilities, his aristocratic background and his personal charm. He served as a captain during the period of the British occupation of Philadelphia, where he married an American wife, Elizabeth Elliot. In 1778, Cathcart raised a force of light infantry known at first as the Caledonian Volunteers, but which eventually was converted to a legion (light infantry mixed with dragoons) and became known as Cathcart's Legion. By 1779, he was a lieutenant colonel, and he led his legion on Sir Henry Clinton's expedition south to take Charleston. He fell ill, however, and turned over command in April to Banastre Tarleton, who of course made the unit famous during the following 18 months. After a short stay in New York, Cathcart returned to England. His subsequent career was stellar: he fought throughout Europe during the wars of the late 18th and early 19th century and became ambassador to Russia. He represented Great Britain at the Congress of Vienna and ended life as an earl.

CATHERINE II (The Great) (1729–1796) Empress of Russia

Catherine, one of the glittering "enlightened" despots of the 18th century, influenced the American Revolution by her foreign pol-

William Cathcart

icy during the early 1780s. She was the well-educated daughter of a minor German prince when sent to Russia at age 15 to become the bride of Peter, heir to the Russian throne. She converted to the Russian Orthodox religion and earnestly cultivated Russian manners and customs. Known almost equally for her intelligence and her promiscuity, she maneuvered herself into a position of power after her weak and dissolute husband became emperor in 1761. Six months after Peter took the throne, Catherine engineered a palace coup that deposed him, and she declared herself empress. Peter was killed soon after, and Catherine began a 34-year reign.

She evidenced interest in reform and liberality during her first years in power, but the threat of internal revolt soured these impulses, and by the time of the American Revolution, she was firmly against any form of action or ideology that might diminish the position of an absolutist monarch. She therefore had no sympathy with the rebellious American colonists; however, she also was eager to advance Russia's international trade, and the British seizure of cargoes from neutral merchant ships on the high seas restricted Russian commerce. In February 1780, Catherine announced the formation of the League of Armed Neutrality, a coalition of Rus-

sia, Sweden and Denmark, which espoused a set of principles allowing free navigation and trade by neutrals. Eventually Portugal, the Two Sicilies and Holland joined the League, but Britain essentially ignored its existence and it was in reality a dead letter. Catherine refused to receive an American envoy and moved on to other matters more vital to Russia's interests. Her greatest foreign policy triumph was in winning access to warm-water ports in the Crimea and annexing a good portion of Poland. She died of a stroke on November 6, 1796. *Further reading:* Oliva J. Lawrence, *Catherine the Great* (Englewood Cliffs, N.J., 1971).

CELORON de BLAINVILLE, Paul Louis (b. 1753) French-Canadian volunteer

Celoron de Blainville was born near Detroit, the scion of a French family that had moved to North America late in the 17th century. His father was a French officer, and the younger Celoron joined the French colors in 1774. At the beginning of the American Revolution, he volunteered for service with the patriots and joined the 1st Canadian Regiment formed by Congress as part of the Continental Army in December 1775 under Colonel James Livingston. He was apparently commissioned as a lieutenant. By the time of General Burgoyne's invasion in 1777, Celoron was attached to Colonel Ebenezer Learned's Massachusetts Battalion, and he was wounded at the battle of Bemis Heights. He subsequently changed units again, and fought at the battle of Monmouth as part of Varnum's Brigade. In February 1779, Celoron transferred to Pulaski's Legion and was named a captain. He moved south with Pulaski and was wounded again at the battle for Savannah. In 1780, he found himself part of the garrison at Charleston, South Carolina and was captured when Sir Henry Clinton took the city. He was exchanged two years later, leaving the American service sometime in 1783. He subsequently served with the French army and French colonial government in the West Indies, primarily on Guadeloupe.

CHALMERS, George (1742–1825) Loyalist attorney, historian

Chalmers was a prolific writer and historian (more properly, perhaps, he was an antiquarian) after the Revolution sent him back to England. He was born in Scotland and came to Maryland in 1763 after education at King's College in Aberdeen and at Edinburgh. He practiced law in

Baltimore and resisted the Revolution to the best of his ability. He met with little success, however, despite his effort to organize a loyalist association in early 1775. Governor Robert Eden refused to supply arms to the association so the members could defend themselves from patriot mobs. Chalmers left for England late in 1775, settling in London, where he was active in the social and intellectual life of the loyalist refugees. He began to publish his views of the American Revolution in 1777. His two largest works on the topic were *Political Annals of the Present United Colonies* (1780) and *Introduction to the History of the Revolt of the Colonies* (1782). In general, Chalmers blamed a weak government for encouraging the seeds of rebellion. He published a host of books and tracts during the rest of his life, including many compilations of official state papers.

CHALMERS, James. Loyalist officer A native of Maryland, Chalmers raised a unit in 1777 designated as the Maryland Loyalists, although it actually was formed in Philadelphia during the British occupation of the city. Chalmers was lieutenant colonel in command. The Maryland Loyalists were sent to Halifax in September 1778 and in December went on to Jamaica. The following month, they went to Pensacola, West Florida as part of the British garrison. The unit was captured when Pensacola fell to the Spanish in 1781. After a short incarceration in Havana, the unit was exchanged en masse and returned to New York. Chalmers left for England in 1783, and his men were sent to Halifax, where the unit was disbanded.

CHAMBERLAIN, William (1755–1828) Soldier, official Chamberlain, a native of Massachusetts, served as a sergeant in the Revolution, although his specific unit is unknown. He lived most of his life in the Vermont region and was a surveyor and farmer in Peacham after the war. His first public office was as clerk to the proprietors of the town in 1785, and he went on to a long string of increasingly elevated posts. He was a delegate to the Vermont House of Representatives and to the state constitutional convention in 1791 when Vermont was admitted to the Union. Shortly thereafter, he was made a brigadier general in the state militia, and he was promoted to major general in 1799—a great leap from his status as an enlisted man during the Revolutionary War. He eventually served as U.S.

congressman from Vermont and as the state's lieutenant governor.

CHAMPE, John (c. 1752–c. 1798) Continental soldier Champe, a sergeant in Light Horse Harry Lee's legion, was at the center of an intriguing might-have-been episode. George Washington desperately wanted to get traitor Benedict Arnold back from the British in the fall of 1780, and he set afoot a plan to kidnap the turncoat from his refuge in New York City. Washington asked Lee to provide an agent for the mission, and the Virginia officer selected Champe, a young noncommissioned officer in the legion cavalry. Champe was from Virginia and apparently was a good soldier who had caught the eye of his commander. Champe was instructed to fake a desertion from the American army at Tappan, New York and to insinuate himself into a position to capture Arnold. Champe left Tappan on October 23 and convinced the British he was a genuine defector. He was assigned to a unit of loyalists and deserters that was forming as part of the expedition to Virginia under Arnold's command (Arnold had received a commission as brigadier in the British army). Champe learned that Arnold visited the garden behind his house every night before retiring (probably to use the privy). Champe's idea was to steal into the garden, nab Arnold and hustle him across the Hudson River to waiting Americans. Unfortunately, on the eve of executing the plan, Champe's unit was ordered aboard a transport ship and the plot was frustrated. Champe was shipped to Virginia and ironically forced to serve under Arnold. The sergeant eventually fled to Lee's forces in Carolina in 1781 and was discharged from service to protect him from possible British retaliation. He reportedly died in Kentucky.

CHAMPION, Epaphroditus (1756–1834) Official, soldier A native of Westchester Parish, Colchester, Connecticut, Champion was a commissary and purchasing agent for the Continental Army during the Revolution. In 1782, he moved to East Haddam, Connecticut and became captain of a regiment of Connecticut militia. By dint of long service, he eventually became a brigadier general of militia by the turn of the century. He was also a prosperous merchant after the Revolution and was elected to the U.S. House of Representatives in 1807, serving for 10 years.

CHANDLER, John (1762–1841) Soldier, official
Chandler was a teenage soldier during the Revolution, serving from 1777 to 1780 and taking part in the battles at Saratoga. He was born in New Hampshire, but he was a U.S. congressman from Massachusetts and was active in the formation of the new state of Maine. He sat in the Maine constitutional convention and then became president of the new Maine state senate. He was commissioned a brigadier general in the U.S. Army during the War of 1812, after which he was appointed to the U.S. Senate from Maine.

CHANDLER, Thomas Bradbury (1726–1790) Loyalist clergyman, writer   Bradbury was one of the principal loyalist Episcopal clergymen to defend the crown in print before the Revolution. He was born in Woodstock, Connecticut and graduated from Yale in 1745 at age 19. He went to Elizabethtown, New Jersey two years later as a paid catechist or lay reader with financial support from the British Episcopal Society for the Propagation of the Gospel, a sponsor of missionaries. In 1751, Chandler went to England and was ordained a priest, returning to become rector of St. John's church in Elizabethtown.

He was a firm loyalist throughout the events leading to the Revolution, and he was an able writer who published several important pamphlets defending the established church and the rights of the crown, including *An Appeal to the Public in Behalf of the Church of England in America* (1767) and *An Address from the Clergy of New York and New Jersey to the Episcopalians in Virginia* (1771). In 1775, Chandler wrote *What Think Ye of Congress Now?* attacking the actions of the patriots and stressing that the growing rebellion resulted from "misinformation and false alarms." With the outbreak of hostilities in Massachusetts in April 1775, Chandler left his family in the rectory at Elizabethtown and fled to England. He remained there for 10 years working on behalf of the missionary society. In 1785, he returned to Elizabethtown; he again took up residence in the rectory and lived a quiet life of semiretirement until his death.

CHARLES III (1716–1788) King of Spain   Charles III is usually judged to have been the most effective Spanish monarch of the 18th century, sharing many of the traits and viewpoints attributed to "enlightened despots" such as Catherine of Russia and Frederick of Prussia. He was the son of Philip V of Spain and his Italian second wife, Elizabeth Farnese, a woman who worked assiduously to find European thrones for her sons since they were at some remove in the line of Spanish succession. Charles became Duke of Parma and king of Naples and Sicily. In 1759, he ascended to the Spanish throne at the death of his half-brother Ferdinand.

Charles embarked on a program of economic and social reform that was mostly successful. His goals were to increase the security and prosperity of the nation through prudent foreign policy and improved fiscal administration. Aided by the able foreign minister Floridablanca, Charles sought to maneuver to Spain's advantage in America. His involvement in the Seven Years' War dealt Spanish hopes in North America a blow with the British victory and Spain's loss of the Floridas, however, and by the time of the American Revolution, Charles was cautious about stepping into the struggle. He was also stridently opposed to the antimonarchical ideas inherent in the American rebellion. Nonetheless, he allowed Spain to be drawn in to the war on a limited basis since it cost little and promised much. The victories of General Bernardo de Galvez in Florida resulted in recovery of these provinces for Spain at the end of the war, and Spanish military expeditions in the Mississippi Valley helped establish a basis for territorial claims. Charles's interest in the American Revolution was almost entirely cynical, and the American decision to conclude a separate peace with England resulted from the Americans' understanding of his position. *Further reading*: Joseph Addison, *Charles the Third of Spain* (1900).

CHARLTON, Samuel (1760–1843) Soldier
Charlton was a black slave sent for enlistment in the Continental Army in place of his white master—a common occurrence during the first years of the war when slave owners used blacks as substitutes. Charlton fought at the battles of Brandywine, Germantown and Monmouth, but his service did him little good: he was forced to return to slavery at the end of his enlistment. He was finally freed by the terms of his master's will and moved to New York City with his wife.

CHASE, Jeremiah Townley (1748–1828) Delegate to Congress, state official, jurist   Born in

Baltimore, Maryland, Chase served on the local committees of correspondence and observation before the Revolution and was a delegate to the Maryland Constitutional Convention in 1776. Three years later, he moved to Annapolis and became a member of the governor's council. In 1783, he was both mayor of Annapolis and a delegate to the Confederation Congress. He became a judge of the Maryland General Court in 1789 and then was made chief justice of the court of appeals, serving until 1824.

CHASE, Samuel (1741–1811) Delegate to Congress, state official, jurist

Chase was one of the controversial figures of the early republic. He was born on the eastern shore of Maryland and studied with his father, a Baltimore clergyman, during his early years. After he was admitted to the bar, Chase set up practice in Annapolis. He was elected to the Maryland assembly from that city in 1764 and served continuously as a state legislator for 20 years.

He was one of the earliest and most strident patriots in Maryland, leading the Sons of Liberty in violent protest against the Stamp Act and eagerly joining the state committee of correspondence and the provincial congresses. He was selected as a delegate to the Continental Congress in 1774. Two years later, he journeyed to Canada with Charles Carroll of Carrollton and John Carroll on an unsuccessful mission to convince French Canadians to join the revolt against Great Britain. On his return to Philadelphia in mid-summer, he found that Maryland was vacillating on the question of independence. He and Charles Carroll hastened to their home state and with the help of William Paca secured the vote of Maryland for the Declaration in July, which Chase signed along with Carroll as the two newly appointed Maryland delegates. Chase served in Congress during the next two years, but his strong language in debate and nasty pen did little to endear him to his colleagues. In 1778, he ran into difficulty when Alexander Hamilton revealed that Chase had tried to use insider information to corner the flour market. He was elected to the federal Constitutional Convention in 1787 but did not attend.

After the war, he tried to combine legal practice and business—unfortunately as it turned out, since he went bankrupt in 1789. Chase is best known for his judicial service, beginning with a seat as chief

François-Jean de Beauvoir, Chevalier de Chastellux

judge of the Baltimore criminal court in 1788 and followed by appointment as the chief justice of the Maryland Superior Court. He was named as an associate justice of the U.S. Supreme Court in 1796, and although an outstanding jurist, he was also an active and sometimes violently partisan politician. In 1804, after a stormy period of controversy over his repressive use of the Alien and Sedition Acts, Chase was impeached by the U.S. House of Representatives, although not convicted in the senate. His escape from retribution for his political activities helped establish the principle of judicial independence in America.

CHASTELLUX, François-Jean de Beauvoir, Chevalier de (1734–1788) French officer, writer

An English-speaking major general and the third-ranking member of Rochambeau's expeditionary force, Chastellux functioned as an important liaison with the Americans, and he later published a valuable multivolume account of his experiences. He was born in Paris and entered French military service as a teenager. He fought in several campaigns during the Seven Years' War, rising to colonel by age 21. When the French expedition to America sailed in 1780, he was a major general but essentially served as a staff officer to Rochambeau. He was a skilled and socially accomplished diplomat who assisted in the conferences with Washington. During his stay in America, Chastellux was stationed at Newport, Rhode Island, but he managed to travel through several of the northern and middle states. He went south to Virginia with the allied armies in

1781 and fought at Yorktown. He returned to France in 1783 and published his *Travels in North America in the Years 1780, 1781, and 1782* in 1786. He died of a sudden fever in 1788. *Further reading: Travels . . . ,* 2 vols., Howard S. Rice, ed. (Chapel Hill, 1963).

CHATHAM, Earl of. See PITT, William.

CHEW, Benjamin (1722–1810) Jurist A man of divided loyalties, Chew was prominent as a judge in Pennsylvania. He was born in Maryland and studied law at the Middle Temple in London; he returned to practice in Dover and New Castle, Maryland until 1754, when he moved to Philadelphia. He was attorney general of Pennsylvania and registrar of the colony until the eve of the Revolution. In 1774, Chew was appointed as chief justice of the Pennsylvania Supreme Court, but he was turned out of office with the collapse of the British influence. He was at best lukewarm toward the Revolution and was put under house arrest by the patriot government of Philadelphia in 1777, although he was allowed to move to confinement in New Jersey later in the year. His mansion near Germantown became a makeshift fort during the battle there in 1777. He returned to his home after the war and served as a judge of the Pennsylvania state courts.

CHIPMAN, Nathaniel (1752–1843) Soldier, jurist, teacher A native of Connecticut, Chipman served in the Continental Army as a lieutenant during the Revolution. He was admitted to the bar in Connecticut in 1779 but apparently moved to Vermont soon thereafter. He served as chief justice of the Vermont Supreme Court in the 1790s and was a U.S. judge in the Vermont district. He taught law at Middlebury College for 40 years.

CHIPMAN, Ward (1754–1824) Loyalist Born in Marblehead, Massachusetts, Chipman graduated from Harvard in 1770. He took refuge inside the British lines in Boston during 1775 and evacuated from the city in 1776, going first to Halifax and then to England. Within a year, he returned to America, taking up a civilian post in New York City with the court of Admiralty. By 1782, he was deputy muster-master general of the British army in New York. He left New York at the end of the war and settled in New Brunswick, Canada, eventually rising to high office as a judge and executive.

CHITTENDEN, Thomas (1730–1797) State official Chittenden was another of the leaders of the "independent state" of Vermont whose loyalties during the Revolution were at times ambivalent. He was born in East Guilford, Connecticut and worked on his father's farm as a boy. As a teenager, he sailed to the West Indies aboard a merchantman, was captured by the French and returned to Connecticut only after several months' imprisonment. He married the next year and moved to Salisbury, Connecticut, where he became a man of some substance, representing his community in the Connecticut assembly from 1765 to 1769 and acting as a local justice of the peace.

He moved to Williston, in the Vermont region of New Hampshire, in 1774 and soon became involved in the attempts of residents there to separate themselves from the rival claims of both New Hampshire and New York. In September 1776, Chittenden attended the convention that drew up a declaration of independence for Vermont and was appointed to the ruling council. He was an associate of the Allen brothers in unsuccessfully petitioning the Continental Congress for recognition of the new state. When their hopes were frustrated by the political influence of New York, Chittenden and others in Vermont proceeded to set up an extralegal government. He was elected governor of the so-called state in the first popular election in 1778 and served continuously (with the exception of one term) until his death in 1797. He was probably involved with Ethan Allen in the near-treasonous plot to separate Vermont and make it a British province—a plan frustrated only by the American military victory at Yorktown. *Further reading:* "Thomas Chittenden," *The Vermonter* 49,6 (June 1944).

CHOISEUL, Étienne François, Comte de Stainville (1719–1785) French minister One of Louis XV's best ministers, Choiseul preceded the Comte de Vergennes as head of foreign affairs. He came to power in the mid-1750s during the Seven Years' War, and although he could not prevent defeat, he did much to strengthen France's military capacity after the war by rebuilding the navy and reorganizing the army. He anticipated the American Revolution and dispatched agents to assess the vigor

Marquis de Choisy

of the colonial resistance to the British rule. He misjudged, however, the pace of the revolution and had concluded by 1770 that actual rebellion was far off. He fell from grace in the same year and was out of office when the American Revolution began.

CHOISY, Marquis de. French officer
Famed in the French army for his defense of Cracow during a previous campaign, Choisy was attached to General Rochambeau's command as a brigadier. He remained in Newport when the main French army marched south in 1781 and saw to the loading and passage of a train of siege artillery on the ships of the Comte de Barras in August. After Choisy arrived at Yorktown, Rochambeau put him in command of the French and American forces on the Gloucester side of the river, hemming in Banastre Tarleton's troops and making an escape by General Cornwallis impossible. After a sharp skirmish between the Duc de Lauzun's cavalry and a large British foraging party, Choisy pushed the allied lines close to the British position and neutralized further attempts at movement by Tarleton.

CHRISTIAN, William (c. 1743–1786) Continental and militia officer
Born near Staunton, Virginia, Christian was a militia officer from a tender age, serving as a captain in the Virginia militia during the Seven Years' War. In the late 1760s, he studied law under Patrick Henry and married Henry's sister, Anne. Christian sat in the Virginia assembly and senate during the mid-1770s and attended the patriot conventions in 1775 before taking part in Lord Dunmore's War on the frontier. He was commissioned by the Continental Congress as lieutenant colonel of the 1st Virginia Regiment in February 1776 and was promoted to colonel in March, but he resigned in July to accept a commission from the state of Virginia as a colonel of militia. He led a punitive expedition against the Cherokee in what is now Tennessee in late 1776, pushing into Indian territory to destroy villages and crops. He forced the Cherokee to agree to a treaty at Long Island (near modern-day Kingsport, Tennessee) in 1777 by which the tribe ceded large tracts of land in the west. After the war, Christian moved to the area of Louisville, Kentucky and settled on lands claimed from Virginia. He was killed in a skirmish with members of the Wabash tribe on the Indiana side of the river.

CHRISTOPHE, Henri (1767–1820) French soldier, King of Haiti
Christophe was surely one of the more interesting figures to fight in the American War for Independence. He was a black slave, born on the island of Grenada, who worked as a cabin boy on a French smuggling vessel and as a servant in an inn at Cap Haitien before he was sold to a French officer; he then became part of the French infantry contingent from Haiti shipped aboard the Comte d'Estaing's ships in 1779 to take part in the joint American-French assault on British-held Savannah. The French army commander at Haiti, the Vicomte de Fontanges, organized an all-black unit of about 545 "Volunteer Chasseurs" as part of the water-borne force. Christophe was only 12, but he apparently served as an orderly and was wounded during the unsuccessful attempt to take Savannah. Some accounts indicate Christophe may have been granted his freedom as the result of his good service at Savannah. He, along with the rest of the survivors, returned to Haiti, and when a massive slave revolt occurred in 1791, Christophe began his rise to the top. He commanded the black rebel armies in the northern part of the island and succeeded in taking control. France was diverted by the momentous events in Europe until 1802, when a French armed unit invaded Haiti and forced Christophe and his armies to flee the capital and take up guerrilla warfare.

By 1811, Christophe regained control of the northern half of the island, and he declared himself king of an independent black nation. He ruled as a monarch until 1820, when an insurrection among his own people and troops prompted him to commit suicide.

CHURCH, Benjamin (1734–c. 1777) Traitor, physician

Church was the first serious traitor to the American cause. Although the final proof of his treachery was not uncovered until the 20th century, he was tried and convicted in 1775 as an informer for the British, and he escaped severe punishment only due to confusion during the first months of the Revolution over what constituted treason against a "nation" that had not yet declared its independence.

Church was born in Newport, Rhode Island and educated well at Boston Latin School and Harvard. He studied medicine privately in Boston and then at the London School of Medicine. He married a British wife while in England, then returned to Massachusetts and set up a practice in Raynham in 1768. He lived well, entertaining often in his fine house, and there has been a suspicion among historians that he was led into treason by a need for money to support his high style of life. He was a poet and orator of some notice in addition to his work as a doctor. Church came to political prominence during the agitation over the Boston Massacre in 1770: he examined the body of Crispus Attucks and published a report of the martyr's injuries, and thereafter, Church wrote and spoke as part of the propaganda effort to keep the memory of the Massacre warm in Boston. He sat on a committee of correspondence with John Adams and Joseph Warren in 1772, and by 1774, it was no exaggeration to say that Church was among the principal leaders of the Massachusetts patriot party, since he was elected to the Provincial Congress and sat in many of the secret meetings of rebels in the colony. Some of his patriot colleagues—chiefly Paul Revere—grew suspicious when royal governor Thomas Hutchinson learned the substance of their meetings, apparently through an informer, but no one seriously challenged Church at that stage. In truth, Church was a paid informer for General Thomas Gage, who assumed the governorship as part of his military command of Boston. Church warned Gage of the arms and munitions the rebels where gathering in the outlying Massachusetts towns, and his reports may well have set off the fateful British expedition

against Lexington and Concord in April 1775. After the battle, Church went to Boston and conferred with Gage in person, passing off the encounter to his patriot friends as a harmless interview. In May, the still-trusting Massachusetts patriots selected Church to carry a petition to Congress in Philadelphia, and he was chosen to greet George Washington when the new general arrived in Massachusetts to take command of the new Continental Army. Washington appointed Church as head of the military hospital at Cambridge, making him in effect the chief surgeon of the army. All the while, Church reported by letter to Gage on the strength and intentions of the rebels, for example telling the British commander six weeks ahead of time that the Americans planned to fortify Breed's Hill and Bunker Hill.

In July 1775, Church made a mistake. He dispatched an enciphered letter to British headquarters with a young woman (possibly his mistress), but the message was intercepted by an American officer and eventually was handed over to Washington. Two amateur cryptographers decoded the letter, which was an incriminating report to Gage from Church, and Washington browbeat a confession from the woman messenger. A search of Church's private papers revealed only that someone had gotten there first and removed any incriminating evidence. Church was arrested and convicted on October 4 by a council of war on charges of carrying on a correspondence with the enemy. However, Washington discovered that he had no authority to punish traitors under the articles of war hastily drawn by Congress, except for removal from the army, forfeiture of pay and whipping. The traditional definition of treason in the colonies was betrayal of the king—what name could be placed on betrayal of a revolt *against* the king? Washington dumped the question back in the lap of Congress, which would have needed to declare the independence of the colonies in order to convict Church of a capital offense. Instead, he was ordered to jail in Connecticut, where he languished in an unhealthy prison in Norwich for several months while Congress considered a change in the definition of treason.

After the British evacuation of Boston, Church returned to Massachusetts and was free for a period, but he was confined again in mid-1776. Neither Congress nor the army could quite decide what to do with him, so in late 1777 or early 1778, they simply let him go. Church boarded a ship and sailed for the West Indies, but the vessel was lost at sea and never heard from again. Proof positive of Church's perfidy came to light 150 years later when his letters to Gage were discovered among the British commander's correspondence files. *Further reading:* Allen French, *General Gage's Informers* (Ann Arbor, 1932).

CILLEY, Joseph (1735–1799) Officer, state official

Cilley was born in Nottingham, New Hampshire and was a farmer, lawyer and merchant. He sat in the New Hampshire Provincial Congress before the Revolution and helped raid the store of cannon and gunpowder at Fort William and Mary near Portsmouth in December 1774, whisking the military supplies out from under the noses of the British. He received a commission as major of the 2nd New Hampshire in 1775 under Enoch Poor. He fought at the battle of Long Island, narrowly avoiding capture, and was at Trenton and Princeton. In 1777, Cilley was promoted to colonel and took over command of the 1st New Hampshire from the disgruntled John Stark, leading the regiment for the next four years. He and his regiment served at Saratoga, wintered at Valley Forge and fought the battle of Monmouth. Cilley was assigned to John Sullivan's expedition against the Iroquois in 1779 and was rewarded by the state of New Hampshire with a commission as brigadier general in the militia. He retired from the Continental service in January 1781. After the war, he was awarded the rank of major general in the New Hampshire state militia. He also served in the state senate and house of representatives and sat on the Governor's Council.

CIST, Charles (Karl Thiel) (1738–1805) Printer

Cist was born Karl Thiel in St. Petersburg, Russia and graduated from the University of Halle in Germany with degrees in medicine and pharmacy. He apparently served in the court of Catherine the Great but unspecified difficulties prompted him to emigrate to Pennsylvania in 1769. He changed his name to "Cist" on taking up a new life in America. Despite his professional training, he worked at the relatively menial business of translation for his first six years in Philadelphia. By 1775, he had learned the printer's trade and established a partnership with Melchior Styner. Cist published one of the first editions of Thomas Paine's *American Crisis* in 1776. The printing business shut down during the British occupation of Philadelphia but resumed in 1778. After the Revolutionary War, Cist continued as a printer and publisher and as a businessman. During the administration of President John Adams, he was the official public printer of the United States with an office and printing shop in Washington, D.C., but he returned to Philadelphia before his death.

CLAGHORN, George (1748–1824) Militia officer, shipbuilder

Claghorn lived in New Hampshire and served as a captain of the Bristol militia at Bunker Hill. Following the war, he established a shipyard at New Bedford, New Hampshire, and in 1794 he was the builder of the U.S.S. *Constitution*, known as "Old Ironsides," one of the new frigates commissioned for a revived national navy. Still in service today, the *Constitution* is the oldest commissioned warship in the world.

CLARK, Abraham (1726–1794) Delegate to Congress

Clark was among the secondary leaders of the Revolution who have gained little notice but who played key roles in forming the new nation. He came from a relatively modest financial and social background without the powerful connections that drove the public careers of many Revolutionary politicians, yet in his long years of service he was (in the words of Ruth Bogin, his modern biographer) an effective "champion of individual liberties, an enemy to every form of privilege, and a protagonist of governmental concern for the lowlier segments of the people." Clark vigorously explored the inherent possibilities of inventing a democracy through his unremitting zeal for egalitarianism.

He was born on his father's farm near Elizabethtown, New Jersey and spent his youth informally learning mathematics and the basics of law. He was apparently never admitted to the bar and had little or no formal education, but by the time he became an adult, Clark was experienced in surveying and the legal business of buying and selling land, and he often assisted his neighbors in settling land disputes. He followed his father into local public office, serving before the Revolution as sheriff of Essex County. He became a member of the New Jersey Committee of Safety in 1774 and served as its secretary, and he was elected to the provincial assembly. In June 1776, Clark was selected as one of the delegates to the Second Continental Congress—the entire New Jersey delegation was replaced at one blow—on the basis of his firm support for independence. He signed the Declaration of Independence later in the summer, and he continued to sit in the Congress throughout the rest of the Revolution. He also served simultaneously in the New Jersey state assembly.

Clark's presence in the Congress presented considerable personal risk, since his family remained at his farm only a short distance from the British forces at Staten Island (one of Clark's sons was captured by the British and held on the infamous prison ship *Jersey* in New York). As a national legislator, Clark was hard-working, but he intentionally avoided the limelight, eschewing speech-making and refusing to write out his positions for publication. He focused consistently on eliminating privilege and guarding against the creation of a new elite. He strongly opposed half pay for Continental officers, for example, believing it would promote a standing army and a professional officer class. At the end of the war, Clark returned to his New Jersey farm, but he was reelected several times during the following years to both the New Jersey legislature and the national Congress. He represented his state at the Annapolis Convention in 1789, but his chronic ill health kept him from his seat at the subsequent Constitutional Convention. Predictably, he opposed the new Constitution until the Bill of Rights was added. He was elected to the new national House of Representatives in 1791 and served two terms. He died from the effects of a sunstroke on September 15, 1794, while still a member of Congress. *Further reading:* Ruth Bogin, *Abraham Clark and the Quest for Equality in the Revolutionary Era, 1774–1794* (Rutherford, N.J., 1982).

CLARK, George Rogers (1752–1818) General

As the outstanding military figure in the West during the Revolution, Clark epitomized the frontier soldier. He was born to a family of farmers near Charlottesville, Virginia and, after receiving a rudimentary education, became a surveyor at age 19. He early turned his eyes toward the western territories of Virginia. Six feet tall, muscular, red-haired, and with sparkling eyes, he emerged as a natural leader during Lord Dunmore's War in 1774, when he served as a captain of militia. He surveyed land

George Rogers Clark

for the Ohio Company and was well known by the outbreak of the Revolution as an advocate of orderly settlement in the West.

In 1776, the American outposts in the "Dark and Bloody Ground" of Kentucky were under constant pressure from Indian raids organized by the British lieutenant governor at Detroit, Henry Hamilton. Clark convinced Virginia governor Patrick Henry and the Virginia Assembly to support a plan to clear the west of British influence. Clark was commissioned as a major in the Virginia militia in 1777, and he moved to organize a force of frontiersmen to march on the British-held settlements in the Illinois country (which were mostly inhabited by French settlers) and, if possible, to capture Detroit itself.

Only 150 men turned up at the planned rendezvous at the Falls of the Ohio (site of present-day Louisville), but Clark pressed on, departing on June 26 by shooting the rapids in the middle of a total eclipse. The small army landed four days later at the mouth of the Tennessee River and marched overland the 120 miles to their first objective, the settlement of Kaskaskia. Clark captured the small garrison without a shot and set about charming the local French and Indians into cooperation. Within a few weeks, he had also secured the settlements at Prairie de Rocher and Cahokia. In August, with the help of the local French who were swayed by both the news of the American-French alliance and Clark's even-handed treatment, Clark's men also occupied the larger settlement of Vincennes. The Illinois country was in American hands.

The British commander, Hamilton, however, did not sit idly in Detroit but set off with a mixed force of redcoats, French volunteers, and Indians on October 7. He recaptured Vincennes on December 17 when the American-led local defenders refused to fight. At least half of Hamilton's Indian forces and his militia then returned home, leaving the British commander with only 35 regulars to defend a makeshift fort. Clark's force at Kaskaskia had likewise dwindled, and the winter season seemed to preclude further action since most of the terrain was flooded and iced over, making movement nearly impossible.

Clark believed surprise was his best weapon, however, so in February 1779 he led his men on a terrible march that found them wading for days through shoulder-deep, ice-cold waters with little to eat. Reaching Vincennes, Clark deployed his small force to make it appear larger than it really was and began a long-range rifle assault on Hamilton's fort. When Hamilton's Indian and French allies wavered, he was forced to capitulate. Clark shipped Hamilton and his few British regulars back to Virginia in custody.

Although he then held the West securely, Clark was never able to mount a full offensive against the principal British base at Detroit. Plans fell through, supplies were delayed, reinforcements were ambushed by Indians, and other mishaps frustrated his scheme of marching north. By the summer of 1780, Clark withdrew to Kentucky, and, although appointed a brigadier general, he could do little more than lead expeditions against hostile Indian villages until the end of the war.

Although he was not yet 30 years old, the great period of Clark's life was over, and everything after the Revolutionary War was a downhill slide. His public reputation suffered from attacks by political rivals, and Clark was soon badly in debt and out of favor with both the Virginia and federal governments. In 1793, Clark attempted to lead an expedition against Louisiana (then in Spanish hands) on behalf of the French, but the U.S. government demanded he withdraw, and he was forced to flee to St. Louis.

He eventually returned to Clarksville, Indiana, just across the river from Louisville, where he lived out his life in relative quiet, serving as a land commissioner, running a grist mill and writing his memoirs. Forced by his debts to live on the grace of his family, he took to heavy drinking and in 1805 suffered both a stroke and amputation of a leg. He died at his sister's home near Louisville in 1818, nearly a forgotten man. *Further reading:* Lowell H. Harrison, *George Rogers Clark and the War in the West* (Lexington, Ky., 1976).

CLARK, Jonas (1731–1805) Clergyman

Clark was the pastor of the First Parish Congregationalist Church in Lexington, Massachusetts from 1755 until his death 50 years later. He was also a close friend and advisor to patriot leaders John Hancock and Samuel Adams, who were staying at Clark's home when General Thomas Gage sent out an armed expedition in April 1775 to capture them. The result was the first battle of the Revolution. A strong supporter of the rebellion, Clark wrote an anti-British tract in 1776 called *The Fate of Blood Thirsty Oppressors and God's Tender Care of His Distressed People.*

CLARKE, Alured (c. 1745–1832) British officer

Clarke commanded important segments of the British infantry in America during the Revolution, although specific details of his service are slim. He rose to great rank and distinction later in life. He probably was the son of Charles Clarke, a baron of the exchequer, by a second wife. Clarke joined the British Army as a teenager in 1759 when he purchased a commission as ensign in the 50th Regiment of Foot. He advanced in rank and experience during the following decade and by 1771 was major in the 54th Regiment, stationed in Ireland. In 1775, Clarke became lieutenant colonel of the 54th, which crossed the Atlantic the following year to take part in the first British attempt to capture Charleston. After the repulse in South Carolina, Clarke's regiment was sent to New York and then stationed in Newport, Rhode Island. He transferred to the 7th (Royal Fusilier) Regiment in 1777 as lieutenant colonel. The Fusiliers went to Philadelphia as reinforcements for the occupation of the city and retreated with the rest of the Royal Army to New York City in 1778, fighting in the desperate battle at Monmouth along the way. In 1779, the regiment raided in Connecticut and then sailed south to assist in the second attempt to take Charleston. In 1782, Clarke became colonel in command of the 7th and probably was in the same year commander of the British garrison at Savannah.

At the end of the American War, the Fusiliers returned to England, but Clarke went to Jamaica to become lieutenant governor. By 1795, he was a major general in India, and he eventually served as British commander in chief on the subcontinent. He continued on the army list for decades longer, and by 1830, as one of the two oldest living generals, Clarke was made a field marshal.

CLARKE, Elijah (1733–1799) Militia commander Clarke was among the best leaders of state militia in the southern theater of the war and was especially prominent during the prolonged and vicious fighting after the British invasion of Georgia and South Carolina in 1779–1780, when he served under and with Andrew Pickens and Thomas Sumter. He was born in South Carolina but lived most of his life in Georgia, principally in Wilkes County. He was without formal education yet had the knack for leading men. By the beginning of the Revolution, Clarke was a colonel in the Georgia militia, and he eventually attained the militia rank of brigadier general. The composition and numbers of his forces changed virtually from week to week as was usual in the Carolina and Georgia theater. Clarke was at several of the skirmishes preceding the battle of King's Mountain, including engagements at Green Spring, South Carolina on August 1, 1780 and at Musgrove's Mill, South Carolina on August 18, 1780, when his men and frontier militia under Isaac Shelby attacked the rear of the loyalist forces under Patrick Ferguson. They failed to surprise Ferguson and were themselves attacked in turn, but they beat off the loyalists while inflicting heavy losses.

One biographer reports that Clarke was wounded at the Musgrove's Mill fight. If so, he apparently recovered rapidly, since within weeks, he appeared with 350 Wilkes County men outside the British-loyalist stronghold at Augusta, Georgia and attacked the fortified house to which most of the enemy had withdrawn. Clarke laid a brief siege against the British, but he lacked a capable artillery officer and the tough-minded British commander, Thomas Browne, refused to surrender. Clarke was forced to leave the scene when a British relief column approached. The attack has been judged as misguided, but it drew off British forces that might have averted the American victory at King's Mountain. In November 1780, Clarke was again in the field, reinforcing Sumter at the battle of Blackstocks against Banastre Tarleton. In May of the following year, Clarke returned to Augusta along with troops

under Thomas Pickens, and the Americans succeeded this time in capturing the British forts and taking Browne prisoner.

After the Revolutionary War, Clarke entered a period of confused scheming, aimed at establishing new settlements in the western part of Georgia. In 1793, he obtained a commission as major general from the French government and joined the infamous Citizen Genet in an attempt to seize lands granted to the Spanish. When this failed, Clarke led a group of white settlers across the Oconee River into Creek Indian lands and tried to proclaim a new territory. He was dissuaded by Georgia state troops, however. He may also have been involved in a scheme to take lands in West Florida. He finally gave up the land adventures and returned to Wilkes County, where he died in 1799.

CLARKE, Richard (1711–1795) Loyalist merchant After graduating from Harvard in 1729, Clarke became a merchant in his native Boston. His firm prospered and by the 1770s was one of the leading mercantile companies of the city. In 1773, Clarke was one of the East Indian Company consignees for the tea dumped by a patriot mob during the Boston Tea Party. He was personally attacked by the Sons of Liberty for refusing to resign as agent for the East India Company. Having enough of rebellious agitation, Clarke went to England in 1775 and became one of the founders of the Loyalist Club. John Singleton Copley, the great loyalist painter, was his son-in-law and lived in Clarke's home in London.

CLARKSON, Matthew (1758–1825) Officer, official Clarkson was a native of New York City. His first military service during the Revolution was as a volunteer aide-de-camp to Benedict Arnold during 1778 and 1779. He then moved to the staff of Major General Benjamin Lincoln, serving until the end of the war. He was captured along with the rest of Lincoln's force at Charleston, South Carolina but was exchanged with Lincoln. Clarkson continued on Lincoln's staff after the Revolutionary War, acting as his assistant when the former general became U.S. secretary of war. Clarkson himself became a major general in the New York state militia, a U.S. marshal and a member of the New York state assembly and senate.

CLAY, Joseph (1741–1804) Official, merchant, delegate to Congress

Born in England, Clay was the nephew of James Habersham, who was a close associate of Georgia royal governor James Wright (Habersham himself served temporarily as governor). The young Clay emigrated to Georgia at the behest of his influential uncle in 1760 and settled in Savannah. With the assistance of his relative, Clay established a highly successful trading business in the colony and within a few years was one of the wealthiest and most prominent men of commerce in Georgia, owning rice plantations in addition to his mercantile interests. He also had a partnership interest in a trading house in Newport, Rhode Island. Despite his close ties to the royal government, Clay was an active patriot from the early days of rebel agitation in Georgia. He helped draw up resolutions from the patriot assembly of Savannah in 1774, and he was elected to the Georgia Provincial Congress in 1775. He was also part of the council of safety that took over administration of Savannah the same year. In 1776, Clay was commissioned as a major in the Continental Army and appointed as deputy paymaster for the southern theater, a post at which he served during the remainder of the war. In 1778, he was elected to the Congress but failed to take his seat. After the Revolution, Clay resumed his mercantile business but also continued in public service as treasurer of the state of Georgia and as U.S. judge for the Georgia District.

CLAYTON, Joshua (1744–1798) Soldier, official, physician

Clayton was born in Dover, Delaware but served during the first year of the Revolution as a major in a Maryland battalion, probably part of Smallwood's Maryland Regiment. Clayton was eventually promoted to colonel and served on George Washington's staff. After the War of Independence, he became prominent in Delaware government, acting as state treasurer and president. In 1792, he became Delaware's first state governor, having previously served as the state's first U.S. senator under the new national constitution.

CLEAVELAND, Moses (1754–1806) Officer, land speculator

Born in Connecticut, Cleaveland graduated from Yale in 1777. He received a commission in the 2nd Connecticut Regiment, organized early that year under Colonel Charles Webb.

Cleaveland, later promoted to lieutenant, served until 1781. After the Revolution he maintained his interest in military affairs, eventually reaching the rank of brigadier in the state militia, although his elevation may have been due more to his political clout than his soldierly excellence. In 1787, he sat as a member of the General Assembly, representing his home county of Canterbury. By the 1790s, he was a significant land speculator and holder of western land grants, and he led a party west to survey the purchase of the Western Reserve Land Company in 1795. He founded the city of Cleveland, Ohio, which bears a variant of his name.

CLERKE, Sir Francis Carr (1748–1777) British officer

Clerke had purchased a commission as ensign in the 3rd Foot Guards in 1770 and served as a captain by the beginning of the Revolution. While his regiment was with the main British force that occupied Philadelphia in 1777, Clerke himself was detached as an aide-de-camp to General John Burgoyne and accompanied the British expedition from Canada. He is best known for the manner of his death: he was mortally wounded at the battle of Bemis Heights on October 7, 1777 by the famous American rifleman Timothy Murphy, who reputedly fired at a distance of 300 yards. Clerke was carried within the American lines and died during the night.

CLEVELAND, Benjamin (1738–1806) Militia officer

Cleveland was born in Prince George's County, Virginia and grew up in Orange County, where he developed a "great fondness" for gambling and horse racing. He moved to the Blue Ridge frontier of North Carolina along with his brother and father-in-law in 1769, becoming a farmer, or at least overseeing farm operations carried on by his relatives' slaves. He was, despite his devotion to leisure pursuits, a vigorous frontier explorer and adventurer. He traveled in 1772 to the Kentucky frontier, crossing the Cumberland Gap and looking over the lush central Bluegrass region until run off by Indians.

Cleveland was a junior officer in the North Carolina militia at the beginning of the Revolution, but he soon moved into leadership. In 1776, he served under General Griffith Rutherford in the so-called Cherokee War and advanced to the rank of militia captain. He also was a member of his local committee of safety, a justice of the county common court and an elected member of the state assembly. He was a vicious militia leader, much feared by loyalists for his quick ways with a rope. His company of "Cleveland's Bull Dogs" terrorized loyalists in North Carolina in much the same fashion as loyalist raiders terrorized patriots. The conflicts between Cleveland and the opposing loyalists had little to do with the Revolution much of the time and often were simply pretexts to raid and pillage among local enemies.

By 1780, Cleveland was a colonel of militia, and he was one of the principal leaders of the American forces that crushed the loyalists under Patrick Ferguson at King's Mountain in October. Cleveland commanded the left flank of the American attack and is reported to have been one of those most anxious to hang captives after the battle. Cleveland lost his land at the end of the Revolution when his title proved defective, and he moved to the western frontier of South Carolina, becoming a local judge renowned for sleeping through the court proceedings. He grew immensely fat in old age and died weighing 450 pounds.

CLINGAN, William (d. 1790) Delegate to Congress

Probably born near Wagontown, Pennsylvania, Clingan lived in Chester County most of his life, taking part in local affairs and representing his neighbors during the Revolution. He was a local justice of the peace for nearly 30 years, from 1757 to 1786. In 1777, he was elected as a delegate to the Continental Congress, and he was one of the first signers of the Articles of Confederation in 1778. He left his seat in Congress in 1779 and took on the task of handling a $20,000,000 loan for the national government.

CLINTON, George (1739–1812) Continental general, governor, vice president

First governor of the state of New York and a general in the Continental Army, Clinton had a checkered military career but was successful as a state government leader. He was born in Little Britain, New York. In 1757, he served as a subaltern under John Bradstreet during the British conquest of Fort Frontenac, and after brief service as a privateer in 1758, he turned to the study of law and began a legal career with admission to the bar in 1764. He became a member of the New York assembly in 1768 and became

George Clinton

Philip Schuyler's rival for leadership of the advocates of revolution and a member of the Livingston family political faction opposing the rival De Lancey family. Elected to the second Continental Congress in 1775, Clinton missed the signing of the Declaration of Independence because George Washington had ordered him to assume command of the defenses of the Hudson Highlands in July 1776. He was appointed brigadier general of the New York militia and in March 1777 assumed the same rank in the Continental Army. His leadership failed to save New York's defenses from Sir Henry Clinton's expedition, leading to the loss of forts Clinton and Montgomery and the destruction of Kingston.

In 1777, Clinton was elected governor of New York in the first election under the new state constitution: he defeated Philip Schuyler in a surprising victory, garnering support from the middle class and small farmers. He assumed his new post with some relief, acknowledging his inadequacies as a military commander. As governor he was occupied with the Border Wars and Indian-loyalist raids. He proved immensely popular as a wartime governor, and he was reelected five times. Clinton opposed the federal Constitution and wrote articles arguing against Alexander Hamilton. As an ally of Aaron Burr and the Livingstons he was again elected governor in 1800 after refusing to run in 1795 following his six consecutive terms. He became vice president of the United States in 1804 and again in 1808, serving with presidents Jefferson and Madison and dying in office. *Further reading:* E. Wilder Spaulding, *His Excellency George Clinton: Critic of the Constitution* (New York, 1938; second ed. 1964).

Sir Henry Clinton

CLINTON, Sir Henry (1730–1795) British general

The longest-serving British commander in chief during the Revolution, Clinton was born in Newfoundland, where his father, Admiral George Clinton, served as governor, and he was raised in New York when Admiral Clinton moved to the governorship there. Clinton was well connected, principally through his cousin the Duke of Newcastle, and on returning to England in 1751 with his father, he became a lieutenant in the Coldstream Guards. His military education came in the German wars of the mid-century. He was promoted to lieutenant colonel in the Grenadier Guards in 1758 and served as aide-de-camp to Prince Ferdinand of Brunswick during the Seven Years' War, taking a wound at Johannisberg in August 1762. In May 1772, he became major general and also began a career as a member of Parliament, assisted by his cousin the Duke. As with all important British general officers of the time, Clinton's vote in Parliament and the amount of political influence he swung had much to do with how he fared in securing good commands and proper rewards. He held a seat in the Commons throughout the American war, but he found it difficult to maintain his standing with the government in the latter years when the power of his patron Newcastle slipped.

The great tragedy of Clinton's life was the death of his wife in August 1772, which left him severely depressed and incapacitated for the following several years. He had recovered sufficiently by early 1775 to be sent out to Boston in the company of fellow generals William Howe and John Burgoyne. He failed to make much impression on commander in chief Thomas Gage, however. Clinton served gallantly in the battle of Bunker Hill—personally leading the final British assault on the patriot barricades—and was made lieutenant general, second in command to Howe, who succeeded Gage. Clinton seldom got along with either his superiors or his subordinates, and the relationship with Howe was no exception. Howe sent him on the Charleston Expedition in 1776, and through a combination of poor planning, ill luck and lack of naval cooperation, the grand assault on the southern American seaport failed miserably. The defeat raised American spirits in the South and allowed Washington to concentrate his forces in the middle colonies. Rejoining Howe and assuming a local rank of full general, Clinton fought well in the battle of Long Island in August. Howe, wanting to be rid of him, sent Clinton to capture Newport, Rhode Island in late 1776, a task he accomplished smoothly, although the triumph was obscured by Washington's nearly simultaneous victory at Trenton. Clinton then returned to England and was greeted by a George Germain who was eager to placate him. He was promoted to permanent lieutenant general and accorded a knighthood.

He returned to New York City in July 1777, where Howe assigned him to the defense of the city, while Howe embarked for Philadelphia. The British grand strategy became completely muddled at this stage, and Clinton was caught in the cracks between rival campaigns: Burgoyne to the north and Howe in Pennsylvania. In October, he captured the Hudson Highlands from the Americans, but he could not push far enough to succor Burgoyne. In May 1778, Clinton succeeded Howe as commander in chief and decided to evacuate Philadelphia, choosing to march overland rather than withdraw by river. He retreated skillfully, encumbered as he was by a huge baggage train and fleeing loyalists, but when Washington brought him to battle at Monmouth, Clinton very nearly lost all—only near-treasonous behavior by American general Charles Lee prevented disaster.

For most of the next two years, Clinton was content to remain in his strong base at New York City and made only small-scale raids. In 1779, he captured Stony Point and Verplanck's Point and sent Tryon to raid on the Connecticut coast. These were solid successes tactically but accomplished little to weaken the Americans. Clinton's great triumph of the war was his successful expedition to take Charleston in 1779 and 1780. He personally conducted the move southward and initiated a change in British strategy that came close to winning half the colonies back to the British cause. Unfortunately, Clinton left Lord Cornwallis in command and returned himself to New York. The result was eventual disaster, when Cornwallis insisted on depleting his strength against Nathanael Greene and finally backed his army into a corner at Yorktown. Clinton could do little to control Cornwallis, whose political star at the moment shone brighter in London than did Clinton's. With the surrender at Yorktown the war was essentially over, and Clinton—who had regularly offered his resignation since 1777—was relieved by Sir Guy Carleton, commander in chief in North America, in 1782.

Clinton received a nasty reception on his return home. Cornwallis escaped censure, and Clinton was nominated as the scapegoat. He was roundly criticized and found it necessary to defend himself in public. In 1783, he published his *Narrative of the Campaign of 1781 in North America*. The following year, he lost his seat in Parliament after quarreling with his cousin, but he was reelected in 1790. He eventually made something of a recovery, and he was promoted to full general in 1793 and in 1794 was made governor of Gibraltar. He died on December 23, 1795 while serving in that post. *Further reading:* William B. Willcox, *Portrait of a General: Sir Henry Clinton in the War of Independence* (New York, 1964); Willcox, ed., *The American Rebellion: Sir Henry Clinton's Narrative of His Campaigns, 1775–1782 . . .* (New Haven, 1954).

CLINTON, James (1733–1812) Continental general

The brother of patriot New York governor George Clinton and the father of politician De Witt Clinton, James was a distinguished man in his own right, serving creditably during the Revolution as a soldier. He was born to a family of Irish emigrants in upstate New York and took part as a militia officer in the British-colonial campaign against Fort Frontenac in 1757 at the beginning of the Seven Years' War. He was elected to the New York Provincial Congress from Ulster County in the spring of 1775 and was appointed as a colonel of the 3rd

James Clinton

New York Regiment in June. His was one of four New York regiments raised in 1775 to protect the state, but all of them, including Clinton's regiment, were dispatched northward with Montgomery's invasion of Canada. Clinton survived the campaign and the disastrous attack on Quebec in December 1775, but the enlistments of his men ran out soon after. In March 1776, he was named as colonel in command of a new regiment of New Yorkers, the 2nd, but he stayed with the regiment only until August when he was commissioned as a brigadier general in the Continental Army. In 1777, he was the defender of Fort Montgomery on the Hudson River when British general Sir Henry Clinton made a half-hearted thrust to join General John Burgoyne. The fort fell to overwhelming British forces, and Clinton barely escaped capture after suffering a bayonet wound.

His greatest contribution to the war effort came in 1779, when he commanded a major portion of the troops assigned to John Sullivan's expedition against the Iroquois in upper New York (some historians label this the "Sullivan-Clinton Expedition"). The campaign to crush the Indians and loyalists who had been raiding New York and Pennsylvania settlements was well organized and well executed, due in large part to Clinton's efforts. His New Yorkers joined three brigades under Sullivan at Athens, Pennsylvania and moved against the mixed British forces under Joseph Brant and the Butlers. On August 27, the Americans cornered the outnumbered opposition and at the battle of Newton (Chemung River) soundly routed the British and Indians. The American force then marched through the Indian homeland, destroying crops and villages and rendering the Iroquois ineffective for the balance of the war. Clinton was assigned as commander of the Northern Department in 1780 and held the northern strongholds while the last months of strategy unfolded. In the fall of 1781, Clinton moved southward with Washington and Rochambeau to Yorktown, where he commanded a brigade in Benjamin Lincoln's division during the siege of Cornwallis' army. After the Revolution, Clinton sat in the New York constitutional convention, voting against the new federal Constitution because it lacked a bill of rights at that stage.

CLOSEN, Baron Ludwig von (Closen-Haydenburg) (c. 1752–1830) French officer

It is often forgotten that many German-speaking soldiers served in the French army and fought in support of the American cause (some estimate as many as one-third of Rochambeau's army was German). Von Closen was one of the more conspicuous German Protestant soldiers who devoted a military career to the service of France. He was born in the Palatinate, near Worms, the son of an aristocratic soldier and a titled mother. Several members of von Closen's family had served in the Royal Deux-Ponts Regiment that had been formed by France in 1757 to fight in the Seven Years' War, and the young baron joined the unit as a sub-lieutenant in 1769. He moved through a series of promotions and postings and was a second captain when the regiment joined Rochambeau's expedition in support of the American war. Von Closen kept a journal during his time in America, which has since proved to be a valuable source of insight and information about the French in America.

Von Closen was a close friend of the lieutenant colonel of the regiment, Comte Guillaume de Deux-Ponts, and immediately after landing with the French force at Newport in July 1780, von Closen was appointed aide-de-camp to the younger Rochambeau, a position that allowed him to travel widely and meet most of the important officials of the day. He was also a serious soldier and skilled draftsman with an inquiring mind. His duties often included carrying dispatches between the French command and Washington's headquarters. Von Closen was with the French army during its maneuvers in the northern theater and moved south when Rochambeau marched to Yorktown. He re-embarked for France with his regiment in late 1782. During the

following years, he served in several other French regiments and remained loyal to the crown during the French Revolution, eventually achieving the rank of major general. He resigned from the army a few days before the fall of the king and returned to his German estates. He lost most of his property during the subsequent European wars but served as a French sub-prefect in Simmern in 1806 and eventually retired to Mannheim. *Further reading: The Revolutionary Journal of Baron Ludwig von Closen, 1780–1783*, Evelyn M. Acomb, ed. (Chapel Hill, N.C., 1958).

CLYMER, George (1739–1813) Delegate to Congress, merchant

A hard-working and dedicated patriot, Clymer was one of the principal financial men of the Congress during the Revolution. He was born in Philadelphia, orphaned when only one year old, and raised by a wealthy merchant uncle, William Coleman, who trained his young ward in business. The elder man eventually left a prosperous firm of which Clymer was a full partner by the time of his uncle's death. Clymer then merged his company with the firm of Meredith & Clymer, and he married the daughter of his senior partner. Not surprisingly, Clymer resisted the British attempts to control the colonial economy by regulatory taxation, and he led Philadelphia businessmen in supporting the growing revolutionary sentiment during the early 1770s. He served on the Pennsylvania Council of Safety and was one of the leaders of the movement that forced tea agents in Philadelphia to resign in 1773.

When the American colonists began to organize a formal government, Clymer stepped forward with his knowledge of commerce and finance to take a leading role: he was appointed one of two Continental treasurers in July 1775, and he helped finance the early days of Congress by converting all his own specie to Continental currency—a rather daring financial vote of confidence for the Revolution. Clymer was appointed as a delegate to Congress in July 1776 as one of the replacements for the four Pennsylvania delegates who had refused to sign the Declaration, and he affixed his name to the historic document, although he had not been a member when it was adopted. He served ably on several committees during his first congressional term and was sent to inspect the northern army on behalf of Congress in the fall of 1776. When Congress fled Philadelphia in the face of Clinton's threatened occupation in late 1776, Clymer stayed behind with George Walton and Robert Morris to conduct the affairs of the government. The British made a special point of destroying Clymer's country home in Chester County the following year after the battle of Brandywine.

He resigned from Congress in 1777, exhausted from working during the occupation, and was not reelected in the fall. He returned to public service in 1780 when elected to a seat in the Pennsylvania legislature and soon thereafter won a second term in the Continental Congress. His financial acumen was not enough to stave off the crushing economic crisis that overtook Congress during the ensuing two years, however. In 1782, he was sent on a tour of the southern states in a vain attempt to get the legislatures to pay up on subscriptions due to the central government. He was again elected to the Pennsylvania legislature in 1784, and he represented his state at the Constitutional Convention in 1787. He was then elected as one of Pennsylvania's representatives to the first U.S. Congress. He served only one term and then was appointed as federal collector of excise taxes on alcohol in Pennsylvania. His public career came to an end in 1795–96 as a presidential commissioner to negotiate an Indian treaty. *Further reading:* Walter H. Mohr, "George Clymer," *Pennsylvania Magazine of History and Biography* 5 (October 1932), 282–85.

COBB, David (1748–1830) Continental officer, physician, jurist

Born in Attleborough, Massachusetts, Cobb lived in Taunton, where he practiced medicine after graduation from Harvard in 1766 and private study in Boston. He was an early patriot, sitting in the Massachusetts Provincial Congress and representing Bristol County at revolutionary meetings. His first military service was as a surgeon in a militia company, but in January 1777 Cobb received a commission as lieutenant colonel and was appointed second in command of Henry Jackson's "additional" infantry regiment that was raised from the Boston region. Cobb apparently served with the regiment during most of the Revolutionary War, fighting at Monmouth and several smaller battles. Jackson's regiment was one of the better state units, absorbing two other Massachusetts volunteer regiments in 1779, and it was eventually incorporated into the Continental Line with full status as the 16th Massachusetts.

In 1781, Cobb was promoted to colonel and assigned as an aide to commander in chief George Washington, whom he apparently served during most of the final two years of the struggle. He was posted to the 5th Massachusetts in January 1783, just months before the dissolution of the Continental Army. Cobb retired along with most of the army's officers in the fall of 1783. Some biographical sketches say he was brevetted to the rank of brigadier general, but he is not mentioned in the promotion lists. He returned to Taunton and became judge of the local court of common pleas, defending his courthouse with an artillery piece during Shays' Rebellion. He was elected as speaker of the Massachusetts House of Representatives in 1789, serving two terms, and then to the U.S. House in 1793 for one term. He then moved to the Maine region of the state and took up farming. In 1802, he was again elected to state office, this time as a senator, and he was lieutenant governor of Massachusetts during 1809. He died in Boston.

COCHRAN, John (1730–1807) Continental medical director

Cochran was the primary medical officer of the Continental Army during the final years of the war, bearing the title of Chief Physician and Surgeon of the Army. He reached his post only after a long struggle among rival physicians and between the central army medical department and individual regimental doctors. He was born in Sadsbury, Pennsylvania to Irish parents and was educated privately by Dr. Francis Allison. He studied medicine with a doctor in Lancaster and gained both medical and military experience during the Seven Years' War as a surgeon's mate with the British army on the expedition against Fort Frontenac. In 1760, Cochran married the widow of Peter Schuyler and doubtless gained some political influence through the connection. He and his wife moved to New Brunswick, New Jersey in the mid-1760s, and he was one of the founders and early presidents of the New Jersey Medical Society. He apparently served as a volunteer physician during the early months of the Revolutionary War.

In general, the organization of medical affairs for the new Continental Army was a disaster. The first chief physician, Massachusetts' Benjamin Church, turned out to be a traitor and was removed from office in 1775. The post then went to John Morgan, who came into conflict almost immediately with regimental surgeons who resented the attempt of Congress to name a general medical director over them. Morgan gave way to William Shippen of Philadelphia, who had to fight not only the regimental surgeons but also the back-room machinations of his rival Benjamin Rush. In early 1777, Cochran and Shippen collaborated on a revised plan of organization for the Continental medical department, which they submitted to Congress in February. Cochran was something of a surprise appointment as the new medical director in April 1777. However, he had the personal confidence of George Washington and had shown considerable diligence in the field rather than devoting his time to political maneuvering as had Rush. Cochran struggled during the rest of the war to improve conditions for the sick and wounded among the Army, a difficult task in light of the low state of medical knowledge, incredibly unhealthy conditions in camp and field, and conflicts over turf between the regiments and his department. However, he did effect improvements in the workings of central army hospitals. After the war, Cochran moved to New York, and in 1790, Washington appointed him commissioner of loans. He retired to Palatine, New York, after a paralytic stroke. His son, John Cochran, was a 19th-century politician, Civil War general, and unsuccessful candidate for vice president. *Further reading:* Morris H. Saffron, *Surgeon to Washington: Dr. John Cochran, 1730–1807* (New York, 1977).

COFFIN, Isaac (1759–1839) Loyalist British naval officer

Coffin was born in Boston to a wealthy family, his father serving as a royal colonial customs officer. He was educated at Boston Latin School until age 14, when he joined the Royal Navy as a member of the crew aboard the *Gaspée* (not the same ship burned by patriots). He remained loyal at the outbreak of the Revolution and was promoted to lieutenant in 1778 and given command of the cutter *Placentia,* in which he fought under Admiral Rodney in the West Indies. However, after taking charge of the 74-gun *Shrewsbury* in 1782, Coffin collided with Rodney over the appointment of junior officers and was forced to stand a court-martial for disobedience. He was acquitted, but the end of the war put him ashore in England. His father was dead and his loyalist family scattered. In 1786, he sailed again as captain of the *Thisbe* but again ran afoul of navy

regulations and lost his command. After a time in Europe fighting for rebels against the Austrian crown, he returned to England. Injuries suffered at sea forced him to administrative duties, but in 1804 he reached admiral's rank and was created a baronet. In 1818, he sat in Parliament and evinced a fondness for the land of his birth through his speeches.

COFFIN, John (1756–1838) Loyalist officer

One of the loyalist Coffin family, John, like his younger brother Isaac, was educated at Boston Latin School before going to sea at a tender age. He was master of a transport ship in 1775 when he was engaged by the British Admiralty to move a full regiment from England to Boston as reinforcements for General Thomas Gage. Two days after arriving, Coffin ferried troops from Boston to the battle at Bunker Hill and himself took part in the fight. In consequence of his bravery he received a field commission as an ensign in the British forces. He was advanced to lieutenant and promised command if he could raise his own loyalist unit. He went to New York about the time the British garrison evacuated Boston and raised the King's Orange Rangers, a mounted rifle company formed of loyalists from Orange County, New York, with Coffin as captain and commander. The unit fought in the New York campaign of 1776 and eventually served in the Charleston campaign of 1779–80, but Coffin himself transferred to the New York Volunteers in 1778. Later in the same year he moved to the southern theater, and he reportedly raised a troop of cavalry in Georgia, fighting at Briar Creek in the spring of 1779 and possibly at Camden in 1780.

Sometime in 1780, Coffin became major of the South Carolina Royals, a mixed force of loyalist dragoons and infantry that had been raised in East Florida. Coffin achieved a considerable reputation for his good showings at Hobkirk's Hill and, particularly, the battle of Eutaw Springs in September 1781. The following month, he was with Lord Cornwallis in Virginia and escaped the surrender at Yorktown, returning eventually to New York City by way of Charleston. When the British abandoned New York, Coffin went to New Brunswick, Canada and started life anew. He accumulated 6,000 acres of farmland and continued on the half-pay list of the British army, finally reaching full general's rank in 1819 by the process of seniority.

Cadwallader Colden

COFFIN, Thomas Ashton (1754–1810) Loyalist British officer

The nephew of loyalist general John Coffin, Thomas was born in Boston and educated at Harvard, graduating in 1772. He, like most of his family, remained loyal to the crown, and in 1775 he moved to Canada where he became the private secretary to Sir Guy Carleton for the duration of the war. Coffin traveled to New York with Carleton in 1782 when the latter was named caretaker commander in chief for the British evacuation. Coffin went with Carleton to England and returned to Canada with his patron in 1786. He subsequently held several important public offices, principally as an inspector or controller of public accounts. He grew wealthy through land deals and moved to England in 1807, where he died.

COLDEN, Cadwallader (1688–1776) Royal official, scientist, physician

Already an old man by the time of the prerevolutionary struggles in New York, Colden defended the rights of the crown vociferously while serving as the last royal lieutenant governor of the colony. He had been born in the previous century in Scotland and emigrated to Philadelphia in 1710 after graduating from the University of Edinburgh and studying medicine in London. He set up a practice in his new home and also carried on a mercantile business. In 1718, he moved to New York with the promise of public office and was named surveyor general. His long career in office included service on the Governor's Council and several minor appointments. He developed a strong interest in science, especially botany, and wrote prolifically on many subjects, ranging from a history of the Indians of New York to physics. He quickly assimilated the new Linnaean system of classification, and he collected and sent to Linnaeus several hundred examples of flora from his rural New York estate. He also published several works on disease and treatment. Overall, he was as distinguished a scientist as the colonies could boast, save for a few others such as Rittenhouse or Franklin.

In 1760, Colden finally attained the office of lieutenant governor on the death of his long-time political rival James De Lancey. Colden took a hard line against colonial rebelliousness during the years leading up to the Revolution. He held the reins of government power several times in New York since the governorship changed rapidly during the period. Colden's sharpest conflict with the unruly Americans came in 1764 when he tried to push through establishment and administration of the Stamp Act. He was burned in effigy by a mob and some of his property was destroyed. In 1774, he received the counsel of the loyalist Joseph Galloway and transmitted a plan for union of the colonies to the British government. With the outbreak of hostilities in 1775, Colden retired to his Long Island estate, where he died two months after the Declaration of Independence was adopted. *Further reading:* Alice M. Keys, *Cadwallader Colden: A Representative Eighteenth Century Official* (originally published 1906; reprint New York, 1967).

COLLIER, Sir George (1738–1795) British naval officer

Collier was one of the few outstanding naval officers to sail American waters during the Revolution, a sharp contrast to the general level of mediocrity in the Royal Navy of the 1770s. He was born in London to an obscure family and entered the navy in 1751. He served in a variety of stations near England and in the East Indies during the Seven Years' War. In 1775, he was sent on a secret mission, never officially explained, to the seas off the American coast, and he was knighted in consequence. He returned to American waters the following year as captain of the frigate *Rainbow* and covered the landing of the British army at New York. Collier then was sent to Halifax as senior naval officer on that station. In the summer of 1777, he captured the new American frigate, the *Hancock*, and destroyed a nascent American expedition at Machias on the Maine coast. When Admiral Gambier withdrew to England in 1779, Collier was summoned to become temporary naval commander in chief at New York with the rank of commodore. He then led a successful raid on Virginia and another on the Connecticut coast, proving himself one of the few naval officers with both initiative and an ability to get along with his counterparts in the Royal Army.

After stopping the planned American Penobscot expedition in its tracks in late 1779, he was replaced in command by the incompetent Admiral Marriot Arbuthnot, and he returned to England. During the following years he further distinguished himself against the Spanish at Gilbraltar, but he resigned from the navy, apparently in disgust, and took a seat in Parliament. He returned to his commission in 1790 and eventually reached the rank of vice admiral through the action of seniority.

COLLINS, John (1717–1795) Delegate to Congress, official

Born in Newport, Rhode Island, Collins was one of the leaders during and after the Revolution of the state that seemed least committed to a central union. Rhode Island was ever reluctant to accede powers to Congress and single-handedly stood off the passage of an impost tax during the last years of the war that might have alleviated the nation's debilitating financial crisis. Collins was a delegate to Congress from 1778 until 1780 and again from 1782 to 1783. He was a proponent of cheap money, and when elected governor of Rhode Island in 1786, Collins acceded to the wishes of the dominant agricultural interests of the tiny state and began to issue paper money. He became the center of attention in 1790 when he broke a tie in the state senate over the issue of calling a state convention to join the federal union—he had finally become convinced of the utility of a central government—but the vote cost him his governorship. He was later elected to the U.S. House of Representatives but failed to take his seat.

COLOMB, Pierre (b. 1754) French volunteer

Born at Nîmes, Colomb (sometimes spelled "Colombe") came to America after service in the French gendarmerie, perhaps as a companion of the Marquis de Lafayette. His actual service record is confused, but he was apparently granted a brevet commission as a captain by Congress in 1777. He may have been assigned before that to the aborted 3rd Georgia Regiment of James Screven, which never really got organized before desertions emptied its

ranks. From the time of his captaincy until 1779, however, Colomb was an aide-de-camp to Lafayette and de Kalb, according to some sources. He may also have fought in the south and may have been captured at Savannah or Sunbury in late 1778 or early 1779. He returned to France in November 1779, serving subsequently during the French Revolution as a commander and brigadier general.

CONANT, William. Militia officer

A resident of Charlestown, Massachusetts, Conant was a friend of Paul Revere and a colonel in the militia. As the Massachusetts patriots awaited a move from the British garrison in April 1775, Revere arranged with Conant and "some other gentlemen" to have them on the alert in Charlestown if and when the British troops began to march out of Boston. The signal to Conant and the others was to be the now famous lanterns in the steeple of the Old North Church— two if the British began to row across the bay; one if the redcoats marched out by the Neck. Conant was to begin spreading the word to the militia when the signal came. On the night of April 18, British commander Thomas Gage ordered an expedition by land, so the signal was hung and Revere rowed across the Charles River. Conant met him at the wharf with a horse. The minutemen were alerted by early morning, and the British column met the first guns of the Revolution at Lexington and Concord.

CONDICT, Silas (1738–1801) Delegate to Congress

Condict was born in Morristown, New Jersey and was the owner of large tracts of land in and around his hometown. He was a member of the state committee of safety and was one of the original members of the New Jersey patriot state council in 1776, serving until 1780. He was elected for a three-year term to Congress in 1781. After the Revolution, he continued in public office as a member of the state assembly. He was speaker of the assembly from 1792 to 1794 and again in 1797. He died in Morristown.

CONNOLLY, John (born c. 1750) Loyalist

During the first months of the Revolution, Connolly attempted to organize a loyalist conspiracy on the western frontier and seize Fort Pitt for the British. He was born in Lancaster County, Pennsylvania, and after training as a physician and seeing service in the West during the Seven Years' War, Connolly settled in West Augusta County, a region disputed between Virginia and Pennsylvania. He was an aggressive land speculator and had much riding on the outcome of governmental disputes over land rights.

Connolly threw his lot with Lord Dunmore, the royal governor of Virginia, and his operations against the Indian settlements around Fort Pitt helped bring on Lord Dunmore's War in 1774. Connolly served as a captain in the Virginia militia during the Indian war and was in command of the Virginia forces at Fort Pitt in April 1775 when the Revolution began at Lexington and Concord. Local patriots, however, relieved Connolly of command, since he was an obvious loyalist and agent of the Virginia governor. In August, Connolly hatched a plan to foment a general Indian and loyalist uprising on the Appalachian frontier, which he would direct, with the ultimate object of taking Fort Pitt for the British. He intended to raise and equip a loyalist regiment at Detroit, gather Indian allies, and sweep down on the Pennsylvania-Virginia frontier. He conferred with Dunmore aboard a British warship at Portsmouth, Virginia and then traveled to Boston, where he got approval of the plan from British commander in chief Thomas Gage. Gage authorized Connolly to offer 300 acres of land to loyalists as a recruiting inducement. The plot was frustrated, however, when Connolly and two companions were arrested by patriots in Frederick, Maryland. The Americans sent Connolly to Philadelphia, and he was held there as a prisoner during 1776 and then moved to Baltimore. In 1780, he was exchanged and returned to New York City.

After a second aborted attempt at organizing another western loyalist uprising, Connolly was assigned to Lord Cornwallis' army in Virginia in June 1781. He was captured and again jailed in Philadelphia. He was finally released in March 1782, and he went to England, where he published a book detailing his adventures as a way to support his claims against the Loyalist Claims Commission. *Further reading:* John Connolly, *A Narrative of the Transactions, Imprisonment, and Sufferings of John C. Connolly* (1783; reprint New York, 1889).

CONTEE, Benjamin (1755–1815) Delegate to Congress, Continental officer   Contee was born in Prince Georges County, Maryland on an estate

called Brookefield. In 1776, he became a junior officer under Mordecai Gist in the famed 3rd Maryland, rising to captain during the war (the regiment was one of the elite units of the Continental Army until it was virtually destroyed at the battle of Camden). Lucky to have survived the war, Contee was elected to the Maryland House of Delegates in 1785. In 1788, he was a delegate to the Confederation Congress, and he became one of the first U.S. congressmen in 1789 with election to the new federal House of Representatives. He declined renomination for the congress in 1790, and after finishing his term of office in 1791, Contee changed careers entirely: He went to Europe, studied theology and was ordained a priest in the Episcopal Church in 1803. He then returned to Maryland and became rector of the Episcopal parish at Port Tobacco, where he lived until his death.

CONWAY, Thomas (1735–c. 1800) European volunteer   Conway was the center of one of the most notorious episodes of the Revolution, the so-called "Conway Cabal." He was born in Ireland but was taken to France at age six and educated there. He trained as a soldier and entered the French army (he was a Roman Catholic and joined many expatriate Irishmen in fighting for France) in 1749. He served as an officer in Germany during the Seven Years' War and had reached the rank of major in the Anjou regiment by 1775, probably as high as a nonaristocratic foreigner with few connections could expect to advance in the army of the French king. Conway then made contact with Silas Deane, who promised the Irishman rank and command in America.

Conway sailed in April 1777 and was appointed a brigadier general by Congress the following month, receiving the command of a brigade of Pennsylvanians under Lord Stirling. He apparently was an able soldier in the field, and his behavior at the battles of Brandywine and Germantown was well praised by his colleagues, including Lafayette and General John Sullivan. However, affairs between George Washington and Congress were at a low state by the end of the year. Before beginning the cruel winter at Valley Forge, Washington and the main army had been twice defeated by the British, and many Congressmen, especially several insistent delegates from New England, began to want Washington taken down a peg, perhaps in favor of Horatio

Gates, who appeared to be a savior after the surrender of General John Burgoyne. Conway entangled himself in this power struggle through his own indiscretion and ambition, but it seems unlikely he was part of any coherent conspiracy against Washington. Conway was, however, eager for higher rank—the same affliction that seized most European volunteers—and he was unhappy that Lafayette's friend Johann de Kalb had been elevated to major general, since back in the French army Conway had outranked de Kalb. Conway petitioned for promotion, but Washington turned him down.

Conway then wrote an ill-considered letter to Gates with an implied criticism of Washington's leadership. The brew thickened when James Wilkinson, the completely disreputable aide to Gates, babbled about the letter to an aide of Lord Stirling. When Washington heard Stirling's version of the letter's contents, the commander in chief immediately dispatched a note to Conway. Gates and Washington's congressional opponents were soon involved in a tangled web of charges, countercharges, and hurt sensibilities. When Congress unilaterally promoted Conway to major general over all the other brigadiers in the army and named him to the new post of inspector general of the army, Washington saw the move as a direct attack. At the same time, Congress created a new board of war that seemed to dilute Washington's authority and named three of his opponents, including Gates himself, as its members. In January 1778, Conway was further elevated when Congress named him as one of the commanders of a proposed expedition to Canada.

By March, the supposed conspiracy to remove Washington had collapsed, or at least the brouhaha had subsided in Washington's mind as the Canadian expedition was called off and the board of war shuffled to the side. Modern historians find it unlikely that Conway was truly a conspirator but rather see him as an ambitious and rash soldier of fortune who failed to catch the nuances of power politics during a stressful time in the relationship of Washington and Congress. Conway, who perhaps realized belatedly that he was caught in a whirlwind, offered his resignation in April and was surprised to have it accepted. In July 1778, he was baited into a duel by General John Cadwalader and was wounded in the exchange. He wrote an affecting letter of apology to Washington, who had by that

stage regained his confidence and refused to respond. When Conway recovered from the injury and returned to France, he rejoined the French army and eventually served with distinction in India, where he was promoted to governor general of all French forces in 1787. He fell victim to the raging politics of the French Revolution in 1790, however, was relieved of command, and had to flee to exile.

CONYNGHAM, Gustavus (c. 1744–1819) Naval officer and privateer

Known to the British as the "Dunkirk Pirate," Conyngham was one of the most daring and successful naval raiders of the Revolution. He was born in Ireland and moved to Philadelphia in 1763 to work for his cousin, Redmond Conyngham, who ran a shipping company. The young man learned navigation and seafaring aboard his cousin's ships and was in command of the brig *Charming Peggy* in 1775 when it was detained in Holland with a cargo of military store. The Dutch seized his ship under pressure from the British government, stranding Conyngham in Europe. However, the American commissioners in France decided to send coastal raiders to harry Great Britain's own doorstep, and they offered a command to Conyngham (the actual commission was lost until the 20th century, and the lack of a paper authority plagued Conyngham with charges of piracy). He took over the lugger *Surprise* in March 1777 and on his first raiding voyage captured a British mail packet and a cargo-laden brig. The British protested loudly to the French government, still nominally neutral, and Conyngham was arrested.

Soon released and with a commission as captain in the Continental Navy, he sailed again from Dunkirk in July aboard the *Revenge*. For two months he raided in the North Sea and all along the British coast so successfully that insurance rates rose among British shippers. He then sailed to the relative safety of a Spanish port, which he made his base of operations for the next several months. Eventually the Spanish pressured him to leave, and he moved to the West Indies, took two prizes off St. Eustatius, and arrived home in Philadelphia in February 1779. During his year and a half of raiding, he had captured 60 vessels from the British—an unparalleled feat by an American sailor during the Revolution.

After the *Revenge* was sold to private owners and refitted as a privateer, Conyngham set off again in search of more prizes, but he was captured in April off the coast of New York. The British were delighted to have him in custody, and since they regarded him as a pirate, they confined him under harsh conditions, first in North America and then successively in Pendennis Castle and Mill Prison in England. However, in November 1779 Conyngham and several companions dug their way out of jail and escaped to the Continent, where he briefly joined John Paul Jones aboard the *Alliance*. Back in America in the spring of 1780, Conyngham was again captured at sea by the British while commanding the *Experiment* and was again sent to Mill Prison at Plymouth. He was exchanged in 1781. After the war he failed to regain his commission in the American navy and became instead a merchant. *Further reading:* Robert W. Neeser, *Letters and Papers Relating to the Cruises of Gustavus Conyngham* (1915; reprint Port Washington, N.Y., 1970).

COOKE, Joseph Platt (1730–1816) Delegate to Congress, militia officer, official   Cooke (whose name is often also spelled "Cook") was born near Stratford, Connecticut. He graduated from Yale in 1750 and was active in local politics during the years before, during and after the Revolution. He represented his town in 30 sessions of the colonial and subsequent state assemblies between 1763 and 1783. He was also a militia officer before the war and continued his role during the Revolution. He was with the Connecticut troops in the New York campaign in 1776 and was one of the state commanders at Danbury, Connecticut when the place was sacked by the British under William Tryon in 1777 (the Connecticut militia performed poorly on the occasion). Cooke resigned his militia commission after the debacle at Danbury and became a member of the state council of safety. After the war, he twice sat as a delegate to the Confederation Congress and was a judge of the probate court for Danbury continuously from 1776 to 1813. He also was a member of the Connecticut Governor's Council in 1803.

COOPER, Sir Grey (d. 1801) British cabinet official   Cooper was British secretary of the treasury through all four cabinets that dealt with the American rebellion. He was born in Newcastle-on-Tyne and educated to the law at the Temple. A successful barrister, he defended the new ministry of Lord Rockingham in print against Charles Lloyd (private secretary to Grenville) and was rewarded

with the post of treasury secretary. He apparently was a good administrator who caused few if any political ripples, since he was successively retained in office by the elder William Pitt, the Duke of Grafton, and finally Lord North. Cooper thus held the office from 1765 to the fall of the North ministry in 1782. He even was named a lord of the treasury by the new coalition government in 1783. He retired from public office thereafter but held a seat in Parliament and spoke often on financial and diplomatic measures. In 1796, he was nominated as a privy councillor.

COOPER, John (1729–1785) Delegate to Congress, state official   Cooper was born in Gloucester County, New Jersey. He was a member of his local county committee of correspondence in 1774 and thereafter moved through a series of patriotic public duties. He sat in the New Jersey Provincial Congress from 1774 to 1776 and helped draft the first New Jersey state constitution. In 1775, he was appointed by the patriot assembly as treasurer of the western part of the state, and the following year, he was named to the state legislative council. In 1776, Cooper was chosen to represent New Jersey in the Continental Congress. He also sat as a judge in the Gloucester County courts in 1779 and again in 1784–85.

COOPER, Myles (1735–1785) Loyalist educator   Cooper was an Englishman by birth; he was educated at Oxford and was a fellow of Queen's College. He sailed to New York as a young man in 1762 at the behest of the Archbishop of Canterbury in order to assist in the administration of King's College (now called Columbia University). He first served as professor of mental and moral philosophy, but he was elected as the second president of the school in 1763 when only 28 years old. He did much to put the college on a regular footing and drafted rules of study and conduct that closely resembled those of the British universities. He founded a medical school as part of King's in 1767.

He returned to Britain for a prolonged visit in 1771, coming back to New York only at the beginning of the Revolution in 1775. He made no secret of his loyalty to the crown and met great opposition from local patriots in New York and from many of the students at the college. He published a pamphlet in support of the royal cause in 1775, which was answered by Alexander Hamilton, who was at the time a student at King's. As passions grew hotter, Cooper's stance became more and more noxious to his educational charges, and in May 1775, the students organized a mob to seize Cooper. He escaped, half-dressed, to a friend's house and eventually took refuge aboard a British ship in the harbor. Thereafter he fled to England, presenting an address at Oxford in December 1776 "On the Causes of the Present Rebellion in America." He was granted two lucrative livings in reward for his loyalty, one in Edinburgh and the other in England.

COPLEY, John Singleton (1738–1815) Loyalist painter

During his American years a portraitist of unrivalled talent, Copley abandoned the New World just before the beginning of the Revolution. He was born in Boston and raised by his mother and stepfather, Peter Pelham, a moderately talented engraver and painter who gave Copley his first instruction. By 1760, Copley had achieved a reputation for his striking portraits, which were executed in an unusually realistic style. His "Boy with a Squirrel," which showed his half-brother Henry Pelham, was exhibited in London in 1766 and caught the notice of Benjamin West, the expatriate American artist who had considerable influence in Britain at the time. Between 1765 and 1774, Copley painted several important revolutionary figures, including now-famous portraits of Paul Revere and Sam Adams. His entire family, however, were loyalists and he was influenced by them and by the tug of the British and European art world. In 1774, he left for England, never to return. He lived with his loyalist father-in-law and launched a career that was initially successful, but he turned away from portraiture toward heroic depiction of historical events. His later years were a period of slow, sad decline from the heights of his early achievements. *Further reading:* Jules D. Prown, *John Singleton Copley* (Cambridge, Mass., 1966).

CORBIN, Margaret Cochran (1751–1800) American heroine

Known as "Captain Molly" and often confused with Molly Pitcher, Corbin was born on the western frontier of Pennsylvania to Scotch-Irish settlers. When she was four years old, her father was killed in an Indian raid and her mother abducted. Corbin was then raised by an uncle. She married John Corbin from Virginia in

1772. At the outbreak of the Revolutionary War, her husband enlisted in the 1st Company of the Pennsylvania Artillery. Margaret accompanied him with the army and was at Fort Washington in November 1776 when her husband's battery tried to stand off an assault by German mercenaries. He was killed in action, and Margaret stepped forward to take his place in serving the gun. She was severely wounded during the battle and was evacuated to Philadelphia after the British victory, lucky nonetheless to have escaped imprisonment in New York. She was debilitated by her wounds, and in 1779, the Executive Council of Pennsylvania took notice of her with an award of $30 and referred her case to the congressional Board of War. On July 6, 1779, the Congress voted Corbin half pay for life and a suit of clothes. She was also officially enrolled in the Invalid Corps (a company of disabled soldiers who could do light duty) and appeared later on the payroll. She retired to Westchester County, New York, where she died. In 1926, her body was moved to a grave at the Military Academy at West Point.

CORNELL, Ezekiel (1732–1800) Delegate to Congress, officer

A mechanic by trade and self-educated, Cornell was born and lived his life near Scituate, Rhode Island. Despite his humble background, he took a leading role in Rhode Island politics and military affairs during the Revolutionary era. He sat in the colonial assembly in 1772 and 1774 and was an aggressive member of the Rhode Island committee of correspondence. He was appointed lieutenant colonel in the odd "army of observation" raised by Rhode Island in the spring of 1775: The unit was to consist of 1,500 men who would defend the colony by observing the British army in Boston, and the Rhode Island troops were to swear allegiance to the king. Once they had joined the other colonial forces at Boston, however, the Rhode Islanders assumed the same status as other New England regiments and were taken into the new Continental Army as the 1st Rhode Island. Cornell served with this unit until it was disbanded in December and most of its men and officers transferred to the 11th Continental Regiment. He served as a senior officer of the 11th during 1776, fighting in New York, and became a deputy adjutant general in October.

Cornell left the Continental Army in December 1776, when the 11th Regiment was dissolved, and became commander of the newly-raised Rhode Island brigade with the state rank of brigadier general. He and his men were part of John Sullivan's large force that attempted to retake Newport from the British in August 1778, and the local men apparently assisted the evacuation of the Americans across the channel from Butt's Hill to Triverton when the campaign failed. In 1780, Cornell resigned from the state forces and was selected as a delegate to Congress. He was twice reelected, even though he was at some odds with the rest of his state over the issue of a strong central government. Rhode Islanders were among the Americans most opposed to any form of national direction, and they frustrated the attempts of Congress to impose a national impost tax to finance the war. After the Revolution, Cornell returned to Scituate and took up farming, never again serving in public office.

CORNPLANTER (1732/40–1836) Indian leader

An important leader of the Seneca tribe, Cornplanter sided with the British during the Revolution, although later in life he established friendly relationships with the United States. He was born in western New York at the Seneca village of Conewaugus on the Genesee River, the son of a white trader named John O'Bail and a Seneca mother. The father abandoned his Native American family and moved to Fort Plain, New York; Cornplanter remained behind and eventually became a war leader of his tribe. He may have participated in raids on the British during the Seven Years' War, but by the outbreak of the American Revolution, he had come to support the redcoats. He led native warriors as part of the mixed force that attacked the Americans at the battle of Oriskany in 1777, and he raided into the settlements of upper New York and the Wyoming Valley of Pennsylvania.

At the end of the Revolutionary War, Cornplanter began a long period of accommodation with the new American nation, participating in treaty negotiations throughout the 1780s and 1790s. He was often opposed in his views by his rival for influence, Red Jacket. Cornplanter visited both presidents George Washington and Thomas Jefferson on behalf of his people. In 1796, he received a grant of land from the state of Pennsylvania in recognition of his peacemaking stance, and by the turn of the century, Cornplanter had amassed considerable holdings, which he made into a Seneca enclave. Late in life

(he probably lived to be over a hundred) a religious vision reversed his pro-white views, and he severed all relations.

CORNSTALK (c. 1720–1777) Indian leader

Cornstalk's murder set off a decades-long conflict between the Shawnee and the Americans. Although born in Pennsylvania, Cornstalk lived most of his life in the Ohio Valley and was a principal chief of the Shawnee, a large and important Algonquian-speaking tribe. He sided with the French during the Seven Years' War, and he raided western Virginia settlements in support of Pontiac in 1763. Cornstalk and his tribe were the focus of Lord Dunmore's expeditions into the Ohio Valley in 1774. Dunmore, the governor of Virginia, had awarded illegal land grants in what is now West Virginia to veterans of the Seven Years' War. When the Shawnee attacked the new white settlements, Dunmore organized a militia force that marched in two columns into the heart of Shawnee territory. After a major battle at Point Pleasant, West Virginia and an attack by Dunmore on the principal Shawnee village at Chillicothe, Ohio, Cornstalk was forced to sue for peace. Scattered attacks against the white settlers continued, however, and in 1777, Cornstalk went to Point Pleasant in an attempt to settle differences. The settlers ignored his flag of truce, seized him and his party (which included the chief's son) and held them hostage in the local jail. When a settler was killed soon after in a raid, a crowd murdered Cornstalk, his son and another Shawnee companion. In part as a result, the Shawnees became implacable foes of white American settlers and remained so until the end of the century.

CORNWALLIS, Charles, Earl (1738–1805) British general

Cornwallis' name is forever associated in the American memory with British defeat and sweet patriot victory. Throughout his long career, Cornwallis enjoyed deep political and court influence, which—aside from his American disaster—he usually returned with sterling service to the crown and the nation. His efforts in the American Revolution, however, were (to say the least) below standard.

He was born in London, the son of the first Earl Cornwallis, and educated at Eton. He joined the Grenadier Guards as an ensign in 1756 and was a student at a military academy in Turin when the

Charles, Lord Cornwallis

call came to join his regiment in a campaign. He fought at the battle of Minden in 1759 under George Germain and began a rapid advance up the ranks thereafter. Cornwallis took his family's seat in Parliament in 1760 and two years later moved to the House of Lords when he became Earl Cornwallis on his father's death. He gained wide experience in the European wars, becoming lieutenant colonel in command of the 12th Regiment of Foot and leading his regiment on the battlefields in Germany. He was not a government supporter but rather part of the loose opposition gathered around Lord Shelburne. Nonetheless, the king and the king's party trusted Cornwallis and heaped honors and offices on him during the 1760s.

By 1776, he was a major general and was assigned to convoy reinforcements to Sir Henry Clinton at Charleston, South Carolina. The assault on the southern American seaport proving a failure, Cornwallis went to New York and was given command of part of the British force that took Long Island and then proceeded to chase Washington out of New York City and across the Hudson River. He performed extremely well in the field during the New York campaign, and General William Howe consequently put Cornwallis in charge of pursuing and crushing Washington's army. Here Cornwallis first demonstrated some of his deficiencies: he was far too leisurely and far too confident in following Washington's retreat through New Jersey, and he assumed that Washington would not venture forth during the winter months. The nasty surprise at

Trenton brought Cornwallis personally to the scene, but he fumbled again in falling for Washington's campfire ruse and let the Continentals advance to Princeton, where they scored another sorely needed victory in early January 1777. Cornwallis returned to England during the first part of the year but was back in America by summer and commanded on the field at the battle of Brandywine in September. He went to England once again in January 1778 for a four-month visit, receiving promotion to lieutenant general while there. By the time he arrived again in Philadelphia, Clinton had replaced Howe as commander in chief.

Relations were never good between Clinton and Cornwallis, and they were not improved by the strong position Cornwallis had with the government at home. Clinton felt threatened, and Cornwallis assumed a stance of critical independence from his commander. Much has been made of the so-called dormant commission Cornwallis held that allowed him to take command if Clinton was incapacitated, although this was mostly a safeguard to keep the German von Knyphausen (who technically outranked Cornwallis) out of the picture in an emergency. Cornwallis did, however, enjoy much more clout in London, especially with Lord George Germain, than did Clinton, and this helped keep tensions between the two generals high. After the battle of Monmouth, where Cornwallis again performed superbly on the field, the British settled into New York and the earl returned to England to nurse his fatally ill wife.

Cornwallis' final appearance in the American war was decisive. He arrived at Charleston in 1780 with Clinton's invasion force. After the city and Benjamin Lincoln's entire American army surrendered in May, Clinton returned to New York, leaving Cornwallis in command in the south. Cornwallis' conduct of the southern campaign during the following year has long been the source of controversy. He was advised (indeed ordered) by Clinton to solidify the British hold on South Carolina and Georgia, both of which lay supine to British control, and to proceed carefully. Cornwallis, however, thought aggression and a march into North Carolina the better strategy, and he used his strong political position to operate independently from Clinton's wishes, communicating directly with Germain and almost ignoring the commander in chief in America. His plan worked at first, and when he crushed

General Horatio Gates at the battle of Camden there seemed to be little to prevent a British sweep toward Virginia.

However, the following months brought Nathanael Greene to command of the American army in the south, and despite Cornwallis' ability to repeatedly if narrowly defeat Greene on any given battlefield, Greene's overall strategy of stifling loyalists and wearing down the British regulars worked in the end. The defeats at King's Mountain and the Cowpens, plus the severe depletion of the battle of Guilford Courthouse, left Cornwallis in a tough spot. His decision to march to Yorktown and garrison the city turned out to be fatal when the French for once beat off the British Royal Navy and Washington made a courageous decision to bring the entire allied army south in a rush. Cornwallis was trapped and no amount of bravery or will power could break the inevitable progression of the siege works that finally forced his capitulation in October. He behaved poorly at the surrender, refusing to appear in person to deliver his sword to Washington, pleading a phony illness.

By odds, Cornwallis should have been the scapegoat of the Revolution, but on his return to England he was absolved of public blame while Clinton bore the onus of the British defeat. Cornwallis' subsequent career was long and successful. He was appointed to command in Bengal in 1786 and not only instituted a series of much-needed reforms of the colonial administration in India but defeated Sultan Tippoo in 1792, adding to the British empire on the subcontinent. In British historical memory, Cornwallis is known mostly for his great achievements in India. He also came to the fore during the Napoleonic wars and as viceroy dealt with the Irish uprising of 1798. He died in India, where he had again been sent in 1805. *Further reading:* Franklin B. Wickwire, *Cornwallis: The American Adventurer* (Boston, 1970); George Reese, ed., *The Cornwallis Papers* (Charlottesville, Va., 1970); Hugh F. Rankin, "Charles Lord Cornwallis: Study in Frustration," in George Billias, ed., *George Washington's Opponents* (New York, 1969), 193–232.

CORNWALLIS, Sir William (1744–1819) British naval officer   The younger brother of British general Charles Cornwallis, William entered the Royal Navy as an 11-year-old boy, catching his first sight of North America soon thereafter aboard the *New-*ark. He served with vigor and reasonable distinction during the Seven Years' War, advancing in rank to commodore in command of a sloop by 1762. He was commander of the *Pallas* in 1774 off the west coast of Africa and during the next two years intercepted several American merchant ships laden with military stores. In 1776, he escorted a large convoy of merchant ships from the West Indies to Britain and was then assigned to a 50-gun ship, the *Isis*, in support of the British forces in America. He changed commands rapidly between 1776 and 1778, finally settling on the *Lion*. He was one of Admiral John Byron's captains at the battle of Grenada in July 1779, and he barely escaped losing his ship to the French under d'Estaing. Cornwallis continued to sail in the West Indies during the remainder of the Revolutionary War, and he had a brush with the fleet carrying Rochambeau's army to Rhode Island in 1780. He also shared in the British fight against Admiral de Grasse at St. Kitts in 1782. After the American conflict ended, he went to India, where his elder sibling was commander in chief. During the Napoleonic Wars, Cornwallis—by then an admiral—did signal duty in blockading the French fleet in Brest.

CORNY, Dominique-Louis Ethis de (1736–1790) French commissary officer   Corny sailed to America in April 1780 along with the Marquis de Lafayette when the latter returned aboard the *Hermique*. Corny had been appointed commissary officer for the French expedition to America, but he was not directly attached to Rochambeau's command. His mission to prepare for the arrival of the main French force was underfunded, but Corny made the best of the situation in Rhode Island, working with Dr. James Craik to set up a hospital on what is now the campus of Brown University in Providence and hiring American merchants to assemble supplies for the French force. Corny returned to France in February 1781 and later participated in the early days of the French Revolution as one of the commissioners sent to open the Bastille on July 14, 1789.

COUDRAY, Tronson de. See TRONSON de COUDRAY, Philippe.

COX, James (1753–1810) Militia officer, legislator   Cox was a native of Monmouth, New Jersey and an officer in the New Jersey state militia during the Revolution. He commanded a company during the battles of Germantown and Monmouth and eventually attained the rank of militia brigadier general. After the turn of the century, he sat in the New Jersey assembly and then was elected to the U.S. House of Representatives for one term.

COXE, Daniel (1741–1826) Loyalist officer and official
A resident of New Jersey, Coxe was prominent among the political leaders of the middle-colony loyalists during the war. He served in the royal New Jersey state assembly as speaker in 1777 and 1778. During the British occupation of Philadelphia, he acted as a commissioner and in 1778 formed and raised the West Jersey Volunteers, of which he was lieutenant colonel but not in actual command (the unit was merged with the New Jersey Volunteers after a few months). He was appointed to the ruling council of the Associated Board of Loyalists as a crony of William Franklin. Coxe was also involved in the operations of British intelligence in 1779, and he acted as a paymaster for Benedict Arnold before the traitor was unmasked. Following the British defeat, Coxe withdrew to England.

COXE, Tench (1755–1824) Loyalist businessman, delegate to Congress, government official
A figure with a strangely convoluted career, Coxe was born in Philadelphia and attended the college there, leaving school before graduation to study law. He failed to pursue a legal career, however, and entered business with his family, where he gained a considerable grasp of finance and economic affairs. Despite his later prominence as a national officeholder, during the Revolution Coxe was a loyalist. He resigned a commission in the Pennsylvania militia in 1776 and went over to the British. In fact, he was with the army of General William Howe when it invaded and seized Philadelphia in 1777. Coxe remained behind, however, in 1778 when Howe withdrew, and he was arrested by the Americans, yet his service with the enemy had small effect on his subsequent career. He was soon paroled and by 1788 was named as a delegate to the Confederation Congress. Coxe was an effective advocate for a strong central government—especially for a sound national fiscal policy—and published *An Examination of the Constitution for the*

United States in support of his position in 1788. He served in the new federal government as assistant secretary of the treasury and then as commissioner of revenue. Originally a Federalist, Coxe was entangled in the splitup of the party during the late 1790s and became a supporter of Jefferson, who appointed Coxe as purveyor of public supplies in 1803. He was also an advocate of developing manufacturing in the new nation and promoted the growing and processing of cotton as an economic staple. *Further reading:* Jacob E. Cooke, *Tench Coxe and the Early Republic* (Chapel Hill, N.C., 1978).

CRABB, Jeremiah (1760–1800) Soldier, legislator
Crabb served as a teenage lieutenant in the 1st Maryland Regiment during the first years of the Revolution. He suffered ill health as a result of the winter at Valley Forge and resigned his commission in 1777. He was elected to the U.S. House of Representatives from Maryland in 1795 but ill health again forced a resignation.

CRAIG, James Henry (1748–1812) British officer
Craig's service in America during the Revolution demonstrated his abilities and presaged a long and distinguished career. He was born at Gibraltar, where his father was a judge, and in 1763 he became an ensign in the 30th Regiment of Foot. He later was aide-de-camp to the lieutenant governor of Gibraltar before assuming a captain's commission in the 47th Regiment, which brought him to America in 1774 as part of the Boston garrison. He was badly wounded at Bunker Hill but recovered in time to serve at Three Rivers and during Sir Guy Carleton's march to Crown Point in 1776. Craig was part of General John Burgoyne's invasion force the following year and was wounded again at the battle of Hubbardstown.

With Burgoyne's surrender, Craig was sent home with dispatches. In December 1777, he received a new appointment as major in the 82nd Regiment—the rank was granted without purchase as reward for bringing Burgoyne's reports to London—and he traveled again to America with the newly raised unit in August 1779. After he took part in the British operations at Penobscot, Maine, Craig and several companies of the 82nd were posted in 1780 to the southern theater where Sir Henry Clinton had seized Charleston. Craig commanded the British post at Wilmington, North Carolina during most of 1781 and used his small number of regulars effectively in conjunction with local loyalists. He was one of the few British southern commanders to squelch patriot partisans, and Wilmington became a secure base for the British to fall back on during the Carolinas campaigning and provided loyalist irregulars such as David Fanning a point of supply and operation. Craig also raided from Wilmington with his regulars in conjunction with the local loyalists. When Cornwallis surrendered at Yorktown, Craig slipped out of Wilmington ahead of an advancing American force and reached the safety of Charleston. His regiment returned briefly to New York in April 1782 and then was disbanded at Halifax a year later.

Craig's career had only begun, however. After an intense study of European military tactics and advance in rank to a major generalship during the 1790s, he took command of the British forces that seized the Dutch Cape colony in South Africa in 1795, securing what was to become a major portion of the British empire. Craig was then sent to India for a tour and back to England, where he became a full general in 1805. After a time as commander in southern Europe, he retired from the active list and became governor general of Canada. While his term there was stormy due to the opposition of French Canadians, he held the province tightly within the British orbit as a new conflict with the United States developed. He resigned in 1811 and died soon after.

CRAIGIE, Andrew (1743–1819) Continental officer, financier   Born in Boston, Craigie was a druggist by profession. During the Revolution he was "apothecary general" to the Continental Army and held a lieutenant colonel's commission. He speculated in government finances and, unlike most who dabbled in national finance during that unstable period, made a considerable fortune, which he invested in real estate around Boston. He entertained often and lavishly at his home in Cambridge in the years following the Revolution.

CRAIK, James (1730–1814) Physician   Craik was born in Scotland on the estate of his father, where by coincidence John Paul Jones's father was a gardener. Craik went to the University of Edinburgh for medical studies and then emigrated to the West Indies in 1750. Within a few years he had resettled in Virginia, and he served as a field physician with the British during the Seven Years' War, attending

Braddock at the general's death. Craik apparently first formed what was to be a lasting friendship with George Washington during the military expedition of 1754. Washington appointed Craik as chief medical officer of the Virginia militia in 1755, and six years later, Craik and Washington traveled to the west to scout lands granted to veterans of the Seven Years' War.

After assuming command of the Continental forces, Washington faced a difficult situation in the medical department. Benjamin Church, the first surgeon general, proved to be a traitor and was turned out almost immediately after taking office. There followed a long and nasty squabble between politically powerful rivals for the medical department, and a permanent division developed between the central medical departments and the individual regimental physicians. Not surprisingly, Washington turned to his old friend Craik to help and appointed the physician as assistant director general of hospitals. Craik apparently kept his ear tuned to political and civilian dissension, and when the so-called Conway Conspiracy seemed to threaten Washington's position as commander, Craik wrote to warn his friend that "base and villainous men, through chagrin, envy, or ambition, are endeavoring to lessen you in the minds of the people." When the French expeditionary force arrived in 1780, Craik aided in setting up hospitals and medical services for the allies in Rhode Island. After the war, Craik returned to Virginia, but he was called back to national service in 1798 by Washington and made physician general of the army. Craik was the attending physician at Mount Vernon on December 14, 1799 when Washington died, and he published an account of the president's last illness.

CRANE, John (1744–1805) Continental officer   Crane was a native of Massachusetts, and as a teenager he served with the colonial militia during the Seven Years' War. He was a member of the pre-Revolution Sons of Liberty in Boston and took part in the Boston Tea Party in 1773. He moved to Providence, Rhode Island in 1774, and shortly before the outbreak of hostilities in 1775, he received a commission in the Rhode Island militia artillery. He led his company to Boston after Lexington and Concord to support the American siege of the city.

When the artillery wing of the Continental Army was organized in 1776, Crane was commissioned as major under Henry Knox. In 1777, Crane was promoted to colonel in command of the 3rd Battalion of Artillery and helped raise the unit, which joined the main Continental Army in the spring of the year. His artillery battalion was one of the most cohesive in the army, comprised almost entirely of Massachusetts men, and was famous for its band of musicians. Crane commanded the battalion throughout the entire war, seeing action in several major engagements, including the Rhode Island campaign, the battles at Saratoga and the defense of Red Bank. In June 1783, when the Continental Army was in the process of disbanding, the corps of artillery was reorganized with Crane as commander of the remnant, which acted primarily as an observation force. He was brevetted as a brigadier general at the same time. Crane relinquished command of the artillery in November 1783, and he retired to civilian life. The Massachusetts legislature granted him a tract of land in the Maine region in reward for his services. From 1790 to 1805, Crane sat as a judge of the Massachusetts Court of Common Pleas. He died in Maine.

CRANE, Stephen (1709–1780) Delegate to Congress

Born in Elizabethtown, New Jersey, which his grandfather had helped found, Crane was a respected local official for many years before the Revolution, serving as sheriff of Essex County, a judge of common pleas and a member of the state assembly. He supported the Revolution from the beginning of agitation in New Jersey and was elected as a delegate to the first Continental Congress in 1774. He also served in the second Congress. He died before the end of the war, while a member of the New Jersey State Council.

CRAWFORD, William (1732–1782) Continental officer, frontiersman

Crawford, a close friend of George Washington, fought well during the war in the east, only to die a hideous death at the hands of Indians on the frontier.

He was born in Virginia and traveled as a young man to the west with George Washington on a surveying expedition. They served together during the Seven Years' War and formed a fast friendship and lifelong business relationship. Crawford settled in the region (southeast of modern-day Pittsburgh) that was disputed between the colonies of Pennsylvania and Virginia, setting up a farm and trading

with the Indians. He also acted as Washington's land agent, helping the future commander in chief to amass huge holdings of prime western land. During Lord Dunmore's War, Crawford commanded Virginia troops as a major and destroyed two Mingo villages near what is now Steubenville. He also established Fort Fincastle at the site of Wheeling, West Virginia.

When not fighting or surveying in the west, Crawford was a justice of the peace, although his office was revoked when Pennsylvania asserted its claim to the disputed territory where Crawford lived. He offered his services to the Committee of Safety in Philadelphia at the outbreak of the Revolutionary War, but since he was identified with the rival land claims of Virginia, the committee turned him down. Instead, Crawford took a commission as lieutenant colonel of the 5th Virginia Regiment in January 1776. By fall, he was colonel in command of the 7th Virginia. Crawford and his men formed part of Washington's main force during the battles in New Jersey in late 1776 and 1777. Crawford served on detached service with a small body of picked light infantry at Brandywine. He then left the main Continental forces and moved again to the west in November 1777, commanding both regulars from Virginia and militia throughout 1778 and 1779, and building several frontier forts.

In 1782, after the fighting against the British along the eastern seaboard had virtually ended, Crawford was persuaded to lead a campaign against the Delaware and Shawnee (and their British-loyalist allies) in the Sandusky region of the Ohio. He set out in June with a force of about 500 militia and volunteers. They intended to surprise their enemy, but they made few efforts to conceal their movements or goal. When Crawford and his men reached the Sandusky villages, they camped on a rise of ground (known later as "Battle Island"), where they came under attack by a smaller force of Indians and the loyalist Butler's Rangers. A lackluster battle continued for two days, with the Americans apparently achieving a slight advantage. However, on the afternoon of the second day, British and Indian reinforcements equipped with field artillery showed up, and the Americans panicked and fled. After a brief stand the next day near Olentangy Creek, Crawford and several companions were separated and captured by the Delaware and taken to a Wyandot village. With the British commander William Caldwell and renegade Simon Girty looking on, Crawford was slowly and horribly tortured to death. The details of the event were reported by one of his companions who survived captivity. *Further reading:* Consul W. Butterfield, *Washington-Crawford Letters* (Cincinnati, 1877) and *An Historical Account of the Expedition Against Sandusky* (Cincinnati, 1873).

CRESAP, Michael (1742–1775) Frontiersman, officer   Cresap was one of many westward-looking colonials who came in conflict with the indigenous natives. He was born in Maryland and schooled in Baltimore. After his early marriage, he became a merchant and importer, but in 1774, he journeyed west to the region of modern-day Wheeling, West Virginia and began to establish a settlement on the frontier. He was soon embroiled in conflict with the Indians, and following a massacre of natives by Americans at Yellow Creek in August 1774, he became one of the leaders of the Virginia militia in Lord Dunmore's War, which is sometimes known as "Cresap's War." He commanded one of the two columns that marched westward and eventually defeated the natives at Point Pleasant. Cresap was accused by Mingo chief Logan in a widely publicized speech of having killed Logan's family and set off a needless conflict. The speech was repeated by Thomas Jefferson in *Notes on Virginia* in 1782 (after Cresap's death) and became the focus of a prolonged dispute. The best evidence shows Cresap to have been relatively innocent and unlikely to have had a hand in killing Logan's relatives.

Cresap's role in the Indian war and his reputation as a frontier fighter, however, helped prompt Congress in June 1775 to commission him as a captain and ask him to raise a company of riflemen for the new Continental Army. He did so with dispatch, recruiting a company of Marylanders, and set out for Boston to join the New Englanders who had formed the first American army around Boston. Covering 550 miles in only 22 days, Cresap's riflemen were the first southern troops to arrive at Boston. Cresap himself was ill, however, and resigned his command in September. He died in New York City on his way home on October 18, 1775. *Further reading:* John J. Jacobs, *A Biographical Sketch of the Life of the Late Captain Michael Cresap* (1826; reprint Cumberland, Md., 1881).

CROMONT du BOURG, Marie-François-Joseph-Maxime, Baron de (1756–1836) French officer   Born at Versailles, Cromont du Bourg volunteered in the dragoons in 1756 and passed through a series of posts in both the dragoons and the infantry before reaching the rank of captain in 1774. He was on half pay in 1776, but he was appointed as an aide-de-camp to General Rochambeau for the American expedition in 1780. He did not sail with the main French force, but delayed his departure until March 1781. He served with Rochambeau's forces at Yorktown and remained in America until 1783. On his return to France he advanced to lieutenant colonel, but he was a firm royalist and decided to emigrate in 1790. He served the Bourbons during the Republic and the first Empire and was rewarded with a colonelcy and honors on the restoration. While on service in America, he kept a valuable diary. *Further reading:* Anne K. Brown and Howard S. Rice, Jr., *The American Campaigns of Rochambeau's Army, 1780–81, 1782, 1783* (Princeton and Providence, 1972).

CROMWELL, Oliver (1753–1853) Continental soldier   Cromwell was born in Columbus, New Jersey and was a free black farmer before the Revolution. He enlisted in the 2nd New Jersey and served for the entire war—nearly seven years—as a private soldier, one of many hundreds of black soldiers in the Continental Army. He was at Trenton, Princeton, Brandywine, Monmouth and the final victory at Yorktown. He received a pension at the end of his service and settled on a farm in New Jersey, living to see his hundredth year as one of the most aged veterans of the war.

CROSBY, Enoch (1750–1835) American spy, soldier   Crosby was a successful spy and undercover agent for the American side during the first years of the Revolution and eventually became, through a circuitous route, the model for James Fenimore Cooper's hero in the early historical novel of espionage, *The Spy*. Crosby was born in humble circumstances in Harwich, Massachusetts and raised in Dutchess County (now Putnam), New York. He became a shoemaker, working in and around Danbury, Connecticut.

When the Revolutionary War began, Crosby enlisted in the local militia and was part of General Richard Montgomery's force that invaded Canada in 1775. He returned to his home after the victory

Enoch Crosby

at Montreal but before the defeat and death of Montgomery at Quebec.

In September of the following year, Crosby decided to reenlist in Washington's army that was in Manhattan. He set off to cross the so-called Neutral Ground of Westchester County and fell in with a loyalist who—mistaking Crosby to be of the same persuasion—revealed he was part of a new loyalist unit forming in the region. Crosby made his way to White Plains and told the story of this encounter to the Committee of Safety and then to John Jay, who headed a special New York committee to detect conspiracy. Jay took Crosby under his wing and directed his movements as an undercover agent. Over the following nine months, Crosby insinuated himself over and over again into loyalist groups, which were then scooped up by the patriots. He estimated later that more than 100 loyalists were caught through his efforts.

Finally, the danger became too great (he was beaten by loyalists and left for dead at his brother's house), and Crosby quit the spy game. In 1779, he enlisted in the 4th New York Regiment, later transferring to the 2nd New York, and served the rest of the war as a private soldier. He returned to his home at the end of the Revolution and became a farmer. When James Fenimore Cooper published *The Spy* in 1822, several people pointed to Crosby as the model for the book's hero, but Cooper denied ever knowing of Crosby. Nonetheless, Cooper eventually admitted to hearing spy stories from John Jay and using them for the basis of his novel.

Further reading: Alice S. Wentzell, "Spy's Literary Role," *Military History* 6,6 (June 1990), 8, 70–75.

CRUGER, John Harris (1738–1807) Loyalist officer

Cruger was one of the better loyalist officers serving the British during the American War. He was a member of a prominent New York family, loyalists all, and both his father and grandfather had been political leaders and mayors of the city. He served on the city council in the 1760s and succeeded his father as mayor in 1764. He married the daughter of the elder Oliver De Lancey, and given all these associations, it was no surprise he chose the side of the crown during the American Revolution.

Cruger was appointed lieutenant colonel and given command of the first battalion of his father-in-law's loyalist brigade when the unit was raised in September 1776 for the defense of New York. He was sent first to Halifax and then south in late 1778, where he and his men helped capture Savannah in December. His battalion was called on again the following year to defend Savannah against the allied assault in October. He was captured in Georgia in June 1780 but soon was exchanged and given command of the key British post at Ninety-Six, South Carolina. Two months later, he came to the relief of the besieged loyalists under Thomas Browne at Augusta, Georgia.

Cruger's greatest feat of arms was in the defense of his post at Ninety-Six in May and June of 1781. He commanded a force of about 550 veteran loyalist infantry, all men who had fought throughout the war, and he had a strong set of fortifications. The Americans, however, were determined to take Ninety-Six, which allowed the British an interior base of operations. A large force under southern commander Nathanael Greene laid siege to Cruger in late May. However, the best efforts of the best American soldiers in the south were unable to dislodge Cruger and his loyalists. Neither the engineering talents of Tadeusz Kosciuzko nor the leadership of Greene nor the dash of Light Horse Harry Lee and William Washington forced Cruger to give up, although his situation was nearing desperation when a relief column approached and the Americans abandoned the effort. Cruger and his men subsequently joined the main British force and fought extremely well at the victory at Eutaw Springs in September. The end for the British cause was in sight, however, and Cruger's final contribution was in helping to defend Charleston during the two years of peace negotiations. His remaining men withdrew first to New York and then to New Brunswick, Canada, where the unit was disbanded in 1783. Cruger had lost all his property in New York to confiscation, and he lived out the rest of his life in England.

CRUMER, Jane. British heroine   Crumer was the wife of a sergeant in the British army serving under General John Burgoyne in the campaign of 1777, and she presumably was an approved camp follower on the ration rolls. During the final days of battle near Saratoga, many wives of British officers and soldiers, including the Baroness von Riedesel and Lady Harriet Acland, were trapped under fire in a foul cellar for several days, along with many children and wounded soldiers. The worst part of the situation was a lack of water, since the refugees' only source was polluted. American sharpshooters picked off anyone who tried to reach the nearby Hudson River. Finally, Crumer took a bucket and strode defiantly to the river, making several trips while the Americans held their fire. Crumer probably saved the lives of many women, children and wounded soldiers with her bravery.

CUMBERLAND, Richard (1732–1811) British official, dramatist   Cumberland was a writer of great industry if only middling talent and is best known as one of the minor English playwrights of the second half of the 18th century; however, he also held government office during the American Revolution and played a role in secret diplomacy with Spain.

He was born at Trinity College in Cambridge, the son of an academical parson. He showed early promise as a dramatist and was supported by sinecures and the relatively lavish income of his father. He was a secretary to Lord Halifax in 1761 and became a clerk at the board of trade in 1762 when Halifax took office as secretary of state. Most of his time was apparently spent writing plays, and for a time at least, he was regarded as a rival of Sheridan.

Cumberland was a political protégé of George Germain, and when the latter became secretary of state for America in 1775, Cumberland received the office of secretary to the board of trade. There is

little evidence he was much occupied by his duties, since his production of dramas did not slack. However, in 1780, Cumberland entered on a secret mission to the court of Spain in the company of Abbé Thomas Hussey, the English Catholic chaplain of the Spanish embassy. Cumberland's task was to negotiate an agreement with the Spanish government for a secret peace with Great Britain. Although nominally in support of the Americans, Spain in fact was distressed at the thought of a new continental rival in America. Cumberland sought to convince Floridablanca, the Spanish foreign minister, that the two imperial powers could divide up western territories between themselves. Spain's military conquests in West Florida by Bernardo de Galvez put Floridablanca in a good negotiating position, but the talks fell apart when Cumberland made it clear that the British would not even discuss giving up Gibraltar.

After his return to England, Cumberland was turned out of office when the board of trade was abolished. He spent the remainder of his life industriously writing plays and translating Greek tragedies. *Further reading:* Samuel F. Bemis, *The Hussey-Cumberland Mission and American Independence* (Princeton, N.J., 1931); Richard Dircks, *Richard Cumberland* (Boston, 1976).

CUMMING, William. Delegate to Congress, attorney, legislator   Although little is known of the details of his life, Cumming was born in Edenton, North Carolina and was admitted to the bar before the Revolution. He was a member of the North Carolina Provincial Congress in 1776 and sat in the state lower house in 1781, 1783, 1784 and 1788. In 1785, he was a delegate from North Carolina to the Confederation Congress.

CUNNINGHAM, Robert (c. 1739–1813) Loyalist officer   Cunningham was born in Ireland and emigrated to the region of Ninety-Six, South Carolina in 1769, becoming a planter and a local judge. He opposed the growing revolutionary sentiment and protested the nonimportation agreements, and with the beginning of the war in 1775, he was seized by the local patriots and sent to Charleston for imprisonment. After his release when Sir Henry Clinton took Charleston in 1780, Cunningham raised a unit of irregular loyalist militia and supported the British during their occupation of the state. Lord Cornwallis appointed him a brigadier general, but he apparently had little effect on military matters during the 1780–81 campaigns. He is reported to have fled American troops after a skirmish at Hammond's Store before the battle of the Cowpens. His estate was confiscated in 1782, and he was refused permission to remain in South Carolina after the war. He resettled in the Bahamas and died at Nassau.

CUNNINGHAM, William (c. 1717–1791) British official

Apparently born in Dublin in the barracks of a company of dragoons, Cunningham was one of the more disreputable British officers because of his conduct as keeper of American prisoners. He came to New York City in 1774 and originally worked as a horse trainer and riding teacher. He must have been vocal in opposition to the Revolution since he fled to the British army in Boston in 1775 and was named as provost marshal by commander Thomas Gage. When the British occupied Philadelphia two years later, Cunningham was put in charge of the prisons. After the British withdrawal to New York City in 1778, he took over administration of the notorious jails and prison ships there. He gained a nasty reputation among patriots for cruelty and inhumane treatment, including intentional starvation of American prisoners. Conditions were indisputably horrible, and thousands died while in his care. Patriot accounts accused Cunningham of hanging 250 prisoners without trial. He moved to England after the war, and several accounts say he was executed in 1791 as a forger.

CUNNINGHAM, William (d. 1787) Loyalist partisan

Often confused with the William Cunningham who was the British provost marshal in New York, this Cunningham was a leader of loyalist irregulars in Georgia and the Carolinas. Little is known of his specific activities, but from his nickname "Bloody Bill" it is reasonable to assume he was embroiled in the vicious, neighbor-against-neighbor partisan warfare that characterized the southern theater, especially after the British invasion of Charleston in 1779–1780. Cunningham may have been associated with David Fanning, another loyalist of evil reputation. Cunningham apparently escaped retribution after the war, since he died in Charleston in 1787.

CURWEN, Samuel (1715–1802) Loyalist

Curwen (whose father spelled the family name "Curwin") was born in Salem, Massachusetts, graduated from Harvard and served as an officer in the colonial militia during the expedition against Louisbourg in French North America in 1744. He studied for the ministry as a young man, but he turned to commerce and prospered as a businessman. He was a royal officeholder before the Revolution, serving as the impost officer at Essex, Massachusetts and as a judge of the Admiralty Court. In 1775, he left Massachusetts for Philadelphia, and later in the year he left his estranged wife behind and fled the colonies for England. He became one of the leaders among the loyalists of London, helping to found the "Brompton Road Tory Club," a social club of New England expatriates.

While not in sympathy with the Revolution and fearful of American independence, Curwen nonetheless pined for his home. He recorded in his journal the ennui, anxiety and discomfort of the exiled American loyalists in London during the Revolution: "Fears about losing pension, and horror of utter poverty. . . . Angry and mortified to hear Englishmen talk of Americans as serfs. Wearied of sights. Sick at heart, and tired of a sojourn among a people, who, after all, are but foreigners. New refugees arrived to recount their losses and sufferings. . . . Continued and frequent deaths among the refugee Loyalists. Pensions of several friends reduced. Fish dinner at the Coffee-house. O for a return to New England!" Curwen particularly disliked the condescending attitude he encountered among native Britons toward Americans. As soon as the war ended, Curwen returned to Massachusetts. He discovered, however, that during his nine-year absence his wife, Abagail, along with his nephew had ruined his finances. Rather than fight publicly with his wife, he turned around and went back to England. In 1794, Abagail died, and Curwen once again returned to his beloved New England, living the remainder of his life in Salem. *Further reading:* Andrew Oliver, ed., *Journal of Samuel Curwen, Loyalist,* 2 vols. (Cambridge, Mass., 1972).

CUSHING, Thomas (1725–1788) Delegate to Congress, state official

Cushing was one of the leading patriots in Boston and Massachusetts during the 1760s, yet he was moderate when the showdown on independence came. He was a prosperous merchant and public official from a family of prosperous merchants and public officials (his father had been speaker of the General Court). Cushing spent the two decades after his graduation from Harvard in 1744 in commerce, an endeavor at which he was highly successful and which colored his political beliefs thereafter.

He first was chosen to sit in the General Court from Boston in 1761, and he became speaker—the position for which he is best known—in 1766. The British measures to raise revenue and control colonial trade aroused his ire, and he took a leading role in the agitations in Boston during the 1760s, serving on committees to oppose restraint of trading and against the Stamp Act. He was elected as a delegate to the convention of Massachusetts towns called to protest British policy and the presence of troops in 1768 and was chosen as chairman. By 1773, Cushing was a member of the Boston committee of correspondence and, as speaker of the General Court, was the official recipient of the infamous Thomas Hutchinson letters sent from London by Benjamin Franklin. He served also in the provincial congresses convened to assume control of the colony.

In 1774, he was selected along with John Adams, Samuel Adams and John Treat Paine as one of Massachusetts' delegates to the first Continental Congress. He was a strong proponent of using nonimportation and nonconsumption tactics to bring Britain around, but he was too moderate to support actual independence. He was sent again as a delegate to the second Congress, but when it became apparent he would not vote for independence, he was replaced by Elbridge Gerry. Cushing returned to Massachusetts and took a place on the state Council. After adoption of the new state constitution, he was elected lieutenant governor, serving until his death.

CUTLER, Manasseh (1742–1823) Clergyman, scientist, land speculator, legislator

Cutler was accomplished and active in several areas during his lifetime. He was born in Connecticut, graduated from Yale at the age of 22 and was admitted to the bar in Massachusetts in 1767. Three years later, he was ordained by the Congregationalists and took over charge of the parish in Ipswich Hamlet, Massachusetts, where he continued as pastor for 52 years. During the Revolution he acted as an army chaplain. Following the war, Cutler helped organize the Ohio Company and traveled to the Ohio Valley in 1786 and 1787, where he founded the city of Marietta. He also helped draft the Ordinance of 1787, under which the western United States was organized. In 1801, he was elected to the U.S. House of Representatives, subsequently serving two terms. He was also an accomplished botanist, gaining fame and honors for cataloging the flora of New England.

CUTTER, Ammi (1735–1819) Physician

Cutter was born in North Yarmouth, Massachusetts in the region that became the state of Maine. He graduated from Harvard in 1752 and then studied medicine in Portsmouth. During the Seven Years' War, Cutter was a surgeon attached to Roger's Rangers, and perhaps he moved to New Hampshire, since in 1758 he was surgeon for New Hampshire troops. In 1777, he was appointed physician-general for part of the army in New York and stationed at Fishkill. He returned to civilian life in 1778 and took up practice again in Portsmouth. He sat in the New Hampshire constitutional convention.

D

DABOLL, Nathan (1750–1818) Mathematician
During the Revolution, Daboll wrote yearly versions of the *New England Almanack*, having discovered mathematical errors in the calculations of an earlier edition by another author. He taught mathematics and astronomy at Plainfield Academy after the war and also gave instruction in navigation. He wrote *Daboll's Practical Navigator*, which was not published until after his death.

D'ABOVILLE, François Marie. See ABOVILLE, François Marie.

DAGGETT, Naphtali (1727–1780) Clergyman
Born in Massachusetts, Daggett passed most of his professional life in Connecticut, attached to Yale College. His first post after ordination by the Presbyterians was at Smithtown, Long Island, but he moved to New Haven to become professor of divinity at Yale in 1756. Ten years later, he became president of Yale, holding that position until 1777, when he returned to teaching. He was one of the defenders of New Haven in 1779 when the British launched a punitive attack against the city in retaliation for raids by Connecticut privateers. Daggett was captured briefly but was released.

DALE, Richard (1756–1826) Naval officer   Dale, born in Norfolk County, Virginia, served on both sides during the Revolution, but he is best known as John Paul Jones's lieutenant. He went to sea at age 11 aboard a merchantman owned by a relative and by 1770 was an apprentice sailor for another Norfolk shipper. In 1776, he was a lieutenant aboard one of the light warships of the tiny Virginia state navy, helping to raid British shipping along the coast. However, he apparently had many loyalist friends, and when one of them took command of a British tender, Dale joined the crew as an officer. The ship and its loyalist crew were captured on a voyage to Bermuda by Captain John Barry and the *Lexington*. In what must have been a dramatic interview, Barry converted Dale to the patriot cause and commissioned him a midshipman in the Continental Navy on the spot.

From then on, Dale served the Revolution. He stayed with Barry and the *Lexington* as master's mate and was captured along with the rest of the crew by the British and thrown into Mill Prison, from which he escaped in February 1778 and made his way to France. Later, he joined the crew of John Paul Jones as first lieutenant aboard the soon-to-be-famous *Bonhomme Richard*. Dale was in the thick of the fight with the *Serapis*, and despite a bad wound, he was the first American officer to board the defeated British ship. He stayed with Jones after their return to France and sailed on the *Alliance* in 1779–80, returning to America in 1781 aboard the *Ariel*. After a tour as first lieutenant on the *Trumbull*, Dale ended his wartime service as a privateer.

Richard Dale

Following the Revolution, Dale was a merchant-man, sailing often to the East Indies. He was appointed as one of the six captains of the reconstituted U.S. Navy in 1794, but he became involved in a dispute over seniority and resigned for a brief period. He came back on active duty after the question of rank was settled by President John Adams, and he commanded a squadron of warships in the Mediterranean in 1801–02.

DALLING, Sir John (d. 1798) British general, official

Dalling influenced the war in America indirectly as military governor of the West Indies. He had served in the Seven Years' War in several major campaigns, including the expedition against Louisbourg, Canada and had commanded a company of light infantry under General Wolfe at Quebec. He went to the West Indies in 1762 as commander of the 43rd Foot stationed in Havana. He was made lieutenant governor of Jamaica in 1767 and became governor 10 years later, after the beginning of the Revolution. The conflicts in the West Indies, of course, exerted a major influence on how the British were able to fight against the patriots to the north, and Dalling's decision to send a large naval and land expedition to Nicaragua and Honduras sapped resources away from the Revolutionary War in 1780 at a crucial time. He was also technically responsible for defending Mobile and Pensacola, which fell to the Spanish during the war. In 1782, he was promoted to lieutenant general.

DALRYMPLE, John (1749–1821) British officer, diplomat

The eldest son of a Scottish peer, Dalrymple served in the American theater first as a captain of the 87th Regiment in the West Indies. In early fall of 1779, he raised a force known as the Jamaica Legion, which he commanded as a major. In October, he led his four companies of 200 men as part of the British invasion of Honduras and Nicaragua and won plaudits for his capture of the Spanish fort at Omoa in the Bay of Honduras. The legion was merged with another unit in February 1780, and Dalrymple apparently returned to his original regiment. In 1781, he took part in the British raid on New London, Connecticut under the command of Benedict Arnold, after which he was sent back to England with dispatches. In January of the following year, he was appointed as minister plenipotentiary to Poland, and he subsequently was named to a similar post at the court in Berlin. He inherited his father's title in 1789, becoming the sixth Earl of Stair.

DALRYMPLE, William (d. 1807) British officer

William Dalrymple (often confused with John Dalrymple) was a career officer in the British army, commanding the 14th Regiment in Halifax, Nova Scotia, when he was ordered by General Thomas Gage to garrison Boston in 1768. He became temporary commander of the regiments unloaded from warships in Boston Harbor and faced the unenviable task of settling a large military presence in a hostile city. The citizens of Boston refused to cooperate in finding housing for the soldiers, so Dalrymple appropriated Faneuil Hall (unfinished at the time) to quarter some of his troops. He remained in command through the time of the Boston Massacre and was not relieved until 1772. As a lieutenant colonel (his "local" rank and his permanent rank differed considerably throughout the war) he was in charge of troops on Staten Island during the New York campaigns of 1776, and he returned to England late in the year. He assumed command of the 14th Regiment in 1777 and was probably with the unit when it went to Jamaica. In 1779, Dalrymple carried dispatches to Sir Henry Clinton at Charleston and for a brief while served as Clinton's quartermaster general, with a local rank of major general. He was listed as colonel in command of the 2nd (Queen's Own) Regiment from 1782 until the end of the war.

D'AMBOISE. See AMBOISE, Chevalier d'.

DANA, Francis (1743–1811) Delegate to Congress, diplomat, jurist   It is no error to call Dana an important political figure of the Revolution, but his potentially most significant diplomatic venture on behalf of the new nation ended in frustration. He was born to a wealthy Massachusetts family, graduated from Harvard and took up the practice of law. He belonged to the Sons of Liberty before the Revolution but was not a fire-eating Boston radical as were many of his associates, such as the Adams cousins. He was selected as a member of the first Massachusetts Provincial Congress, but instead of taking his seat, Dana set out on a personal mission of reconciliation with the mother country. He went to England and through family connections laid pleas for healing before several officials. He was utterly rejected, and after 18 months, he returned to America, convinced that independence was inevitable. He was elected to the Massachusetts Council in 1776 and then as a delegate to the Congress. He served there vigorously, just missing appointment to France in place of Silas Deane, and sat on several important committees, including the one that helped reorganize the army in 1777–78.

In 1779, Dana left Congress and traveled to France as secretary of the legation of John Adams to seek a peace negotiation with Britain. While Dana was in France, Congress decided to send a representative to the court of Catherine the Great, who had put in place the League of Armed Neutrality in protest of the British high-seas policy of seizing cargos destined for rebel hands. Catherine, however, was unlikely to accept a ministry from the upstart Americans, so Dana traveled to St. Petersburg ostensibly as a private citizen. He carried official credentials but was instructed to bide time until the proper moment to declare himself an envoy. The time never came, despite a long and lonely year and a half in the bleak Russian capital. Dana did attempt once to present his credentials, but he was turned away by oblique excuses. He returned to America in December 1783. After the war, he was appointed as a justice of the Massachusetts Supreme Court, a post in which he served for most of the rest of his life, becoming chief justice in 1791. He was an iron-bound Federalist and strongly supported such radical measures as the Alien and Sedition Acts. He was the grandfather of the 19th-century writer Richard Henry Dana.

DANE, Nathan (1752–1835) Delegate to Congress, attorney   Born in Ipswich, Massachusetts, Dane spent the first years of the Revolution as a student at Harvard, from which he graduated in 1778. He then studied law and was admitted to the bar in 1782, also immediately taking a seat in the Massachusetts General Court. From 1785 to 1787, Dane was a delegate to the Confederation Congress. He is known best, however, for his subsequent work as a legal codifier. After two years as a judge of a county court of common pleas, he was named in 1795 as commissioner to revise the laws of the commonwealth. His eight-volume *General Abridgement and Digest of American Law* was published in 1823. He was also a strong supporter of Harvard College and established a professorship of law named for himself.

DARKE, William (1736–1801) Officer   Born in Pennsylvania, Darke served as a corporal in the Seven Years' War, but he had moved to Virginia by the 1770s. He was a captain in a Virginia militia company and was captured by the British at the battle of Germantown in 1777. He was held aboard one of the infamous British prison ships in New York Harbor for three years but was exchanged in 1780. The following year he helped recruit for the reorganized 1st Virginia Regiment, which was originally planned to include 6,000 men but ended up with only a small number of troops when the British invasion of Virginia disarranged plans. Darke, by then a lieutenant colonel, was apparently one of the officers in the two temporary battalions of the 1st Virginia that actually served, seeing duty with the Continental Army at the siege of Yorktown. After sitting in the Virginia constitutional convention after the war, Darke was recommissioned in 1791 and was wounded in a battle with the Miami Indians during frontier warfare. He eventually received a commission as a brigadier general.

DARRAGH, Lydia Barrington (1729–1789) American heroine   The subject of a story that is clouded in its authority, Darragh was a memorable patriot woman no matter what the veracity of her legendary deeds. She was born in Dublin, the daughter of a Quaker household, and married at age 24. She and her husband emigrated soon after the wedding to Philadelphia, where Darragh became a well-known midwife and nurse. In 1766, she advertised that she planned to open an undertaking parlor. It appears that she supported her family—she bore nine children, five living to adulthood—by her work.

During the British occupation of Philadelphia, she reputedly "saved" Washington's army by an act of intelligence gathering. Her home was opposite General William Howe's headquarters, and according to the story, a group of British officers used her house to plan an attack on Washington at Whitemarsh. Darragh overheard the conference and, using the subterfuge of fetching flour from a country mill, set out to warn the commander in chief. Along the road, Darragh met an American officer friend and passed on the message of the impending attack. Washington prepared his forces, and the British were frustrated.

This story did not appear until 1827 and it has been examined several times without achieving much substantiation. The memoirs of Elias Boudinot, who was in charge of American intelligence, seem to refute the Darragh saga, which was based originally on a family story. It is perhaps just as interesting to note Darragh's ability to maintain a business in Revolutionary Philadelphia—her husband died in 1783—and her struggles with her local Friends meeting, which expelled her for a period due to her family's involvement in the war (her son served as an officer). She left an estate in excess of £1,600 on her death in 1789.

DARTMOUTH, William Legge, Earl of (1731–1801) British official

The stepbrother of Lord North, Legge inherited his title as second Earl of Dartmouth from his grandfather. He was well educated in the fashion of an 18th-century English aristocrat at Westminster School and Trinity College, Oxford. He took his seat in the House of Lords after assuming the title in 1750. He served in the government in 1765 and 1766 as president of the board of trade and in 1772 returned to the same office and as secretary of state for the American colonies.

Although he held a seemingly key office during the crucial years of dispute with the American colonies, he in fact exerted a smaller influence than

Earl of Dartmouth

his position might indicate. The government during these years was in considerable turmoil, and the position of secretary of state—divided in two—was sapped of power by bickering and wrangling over who had specific authority and who would control patronage. Dartmouth was by temperament unwilling to keep up a long internecine battle over his privileges, and he left much of the actual administration of duties to his juniors. He also dithered in his attitude toward the Americans, for a long time being unable to make up his mind about the soundness of their complaints and what should be done from the government's point of view. In fact, his resignation in November 1775 was prompted by his reluctance to prosecute an actual war against the colonial rebels. He thereafter received places of honor but no political office, although he came to support firmness against the Revolution. Dartmouth had a reputation as a pious Methodist and took a strong interest in the Indian mission school set up in New Hampshire by Eleazar Wheelock. His contributions to the school were acknowledged in 1769 when it was named Dartmouth College in his honor. *Further reading:* B. D. Bargar, *Lord Dartmouth and the American Revolution* (Columbia, S.C., 1965).

DAVENPORT, Franklin (1755–1832) Militia officer, legislator

Born in Philadelphia, Davenport was admitted to the bar in New Jersey during the first year of the Revolution. He began his military career as a private in the New Jersey militia but was commissioned in 1776 and fought at the battles of

Trenton and Princeton during Washington's New Jersey campaign. Later in the war, he was a quartermaster for the New Jersey troops. He continued in the militia and was made a brigadier general in 1796. By the end of the century, Davenport was also a prominent politician, and he served as both U.S. senator and congressman from New Jersey.

DAVENPORT, James (1758–1797) Official, jurist   Davenport was born in Stamford, Connecticut and graduated from Yale at age 19. During the Revolution, he worked in the commissary department of the Continental Army. Following the war, he held several political and judicial posts, becoming a member of the U.S. House of Representatives shortly before his death.

DAVENPORT, John (1752–1830) Soldier, official   A native of Stamford, Connecticut and a graduate of Yale, Davenport briefly taught at the New Haven college before taking up the practice of law in his hometown. During the first years of the Revolution he worked in the commissary department, but he was commissioned as a major in 1777. He was simultaneously a member of the Connecticut House of Representatives. Davenport later served a long term as a member of the U.S. House of Representatives, from 1799 until 1817.

DAVID, Ebenezer (c. 1751–1778) Army chaplain and surgeon's mate   David was the son of a Philadelphia tailor and part-time preacher of the small Seventh-Day Baptist sect. He attended Philadelphia Academy and then went to Rhode Island to become a student at Rhode Island College (later to become Brown University), first in Warren and then in Providence when the school moved there in 1770. He graduated in 1772 and immediately began work as a teacher of Latin in a preparatory school attached to the college. David also studied for the ministry and formed an attachment to the Seventh-Day Baptist congregation in Newport. He was licensed as a preacher in Newport in 1773 and ordained in May 1775.

He joined Varnum's Rhode Island Regiment during the siege of Boston, succeeding John Murray as a chaplain, and when the Rhode Island regiment was taken into the Continental Army, David received a commission as its chaplain and as chaplain of the 25th Continental Regiment of Massachusetts,

serving both units simultaneously. He was with the army during the New York campaign of 1776 and served in the Hudson Highlands.

In early 1777, David returned to Providence to study medicine, intending to switch from religious duties to the medical service. In May 1777, he returned to duty as a chaplain with the 2nd Rhode Island. After serving with the regiment during the defense of the Delaware River forts, David went into winter quarters with the army at Valley Forge, apparently in a dual role as chaplain and surgeon's mate. He was assigned to an army hospital in Lancaster, Pennsylvania during the winter; he contracted a fatal illness from his patients and died in March 1778. A series of his letters to prominent Rhode Island patriot merchant Nicholas Brown that vividly describe army life was preserved among Brown's business correspondence and published in 1949. Further reading: Jeanette B. Black and William G. Roelker, eds., *A Rhode Island Chaplain: Letters of Ebenezer David to Nicholas Brown, 1775–1778* (Providence, 1949).

DAVIDSON, George. Militia officer   Although he briefly held a Continental commission, Davidson primarily served as an officer of the North Carolina back-country militia. His most notable service was as leader of one of the few coherent American fighting forces left in the Carolinas after the British seizure of Charleston in 1780. He commanded about 70 riflemen in two companies under Colonel William Davie; the companies surprised part of Banastre Tarleton's cavalry near Wahab's Plantation, North Carolina on September 21, 1780 and routed the British, a rare example of American success at the time.

DAVIDSON, William Lee (1746–1781) Continental officer, militia general   Born in Lancaster County, Pennsylvania, Davidson moved with his family to North Carolina in 1750. He was a member of the Rowan County Committee of Safety in 1775 and then was commissioned as major of the 4th North Carolina Regiment in the following year. His conduct at the battle of Germantown won Davidson a promotion to lieutenant colonel of the 5th North Carolina, and he transferred twice more, ending up with the 1st North Carolina Regiment. The entire North Carolina contingent of the Continental Line was sent south in November 1779 to help defend the state against Clinton's and Cornwallis' invasion, but Davidson tarried too long during a visit home and failed to reach Charleston before the city fell and his unit was captured.

Adrift from his Continentals, Davidson turned to militia warfare and became one of the principal leaders in North Carolina over the following year. Commissioned a brigadier general of militia, he raised and commanded a battalion of light infantry that fought at Ramsur's Mill, and he was badly wounded at Coulson's Mill in the summer of 1780. His militiamen were good fighters and he led them well, showing unusual cooperation with other militia leaders such as William Davie and eventually with Nathanael Greene when the latter assumed command of the southern theater. In December 1780, Davidson joined forces with Daniel Morgan, but he missed the battle at the Cowpens while off recruiting more militia. The following month, Davidson was assigned by Greene to hold the fords of the Catawba River against Cornwallis. At Cowan's Ford on February 1, 1781, Davidson's men pushed back the first attempt of the main British army to cross the river but were outflanked and defeated. Davidson himself was killed while trying to make a stand. Davidson College was named in his honor, and a memorial to him was eventually erected at Guilford Courthouse. *Further reading:* Chalmer G. Davidson, *Piedmont Partisan: The Life and Times of Brigadier General William Lee Davidson* (Davidson, N.C., 1951).

DAVIE, William Richardson (1756–1820) Militia officer, official

One of the better partisan militia fighters in the Carolinas during the Revolution, Davie was born in England and came with his parents to the Waxhaw settlement of South Carolina at age seven. He was brought up by his uncle, a Presbyterian clergyman. Davie went north to college, graduating from Princeton with honors in 1776, and then returned south to Salisbury, North Carolina, where he began the study of law. The war soon intervened, however, and he took up arms as a militia officer in 1777 under General Allen Jones. Davie was a natural cavalryman, however, and raised his own troops of mounted militiamen. He was part of Pulaski's Legion during 1779 and was badly wounded during Benjamin Lincoln's unsuccessful attack on the British at Stono Ferry outside Charleston in June.

William R. Davie

He recovered, but meanwhile Lincoln surrendered Charleston to the British. Davie then began operations in the Carolinas as one of the several American partisans who made life difficult for the British occupiers, establishing a reputation for dash, courage and good judgment. At Wahab's Plantation, North Carolina in September 1780, he attacked a British post with his mounted troops and a company of riflemen. Davie routed the enemy in a skillful engagement and captured a significant number of horses and supplies, providing the American cause with one of its few bright spots during the months after Lincoln's surrender. Five days later, Davie and only 20 dismounted cavalrymen behind a stone fence stood off Cornwallis' entire army as it advanced toward Charlotte.

With the advent of Nathanael Greene to command of the southern theater, however, Davie's role changed drastically. Greene planned a mobile campaign in a region badly depleted of food and supplies for his army, and the new commander desperately needed someone who could feed the troops while the game of thrust and parry with the British went on. Greene selected Davie, who bitterly protested being turned into a commissary (he knew it was a huge challenge and a thankless job). Davie took the job nonetheless, and during the following months his efforts kept Greene's forces in the field and allowed the commander to ultimately force Cornwallis into his fatal position in Yorktown.

At the end of the Revolution, Davie moved to Halifax, North Carolina, married, and began a long term in public office as a legislator and judge. He

Scene at Concord's North Bridge where Isaac Davis was killed

served in the state legislature almost continuously for more than a decade and sat on the circuit bench. He also found time to interest himself in public education and was largely responsible for the establishment of the University of North Carolina. In 1797, as new war clouds gathered, he assumed command of the state militia, and he was commissioned a brigadier general in the U.S. Army in 1798 during the crisis with France. In the same year, he was elected governor of North Carolina, and in 1799 he was appointed peace commissioner to France. He was a vigorous opponent of Jefferson, however, and left public office after 1800, retiring to a plantation in South Carolina. *Further reading:* Blackwell P. Robinson, *William R. Davie* (Chapel Hill, N.C., 1957).

DAVIS, Isaac (1745–1775) Militia officer   Davis won immortality in American history in the early morning hours of April 19, 1775 when, as captain, he led his company of Acton, Massachusetts minutemen down from the hill overlooking the North Bridge in Concord toward the redcoats. The British soldiers holding the bridge, nervous from the nasty fight a few hours earlier in Lexington, immediately opened fire, and Davis was killed along with two others of his militia company. His body was carried to his home and laid out by his widow. He thus became one of the first casualties of the War for Independence.

DAWES, William (1745–1799) Courier, soldier   Although his compatriot, Paul Revere, is better known, Dawes was the most successful rider dispatched to rouse the countryside against the British advance toward Lexington and Concord in April 1775. He apparently was a native of Boston and a tanner by trade, who had been involved in the prerevolutionary activities of the city and had served patriot leader Dr. Joseph Warren as a courier. Tension mounted in the city during the spring of 1775, and rebel leaders feared an expedition by the British to seize arms and perhaps capture Samuel Adams and John Hancock, who were in hiding. Warren asked Dawes to stand alert for a mission. When Warren learned of the British plans to march to Lexington and Concord during the evening of April 18, he called in Dawes and dispatched him with the warning along a land route, past the British sentries on Boston Neck and out the road to Lexington. Revere was to row across the water to Charlestown and thence take horse to warn Hancock and Adams. Dawes managed to pass the guards and rode hard through the night. He reached Lexington soon after Revere, and both of them, joined by Dr. Samuel Prescott, headed for Concord shortly after midnight. They ran into a British patrol, and although Revere was captured, Dawes put spurs to horse and escaped to alert the neighborhoods along the way and call out the minutemen of Concord. After his historic adventure, Dawes apparently served as a private soldier during the siege of Boston and then retired to Worcester and became a commissary for the army. After the Revolution, he returned to Boston and ran a grocery business.

DAWSON, John (1762–1814) Delegate to Congress   Too young to have had much active participation in the Revolution itself, Dawson represented his native Virginia during the days of the early Republic. He attended Harvard during the latter years of the war, graduating in 1782. He served in the Virginia legislature during the 1780s and in 1788 was a delegate to the Confederation Congress. Elected to the U.S. House of Representatives in 1797 after the subsequent change to the new form of federal government, Dawson sat in Congress for 17 years. He proposed the amendment to the Constitution that provided for separate election of a president and vice president after the debacle of the election of 1800. During the War of 1812, he was an aide to Andrew Jackson.

DAYTON, Elias (1737–1807) Continental officer

Dayton was the sort of senior officer that the Continental Army could have used more of: a brave and good leader, steadfast in supporting the central goals of the overall war. He was born in Elizabethtown, New Jersey and was an apprentice mechanic in his youth. He saw extensive service during the Seven Years' War as an officer of the New Jersey colonial militia under General Wolfe at Quebec and three years later in Pontiac's War. He became the proprietor of a general store in Elizabethtown after fighting with the British against the French and Indians, serving locally as an alderman. In 1774, Dayton joined the local Committee of Safety, and in October 1775, he acted as muster master for New Jersey troops.

Although he might well have become a general in the state militia, Dayton chose to serve as a Continental officer throughout the entire war. He received a commission as colonel from Congress in January 1776 and raised the 3rd New Jersey Regiment that formed part of the Continental Line (the original enlistments ran out in November 1776 and the regiment was re-formed, serving intact until 1781). He, along with Lord Stirling, personally led a group of volunteers in small boats that captured the British transport-supply ship *Blue Mountain Valley* in January 1776. In May, Dayton led his new regiment into northern New York state, where he rebuilt Fort Stanwix and established Fort Dayton. The regiment joined the main army in winter quarters at Morristown in early 1777 and fought at Brandywine and Germantown, where Dayton had horses shot from under him according to some accounts, and then the following year (after the winter at Valley Forge) they fought at Monmouth.

During 1777, Dayton also took on duties as a spymaster for Washington and ran an extensive ring of agents operating on Manhattan and Staten Island. He joined John Sullivan's expedition against the Iroquois in 1779, after having refused a seat in Congress when elected the previous year to replace John Neilson. In 1780, the 3rd New Jersey was stationed near Dayton's home and helped repulse the advances by Baron von Knyphausen from New York. He was due to transfer command to the 2nd New Jersey in place of Israel Shreve in January 1781 but was still with the 3rd when the mutiny of the New Jersey Line occurred. He helped put down the uprising and then took over the new regiment in

March. During the summer, he and his Continentals shouldered arms and marched with Washington south to Virginia, where he commanded an entire brigade of 1,300 men during the siege of Yorktown. The 2nd New Jersey was disbanded in January 1783, and Dayton was appointed a brigadier general and retired at the same time. After the war, he returned to Elizabethtown but continued in public service, sitting in the state legislature, taking a commission as major general in the state militia and representing New Jersey in the Congress of 1787–88.

DAYTON, Jonathan (1760–1824) Continental officer, official

The son of Elias Dayton, Jonathan served with his father's regiments during most of the Revolutionary War and achieved notoriety later as a political official. He graduated from the college at Princeton in 1776 at age 16 and immediately joined his father's 3rd New Jersey Regiment as an ensign. He then advanced to regimental paymaster and eventually to the rank of captain. He was aide-de-camp to John Sullivan during the Iroquois campaign in 1779. He was captured at his hometown in October 1780 but was exchanged soon thereafter. He transferred regiments with his father in 1781 when the elder Dayton took over command of the 2nd New Jersey, and he served as a captain at Yorktown.

Admitted to the bar, he moved into politics after the war, sitting in the New Jersey assembly and as speaker of the house. His father was elected to the federal Constitutional Convention in 1787 but declined in favor of Jonathan, who then served as the youngest member of the Convention, during which he supported adoption of a new form of government. He was elected to the first Congress under the Constitution but declined to serve. When elected again, two years later, he took his seat and remained in the U.S. House of Representatives for four terms, becoming Speaker of the House during the Fifth Congress. In 1799, he moved over to the U.S. Senate for one term.

His national public career came to a shuddering halt, however, when he was indicted for treason along with Aaron Burr in 1807. He had been a partner with Burr in land speculation in the west and was accused of complicity in Burr's conspiracy. Dayton's case was never tried.

Silas Deane

DEANE, Silas (1737–1789) Delegate to Congress, diplomat

A member of both the first and second Continental Congresses, Deane served as an American diplomat in Europe during the Revolution and was at the center of one of the nation's first severe political controversies. He was born in Groton, Connecticut, the son of a blacksmith; he graduated from Yale in 1758 and opened a law practice in Wethersfield in 1762. Two fortuitous marriages brought him comparative wealth and influence.

Before the Revolution, he was deeply involved in complex financial deals and land speculation with several prominent Connecticut politicians and merchants. Deane supported the patriot cause, leading opposition to the Townshend Acts in the Connecticut General Assembly in 1772 and serving as secretary of the committee of correspondence in 1773. He represented Connecticut in the Continental Congresses from 1774 until 1775, when he was not reelected, having fallen from political grace at home. However, the Congress had decided to seek foreign aid in France and selected Deane to negotiate with the French government, making him the United States' first diplomat. He was charged by two separate committees of Congress to procure supplies, an opportunity for a man of his loose business ethics to enrich himself.

His greatest mistake was entering a commercial conspiracy with Edward Bancroft, who, unknown to Deane (or any other Americans), was in the pay of the British. Bancroft and Deane manipulated purchases in France to their own financial gain and devised a skein of financial deals—including using inside knowledge to play the British stock market—

they hoped would make them rich. All the while, Bancroft was passing American secrets to his British masters. Despite his illicit personal gains, Deane did procure important matériel for the Revolution, and he was hand-in-glove with Caron de Beaumarchais in setting up the dummy Hortalez et Cie, a company that funneled crucial goods to the colonies.

Deane also directed a flow of military volunteers to the Continental Congress. He disingenuously believed any European officer who presented himself as a military expert and forwarded all uncritically to Philadelphia with recommendations for high rank. While a few of these volunteers, such as Lafayette and de Kalb, proved to be stalwarts, most were worthless at best and some positively harmful. Deane's lack of discrimination did little to establish his good judgment in Congress.

In the fall of 1776, Congress sent Arthur Lee and Benjamin Franklin to join Deane in Paris, and trouble began almost at once. Lee was a malevolent, suspicious man, and he soon launched a series of accusations against Deane, claiming that Deane was a corrupt profiteer. Ironically, he had no evidence whatsoever and based his charges on personal paranoia and malice: neither he nor anyone else at the time had proof of Deane's peculations with Bancroft. Lee had powerful friends in Congress, however, and by 1777 a severe split developed in Philadelphia between pro-Deane and pro-Lee factions. For many months the other business of the Congress either came to a halt or was viewed through the lens of the controversy. Deane was recalled to answer an inquiry—Beaumarchais's payments were suspended and he probably suffered most from the affair—and was ultimately cleared, but he was dropped from service. He returned to Europe and continued to connive with Bancroft, but things turned increasingly sour. He wrote a series of letters that urged reconciliation with the British, which Bancroft secretly turned over to the government in London. The British authorities pretended to have intercepted the letters and had them published in New York in Rivington's *Gazette*. Deane was now seen in America as a traitor, and he descended into abject poverty, living miserably in Ghent and then London. He died as he took ship to begin a trip to Canada. The full extent of his dealings and the perfidy of Bancroft were not revealed until nearly 200 years later. *Further reading:* Julian Boyd, "Silas

Deane: Death by a Kindly Teacher of Treason?" *William and Mary Quarterly*, 3rd ser., 16 (1959), 165–87; 319–42; Coy N. James, *Silas Deane: Patriot or Traitor?* (East Lansing, Mich., 1975).

DEARBORN, Henry (1751–1829) Continental officer, official   Dearborn served well in several campaigns during the Revolution, but he proved decades later to be a disaster as secretary of war and commander during the War of 1812. He was born in New Hampshire and trained as a physician. In 1772, he set up his practice at Nottingham Square, New Hampshire and raised a local militia company. When the British were chased back from Lexington and Concord in the spring of 1775, Dearborn and his men marched to Boston and joined John Stark's regiment of New Hampshiremen in time to fight at Bunker Hill. Subsequently, Dearborn volunteered for Benedict Arnold's expedition to Canada, where he was captured during the American defeat in front of Quebec in December 1775. He was held by the British until March 1777. On his release, he became a major in the 3rd New Hampshire under Alexander Scammell (who became Dearborn's good friend). During the summer of 1777, Dearborn organized a light infantry battalion of 300 men picked from the main northern army. This was an elite unit, one of the best trained and equipped in the entire American force. Dearborn's Light Infantry was attached to Daniel Morgan's Rifle Corps and fought extremely well at Saratoga under Dearborn's leadership. Promoted to lieutenant colonel, Dearborn was part of John Sullivan's campaign against the Iroquois in 1779 and then served on Washington's staff as an assistant quartermaster general through the Yorktown campaign.

Following the Revolution, Dearborn moved to Maine and filled a series of military and public offices. By 1790, he was a major general of militia and U.S. marshal. In 1793, he was elected to the U.S. Congress from Massachusetts. He was chosen by Thomas Jefferson to be secretary of war and served during both of Jefferson's terms. With the War of 1812, Dearborn was appointed the senior major general of the U.S. Army and placed in command of the the northeast. He was a complete flop and is usually blamed for much of the ineptitude with which the war was fought by the Americans. He was eventually relieved of command but not soon enough to prevent several American defeats

brought on by his incompetent preparations. James Madison attempted to make Dearborn secretary of war in 1815, but the nomination was rejected by the U.S. Senate. *Further reading:* Henry Dearborn, *Revolutionary War Journals . . .* , H. H. Peckham, ed. (Ann Arbor, Mich., 1939).

DE BARRAS, Louis. See BARRAS, Louis, Comte de.

DECATUR, Stephen (1752–1808) Naval officer   Father of one of America's most famous naval officers of the same name, the elder Decatur was born in Rhode Island. He was a privateer during the Revolution. Afterward, he owned merchant ships operating from Philadelphia. In 1798, he was commissioned as a captain in the U.S. Navy, and he commanded a squadron during the undeclared naval war with the French at the end of the century.

DE GRAAF, Johannes. See GRAAF, Johannes de.

DE GRASSE, Comte. See GRASSE, Comte de.

DE HAAS, John Philip (1735–1786) Continental general   De Haas was the mystery general of the Continental Army during the Revolutionary War. He was born in Holland and came to Lancaster County, Pennsylvania at age two with his family. He served with the Pennsylvania militia during the Seven Years' War and as a local magistrate from the end of that conflict to the beginning of the Revolution. In 1775, de Haas raised a company of patriot militia and received an appointment as a major. Soon after elements of the Pennsylvania infantry militia were taken into Continental service in November 1775, de Haas was commissioned as colonel in command of the new 1st Pennsylvania Regiment. The unit with de Haas at its head went north with Benedict Arnold's expedition to Canada. After serving through the messy campaign around Montreal and subsequently at Fort Ticonderoga, the regiment returned to its home state. The Pennsylvania regiments were reorganized in October 1776, and de Haas emerged as colonel of the new 2nd. Then the mystery begins.

In February 1777, he was promoted to brigadier general, although he apparently failed to acknowledge the new appointment. According to one biographical source, De Haas resigned his commission suddenly and without offering a reason. The official army record (such as it is), however, shows him not retiring until November 1783, when most of the Continental officers left the service, and—even more inexplicable—he was recorded to have been promoted to brevet major general in September 1780. There is no account of his actual activities as a Continental general after mid-1777, however, although he is alleged to have commanded a militia company on the western frontier of Pennsylvania in 1778 and then moved to Philadelphia the following year.

DE LANCEY, James (the Elder) (1732–1800) Loyalist officer

James De Lancey—known usually in biographical accounts as "the Elder"—was the nephew of Oliver De Lancey the Elder and the son of James De Lancey (Oliver the Elder's brother), who had been New York lieutenant governor and chief justice. He was, therefore, the grandson of Stephen (Étienne) De Lancey, the original Huguenot emigrant founder of the clan in America. The De Lancey family relationships were confusing, especially with the Jameses. This James—like his cousin Oliver the Younger—was educated in England and joined the British army, serving in North America during the first part of the Seven Years' War. On the death of his father in 1760 however, James inherited much of the family wealth and position in New York, and he left the army to assume a place as family leader and public figure. He also was known for importing some of the first thoroughbred race horses to America and is often referred to as the "father of the New York turf." Along with the rest of his kin, he resisted the patriot movement (often embodied by the social and political rival family of the Livingstons) and tried unsuccessfully to fight the mounting pressure against the crown in New York. In early 1775, he could no longer control the Council or Assembly in New York, so he sold out his horse farm and left for England, where he was a principal member of the loyalist claims commissions after the war.

DE LANCEY, James (the Younger) (1746–1804) Loyalist officer

Not, as might be supposed by his historical designation as "the Younger," the son of James De Lancey the Elder, but rather a cousin. This James was the son of Peter De Lancey, who was a brother of Oliver the Elder and James the

New York lieutenant governor. He was therefore the nephew of Oliver the Elder and a cousin of Oliver the Younger. To make the relationships even more complex, James the Younger's mother was the eldest daughter of Cadwallader Colden, who was a rival of the De Lancey clan for political office in New York and who succeeded James De Lancey (James the Younger's uncle) as lieutenant governor of the colony. James the Younger became, perhaps, the most notorious of all the De Lanceys during the Revolution. He commanded a troop of loyalist brigands, known as "Cowboys" after their habit of stealing cattle, who roamed the so-called Neutral Ground of Westchester County, New York, north of Manhattan. James preferred to call his force De Lancey's Horse or the Westchester Refugees. Whatever the name, the company helped turn the region into a lawless territory where enemies and the innocent alike traveled or lived at their peril. The rules of warfare applied little, and the stories of terror, murder and thievery were legion—although De Lancey had to share the dishonors with the even worse raiders of Cortlandt Skinner's band of horsemen (Skinner was also connected to the De Lanceys by marriage). James the Younger fled to Nova Scotia at the end of the Revolutionary War and became a respectable citizen, farming peacefully and holding office as a member of the council and assembly.

DE LANCEY, Oliver (the Elder) (1718–1785) Loyalist general

One of the more important loyalists in America during the Revolution and the highest-ranking loyalist soldier, the elder Oliver De Lancey headed his wealthy and powerful family after the death of his brother, James, in 1760. His father, Stephen (or Étienne as he was originally known), was a French Huguenot who had migrated to New York in 1686 and married Anne Van Cortlandt, cementing a relationship with the powerful Dutch clans of the colony. The union prospered, and their children vied for control of New York through their political connections, public offices and great wealth.

Oliver was the youngest son of Stephen and Anne. He took part in the family mercantile business and first took up arms during the Seven Years' War when he recruited and commanded volunteers from New York. He moved then to a series of public offices, although he remained in the political shadow of his brother, who was chief justice and lieutenant governor of the colony and the leader of the family. On James's death, Oliver moved to the front at a time when dissent in America began to grow. By most accounts, he was intemperate and less politically adroit than his brother had been, and he was prone to make enemies. Much of the De Lancey family influence came through complex marriage and business relationships both in the colonies and in Great Britain, and the family ties assured Oliver of a voice in most public matters. The entire family was—unsurprisingly—loyal to the crown and came into ever more intense conflict with the rising forces of patriotism, including their "natural" rivals in New York, the Livingstons. With the outbreak of the War for Independence, Oliver stepped forward to raise loyalist troops, eventually recruiting and nominally commanding three battalions. He was commissioned a brigadier general in the British army, which made him the senior loyalist officer by rank and date of appointment. De Lancey's New York Volunteers fought both in defense of the family's home colony and in the south. Oliver himself remained in New York City during the war. Patriots raided and nearly destroyed his estate in 1777, and in 1779, the patriot government of New York confiscated all his property. With the final defeat of the British cause, Oliver moved to England; he received a large settlement for his lost property, but he died two years later.

DE LANCEY, Oliver (the Younger) (1749–1822) Loyalist officer

The son of Oliver the Elder, the younger De Lancey was a career soldier in the British army and served with considerable distinction during the American War. He was born to the notable De Lancey clan in New York City but was sent to Britain for his education. He joined the army as a coronet of the 14th Dragoons in 1766. By 1774, he was a captain of the 17th Dragoon regiment, which remained his unit for almost the next half-century. He was sent to America ahead of the 17th in 1775 and made arrangements for its transfer. He fought with his men at the battle of Long Island and commanded the key movement that secured Jamaica Pass for the British attack. De Lancey and the 17th (one of only two regular British cavalry units in America during the war) served at White Plains and Monmouth during the subsequent months.

In 1778, De Lancey was promoted to major and appointed as adjutant general to Sir Henry Clinton in place of the captured spy John André. He also took over André's function as British spymaster and reorganized the British secret service wing, trying unsuccessfully to get several American generals to defect and to promulgate mutiny among the enlisted ranks of the Continental Army. He also sailed south with Clinton's expedition to take Charleston in 1780. He was promoted to lieutenant colonel in 1781 and made adjutant for the entire British force in North America. After the British withdrawal in 1783, he returned to England and sat on the commission to settle loyalist military claims. His career continued to move upward steadily during the ensuing years, and he retired with the rank of full general in 1812, having served as barracks master general, colonel of the 17th and in Parliament.

DEMONT, William. Continental officer, traitor

Demont was a native of England who had settled in Pennsylvania. He was commissioned into the 5th Pennsylvania in January 1776 as an ensign and was appointed adjutant to commanding general Robert Magaw by the Pennsylvania Committee of Safety in late September. The 5th was part of the garrison and Magaw the commander of Fort Washington, the American stronghold on Manhattan. Demont defected to the British on November 3, taking with him detailed plans of the fort. Having pushed George Washington's army to the north, the British turned and attacked Fort Washington, taking it easily and capturing thousands of troops and many supplies. Demont was with the British in 1777 when they occupied Philadelphia, but he returned to England in 1780 and pressed a claim for payment for his services. He was finally awarded £60 in 1792.

DENISON, Nathan (1740–1809) Militia officer

Born in London, Connecticut, Denison moved to the Wyoming Valley, an area disputed between Connecticut and Pennsylvania, as one of the leaders of the Connecticut contingent in the region. He shared influence with Zebulon Butler—both were justices of the peace—and was one of the commanders of the force that tried to defend the settlements against the British-Indian raid by John Butler that resulted in the so-called Wyoming Valley Massacre in 1778. Denison held a commission as colonel in the Connecticut militia at the time.

DENNY, Ebenezer (1761–1822) Continental officer

One of the most-quoted eyewitnesses to the defeat of the British at Yorktown, Denny was born in Carlisle, Pennsylvania and served as a junior officer in the Continental Army. His father served in the Seven Years' War and ran a store in Carlisle, where the young Ebenezer worked as a clerk. The father raised a company of militia at the beginning of the Revolution but was killed at Crooked Billet. Ebenezer's first service was aboard a privateer, and in 1781 he was commissioned as an ensign in Anthony Wayne's 1st Pennsylvania regiment and marched south with Wayne's Pennsylvanians to join forces with the Marquis de Lafayette. He fought in the front line with Wayne at the battle of Green Spring when the 1st Pennsylvania made its breathtaking charge in the teeth of virtually the entire British army. Denny, by then a lieutenant, moved with his unit to Yorktown and served in the siege trenches, during which time he kept a daily journal. On October 17, 1781 he recorded a signal event:

> In the morning, before relief came, had the pleasure of seeing a drummer mount the enemy's parapet, and beat a parley, and immediately an officer, holding up a white handkerchief, made his appearance outside their works; the drummer accompanied him, beating. Our batteries ceased. An officer from our lines ran and met the other, and tied the handkerchief over his eyes. The drummer sent back, and the British officer conducted to a house in rear of our lines. Firing ceased totally.

After the Revolution, Denny fought again with General Harmar in the Indian Wars and eventually became a prosperous banker and insurance company owner in Pittsburgh, where he served as mayor in 1816. His Revolutionary War journal was published in 1859. *Further reading:* Ebenezer Denny, *Military Journal of Maj. Ebenezer Denny* (Philadelphia, 1859; reprint New York, 1971).

DENT, George (1756–1813) Soldier, official

Most of Dent's Revolutionary War service was in the Maryland militia. A native of Charles County, he served first with his local company as a lieutenant. In 1776, when the Flying Camp was organized as a mobile reserve corps, Dent was part of Maryland's contingent. He was promoted to captain in 1778. Following the Revolution, Dent was speaker pro tem of the Maryland house of representatives and then president of the state senate. He served three terms in the U.S. House as representative from Maryland. In 1801, he was appointed as U.S. marshal for the District of Columbia, although he served only one year before moving to Georgia.

DE PEYSTER, Abraham (1753–c. 1799) Loyalist officer

One of three loyalist brothers to serve on the British side during the Revolution, Abraham was born in New York. His family had emigrated to America in the late 17th century (originally French Protestants, they had fled first to Holland) and had become one of the wealthy and influential clans in the colony. His father had made a fortune as a New York City merchant. Abraham joined the loyalist King's Rangers during the Revolution and was second in command to Patrick Ferguson at King's Mountain, when the unit was virtually destroyed by American frontier militiamen and Ferguson was killed. De Peyster surrendered the remnant of the loyalist force at the end of the battle. After the war, he emigrated to New Brunswick, Canada, serving as treasurer of the province and colonel of the local militia.

DE PEYSTER, Arent Schuyler (1736–1832) Loyalist officer

Born in New York City, Arent was the uncle of the three De Peyster brothers who also served as officers for the British. He was a longtime soldier; he joined the 8th Regiment of Foot in 1755 and remained with this regiment for his entire regular army career. He fought in the Seven Years' War, part of the time under his uncle, Peter Schuyler. During the Revolution he served with the 8th in Upper Canada, where it garrisoned British posts at Detroit and Michimackinac. In 1781, he became colonel of the 8th Regiment in command of these posts, where he dealt extensively with the western Indian tribes and successfully kept most of them in the British orbit. After the war, he moved to Scotland.

DE PEYSTER, Frederick. Loyalist officer

Born in New York, Frederick was the brother of Abraham and James and like them was an officer in the British forces during the Revolutionary War. He held a commission in the New York Volunteers, raised in

Halifax in early 1776, and distinguished himself in leading the storming party that took Fort Montgomery in 1777. Following the Revolution, he joined his siblings in New Brunswick, Canada, but he returned to the United States sometime before his death, which probably occurred in the late 1790s.

DE PEYSTER, James (d. 1793) Loyalist officer

Perhaps the youngest of the De Peyster brothers (their birth dates are uncertain), James was a lieutenant in the King's American Regiment, which had formed in New York in 1776, entering military service at about 19 years of age. The King's Regiment (later renamed the 4th American Regiment) served in campaigns in New York and in the south after 1780. After the war, James received a commission in the British army as a lieutenant of artillery; he was killed in action in 1793 near Menin in Flanders.

DESPARD, Edward Marcus (1751–1803) British officer

Despard, one of the last men ever sentenced to be hung, drawn and quartered, served in the West Indies and Central America during the American Revolution. He was an Irishman and had entered the British army in 1766. He served as an engineer in Jamaica from 1774 to 1779, when he was assigned to the expedition Sir John Dalling sent to Honduras and Nicaragua; Despard was a companion of Horatio Nelson on the adventure. He was then named governor of the Mosquito Coast and he captured the Spanish outpost at Black River in 1782. He was appointed governor of the British settlement of woodcutters in Yucatán in 1784, but he eventually ran afoul of other local officials and was recalled to England. He found himself stuck in the toils of the government bureaucracy and made such a nuisance that he was arrested several times between 1790 and 1800. Embittered by his treatment and perhaps a little deranged, he began a plot to seize the Tower of London, take over the Bank of England and assassinate King George III. He was arrested along with 40 Irish laborers and soldiers and tried on charges of high treason. He and six others were sentenced to the ultimate and traditional punishment. He was executed on February 21, 1803 by hanging and his head was cut off, but the rest of the mutilations were foregone.

DESPARD, John (1745–1829) British officer

The brother of Edward Marcus Despard, John was a career British officer who served in the American War and eventually went on to high rank. He was born in Ireland and joined the British Army in 1760, serving in European campaigns during the Seven Years' War. He went to Quebec in 1793 as a lieutenant in the Royal Fusiliers but returned to England the following year to recruit. He was back in Quebec when the Revolution started in 1775, and he was one of the British force that surrendered in November at St. John's in Newfoundland. He was exchanged a year later, went to New York and was promoted to captain. Despard led troops during the Hudson Highland campaign of 1777 and helped take Fort Montgomery. In 1778, he was transferred as a major to command of loyalist troops. Sir Henry Clinton appointed Despard as deputy adjutant general of the expedition to take Charleston in 1779, and he served the rest of the war in the southern theater, falling into American hands again with Lord Cornwallis' surrender at Yorktown. Despard was released on parole the following year and resumed his career. He was a colonel of his regiment by the late 1790s and was made brigadier general and then major general in rapid succession in 1798. He was commandant of troops on Cape Breton during the time his brother was arrested and executed for high treason. He attained the rank of full general before his retirement in 1814.

D'ESTAING, Comte. See ESTAING, Comte d'.

DESTOUCHES, Charles-René-Dominique Sochet, Chevalier. French naval commander

Destouches, the oldest naval captain of the squadron, commanded one of the ships under Admiral Ternay that carried Rochambeau's expeditionary force to America in 1780. He assumed command of the French squadron when Ternay died in Newport in December. In March 1781, he sailed out of Newport, bound for Chesapeake Bay on a mission to contact and aid Lafayette in Virginia. Despite a day and a half's head start, Destouches reached the capes off the mouth of the bay after a British squadron from New York under Arbuthnot. The two forces, equally matched at eight ships each, fought a brief, inconclusive encounter off the capes on March 16. Destouches turned around and sailed back to Newport, leaving the British once again in control of the important sea-lanes on the southern coast. Two months later, Destouches was replaced in command by Admiral Barras.

DEUX-PONTS, Christian, Count de Forbach, Marquis de (b. 1752) French officer

The eldest of the two Deux-Ponts brothers who shared virtually the same name, used nearly identical titles, served in the same French regiment and are often confused with one another, Christian commanded the Royal Deux-Ponts Regiment that was part of Rochambeau's expeditionary force. The unit was comprised mostly of German-speaking soldiers and had been recruited from a Germanic duchy ruled by Christian's father, also named Christian. The younger Christian (along with his brother Guillaume) was the product of a morganatic marriage between the duke and a French dancer, so he could not inherit the title or the duchy. He and his brother, however, both used the identical but meaningless courtesy titles of Count de Forbach and Comte de Deux-Ponts. Christian entered the French Royal Army as a lieutenant in 1768 at the age of 16 and was named colonel of the Deux-Ponts Regiment in 1772, although he did not actually take command until 1775 or perhaps even later. He arrived with his regiment in Newport in 1780, along with the rest of Rochambeau's main force, and spent until mid-1781 at Providence. He remained in America after Yorktown, returning to France in 1783. The French Revolution turned him out of his place in the army, and he took service in the army of Bavaria during the ensuing European wars.

DEUX-PONTS, Guillaume, Count de Forbach, Comte de (b. 1754) French officer

The younger of two German-speaking brothers who served in the Royal Deux-Ponts Regiment of the French expeditionary force, Guillaume is the better known because of a feat of arms at Yorktown and the journal he kept of his experiences in America during the Revolution. He is often confused with his brother Christian, as he was even by contemporaries among his American colleagues.

Deux-Ponts joined his brother's regiment in the early 1770s and was the unit's second in command with the rank of lieutenant colonel when he arrived in Rhode Island in 1780. During the siege of Yorktown, Deux-Ponts personally led the French attack on Redoubt No. 9 on the evening of October 14, 1781. In a conspicuous display of bravery, he and

Guillaume, Comte de Deux-Ponts

his comrades stormed the British strong point in the fortifications and seized the key position from its defenders. Deux-Ponts, in a Gallic comment, wrote of the occasion: "That moment seemed to me very sweet, and was very elevating to the soul and animating to the courage." He was wounded during the action when a musket ball ricocheted near his face as he looked over the parapet. He returned to France shortly after Cornwallis' surrender. The French Revolution dislocated his career, and he went to the Bavarian court along with his brother, where he served as captain of the bodyguard of the King of Bavaria. *Further reading:* Comte Guillaume de Deux-Ponts, *My Campaigns in America: A Journal Kept by Count William de Deux-Ponts, 1780–81,* Samuel A. Green, trans. (Boston, 1868).

DE WEES, Samuel (b. 1760) Soldier

An enlisted man who left an enlightening memoir of his service as a teenager during the Revolution, De Wees was born near Patton's Furnace in Berks County, Pennsylvania. His father was a poor maker of leather breeches and a part-time collier in the local mines. At age five De Wees was bound out by his father to a Quaker farmer, who according to De Wees was an evil taskmaster and child beater. At the beginning of the Revolutionary War, De Wees joined his father and brothers in the enlisted ranks of a Pennsylvania regiment, acting as a fifer and caring for the wounded (a typical battlefield assignment for bandsmen or regimental musicians). He was a hospital attendant at the battle of Brandywine in September 1777 and wrote later of his impressions: "To hear the wild and frantic shrieks of the wounded, the groans of the dying, and to see the mangled and bloody state of the soldiers upon the arrival of the wagons,—to see the ground all covered over with the blood, and blood running in numbers of places from the wagon bodies, was enough to chill the blood in the warmest heart. . . ." De Wees was apparently attached to the 11th Pennsylvania Regiment at the time of Brandywine, but soon after the battle his father died of smallpox and the young man was again bound out to the same Quaker. Later in the year, he returned to the regiment as a "waiter" for the commander, Colonel Richard Humpton. The 11th was merged into the 10th Pennsylvania in mid-1778. After the war, De Wees moved to Maryland, and he later served in the Maryland militia during the Indian wars. *Further reading:* Samuel De Wees, *A History of the Life and Services of Samuel De Wees . . . ,* John S. Hanna, ed. (Baltimore, 1844).

DE WITT, Charles (1727–1787) Delegate to Congress, editor, state official

Born at Kingston, New York, De Witt was the editor of the *Ulster Sentinel* as well as a member of the colonial assembly before the Revolution. He was active in local patriot affairs in 1775 and 1776, sitting on the committee of safety and attending the New York Provincial Congress. In 1784, De Witt was selected as a delegate from New York to the Confederation Congress. He helped draft the state constitution for New York.

DE WITT, Simeon (1756–1834) Cartographer

De Witt provided valuable mapmaking services to George Washington, particularly during the crucial campaigns of 1781. He was born in Ulster County, New York, the son of a physician of Dutch descent and a French Huguenot mother. He studied privately in Schenectady, New York and then went to Queen's College (now Rutgers) in New Jersey, but the Revolutionary War interrupted his studies (he was later awarded a degree retroactive to 1776). He returned home, but in 1777, he joined a local volunteer militia company and fought in the American campaign that defeated Burgoyne. After the British surrender at Saratoga, De Witt went back to private study of mathematics and surveying.

In July 1778, De Witt was recommended by his uncle, General James Clinton, to become an assistant to Robert Erskine, who had just been named the official cartographer to the Continental Army. Few reliable maps of the colonies existed at the beginning of the Revolution, and the British had almost the only military maps. American commander in chief George Washington had asked Congress to appoint a competent mapmaker, and Erskine—a recent emigrant from Scotland—was chosen. The new official cartographer offered De Witt a salary of two dollars a day and the use of a horse, and the young man accepted. He worked as Erskine's assistant for the following two years, making maps and surveys as requested by Washington. In October 1780, Erskine died, and De Witt succeeded him as Geographer and Surveyor-General of the Continental Army.

In August 1781, Washington directed De Witt to survey and prepare maps for the march south to Virginia. De Witt carried out the assignment brilliantly and in a matter of weeks provided the commander in chief with maps accurate enough to guide the allied French and American forces to victory in the south. De Witt himself was present with the army before the fortifications at Yorktown. De Witt retired from service along with the rest of the Continental Army in 1783. The maps he had prepared for the military comprised the best and most detailed maps available for large portions of the new nation, and De Witt asked Congress to publish his work. Unfortunately, Congress was flat broke and turned down the request. De Witt returned to New York and continued working as a surveyor and mapmaker—he had been previously named surveyor general of the state—for the next 50 years. He produced a comprehensive map of New York state in 1802, which was the basis for regional cartography for several generations. *Further reading:* Walter W. Ristow, *Simeon De Witt: Pioneer American Cartographer* (Washington, D.C., 1969).

DICK, Samuel (1740–1812) Delegate to Congress, physician, militia officer, Continental surgeon

Born in Maryland, Dick went to Scotland for a formal education in medicine. He returned to America in 1770 and settled into a practice in Salem, New Jersey. He sat in the New Jersey Provincial Congress of 1776 and was appointed colonel of the Salem County militia during the same year. His active field service during the war, however, was as an assistant surgeon on the Canadian expedition of 1776. He was a member of the state

John Dickinson

assembly in New Jersey and in 1778 was appointed collector of customs for the western district of the state. He was sent as a delegate to the Confederation Congress in 1784 and 1785. He was also a delegate to the state convention to consider the federal constitution and was a surrogate judge in his home county from 1785 until 1804.

DICKINSON, John (1732–1808) Delegate to Congress, militia officer and soldier, state official

Dickinson was one of the important moderates before the actual break with England—a break he consistently opposed—and was widely admired then and since for his writing, yet once the Revolution got under way in earnest, Dickinson's position lost most of its relevance and he his influence. He served two colonies during his career: Pennsylvania and Delaware.

Born in Talbot County, Maryland, he studied law in Philadelphia and subsequently at the Middle Temple in London from 1753 until 1757. He opened a law practice in Philadelphia and became a member of the Delaware assembly in 1760. Two years later, he moved to the Pennsylvania legislature, but since he supported the proprietary colonial government in opposition to Franklin and Galloway, he lost his seat in 1764 and did not return until 1770. In 1765, the legislature appointed him to the Stamp Act Congress, where he drafted the declaration requesting repeal of the Stamp Act. He was consistent in his view of the dispute with Britain: Dickinson be-

lieved in the long-established rights of Englishmen; the attempts to tax and restrict the colonials were therefore violations and innovations that should be opposed, but not to the point of violence or separation. Responding to the Townshend Acts of 1767, Dickinson published *Letters from a Farmer in Pennsylvania*, which in masterful prose disputed England's right to tax the colonies and advocated nonimportation of goods from Great Britain but at the same time urged conciliation. In 1774, he served as chairman of the committee of correspondence and was selected as a delegate to the first Continental Congress. Ever the advocate of remaining within the British fold, he drafted the unsuccessful Olive Branch Petition of 1775.

As an advocate of reconciliation and peace he voted against the Declaration of Independence, but nonetheless once it was passed, Dickinson turned out to fight—which was more than most congressmen did. He was a colonel of Philadelphia militia and led his troops during the campaign in New Jersey, although he resigned soon after when he lost his seat in Congress. He was elected to Congress again in late 1776, from Delaware this time, but declined to take his seat and withdrew to his farm in Delaware. He apparently served as a private soldier in a militia company at the battle of Brandywine but then took a commission as a brigadier general of militia. He was again elected to Congress from Delaware in 1779 but served only a short while before resigning. In 1781, he became president of the Supreme Executive Council of Delaware, and from 1782 to 1785 he served as president of the Supreme Council of Pennsylvania. In 1786, he was president of the Annapolis Convention, and Delaware sent him as a representative to the constitutional convention in 1787. In a series of letters signed "Fabius," he advocated adoption of the Constitution. Dickinson died in Wilmington, Delaware. Dickinson College, which he helped to found in 1783, is named in his honor. *Further reading:* Michael E. Flower, *John Dickinson: Conservative Revolutionary* (Charlottesville, Va., 1983); David L. Jacobson, *John Dickinson and the Revolution in Pennsylvania, 1764–1776* (Berkeley, Calif., 1965).

DICKINSON, Philemon (1739–1809) Militia general, delegate to Congress

Dickinson, the brother of John Dickinson, was an active and effective militia commander in the northern theater, one of the few militia officers to make strong contributions to Washington's campaigns over a long period of time. He was born in Maryland, where his father had large estates, and was educated at the College of Philadelphia (the University of Pennsylvania). He read law with his distinguished elder brother, but early in his adult life he managed his father's lands in Delaware and Maryland.

At the beginning of the Revolution, Dickinson lived on his own estate near Trenton. He was appointed as colonel of one of the battalions raised by New Jersey in early 1775 and in October was commissioned as brigadier general of the state militia. He also was elected as a member of the New Jersey Provincial Congress in 1776. He seldom led trained or seasoned troops during the war but used whatever volunteers came to hand. He was an aggressive raider and often provided good reconnaissance for the Continental Army and harassed British movements. In 1776 and 1777, Dickinson led successful raids against British foraging parties, most notably in January 1777 when he captured 40 wagons and 100 British horses near Somerset, New Jersey. He resigned briefly in the same year but was named major general and commander of New Jersey militia in June. He raided Staten Island in 1778, and his militiamen scouted the advance of the British army from Philadelphia in 1778 and provided the first contact and reports prior to the battle of Monmouth after destroying bridges and roads in front of Clinton's column. A year later, he nipped at the edges of Baron von Knyphausen's advance toward Springfield.

He was elected to Congress in 1782 as a delegate from Delaware, where he owned considerable land. At the end of the war, Dickinson served on the New Jersey Council, although he was defeated several times by William Livingston for the office of governor. In 1785, he served as one of the members of the commission to select a site for the new national capital, and in 1790–93 he became a U.S. senator, filling an unexpired term when William Paterson became New Jersey governor.

DICKSON, Joseph (1745–1825) Soldier, legislator

Dickson was a North Carolina cotton and tobacco planter who sat on the local Rowan County Committee of Safety before the Revolution. In 1775, he is reported to have been commissioned as a captain in the Continental Army, but without mention of which unit. In 1780, he was acting as an officer with back-country militia and led troops at the battle of King's Mountain. One biographical writer claims Dickson was a brigadier general by the end of the war, but there is no mention of his name among brigadiers appointed to the Continental Army, so the commission was probably in the state militia. Dickson served in the North Carolina senate following the Revolution and was elected to the U.S. House of Representatives in 1801. At the end of his term in Congress, he moved to Tennessee, set up a plantation north of Murfreesboro and served in the Tennessee House of Representatives as speaker.

DIGBY, Robert (1732–1814) British admiral

Digby was the last British naval commander in chief of the American station, but he arrived after the war was in effect over. The grandson of a baron and the younger brother of an earl, he commanded a 60-gun ship of the line, the *Dunkirk*, during the Seven Years' War, taking part in the battle at Quibiron Bay in 1759. Like most senior British commanders, he also sat in Parliament. In 1778, he moved to a larger ship, the *Ramillies*, and was in the engagement off Ushant, which eventually led to his involvement in the court-martial of Admiral Hugh Palliser and the latter's quarrel with Admiral Keppel. Digby progressed then to second in command of the Channel Fleet and of the expedition in 1779 to relieve Gibraltar. He was assigned in August 1781 as commander in America, but he arrived at New York aboard the *Prince George* just as his predecessor, Thomas Graves, was departing with a fleet for the Chesapeake to meet Admiral De Grasse and the French. Digby allowed Graves to continue in command and remained in New York. Graves was unsuccessful, however, Cornwallis subsequently surrendered, and warfare in North America came to an end, so Digby had little to do and few ships to command. He returned to England in 1783 and eventually reached the rank of full admiral in 1794.

DONOP, Carl Emil Kurt von, Count (1740–1777) German mercenary officer

A brave soldier but a poor tactician, von Donop commanded the German jaeger corps hired by the British from Hesse-Cassel. He arrived with four battalions of jaegers and grenadiers at Long Island in August

1776 with other German troops under von Hiester in time to join the fight against Washington in New York. With the American withdrawal through New Jersey, von Donop was assigned by British commander William Howe to garrison the outpost towns near the Delaware during the winter. He was near Bordentown in late December when Washington destroyed Rall at Trenton, and von Donop prudently withdrew his force to Princeton at news of the American victory. In October of the following year, von Donop was detached from the main British army and sent to take Fort Mercer at Red Bank, New Jersey, one of the Delaware River forts still in American hands. The strong point was thinly held by Rhode Islanders under Christopher Greene, but the fortifications were good—a new interior wall reduced the area the defenders needed to cover—and Greene was a fine commander. Von Donop showed either contempt for his foe or poor judgment in his attack. He sent half his force to assault from one direction and led the second division himself against the wall of the fort. He arrived at the base of the fortifications and discovered he had no ladders to make the final climb. At that point the Americans opened fire at close range and virtually annihilated the Germans. Von Donop took a mortal wound in the leg.

DOOLITTLE, Amos (1754–1832) Engraver Born in Cheshire, Connecticut, Doolittle lived most of his life in New Haven. He served in a militia unit during the Revolution but was best known for his engravings of patriot images. In 1775, he executed four copper-plate engravings of the "Battle of Lexington and Concord" and later engraved illustrations featuring portraits of Washington, Jefferson and John Adams.

DORCHESTER, Lord. See CARLETON, Guy.

DOUGLAS, William (1743–1777) Officer Douglas was born in Plainfield, Connecticut and received a commission in 1775 as a major of the state militia. Having previously fought in the battles of Long Island, White Plains and Harlem Heights, he took command as colonel of the 6th Connecticut Regiment of the Continental Line when the unit was organized in January 1777. Later in the same year, Congress appointed him commodore of Lake Champlain, but he died within a few months from tuberculosis.

DOWNER, Eliphalet (1744–1806) Naval surgeon Born in Connecticut, Downer practiced medicine in Brookline, Massachusetts before the war. He served as a surgeon aboard the privateer *Yankee* and was captured by the British and transported to prison in England. He escaped to the Continent in 1777 and again sailed as a surgeon, this time aboard the sloop *Dolphin*. While serving on the *Lexington,* he was captured again and again escaped. In 1779, he was a surgeon on the ill-fated Penobscot Expedition.

DOXTADER, John. Loyalist raider Doxtader led loyalist and Indian raids in the border region of New York state in 1781. He surprised the settlers of Currytown, New York, near Canajoharie, on July 9 and burned the town while the inhabitants hid in nearby fields. However, the following day he was assaulted at his camp at Sharon Springs by Americans under Marinus Willet and Robert McKean. Although outnumbered nearly two to one, the Americans drew Doxtader and his men out of their positions and killed 40 with a devastating double flank attack. Doxtader fled the scene.

DOYLE, John (c. 1750–1834) British officer Born in Ireland, Doyle entered the British army in 1771, and in 1775, he went to Boston with the 40th Regiment as part of the reinforcement for the garrison. He fought in the campaign in New York and is reported to have personally rescued James Grant (then lieutenant colonel of the 40th) during a battle at Brooklyn. Doyle continued service through the battles of Brandywine and Germantown. He met Lord Rawdon in 1777 and assisted him in raising the Volunteers of Ireland (eventually designated the 2nd American and then the 105th Regiment) from among loyalists of Irish descent. Doyle was a captain of the new unit at Monmouth and went south with the Volunteers when they were assigned to the expedition against Charleston in 1779. He was promoted to major during the campaign against American partisans in the Carolinas in 1780 and 1781 and served with distinction at Camden and Hobkirk's Hill. After the Revolution, he returned to Ireland and sat in the Irish Parliament. He eventually became a distinguished British commander, rising to the rank of full general before his death and taking a leading role in several campaigns during the wars against the French.

DRAPER, Margaret (c. 1730—1807) Loyalist publisher

The wife of loyalist Boston newspaper publisher Richard Draper, Margaret took over his strongly pro-British *Massachusetts Gazette and Boston News Letter* on his death in 1774. She continued the paper's vigorous loyalist editorial policy until the withdrawal of the British forces in 1776. During the siege of the city by the Americans, hers was the only paper published in Boston. She emigrated to England by way of Halifax.

DRAPER, Mary. Patriot

Mary Draper lived near Dedham, Massachusetts. Her role in the Revolution was small in the overall scheme of the struggle, but she must have been typical of many such otherwise anonymous women who contributed to the American cause. She was a farm wife whose prosperous husband was a captain in the rural militia. When, in April 1775, the British sent an expedition against the patriots that resulted in the first skirmishes at Lexington and Concord, Captain Draper seized his weapon and joined the hundreds of minutemen who flocked to harass the British retreat. Meanwhile, Mary Draper set up a roadside buffet for militiamen who passed by on their way to the fight. She, her daughter and the household servants prepared and handed out bread, cheese and cider to any and all amateur soldiers who traveled the road that day toward Boston with muskets in hand. As a 19th-century writer described the scene: "Thus were the weary patriots refreshed on their way."

DRAYTON, William Henry (1742—1779) Delegate to Congress, jurist

An officeholder under the royal colonial government, Drayton became one of the most active patriots in South Carolina in the months just before the Revolution. He was born on an estate near Charleston (the nephew of royal lieutenant governor William Bull on his mother's side) and went to England for his education. He attended Westminster School and graduated from Oxford. On his return to South Carolina, Drayton married and began the practice of law in 1764. He soon moved into important positions in the colony, sitting in the assembly. He at first opposed the resistance in the colony to the crown, writing a

pamphlet that condemned the nonimportation agreements. During a 1770 visit to England, Drayton was received warmly by the government, which viewed him as a defender of the royal cause, and he was appointed as a royal privy councillor for the colony and as a member of the Governor's Council.

After his return to Charleston, however, Drayton came to realize he would likely be superseded by officials sent out from Great Britain, and he began to protest publicly about the inequity of depriving native Americans of power in the colonies. As a result, he was removed from office, and he turned into an ardent patriot. Drayton began to organize resistance and even toured the back country to rally support for opposition to the royal government. He was elected president of the South Carolina Provincial Congress in November 1775 and argued vigorously for South Carolina's participation in the war of rebellion. The following March, he was appointed as chief justice of South Carolina under the new state government. He was sent to Congress as a delegate in 1778 and was most noted there for chairing a committee that dealt with George Johnstone of the Carlisle Commission. Drayton died in Philadelphia of typhoid while sitting in Congress. *Further reading:* William M. Dabney and Marion Dargan, *William Henry Drayton and the American Revolution* (Albuquerque, N.M., 1962).

DUANE, James (1733—1797) Delegate to Congress, attorney, land speculator

Duane was a leader of the conservative faction in Congress and an effective politician who urged that the Revolution move slowly and deliberately. A native of New York City and the son of a well-to-do merchant, he studied law privately and set up a practice in New York in 1754. He was immensely successful as a lawyer, building a reputation as one of the city's leading advocates and as being unafraid to cross legal swords with the royal government. He was cautious about extralegal protests, however, and helped quiet mob violence during the Stamp Act crisis in 1765.

Duane never really wavered in his support of the patriot cause, but he almost always wanted measures to proceed at a deliberate pace with all options being examined before taking judgment. He might well be described as a prudent patriot. He was strongly in favor of the nonimportation agreements and when the time came to declare himself, he did not hang back. He was appointed to the New York Committee of Correspondence in May 1774, and he joined the subsequent patriot committees as soon as they were formed. In July 1774, Duane was selected as one of the five New York delegates to the first Continental Congress, despite some opposition from the more radical elements among New York patriots. During the first session of Congress he called for moderation and supported Joseph Galloway's plan for compromise with the royal government. He also did a good deal of valuable committee work. The New York Provincial Congress selected Duane to serve again when the Continental Congress was called for a second time, and he served almost continuously until the end of the war. He maintained his moderate views all the while, which in 1781 got him in trouble when a local Philadelphia paper accused him of wavering loyalty. Statements in his support came from all the prominent politicians of New York and the New York assembly gave him a vote of confidence, so the accusations soon disappeared.

While in Congress, Duane used his influence in typical 18th-century fashion to further his personal economic interests. He was an owner of large tracts of land in the Vermont section of New Hampshire that was long in dispute between settlers there and the hated "Yorkers." Duane defended the claims of New York owners in the courts and did much to frustrate the efforts of Vermonters to establish a separate state. New Hampshire agreed to Vermont's separation, but Duane and other politically powerful New Yorkers stalled congressional recognition until long after the Revolution, hoping to firm up their land titles. His delaying tactics only prolonged the controversy, however, and he eventually lost most of the land he claimed in Vermont when the region finally became a state in 1791.

At the end of the Revolution and the evacuation of New York City by the British, Duane was appointed to the new Council of Governor Clinton and became mayor of the city. He also served as a judge and was appointed as justice of the first federal district of New York when a new court system was established under the Constitution in 1789. Late in life he moved to an estate in Duanesburg, part of his large holdings in the Mohawk Valley. *Further reading:* Edward P. Alexander, *A Revolutionary Conservative: James Duane of New York* (New York, 1938).

DUBUYSSON, Charles François, Vicomte (1752–1786) French volunteer officer

A veteran officer of the French Army, Dubuysson came to America after his discharge from French service in 1777 with Lafayette and de Kalb. He received a commission as a major in October 1777 and became de Kalb's aide-de-camp. Promoted to lieutenant colonel in 1778, Dubuysson was at de Kalb's side at the battle of Camden, when the general was mortally wounded in a futile stand after Horatio Gates had fled the scene, and Dubuysson himself was severely wounded. He wrote to American generals Smallwood and Gist after de Kalb's death, passing on the general's dying gratitude for their stand on the field at Camden. Dubuysson's own health was broken by his wounds, however, and he returned to France where he eventually died several years later of the long-term effects of his injuries.

DUCHE, Jacob (1738–1789) Clergyman, turncoat loyalist

Duche performed one of the more public if relatively harmless feats of turnabout during the Revolution. He was the son of a prosperous Philadelphia merchant and was among the first students at the new College of Philadelphia, graduating in 1757. He went to England for a year at Cambridge University and returned to Philadelphia as a deacon in Anglican orders. A fine speaker, he taught oratory at his alma mater and assisted in the yoked parishes of Christ Church and St. Peters until 1762, when he went to England again for full ordination to the priesthood. Back in Philadelphia and married, he won a large following as a popular preacher.

In 1776, Duche became rector of the two churches in Philadelphia and was appointed in July as the chaplain to the Continental Congress. His public utterances and privately expressed sympathy all seemed to be with the patriot cause, and his popularity made him a good political choice to offer prayers over the deliberations of the congressmen. He held the post only until October, however, when he resigned. When the British occupied Philadelphia the following year, Duche was arrested as a patriot and held briefly. On October 8, 1777, he wrote a long letter to George Washington in which he damned Congress, the army and the entire American enterprise. Duche insulted most of the New England delegates and declared that the officers and men of the army had neither courage nor principle. He urged Washington to rescind the Declaration of Independence and negotiate for peace. Washington was astounded by the letter and immediately released it to Congress, which made the text public in all the colonies. Duche was everywhere denounced as a traitor. Two months later, he sailed for England, where he became the chaplain and secretary of an insane asylum. The Pennsylvania legislature proscribed him and confiscated his property. In 1792, however, the laws of banishment were rescinded, and Duche returned to Philadelphia, where he died.

DUDLEY, Ambrose. Militia officer

Dudley, a colonel of Virginia militia, was taken by surprise outside of Charles City Court House in January 1781 by a cavalry troop under John Simcoe during Benedict Arnold's campaign in Virginia. Even though Dudley's force outnumbered the British by at least three to one, he was routed after a brief skirmish and his men scattered.

DUER, William (1747–1799) Delegate to Congress, land speculator

One of the speculative high rollers of the Revolutionary period, Duer was born in England to a wealthy family that owned large plantations in the West Indies. He attended Eton, then served in the British army in India, although he resigned in the mid-1760s when he inherited his father's wealth. He traveled to North America in 1768 to purchase lumber (he had a contract to supply masts and timber to the Royal Navy) and was persuaded by Philip Schuyler to purchase forest lands along the upper Hudson. He emigrated to New York permanently in 1773.

Despite his recent arrival, Duer was a patriot and threw himself into the ferment of the times with vigor. He was a delegate to the New York Provincial Congress in 1775 and the state constitutional convention the following year. He also joined the New York Committee of Public Safety and held a militia commission, although he apparently never actually served in a military role. In 1777, Duer was selected as one of New York's delegates to the Continental Congress, where he served for two years as an active and vocal member. He supported Washington during the so-called Conway Cabal controversy despite an illness that kept him away from congressional sessions. He resigned from Congress in 1779—the same year he married American general Lord

Stirling's daughter Catherine (known as "Lady Kitty")—in order to expand his business interests, but he maintained a public role as a judge and commissioner to look into conspiracies in New York.

His financial empire grew rapidly at the end of the Revolution, and by the mid-1780s he was a very rich man with land holdings throughout New York and New England and interests in several banking concerns. One of his largest schemes was the Scioto Company, a rather grandiose venture to buy western lands from the government and sell them to foreign investors. Not surprisingly, Duer supported a strong central government and the fiscal policies of Alexander Hamilton, who was his close friend. With the establishment of a new federal government in September 1789, Duer was appointed assistant secretary of the U.S. Treasury under Hamilton, but he served only six months before resigning. He continued to expand his financial holdings over the following two years, but in 1792 disaster struck. Duer was accused of irregularities while in office as assistant secretary and was sued by the federal government. His entire business empire collapsed at a stroke and he was thrown into prison as a debtor. He never recovered from the blow and died in prison seven years later.

DULANY, Daniel (the Younger) (1722–1797) Loyalist attorney, writer

A powerful writer and recognized even by his opponents as one of the best lawyers in the colonies, Dulany early supported colonial rights against British taxation but turned loyalist with the actual coming of the Revolution. He was the oldest son of Daniel Dulany the Elder, who had come to America early in the century and established a highly prosperous legal practice and business empire in Annapolis, Maryland.

The younger Dulany went to England for his education at Eton, Cambridge and the Middle Temple. He returned to Maryland in 1747 and embarked on a brilliant career as an attorney and public official. He was a gifted speaker and writer, and he rapidly established a reputation as a superb advocate. He built on the wealth accumulated by his father and by the 1760s was one of the foremost citizens of the colony, sitting in the assembly and on the colonial Council and holding the office of attorney general.

He was opposed to the Stamp Act and wrote a well-reasoned pamphlet in 1765 called *Considerations* on the Propriety of Imposing Taxes in the British Colonies for the Purpose of Raising a Revenue by Act of Parliament, in which he refuted the notion that the American colonies benefited from virtual representation in Parliament and claimed they should therefore be free of taxation. The pamphlet gave Dulany a place as a defender of colonial liberties, but he was no radical revolutionary, and as the rebellious fever in Maryland heated, he moved more and more toward the loyalist side. In 1770, after the Maryland legislature passed laws reducing the income of royal officials, Dulany wrote a series of published letters under the name "Antilon" that attacked the right of the colony to denigrate the royal prerogatives. The opposing view was taken by Charles Carroll of Carrollton writing as "First Citizen." The literary debate damaged Dulany's standing in Maryland and drove him into political exile as an overt loyalist. He retired to an estate near Baltimore and much of his wealth was confiscated in 1781. *Further reading:* Aubrey C. Land, *The Dulanys of Maryland: A Biographical Study of Daniel Dulany the Elder (1685–1753) and Daniel Dulany the Younger (1722–1797)* (Baltimore, 1955).

DUMAS, Charles William Frédéric (1721–1796) Dutch diplomat

Dumas was a strange character who became involved in American affairs in Europe during the Revolution. He was born in the German principality of Ansbach to French émigré parents. He may have lived in Switzerland for a time, and he arrived in the Netherlands about 1750. He was a man of considerable erudition who made his living as a sort of free-lance tutor and translator. He was also a romantic and a great letter writer.

During the early 1770s, Dumas established a copious correspondence with many leaders of the American Revolution, impressing men like Benjamin Franklin and John Adams with his depth of learning and his fervor for the American cause. Based on their pre-Revolution exchange of letters, Franklin decided Dumas would be useful as a representative of the colonies to the government at The Hague, so in 1775 Franklin wrote to Dumas with a congressional appointment as the American Agent to the Dutch Republic. Dumas embraced the role with abandon, and his subsequent letters reveal a highly romanticized attachment to a fuzzy vision of America and the possibilities of the Revolution. For a short while, Dumas cloaked his activities on behalf

Mathieu, Comte de Dumas

of America, but by the fall of 1776, the British knew all about his position. Dumas assisted Adams when the latter appeared in Holland to ask for Dutch support and loans, and he kept up a brisk correspondence with Franklin in Paris. The effectiveness of his efforts seems doubtful (most American diplomats regarded him as something of a busybody), but his commitment was irreproachable: he even took an oath of allegiance to the United States in 1782 and moved into the American embassy at The Hague. *Further reading:* J. W. Schulte Nordholte, *The Dutch Republic and American Independence* (Chapel Hill, 1982).

DUMAS, Mathieu, Comte de (1753–1837) French officer

Of obscure origins (not even explained in his memoirs), Dumas entered the French army in 1773 and served as a captain, apparently with engineer training, as part of General Rochambeau's expeditionary force to America. During the months before the movement to Yorktown, Dumas was an aide-de-camp to Rochambeau, but he received a field assignment during the siege and fought in the trenches as an engineering officer. After the surrender of Lord Cornwallis, Dumas remained in America for several months, not leaving until December 1782. During the French Revolution, he supported the king and was forced to flee the country during the Terror. He returned during the reign of Napoleon and served the empire as a soldier and an administrator.

DUNBAR, Moses (1746–1777) Loyalist officer

Born in Plymouth, Connecticut, Dunbar became known in Tory circles as the "loyalist Nathan Hale" after his execution at the hands of the state of Connecticut. At the time of the Revolution, he lived in Bristol, and he apparently recruited loyalists locally under a commission from Sir William Howe. He was arrested and tried by the Connecticut Superior Court in January 1777. He escaped briefly from jail but was caught and hung at a public execution on March 19. His widow fled to the British, remarried and eventually returned to Bristol after the war.

DUNDAS, Thomas (1750–1794) British officer

Perhaps from the Scottish outer islands (his father sat in Parliament for Orkney and Shetland), Dundas entered the British army in 1766 and was a major of the 65th Foot during his first assignment in America during 1776. He returned to Scotland the following year and became lieutenant colonel of the 80th Foot, a new regiment raised in Edinburgh. He arrived in New York with his new unit in August 1779 and contracted a near-fatal case of fever. He was dispatched to Virginia with Benedict Arnold in 1780, and he carried with him a secret commission from British commander in chief Sir Henry Clinton that authorized him and Major John Simcoe to take charge if Arnold should falter (none of the British really trusted Arnold). Dundas moved under the command of Cornwallis in 1781 and commanded a brigade at the battle of Green Spring. He retreated to Yorktown with the rest of Cornwallis' army and was commander of the British position on the Gloucester side of the river. He and Major Alexander Ross conducted negotiations on the terms of surrender on behalf of Cornwallis. After the American Revolution, Dundas advanced to the rank of major general and took part in the British capture of Martinique, St. Lucia and Guadaloupe from the French in 1794. He died of a fever on Guadaloupe. When the French retook the island, they dug up his body and exposed it to the elements and carrion-eating birds.

DUNLAP, John (1747–1812) Printer

A native of Ireland, Dunlap emigrated to Philadelphia as a boy in 1757, where he apprenticed to his uncle. He opened his own print shop in 1766 and began publishing the *Pennsylvania Packet* in 1771. He was active in the local Philadelphia militia as one of the officers of a troop of the Philadelphia City Cavalry. He is believed to be one of the printers who prepared the public version of the Declaration of Independence for distribution in July 1776. In 1778, he was an official printer to the Congress. He served after the Revolution on the Philadelphia Common Council and in the militia during the Whiskey Rebellion.

DUNMORE, John Murray, Earl of (1732–1809) Royal governor

One of the more contentious of the royal governors, Dunmore resisted the rebellion in Virginia with all his might but with little success. He was born into a noble Scots family (descended from the Stuarts) and inherited his title in 1756. He was chosen as one of the Scots peers to sit in the British House of Lords in 1761 and moved to London, where he partook of the rich political and social life of the capital.

In 1770, he was named as royal governor of New York and took up his post in October. Before a year was out, however, he was promoted to the post of royal governor of Virginia (the best plum in the colonies for a British official) and moved with his family to the governor's palace at Williamsburg. Despite a good beginning among the planter politicians of Virginia, Dunmore soon butted against the growing dissatisfaction and rebellion in the colony. A strong anti-British faction led by Patrick Henry succeeded in gathering surprising support in Virginia for the position of the radicals in Massachusetts, and in 1773, the House of Burgesses decided to set up a committee of correspondence to communicate with dissidents in other colonies. Lord Dunmore's response was to dissolve the legislature. He did the same a year later when the burgesses voted a day of fast and mourning in response to the punitive Boston Port Bill.

As tension continued to grow, Dunmore launched what may have been a diversionary measure by setting afoot an expedition against the Indians to the west. In September 1774, Dunmore led a large militia force into what is now West Virginia, intent on quelling the Shawnee led by Cornstalk. The colonial forces split, and on October 10 the column commanded by Colonel Andrew Lewis decisively defeated the Shawnee at Point Pleasant. Dunmore negotiated a settlement, bringing what is known as Lord Dunmore's War to a quick conclusion but not before providing valuable military experience for the Virginia militia, most of whom soon served on the patriot side in the War for Independence.

Back in Williamsburg, Dunmore found that the patriot tide was running high. He took vigorous action in April 1775 after the burgesses responded to Patrick Henry's "give me liberty or give me death" speech. Dunmore seized the colony's supply of gunpowder, which was in turn retaken by the Hanover County militia under the command of Henry. On June 1, Dunmore fled the colonial capital with his family for the safety of HMS *Fowey*. The conflict was fairly joined thereafter, and Dunmore attempted to stop the rebellion through force, although he had few resources at hand. He declared martial law and issued statements urging the colony's black slaves to rebel and form an army for the loyal British cause. He could have done little else more calculated to spread fear and loathing among the white slaveholders of Virginia, to whom the specter of a black uprising was the ultimate bugaboo. Dunmore assembled a military force, including a unit of black slaves known as Dunmore's Ethiopians, and on December 9 fought a battle with Continentals and militia under Colonel William Woodford at Great Bridge. The result was a disaster for Dunmore, who handled the fighting abysmally, and the patriot victory snuffed out British and loyalist resistance in Virginia for years to come. In January 1776, Dunmore ordered the destructive bombardment of Norfolk by the small British fleet and tried to follow with a drive toward the Chesapeake, but he was again defeated at Gwynn's Island in July and the British presence in Virginia was at an end for the time being. Dunmore withdrew his fleet, taking with it significant numbers of loyalists. He returned to England by way of New York. In 1787, after the American War, he was appointed governor of the Bahamas, serving until 1796. *Further reading:* James A. Hageman, *Lord Dunmore: Last Royal Governor of Virginia* (1974).

DUPLESSIS, Thomas. See PLESSIS, MAUDIT du.

DUPORTAIL, Louis Le Beque de Presle, Chevalier (1743–1802) French volunteer, Continental general   One of the more useful French volunteers and known to his American colleagues simply as General Duportail during his service in the Continental Army, Duportail was an aristocrat born in Pithiviers, France. In 1762, he became a

lieutenant and a student at the school of engineering at Mézières, graduating three years later. He was promoted to captain in 1773.

When Benjamin Franklin requested that the French government provide trained military engineers to help the American cause, Duportail was one of four the foreign ministry chose. Duportail reported for duty in the Continental Army on February 13, 1777; in July, he was made colonel of engineers backdated to February, and in November, he became a brigadier general and chief of engineers for the army. Duportail served in the Philadelphia campaign and was in charge of upgrading the forts on the Delaware River. He stayed with Washington through the winter encampment at Valley Forge and the campaign at Monmouth, and in June 1778 he was sent to strengthen the defenses at Philadelphia. In 1779, Duportail served in the Hudson Highlands and received the new title commandant of the Corps of Engineers and Sappers and Miners. In March 1780, he was put under Benjamin Lincoln's command but reached Charleston too late to be of significant service. Taken prisoner at the fall of Charleston in May 1780, Duportail was exchanged in October and eventually joined Washington for the Yorktown campaign. He was promoted to major general in November 1781.

Resigning from the Continental Army in October 1783, Duportail returned to France and assumed the post of brigadier general of infantry. In November 1790, Duportail became minister and secretary of state for war, a post he held for only a year. In January 1792, he was promoted to lieutenant general and given command of the Moulins region; but being a supporter of Lafayette, who was then under political suspicion, he was prevented from assuming this post. Charged with political disloyalty, he went into hiding for two years. He escaped to America, where he settled on a small farm near Philadelphia. Duportail's name was removed from the proscribed list in June 1797, but he died aboard ship while returning to France in 1802 and was buried at sea.

DURKEE, John (1728–1782) Officer   Durkee was born in Windham, Connecticut. He was an innkeeper and local justice of the peace in Norwich and served in the colonial legislature. During the Seven Years' War, he held the rank of major in the Connecticut militia. During the prewar agitation,

Durkee was an active patriot in the Sons of Liberty and a committee of correspondence. He was commissioned as a major in the Continental Army in 1775, eventually becoming colonel in command of the 4th Connecticut Regiment in 1777 and then commander of the reorganized 1st Connecticut in 1781.

DuSIMITIÈRE, Pierre Eugène (1726–1784) Artist, naturalist

DuSimitière was born in Switzerland and lived for several years in the West Indies before emigrating to New York City in 1765. He moved to New Jersey and finally settled in Philadelphia. He was an accomplished portraitist as well as a naturalist, and he became the curator of the American Philosophical Society in Philadelphia, a post he held during the Revolution. DuSimitière is best remembered for the portraits he painted (most of them subsequently engraved for wide distribution) of the major figures of the Revolution. The collection is one of the most complete by a contemporary artist.

DUVALL, Gabriel (1752–1844) Soldier, jurist, official

Duvall was born in Prince Georges County, Maryland. During the Revolutionary War he was a muster master and commissary for Maryland, and he then enlisted as a private in the state militia and saw action at Brandywine. Unusual for an enlisted militiaman, he was also a high-level politician, serving on the Maryland Governor's Council in 1783 and 1784. He moved from there to the state assembly and the U.S. House of Representatives. He was also the chief justice of Maryland and the comptroller of the U.S. Treasury. In 1812, Duvall was appointed as an associate justice of the U.S. Supreme Court, serving 22 years on the highest bench in the land.

DWIGHT, Timothy (1752–1817) Educator, clergyman, writer

Born in Northampton, Massachusetts, Dwight became one of the nation's most influential early educators and writers. He graduated from Yale in 1769 and took the post as headmaster of Hopkins Grammar School in New Haven, Connecticut. From 1777 to 1779, Dwight served as chaplain of Parsons' Connecticut Brigade. He returned in 1781 to Massachusetts and sat in the legislature until his ordination to the ministry of the Congregational Church in 1782. After the Revolution, Dwight began to publish epic poetry and other writings which earned him a place among the group of writers known as the "Hartford Wits." He became president of Yale in 1795 and served until his death 22 years later.

DYER, Eliphalet (1721–1807) Delegate to Congress, land speculator, jurist

A native and lifelong resident of Windham, Connecticut, Dyer was one of the principal speculators in the Wyoming Valley and a sponsor of the Connecticut settlement there. He graduated from Yale and opened a law practice in Windham in 1746. He was elected to the General Assembly the following year and served there continuously for 15 years. In 1753, he formed the Susquehanna Company to buy land in the isolated Wyoming Valley and negotiated a purchase from the Iroquois. Land titles in the region were disputed, however, and there ensued a long conflict over who owned land and who had political rights. Dyer promoted settlement by Connecticuters, but rivals from New York frustrated his efforts to gain control. He went to England in 1769 in an attempt to confirm his titles, but he failed, as did a commission on which he sat in 1773.

Meanwhile, Dyer became an active patriot, serving as a Connecticut delegate to the Stamp Act Congress in 1765. He was appointed a judge of the Connecticut Superior Court in 1766 and used his public position to further the patriot cause. He was selected as one of his colony's delegates to the first Continental Congress in 1774 and sat on the Connecticut Committee of Safety. Declining an appointment as a brigadier of the state militia, Dyer remained in Congress and hoped to use his influence to settle his Wyoming Valley land claims when the issue came before the body in 1782. He lost decisively when a congressional commission ruled against the Connecticut interests. Following the Revolution, Dyer was chief justice of the Connecticut Supreme Court.

E

EARLE, Ralph (1751–1801) Artist   Earle was born in Massachusetts, but he was best known for painting done while living in New Haven, Connecticut (where he worked as a portraitist before the Revolution). He gained a considerable reputation for his battle scenes of the war. He went to England in 1779 and worked as a portraitist, but sometime in the 1780s, he returned to America and painted in Massachusetts, Connecticut and New York.

EDEN, Robert, Sir (1741–1784) British royal governor   The final royal governor of Maryland, Eden was one of the more affable British officials in North America and left little rancor. The elder brother of William Eden, Sir Robert Eden was born in the north of England and entered the British army at age 14, seeing considerable service during the Seven Years' War. He married well—to Caroline Calvert, the sister of Lord Baltimore—and in 1768 was appointed governor of Maryland. He arrived in Annapolis in June of the following year, just in time to dissolve the colonial assembly before it could pass a protest against the Townshend Acts. He kept a mature balance in colonial politics, writing: "It has ever been my endeavor by the most soothing measures I could safely use, and yielding to storm, when I could not resist it, to preserve some hold of the helm of government, that I might steer as long as should be possible, clear of those shoals which all here must, sooner or later, I fear, get shipwrecked on."

Despite his evenhanded views toward the colonists' position and his mild defense of Maryland in reports to the government in London, he was correct to believe he could not survive the coming storm. One of his letters to Lord George Germain in early 1776 was intercepted and was interpreted by radicals to be anticolonial. The Continental Congress ordered his arrest, but the Maryland Committee of Safety demurred. Soon after this episode, however, Eden was ordered by London to admit armed forces to the colony, and in consequence he was asked by the patriots to leave. He did so peaceably (Maryland avoided almost all violence during the Revolution) in June 1776. After the war, he returned to settle a property claim and died suddenly in Annapolis. *Further reading:* Bernard C. Steiner, *Life and Administration of Sir Robert Eden* (Baltimore, 1898).

EDEN, William (1744–1814) British official   William Eden, brother of Maryland royal governor Sir Robert Eden, was the principal British spymaster for the Continent during the early part of the American War and a member of the infamous Carlisle Commission. He was educated at Eton (where he befriended Lord Carlisle) and Oxford before taking up the practice of law in London. He entered the government in 1774 as undersecretary of state and assumed responsibilities for British intelligence when the Continental Congress sent representatives to Paris. His principal spies among the Americans were Paul Wentworth and Dr. Edward Bancroft, both of whom were successful at infiltrating the heart of the American delegation. Eden often knew the contents of Silas Deane's, Benjamin Franklin's and Arthur Lee's discussions and letters long before officials in America. In 1778, Eden was named as one of the three members of the Carlisle Commission, headed by his school chum, and was sent to America to negotiate with Congress and to derail the Franco-American alliance. Eden's four-months-pregnant wife Elizabeth, daughter of loyalist New York lieutenant governor Andrew Elliot, went along on the voyage, and Lord Cornwallis was a passenger on the trip. When Eden and his fellow commissioners arrived in Philadelphia (still in British hands at the time), they found that Congress had resolved not to meet them. Eden probably had a part in the clumsy attempts that followed to bribe several congressmen and that resulted in a complete collapse of the mission. He and the others returned to England empty-handed. Following the Revolution, Eden went on to an illustrious career as a politician and was created Lord Auckland in 1793.

EDES, Benjamin (1732–1803) Editor, publisher

A native of Massachusetts, Edes founded the *Boston Gazette and Country Journal* in 1755 in partnership with John Gill. His paper was one of the most vociferous supporters of the pre-Revolution agitation in Boston and New England. Edes published editorials and propaganda by the radical leaders of Boston, including Samuel Adams and John Hancock. He was an active patriot himself as a member of the Sons of Liberty, and he is reputed to have been part of the Boston Tea Party in 1773.

EDWARDS, Pierpont (1750–1826) Delegate to Congress, jurist, official

Edwards was the eleventh and youngest child of famed New England preacher Jonathan Edwards and was brought up among the Stockbridge Indians, to whom his father served as a missionary. Throughout his life Edwards displayed an antipathy to organized religion and the Congregationalist Church in particular. He graduated from the College of New Jersey at Princeton in 1768 and set up in the practice of law in New Haven, Connecticut three years later. He reputedly served briefly while in the Connecticut militia during the war but was mostly occupied in his law practice and as a state legislator in 1777. He also

served in the legislature after the war and was a delegate to the final Confederation Congress in 1787–88. He served in several judicial posts and was an active politician in support of Jefferson and the Republicans after the turn of the century.

EGLESTON, Joseph (1754–1811) Officer

Egleston was born in Virginia and attended William and Mary, graduating in 1776 just as the war began in earnest. He became paymaster of the Continental Dragoons in March 1777, resigning eight months later. The following year, Egleston was commissioned a lieutenant in Henry Lee's Dragoons (soon to become Lee's Legion). He was captured by the British in 1780 at Elizabethtown, New Jersey but was exchanged and joined Lee in the Carolinas. He was noted for distinguished action at several battles, including Guilford Courthouse and Eutaw Springs. He ended the war as a major. He served several terms in the Virginia legislature following the Revolution and was a U.S. Congressman from his home state from 1798 to 1801.

ELBERT, Samuel (1740–1788) Continental officer, state official

Although himself a reasonably good officer, Elbert received little help for his hapless campaigns in the far southern theater of the war. He was born in South Carolina, orphaned early in life, and moved to Savannah, Georgia, where he became a prosperous merchant and Indian trader. He was active in the halting revolutionary movement in Georgia (many patriots in the youngest colony feared Indian attacks if they declared for the Revolution), serving as a Son of Liberty and on the first council of safety in 1775. He was a delegate to the Georgia Provincial Congress and was appointed to the committee that dealt with military affairs.

Elbert was commissioned as a lieutenant colonel in the Continental service in January 1776 and was sent on an expedition to seize East Florida. The campaign was hopelessly under-supported, and after taking Amelia Island, Elbert discovered that he had too few supplies to continue the effort against British positions on the mainland. He withdrew to Savannah and took over command of Continental forces in Georgia from Lachlan McIntosh. When General Robert Howe arrived in Georgia as the ranking Continental officer, he sent Elbert south to the Floridas again, and again Elbert was ill-equipped for a long campaign, although he succeeded in taking Fort Oglethorpe near Frederica. He and his men were recalled to Savannah and took part in its unsuccessful defense in 1778. In March 1779, Elbert and 100 of his Georgia Continentals formed part of the force assembled at Briar Creek under the incompetent American general John Ashe, who allowed British lieutenant colonel Mark Prevost to catch his entire force unprepared with its back to a swamp. Elbert and his men stood firmly against the British assault but were overwhelmed, and Elbert was wounded and captured. He was not exchanged until more than three years later, but he was free in time to command a brigade at the siege of Yorktown. He was brevetted a brigadier general at the time of his discharge in 1783. Following the war, he declined election to Congress but accepted the governorship of Georgia in 1785. *Further reading:* Charles C. Jones, *The Life and Services of the Honorable General Samuel Elbert of Georgia* (Cambridge, Mass., 1887).

ELLERY, William (1727–1820) Delegate to Congress, government official

One of the lesser-known congressional figures, Ellery was born in Newport, Rhode Island to a well-to-do merchant family. He graduated from Harvard and dabbled in commerce and public service (he was a naval officer of the colony and clerk for the General Assembly) before turning to the practice of law. He was active locally in several patriot committees and was selected as a delegate to the Continental Congress in May 1776 by the Rhode Island legislature. Although never prominent in congressional affairs, Ellery served almost continuously until 1786 and built up seniority and a solid if unspectacular record as a national legislator. He signed the Declaration of Independence in August 1776, although he thought the document to be the delegates' "death warrant." His primary role in Congress was on the committees that attempted to create and maintain a Continental Navy. In 1785, Ellery declined appointment to the Rhode Island Supreme Court in order to remain in Congress, but he resigned the following year to become commissioner of Continental loans in Rhode Island.

His own fortunes had suffered during the British occupation of his home city, and his house and business had been destroyed. He lived quietly and prosperously in the decades after the Revolution,

holding an appointment as collector of customs in Newport for 30 years. At his death at age 92 he was the second oldest living signer of the Declaration, survived only by Charles Carroll of Carrollton. The theologian William Ellery Channing and the writer Richard Henry Dana Sr. were his grandchildren. *Further reading:* William M. Fowler, *William Ellery: A Rhode Island Politico and Lord of the Admiralty* (Metuchen, N.J., 1973).

ELLIOT, Andrew (d. 1830) Loyalist official

Born in Scotland, Elliot emigrated to America in 1746. He long served the crown before the Revolution, and he remained in high office in New York throughout most of the war. During the 10 years before the outbreak of hostilities, he was collector of customs in New York City. When the British army occupied the city, he continued as customs officer and added many other ceremonial and functional offices, including duties as receiver general, superintendent of police and lieutenant governor. Elliot got on well with General William Howe, but when Sir Henry Clinton assumed the duties of commander in chief, Elliot's star rose even higher. His daughter, Elizabeth, was married to William Eden, one of the Carlisle peace commissioners and an influential British politician. At Eden's urging, Clinton appointed Elliot to the New York Council. Elliot also served as one of the three negotiators, led by General James Robertson, who tried to work out an exchange for Major John André after the spy's capture. Elliot was acting governor of New York from April 1783 until the final British evacuation in the fall. When the Americans regained control of New York, Elliot's property was seized. He and his family moved to England, where he received an annual pension of £480 for his services in America.

ELLIOT, John (d. 1808) British naval officer

Brother of New York lieutenant governor Andrew Elliot and uncle of the wife of William Eden, John Elliot was the commodore of the *Trident*, which carried Eden, Eden's wife Elizabeth (Elliot's niece), and the Carlisle Peace Commission to America in 1778. Elliot served as second in command to Admiral Richard Howe during the two-month stay of the commission. After his return to England, he took command of the *Edgar* and served with distinction under Admiral Sir George Rodney at the battle off Cape St. Vincent in January 1780. He commanded the Channel Fleet during the final two years of hostilities with the Americans and became governor of Newfoundland in 1786. He hoisted his flag as admiral in 1795 but had no further employment from the Admiralty.

ELLIS, Welbore (1713–1802) British official

Ellis was a veteran British politician and minister. The son of a bishop, he was educated at Westminster School and Oxford, and he served as a lord of the Admiralty and secretary for war before the American Revolution. He was out of office during the long administration of Lord North, but he came in as secretary of state in the new government after North's fall in February 1782, replacing Lord George Germain. He resigned when Rockingham came to power the next month.

ELLSWORTH, Oliver (1745–1807) Delegate to Congress, jurist

Beginning his career as an impoverished Connecticut country lawyer, Ellsworth became chief justice of the U.S. Supreme Court. He was born in Windsor, Connecticut and was intended by his father for the pulpit, but he left Yale after his sophomore year, graduated instead from Princeton, and soon thereafter threw over divinity for the law. His first years as an attorney in Windsor were bleak, however. He made a grand sum of three pounds in legal fees during his first three years in practice and had to resort to farming and woodcutting to support his wife.

He was a representative to the General Assembly, however, and he used this office and a move to Hartford to renew his career. After a few years in Hartford, Ellsworth had the largest legal practice in the colony and was a rich man. He entered patriotic activities in 1775 as a member of a commission to collect debts for Connecticut from the Continental Army and Congress. In 1777, he was selected to represent Connecticut in Congress, and he served there on a host of committees until 1783. He was a vigorous drafter of legislation and apparently worked hard at the duties of a legislator. He was appointed to the Connecticut Council of Safety in 1779, and he served as state's attorney and as a justice of the court of appeals. Ellsworth was prominent as a delegate to the federal constitutional convention in 1787 and strongly supported the new form of government when it came to the vote in his home state. He was selected as one of Connecticut's

first U.S. senators, serving from 1789 until 1796, when he was named as chief justice of the U.S. Supreme Court. His term as the highest judge of the land was not noted for brilliance, and his reputation probably suffered from being the immediate predecessor of John Marshall. He resigned from the court after three years and served briefly as a commissioner to France. *Further reading:* William G. Brown, *The Life of Oliver Ellsworth* (New York, 1905; reprint 1970).

ELMER, Jonathan (1745–1817) Delegate to Congress, physician, official

Elmer was born in Fairfield, New Jersey and graduated from the new medical school in Philadelphia in 1769 as one of the first physicians to be trained formally in the colonies. He practiced medicine before the Revolution in Bridgeton, New Jersey and held local office as a high sheriff and surrogate justice of the county. In 1775, Elmer was elected as captain of a local militia company of light infantry, but he never served in the field. Instead, he turned to politics and was sent as a delegate to the Continental Congress in 1777–1778 and again from 1781 to 1783. He was also a delegate to the Confederation Congress after the Revolution in 1787–1788. Following the establishment of the new federal government, Elmer was chosen as a U.S. senator from New Jersey, sitting from 1789 to 1791. He then returned to his home and sat intermittently as a judge of common pleas until shortly before his death.

ELPHINSTONE, George Keith (1746–1823) British naval officer

Rising to great prominence during the later Napoleonic wars, Elphinstone was one of the more effective junior commanders of the Royal Navy during the American Revolution. He was born in Scotland to a family of seafarers and sailed to China in 1767 aboard a ship captained by his brother. By the outbreak of the war in America, Elphinstone was captain of a frigate, the *Perseus*, which came to North American shores on convoy duty in 1776. He battled American privateers and blockade runners during the first years of the conflict, and he proved capable of cooperating effectively in joint land-sea operations, one of the weaknesses of other Royal Navy officers.

In 1779, he sailed from New York as part of Sir Henry Clinton's expedition to capture Charleston, South Carolina. The trip was miserable, with foul weather all down the long eastern American seaboard, but the force finally reached the intermediate destination of Savannah after a 38-day voyage. Elphinstone was familiar with the Charleston area and guided the fleet to a landing in February near North Edisto Inlet. He and Clinton worked well together, and Elphinstone was responsible for the naval operations that landed Clinton's main force above the city, cutting off the escape of the American army. Elphinstone returned to England later in 1780. He took command of the 50-gun *Warwick* and sailed back to American waters to continue blockade and commerce raiding duties.

Following the American war and a 10-year hiatus in his career due to ill health, Elphinstone returned to duty as a rear admiral when Britain was threatened by the naval wars of the French Revolution. He helped quell the naval mutinies of 1797 and was then given command of the Mediterranean fleet. In 1801, he and Sir Ralph Abercromby conducted the successful amphibious operation that defeated the French forces remaining in Egypt. During the balance of the wars with Napoleon, Elphinstone held the key commands in the North Sea and of the Channel fleet. He died rich in prize money and honors.

ENOS, Roger (1729–1808) Continental and militia officer

Born in Simsbury, Connecticut, Enos served as a colonial officer during the Seven Years' War and was a veteran soldier and major of the 2nd Connecticut Regiment at the outbreak of the Revolution in the spring of 1775. Promoted to lieutenant colonel, Enos commanded the 2nd Connecticut on the march north to Canada as part of Benedict Arnold's expedition. Like many of the New England troops on the horrible trek across the north woods, Enos and his men suffered severely from lack of supplies and the difficulties of an ill-organized movement over nearly impassable territory. At some stage, Enos ordered his regiment to leave the column and return home. In December 1775, he was court-martialed for leaving without orders, but he was acquitted. Nonetheless, he resigned his Continental commission and became a colonel in the Connecticut militia. In 1780, Enos moved to the Vermont region and became brigadier general of all Vermont militia. He was active in the political efforts to establish Vermont as a separate state (efforts frustrated until 1791 by the claims of New York).

ERSKINE, Robert (1735–1780) Mapmaker, engineer

Erskine provided crucial cartographic services to Washington's army during the Revolutionary War. He was born in Scotland, the son of a parson, and trained as an engineer. He moved to London and attempted to become a merchant, but his enterprises failed and Erskine only narrowly escaped debtors' prison. He turned to the study of hydraulics and was elected to the Royal Society on the strength of inventing a new centrifugal hydraulic engine. In 1771, he came to Rosewood, New Jersey as the representative of a British investor who owned the American Iron Company with mines and manufacturing facilities in the area. When the Revolution began four years later, Erskine became a firm patriot, organizing his ironworkers into a county militia company.

Among Erskine's talents was mapmaking, a rare and badly needed skill in the colonies. Most maps available to patriots were local in scope and suspect in accuracy. The only decent military maps were unpublished, hand-drawn copies in the possession of the British. By 1777, it was clear to George Washington that he and his commanders needed better maps, especially of the vital region between the Delaware River and the Hudson Highlands. Washington proposed to Congress in January 1777 that something concrete be done to remedy the situation, and six months later, he appointed Erskine as geographer and surveyor general of the Continental Army. Erskine hired an assistant, Simeon De Witt, and began immediately to survey the key areas of the middle states and prepare maps based on personal observation. Although his work was not entirely accurate by modern standards, Erskine produced during the next three years a series of more than 200 maps of New York, New Jersey, Connecticut and Pennsylvania. In 1780, Erskine contracted a fatal illness while working in the field and died, leaving the completion of his task to De Witt. *Further reading:* Albert H. Heusser, *George Washington's Map Maker: A Biography of Robert Erskine* (New Brunswick, N.J., 1966).

ERSKINE, William (1728–1795) British officer

Born in England, Erskine joined the British Royal Army as a teenager and by the end of the Seven Years' War was a highly experienced combat leader, having fought throughout Germany and with particular distinction at the battle of Elmendorf. He was a brigadier general by 1776 and commanded a brigade under General William Howe at the battle of Long Island in August 1776. The following year he was second in command to Governor William Tryon on the raid against towns on the Connecticut coast. For most of the war, however, Erskine was a high-level staff officer, and he acted as quartermaster general for Sir Henry Clinton when the latter took over as commander in chief in 1778. In the same year, Erskine was made the ceremonial colonel of a new regiment, the 80th Royal Edinburgh Volunteers, a post that involved no service but considerable income. He also took the field on occasion, as in 1778 when he commanded brief expeditions from the British base in New York City. He resigned as quartermaster general in 1779 and returned to England. He was made major general in the same year and was given the colonelcy of the 26th Cameronians in 1783. Erskine later commanded troops in the Flanders campaign.

ESTAING, Charles Henri Hector Théodat, Comte d' (1729–1794) French admiral

Although he was the principal French naval officer in American waters during an important period of the Revolution, d'Estaing was seldom effective. He was born in the Auvergne region and early entered military service, becoming a colonel while still a teenager and a brigadier general by age 27. As was common in the French service, his initial experience was as a land soldier but he also received significant commands at sea. He served in India, where he was captured and paroled by the British in 1759, captured again, and imprisoned at Portsmouth for parole violations. He was promoted to lieutenant general in 1763 and to vice admiral in 1777.

He was selected to command the French fleet sent to American waters in 1778 as the first significant French military force to fight in the Revolution. Unfortunately, his voyage from Toulon took nearly three months and he missed the opportunity to engage the British at the mouth of the Delaware, where much of Sir Henry Clinton's force was evacuating Philadelphia by sea—the first of several misadventures. Following the British to New York, d'Estaing dithered over whether his ships could cross the bar into Sandy Hook, and he eventually sailed away without making any attempt to attack. In August 1778, d'Estaing took part in what turned

Charles, Comte d'Estaing

out to be a disastrous Franco-American attempt to take Newport, Rhode Island. He failed to get along with the American commander, General John Sullivan, and d'Estaing's prickly European formality and snobbish attitudes led him to not only disparage Sullivan and the American troops but to bolt the scene at the first appearance of a British squadron and a storm. The dismal failure of the French navy to carry out planned land-sea operations and its tendency to leave in the middle of a campaign were, lamentably, characteristic for much of the war.

After Newport, d'Estaing sailed his fleet to the West Indies, but he was stymied there for the most part by British admiral John Byron. In September 1779, d'Estaing tried again when he sailed with a large land and sea force to Savannah, which was then in British hands. Although his force was greatly superior in numbers, d'Estaing failed to coordinate well with the American forces and foolishly let British general Augustine Prevost have sufficient time to ready his defense. Although he showed personal bravery in the assaults on the city, d'Estaing was largely responsible for the bloody repulse administered by the British. Following his repeated failure, d'Estaing returned to France in 1780. He was appointed to command a new combined French-Spanish fleet in 1783, but the war ended before he put to sea. With the coming of the French Revolution, d'Estaing remained loyal to the royal family, and his testimony on behalf of the queen resulted in his own condemnation and execution in April

1794. *Further reading*: Alexander A. Lawrence, *Storm over Savannah: The Story of Count d'Estaing and the Siege of the Town in 1779* (Athens, Ga., 1951).

ETTWEIN, John (1721–1802) Clergyman

Ettwein was one of the leaders of the Moravian sect in America. He was born in Germany and was a shoemaker before his conversion to the Moravian faith. He then became a missionary and emigrated to North America in 1754. He lived in North Carolina during the early 1760s but settled in Bethlehem, Pennsylvania in 1766 as an assistant to the local Moravian bishop. His loyalty was suspect early in the Revolution, and Ettwein was arrested by patriot authorities but soon was released. He then served as a chaplain to the army hospital in Bethlehem during 1776 and 1777. Ettwein was chosen by his denomination as an unofficial representative to the Continental Congress. In 1784, he became a bishop, serving until shortly before his death.

EUSTIS, William (1753–1825) Physician, official

Eustis was born in Cambridge, Massachusetts and graduated from Harvard in 1772. He studied medicine privately with Dr. Joseph Warren, one of the colony's leading patriots, and tended the wounded after the battle of Bunker Hill. Eustis served during the war as a surgeon at a hospital located in the former home of New York loyalist Beverly Robinson near West Point. After the war, he returned to his medical practice in Boston, but he began a political career in 1788 with his election to the Massachusetts state legislature and then to the U.S. Congress (after several failed attempts) in 1800. In 1807, President Thomas Jefferson named Eustis as U.S. secretary of war. This turned out to be a disastrous appointment and Eustis was blamed all-round for the failures of the military during the War of 1812. He nonetheless continued in political life and was elected governor of Massachusetts in 1823. He died from pneumonia shortly after taking office for a second term as governor.

EVANS, John. Delegate to Congress, jurist

Apparently a native of Delaware, although there is no record of his birth or death, Evans sat in the Delaware Assembly in 1774, 1775 and 1776. He was a delegate to the state constitutional convention in 1776 and was selected as one of the new state's delegates to the Continental Congress in November. He was in poor health, however, and declined to serve, although his credentials were presented in December. He withdrew as a delegate, never having appeared in Philadelphia. He was made a justice of the state supreme court the following year.

EVELEIGH, Nicolas (c. 1748–1791) Delegate to Congress, Continental and militia officer, government official

Although he was born in Charleston, South Carolina, Eveleigh was taken to England by his parents when he was seven years old and was educated there. He did not return to Charleston until 1774, but he was a firm patriot. In 1775, with the organization of troops for the defense of South Carolina, Eveleigh received a commission in the 2nd South Carolina Regiment, which was eventually taken onto the list of the Continental Army. At first, however, the South Carolina regiments served as state troops, and they were reorganized only a month before their defense of Charleston against an attempted invasion by Sir Henry Clinton in 1776. Eveleigh was at Fort Sullivan in the seaport's harbor on June 28 when the Americans repulsed the British fleet and frustrated the invasion. Eveleigh apparently did not accompany the new 2nd South Carolina when it marched north to join the main army of George Washington. In April 1778, he was named colonel of militia and deputy adjutant general for South Carolina and Georgia, but he resigned his military offices in August. He took a seat in the South Carolina assembly in 1781 and was named as a delegate to the Continental Congress later in the same year. With the establishment of the new federal government in 1789, Eveleigh was appointed as the first U.S. comptroller, and he died while serving in Philadelphia.

EWALD, Johann von (1744–1813) German mercenary officer, diarist

Ewald wrote one of the most valuable diaries left by any of the Hessian officers, and he was a notable battlefield leader who later wrote extensively on partisan military tactics based on his experiences in America. Despite the "von" in his name, he was not of noble birth, a fact that eventually disqualified him from promotion in his native Hesse.

He joined the army at age 16 and fought during several European campaigns of the 1760s. By 1774, having written a well-received manual on military tactics, Ewald was a captain of the second company of jaegers dispatched to America under the contract of the British government with the landgrave of Hesse-Cassel. Ewald and his detachment arrived in New York in October 1776 and immediately plunged into combat. The jaegers—armed with short-barreled rifles and trained in fighting among dense cover and forests—were among the best German troops employed by the British, and Ewald was obviously one of the better officers. He formed a close association with Lord Cornwallis and enjoyed the British general's good opinion and patronage during the ensuing years in America.

Ewald and his jaegers distinguished themselves many times during the 1777–78 campaigns in New Jersey and Pennsylvania, particularly at Brandywine (where Ewald led the envelopment by the British of Washington's right wing) and Monmouth. In 1780, Ewald was sent to the Carolinas as part of the British expedition against Charleston, and his subsequent eyewitness account of the siege and capture of the city is among the best contemporary writing on the topic. In 1781, he was with Arnold's force in Virginia and then was attached to Cornwallis' army that surrendered at Yorktown. He was paroled to Long Island after the American victory and almost died there from dysentery. He returned to Hesse in 1784.

For the following four years he served at the same rank and grade while writing extensively and gaining a reputation as one of Europe's experts on partisan warfare. His advancement in Hesse-Cassel having been blocked by lack of social connections, Ewald reluctantly left the service of his homeland in 1788 and received an appointment as an officer in the Danish army. He subsequently rose to the rank of major general and was granted a Danish title of nobility. He commanded key positions during the Napoleonic wars. The part of his diary covering the capture of Charleston was first published in 1938; his full diary came to light only after World War II. *Further reading:* Bernhard Uhlendorf, *The Siege of Charleston . . .* (Ann Arbor, Mich., 1938); Johann von Ewald, *Diary of the American War: A Hessian Journal,* Joseph P. Tustin, ed. (New Haven, Conn., 1979).

EWING, James (1736–1805) Militia officer, official Ewing was a native Pennsylvanian and served as a lieutenant in the colonial militia during the Seven Years' War. He was a member of the Pennsylvania assembly from 1771 to 1775. In 1776, he was commissioned as a brigadier general of Pennsylvania militia, but there is no record of actual field service during the war. He later sat in the state senate.

F

FAIRFAX, Bryan (d. 1802) Loyalist, clergyman
A member of a prominent Virginia family, Bryan Fairfax was a life-long friend of George Washington, despite loyalist leanings. He was originally a mild supporter of the patriot cause in Fairfax County, but he broke with the growing local anti-British sentiment in 1774 because he opposed the use of force in resisting the crown. Fairfax lived quietly during the war, serving as an Episcopal minister in the city of Alexandria. He was one of the first Anglican clergymen to embrace the new American Protestant Episcopal Church when it was organized in 1789. In 1781, following the death of a British relative, he inherited the title of Lord Fairfax of Cameron.

FAIRFAX, Thomas, Lord (Baron Fairfax of Cameron) (1693–1781) Loyalist Lord Fairfax was an unusual beast in revolutionary America: the putative proprietor of an incredibly huge tract of land and a resident peer of the realm in the New World. He descended from the Culpeper family who came into wealth and title during the Restoration. One of the gifts of Charles II to Thomas's ancestor was title to all of the ''Northern Neck'' of Virginia, roughly 5 million acres of land between the Potomac and the Rappahannock rivers. Thomas, who was born in Kent, was educated at Oxford early in the century, served in the Horse Guards and was a courtier of George I. He had long been in retirement from public life when he came to Virginia in 1735 to negotiate with the colonial legislature about challenges to his land titles. He apparently liked Virginia, since he emigrated permanently in 1745. Although in theory he was the owner of much of the colony, Fairfax took no part in colonial affairs, other than social, and he withdrew to an estate in the Shenandoah Valley, where he lived an unostentatious bachelor life. He was—not surprisingly—loyal to the crown during the Revolution, but he was entirely quiet about his sympathies and remained unmolested until his death shortly after the surrender at Yorktown. The Fairfax proprietary was confiscated, but the title passed to a collateral branch of the family in Alexandria, making Bryan Fairfax, a nephew at long remove and an otherwise unassuming parson, the eighth Baron Fairfax. *Further reading:* John E. Cooke, *Fairfax: or, the Master of Greenway Court . . .* (New York, 1868).

FANNING, David (1755–1825) Loyalist partisan leader Had he been a patriot instead of a loyalist, Fanning might well be remembered as the equal of such famous American fighters as Francis Marion, Thomas Sumter and Andrew Pickens. He was a persistent thorn in the side of the Americans during the vicious back-country civil war that raged in North and South Carolina, especially between the fall of Charleston in 1780 and the defeat of Cornwallis more than a year later. Fanning also wrote in later life almost the only useful narrative of the partisan war as seen from the loyalist side.

He was born in Amelia County, Virginia, orphaned in North Carolina at nine years of age and bound out by the local court to a harsh guardian. He suffered from a disfiguring scalp disease as a boy and wore a silk skull cap the rest of his life to hide his scarred head. Fanning moved to the western section of South Carolina in 1773 and became an independent farmer and Indian trader, learning all the back-country routes and hideaways. In early 1775, he was accosted by a band of "patriot" partisans who stole his trade goods—an incident he blamed for his decision to become a loyalist and indicative of the way local animosities colored the Revolution in the Carolinas. After rejecting a test oath of allegiance to the patriot cause in July 1775, Fanning joined a loyalist militia band under Robert Cunningham near Ninety-Six, South Carolina, but the loyalists in general were weak at this stage of the Revolution and Fanning was soon on the run. According to his own account, he was captured and either was released or escaped 14 times over the following three years. For a period in 1779 he was at peace with the patriots and even acted as their guide on occasion.

The successful British invasion of South Carolina in 1780, however, revived loyalist fortunes, and Fanning gathered a force under his command at a headquarters near Cox's Mill. From this stronghold he raided all over the Carolinas during the next year and a half, attacking patriot settlements and fighting miscellaneous bands of patriot militia. While they had success against other loyalist partisans, the Americans always seemed to arrive too late with too little to defeat Fanning, who moved quickly and struck hard. His most spectacular adventure was on September 12, 1781, when he captured nearly the entire patriot government of North Carolina—including the governor, the council, several legislators and many Continental officers—in a raid on Hillsborough. He was wounded the following day in a large battle near Lindley's Mill, but he escaped with his prisoners.

The fall of Yorktown sounded the knell for the Carolina loyalists, however, and by early in 1782, Fanning was ready to make peace. He married in April, disbanded his forces and fled to Charleston. From there Fanning and his young wife went to East Florida. After the peace treaty handed Florida back to the Spanish, Fanning evacuated to New Brunswick, Canada, where he sat in the provincial

Edmund Fanning

parliament and, except for an episode in 1801 when he was arrested, lived out his life in relative quietude. He wrote his narrative in 1790, although it was not published until the mid-19th century. *Further reading:* Lindley S. Butler, ed., *The Narrative of Colonel David Fanning* (Charleston, S.C., 1981).

FANNING, Edmund (1739–1818) Loyalist official, soldier   Fanning was a prominent loyalist in two states. Born on Long Island and educated at Yale, he moved to North Carolina in the early 1760s. He there became a close friend and associate of Governor William Tryon and was appointed to several lucrative offices in the colony, which he apparently used shamelessly to line his own pockets. Fanning was one of the major objects of public ire during the Regulator outbreak, although his evil reputation may have been due more to his close ties to Tryon than to any actual cruelty or depravity. He was seized and beaten by a Regulator mob in 1770, and his house was destroyed the next day. Fanning thereupon fled to New York, where Tryon had been appointed governor. He continued to stand high in the governor's favor, acting as his private secretary and receiving several well-paid official appointments. At the beginning of the conflict with the rebels, Fanning raised his own regiment of loyalist troops, known as the Associated Refugees or the King's American Regiment of Foot. He commanded the regiment throughout the Revolutionary War, serving in Rhode Island, New York and South Carolina. Fanning was twice wounded and gained a reputation among the British as a competent soldier. He moved to Nova Scotia following the Revolution and again repeated the pattern of officeholding. He sat on the provincial council and became lieutenant governor of Nova Scotia and subsequently of Prince Edward Island. He also held a commission in the British army, and by the process of seniority, Fanning advanced to the rank of full general by 1808. From 1813 onward, he lived in England.

FANNING, Nathaniel (1755–1805) Naval officer, privateer

The author of one of the best first-person accounts of naval service with John Paul Jones and the famous engagement of the *Bonhomme Richard* and the *Serapis,* Fanning was an adventuresome junior naval officer and privateer during the Revolution. He was born in Stonington, Connecticut, the nephew of Edmund Fanning. Like others among his eight siblings, Fanning went to sea early and by the time of the Revolution was an experienced sailor. He was a privateer aboard the *Angelica* in 1778 when he was captured by the British in what proved to be only the first of several imprisonments. He was put in Forton prison and held until June 1779, when he was exchanged to France. John Paul Jones had just come into command of the converted merchantman renamed *Bonhomme Richard,* and Fanning signed on as a midshipman and as Jones's clerk. He observed the subsequent voyage and his captain closely, including the fight to the death with the *Serapis* off Flamborough Head during which Fanning commanded the maintop. Fanning's opinion of Jones was considerably less flattering than some, and he delineated in his narrative Jones's callousness, egotism and brutal treatment of his crews. Nonetheless, Fanning transferred with Jones to the *Alliance* and subsequently to the *Ariel.*

In December 1780, Fanning and other officers refused to serve any longer with Jones, and Fanning left to become an officer on a French privateer. He was again captured by the British in May 1781, was released, and was captured twice more before the end of the war. He had meanwhile become a French subject, but he returned to America in 1784 and assumed citizenship, working as a merchant seaman. In 1804, he received a commission as a lieutenant in the revived U.S. Navy, but he died the following year of fever while on duty aboard a gunboat assigned to patrol off the Carolinas and Georgia. *Further reading: Narrative: The Memoirs of Nathaniel Fanning, An Officer of the American Navy, 1778–1783, by Himself* (New York, 1806; reprint 1913).

FARMER. See BILLOPP, Christopher.

FARMER, Ferdinand (1720–1786) Clergyman

Born in Swabia under the original family name of Steinmeyer, Farmer was one of the principal Roman Catholic missionaries in the colonies (outside Maryland). A Jesuit, he came to Pennsylvania in the 1750s and served a mission in Lancaster and then Philadelphia. In 1775, he organized one of the first Roman Catholic congregations in New York City. During the Revolution, Farmer was offered the post of chaplain to the company of Roman Catholic loyalist volunteers, but he refused. He was also an amateur astronomer and mathematician and a member of the American Philosophical Society in Philadelphia.

FARRAGUT, George (1755–1817) Naval officer

The father of "Damn the Torpedoes" David Farragut of Civil War fame, George was born a British subject on Minorca to a British father and a Spanish mother. He first went to sea aboard a merchantman in the Mediterranean at age 10. He moved to America in 1776 and became an officer on a privateer. In 1778, he received a commission in the South Carolina state navy. He also fought on land during the war, at Savannah in 1779 and again at Charleston in 1780. Farragut apparently escaped capture with the fall of Charleston and was a volunteer at the battle of the Cowpens and an artilleryman in the North Carolina militia. He is also reported to have raised and commanded a troop of cavalry late in the war. Following the Revolution, he was first a merchant mariner and then was commissioned as a sailing master in the U.S. Navy.

FAY, Jonas (1737–1818) Physician, officeholder

Fay was one of the officials of the "state" of Vermont during the period when the disputed Hampshire Grants region declared its independence. He was born in Massachusetts, but about 1760, following service in the Seven Years' War, he settled in Bennington. He soon became a partisan of the Vermonters and was selected in 1772 to petition New York governor William Tryon on behalf of the settlers in the Hampshire Grants (New York claims were ever the sticking point until 1791).

He served as secretary for the conventions held in Vermont to deal with the conflicts during the mid-1770s. In 1775, he acted as surgeon to the Green Mountain Boys on the expedition to take Fort Ticonderoga, and he may have served at other times during the war as a surgeon with Vermont militia. He was appointed in 1776 to present Vermonter claims to the Continental Congress, a cause that failed in the face of New York resistance. In 1777, Vermont drafted a constitution and began to act like an independent state, and Fay became a member of the governing Council of Safety. He probably had a hand in the treasonous plan of Ethan Allen to give up the region to the British in 1781. In 1782, he became a justice of the Vermont Supreme Court.

FAYSSOUX, Peter (1745–1795) Physician
Fayssoux was born in Charleston, South Carolina and received a medical degree from the University of Edinburgh, making him one of the better-educated doctors in the colonies. He was an active prewar patriot in Charleston and a member of the South Carolina assembly. He was appointed as senior physician to the state militia and for a time in 1781 was on the medical staff of the Continental Army under Nathanael Greene as chief physician of the Southern Department. Following the war, Fayssoux was the founder and first president of the South Carolina medical society.

FEBIGER, Christian (1746–1796) Continental officer   Born and educated in Denmark, Febiger saw action in nearly all the important campaigns in the north during the first years of the Revolution. As a young man he served on the staff of his uncle, the Danish governor of the West Indian island of Santa Cruz, and in 1772 toured the American colonies, settling in Massachusetts. With the outbreak of warfare at Lexington and Concord, Febiger immediately volunteered for duty with the Essex and Middlesex militia and fought at Bunker Hill. He was commissioned into the force assembled under Benedict Arnold in the summer of 1775 and went north to Canada as Arnold's brigade major. He was captured in the unsuccessful attack on Quebec in December and was held by the British until January 1777. Following his exchange he became lieutenant colonel of the 11th Virginia under Daniel Morgan. He fought at Brandywine, was promoted to full colonel afterward and served at both Germantown and Monmouth. In July 1779, Febiger was given command of a light infantry regiment under Anthony Wayne and assigned to the attack on Stony Point. He personally led one of the silent assault columns that took the post from the British in one of the war's small but impressive American victories. He then was assigned to Philadelphia and funneled supplies south to Nathanael Greene's army in the Carolinas. His last military duty was in Virginia in 1781. At his mustering out of the Continental Army in September 1783, Febiger was brevetted to the rank of brigadier general. He settled in Philadelphia and became treasurer of the state in 1789.

FELL, John (1721–1798) Delegate to Congress, merchant   Fell was born and raised in New York City, becoming a merchant with a considerable fleet of ships by the early 1760s when he moved to Bergen County, New Jersey. With the approach of the Revolution, Fell took a large role in the patriot movement and was one of the more aggressive leaders in the crucial region of Bergen County. He was chairman of the local committee of safety and of the committee of correspondence. He was the leading delegate from his county to the New Jersey Provincial Congress in 1775. Known locally as a vociferous persecutor of loyalists, he was himself captured by pro-British raiders in April 1777 and held under harsh conditions at the provost jail in New York. He was paroled in January 1778 and eventually was exchanged later in the year. In 1778, Fell was selected as a delegate from New Jersey to the Continental Congress, where he served until 1780. He was a hard-working but obscure member of the body, sponsoring few motions and speaking seldom, but he was assiduous in committee work. A decade after the Revolution, he moved back to New York City and thence to Dutchess County, where he died. He left a journal of his experiences as a delegate to Congress, which has since been published. *Further reading:* Donald W. Whisenhut, ed., *Delegate from New Jersey: The Journal of John Fell* (Port Washington, N.Y., 1973).

FERGUSON, Elizabeth Graeme (1737–1801) Poet, translator   Ferguson was born in Philadelphia to a prosperous and politically powerful family. In her youth she was engaged for several years to William Franklin, the illegitimate son of Benjamin and the eventual loyalist governor of New Jersey.

Her major work of translation was of *Télémaque* from French into English. She lived in England during the late 1760s but returned to Philadelphia and acted as hostess in her father's home after the death of her mother, making the residence a center for literary life in the city. In 1775, she married Henry Hugh Ferguson, who turned out to be a loyalist. During the British occupation of Philadelphia, Henry acted as commissary of prisoners and then fled to England, leaving Elizabeth behind. She protested the state's confiscation of her inheritance along with her husband's property, but to no avail. Part of her property was returned by the Pennsylvania legislature in 1781.

FERGUSON, Hugh Henry (b. 1748) Loyalist official

A native of Scotland, Ferguson moved to Pennsylvania in 1769 and set himself up as a planter. He married into a prominent family of officeholders. The grandfather of his wife, Elizabeth Graeme, had been one of the proprietary governors of the colony. Ferguson himself served as justice of the peace and judge of the Court of Common Pleas. He left for England in 1775 at the beginning of the war but returned in 1777 and served as a volunteer with the British army. He was commissary of prisoners in Pennsylvania for the British during their occupation of Philadelphia in 1777 and 1778. He separated from Elizabeth in 1778 because of political differences, and he then returned to Britain. His wife remained behind and fought confiscation of her property, which she had inherited from her family but was held in her husband's name.

FERGUSON, Patrick (1744–1780) British officer

An intelligent, active and innovative officer, Ferguson was fated to be at the center of much dramatic action during the American Revolution. Despite his failure at King's Mountain, where he paid the soldier's ultimate price, Ferguson's invention and use of the breech-loading rifle made him one of the few officers of his day to understand the potential impact of new military technology.

He was born in Scotland to a good family of military heritage (his uncle was a major general) and joined the Scots Greys as a teenager in 1759 after training at a military school in London. He fought in the European campaigns, notably at the battle of Minden in 1760, and then purchased a captaincy in the 70th Regiment of Foot in 1768,

serving in the West Indies with his new unit. Poor health removed him from active duty during the early 1770s. However, about 1774, while convalescing in Scotland, Ferguson became interested in the idea of devising a practical breech-loading rifle for infantry. By 1776, he had perfected his design and, in a remarkable demonstration to British army commanders at the Woolwich arsenal, showed that the new weapon could be fired with astonishing accuracy and speed: He fired up to six rounds a minute in a drizzling rain, hitting his target consistently at 100 yards and reloading while flat on his back.

A hundred of the new weapons were ordered up from the ordnance works, and Ferguson, promoted to major, was commissioned to raise a corps of riflemen. He landed with his men in New York in March 1777. Unfortunately, no one had consulted British commander in chief William Howe about the new unit with its unusual weaponry, but Howe accepted Ferguson's services for the time being. Ferguson and his men made their greatest impression at the battle of Brandywine, where they were put in the van of Baron von Knyphausen's diversionary demonstration against the American strong points and penetrated deeply against strong opposition. At one stage, Ferguson, who was reputed to be the best marksman in the British army, had General George Washington within voice range and directly under his rifle sights, but he forebore to kill Washington, whom he termed "an unoffending individual who was acquitting himself very cooly of his duty." During the latter stages of the battle, Ferguson's elbow was shattered by an American musket ball. While he recovered from his severe wound—learning to use his left hand in place of his right—Howe disbanded the rifle company and put the unique weapons in storage. The commander was apparently piqued to have under his command a conspicuous unit about which he had not been consulted, despite its demonstrated effectiveness.

Ferguson returned to duty in 1778 under the new British commander Sir Henry Clinton and worked closely with Clinton during the next two years. Ferguson transferred in 1779 to the new 71st Fraser Highlander regiment and sailed south in command of a battalion of the Highlanders as part of Clinton's expedition against Charleston. He fought extremely well during the campaign that seized the port city and was subsequently detached to command a force of loyalists—part local militia and part trained veterans from the north. In the late summer of 1780, Ferguson set off into the Carolina back country with a mobile force of 1,100 men, intent on crushing patriot resistance. He jockeyed for position with American militia that assembled from the western regions (the "over mountain men") and after marches and countermarches established his army of loyalists atop King's Mountain in the first week of October, apparently determined to make a stand and defeat the backwoodsmen. The ensuing battle on October 7, 1780 was a disaster for the British cause. Ferguson's loyalists found themselves trapped in the open ground of their campsite along the ridge, and the American riflemen took advantage of the wooded slopes to pick off and then rush their opponents. Ferguson, the only British officer in the battle, futilely tried to rally his men, dashing back and forth on horseback while clad in a conspicuous checkered shirt and blowing a silver whistle. He was cut down—rather ironically—by rifle fire and buried on the battlefield. *Further reading:* David Patten, "Ferguson and His Rifle," *History Today* 28 (July 1978), 446–54; Richard Hargreaves, "The Man Who Didn't Shoot Washington," *American Heritage* 7 (December 1955), 62–65.

FERGUSON, Robert. Loyalist   A native of Rhode Island, Ferguson was only a teenager when the Revolution began. He served the British army throughout the entire war, first as a clerk and then as a "conductor" of artillery (probably a civilian contract teamster). He is reputed to have supplied Sir Henry Clinton with maps and information about Rhode Island. Ferguson left America in 1783 at the end of the war and settled in England.

FERMOY, Matthias Alexis Roche de (born c. 1737) French volunteer   A terrible officer who entered American service at elevated rank, Fermoy was born on Martinique in the West Indies. He claimed to be a colonel of engineers when he came to America in 1776, which if true made him just the sort of officer the Continental Army had need of. Congress commissioned him immediately as a brigadier general and he was given charge of an important part of Washington's assaulting army at Trenton. He performed reasonably well during the battle against Rall's Hessians, helping to block their escape from encirclement. This was the last time Fermoy was competent on a battlefield, however. When

Hans Axel Fersen

sent by Washington to delay the expected British advance from Princeton, he disappeared from the scene. Fermoy cemented his reputation with his performance after joining Philip Schuyler's army in New York to oppose General John Burgoyne. Fermoy was in command of Mount Independence, part of Fort Ticonderoga and was ordered to conduct a secret nighttime withdrawal. He failed to issue the necessary orders before retiring for a night's sleep on July 5, 1777, and when he roused himself in the early morning hours, he set fire to his quarters, thereby alerting the British forces that an escape was in the making. He may have been drunk during the key hours of the night.

In the typical manner of the many disreputable European adventurers who so graciously offered their service to the American Revolution, Fermoy followed up his debacle with a demand for higher rank and a larger command. Congress turned him down flat, and he resigned in early 1778.

FERSEN, Hans Axel, Count von (1755–1810) French officer   Another of the foreign officers serving in the French expeditionary force, Fersen was a Swede of noble birth who had attached himself to the French court at Versailles. Rumors made him the lover of Marie Antoinette, but whatever the source of his preferment, he became a colonel of the Royal Army. He was appointed as aide-de-camp to General Rochambeau and sailed for America in the spring of 1780. Fersen served with the French headquarters throughout the campaign of 1781 and was cited for bravery at Yorktown. He returned to Europe in 1783 at the withdrawal of the French forces. Thereafter he served for a time at the court of his native land, but he returned to France during the outbreak of the French Revolution, apparently in an attempt to save the royal family from the guillotine. Following the execution of the king and queen, Fersen went back to Sweden and became a diplomat. He was killed by a mob during a revolutionary riot in 1810.

FEW, William (1748–1828) Delegate to Congress, militia officer, legislator, jurist   Few was born in Maryland but moved with his family to the Orange County region of North Carolina when he was 10 years old. His father and brothers were involved in the Regulator uprising (one brother was hanged as a rebel in 1771 after the defeat of the Regulators at the battle of Almance), and the family moved again to Georgia, where William passed the bar in 1776 and began a law practice. He was active in the politics of revolutionary Georgia, sitting in the house of representatives in 1777, 1779 and 1783, as well as serving as a local judge and surveyor general for Richmond County. Few held a commission as a lieutenant colonel in the local county militia and was part of the ill-fated expedition against British-held East Florida in 1778. In 1780, he was selected as a delegate to Congress from Georgia; he served until 1782 and returned to the body after the war in 1786.

In addition, Few was on the Georgia state executive council during the Revolution and for a time acted as a commissioner to deal with western Indian tribes for the Continental Congress. He was a member of the federal constitutional convention and was chosen as one of the first senators from Georgia under the new national government in 1789. Defeated for the U.S. Senate seat in 1795, he became a judge of the U.S. circuit court in Georgia. In 1799, Few moved to New York City and became a successful businessman in addition to sitting in the state legislature and holding several public offices, including a post as federal commissioner of loans

in 1804. *Further reading:* Josephine Mellicamp, "William Few, Jr.," in *Senators from Georgia* (Huntsville, Ala., 1976).

FISH, Nicholas (1758–1833) Militia and Continental officer   Fish was born in New York City and attended Princeton before studying law in his native city. He formed a close friendship as a young man with Alexander Hamilton (Fish named his eldest son, a future U.S. secretary of state, after Hamilton) when the latter was a student and ardent patriot debater at King's College. In 1775, Fish became a lieutenant in a New York militia regiment, fighting eventually in the battle on Long Island. He received a Continental commission as a major of the 2nd New York in 1776 and was present at the battles at Saratoga and on John Sullivan's 1779 expedition against the Iroquois. His most important battlefield service was at Yorktown as Hamilton's second in command. Fish was among the officers leading the attack on the British redoubt just before the surrender. Following the Revolution, Fish served as adjutant general of New York and was a supervisor of revenue in New York for the federal government and a city alderman. A strong Federalist, he was closely involved in New York City politics and society during the latter decades of his life.

FISKE, John (1744–1797) Naval officer   Born in Salem, Massachusetts, Fiske was a member of the local committee of safety before the Revolution. He commanded the brigantine *Tryannicide* in 1776 and then the *Massachusetts* the following year as part of the American effort to harass British shipping in European waters. He returned to the business of merchant shipping after the war but continued an interest in military affairs. In 1792, he was a major general of the state militia.

FITHIAN, Philip Vickers (1747–1776) Clergyman, tutor   Fithian was born in New Jersey and graduated from the college at Princeton in 1772. As a way to earn money for studies in divinity, he took a post as a private tutor to the children of Robert Carter II, a rich Virginia plantation owner, staying at the Carter mansion for 10 months during 1773 and 1774. His surviving letters, written from the perspective of a northern Calvinist, give insight into the daily life on a great Virginia plantation. On his return to New Jersey, Fithian received his license to preach and supplied pulpits in New Jersey for a period before traveling on a missionary journey for the Presbyterians into the frontier sections of Pennsylvania and Virginia. Early in 1776, he joined Nathaniel Heard's brigade of the New Jersey militia as a chaplain. He was at the battle of White Plains; he contracted an illness from exposure and died near Fort Washington on October 8. *Further reading:* Franklin Parker, "Philip Vickers Fithian: Northern Tutor on a Southern Plantation," *Journal of the West* 4 (January 1965), 56–62; Hunter D. Farish, ed., *Journal and Letters of Philip Vickers Fithian, 1773–1774: A Plantation Tutor of the Old Dominion* (Williamsburg, Va., 1943; reprinted 1957).

FITZGERALD, John. Continental officer A native of Ireland, Fitzgerald had settled in Virginia before the Revolution. He served during the crucial period of the war in the middle colonies (1776 to 1778) as one of George Washington's aides-de-camp. At the battle of Princeton when Washington rode his horse to the front of the battleline between the two opposing forces in order to rally the Americans at a crucial point in the fight, it appeared the commander in chief would be killed by the next British volley. Fitzgerald reportedly covered his eyes to avoid the sight of his general being cut down, but Washington escaped harm. At the battle of Monmouth in June 1778, Fitzgerald carried urgent but ignored messages from Washington to Charles Lee and was himself wounded in the latter stages of the fight. Following the war, Fitzgerald returned to Alexandria, Virginia and was associated with Washington in promoting the Potomac Navigation Company.

FITZHUGH, Peregrine. Continental officer Possibly related to congressman William Fitzhugh, Peregrine was from Virginia and a lieutenant colonel. He served as one of nine aides-de-camp to George Washington at Yorktown in 1781 and apparently was part of the commander in chief's official military family until 1783 and the dissolution of the army.

FITZHUGH, William (1741–1809) Delegate to Congress Born in King George County, Virginia, Fitzhugh was a planter and farmer. He was a member of the Virginia Constitutional Convention in 1776 and sat in the House of Delegates from 1776 to 1777 and again from 1780 to 1781. In 1779 and 1780, he was a delegate from Virginia to the Continental Congress.

FITZROY, Augustus Henry. See GRAFTON, Duke of.

FITZSIMONS, Thomas (1741–1811) Delegate to Congress, businessman, legislator FitzSimons was born in Ireland and emigrated to Philadelphia sometime during his youth. He became a merchant and solidified his business career with marriage to Catherine Meade, sister of another merchant, Robert Meade, in 1761. FitzSimons and his brother-in-law operated an extensive trading company under the name George Meade & Company. Throughout his subsequent career, FitzSimons could be counted on to support the political position that would most favor commerce and a strong central economy. He raised a militia company during the war and is reported to have taken the field during the New Jersey campaign of 1777. His major revolutionary activities were civilian, however. He was a member of the board of the Pennsylvania Navy and served in the state legislature as well as contributing funds to support the Continental Army. In 1782, FitzSimons was selected as a delegate to Congress, where he supported payment of all national debts, including monies owed to Continental officers, and the imposition of import tariffs. He was one of the organizers of the bank chartered by Congress in 1781. During the federal constitutional convention he represented Pennsylvania and pushed for a strong central government. He then became an ardent Federalist, hoping to put Hamilton's policies into effect.

FLEMING, William (1736–1824) Delegate to Congress, state official, jurist Born in Cumberland County, Virginia, Fleming graduated from the College of William and Mary in 1763 and subsequently was admitted to the bar. He sat in the House of Burgesses during the crucial years between 1772 and 1775 and attended the revolutionary conventions of 1775 and 1776. During the first years of the war, he was a member of the Virginia House of Delegates. In 1779, Fleming was selected as one of his state's delegates to the Continental Congress. Following the war, he became a judge on a court of appeals, holding his place on the bench for 35 years.

FLEURY, Marquis de Teissedre de. See TEIS-SEDRE de Fleury, Marquis de.

FLORA, William (1755–1820) Continental soldier Flora was a free black citizen of Portsmouth, Virginia at the outbreak of the war. He spurned royal governor Lord Dunmore's call for blacks to join the crown, enlisting instead in the 2nd Virginia Regiment under Colonel William Woodford. Flora drew notice for his bravery at the battle of Great Bridge in 1775 when he was one of the last sentries to retreat within the American lines. Ironically, he fought members of Dunmore's black "Ethiopian" regiment during the battle, which the British lost. Flora served through the entire war and was present at the surrender at Yorktown. He afterward operated a successful livery stable and was able to buy the freedom of his wife and children. In 1806, Flora received a 100-acre land grant for his Revolutionary War service, and he is reported to have volunteered at an advanced age for duty during the War of 1812.

FLOWER, Benjamin (1748–1781) Continental officer An officer from Pennsylvania, Flower was made commissary for the ill-fated Flying Camp formed in the summer of 1776 at George Washington's request as a mobile reserve for the anticipated battles in New York and New Jersey. The Flying Camp idea failed miserably and in the following January, Washington reassigned Flower (by then a colonel) to form a regiment of artillery artificers. Flower gathered officers and men who were also skilled workmen and created a specialized unit that included carpenters, blacksmiths, wheelwrights, tinners, harnessmakers, farriers, coopers and nailers. Two companies were designated as "laboratory" units working at depots in Carlisle and Springfield and a third was a field unit designed to service the army's artillery during a campaign. Known as Flower's Regiment, the artificers acted more or less as ordnance workers to develop, test and maintain artillery. Flower died in April 1781, by which time the artificer regiment had dwindled through the attrition imposed by several army reorganizations.

FLOYD, William (1734–1821) Delegate to Congress, militia officer, official Floyd was a man of faint public notice who nonetheless served his country in Congress during almost the entire Revolution. He was the eldest son of a family of prosperous farmers on Long Island, New York, and at age 20, with little education or training, he inherited his family's lands. He built them into a rich holding and by the time of the Revolution was a wealthy man with considerable local influence: he was a colonel in the Suffolk County militia and held several local offices. In 1774, Floyd was sent to the First Continental Congress as a delegate from Long Island, and he returned to the ensuing Second Congress, sitting until late 1776. While a delegate he signed the Declaration of Independence and served quietly on several important committees. From 1777 to 1779, when he returned to Congress for a third time, he served on his local council of safety and in the New York state senate.

His estates on Long Island were usurped by the British and their loyalist allies after the summer of 1776, and Floyd's family was forced to flee to Middleton, Connecticut for the duration of the conflict. His home and lands were nearly destroyed during the war, and his first wife died in exile in 1781. He left Congress at the conclusion of the Revolution in 1783 and returned to Long Island to rebuild his fortunes. In 1789, Floyd was elected as one of New York's first representatives to the new federal congress, but he served only one term and was defeated for reelection in 1790. Three years later, he purchased land in the Mohawk Valley near Rome, New York and moved with a second wife and several children to begin a new life. He eventually accumulated a large holding of land and lived out his days on an estate near Westernville, New York.

FOLSOM, Nathaniel (1726–1790) Delegate to Congress, militia officer Folsom was born in Exeter, New Hampshire and was a veteran of the Seven Years' War, during which he served on the Crown Point expedition. He was active during the years before the Revolution in the colonial militia and was the major general in command of all New Hampshire troops at the outbreak of the war. He was superseded in his militia duties after the siege of Boston by John Sullivan. He was one of New Hampshire's delegates to the first Continental Congress in 1774, and he was sent again to subsequent congresses in 1777–78 and 1779–80. He sat in the Provincial Congress in 1775 and later served as a state legislator and judge of common pleas.

FONTANGES, Vicomte de (1740–1822) French general

Fontanges was a career soldier of France. He entered the army in 1756 and fought during the Seven Years' War in Europe, advancing to the rank of captain. In 1775, he transferred to the navy and colonial service and was appointed a major with an assignment in the West Indies at Santo Domingo. He was a major general in 1779 when d'Estaing sailed with a large fleet to invest the British at Savannah, Georgia. Fontanges commanded the land forces, which may have numbered as many as 3,500, including many black troops recruited from the slave population of Santo Domingo. The French landings in September were poorly coordinated, and d'Estaing and Fontanges refused to confer with the American commanders during the ensuing siege and negotiations with the British. Fontanges was wounded on October 7, two days before the futile main assault by the Franco-American force. After the French army and fleet withdrew, Fontanges resumed his duties at Santo Domingo. He fled the island during the subsequent slave uprising and returned to France.

FORBES, James (c. 1731–1780) Delegate to Congress, local official

Born near Benedict, Maryland, Forbes was a justice of the peace and a local tax commissioner, although little is known of the details of his life. He sat in the state general assembly in 1777 and was appointed as a delegate to the Continental Congress the following year. He died while serving in Philadelphia and was buried there.

FORMAN, David (1745–1797) Militia and Continental officer

Forman was closely associated with his native Monmouth County, New Jersey throughout the war. His family had originally come to New York in the previous century as religious dissenters and had settled in New Jersey sometime early in the 1700s. Forman was a militia commander in Monmouth County at the beginning of the war, and he apparently served during the New York campaigns of 1776. He came to the attention of George Washington after suppressing a loyalist uprising in Monmouth County in November 1776, and the commander in chief asked him to raise one of the "additional" regiments authorized by Congress. Forman received a commission as colonel in the Continental Army in January 1777 and recruited his regiment from New Jersey and Maryland. A few months later, he received a commission from New Jersey as brigadier general of state militia, and he commanded militia troops at Germantown in October but resigned the state commission in a dispute with the legislature in November. Although the Continental regiment bearing his name continued to serve until it was broken up and incorporated into other units in 1778 and 1779, Forman himself was detached and made a staff officer to General Charles Lee, which created a frustrating experience for Forman during the battle of Monmouth.

For the rest of the war, Forman remained in and around Monmouth County, conducting a vicious and prolonged campaign against the Associated Loyalists. He was known among his foes as "Devil David" and was reputed to be ruthless in persecution of loyalists. Following the war, he moved to Maryland and then to Tennessee. Felled by a stroke in New Orleans, he was sailing to New York when captured by a British privateer, and he died at sea.

FORREST, Uriah (1756–1805) Delegate to Congress, militia officer

Forrest was born near Leonardtown, Maryland and served actively as an officer of the Maryland militia during the Revolution. He was wounded at the battle of Germantown and after the battle of Brandywine lost a leg. Following the war, he was sent as a delegate from Maryland to the Confederation Congress, serving in 1786 and 1787. After the new federal government was established, Forrest was elected as a U.S. representative from Maryland in 1793, but he resigned before completing his term. He had meanwhile risen to the rank of major general in the state militia. From 1800 until his death he worked as a clerk in the circuit court for the District of Columbia.

FOSTER, Abiel (1735–1806) Delegate to Congress, clergyman, legislator

Born in Andover, Massachusetts, Foster graduated from Harvard in 1756, studied theology and was ordained to the ministry. He took a parish in Canterbury, New Hampshire in 1761 and served there until midpoint of the Revolution. Meanwhile, he was active in the patriot organizations of New Hampshire, sitting in the provincial congress at Exeter in 1775. In 1779, Foster left his parish and began a long period of public office. He was elected to the state house of representatives and served until 1783, when he went to the Confederation Congress as a delegate from

New Hampshire. He simultaneously served as a judge of his local court of common pleas. With the inauguration of the new federal government, Foster was elected as U.S. representative from New Hampshire to the first congress. After a return to the state senate from 1791 to 1794 (he was president of the body), he was reelected to the U.S. Congress for two more terms.

FOX, Charles James (1749–1806) British politician and officeholder

Fox was one of the glittering names of British politics during the second half of the 18th century, a man who all acknowledged to be a brilliant orator but hopelessly dissolute in his personal life and unable to accomplish much outside his role as the leader of the opposition. He was (typically) out of office during most of the American Revolution and came mostly by default to be a vocal supporter of the colonial cause.

He was born into an aristocratic family and educated at Eton and Oxford, but his early life was devoted almost exclusively to learning the ways of an 18th-century rake. He loved gambling, the company of women and strong drink, but he also loved politics and had a command of the language when on his feet that made him a spellbinder in debate and speechmaking. He first went to Parliament (from a rotten borough) in 1768. He initially supported the royal party and was allied with Lord North, who appointed Fox a lord of the Admiralty in 1770. But Fox had virtually no political principle other than that which could be devised for the moment, and when he took up the cause of John Wilkes, Fox put himself in opposition to the king's party. The strait-laced George III also disliked Fox's flamboyant style of living, reason enough in the times to make Fox an outsider while the king's party held a majority.

Fox was dismissed from office in 1774 and spent the following nine years as the leader of the so-called Rockingham Whigs in the House of Commons. Until then, he had been completely indifferent to the issue of the American colonies, but he seized on the war as a pretext to criticize North (his previous friend and ally) and the king's party. Throughout the eight years of the Revolution, Fox again and again spoke eloquently in the House against the war, providing quotation after quotation in the service of the American patriots. When the war was lost and North finally had to resign, Fox

played the role of government maker and became one of the secretaries of state in the Rockingham government that took over from North in 1782. Rockingham's death shattered the arrangement, and after a brief government under Shelburne, Fox formed a new coalition with Lord North and took office again in early 1783. The government was turned out by the end of the year, and Fox again assumed leadership of the opposition. He returned to the government for a few weeks just before his death. *Further reading:* John W. Derry, *Charles James Fox* (New York, 1972); I. R. Christie, ''Charles James Fox,'' *History Today* 8 (February 1958), 110–18.

FRANCIS, Philip (1740–1818) Writer, British official

Almost certainly the author of the ''Junius'' letters, Francis was a British government official before the Revolution who anonymously attacked his own government and king. He was born in Dublin and educated at St. Paul's school in London. He came under the patronage of Lord Holland as a teenager and wrote anonymous pamphlets for Holland while serving as a junior clerk in the secretary of state's office. Francis became first clerk of the War Office in 1762. Between 1769 and 1772, there appeared in the British press a series of vicious letters attacking the government and George III. The author used the pen name Junius and demonstrated not only an unrestrained invective but an inside knowledge of government affairs. The letters caused an ongoing sensation and if discovered, the identity of the author would have opened him to severe prosecution. Among other matters, Junius rated the British government and the king on American policy. No absolute evidence has ever been found to tie Francis to authorship of the letters, but the identification seems more than circumstantially certain. He left the War Office in 1772 and was appointed in 1774 to the Council of Bengal. While in India he became a deadly opponent of governor general Warren Hastings and worked for Hastings' impeachment during the 1780s. He was wounded in a duel with Hastings but recovered and returned to England. *Further reading:* Romney Sedgwick, ''The Letters of Junius,'' *History Today* 19 (June 1969), 397–404.

FRANCISCO, Peter (c. 1760–1831) Continental soldier

One of the most colorful figures of the Revolution, Francisco was a giant of a man—reportedly six feet, six inches in height and weighing 260 pounds—and a nearly incredible hand-to-hand fighter on many battlefields. Adding to the romantic aura was his mysterious appearance on the Virginia shore as a four-year-old, apparently having been abandoned on the beach by a sailing ship. Some have speculated he was Portuguese and may have come from a noble family, but no one knows his origins. He was raised in the household of Judge Anthony Winston, a relative of Patrick Henry. He joined the 10th Virginia Regiment in 1775 when about the age of 15. He was wounded at the battle of Brandywine and was befriended by the Marquis de Lafayette when both men were treated for injuries. He then fought at the battles of Germantown and Fort Mifflin before receiving another wound at Monmouth. By this time his fame had spread in the Continental Army. He wielded a specially-made five-foot broadsword (which survives in a Virginia museum collection) and habitually closed with the enemy to hack about him—a tactic that resulted in many wounds for Francisco and many casualties among the opposition.

In July 1779, Francisco was one of the men in the suicide squad in the attack on the British fortifications at Stony Point, where he was wounded by a severe bayonet slash. He was back in action within weeks, however, and wielded his medieval weapon during the attack at Paulus Hook, New Jersey, reportedly killing two grenadiers. In 1780, Francisco was back in the southern theater as a militiaman under Colonel William Mayo. At the battle of Camden, he rescued Mayo from the British and then dragged a 1,000-pound cannon from the field to save it from capture. In August 1781, Francisco was a member of a mounted partisan troop fighting in conjunction with Colonel William Washington's dragoons. At Guilford Courthouse, he took two more bayonet wounds but was reputed to have killed 11 of his enemy—a feat that earned him the name "Goliath of Guilford" among his contemporaries. He was found wounded lying among a heap of his dead and dying foes in a scene worthy of Celtic or Nordic saga. After more adventures and feats of strength and daring, Francisco retired from combat with the British surrender at Yorktown. After the war, he transformed himself into a country squire with property awarded for his service and from his new wife's dowry. He married three times and fathered six children. In 1823, he moved to

Richmond, Virginia and became sergeant at arms for the House of Delegates (one suspects that the body kept good order under his eye). In 1824, Francisco accompanied Lafayette on the latter's triumphal tour of Virginia.

FRANKLIN, Benjamin (1706–1790) Delegate to Congress, diplomat

Franklin had so many parts that he defies summary: printer, author, editor, inventor, scientist, politician, diplomat. Franklin was nearly 70 when the Revolution began but he had the energy to spark the movement for independence, serve in organizing the first months of a revolution, represent America in Paris during the entire war, and negotiate the peace treaty with enough left over to play a significant role in devising the new Republic while in his eighth decade.

Born in Boston, he had little formal schooling before going to work in his father's tallow shop and then as an apprentice printer with his brother James. In 1723, he ran away to Philadelphia, arriving with only one Dutch dollar and a copper shilling, but by 1730, he was sole owner of a printing business and the *Pennsylvania Gazette*. In 1727, Franklin founded a debating society, the Junto, and in 1732, he set up a circulating library and also began to publish *Poor Richard's Almanac*, which he continued to edit until 1757. In 1743, the Junto was transformed into the American Philosophical Society. Franklin also was the primary force in establishing Philadelphia's first fire company and an academy that eventually became part of the University of Pennsylvania.

His domestic life revolved around a common-law wife, Deborah Read, by whom he had at least two illegitimate children. His son William, probably a result of the union with Read, although the precise facts of William's parentage have never been clearly established, became Franklin's close companion. By the 1740s, Franklin had amassed a sufficient fortune to turn over the printing business to his partner and devote his energies to scientific pursuits, essentially retiring from business for the rest of his life. His *Experiments and Observations on Electricity*, published in 1751, established his reputation in Europe as a scientist.

Elected to the Pennsylvania Assembly in 1751, Franklin served in that body through 1763. The British government appointed him deputy postmaster general of the colonies in 1753, a position he held until 1774. At the outset of war with France in

Benjamin Franklin

1754, Franklin attended the Albany Convention and submitted a proposal that became a precedent for the eventual American union. The Pennsylvania Assembly sent Franklin to London as its agent during the years 1757–62 and again for 1764–75. He also served as agent for Georgia and Massachusetts. He allied himself at home with James Galloway and worked—unsuccessfully—to abolish the power of the Penn family proprietorship, an end that was not accomplished until the Revolution. Though initially a strong supporter of American ties to the crown, Franklin became an outspoken advocate of American dissent during his second tour in England, asserting that Parliament should have no authority over the colonies and speaking out against the Stamp Act in the House of Commons in 1766 (even though at first he had tried to get two of his friends positions as stampmasters).

He returned to Philadelphia in 1775 as a supporter of revolution and was immediately selected to serve in the Continental Congress. His work there encompassed many areas; the most famous was probably his membership on the committee to draft the Declaration of Independence. Franklin also drafted articles of confederation, set up the first U.S. post office and served on the three-man mission to win over Canada. His son, William, had meanwhile become royal governor of New Jersey and was arrested by patriots when he remained loyal to the crown. Father and son split over the Revolution and were never reconciled (Benjamin took over the upbringing of William's illegitimate son, William Temple Franklin).

In September 1776, Congress named Franklin as one of three commissioners to the court of France, and he left in December for Paris, where he was charged to negotiate a treaty of alliance, raise loans and secure supplies. In Paris, Franklin became a diplomatic wonder. He put on a rare public show, playing simultaneously the roles of New World rustic and European sophisticate. His personal charm and keen understanding of the European situation allowed Franklin to essentially achieve his diplomatic goals, despite horrendous obstacles, not the least of which was difficulty with his fellow commissioners Arthur Lee and Silas Deane (and the infiltration of the American mission by British agents, principally Dr. Edward Bancroft). The quarrels between Lee and Deane and Lee and Franklin resulted in the dismissal of the two other commissioners and the appointment of Franklin in 1778 as American minister plenipotentiary.

Franklin meanwhile had adroitly brought about a full French alliance on the heels of General John Burgoyne's defeat, and thenceforth his standing at the court reached full flower. The victory of the allied armies at Yorktown set afoot negotiations for peace with Britain, and in the end Franklin decided (or rather was forced) to go it virtually alone, separating the interests of the United States from those of France—despite a treaty obligation to the contrary—and moving toward a separate treaty. The formal Treaty of Paris, not signed until 1783, resulted from the work of Franklin, John Adams and Henry Laurens.

Franklin finally returned to Philadelphia in the fall of 1785 and was soon elected president of the Supreme Executive Council of Pennsylvania, holding that post for three years. In 1787, he also became president of the Pennsylvania Society for Promoting the Abolition of Slavery and a member of the Constitutional Convention representing Pennsylvania. Although none of his major proposals was approved for inclusion in the Constitution, he urged its unanimous adoption. In recognition of his achievements Harvard, Yale, Oxford, William and Mary and St. Andrews all awarded him honorary degrees. Franklin had begun the writing of his *Autobiography* while in London, but it remained incomplete at the time of his death. *Further reading:* Leonard W. Labaree, et al., eds., *The Papers of Benjamin Franklin*, multivolume (1959–); Carl Van Doren, *Benjamin Franklin* (New York, 1938); Ralph Ketcham, *Benjamin Franklin* (New York, 1965); Ronald W. Clark, *Benjamin Franklin: A Biography* (New York, 1983).

FRANKLIN, William (1731–1813) Loyalist royal governor

Franklin was the illegitimate son of Benjamin Franklin and during his early life was a close companion of his illustrious father, but he became perhaps the best-known loyalist leader during the War for Independence. He was openly acknowledged by the elder Franklin but his mother's true identity has never been certifiably discovered. Benjamin lived with Deborah Read as man and wife in Philadelphia at the time of William's birth, but the stormy relationship between William and Deborah casts doubt on her parenthood. Benjamin resolutely refused to name the mother. William was raised in the Franklin household, however, and given every advantage of education and rearing.

During the first three decades of his life, he was very close to his father and acted as a companion and assistant in Benjamin's political, financial and scientific affairs. In 1746, while only a teenager, William joined a colonial militia troop for a planned expedition against Canada, but the venture was called off. He accompanied his father as part of a delegation to negotiate for Indian lands and acted as an aide during the Albany Congress in 1752. With Benjamin's influence, William became clerk of the Pennsylvania Assembly and then postmaster for Philadelphia. In 1757, Benjamin was appointed as agent in London for the colony of Pennsylvania, and William went to England with his father. He moved into Benjamin's London residence, studied law at the Middle Temple and was admitted to the English bar.

William apparently moved easily among the political and social elite of London, and among his friendships was one formed with the Earl of Bute, still the royal favorite at the time. In a surprising, even astounding, turn of events in 1762, William was named as the royal governor of New Jersey. While in England, William himself had fathered an illegitimate son, called William Temple Franklin, who was removed from his mother's custody and raised in part by his grandfather. Shortly before leaving England, William married Elizabeth Downes, the daughter of a rich West Indies planter. He arrived in America in 1763 and took up his office in New Jersey with considerable pomp and ceremony. His first 10 years as royal governor went relatively well: he was an able official and took his duties seriously. However, as the revolutionary crisis grew, William's sympathies turned more and more on his loyalty to the crown.

By 1775, William and Benjamin were almost completely estranged over political issues, and William resolved to hold New Jersey in the British orbit as long as possible. There was little he could do, however, to prevent the patriots from taking control. In June 1776, the New Jersey Provincial Congress ordered his arrest. He was confined to his house in Burlington, New Jersey, and then on order of the Continental Congress was placed in harsh confinement in Connecticut. While he was in prison, Elizabeth sickened and died, and the patriot authorities refused to allow William to visit her—a fact that embittered him greatly.

William was exchanged in 1778 for John McKinley, the patriot governor of Delaware, and went to British-occupied New York City, where he set about organizing a quasi-military loyalist organization called the Board of Associated Loyalists, of which he was president. The Associated Loyalists were at their worst nothing more than gangs of vicious thugs who preyed on friend and foe throughout the contested no-man's-lands in parts of New Jersey and New York. At best, they provided valuable intelligence for the British and served to keep the general patriot population under control. For three years, Franklin and the Associated Loyalists spread fear and trembling. In 1782, however, they overstepped the limits when they illegally executed Joshua Huddy and set off a major international incident. British commander in chief Sir Henry Clinton ordered the group disbanded, and William Franklin's role in America came to an end. He left for Great Britain the following year, where he was awarded a paltry £1,800 for his lost property and a pension of £800 annually—small reward for his efforts on behalf of the crown. In 1784, he wrote a mildly conciliatory letter to his father, but the two were never really reconciled, although they met briefly in 1785 when Benjamin was on his way home from France with William Temple. *Further reading:* Sheila Skemp, *William Franklin: Son of a Patriot, Servant of a King* (New York, 1990); Larry Gerlach, *William Franklin: New Jersey's Last Royal Governor* (Trenton, N.J., 1975).

FRANKS, David (1720–1793) Loyalist merchant

Born in New York as the third generation of a

Jewish merchant family (and related at a distance to both Isaac and David Salisbury Franks), David Franks had strong connections to the British. His sister Phila married loyalist Oliver De Lancey, and Franks himself had acted as a contractor for the British forces in North America during the Seven Years' War and supplied British garrisons on the Mississippi afterward. At the beginning of the Revolution, Franks lived in Philadelphia with his wife, who was Christian. He was appointed by Congress as a commissary for British prisoners (supplying food and clothing to captured Britons at British expense), but he was suspected of loyalist sympathies and arrested in 1778 on the basis of an intercepted letter. He was released but was arrested again in 1780 and expelled from Pennsylvania. Franks and his family arrived in England in 1782, and he received a small settlement from the loyalist claims commission in London. At some point before 1792 he returned to Philadelphia. Franks died there in 1793 during an epidemic of yellow fever.

FRANKS, David Salisbury (1743–1793) Continental officer, diplomat   Franks was born in Philadelphia to a prominent Jewish mercantile family but moved with his father to Montreal in 1769. The elder Franks remained loyal to the British crown, but David was open in his support of the revolt to the south and was briefly imprisoned as a leader of sedition by Governor Guy Carleton. When American forces under Richard Montgomery captured Montreal in 1775, Franks joined them as unofficial paymaster, and he accompanied the American retreat southward in 1776 after the disaster at Quebec. He had met Benedict Arnold in Montreal and attached himself to Arnold's military establishment as an aide-de-camp with the rank of major. He served with Arnold during the campaign against General John Burgoyne in 1777 and was his aide while Arnold was commander in Philadelphia, with brief detachments as a liaison with the French admiral d'Estaing in 1778 and as an aide to Benjamin Lincoln in South Carolina in 1779. Franks returned to Philadelphia to testify at Arnold's court-martial and then moved with the general to West Point.

Franks was serving as one of two aides to Arnold when the traitor was revealed and fled to the British lines. Franks was absolved of knowledge or complicity in Arnold's plot, but his military career was

effectively ended, although he continued on the army rolls as a lieutenant colonel until 1783. After 1781, however, Franks was employed as a minor diplomat, originally under the patronage of Robert Morris. He mainly acted as a courier between America and Europe, carrying papers and messages to Paris and Madrid. Despite his ambitions, Franks never received a regular diplomatic appointment, although he continued to serve until 1787, principally with American consul general Thomas Barclay in Marseilles. Franks was turned down in his application in 1790 to be taken into the consular ranks. He had a brief association with the Scioto Land Company and was appointed an assistant cashier to the Bank of North America in 1791. He died of yellow fever in 1793. *Further reading:* Jacob Marcus, ed., *Memoirs of American Jews, 1775–1865* (New York, 1955), 45–49.

FRANKS, Isaac (1759–1822) Soldier   Franks was born in New York and was very distantly related to David Franks and David Salisbury Franks. Despite his Jewish family background, Isaac was apparently a practicing Christian. He volunteered at age 17 as a soldier in a short-term regiment for the battles against the British on Long Island. He was captured on Manhattan but escaped to New Jersey in a leaky rowboat. He there joined the quartermaster division as an assistant foragemaster for Washington's main army. He eventually was promoted to foragemaster and assigned to West Point, where he received a commission as ensign in a Massachusetts regiment in 1781. He resigned the following year, married, and moved to Philadelphia, where he became a financial broker. In 1794, the former enlisted man received a commission as a lieutenant colonel in the state militia. The previous year he had lent his large house at Germantown to President George Washington, who needed a residence outside Philadelphia in order to escape an outbreak of yellow fever.

FRASER, Simon (1726–1782) British officer   The eldest son of Lord Lovat and not to be confused with other British officers of the same name, this Fraser did not serve in America during the Revolution, but raised the 71st Regiment of Foot, known as Fraser's Highlanders, a unit that played important roles in many Revolutionary War battles. He was a prominent Jacobite during the Highlander uprisings in 1745 but received a full pardon and had a distinguished career during and after the Seven Years' War as a British officer. He was a major general in 1775 when he formed the 71st.

FRASER, Simon (1729–1777) British officer

One of the three Simon Frasers connected prominently with the British army during the Revolution, this Fraser was not closely related to the Simon Fraser of Lovat and did not serve in that officer's new 71st Fraser Highlanders. Rather, he was a career officer who began service in 1755 in the Royal American Regiment. He did serve in the first regiment called the Fraser Highlanders (the 78th) during the Seven Years' War, but he was a lieutenant colonel of the 24th Regiment of Foot when he went to Canada in 1776 as part of the reinforcements sent to Sir Guy Carleton under the command of General John Burgoyne. Fraser led a successful campaign to defend the British position at Three Rivers in June 1776 and was given the local rank of brigadier general. The following year, Fraser was one of Burgoyne's principal officers when the march from Canada was launched with the intent of splitting the American colonies. Fraser commanded part of Burgoyne's advanced force and fought well at Hubbardstown in July. He led his command at the first battle near Saratoga (Freeman's Farm) and played a prominent role at the second battle (Bemis Heights) on October 7 until, near the end of the early phase of the fighting, Fraser was singled out by the American marksman Timothy Murphy and cut down by a rifle ball at long range. He died the following morning and was buried on the field.

FRASER, Simon (1738–1813) British officer

A younger cousin of the Simon Fraser of Lovat, this Simon Fraser served in the American war as an officer of the 71st Fraser Highlanders, raised by his cousin in 1775. He had previously served in the 78th Regiment, also known as the Fraser Highlanders. He was a major during the American Revolution, fighting with distinction at Hobkirk's Hill. He retired at the end of the war but returned to duty in 1793 with a third regiment called the Fraser Highlanders—the 133rd—which he helped raise. He achieved the rank of lieutenant general during the Napoleonic wars.

FREEMAN, Jordan (d. 1781) Soldier

Freeman, a black man, was probably an orderly to Lieutenant Colonel William Ledyard, who commanded the American defenders of Fort Griswold at New London, Connecticut against an assault by vastly superior numbers of British under Benedict Arnold on September 6, 1781. Arnold's force of loyalists and regulars had swept into New London, burned and plundered, and then turned back to take the American fort on the banks of the Thames River. Freeman and fewer than a hundred other Americans put up a fierce but futile resistance. Freeman reportedly killed the leader of the British assault, a Major Montgomery, with a spear but was himself killed either during the hand-to-hand combat on the fortifications or during the massacre of the American defenders that took place after the surrender.

FREEMAN, Nathaniel (1741–1827) Militia officer, physician, lawyer

As a young man, Freeman studied medicine with a doctor in Connecticut, but he returned to his native Sandwich, Massachusetts to read law with his uncle. He then took up practice of both professions. He was a member of the local committee of correspondence and a delegate to one of the provincial congresses in 1775. Freeman served as lieutenant colonel and colonel in the local militia regiment, and his unit was part of the disastrous expedition against the British in Rhode Island in 1778. Following the action at Newport, Freeman was elected to the Massachusetts legislature. He continued in the militia after the Revolution, eventually reaching the rank of brigadier general.

FRELINGHUYSEN, Frederick (1753–1804) Delegate to Congress, militia officer, official

A native of Somerville, New Jersey, Frelinghuysen graduated from Princeton in 1770 and became a lawyer. He was a representative from Somerset County to the patriot provincial congress in 1775. With the coming of outright warfare, he entered the state militia and served during several of the important battles in the middle states—including Trenton and Monmouth—as a captain of New Jersey artillery (from 1776 to 1778) and as an aide-de-camp to General Philemon Dickinson. He then turned to public office and was chosen as one of New Jersey's delegates to Congress in 1778, serving again as a delegate in 1783. Frelinghuysen was also a member of the New Jersey Legislative Council in 1782 and sat in the General Assembly off and on for several years after the Revolution. In 1790, he received a commission as a brigadier general during an Indian campaign in the west, and he was elevated to major general of state militia during the Whiskey Rebellion of 1794. He was U.S. senator from New Jersey from 1793 to 1796, when he resigned.

FRENEAU, Philip Morin (1752–1832) Poet, privateer, journalist

Considered by literary historians to have been the first really good American poet and a precursor of the Romantic movement, Freneau was an active participant in the Revolution and the political life of the early Republic. He was born in New York to a family of Huguenots (his father spelled his last name "Fresneau") and entered Princeton (known then as the College of New Jersey) in 1768. He was a classmate of James Madison and Hugh Henry Brackenridge, and Freneau wrote a patriotic poem called "The Rising Glory of America" with Brackenridge shortly after their graduation in 1771. Freneau dabbled briefly in teaching school but devoted most of his energies to writing poetry and the study of theology. In 1775, he published a series of satirical poems on the British, which established his place as a literary patriot.

He sailed in February 1776 to the West Indies and served for two years as a secretary at Santa Cruz in the Virgin Islands. He also visited other islands in the Caribbean and perhaps served aboard American privateers in the region. He began a voyage back to the United States in July 1778 but was captured at sea by the British. After his release, Freneau settled in Philadelphia, joined the New Jersey militia as a private and began to publish a newspaper, *The American Independence*. Over the remaining years of the Revolution, Freneau divided his time between writing, journalism and the sea, publishing several of his best and most remembered poems, as well as many essays, and sailing on merchant ships and privateers. In May 1780, he was captured aboard the privateer *Aurora* and confined by the British in the infamous prison ships in New York harbor, where his health declined rapidly. After his release in 1781, he wrote two poems about the experience.

He continued his dual careers as poet and sailor after the Revolution, adding political journalism and minor public offices. His first full volume of verse was published in Philadelphia in 1786. He allied himself with Thomas Jefferson and in 1791 became editor of the highly political *National Gazette*, an anti-Federalist paper that vexed both Alexander Hamilton and George Washington (who called the poet "that rascal Freneau"). Throughout much of the rest of his long life, Freneau continued to alternate between journalism and seafaring. He moved to a farm in New Jersey in 1824, and his last poem (on the battle of Monmouth) was published in a Trenton newspaper in 1827. He died in 1832 when caught in a blizzard near his rural home. *Further reading:* Philip M. Marsh, *The Works of Philip Freneau: A Critical Study* (Metuchen, N.J., 1968); Samuel E. Foreman, *The Political Activities of Philip Freneau* (Baltimore, 1902); Mary S. Austin, *Philip Freneau: The Poet of the Revolution* (New York, 1901).

FROST, George (1720–1796) Delegate to Congress, jurist

Frost was born in Newcastle, New Hampshire. He spent 20 years as a sea captain and then in 1760 returned to Newcastle for 10 years before resettling in Durham, New Hampshire. In 1773, Frost became a judge of the county court of common pleas, a post he held until 1791. From 1777 to 1779, he was a delegate from New Hampshire to the Continental Congress, and during the last three years of the Revolution he sat on the New Hampshire executive council.

FRYE, Joseph (1711–1794) Continental general

Frye was in his mid-sixties when the Revolution began and apparently long past his prime as a soldier. A native of Andover, Massachusetts, his record in the colonial wars had been outstanding, and he had moved in the 1760s to the Maine region following nearly 20 years of army service. The Massachusetts Provincial Congress granted him a commission as major general of militia in June 1775, and he was appointed a brigadier in the Continental Army in January 1776. He was hopeless as an active officer, however, seldom leaving his quarters, and as commander in chief George Washington maneuvered his retirement within three months.

G

GADSDEN, Christopher (1724–1805) Delegate to Congress, state official, general   Gadsden was the principal leader of the patriot forces in South Carolina and one of the earliest advocates of independence. He was born in Charleston, the son of a British merchant fleet officer and collector of the port. Gadsden was sent to England for his early education, then apprenticed to a Philadelphia mercantile house on his return. He also served two years as a purser aboard a British warship before setting up as a merchant and planter in South Carolina. Before the age of 30, he was a prosperous and influential member of South Carolina's mercantile society. He entered politics with a seat in the assembly in 1757, and he enjoyed a wide popularity among the mechanics and trading clerks of Charleston who formed the basis for his political power.

Difficulties with the royal governor in 1762 pushed Gadsden toward dissatisfaction with British rule, and with the Stamp Act crisis three years later, he began to assume the role of spokesman for anti-British sentiment, speaking at the Stamp Act Congress for colonial unification and against the power of Parliament. By the early 1770s, Gadsden was the acknowledged leader in South Carolina of the more radical patriot faction, although his interests were firmly on the side of an orderly resistance to the crown. He represented South Carolina in the first Continental Congress in 1774 and was appointed the first colonel of the South Carolina Continental regiment raised the following year after the out-

break of armed hostilities. He was sent as a delegate to the second Congress in 1775, where he acquired a reputation as a fire-eater who wanted to attack the British in Boston, but he left Philadelphia in January 1776 to take command of troops for the defense of Charleston against the first British attempt to take the city. He played little role in beating off the British, however, and never really functioned in the field as a military commander, despite promotion to the rank of brigadier general. In fact, his only contribution was to quarrel with General Robert Howe, with whom Gadsden fought an inconclusive duel.

He did achieve considerable notoriety in February 1776 by proposing to the South Carolina Provincial Congress that the colonies declare independence. In 1778, Gadsden was a driving force in the South Carolina constitutional convention, but in the course of the debates he came crosswise with the powerful Rutledges and managed to severely erode his political position. In fact, he was thereafter shunted aside into meaningless offices for the most part.

He served as lieutenant governor of the state in 1780, when Sir Henry Clinton made a second attempt to seize Charleston. Shut up in the town with other civil officeholders and commanding general Benjamin Lincoln, Gadsden demanded that the army try to hold out against the British—a futile and damaging position that helped bring on the disastrous surrender. He was captured by Clinton and paroled, and then was rearrested and sent to St. Augustine by Lord Cornwallis after Clinton returned to New York. He was held in prison for 10 months in close confinement. He declined election as governor of South Carolina in 1782 and served instead as a member of the legislature. Most of the remainder of his life was devoted to business, although he sat in the state conventions that ratified the federal constitution and wrote a new state constitution. *Further reading:* Richard Walsh, ed., *The Writings of Christopher Gadsden, 1746–1805* (Columbia, S.C., 1966).

GAGE, Thomas (1721–1787) British general

The last royal governor of Massachusetts and the British commander in chief in America from 1763 to 1775, Gage was born in Firle, England, the descendant of a French nobleman who arrived in England with William the Conqueror. He was educated at Westminster School and in 1740 was commissioned an ensign. His military career before the American Revolution was extensive and on the whole successful. He fought at Fontenoy and Culloden in 1745 and took part in the Low Countries campaign of 1747–48. Gage thereafter became an officer of the 44th Regiment, and in 1751, he was promoted to lieutenant colonel.

When the Seven Years' War began, Gage's regiment was ordered to America, and he served in General Edward Braddock's disastrous Pennsylvania campaign of 1755, becoming an acquaintance of George Washington during the expedition. In 1758, Gage was wounded during the unsuccessful attack on Fort Ticonderoga; he was later promoted to brigadier general, and in the same year he married. After the French surrender, Gage became governor of Montreal and a district that encompassed Crown Point and an area reaching to the shores of Lake Ontario. In 1761, he was promoted to major general, and in 1763 he became commander in chief in America, assuming his post in New York City.

As rebelliousness rose in Massachusetts, Gage traveled to Boston and enhanced its garrison, but in 1773, he and his family returned to England. He was sent back to America the following year as both commander in chief and governor of Massachusetts, serving during the events leading to the battles at Lexington, Concord and Bunker Hill. His position was a difficult one, but he did little to stifle the organization of the provincial congresses and a strong patriot militia outside Boston, preferring to remain snug inside the city. He sent the fatal expedition to Lexington and Concord only under pressure from London, and the subsequent battle at Breed's Hill was a sobering event for the British—the butcher's bill of officers and men shocked everyone. Nonetheless, most critics voiced the opinion that if Gage had shown more energy in mid-1775, the rebellion might have been crushed at its beginning. Instead, he allowed the New England militiamen to form an army and then watched as Washington took command. Gage bore the full brunt of blame, and in late 1775, he was recalled to England. Completely out of favor with the government, he struggled to make ends meet, until he was appointed to the staff of Jeffrey Amherst in 1781. In 1782, he was made a full general, but he had no further assignments. *Further reading:* John R. Alden, *General Gage in America* (Baton Rouge, La., 1948).

GAINEY, Micajah. Loyalist partisan

Gainey lived on the Little Pedee River in South Carolina and led a troop of loyalists against the patriots of the region, often crossing swords with American Francis Marion. Gainey was defeated by Marion at Port's Ferry, South Carolina in August 1780 but continued operations for another year. In 1781, he made peace with the patriots and broke up his loyalist force.

GALLOWAY, Joseph (c. 1731–1803) Delegate to Congress, colonial official, loyalist

Galloway represented the most public case of an important colonial politician who was in close sympathy with the American cause but who could not tear himself away from allegiance to the crown. He worked mightily and long to preserve the colonies within some suitable imperial structure yet failed when overtaken by the force of rebellion.

Born in Maryland to a wealthy merchant and land-owning family, he went to Philadelphia to study law and settled there as one of the city's most successful lawyers. His marriage to Grace Growden in 1753 improved his financial and political position (her father was speaker of the colonial assembly). In the mid-1750s Galloway formed a close friendship and political alliance with Benjamin Franklin, and he worked with him for 20 years until the Revolution drove them apart. Galloway entered the assembly in 1756, sitting continuously until 1775 and acting as speaker—a powerful position—from 1766 to 1774. He and Franklin were united in an attempt to change the structure of the colonial government, hoping to rid Pennsylvania of the power of the proprietary Penn family and convert the colony to a royal government.

During the early years of the crisis with Great Britain, Galloway strongly supported the complaints of the patriotic colonists, especially since he wholeheartedly represented the interests of the wealthy merchant class. However, he was convinced that a new relationship between America and Britain could be devised, resting on the foundation of the British constitution and common law. He and Franklin grew farther and farther apart as Franklin was pushed by events into a more radical stance. In 1774, Galloway was selected as a delegate to the first Continental Congress, and he submitted a compromise plan of union, which he thought might preserve the peace. His plan called for an appointed president general in the colonies and a grand council to be elected by the colonial assemblies. The colonial government would be able to regulate trade and civil affairs and could veto acts of Parliament that might affect all the colonies. This plan had a good deal of charm for the more conservative elements in the first Congress, and after lengthy consideration it was defeated by only one vote.

Frustrated with the rejection and fearful of mob violence in Philadelphia, Galloway withdrew from the city and declined appointment to the second Congress in 1775. He eventually left for the refuge of British-held New York. Granted a pension by the government in London, Galloway tried to convince General William Howe to support a loyalist army, but was mostly ignored. In 1777, when Howe occupied Philadelphia, Galloway was installed as one of the loyalist civil authorities. He withdrew when the British abandoned Philadelphia in 1778, and he sailed for England. In Britain he spoke and wrote against the conduct of the war by Howe and continued until the end of the conflict to lobby for conciliation and union. His extensive property was confiscated after the Revolution by Pennsylvania and his petition to return in 1793 was turned down. *Further reading:* Ernest H. Baldwin, "Joseph Galloway: The Loyalist Politician," *Pennsylvania Magazine of History and Biography* 26 (1902), 442; Benjamin H. Newcomb, *Franklin and Galloway: A Political Partner-*ship (New Haven, 1972); Julian Boyd, *Anglo-American Union: Joseph Galloway's Plans to Preserve the British Empire, 1774–1788* (Philadelphia, 1941).

GALVAN, William de. French volunteer

Little is known about Galvan's background before he turned up in America in 1779 and applied to Congress for a commission. He was made an officer in the Continental Army in January 1780 and the following spring was assigned to the Marquis de Lafayette as a major. Lafayette sent him to Cape Henry to stand lookout for the French fleet bringing General Rochambeau's army to America—no one was certain where the fleet would land. Afterward, Galvan served with Lafayette's light infantry corps in Virginia, winning praise for his actions at the battle of Green Spring, where he reportedly captured a British gun. He also served as a division inspector under von Steuben at Yorktown.

GALVEZ, Bernardo de (1746–1786) Spanish official

The Spanish governor of Louisiana and Florida during the Revolution, Galvez came from a distinguished family, his father having been viceroy of New Spain and his uncle minister general of the Indies. Galvez served with the Spanish army in Portugal, Algiers and New Spain and attended military school at Ávila. He was sent to Louisiana with the rank of colonel, and in 1777, when he was only 31 years old, Galvez became governor. He pursued policies that weakened the British in the region, seizing British privateers and supporting the American agent Oliver Pollock's efforts in New Orleans to obtain supplies for the rebels.

After Spain entered the war more or less on America's side, Galvez proved to be an energetic commander and captured British outposts on the Mississippi River, including Baton Rouge and Natchez. In 1780, he took Mobile, which had been set up by the British as an outpost of their forces at Jamaica. In 1781, Galvez attacked the main British post in West Florida at Pensacola, surrounding the garrison under General John Campbell with a besieging army 10 times the size of the British force. The British held out longer than expected (especially considering the ragtag composition of Campbell's troops), but a stray Spanish shell landed in the British powder magazine, killing a hundred men and destroying one of the main redoubts. Campbell was forced to surrender.

Galvez's military successes resulted in the British ceding of both East and West Florida to Spain after the war in the Treaty of Paris, giving Spain control not only over the Floridas but also over the mouth of the Mississippi. At the conclusion of peace, Galvez returned to Spain and in 1783–84 was an advisor on policy affecting the future of the Florida and Louisiana territories. He was made major general, awarded Castilian titles of nobility, and appointed captain general of the Floridas and Louisiana. In 1785, Galvez was appointed viceroy of New Spain. Barely 40 years old, he died of a severe fever while in Mexico in 1786. *Further reading:* John W. Caughey, *Bernardo de Galvez in Louisiana, 1776–1783* (Berkeley, Calif., 1934).

GALVEZ, José de (1729–1786) Spanish official

The uncle of Bernardo de Galvez, José was probably the most important colonial administrative official in New Spain during the era of the American Revolution. He was appointed as *visitador* with wide discretionary powers in 1765 by Charles III with a commission to reform the administrative structure in the Spanish colonies. He submitted his recommendations in 1771 on his return to Spain, and they had wide-reaching effects. He was appointed minister general of the Indies in 1775 and took up residence in the New World, supporting his nephew's conquests during the war.

GAMBIER, James (1723–1789) British admiral

Perhaps the worst of a sorry lot of British naval commanders in America during the Revolution, Gambier was judged incompetent by his contemporaries as well as by historians since. He was apparently chosen for duty in North America for political reasons by Lord Sandwich, the first lord of the Admiralty, since his naval career was anything but distinguished. Gambier became a naval officer in the early 1740s, serving in the Mediterranean as a lieutenant by 1743. His first command was a sloop in 1746, and he moved on to command a succession of ships during the Seven Years' War, but at the end of the conflict with the French, he was relegated to commanding a guardship.

During the first years of the American Revolution, Gambier was in charge of victualling at Portsmouth. Nonetheless, in 1778, he was named as second in command to Lord Howe and successively John Byron on the North American station. When these senior admirals were absent, Gambier took nominal command of the navy. He was regarded by Sir Henry Clinton, the overall commander in chief, as a fool, and Gambier's whining correspondence does nothing to alleviate this opinion. He was recalled in 1779, and one observer commented that his replacement was the cause for "universal joy of all ranks." By the inexorable mechanism of seniority, Gambier reached vice admiral's rank but was forced into retirement in 1784 after briefly serving as commander at Jamaica. *Further reading:* William B. Willcox, "Arbuthnot, Gambier, and Graves: 'Old Women' of the Navy," in George Billias, *George Washington's Opponents* (New York, 1969).

GANNETT, Deborah. See SAMPSON, Deborah.

GANSEVOORT, Leonard (1751–1810) Delegate to Congress, legislator, jurist

The younger brother of Peter Gansevoort, Leonard served the civilian side of the patriot movement in New York. Born in Albany to a family of merchants and brewers, he studied law in New York City but returned to Albany to set up a practice in 1771. A member of the early provincial congresses in New York in 1775 and 1776, Gansevoort was president of the patriot congress that met in 1777, thus making him virtually the chief American executive in the state for a brief period. He continued in local offices during the war, acting as clerk of Albany County and city recorder, and he was a member of the New York assembly in 1778 and 1779. Gansevoort held a commission in the local militia company of light horse but saw no active field service. In 1788, following the war, he was sent as a delegate to Congress. His final public offices were judgeships of local courts in Albany. *Further reading:* Alice P. Kennedy, *The Gansevoorts of Albany: Dutch Patricians in the Upper Hudson Valley* (Syracuse, N.Y., 1969).

GANSEVOORT, Peter (1749–1812) Continental officer

Gansevoort was a member of a prominent Dutch family of Albany, New York and the brother of Leonard Gansevoort. He was appointed as a major of the 2nd New York Regiment in June 1775 and marched with Richard Montgomery's force on the Canadian invasion. On his return from the unsuccessful campaign, Gansevoort was promoted to lieutenant colonel and given command of Fort George. By the spring of 1777, he was colonel of

Peter Gansevoort

the 3rd New York and with about 550 of his men held the garrison at Fort Stanwix, which lay in the path of the force under British Lieutenant Colonel Barry St. Leger that was marching to join General John Burgoyne around Albany. Gansevoort had wisely repaired the dilapidated fort and gathered all reinforcements inside the walls. Despite St. Leger's greatly superior numbers, he had no heavy artillery and could not batter his way in. A display of St. Leger's Indian troops (who made up the bulk of his force) convinced Gansevoort and the rest of the Americans that determined resistance was preferable to surrender or capture at the hands of the Indians. Gansevoort's defense of the fort was skillful, and when St. Leger moved most of his fighters away to ambush an American relief column under Nicholas Herkimer at Oriskany on August 6, a detachment from the fort sallied out and destroyed the British camp and supplies. Bucked up by his strong second in command, Marinus Willet, Gansevoort defiantly rejected a second demand by St. Leger to surrender. The British abandoned the siege at news of a column advancing under Benedict Arnold.

The defense of Stanwix earned Gansevoort a high reputation and the thanks of Congress, but it also marked the apex of his active military career even though he was only 28. After a short assignment to Albany, he married and returned to command at Fort Stanwix in 1778. He had charge of the garrison at Saratoga in 1780 and later at Albany again. He received a commission as a brigadier general of New York militia in 1781 and was promoted to major general the following year, but he had no significant commands. Many years after the Revolution—in 1809—he was commissioned a brigadier general in the regular army, but there is no evidence of active duty before his death. *Further reading:* Alice P. Kennedy, *The Gansevoorts of Albany: Dutch Patricians in the Upper Hudson Valley* (Syracuse, N.Y., 1969).

GARDINER, John (1747–1808) Delegate to Congress, militia officer, legislator Born in South Kingstown, Rhode Island, Gardiner farmed near Narrangansett before the war. He was a captain in a militia unit known as the Kingstown Reds in 1775 and 1776. He sat in the Rhode Island legislature after the Revolution as a member of the cheap money party that dominated state politics and did much to frustrate the formation of an effective central government for the newly independent United States. In 1789, he was named as a delegate to the final Confederation Congress.

GARDNER, Caleb (1739–1806) Militia officer, merchant A native of Newport, Rhode Island, Gardner was a prosperous trader and, apparently, a cosmopolite. He was an officer in the Rhode Island militia and a member of the state assembly during the war. His most notable service, however, was as translator and liaison with the French expeditionary forces that lodged in Newport for much of 1780 and 1781. He is credited with guiding the French fleet into the harbor and thereafter working in close relationship with generals Rochambeau and Washington.

GARDNER, Joseph (1752–1794) Delegate to Congress, militia officer, physician Gardner was born in Chester County, Pennsylvania and set up a medical practice there before the Revolution. In 1776, he raised a company of militia and served as captain in addition to his membership on the local committee of safety. He was a member of the Pennsylvania Assembly from 1776 to 1778 and sat on the Supreme Executive Council in 1779. In 1784 and 1785, he was a delegate from Pennsylvania to the Confederation Congress. Following his years in public office, he returned to medicine, setting up a practice in Philadelphia. Two years before his death, Gardner moved to Elkton, Maryland.

GARTH, George (d. 1819) British general Garth entered the Royal Army in 1755 and was a colonel by 1779 when he was given the local rank of major general and assigned as second in command to William Tryon for the British raid on the Connecticut coast. Garth and Tryon successfully attacked several towns, including New Haven, which they burned and plundered in retaliation for Connecticut raids on British shipping. Garth was captured at sea by the French while he was on his way south to take command in Georgia later the same year. He was eventually exchanged and served in the West Indies. He reached the rank of full general before retiring.

GATES, Horatio (1728–1806) Continental general

Gates's reputation, despite attempts at resuscitation, remains among the lowest of all senior American commanders of the Revolution. While he must certainly be allowed credit for his triumph at Saratoga, nothing can wipe away the degradation of his flight from the field at Camden.

Born in England, the son of a housekeeper for the Duke of Leeds, Gates joined the British army at an early age and served in North America during the Seven Years' War, with General Edward Braddock in the unsuccessful effort to capture Fort Duquesne in 1755 and later in Martinique. He retired from the army at half pay in 1765 with the rank of major. In 1772, helped by George Washington, he settled on a farm in Virginia. Siding with the patriots, Gates entered the Continental Army when it was organized in June 1775 as Washington's adjutant general with the rank of brigadier general, and his military experience in the Royal Army was invaluable in setting up a new military force from scratch. In May 1776, he was promoted to major general and sent to the Northern Department to serve under Philip Schuyler. Their relationship was adversarial from the beginning and came to be the focus of a severe rift between the New Englanders, who favored Gates, and the New Yorkers, who supported Schuyler. For several months, Gates and Schuyler were at the center of complex changes in command ordered by Congress—where the award of command became a political issue, as did most of Gates's subsequent military assignments—with Washington more or less on the sidelines.

By the end of the year, Gates rejoined Washington for the New Jersey campaign, but in the spring of 1777, Congress sent Gates to be commander at Fort Ticonderoga, ostensibly in preparation to succeed Schuyler as commander of the Northern Department. However, Congress then reneged, and Gates traveled to Philadelphia to protest his treatment before the delegates. After Ticonderoga fell to the British, Gates again went to New York state and in August finally replaced Schuyler as commander of the Northern Department. He took over a large army that stood in the path of Burgoyne's invasion.

Horatio Gates medal

While it may be argued that Gates did little except set up in a good defensive position at Saratoga and that he quarreled with his best generals—notably Arnold, who was the battlefield hero of the subsequent fighting near Saratoga—Gates was in command and quite rightly allowed Burgoyne to batter himself to death at Freeman's Farm and Bemis Heights. Gates's ill-considered agreement to the infamous Convention rather than a simple surrender led to endless problems, but the idea may have seemed reasonable at the time.

It was perhaps ultimately Gates's worst fortune to have been hailed as a hero just at the time that Washington suffered another in a long series of defeats. The obvious but illusory contrast between the two generals led many congressmen, most of whom failed to understand the simplest military truths, to champion Gates. The contrast also fostered a movement to make Gates commander in chief, replacing Washington. The backroom scheming was complex and nasty and led Congress to appoint Gates president of the board of war created in October 1777. The so-called Conway Cabal to discredit Washington and elevate Gates collapsed, however (few Americans of the time could withstand the withering personal censure of Washington, no matter how politically brave they seemed in private). After reestablishing his working relationship with Washington, Gates resumed command of the Northern Department in April 1778, and later that year he became commander of the Eastern Department in Boston.

In July 1780, without consulting Washington, Congress appointed Gates commander of the Southern Department, marking one of the most disastrous civilian decisions about military affairs in American history. Gates's performance was scarcely to be believed. He took over an army in a low state but remained blind to the small size of his force and the fact that it was ill-fed and ill-prepared to fight, and he rushed headlong into a confrontation with the British at Camden. Worse was to come. Not only did Gates carelessly allow militia to be placed in crucial positions on the front line, but he himself refused to come close to the field, preferring to establish himself well to the rear and ignoring pleas from his staff to take command. When the militia broke and panicked in the first moments of the battle, Gates simply turned tail and ran. In a

Horatio Gates portrait

miserable display of personal cowardice (despite the claims of his apologists), Gates commandeered a fast horse and rode as hard as he could away from the sound of the guns. He ended the day 60 miles away in Charlotte and continued hell-bent for the following two days, reaching Hillsboro, North Carolina, on the third day after the battle. His second in command, the Baron de Kalb, died the same day from 11 wounds suffered on the field. In total disgrace, Gates retired to his farm and for two years tried to get a Congressional inquiry to clear his name. Remarkably, he was neither court-martialed nor condemned by an official inquiry, and he was allowed to return to the army at Newburgh in 1782 for the last year of the war. In 1783, Gates retired once again to his farm. His wife died in 1784, and he remarried in 1786. In 1790, Gates freed his slaves and moved to New York City, serving in the New York legislature in 1800–01. *Further reading:* Paul D. Nelson, *General Horatio Gates: A Biography* (Baton Rouge, La., 1976).

GEDDES, George. American privateer

Geddes sailed during the Revolution as a privateer out of Philadelphia. In 1779, he commanded a 10-gun brig, the *Holker*, under a commission from the state of Pennsylvania, and he captured a significant store of artillery and military supplies when he took the British ship *Diana*. By 1781, Geddes commanded one of the more powerful privateers, the *Congress*,

George III

with 24 guns and a crew of 200. In September 1781, he surprised a British 16-gun sloop, *Savage*, off the coast of Georgia where it had been raiding along the shore. After a long night chase, Geddes caught the smaller ship and pounded it into surrender, killing the British captain during the battle. Unfortunately for Geddes, a British frigate captured both the *Congress* and his prize before the privateer could reach a friendly port. The *Congress* was taken into the British service as the *Duchess of Cumberland*.

GELSTON, David (1744–1828) Delegate to Congress, state official

Born in Bridgehampton, New York, Gelston was an active patriot as a member of three provincial congresses between 1775 and 1777. In the latter year, he became a member of the state assembly and attended the state constitutional convention. He continued in the legislature until 1785, serving as speaker during his last year. He was one of New York's delegates to the final Confederation Congress in 1789. He continued in public office as a member of the state council, senator, canal commissioner and judge of a surrogate court. In 1801, Gelston was appointed customs collector for the Port of New York, a post he held for the following 19 years.

GEORGE III (1738–1820) King of Great Britain and Ireland

Grandson of George II and his successor as king, George William Frederick ascended to the throne in 1760 when he was 22. His image in the United States has never been the same since Thomas Jefferson cataloged his despotic transgressions in the Declaration of Independence, but the truth is, George was a capable man who was bent on enjoying all his prerogatives, controlling his government insofar as he could, and maintaining the power and dignity of the throne and Great Britain. The rebelliousness of the American colonies seemed to him to impinge on nearly all these goals, and his reaction was predictably stubborn, yet he was far from an ogre or an absolute monarch. He was also a chronically sick man, afflicted with a rare genetic disease (porphyria) that also beset his offspring and his European cousins, although his severest symptoms did not appear until after the American Revolution. He had an emotionally impoverished childhood and emerged into early adulthood closely attached to his tutor and confidant, the Earl of Bute. George was not entirely unprepared to take the throne, however. He was the first of the Hanoverians to be really an Englishman (English was his first language and unlike his grandfather, he spoke

George III

with no foreign accent), and he was reasonably well educated. Moreover, he was industrious, hard-working and completely upright in his own morality.

His main task after taking the throne was to gain as much control of the political process as he could, wresting power from the so-called Whigs. He set about diminishing the Whigs, terminating the government of William Pitt the elder and searching for a chief minister he could trust—Bute proving early to be a poor minister and immensely unpopular. He also succeeded in controlling the terms of the Treaty of Paris of 1763 that brought an end to the Seven Years' War. George skillfully employed the best political weapons at his disposal: money and honors.

The entire governmental and political system of England (and to a large extent colonial America) revolved around buying support with outright grants of cash, purchase of Parliamentary seats or the award of places that carried with them both prestige and government income. The king could control the votes of Parliament by controlling the income and places of those who voted, and he learned how to do so very well indeed. The result was a fantastic web of what later generations (and many at the time) viewed as corruption. Merit had little to do with office and political power almost everything. The king's 10-year struggle to gain control over Parliament resulted in 1770 in the installation of Lord North, who was doggedly loyal to George III, as prime minister.

But the repressive policies toward the American colonies the king effected through the North ministry, of course, backfired. George and North could scarcely imagine that the attempts to raise money from the colonies and to assert what they saw as perfectly legitimate prerogatives would rekindle a long-smoldering feud and eventually lead to open defiance and warfare. Once the issues were joined, however, the stubborn George would not back down until the very end. Even after news of the British defeat at Yorktown reached London, George III stalled North's resignation until the following spring. He finally and reluctantly authorized peace negotiations to end the American Revolution, and he tried to find amenable ministers during a quick succession of governments in 1782 and 1783. Following conclusion of the Treaty of Paris, the king appointed

After a reading of the Declaration of Independence, New York troops tore down an equestrian statue of George III. The statue was later melted down into bullets for the American army.

William Pitt the Younger prime minister in December 1783, bringing long-term stability.

In the fall of 1788, however, the symptoms of insanity induced by his congenital malady (they had first appeared in 1765) overwhelmed the king, rendering him mad; but he recovered, and with the outbreak of the French Revolution, his popularity among the people revived. Shorter periods of insanity occurred in 1801 and 1804, and the disgusting behavior of his own family—especially his two profligate eldest sons—increased his stress. In 1810, after the death of his favorite daughter, he slipped into permanent dementia and the Prince of Wales assumed the role of regent. George III's final decade was spent as a blind, deaf madman. *Further reading:* Allen Andrews, *The King Who Lost America: George III and Independence* (London, 1976); J. Steven Watson, *The Reign of George III, 1760–1815* (Oxford, 1960).

GERARD, Conrad Alexandre (1729–1790) French diplomat

Born in Alsace, Gerard entered the French diplomatic service in 1753 after education at the University of Strasbourg. He passed through a series of increasingly important assign-

Conrad Gerard

ments but was essentially an obscure career diplomat until the ascension of the Comte de Vergennes to the foreign ministry in 1774. Gerard was Vergennes's favorite and subsequently was named as the first French minister plenipotentiary to the United States when France signed an alliance with the new nation in 1778. He served in Philadelphia until 1780. *Further reading:* John J. Meng, ed., *Despatches and Instructions of Conrad Alexandre Gerard, 1778–1780* (Baltimore, 1939).

GERMAIN, George Sackville, Lord (1716–1785) British official

Germain was the British cabinet officer most responsible for the conduct of the war in America. The son of the first Duke of Dorset (lord lieutenant of Ireland during the reign of George II), Germain attended the Westminster School and received a degree from Trinity College, Dublin, in 1734. In 1737, he was made a captain in the Irish 7th Horse Regiment, and in 1740 he became a lieutenant colonel of the 28th Foot Regiment. He became a member of Parliament in 1741. He fought as commander of his regiment in the Low Countries and was wounded at the battle of Fontenoy in May 1745. The following year he became commander of the 20th Foot Regiment and, in 1749, of the 12th Dragoons. Then, in 1750 he became colonel in command of his original regiment.

Germain served as his father's personal secretary and secretary of war during his father's second stay in Ireland in 1751–56. In 1755, Germain was promoted to major general and assigned as the Duke of Marlborough's second in command in Hanover under Prince Ferdinand, assuming command when Marlborough died in September 1758. His nearly uninterrupted military rise came to an abrupt halt at the battle of Minden in 1759. He was judged to

have been slow to bring up the British cavalry, especially in the opinion of George II, who undertook a personal campaign against Germain. Germain was court-martialed and judged unfit for military service. He was out of the army and stained with a black mark that he worked the rest of his life to erase.

It was in 1770 that he took the name Germain upon inheriting property from Lady Betty Germain and began a remarkable public recovery as a politician and minister. He allied himself with Lord North, and in November 1775, Germain became secretary of state for the colonies and also lord commissioner of trade and plantations, so that—ironically for a cashiered general—he was in control of all British forces prosecuting the war against the Americans throughout the Revolution.

During the war he had many conflicts with generals Howe, Carleton and Clinton, whereas he strongly favored Burgoyne and Cornwallis. He has been often blamed for the overall poor showing of British arms during the war and especially for his policies that contributed to the British defeat; however, in fairness his strategies were basically sound. The difficulties of conducting a long war so far from home base were underestimated and more than any government or army could be expected to overcome. When the French entered the war in 1778, the supreme advantage of seaborne mobility that had served the British so well up to that point was never quite the same, and it vanished entirely off

Lord George Germain

the Virginia Capes in the Fall of 1781. Nonetheless, Germain was negligent in controlling and coordinating the invasion plan of Burgoyne in 1777, and his indulgence of Cornwallis in 1781 contributed greatly to the latter's fatal mistakes in the south.

Germain resigned with the fall of the North government in February 1782 and was given a peerage as Viscount Sackville. In 1783, he retired to his country home in Sussex in poor health, and he died a year and a half later. *Further reading:* Alan Valentine, *Lord George Germain* (New York, 1962); Gerald S. Brown, *The American Secretary: The Colonial Policy of Lord George Germain, 1775–1778* (Ann Arbor, Mich., 1963).

GERRY, Elbridge (1744–1814) Delegate to Congress, state official, vice president

Gerry had a long, complex career in public office, filled with flip-flop changes of stance; his mind seemed incapable of consistency. He was born in Marblehead, Massachusetts to a merchant family and after graduation from Harvard in 1762 joined the family business of exporting dried cod to the West Indies and Europe. He was very successful as a merchant and an acute businessman, which led naturally to an interest in preserving colonial economic rights—especially fishing rights—in the face of British attempts to milk the American economy. He took a seat in the Massachusetts legislature in 1772 and soon associated himself with Sam Adams, becoming a leader of the radical faction in colonial politics. He was a member of the Marblehead Committee of Correspondence and then was named additionally to the Massachusetts committee. He used his mercantile connections in Marblehead to funnel supplies to Boston after the British Parliament passed the Boston Port Bill in an attempt to cut off the city after the Boston Tea Party.

Gerry attended the provincial congresses in Massachusetts and sat on the council of safety with specific responsibility for finding supplies and building up the colony's stock of arms and military equipment. When General Thomas Gage launched the British expedition toward Lexington and Concord in April 1775, Gerry narrowly escaped capture at Menotomy. The following year, he was sent to the Continental Congress, where he voted for independence but did not sign the Declaration until September. He was appointed to the congressional committee that dealt with finance and added a great

Elbridge Gerry

deal through his business expertise; however, the strange inconsistency of his viewpoint began to appear as he vacillated from one side to the other on the question of half pay for the army. He voiced an almost pathological fear of a standing army but at other times claimed that the Congress owed half pay as a sacred obligation. At times he seemed to be a supporter of George Washington, yet he also supported Thomas Conway during the so-called Conway Cabal and was a member of a congressional committee that strongly criticized Washington's plans in 1778. He was involved in supplying the Continental Army throughout the first four years of the war as a private businessman, while at the same time chairing the finance committee of Congress that regulated the commissary work. In 1780, he quarreled with fellow congressmen over a relatively minor change in the price formulas for supplies, and he withdrew to Massachusetts for the next three years although he was still officially a delegate. He spent the last three years of the Revolution as a merchant and owner of privateers.

His extended career after the Revolution nearly defies summary in light of his frequent changes of viewpoint. At first he advocated a strong federal government, and then he refused to support the new Constitution. He was elected to the first U.S. Congress as an anti-Federalist but behaved in office as a Federalist. His strangest behavior came in 1797 as a member of the commission sent to France. He was completely manipulated by French foreign minister Talleyrand during the so-called XYZ Affair and came away badly discredited. He also lost races for the governorship of Massachusetts three times but was elected in 1810. During his term as governor he achieved lasting fame for his involvement in manipulating voting districts—a practice that came to be known as Gerrymandering. In 1813, Gerry was elected as vice president to James Madison. He died in office in Washington, D.C. *Further reading:* George A. Billias, *Elbridge Gerry: Founding Father and Republican Statesman* (New York, 1976).

GERVAIS, John Lewis (d. 1798) Delegate to Congress, state official

Born in France and educated in the German state of Hanover, Gervais emigrated to South Carolina in 1764. He became a planter and by the time of the Revolution was influential in politics. He attended the South Carolina patriot provincial meetings of 1775 and 1776 and was a member of the council of safety. In 1778, he was appointed deputy postmaster for South Carolina, and in 1780, he helped raise troops for the unsuccessful defense of the state against the British invasion of that year. During 1781 and 1782, Gervais was president of the state senate. He was sent as a delegate to the Confederation Congress in 1782 and 1783.

GIBAULT, Pierre (1737–1804) French-Canadian clergyman

Gibault played an important if disputed role in George Rogers Clark's conquest of the Illinois Territory in 1778. He was born in Quebec and may have lived on the Illinois frontier as a child. He attended seminary in Quebec and was ordained a priest by Bishop Jean-Oliver Briand around 1766 at a relatively advanced age. Briand sent Gibault to the western frontier in 1768, naming him vicar general with his seat at Kaskaskia. When George Rogers Clark invaded the Illinois country in 1778, taking Kaskaskia almost without a blow, Gibault appealed to the American commander for tolerance. According to some accounts, Gibault practically changed allegiances when Clark guaranteed the sanctity of the Catholic churches. Gibault reportedly urged the local French *habitants* to support the Americans and even delivered messages to the French at Vincennes. Gibault's role in Clark's victories has been somewhat obscured by the conflicting testimony after the fact.

In 1780, Bishop Briand suspended Gibault from ecclesiastical office, probably as the result of charges of disloyalty brought by the British, but the exact nature of Gibault's offense was not specified. Gibault himself vehemently denied complicity with the Americans, but the authorities in Virginia (under whose commission Clark had invaded the west) publicly acknowledged the priest's role in convincing the French in Illinois to change sides. Whatever he did or did not do to aid Clark, Gibault had a difficult time after the Revolution. He was separated from the church in Canada but was not viewed with favor by John Carroll, new Roman Catholic bishop for America. Gibault moved into Spanish territory across the Mississippi River and spent his remaining days under the ecclesiastical authority of the Spanish church. *Further reading:* Joseph P. Donnelly, *Pierre Gibault, Missionary, 1737–1802* (Loyola University Press, 1971); Walter Havinghurst, "A Sword for George Rogers Clark," *American Heritage* 13 (October 1962), 56–64.

GIBBONS, William (1726–1800) Delegate to Congress, state official

Although born in South Carolina near Bear Bluff, Gibbons lived his adult life in Georgia, where he became a leading rice grower near Savannah. He was a member of the more radical Georgia revolutionary faction and helped to organize the colony's participation in the rebellion during the early years of resistance to the crown. In 1774, he was a member of the Sons of Liberty, and he was one of the radicals who broke into the royal powder magazine in Savannah in May 1775 after hearing the news of Lexington and Concord. Gibbons was a leader during 1775 in forming the provincial congress that contested for control of the colony with royal governor James Wright, and he was a member of the committee of safety. From 1777 to 1781, Gibbons served on the executive council that assumed responsibility for governing Georgia on behalf of the patriots. Along with service in the Georgia House of Representatives during the 1780s, Gibbons was also the state's delegate to the Confederation Congress from 1784 to 1786.

GIBSON, George (1747–1791) Continental and militia officer

Born in Lancaster, Pennsylvania, Gibson was brought up on the frontier. He was apprenticed to a Philadelphia mercantile house at age 15 and gained trade experience as a supercargo on voyages to the West Indies. Before the Revolution, he operated a trading post at Fort Pitt in partnership with his brother John and fought in Lord Dunmore's War in 1774. He organized a company of back-country militia in 1775, which was attached to Colonel Hugh Mercer's brigade at Williamsburg, Virginia. Gibson's most famous exploit during the war was an expedition down the Mississippi to New Orleans in July 1776. He and 25 men disguised as traders purchased 10,000 pounds of gunpowder from the Spanish and carried it back upriver under the noses of the British. He was appointed as colonel of the 1st Virginia Regiment in 1777 and served in the New Jersey theater. In 1779, he was relieved from field duty and put in charge of a British prisoner of war camp near York, Pennsylvania until the end of the war. He turned to farming near Carlisle, Pennsylvania until 1791, when he volunteered for Arthur St. Clair's expedition against the western Indians. Gibson was killed in a skirmish on the Wabash River on December 14.

GIBSON, John (1740–1822) Continental officer   The brother of George Gibson, John held several relatively high commands during the Revolution. He was born in western Pennsylvania and was an Indian trader at Fort Pitt before the war. He was captured during Pontiac's War in 1763 but was released or escaped the following year. He fought in Lord Dunmore's War in 1774 and was named the following year as an agent of Virginia to the western Indians. In 1776, Gibson was commissioned as lieutenant colonel of the 13th Virginia Regiment, and he transferred to the 6th Virginia a year later as colonel. He was part of Lachlan McIntosh's futile expedition against western Indians and loyalists in 1778, taking command of Fort Laurens when McIntosh retreated to Fort Pitt. He became commander of the 9th Virginia in September 1778 and was named as second in command to George Rogers Clark for an expedition against Detroit that never got off the ground. In February 1781, Gibson was made commander of the 7th Virginia and posted to Fort Pitt, but he was superseded there and retired from active duty in March 1782. When the Continental Army was dissolved in the fall of 1783, Gibson received a brevet as brigadier general. He continued in the militia after the war and reached the rank of major general. *Further reading:* Charles

Hanko, *The Life of John Gibson, Soldier, Patriot, Statesman* (1955).

GILBERT, Benjamin (1755–1828) Continental soldier   Serving during the war as a private soldier and a lower-ranking officer, Gilbert left both a diary and a collection of letters that recorded the day-to-day experiences of a member of the Continental Army. He was born in Brookfield, Massachusetts to a family of ordinary means and a slight military tradition (both his father and brother served in the Seven Years' War and were members of the local militia).

Gilbert was a fifer in the Brookfield militia company of Jonathan Barnes and marched off on April 19, 1775 to fight the British retreating from Lexington and Concord. He subsequently enlisted in Ebenezer Learned's Regiment and fought at Bunker Hill. With the reorganization of the army in 1776, Gilbert joined the 5th Massachusetts (serving under Captain Daniel Shays) and took part in the campaign the following year against General John Burgoyne. He received a commission as an ensign in December 1779 and reenlisted the following month. During the remainder of the war, Gilbert served as a recruiter and was on duty in the Hudson Highlands. He became a lieutenant in the 3rd Massachusetts in the summer of 1783, a few months before his discharge.

During much of his active Revolutionary War service, Gilbert kept a relatively detailed diary of his experiences in which he transcribed many of the letters he sent to family and friends. His private writing shows the everyday life of the soldier, covering such topics as food, clothing, drinking, sex, illness, Freemasonry and many other details. Following the war, Gilbert purchased a farm in Oswego County, New York and settled into a peaceful existence as a married man and a farmer. He eventually served as a sheriff, a town supervisor and a justice of the peace. *Further reading:* Rebecca D. Symmes, ed., *A Citizen Soldier in the American Revolution: The Diary of Benjamin Gilbert in Massachusetts and New York* (Cooperstown, N.Y., 1980); John Shy, ed., *Winding Down: The Revolutionary War Letters of Lieutenant Benjamin Gilbert of Massachusetts, 1780–1783* (Ann Arbor, Mich., 1989).

GILBERT, Thomas (c. 1714–1796) Loyalist organizer   Born in Taunton, Massachusetts to a family that had lived in the colony since the mid-17th century, Gilbert was an officer during the Seven Years' War and received half pay for his service. He farmed near Freetown, sat in the House of Representatives, and supported the crown from the beginning of conflict with American patriots. In 1774, he opposed sending delegates to the Continental Congress, for example, and he prevailed on Freetown to protest the dumping of tea into Boston Harbor. In consequence, he became very unpopular with his neighbors and was assaulted verbally by mobs several times. In early 1775, acting at the urging of General Gage in Boston, Gilbert began to organize a loyalist Massachusetts militia, recruiting 300 men to the cause. His efforts came to naught, however, when he was proscribed by the provincial congress in May 1775 and his militia threatened with destruction by the patriots. He had to flee to the safety of Boston. Gilbert evacuated with the British army to Halifax in 1776, although he apparently served with the British army as a civilian during the war. In 1783, he settled in Nova Scotia, his property in Massachusetts having been seized.

GILL, John (1732–1785) Publisher

Gill was a partner of Benjamin Edes in publishing the *Boston Gazette and Country Journal,* which they founded in 1755. For a time, they were also the official printers for Massachusetts, but the partnership broke up in 1775. Their newspaper, however, had by then served well as a forum for radical patriotism: Gill was arrested by the British for publishing sedition, but he was held only a short while. In 1776, Gill began the *Continental Journal and Weekly Advertiser,* which he continued to edit and publish throughout the Revolution.

GILMAN, John Taylor (1753–1828) Delegate to Congress, state official

The brother of Nicolas Gilman, John was born in Exeter, New Hampshire and was a merchant and shipbuilder, joining his father's business as a teenager. During the war he was deputy treasurer of New Hampshire and he became treasurer in 1783, serving until 1794. He also sat in the New Hampshire legislature from 1779 to 1781. In 1782, Gilman was selected as one of the state's delegates to the Confederation Congress. After the passage of the new federal constitution, Gilman was elected governor of New Hampshire as a Federalist. He was in the governor's chair from 1794 until 1805 and again from 1812 until 1813. While governor he opposed the formation of any banks in the state except the one of which he was president.

GILMAN, Nicolas (1755–1814) Delegate to Congress, militia officer, state official

The younger of the two prominent Gilman brothers of New Hampshire, Nicolas served in a militia unit during most of the war. Following the peace and his return to his native Exeter, Gilman entered politics and was selected as a delegate to the Confederation Congress during 1786 and 1788. He was also a delegate to the federal Constitutional Convention in 1787 and was subsequently elected as a U.S. representative from New Hampshire as a Federalist, serving from 1789 until 1797. He switched to the Jeffersonian side of national politics in 1804 and was appointed to the U.S. Senate in 1805, a post he held until his death nine years later.

GIMAT, Jean-Joseph Sourbader de (b. 1743) French volunteer

A native of Gascony, Gimat joined the French Royal Army in 1761 as a junior officer and served until 1776, when he accompanied the Marquis de Lafayette and Baron de Kalb to America. He had been part of the deal struck between Lafayette and the American envoy Silas Deane to have the Congress grant commissions and commands to the Frenchmen. In July 1777, Gimat received the rank of major in the Continental Army and retroactive pay and seniority as of the previous year. He acted as an aide-de-camp to Lafayette until January 1779, when he temporarily returned to France. He sailed back to America with Lafayette in the fall of 1780 and was given command of a light infantry regiment under Lafayette for the movement into Virginia. Gimat served with distinction during the campaign, especially at the battle of Green Spring in July 1781. At Yorktown, he just missed glory when Alexander Hamilton preempted his command of the American forces designated to assault Redoubt Number 10. Nonetheless, Gimat was wounded during the siege and subsequently commended for distinguished service. He returned to France in the following year and resumed his commission in the French army, rising to colonel. He later was assigned to the West Indies and made governor of St. Lucia.

GIRTY, Simon (1741–1818) Loyalist turncoat

One of the most feared and hated figures of the frontier during and after the American Revolution, Girty earned the revulsion that attached to white leaders who participated in the brutal style of Indian warfare, and he gained additional opprobrium as a turncoat traitor.

He and his brothers (whose activities are often confused with Simon's) were born in western Pennsylvania. During the Seven Years' War, Indians killed his parents and captured Girty. He lived among the Seneca from 1756 to 1759, learning their culture and language. After his release, Girty served the British as a scout and interpreter, taking part in Lord Dunmore's War in 1774. By 1776, he was a junior officer in the Virginia militia, but he went over to the British side in 1779 and began the activities that earned him the name "The Great Renegade." He was active mostly in the Ohio Valley and led or participated in many Indian raids against American settlers over the next several years. To some degree, he answered to British authorities in Detroit, but discipline was loose. Girty's most nefarious actions may have been his involvement in the hideous death of American colonel William Crawford, who was captured and burned to death by Indians under Girty's command in June 1782. Later in the same summer, Girty led a large force of Indians and loyalists in a raid into the Kentucky territory, and he skillfully ambushed a group of settlers at the battle of Blue Licks on August 9. He moved to Detroit at the end of the war, where he worked for the British. He took part in the Indian wars of the 1790s, helping to defeat Arthur St. Clair in 1791 and serving with the Indians who lost to Anthony Wayne at Fallen Timbers in 1794. Girty moved to Canada when the British gave up Detroit. *Further reading:* W. Butterfield, *History of the Girtys* (Cincinnati, 1890); Thomas Boyd, *Simon Girty* (New York, 1928).

GIST, Mordecai (1743–1792) Continental general

During most of the war Gist commanded Maryland Continentals, who were among the best units on any battlefield where they appeared. He was born near Reisterstown, Maryland (the family name was originally "Guest") and was a shipper and businessman in Baltimore at the beginning of the Revolution, serving as captain of a local militia unit, the Baltimore Independent Company.

Mordecai Gist

In January 1776, Gist was commissioned as a major in the 1st Maryland Regiment that was raised and commanded by William Smallwood. The Marylanders went north to join the main Continental Army, and the 1st won laurels at the battle of Long Island in August 1776 under Gist's direct command when they fought valiantly and well as part of Lord Stirling's stand against the British regulars in the mismanaged battle. After the battle of White Plains, where Colonel Smallwood was wounded, Gist was given a promotion to colonel and transferred to the 3rd Maryland, which he led at Germantown the following year. He returned to the South after the New Jersey and Pennsylvania campaigns and in 1779 was promoted to brigadier general and given the 2nd Maryland Regiment.

By this stage of the war, the Maryland regiments had proven themselves among the few Continental units capable of standing toe-to-toe with the British regulars, and they had been at the heart of most of the key battles in the north. They now fell under the command of Horatio Gates, however, which led to their near annihilation. At the battle of Camden, Gist and the 2nd Maryland were placed with Baron Johann de Kalb at the center of the line. When the feckless militia on their flank broke and ran, the Marylanders were in the midst of a maelstrom. The fierce fighting ended with high bravery from Gist and his men, but debilitating casualties and crushing defeat. Gist received the thanks of Congress (which was shamefaced at appointing the cowardly and inept Gates to command) for his part at Camden, but the Marylanders were destroyed as a cohesive fighting force. Gist spent the next months in recruiting and supplying Nathanael Greene's army in the Carolinas. He retired in November 1783 and bought a plantation near Charleston, South Carolina. *Further reading:* K. W. Blakeslee, *Mordecai Gist and His American Progenitors* (1923).

GIST, Nathaniel (d. 1796) Continental officer

Probably a cousin of General Mordecai Gist, Nathaniel was authorized in January 1777 by George Washington to raise a ranger corps of four companies for Continental service. Commissioned colonel of the unit, Gist raised two companies in his native Maryland and two in Virginia. The rangers were combined with Thurston's Additional Regiment in January 1779. Gist (and presumably most of his men) was captured at the fall of Charleston in May 1780, and the ranger corps officially disbanded in November of the same year. He retired from service in January 1783.

GLEN, Henry (1739–1814) Legislator

Born in Schenectady, New York, Glen was a member of several provincial congresses between 1774 and 1776. During the Revolutionary War, he was a deputy quartermaster general. After the war, he sat first in the New York State Assembly and then was elected to the U.S. House of Representatives for three terms.

GLOVER, John (1732–1797) Continental general

Glover was a competent, reliable leader who played a key military role at several points in the Revolutionary War, especially at the head of his colorful regiment of Marblehead Mariners during the campaigns of 1776. He was born in Salem, Massachusetts but moved at an early age to the sea village of Marblehead. Starting as a shoemaker, he became a well-to-do fisherman, shipowner and merchant. He was also active as an officer of the local militia, reaching the rank of captain by 1773. Glover was relatively slow to be swept up by revolutionary fervor, however, and he spent much of his time on private and business affairs until shortly before the final breach with the mother country. In 1773 and 1774, for example, he was much occupied with an attempt to open an inoculation hospital in Marblehead, a project that failed in the face of local opposition. Nonetheless, he was a member of Marblehead's committee of correspondence.

In April 1775, Glover was commissioned a colonel by the Provincial Congress, and he organized

John Glover

the 21st Massachusetts Regiment, also known as Glover's Massachusetts Battalion, made up of fishermen and seafarers from Marblehead. Outfitted in short blue jackets and loose, nautical trousers, the men of the 21st were expert in handling small craft in all conditions. Moreover, they formed a close-knit unit and knew the value of working together as disciplined crews. Glover's men first were stationed at Marblehead but moved to Boston after Washington took command of the new Continental Army, of which they became a part. The Mariners were reorganized in January 1776 as the 14th Continental Regiment, one of the original units of the Continental Line. Washington had earlier given Glover the task of organizing a small fleet of privateers to harass British transport and supply shipping around Boston. The effort could do little more than nip at the heels of the Royal Navy, but some of Glover's men captured the *Nancy*, an ordnance brigantine, in November 1775, delivering a large store of arms and goods to the American cause.

Glover's Mariners proved their unique worth in August 1776. Washington had allowed almost his entire army to be bottled up by the British on Long Island and was under heavy attack by Sir William Howe's naval and land forces. A defeat at the hands of Howe's superior numbers threatened to destroy the Continental Army and end the Revolution. During a howling storm that kept the British squadron temporarily from beating upriver to cut off an American escape, Washington called on Glover and the Marbleheaders. Requisitioning all available craft, Glover's men began in the dark to ferry the army and its supplies across the rough waters of the river, aided by the 27th Massachusetts from Salem. By morning, Washington's force was safely on the New York shore.

Glover and his Massachusetts men were capable of more than rowing boats, however. They performed heroically on land as well at Kip's Bay, New York and especially at the battle of Pell's Point in October 1776, when 750 of Glover's men stalled the British attempt to trap Washington's army. The Mariners stood off almost 4,000 British and German troops and inflicted heavy casualties while Washington withdrew to White Plains.

Glover and his Mariners secured their place in American history two and a half months later, on Christmas Day, 1776. Gathering on the Pennsylvania shore to which Washington had fled after defeat in New York, the Mariners loaded the army onto borrowed craft—large Durham boats that held an entire company of infantry—and rowed across the Delaware River in the middle of a bitter winter storm, fending off ice with poles and oars. Despite the darkness and fierce weather, by morning Washington's men had disembarked on the New Jersey shore, ready to surprise the German mercenaries in their winter quarters at Trenton. Glover's men not only pulled their oars through the night, but they formed up and advanced as part of Washington's force, blocking the Hessian escape route. After the victory, the Mariners marched back to the river, took to their boats again, and moved the American army and 900 prisoners back safely to the Pennsylvania side, despite subzero temperatures and an ice-clogged river, completing one of the more remarkable exploits in American military annals. The enlistments of the mariners of the amphibious regiment ended, however, with the new year, and Glover's unit broke up during the following weeks.

Glover himself went back to Marblehead to tend to his sick wife (she died the next year). He turned down a commission as brigadier general in February 1777, but he eventually decided to rejoin the fight and accepted the new rank in June. He was attached to the command of General Philip Schuyler and then General Horatio Gates in New York and fought during the defeat of General John Burgoyne. One of his duties after the surrender at Saratoga was to escort Burgoyne's defeated army to Cambridge. He then was assigned to the ill-fated attempt to capture Newport, Rhode Island in 1778 as commander of one of the Continental brigades under the Marquis de Lafayette. After a brief tour as commander at Providence, Glover moved to West Point with a brigade. He remained in the Hudson Highlands during the balance of the war except for a recruiting trip to Massachusetts in 1782. Citing ill health, he retired in 1782, noting somewhat bitterly that he had received no pay since 1780. He was brevetted as a major general in 1783.

He returned to Marblehead and his second wife (he had remarried in 1781), and during the postwar period, Glover carried on his maritime business and fulfilled his civic duties as a selectman of the town, a member of the Massachusetts constitutional convention and a representative to the General Court. *Further reading:* George A. Billias, *General John Glover and His Marblehead Mariners* (1960).

GOLDSBOROUGH, Robert (1733–1788) Delegate to Congress, attorney

Goldsborough was born and lived most of his life in Cambridge, Maryland. He graduated from the College of Philadelphia (later to become part of the University of Pennsylvania) in 1760 and went to England to study law at the Middle Temple. He returned to Cambridge in 1764 and set up a practice. Elected to the Maryland legislature, he also served as the colony's attorney general from 1766 to 1768. He was an early patriot in Maryland and one of the colony's first delegates to the Continental Congress in 1774 and 1775. He also served on the state committee of safety and in the first Maryland state senate.

GOODRICH, Elizur (1734–1797) Clergyman

Goodrich was pastor of the Congregational Church in Durham, Connecticut for more than 40 years, beginning in 1756 at age 22 and continuing until his death. During the Revolution he held that American patriotism was a religious duty, and from his pulpit he urged his parish members to active participation in the war.

GORDON, James (1739–1810) Militia officer, legislator

Gordon arrived in New York from his native Ireland at age 19. He lived in Schenectady and traded with the nearby Indian tribes before the

Revolution. He was a lieutenant colonel in the Albany County militia and spent some time during the war as a captive of the British in Canada. In addition to service in the New York assembly and senate, he was U.S. congressman from the state for two terms from 1791 to 1795.

GORDON, William (1728–1807) Clergyman, historian

Born in Hertfordshire, England, Gordon became one of the most important early historians of the American Revolution, and his work, although previously discredited, is now regarded as an excellent source of both information and contemporary interpretation.

He was educated to the cloth in an independent academy in London and preached for nearly 20 years in English dissenting chapels. He was seized with a great fervor for the cause of the American colonies, however, and in 1770, he emigrated to Massachusetts, where he became pastor of the Third Congregational Church in Roxbury. He was never a popular figure among his parishioners, but he was an ardent patriot, preaching anti-British sermons, writing for the newspapers and cultivating the friendship of leading Massachusetts rebels. He resolved within two months of the battle of Lexington and Concord to write a comprehensive history of the revolt and set about interviewing as many of the principal participants as he could. He also borrowed manuscripts, clippings and letters on which to base his account of the Revolution. He was a man of forthright opinion, however, and he made many enemies with intemperate remarks.

After the end of the war, while writing his magnum opus, Gordon apparently quarreled with a few too many of his parishioners, and in 1786 he returned to England, where he hoped to publish his history of the American Revolution. He initially met frustration: the printer refused to print the work on the grounds it was too pro-American and libeled too many British public figures. The manuscript apparently went through two major revisions, some at the hands of others, before Gordon saw it published in 1788 in four large volumes as *The History of the Rise, Progress, and Establishment of the Independence of the United States of America: Including an Account of the Late War; and of the Thirteen Colonies, From their Origin to that Period.* The history found few buyers in Great Britain but sold well in the United States. Historians in the early 20th century

discredited Gordon's work and accused him of plagiarizing much of it from Edmund Burke's *Annual Register* (a charge that could be accurately made against many early histories of the Revolution), but later study has shown the borrowing to have been slight and insignificant. Gordon's own partisanship for the American cause had waned considerably by the time his history was published and he returned to the pulpit at a parish in Huntingdonshire. He died in poverty in Ipswich in 1807. *Further reading:* George W. Pilcher, "William Gordon and the History of the American Revolution," *The Historian* 34 (May 1972), 447–64.

GORHAM, Nathaniel (1738–1796) Delegate to Congress, state official

Gorham was born in Charlestown, Massachusetts and apprenticed as a teenager to a merchant in New London, Connecticut. He returned to his native town and eventually became a prosperous businessman, sitting in the Massachusetts colonial legislature during the tumultuous years of 1771 to 1775. He was a member of the patriot faction and was one of the delegates who formed the extra-legal Massachusetts Provincial Congress in 1774 and 1775. During the Revolution, Gorham was a member of the state board of war and was active in the Massachusetts state constitutional convention of 1779 and 1780. He was speaker of the Massachusetts General Court three times between 1781 and 1785. His first term as a delegate to the Confederation Congress was in 1782 and 1783. He returned to the congress in 1785 and was selected as president in June 1786. When the convention met in 1787 to consider altering the Articles of Confederation in favor of a new federal constitution, Gorham presided for three months and then was active and influential in passing ratification of the new plan of government in Massachusetts. He had meanwhile continued his business activities, incorporating the Charles River Bridge company in 1785. He made a grand bid for fortune when New York ceded 6 million acres of land to Massachusetts as part of the federal settlement. Gorham and his partner got title to the land, but disputed claims resulted in wiping him out financially. He died of apoplexy in the midst of the land debacle.

GOSTELOWE, Jonathan (1744–1795) Officer, cabinetmaker

Gostelowe was a Philadelphia

cabinetmaker of considerable renown in his day, eventually becoming head of the local cabinetmakers' guild. During the Revolution he served as a major in the Continental artillery and later became the chief military commissary in Philadelphia. He continued in the state militia after the war.

GOULD, Paston (d. 1783) British general

Gould had nominal command of the southern theater during part of the latter stages of the war, but he did little of note himself. He had served since 1755 and was a colonel when he arrived in Charleston in June 1781 with reinforcements from Ireland. As a local brigadier general he was the ranking officer in the region. He was advanced to the local rank of major general in September. He retired due to ill health the following year and died soon after.

GOUVION, Jean Baptiste (1747–1792) French volunteer

Gouvion was one of the French military engineers sent by Franklin, at the request of Congress, to aid the American cause. He had joined the French army in 1769 and trained as an engineer at the military school at Mézières. When he reached America in 1777, he was on leave from his assignment in the French army. Gouvion received the rank of major of engineers in the Continental Army and was promoted to lieutenant colonel by the fall of the year. While few details of his activities are clear, several accounts mention him in connection with the design and construction of fortifications at Verplanck's Point and West Point, and he served at Yorktown. In 1781, shortly after the surrender of Lord Cornwallis, Gouvion was brevetted to the rank of colonel and given leave to return to France. He commanded troops under the Marquis de Lafayette during the French Revolution and was killed in battle in 1792.

GRAAFF, Johannes de. Dutch colonial official

De Graaff was governor of the Dutch West Indies island of St. Eustatius, which served as the major entrepôt for arms and supplies for the Americans during the Revolution. He became governor in September 1776, just as the Revolution gathered steam, and he allowed the American merchants and privateers to use his tiny island almost without restriction, much to the vexation of the British who strove mightily to shut down the flow of goods. De Graaff was not only in sympathy with the American Rev-

Henry Fitzroy Augustus, Duke of Grafton

olution, he personally profited from the war traffic during his years as governor. He was the object of a great deal of diplomatic pressure from the British and the target of criticism from his political enemies in Holland, but neither seemed to bother him very much. The British were most enraged by an incident on November 16, 1776, when De Graaff allowed the signal gun of Fort Orange on the island to fire a salute to the new American flag flown by the *Andrew Doria*. After a storm of British protests, the Dutch government called De Graaff home but cleared him of all charges and sent him back to govern his island. His continued support of American smuggling and privateering finally proved too much for the British in 1780 and they declared war on the Dutch Republic. A British force captured St. Eustatius the following year, and De Graaff was deposed.

GRAFTON, Augustus Henry Fitzroy, Duke of (1735–1811) British politician

The grandson of the second Duke of Grafton, Henry Augustus Fitzroy inherited the title in 1757 after graduation from Cambridge. He had entered Parliament the previous year, and he rose very rapidly to wield considerable power after he vociferously opposed the governments of Lord Bute. In 1765, Grafton became secretary of state under Rockingham and then first lord of the Treasury in the succeeding government of Lord Chatham (William Pitt the Elder). Chatham's illness placed Grafton in the role of acting prime minister, but the government was weak and tottered during much of its life. Grafton came under a series of vicious attacks through a series of letters published anonymously under the name "Junius," which added to his political woes. He and the government resigned in 1770, opening the way for Lord North's long reign. Grafton accepted the post of lord privy seal in 1771 but took little active part in the government. He came to be a proponent of conciliation with the American colonies, and he resigned the privy seal in 1775 over this issue. He returned briefly to office in the short government of Rockingham in 1783, retiring from public life with Rockingham's death and the change in ministers. *Further reading:* Bernard Falk, *The Royal Fitz Roys: Dukes of Grafton through Four Centuries* (New York, 1950).

GRAHAM, John. Loyalist official   Graham was a native Briton who arrived in Georgia in 1753 as a merchant. As he grew wealthy (his pre-Revolution estate was estimated at more than £70,000), he took up life as a planter, and he held several offices in the colony before the Revolution, including the lieutenant governor's post. He was also a member of the Governor's Council that was imprisoned en masse by patriots in 1776, but he escaped by canoe to the safety of a British ship. He and his family went to Great Britain, but he returned to Georgia in 1779 as part of the British reinvasion of the state. In 1781, Graham traveled the Georgia back-country settlements, hoping to quell support for the American cause. He commanded a company of loyalist militia in 1782 but evacuated to England at the end of the year.

GRAHAM, Joseph (1759–1836) Militia officer
Graham was born in Pennsylvania but moved with his family to South Carolina and then to Mecklenburg County, North Carolina. The historical sources conflict over his early Revolutionary War service: In 1778 he was either a lieutenant in the North Carolina rangers or a sergeant in the 4th North Carolina Continentals. In 1780 he was appointed as adjutant of a militia regiment and later became captain of a troop of mounted infantry. He and his men were part of Colonel William Davie's small force that blocked the advance of the entire British army under Lord Cornwallis at Charlotte, North Carolina, on September 26, 1780. Graham is reported to have received nine wounds during the sharp skirmish.

After recovering, Graham raised a dragoon company as a major. He resigned in 1781 and turned to trade. In later life he wrote a useful account of his part of the Revolution. *Further reading:* "General [sic] Joseph Graham's Narrative of the Revolutionary War in North Carolina in 1780 and 1781," in William H. Hoyt, ed., *The Papers of Archibald D. Murphy* (Raleigh, N.C., 1914).

GRANT, James (1720–1806) British general
Born in Scotland, Grant entered military service as captain in the 1st Battalion of the Royal Scots in the fall of 1744, serving at the battles of Fontenoy and Culloden. He became a major in the 77th Highlanders in February 1757 and led an 800-man unit to defeat at Fort Duquesne in September 1758, after which he was taken to Montreal as a prisoner. Grant was nevertheless promoted to lieutenant colonel in 1760, and in 1761 he commanded an expedition against the Cherokee. When Britain gained possession of the Floridas at the end of the Seven Years' War, Grant was made governor, a post he held until 1771, when he returned to England because of illness. The following year he was in command of the 40th Foot Regiment in Ireland. In 1773, Grant became a member of Parliament.

In December 1775, he was made a colonel in the 55th Foot Regiment, and the next year he returned to America as a brigadier general, arriving in Boston with generals Howe, Burgoyne and Clinton. He fought at Long Island in August 1776 and then succeeded Lord Cornwallis as commander of British posts in New Jersey, where he was in charge when Washington successfully attacked Trenton and Princeton. Grant served at Brandywine and Germantown. In 1778, he led the unsuccessful effort to trap the Marquis de Lafayette at Barren Hill and also was unsuccessful at protecting the rear of Clinton's army at the battle of Monmouth. In December of that year, he was sent with a detachment of Clinton's troops to the West Indies and captured St. Lucia. Grant served well as commander in the West Indies and returned to England in the late summer of 1779. He was promoted to lieutenant general in 1782 and full general in 1796. Grant served again in Parliament from 1787 until 1801.

GRANT, James (d. 1776) British officer   Easily confused with the British general of the same name, this James Grant was a veteran of the Seven Years'

War and the commanding colonel of the 40th Regiment of Foot when it was sent to garrison Boston in 1775. After the evacuation of the Massachusetts city, the regiment went to Halifax and then landed at New York in the summer of 1776. Grant was mortally wounded while leading his troops at the battle of Long Island in August.

GRASSE, François Joseph Paul, Comte de (1722–1788) French admiral

De Grasse was one of the more able French naval commanders; his decision to sail to Virginia in the fall of 1781 (and to fight once he arrived) was crucial to the allied victory over Lord Cornwallis. An aristocrat born into one of France's oldest families, de Grasse attended the naval school at Toulon when he was only 11, and at age 12 he became a page with the grand master of the Knights of Saint John at Malta. His naval career was upward and steady in the decades before the American Revolution. In 1740, he served in the War of Jenkins' Ear, and in May 1747, he was captured during a battle off Cape Finisterre and spent three months as a prisoner in England—putting his period of confinement to good use to study British society and naval affairs. He subsequently served in India, the West Indies, Morocco and throughout the Mediterranean. In 1774, de Grasse became commander of the Marine Brigade stationed at Saint-Malo, and in 1775 he voyaged to Haiti. In 1778, he was made a commodore and commanded a force at the battle of Ushant.

De Grasse's involvement in the American war began as a commander of a squadron under d'Estaing in the battles against Admiral Byron's fleet off Grenada and during the unsuccessful assault on British-held Savannah in 1779. For a short time he was in command of the French fleet in the West Indies, but he returned home due to ill health, arriving in Cádiz in October 1780. In March 1781, he was promoted to rear admiral and set sail with a powerful squadron of 20 ships of the line, bound for the West Indies. Throughout the alliance with the American colonists, French naval commanders had failed to coordinate with land operations and had often refused to engage British squadrons at crucial moments. De Grasse proved himself a better man in August 1781, when he set out from the West Indies with his squadron of warships and a convoy of transports carrying 3,000 troops. He arrived off the coast of Virginia on August 26 and with no British

François, Comte de Grasse

opposition in sight began to unload his troops. On September 5, the British under Admiral Thomas Graves appeared off Chesapeake Bay. De Grasse's decision to give battle was one of the key moments of the Revolution and perhaps may be credited with allowing the war to be won. Sailing out with a superior number of warships, de Grasse engaged the British in a relatively lackluster battle, breaking off after several hours of inconclusive fighting. The two forces circled and feinted, with the British finally sailing back toward New York on September 14. While not a resounding triumph, the action left Cornwallis and his army stranded at Yorktown and a huge allied army poised to defeat him. As long as de Grasse controlled the sea-lanes, Cornwallis was at the mercy of the allies, and the British surrender on October 19 effectively ended the war.

Fearing the hurricane season and in accord with an agreement with the Spanish, de Grasse returned to the West Indies, although George Washington pleaded for further operations against the British garrisons along the southern coast. In February 1782, de Grasse captured St. Kitts from the British, but in April he was defeated at sea and taken prisoner. While a captive in London he had several conversations with Lord Shelburne that led to his serving as an intermediary in the preliminary peace negotiations. On his return to Paris, de Grasse became involved in a long and politically complex controversy over his defeat in the West Indies, but he was exonerated by a tribunal in May 1784. Following his death in Paris, French revolutionaries destroyed his country estate, and his children escaped to America, where they received grants from Congress in recognition of their father's contribution to American independence. *Further reading:* Charles L. Lewis, *Admiral de Grasse and American Independence* (Annapolis, 1945; reprint New York, 1980).

GRATZ, Barnard (1738–1811) Merchant

Gratz was born in Germany, learned the mercantile trade at the counting house of his cousin in London and arrived in Philadelphia in 1754 to work for fellow Jewish merchant David Franks, principally in the fur trade with western Pennsylvania. After a brief partnership with Benjamin Clava, Barnard went into business with his brother, Michael. Despite the fact that their trade centered on doing business in Europe, they signed the nonimportation agreements in 1765. Gratz was one of the most prominent members of the Jewish community in Philadelphia during the revolutionary period and laid the cornerstone of the first synagogue in the city in 1782.

GRATZ, Michael (1740–1811) Merchant

The younger brother of Barnard Gratz, Michael was also born in Germany and worked at a cousin's mercantile house in London. He traveled extensively before arriving in Philadelphia in 1756. After three years working for David Franks, Gratz began a partnership with his brother under the name B. & M. Gratz. In addition to fur trading, the company acquired large tracts of western lands. He moved to Virginia during the Revolution.

GRAVES, Samuel (1713–1787) British admiral

The elder cousin of Thomas Graves, Samuel was also a long-serving Royal Navy officer by the coming of the War for Independence. He commanded the *Duke* from its engagement at the first battle of Quibiron Bay in 1759 until he was able to fly his flag as admiral in 1772. He was named as naval commander of the American station in 1774 and reached Boston in July to find Thomas Gage and the British garrison faced with an increasingly hostile set of colonists and much trouble along the New England coast. There was little Graves could do since the situation called for an efficient force of small coastal ships, which he did not have. He was replaced early in 1776 by Richard Howe and was

not employed again by the Admiralty. *Further reading:* William B. Willcox, "Arbuthnot, Gambier, and Graves: 'Old Women' of the Navy," in George A. Billias, *George Washington's Opponents* (New York, 1969).

GRAVES, Thomas (c. 1725–1802) British admiral

A member of a British naval family (his father was a captain and his cousin was Admiral Samuel Graves), Thomas probably entered service at the traditional young age. By 1756, he commanded a frigate, and he was court-martialed for failure to engage a French East Indiaman off the French coast in December of that year. He was reprimanded but continued in service, reaching admiral's rank through the inevitable action of seniority in 1779.

He played an important part in the American naval war after sailing with six ships of the line to New York in July 1780. He arrived only days after the French squadron under de Ternay had landed the French expeditionary force at Newport—thereby missing an opportunity to frustrate the Franco-American alliance. After duty at New York and fighting in the inconclusive naval battle of Chesapeake Bay in March 1781, Graves became temporary commander of British naval forces when Admiral Marriot Arbuthnot returned to England. Graves worked reasonably well with army commander in chief Sir Henry Clinton (who had not had a good rapport with Arbuthnot), but in the end he did little to advance the British cause.

His crucial action was off the Chesapeake Capes in September 1781. Graves had sailed from New York with a fleet of 19 ships. His mission was to relieve Lord Cornwallis, who had penned his troops up at Yorktown, and prevent the French under Admiral de Grasse from landing troops and a siege train. Unfortunately, Graves arrived too late again. The French were already in position and unloading when Graves's ships hove into view off the mouth of the Chesapeake. In an unusual display of aggressiveness, de Grasse led his 24 ships of the line out to do battle on September 5. Although Graves held the vital windward advantage, the ensuing battle was inconclusive—the British inflicted damage but took it as well. After feinting and dodging with the French the following day, Graves withdrew and sailed back to New York, leaving the

GREATON, John (1741–1783) Continental officer, merchant   197

French navy in command of the local seas and Cornwallis to his fate.

Graves organized another relief expedition the following month but turned back when he learned soon after putting to sea that Cornwallis had surrendered. In November, he left for the West Indies, where he was assigned to convoy to England a French treasure captured by Admiral Sir George Rodney, a task that was frustrated by bad weather. Graves subsequently served during the naval wars with France and was distinguished at the battle of the First of June in 1794. He was rewarded with an Irish peerage and died as Baron Graves. *Further reading:* French E. Chadwick, ed., *The Graves Papers and other Documents* (1916, reprint New York, 1968); William B. Willcox, ''Arbuthnot, Gambier, and Graves: 'Old Women' of the Navy,'' in George A. Billias, *George Washington's Opponents* (New York, 1969).

GRAVIER, Charles. See Vergennes, Comte de.

GRAY, Harrison (1711–1794) Loyalist official Gray was receiver general (treasurer) of Massachusetts before the Revolution. He is said to have waffled publicly in his loyalties, suiting his cant to the political preferences of the audience. He was proscribed and banished by the patriot assembly, and his property was confiscated. In 1776 he left with the British evacuation of Boston for Halifax along with his family, and he moved on to England the same year.

GRAYDON, Alexander (1752–1818) Continental officer, writer Not much of a soldier but remembered for his writing, Graydon was born, raised and educated in Philadelphia. He was apparently none too serious in his approach to life and had a reputation as a dissipated and indolent young man who was too lazy to pursue the profession of law for which he was trained. He was commissioned as a captain in the Continental Army in January 1776 and undertook a courier mission to General Philip Schuyler in upstate New York the following May. In August, Graydon was with his regiment at the battles in New York and was captured at Harlem Heights. He was held by the British in easy confinement until the spring of 1777, when he was paroled. He returned to Philadelphia, married and gave up the military life despite an official

exchange in 1778 that would have allowed him to return to duty. He moved to Harrisburg after the war, and in 1811 he published his *Memoirs of a Life . . . ,* which is still consulted for insight into his times.

GRAYSON, William (c. 1736–1790) Continental officer, delegate to Congress Grayson was born in Virginia and attended the College of Philadelphia (which became part of the University of Pennsylvania). He was a lawyer in Dumfries, Virginia at the beginning of the Revolution, and in August 1776, he was commissioned as a lieutenant colonel and made an aide-de-camp to commander in chief George Washington. In January of the following year, Grayson was authorized by Congress to raise one of the "additional" regiments for the Continental Army. He recruited men from both Maryland and Virginia and assumed command of what was known as Grayson's Regiment with the rank of colonel. He and his regiment served in several of the important battles during the northern campaigns, including Brandywine, Germantown and Monmouth.

In the spring of 1778, Grayson served on a commission to deal with British commander William Howe on the topic of prisoners. His regiment was combined with Nathaniel Gist's ranger corps in 1779, and Grayson resigned his commission to become a member of the congressional board of war. Grayson left Philadelphia in 1781· and returned to Dumfries, where he resumed his legal practice. He was selected as a delegate to Congress in 1785, after sitting first in the Virginia House of Delegates. During the debates over the proposed federal constitution, Grayson opposed ratification due to his interests in western lands. Despite his resistance to the new form of national government, he was selected as one of the first U.S. senators from Virginia in 1789.

GREATON, John (1741–1783) Continental officer, merchant Greaton was born in Roxbury, Massachusetts and was a merchant and trader before the Revolution. He joined the Sons of Liberty in 1774 and was elected a lieutenant of the local militia about the same time. After the battles of Lexington and Concord, Greaton was commissioned into the new Continental Army and advanced rapidly in rank. In July 1775, he was made lieutenant colonel and second in command of Colonel William Heath's Massachusetts Battalion, one of the 12 original battalions authorized by the legislature to defend the colony. He remained with Heath's unit when it was assigned to the expedition sent to Canada in the fall but transferred after returning in December to the 24th Continental Regiment as commanding colonel. He fought during the New Jersey campaigns as colonel of the 3rd Massachusetts, the regiment he headed until the end of the war. For a while in 1777, Greaton was the senior ranking officer in the northern department as the army gathered itself to oppose General John Burgoyne. He failed to win further promotion, however, perhaps because of political intrigue in the Congress. He was one of the officers that petitioned Congress in late 1782 over the matter of compensation and retirement pay. In 1783, when the war had been over for many months, Greaton was finally promoted to brigadier general. He retired in November and died the following month.

GREEN, Francis (1742–1809) Loyalist   The son of a Massachusetts colonial official, Green served as a junior officer in the British army during the Seven Years' War and saw action at the capture of Louisbourg, Nova Scotia and in the West Indies. He went to England in 1765, sold his commission, and returned to Boston and became a merchant. He disliked the British government's attempts at mercantile domination of the American colonies, but Green could not abandon the idea of the legitimacy of the crown and what he called the "old Constitution." In 1774, he was assaulted and harassed by patriot mobs in Windham and Norwich, Connecticut while on a business trip. He withdrew to the safety of Boston and evacuated to England via Halifax with the British retreat in 1776. He moved to Nova Scotia in 1784 and became a judge of the Court of Common Pleas. In 1796, after a 20-year absence, he moved back to Massachusetts, having become convinced that "at this period his country was respectably Federal." He was a pioneer in the teaching of deaf mutes, an interest aroused by the affliction of his son, and he established a school for deaf mutes in London and wrote *The Art of Imparting Speech* in 1783, one of the earliest such texts.

GREEN, John (d. 1793) Continental officer   An officer from Virginia, Green advanced in rank during the first years of the war, moving from captain in 1775 to colonel of the 10th Virginia Regiment in 1778. Later in that year, he took over the 6th Virginia when it was formed from elements previously part of the 1st and 2nd Virginia Regiments. He was nominally in command of the 6th for the rest of the war, but most of his troops were captured at Charleston in 1780, and the 6th ceased to exist in any real sense. Green helped pull together a few troops in Virginia during 1781 and formed a makeshift force known as the 1st Virginia Battalion. He was given charge of covering the army's retreat at Guilford Courthouse, which he did with considerable skill.

GREENE, Christopher (1737–1781) Officer   A Rhode Islander and a distant relative of General Nathanael Greene, Christopher commanded Continental troops ably in several important Revolutionary campaigns and battles. He had served in the Rhode Island assembly before the Revolution and worked at his family's manufacturing business in Warwick, Rhode Island. He was a member of the Rhode Island patriot militia known as the Kentish Guards at the beginning of the war.

In May 1775, Greene received a commission as major in James Varnum's newly organized 1st Rhode Island Regiment, a unit formed to join the patriots laying siege to Boston. The 1st Rhode Island was absorbed into the new Continental Army in June 1775. In the fall of the year, Greene volunteered to serve with Benedict Arnold on the American expedition to take Canada, receiving a promotion to lieutenant colonel commanding one of Arnold's battalions. He was captured at the battle at Quebec on New Year's Eve and was held prisoner by the British until the following August. On his return to Rhode Island, Greene was given command of a reorganized 1st Rhode Island Regiment that included several units comprised of black soldiers.

Greene was in charge of Fort Mercer at Red Bank, New Jersey in the fall of 1777, and he conducted a brilliant defense of the post against a large force of German mercenaries under Colonel von Donop. Greene's men repulsed the Hessian assault, killed a high percentage of the German troops and mortally wounded the German commander. Greene was forced to withdraw, however, on the following day in the face of the advance of the main British army headed toward the occupation of Philadelphia. Greene received a sword of honor from Congress for his efforts at Red Bank. In 1778, he took part in the battle near Newport in August, commanding black troops valiantly but futilely as part of John Sullivan's Rhode Island campaign. Greene served with the main Continental Army until 1781, when he was given command of forces in Westchester County, New York that were to help pin Sir Henry Clinton's troops in New York City. On May 14, a group of Oliver De Lancey's loyalist irregulars surprised Greene at his headquarters at Croton River, New York. Greene was killed and his body was mutilated by the Tories—a sad and savage end to his career.

Nathanael Greene

GREENE, Nathanael (1742–1786) Continental general

The best American military strategist of the war, despite his failures to actually win on the battlefield, Greene was probably the outstanding patriot general of his age. He was born to a Quaker family in Warwick, Rhode Island and worked as a young man in his father's iron foundries. He was a well-read autodidact with a particular interest in military affairs. In 1770, he moved to Coventry to take over a new foundry and at the same time was elected to the Rhode Island legislature, serving for two years and returning in 1775.

In September 1773, Greene was turned out by his Quaker meeting for attending a military parade. Within a year, he had helped organize a stylish militia unit, called the Kentish Guards, but was himself denied a commission on account of a game knee. However, when the actual fighting started in 1775, Greene was immediately commissioned as the youngest brigadier general of the new Continental Army and was given command of three Rhode Island regiments, which he led to Boston to join the siege of the British. He moved with the main army to New York in mid-1776, but a sudden fever prevented him from participation in the battle of Long Island. Promoted to major general in August, he petitioned General George Washington to be allowed to defend Fort Washington, and the British scored one of their greatest victories when the ill-designed fort fell in November.

Greene then showed great skill and ability during the subsequent battles in New Jersey and Pennsylvania, beginning at Trenton, where he commanded a column, through Germantown, where he led the deep penetration of the British lines and might have

carried the day if he had not been fired on by friendly troops in the confusion of the battle.

Washington had come to rely on Greene, and in February 1778, the commander in chief persuaded Greene to take the assignment as quartermaster general of the army. This was a thankless and extremely difficult task, and one Greene thought beneath his abilities, but he agreed to assume the post, and over the following two years he managed to bring some order and consistency to the matter of army transportation and supplies—meanwhile enriching himself from healthy commissions. When he came under criticism from Congress in 1780 at the behest of his former rival as quartermaster, Thomas Mifflin, Greene resigned in disgust and returned to field duty in the Hudson Highlands.

His great opportunity arrived in late 1780. Horatio Gates, appointed to command in the south by Congress without consulting Washington, had led his army to total defeat at Camden and had personally fled the battle scene. Shamefaced, the Congress asked Washington for a new commander, and Greene was the choice. He hastened south and took command of a small, poorly supplied army that faced a large force of British regulars and loyalists under Lord Cornwallis. The following campaign showed Greene at his finest. He settled on a war of speed and attrition, encouraging back-country partisans to harass and nip at the British army and its numerous outposts, while Greene led Cornwallis a merry chase throughout the fall and winter. He daringly split his small army but never allowed the British to catch either part at a disadvantage. Greene fought three major battles in the Carolinas—Guilford Courthouse, Hobkirk's Hill and Eutaw Springs—and he lost all of them, albeit by a narrow margin in some cases. His tactical sense and ability to control a battle on the field were secondary to his strategic acumen. Despite the futility of repeated formal defeat, his overall campaign weakened the British army to the point of near collapse. The term "Pyrrhic victory" might have been coined for what Cornwallis experienced at Greene's hands. As Greene wrote in his most famous statement: "We fight, get beat, rise and fight again." Greene's campaign finally turned Cornwallis toward Yorktown and final defeat. After the war, Greene suffered financial reverses and moved to Georgia to the former estate of a loyalist which had been given to him by the state legislature. He died of a sunstroke in 1786. *Further reading:* Theodore G. Thayer, *Nathanael Greene: The Strategist of the American Revolution* (New York, 1960).

GREENMAN, Jeremiah (1758–1828) Continental officer

A native of Newport, Rhode Island, Greenman joined the Rhode Island troops in 1775 as a private and was part of Benedict Arnold's expedition to Quebec, where he was captured. After his release, Greenman returned to Rhode Island and reenlisted as a private, advancing to sergeant's rank by the end of 1777. In 1779, he received a commission as ensign. He was promoted to lieutenant in 1780 and became regimental adjutant for the combined Rhode Island Continental Regiment, serving until the dissolution of the army in 1783. During his eight years of service, Greenman kept a diary that was later published. Following the war, he returned to Newport and, after a failed venture as a storekeeper, turned to the sea. He eventually became the master of merchant ships sailing out of the Rhode Island port of Providence. In 1791, Greenman received an appointment as second mate aboard a federal revenue cutter. He immigrated with his family to Ohio in 1806. *Further reading:* Robert C. Bray and Paul E. Bushnell, eds., *Diary of a Common Soldier in the American Revolution, 1775–1783)* (DeKalb, Ill., 1978).

GREENWOOD, John (1760–1819) Soldier, dentist

Greenwood was an apprentice cabinetmaker in Massachusetts before the Revolution. He was a rifleman and scout during the war and afterward moved to New York City and became a dentist. He

George Grenville

is reported to have invented a foot-power dental drill for fabricating porcelain false teeth. Greenwood's most famous patient was George Washington, a man afflicted during most of his adult life with bad teeth due to poor dentistry.

GRENVILLE, George (1712–1770) British official

Responsible for the revenue acts that bore his name and helped spark the American Revolution, Grenville was a typical British politician of the mid-18th century. He graduated from Eton and Oxford and became a lawyer. Entering Parliament in 1741, he rose steadily in the ranks, assisted by the patronage of his brother-in-law, William Pitt the Elder. Grenville became a treasury lord in 1747 and moved through a succession of offices, including posts as treasurer of the navy, privy councillor, secretary of state and first lord of the Admiralty. In 1763, he took office as first lord of the treasury and chancellor of the exchequer and was faced with finding ways to pay the huge debt amassed during the Seven Years' War and ways to pay for the administration of the much-expanded British empire in North America. The subsequent Grenville Acts, including the Stamp Act, the Sugar Act and the Navigation Act, inflamed passionate opposition in the American colonies and led to the formation of the first organized resistance to British authority. Grenville fell from power in 1765, when Lord Bute was replaced as prime minister by Rockingham. He died five years before the outbreak of armed hostilities in America.

GREY, Charles (1729–1807) British general

Known as "No Flint" after the assault at Paoli in 1777, Grey was one of the best British generals to fight in America, and he also wielded considerable political influence with the government in London. He had a sterling military career long before the coming of hostilities in the colonies.

He joined the British army as an ensign in 1748 and served with increasing distinction throughout the following decade and a half. In 1752, Grey was a lieutenant with the 6th Regiment at Gibraltar. He raised an independent company in 1752 and became part of the 20th Regiment. During the battles of Minden and Campen in 1759, he was wounded, and two years later, he was appointed as a lieutenant colonel in command of the new 98th Regiment of Foot and led his unit at Belle Isle and Havana. Grey retired on half pay in 1763 at the end of the war with France, but he gained influence at court and served as an aide to the king (with a promotion to full colonel) in 1772.

He was dispatched to North America in 1776 with the local rank of major general. Grey's notoriety among Americans was earned by his exceptionally skillful assault on the camp of General Anthony Wayne at Paoli, Pennsylvania on the night of September 21, 1777. Grey carefully planned the attack and prepared his men with precise instructions for the night operation. He decreed that all flints be drawn from the British muskets to prevent premature firing that might alert the American sentries. The assault was by bayonet alone, and Grey succeeded in taking Wayne's force entirely by surprise: The British attackers inflicted 150 casualties on a force totalling 500 and took more than 70 prisoners. The stunned Americans claimed the attack was a massacre, but it was simply a skilled and murderously effective military operation, carried at the brutal point of the bayonet. Grey repeated his triumph almost exactly at Tappan, New York a year later, when a similar surprise bayonet attack destroyed the American regiment of George Baylor (Grey was again accused of a massacre, but the charge was without basis). Late in 1778, Grey was appointed to the lucrative and ceremonial post of colonel of the 28th Foot. He returned to Britain in

1782 and filled a series of increasingly successful and important posts, being made a full general in 1794 after fighting against the French. He was eventually elevated to the peerage and ended his life as Earl Grey.

GRIDLEY, Richard (1711–1796) Continental officer

Gridley was born in Boston and had a distinguished career as an engineer and artillerist during the colonial wars. He studied mathematics as a young man and worked as a surveyor and civil engineer until 1745, when he was commissioned by the British as a lieutenant colonel to head the artillery train on the first expedition against Louisbourg, Nova Scotia. He served during all of the ensuing campaigns against the French, building western forts and commanding artillery as the chief military engineer and gunner for the British army in North America. He retired at the end of the Seven Years' War and was awarded a land grant on the Magdalen Islands, along with land in New Hampshire, valuable fishing rights and half pay. In 1772, he began iron-ore smelting near Sharon, Massachusetts.

With the beginning of the Revolution, he came out of retirement, despite advanced age, and was appointed as a major general in the Massachusetts militia and put in charge of artillery. He helped plan construction of the hasty fortifications at Breed's Hill and was wounded at the following battle. Gridley was appointed chief engineer of the newly-formed Continental Army in the summer of 1775 (his Massachusetts artillery regiment was absorbed into the Continental Army at the same time), and he was made head of artillery for the army. He apparently was past his prime, however, and after protests by other officers about his shortcomings, Gridley was removed from the artillery command in November 1775 in favor of Henry Knox. He retained his title of chief engineer for most of the war, but his main employment was the manufacture of mortars at his ironworks. He was not asked to participate in celebrating the end of the Revolution in Boston because he had become a Universalist and was considered "not . . . a Christian."

GRIFFIN, Cyrus (1748–1810) Delegate to Congress, jurist

Born in Virginia, Griffin went to Scotland to study law, graduating from the University of Edinburgh and then moving to London for study at the Middle Temple. In 1770, he eloped with Lady Christina Stuart, the eldest daughter of an English earl. In 1774, he and his wife were back in Virginia, but Griffin was not a strong believer in independence, and he took a slow road to patriotism.

In December 1775, he sent a plan for reconciliation to Lord Dartmouth, but it was of course too late for such well-meaning ideas. Once the revolutionary die was cast, Griffin turned his energies to building a viable American nation. Following two years in the Virginia state legislature, he went to the Continental Congress as a delegate from Virginia in 1778. By 1781, however, he had tired of the factionalism and increasing self-interest evident in the Congress, and he returned to Virginia. There he accepted an appointment to the Court of Appeals in Cases of Capture, a court set up by Congress to mediate disputes between states and which was a precursor of a federal judiciary. His evenhanded conduct of the affairs of the court helped at least in some measure to smooth the way for wide acceptance of a national court system. In 1787, he was returned to the Congress as a delegate, and he presided over the final sessions of the body in 1788 and 1789. He was then appointed to the new U.S. District Court and sat on the federal bench until his death.

GRIMKE, John F. (1752–1819) Officer, jurist
Grimke was a native of Charleston, South Carolina. In 1776, he joined the 4th South Carolina Regiment, known as the South Carolina Artillery, as a captain, and he eventually advanced to the rank of lieutenant colonel. The unit was an all-volunteer regiment recruited in the state for coastal defense but considered as part of the Continental Army. Grimke also was deputy adjutant general for South Carolina. He was captured along with his entire regiment when Sir Henry Clinton took Charleston in 1780. Grimke was paroled a year later and took a seat in the South Carolina House of Representatives. He was a delegate to the South Carolina convention that ratified the federal constitution, and in 1799, he became senior associate of the state superior court. He is perhaps best remembered as the father of Angelina and Sarah Grimke, two of his 14 children, who became the early 19th century's most famous feminist writers and thinkers.

GRYMES, John Randolph (1746–1820) Loyalist officer
Grymes, a Virginian, raised and commanded a troop of loyalist cavalry under Lord Dunmore in 1776, actions for which his estate was seized by the patriots. He subsequently joined the Queen's American Rangers. He resigned his commission in 1777 and emigrated to England the following year. He was appointed as the agent for prosecuting loyalist claims in Virginia after the war. He lived most of the rest of his life in England, where he married the niece of Peyton Randolph.

GUICHEN, Luc Urbain de Bouexic, Comte de (1712–1790) French admiral
Guichen's career during the American Revolution was mediocre at best. He had joined the French navy in 1730 and achieved captain's rank after 26 years of service. He was a rear admiral by the first battle of Ushant in 1779, and he commanded a French squadron in the West Indies the following year when he engaged the British squadron of Admiral Sir George Rodney in an inconclusive fight off Martinique. Guichen never came close to beating Rodney, but he did fend off the British attempt to take French bases and possessions. Guichen fared less well in September 1780 when a convoy he escorted was surprised off Ushant by a smaller British squadron commanded by Richard Kempenfelt, and virtually all the French ships were captured or destroyed.

GUNBY, John. Continental officer
Gunby commanded some of the very best American troops of the war as colonel of the Maryland Line. He began the war as a captain of an independent company of Marylanders that was incorporated into the 7th Maryland Regiment in December 1776. The following month, Gunby became commanding colonel, and he continued with the 7th through the disastrous battle at Camden in 1780, although he was not in action himself at the battle. The losses from Camden nearly destroyed the Maryland contingents in the Continental service, and in January 1781 the remaining men from the 1st Maryland and companies from new Maryland levies were combined into a new 2nd Maryland with Gunby in command. The unit (often referred to as the 1st Maryland in accounts of those battles) fought at Guilford Courthouse and Hobkirk's Hill. Gunby was blamed for the American loss at Hobkirk's Hill after he withdrew his regiment from the line in

order to re-form at a crucial moment in the battle. The Marylanders' strength dwindled even more after the end of active hostilities in 1781, and Gunby's last command was of the Maryland Battalion, made up of the few men still on the Continental rolls during 1783. He was brevetted as a brigadier general when he was mustered out in December 1783.

GWINNETT, Button (c. 1735–1777) Delegate to Congress, merchant-planter, state official

One of the more obscure signers of the Declaration of Independence and beloved of latter-day autograph collectors (because of the scarcity of his signature), Gwinnett was born in England, the son of a Welsh parson. He became a merchant at Bristol and then Wolverhampton, trading with the American colonies. He emigrated to Savannah, Georgia in the mid-1760s (perhaps with an intermediate stop in Charleston, South Carolina) and set up a trading house. His fortunes in America were never good, however, and he made his financial position even more precarious by borrowing heavily to purchase St. Catherine's island off the coast of Georgia near Sunbury and setting up a large plantation. From then on Gwinnett struggled against financial failure (he lost ownership of his island in 1773 but retained a home there) while becoming ever more deeply involved in the politics of revolutionary Georgia.

Sunbury was the center of radicalism in Georgia, owing to a large number of transplanted New Englanders, including Gwinnett's friend Lyman Hall. The rest of the colony was very slow to enter the revolutionary fray, with a strong conservative faction opposing the Sunbury patriots and other segments of the population fearful of Indian threats from the western frontier. These factionalisms were exacerbated by vicious personal conflicts among the leading politicians of the colony. Gwinnett held local offices and sat in the colonial assembly from 1769 to 1771, but he was forced to devote most of his energies between 1771 and 1776 to his personal business. In 1776, however, he was appointed to serve as a delegate to the Continental Congress (the colony had failed to send delegates to the first sessions). He arrived in Philadelphia in May 1776, took part in the debates over independence, signed the Declaration, and departed in August.

Back in Georgia, Gwinnett hoped to be named brigadier general of Georgia troops, but he lost the appointment to Lachlan McIntosh, setting off a continuing conflict between the two rivals for power and position. Frustrated in his ambition to gain a military post, Gwinnett nonetheless became speaker of the Georgia Assembly and, when the chief executive died, Gwinnett was named as acting governor and commander in chief of the state. His office lapsed after only two months, however, and he was defeated for renomination. (He had been reelected as a delegate to Congress but remained in Georgia.) While acting governor, Gwinnett had arrested McIntosh's brother and quarreled with the general over a botched expedition to Florida. The conflict came to a head in the assembly when McIntosh called Gwinnett a scoundrel on the floor of the gathering. Gwinnett challenged McIntosh to a duel and was mortally wounded in the meeting on May 16, 1777. He was probably buried in Colonial Park Cemetery in Savannah, although the exact location of his grave is uncertain. *Further reading:* Charles F. Jenkins, *Button Gwinnett* (New York, 1926).

H

HABERSHAM, James (1712–1775) Loyalist official, merchant By the time of the Revolution, Habersham had long been Georgia's leading merchant and one of the colony's wealthiest and most influential men. Born in England, he came to Georgia as a young man, the companion of the evangelist George Whitefield. Landing in Savannah in 1738, only a year after Georgia was established, Habersham founded a school for destitute children and helped establish the Bethesda Orphanage with Whitefield, running the orphanage personally for three years.

He left behind benevolent works in 1744 and turned to commerce, at which he grew wealthy as one of the founders of Harris & Habersham, the principal mercantile company in the colony. He pushed through legalization of the slave trade and helped to alter Georgia's economy toward rice and cotton agriculture based on black slave labor. He amassed large land holdings in addition to his trading interests. Habersham, like most wealthy colonials, held several public offices, and he was a close friend of the royal governor, James Wright. Habersham acted as governor while Wright was in England during 1771–73.

The agitation in the colonies against Great Britain caused him consternation and pain (his sons became prominent patriots), and in 1775, he wrote to a friend in London: "The people on this Continent are generally almost in a state of madness and desperation; and should not conciliatory measures take place on your side, I know not what may be the consequences. . . . May God give your Senators wisdom to do it, and heal the breach; otherwise, I cannot think of the event but with horror and grief. Father against son, and son against father, and the nearest relations and friends combating with each other! I may perhaps say the truth, cutting each other's throats. Dreadful to think of, much worse to experience." He left Georgia in 1775 to visit New Jersey and died while there.

HABERSHAM, John (1754–1799) Delegate to Congress, Continental officer The son of James and the younger brother of Joseph, John Habersham was born near Savannah, Georgia on his father's estate, "Beverly." He graduated from Princeton and returned home to become a merchant. Like his brother (and unlike his loyalist father), John was a patriot. After the 1st Georgia Regiment was authorized by the Continental Congress in November 1774 as a unit to defend the colony, Habersham received a commission as a lieutenant the following January. The 1st Georgia barely managed to achieve an existence and even at its highest point was drastically understrength, but Habersham appeared on its rolls as an officer throughout the war. He was promoted to captain in May 1776 and to brigade major in late 1777 (his brother Joseph was colonel of the regiment from September 1776 to March 1778). He was made major of the unit in April 1778 but was captured by the

Joseph Habersham

British in the fall of Savannah in December. He was exchanged and paroled but was captured again at Briar Creek in March 1779. Again exchanged, he apparently avoided capture with the handful of remaining members of the 1st Georgia who were taken by the British at Charleston in 1780. In 1785, Habersham was selected as a delegate to the Confederation Congress, serving through the following year. In addition to appointments as an Indian agent and boundary commissioner, Habersham was collector of customs at Savannah during the 1790s.

HABERSHAM, Joseph (1751–1815) Patriot leader, government official

Joseph was one of the patriot sons of James Habersham the loyalist leader, and he was in the forefront of the rebellion in Georgia that expelled his father's close friend and patron, royal governor James Wright. Joseph was born in Savannah, where his father was a wealthy merchant and influential member of the colonial government. He went to New Jersey for his early education and attended Princeton. In 1768, his father sent him to England, where he worked as a merchant for three years before returning to Savannah. He went into the business of trade in Georgia and was himself a prosperous merchant as a partner in Joseph Clay & Company by the approach of the Revolution.

He was one of the first members of the Georgia Council of Safety and helped seize gunpowder from the royal arsenal in Savannah in the summer of 1775. Habersham helped organize the first pro-

vincial congress in Georgia in July 1775, and the body kept up an uneasy peace with Governor Wright until the following January, when British troops arrived. Habersham organized the capture and arrest of Wright (who subsequently escaped) and effectively took control of the colony on behalf of the provincial congress. Habersham received a commission as an officer of the 1st Georgia the same month and served until 1778, when he resigned. He moved to Virginia in late 1778 when the British captured his home city. Following the war, Habersham sat in the Georgia legislature, and in 1795 he was named as U.S. postmaster general. He served until 1801, when he resigned to return to business in Georgia.

HALDIMAND, Frederick (1718–1791) British general

Although he occupied important official positions during much of the American Revolution, as a foreigner, Haldimand was never quite trusted by British officialdom and was seldom allowed much rein. He was a native Swiss and had fought as a mercenary officer during the European wars of the early 1750s. In 1756, he was recruited by the British as a senior officer for the 62nd Royal American Regiment, which was to be raised in North America for campaigning against the French. From 1758 onward, Haldimand served in North America and proved himself an able soldier. He was nominally second in command to General Thomas Gage and assumed command of New York when Gage was absent in England from 1773 to 1775. The government recalled Haldimand to England in 1775 to take him out of the line of command succession in America when it became probable that a war would be fought against the American colonists. He was appointed commander in Florida the following year and served there until 1778, when he was named to succeed Sir Guy Carleton as governor and commander of Canada. He directed raids by mixed troops against New York, and in 1780–81, Haldimand negotiated with Ethan Allen to take over the "state" of Vermont, a plot that was frustrated only by the surrender of Lord Cornwallis at Yorktown. Haldimand was removed in 1784 and returned to England.

HALE, Nathan (1755–1776) American spy

An American hero because of his capture and execution as a spy, Hale was born in Coventry, Connecticut, one of nine sons of a farmer. He graduated from Yale in 1773 and thereafter taught school, first in East Haddam and then in New London, until the Revolution began. In July 1775, Hale was commissioned as a lieutenant in the 7th Connecticut militia. In January of the following year, he became a captain in the 19th Continental Regiment and then participated in the siege of Boston. In April, he arrived in New York City. He is believed to have been a member of a group of seamen from his company who captured a British supply sloop the next month. Hale served in the Battle of Long Island and was with Washington on the retreat from Brooklyn.

Thomas Knowlton chose Hale as commander of a company of his rangers, and when Washington requested that a captain from the rangers volunteer to gather intelligence before the battle of Harlem Heights, Hale accepted the duty. Disguised as a Dutch schoolteacher, he left the American encampment at Harlem Heights in September 1776 and made his way to Long Island, where he gathered the desired information about the disposition of British forces. But while returning to his own lines on the night of September 21 he was captured, perhaps having been betrayed by a loyalist relative. Hale was taken to William Howe's headquarters, where incriminating documents were found when he was searched. Since he was in disguise instead of uniform, Howe ordered that he be hanged for spying the very next day. Having written letters to his brother Enoch and to Knowlton, who he did not know was already dead, Hale went to the gallows with composure. A witness reported that he made a brief speech ending with: "I only regret that I have but one life to lose for my country." *Further*

The hanging of Nathan Hale depicted in an illustration published in Harper's Weekly *in October 1880.*

reading: Morton Pennypacker, *The Two Spies: Nathan Hale and Robert Townsend* (New York, 1930).

HALL, John (1729–1797) Delegate to Congress

Hall was an attorney, born near Annapolis, Maryland, where he also practiced. He was a member of the Maryland Council of Safety and a delegate to the provincial conference of 1775. He was selected as a delegate to the Continental Congress in the same year and returned in 1777, 1780, 1783 and 1784. Following his public service, he returned to Annapolis and practiced law until his death.

HALL, Lyman (1724–1790) Delegate to Congress, clergyman, physician

Hall was one of the principal rebels of the early days of the Revolution in Georgia, but he was a native of Wallingford, Connecticut and had begun his career in New England before moving south.

He graduated from Yale in 1747, studied theology with an uncle, and was ordained as a Congregationalist preacher in 1749. He served a congregation in Fairfield, but from the beginning of his ministry he was at odds with his parishioners, perhaps over matters of theology. Whatever the cause of his difficulty, in 1751 he was dismissed from his post on charges of immorality. He confessed his guilt and was reinstated as a minister in the area. Hall was apparently disillusioned with the church, however, and he turned to the study of medicine. He at first returned to Wallingford as a doctor but then emigrated south to Dorchester, South Carolina to live among a group of transplanted New Englanders. After a brief stay in Dorchester, he moved on to an even larger New England colony around the seaport of Sunbury, Georgia, in St. John's Parish.

His new home was the most prosperous section of Georgia and the most radical politically. As the storm clouds of rebellion gathered in the other American colonies, the Sunbury district stood almost alone in Georgia in favor of the patriot cause. Most of the colony was under the thumb of loyalist-leaning administrators or westerners who feared Indian warfare. Hall attended patriot meetings in Savannah (where there were also a few rebels) in 1774, but the provincial congress failed to join the other colonies and neglected to elect delegates to the Continental Congress. In March 1775, St. John's Parish held its own meeting and designated Hall as an unofficial delegate to Philadelphia. He arrived in May and was admitted by the Congress as a nonvoting member.

Georgia was finally persuaded to join the other 12 colonies during the summer of 1775, and Hall was confirmed as one of three official delegates. He continued in Congress until 1777, signing the Declaration of Independence in the summer of 1776. When Georgia fell to a British invasion in 1778, Hall's home and holdings were destroyed, and he moved his family north. He returned to Georgia in 1782 following the British evacuation. He was elected to the state legislature and became governor in 1783. His last public offices were as a local judge. He spent much of his energies in his later years working to establish a state university for his adopted state.

HALL, Prince (1735–1807) American soldier, activist

Hall was born, probably into slavery, of unknown parents. He is recorded as a child to have been the property of William Hall of Boston, and he lived and worked in Boston as a leather craftsman in the years before the Revolution. In 1770, he received his freedom. Diligent research by several historians and biographers has failed to establish the details of his early life, but it is likely he was one of the several Prince Halls who appear on the Massachusetts muster rolls during the Revolution. Some accounts put Hall at the battle of Bunker Hill, but documents show he at least supplied leather goods—drum heads—to the Massachusetts artillery.

His greatest fame came from his efforts as an early social organizer and activist for black rights. He was the moving spirit and founder of the first black masonic lodge in America, African Lodge No. 1, which received an official charter in Boston in 1787 with Hall as Master. The lodge had existed for several years before receiving recognition by masonic authorities (it began as a small group attached to the British army lodge just before the war), and Hall and other free blacks in Boston used the mechanism of the fraternal order as a means to organize. Over a period of several years, they presented a series of petitions to the Massachusetts authorities asking for the abolition of slavery and the granting of civil rights to black citizens. Hall continued to speak, organize and write on behalf of black rights until his death shortly before the abolition of the African slave trade in America. *Further reading:*

Charles G. Wesley, *Prince Hall: Life and Legacy* (Washington, D.C., 1977).

HALLOWELL, Benjamin (Carew) (d. 1834) Loyalist naval officer

Hallowell, who used the name Carew later in life, was the son of a Boston loyalist official. He entered the Royal Navy during the Revolution in 1781 as a lieutenant and served with Sir George Rodney's fleet against Admiral de Grasse. Following the Revolution, he continued a naval career that led to honors and promotion. He commanded ships in several of the signal naval engagements between Great Britain and France over the next decades, including the battles of Cape St. Vincent and the Nile. He eventually became an Admiral of the Blue and a knight. He inherited the estate of the Carew family and adopted that name.

HAMILTON, Alexander (1757–1804) Continental officer, delegate to Congress, official

An officer during the Revolution and a principal architect of the new Republic, Hamilton was born to a Scottish merchant and his Huguenot mistress (she was divorced but legally precluded from remarrying) at Nevis in the British West Indies. His mother died in 1768 estranged from his father and thus leaving Hamilton effectively orphaned. He had been tutored by his mother and a Presbyterian minister in St. Croix and knew French fluently.

Hamilton went to work as a clerk in St. Croix, but in 1772, his aunts provided him funds to travel to New York and enroll in King's College (now Columbia). A precocious student and a vocal patriot, Hamilton wrote a series of cogent pamphlets opposing British policies, and in 1775 he formed a volunteer company. In March 1776, Hamilton was commissioned a captain in the Provincial Company of New York Artillery. In this role he served well in the battles of Long Island, Harlem Heights, Trenton and Princeton. In March 1777, Hamilton was appointed secretary and aide-de-camp to Washington with a promotion to lieutenant colonel—he was then only 20. He held this post for nearly four and a half years, and he was regarded by Washington as a trusted adviser with a solid grasp of military and political affairs.

In December 1780, Hamilton married Elizabeth Schuyler, a member of one of the most powerful families in New York. Leaving service with Washington after a rift in July 1781, Hamilton assumed

Alexander Hamilton

command of a battalion under the Marquis de Lafayette and fought with special distinction in the Yorktown campaign. He left military service with the final dissolution of the Continental Army in December 1783.

Hamilton served in the Congress in 1782–83 and thereafter practiced law in New York. His efforts at the Annapolis Convention in 1786 helped lead to the federal constitutional convention in 1787, at which Hamilton served as a delegate from New York and advocated a strong central government. He worked hard for ratification, joining John Jay and James Madison in writing the *Federalist* papers and helping to secure ratification by the New York convention. In 1789–95 he served as the nation's first secretary of the treasury. He was a powerful member of Washington's cabinet and a strong advocate of Federalism. Hamilton resigned in January 1795 to return to his law practice in New York, but he continued to advise Washington and helped to write his Farewell Address of 1796.

In 1798, with war between the United States and France threatening, Hamilton was commissioned a brigadier general and appointed inspector general of the army. Hamilton's political maneuverings alienated President John Adams and contributed to Adams' defeat in 1800, when Aaron Burr and Thomas Jefferson tied as finalists for the presidency. Though Hamilton opposed Jefferson both politically and personally, he helped secure the presidency for him. In 1804, he also helped to defeat the movement to elect Burr as governor of New York. The resulting enmity between the two men led to their duel at Weehawken Heights, New Jersey on July 11, 1804.

Hamilton died the next day in New York from the wounds he received. He was buried in Trinity Churchyard. *Further reading:* Forrest McDonald, *Alexander Hamilton: A Biography* (New York, 1979); John C. Miller, *Alexander Hamilton: Portrait in Paradox* (New York, 1959).

HAMILTON, Henry (d. 1796) British officer   A veteran who had served at the battles of Louisbourg, Nova Scotia and Quebec and in the West Indies, Hamilton was lieutenant governor of Canada and commandant at Detroit during the years 1775 to 1779. Although the forces at his command included only a few regulars from the 8th Regiment, Hamilton recruited Indians and renegades, including Simon Girty, to assist in attacks on American frontier settlements. He received orders to undertake the attacks in June 1777, but following an attack on Wheeling (in what is now West Virginia) in September, his Indian forces joined General John Burgoyne's expedition. So it was not until early 1778 that Hamilton was able to launch a concerted effort against the settlers. The campaign of George Rogers Clark disrupted these efforts, leading to Hamilton's march to retake Vincennes. Clark captured him in February 1779. Detained as a prisoner at Williamsburg, Virginia for several months, Hamilton was then paroled and sent to New York. Hamilton was nicknamed the "Hair Buyer" by the Americans, who believed that he offered payments to the Indians for the scalps of settlers, although no proof exists that he did. Hamilton became lieutenant governor of Quebec in 1784, serving for a year. In 1790–94, he was governor of Bermuda, and he then served for a year as governor of Dominica. *Further reading:* John D. Barnhart, *Henry Hamilton and George Rogers Clark in the American Revolution* (Crawfordsville, Ind., 1951).

HAMILTON, John (d. 1817) Loyalist officer
Hamilton was a resident of both North Carolina and Virginia, with property and mercantile interests in both. He apparently traveled often between the two colonies before the Revolution. He remained loyal to the crown and actively raised loyalist troops in North Carolina. He was lieutenant colonel and commander of the North Carolina Loyalist Volunteers and later served with the Royal North Carolina Regiment. Unlike so many other loyalist soldiers, he was respected among his patriot foes as a humane and worthy opponent. Although both North Carolina and Virginia attainted him a traitor and seized his property during the war, he returned to Norfolk, Virginia at the conclusion of the Revolution and served as British consul, working to settle British and loyalist claims.

HAMMON, Jupiter (1711–c. 1800) Slave poet
Hammon was born a slave, the property of a Long Island, New York merchant named Henry Lloyd. He was apparently taught to read and write at an early age, perhaps at the village school in Oyster Bay near the Lloyd family mansion. Scattered references in Hammon's writings indicate he was allowed use of his master's library. Hammon was the first black American to publish a poem when his broadside, *An Evening Thought . . .* , appeared in 1760. During the Revolution, Hammon moved with his new master, John Lloyd Jr., to Hartford, Connecticut when the British invaded New York and Long Island. Hammon's wartime writing was all published in Hartford. The consistent themes of his writings were religious, and his exhortations to his "brothers and sisters" for moral behavior perhaps played a role in his freedom to publish. Hammon's other significant works were *A Winter Piece . . .* (1782) and *An Address to the Negroes of the State of New York* (1787). He died still the property of the Lloyd family.

HAMMOND, Samuel (1757–1842) Soldier, official   Born in Virginia, Hammond served all over the south before his career ended. His first military post was as a private volunteer in Lord Dunmore's War. During the first four years of the Revolution, Hammond was an officer in the Virginia militia, but he was commissioned as a captain in the Continental Army in 1779 and eventually reached the rank of major. He took part in several of the significant battles in the southern theater during the last years of conflict, including King's Mountain, Cowpens and Eutaw Springs. He moved to Georgia following the Revolution and there sat in the state legislature and fought as a militia officer against the Cherokee. From 1803 until 1805, Hammond was one of Georgia's representatives to the U.S. Congress. He then moved to Louisiana after that territory came into the possession of the United States and became first military and civilian commandant of the northern district and then judge of the Court of Common

Pleas. His next post was as president of the Territorial Council of Missouri. He also served subsequently as surveyor general of South Carolina and secretary of state of Louisiana. He died in his native state.

HAMPTON, Wade (c. 1751–1835) Officer, official

Hampton was born in Virginia and lived near modern-day Spartanburg, South Carolina at the outbreak of the Revolution. His parents, a brother and a nephew were killed by Cherokee Indians in July 1776, but Hampton escaped and took up service as a junior officer in the 1st South Carolina Regiment. He performed a political turnabout in 1780 and declared allegiance to the crown, but he renounced that position a year later and joined the partisan forces of Thomas Sumter. He was commissioned as a colonel and fought well at the battle of Eutaw Springs. Following the war, he served in the U.S. House of Representatives. In 1808, he returned to a military career, eventually becoming a major general during the War of 1812. He resigned his commission in 1814 and moved to Mississippi, where he owned large tracts of land.

HANCOCK, John (1737–1793) Delegate to Congress, merchant, governor

Hancock was an important figure of the early days of the rebellion, but he more or less withdrew from the national scene after 1776 and failed thereafter to play much of a role except within his own state.

Hancock was born in North Braintree (now Quincy), Massachusetts. Orphaned as a youngster, he was adopted by his uncle Thomas Hancock, Boston's wealthiest merchant. He attended Boston Latin School and graduated from Harvard in 1754. In 1763, he was made a partner in Thomas Hancock & Company, and the next year he inherited the firm at the age of 27, making Hancock by all accounts the richest man in Boston. He favored the patriots' views and circumvented the excises imposed by the Stamp Act by practicing smuggling. In 1768, the British authorities seized his merchant ship *Liberty* and its cargo of Madeira because he had failed to pay duties. The prominence he gained as a result of this episode led to his being elected in 1769 to the Massachusetts General Court, in which he served until 1774.

In 1770, Hancock became head of the Boston town committee formed to investigate the Boston

John Hancock

Massacre. He also formed a political alliance with Sam Adams and assumed a leadership role among Massachusetts patriots. His wealth guaranteed him a place in any council, and Hancock assiduously cultivated political popularity, even among the "lower orders" who might not have been expected to lend him support. His social position made his political activities conspicuous—he was selected as president of the extralegal Massachusetts Provincial Congress in 1774—and the British authorities focused on him and Sam Adams as the two chief rebels, excluding them specifically from their offers of amnesty in 1775. He and Adams fled Boston for the safety of the rural villages, and the fateful expedition sent by General Thomas Gage to Lexington and Concord on April 18, 1775 had as one of its main objectives the arrest of Hancock. He was then elected as a delegate to the Continental Congress and became president in May 1775.

Hancock's main political ability was arousing popular support for himself, in part through lavish expenditures. His larger than average ego and his rather haughty manner did not endear him to his fellow congressmen. He showed little in the way of leadership and is generally judged by historians to have been only of middling intellect. Despite a complete lack of military experience, Hancock expected to be named as commander in chief of the new Continental Army, and he was permanently miffed when the appointment went to Washington. Hancock's place in American history, however, was secured in 1776 by the manner in which he signed the Declaration of Independence. Only Hancock and Charles Thomson, secretary of the Congress, signed the first broadside copy of the Declaration on July 4, 1776, and at the more formal signing in August, Hancock wrote his name in huge letters, according to legend with the comment that he did so to let King George read the signature without his spectacles.

He resigned the presidency of Congress in 1777 and repaired to Boston, seldom thereafter taking much part in national affairs, although he remained a delegate in name until 1780. His main attentions were in his home state, where he continued to build his popular political base. In 1778, he briefly took the field as a major general of militia during the assault on Newport. In 1780, Hancock was elected as the first state governor of Massachusetts, a position he held steadily for the rest of his life, save between 1785 and 1787, when he resigned—allegedly for ill health—to avoid dealing with Shays' Rebellion. In 1785, he was nominally elected to Congress again and chosen president, but he never appeared in person to take his seat. *Further reading:* William Fowler, *The Baron of Beacon Hill: A Biography of John Hancock* (Boston, 1979); Herbert S. Allan, *John Hancock: Patriot in Purple* (New York, 1948).

HAND, Edward (1744–1802) Continental general, delegate to Congress, government official   Hand was another of the recent emigrants to America who served the revolutionary cause well as a soldier. He was born in Ireland and studied medicine at Trinity College in Dublin. He came to the American colonies in 1767 as a surgeon's mate in the 18th Royal Irish Regiment of the British army. He was commissioned as an ensign in 1772, but in 1774, Hand resigned from the Royal Army and took up practice as a physician in Philadelphia.

After the beginning of armed hostilities in the spring of 1775, the Continental Congress requested Pennsylvania, Virginia and Maryland to raise rifle companies, and Hand was commissioned as lieutenant colonel of the Pennsylvania Rifle Regiment (sometimes known as Thompson's Rifle Battalion). The Pennsylvanians marched to join the siege of Boston during the summer. Hand was promoted to colonel of the regiment in March 1776 (the unit was redesignated for a short period as the 1st Continental) and led his men well at the battles of Long Island and White Plains during the summer. In

January 1777, Hand and his rifle regiment stood off the approaching army of Lord Cornwallis and allowed George Washington time for a victory over a smaller British force at Princeton. The Pennsylvania riflemen had meanwhile been rearmed with muskets and reorganized as the 1st Pennsylvania Regiment of the Continental Line, with Hand as colonel. He left his command in April, however, when promoted to brigadier general on the strength of his performance in the New Jersey campaign.

Hand's subsequent military career was less successful. He was assigned to Fort Pitt with a mission to organize militia and march against the British frontier command post at Detroit. The expedition was a failure, and Hand turned back without accomplishing much, a venture that damaged his reputation. He was replaced as commander at Fort Pitt and sent to Albany, New York in November 1778. The following year, Hand commanded part of John Sullivan's expedition against the Iroquois. In August 1780, Hand took over command of a newly organized light infantry brigade, but in January 1781, he was named adjutant general to Washington. When mustered out of the Continental Army in 1783, Hand received a brevet as major general. He moved to Lancaster, Pennsylvania and resumed his medical practice but was soon involved in politics. He was elected as a delegate to the Confederation Congress in late 1783 and served through 1784. Thereafter he sat in the Pennsylvania assembly and attended the constitutional conventions of the late 1780s. In 1791, Hand was appointed federal inspector of revenue, serving until the election of Jefferson (Hand was a staunch Federalist and thus was turned out by the new president). During the war scare of 1798, he was temporarily commissioned as a major general. He died of apoplexy in 1802 while embroiled in an investigation of his accounts as revenue inspector.

HANGER, George (c. 1751–1824) British/German officer   Hanger was the youngest son of a British peer and was educated at Eton and the university at Göttingen in Germany. He joined the British Royal Army as an ensign in 1771 but resigned in a dispute over promotion in 1776 and took service under the landgrave of Hesse-Cassel. He was assigned to the jaeger corps of the Hessian mercenaries that came to America in 1776. In July 1778, Hanger took command of a new jaeger com-

pany raised by drawing two men each from the existing mercenary regiments, but the unit was disbanded in November. A year later, he raised another new company and sailed with his men on Sir Henry Clinton's expedition against Charleston. Hanger served as one of Clinton's aides-de-camp during the campaign in the south in 1779 and 1780 and then became a major in Banastre Tarleton's British Legion, apparently effecting a transfer to the British army list. He retired from the armed forces on half pay on his return to England. His subsequent career was checkered: he was arrested in 1798 and put in debtor's prison but was released the following year. He was a companion of the prince regent but eventually lost favor as being too eccentric and coarse even for the future George IV, who was himself less than a moral paragon.

HANSON, Alexander Contee (1749–1806) Jurist

A lawyer in his native Annapolis, Maryland before the Revolution, Hanson was a family friend of George Washington and served as Washington's private secretary for a brief period. He was appointed as an aide-de-camp to Washington but did not serve due to illness. In 1776, Hanson became one of the first judges of the general court of Maryland under the new state constitution, and he served as chancellor of the state after the Revolution.

HANSON, John (1721–1783) Delegate to Congress

Born in Mulberry Grove, Maryland, Hanson was an early advocate of independence and the patriot cause. He served as a member of the Maryland House of Delegates from 1757 until 1773, and he was a member of the committee that drew up the instructions for Maryland's delegates to the Stamp Act Congress in 1765. Hanson signed the nonimportation agreement Maryland adopted as a response to the Townshend Acts in 1769. He also supported the Association of Maryland, which sanctioned armed resistance to the British, in 1774. Hanson served as treasurer of Frederick County in 1775 and established a gun-lock factory in Frederick. He was very active in raising troops and finding armaments for the Continental Army. In June 1780, Hanson began service as a delegate to the Continental Congress, and he worked hard to convince others to ratify the Articles of Confederation, persuading authorities from Virginia and other states to relinquish their claims on western lands. In No-

vember 1781, Hanson was elected the first president of the Confederation Congress, serving a one-year term before retiring from public service. *Further reading:* J. Bruce Kremer, *John Hanson of Mulberry Grove* (New York, 1938).

HARADEN, Jonathan (1744–1803) Naval officer, privateer

A native of Gloucester, Haraden was a commissioned officer in the Massachusetts state navy during the first years of the war. He served aboard the *Tyrannicide* when it cruised in British waters during 1777. He left the state navy the following year and became a privateer in command of the *General Pickering*, successfully raiding British shipping off the American coast. He was captured at St. Eustatius in 1781 but escaped the following year and continued as a privateer until the signing of the peace treaty in 1783.

HARDENBERGH, Jacob Rutsen (1736–1790) Clergyman, educator

Hardenbergh was a leader of the Dutch Reformed Church in America during the age of the Revolution. In 1758, he became one of the first Dutch Reformed clergymen to be ordained in America, and he led a movement to establish an independent branch of the church in the colonies, an effort that was rebuffed by the parent establishment in Holland. He turned his efforts toward education in 1766 and received a royal charter for Queen's College, the New Jersey school that eventually became Rutgers. He was a strong supporter of the rebellion and sat as a delegate to the New Jersey Provincial Congress. After the war, he became president of Queen's College.

HARDY, Samuel (1758–1785) Delegate to Congress

A native Virginian, Hardy graduated from the College of William and Mary during the midst of the war in 1778. He was not admitted to the bar until 1781—while the final months of the conflict raged in his home state—and he soon moved into public life as lieutenant governor of the state. In 1783, Hardy was sent to the Confederation Congress as a delegate. He served until 1785, supporting a central government at a time when the Confederation was faltering.

HARING, John (1739–1809) Delegate to Congress, jurist

Haring was born in Tappan, New York but moved to New York City, where he studied law and opened a practice in the city and in Rockland County. He was selected as a delegate to the Continental Congress in 1774 and 1775, and he was returned to the Confederation Congress after the end of the war in 1785. He was president pro tem of the second and third New York provincial congresses between 1775 and 1777. During most of the actual war, Haring sat as a judge in Orange County, New York, and in 1781–82, he was also a member of the state senate. He opposed the new federal constitution and voted against adoption in the New York convention of 1788.

HARMAR, Josiah (1753–1813) Continental officer

Harmar is best known for his military activities after the Revolution. He was born in Philadelphia and educated at a private Quaker school. In October 1776, he became a major in the 3rd Pennsylvania Regiment, and he passed through a long series of assignments and transfers among the Pennsylvania regiments during the war, ending as colonel of the 1st Pennsylvania in 1783, when the bulk of the Continental Army was discharged. He served primarily with Washington in the north, but he also campaigned with Nathanael Greene in the Carolinas after 1780. Only a few troops were retained on active duty after the war (not only because Congress feared a standing army, but also because there was no treasury to support much more than a company-strength establishment), but a commander was needed, and Harmar was selected as Lieutenant Colonel Commandant of the United States Infantry Regiment and Commander of the Army.

He proved to be not very good as a commander of even such a tiny force. His major responsibilities—carried out as a brevet brigadier general after 1785—turned out to be on the Ohio frontier, where friction between white settlers and the resident Indians gradually increased. Harmar was unsuccessful in removing settlers from restricted areas, and by 1790 he was faced with nearly a full-scale war. He led a force of poorly equipped frontiersmen into the interior of Ohio in 1790, and while not quite defeated, his expedition was badly mauled and retreated with little accomplished. He relinquished the frontier command to Arthur St. Clair and returned to Pennsylvania, where Harmar became adjutant general of the state until 1799. *Further reading:* Howard H. Peckham, "The Papers of General Josiah Harmar," *Michigan Alumni Quarterly* 43 (Winter 1937), 428–32.

HARNETT, Cornelius (c. 1723–1781) Delegate to Congress

Harnett was one of the primary revolutionaries in North Carolina during the early days of the rebellion. He was born in rural North Carolina, inherited considerable property and became a merchant in Wilmington. He held several local offices and represented Wilmington in the colonial assembly from 1754 until the dissolution of the royal government in 1775, a change he did much to effect. He was one of the most vigorous opponents of the Stamp Act, heading the Cape Fear Sons of Liberty in 1765 and 1766 and acting as chairman of the meetings in 1769 that adopted nonimportation agreements. He was also an organizer and subsequently a member of the North Carolina Committee of Correspondence. He was away during the first provincial congress in North Carolina but sat in the following four, serving as president of the congress held in late 1776. He was also head of the Wilmington committee of safety.

As president of the provincial council in late 1775 and early 1776, Harnett was responsible for moving North Carolina onto a war footing, and as a consequence he was named specifically as an outlaw by the British when they attempted an invasion of North Carolina in 1776. Having sponsored a motion in the provincial congress to vote for independence in the Continental Congress in April 1776, Harnett himself was selected as a delegate to the Philadelphia body a year later. He served in Congress, signing the Articles of Confederation, until 1780. He returned to his home in Wilmington, but when Sir Henry Clinton succeeded in a second invasion of North Carolina, Harnett was captured and held under the old indictment. He died while a prisoner on parole in Wilmington. *Further reading:* David T. Morgan, "Cornelius Harnett: Revolutionary Leader and Delegate to the Continental Congress," *North Carolina Historical Review* 49 (July 1972), 229–41.

HARRIS, Sir James (1746–1820) British diplomat

A school companion of Charles James Fox and William Eden, Harris was tied to their political party for much of his career. He was well traveled and a good linguist when he was appointed as secretary of the British embassy in Madrid in 1767. Because he made a success of his mission there when left as chargé d'affaires and was in a strong political position at home, he was appointed to the court in Berlin in 1772. In 1777, Harris was named as British ambassador to the court of Catherine the Great of Russia. He served in St. Petersburg until 1783 (he was knighted while on the post), attempting to prevent Catherine from damaging British interests during the prolonged struggle with America and France. He was not able to stop her formation of the League of Armed Neutrality, however, even though it had little actual effect on events. He left Russia in 1783 and passed through a succession of other diplomatic posts during his long career, rising and falling with the political fortunes of his party. In 1788, he was created as Baron Malmesbury, a title eventually elevated to an earldom. *Further reading:* Isabel de Madariaga, *Britain, Russia, and the Armed Neutrality of 1780: Sir James Harris' Mission to St. Petersburg during the American Revolution* (New Haven, Conn., 1962).

HARRISON, Benjamin (1726–1791) Delegate to Congress, planter, state official
Harrison was born on his family's estate in Virginia, the fifth in line to bear the name and the scion of one of the most prominent planter families in the colony. He attended the College of William and Mary in Williamsburg, but when his father died, Harrison left before graduating to assume management of his family's estates. He was one of the more conservative patriots in Virginia and had been only lukewarm in supporting the more vigorous rebels such as Patrick Henry during the Stamp Act crisis. However, as the time of decision drew closer, Harrison threw his considerable weight to the side of the patriots.

He was one of the most powerful members of the House of Burgesses, serving frequently as speaker, and when he began to take part in committees of correspondence and provincial congresses in 1774, the anti-crown forces in Virginia gained strength. He was selected as one of Virginia's delegates to the first Continental Congress in 1774, and he continued to represent the state until 1777. Harrison was better known for his conviviality in Philadelphia than for his legislative activity (he was nicknamed the "Falstaff of Congress" on account of his girth and love of parties), but he served ably on several committees and achieved his greatest honor as chairman of the committee of the whole

that introduced the Declaration of Independence in mid-1776. He also sat on military, financial, naval and foreign affairs committees.

Harrison returned to Virginia in 1777 and became speaker of the lower house. He became governor in 1781 and served three terms as chief executive. He objected to the new federal constitution on account of the lack of a bill of rights, but he proved a supporter of the new government when it was approved. His son William Henry Harrison and his great-grandson Benjamin Harrison became presidents of the United States.

HARRISON, Robert H. (1745–1790) Officer, jurist
Harrison was a native of Maryland who served on George Washington's staff during the early years of the Revolution. A letter from British adjutant Major John André written at Philadelphia in 1777 mentions Harrison as having been sent by Washington to negotiate an exchange of prisoners. Following the Revolution and the establishment of the new federal government, Harrison declined appointment to the U.S. Supreme Court in favor of retaining his seat as justice of the Maryland state general court.

HARRISON, William, Jr. Delegate to Congress
Although his birth and death dates are unknown, Harrison was probably quite young during the actual Revolution, and there is no record of his activities. He was born in Maryland and represented the state in the Confederation Congress from 1785 to 1787. By trade, he was a shipbuilder, and during the War of 1812, he served as a lieutenant of dragoons in the Maryland militia. In 1813, he was a justice of the local court in St. Michaels, Maryland, where he operated his shipyard.

HARROD, James (1742–1793) Frontiersman
Harrod, born on the frontier, was brought up in the nether regions of Pennsylvania and fought as a private in the Seven Years' War. In 1773, he explored down the Ohio River as far as the present-day site of Louisville, and he returned the next year with 30 men to a spot near the Kentucky River he called Harrodsburg. After a pause to fight at the battle at Point Pleasant (part of Lord Dunmore's War), Harrod established the first permanent settlement in Kentucky, although he soon came into conflict with Richard Henderson's Transylvania

Company. During the Revolution, Harrod fought in several campaigns against the western Indian tribes. He sat in the Virginia legislature (Kentucky became a formally organized county of the state during the Revolution) in 1779 and again in 1784. He disappeared while on a solitary hunting trip in 1793.

HART, John (1711–1779) Delegate to Congress, legislator   Hart paid dearly for his role in the Revolution and his brief moment in the historical spotlight, demonstrating an oft-forgotten aspect of the rebellion: Politicians and civil leaders ran great personal risk in supporting independence. He was born in Stonington, Connecticut but moved with his parents when only a year old to the Hopewell region of New Jersey. He had little or no formal education and was raised to become a farmer. Known locally as "Honest John," Hart prospered, and in the decades before the Revolution, he accumulated a grist mill, a fulling mill and a saw mill—in addition to a very large family of 13 children. Not surprising for a man of such substance, Hart also held many local offices, and he sat in the New Jersey legislature for 10 years and was a judge of the court of common pleas. He opposed the royal government in New Jersey on the issues of taxation and the quartering of troops.

Hart was a delegate to the first provincial congresses in New Jersey and chaired a session in 1776. He also was a member of the colony's committees of correspondence and safety. In June 1776, Hart was selected as one of the wholesale replacements for the New Jersey delegation to the Continental Congress. He took his seat in time to vote for independence in July and to sign the Declaration in August, immediately after which he returned to the new state legislature of New Jersey and became speaker of the lower house. When the British army swept through New Jersey in the fall of 1776, Hart's farms and livestock were destroyed and he was forced to flee personally to the safety of the nearby hills, where he lived as a fugitive for several months. On his return, he discovered that his wife had died and his family had scattered. His health permanently damaged, Hart retired from public life after a brief time on the state committee of safety, and he died the following year.

HART, Myer (d. 1795) Frontier merchant   Hart was a founder in 1750 of Easton, Pennsylvania, a frontier town populated by 11 families; several of them, like Hart, were Jewish. He kept the local store and with growing prosperity became an innkeeper as well and one of the region's wealthiest residents. During the first years of the Revolution, Hart acted as an agent for David Franks in caring for British prisoners held at Easton. He lost all of his property shortly after the end of the Revolution.

HART, Nancy (b. c. 1735) Legendary heroine   The greatest of the revolutionary heroines of the south, at least in legend, Hart was probably born in Pennsylvania but moved to South Carolina and then Georgia with her husband and family by the time of the Revolution. It is impossible to separate fact from fancy in the stories spawned about her activities as a loyalist-hating backwoods patriot, since there is no documentation and only hearsay to go on. However, several episodes were well known and circulated in her own lifetime and circumstantial evidence supports at least some of the anecdotes. The back country of Georgia was a place of vicious fighting between patriot and loyalist after the British took Savannah in 1778. Hart reputedly fought with her husband at the defeat handed the loyalists at Kettle Creek in February 1779, and thereafter was assiduous in tracking down loyalists and bringing them to rough justice. She is credited with gathering intelligence on British and loyalist movements, and in her most famous episode, she reportedly killed two loyalists who sat at her dinner table and delivered their four companions for hanging in her front yard. Following the war, she moved to Brunswick, Georgia with her husband, who was a local official. When Hart became a widow, she moved to Kentucky, and she died there sometime after 1820.

HARTLEY, David (1732–1813) British politician, diplomat, writer   Hartley was a member of the parliamentary opposition during the American war, speaking and writing against British policy toward the former colonies, but he became the British representative who signed the final peace treaty. He graduated from Oxford in 1747 and studied law at Lincoln's Inn during 1759. While in London, Hartley met Benjamin Franklin and the two became lifelong friends and correspondents; their relationship may have influenced Hartley's views on the Revolution. He sat in Parliament from 1774 to 1780 and again from 1782 to 1784 as a member of the Rockingham faction. In 1778, Hartley published *Letters on the American War,* urging reconciliation and a change in British policy. When the North government fell after the defeat of Lord Cornwallis and the Rockinghamites came to power, Hartley was appointed as plenipotentiary to conclude a treaty with Franklin, who represented the United States in Paris. He continued to write during the remainder of his life, usually on political topics. *Further reading:* George Gumridge, *David Hartley, M.P., an Advocate of Conciliation* (Berkeley, Calif., 1926).

HARVIE, John (1742–1807) Delegate to Congress, official

Born in Albemarle County, Virginia, Harvie was a lawyer before the Revolution. He attended the Virginia patriot assemblies in 1775 and 1776 and helped write the declaration of rights and the documents specifying the form of government for the new state. He also held a commission as a senior officer in the Virginia militia at the beginning of the war but apparently never took the field. From 1777 to 1779, Harvie served as one of Virginia's delegates to the Continental Congress. He acted during the war as an Indian agent for the state and as a purchasing agent and land registrar. After the war, Harvie was mayor of Richmond.

HASLETT, John (d. 1777) American officer

Haslett was born in Ireland and was a prosperous physician in Kent and Sussex counties in Delaware by the time of the Revolution. He was colonel of the state militia and was named as commander of the Delaware Regiment raised for Continental service in early 1776. Along with the Marylanders, the Delaware troops became the hard core of the Continental Army, capable of standing in open battle with the best the British could muster. Haslett led the unit north to join Washington's army in New York but was himself absent on court-martial duty during the battle of Long Island in August 1776. He was at the head of the Delaware unit at White Plains, however. Haslett was killed on January 3, 1777 during the battle of Princeton.

HASWELL, Anthony (1756–1816) Publisher

Haswell was born in Portsmouth, England and emigrated to the American colonies in 1769. He lived in Massachusetts at the beginning of the Revolu-

tion, where he published the *Massachusetts Spy* in 1777. In 1781, Haswell changed his base to Hartford, Connecticut and published the *New England Almanack for 1781.* It was back to Massachusetts the following year, and in 1783, he moved to the Vermont section of New Hampshire and issued the *Vermont Gazette.* One of his biographies says he "saw action" during the Revolution, but no details are supplied. He was postmaster general of Vermont in 1784 and apparently continued to publish various newspapers in Vermont for several decades after the end of the war. In 1800, he became one of the first publishers to be politically prosecuted by the Federalists under the Alien and Sedition Acts, receiving a stiff fine and two months in prison.

HATHORN, John (1749–1825) Militia officer, delegate to Congress, legislator

Hathorn was born in Wilmington, Delaware but lived his adult life in New York. He was by profession a surveyor and schoolteacher. A captain of the colonial militia before the Revolution, he was named colonel of the 4th Orange County Militia Regiment in early 1776 and served throughout the war. He was also intermittently a member of the state assembly, including two terms during the years of the Revolution. After the end of hostilities, Hathorn served in the state senate and on the state council, and in December 1788 he was elected as a delegate to the Confederation Congress, but the new federal constitution went into effect before the next session could meet. Hathorn nonetheless was elected as a New York representative to the first U.S. Congress and returned again in 1795, although he was defeated in three other attempts to keep or regain his congressional seat.

HAUSSEGGER, Nicolas. Continental officer

Little is known about Haussegger's personal history, and his actions during the war are tinged with mystery. He was a Pennsylvanian of German extraction who was appointed a major in the 4th Pennsylvania Battalion in January 1776. In June, Congress authorized the raising of a new German Battalion to be recruited from among German settlers in Pennsylvania and Maryland. Haussegger was named colonel and commanded the unit (which later in the war became part of the 8th Maryland). During the first days of January 1777, Haussegger's regiment was assigned as part of the covering force outside Trenton, New Jersey, where Washington was hoping to concentrate his troops to follow up the victory over the Hessians during the previous week (the Continental Army had nearly dissolved due to the expiration of enlistments on December 31). When the British appeared on the road from Princeton and pushed forward a feeble assault, most American units fought well in a delaying action, but the German Regiment broke under minimum pressure and Haussegger himself surrendered. He was paroled to his home in Lancaster County but was viewed with suspicion by the American high command. He eventually went over to the British— probably after 1779—and historians have long believed he was a traitor while in command at Trenton, but no hard evidence has ever surfaced.

HAWKINS, Benjamin (1754–1816) Delegate to Congress, official

Hawkins was a native of North Carolina. He attended the college at Princeton from 1773 to 1776 and left to become a French interpreter for George Washington. He then moved back to North Carolina and became a member of the legislature. In 1780, he worked to find military supplies for the state in the face of the British invasion. The following year, Hawkins was selected as a North Carolina delegate to the Confederation Congress, serving until the end of the war and returning in 1786. Beginning in 1785, he was the principal agent of the state in dealing with the western Indians, primarily the Creek and Cherokee. He was appointed as one of the first U.S. senators under the new federal Constitution in 1789. After he left the Senate in 1795, Hawkins again became an Indian agent, dealing with all the tribes south of the Ohio River.

HAWLEY, Joseph (1723–1788) Lawyer

A native of Northampton, Massachusetts, Hawley was an influential local lawyer and official, serving as chairman of the board of selectmen for more than 40 years. During the 1750s, he was active in the state militia, rising to major, and sat intermittently in the Massachusetts General Court. During the Revolution, Hawley was "a leading proponent" of the rebellion in the Connecticut River Valley, but in 1780 he refused to take a seat in the Massachusetts Senate, which convened with a religious oath, because he wanted to keep church and state separate.

HAYES, Joseph (d. 1781) Militia officer

Hayes was a native of South Carolina and commanded a militia force as a colonel during the fierce partisan warfare in the Carolinas during 1780 and 1781. He and his men were defeated by the notorious loyalist partisan leader "Bloody Bill" Cunningham at an action near Hayes' Station, South Carolina on November 9, 1781. Hayes was killed in the fighting.

HAYNE, Isaac (1745–1781) Militia officer

The circumstances of Hayne's death at the hands of the British set off a controversy that continued after the Revolution. He was a planter and horse breeder in the Colleton District of South Carolina and was involved in the vicious fighting between patriots and loyalists during the early 1780s. He was also a partner in ownership of an iron works that supplied ammunition to the North Carolina Continentals until it was destroyed by a loyalist raid.

Hayne was an officer in the local militia at the beginning of the war, but he resigned in a dispute over rank and reenlisted as a private. He was serving in one of the city's outposts when Charleston fell to Sir Henry Clinton in May 1780, and he was captured. He was released on parole and returned to his home, only to be summoned by the British to Charleston in 1781 and told to sign an oath of allegiance. He apparently did so with the proviso that he would not serve under arms for the enemy. When he was subsequently ordered to report for duty with the British army, Hayne considered his parole to be broken, and he joined the South Carolina militia as a colonel.

In July 1781, Hayne captured the loyalist turncoat Andrew Williamson but was in turn surprised by a British force under Colonel Nisbet Balfour and captured himself. Taken to Charleston, Hayne was accused by Nisbet and Lord Rawdon, the ailing British commander, of breaking parole and spying for the Americans. He was hung without trial after an informal hearing on August 4, 1781. Hayne's summary execution outraged patriots and touched off a long-standing wrangle over who had been responsible for the order to kill Hayne and whether legal niceties had been observed. For patriots, Hayne became a martyr—the Ethan Allen of the South. *Further reading:* David Bowden, *The Execution of Isaac Hayne* (1977).

HAYNES, Lemuel (1753–1833) Soldier, clergyman

Haynes was one of the best-known black

men in New England during his long career as a churchman serving white congregations. He was born in West Hartford, Connecticut in 1753, the son of a white mother and an unknown black father. His mother cast the mixed-race infant aside, and Haynes was raised as a bound servant by David Rose in Granville, Massachusetts from the age of five months. He worked on Rose's farm, but Haynes's obvious quick intelligence prompted Rose to allow him to be educated in the local common schools.

While still a boy, Haynes displayed the ability to preach effectively. He completed his term of service in 1774 and joined the local minuteman militia company. He fought in the battles of Lexington and Concord in April 1775, about which Haynes wrote a verse sermon, and served with Captain Lebbeus Ball's militia company during the siege of Boston. Haynes also was attached to the hastily formed expedition of Ethan Allen and the Green Mountain Boys that took Fort Ticonderoga. Haynes then settled in Wintonbury, Connecticut, where he taught school and studied language and theology on his own. In 1780, after passing an examination by a group of Congregationalist ministers, Haynes was appointed as pastor of a white church in Middle Granville. He married a young white schoolteacher in 1783. He meanwhile had acquired a wide reputation as a preacher, touring pulpits in Vermont and Connecticut. He was ordained in 1785 by the ministerial association of Litchfield, Connecticut and called to the pulpit of the white church in Torrington. Despite his powerful preaching style, Haynes was turned out of Torrington after two years and moved on to the church at Rutland, Vermont, where he remained for 30 years.

He was not only famed as a powerful preacher, but Haynes also was a strong supporter of the Federalist party and publicly wrote and spoke against the Jeffersonians. In 1818, after three decades with Haynes as its minister, the Rutland congregation turned against him, in part because of his unflinching criticism of the War of 1812 and the ruling political party, and he was again dismissed. Haynes commented that the congregation was so "sagacious" that after 30 years they had finally discovered he was black and would not suit. Despite his advanced age, Haynes took a new post at Manchester, Vermont, but he moved on after two years to Granville, New York, where he died. Long after his death, a manuscript in his hand (written during the

Revolution) was discovered that argued forcibly and cogently against slavery and pointed out the "undeniable right to his liberty" of the black in a nation fighting for freedom. *Further reading:* Ruth Bogin, " 'Liberty Further Extended': A 1776 Antislavery Manuscript of Lemuel Haynes," *William and Mary Quarterly,* 3d ser., 40 (January 1983), 85–105.

HAYS, Mary Ludwig ("Molly Pitcher") (c. 1754–1832) Legendary heroine

The name "Molly Pitcher" has been attached to several women reputed to have fought side by side with men in the Revolution, but the leading candidate for the honor is Hays, a domestic servant from Carlisle, Pennsylvania. The daughter of German immigrant parents, Mary Ludwig married John Hays, a barber, and went along when he enlisted as gunner in a Pennsylvania regiment in 1775. By 1778, she was apparently an established camp follower, seeing to washing, cooking and nursing for the troops in the field. On June 28, during the battle of Monmouth, she was carrying water to the front lines (hence the nickname "Molly Pitcher") when her husband fell wounded or exhausted at his gun. According to legend, Mary took his place as cannon loader for the rest of the fight, helping to keep the gun in action.

After the Revolutionary War, Mary and her husband returned to Carlisle, where she worked as a cleaning woman. Following Hays's death, she married John McCauley. In 1822, the Pennsylvania legislature voted her a payment of $40 and an annuity "for her services during the revolutionary war." Described by contemporaries as an uncouth, tobacco-chewing, foul-mouthed character—the perfect picture of an old trooper—she was also known to be warm-hearted and generous. She died in 1832 and was buried in the Old Graveyard at Carlisle. Her story was revived during the centennial celebration in 1876, and a tombstone was added to her grave. Further markers were added subsequently, and a battle monument at Monmouth shows her with cannon and water pail. *Further reading:* John B. Landis, "Investigation into the American Tradition of Women Known as 'Molly Pitcher,' " *Journal of American History* (First Quarter, 1911).

HAZARD, Jonathan (1744–c. 1824) Delegate to Congress, Continental officer

Known to contemporaries as "Beau" due to his natty appear-

Mary Ludwig Hays ("Molly Pitcher")

ance, Hazard was born in Newport, Rhode Island and was a politician of considerable influence during and immediately after the Revolution. He was elected to the new state house of representatives in 1776, and he served as paymaster for Rhode Island Continentals during 1777, seeing field service with the main army in New Jersey. He returned to politics, however, and again took a seat in the state assembly. He was appointed to the Rhode Island council of war in 1778. Hazard was one of the leaders of the agricultural party in Rhode Island, which did much to frustrate the formation of a strong national government, and in 1786 he successfully led the fight in the state legislature for paper money. Despite his general opposition to a national government, he was elected as a delegate to the Confederation Congress in 1787, but he failed to take his seat. Elected again the following year, Hazard did serve a second term in the Congress during its waning days. His power in Rhode Island faded, however, during the 1790s, when he was again a member of the legislature. In 1805, he moved to a Quaker settlement in Oneida County, New York.

HAZEN, Moses (1733–1803) Continental general
Born in Haverhill, Massachusetts, Hazen served during the Seven Years' War and from 1771 until 1773 was an officer in the British 44th Regiment of Foot. He resigned from the British army, however, to settle near St. John's in Newfoundland, becoming a wealthy merchant and landowner.

The aborted American invasion of Canada in 1775 created something of a dilemma for Hazen's loyalties (he was viewed suspiciously by both sides), but he ultimately settled on the Americans and aided the retreat of the defeated army. He made his way to Albany and in January 1776 was authorized by Congress to raise a regiment. The 2nd Canadian Regiment, usually known as Hazen's Regiment, was made up mostly of Canadian refugees and became a dumping ground for foreign officers as the Revolution wore on. After creditable fighting in the New York and New Jersey campaigns of late 1776 and early 1777, Hazen's career tapered off. He pressed—naturally enough—for renewed operations to take Canada, but his plans came to naught, especially after Congress in a rare show of wisdom cancelled a proposed operation against Canada in 1778. He was brevetted as a brigadier general in June 1781 and commanded a brigade under the Marquis de Lafayette at Yorktown. He settled in Vermont after the war. *Further reading:* Allan Everest, *Moses Hazen and the Canadian Refugees . . .* (Syracuse, N.Y., 1976).

HAZLEWOOD, John (c. 1726–1800) State naval officer

Hazlewood was born in England, emigrated to Philadelphia, and before age 20 was a merchant sea captain commanding ships in the trade between Philadelphia and London. In July 1775, he was recruited by the Philadelphia Committee of Safety to help devise and install defenses on the Delaware River to protect the port of Philadelphia from the British fleet. The best the patriots could manage was to put a small force of fire rafts on the water and sink log obstructions in the channel. Hazlewood was given command of the rafts, which mercifully did not have to face the British for two more years. In September 1777, however, he was made commodore of the Pennsylvania state navy and assigned to keep General William Howe from invading Philadelphia by water. Hazlewood's defenses were no match for the combined British land and river campaign, and he was barely able to evacuate some of his small vessels without harm. Hazlewood retained his rank as commodore after the British withdrawal from Philadelphia in 1778, even though the state navy was disbanded. In 1780, he became commissioner of purchases for the Continental Army in Philadelphia, and he returned to private business after the war. *Further reading:* J. G. Leach, "Commodore John Hazlewood, Commander

of the Pennsylvania Navy in the Revolution," *Pennsylvania Magazine of History and Biography* (April 1902).

HEARD, Nathaniel. Militia officer

Heard was a colonel of New Jersey militia early in the war and led five regiments of New Jerseyans to join Washington's main army in New York in the summer of 1776. He participated in the loss at Long Island and retreated to Harlem Heights. When Washington retreated across New Jersey in the fall, Heard refused to bring his militia in as reinforcements, and when their enlistments expired on November 30, the New Jersey troops went home, leaving Washington unsupported to deal with the British. Heard was eventually made a brigadier general of militia.

HEATH, William (1737–1814) Continental general

Heath was born in Roxbury, Massachusetts, where his ancestors had settled in 1636. He was a delegate to the Massachusetts General Court in 1761 and also in 1771, serving from then until the British dissolved the assembly in 1774. In 1765, Heath joined the Ancient and Honorable Artillery Company of Boston. In 1774–75, he served as a member of the committee of safety and of the Massachusetts Provincial Congress, which appointed him brigadier general in February 1775.

Following the British retreat from Lexington and Concord, Heath was the first American general to appear, ordering deployment of troops to begin the siege of Boston. He also organized American forces at Cambridge before the battle of Bunker Hill. In June 1775, he was appointed as one of the original brigadier generals of the Continental Army, satisfying the political distribution of rank by Congress. In March 1776, he led the first detachment of Massachusetts Continentals to New York, where he served as Israel Putnam's second in command. In November, he was put in charge of the troops defending the Hudson Highlands. After leading an unsuccessful attack against Fort Independence in January 1777, he was censured by Washington, who denied him other field commands for the rest of the war.

As successor to Artemas Ward in command of the Eastern Department, Heath had brief custody over General John Burgoyne and the Convention Army. In June 1779, he was placed in command of the troops on the east side of the lower Hudson River, and he remained at this post until the end of the war except for a three-month sojourn in Providence to manage the arrival of the Comte de Rochambeau and his troops from France. Heath returned to Roxbury in July 1783. In 1788, he served in the Massachusetts convention that ratified the Constitution, and he was a member of the state senate in 1791 and 1792. In the latter year, he also served as a member of the probate court in Norfolk. Elected lieutenant governor in 1806, Heath declined to serve. *Further reading:* Rufus R. Wilson, ed., *Heath's Memoirs of the American War . . .* (New York, 1904).

HECK, Barbara (1734–1804) Loyalist religious leader   Heck was known as the "mother of Methodism" in America. She was born in Ireland and emigrated to the American colonies around 1760. In 1766, she became one of the colonies' most active evangelists for the Wesleyan movement. She was responsible for the first Methodist chapel in America and founded a Wesleyan Society in New York. Heck was, however, a firm loyalist, and she departed for Canada at the beginning of the Revolution.

HECKENWELDER, Johann Gottlieb (1743–1823) Religious missionary   Born in England, Heckenwelder came to America in 1754 and became a sometime missionary and trader to the Indians of Pennsylvania along the Susquehanna River. He was adept at several Indian languages and learned a good deal about the customs and life of several tribes. Eventually he became a full-time missionary to a group of natives who had converted to Christianity, helping to settle them in Ohio at Gnadenhutten. He was seized by the British in 1781 and accused of spying for the Americans. After a brief captivity, however, he was released and returned to his missionary endeavors. He continued to live and work among the Indians for the rest of his life, aiding them in dealings with the new American government.

HECTOR, Edward (c. 1744–1834) Soldier   Hector, a black man, was a private in the 3rd Pennsylvania Artillery and was noted for his heroism at the battle of Brandywine in 1777. In charge of an ammunition wagon, Hector brought his team and equipment out from beneath a British advance that had scattered his battery, refusing to abandon his responsibility in the face of fire. He was denied a

pension by the Pennsylvania legislature but was awarded a $40 "donation" shortly before his death at age 90.

HEISTER, Leopold Phillip von (1707–1777) German mercenary commander   Von Heister led the first contingent of German mercenaries to America as commander in chief of the Hessian troops. He sailed from Spithead in May 1776 with 7,800 German mercenaries and 1,000 British troops. Arriving in Halifax, von Heister discovered that British commander in chief William Howe had already sailed for New York. Von Heister and his troops joined the British force there on Staten Island in July. Von Heister led the center of the British attack during the battle of Long Island, showing for the first time how effective the Germans were to be in the war, and personally accepted the surrender of Lord Stirling. He commanded the German troops at the battle of White Plains in October 1776. Von Heister technically outranked all British officers except Howe, but Sir Henry Clinton (second in command to Howe at the time) held a secret dormant commission as a full general that would have allowed him to supersede von Heister if Howe had been incapacitated or killed. Von Heister and Howe did not get along well, and following the disastrous Hessian defeat at Trenton in December 1776, von Heister was recalled and replaced by Baron Wilhelm von Knyphausen. Von Heister died in November 1777 a few months after his return to Hesse-Cassel.

HELM, Leonard. Militia officer   Helm was one of George Rogers Clark's subordinate officers on the western campaign in 1778. He was dispatched by Clark to take possession of the post at Vincennes when French allies reported the place was almost undefended. Helm had a very small force of only a few men, but he succeeded in occupying Fort Sackville at Vincennes with no difficulty. Unfortunately for him, British lieutenant governor Henry Hamilton bestirred himself to counter Clark's invasion and marched on Vincennes with about 200 troops, ignoring the onset of winter weather. When Helm received reports of Hamilton's approach in mid-December, he sent out all but one of his men to alert Clark at Kaskaskia. The party was captured by Hamilton's scouts, however, and when the British appeared at Vincennes, Helm was forced to surrender. He was freed and returned to duty when Clark retook Vincennes in February 1779.

HEMPSTEAD, Stephen. Continental soldier

A sergeant in a Connecticut regiment, Hempstead accompanied American spy Nathan Hale on the first leg of Hale's fatal journey to New York. He also served in 1781 in the American defense of New London against Benedict Arnold's raid and wrote an account of his experiences. *Further reading: Narrative of Jonathan Rathburn with Accurate Accounts of the Capture of Groton Fort, the Massacre that Followed, and the Sacking and Burning of New London . . . with Narratives by Rufus Avery and Stephen Hempstead, Eyewitnesses of the Same* (New London, 1840; reprint, New York, 1971).

HEMSLEY, William (1737–1812) Delegate to Congress, planter, legislator

Hemsley was born on an estate near Queenstown, Maryland and became a planter on the Eastern Shore. He held several local offices before the Revolution, including surveyor of Talbot County and provincial treasurer of the Eastern Shore. From 1779 to 1781, he sat in the state senate, and in 1782, he was sent to the Confederation Congress as a delegate. On his return to Maryland the following year, he resumed his place in the senate and continued to operate his plantation.

HENDERSON, Richard (1735–1785) Land speculator, colonizer

Henderson, born in Virginia, was one of the most ambitious land speculators of the Revolutionary period. His family moved to North Carolina when he was a child, and he grew up in that colony, becoming a lawyer. By 1768, he was an associate justice of the North Carolina Superior Court and already in business with Daniel Boone and others as speculators in western lands. The field was an open one: whoever could first prove claims in the west stood to make a fortune. He founded Richard Henderson and Company in 1764 and then what came to be known as the Transylvania Company (a Latin name meaning "over the mountains"), which Henderson and his associates hoped would be the basis for a large proprietary colony in what is modern-day Kentucky. The difficulty, however, was in getting the claims confirmed. Henderson at first sought titles from the British home government, but the colonial admin-

istrations in Virginia and North Carolina, controlled in both cases by rival land speculators, contested Henderson's claims.

The beginning of the Revolutionary War stifled the Transylvania Company's bid for legitimacy. By 1779, Henderson had shifted his attention farther south to what is now part of Tennessee. He managed to successfully begin a colony in the area of modern-day Nashville. He was elected to the North Carolina legislature during 1781 and was appointed to the state council the following year.

HENDERSON, Thomas (1743–1824) Physician, soldier, official

Henderson was born in Freehold, New Jersey, graduated from the College of New Jersey (Princeton) and received training as a doctor, joining the New Jersey Medical Society in 1766. He was active in local revolutionary committees in 1774, and he served as an officer in the local militia. In 1776, he obtained a commission as a major in the Continental Army. The following year, when one of the "additional" regiments was raised in New Jersey and Maryland by Colonel David Forman, Henderson became the unit's lieutenant colonel. Forman's Regiment was broken up in July 1778, 18 months after it formed, and Henderson apparently did not transfer, as did the unit's other officers, to Spencer's Regiment, or if he did, he served only a short while. He also sat on the New Jersey Provincial Council and as a surrogate judge in Monmouth County. After the Revolution, he moved through a series of judicial offices and, as a member of the state council in 1794, became acting governor. In 1795–97, he was one of New Jersey's representatives to the U.S. Congress.

HENDERSON, William (1748–1787) Officer

Henderson was born near Williamsborough, North Carolina and moved to Pacolet, South Carolina, where he was a merchant before the Revolution. With the outbreak of the war, he became a lieutenant colonel in a South Carolina regiment. He was part of Benjamin Lincoln's command at Charleston in the spring of 1780 and on the morning of April 24 led a force of 200 Virginians and Carolinians on a sortie against the approaching British siege lines. He succeeded in overrunning the first line of works but was repulsed at the second. The sortie was brave and well conducted but did little to slow the British advance. Henderson was captured when the city surrendered in May. He was exchanged the following year and joined the army of Nathanael Greene near Ninety-Six as a lieutenant colonel of South Carolina militia. He led 73 men as Greene's advance guard at the battle of Eutaw Springs in September, taking a wound during the fighting. He died after the war, having returned to Pacolet.

HENRY, James (1731–1804) Delegate to Congress, attorney, legislator, jurist   Born in Assomac County, Virginia, Henry went to Scotland for his education, graduating from the University of Edinburgh. He returned to his home colony and opened a practice of law. From 1772 to 1774—a turbulent time—he served in the House of Burgesses. He then became a member of the new state house of delegates, sitting until 1780, when he was sent to the Continental Congress for one term. Henry became a judge during the late 1780s, sitting until four years before his death.

HENRY, John (1750–1798) Delegate to Congress, attorney, state official   Henry was born in Dorchester County, Maryland and graduated from the College of New Jersey (now Princeton) in 1769. He spent the following six years in England, studying law at the Middle Temple. He returned to Maryland on the eve of the Revolution and was elected to the general assembly, where he served for two years. In 1777, Henry was sent as a delegate to the Continental Congress. He was a strong proponent of George Washington and was appalled at what he considered the waste of money and supplies by the Congress—resources Henry thought should be conserved for building up the Continental Army. He worked on several congressional committees to raise funds and find supplies for the troops. He returned to Maryland and a seat in the state senate in 1780. Reelected to the Confederation Congress in 1785, he helped write the Northwest Ordinance, one of the enduring accomplishments of the Confederation period. After the establishment of the new federal government, Henry was elected by the Maryland legislature as the first U.S. senator from the state, and he was reelected in 1795. He resigned from the Senate in 1797 to become governor of Maryland. He died after a single one-year term. *Further reading: Letters and Papers of Governor John Henry* (Baltimore, 1904).

HENRY, John Joseph (1758–1811) Continental soldier   Henry was born in Lancaster, Pennsylvania and was apprenticed as a lad to his uncle William, a gunsmith, and taken for a brief stay at Detroit. He returned home, however, and in 1775 at age 16 ran away to join Benedict Arnold's expedition to Quebec as a private soldier. He survived the rugged march into Canada but was captured by the British in January 1776 and imprisoned for nine months. His health was apparently broken by the experience and he spent the next two years convalescing at his home. He recovered enough to begin the study of law and began practice in 1785. In 1793, Henry was appointed as president of the second judicial district of Pennsylvania, a post at which he served until shortly before his death. During his later years, he wrote an account of the Quebec expedition that has been widely quoted and reprinted since. *Further reading: An Accurate and Interesting Account of the Hardships and Sufferings of That Band of Heroes, Who Traversed the Wilderness in the Campaign against Quebec in 1775* (Lancaster, Pa., 1812; reprinted under various titles: Albany, 1877; New York, 1968).

HENRY, Patrick (1736–1799) State official, orator   For Virginians of his time and for most Americans since, Henry was the voice of the Revolution, his oratory ringing through the halls and down the ages. Even though he proved less adept at managing affairs after the break with Britain, Henry was crucial in setting off the War for Independence.

He was born in the frontier area of Hanover County, Virginia and educated by his father and uncle. When he was 15 Henry became a store clerk, and at 16 he opened his own store in partnership with his brother. At 18, he married (this and a second marriage produced 17 children) and began farming, but a disastrous fire forced him back into storekeeping. Heavily in debt, he obtained a law license in 1760 after a very cursory study of the law and began a highly successful legal career. Few authentic versions of his speeches survive—even the most famous are known only by hearsay and second- or third-hand reports—but the impact of his voice can be observed over and over again in the subsequent actions of his listeners. His great success as an advocate was due to his ability to

Patrick Henry

sway a court with oratory, and this stood him in good stead his entire life.

Despite being viewed as a back-country rustic, Henry made a great splash in Virginia politics in 1763 in the so-called Parsons' Cause case, in which he argued that by disallowing a Virginia law the king had violated the compact between the crown and its subjects and thereby forfeited claims to his subjects' obedience. In 1765, Henry became a member of the Virginia House of Burgesses and championed Virginia's legislative autonomy, advocating seven resolutions that comprised a radical response to the Stamp Act. His supporting speech stirred his listeners and may have ended with the statement: "If this be treason, make the most of it." The resolutions evoked widespread agitation and established his renown throughout the colonies.

In 1774, after Lord Dunmore dissolved the House of Burgesses, Henry led the delegates in meetings at the Raleigh Tavern. In his best-remembered speech, delivered in March 1775, Henry pressed home a point that may have clinched the beginning of the Revolution. He refused to separate the interests of the southern colonies from those of Massachusetts. There was, he maintained, an equal threat to both. He argued for armed resistance to the crown and uttered the immortal words: "I know not what course others may take; but as for me, give me liberty or give me death!"

Oddly enough for a man of such impassioned oratory, Henry wanted to go slowly in making a final break from Britain, and as a delegate to the

Continental Congress from 1774 to 1776 he opposed complete independence from Britain, and this eventually cost him a role as a national leader—most of his subsequent activities were in Virginia. Henry was appointed colonel of the first regiment formed in Virginia, but he resigned when he was precluded from command by his political opponents. In May 1776, he helped draft the Virginia constitution, and he became the first governor at the end of June, serving until the summer of 1779. His record as war governor was good, although he faced no actual British military assault until late in his term. He authorized George Rogers Clark's expedition into the Northwest Territory and he did much to supply the war effort. In the last months of his tenure as governor, Virginia was ravaged by a series of British coastal raids. Henry was succeeded by Thomas Jefferson and retired to Henry County southwest of Richmond. His relationship with Jefferson was an up and down affair, and in 1781 Henry supported a faction seeking an investigation of Jefferson's conduct as governor, generating hostility between the two men that lasted until the end of his life. Henry served again as governor from 1784 to 1786.

As a delegate to the Virginia Convention in 1788 he opposed ratification of the federal constitution on the principle of states' rights but was instrumental in the adoption of the Bill of Rights. During the 1790s, Henry concentrated on his law practice, and he declined offers from Washington to become secretary of state and chief justice. In January 1799, he acceded to Washington's request that he campaign for a seat in the Virginia House of Delegates as a Federalist, thus changing political sides and opposing his former allies. Although he defeated John Randolph for the seat, Henry died of cancer before he could be sworn in. *Further reading:* Robert D. Meade, *Patrick Henry*, 2 vols. (1957–1969); Richard R. Beeman, *Patrick Henry: A Biography* (New York, 1979). William Wirt Henry, *Patrick Henry: Life, Correspondence, and Speeches*, 3 vols. (New York, 1891).

HENRY, William (1729–1786) Delegate to Congress, gunsmith, inventor A native of Pennsylvania, Henry moved to Lancaster when a teenager and was apprenticed to a gunsmith, learning the craft so well that he became one of the most renowned makers of firearms in a colony noted for riflemakers. He was a partner in a gun-making firm by age 21 and supplied large numbers of weapons

Nicolas Herkimer

for the British during the colonial wars, serving personally as an armorer on the frontier. During the early 1760s on a trip to England Henry met Isaac Watt, and thereafter he experimented with steam engines, designing one of the early, albeit unsuccessful, steam-driven boats in 1763. He held local office and sat in the Pennsylvania assembly in 1776. During the war, Henry was a commissary officer and a member of the council of safety. In 1784 and 1785, he was a delegate to the Confederation Congress. He also is credited with the invention of a screw auger and a steam-heating system.

HERKIMER, Nicholas (1728–1777) Militia general
Herkimer was born to German immigrants who settled in the Mohawk Valley near the present-day city of Herkimer, New York. As a lieutenant in the militia during the Seven Years' War he served as commander of Fort Herkimer in 1758. An active patriot in Tryon County, Herkimer served as head of the county's committee of safety, and in 1776, he was made brigadier general of the New York militia and charged with defending the state against attacks by loyalists and Indians. In July 1777, Herkimer conferred with Joseph Brant in an unsuccessful effort to obtain the neutrality of the Mohawks. In early August, he marched to relieve Fort Stanwix, which was under attack by Barry St. Leger, but Herkimer's column was ambushed by loyalists and Indians at Oriskany on August 6. Herkimer was

severely wounded and reportedly directed the battle while propped against a tree. Ten days later he bled to death following amputation of his leg by a French surgeon serving with Benedict Arnold's relief force.

HERON, William (1742–1819) Double agent
Known as "Hiram the Spy," Heron played a double game as an intelligence source for both the British and Americans, although like several other Revolutionary War spies, his perfidy was undiscovered in his own lifetime. He was a native of Ireland who emigrated to Redding Ridge, Connecticut, where he worked as a schoolmaster and surveyor before the Revolution. He held several local offices and was sent to the Connecticut Assembly several times between 1778 and 1782. He was a friend of many Continental officers, including his neighbor, General Samuel Parsons. In 1780, using a pass from Parsons, Heron traveled to British-occupied New York with a letter from Benedict Arnold to "John Anderson" (Major John André). Heron established his bona fides with Parsons by supplying the general (and eventually George Washington) with tidbits of intelligence about the British, based on frequent trips to Manhattan; however, at the same time, Heron reported regularly to the loyalist British intelligence officer Oliver De Lancey, handing over lists of French and American troop strength and minutes from the Connecticut Assembly. He received cash payments from the British and was apparently an agent solely for profit, playing one side against the other for his own personal gain. He was unsuspected and lived out the remainder of his life on good terms with his neighbors, being returned several times to his seat in the legislature after the Revolution. His true role was revealed more than a century later when British official papers came to light.

HEWAT, Alexander (1745–1829) Loyalist clergyman, historian
Hewat was born in Scotland and graduated at age 18 from the University of Edinburgh. He then came to South Carolina, where he became pastor of the First Presbyterian Church in Charleston at the tender age of 22. With the coming of the Revolution in 1775, Hewat resigned his post and returned to the British Isles. In 1799, he published one of the early histories of Georgia and South Carolina, the two-volume *Historical Ac-*

count of the Rise and Progress of the Colonies of South Carolina and Georgia.

HEWES, Joseph (1730–1779) Delegate to Congress, legislator, merchant

Hewes was the son of a well-to-do Quaker family of Kingston, New Jersey. He worked as a boy in a Philadelphia merchant house and was master of his own highly successful business there before the age of 30. He moved to Edenton, South Carolina in 1760 and enjoyed great prosperity as a shipper and merchant in the thriving seaport town. He was a leader of revolutionary agitation in South Carolina from the early days, supporting nonimportation, for example, despite his merchant's natural inclination otherwise. He sat continuously in the state assembly from 1766 until the dissolution of the royal government.

Hewes was a member of the South Carolina Committee of Correspondence and attended all the provincial congresses. Sent as one of the colony's original delegates to the Continental Congress, he served until 1777, when he was defeated for reelection. He was at first opposed to independence, albeit a strong supporter of rebellion, and he remained unconvinced until the last moment when he underwent, according to John Adams, an on-the-spot conversion and signed the Declaration. He was influential in the committee work of Congress, especially the committee to form a Continental navy. He championed the cause of a new friend, John Paul Jones, but was overruled by Adams (who called in political debts garnered through New England's support of Washington for commander in chief of the land forces) and could get no better than a senior lieutenancy for Jones. Hewes had, of course, by this time abandoned his Quakerism. He returned to South Carolina in 1777 after losing his seat in the Congress and returned to a place in the state legislature. In 1779, he was again chosen as a delegate to Congress, but he died in Philadelphia in November a few weeks after taking his seat.

HEYWARD, Thomas, Jr. (1746–1809) Delegate to Congress, militia officer, state official

Born on his father's plantation in South Carolina near the Georgia border, Heyward inherited great wealth and estates and became a rich planter as well as a lawyer after study at the Middle Temple in London. By 1771, he was master of a large estate north of Savannah and had become a member of the South Carolina legislature, which was already embroiled in conflict with the royal government. He attended the first South Carolina provincial congresses and helped write the state constitution. He was sent to the Continental Congress in 1776 and there signed the Declaration of Independence. In 1778, Heyward returned to South Carolina. As a captain of a militia artillery unit, he helped defend Port Royal Island in February 1779, receiving a wound during the action. In 1780, the British invaded South Carolina in earnest, destroying Heyward's estate on the way to lay siege to Charleston. He was captured with the fall of the city, one of only three signers of the Declaration to fall into British hands. He was held prisoner in St. Augustine, Florida until July 1781. Following the war, Heyward reclaimed his estates and lived the remainder of his life on his plantation, serving also as a circuit judge.

HICKEY, Thomas (d. 1776) Continental soldier

Hickey was a private soldier in the Continental Army and a member of George Washington's Life Guard, a unit formed at the beginning of the New York campaign in 1776 and assigned to headquarters security, when he was arrested with a companion and charged with passing counterfeit money. He incautiously boasted to fellow prisoners that he was part of a conspiracy to turn against the American cause. He was brought before the provincial congress of New York on trial and was condemned to death for mutiny and sedition. Based on Hickey's testimony, American officials suspected a massive plot by British royal governor William Tryon, who was ensconced aboard a warship in the harbor, to suborn and bribe hundreds of patriots. A certain hysteria tinged the subsequent investigation, but only 13 were arrested and carted off to confinement in Connecticut as a result. Hickey was hanged before a huge throng—Washington turned out most of the army for the spectacle—on June 15, 1776.

HIESTER, Daniel (1747–1804) Militia officer, official

Hiester was a tanner and farmer in Pennsylvania, his native state. He was also a member of the Pennsylvania Assembly from 1778 to 1781 as well as an officer—first colonel and then brigadier general—in the state militia during the American Revolution. Following the war, Hiester served as a member of the Supreme Executive Council, and in

1789, he became one of Pennsylvania's representatives to the U.S. Congress. He then moved to Maryland and was elected again to the House of Representatives from his new state. He died in Washington, D.C. at the end of his second Maryland congressional term.

HIESTER, Joseph (1752–1832) Officer, state official

Born in Berks County, Pennsylvania, Hiester was chosen as a delegate to the 1776 provincial conference. He then entered the Continental Army as an officer, serving as a company commander under Colonel Henry Haller at the battle of Long Island and eventually achieving the rank of lieutenant colonel. His main efforts were political, however, and he sat continuously for 10 years in the Pennsylvania Assembly, beginning in 1780. He served during two widely separated periods as U.S. representative from Pennsylvania, in 1797–1805 and again in 1815–1820. Following his last term in Congress, he was governor of Pennsylvania for five years.

HIGGINSON, Stephen (1743–1828) Delegate to Congress, official

Born in Salem, Massachusetts, Higginson was one of the host of Massachusetts privateers during the war. In 1782, he took a seat in the Massachusetts Assembly and was selected as a delegate to the Confederation Congress. He was also appointed as a lieutenant colonel of the state militia and helped suppress Shays' Rebellion in 1786. He was a leading Federalist in Massachusetts during the 1790s and wrote an anonymous tract in support of Jay's Treaty in 1795.

HILL, James (1734–1811) Officer, state official

Although born in Maryland, Hill lived most of his life in New Hampshire. He was a shipwright by trade. In 1775, he joined the Continental Army as a junior officer, serving first under John Sullivan. He was promoted to lieutenant colonel in 1778 and assigned to the command of Horatio Gates in the campaign against General John Burgoyne. After the War for Independence, Hill continued in the state militia, becoming a brigadier general in 1788. He also sat in the New Hampshire Provincial Congress during the Revolution and as a member of the legislature afterward. He fathered 17 children.

HILL, Whitmell (1743–1797) Delegate to Congress, legislator, militia officer

Born in North Carolina, Hill (whose first name is variantly spelled "Whitmil" and "Whitmel") graduated from the College of Philadelphia in 1760. He served as a colonel of North Carolina militia during the war and was a delegate to the colony's revolutionary assemblies. He served in the state lower house in 1777 and in 1778 was selected as a delegate to the Continental Congress, where he sat until 1780. He was simultaneously a member of the North Carolina state senate. He served a final term in the state senate in 1785 before retiring from public life.

HILL, William (1741–1816) Businessman, militia officer

Hill was born in Ireland and moved to York County, South Carolina by way of Pennsylvania. He amassed a considerable land holding, including rich iron ore deposits, and with the beginning of the Revolution he set up an extensive ironworks called Aera Furnace, capitalized in part by a loan from the South Carolina treasury. Hill turned out finished implements and weapons from his iron foundry, supplying most of the cannonballs for the defense of Charleston in 1780. When the British took control of South Carolina after the fall of Charleston, they burned Hill's ironworks and his home. He then turned to fighting under the command of partisan general Thomas Sumter, serving as a lieutenant colonel in many engagements with the British and loyalists, including Williamson's Plantation, Hanging Rock, King's Mountain, Fishdam Ford and Blackstock's Plantation. Following the Revolution, Hill rebuilt his ironworks and served in the South Carolina legislature. In 1815, he wrote a memoir of his Revolutionary service. *Further reading: A. S. Salley, Jr., ed., Colonel William Hill's Memoirs of the Revolution (Columbia, S.C., 1921).*

HILL, Wills. See HILLSBOROUGH, Earl of.

HILLEGAS, Michael (1729–1804) Businessman, government official

Hillegas was born in Philadelphia, the son of a prosperous German immigrant merchant. After schooling Hillegas entered his father's business, which he inherited at the elder man's death in 1762, and made a fortune in sugar refining and iron manufacture. He sat in the Pennsylvania assembly and was a member of several commissions, including one to settle and audit public accounts. He participated in early patriot activities such as the Philadelphia committee of observation and was treasurer of the local committee of safety. In June 1775, he and George Clymer were jointly appointed by the second Continental Congress as treasurers of the united colonies. Slightly more than a year later, Clymer was selected as a delegate to Congress, and Hillegas was named as sole treasurer, a post he filled until 1789. He aided the Revolution with his own money during the war, lending funds to the nearly bankrupt central government. Much of his wealth survived the Revolution intact, however, and he continued to live and work as a businessman until his death.

HILLHOUSE, James (1728–1816) Soldier, official   Graduated from Yale at age 19, Hillhouse was immediately admitted to the bar in Connecticut and began a career in politics, sitting in the Connecticut House of Representatives. He served in the militia as a lieutenant of the New Haven Volunteers early in the war, and in 1779, when General William Tryon attacked New Haven and vicinity, Hillhouse was one of the Governor's Foot Guards that mounted a futile defense. He was elected to the U.S. House of Representatives in 1791 and became a U.S. senator in 1796. He was president pro tem of the Senate for nine years.

HILLSBOROUGH, Wills Hill, Earl of (1718–1793) British official   Son of an Irish peer, Hill served in the Irish government and then in the English House of Commons until created a British peer in 1756, when he moved to the Lords. He became president of the board of trade in 1763 and for many years thereafter was never far from the seat of power, filling several offices. He took over as secretary of state for the colonies in 1768 and had direct responsibility for administration of government policy in America. He worked closely with Massachusetts royal governor Francis Bernard and in general backed the use of repressive coercion against Boston, personally ordering the movement of troops to garrison the city. He resigned in 1772, and although out of office during the war, he continued to press for the strongest measures during Parliamentary debate.

HINDMAN, William (1743–1822) Delegate to Congress, official   Born in Maryland, Hindman studied at the College of Philadelphia and after graduation in 1761 went to London for legal training

at the Inns of Court. He was admitted to the Maryland bar in 1765. With the coming of the Revolution, he served in the Maryland Senate, beginning in 1777 and leaving in 1784 to become a delegate to the Confederation Congress, where he remained until shortly before the body passed from existence. He continued in public life as a member of the Maryland Governor's Executive Council and was elected as a U.S. representative, beginning with the second federal congress in 1793 and remaining until 1799. He also served briefly as U.S. senator from Maryland in 1800.

HINRICHS, Johann (d. 1834) German mercenary officer   Hinrichs came to America as a lieutenant of the jaeger corps, one of the first German units to arrive. He fought in most of the major engagements of the New York campaign, during which he was wounded severely, and afterward was promoted to captain. Few details of his life are known, but he was apparently well read and educated, and he evidenced a lively interest in the geography, natural history and society of the American colonies. At least briefly, he entertained thoughts of remaining in America. In 1780, he was sent south and took part in the siege of Charleston, an experience of which he wrote extensively in a diary (since published). Returning to Europe, he entered the service of Prussia and eventually retired with a title of nobility and the rank of lieutenant general. *Further reading:* Bernhard A. Ulendorf, ed., *The Siege of Charleston . . .* (Ann Arbor, Mich., 1938).

HINTON, John. Militia officer   Hinton was a colonel in the North Carolina back-country militia in the early days of fighting in the state and a member of the North Carolina Provincial Congress in 1775 and 1776. The Provincial Congress rallied patriot support against Governor Josiah Martin in late 1775 and fielded an army in early 1776 to oppose a force of recent-immigrant Highlander loyalists that assembled to aid a British invasion. Hinton was one of the leaders of the patriot militia that defeated the Highlanders at Moore's Creek Bridge in February 1776, crushing all effective loyalist opposition in the state for several years and frustrating British hopes of controlling the South until late in the war.

HOBART, John Sloss (1738–1805) Jurist, legislator   Hobart was born in Fairfield, Connecticut, the son of a parson descended from a long line of New England preachers. He graduated from Yale in 1757 and inherited an estate on Long Island from his mother. Living between New York City and Huntington, Long Island, Hobart was active in the prerevolutionary agitation in the New York colony. He served on the Suffolk County Committee of Correspondence in 1774 and attended all the provincial congresses in New York from 1774 until 1777. In the latter year, he was on a committee to plan a new form of government for the state. He had no legal training, but in May 1777 Hobart was appointed as justice to the new state supreme court, a post he held for two decades. He retired from the supreme court in 1798 and briefly filled the unexpired term of Philip Schuyler in the U.S. Senate before being named as judge of the U.S. district court for New York. He died in office.

HOGUN, James (d. 1781) Continental officer

A native of Ireland, Hogun came to Halifax County, North Carolina around 1751. He was on the local committee of safety in 1774 and represented his county in the state provincial congresses of 1775 and 1776. In the latter year he was appointed major of the Halifax militia and in November was commissioned by Congress as colonel commanding a new regiment, the 7th North Carolina. He led his troops north to join the main army of Washington and took part in the battles of Brandywine and Germantown, where he caught the notice of members of Congress. When the congressmen ordered the formation of new regiments in North Carolina during 1778, Hogun received the assignment to recruit a new unit: He returned south, raised a regiment and led it north to White Plains in August. In January 1779, Congress appointed Hogun as a brigadier general, promoting him over the head of Thomas Clark, who had received the recommendation from the North Carolina legislature. In March, Hogun briefly assumed command of the garrison at Philadelphia (taking over from Benedict Arnold), but in November he was ordered to march a brigade of North Carolina Continentals to Charleston to help defend the city against Clinton's expedition. The journey took three months and was hard going during winter. Hogun reached the city in time to add his strength to the defense but was captured with the surrender. He was imprisoned with his men at Haddrell's Point and died from the hardships of captivity in January 1781.

HOLKER, John (1745–1822) French official

Holker was the son of a Scots Jacobite who fled to France in 1745 after the failed rebellion in the Highlands. The father gained a title and considerable wealth by revealing the manufacturing secrets of the British textile trade to the French. John Holker, born in England, became a French commercial agent and was named during the Revolution as consul in Philadelphia with special responsibility for the French navy (which ran the consular service). He combined public and private business to a degree that later generations would find unethical, although it was common enough in his day. During the course of his official duties he made a huge personal fortune by trading in goods and playing the currency exchange rates. He was supposed to aid in financing the French expedition—which had a terrible problem in finding enough hard money or worthwhile currency to pay troop salaries and bills for supplies—but he cannily played off the two markets for discounted American paper money between Philadelphia and Boston to the detriment of Rochambeau's army and the French fleet in North America. He also acted as the private agent for French trading companies and did business with the Continental Army on his own. Holker was deeply involved in financial schemes with Robert Morris and seems to have paid much more attention to his own affairs than to the needs of the French military. At times he refused to honor bills of credit from the navy or the army, and he submitted inflated claims for his services while depressing the market in American paper money by flooding the discount exchange with currency he received as payment from Rochambeau. He also bought inferior horses and sold them at premium prices to the French cavalry. In 1781, the French government tired of his peculations and commanded that he desist from all personal business. Holker resigned his post as consul and eventually returned to France a wealthy man.

HOLLAND, James (1754–1823) Soldier, official

During the Revolution, Holland was an officer in the North Carolina militia and eventually received a commission in the Continental Army. At the same time, he served in political office as a sheriff of

Tryon County. After the war, he continued in a series of public positions as member of the state legislature and the North Carolina constitutional convention in 1789. At the relatively advanced age of 39 Holland was admitted to the bar and took up the practice of law. From 1795 to 1797 and again from 1801 to 1811, he represented North Carolina in the U.S. Congress. He then moved to Tennessee and became a farmer.

HOLLAND, Samuel. British and loyalist officer

Holland lived most of his American years in New York, where he had arrived in 1756 as a lieutenant in the 60th Regiment of the Royal Army, having obtained his commission through the influence of Governor Thomas Pownall. Holland held a succession of official places in the colonies over the subsequent two decades. By the time of the Revolution he lived in Perth Amboy, New Jersey and was surveyor general of the Northern District of North America. The Americans tried to recruit him as chief engineer or chief of artillery, but Holland remained loyal. He acted for several months as an agent of New York governor William Tryon but in November 1775 went to England. He returned to America the following year as an aide-de-camp to a Hessian general. In 1777, Holland raised his own corps of guides and pioneers, presumably from among American loyalists. He went to Canada in 1778, where he served as muster master of the Hessian troops. Following the war, he became surveyor general of Quebec.

HOLLENBACK, Matthias (1752–1829) Soldier, jurist

Hollenback was born in Lancaster County, Pennsylvania and moved to the Wyoming Valley as a teenager. He held a commission as ensign in the Connecticut militia in 1775. In August of the following year, Hollenback joined the independent company of Captain Robert Durkee that was raised from among Wyoming Valley men in response to a call from the Continental Congress. The unit became part of the Continental Army in January 1777, and as one of its junior officers, Hollenback saw action at the battles of Brandywine and Germantown. After the Revolution, Hollenback established a trading post in the Susquehanna Valley and amassed a considerable land holding. Following service as a local justice of the peace, he became an associate

justice of the Pennsylvania Supreme Court, holding office from 1791 until his death.

HOLT, John (1721–1784) Printer, publisher

Born in Williamsburg, Virginia, Holt lived there for the first part of his life, but declining business fortunes prompted him to move to New York in 1754, where he took up the printing trade as a junior partner of James Parker. In 1755, Holt moved to New Haven, Connecticut and started the colony's first paper, the *Connecticut Gazette*. He also served as deputy postmaster in New Haven. In 1760, it was back to New York, where Holt began the *New York Journal* two years later. He was an active opponent of the Stamp Act and during the 1760s and 1770s printed many of the political broadsides and pamphlets supporting the patriot cause in New York. He fled the city in the summer of 1776, just ahead of the British occupation. Back in Connecticut, Holt started a new paper and became the public printer for the state. The British raid on Danbury chased him once again in 1777, and he moved to Poughkeepsie, New York. He returned to New York City after the British withdrawal in 1783 and published the *Independent New York Gazette* until his death a year later. *Further reading:* Victor H. Paltsits, "John Holt—Printer and Postmaster: Some Facts and Documents Relating to His Career," New York Public Library *Bulletin* 24 (1920), 494.

HOLTEN, Samuel (1738–1816) Delegate to Congress, physician, official, jurist

Holten was born in Salem Village, Massachusetts, and after private medical training he set up his first practice in Gloucester around 1756, while still in his teens. Two years later, he returned to his native town, which had been renamed Danvers. He was a member of the Massachusetts General Court during the years of dispute with the royal government, first taking a seat in 1768. He was an active participant in the provincial congresses of 1774 and 1775 that created a patriot government in opposition to the crown, and he essentially abandoned medical practice for public life during the Revolution. He was a member of the Massachusetts Committee of Safety in 1776 and within two years began a long period of representing Massachusetts in the Continental and Confederation congresses. He was a delegate in 1778–80, 1782–83, 1784–85 and 1786–87. He was elected to the U.S. House of Representatives in

1793, after the formation of a new federal government, but served only one term. He spent the next 19 years as judge of the Essex County Probate Court, leaving the bench shortly before his death.

HOLTZENDORF, Louis-Casimir, Baron de (b. 1728) Continental officer

One of the first to volunteer from France for service in America, Holtzendorf was a German-speaking native of Prussia and had served on the Prussian general staff. In 1776, he was in Paris and negotiated with Silas Deane for a commission from Congress. Holtzendorf arrived in America late in the year and received the rank of lieutenant colonel. He served during the battles in Pennsylvania in 1777 at Brandywine and Germantown but is not listed as commanding any specific units. He resigned his commission and returned to France in mid-1778.

HONEYMAN, John (c. 1730–c. 1823) American spy

Honeyman was born in Ireland and emigrated to America in time to serve in the Seven Years' War, following which he moved to Philadelphia and became a weaver. In the fall of 1775, when George Washington was retreating across New Jersey, Honeyman volunteered as a spy for the American cause. He moved to Griggstown, New Jersey and in the guise of a butcher and cattle trader moved back and forth across British lines, gathering information on troop strength and dispositions for Washington. His most important service was in December. After allowing himself to be arrested by the Americans as a suspected loyalist (as a means of reaching Washington), Honeyman gave the commander in chief a complete picture of the Hessian forces at Trenton and an accurate plan of the town, information that aided Washington's plan for a surprise assault. Honeyman returned to the British lines before the battle and reported the disinformation that Washington was disorganized and unlikely to be aggressive. Following the war, Honeyman moved to Lamington, New Jersey and became a farmer. *Further reading:* Leonard Falkner, "A Spy for Washington," *American Heritage*, 8 (August 1957), 59–64.

HOOD, Samuel (1724–1816) British admiral

Never in command of the fleet in American waters but always a second in command to lesser men, Hood emerged from the American war with his good reputation intact, yet he was denied any sterling victory. He was unusual in his naval career in that he had no powerful patron or political connection, unlike most officers who rose to high rank and command. He went to sea—along with his brother, who also became a British admiral—in 1741. After serving as a lieutenant both at sea and ashore, he was appointed master and commander of the *Jamaica* and spent two years in American waters, much of it around Charleston, South Carolina. He won distinction as a frigate commander during the Seven Years' War.

In 1767, Hood was made commander in chief of the British squadron in America, but this was a small command and much of his time was spent in transporting troops to quell patriots in Boston. He rotated back to England in 1770. After duty on a guardship and patrolling the English Channel, Hood resigned in 1778 and took a civilian post as resident commissioner for the Royal Navy at Portsmouth. In 1780, Hood was made a baronet, promoted to rear admiral, and sent to the West Indies as second in command to George Rodney. He was a superior strategist and fighter, but Rodney's direction stifled Hood's abilities. Hood sailed north in 1781 to join Admiral Thomas Graves against the French fleet of Admiral de Grasse. At the battle of the Capes in September Hood was again relegated to a subordinate position and could do little to change the ineffectual outcome of the engagement. The following year, Hood played a significant role in Rodney's defeat of de Grasse at the Battle of the Saints and was rewarded with an Irish title. He returned to England and served through the first years of the naval wars with France in the 1790s. *Further reading:* Daniel A. Baugh, "Sir Samuel Hood: Superior Subordinate," in George A. Billias, *George Washington's Opponents* (New York, 1969).

HOOPER, William (1742–1790) Delegate to Congress, attorney

Hooper was born in Boston and groomed by his family for the Episcopal priesthood (his father was a Congregationalist parson turned Anglican). He attended Boston Latin School and then graduated from Harvard in 1760 at age 18. However, he turned his back on the church and studied law with radical James Otis, a decision that alienated him from his family. He moved to Wilmington, South Carolina in 1764, married, and established a flourishing legal practice. He also began a political career, serving as deputy attorney general of the colony in 1770 and 1771. During the Regulator uprising, Hooper was an ally of royal governor William Tryon, and although not himself a military man, Hooper was with the government forces at the battle of Alamance when the back-country Regulators were defeated. Hooper soon developed major differences with Tryon and the royal government, however, perhaps influenced by his early association with Otis and the Boston radical party.

Elected to the South Carolina assembly in 1773, Hooper supported a bill to make English debtors answerable to the colonial legislature, published a series of newspaper articles against the government and found himself disbarred. He then threw all his weight on the side of the rising rebellion. He was a member of the committee that called the first extralegal provincial congress in South Carolina in 1774 and was selected as a delegate to the first Continental Congress. Hooper represented South Carolina in Philadelphia for three years, exhibiting a flare for oratory and signing the Declaration of Independence. He resigned in 1777 to return to his home and his faltering law practice, although he continued to act in political affairs as a member of the state legislature. The British invasion of South Carolina in 1780 ruined him. He was away from Wilmington when the British took the city, and Hooper was cut off from his family and property. After nearly a year of living on the charity of friends, he returned in 1781 to find nothing left. He moved with his family to Hillsboro, but he never regained his former political influence.

HOPKINS, Esek (1718–1802) Continental naval officer

The first commander in chief of the Continental Navy, Hopkins was born on a farm near Providence, Rhode Island, now part of Scituate. He went to sea in 1738, succeeding as a captain and later, during the Seven Years' War, as a privateer. He retired to the family farm in 1772. His brother Stephen was the most prominent politician in Rhode Island, so Hopkins was interested in local politics. In October 1775, he became brigadier general and was appointed to command the state militia.

As a delegate to the Continental Congress and a member of its marine committee, Stephen maneuvered Esek's appointment in December as commander in chief of the newly created navy, while Esek's son John was made a captain. Hopkins encountered difficulties in equipping and finding crews for the few ships that were available to him, but he finally made up a flotilla and prepared to sail against the might of the Royal Navy. Given the daunting assignment of clearing the Chesapeake Bay and the Carolina and Rhode Island coasts in February 1776, Hopkins thought better of challenging the British and instead sailed to the West Indies and captured Nassau in March. He rather easily took the British posts at Nassau, but to his dismay, Hopkins discovered that the hoard of supplies and matériel he hoped to capture was nowhere to be found—most had been sent away before the American flotilla arrived. Hopkins' great adventure was to do little more than sail in, stay a while and sail away. On his return, Hopkins' squadron encountered HMS *Glasgow* but failed to capture it, even though Hopkins had superior force. Congress was justifiably miffed that Hopkins had unilaterally changed his mission—although a loophole in his orders made it barely possible—and ordered an investigation, which censured Hopkins for insubordination. Congress suspended Hopkins from command in March 1777, and finally dismissed him in January 1778. Hopkins served as a deputy in the Rhode Island General Assembly from 1779 to 1786. From 1782 until 1802, he was a trustee of Brown University. He also served as collector of imposts in 1783.

HOPKINS, John Burroughs (1742–1796) Naval officer, privateer

Hopkins was born in Providence, Rhode Island, the eldest son of Esek Hopkins. Like his father, John Burroughs served in the Continental Navy during the Revolution, being named one of the four original captains by Congress in 1775 and given command of the 14-gun brig *Cabot*. He sailed as part of his father's squadron to Nassau in early 1776. In April, his ship led the American vessels in the fight with the *Glasgow* near Block Island, and Hopkins was wounded and his ship heavily damaged during the encounter. He was named to the new frigate *Warren* the following year and slipped out of the Providence River past the British blockade in March to take two prizes before putting in at Boston. His best effort was in 1779, when he led a small squadron of American ships on a six-week cruise off the Virginia capes. The squadron captured a loyalist privateer out of New York, seven ships of a nine-vessel convoy, and the 20-gun British warship *Jason*. Hopkins brought his prizes into port at Boston and Portsmouth but then quarreled with the naval committee of Congress over whether he had exceeded his instructions, and he resigned from the navy. He returned to sea as a privateer in 1780 and was captured by the British but was soon released. His final voyage of the war was in 1781 as captain of a Rhode Island privateer.

HOPKINS, Samuel (1753–1819) Soldier, official

Hopkins was born in Albemarle County, Virginia. During the first years of the Revolutionary War he apparently served with the Continental Army in the northern theater, but his unit and position are not known. In 1780, however, he was a lieutenant colonel of the 10th Virginia Regiment under William Davies, and along with fragmented detachments of other Virginia enlisted men and officers, Hopkins was captured at the fall of Charleston in May. Following the war, Hopkins moved to Kentucky and became first a judge and then a member of the Kentucky legislature. During the War of 1812, he was commissioned as a major general and was appointed commander in the west. He served as U.S. representative from Kentucky from 1813 until 1815.

HOPKINS, Stephen (1707–1785) Delegate to Congress, government official

Like his friend Benjamin Franklin, Hopkins was a generation older than most of the men who made the American Revolution, and he had been a political power in his native Rhode Island for decades before the colonies declared independence. He was a largely self-made man, rising from modest circumstances. He was born near Providence and received little education, and in his youth he was a farmer and surveyor in the town of Scituate. He began to fill local offices there in the early 1730s and was sent to the colonial assembly, where he sat almost continuously until the early 1750s. He began a merchant marine shipping business in nearby Providence with his brother Esek in 1740 and moved there two years later. He shifted his focus to jurisprudence to some degree in the 1750s, becoming first assistant justice and then chief justice of the colonial superior court.

As a charter colony, Rhode Island elected its own governor, and Hopkins held the office several times between 1755 and 1767, usually contesting the post with his chief political rival, Samuel Ward. In general, Hopkins was the champion of the more radical faction in Rhode Island politics and Ward the representative of the more aristocratic conservatives, with further tension arising from the economic rivalries between Hopkins' Providence and Ward's Newport. It was a natural step for Hopkins to become a strong supporter of colonial independence. He attended several inter-colonial meetings during the 1760s, and by the early 1770s, he was a vocal opponent of the crown in America, having published a widely circulated pamphlet in 1764. He was selected as one of Rhode Island's delegates to the first Continental Congress in 1774 and served until 1776, signing the Declaration of Independence in the latter year. His most influential congressional post was as head of the committee on the navy, and he used his power to have his brother Esek appointed a commodore and commander in chief of the new Continental Navy (a selection that proved less than fortunate), and he wrangled a coveted place on the captains' list for his nephew. Nearing his 70th birthday, Hopkins resigned from Congress in 1777 and returned to Providence. He continued to sit in the Rhode Island assembly for three more years but retired from public life in 1780.

HOPKINSON, Francis (1737–1791) Delegate to Congress, writer, official, jurist

Hopkinson was a man of many parts and several careers. He is remembered best for his writing during the Revolution, but he also was a signer of the Declaration of Independence, a judge and one of America's first musical composers. He was born in Philadelphia and was the first student to graduate from the University of Philadelphia (later part of the University of Pennsylvania). He studied law with Benjamin Chew and was admitted to the bar in 1761, but his early career was as a collector of customs and a largely unsuccessful businessman. He went to England in 1767 to seek an office through patronage— he was a distant relative of Lord North—but came away empty-handed. After trying business again and serving as a customs collector in Delaware, he married the daughter of Joseph Borden and moved to Bordentown, New Jersey (named after his father-in-law), where he finally set up a successful legal practice.

Hopkinson had a facile pen and during the pre-revolutionary period produced several allegories, pamphlets and poems supporting the patriot cause, most notably *A Pretty Story* and *The Prophecy*. After sitting on the New Jersey governing council and in the colonial legislature, Hopkinson was named as a delegate to the Continental Congress in 1776. He served only a few months but was on hand in the summer to sign the Declaration. He was named to the Pennsylvania navy board during the war and served as treasurer of loans for the state. He also continued to write on political topics, including several pamphlets that received wide circulation. His most popular work was the humorous poem "The Battle of the Kegs" in 1778, which farcically celebrated David Bushnell's attempt to sink British shipping on the Delaware River with mines floated downstream in barrels. Hopkinson also wrote one of the first American attempts at opera, *The Temple of Minerva*, in 1781. Following the war, Hopkinson became a jurist, sitting as a judge of the circuit court while continuing to write and publish on a variety of topics. He also claimed to have been the principal designer of the Stars and Stripes. He died of apoplexy. *Further reading:* George E. Hastings, *The Life and Works of Francis Hopkinson* (Chicago, 1926; reprint 1968).

HORNBLOWER, Josiah (1729–1809) Delegate to Congress, engineer, official

Hornblower was born in England, where his father was a highly skilled engineer. The young man was well schooled by his father in the design and construction of steam engines, which was at the time an infant but closely guarded technology. In 1753, Hornblower was brought to New Jersey by John Schuyler and hired to assemble a smuggled steam engine at Schuyler's copper mine on the Passaic River near Belleville. Two years later, Hornblower married an American and settled down as manager of the mine. He became relatively prosperous, leased the mine and became proprietor of a ferry. He joined the patriot political movement in 1776 as a member of a committee of safety. He was elected to the New Jersey assembly in 1779 and was chosen speaker in 1780. From 1781 to 1784 he sat on the state ruling council. He was sent to the Confederation Congress as a delegate in 1785. Following the war, he took up farming and experimented with steam-driven river craft, and he sat as a judge of the county court of common pleas.

HORRY, Daniel Huger. Continental officer

Probably related to Peter and Hugh Horry (and perhaps to the South Carolina Huger family), Daniel received a commission as a captain in the 2nd South Carolina Regiment in mid-1775. The regiment was one of two authorized by the South Carolina Provincial Congress and officially adopted by the Continental Congress as part of the Continental Army but which served only in defense of the state. Horry commanded a company of the 2nd in defense of Charleston in 1776. In 1779, he was appointed by the South Carolina government to raise a regiment of light dragoons (known as Horry's Dragoons) to defend the state against the second British invasion. He commanded the unit with the rank of lieutenant colonel. Horry's Dragoons were never officially taken onto the rolls of the Continental Army, but they fought side-by-side with the Continentals in South Carolina and most accounts list them as part of the national army. Horry and his mounted troops served in the second defense of Charleston and were captured when the city fell in 1780. He subsequently took an oath of loyalty to the crown and withdrew from further military service.

HORRY, Hugh. Militia and Continental officer

A South Carolinian, Hugh was the brother of Peter Horry and probably was related to Daniel Huger Horry. He was a major and then lieutenant colonel of the 2nd South Carolina Regiment that was formed in 1779 when the Continental regiments of South Carolina were reorganized. The 2nd was captured at the fall of Charleston in May 1780, but Horry apparently escaped or was not with his unit in defense of the city. Horry joined Francis Marion when the great partisan leader was named as brigadier general of South Carolina militia, and he commanded the infantry regiment of Marion's brigade during the summer of 1780. Horry played a key role in the action at Nelson's Ferry in August when Marion rescued 150 captured Continental troops from the British.

HORRY, Peter. Continental and militia officer

The brother of Hugh Horry, Peter Horry was a captain and then major in the 2nd South Carolina Regiment early in the war, but he later became an officer under Francis Marion during the partisan campaigns in the Carolinas. Some sources give his militia rank as colonel, others as brigadier general. He was wounded at Eutaw Springs in 1781. Much later in life he wrote a narrative of Marion's activities during the Revolution which he gave to the infamous Parson Weems, who turned the factual account into a highly romanticized biography of Marion. Horry vehemently disclaimed all connection with the book, although his name appeared on the title page.

HOSMER, Titus (1737–1780) Delegate to Congress, official, jurist

Born in Middletown, Connecticut, Hosmer (whose name is sometimes given as "Hosmus") graduated from Yale in 1757 and then studied law. He set up a practice in Middletown after admission to the bar in 1760. He took a seat in the General Assembly in 1773 and continued to serve through the beginning of the Revolution, until 1778, acting as speaker in 1777. He also was a member of the state committee of safety and was selected as a delegate to Congress in 1778. When Congress created a national court of maritime appeals in 1780, Hosmer was made one of the judges, but he died soon after taking office.

HOTHAM, William (1736–1813) British naval officer

Hotham was born to an aristocratic family and sent to sea in 1751 after training with the Royal Navy at Portsmouth. He advanced rapidly and commanded small ships in many successful engagements during the wars against France. By 1776, Hotham flew the broad pennant of a commodore and was dispatched to New York as second in command to Admiral Richard Howe. He was in charge of the naval portions of the landing at Kip's Bay in September 1776, and during the British occupation of Philadelphia, he was the senior naval officer at New York and provided the ships and naval direction for Sir Henry Clinton's brief probe up the Hudson River. He fought the French fleet most credibly off Newport in 1778, after which he withdrew to the West Indies. In later life, he became an admiral and was elevated first to the Irish peerage and eventually made a British baronet.

HOUDIN, Michel-Gabriel (d. 1802) French-American officer

Houdin served as a lieutenant in the 15th Massachusetts Regiment under Colonel Timothy Bigelow, beginning in January 1777 when the unit was formed. He was active in the campaign against General John Burgoyne, wintered at Valley Forge and fought at Monmouth. In 1779, Houdin was promoted to captain and transferred to the 5th Massachusetts under Rufus Putnam. He ended his service in the 2nd Massachusetts in 1783. The following year he returned to France, but he later resettled in America.

HOUSTON, William Churchill (c. 1746–1788) Delegate to Congress, militia officer, state official, teacher, attorney

Born in South Carolina, Houston went north to the College of New Jersey (Princeton) for his education and lived the rest of his life in his adopted state. He graduated in 1768 and immediately began teaching at the college grammar school. By 1771, he was a professor of mathematics and natural philosophy at Princeton, and he remained on the faculty throughout the war, despite his many other activities. He held a commission in the local county militia in 1776 and is reported to have served in the field during the New Jersey campaigns.

His major contributions to the Revolution were on the political side, however. He was appointed a delegate to the second Continental Congress in 1775 and acted as deputy secretary of the body during his two-year stay. He was a member of the New Jersey Provincial Congress in 1776 and sat in the state assembly after leaving Congress in 1777. The next year, Houston was on the state council of safety, and in 1779, he returned to Congress as a delegate. During the same period he somehow found the time to study the law, and he was admitted to the bar in 1781. From 1782 to 1785, he was a receiver of taxes in New Jersey on behalf of the Congress (he turned down appointment in 1781 as comptroller for the Congress). Houston resigned his post on the faculty at Princeton after commencement in 1783 and focused his professional life on his law practice. He served a third time in Congress in 1784 and 1785 and was a delegate to both the Annapolis and Philadelphia constitutional conventions. He died of tuberculosis while on his way to seek recovery in a southern climate.

HOUSTOUN, John (1744–1796) Delegate to Congress, state official

Houstoun was one of the early revolutionaries in Georgia, a colony rife with political dissension during most of the revolutionary period, and he held office as governor during most of the war but played only a minor role in vital affairs. He was born in Waynesboro and began a law practice in Savannah after admission to the bar. Savannah harbored one of the few enclaves of rebels in the colony—it was much overshadowed by the transplanted New Englanders of the Sunbury district and radical agitators in the back country—and Houstoun helped form one of the first chapters of the Sons of Liberty. He was selected as one of the first official delegates to the Continental Congress from Georgia in 1775 after sitting in the colonial provincial congress. The politics and condition of the civil government in Georgia were much confused during the first years of the Revolution, with the military, which fumbled attempts to use the state as a base for invading British Florida, exerting much control. Houstoun was elected governor—a weak office—in 1778 but the British had already invaded and seized control of Savannah. Houstoun became chief justice of Georgia after the war and ran unsuccessfully for another term as governor in 1787. He was elected mayor of Savannah in 1789 and 1790 and sat as a judge of the state superior court in 1792.

HOUSTOUN, William (1755–1813) Delegate to Congress, attorney

Not to be confused with William Churchill Houston of New Jersey, this William Houstoun (the spelling of the names was often interchangeable in the 18th century) was a lawyer from Georgia and a minor delegate to the Confederation Congress. He was born in Savannah and educated in England at preparatory schools. He was still in Britain at the beginning of the Revolution and was admitted to legal studies at the Inner Temple in 1776 when he was 21. He returned to Savannah before the end of the war, however, and was elected to Congress in 1784, sitting until 1786. He acted as an agent in a boundary dispute with South Carolina and sat in the federal constitutional convention in 1787, declining to sign the document. He died in Savannah but was buried in New York City.

HOWARD, Frederick. See CARLISLE, Earl of.

HOWARD, John Eager (1752–1827) Continental officer, delegate to Congress, government official

One of the Continental Army's best field officers, Howard was a mainstay of the American southern campaigns in 1780 and 1781 as a commander of the redoubtable Maryland Continentals. He was born on a country estate near Baltimore and received an education at home from private tutors.

John Eager Howard

He entered the military as captain of the 2nd Maryland Battalion, organized in mid-1776 as part of the Flying Camp strategic reserve, and fought at the battle of White Plains. In February 1777, Howard was commissioned as a major in the 4th Maryland, with which he served at Germantown. In March of the following year, he transferred to the 5th Maryland as a lieutenant colonel, taking part in the battle of Monmouth in June. The Marylanders moved to the southern theater in 1780 and individual regiments were virtually destroyed at the debacle at Camden. Remnants of former units were combined, however, into a Maryland detachment, and Howard had field command of a group of these veterans whose combat experience was not exceeded by any other soldiers of the Continental Army. Howard and his men were more than a match for the finest British troops, and they were probably the best among American forces at the bayonet attack, a primary battle tactic that had been the sole province of the British early in the war.

Howard's finest moments were at the battle of Cowpens in January 1781. He and his Marylanders held the reserve positions behind the militia, and when Tarleton's British infantry launched a headlong chase of the retreating American amateurs, Howard met them with a deft maneuver and then a hardy bayonet charge that shattered the British assault and assured a complete victory for the Americans—one of the few clear-cut battlefield victories of the southern campaign or of the entire war for that matter. Howard received the thanks of Congress and a medal for his crucial role at Cowpens. He also led his men at the ensuing battles at Guilford Courthouse, Hobkirk's Hill (saving Nathanael Greene's army from disaster with another bayonet charge) and Eutaw Springs. As one observer has pointed out, merely to have participated in so many crucial battles was unusual, but to have been distinguished in nearly all was remarkable.

After the Revolution, Howard entered a long period of public service. He was a delegate to the Confederation Congress in 1788 and served as governor of Maryland from 1789 until 1791, when he moved to the state senate for a four-year stint. In 1796, he was elected to fill a vacancy in the U.S. Senate, serving until 1803 and acting as president pro tem during part of that period. As a Federalist, he fell from power after the turn of the century, but he had previously declined appointments as secretary of war and brigadier general. He was the unsuccessful Federalist candidate for vice president in 1816.

HOWE, Richard, Viscount (1726–1799) British admiral

Popularly known as "Black Dick" because of his swarthy complexion, brother of William Howe, and commander in chief of the navy in America during the years 1776–78, Howe was born in London. He began his naval career at the age of 14 serving on an around-the-world voyage with Admiral George Anson, but his own ship was forced to return home because of damage after rounding Cape Horn. Howe served in the West Indies in 1742 and was promoted to lieutenant. He served in American waters during the Seven Years' War as captain of the *Dunkirk*. When his elder brother, George, died at Fort Ticonderoga in 1758, Howe inherited the Irish title of viscount. In 1762, he entered Parliament, and in 1763 and again in 1765, he served on the Admiralty board, and from the latter year until 1770 he was treasurer of the navy.

Howe was promoted to vice admiral in December 1775, and the following February, he was appointed commander of the navy in America, where his brother William was military commander in chief. The two brothers were also empowered to negotiate a peace settlement with the colonies—a futile endeavor despite their sympathy for the Americans. Howe provided naval support during the New York campaign. Disgruntled over what he regarded as inadequate support from London and also over the arrival of the Carlisle Peace Commission in 1778,

Richard, Lord Howe

Howe resigned but stayed on long enough to defend New York and thwart the French-American attack on Newport in August 1778. When Admiral Byron arrived, Howe returned home, refusing to serve again as long as Lord Sandwich headed the Admiralty. When the Rockingham government came to power in March 1782 and Lord Sandwich retired, Howe accepted command of the navy in the British Channel and succeeded in relieving the British garrison on Gibraltar. Except for several months in 1783, Howe served as first lord of the Admiralty from January 1783 until August 1788. When war with France broke out in 1793, Howe again took command of the navy in the Channel, performing very effectively in 1794 despite his age. In 1797, he was sent to terminate the naval mutiny at Spithead, his last service. Howe was awarded the British title of viscount in 1782 and became Baron and Earl Howe in 1788. *Further reading:* Troyer Anderson, *The Command of the Howe Brothers During the American Revolution* (New York, 1936); Ira D. Gruber, *The Howe Brothers and the American Revolution* (New York, 1972).

HOWE, Robert (1732–1786) Continental general, planter

Born in Bladen County, North Carolina and educated in Europe, Howe amassed a fortune before the Revolution as owner of a rice plantation. He served as justice of the peace for Bladen County in 1756 and in the same capacity for Brunswick County in 1764. From 1764 until 1775, he was a member of the North Carolina Assembly. Howe was militia commander of Fort Johnston in 1766–67 and again from 1769 until 1773. After his

Robert Howe

second tour in this post he was made a colonel of artillery and served in Governor William Tryon's expedition against the Regulators. In 1774, he served as delegate to the provincial congress that met in New Bern, was a member of the North Carolina Committee of Correspondence and helped raise and train militiamen.

After the Revolution began, he was commissioned a colonel in the 2nd North Carolina Regiment. In January 1776, he fought ably in the actions that drove Lord Dunmore out of Virginia, earning him an appointment as a brigadier general in the Continental Army. In the fall of 1777, he was promoted to major general and placed in command of the Southern Department. His expedition against the British at St. Augustine, Florida, however, was a complete failure. He was replaced as southern commander by Benjamin Lincoln in September 1778 but continued in command in Georgia. With the British capture of Savannah in December he was recalled to the North, exonerated of fault at Savannah by a court-martial and placed in charge of Benedict Arnold's court-martial for misconduct as commander in Philadelphia. Washington then put him in command of West Point and outposts in the Hudson Highlands in February 1780. He was succeeded in August by Benedict Arnold, and in September, after Arnold's flight, Howe served with the board of officers that recommended Major John André be hanged. In January 1781, Howe commanded the troops that suppressed the mutiny of Pennsylvania and New Jersey soldiers, and in 1783, he led his troops in dispersing the mob that had

driven Congress from Philadelphia. Howe returned to his rice plantation that same year, but in 1785, Congress appointed him to help with the boundary negotiations being conducted with the Indians. He was elected to the North Carolina legislature in 1786 but died before he could take his seat.

HOWE, William (1729–1814) British general

Howe was commander in chief of British forces, brother of Admiral Richard Howe, and an aristocrat by birth (the Howes' grandmother had been George I's mistress). He was educated at Eton, and he became a cornet in the Duke of Cumberland's Light Dragoons in September 1746 and a year later was promoted to lieutenant. Howe joined the 20th Regiment of Foot in January 1750 and became a captain in the spring of that year. In January 1756, he became a major in the 58th Regiment, attaining the rank of lieutenant colonel by the end of 1759. Howe's record during the Seven Years' War was scarcely excelled by any other British soldier, and it formed the basis for the high regard in which he was held by the government at the beginning of the American Revolution. He commanded his regiment at Louisbourg, but he gained most fame for leading Wolfe's troops onto the Plains of Abraham for the victory at Quebec. He also helped to capture Montreal in 1760. The next year, he fought at Belle Isle, and in 1762, he assisted in the capture of Havana.

In 1758, Howe succeeded his eldest brother, George, who had been killed at Ticonderoga that year, as member of Parliament representing Nottingham, holding his seat until 1780. In Parliament he strongly opposed the government's repressive policies towards the Americans and established himself—along with his brother Richard—as sympathetic to the cause of the American colonials. Howe was promoted to major general in 1772, and in February 1775, he was ordered to America. Arriving with fellow major generals Burgoyne and Clinton aboard the *Cerebus*, Howe assumed responsibility for the attack on Bunker Hill and Breed's Hill in June. He commanded the battle on the British side, and although it was a victory, the severe cost in casualties (especially among the officers) may have led him to be overly cautious in later campaigns (although this criticism has often been overdone in the history books). With Thomas Gage an obvious failure as commander in chief, the North government named Howe as the new commander in Boston in October and confirmed him as commander in chief of British forces in the colonies the following April. The British position in Boston was untenable, however, especially after Washington fortified the Dorchester Heights, and Howe evacuated Boston early in 1776 to move to New York.

His subsequent summer and fall campaign was a brilliant success and demonstrated the superiority of trained armies over the game but inexperienced Continental forces. While the Americans fought well in detail, their officers failed again and again to demonstrate good tactics, and in a series of sharp battles Howe chased Washington completely out of New York and seized a huge number of arms and men at Fort Washington. Victory seemed inevitable at this stage, and Howe appeared to need only to catch Washington in New Jersey to finish off the Revolution. Howe's lack of hard driving and the complacency of his subordinates, however, allowed Washington to turn the tables with bold strokes at Trenton and Princeton, and the great moment for the British passed. Howe himself was later accused of indolence, and it was charged that he preferred to remain amid the comforts of New York City (including the arms of his mistress, who was also the wife of Howe's commissary) rather than conduct a second vigorous campaign.

In 1777, Howe's plans focused on taking Philadelphia, which he did after again demonstrating the deficiencies of American generalship by winning at Brandywine and Germantown. But holding Philadelphia gained little, and Howe felt inadequately supported by the British administration and was weary of fighting against people he may have essentially agreed with, so he submitted his resignation. After being given an extravagant send-off by his men and officers in the form of the infamous party known as the Mischanzia, Howe turned over command to Sir Henry Clinton and sailed for England in May 1778. There he found himself in a political maelstrom and was forced into a nasty public feud with Burgoyne. In May 1779, following agitation in Parliament, a formal inquiry into the conduct of William and his brother Admiral Lord Richard Howe began; it ended inconclusively in June. In 1782, Howe was appointed lieutenant general of the ordnance, and in 1793 he was promoted to full general. In 1799, he succeeded to the Irish title of viscount upon the death of Richard. Howe resigned as general of ordnance in 1803 because of

health problems—a long, painful illness leading to his death 11 years later. *Further reading:* Troyer Anderson, *The Command of the Howe Brothers During the American Revolution* (New York, 1936); Bellamy Partridge, *Sir Billy Howe* (New York, 1936); Ira D. Gruber, *The Howe Brothers and the American Revolution* (New York, 1972).

HOWELL, David (1747–1824) Delegate to Congress, educator, jurist

Howell, who was born in Morristown, New Jersey, was associated most of his life with Brown University. He attended an academy in Hopewell, New Jersey and then graduated from the College of New Jersey (which became Princeton) in 1766. Two years later, he was admitted to the bar. Howell was a friend of James Manning, the new president of Rhode Island College, and became one of the school's first teachers in 1766. The college moved to Providence and was later renamed Brown University. During the Revolution, Howell served as professor of natural philosophy and mathematics, and he also taught languages, until classes were suspended in 1779 due to the war. In 1780, he became a judge of the court of common pleas, and from 1782 to 1785, Howell was a delegate to the Confederation Congress. He filled several important judicial offices during the remainder of his long career, including a place as judge of the U.S. District Court for Rhode Island after the turn of the century. Although no longer an active teacher, he held a ceremonial appointment as a professor of jurisprudence at Brown from 1790 until his death and was acting president in 1791 and 1792.

HOWELL, Richard (1754–1802) Soldier, official

Born in Newark, Delaware, Howell lived during his adult life in New Jersey. He served as an officer in the New Jersey militia during the Revolutionary War, taking part in the expedition to Quebec in 1776 and receiving a wound at Brandywine. In 1779, Howell joined the bar in New Jersey and began a career in public office. He became governor of the state in 1793, serving until 1801 and leading state troops during the Pennsylvania Whiskey Rebellion.

HOWLEY, Richard (1740–1784) Delegate to Congress, state official

Howley (whose name was also spelled "Howly") was a lawyer and rice planter from St. John's parish in Georgia. He moved to St. Paul's parish in 1779, entered the state assembly, and was elected by his fellow legislators as governor of the state, but since the British had military control of Georgia and since local political rivalries had nearly destroyed any semblance of organization in Georgia, Howley barely functioned as an executive. His main duties were in Philadelphia as one of Georgia's three delegates to the Congress. He returned to Georgia after the defeat of the British under Lord Cornwallis at Yorktown and served for four months as chief justice of the supreme court.

HUCK, Christian (d. 1780) Loyalist officer

Originally a lawyer of Philadelphia, Huck (also spelled "Hucke" or "Huyck") gained notoriety in South Carolina as a particularly vicious and foul-mouthed loyalist partisan and raider. He was a captain of dragoons under Banastre Tarleton and commanded outposts around Camden, North Carolina. Huck apparently hated Presbyterians above all other patriots and went out of his way to oppress this particular religious denomination. His command of profane invective must have been remarkable, since he was known among his opponents— none too gentle of language themselves—as the "Swearing Captain." He is reputed to have said, "God Almighty was turned rebel; but if there were twenty Gods on their side, they should all be conquered," a comment that apparently shocked even the sometimes irreverent patriot partisans of the Carolinas. Huck died in battle at Williamson's Plantation, South Carolina in July 1780, when a rebel force surprised his Tories as they plundered a captured house.

HUDDY, Joshua (d. 1782) American partisan and privateer

Huddy was one of the American partisans who warred with Tory irregulars in and around New York during most of the Revolution. His home was Monmouth County, New Jersey, and he commanded a privateer with a crew of 14 that was the terror of the loyalists. Both sides in the region fought a lawless, bitter and brutal warfare for years, with little respect for persons or rules. He was captured by the British in a surprise attack in March 1782 and was carted off to confinement in New York. On April 12, a group of loyalists, acting on the orders of the board of the Associated Loyalists, requested and received custody of Huddy.

They claimed they wanted to exchange him for one of their own prisoners held by the patriots. Instead, they ferried Huddy across the Hudson River and hung him to the nearest tree, leaving a sign pinned to his body that he had been executed in vengeance. The affair set off an international incident in which an innocent young British officer captured at Yorktown, Charles Asgill, nearly paid with his life for the loyalists' brutality. In the end, Asgill was saved only by the intervention of the French court. *Further reading:* Katerine Mayo, *General Washington's Dilemma* (New York, 1938).

HUGER, Benjamin (1746–1779) Officer

One of the Huger brothers of South Carolina, Benjamin sat in the colonial assembly before the Revolution and was a member of the provincial congress in 1775. He received a commission in late 1775 as a lieutenant in the South Carolina Artillery (which became the 4th South Carolina Continentals) when the unit was raised to man coastal defenses. In September of the following year, Benjamin joined his brother Isaac's new regiment, the 1st South Carolina Rifles (listed as the 5th South Carolina Regiment on the rolls of the Continental Army). Benjamin became a friend of the Marquis de Lafayette when the young Frenchman landed in South Carolina in 1777 and found refuge at Huger's plantation. Benjamin was killed by friendly fire near Charleston in May 1779.

HUGER, Daniel (1741–1799) Delegate to Congress, planter

The eldest of the South Carolina Huger brothers, Daniel was the least active in the Revolution. He was a planter and a member of the colonial assembly before the war and sat on the executive council in 1780. However, he accepted the protection of the new government when the British took Charleston in 1780 and remained on the sidelines until after the end of hostilities. He was sent as a delegate to the Confederation Congress from 1786 to 1788, and after the establishment of the new federal government, Huger was elected as one of South Carolina's first representatives to the U.S. Congress, serving from 1789 until 1793.

HUGER, Francis (1751–1811) Continental officer

The youngest of the five Huger brothers of South Carolina, Francis—like his siblings—was educated in Europe. He served in the defense of

Charleston's Fort Sullivan under William Moultrie in 1776 as a captain of the 2nd Carolina Regiment. Later, as a lieutenant colonel he was a deputy quartermaster for the Southern Department, but he resigned in 1778 before large-scale operations began in the South, retiring to his plantation on the Cooper River.

HUGER, Isaac (1743–1797) Continental and militia officer

The highest-ranking soldier among the Huger brothers, Isaac shared the same education in Europe. He fought in the Cherokee War in 1760 as a lieutenant of South Carolina militia and so had some military experience before the Revolution. He was a member of the South Carolina Provincial Congress in 1775 and was elected to the congress again in 1778, although he was on active military duty at the time and probably did not take his seat. He was commissioned as a Continental officer in 1775—lieutenant colonel of the 1st South Carolina—and sucessively was promoted to colonel and brigadier general by early 1779. Like most of the South Carolina Continentals, he did not serve outside the immediate southern theater. He was badly wounded at Stono Ferry in June 1779 but recovered in time to command the Carolina and Georgia militia at the unsuccessful American assault on Savannah the following October.

His most ignominious defeat was at Monck's Corner in April 1780. He had almost the only coherent American military force in the field at the time since Benjamin Lincoln's army was nearly sealed into Charleston by Sir Henry Clinton. Clinton sent Banastre Tarleton to bag Huger, and so he did, surprising and routing Huger, who had failed to prepare his sentries and troop dispositions properly. Huger performed much better as part of Nathanael Greene's army at Guilford Courthouse in March 1781, where he was again wounded while leading Virginia Continentals. At the battle of Hobkirk's Hill, South Carolina the following month, Huger commanded Greene's right wing in another of those infamous Pyrrhic victories won by the British during the Carolina campaign. With most of the active fighting at an end after the fall of 1781, Huger retired from duty and sat in the South Carolina General Assembly.

HUGER, John (1744–1804) State official

The third of the Huger brothers, John was born at the family plantation, "Limerick," in South Carolina. He served primarily as a civilian official during the Revolution, although he had been an ensign during a campaign against the Cherokee in 1760. He sat in the provincial congress in South Carolina and was named to the colonial council of safety that took control of the colony from royal officials and acted as an executive council until the new state constitution was passed. Huger became the first secretary of state of South Carolina and served during most of the Revolution. Following the war, he returned to private life as a rice planter.

HULL, Agrippa (1759–c. 1838) Continental soldier

Hull was born as a free black in Northampton, Massachusetts and lived as a boy in Stockbridge. He enlisted in a Massachusetts regiment in May 1777 and served as an orderly to General John Paterson for two years. He then became an orderly for the Polish volunteer officer Tadeusz Kosciuszko and served with him during the rest of the war, including the entire southern campaign. While in South Carolina during 1781, Hull was a surgeon's assistant. He was discharged at West Point, New York in the summer of 1783 and returned to Stockbridge, where he lived the rest of his life, farming and doing odd jobs. He traveled to New York in 1797 for a reunion with the visiting Kosciuszko.

HULL, William (1753–1825) Continental officer

Hull became one of the goats of the American military during the War of 1812 but served more than adequately as a young man during the Revolution. He was born in Connecticut and was admitted to the bar in 1775 in Litchfield after graduating from Yale three years before.

His legal career was immediately interrupted, however, by the beginning of the war. As a captain of militia, Hull joined the army at Boston in July 1775 and within weeks received a commission in the 7th Connecticut Regiment. He eventually reached the rank of lieutenant colonel (1779) and saw action at many of the major battles of the northern theater, including White Plains, Trenton, Princeton, Saratoga and Monmouth. During the latter stages of the war, Hull was stationed in New York as part of the Continental force that nipped at the British in New York City. His most prominent action was to lead a raid on the loyalist stronghold at Morrisania, New

York in January 1781, when he damaged the supply base of Oliver De Lancey.

He again took up law after the Revolution and became a political partisan of Thomas Jefferson during the days of the early Republic. Jefferson appointed Hull as the governor of Michigan Territory in 1805. With the advent of war with the British in 1812, Hull was commissioned as a brigadier general and launched a mismanaged invasion of Upper Canada. He was driven back and surrendered his entire force to the British at Detroit without resistance. The court-martial that followed nearly resulted in his execution for cowardice and treason. In the end, he was merely cashiered.

HUMPHREYS, Charles (1714–1786)

Delegate to Congress. A Quaker, Humphreys was born in Haverford, Pennsylvania and was a miller by trade. He attended the colonial legislature in the decade before the Revolution and was selected as a delegate to the first and second Continental Congresses; however, he voted against the Declaration of Independence because he saw it as an incentive to continue the war, which he opposed on religious grounds.

HUMPHREYS, David (1752–1818) Continental officer, poet, diplomat

One of the group of New England writers known as the Connecticut (or Hartford) Wits, Humphreys was also a great personal favorite of George Washington. He was the son of a Derby, Connecticut parson and attended Yale, graduating in 1771. He worked as a tutor at the Frederick Philipse manor in upper New York before the Revolution and was commissioned as a captain in 1776. He served as an aide-de-camp to Israel Putnam in 1778, and in 1780, Humphreys became an aide to George Washington, with whom he maintained a close association for many years thereafter. Following the end of the war, Humphreys was appointed as secretary to the American commission in Paris and began a diplomatic career that made him the first American minister to Portugal in 1790 and the minister to Spain in 1794. He meanwhile published a growing body of poetry (much of it on patriotic themes) and essays which gained him a wide reputation. Humphreys wrote a celebratory biography of Israel Putnam in 1788 while serving as Washington's secretary at Mount Vernon. *Further reading:* Francis L. Humphreys, *The Life*

David Humphreys

and Times of David Humphreys . . . , 2 vols. (1917; reprinted 1971); Edward M. Cifelli, *David Humphreys* (Boston, 1982).

HUMPHREYS, James, Jr. (1748–1810) Loyalist publisher

Native to Philadelphia, Humphreys studied medicine after attending the College of Philadelphia, but he disliked the healing profession and apprenticed himself to William Bradford to learn the printer's trade. In 1770, Humphreys set up his own printing house in Philadelphia. He founded a pro-British newspaper, the *Pennsylvania Ledger,* in 1775 at the beginning of the Revolution. He was soon forced out of business by local patriots and received anonymous threats of violence should he fail to leave Philadelphia. He apparently withdrew to New York but returned when Philadelphia was taken by the British in 1777. Humphreys started up his paper again during the occupation but had to desist with Sir Henry Clinton's withdrawal in 1778. Humphreys himself fled again to New York City in the wake of the British army. With the end of the war, he emigrated for a brief time to England and finally settled in Nova Scotia, where he published the *Nova Scotia Packet.*

HUMPTON, Richard (c. 1733–1804) Continental officer

Born in Yorkshire, England, Humpton served in the British army in the West Indies during the Seven Years' War and afterward settled in Pennsylvania. In July 1776, he was appointed as a lieutenant colonel of the ill-fated Flying Camp (organized from the militias of several middle states as a strategic reserve for Washington's New York campaign). In October, he became colonel of the 11th

Pennsylvania Regiment. During Washington's retreat across New Jersey, Humpton was responsible for scouring the Delaware River of all small craft that might be used by the British to pursue the Continental Army. Humpton's efficiency at this task helped foil the British plan to catch Washington and made possible the American counterstroke at Trenton in late December. He later commanded the 10th, 6th and 2nd Pennsylvania Regiments. Shortly before mustering out of the army in the fall of 1783, Humpton received his brevet as brigadier general.

HUNT, Isaac (1742–1809) Loyalist writer   Hunt was born in the West Indies but moved at an early age to Philadelphia, where he was educated at the Philadelphia Academy. He wrote and published satirical essays under the pen name "Isaac Bickerstaff" during the 1760s and early 1770s, and he was a member of the Pennsylvania bar. His political sentiments were pro-British, and since he made no secret of his leanings, he found himself in trouble with the patriots of Philadelphia. He was seized by a mob in 1775 but escaped unharmed. Hunt then removed himself to the West Indies and eventually to England, where he was ordained as a priest in the Episcopal Church. His son, Leigh Hunt, became one of England's important writers during the 19th century.

HUNTER, Andrew (1751–1823) Clergyman, educator   Hunter was born in the colony of New York and graduated from Princeton (known then as the College of New Jersey) in 1770. He was a Presbyterian and began to preach officially in 1774, when he made a trip to Virginia as a missionary. He was active in rebellion during the same year and took part in a miniature "tea party" in Greenwich, New Jersey, where East India Company tea was burned by a patriot mob. He was appointed as a military chaplain by the New Jersey Provincial Congress in 1776, and he apparently served with the 2nd New York Regiment under Philip Van Cortlandt. After the war, Hunter filled parish posts in New Jersey. He became a professor of mathematics and astronomy at Princeton (where he had previously sat as trustee) in 1804. His final post was as a teacher for the U.S. Navy in Washington, D.C.

HUNTER, Elijah. American spy   Hunter was a captain in the New York militia and acted as a double agent for the Americans, moving back and forth between American and British lines around New York City. He worked under the control of Colonel Elisha Sheldon, the American commander at Lower Salem, and he apparently was thought by the British to be spying for them.

HUNTINGTON, Benjamin (1736–1800) Delegate to Congress, attorney, official   Huntington was born in Norwich, Connecticut and became one of several politically active Connecticut Huntingtons. He graduated from Yale at the relatively advanced age of 25 and took up surveying for several years before reading for the law. During the late 1760s, he was a practicing attorney in Norwich. His career as a public official began in 1771, when he became a delegate to the Connecticut legislature, where he continued to sit throughout the early days of the Revolution, serving as clerk in 1776 and 1777 and as speaker of the house in 1778 and 1779. In 1780, Huntington was sent as a delegate to the Continental Congress, and he stayed for eight years, until the last months of the Confederation Congress in 1788. He was also simultaneously a state senator. He was elected as one of Connecticut's first U.S. representatives in 1789. He served only one term in the Congress, however, and returned to Connecticut in 1793 to take a seat on the state superior court.

HUNTINGTON, Ebenezer (1754–1834) Soldier, official   A native of Norwich, Connecticut, Huntington graduated from Yale at the beginning of the Revolutionary War in 1775. By 1781, he was a lieutenant colonel commanding a battalion of light infantry under the Marquis de Lafayette in the Virginia campaign, and he led his Connecticut and Massachusetts troops at Yorktown. In 1798, he was commissioned as a brigadier general in the regular U.S. Army, but he left military service in 1800 at the end of the crisis between the United States and France. He twice represented Connecticut in the U.S. Congress.

HUNTINGTON, Jabez (1719–1786) Militia officer, state official   Huntington was a wealthy and socially prominent merchant of Norwich, Connecticut. He graduated from Yale in 1741 and returned to his native town to build a prosperous West Indies trade. In the decades before the Revolution, he served in many local and colony-wide offices, and he was an officer in the colonial militia, eventually rising to lieutenant colonel. A judge and former speaker of the colonial assembly, Huntington joined the patriot Connecticut Committee of Safety in May 1775 and served during the next four years. Although not active in the field, he remained an officer of the state militia after the outbreak of hostilities, and in 1777, with the death of David Wooster, Huntington became major general in command of all Connecticut militia. He was overcome with a nervous disease in 1779 and remained an invalid until his death.

HUNTINGTON, Jedediah (1743–1818) Continental officer

Although he held high rank and significant commands during most of the Revolutionary War, Huntington saw little combat himself. He was the son of Jabez Huntington of Norwich, Connecticut and a graduate of Harvard, and he shared in his father's lucrative West Indies merchant trade before the rebellion. He was a member of the colonial militia and the Sons of Liberty in 1775 when hostilities began. He marched to Cambridge as colonel of the 20th Connecticut militia regiment and took part in the siege of Boston. In July 1775, he was named as colonel in command of the 8th Connecticut Regiment of the new Continental Army, but he moved to the 17th Connecticut in December. He was ill or absent during the New York campaigns, although his regiment fought as part of Washington's army during the summer of 1776. Huntington took command of the 1st Connecticut Regiment in January 1777 and received a promotion to brigadier general five months later. The rest of his wartime career was taken up with assignments in Philadelphia and at posts in the Hudson Highlands. He was breveted a major general before his mustering out in 1783. Six years later, he was appointed the customs collector for the port of New London, a post he held for 26 years.

HUNTINGTON, Samuel (1731–1796) Delegate to Congress, state official

Although plagued by ill health most of his adult life, Huntington held key political offices both in his native Connecticut and on the national level. He was born into humble circumstances in the village of Windham (since become Scotland), Connecticut. As a boy, he was apprenticed to a cooper, but he was bright and ambitious and educated himself by reading. He studied law on his own and was admitted to the bar in 1758, setting up a practice in Norwich soon after. By the 1760s, he was a public figure, taking a seat in the legislature and becoming a king's attorney the following year. He was a judge of the superior court from 1774 through the Revolution (a position held open for him while he actively served in other offices). He was already one of the leaders of the revolutionary movement in Connecticut when he entered the upper house of the legislature in 1775. He was named as a delegate to the Continental Congress in 1776, and he continued (with frequent interruptions to recover his health) until 1783. Huntington was a vigorous committeeman when health allowed him to attend Congress, and he was selected as president of the Congress in September 1779, replacing John Jay. Despite his fragile physical state, Huntington held the presidency through a crucial period, until 1781. He retired to Connecticut for a long period of convalescence, returning briefly to Congress in 1783. He then filled a series of state offices, including terms as chief justice of the superior court and lieutenant governor. He was elected governor of Connecticut in 1786 and died still in office 10 years later.

HUSSEY, Thomas (1741–1803) British clergyman

Hussey was an Irish Catholic, trained to the priesthood in Europe, who served as a diplomatic agent during the American Revolution. He was appointed Roman Catholic chaplain of the Spanish embassy in Britain in 1767, putting him in a delicate position at the court. He was at once associated with the British government and the agent of a foreign power. When Spain entered the American war, more or less in support of the colonies but really looking to its own interests, Hussey was recruited by the British government to help pry Spain away from the alliance with France and the Americans. He worked—unsuccessfully as it turned out—with British agent-diplomat Richard Cumberland in Madrid. Hussey subsequently returned to Britain and began to work politically on behalf of Catholic rights in Ireland. He was eventually made a bishop and the first president of the new Catholic university at Maynooth in Ireland. *Further reading:* Samuel F. Bemis, *The Hussey-Cumberland Mission and American Independence* (Princeton, 1931).

HUTCHINS, Thomas (1730–1789) Engineer, mapmaker

Hutchins was born in the colonies,

in Monmouth County, New Jersey. During the Seven Years' War, he was an officer in the Pennsylvania militia and an engineer for the fortifications at Fort Pitt on the western frontier and at Pensacola in Florida. By the beginning of the Revolution, he was well known as both an engineer and a geographer. The British offered him a commission as a major, but Hutchins turned them down, which resulted in his imprisonment on a charge of treason. He was released by the British in 1780, and he went to France, where he met Benjamin Franklin. On Franklin's recommendation, Hutchins returned to America and took an appointment as chief mapmaker to the Southern Department under Nathanael Greene—an important post during Greene's highly mobile campaign against the British in North Carolina. In 1783, Hutchins was appointed to set the boundary between Virginia and Pennsylvania, and from 1785 to 1789, he surveyed western lands ceded to the central government by the states.

HUTCHINSON, James (1752–1793) Physician, educator

Born in Pennsylvania, Hutchinson went to England for his medical education and studied in London. Despite the difficulties of travel during the Revolution, he managed to return to America in 1777 and served as a surgeon with the Continental Army. In 1778, he was appointed as surgeon general of Pennsylvania, a post he held until the end of the Revolution. He later joined the faculty of the University of Pennsylvania, the foremost medical school in the early United States, as a professor of chemistry, and he helped found the Philadelphia College of Physicians.

HUTCHINSON, Thomas (1711–1780) Royal governor

Hutchinson was the principal royal authority in Massachusetts during the period immediately preceding the American Revolution and was the focus of most of the agitation by the Boston radicals. He was in many ways an admirable figure—intelligent, cultured and capable—but he was fated to be blamed for much. Born in Boston to a wealthy family, he was the descendant of 17th-century religious rebel Anne Hutchinson.

He graduated from Harvard in 1727 and began a career as a merchant and financier at which he was extremely successful, amassing a large new fortune on top of inherited wealth. By middle age, Hutchinson had widespread financial interests and had

Thomas Hutchinson

begun to accumulate public offices that brought him even more wealth and political power. He sat in the colonial assembly intermittently from 1737 to the late 1760s, often acting as speaker. In 1749, he devised a scheme to use funds issued by the crown (to repay Massachusetts for the Louisbourg expedition) to retire the colony's paper currency—a move that benefited the property-owning and creditor elements of society. He was prominent in the Albany Congress in 1754, and in 1758, Hutchinson was named as royal lieutenant governor of Massachusetts, a post he held until 1771. He was also a judge of several courts, beginning in 1752, although he had no legal training. By 1760, he was chief justice of the Massachusetts Superior Court of Judicature, the highest court in the colony, as well as lieutenant governor.

The latter post was extremely powerful, since Hutchinson was the most stable part of the colonial royal administration while governors came and went. He often ruled as acting governor in the absence of a top official, and he exerted power as a member of the Governor's Council. As seems natural given his position, he was an unwavering supporter of British government control of the colonies, although he questioned the practical wisdom of the Stamp and Sugar acts. Nonetheless, he did all he could to enforce the odious measures and soon found himself to be the chief butt of contention with Boston radicals led by Sam Adams. A mob rampage in 1765 over the Stamp Act destroyed Hutchinson's elegant house and set the tone for the continuing struggle.

Hutchinson was also a historian and published a multi-volume history of the colony.

In 1771, Hutchinson was finally appointed royal governor when Francis Bernard was removed as too weak-willed. The climax of Hutchinson's disputes with the radicals came over the Tea Act. He and his family had significant personal investments in tea, and this financial incentive gave added weight to his policy of trying to force through the landing of the taxed substance. The Boston Tea Party in December 1773 began to undermine the confidence of the British government in Hutchinson's ability to cope, and when a series of his private letters were published by the rogue legislature (they had been procured by Benjamin Franklin in London and sent secretly to Speaker Thomas Cushing), Hutchinson's position deteriorated rapidly. He was recalled to London in 1774 and replaced by a military governor, General Thomas Gage. At first, Hutchinson hoped to return to Boston when order was restored, but the chance faded and he remained on the sidelines in England until his death. *Further reading:* Bernard Bailyn, *The Ordeal of Thomas Hutchinson* (Cambridge, Mass., 1974); John R. Galvin, *Three Men of Boston* (New York, 1976); William Pencak, *America's Burke: The Mind of Thomas Hutchinson* (Washington, D.C., 1982).

HUTSON, Richard (1748–1795) Delegate to Congress, jurist

A native of Prince William Parish, South Carolina, Hutson attended the College of New Jersey (eventually to become Princeton) and returned to South Carolina to study and then practice law. He served in the state assembly in 1776 and in 1778 was selected as a delegate to the Continental Congress, where during his one-year term he signed the Articles of Confederation. He was a member of the South Carolina Assembly from 1779 to 1782, the period during which the British assaulted, took and held Charleston, throwing local patriot officials into prolonged disarray. Following the war, he sat as a judge on the state court of equity.

HYLER, Adam. American partisan

Hyler was an effective irregular fighter in New Jersey between 1776 and 1778. He operated by boat out of a safe anchorage at Egg Harbor, New Jersey (near present-day Atlantic City) that was a haven for American privateers. Hyler held much of the coast between Egg Harbor and Staten Island in thrall by means of small but swift raids. Loyalists of the region were compelled to pay him tribute, and British commerce moved at its peril. A British raid in 1777 destroyed Hyler's small fleet, but he soon replaced it and continued to raid almost at will. Egg Harbor was difficult to approach overland and was protected from larger ships by a sand bar. In addition, a maze of creeks and islets made it difficult for an enemy to find Hyler's crews and boats. He captured several British warships, including a corvette off Coney Island, and he raided successfully ashore, even venturing into New York City proper. The British finally attacked Egg Harbor in strength in October 1778, and Major Patrick Ferguson succeeded in destroying Hyler's base of operations. *Further reading:* Fred J. Cook, *What Manner of Men* (New York, 1959); Andrew A. Zellers-Frederick, "Privateer's Haven," *Military History* 8, 2 (August 1991), 8, 72–76.

HYNSON, Joseph. British spy

Hynson was a sea captain from Maryland who was recruited by loyalist Reverend John Vardill as a spy for the British diplomatic intelligence service in 1777. Hynson outfitted a packet ship that was to serve as a fast means of communication between the American commissioners in Paris and Congress in Philadelphia. He was secretly in the pay of the British, however, and he turned over the contents of a dispatch pouch from Benjamin Franklin and Silas Deane to the British while forwarding to Congress a wad of blank papers. He received £200 from the British for his services. *Further reading:* Samuel F. Bemis, "British Secret Service and the French-American Alliance," *American Historical Review* 29 (April 1924), 474–95.

HYRNE, Edmund (1748–1783) Officer

Hyrne was a company commander in the 1st South Carolina Regiment, formed in 1775. The regiment was technically part of the Continental Army but served in the South and more or less remained under the control of state officials. The 1st South Carolina helped defend Charleston in 1776 against the first British attempt to take the key southern port. By 1779, Hyrne had reached the rank of major, and he was appointed as deputy adjutant general for the Southern Department. He was cited for bravery in 1780, and in the following year, he became an aide-de-camp to Nathanael Greene. He died at the end of the Revolution while living on his plantation in his native state.

I

ILSLEY, Daniel (1740–1813) Merchant, official
Born in Falmouth, Massachusetts, in the section of the colony that eventually became the state of Maine, Ilsley was a shipper and owner of a distillery before the Revolution. He joined the local committee of correspondence and helped muster men for the army during the war, himself holding a militia commission as a major. He served in the Massachusetts state convention that ratified the U.S. Constitution in 1788, and after the turn of the century, he was elected to the U.S. House of Representatives. He died in Portland.

INGERSOLL, Jared (1749–1822) Delegate to Congress, official jurist Born in New Haven, Connecticut and a graduate of Yale, Ingersoll moved to Philadelphia and practiced law there from 1773 onward. He was a delegate to Congress in 1780, but his major public service came during the years of the early Republic, when he was attorney general for the state of Pennsylvania and argued several important cases before the new U.S. Supreme Court. He was an unsuccessful nominee for the national vice presidency as a Federalist in 1811, returning to his state attorney general's post afterward. During his final years, he sat as a presiding judge in the city courts of Philadelphia.

INGLIS, Charles (1734–1816) Loyalist clergyman and writer Inglis, a native of Ireland, was assistant rector of Trinity Church in New York City.

As with many Episcopal clergy in America, Inglis remained loyal. He published a retort to Thomas Paine's *Common Sense* called *The Deceiver Unmasked or Loyalty and Interest United . . .*, and even under duress he refused to alter the form of the prayers for the crown when the American army occupied New York in 1776. He escaped to Long Island in August 1776, but he returned after the British retook the city only to find his church burned to the ground, an act he blamed on American troops. He remained in New York City during the rest of the war, becoming rector of Trinity in 1777. With the British evacuation in 1783, he removed to Canada, and he was appointed bishop of Nova Scotia in 1789.

IREDELL, James (1751–1799) Jurist Born in England, Iredell was a royal official before the Revolution, but he espoused the American cause with the coming of the conflict. He had served in North Carolina as an inspector of customs, but he accepted the post of judge of the Superior Court of North Carolina in 1777 as part of the new government. Two years later, he became attorney general of the state. During the postwar era, Iredell was a strong supporter of a central government and the proposed federal Constitution. He was a leader in the North Carolina convention and wrote a rebuttal to the widely publicized criticisms of Virginia's George Mason. When the new national government came into being, Iredell was appointed as one of the first associate justices of the new U.S. Supreme Court, serving nine years until his death in 1799.

IRVINE, William (1741–1804) Continental general, delegate to Congress, physician

Born in the north of Ireland, Irvine studied at Dublin University and was trained as a physician. He served as a surgeon on a British man-of-war and then in the Seven Years' War in America. He resigned from the British service at the end of the conflict with the French and remained in the colonies, establishing a medical practice in Carlisle, Pennsylvania. He was a member of the Pennsylvania provincial congress in 1774.

In January 1776, Irvine was appointed as colonel of a new Pennsylvania regiment—the 6th—and ordered north with the army sent to relieve the failed Canadian invasion force, which was in the process of fleeing from Quebec. He was part of the American force defeated at Three Rivers in June and taken captive. He was soon paroled, and thus set free, but he was not formally exchanged until 1778 and had to remain inactive until then. In the meantime, the 6th Pennsylvania was dissolved and re-created as the 7th with Irvine as commanding colonel, even though he was barred from actually taking charge for more than a year. In 1779, Irvine was promoted to brigadier general as part of the division of Pennsylvania Line regiments under Anthony Wayne.

The Pennsylvania regiments underwent considerable depreciations after the mutiny of 1781, and Irvine was shunted aside during the reorganizations that preceded the march south to lay siege to Lord Cornwallis and was sent instead to the western frontier as commander of Fort Pitt. His tenure there was not successful—he had few troops and not much in the way of supplies—and he resigned in 1783. He became a land agent after the war and in 1787 was elected as a delegate to the Confederation Congress. After the establishment of a new federal government, Irvine served as a U.S. representative from Pennsylvania.

IZARD, Ralph (1742–1804) Diplomat, delegate to Congress

A convinced patriot despite his position in life, which would have made him a likely loyalist, Izard was born on a plantation near Charleston, South Carolina into one of the colony's richest families. His paternal grandfather had been a founder of the colony, and his mother's father was governor. Izard himself married Alice De Lancey, the daughter of New York's Peter De Lancey. Izard's father died when he was seven, and at age 12 he was sent to England for education. He returned to manage his inherited indigo and rice plantations in 1764 but went back to England in 1771 with the intent of remaining permanently. However, he disagreed completely with the crown and his loyalist relatives in the matter of the Revolution, so he removed himself and his family to Paris in 1776.

In May 1777, he was appointed by the Continental Congress as envoy to Tuscany, but it was an empty assignment since Tuscany refused to receive a representative of the rebellious American colonies. Izard stayed on in Paris, attaching himself preemptively to the American mission there. He worked closely with Arthur Lee but soon developed a feud with Benjamin Franklin. Izard claimed a role for himself in negotiating with the French court that Franklin failed to recognize. He also demanded that he be paid his salary as a diplomat from funds raised in France and that his private trade goods be exempt from duties. His hauteur did not sit well with Franklin, who brushed the aristocratic Izard aside. He was recalled by Congress in mid-1779. Although he received some sympathy from Congress on his arrival in Philadelphia, Izard's diplomatic career was over. He was elected as a delegate to Congress in 1782 and 1783, sitting during the time when the body's fortunes were ebbing low. After the establishment of the new federal government in 1789, Izard was sent as a U.S. senator from South Carolina and served until 1795, when he retired from public life. *Further reading:* Anne Deas, ed., *Correspondence of Mr. Ralph Izard of South Carolina . . .* (1844; reprinted New York, 1976).

J

JACKSON, Andrew (1767–1845) Soldier, president   Jackson's unfortunate experiences as a child during the Revolution doubtless did much to form his powerful, self-willed personality that came to have a dramatic effect on the history of the nation when he reached the pinnacle of political power during the early 19th century. He was born in the back-country Waxhaws settlement of South Carolina to a family of recent Irish immigrants. His father died when Jackson was two years old, and he lived along with his two brothers and mother on the sparse charity of relatives. The beginning of the Revolutionary War when he was nine years old involved vicious strife in the remote South Carolina districts. One of Jackson's brothers was killed in 1779, and Jackson and his remaining sibling fought in the engagement at Hanging Rock in August 1780, although Jackson was only 13 years old. They were both captured by the British and thrown in prison, where Jackson caught smallpox, a disease that disfigured him. His brother subsequently died—probably from the effects of disease and prison—and Jackson's mother succumbed to a fever while nursing prisoners in British-held Charleston in 1781. At age 14, Jackson was completely alone in the world, a veteran of the nasty semi-civil war in South Carolina, and permanently embittered against the British.

His rise to power began with reading for the law and admission to the bar in 1787. He then moved to Tennessee, where he was elected to Congress and served as a supreme court judge. He came to national fame during the War of 1812 when he defeated the British at the battle of New Orleans in 1815. After serving as military governor of Florida and in the U.S. Senate, Jackson ran for president in 1824 but was cheated of victory by legerdemain in the electoral college. He won the presidential election of 1828, and his administration set an entirely new tone in national politics, ending the dominance of the more genteel Virginia and New England traditional leadership. His presidential terms were fraught with explosive issues such as the tariff, the national bank and the states' rights nullification controversy. He retired to his mansion outside Nashville in 1838, having left his stamp permanently on American history. *Further reading:* Robert V. Remini, *The Life of Andrew Jackson* (New York, 1988); Burke Davis, *Old Hickory: A Life of Andrew Jackson* (New York, 1977).

JACKSON, David (1747–1801) Delegate to Congress, physician   Born in Oxford, Pennsylvania, Jackson graduated from the College of Philadelphia in one of its early medical classes in 1768 and set up practice in Philadelphia. He was a manager of the army lottery for the Continental Congress in 1776 and 1777 and served a short tour as a surgeon and quartermaster for the Pennsylvania militia in 1779. Following the war in 1785, he was a delegate to Congress representing Philadelphia.

He was a trustee of the University of Pennsylvania, which was created in part from his alma mater.

JACKSON, Hall (1739–1797) Physician

Jackson was probably the leading medical man in New Hampshire before and during the Revolution. He was born in Hampton, New Hampshire and studied initially with his father, also a doctor. The younger Jackson also studied in England, and although he did not take a degree from a British medical school, he attended lectures at London hospitals. Jackson returned to Portsmouth, New Hampshire and set up a practice. He assisted in treating victims of a smallpox epidemic in Boston in 1764 and established a smallpox hospital near his own town. He volunteered his services to the patriots immediately upon the outbreak of hostilities with Great Britain. He tended the wounded from the battle at Bunker Hill and Breed's Hill, and later in 1775 he received a vote of gratitude from the Provincial Congress of New Hampshire and was appointed as chief surgeon to New Hampshire troops. He was one of the founders and charter members of the New Hampshire Medical Society and was voted honorary membership in the Massachusetts Medical Society.

JACKSON, Henry (1747–1809) Continental officer

Jackson commanded the 16th Massachusetts Regiment (one of the "additional" Continental regiments raised in January 1777) during the unsuccessful assault on Newport in 1778. He transferred as a colonel to command of the 4th Massachusetts in early 1783 and led his regiment into New York City on the heels of the British evacuation in November. He then received a brevet rank as brigadier general, but functionally he was colonel of the 1st American Regiment, which was the only infantry unit in commission after November 1783 and the dissolution of the Continental Army. He left the regular service in early 1784 when the standing army had been reduced to a handful of men. He also held the rank of major general in the Massachusetts militia from 1772 until 1796.

JACKSON, James (1757–1806) Soldier, official

Born in Great Britain, Jackson emigrated to Georgia in 1772 at age 15. Despite his youth, he sat in the first Georgia state constitutional convention in 1777. As a lieutenant colonel with a Continental commission, he raised Jackson's Georgia Legion in June

James Jackson

1781. The unit was a mixed force of infantry and mounted dragoons, numbering at first about 300 men. Jackson was commander of the Legion, which was not part of the regular Continental Army nor pure militia, but rather a hybrid organization raised and paid for by the state of Georgia but nominally under the command of a Continental officer. The Legion was disbanded in August 1782 after falling below strength: there were only 40 horsemen left when the unit dissolved. Jackson transferred his military interests to the state militia after the war and became a brigadier in the Georgia forces in 1786. He then began a political career, serving as U.S. representative in the first national Congress in 1789. He moved over to the U.S. Senate for one term, and from 1798 to 1801, Jackson was governor of Georgia. He went back to the Senate following his gubernatorial term and remained in office until his death.

JACKSON, Jonathan (1743–1810) Delegate to Congress, merchant, state official

A Boston native, Jackson graduated from Harvard in 1761 and moved to Newburyport, Massachusetts, where he became a merchant. He sat in the crucial 1775 provincial congress in Massachusetts and in 1777 was a member of the state lower house. He served one term in 1782 as Massachusetts' delegate to the Confederation Congress. He filled several state offices during the decades after the Revolution: in 1789, he was a state senator and U.S. marshal; from 1802 to

1806, he served as treasurer of the state. He prospered in business during the same period and was president of the Massachusetts State Bank and head of the Harvard College corporation.

JACKSON, Michael (1734–1801) Continental officer

Jackson was born in Newtown, Massachusetts and served in the Seven Years' War as a lieutenant. He was captain of his local minuteman company and led his men during the harassment of the British retreat on April 19, 1775 following Lexington and Concord. In June, he joined Gardner's Massachusetts Regiment and was wounded at the subsequent battle of Bunker Hill. Jackson was promoted to lieutenant colonel in January 1776 and assigned to the 16th Continental Regiment (a Massachusetts unit). When the 8th Massachusetts was created in November 1776, Jackson became its original colonel and commander, serving with it until 1783, when the unit (including by that stage elements of the 3rd Massachusetts) was disbanded. Three months before the discharge of his regiment, Jackson received a brevet as brigadier general.

JACKSON, Richard (d. 1787) British politician and official

Jackson, an Irishman and a prominent attorney (known as "Omniscient Jackson" for his knowledge of the law), served as a member of Parliament from 1768 to 1784 and was private secretary to George Grenville during the mid-1760s. During the same period, he was also the designated agent in London for several American colonies, including Massachusetts, Connecticut and Pennsylvania, and despite the apparent conflict of interest (a factor that seldom troubled 18th-century office-holders) he helped Benjamin Franklin present the case to Grenville against Parliamentary taxation of the colonies in 1765. He generally opposed the American war and refused at the last minute to serve on the peace commission of Lord Carlisle on the grounds it was not a sincere attempt at reconciliation. He became a close associate of Lord Shelburne and took office briefly under Shelburne's ministry of 1782–83.

JACKSON, Robert (1750–1827) British army physician

Later in life an important reformer of the British military medical service, Jackson had an adventurous time during the American war. Born in Scotland, he studied medicine in Edinburgh and sailed twice as a surgeon on whaling vessels to finance his education but failed to take a degree before running out of money and moving to Jamaica in 1774. In 1780, Jackson went to New York and applied for a position with a militia unit, but he was appointed instead as an ensign and surgeon's mate in the 71st Fraser Highlanders. He was with the Highlanders as part of Banastre Tarleton's force in January 1781 when it met Daniel Morgan's men at the Cowpens. When Tarleton's horse went down during the battle, Jackson offered his own mount to his commander and calmly walked toward the American lines with a white handkerchief held aloft on his cane. He identified himself as a surgeon and offered to treat the British wounded. Morgan paroled the enemy casualties and allowed Jackson to care for them. In 1782, Jackson was back in England, and marriage to a wealthy woman allowed him to finally finish his education in 1786. During the 1790s, Jackson vigorously protested the miserable state of medical care in the British army and after a long struggle reformed the service by introducing competent physicians and modern methods.

JACKSON, William (1759–1828) Soldier, official, journalist

Born in Cumberland, England, Jackson emigrated to Pennsylvania before the Revolution. He was a lieutenant in 1778 on the expedition led by General Robert Howe against the British at St. Augustine in East Florida, a venture that failed miserably when state militia commanders refused to take orders from Continental officers. Jackson eventually was promoted to major and became an aide to General Benjamin Lincoln. When Lincoln was appointed secretary of war by the Confederation Congress in 1782, Jackson served as his assistant. He acted as secretary to the national Constitution Convention in Philadelphia, and when George Washington took office as the first president of the United States, Jackson became one of his secretaries, serving for the first two years of Washington's initial term. From 1796 until 1801, Jackson worked as a customs official in the port of Philadelphia, but he abandoned public office in the latter year and founded a newspaper called *The Political and Commerce Register*, which he edited until his retirement in 1817.

JAMES, Jacob. Loyalist officer

Born in America, James was a pub-keeper in Goshen, Pennsylvania at the beginning of the Revolution. He joined the British army in September 1777 and recruited guides for the army, a role he himself sometimes fulfilled. He also stole horses for the army from the countryside surrounding Philadelphia and kidnapped patriots. In 1778, he raised a troop of dragoons that was attached to Tarleton's British Legion, and he served as its captain during the balance of the war. He was captured in North Carolina in 1780, but was apparently exchanged. At the end of the Revolution, he emigrated to England, leaving behind his wife and five children.

JAMESON, John. Continental officer

Jameson's moment in the historical limelight came in 1780, when he commanded the American outpost at Lower Salem, New York. The captured spy John André, still maintaining his fictional identity as "John Anderson" under a pass from Benedict Arnold, was delivered by militiamen to Jameson's custody. Confused by the papers André carried and under orders from Arnold (his commander) to forward any person answering to the name John Anderson, Jameson dispatched the documents to George Washington at Danbury and sent André under escort toward Arnold's headquarters at West Point, preceded by a messenger. Although Jameson soon recalled André and thus prevented the spy's escape, the messenger's forewarning allowed Arnold to slip away just ahead of capture.

JAQUETT, Peter (d. 1834) Continental officer

Jaquett was a junior officer in the famed Delaware Regiment of the Continental Army during 1776 and was promoted to captain in 1777. After the battle of Camden when the doughty Delawares were nearly annihilated, Jaquett took command of one of the remaining companies that was folded into the 1st Maryland. He is reported to have fought at the side of Baron de Kalb during the fierce action at Camden. Jaquett received a brevet as major when he mustered out in 1783.

JARVIS, Abraham (1740–1813) Clergyman

One of the most prominent Episcopal clergymen in New England during the Revolutionary period, Jarvis was born in Connecticut and graduated from Yale in 1761. He then went to England and was ordained as an Anglican priest in 1764. On his return to Connecticut, he became a leader in the

church and in pre-Revolution patriotic activities in the Episcopal sect. During the war, he suspended public worship rather than read the required Anglican prayers for the king. In 1783, he was secretary of a secret meeting to organize an Episcopal Church in America and concurred in the decision to send Samuel Seabury to England for consecration as Bishop of Connecticut. In 1797, Jarvis himself succeeded to the episcopacy of his native state.

JASPER, William (c. 1750–1779) American soldier

Jasper was from a humble background, probably born near Georgetown, South Carolina, but he became one of the best-known heroes of the Revolution in the South and his name was subsequently spread across the map of the United States.

He joined a company raised by Francis Marion as private in July 1775, rising soon to the rank of sergeant. He was one of the troops assigned to the defense of Fort Sullivan at Charleston in 1776 under William Moultrie. During the naval bombardment of the fort, Jasper climbed up on the fortifications to recover a flag struck down by the British fire and remounted it on a staff. Jasper's act of personal bravery was acknowledged by South Carolina governor John Rutledge with the award of a sword and the offer of a commission. Jasper took the sword but turned down the commission in favor of a post as roving backwoods scout. He roamed the swamps of South Carolina and brought back intelligence for Moultrie and Marion. According to legendary accounts, he was often accompanied by a friend named Newton, although no documentary evidence has ever been found to substantiate Newton's existence.

On October 6, 1779, Jasper was killed while defending the fortifications at Savannah, Georgia against a British attack. By an inexplicable folkloric mechanism, Jasper and Newton became favorite place-names throughout the United States, often linked by proximity such as towns named Newton in counties named Jasper. There is also a monument to Jasper in Savannah and a redoubt at Fort Sullivan (now called Moultrie) is named in his honor. *Further reading:* Lou Ann Everett, "Myth on the Map," *American Heritage* 10 (December 1958), 62–64.

JAY, Sir James (1732–1815) Physician

The elder brother of John Jay, James had an interesting career. He was born in New York City and went to Edinburgh for medical education. After a brief at-

William Jasper

JAY, John (1745–1829) Diplomat, delegate to Congress, jurist

Although somewhat overshadowed by the more famous names of the age, Jay was an important figure during the Revolution and early Republic. He was born in New York City to a wealthy and influential family of merchants, descended from Huguenot stock. He graduated from King's College (now Columbia University) in 1764 and then studied law. After his admission to the bar in 1768, Jay became one of the more successful and energetic young attorneys of the city. His marriage to the daughter of William Livingston (future patriot governor of New Jersey) only solidified Jay's position in the power structure of New York.

He took little part in the prerevolutionary activities in the colony, spending most of his energies until 1774 on his law practice. His first public role was as secretary to the New York committee of correspondence, on which he represented the conservative faction that was interested in preserving the rights and privileges of property and that feared mob rule. As the Revolution gained momentum, however, Jay moved toward a more moderate position. He was selected to represent New York in the first and second Continental Congresses, and he generally supported independence, although he was absent from the actual debates and passage of the Declaration in the summer of 1776. Jay headed a local committee of observation in New York that dealt with intelligence agents during 1776, and he held the rank of colonel in the state militia but never served actively in a military role. He helped draft the constitution for the new state of New York and sat as chief justice until 1779.

Jay returned to the Continental Congress in December 1778 and was elected president. He was deeply involved in the debates in Congress over foreign policy, and in the fall of 1779, he was named as minister to Spain. Jay's diplomatic career was thus launched with a difficult assignment. Spain was an ally of France in the war against Britain but disdained any formal affiliation with the upstart American colonies, realizing that the infection of rebellion might spread to its own colonies in New Spain and that the interests of an independent United States would conflict sharply with Spanish interests in the Floridas and along the Mississippi. Spain's main goal was to win back Gibraltar from the British. Jay found himself on the outside looking in when he arrived in Madrid in January 1780. The

tempt at a practice in New York, he returned to England in 1762, principally as a fund-raiser on behalf of King's College (now Columbia University). He succeeded in raising £10,000 and was knighted by George III when he presented an address to the king from the college board of governors in 1763. There was trouble over collecting the money, however, and Jay fell out with the college. He remained in Britain during the prerevolutionary years and reportedly invented an invisible ink later used by American intelligence agents (perhaps by his brother who headed an intelligence committee in New York). Jay returned to America in 1778, lent $20,000 to the clothier-general of the Continental Army in Boston and sat in the New York state senate until 1782. He then apparently hit on a scheme to deal with the British. He allowed himself purposely to be captured in New Jersey and presented a plan for reunion to British and loyalist authorities. His offering was rejected and he was released, although his adventure ruined his credibility among the patriots. He went to England and practiced medicine there until late in his life, when he returned to New Jersey.

John Jay

Spanish refused to formally recognize him and his mission, although they were willing to continue to provide supplies and some money. Two years of effort produced little more than a loan of $170,000.

In 1782, the Congress named Jay as one of the commissioners to negotiate a peace with Britain, and he left for Paris to join Benjamin Franklin and John Adams. Between them, Jay and Adams convinced Franklin that France's interests (now that the war was over) could never coincide sufficiently with America's, and the commissioners settled a separate peace with Britain. Jay returned to New York City, refused appointment as minister to England, and resumed his long-interrupted law practice, but his respite from public service was short-lived. In 1784, he was named by Congress as foreign minister. Serving until 1790, Jay found the task of conducting foreign affairs for a loose and quarreling confederation of states to be an almost impossible challenge, and he became a firm advocate of a strong central government. He was prevented by local politics from serving at the federal constitutional convention in Philadelphia, but he threw himself into the struggle for ratification, writing five of the *Federalist Papers* (only a recurring bout of ill health prevented him from contributing more).

With the formation of the new central government, Jay was named as the first chief justice of the U.S. Supreme Court, taking office in March 1789, and he established most of the early procedures for the Court. His most notorious and controversial role in the new nation's affairs was on the diplomatic side, however. While still chief justice, Jay was appointed in 1794 to negotiate with the British. Despite the provisions of the previous peace treaty, the British had held on to forts in the West and had obstructed American commerce. Jay devised a new treaty that fell short of providing all that some American interests wanted yet gained a good deal for the young republic and avoided a renewed conflict. The so-called Jay's Treaty set off a hot debate before it was ultimately ratified, and Jay's national standing suffered. He resigned as chief justice in order to accept the governorship of New York, a post to which he had been nominated and elected while in England negotiating his treaty. After two terms, he declined renomination in 1800 and also turned down reappointment as chief justice of the nation's high court. Jay withdrew from public life and spent his remaining 28 years in retirement on his farm in Westchester County. *Further reading:* Donald Smith, *John Jay: Founder of a State and Nation* (New York, 1968); Richard B. Morris, *John Jay: The Nation and the Court* (Boston, 1967); Robert B. Morris, ed., *John Jay: The Making of a Revolutionary* (New York, 1975); Frank Monaghan, *John Jay: Defender of Liberty* (New York, 1935).

JEFFERIES, John (1745–1819) Loyalist officer, physician

Born in Boston, Jefferies attended Harvard, graduating in 1763, and went to Scotland for medical training. He received a degree from the University of Aberdeen in 1769 and entered the service of the Royal Navy as an assistant ship's doctor. In 1774, he transferred to the army with the rank of surgeon major. During the first part of the war in America, he was surgeon general for British forces in Nova Scotia. When Sir Henry Clinton took Charleston, South Carolina in 1780, Jefferies was assigned as surgeon general for the South. After the war, he became a pioneer in the new art of hot-air ballooning. He made the first airborne crossing of the English Channel on January 7, 1785, traveling in a balloon from Dover to Ardes, France. He later returned to America and died in Boston.

JEFFERSON, Thomas (1743–1826) Delegate to Congress, governor

Had Jefferson died the instant he lifted his pen from finishing the Declaration of Independence, he would still be immortal. That his career was long and he lived another 50 years only solidified his place in the American pantheon. However, after the first part of the Revolution,

Jefferson contributed relatively little to the War for Independence, and his record as war governor of Virginia was mediocre at best. Notwithstanding, Jefferson was one of the most versatile men of his era: statesman, philosopher, scientist, diplomat, politician, architect and farmer.

Born in Albemarle County, Virginia, Jefferson was related to the Randolphs, one of the colony's most prominent families, through his mother Jane Randolph, and he was a distant relative of the Lees and the Marshalls. His father was a surveyor who drew up the first accurate map of Virginia, served as a burgess and left Jefferson 2,750 acres of land at his death in 1757. Jefferson graduated from the College of William and Mary in 1762. He was licensed in 1767 to practice law, a career he pursued for only seven years. In 1769, Jefferson was elected to the Virginia House of Burgesses, serving until his election to the Continental Congress in 1775. Publication in 1774 of his *Summary View of the Rights of America,* a radical attack on the crown, made him a leading revolutionary figure, and after election to Congress, he was the clear choice in 1776 to draft the Declaration of Independence.

Consequently, following his absence from the Congress from late December until mid-May 1776, Jefferson was appointed in June to a committee to write the declaration, which turned out to be almost entirely his work. In its rolling phrases, Jefferson captured the great ideas of the Enlightenment as they were to be made concrete in the American Revolution, providing an intellectual blueprint for a new nation—wedding philosophical principle to a theory of government—and setting a standard by which all subsequent political manifestos must be judged. It was a magnificent achievement.

Although reelected to Congress and offered a post as one of the commissioners to represent the United States in Paris, Jefferson chose instead to return to Virginia and pursue reforms there. He became a member of the House of Delegates in October 1776 and was chosen to serve on a five-man board to revise the laws of the state. In June 1778, the board proposed 126 bills, of which 100 were eventually approved, achieving Jefferson's objectives of abolishing primogeniture, entail and an established church. In June 1779, Jefferson succeeded Patrick Henry as governor of Virginia. But he proved inept as a wartime leader when the British invaded in 1781, forcing the government to

Thomas Jefferson

flee Richmond in May and to reassemble at Charlottesville while Jefferson himself went home to his estate at Monticello. He narrowly escaped capture by Banastre Tarleton's raiders on June 4 and was forced to flee ignominiously. He in effect gave up the governorship just as his term expired. The legislators chose Thomas Nelson Jr. in his place and ordered an investigation of his conduct. The investigating committee reported in December that there were no grounds for censuring Jefferson, who nevertheless suffered a loss of public esteem.

During the years 1781–83, he worked on his *Notes on the State of Virginia.* Jefferson's wife died in September 1782, and he was appointed as a peace commissioner in November but never was needed in France because of the pace of the negotiations. Elected to Congress in June 1783, Jefferson drafted an ordinance in March 1784 that formed the precedent for the Ordinance of 1787 and called for a ban on slavery in the western territories after 1800. In August 1784, he was in Paris to assist Benjamin Franklin and John Adams in negotiating treaties of commerce with France. He succeeded Franklin as minister to France the following year, when he also negotiated a treaty of commerce with Prussia. Jefferson returned home in the fall of 1789 and accepted appointment as Washington's secretary of state, beginning his duties in March 1790 and continuing in the post until December 1793.

In 1796, he was elected vice president when John Adams won the presidency. And in 1800, he became president following a tie vote between himself and Aaron Burr and his selection by the House of Representatives. Jefferson was the first president to

Monticello, Virginia, home of Thomas Jefferson

be inaugurated in Washington, D.C., which became the seat of the government in 1800. His achievements as president included the Louisiana Purchase in 1803 and the subsequent Lewis and Clark Expedition. He was reelected in 1804. Leaving the presidency in 1809, Jefferson spent the remainder of his life at Monticello. He served as president of the American Philosophical Society from 1797 until 1815. He was responsible for founding the University of Virginia in 1819 and was the architect of the school's original buildings. The Embargo of 1807, Jefferson's own achievement, destroyed his finances, forcing him to sell his 10,000-volume library to the government in 1815—it formed the original Library of Congress. In 1819, he again suffered a severe financial reversal. By a remarkable historical coincidence, Jefferson died precisely on the 50th anniversary of the signing of the Declaration of Independence, followed in death on the same day by John Adams. *Further reading:* Dumas Malone, *Jefferson and His Time,* 6 vols. [see esp. vols. 1–3] (Boston, 1948–1981); Merrill D. Petersen, *Thomas Jefferson and the New Nation: A Biography* (New York, 1970); Gary Wills, *Inventing America: Jefferson's Declaration of Independence* (Garden City, N.Y., 1978); Noble E. Cunningham, *In Pursuit of Reason: The Life of Thomas Jefferson* (Baton Rouge, La., 1987); Julian P. Boyd, et al., eds., *The Papers of Thomas Jefferson,* multivolume (Princeton, N.J., 1950–   ).

JENIFER, Daniel of St. Thomas (1723–1790) Delegate to Congress Jenifer, whose compound first name was not a descriptive distinction in the style of the time but rather his actual given name, was born in Maryland and inherited im-

mense wealth. A lifelong bachelor, he held several public offices under the crown but with the approach of the Revolution became a convinced patriot, favoring a strong central government for the former colonies. He went directly from sitting on the council of the royal governor to heading the revolutionary Maryland Council of Safety in 1775. He became president of the senate when a new state government was organized in 1777. He was sent to Congress the following year and served until 1782, taking part in the committees on the admiralty and on western lands. He was not prominent as a delegate, but he consistently worked to strengthen the power of the central government and supported giving Congress the power to tax. He returned to his Maryland estates after the war and twice ran unsuccessfully for governor.

JERRY (d. 1775) Loyalist A free black man, apparently born in South Carolina and about whom little biographical detail is known, Jerry remained loyal to the crown and volunteered his services to the British as a ship's pilot. He also tried to foment a rebellion among black slaves in the colony, urging them to join the British, and when captured by white patriot South Carolina authorities in August 1775, he was hanged.

JOHNSON, Guy (c. 1740–1788) Loyalist officer and official Born in Ireland, Johnson came to North America around 1756 under the patronage of his uncle, Sir William Johnson. He lived at Johnson Hall, the elder Johnson's large Mohawk Valley estate in New York, and served as secretary to his uncle, who was British superintendent of Indian affairs. He married Sir William's daughter Mary in 1763 and set up his own establishment at Guy Hall. In 1773, Johnson was elected to the New York assembly, and he held a commission in the New York colonial militia. On the death of his patron in 1774, Johnson suceeded to the office of superintendent of Indian affairs. He fortified Guy Hall but withdrew to Canada in 1775. After a brief period of organizing loyalist and Indian troops, Johnson went to England. He returned to New York City in 1776 and remained there for two years, taking little part in the war. In his absence from the northern border, most of the leadership initiative passed to the Butlers and to Joseph Brant. When Johnson moved to Quebec in 1779, he took a small role in directing border raids, but for the most part his activities were minor during the war despite his official position. He was replaced as superintendent by his cousin Sir John Johnson in 1782, and he removed to England, spending the rest of his life seeking compensation for his lost North American property.

JOHNSON, Henry (1748–1835) British officer

Johnson was a veteran of the 28th Regiment of Foot, having served during the Seven Years' War in the West Indies. He came to America in 1775 as major of the 28th. In October 1778, he was made lieutenant colonel of the 17th Foot. Left in command of the post at Stony Point, New York in July 1779, Johnson was completely routed by the daring American attack directed by Anthony Wayne. Johnson was subsequently court-martialed but apparently was acquitted (no record of the trial survives) and returned to duty with the 17th. He served in Canada and Ireland in later decades and eventually became a full general and a baronet.

JOHNSON, Sir John (1742–1830) Loyalist official

Sir John was the son of Sir William Johnson and Catharine Weissenberg; he was born in New York's Mohawk Valley at his father's estate. He was brought up on the frontier but sent to Philadelphia for education. He fought with his father during the colonial wars with the French and was at his father's side during Indian conferences of the early 1760s. In 1765, Johnson went to England and was knighted (mostly in deference to his father). He returned to New York in 1773 and inherited Sir William's title and estates in 1774.

When he began to fortify Johnson Hall and gather large numbers of Indians and loyalists in 1776, the American Congress grew alarmed and ordered General Philip Schuyler to prevent the establishment of a powerful British post in the Mohawk Valley. Johnson agreed after negotiations to disband his forces and remain peaceful. In May 1776, however, he abandoned his pregnant wife (who was taken hostage to Albany) and fled to Canada. He organized a regiment of loyalists known as the Royal Greens and led it as part of Barry St. Leger's expedition in 1777 but played only a small role in the battles around Fort Stanwix. During the following two years, Johnson directed Indian and loyalist raids against the valley settlements in New York, although his influence was eclipsed for some time by the Butlers

and his cousin (and brother-in-law), Guy Johnson. In 1782, Sir John was commissioned by the British government as superintendent of Indian affairs, replacing Guy. His main activities were to help settle loyalists in Canada after the Revolution and conduct negotiations with the tribes.

JOHNSON, Michael. See ATTUCKS, Crispus.

JOHNSON, Thomas (1732–1819) Delegate to Congress, militia general, governor, jurist

Born in Calvert County, Maryland as one of 12 children, Johnson studied law and set up a practice in Annapolis in the early 1760s. He was a leader among the opposition to the Stamp Act as a member of the Maryland assembly and 10 years later was among those who organized the revolutionary provincial congress in Annapolis. The body chose him as one of Maryland's delegates to the first Continental Congress in 1774 and reappointed him to the second Congress the following year. Johnson was selected by his congressional colleagues to enter George Washington's name as a nominee for commander in chief of the Continental Army, which he did in June 1775. He was an active member of Congress, but like many delegates, Johnson also spent considerable time guiding the political fortunes of his home state. He was absent in Maryland, for example, during the adoption of the Declaration of Independence. In 1776, he was appointed as a brigadier general of the state militia and raised 1,800 men, whom he led to join the main army in New Jersey in early 1777. He was on duty at Basking Ridge when elected as the first governor of Maryland by the legislature. He served as governor until late 1779 and then moved to a seat in the lower house of the legislature.

His judicial career began in 1790 when he accepted an appointment as chief judge of the general court of Maryland, having declined an appointment as U.S. district judge under the new federal constitution. In 1791, Johnson was named by President Washington to fill a vacant seat as associate justice of the U.S. Supreme Court. He resigned because of poor health in February 1793 and declined an offer from Washington to become secretary of state two years later. He meanwhile served as one of the commissioners to establish the new federal capital at Washington, D.C. *Further reading:* Edward Delaplaine, *The Life of Thomas Johnson* (New York, 1927).

Sir William Johnson

JOHNSON, Sir William (1715–1774) British official

Although he died on the eve of the American Revolution, Johnson's influence among the Six Tribes of the Iroquois confederation was the basis for much of Britain's power in the North during the conflict. He was the most successful and powerful white figure in Indian colonial affairs in the decades before his death. Many of the personal details of his biography are obscure, but he was born in Ireland of Anglo-Irish stock and apparently came to North America in 1738 under the patronage of his uncle, Admiral Sir Peter Warren, who had married into the New York De Lancey family and wanted Johnson to manage a large land holding in upper New York. Johnson moved to the Mohawk River Valley—his home for the rest of his life—as a trader. He established close relations with the Mohawk tribe almost immediately and within a few years was the most important trader with the Mohawk and their Iroquois allies. Johnson formed a liaison with a young indentured German maidservant, Catharine Weissenberg, with whom he had three children (including John Johnson, William's eventual heir), although the couple were not married until Catharine lay on her deathbed.

Johnson melded himself closely into the culture of the Mohawk, and he became the most trusted white man in Indian eyes, coming to be regarded virtually as one of their own. He also began to amass large tracts of land through purchase and gifts, resulting in an eventual holding that was one of the largest in the northern colonies. Johnson's power and influence were recognized by the British government, and he eventually was granted formal powers. He cemented the alliance of the Iroquois tribes with the British during the wars with the French, most notably as commander of British colonial forces in the defeat of French Baron Dieskau in 1755. After the successful campaigns against the French, Johnson held a major general's commission, was created a baronet and became British superintendent of Indian affairs; his power in the upper colony was virtually unchallenged. Meanwhile, he had married by Indian ceremony a young woman named Molly Brant, who held forth at the baronial hall Johnson had built at Johnstown. Her brother, Joseph Brant, was practically adopted by Johnson and was educated to leadership along with Johnson's nephew, Guy Johnson, and William's son John. The Mohawk and other tribesmen of the confederation flocked to Johnson Hall during the late 1760s, looking to Sir William for leadership. By the time of his death in 1774, Johnson had so consolidated his hold on the tribes that they remained in the British orbit throughout the subsequent war with the rebellious colonies. *Further reading:* James Flexner, *Sir William Johnson of New York* (New York, 1959); Milton Hamilton, *Sir William Johnson: Colonial American* (Port Washington, N.Y., 1976).

JOHNSON, William Samuel (1727–1819) Delegate to Congress, attorney, educator

A native of Stratford, Connecticut, Johnson was a loyalist or near-loyalist during the first years of the Revolution but became a delegate to Congress immediately after the formal end of the conflict. He was the son of Samuel Johnson, one of the most prominent Episcopal clergymen in America and president of King's College in New York.

The younger Johnson was groomed for the priesthood, but after graduation from both Yale and Harvard, he turned to the law, reading on his own to qualify before the bar. He was a skillful attorney and built a large practice by the 1760s. He sat first in the lower house of the Connecticut colonial legislature and then moved to the upper house. The contradictions in his attitude toward the crown were demonstrated during the Stamp Act crisis: he was a friend of Jared Ingersoll, who was one of the stamp collectors, but he also attended the Stamp Act Congress. Johnson's personal associations with royalists—his father and several relatives foremost among them—were close and numerous but he inclined toward the political position of the patriots. In 1767, he went to England as colonial agent for Connecticut, remaining there until 1771. He was selected as one of Connecticut's delegates to the first Continental Congress in 1774, but he declined to serve, fearing (correctly) that such a congress would impel the colonies more rapidly toward independence. After the clash of arms at Lexington and Concord, the more radical factions took control of Connecticut government, and Johnson came under suspicion for corresponding with the enemy, which may have been little more than honest attempts to communicate with his friends who were now on the other side. He retired from public life in 1775, but in 1779 he was again accused of dealing with the British. He was arrested for a short period but gained his release by taking an oath of loyalty to the new state of Connecticut.

After the end of the war, Johnson regained most of his good standing, and in 1784 he was selected as a delegate to the Confederation Congress, where he served until 1786. In 1787, he was named as the first lay president of Columbia College, the former King's College, which had been controlled by the Episcopalians and of which his father had been head before the war. Johnson was one of the most active delegates to the federal constitutional convention in 1787, exerting his considerable oratorical skills in the cause of a strong central government. He was sent to the U.S. Senate in 1789 and sat until his resignation in 1791. *Further reading:* Elizabeth McCaughey, *William Samuel Johnson: Loyalist and Founding Father* (New York, 1980).

JOHNSTON, Augustus (1730–1790) Loyalist official A native of New Jersey, Johnston served in a variety of offices in Rhode Island before the Revolution. During the 1750s, he worked in the General Assembly, and he was attorney general of the colony from 1757 to 1766. He was designated as a stamp distributor in 1765 during the Stamp Act Crisis, but he was forced by public pressure to refute his office. With the coming of the Revolution in 1776, he remained loyal to the crown, refusing to sign an oath to the new state of Rhode Island, and his property was confiscated.

JOHNSTON, Samuel (1733–1816) Delegate to Congress, state official Born in Scotland, Johnston arrived in North Carolina at age three when his parents came to America with his uncle, Gabriel Johnston, who was to become the new governor of the colony. He was sent to New Haven, Connecticut for an academy education but returned to North Carolina and settled on an estate near Edenton, becoming a lawyer. He was a long-time royal officeholder in the colony, serving in a variety of posts. Nonetheless, Johnston was a convinced patriot and served on the North Carolina Committee of Correspondence in 1773 and was a delegate to the first four provincial congresses. As a leader of the conservative revolutionary faction, he acted on the council of safety and as paymaster of troops. He disagreed, however, over the question of extending voting rights to the less propertied—he feared the mob his entire life—and he was defeated for a seat in the fifth provincial congress, which was to draw up a state constitution. In 1780, Johnston was elected as a delegate to the Congress, taking his seat there about the time the British seized military control of most of the southern states. He was elected under the new Articles of Confederation as president of Congress the following year but declined the office. After the Revolution, he was elected governor of his state and twice reelected, resigning in 1789 to fill a vacancy in the U.S. Senate. He was president of both North Carolina conventions on the federal constitution. His final office was as justice of the state superior court.

JOHNSTONE, George (1730–1787) British officer and official Johnstone, born in Dumfries, Scotland, the son of a Scots aristocrat, went to sea as a teenager in the mid-1740s. He was commissioned as a lieutenant in the Royal Navy in 1755 and served with considerable personal bravery in several engagements. He was, however, a contentious and intemperate man, given to issuing frequent challenges to the duel. In 1757, Johnstone was court-martialed for insubordination and disobedience and found guilty but was let off in light of his good service record. Despite this blot in his copybook, Johnstone was promoted to post captain in 1762, but he was forced onto half pay after an accident (he fell off a cliff and injured his foot).

His political connections were good, and in 1763 he was named as the British governor of West Florida, which was new territory coming to the British as a result of the Seven Years' War. He relinquished the post after four years and returned to Britain, where he was elected to Parliament the following year. He was noted in the House for "intemperate" utterances, one of which led to an inconclusive duel in late 1770 with Lord George Germain. He sat in Parliament throughout the first years of the war and in 1778 was appointed as one of the members of the Carlisle Commission sent to deal with the American Congress. His clumsy attempts to bribe congressional delegates were made public, and Congress formally voted to refuse to deal with him, forcing his resignation from the commission. Johnstone seemed impervious to blame, however, and his reward for botching the peace negotiations was an appointment as commodore of a naval squadron. He was moderately successful at sea but retired in 1779 to resume his place in Parliament, where he became an opponent of the administration in India. Ill health forced his withdrawal from the public scene in 1785. *Further reading:* John Born, *Governor Johnstone and Trade in British West Florida* (Wichita, Kan., 1968).

JONES, Allen (1739–1798) Militia general, delegate to Congress

The elder brother of Willie Jones, Allen was likewise born in North Carolina. He was educated in England and returned to live in the Halifax district of North Carolina, with which he was associated for most of his life. He served in the colonial legislature before the Revolution and was a member of all five provincial congresses as well as the local committee of safety. In 1776, Jones was appointed as brigadier general of the Halifax militia, but he did not lead troops in the field, his main contribution to military affairs being a strong objection in 1778 to sending North Carolina militia to fight in South Carolina. He was a member of the state senate during most of the war and was selected as a delegate to the Continental Congress in 1779 and 1780. Following the Revolution he advocated leniency toward former loyalists and upheld the rights of property, a great deal of which he himself owned.

JONES, David (1736–1820) Clergyman

Jones was born in Delaware and educated in New Jersey. He was a Baptist, ordained in 1766 in Freehold, New Jersey, where he served a parish until he moved to Chester County, Pennsylvania in 1775. He was a vociferous patriot, preaching rebellion

David Jones

from his pulpit, and he acted as chaplain to Anthony Wayne's Pennsylvania regiments from 1776 to the end of the war (he returned to duty as a chaplain during the War of 1812, although he was by then in his mid-seventies). He moved to Bucks County in 1786 but returned to his former parish, the Great Valley Baptist Church in Chester County, in 1792 and continued as pastor there until his death.

JONES, George (1766–1838) Official

Jones was a native of Savannah, Georgia and was taken prisoner by the British in 1780 (when he was only 14 years old) and held for a year. Following the Revolution, he became a physician and held a long series of local, state and national offices during his public career. He was mayor of Savannah, sat in the Georgia legislature, was a circuit court judge and briefly was a U.S. senator.

JONES, John Paul (1747–1792) Continental naval officer

Jones is indisputably the great naval hero of American history, based mainly on his astounding single-ship victory over the *Serapis* in 1779. It was a hard task to win a lasting reputation as a captain of the minuscule Continental Navy during the American Revolution—the few small American ships were but so many flies to be swatted by the Royal Navy—but Jones did so through superior seamanship and his indomitable fighting will. He was not an admirable person otherwise, but his combat record can never be gainsaid.

He was born in Kirkcudbrightshire, Scotland, as John Paul (he added the name Jones in 1773) and was apprenticed to a shipowner in Whitehaven at age 12. After his employer went bankrupt, Jones joined the crew of a slave ship, and at 19 he was first mate on the slaver *Two Friends* in the trade between Jamaica and the coast of Guinea. Leaving this service, he booked passage on a ship to England of which he took command when both the captain and first mate died of fever. As reward the owners gave him the ship's crew, 10 percent of the cargo, and command of their merchant ship *John*, whose home port was Dumfries. Jones captained the ship on two voyages to the West Indies in 1769 and 1770, but on the second voyage he flogged the ship's carpenter to death and was arrested for murder upon his return to Scotland. He was cleared of the charge, and in 1773, he became master of the *Betsey* out of London. However, in Tobago he killed another man—the leader of a mutiny by his crew—and to avoid a trial he sailed in secret for America, where he assumed the name Jones.

Unemployed when the Revolution began, Jones went to Philadelphia, where he was hired to help fit out the *Alfred*, the first ship purchased by Congress for the Continental Navy. He had some influence in Congress by virtue of his friendship with Robert Morris and Joseph Hewes but not enough to win a prized captain's commission, and Jones had to settle in December 1775 for the rank of first lieutenant on the *Alfred*. In 1776, however, he was given command of the *Providence,* and following his successes with this ship, Jones was made captain and provided with a small squadron with which to pursue the capture of more British shipping. In June 1777, Jones was given command of the *Ranger* and was sent to France to take command of the *Indien,*

only to discover the ship was being given to France. He sailed in the *Ranger* from Brest in April 1778 for a series of coastal raids on Scotland, taking prizes as he cruised. The raid had little real effect on British shipping or the course of the war, but the psychological impact was great on the British, who saw their home island attacked directly by armed Americans.

Returning to France as a hero, Jones was given command of the decrepit 42-gun French ship *Duras*, which he renamed *Bonhomme Richard* in honor of Benjamin Franklin, who had pleaded Jones's cause in France. Jones sailed again on a raiding cruise with a small flotilla in August 1779. On the evening of September 23, Jones encountered the 44-gun *Serapis* off Flamborough Head and moved to begin an engagement. Even discounting all the legend that has since encrusted the fight (Jones probably never said "I have not yet begun to fight"), the resulting battle was one of the great ship-to-ship engagements in naval history. By any rational measure and by the acknowledged customs of the time, Jones lost the fight, but despite heavy losses among his crew (50 percent casualties) and a battering that left his ship sinking rapidly beneath him, Jones simply refused to admit defeat. After more than two hours of savage fighting—the two ships were lashed together and the killing took place at point-blank range—British captain Richard Pearson finally struck his colors. Jones had to abandon the *Richard* and took possession of the *Serapis.*

Despite his victory, Jones was frustrated by British pressure on the Dutch, who expelled the Americans from safe ports, and by the American policy of turning most of their ships over to the French.

John Paul Jones medal

A contemporary British print illustrating what was probably an apocryphal incident, that of John Paul Jones shooting a sailor who had attempted to strike his ship's colors during a battle.

Moreover, the insane Pierre Landais (who had done his best to sink Jones during the *Serapis* engagement) commandeered the *Alliance,* the last remaining American man of war in French waters. Left no choice, Jones sailed for America in December 1780. In 1781, Congress made him commander of the navy's largest ship, *America,* but upon its completion, the ship was turned over to the French. After the Continental Navy was decommissioned, Jones returned to France as an American agent to claim the prize money for the ships he had captured. Louis XVI made him a chevalier, and during his final visit to the United States in 1787 Congress awarded him a gold medal, the only one awarded to an officer of the Continental Navy. In 1788, Jones accepted Catherine the Great's request that he serve in the Russian navy against the Turks, but his service in May in the Black Sea was unrewarding. He left Russia in September 1789, returning to Paris, where he died three years later. *Further reading:* Samuel Eliot Morrison, *John Paul Jones* (Boston, 1963).

JONES, Joseph (1727–1805) Delegate to Congress, legislator, jurist

An uncle of James Monroe, Jones was born in Virginia. He studied law in England at the Inner and Middle Temples and was admitted to the British bar in 1752. He served in the House of Burgesses in the early 1770s and joined the King George County Committee of Safety in 1774, moving on to the colony-wide committee the following year. He was a delegate to all of the Virginia patriot conventions and during the war sat in the House of Delegates almost continuously, save during 1777 and 1778, when he was a delegate to the Continental Congress. While he held the rank of major general in the Virginia militia, Jones confined his wartime activities to the political and judicial fronts, acting as a judge of the state general court when not in the legislature. He was reappointed to the bench in 1789 and served until his death.

JONES, Noble Wimberley (c. 1724–1805) Delegate to Congress, legislator, physician

Jones was born in England, near London, and trained as a physician. He came to Georgia in the early days of the colony—about 1748—and set up a practice in Savannah. He was a prominent colonial legislator in the decades before the Revolution, sitting in the assembly for 19 years, beginning in 1755. In 1768 and 1769, Jones was speaker of the lower house. He was a member of the Georgia Council of Safety and a delegate to the first halting provincial congresses in Georgia (a colony very slow to join the others in taking formal steps to organize against the crown). Jones was one of the colony's first delegates sent to the Continental Congress when Georgia finally chose representatives in 1775. He was returned to Congress from 1781 to 1783. He also continued to serve as a legislator in Georgia during most of the war. He became president of the state medical society and presided over the state constitutional convention in 1795.

JONES, Thomas (1731–1792) Loyalist jurist, historian

A native of New York, Jones studied law with his father, a noted attorney and jurist himself, and graduated from Yale in 1750. His fortunes were made with his marriage in 1762 to Anne De Lancey, daughter of the chief justice of New York and a member of the wealthiest and most politically powerful clan in the colony. The couple built a mansion on Manhattan island and settled into a life among the city's elite. In 1773, Jones was appointed as a judge of the Supreme Court, taking over the spot held previously by his father.

With the advent of the Revolution he came immediately into conflict with the patriots of the region. He was arrested by authority of the New York Provincial Congress in June 1776 but was paroled, only to be arrested again in August. He was held prisoner in Connecticut until December, when he was again paroled and returned to his home in New York. He spent the following three years quietly working on a history of the Revolution. In November 1779, he was seized by a small raiding party of patriots from Connecticut, which stole up on Jones's house during an evening party and spirited him away under the noses of the British troops in the area. The Americans wanted Jones as bait to exchange for General Gold Selleck Silliman, who had been taken by the British earlier in the year. Jones suffered in confinement until the exchange took place in April 1780. He left with his family in June for Jamaica and went on to England the following year. Except for a brief visit to New York, he lived the rest of his life in Britain. His book, *A History of New York During the Revolutionary War*, was not published for nearly a century, and it is one of the only histories written from the loyalist point of view.

JONES, William (1753–1822) Continental officer, state official

Jones was born in Newport, Rhode Island and was commissioned a lieutenant in the Rhode Island regiment at the beginning of the war. He was promoted to captain and served at Harlem Heights, White Plains and Princeton. He resigned in 1777 and returned to Rhode Island, but the following year, he was named as captain of marines aboard the 28-gun frigate *Providence,* where he served for the remainder of the war. The ship carried dispatches to the commissioners in France, and Jones was sent from the port of Nantes to Paris with the documents. After raiding British shipping along the northern coast following Jones's return to America, the *Providence* was assigned in 1780 to help defend Charleston, South Carolina. Jones and his marines were sent ashore to reinforce the garrison and were captured when Sir Henry Clinton took the city by siege. Jones was paroled and returned to Rhode Island, where he took up the hardware

business. After the turn of the century, he was elected to the state legislature, and in 1811, he became governor, serving until 1817.

JONES, William (1760–1831) Soldier, privateer, government official

Born in Philadelphia, Jones volunteered as a teenage soldier in 1776 and fought at Trenton and Princeton, although with what unit is unknown. Later in the war, he sailed as an officer on a privateer and was reported to have been twice wounded and captured. After the Revolution, he moved to Charleston, South Carolina, where he was a merchant. He returned to Philadelphia in 1793 and was elected to the U.S. House of Representatives eight years later. In 1813, Jones became secretary of the navy under James Madison, and he also served as acting secretary of the U.S. Treasury for part of the same period. He resigned in 1814. Two years later, he was chosen as first president of the second U.S. national bank, but he was completely inept and was forced to resign amid disgrace and scandal in 1819. His name was later cleared to some extent when he was shown to have been merely ignorant of finance and lacking in administrative ability rather than venal.

JONES, Willie (1740–1801) Delegate to Congress, planter, state official

Jones, whose first name was not a diminutive of "William" but rather a variant spelling of "Wylie," was the son of a former North Carolina attorney general and, like his brother Allen, was educated at Eton. He became a wealthy planter and squire, with considerable land, slaves and property. He was an ardent patriot, beginning in 1774 as a member of his local committee of safety. He was elected to all five provincial congresses from the Halifax district, but he failed to serve in the fourth since he was at the time acting as southern superintendent of Indian affairs for the Continental Congress. He was a power in North Carolina politics during the Revolution as head of the statewide committee of safety in 1776 and subsequently as the first ex-officio governor of the new state. He was the leader of the more democratic faction in the state and drew his influence from wide popular support. He sat as a member of the lower house of the North Carolina legislature from 1777 to 1780, when he was sent as a delegate to the Continental Congress. He opposed the federal constitution—declining to take his seat at the Philadelphia convention—and his fight against its ratification in North Carolina eventually shattered his political power. He retired from public life in 1789 and managed his estates.

JULIET, Gustav. German mercenary turncoat

Juliet came to America as a German mercenary in the contingent sent by the landgrave of Hesse-Cassel. After he deserted the British side and applied to the Continental Congress for employment in the American army, Juliet was appointed as a lieutenant in Pulaski's Legion, a unit formed to a considerable degree from similar deserters. In October 1778, Juliet was serving with Pulaski's men, under the command of the Baron von Bose, at Little Egg Harbor, New Jersey, a refuge for American privateers and raiders. After a quarrel with von Bose, Juliet again deserted and went back to the British, providing detailed information about the disposition of the defenses of the American post. On October 15, Juliet guided a British force under Major Patrick Ferguson to the edge of the American camp, which was destroyed in the ensuing fight.

Juliet failed to gain much by his double defection, however. Despite using an assumed name among the British, he was recognized and imprisoned as a deserter. *Further reading:* Andrew A. Zellers-Frederick, "Privateer's Haven," *Military History* 8, 2 (August 1991), 8, 72–76.

JUNGKENN, Friedrich Christian Arnold, Baron von (1732–1806) Hessian official

Jungkenn was a veteran soldier of the Prussian service and a long-time retainer of Prince Friedrich of Hesse-Cassel. When the latter became landgrave of Hesse-Cassel in 1760, Jungkenn took a commission in the Hessian army and served at the court. By 1780, he was a major general and minister of state, charged also with the duties of minister of war. The Hessian mercenaries rented to Great Britain by the landgrave reported to Jungkenn, and a collection of their letters and diaries provides considerable insight and information about the Revolution. *Further reading:* Bernard A. Uhlendorf, ed., *The Siege of Charleston* (Ann Arbor, 1938).

K

KALB, Johann de (1721–1780) Continental volunteer general, French agent Known to the Americans as "Baron de Kalb" (a spurious title), de Kalb was born into a peasant family named simply Kalb in Huttendorf, Bavaria. He left home at age 16, and in his early twenties he surfaced as a lieutenant named Jean de Kalb in a French infantry unit. De Kalb served through the War of the Austrian Succession from 1740 to 1748 and rose to the rank of major by 1756, the beginning of the Seven Years' War, in which he fought with distinction. In 1764, he married an heiress, and in 1765, he retired from the military.

During the early months of 1768, de Kalb traveled in the American colonies as a secret agent for Étienne Choiseul, the French foreign minister. After Louis XVI took the throne in 1774, de Kalb returned to military service and was commissioned a brigadier general in November 1776. Desiring to serve in America, he became one of Silas Deane's recruits in Paris, and in April 1777 he sailed for the United States along with the Marquis de Lafayette. The pair of volunteers met a poor reception in Congress, which at this stage of the war had begun to have its fill of European adventurers, especially anyone sent by Deane. Ironically, Lafayette and de Kalb were the two most valuable European soldiers to offer their services to the American Revolution, but their timing was poor. On top of that, Congress failed to believe in de Kalb's assumed title and at first refused to grant him a commission. He was preparing to return to France when Congress relented and appointed him major general in September 1777.

He joined Washington in November, spending the winter at Valley Forge, but received no genuine assignment. Finally in April 1780 he was given a task matching his rank: the relief of Charleston. Unfortunately, it was also a task beyond accomplishment. He advanced toward the doomed city with a force of good American troops, mostly Marylanders and Delawares, but found little help along the way from either the civilian governments or state militias. His men nearly starved before learning of Charleston's fall. To his even greater misfortune, de Kalb then came under the command of Horatio Gates, who had been named by Congress as commander of the Southern Department. Gates ignored de Kalb's advice and led the army on to a battle at Camden for which it was ill-prepared. On August 16, 1780, de Kalb set a standard for personal bravery on the field. He commanded the solid right side of the American front line, and when the state militia fled in panic, his position was hopeless. Nonetheless, he stood with sword in hand and fought with his men until overcome. He suffered severe wounds—nearly a dozen—and was carried from the field in mortal condition. He died three days later at Camden.

KEAN, John (1756–1795) Delegate to Congress, merchant Born in Charleston, South Car-

Johann de Kalb

olina, Kean was a merchant in the thriving seaport before the war. He was captured by the British when they took the city in 1780. Following his release, he was named as one of the members of a commission to audit the accounts of the Continental Army. In 1785, he was selected as a delegate to the Confederation Congress from South Carolina, and he served until 1787. With the coming of the new federal government, President George Washington named Kean as cashier in the Bank of the United States. He died while serving in this post in Philadelphia.

KEARNEY, Dyre (d. 1791) Delegate to Congress   Very little is known about the personal biography of Kearney, other than that he was born in Kent County, Delaware and practiced law in Dover after admission to the bar in 1784. He sat as a delegate in the final Confederation Congresses in 1787 and 1788, and then returned to his lawyering in Dover. He died in November 1791.

KEITH, Lord. See ELPHINSTONE, George Keith.

KELLY, Hugh. Loyalist officer   A native of Ireland, Kelly emigrated to Maryland in 1774. Intending at first to settle over the mountains, he purchased 450 acres of land along the Monongahela River in Virginia the following year. However, he was still living in Maryland as a manufacturer of linen when the war broke out, and he decided to join the British cause. His life as a soldier and leader of irregulars for the British was adventurous, at least according to his own testimony. He claimed to have helped organize 1,900 loyalists in Maryland, Virginia and

Pennsylvania in addition to raising a smaller force over the Alleghenies near the Red Stone Settlement. In 1780, he conspired with officers of the Convention Army, then in Virginia, to raise a loyalist force named "The Maryland Retaliators" to aid Lord Cornwallis. He was captured in February 1781 and scheduled to be hung without trial, but the decree was reprieved. He either escaped or was released and hid in Virginia until the British defeat at Yorktown. Disguising himself as a Dunkard with a long beard, he made his way to New York City, where he formally joined the British army as a captain of guides. He also served as a barracks master in Brooklyn. With the final evacuation of New York, he left for England.

KEMBLE, Peter (1704–1789) Loyalist, merchant   One of the leading merchants of New York and New Jersey, Kemble was born in Smyrna, Turkey, the son of a British trader and a Greek mother. He came to America in 1730. He not only became well-to-do from his mercantile successes, but his family connections by marriage were of the best: the De Lanceys, the Schuylers and the Van Cortlandts, all important families in New York on both sides of the Revolutionary conflict. Kemble's son, Stephen, was a distinguished British officer, and his daughter, Margaret, was married to General Thomas Gage. Kemble remained in America during and after the Revolution, despite his obvious loyalist leanings. His mansion near Morristown, New Jersey became George Washington's headquarters while the Continental Army lay in winter quarters during 1780.

KEMBLE, Stephen (c. 1730–1822) Loyalist officer   Kemble was the son of wealthy New Jersey merchant Peter Kemble. His military career in the British army was bound closely to the fact that General Thomas Gage was his brother-in-law. Kemble's first commission was as an ensign in Gage's regiment in 1757 (a year before Gage married Kemble's sister). Kemble served with Gage throughout the Seven Years' War, and by 1772, he was Gage's deputy adjutant general and a major. Kemble remained in America after Gage was recalled to England in 1775 and served as adjutant for generals Howe and Clinton. One of his primary duties was to run the British spy network, but when Benedict Arnold made contact with the British high command, Sir Henry Clinton wanted young Major John André to handle the affair, so a complex deal—typical of the commercial nature of the British army in the 18th century—was worked out whereby André received a promotion but paid the additional salary to Kemble so that the latter would give up his post as adjutant. Kemble received an appointment as lieutenant colonel in the 60th Regiment and left for the West Indies. He served in the army into the 1790s but in 1805 returned to New Jersey as a civilian and lived in his native state until his death.

KEMPENFELT, Richard (1718–1782) British admiral

A long-time British naval officer, Kempenfelt (the son of a Swedish retainer of James II) was an admiral by the time of the American Revolution. He did not serve in the American theater, but his dashing victory over the French admiral de Guichen off Ushant in December 1781 destroyed or captured most of a vital French convoy headed toward the West Indies. Kempenfelt took 20 prizes out from under the nose of de Guichen, who commanded a much superior force. Kempenfelt was drowned in a freak accident in 1782 when his ship the *Royal George* broke up and sank suddenly while under repair at Spithead.

KENTON, Simon (1755–1836) Frontiersman

Kenton was born in Virginia and ran away from his home in 1771 when he thought he had beaten to death a rival for the hand of a local girl. He changed his name to Butler and began a series of treks into the Kentucky territory, a bountiful but dangerous region just beginning to be opened to white settlement. After several adventurous trapping and hunting expeditions, Kenton settled briefly at Limestone on the Ohio River, the site of modern-day Maysville, Kentucky. By 1774 and the outbreak of Lord Dunmore's War, Kenton had a reputation as one of the best scouts and rifle shots on the frontier, and he was a friend of both Daniel Boone and Simon Girty. Kenton scouted for the Americans during Lord Dunmore's War, but he took little part in the Revolution until 1778, when he accompanied George Rogers Clark west as a scout. After serving with Clark, Kenton returned to Kentucky. In 1778, he learned that the man he thought he had killed in Virginia was alive, so he reverted to his true name, married and openly settled at Maysville. In the years after the Revolution he amassed large land

Simon Kenton

holdings in Kentucky and Ohio, where he eventually moved, but he lost all his property due to imperfect titles (he was illiterate and had little understanding of legal affairs). Kenton received a commission as a brigadier general of Ohio militia in 1805, and he fought at the Battle of the Thames during the War of 1812. He died penniless on a farm near Zanesville, Ohio. *Further reading:* Edna Kenton, *Simon Kenton: His Life and Period* (1930; reprinted New York, 1971); Thomas Clark, *Simon Kenton, Kentucky Scout* (New York, 1943).

KEPPEL, Augustus (1725–1786) British admiral

Although he did not personally serve in the American theater, Keppel had a major influence on British naval strategy during the war. He was the second son of a British earl and had gone to sea at age 10. His career in the Royal Navy was long and relatively distinguished by the time of the American Revolution, but he had also involved himself in politics on the side of the opposition and thus was the focus of more than military attention. Although a bitter foe of Lord Sandwich, first lord of the Admiralty, Keppel was promoted to admiral of the blue in 1776 and given command of the Channel Fleet. The British feared a French invasion and were undecided as to strategy. This indecision allowed a French fleet under d'Estaing to escape from Toulon in 1778, and Keppel was ordered to defend against a similar French breakout from Brest. After much shuffling of ships in and out of port, Keppel met the French fleet under d'Orvilles off Ushant in July 1778. The resulting battle was inconclusive, but the French were driven back into port. Keppel was then accused of mismanagement and brought to court-martial on charges by his third in command, Charles Palliser, a political ally of Sandwich. Keppel was ultimately acquitted, but the trial and the political struggle virtually paralyzed the Royal Navy for several months and weakened the British naval command structure for years to come. Keppel retired from the fleet and returned to Parliament as a vocal opponent of Lord North's government. He served as first lord of the Admiralty in the brief Rockingham government in 1782.

KEY, Philip Barton (1757–1815) Loyalist officer, U.S. congressman, jurist   Key had a very unusual career: Service as an officer in a British loyalist regiment during the Revolution did not bar him from becoming a prominent U.S. judge and legislator. He was born in Charlestown, Maryland and in 1778 joined the Maryland Loyalist Regiment as a captain under Lieutenant Colonel James Chalmers. The unit had been organized the year before during the British occupation of Philadelphia but had withdrawn to New York when Sir Henry Clinton had abandoned the American capital. Key apparently went with his unit to Halifax, Nova Scotia in December and then on to Jamaica and to Pensacola, where he remained until the fall of the British post in May 1781. The entire regiment was captured by the Spanish and transported to prison in Havanna. The officers and men of the loyalist Maryland unit were paroled by the Spanish after only a month in Cuba, and they were transported to New York City, where they remained until the end of the war. After the regiment was disbanded in New Brunswick in 1783, Key made his way to England and studied law at the Middle Temple. He returned to Maryland in 1785 and was admitted to the bar. By 1794, he was a member of the Maryland House of Delegates, serving there until 1799. He then took an appointment as chief justice of the Fourth U.S. Circuit Court. In 1805, Key was counsel for U.S. Justice Samuel Chase in his impeachment trial before the Senate. Key's last major post was as U.S. representative from Maryland from 1807 to 1815. He died while in office and was buried in Washington, D.C.

KILTY, William (1757–1821) Soldier, jurist   Kilty was born in London, England and educated in France, apparently as a physician. He emigrated to

Maryland shortly before the Revolution, around 1774. In 1778, he enrolled in the 4th Maryland Regiment (one of the original elite Maryland units in the Continental Line) as a surgeon's mate. After the war, he became a lawyer and compiled the laws of Maryland in 1800. He was named as chief justice of the Circuit Court of the District of Columbia in 1801. In 1806, Kilty became chancellor of Maryland, serving until his death.

KING, Rufus (1755–1827) Delegate to Congress, legislator, diplomat   King, who became one of the principal Federalists during the early republic, was born in the Maine section of Massachusetts. He graduated from Harvard in 1777 and studied the law. In 1779, he briefly served in the war as an aide to John Glover, but most of his important career came after the Revolution. He sat in the Massachusetts General Court from 1783 to 1785 and for part of that time was simultaneously a delegate to the Confederation Congress. He was a member of the federal constitutional convention and subsequently was chosen as U.S. senator from New York, where he moved in the mid-1780s. He resigned his senate seat in 1796 to become minister to Great Britain, remaining there until 1803. He ran unsuccessfully as the Federalist candidate for vice president in 1804 and returned to the senate in 1813 for a 12-year stint. He meanwhile failed to win election as governor of New York and as the Federalist candidate for president in 1816. After leaving the senate in 1824, King was again appointed minister to England, leaving the post shortly before his death. *Further reading:* Robert Ernst, *Rufus King: American Federalist* (Chapel Hill, N.C., 1968).

KINLOCH, Francis (1755–1826) Delegate to Congress, militia officer, attorney   Kinloch was born in Charleston, South Carolina and went to England in 1768 for education. After attending Eton, he studied at Lincoln's Inn, and he was admitted to the bar about the time the Revolution began in America. He traveled on the Continent during the first years of the conflict but returned home in 1777 and volunteered as a militia officer. The details of his service are vague, but he apparently participated in the defense of Savannah in 1779, where he was wounded, and the defense of Charleston in 1780. He was also a member of the lower legislative house in North Carolina during 1779. In 1780 and 1781, while the British seized control of his home, he represented South Carolina as a delegate to the Congress. He became a rice planter after the war, taking time to sit in several constitutional assemblies.

KINSEY, James (1731–1805) Delegate to Congress, jurist
Born in Philadelphia, Kinsey became a lawyer with a practice in both Pennsylvania and New Jersey. He lived in Burlington, New Jersey. He sat in the New Jersey assembly between 1772 and 1775 and was a member of the Burlington County committee of correspondence in 1774. He was selected as a delegate to the first and second Continental Congresses but resigned in November 1775. He became chief justice of the New Jersey Supreme Court in 1789, holding the post for 14 years.

KIRBY, Ephraim (1757–1804) Soldier, official
Born in Litchfield County, Connecticut, Kirby served as a private for three years during the Revolution, seeing action at Brandywine, Germantown and Monmouth. In 1782–83, he was an ensign in the Rhode Island militia. Following the Revolution, he became a lawyer and officeholder. In 1803, he was named as the U.S. commissioner on the Spanish Boundary and moved to Mississippi, where he died.

KIRKLAND, Moses. Loyalist officer
Kirkland was a prosperous planter in the region of Ninety-Six, South Carolina and at first appeared to support the patriot cause. He was a member of the Assembly in 1775 but withdrew, according to his account, when the body resolved to send delegates to the Continental Congress. Other reports say he was disappointed when he failed to receive a suitable military commission from the Assembly. Whatever the source of his disaffection, Kirkland led his local troop of about 90 back-country rangers over to the British side. He eventually fled South Carolina for Florida and thence attempted to travel to Boston, but he was captured and imprisoned in Philadelphia. He escaped from jail and joined Lord Dunmore's fleet. He next served with Sir William Howe on Staten Island. In 1777, Howe sent Kirkland south to East Florida, where he became a deputy to John Stuart, the southern British Indian superintendent, and helped organize Indian support of Prevost's campaigns. At one stage, Kirkland was captured by

the French, but he again managed to escape. In 1780, he was appointed to command of a loyalist regiment at Ninety-Six. He evacuated to Jamaica in 1782, after the British defeat. He died while on the way to England to press his claims for the loss of his property in South Carolina to patriot confiscation.

KIRKWOOD, Robert H. (1746–1791) Continental officer
Kirkwood was one of the most under-ranked and unrewarded officers of the Continental Army. He commanded some of the finest troops of the war, but for purely legalistic reasons was never more than a mere captain while serving in the field. He was born in New Castle County, Delaware and was a farmer at the beginning of the Revolution. He was commissioned as a lieutenant in the Delaware Regiment in January 1776. This unit—the only one from the small state—became one of the best fighting forces of which the American army could boast, rivaled only by the neighboring Marylanders. Kirkwood fought at Long Island, Trenton and Princeton at the head of his company. In 1780, the Delawares were sent south to form part of the army under the foolish and cowardly Horatio Gates: the result was a brave but disastrous stand at the battle of Camden that killed all the senior officers and reduced the regiment to fewer than 200 men. Kirkwood inherited command as the surviving senior captain, and he led his tiny force in all the major battles of Nathanael Greene's decisive southern campaigns, but because the unit was so small he could not be promoted to any rank higher than captain. He was awarded a token brevet as major when mustered out of the army in 1783. Kirkwood moved to Ohio after the war, claiming lands awarded to him by the state of Virginia. He was commissioned as a captain in the 2nd U.S. Infantry when a new force was raised to fight the Indians in the West, and he was killed in November 1791 while part of Arthur St. Clair's disastrous campaign. *Further reading: The Journal and Order Book of Captain Robert Kirkwood of the Delaware Regiment of the Continental Line* (1910; reprinted Port Washington, N.Y., 1970).

KNOWLTON, Thomas (1740–1776) Militia and Continental officer
Knowlton was born in West Boxford, Massachusetts but raised on a farm near Ashford, Connecticut. He served in the Seven Years'

War as a sergeant, ensign and lieutenant and returned to farming after 1763. He remained active in the local militia, however, and was captain of the Ashford company that joined the American forces gathered around Boston in the spring of 1775. At the battle of Bunker Hill Knowlton and his company were assigned a key spot on the left of the American fortifications, joining John Stark's men in building flimsy, grass-filled, split-rail breastworks to defend the flank. Knowlton and his men repulsed the British attacks during the battle and allowed evacuation of the main works when American ammunition ran out. In January 1776, Knowlton received a Continental commission as major of the 20th Continental Regiment and six days later led a raid on Charlestown that caused considerable embarrassment to the British (Howe and his commanders were in the midst of a performance of a burlesque of the Americans and had to make a hasty exit when the alarm was sounded—many theatergoers thought it part of the play). In August, Knowlton was promoted to lieutenant colonel. He fought in the battle of Long Island and afterward organized a body of light infantry "rangers." He was killed at Harlem Heights on September 16, 1776 when an attempted flank attack on the British failed.

KNOX, Henry (1750–1806) Continental general, government official

A self-taught soldier, Knox commanded the Continental artillery throughout the war of the Revolution. Born in Boston, he became the sole supporter of his widowed mother when only 12 years old. Showing the same self-reliance he later demonstrated as a soldier, Knox went to work in a bookstore. By age 21, he owned his own shop—the London Book-Store. Even in his early days he was a huge man—by the end of the war he weighed 300 pounds—but he was energetic and very good at managing men.

Knox had read extensively in the fields of military history and science, and by the outbreak of the war in 1775, he was second in command of a Boston militia unit. Although he had no actual experience, he received a commission as a Continental colonel in November 1775 and was ordered to put together a force of artillery for the army. Knox subsequently commanded the artillery for the main army until after the end of active fighting. He formed a lasting, close relationship with George Washington, and the commander in chief relied heavily on his chief of

artillery. Knox's first great feat of the war was to transport the captured artillery from Fort Ticonderoga to Boston during the winter of 1775. Washington's army had the British penned in Boston, but without siege guns, there was little hope of dislodging them. Knox went to Ticonderoga, organized the building of sleds and supervised moving 60 heavy guns across 300 miles of tough countryside. When he arrived at Boston, the placement of the guns forced the British to evacuate.

Knox slowly learned the practical skills of an artillery commander and supported Washington's army with his guns during the battles of Long Island. He performed with distinction at Trenton and was appointed a brigadier general two days later. Knox commanded the Continental artillery during the rest of the New Jersey campaign and at the battles of Brandywine, Germantown and Monmouth. In the fall of 1781, he was in charge of the American siege artillery at Yorktown that battered Lord Cornwallis' forces into defeat. Following the British surrender, Knox moved back north and took command of the American post at West Point. He was promoted to major general in 1782 and briefly became commander in chief of the remnant army at Washington's resignation in late 1783. After the war, Knox was appointed secretary of war under the Articles of Confederation, and at Washington's election as president, Knox became the first secretary of war under the Constitution, serving until 1794. He retired from public life in that year and indulged himself—alternating residences between New York and Philadelphia—in a luxuriant style of living, having grown rich from his wife's inheritance. He died at the early age of 56 when a chicken

Henry Knox

Henry Knox's troops hauling British artillery captured at Fort Ticonderoga to Boston.

bone lodged in his intestines. *Further reading:* North Callahan, *Henry Knox: General Washington's General* (New York, 1958).

KNOX, William (1732–1810) British official

Knox was one of the American "experts" in British government circles. Born in Ireland, he sailed to America in 1757 as an official in the retinue of Georgia governor Henry Ellis, serving at Savannah until 1761. Shortly after his return to England, Knox was appointed colonial agent for Georgia and East Florida, and he consulted with the government of Lord Bute on American affairs. He unsuccessfully proposed the creation of a colonial aristocracy and parliamentary representation for the American colonies. He was dismissed as agent by the Georgia assembly in 1765 after writing a pamphlet in defense of the Stamp Act, which Knox thought to be the least objectionable form of colonial taxation. He was called to testify before a House of Commons committee on the state of the American colonies in 1765, and five years later when the government structure was changed to include a separate secretary of state for America, Knox was appointed as undersecretary. He served in the post during most of the Revolution, until 1782. He offered advice to Lord North on conciliation measures in 1776, but on the whole, Knox supported strong measures against the rebellion. He continued to be consulted on American affairs even after his dismissal with the fall of

North's government, and in 1786, he was made attorney to press for the claims of Georgia loyalists.

KOSCIUSZKO, Tadeusz (1746–1817) Continental general

Born in Poland (in a region that was then part of the Grand Duchy of Lithuania) and well trained as a soldier, Kosciuszko was one of the more effective European volunteer military men to serve the American patriot cause. He was orphaned as a boy, but managed to attend both the royal military school in Poland and the French school of engineering and artillery: Thus, he was skilled in several areas needed by the amateur Continental Army. He came to America in 1776 on his own accord and was commissioned by Congress as a colonel of engineers. He was assigned to the command of Horatio Gates and planned the entrenchments at Saratoga, which played an important role in Gates's victory over General John Burgoyne. Kosciuszko became a close friend of Gates and went south to join him in 1780 after planning the defenses of the American fort at West Point on the Hudson. Kosciuszko arrived in Carolina after Gates's disaster at Camden; however, he remained on the staff of Nathanael Greene and had charge of Greene's transportation during the race for the Dan River crossings ahead of Lord Cornwallis. In 1781, Kosciuszko was in charge of engineering at the siege of Ninety-Six, South Carolina, but he failed to take the British post. During the following months, he served Greene as a commander of cavalry. In 1783, he was made a brigadier general, and the next year he returned to Europe.

The rest of his life was devoted to the cause of Polish independence. He led a futile campaign against

Tadeusz Kosciuszko

the invading Russians in 1792 and then moved to Paris. He was captured by the Russians in 1794 after another unsuccessful uprising. On his release he came again to the United States, where he received a lump sum payment and land in Ohio. He returned to Europe in 1798. Kosciuszko's memory was later honored by several place-names in the West, including a county in Iowa. *Further reading:* Miecislaus Haiman, *Kosciuszko in the American Revolution* (New York, 1943; reprinted 1975).

KNYPHAUSEN, Wilhelm, Baron von (1716—1800) German mercenary general   A tough and competent professional soldier, Knyphausen was the senior German military figure in America during much of the war. He had served in the Prussian army since the mid-1730s and held the rank of lieutenant general (the equivalent of an American brigadier) in 1776, when he sailed for America in command of 4,000 mercenaries from Hesse-Cassel.

He arrived in place too late to take part in the battle of White Plains, but thereafter he took important roles in the subsequent British campaigns in New York and New Jersey. When General Leopold von Heister was replaced as senior German officer after the debacle at Trenton, Knyphausen took his place. He led half of Howe's army at the battle of Brandywine and escorted the baggage train during the British movement from Philadelphia to New York in 1778. His role increased in 1779 when Sir Henry Clinton went south to conduct the campaign against Charleston. Knyphausen assumed command of the British forces in New York City during Clinton's absence, and he launched several movements into New Jersey against the Americans, although with only moderate success. His health began to fail in 1781, and with Clinton's return, Knyphausen took a lesser role. He returned to Europe and retired in 1782. Subsequently, he served as military governor of Cassel.

LA BALME, Augustin, Mottin. See MOTTIN de la Balme.

LACY, Edward, Jr. Militia officer Lacy was a South Carolina back-country militia leader who brought his troop of 300 or so partisans to join the battle at Williamson's Plantation near Brattonville, South Carolina on July 12, 1780. Loyalist Captain Christian Huck had captured several patriots at the home of American Captain James McClure and had about 100 men camped on the farm. Lacy, who lived nearby, confined his own father—a loyalist—to his bed by strapping the old man down, thus preventing a warning to the enemy. Lacy and other militia officers led a dawn assault that killed Huck and killed, wounded or captured all but 12 of the loyalists. The victory added much to patriot strength in the back-country campaign.

LACEY, John (1755–1814) Militia officer, state official Lacey was born into a Quaker family in Bucks County, Pennsylvania and worked in his father's grist mill as a boy. In February 1776, over the objections of his family and at the cost of a breech with his pacifist sect, Lacey joined the Pennsylvania militia with the rank of captain and raised an infantry company. He led his men north during the fall of 1776, returning to Pennsylvania in December. During a few weeks in the spring of 1777, Lacey acted as a county "sub-lieutenant" to organize militia in Bucks County, but he was commissioned a lieutenant colonel in May and operated locally as commander of roving militia. In January 1778, Lacey became a brigadier general of state militia (at the tender age of 23), but since the British held Philadelphia few militiamen volunteered for his command. His only notable action was at Crooked Billet, Pennsylvania in 1778. Lacey and about 60 militiamen had been stationed at the village in order to harass the British supply lines. Lacey awoke on May 1 to find himself surrounded by nearly 700 British and loyalist troops. He retreated through the nearby woods but lost nearly half his men. Lacey had apparently had enough and resigned 10 days later. He was called back to duty in 1780 and 1781 but took no part in the field. He had been meanwhile elected to the state assembly in 1778, and he was appointed to the Supreme Executive Council in 1779. Following the war, he moved to New Jersey and became a manufacturer of iron. *Further reading:* William Davis, *Sketch of the Life and Character of John Lacey, a Brigadier General in the Revolutionary Army* (Doylestown, Pa., 1868).

LAFAYETTE, James Armistead. American spy James Armistead was a slave of William Armistead of New Kent County, Virginia when the Marquis de Lafayette began a 1781 campaign in the state to neutralize the British army. James Armistead volunteered to act as an intelligence agent for the Americans, since he was able to slip in and out of British lines without arousing suspicion. The Marquis de Lafayette testified after the war to the effectiveness of the spy's reports. In 1786, the state legislature of Virginia granted Armistead's freedom, recompensing his owner at the going auction price for slaves, and the newly freed man took the name of his military patron. In 1819, James Lafayette was granted a small lump sum and an annual pension of $100 by the state of Virginia. When the Marquis de Lafayette made his triumphal tour of the United States in 1824, James Lafayette greeted him in Richmond.

LAFAYETTE, Marie Joseph de Motier, Marquis de (1757–1834) Continental general, French volunteer

The best-known and most prominent of the Frenchmen who served the American Revolution, Lafayette became a hero to the American public as a result of his glamor and his highly visible role in the war. He was born to a wealthy, aristocratic family but was orphaned at an early age. He entered military service while a teenager, having married at age 16, but was an inexperienced soldier when smitten with the romantic notion of helping to free the Americans from the trammels of Great Britain. He and his mentor, the spurious "baron" de Kalb, persuaded American envoy Silas Deane to guarantee them commissions as major generals. They sailed for America in 1777, reaching Philadelphia in August. After some grumbling, Congress granted the commission but awarded no actual command to the 19-year-old Frenchman.

Fortunately for Lafayette, George Washington took an instant liking to the amiable youth and ever after shepherded his career in America. Lafayette fought at Brandywine as a volunteer on Washington's staff and took a wound that provided a sign of his earnestness. In late 1777, Congress appointed him to command a division of Virginia light infantry. At the battle of Monmouth, Lafayette commanded on the field with reasonable distinction. He then had charge of two brigades in the near-fiasco of the first French-American venture at Newport. When it began to appear that France might genuinely support the American Revolution with troops, Lafayette returned to France to lobby for a major French expedition to the New World. He returned in April 1780, just ahead of Rochambeau's expeditionary force. While he wished to play a central role in liaison between Rochambeau and Washington, the French commander kept Lafayette

Marquis de Lafayette

at arm's length. Washington gave the "boy" command of an army in Virginia with orders to stop British depredations, and Lafayette was successful in holding the armies of Arnold, Phillips and subsequently Cornwallis at bay, although he achieved no major victories. Perhaps his best showing in the field was at Green Spring when he extricated Anthony Wayne's Pennsylvanians from Cornwallis' trap. During the late summer of 1781, Lafayette pinned Cornwallis at Yorktown while Washington and Rochambeau moved south from New York. He commanded one of the three major American divisions during the siege and defeat of Cornwallis.

He returned to France within two months of the surrender at Yorktown. His career as a revolutionary in France was mixed. He served in several assemblies and had command of a French army in 1792 when he was condemned by a radical faction and forced to flee. He spent several years as a prisoner of the Austrians and Prussians but was freed by Napoleon. He turned down an offer to become American governor of Louisiana, but he did accept a grant of money and extensive lands from the United States.

In 1824, Lafayette returned to America for a year-long triumphal tour, during which he was hailed by Americans as a symbol of French support for the Revolution nearly 50 years previous. The many place-names in his honor found on the map of the United States and the words of General John Pershing ("Lafayette, we are here!") on landing the American

Expeditionary Force in France during World War I, nearly 160 years after the American Revolution, are testament to Lafayette's influence. *Further reading:* Louis R. Gottshalk, *Lafayette Joins the American Army* (Chicago, 1937) and *Lafayette and the Close of the American Revolution* (Chicago, 1941); Oliver Bernier, *Lafayette: Hero of Two Worlds* (New York, 1983); Stanley J. Idzerda, ed., *Lafayette in the Age of the American Revolution: Selected Letters and Papers, 1776–1790* (Ithaca, N.Y., 1977).

LAMB, John (1735–1800) Continental officer

Lamb was the son of a British criminal who moved his family to New York City after serving a sentence of transportation in Virginia. The father was a maker of optical and mathematical instruments, and the young Lamb followed the same trade. By the 1760s, the family had branched into the mercantile business as wine merchants and were relatively prosperous.

Lamb was one of the most vigorous radicals in New York City before the Revolution and shared with Isaac Sears the role of chief rabble-rouser. In 1765, he spoke and wrote against the Stamp Act and helped organize the city chapter of the Sons of Liberty. He kept up a flood of anonymous writings against the crown and colonial authorities, and in 1769, he publicly spoke against the legislative assembly, which called him to book but could not find enough evidence to convict him for criminal libel. When the news of the clash of arms at Lexington and Concord reached New York City in 1775, Lamb and Sears led patriots in the seizure of the customs house and the harbor. In July 1775, Lamb

John Lamb

received a commission as captain of the New York Independent Company of Artillery and joined the army upstate preparing for an invasion of Canada. He roused the displeasure of commanding general Philip Schuyler (a New York patrician) by continued agitation among the northern army. Lamb and his unit were part of the futile assault on Quebec City on the last day of 1775, and Lamb was wounded and captured by the British defenders. He was paroled soon after and was promoted to commandant of artillery for the northern army but could not actively serve until formally exchanged in January 1777.

Lamb was then commissioned as colonel of the 2nd Continental Artillery Regiment, making him one of the principal officers of that branch of the army. In April 1777, Lamb was wounded during fighting near Danbury, Connecticut. During 1779 and 1780, he commanded the artillery at the key Hudson River post of West Point. When Washington moved the main army south to Yorktown in 1781, Lamb's regiment was part of Henry Knox's artillery brigade, and he performed with distinction during the victorious siege of Cornwallis' army in Virginia. He was breveted brigadier general on his departure from the army in the fall of 1783. Lamb returned to New York, and although he was a vigorous opponent of the new federal constitution, he was appointed customs collector by the new president, George Washington. Unfortunately for Lamb, one of his assistants looted the accounts, and Lamb had to sell all his property to make them good. He died in poverty. *Further reading:* Isaac Q. Leake, *Memoir of the Life and Times of General John Lamb* (1857; reprinted New York, 1971).

LAMB, Roger (1756–1830) British soldier

Lamb, born in Dublin, served as a sergeant in America and afterward wrote two works that have since been regarded as the best eyewitness accounts of the war from the private British soldier's vantage point. He was part of General John Burgoyne's expedition in 1777 as a noncommissioned officer in the Royal Welch Fusiliers. He was captured after Burgoyne's surrender but escaped with two companions. In 1780, he sailed with Sir Henry Clinton's invasion of South Carolina and subsequently fought in the southern theater—carrying the regimental colors at the battle of Camden—until Cornwallis' surrender at Yorktown. He again escaped and made his way to British headquarters in New York City, where he was made a clerk. After the British withdrawal, Lamb returned to Dublin and became a teacher. In 1809, he published *An Original and Authentic Journal of Occurances During the Late American War . . .* and in 1811 followed with *Memoir of His Own Life. Further reading:* Robert Graves, *Sergeant Lamb's America* (reprinted 1986).

LAMBERT, Latham (d. 1781) Militia soldier
Lambert was a black farm worker (possibly a freeman) from near New London, Connecticut who volunteered as one of the defenders of tiny Fort Griswold during Benedict Arnold's raid on September 6, 1781. After ravaging the town of New London, Arnold's large force of loyalists and British regulars turned on Fort Griswold, taking the place by storm. When American commander Lieutenant Colonel William Ledyard surrendered his sword, he was immediately run through with his own weapon. Lambert, still armed and standing nearby, stabbed the loyalist officer who had attacked Ledyard, thereby setting off a melee and subsequent massacre of the defeated American defenders. Lambert probably died from multiple bayonet wounds. He was one of 70 to 80 Americans killed after surrendering that day.

LANDAIS, Pierre (c. 1731–1820) French and American naval officer
A man whose mental instability was his chief characteristic, Landais was entrusted with one of the more significant commands in the Continental Navy during the war. He was born in Saint-Malo and entered French naval service at an early age. He was wounded and captured briefly by the British in 1762, and he sailed with Bougainville in 1766 on the famous around-the-world voyage.

Landais left the French service in 1777 and sought a commission in the new American navy from Silas Deane in Paris. Landais arrived in Portsmouth, New Hampshire in December and went to Philadelphia, where Congress commissioned him captain of the *Alliance,* one of the best new ships in the American fleet. He sailed back to France with the Marquis de Lafayette as a passenger, but the voyage was a harbinger of things to come: the crew mutinied under Landais's strict and capricious command. With the mutineers in a French prison, Landais proceeded under orders of Benjamin Franklin to join John Paul Jones's squadron. The *Alliance* was to act as primary support to Jones's *Bonhomme Richard,* but Landais's inexplicable behavior manifested itself during the fabled battle between the *Richard* and the British *Serapis* on September 23, 1779. While Jones was engaged in a hull-to-hull death struggle with the *Serapis,* Landais appeared on the scene and proceeded to pour broadsides into the American flagship, killing several men and officers and holing the *Bonhomme Richard* beneath the water line. Jones refused to quit, however, and eventually transferred his command to the *Serapis* while the *Bonhomme Richard* sank.

Jones was outraged at Landais's perfidy, but Franklin in Paris feared for political reasons to remove a French officer, and Landais retained his command. Moreover, he literally took over the *Alliance* by force when Franklin ordered him to relinquish command to Jones. Nothing could dislodge Landais short of an armed boarding party, so the authorities acquiesced in letting him sail for America with commissioner Arthur Lee on board. The voyage was almost surreal. Landais went further and further over the edge of instability. At one point he threatened Lee with a carving knife when the Frenchman thought Lee was taking too good a morsel from a platter of turkey. When he refused to allow the crew to stop and fish in order to replenish the supply of food, the officers and men mutinied and relieved Landais of command on the grounds he was mentally incapable. Both Landais and the chief officers subsequently were court-martialed. The verdict against Landais was delivered in January 1781: he was removed from command and cashiered from the American service. After living in New York City for several years, Landais returned to France and resumed a naval career under the regime of the French Revolution, eventually rising to the rank of vice admiral. He moved back to New York in 1797 and died there. *Further reading:* Richard B. Morris, ''The Revolution's Caine Mutiny,'' *American Heritage* 11 (April 1960), 10–13.

LANDSDOWNE, Marquis of. See SHELBURNE, Earl of.

LA NEUVILLE, Chevalier de. See PENOT LOMBART.

LANGDON, John (1741–1819) Delegate to Congress, state official, merchant

Born in Portsmouth, New Hampshire, Langdon was a highly successful merchant by his early thirties, when he was caught up in the Revolution. In 1774, he took part in the patriot raid on the British fort at Portsmouth and helped seize gunpowder and arms. He sat in the New Hampshire legislature in 1775 and again from 1777 to 1781, serving as speaker for most of the time. He was sent to Congress as a delegate for two terms—1775 to 1776 and 1786 to 1787. During the War for Independence, Langdon was a prize agent for the state of New Hampshire and was closely involved in naval affairs, building several ships. In the face of General John Burgoyne's invasion from Canada in 1777, Langdon organized and helped finance New Hampshire militia under John Stark, and he personally led a militia unit at the battles at Bennington and Saratoga. With the establishment of a new federal government, he was selected as one of the first U.S. senators from New Hampshire, serving until 1801. He refused several federal offices in favor of running for the governorship of his home state, which he won in 1805.

LANGDON, Samuel (1723–1797) Clergyman, college president

Langdon was born in Boston and graduated from Harvard at age 17. In 1747, after brief service in the New Hampshire colonial militia, he became assistant pastor to a congregation in Portsmouth, New Hampshire. He was soon ordained and took over as head of the church, where he remained for 27 years. During much of the Revolution, Langdon was president of Harvard, serving from 1774 until 1780. He then took a church in Hampton Falls, New Hampshire. He sat as a member of the state convention that ratified the new federal constitution in 1788.

LANGDON, Woodbury (1739–1805) Delegate to Congress, merchant

A native of Portsmouth, New Hampshire and the older brother of John Langdon, Woodbury was a well-to-do merchant in the years before the Revolution. He was slow to take up the patriot cause, however, and for several years resisted political action that might have damaged his profits. In 1769, for example, he worked against the nonimportation agreements. Despite his conservatism, he became a member of several provincial patriot assemblies in New Hampshire at the beginning of the Revolution. He went to England when hostilities broke out, however, to see to his commercial interests. He returned in 1777 and was captured by the British on landing in New York City. He escaped from confinement, returned to New Hampshire and was selected as a delegate to the Continental Congress in 1779. He left the body the following year and, although elected again three times, he refused to take his seat. He held several state offices, including a place on the bench of the superior court, but was impeached in 1790 for neglect of duty.

LANGLADE, Charles-Michel de (1729–c. 1800) French-Indian leader

A somewhat mysterious figure during the American Revolution, Langlade was the son of Augustin Mouet de Langlade, a French trader. His mother was a member of the Ottawa tribe. Langlade himself was educated in white schools, probably by the Jesuits at Mackinac, but lived most of his life among his Indian relatives. He fought for the French during the Seven Years' War and apparently organized Indian troops that took part in the French victories at Pickawillany, Ohio and at Fort Duquesne. He switched allegiance to the British after 1763. During the Revolution he helped supply Indian troops to several British campaigns, but his personal role is unclear. Some accounts put him in command of most of the Great Lakes tribesmen on the Burgoyne expedition. He established a settlement at Green Bay and became known as the "Father of Wisconsin."

LANGWORTHY, Edward (1738–1802) Delegate to Congress, teacher, writer

Langworthy was an orphan, born near Savannah, Georgia. He was brought up and educated in the Bethesda Orphan Home, and his first job was as a teacher in the orphanage academy. In 1774, he was apparently undecided about revolutionary issues (as were many in Georgia) since he signed a loyalist petition, but by the following year, Langworthy had become a patriot. He served as secretary for the local council of safety and moved on to be secretary to the state provincial conventions. In 1777, he was sent as a delegate to the Continental Congress. He was a relatively obscure member until joining North Carolinian Thomas Burke in leaving the hall on April 10, 1778 to rob the body of a quorum and prevent passage of an offensive letter to commander in chief

George Washington. Langworthy returned sheepishly to the meeting, but Burke did not. Langworthy left Congress abruptly in April 1779 after opposing Henry Laurens on the issue of the Newfoundland fisheries. Laurens pointed out that Langworthy's term had technically expired the previous February. After the war, Langworthy wrote the first biography of General Charles Lee, whose papers he had obtained in the mid-1780s. He meanwhile had moved to Baltimore, where he was a teacher and a clerk in the customs house.

LANSING, John, Jr. (1754–1829) Delegate to Congress, legislator, jurist

Born in Albany, New York to a family of Dutch descent, Lansing studied law in both Albany and New York City and was admitted to the bar in Albany in 1775. He served as a civilian secretary to General Philip Schuyler during 1776 and 1777 and then returned to his law practice in Albany. He was elected to the New York legislature in 1780, subsequently serving six terms. In 1784 and 1785, Lansing was a delegate to the Confederation Congress. He was one of three New York delegates to the constitutional convention in 1787, but he opposed the new federal government and worked against adoption. He began his long judicial career in 1790 as a justice of the New York Supreme Court, rising to chief justice in 1798. He served as chancellor of New York from 1801 until 1814, when he resumed the private practice of law. He disappeared mysteriously in December 1829 while on his way to mail a letter during a visit to New York City, and some evidence points toward murder.

LAUMOY, Jean Baptiste, Chevalier de (1750–1832) French volunteer

Laumoy was one of the four French army engineers sent to assist the American cause in 1777—the patriots had no military men trained to build fortifications or undertake sieges. He joined Duportail, Gouvion and La Radière as volunteer engineers in American service. Laumoy was the son of an army officer and had first joined the Royal French Army in 1760. He was a major by the time he sailed for America, where Congress awarded him a commission as a colonel of engineers. He first served under the Marquis de Lafayette and endured the hard winter at Valley Forge. He was wounded at the engagement at Stono Ferry in 1779 and was captured by the British with the fall of Charleston in 1780. He was not exchanged

until late 1782. Before he returned to France, Laumoy was breveted to brigadier general's rank. After rejoining French service he was assigned to the West Indies, but he returned to his home during the French Revolution. He was an ally of Lafayette and was forced to flee France in 1792, coming again to America until it was safe for him to go back to France, which he did in 1801.

LAURANCE, John (1750–1810) Continental judge advocate, delegate to Congress, legislator, jurist

A native Englishman, Laurance emigrated to New York at age 17. He was admitted to the bar in 1772 and then married Elizabeth McDougall, the daughter of Alexander McDougall. Laurance received a commission as a lieutenant in the 4th New York Regiment in the summer of 1775 and went on the unsuccessful invasion of Canada with his unit. After his return, his father-in-law was promoted to the rank of brigadier general, and Laurance became his aide-de-camp. In April 1778, he was appointed as judge advocate general—chief military lawyer—on commander in chief George Washington's staff, serving until 1782. His most famous case was the prosecution of Major John André. Following the war, Laurance returned to the practice of law, and he was sent as a delegate from New York to the Confederation Congress between 1785 and 1787. He subsequently served in the new federal government (which he enthusiastically supported) as a U.S. representative and senator. He was also a U.S. district judge.

LAURENS, Henry (1724–1792) Delegate to Congress, diplomat

Born in Charleston, Laurens was one of the principal men of South Carolina and one of its wealthiest merchants, dealing in slaves, rice, indigo and wine before the Revolution. He visited England in the early 1740s to study commerce but returned to his home and sat in the South Carolina colonial assembly, beginning in 1757, and he led militia against the Cherokees in 1761.

Despite a second period of residence in Britain from 1771 to 1774 (or, perhaps, because of it), Laurens became a patriot during the early and mid-1770s, although he was moderate in his stance toward independence. He served on the committee of safety, wrote extensively in support of the patriot cause, and chaired the South Carolina provincial congress in 1775. South Carolina selected him as a delegate to the second Continental Congress in 1777. He was

Henry Laurens

elected president of the South Carolina colonial assembly the following year and was an exceptionally hard-working administrator, often putting in 20-hour days, but his implacable opposition to Silas Deane put him in the midst of the Deane-Lee political rift, and he resigned in 1778.

Congress nonetheless selected him in 1779 as an emissary to Holland. He sailed for Europe in 1780 with a draft treaty with the Netherlands and a mission to secure a large loan. The British captured his ship, however, and Laurens was imprisoned in the Tower of London under the harshest conditions. He suffered miserably and became increasingly ill, but he declined British offers of pardon in return for cooperation. He was finally released in late 1781 and exchanged for Lord Cornwallis. While he was in prison, Congress named him one of the peace commissioners. He arrived in Paris to join the commission only days before the preliminary treaty was signed. During 1782 and 1783, Laurens acted as an unofficial ambassador to Great Britain. He returned to the United States thereafter, retired from politics, and lived in South Carolina, where he attempted to repair his lost fortunes. *Further reading:* David D. Wallace, *The Life of Henry Laurens . . .* (New York, 1915).

LAURENS, John (1754–1782) Continental officer

The son of prominent revolutionary politician and diplomat Henry Laurens, John was born in South Carolina and sent to Europe for education.

He was a student at the Middle Temple in London at the beginning of the war and remained there at his father's request until 1777, when he finally sailed for home to fulfill his wish to fight for the Revolution. He became a volunteer aide-de-camp to George Washington, serving as a secretary and translator since he was fluent in French. He fought in the battles of Brandywine, Germantown and Monmouth, and after the latter engagement, Laurens challenged General Charles Lee to a duel because of Lee's disparaging comments about Washington. Lee was wounded in the subsequent meeting.

In 1779, Laurens was commissioned as a lieutenant colonel and formally appointed to Washington's staff, acting as a liaison with the French army in Rhode Island; however, he soon went back to the southern theater to help defend his home state against the renewed British campaign. He was part of the unsuccessful Franco-American attempt to retake Savannah and the following year he was captured when Charleston fell to Sir Henry Clinton. Unlike most of the American officers taken prisoner in May 1780, Laurens was exchanged and thus was able to resume his duties. He was selected by Congress for a mission to France, and he helped Benjamin Franklin pry loose a promised loan from the French government in 1781. Laurens returned to Boston later in the year with supplies and much-needed cash for Congress.

He then rejoined the main army and marched south with Washington to attack Lord Cornwallis at Yorktown. During the siege, Laurens distinguished himself as one of the officers at the head of the storming party that took a key British redoubt, and he was appointed to negotiate terms of surrender with the British. Rather ironically, Lord Cornwallis was exchanged for Laurens' father, who had been captured on a diplomatic mission and held in the Tower of London. Following the British defeat at Yorktown, the war was essentially over, but the British still held Charleston and Savannah, and Laurens returned to South Carolina to serve under Nathanael Greene, who was charged with keeping the enemy hemmed into coastal enclaves. Sent out to stop a British foraging party on August 14, 1782, Laurens was killed in an ambush during one of the last fights of the war. *Further reading:* Robert W. Weir, "Portrait of a Hero," *American Heritage* 27 (April 1976), 16–19; Sara B. Townsend, *An American Soldier: The Life of John Laurens* (Raleigh, N.C., 1958).

Duc de Lauzun

LAUZUN, Armand-Louis de Gontaut-Biron, Duc de (1747–1793) French officer

Lauzun commanded the French cavalry wing during the latter stages of the Revolution. He had entered the army in 1761 and came to notice in 1779, when he temporarily seized a British post in Senegal. He was appointed colonel of hussars in 1780 and began to raise his own regiment, but he failed to bring it up to strength before the French expeditionary force to aid the Americans was set on foot. Nonetheless, Lauzun was promoted to brigadier and sailed for the United States in April 1780. He was given command of most of the available French mounted troops, although they did little except fritter away their time at Lebanon, Connecticut for more than the next year. Washington was in no position to make any serious moves against the British in New York City, with or without French support, so Lauzun's horsemen accomplished little beyond a few tentative missions on the edge of the British-held territory.

In the fall of 1781, however, the decisive moment came, and the combined French and American armies marched southward to catch Lord Cornwallis. Lauzun was assigned to the Gloucester side of the James River after reaching Virginia, where his task was to keep Banastre Tarleton penned into the town. He did so skillfully—cooperating well with American troops—and a series of sharp clashes quieted Tarleton while the siege guns on the other side of the river pounded Cornwallis into surrender. Lauzun had the honor of carrying the dispatches of victory to France, but he returned to America the following summer and was placed in command of the remaining French troops when Rochambeau departed. He remained until the final French withdrawal in 1783. Soon after his return to France, Lauzun was swept up in the Revolution, and he commanded several armies for the new government before falling under suspicion. He died under the guillotine on the last day of December 1793.

LAW, Andrew (1749–1821) Composer, clergyman

Law was an active church-music composer and singing teacher at the time of the Revolution. He was born in Connecticut and graduated from Rhode Island College (later Brown University) in 1775. He had previously published a hymnal, *A Select Number of Plain Tunes Adapted to Congregational Worship*, in 1767. He published two more musical books, one a primer, in 1780. Law copyrighted his songbooks with the Connecticut Assembly and patented a new method to print music, using shaped notes to make singing easier for congregations. Ordained as a Congregationalist in 1787, Law served parishes in Philadelphia and Baltimore and later taught singing in Massachusetts.

LAW, Richard (1733–1806) Delegate to Congress, jurist

A native of Milford, Connecticut and probably a cousin of Andrew Law, Richard graduated from Yale in 1751 and was admitted to the bar two years later, setting up a practice in New London. He became a local justice of the peace in 1765 and was sent as a representative to the Connecticut General Court during the same year. He was chief judge of the New London County Court from 1773 to the end of the Revolution in 1783. He was also a member of the patriot government of the new state after serving on the Connecticut Council of Safety, and he sat on the Governor's Council for 10 years, beginning in 1776. Law was a delegate to the Continental Congress in 1777 and to the Confederation Congress from 1781 to 1782. In 1784, he began a 22-year stint as mayor of New London, and he simultaneously sat as a justice of the Connecticut Supreme Court. In 1789, he was appointed as a U.S. district judge for Connecticut under the federal constitution. Along with Roger Sherman, Law codified the statutes of Connecticut in 1784.

LAWSON, Robert (d. 1805) Continental and militia officer Probably a native of Virginia, although little is known of his personal history, Lawson was commissioned a major in the 4th Virginia Regiment in early 1776. He became lieutenant colonel in August 1776, and sometime between April and August of the following year, Lawson assumed command of the regiment as a colonel. He resigned from the Continental service in December 1777 but appeared again in 1779 as a brigadier of Virginia militia. Several accounts of the battle of Guilford Courthouse list him as the commander of the Virginia militia that formed the second line of Nathanael Greene's dispositions for the battle.

LEAMING, Thomas (1748–1797) Militia officer, lawyer Leaming was from the Cape May region of New Jersey. In 1776, he sat as a member of the New Jersey Provincial Congress and raised a company of militia from his home territory. As a militia officer, Leaming took part in the battles of Trenton, Princeton, Germantown and Brandywine. Sometime during 1777, he left the militia and formed a business company that sponsored privateers, proving successful in taking a large number of prizes by the end of the war. He was admitted to the bar in Philadelphia after the Revolution (he had previously read law with John Dickinson) and set up a practice there. He died from yellow fever in 1797.

LEARNED, Ebenezer (1728–1801) Continental and militia officer Learned was born and lived his life in Oxford, Massachusetts. He served in a company of Oxford militiamen during the Seven Years' War and was active locally in prerevolutionary committees. He represented Oxford at the Massachusetts Provincial Congress of September 1774 and again in January 1775. He arrived at Cambridge with his local company on April 21, 1775 and took

up a position as part of the "Boston Army" that gathered spontaneously to hem the British into the city. With the formation of the Continental Army, Learned was commissioned as colonel of the 3rd Regiment and received the British officer sent out to tell Washington of General William Howe's decision to evacuate Boston. Learned was the first man into the city, opening the gates with his own hands. His regiment was ordered to New York in May, but Learned resigned his commission and returned to Oxford. In April 1777, he was commissioned by Congress as a brigadier general and assigned to the northern army under Philip Schuyler and then Horatio Gates. After doing little of note during the campaign against General John Burgoyne, Learned again resigned.

LE BEQUE DE PRESLE. See DUPORTAIL, Louis.

LEE, Andrew. Militia officer, spy Few details are known, but Lee was apparently a resident of Pennsylvania, a graduate of Harvard, and a captain in the state militia during the Revolution. He reportedly worked as a spy and, disguised as an escaping British prisoner of war, discovered and exposed a series of British "safe" houses in Pennsylvania during 1781.

LEE, Ann (1736–1784) Religious leader "Mother" Ann Lee was the charismatic founder of the Shaker sect. She was born and raised in the slums of Manchester, England and during the 1760s claimed to have received a vision from God that nominated her as the new messiah, a feminine version of Jesus Christ. She and her small group of followers emigrated to New York City in 1774, but they nearly starved to death before they decamped to a swampy settlement called Watervliet in upstate New York near Albany in 1776. Her religious teachings and the practices of her followers seemed radical to her patriot neighbors, who harbored suspicions anyway about a group of recent British emigrants who claimed to be pacifists but who had moved en masse to the New York frontier and set up a colony directly along the pathway of potential British invasions from Canada. Lee and her followers were harassed constantly by local authorities and mobs, even though they had no political ambitions and in fact were moving toward a doctrine of withdrawal from the "world." Lee was jailed several times during the Revolution, in part because she and her coreligionists refused to take oaths of allegiance as a matter of religious policy. She died following a prolonged proselytizing tour of New England in 1784. *Further reading:* Nardi Reeder Campion, *Mother Ann Lee: Morning Star of the Shakers* (Hanover, N.H., 1990).

LEE, Arthur (1740–1792) Diplomat, delegate to Congress

Lee was one of the more unpleasant and certainly one of the most disruptive personalities of the Revolution. He was a spiteful, paranoid obstructionist who did almost no good and much ill for the American cause. He was the brother of Richard Henry, Francis Lightfoot, William and Thomas Ludwell Lee, making him a cousin of the other branch of the Virginia Lee clan (including "Light-Horse Harry," Charles and Richard Bland Lee).

Arthur was born at his family's estate in Westmoreland County, Virginia and was taken under the wing of his eldest brother, Philip Ludwell, when their father died around 1750. The boy was sent to England for education, and he attended Eton School and then studied medicine at the University of Edinburgh. He graduated with a degree in 1764 and returned home to Virginia for a brief period of medical practice at the colonial capital at Williamsburg. He abandoned medicine, however, after two years and returned to London to study law at the Inns of Court. Although he clearly identified himself as an American, Lee involved himself in British politics and would likely have been happy to find a place in public office. His major political activities were in support of John Wilkes, who was turning the British government on its head at the time, and he also wrote a series of anonymous, published "letters" (in the manner of Junius) excoriating the crown. Lee had already published 10 political essays known as the "Monitor Letters" shortly before his return to Britain.

One of his political strengths throughout the revolutionary era was his strong personal ties to important American politicians, and in 1770, he used the good opinion of Sam Adams and others in Massachusetts to have himself appointed London agent for the embattled northern colony. Lee was still in London when the War for Independence began in 1775, and he was appointed by the Secret Committee of Congress as one of the three American commissioners—joining Benjamin Franklin and Silas Deane—who were to serve as the chief diplomatic mission to France. Here, Lee's full powers of disruption and paranoia came to fruition. He soon began to express an extreme distaste and suspicion of Deane, motivated at least in part by jealousy over Deane's apparent success in helping to organize the flow of French supplies to the colonies under the dummy company of Hortalez et Cie. Deane was, of course, not squeaky clean and was under the influence of the commission's secretary, Edward Bancroft, who was himself in the pay of the British, but Lee's long campaign against Deane was conducted with not a shred of knowledge of these facts and seems to have been based solely on Lee's inveterate hostility and suspicion toward his colleagues.

Lee himself was dispatched to Spain in early 1777 with the mission of securing money. He was not received by the Spanish court, which was holding the American colonists at arm's length, but he did manage to obtain the needed financial aid through an intermediary. He then went to Berlin on a similar mission, but he failed entirely to gain either recognition or monetary support. Back in Paris by mid-1777, Lee began a campaign of vilification and accusation against Deane, and to a lesser extent against Franklin, that resulted in a long, drawn-out controversy in the Continental Congress that did much to weaken if not paralyze the body for nearly two years. In a series of letters to his friends in Congress, Lee accused Deane of peculation and corruption (which was, indeed, true, but Lee had no evidence or proof and based his attacks on personal misanthropy). Deane was recalled and subjected to an investigation, which ultimately cleared him, while Lee remained in Paris to harass Franklin. For a period of many months, almost all matters before Congress were colored by the split among the delegates between pro-Deane and pro-Lee forces. After a long wrangle, Congress finally decided in the spring of 1779 that matters could not continue, and Lee was recalled and dismissed, leaving Franklin in sole charge of diplomacy in Paris for the time being.

Lee's influence was basically at an end. He returned to Virginia and a seat in the legislature, and in 1781, he was sent as a delegate to the Congress, but he no longer had the power to set the government awry with his accusations. He served on the functionless treasury board during the last years of the Confederation but essentially was out of public life. He spent his remaining years on his estate in Virginia. *Further reading:* A. R. Riggs, *The Nine Lives of Arthur Lee, Virginia Patriot* (Williamsburg, Va., 1976); Louis W. Potts, *Arthur Lee: A Virtuous Revolutionary* (Baton Rouge, La., 1981).

LEE, Charles (1731–1782) Continental general

Lee was one of the enigmas of the American Revolution. He was an experienced and apparently competent soldier who—contrary to his background—volunteered for service against the crown, yet he proved to be a weak commander and a treacherous colleague. He was born in Britain to a military family and was educated in England and Switzerland. Embarking on a career in the British army, he joined his father's regiment in 1747, and in 1751, he received a commission as lieutenant in the 44th Regiment of Foot.

His first trip to America was with the 44th as part of Edward Braddock's expedition in 1755, and he fought during much of the Seven Years' War in North America. He returned to England in 1761, transferred to the 103rd Regiment as a major, and served under Burgoyne in Portugal before retiring on half pay as a lieutenant colonel when his regiment was disbanded in 1763. In 1765, Lee went to Poland, where he served as a soldier of fortune off and on until 1770. He moved to America in 1773 and purchased an estate in what is now West Virginia. With the beginning of the war, he petitioned the Continental Congress for a commission in the new Continental Army, and impressed with his credentials, the body appointed him a major general. After serving with little distinction in the New York campaign, he accepted command of the Southern Department in 1776 and directed the successful defense of Charleston against a British invasion.

He was an ambitious man whose jealousy of Washington—whom Lee regarded as a rank amateur—got him into difficulty. During the New Jersey campaign in 1776, Lee failed to support Washington as requested and to many it appeared he actually hoped Washington would fail, presumably with Lee as the next in line to become commander in chief. Lee was guilty of writing several letters to politicians that betrayed his contempt for Washington. On December 13, 1776, Lee was captured at Basking Ridge by a British raiding party and taken as a prisoner to New York. During his confinement, he proposed to General William Howe a plan to defeat

Charles Lee

the rebels by splitting the middle colonies—evidence of his perfidy did not, however, come to light until the mid-1800s. Lee was exchanged in time to take command of part of the army at Monmouth, where he failed so miserably to support Washington at a crucial moment—ordering an inexplicable retreat—that he was charged with disobedience and misbehavior. The court-martial found him guilty and suspended him from command for a year. At the end of his sentence, he wrote such an offensive letter to Congress that the body dismissed him from the service of the nation. He retired to his estate in the Shenandoah Valley. While his actions at Monmouth can be seen as near-treasonous, the consensus of historians is that Lee did not intend overtly to betray the American cause at that stage, but rather harbored a profound lack of confidence in his troops' abilities, which, when wedded to his personal ambitions to take a leading role in arranging a peace, led him astray. *Further reading:* John R. Alden, *General Charles Lee: Traitor or Patriot?* (Baton Rouge, La., 1951).

LEE, Charles (1758–1815) Jurist, government official

The brother of Henry (and therefore cousin to the Westmoreland County Lees), Charles Lee took only a minor role in the Revolution, although he became a prominent jurist during the first years of the new Republic. He was born in Virginia and graduated from the College of New Jersey (Princeton) in 1775 on the eve of the war. From 1777 until 1789, he was a "naval officer" of the state of Virginia, although his exact duties—if any—are unclear. Following the war, Lee formed a political alliance with George Washington and was the president's strong supporter during the late 1780s and 1790s. Lee was a customs inspector at Alexandria, Virginia for several years, and in 1795, he was appointed by Washington as attorney general of the United States. As a Federalist, Lee was doomed to leave office with the new administration in 1801, but he received one of the infamous appointments as a "midnight judge" when President John Adams packed the federal bench just before leaving office. Lee lost his post when the new Congress repealed the Judiciary Act in 1802, and he turned to private law practice.

LEE, Ezra (1749–1821) Continental soldier, first submariner

Lee was a native of Lyme, Connecticut and served as a sergeant in one of the Connecticut regiments when he was selected in 1776 to be both captain and crew of the world's first attack submarine, David Bushnell's *American Turtle*. The ingenious craft incorporated all of the necessary mechanisms and technology of a successful underwater warship but in a crude form that subjected the operator to prolonged physical and psychological stress. The inventor himself was too frail to operate the submarine, and his brother, Ezra Bushnell, who had run the craft during tests, fell ill, so Sergeant Lee was trained to take over. He was enclosed in a small oak spheroid with his head thrust up into a conning tower. He controlled ascent and descent by means of turning a paddle mechanism and hand pumping air in and out. Forward motion underwater required peddling to turn an external screw—similar to riding an underwater bicycle.

Lee launched his attack on the 64-gun British frigate *Eagle* on September 6, 1776 and with great effort succeeded in bringing his craft into position under the hull of the enemy ship. Unfortunately, the screw mechanism by which he was to attach a clockwork underwater bomb failed. The inventor had neglected a basic law of physics which prevented the wood screw from penetrating the ship's hull: it merely pushed the small submarine away. Frustrated, Lee cut loose the explosive, which went off with a loud but harmless bang, and escaped. A later attempt against the British frigate *Cerberus* was nearly as fruitless, although a nearby schooner was damaged. The *Turtle* was lost at sea before a third attempt. Sergeant Lee returned to duty with his

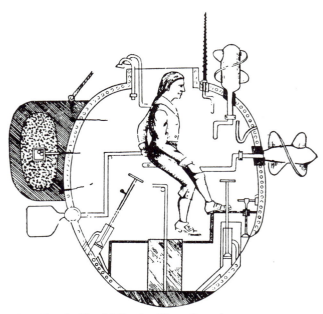

Ezra Lee in David Bushnell's submarine

regiment, fighting at Trenton, Brandywine and Monmouth.

LEE, Francis Lightfoot (1734–1797) Delegate to Congress, planter

Francis Lightfoot was one of the brothers of the "Stratford" branch of the Virginia Lees—making him the sibling of Arthur, Richard Henry, William and Thomas Ludwell—and an ardent patriot, although he was more retiring in public manner than others of his family. He was born and educated at Stratford in Westmoreland County, and he became a planter on an inherited estate in Loudoun County near Leesburg (named for him and his brother Richard Henry) in 1750 when his father died. He took a seat in the House of Burgesses in 1758, holding it until the Revolution. In 1769, Lee married Rebecca Tayloe and moved to a new estate provided by her father in Richmond County. He eagerly supported the prerevolutionary agitation in Virginia, beginning with opposition to the Stamp Act, and he was an important organizer during the final months before the actual ouster of the royal government. He helped to set up the Virginia Committee of Correspondence in 1773, and he attended provincial congresses in 1774 and 1775. Lee was selected in 1775 as a delegate to the Continental Congress, replacing Patrick Henry, and he served quietly but effectively until 1779, signing the Declaration of Independence and the Articles of Confederation. He was not an orator, however, and despite his effective committee work, he was much in the congressional shadow of his more flamboyant elder brother Richard Henry Lee, who served in Philadelphia at the same time. Lee withdrew from Congress in 1779, and apart from service in the Virginia legislature, he essentially avoided office for the remainder of his life, preferring a quiet existence on his estate. *Further reading:* Alonzo T. Dill, *Francis Lightfoot Lee: The Improbable Signer* (Williamsburg, Va., 1977).

LEE, Henry (1756–1818) Continental officer, delegate to Congress, governor

Lee, known forever since by the nickname "Light-Horse Harry," earned a deserved reputation as the best cavalry and dragoon leader of the Revolutionary War and perhaps the best in American history—a superb combat soldier who wore himself out in the service of his country. He was a cousin of the Westmoreland County branch of the Lee family (Arthur, Richard Henry, Francis Lightfoot, William and Thomas Ludwell) and the brother of Charles Lee (Henry married his own cousin, Matilda, who was daughter of another of the Westmoreland brothers, thus creating an even more complex family tree).

Lee was born at his family's estate of Leesylvania in Prince William County and graduated from Princeton (then called the College of New Jersey) in 1773. He was preparing to go to England to study law when the war began. Appointed a captain of Virginia cavalry in Bland's Regiment, he was with Washington's army in the North during the spring of 1777 when he caught the eye of the commander in chief. Even though Washington was a Virginia gentleman—like Lee—and might have been expected to value horses and horsemen, he had little affection for cavalry and found few uses for them. For the most part, Washington acquiesced when Congress awarded independent cavalry commands to its favorites. During 1777, however, Washington was pressed to keep track of the British movements in Pennsylvania and New Jersey, so for the time being he needed cavalry officers like Lee. In reward for several adroit actions against the British, Lee was named in January 1778 by Congress (with Washington's blessing) to command a special elite force of dragoons and infantry, which came to be known after 1780 as Lee's Legion.

Under his leadership the Legion became one of the truly outstanding units in all of the American army. The Legion combined several kinds of troops, including some true cavalry that fought from horseback, but was built around dragoons, mounted infantry and light foot infantry. The units (usually three mounted and three foot) were designed to move swiftly and strike hard, which they learned how to do effectively by war's end. Lee was allowed to recruit his men and officers from other regiments, and he assembled an elite group that was extremely well equipped and well mounted. His first great victory was at Paulus Hook, New York in August 1779, an action that won Lee the thanks of Congress and one of the few medals awarded by the national government during the war.

Lee was promoted to lieutenant colonel in November of the same year. Washington then sent Lee and his Legion south in 1780 to join Nathanael Greene in the southern campaign. Throughout the following two years, Lee was everywhere in the southern theater and took part in nearly every important action. His men acted both as the mobile core of the American army and as partisans, raiding British outposts in the Carolinas, often in conjunction with the forces of Francis Marion or Thomas Pickens. Lee with his Legion proved to be the equal of Banestre Tarleton, his British counterpart who had wreaked complete havoc in the Carolinas until Lee's appearance. Lee (along with William Washington) did much to save Greene's army at the battle of Eutaw Springs in 1781. Lee was detached from Greene's command in the early fall of 1781 and joined the main allied army at Yorktown, where he

Henry ("Light-Horse Harry") Lee

probably operated against Tarleton on the Gloucester side of the river. He rejoined Greene in the Carolinas but in February 1782, Lee—still a lieutenant colonel but deserving of far higher rank and honor—withdrew from active command, apparently a victim of battle fatigue. His wartime experiences had compressed a lifetime of stress and imposed it on a very young man, and the result was a long-lasting emotional and physical diminution.

Lee married Matilda and after the war entered Virginia politics, sitting in the legislature and representing his state in the Confederation Congress from 1785 to 1788. He remarried in 1793 after Matilda's death and served as Virginia's governor from 1792 to 1795, leaving his executive post temporarily in 1794 to command the army that put down the Whiskey Rebellion. His life then turned sad and sour, however. He failed as a businessman, and his finances deteriorated drastically. In 1808, he was imprisoned for debt and wrote his fine *Memoirs of the War in the Southern Department of the United States*—one of the best accounts of the war by a participant—while in jail. He was injured by a mob in Baltimore in 1812 while helping to defend a friend's press. A broken man, he left the United States in 1813 and moved to the West Indies, seeking peace and health. He died at Cumberland Island, Georgia while on the way back home. In 1913, Lee's remains were moved to the campus of Washington and Lee University. The fifth child of his second marriage was Robert E. Lee, the greatest American general of them all. *Further reading:* Charles Royster, *Light-Horse Harry Lee and the Legacy of the American Revolution* (New York, 1981); Henry Lee, *Memoirs of the War in the Southern Department of the United States*, 2 vols. (1812; reprinted New York, 1970).

LEE, Richard Henry (1732–1794) Delegate to Congress, legislator, planter

Lee was the most effective legislator among the remarkable set of Lee brothers—including Arthur, Francis Lightfoot, William and Thomas Ludwell—descended from Thomas and Hannah Lee of Westmoreland County, Virginia. He was at the center of the Revolution in his native colony and played an important role in the Continental Congress. He was born on the family estate and sent to England for education, returning to Virginia in 1751 after attending Wakefield School and touring Europe. He lived for a time at the

Richard Henry Lee

principal family seat of Stratford, but after his marriage in 1757, Lee moved to a new plantation nearby. As a matter of course he took a seat in the House of Burgesses.

Throughout the agitations of the 1760s and early 1770s, Lee was at the forefront of patriotic movements in Virginia. Although a colonial aristocrat and a thoroughly typical member of the planter class, he opposed the policies of the British ministries and the king (against whom he proposed especially to focus revolutionary rhetoric) with great vigor, bringing to bear his considerable oratorical and organizational talents. He allied himself in the 1760s with Patrick Henry and seldom deviated from the alliance throughout his public career. Lee organized the Westmoreland Association of local planters in 1766 as an economic boycott against the British and moved from there to opposition to the Townshend Acts and a proposal that disaffected colonists should set up committees of correspondence as a method of mutual support. He led the formation of the Virginia Association in 1769 after the dissolution of the Burgesses, and after a quieter period during the early 1770s, Lee joined Henry and Jefferson to bring Virginia vocally into support of Boston and Massachusetts in 1774—a meaningful expression of the alliance of southern and northern colonial interests. He was selected as one of the initial delegates to the Continental Congress in 1774, and he served until 1779, when he was forced to withdraw for reasons of health. He was a good and effective legislator, forming a close relationship with the Adamses of Massachusetts and using his speaking skills to the fullest. Lee was one of the early proponents of independence, and on instructions from home he entered the resolution on June 7, 1776 that led to the Declaration of Independence. He himself was absent in Virginia during the drafting and adoption of the document, but he signed the Declaration later in the fall when he returned to duty in Philadelphia.

After his withdrawal as a delegate to Congress in 1779, Lee served in the Virginia legislature. He was once again elected as a delegate to Congress after the war, and he acted as president in 1784. He understood all too well the deficiencies of the Articles of Confederation, but he opposed the new federal constitution because it lacked a bill of rights, and he refused to represent Virginia at the national convention in 1787. When elected to the new U.S. Senate in 1789, Lee worked for adoption of the first 10 amendments to the Constitution, and he resigned from office a year after their adoption. He died on his plantation a year later. *Further reading:* Oliver Chitwood, *Richard Henry Lee, Statesman of the Revolution* (Morgantown, Va., 1967).

LEE, Thomas Ludwell (1730–1777) Legislator

One of the less prominent of the Lee brothers of Westmoreland County, Virginia, Thomas Ludwell participated mainly in local and state affairs, leaving the national and international scene to Arthur, Francis Lightfoot, Richard Henry and William. He was a lawyer and, of course, a member of the House of Burgesses. He was active in revolutionary meetings, however, as a delegate to the conventions of 1774 and 1775, and he served on the committee of safety. After the organization of a new state government in Virginia, Lee became a judge of the general court,

but he died at a relatively young age in the midst of the Revolution.

LEE, Thomas Sim (1745–1819) Delegate to Congress, governor, militia officer

A member of the Maryland branch of the Lee family (a split occurred in 1700 when Philip Lee, Thomas Sim's grandfather, moved from Virginia) and born near Upper Marlboro in Prince Georges County, Thomas Sim Lee was a man of property, although he was relatively obscure until the Revolution. He held local offices only until 1777, when he sat on the provincial council. He served in a local militia unit as a major, but there is no record of his field duty. In 1779, Lee was selected by the state legislature as governor of Maryland. He held the post during the balance of the war, until 1783, and devoted most of his energies to providing troops and supplies to the American cause. He was sent as a delegate to the Confederation Congress in 1783 after leaving the governor's office. He was again elected governor in 1792, serving until 1794. He declined several other posts, including service at the federal constitutional convention and in the state senate. He was elected governor for a third time in 1798, but he again declined to serve and remained in retirement from public life.

LEE, William (1739–1795) Diplomat, merchant

Brother of Arthur, Richard Henry, Francis Lightfoot and Thomas Ludwell Lee, William served as a particularly inept diplomat for Congress in Europe during the first years of the Revolution and colluded with Arthur in bringing on the controversy with Silas Deane. He was born, like his siblings, on the family estate in Westmoreland County, Virginia, but little is known of his education or early life. In 1768, he went to London with Arthur and there became a merchant. He involved himself along with his brother in the politics of the city, supporting John Wilkes and emerging as one of the popular figures among the antigovernment forces of London. He also allied himself to Stephen Sayre, an erstwhile colonial agent, and managed in 1773 to have himself appointed sheriff of London and alderman, an unusual position for an American.

Through the influence of his elder brother Richard Henry, Lee was appointed in 1777 as a commercial envoy to Nantes, France, but he spent little or no effort on this mission and chose instead to remain in Paris and conspire with Arthur against the other American commissioners, Benjamin Franklin and Deane. He was as much embroiled in the Deane controversy as Arthur, but was not quite so public in his statements. In May 1777, Lee was directed by Congress to establish missions to the courts at Berlin and Vienna, but he was entirely rebuffed and was not even allowed to enter either capital. He displayed his capacity for mischief when—unauthorized by Congress—he contacted a minor Dutch official and drew up a completely irregular "treaty" of commerce, which when later discovered by the British among the papers of the emissary Henry Laurens provided the pretext for a declaration of war by Great Britain on Holland and the subsequent loss of Dutch supply bases in the West Indies. When the Deane controversy was finally decided in Congress during 1779, Lee was dismissed from his diplomatic appointment. He remained in Europe until 1783, then returned to Virginia. *Further reading:* Worthington C. Ford, ed., *Letters of William Lee, 1766–1783* (1891; reprinted New York, 1968).

LEGGE, Francis (1719–1783) British official A relative of the Earl of Dartmouth, Legge was a controversial colonial official. He was appointed governor of Nova Scotia in 1773 and quarreled with nearly everyone in the province during his administration. In 1775, he raised a thousand-man force in defense against the attempted American invasion. He was recalled to England in 1776.

LEGGE, William. See DARTMOUTH, Earl of.

LEIGH, Sir Egerton (d. 1781) Loyalist official Leigh was attorney general of South Carolina under the crown and, as a member of the colonial office-holding elite, remained loyal. His father had also held high office as chief justice of the colony. Leigh sat on the Governor's Council and was, in addition, surveyor general, enjoying an annual allowance from the British government of £600. He was made a baronet in 1772 or 1773 and continued to serve as a British official until his death.

LEIPER, Thomas (1745–1825) Soldier, businessman Leiper emigrated to America from his native Scotland in 1763, first to Maryland and two years later to Philadelphia, where he became a man-

ufacturer of snuff and other tobacco products. He was active in opposing the British through 1773 and 1774, and at the outbreak of the Revolution, he joined the Philadelphia City Cavalry. The unit, sometimes known as the Philadelphia Light Horse, was an elite militia force whose membership was drawn from "gentlemen of property" in Philadelphia. Leiper rode with the first troop, one of three in the company. The Philadelphia City Cavalry was not just for show—the company was a well-mounted reconnaissance unit that often carried dispatches for the Congress or the Continental Army and acted as scouts. In 1776 and 1777, Leiper and his fellow cavalrymen fought in the field with the Continental Army, seeing action at Trenton, Princeton, Brandywine and Germantown. After the war, Leiper expanded his business to include a stone quarry and, eventually, banking. An Anti-Federalist, he served as president of the Philadelphia Common Council for several years after the turn of the century.

L'ENFANT, Pierre Charles (1754–1825) Continental officer, architect, city planner Responsible for the grand, if unrealized, design of the nation's capital city, L'Enfant served ably as a volunteer soldier during the war before turning his hand to visionary architecture and planning. He was the son of a minor French painter and was apparently a trained engineer in 1776 when he negotiated an agreement for a commission with Silas Deane in Paris. L'Enfant arrived in America in 1777, and he received the promised commission from Congress as a lieutenant of engineers in time to winter at Valley Forge. He was promoted to captain in 1778 and served on the staff of General von Steuben until he transferred to the southern theater. L'Enfant served under John Laurens during the French-American attack on Savannah in October 1779, where he was badly wounded while leading an assault column. He recovered slowly at Charleston and was still a semi-invalid when captured with the rest of the city's garrison in May 1780. He remained a prisoner of the British for 18 months, gaining release and exchange in January 1782. He returned to the North and was promoted to major in mid-1783.

After he was mustered out of the army in early 1784, L'Enfant remained in America, hoping to develop his artistic and design skills into a profession.

He won a commission to design the regalia of the Society of Cincinnatus (formed by ex-officers of the Continental Army) and was occupied during the late 1780s in the design of ceremonial structures and building renovations in New York City. His greatest commission was to design the new federal capital city proposed for a wilderness site in Virginia. At the behest of George Washington, L'Enfant submitted a plan in 1791, incorporating an elegant and grand vision of the central seat of government. Although much of the plan exists today only in the drawings of L'Enfant, the basic outlines of central Washington, D.C. reflect his ideas—most notably the characteristic circles overlaying a basic grid pattern with a dominant avenue connecting the executive and legislative branches.

Despite his talents as a designer, L'Enfant was not a good practical builder. His disregard for the realities of creating a city amid the marshes and his failure to placate the speculators and politicians who wanted to control the future of the capital soon got him in trouble. In truth, there was only a fraction of the money available needed to realize his scheme, and L'Enfant basically ignored this problem. He was dismissed as supervisor of building after only a few months. He drifted from job to job for the next several years and spent much of the rest of his life attempting to collect a huge claim against the federal government for his services. He refused an offer in 1812 to teach engineering at the new military school at West Point. L'Enfant died nearly penniless, living on the charity of a friend. In 1909, his body was removed from a pauper's grave and reinterred in Arlington Cemetery. *Further reading:* Hans Caemmerer, *The Life of Pierre Charles L'Enfant* (reprinted New York, 1970).

LEONARD, Daniel (1740–1829) Loyalist lawyer, writer

Born in Norton, Massachusetts, Leonard graduated from Harvard and practiced law in Taunton before the Revolution. He sat in the General Court from 1770 to 1774 and was a spokesman for the royal cause. He was also adept with the pen, publishing a series of articles in 1774 and 1775 under the name "Massachusettensis," to which John Adams addressed his "Novanglus" writings in reply. Leonard was fond, as were most political writers of the day, of elaborate metaphor. "I saw a small seed of sedition," he wrote, "when it was implanted: it was a grain of mustard. I have watched the plant, until it has become a great tree; the vilest reptiles that crawl upon the earth are concealed at the root; the foulest birds of the air rest in its branches." In 1775, Leonard moved inside the British lines in Boston, serving as a customs commissioner until the evacuation in 1776, when he went first to Halifax, Nova Scotia and then to England. He was appointed chief justice of Bermuda in 1782, a post he held for 24 years. He died in London.

LEONARD, George (1742–1826) Loyalist

Leonard was active throughout most of the Revolution in the Associated Loyalists, which he first joined in 1775 during the siege of Boston. He evacuated with the British forces to Halifax in 1776 but returned to the colonies later as an agent of the Associated Loyalists in Rhode Island. He was a director of the loyalist group from 1780 to 1782 and was active around New York City. He left for Halifax in 1783 and there became an agent for resettling American loyalists after the peace. He sat on the Nova Scotia Governor's Council for more than three decades.

L'EPINE (d. 1782) French volunteer

Outside the mold of most of the French volunteer officers, L'Epine was not of noble birth and had scant military background. He was the son of a watchmaker and the nephew of the financier and author Caron de Beaumarchais. His purpose in coming to America was as much commercial as bellicose. He arrived in 1777 and was commissioned by Congress as a brevet captain (he eventually received rank as a major). Even though he served as an aide-de-camp for de Kalb and von Steuben, he apparently spent much of his time traveling through the states, selling copies of his uncle's literary works, having brought a stock with him. He returned to France in December 1778 and died from injuries received in an accidental house fire.

LESLIE, Alexander (c. 1740–1794) British general

Relatively obscure despite his service in America at high rank during the entire war, Leslie was lieutenant colonel of the 64th Regiment of Foot stationed at Halifax, Nova Scotia in 1775 when he was ordered to reinforce the British garrison at Boston. He led an expedition in February to Salem, Massachusetts, and this expedition served as a precursor to the march on Lexington and Concord.

Promoted to brigadier general, he commanded the British light infantry during the New York campaign in 1776, taking part in the battles at Harlem Heights and White Plains. He demonstrated little tactical or strategic acumen, although displaying considerable personal bravery. When the British chased Washington through New Jersey late in the year, Leslie was detached to hold an outpost at Maidenhead, but he failed to post adequate scouts and Washington, on the way to Princeton in January 1777, managed to march the entire American army within three miles of Leslie's position without alerting the British general.

In 1779, Leslie was promoted to major general and given command of the 64th. He and his regiment in 1780 formed an expedition to the Chesapeake in support of the British campaign in the Carolinas. He joined Lord Cornwallis in January 1781 and subsequently commanded the British right wing at the battle of Guilford Courthouse in March. Leslie personally returned to New York in July 1781 and remained there until after the British surrender at Yorktown. In November, he sailed to Charleston and assumed command of British forces in the southern theater, although little was left for him to do except hold on to a few bases until the inevitable peace came. He supervised the final British evacuation of Charleston in late 1782.

LEVY, Aaron (1742–1815) Merchant   Born in the Netherlands, Levy immigrated to America in 1760, settling in Philadelphia where he became a trader with the frontier towns in Northumberland County. He was part of the significant network of Jewish merchants in the city that tied the frontier to the business centers of Europe. He was also a major land speculator and amassed very large tracts during and after the Revolution. He was probably at the height of his prosperity during the years of the War for Independence, and he made large (unrepaid) loans to the Continental Congress in support of the American cause, often acting through the agency of his associate the financier Robert Morris. He founded the city of Aaronsburg in 1786, but the place failed to thrive, perhaps because it became known as "Jewstown" among prospective settlers. Levy's prosperity declined after the war, and he lost much in the collapse of Morris' financial empire.

LEW, Barzillai (1743–1793) Continental soldier   Lew was born in Massachusetts, the son of a free black father who had emigrated from Haiti. The younger Lew was a cooper by trade and a veteran of the Seven Years' War, in which he fought as a volunteer with a Massachusetts colonial militia company. In May 1775, a month after the beginning of open warfare, Lew enlisted in a Massachusetts regiment, and in June he fought at the battle of Bunker Hill and Breed's Hill. He served the entire war as an infantryman and a fifer. During the later years of the war, he is reported to have organized an all-black unit of guerrilla fighters.

LEWIS, Andrew (1720–1781) Continental general   Born in Ireland, Lewis was brought to frontier Virginia as a child by his father, who fled his homeland after killing his landlord in a quarrel. The family settled near Staunton, Virginia, which the elder Lewis helped to found. Andrew grew up to be relatively prosperous. During his early adulthood, he fought the Indians on the frontier, and he also served with the British colonial forces during the wars with France in North America. He was with George Washington at Fort Necessity and was later part of Edward Braddock's army, although Lewis was absent during Braddock's disastrous defeat. He was less fortunate in 1758 while on a reconnaissance with Major James Grant, and he was captured and held prisoner at Montreal. His most notable fighting was during Lord Dunmore's War in 1774, when Lewis led the main column of the Virginia army against the Indians, winning a signal victory at Point Pleasant and thereby cementing his reputation as a successful frontier soldier. He attended the Virginia revolutionary assemblies in March and December 1775, and in March 1776, he was commissioned a brigadier general by the Continental Congress. He took command of American forces at Williamsburg, Virginia and was responsible for chasing Governor Dunmore from Gwynn Island in July, a feat that helped rid Virginia of British power until late in the Revolution. Unfortunately, Lewis was not immune to the jealousy and egotism rampant among American general officers early in the war. When he was passed over for major general in February 1777, Lewis was so offended that he resigned his commission—allegedly for reasons of health—and withdrew from national military affairs. He continued as an officer in the Virginia militia until his death but participated in no significant actions.

LEWIS, Fielding (1725–c. 1782) Official, manufacturer

Fielding was doubly related to George Washington—he married Washington's cousin Catherine in 1746, and after her death in 1750, he married Washington's sister Betty. He was a close associate of Washington for most of his life. Born into a wealthy Virginia family, Lewis was best known for the building of a magnificent mansion called "Kenmore" at Fredericksburg, Virginia. He was a representative to the Virginia Burgesses from 1760 to 1770, and with the coming of revolutionary agitation, he was active in local affairs as a member of the committee of correspondence. He was fragile of health and declined to serve in the military; however, during the war he ran a small arms factory for the state, augmenting the operation's budget with his own fortune. *Further reading:* Russell Bastead, "Kenmore in Fredericksburg, Virginia," *Antiques* (March 1979), 535–61.

LEWIS, Francis (1713–1803) Delegate to Congress, merchant

Lewis was born in Wales and raised by relatives after his parents died while he was still young. He entered trade in London and in 1738 emigrated to America, where he set up mercantile businesses in both Philadelphia and New York City, alternating his residence. He was a vigorous businessman, personally sailing to trade in Europe and Africa, and he prospered greatly. He served during the colonial wars, first as a volunteer aide-de-camp and then as a clothing contractor for the British forces. He was captured by Indians and handed over to the French, who eventually exchanged him. Lewis received a substantial land grant from the British crown as compensation for his service, and he turned it into even more wealth. He retired from business in 1765 and moved to Long Island.

Lewis was an active patriot during the early 1770s, a member of the Sons of Liberty in New York and of the revolutionary committees. He was sent to Congress as a delegate in 1775, and although prevented from voting for independence by instructions from home, he signed the Declaration in August 1776. He sat on the naval committee in Congress and helped organize supplies for the army. When the British invaded New York and Long Island in

1776, they destroyed Lewis' home and took his wife prisoner. Although she was exchanged, the experience ruined her health and led to her death in 1779. Lewis was deeply affected and resigned from Congress, although he continued to sit on the admiralty board.

LEWIS, Morgan (1754–1844) Continental officer, state official

Lewis was the son of Francis Morgan and was raised at Elizabethtown, New Jersey. He graduated from the college at Princeton in 1773 and was a law student when the Revolution began. He first served as a volunteer of militia around Boston in 1775 but was commissioned as a major in the 2nd New York Regiment when the unit was organized as part of the Continental Army in early 1776. Later in the year, he was promoted to colonel and designated as deputy commissary general of the northern army. He was chief of staff to General Horatio Gates during the campaign against General John Burgoyne in 1777. His most impressive fighting was against a loyalist-Indian raiding party under Sir John Johnson and Joseph Brant at Klock's Field, New York, in October 1780.

He completed his legal studies after the war and entered New York politics (he became Robert R. Livingston's son-in-law in 1779) as an Anti-Federalist. He served as attorney general of the state and justice of the supreme court. Lewis was elected governor of New York in 1804 but missed reelection in 1807. He returned to military duty during the War of 1812 as a quartermaster on the Niagara frontier with the rank of major general. *Further reading:* "General Lewis Morgan," *New York Historical Quarterly* 38 (1954), 429–30.

L'HOMMEDIEU, Ezra (1734–1811) Delegate to Congress, attorney

Born on Long Island to a French Huguenot family, L'Hommedieu graduated from Yale in 1754 and became a lawyer. He was an unobtrusive but consistent member of most of the revolutionary bodies in New York, including the provincial congresses from 1775 to 1777 and the state assembly in 1777 and 1778. He was delegate to the Congress from New York for four terms, from 1779 until 1783, but made little independent mark while serving. After the Revolution he served again in the state assembly, and he is credited as one of the sponsors of the legislation that founded the state university of New York.

LILLINGTON, John Alexander (c. 1725–1786) Militia and Continental officer   Lillington (who sometimes signed his name "Alexander John") was born in Barbados, where his father was a British officer and a member of the royal council. He came to North Carolina in 1734 with his father to take up residence on land near Wilmington that had been secured decades earlier by his grandfather. Lillington was a delegate to the North Carolina Provincial Congress in August 1775 and was appointed colonel of the Wilmington district militia. He was one of the principal patriot leaders at the battle of Moore's Creek Bridge in February 1776, when the back-country militia extinguished the loyalist threat by destroying the brave but foolhardy North Carolina loyalist Highlanders. He was commissioned as colonel of the 6th North Carolina Continental regiment in April but resigned after only a month to serve as a brigadier general in the state militia. He was at the battle of Camden and probably saw his militia break and run during the early stages of the battle. The town of Lillington, North Carolina was named in his honor.

LILLINGTON, John. Militia and Continental officer   The son of John Alexander Lillington, this officer left college in Philadelphia at the beginning of the war and returned to fight in his home state of North Carolina. He was commissioned a lieutenant in the 1st North Carolina in September 1775 but resigned in May of the following year to take a post as colonel in his father's militia brigade.

LINCOLN, Benjamin (1733–1810) Continental general   Lincoln experienced both extreme highs and lows during his service to the Revolution. He was a native of Hingham, Massachusetts and a moderately prosperous farmer who was much involved in militia affairs before the war. When hostilities began he was a brigadier of the Massachusetts militia, and he was given responsibility for militia troops around Boston and subsequently at New York City. Although he held no previous commission in the Continental Army, he was appointed as full major general in February 1777, an act that outraged many ahead of him on the seniority list (including Benedict Arnold).

Lincoln was ordered to New England in August 1777 and managed, despite disagreements, to prompt the recalcitrant militia to undertake the attack on

Benjamin Lincoln

Friedrich Baum's combined forces at Bennington. He then repaired to Saratoga, where he commanded the defenses at Freeman's Farm. During the latter stages of the engagement he suffered a bad wound and was invalided for several months. In September 1778, Congress appointed him to command the Southern Department, neglecting to consult Washington first. Lincoln found a difficult situation in the South. He arrived too late to do anything about the British seizure of Savannah, and he allowed himself and most of his army to be bottled up in Charleston. A good campaign by Sir Henry Clinton forced Lincoln—who had been to some degree intimidated by civilian authorities into staying cooped up—to surrender the city in 1780, marking one of the worst American defeats of the war. Lincoln was taken prisoner, although he was paroled before the end of the year. In 1781, Lincoln was given charge of the American army during its march south to invest Yorktown, and he commanded one of the three divisions of the army during the siege. He stepped forward to accept the British gesture of surrender at Yorktown. A few weeks later, Lincoln was appointed by Congress as the nation's first secretary at war, a post he held until the formal end of the war in 1783. He returned to Massachusetts, where he held several government offices in later years, and in 1787 he commanded the troops sent against Shays' Rebellion.

LINDSAY, Alexander. See BALCARRES, Earl of.

LINN, James (1749–1821) Militia officer, official   Born in New Jersey, Linn passed the bar in

1772, three years after graduation from the college at Princeton, and began the practice of law in Trenton. He was a judge of the court of common pleas, and in 1776, he demonstrated his patriotism by serving in the New Jersey Provincial Congress. He was also an officer in the Somerset County militia, although there is no information on any service in the field during the war. He sat on the New Jersey Council in 1777. After the Revolution, Linn moved on to a series of public offices: in the 1790s he again served on the state council; he represented New Jersey in the U.S. Congress for one term from 1799 to 1801; and he was U.S. supervisor of revenue during the Jefferson administration. After leaving the federal government at the end of Jefferson's presidency, Linn became secretary of state of New Jersey, holding his final office for 11 years.

LINN, John (1763–1821) Soldier, government official

Born in Warren County, New Jersey, Linn moved with his parents to Sussex County, where he attended the common schools. He was a teenage soldier during the Revolution and served as a private and then a sergeant in the 1st New Jersey Regiment. He did not enter public office until long after the war, taking a seat in the New Jersey general assembly in 1801 and becoming a judge of the court of common pleas four years later.

LIPPINCOTT, Richard (1745–1826) Loyalist officer

A captain of the New Jersey Associated Loyalists, Lippincott was responsible for the hanging of patriot Captain Joshua Huddy in April 1782, an act that set in motion the complex Huddy-Asgill affair. Acting under the orders of the board of the Associated Loyalists (probably with the direct involvement of Governor William Franklin), Lippincott took possession of Huddy, who had been captured by the British a month earlier, and was to convey him from New York to the Jersey side of the Hudson River and exchange him and two others for captured Associators. Instead, Lippincott and his men hung Huddy and placed on the swinging body a note saying that the act was in retaliation for the patriot killing of loyalist Phillip White. American commander in chief George Washington demanded that Sir Henry Clinton give up Lippincott as a murderer, but the British commander refused. Clinton did, however, court-martial Lippincott for his part in the affair, but the captain was acquitted

on the grounds that he was only following orders from the board of the Associated Loyalists. Lippincott emigrated first to England after the war and in the 1790s moved to Canada, where he died.

LITTLE, George (1754–1809) State naval officer

Little was a commissioned officer of the Massachusetts state navy, one of the tiny state operations that sought to harass the vastly greater British Royal Navy. The state navy was itself in competition with a huge number of privateers—Massachusetts commissioned 600 private sea adventurers during the Revolution. Little entered the Massachusetts navy in 1778 as a second lieutenant and served as first officer on the *Hazard*. The following year, he was promoted to captain and given command of the *Winthrop*. He received his discharge in 1780. After a long postwar hiatus, Little returned to naval warfare in 1799 when he was commissioned as a captain in the revived U.S. Navy and fought the French during the undeclared naval conflict at the end of the century, capturing several prizes.

LIVERMORE, Samuel (1732–1803) Delegate to Congress, legislator

Livermore was born in Massachusetts and lived his adult life in a remote region of New Hampshire, which did not prevent him from filling important public offices during the early years of the republic. He graduated from the College of New Jersey (Princeton) in 1752 and passed the bar four years later. After a brief practice in Waltham, Massachusetts, he moved to Portsmouth, New Hampshire. Livermore moved successively farther from the eastern settlements before the Revolution, first to Derry and then to Holderness, which was almost inaccessible for part of the year. He owned a large estate and ran it virtually as a personal fiefdom, dispensing economic favor and justice to his employees and tenants. He became attorney general of New Hampshire, despite his isolation, in 1776 and was selected as a commissioner to negotiate the issue of the New Hampshire Grants in 1779. He took little part in the first years of the Revolution, preferring to remain on his estates. In 1780, Livermore moved into the public arena as a delegate to Congress. He sat twice in the body, returning in 1785. He meanwhile had become chief justice of the state supreme court. He was elected as a U.S. representative in 1789 and 1791, and to the U.S. Senate in 1792.

LIVINGSTON, Abraham. Continental officer
A member of the Canadian branch of the Livingston family, Abraham was the brother of James and Richard Livingston. He served as a captain in his brothers' regiment of Canadian volunteers organized in December 1775 to support Richard Montgomery's invasion of Canada.

LIVINGSTON, Henry Beekman (1750–1831) Continental officer
The son of the elder Robert R. Livingston, Henry Beekman Livingston was born at Clermont, New York. In June 1775, he raised a company of infantry in his home state and served as captain in the 4th New York Regiment. His first significant duty was as aide-de-camp to General Richard Montgomery (his brother-in-law) during the 1775 invasion of Canada. He led the capture of the British post at Chambly and was recognized by Congress with a sword of honor, awarded before the debacle in December in which Montgomery died. The following year, Livingston became aide-de-camp to Philip Schuyler and was promoted to colonel. At the battle of Monmouth in June 1778, Livingston performed admirably, rallying his men behind a hedgerow and establishing a holding position that allowed Washington to stop the rout of the American army. In August of the same year, Livingston was one of the commanders of light infantry at Newport, Rhode Island and again distinguished himself on the battlefield. He resigned his commission in January 1779, although one historical source says he was made a brigadier at the end of the war. He spent the latter part of his life on an inherited estate at Rhinebeck, New York.

LIVINGSTON, Henry Brockholst (1757–1823) Continental officer, jurist
Born in New York City, Henry Brockholst Livingston was the only son of New York governor William Livingston. He graduated from the college at Princeton in 1774 and entered military service in 1775 as an aide to Philip Schuyler with the rank of captain. He eventually was promoted to lieutenant colonel of the 3rd New York Regiment and acted in 1776 as an aide to Arthur St. Clair. In 1777, Livingston was on Benedict Arnold's staff and took part in the campaigns against General John Burgoyne. The following year, along with his cousin Henry Beekman Livingston, he served with distinction on the expedition against the British at Newport, Rhode Island. In 1779, Livingston took a leave of absence from the army to act as private secretary to his brother-in-law John Jay during the latter's mission to Spain. Livingston was captured by the British during his return voyage to America in 1782 and sent to New York, where he was released on parole. Unable to serve in the army under the conditions of his release, Livingston moved to Albany and studied law. He was admitted to the bar in 1783. After the war he established a successful legal practice and was active in politics as an Anti-Federalist and supporter of Jefferson. In 1806, Livingston was named as an associate justice of the U.S. Supreme Court.

LIVINGSTON, James (1747–1832) Continental officer
The brother of Abraham and Richard Livingston and a distant relative of the New York Livingstons, James was born in Montreal. During the American invasion of Canada in 1775, James raised (by the authority of the Continental Congress) a small regiment of Canadians for service to the American cause. He was colonel and commander of the unit, known as the 1st Canadian Regiment. Livingston helped capture the British post at Chambly during the campaign against St. John's, but after Richard Montgomery's defeat at the gates of Quebec in December 1775, he turned back with the rest of the American army. He served in the northern army against General John Burgoyne and was in command of Stony Point and Verplanck's Point in 1780. The 1st Canadian was disbanded in January 1781 with most of the remaining men transferring to Moses Hazen's Canadian regiment. Livingston resigned from the army when his unit dissolved, and he settled in New York state.

LIVINGSTON, Peter Van Burgh (1710–1792) Merchant
Born of Dutch ancestry in Albany, New York, Livingston was a successful New York City merchant who was active in civilian patriot affairs during the Revolution. He graduated from Yale in 1731 and moved to New York City soon thereafter. During the Seven Years' War, Livingston not only supplied arms and foodstuffs to the British and colonial forces, but he also organized and financed privateering ventures against the French. His business prospered, but he resented the attempts by the British government after the Seven Years' War to control the colonial economy and demonstrated his stance by signing and supporting the nonim-

portation agreements following the Sugar Act in 1764. He was closely involved in revolutionary activity as the final breach with Great Britain approached in the mid-1770s. Livingston was one of the New York Committee of Fifty-One that selected delegates to the first Continental Congress in 1774 and was a moving force in the provincial governments set up by New York patriots in 1775, acting as chairman of the Provincial Congress.

LIVINGSTON, Philip (1716–1778) Delegate to Congress

A member of the wealthy and politically active New York Livingston family, Philip was the fifth son of Philip Livingston Sr. and Catherine Van Burgh Livingston, and therefore the nephew of Peter Van Burgh Livingston and the cousin of William Livingston. He built on his family money through profitable privateering during the colonial wars, establishing himself in New York City in preference to his family homes in and around Albany, the region where he had been born. He was an important figure in New York City politics and cultural affairs before the Revolution (he was a strong supporter of King's College and many societies and hospitals). He was also an early patriot, sitting in the Stamp Act Congress in 1765 and representing the more conservative faction of the rebellion. He opposed the radical Sons of Liberty as being too violent, but Livingston did not flinch from the movement toward independence. He was a member of the revolutionary committees that seized control of government in New York in 1774 and 1775 and was selected as a delegate to the first Continental Congress. He returned as a delegate to the new Congress in 1775. He was away during the vote for independence (his delegation was under orders to vote against) but he signed the Declaration on August 2. His homes in New York were seized by the British after they took control in 1776, and Livingston lost much of his accumulated property to confiscation. He died while still sitting as a delegate.

LIVINGSTON, Richard (d. 1786) Continental officer

A brother of Canadians James and Abraham Livingston, Richard also served in the 1st Canadian Regiment organized by his brother in 1775 as part of the American invasion of Canada. He was commissioned as lieutenant colonel of the unit and served until his capture by the British at Fort Mont-

gomery in 1777. He resigned after his release in November 1779.

LIVINGSTON, Robert R. (the Elder) (1718–1775) Jurist

One of the multitude of Robert Livingstons of New York, Robert R. adopted a middle initial to distinguish himself from his cousins with the same first name (his first son was also called Robert R.). An attorney, he served in the New York assembly from 1758 to 1768 and as a judge. A particular opponent of New York lieutenant governor Cadwallader Colden, Livingston often opposed the policies of the British government in regard to the colony and took an active role in prerevolutionary agitation, especially during the Stamp Act crisis, but on the whole he favored reconciliation rather than rebellion. He died eight months after the beginning of armed hostilities.

LIVINGSTON, Robert R. (the Younger) (1746–1813)

The son of Robert R. Livingston, the brother of Henry Beekman Livingston, the nephew of Peter Van Burgh Livingston, and the cousin of Philip and William Livingston, this member of the wealthy and powerful family was born in New York City. He graduated from King's College in 1765 and passed the bar in 1770. He practiced law with John Jay, a relative by marriage and a college classmate, but the beginning of the Revolution took him into office in 1775 as a delegate to the Continental Congress. He continued to serve intermittently in Congress until 1785, varying his duties there with activity in New York as a member of revolutionary committees and conventions. He was appointed as a member of the committee to draft a declaration of independence, but since he thought the time not yet ripe for such a move, he declined to vote for and failed to sign the eventual document.

In 1777, he became chancellor of the state of New York, holding the appointment until 1801. In 1781, he was named by Congress to be secretary of the department of foreign affairs, and he devoted a great deal of energy to the task, although Congress made his duties difficult. He resigned in June 1783 after taking an important role in working out the formal peace treaty with Britain. He became a leader of the New York Federalists during the late 1780s and chaired the state convention that ratified the new constitution. However, he quarreled with the new government (as chancellor he had sworn in

Robert Livingston (the Younger)

George Washington as the first U.S. president) and went over to the Republicans, allying himself with the Clinton family faction. He was named as minister to France by President Thomas Jefferson in 1801, and he helped negotiate the Louisiana Purchase. He retired from public life in 1804 and devoted his energies to agricultural experiments and the development with Robert Fulton of a practical steamboat—securing a monopoly for steam travel on the Hudson River in 1807. *Further reading:* George Dangerfield, *Chancellor Robert R. Livingston of New York, 1746–1813* (New York, 1960).

LIVINGSTON, Walter (1740–1797) Delegate to Congress, commissary Another of the New York Livingstons, the nephew of Philip, Walter was a judge of Albany County when he attended the New York revolutionary conventions in 1775. He became a commissary for stores and provisions in the same year, serving until he resigned in the fall of 1776. He was elected to the state assembly the following year and remained in that body until 1779. He was sent as a delegate to the Confederation Congress in 1784 and became commissioner of the U.S. treasury (of which barely any existed at the time) in 1785. He died in New York City.

LIVINGSTON, William (1723–1790) Delegate to Congress, militia general, governor The elder brother of Philip Livingston, the cousin of Robert R. and Henry Beekman Livingston, and the father of Henry Brockholst Livingston (not to mention becoming the father-in-law of John Jay), William was born in Albany, New York and raised by his maternal grandmother. He spent a year at age 14 as a missionary to the Mohawk Indians as a means to prepare him for a career as a fur trader or western land speculator. He graduated from Yale in 1741 and turned from business toward the law, studying in New York City with James Alexander, Lord Stirling's father, and William Smith. He was a close friend of John Morin Scott and William Smith Jr. while they were all young attorneys during the late 1740s and early 1750s. He opposed the Anglican establishment in New York and during the 1760s wrote several harsh essays and satires against the leading figures of the church and government, principally the De Lanceys. He was more radical in his revolutionary tendencies than most of his relatives and for a while he served as a bridge between their relatively patrician view of rebellion and the more violent factions in New York represented by the Sons of Liberty. Moving to Elizabethtown, New Jersey in 1772, he joined revolutionary committees and in 1774 was sent to the first Continental Congress as a delegate. He remained in Congress until June of 1776. He was also a brigadier general of

William Livingston

New Jersey militia, but he left military duties when elected governor of New Jersey in 1776, an office he held until his death.

LIVIUS, Peter (1729–1795) Loyalist jurist

Livius was born in England but moved to New Hampshire, where he practiced law, served on the Council, and was briefly chief justice of the colony. He was a contentious person and lodged charges against the governor of New Hampshire, which were dismissed by the British Board of Trade. Loyal to the crown, he moved to Quebec in 1777 and was appointed chief justice of Canada. He fell into a dispute there with Sir Guy Carleton, the governor general, who removed Livius from office temporarily.

LLOYD, Edward (1744–1796) Delegate to Congress, legislator

Lloyd lived in Talbot County, Maryland and served in local offices and in the legislature almost continuously from 1771 onward. He was one of the Talbot County Committee of Correspondence in 1774, and he also sat on the Maryland Executive Council after adoption of a state constitution. In 1781, Lloyd moved from the lower house to the state senate, remaining for 15 years, until 1796. During 1783 and 1784, he was also a delegate to the Confederation Congress.

LOCHRY, Archibald. Militia officer

Lochry was a colonel of Pennsylvania militia in August 1781 when he set forth with a company of about a hundred volunteers to join George Rogers Clark in Indiana. His advance party was captured by Joseph Brant, however, and Brant learned of Lochry's destination. Lochry and his men walked into an ambush on August 24 near the confluence of the Ohio and Big Miami rivers. Nearly the entire force was killed or captured. Lochry was taken prisoner and was killed later in the day.

LOCKE, Francis. Militia officer

Locke was a leader of back-country militia in North Carolina during the 1780–81 campaigns against the British after the fall of Charleston. In June 1780, he assembled 400 men near Mountain Creek and advanced on a loyalist force under Colonel John Moore. The ensuing disorganized but vicious battle near Ramsour's Mill was directed by Locke as best he could

under the circumstances. His men were not trained as soldiers and paused after their first flush of victory to loot (a common enough occurrence in militia engagements in the Carolinas). Locke barely managed to repulse a counterattack, but he ultimately drove Moore's men from the field with severe casualties.

LOCKE, Matthew (1730–1801) Legislator, militia official

Born in Ireland, Locke came to North Carolina around 1752 and settled near the town of Salisbury. He served intermittently in the North Carolina legislature before, during and after the Revolution, sitting for five terms in total. He was a member of his local committee of safety and represented Salisbury in the North Carolina provincial congresses of 1775 and 1776. His military service was as a paymaster (with the rank of brigadier) for the state militia during the war. In 1793, he was elected to the U.S. Congress as a representative from North Carolina.

LOGAN (c. 1725–c. 1780) Indian leader

Logan, also known as "Mingo" and "John Logan," was the son of a Cayuga woman and a Cayuga or French father, but he was raised by the Oneida. He was born in Pennsylvania and took the name he was known by among whites from James Logan, a Pennsylvania colonial official. Moving to the Ohio Valley around 1770, Logan was an ally of Cornstalk during Lord Dunmore's War, following the massacre of Logan's entire family by white settlers. He led raiding parties throughout the Appalachian region and refused to attend the peace conference with Dunmore. During the American Revolution, Logan supported the British with raids on American frontier settlements. He was killed in a quarrel with a nephew.

LONG, Pierse (1739–1789) Delegate to Congress, Continental officer

Born in Portsmouth, New Hampshire, Long was a shipping merchant, and during the Revolution, he served as an officer in the 1st New Hampshire Regiment (apparently as a colonel, although the regiment was commanded by others). He became a delegate to the Confederation Congress after the war in 1785 and attended the state convention that ratified the new federal constitution in the summer of 1788. He was appointed as customs collector for Portsmouth but was too ill to take his office and died soon thereafter.

LORING, Joshua, Jr. (1744–1789) Loyalist official
Born in Boston, the son of a wealthy former British naval officer and privateer, Loring lived in Dorchester, Massachusetts. He served in the British army, retiring as a lieutenant in 1768 with a land grant of 20,000 acres in New Hampshire. He held several lucrative offices before the Revolution, including the posts of permanent sheriff of Suffolk County and deputy surveyor of the King's Wood in North America. He married Elizabeth Lloyd of Boston in 1769. The couple sailed for Canada from Boston with the British evacuation fleet in 1776. After the British occupied New York, the Lorings moved to the city, where Elizabeth openly became the mistress of commander in chief General William Howe. The name of "Mrs. Loring" became notorious. Loring himself was appointed as British commissary of prisoners, a post calculated to produce a maximum profit from graft and corruption and doubtless a payoff from Howe. Within another year, Elizabeth left for England; Loring followed in 1782.

LOSSBERG, Friedrich Wilhelm von (born c. 1720) German mercenary officer
This von Lossberg is not to be confused with Major General H. A. von Lossberg, who commanded the Fusilier Regiment von Lossberg (Alt) also from Hesse-Cassel. Friedrich Wilhelm was a native of Thuringia who came to America as colonel in command of the Hessian Leib Infantry Regiment. He commanded a brigade at the taking of Newport, Rhode Island in 1776 and also during the defense of Newport two years later. In 1780, he took command of the Lossberg Regiment (Jung)—a confusing nomenclature, but a different regiment than the one mentioned above. When Baron von Knyphausen finally succeeded in getting permission to withdraw and return to Germany in 1782, Friedrich von Lossberg was appointed as the new commander in chief of German forces in America. The active war was in fact long over, and his duties were mainly to see to the safe return of the German troops to their home principalities.

LOTT, Abraham (1726–1794) Loyalist official
Lott was the royal treasurer of the colony of New York. During the Revolution, he maintained his

Louis XVI

office under the British occupation despite the claims of the rival patriot government. He was robbed by patriot partisans in 1781, when a raiding party took £600 and two black slaves from his house. He stayed in New York after the war.

LOUGHBOROUGH, Lord. See WEDDERBURN, Alexander.

LOUIS XVI (1754–1793) King of France
As a young monarch, Louis showed relative sympathy to the American cause between 1776 and 1778, when the French alliance was formally agreed to. He came to the throne in the first year of fighting in America, and although somewhat cautious, he allowed his minister Vergennes to authorize a large subsidy to the American rebels and acquiesced in the sending of supplies by Beaumarchais through Hortalez et Cie. Louis was by no means an uninformed or unintelligent monarch, but at first he was restrained by the influence of his more cautious ministers and by the need to preserve the interests of the Bourbon monarchy of his cousin in Spain. With the American victory at Saratoga, however, the chance for revenge appeared, and Louis agreed to the alliances of war and trade with the United States. He was apparently as charmed as other Frenchmen were by Benjamin Franklin. His own life ended, of course, on the scaffold in 1793—he was the last monarch of the ancien régime, a victim of the astounding events

of the French Revolution. *Further reading:* Eugene Lever, *Louis XVI* (Paris, 1985).

LOVELL, James (1737–1814) Delegate to Congress, teacher

Lovell, the son of John Lovell and father of James Lovell Jr., was born in Boston and trained at the South Grammar School (later renamed Boston Latin School), of which his father was head. He was a bright student and a good speaker, graduating from Harvard in 1756 and becoming a teacher at South Grammar. He spent a decade and a half uneventfully teaching languages and mathematics, until April 1771, when he was chosen to deliver the main oration at the anniversary memorial of the Boston Massacre. His public speech brought him sharply to the attention of the British, who kept an eye on him until 1776, when General William Howe evacuated Boston and Lovell was arrested as a spy and carted off to Halifax, Nova Scotia (where his loyalist father had previously fled). Lovell was released in the fall of 1776 and returned to a hero's welcome in Boston. He was immediately elected as a delegate to the Continental Congress.

As a congressman, Lovell was full of energy but was a gross intriguer. He fell under the spell of Horatio Gates (not the only congressman to do so) and became Gates's greatest supporter and by default Washington's harshest congressional critic. After the British victories at Saratoga, Lovell urged Gates to go over Washington's head and himself became deeply, although transparently, involved in the Conway Cabal aimed at removing Washington as commander in chief. Lovell also was the principal congressman assigned to deal with the horde of French officers who came seeking commissions and commands—he combined a fluid command of French with a strident dislike of the people—and he developed an extreme antipathy toward the French glory-seekers and Silas Deane and Benjamin Franklin, whom Lovell blamed for sending them to America. He was also virtually the only consistent member of the foreign relations committee and exerted an undue influence by simply staying on the job. Lovell apparently hoped to have Franklin ousted in favor of himself, although he had exhibited no diplomatic skills whatsoever. His intrigues came to naught, and in 1782, he resigned his seat in Congress and returned to Boston to become collector of continental taxes. He held public offices under the new federal constitution, principally as an officer of the port of Boston.

LOVELL, James, Jr. (1758–1850) Continental officer

Son of patriot congressman James Lovell and grandson of loyalist schoolmaster John Lovell, James Jr. graduated from Harvard during the second year of the war and joined the Continental Army in May 1777 as an ensign. He became adjutant of Henry Jackson's Massachusetts Regiment in 1779 and transferred to Light-Horse Harry Lee's battalion of light dragoons in 1780, serving in it as adjutant until the end of the conflict.

LOVELL, John (1710–1778) Loyalist educator

The senior Lovell graduated from Harvard in 1728 and became the headmaster of the South Grammar School (later Boston Latin) in 1734, holding the post for more than 40 years, until the school was dissolved by the British in April 1775 at the beginning of the Revolution. During the course of his pedagogical career, Lovell taught many students destined to become prominent Boston patriots, including Samuel Adams, John Hancock and Henry Knox. His own son, James, became a delegate to the Congress and his grandson, James Jr., a Continental officer. John, however, stayed loyal to the crown and evacuated from Boston to Halifax, Nova Scotia (where James, ironically, was a prisoner of the British) in 1776.

LOVELL, Solomon (d. 1801) Militia general

Lovell was a brigadier general of Massachusetts militia who shared command of the ill-conceived and disastrously executed expedition against the British base at Penobscot in July and August 1779. Lovell and Peleg Wadsworth set forth with the support of Continental Navy captain Dudley Saltonstall to seize a post that British colonel Francis McLean was building at Penobscot as a base for raiding and to protect the approaches to Nova Scotia. The American expedition was a fiasco, due largely to Lovell's dithering after reaching the point of attack. British reinforcements arrived before the Massachusetts men could get off the mark, and they were forced to abandon their ships and flee on foot across the wilderness. While several other officers (including Paul Revere) were court-martialed for the incident, Lovell was not only absolved but was praised by an embarrassed Massachusetts government that wanted to save face.

LOW, Isaac (1735–1791) Delegate to Congress, loyalist

Born in New Jersey, Low exemplified loyalists who went to the brink of rebellion, but pulled back at the last instant. He was a highly successful merchant and banker in New York in the years before the outbreak of revolutionary fervor. He was a delegate from New York to the Stamp Act Congress and a strong supporter of the nonimportation agreements, serving on a committee of inspection to enforce the embargo on trade with Britain. He was also a prominent member of the Committee of Fifty, set up to correspond with patriot groups in other colonies. In almost all of his public utterances, he defended the right of the American colonies to chart their own course, although he spoke against what he considered the illegal dumping of tea. In 1774, he was selected as one of the representatives of New York to the first Continental Congress. At home, he sat in the provincial congress and was president of the New York Chamber of Commerce. With the outbreak of violence in 1775, however, he reversed his position and abjured independence. He was arrested briefly in 1776 on charges of treason, and his property, valued at more than £14,000, was confiscated. He fled to the British in late 1776 and emigrated to England in 1783 when the Royal Army finally abandoned New York City.

LOWELL, John (1743–1802) Delegate to Congress, legislator, jurist

A native of Newburyport, Massachusetts, Lowell graduated from Harvard in 1760 and then studied law in the Boston office of Oxenbridge Thacher. He set up a practice in Newburyport and during the early 1770s, he served as a local selectman and represented his town in the provincial congresses. He moved to Boston in 1777 and was a member of the General Court and the state constitutional conventions. In 1782 and 1783, Lowell was sent as a delegate to the Confederation Congress, while also sitting as a judge of one of the special admiralty courts. Under the new federal constitution in 1789, he became a U.S. district judge for Massachusetts and eventually chief judge of the First U.S. Circuit.

LOWNDES, Rawlins (1721–1800) State official

Born in the West Indies, Lowndes was a prominent South Carolina officeholder before the Revolution. He was provost marshal of the colony, a member of the legislature (speaker of the lower chamber) and a justice of the court of common pleas. Despite his ties to the crown, he was an ardent patriot and was active as a member of the provincial congresses in South Carolina and served on the colony-wide committee of safety. Lowndes was named to the revolutionary legislative council in 1776 and acted as state president during the crucial years of 1778–79. After the war, he represented Charleston in the state senate.

LUDINGTON, Sybil (1761–1839) American heroine

Ludington's accomplishment was similar to that of William Dawes, who roused the countryside against the British advance toward Lexington and Concord. She lived in Fredericksberg, New York and was the daughter of a local militia officer. On April 26, 1777, when New York governor (and British general) William Tryon made his assault on the American post of Danbury, Connecticut, which lay south of Ludington's home, she volunteered to alert the militia of the countryside. She rode a 40-mile circuit during the night, sounding the alarm throughout Putnam County. Unfortunately, her exertions came to little, since Tryon brushed aside the American militia. She married a lawyer in 1784 and moved to Unadill, New York.

LUDLOW, Gabriel George (1736–1808) Loyalist

The younger brother of George Duncan Ludlow, Gabriel was a justice of the peace in Queens County, New York, before the Revolution and a colonel in the colonial militia. During the war, Ludlow served in De Lancey's Long Island Brigade of Loyal Americans, reaching the rank of colonel. He emigrated to New Brunswick following the British withdrawal from New York, and he served the crown in Canada as judge of the Vice-Admiralty Court, president of the Council and eventually as commander in chief of New Brunswick.

LUDLOW, George Duncan (1734–1808) Loyalist jurist

A native of New York, Ludlow was an apprentice apothecary in his youth before he turned to the study of law. Despite a speech defect, he made a success of his new profession, rising to be a judge of the New York Supreme Court by the time of the Revolution. During the American occupation of the city, Ludlow withdrew to Queens County, but he returned to assume office under the British after Washington's army was pushed out in 1776. He was appointed superintendent of police on Long Island and continued to serve as a jurist throughout the war. Ludlow sat for a time on the board of the Associated Loyalists, but he resigned in protest over the murder of Captain Joshua Huddy. He was nearly captured by American raiders in 1779 but escaped by hiding on the roof of his house. In 1783, he left for New Brunswick, where he lived the rest of his life, serving on the Council there and as chief justice of the Supreme Court.

LUDWICK, Christopher (1720–1801) Baker
Ludwick was born in Hesse and led an adventurous life before coming to America. He learned the trade of baking from his father, but during his youth he soldiered against the Turks and as a member of the army of the King of Prussia. He served aboard a British East Indiaman as a baker, lived briefly in London, and sailed again as a merchant seaman to the West Indies. He settled in Philadelphia in 1754 and established a prosperous baking business in the city, eventually accumulating considerable property. With the coming of the Revolution, he proved invaluable for both his professional skills and his Hessian background. In 1776, Ludwick crossed the British lines to Staten Island in the guise of a deserter and proselytized for America among the Hessian mercenary troops stationed there. He persuaded several hundred to defect. The following year, Ludwick was named as superintendent of baking for the Continental Army. He continued to prosper after the war, despite the loss of his home at Germantown to British depredations. Known throughout his life for private philanthropy, Ludwick left his estate to provide for the free education of children in Philadelphia.

LUZERNE, Anne-César de la (born c. 1743) French diplomat
Luzerne became the second French minister to the United States in 1779, succeeding Conrad Gerard. Although he spoke little or no English on his arrival, he charmed many members of Congress who held him in considerable esteem, and the importance to America of French support added to his position in Philadelphia. He exerted great influence on American affairs, espe-

cially in regard to the French military alliance. He left America in 1784 and returned to France.

LYNCH, Charles (1736–1796) Militia officer, official
The man whose name became synonymous with extra-legal mob punishments—"lynch law" derived from his actions as an informal judge, although he imposed no penalties worse than whipping—Lynch was born near the modern-day site of Lynchburg, Virginia. (The city was named for his brother.) Lynch's Irish father had come to the colony as an indentured servant but had married his Quaker master's daughter and prospered thereafter. The younger Lynch sat in the Virginia House of Burgesses before the Revolution and was active in organizing against the royal government and attended the Virginia state constitutional convention in 1776. In 1778, he was appointed as a colonel of Virginia militia and became leader of one of the most effective militia units of the war, a group of 200 Virginia riflemen most of whom were veterans of Continental service. He joined Nathanael Greene's army in the Carolinas in 1781, and the Virginia unit performed superbly at the battle of Guilford Courthouse, helping to anchor the right of the main battleline along with the Delaware regulars. Lynch and his men fought with Greene throughout the rest of the southern campaign. During 1779 and 1780, Lynch presided over back-country courts that, strictly speaking, had no legal basis. However, he had been a local justice of the peace and the war had so disarranged normal government that no formal courts could be constituted. He was apparently evenhanded in his decisions, which bore little relation to the sort of public violence that came to be associated with "lynching" in the 19th and 20th centuries.

LYNCH, Thomas, Sr. (1727–1776) Delegate to Congress, planter
Lynch, whose father had discovered how to cultivate rice in the alluvial flood plain of South Carolina, was born on his family's estate in Berkeley County and inherited large plantation holdings. He sat in the colonial assembly intermittently during the 1750s and 1760s and became an ardent patriot, representing South Carolina at the Stamp Act Congress. In 1774, he was selected as one of the colony's delegates to the first Continental Congress, and he returned as a delegate to the second Congress in 1775. Unfortunately, he

suffered a stroke in 1776 and was unable to continue his duties, despite the assistance of his son, Thomas Jr., who had been appointed as an extra delegate just to care for Thomas Sr. While traveling home in December 1776, Lynch died of a second stroke in Annapolis, Maryland.

LYNCH, Thomas, Jr. (1749–1779) Delegate to Congress, planter

A man plagued by misfortune, Lynch was the only child of Thomas Lynch Sr. He grew up and got his early education on his father's rice plantations in South Carolina but went to England in 1764 to attend Eton and Cambridge. He studied law in London but decided to become a planter on his return to his home colony in 1772. He married and settled on a plantation given to him by his father. He was drawn into the revolutionary activities in South Carolina and sat in the provincial congresses and the first state assembly. In 1775, he volunteered as a captain in the 1st South Carolina Regiment, although his father, by then a delegate to the Continental Congress, hoped to secure a higher rank for his son. On a recruiting trip, Lynch contracted a fever that debilitated him for the rest of his short life. Early the following year, his father suffered a stroke while in Philadelphia, and Thomas Jr. was appointed as an extra delegate to Congress in order to act as his father's aide. He was present for the adoption of the Declaration of Independence and signed the document in August—one of the youngest delegates to do so. In December, he started home with his ailing father, but the elder Lynch died on the way at Annapolis. Thomas Jr. never recovered his health, and was lost at sea with his wife while headed for southern France in 1779.

LYON, Matthew (1750–1822) Soldier, official

The peripatetic Lyons was born in Ireland and moved to New Hampshire as a teenager. He lived in the Vermont section of the colony and participated in the agitation to have the region declared a separate entity, a tug of loyalties that afflicted many from the New Hampshire Grants. He was part of the Green Mountain Boys militia and served both in the capture of Fort Ticonderoga and Seth Warner's expedition to Canada in 1775. The following year, Lyon was paymaster for the Vermont militia. He settled in Arlington, Vermont in 1777. From 1779 to 1796—the long period of ferment in the region—he was a representative to the Vermont House of Representatives. He became a relatively successful businessman at the same time, building several lumber mills and starting a newspaper in Fair Haven, a town he founded. In 1797, Lyon was elected to the U.S. House as a representative of Vermont, and he served two consecutive terms. At the end of his congressional stint, Lyon moved to Kentucky and was elected to the U.S. House again from his new state, after first serving in the Kentucky legislature. In 1820, at the age of 70, he moved again, this time to the Arkansas frontier, where he was appointed as the official trader to the Cherokees. He died and was buried in Sparda Bluff, Arkansas Territory, but in 1823, his body was removed to Eddyville, Kentucky.

M

McALLISTER, Archibald (d. 1781) Continental officer First commissioned as a lieutenant in the Maryland battalion of the Flying Camp strategic reserve in 1776, McAllister served as a junior officer in several Maryland regiments until 1779. On August 19 of that year, he led one of the advance parties in the American assault on the British fortification at Paulus Hook, New Jersey, swarming through the defenses at the head of a virtual suicide squad and entering the stronghold first. He was brevetted to captain's rank for his daring deed.

McARTHUR, Archibald. British officer Probably of Scots origin, McArthur was a captain in the 54th Regiment of Foot before the American war and was appointed as major of the new 71st Fraser Highlanders when the unit was formed in 1777. He was captured in the British defeat at Cowpens in 1781 but was exchanged and made lieutenant colonel of the 60th (Royal American) Regiment.

McCLENACHAN, Blair (d. 1812) Businessman, legislator McClenachan was a native Irishman who established a successful business career in Philadelphia before the Revolution as a banker, shipper and merchant. He was one of the founders of the famous Philadelphia City Cavalry, a well-equipped and active company of cavalry drawn from well-to-do Philadelphians. The cavalry performed well during the war, serving mainly as a reconnaissance and courier detachment (members often carried dispatches for Congress) and in the field during Washington's New Jersey campaign of 1777. It was funded entirely by its own members and did not draw on Congress for supplies or money. McClenachan himself contributed significant amounts to aid the American cause and often extended credit to Congress in 1780 at a time when the central government was virtually broke. After the Revolution, he sat in the Pennsylvania House of Representatives, and in 1797, he was one of the state's representatives to the U.S. Congress.

McCLENE, James (1730–1806) Delegate to Congress McClene was born in New London, Pennsylvania and moved to frontier Cumberland County when he was 24. He served in the Pennsylvania constitutional convention in 1776 and took a seat in the state house of representatives the same year. During 1778 and 1779, he was a member of the ruling Pennsylvania Supreme Executive Council. In 1779 and 1780, McClene represented Pennsylvania in the Continental Congress, and he served intermittently in the state legislature after the war.

McCOMB, Eleazer (d. 1798) Delegate to Congress, state official, businessman There is no record of McComb's birth or early life, but he appears in 1779 as an appointee to the Delaware Privy Council, having served previously as a captain in the Delaware militia, probably from Dover, where he lived. He was sent to the Confederation Congress as a delegate in 1783 and 1784. In 1787, he was auditor of accounts in Delaware, and he moved to Wilmington in 1792 while still holding that office. He turned to private business thereafter, running a commercial shipping company and becoming in 1795 a director of the Bank of Delaware.

McCREA, Jane (c. 1754–1777) Loyalist

McCrea, although a loyalist, became the focus of an American propaganda campaign after her death at the hands of General John Burgoyne's Indian auxiliaries in July 1777. The certain facts of her background and death are obscured by legend, myth and conflicting contemporary accounts, but she was probably born in New Jersey to the family of a parson. By the time of Burgoyne's invasion from Canada in 1777, McCrea lived with her brother in the Hudson River region between Saratoga and Fort Edward. She was engaged to Lieutenant David Jones, a loyalist officer serving with Burgoyne. In July, McCrea left her brother (who may have moved to Albany ahead of the British) and joined Mrs. Sarah Fraser McNeil, a distant relative of British general Simon Fraser, at the nearly abandoned Fort Edward. The two women were captured by a band of Indians scouting ahead of Burgoyne's main force. Apparently the group headed toward Burgoyne's headquarters with the two women as captives, perhaps intent on turning them in for a reward. At some point along the journey, McCrea was killed and scalped. Her captors hid the body in a ravine and continued on to the British camp. (Some accounts claim McCrea died from wounds suffered when the fleeing party was fired on by American pursuers.)

The young woman's distinctive blond scalp was recognized at the camp by her fiancé, but Burgoyne refused to take any action against the Indians—a Wyandotte named Panther was judged to be the murderer—for fear of alienating the Indian auxiliaries he needed for his invasion. When American general Horatio Gates, newly appointed to command of the army opposing Burgoyne, learned of McCrea's death, he issued a strong personal condemnation of Burgoyne's lack of action and used the incident to stimulate fears of Indian warfare and to help rally militia to the American cause. American propagandists at the time and since have pointed to Jane McCrea as a typical victim of Indian brutality and British indifference. *Further reading:* James Hol-

den, "The Influence of the Death of Jane McCrea on the Burgoyne Campaign," New York State Historical Association *Proceedings* 12 (1913), 249–310.

McDONALD, Allan or Alexander. Loyalist officer

McDonald, the husband of the celebrated Jacobite heroine Flora McDonald, emigrated with his wife to North Carolina in 1771. As with most of the Highlanders who lived in the colony, he was more attracted to the Hanoverian crown than to the rebel cause. He accepted a commission from the British and was one of the leaders under Donald McDonald of the Highland loyalists who virtually reenacted the military futility of the Scots' battle of Culloden at Moore's Creek Bridge, North Carolina in February 1776. He was captured at the defeat and held in Virginia. He eventually joined his wife in re-emigrating to the British Isles, where he received half pay for his role in the Revolution.

McDONALD, Donald (b. 1712) Loyalist officer

A veteran of the Jacobite rebellion and the battle of Culloden 30 years before the American Revolution, McDonald had settled in North Carolina near Cross Creek with several hundred other Scots Highlanders and their families. They had no love for the Crown of Hanover, but they loved their Ulster and Lowland Scot neighbors in America even less, so when royal governor Josiah Martin called for a rising of loyalists in conjunction with Sir Henry Clinton's 1776 expedition against Charleston, McDonald raised a force of his fellow Highlanders and prepared to challenge the patriots. Bedecked with kilts, claymores, bagpipes and all the regalia of their homeland, the Highlanders confronted a strong patriot force at Moore's Creek Bridge in February 1776. McDonald himself was ill and not on the field when the Highlanders launched a completely futile (albeit brave) attack. The patriots nearly wiped out McDonald's men, and he was captured. He was held in Philadelphia until exchanged and returned to England.

McDONALD, Flora (1722–1790) Loyalist

She was one of the great heroines of the Jacobite Highlanders for her exploit as a young woman when, after the battle of Culloden in 1746, she helped Bonnie Prince Charlie escape to the Isle of Skye disguised as her maid. She was thrown in the Tower of London for her effort but was released when she told George II she would have done no less for him. She married Allan (or Alexander) McDonald and moved to North Carolina in 1771, joining a large contingent of emigrant Highlanders in the back country of that colony. She and her husband chose the British side, and after the defeat of the loyalist Highlanders at Moore's Creek Bridge and the capture of her husband, she returned to Great Britain. She is buried on the Isle of Skye and is still remembered by die-hard Jacobites.

McDOUGALL, Alexander (1732–1786) Continental general, delegate to Congress

McDougall was born at Islay in the Inner Hebrides and was brought to New York as a child. By his early twenties he was a privateer, sailing against the French during the Seven Years' War. He then became a storekeeper and merchant in New York City. He was vigorous—to say the least—in his opposition to the British economic measures against the colonies during the 1760s, and he became one of the leaders of radical opposition. He was arrested in 1770 and accused of libel for anonymously writing a fiery pamphlet called *A Son of Liberty to the Betrayed Inhabitants of the City and Colony of New York.* The chief witness against McDougall—the pamphlet's printer—died before the case came to trial, but McDougall was kept in jail on contempt charges for more than a year. He put himself at the head of protests during 1774 and 1775.

After the actual coming of the war, McDougall was commissioned as colonel of the 1st New York Regiment in June 1776 and fought during the New York campaign and at Germantown the following year. Promoted to major general in the fall of 1777, he spent most of the rest of the war as commander in the Hudson Highlands, the vital area that the Americans had to retain to keep from losing all control over the war in the upper colonies. He replaced Benedict Arnold as commander of West Point on the latter's defection in 1780. In 1781 and 1782 McDougall represented New York as a delegate to Congress, but afterward he returned to active army duty, only to stand court-martial for insubordination to General William Heath. He was acquitted and continued to serve until the dissolution of the Continental Army in 1783. He later served in the state senate and again as a congressional delegate from New York in 1784 and 1785.

Before his death, McDougall helped organize the Bank of New York.

McDOWELL, Joseph (1756–1801) Militia officer, state official

McDowell was born on his family's estate, Quaker Meadows, in Burke County, North Carolina. He served in his brother's militia regiment in 1776 on an expedition against the Cherokee and fought at Ramsour's Mill and Musgrove's Mill in 1780. He was apparently in command of his brother's militia in October 1780 as a major and brought a considerable force to join the over-mountain men at the battle of King's Mountain. He was also present with several hundred mounted militia at the battle of the Cowpens the following January. After the Revolution, McDowell served in the North Carolina house and senate, and he was elected to the U.S. House of Representatives for a term from 1797 to 1799. He was known to contemporaries as "Quaker Meadows Joe" to distinguish him from a cousin.

McGILLIVRAY, Alexander (1759–1793) Indian leader

McGillivray was a leader of one of the large Creek tribal factions and was involved in the American Revolution. He was born in what is today Alabama at the trading post of his father, Lachlan McGillivray, a Scots trader. His mother was of mixed French and Creek origin. McGillivray received a good education in Charleston, South Carolina, where he studied with the Reverend Farquhar McGillivray (a relative), and in Savannah. When the Revolutionary War began, McGillivray's father returned to the British Isles, bequeathing to his son lands in Georgia. The younger man was already a leader among the Creek. The patriot government of Georgia confiscated his property, in part because the elder McGillivray was considered a loyalist, and this helped drive the young chief into the arms of the British. He was commissioned a colonel and organized and led forays against American frontier settlements. Following the war, McGillivray signed a treaty with the Spanish and accepted a colonel's commission from them. In 1784, however, the state of Georgia agreed to pay him reparations for his confiscated land, and McGillivray began to incline toward an alliance with the new American nation. He signed a treaty in 1790 by which the Creeks' claims to generous land boundaries were recognized. In return, he was awarded a secret commission in the

U.S. Army as a brigadier general and paid an annuity of $1200.

McHENRY, James (1753–1816) Continental officer, army surgeon, delegate to Congress, government official

McHenry was born in County Antrim, Ireland and emigrated to Philadelphia as a teenager, apparently having attended Dublin University. He studied further at the Newark Academy and then joined his brother in the importing business in Baltimore. He meanwhile also studied medicine under Benjamin Rush and was a qualified surgeon by the beginning of the Revolution. He volunteered his services to the army at Boston in 1775 and in January of the following year, he was named to the medical staff of the military hospital at Cambridge, benefiting no doubt from his connection to Rush, who held much political sway in medical affairs. In August 1776, McHenry was appointed as surgeon of the 5th Pennsylvania. Unfortunately, McHenry was at Fort Washington, New York when the entire garrison fell to the British in November 1776. He was paroled in a matter of months but was not exchanged until March 1778.

He abandoned medicine in May of that year when he became secretary to commander in chief George Washington, whom he served until 1780, when he transferred to the personal staff of the Marquis de Lafayette. McHenry received a commission as a major in the Continental Army in 1781, having been technically a civilian until then. In the same year, he was elected to the Maryland state senate, and in 1783 he was sent as a delegate to the Confederation Congress, holding his seat until 1786. He supported the proposed federal constitution and was a delegate to the Philadelphia convention. In 1796, Washington named McHenry as U.S. secretary of war (replacing Timothy Pickering), and he carried over into the administration of John Adams. However, McHenry was a supporter of Alexander Hamilton and a member of the group of cabinet members who turned against Adams. He was asked to resign by the new president in 1800, and he returned to his businesses in Baltimore. Fort McHenry in Baltimore harbor, the inspiration for the writing of "The Star-Spangled Banner" during the War of 1812, was named for McHenry while he was secretary of war. *Further reading:* Bernard C. Steiner, *The Life and Correspondence of James McHenry, Secretary of War under Washington and Adams* (Cleveland, 1907).

McINTOSH, John (1755–1826) Continental officer

Born in Georgia, McIntosh served during the Revolution in his native state and in the Carolinas campaigns. He was the nephew of American general Lachlan McIntosh, and when his uncle took command of the 1st Georgia in January 1776, the younger McIntosh received an appointment as a captain, although the regiment never raised the required men and really never functioned as a unit of the Continental Army. In April 1778, he was named as lieutenant colonel of the 3rd Georgia, but this unit also never really functioned due to failure to recruit enough men. Both of McIntosh's major appointments existed, therefore, only on paper. He did fight, however, at the defense of Fort Morris at Sunbury, Georgia in 1778, refusing to surrender to a British demand. He was captured at Briar Creek in 1779 and exchanged a year later. He moved to the Floridas after the war and was embroiled in trouble with the Spanish, being arrested and held for a year in Havana. During the War of 1812, McIntosh saw duty as a militia officer.

McINTOSH, Lachlan (1725–1806) Continental general

McIntosh was a figure of some controversy during the Revolution. He was born in Scotland and came to America with his parents as a boy, settling in the new colony of Georgia as part of a group of immigrant Highlanders. In 1748, McIntosh moved to Charleston, South Carolina, and he apparently worked in Henry Laurens' counting house. When the Georgia Provincial Congress convened in Savannah in July 1775 in a timid movement toward rebellion, McIntosh was a delegate from St. Andrew's Parish. He was commissioned in January 1776 as a colonel of the 1st Georgia Battalion, which was to be raised in the colony as part of the Continental Army. McIntosh was never able to recruit many men, however, and turned over command to Joseph Habersham in September with only a handful of troops on the active roll. McIntosh himself was immediately awarded a commission as brigadier general by the Continental Congress, nosing out Georgia's delegate to Congress, Button Gwinnett, for the honor and exacerbating a political and personal conflict between McIntosh and Gwinnett that came to a head in May

Lachlan McIntosh

1777 with a duel. Both men were wounded, but Gwinnett died while McIntosh recovered. He was more or less spirited away from the South before Gwinnett's political allies could take revenge and was sent north to join the main Continental Army at Valley Forge.

In the spring of 1778, McIntosh was appointed to command the Western Department, but he did poorly—failing to engage any Indians on the frontier—and was relieved in March 1779. Sent again to the South, in May McIntosh commanded South Carolina troops in the French-American attempt to retake Savannah from the British. His performance was apparently better than during his previous commands, and he gave good if ignored advice to attack sooner rather than later. He then joined Benjamin Lincoln's army in Charleston and was captured when Clinton took the city in May 1780. While a prisoner, McIntosh was suspended from rank by Congress at the insistence of his political enemies, principally Georgia delegate George Walton, but Congress reversed itself in July 1781 and not only restored McIntosh but brevetted him to the rank of major general. McIntosh was paroled by the British in February 1782 and returned to Georgia a year later. *Further reading:* Harvey H. Jackson, *Lachlan McIntosh and the Politics of Revolutionary Georgia* (Athens, Ga., 1979).

McKEAN, Thomas (1734–1817) Delegate to Congress, official

McKean may have been the champion officeholder of the Revolutionary period, occupying major positions in two states and the

national government concurrently. He was born in Pennsylvania, the son of a farmer and tavern keeper in Chester County. His roots near the intersection of Delaware, Pennsylvania and New Jersey were reflected in his subsequent career, during which he seemed to be a resident of several places at once. He had his early education in Pennsylvania but went to New Castle, Delaware to read law and work as a law clerk until he was admitted to the bar in 1755. In 1758, he spent a year in London, studying at the Middle Temple. His subsequent law practice covered portions of all three states. McKean's first public services were confined to Delaware, where he served in many local and colony-wide capacities, mostly having to do with legal matters, as well as sitting in the colonial assembly from 1762 until 1772. He was associated with Caesar Rodney, with whom he revised the laws of Delaware in 1762. He cemented his New Jersey relationships the following year when he married Mary Borden, making him the son-in-law of Joseph Borden of Bordentown and the brother-in-law of Francis Hopkinson (McKean remarried in 1774 after Mary's death).

McKean was a vociferous patriot from early in the rebellion. He was outraged by the Stamp Act and took a leading role in opposing it in the Stamp Act Congress and as a local legal official. He moved to Philadelphia in 1774 but continued to sit in the Delaware legislature, and he was selected as a delegate to the first Continental Congress from Delaware in 1774. He represented Delaware in Philadelphia until he was turned out by a conservative faction in late 1776, and he played an important role in passing the Declaration of Independence in the summer of 1776. McKean and George Read were the only two Delaware delegates in Philadelphia during the debate on independence, since Caesar Rodney had returned to Dover. When he and Read split on the issue, McKean dispatched an urgent message to Rodney, who subsequently made his famous dash to Philadelphia in time to help swing the vote. McKean belatedly signed the Declaration in January 1777, many months after most signers had affixed their names and at a time when he was technically no longer a delegate.

From late 1776 until 1778, McKean returned to his seat in the Delaware legislature, becoming speaker, and when the British invaded, he was briefly the president of the state although he was on the run from capture much of the time during the three months in 1777 when he was chief executive. During the same period, he was appointed a justice of the Pennsylvania Superior Court, and he held that office simultaneously with his posts in Delaware (in fact, he remained a Pennsylvania judge until 1799). In January 1778, he relinquished the office of president of Delaware but was reelected as one of Delaware's delegates to Congress. He represented Delaware until 1783, and he was briefly president of the Congress—technically chief executive of the United States—in 1781.

After the conclusion of the peace, McKean shifted most of his focus to Pennsylvania. He was initially a strong Federalist and supported the new constitution in the state convention of 1789; however, he switched to the Jeffersonians in the late 1790s and was elected governor of Pennsylvania in 1799 as a member of the new "party." His nine-year tenure as governor was stormy, and he was nearly impeached before retiring from office in 1808. *Further reading:* John M. Coleman, *Thomas McKean: Forgotten Leader of the Revolution* (Rockaway, N.J., 1975); G. S. Rowe, *Thomas McKean: The Shaping of an American Republicanism* (Boulder, Colo., 1978).

MACKENZIE, Frederick (d. 1824) British officer

Mackenzie was born in Ireland, the son of a Huguenot family that had fled France for Ireland after the revocation of the Edict of Nantes. His father was a merchant in Dublin. Mackenzie became an officer of the Royal Welch Fusiliers in 1745 and came to Boston in the early 1770s as part of the prewar British garrison. In 1774, he was promoted to captain and served as adjutant of his regiment. On the night of April 18, 1775, Mackenzie was assigned as part of the British force ordered to march to Lexington and Concord. His diary description of the subsequent retreat from Concord is almost the only detailed account from the British side and has been an essential source for historians ever since. Mackenzie missed the actual engagements in the two villages, but he recounted in his diary the harassing attacks of the American militia during the costly British withdrawal toward Boston during April 19. As he wrote: ". . . numbers of armed men on foot and on horseback, were continually coming from all parts guided by the fire, and before the column had advanced a mile on the road, we were fired at from all quarters, but particularly from the houses on the roadside, and the adjacent stone walls."

Mackenzie served for a period in Halifax, Nova Scotia during 1776 and then moved to British-held New York City as an adjutant. He was promoted to major in 1780 and eventually reached the rank of lieutenant colonel of the 37th Regiment of Foot after the war. On returning to Great Britain, Mackenzie retired from active field duty but trained volunteers during the Napoleonic Wars and was an assistant barracks-master general at army headquarters as well as secretary of the Royal Military College. His diary was published in the 20th century. *Further reading:* Allen French, ed., *The British Fusilier in Revolutionary Boston: Being the Diary of Lieutenant Frederick Mackenzie . . .* (Cambridge, Mass., 1926).

McKINLY, John (1721–1796) State official

McKinly was born in northern Ireland and trained as a physician. He emigrated to Wilmington, Delaware as a young man and not only established a successful medical practice but took a prominent hand in public affairs as a local official, serving as sheriff and chief burgess for Wilmington between 1759 and 1776. In the early 1770s, as the agitation against Britain grew, McKinly was appointed to the Delaware Committee of Correspondence and was a leader of pro-patriot forces. He was appointed as president and commander in chief of Delaware in February 1777, making him chief executive of the state. Unfortunately, his office also made him the object of a British expedition against Wilmington in September 1777, when after their victory at nearby Brandywine the British sent a force to take Wilmington and seize McKinly. He was captured and hauled off to Philadelphia and thence to New York City when Sir Henry Clinton retreated from Pennsylvania in the summer of 1778. McKinly was released on parole in August but could not return to duty until formally exchanged. He went immediately to Philadelphia, where he won the agreement of Congress to exchange himself for loyalist New Jersey governor William Franklin. McKinly returned to Wilmington after the exchange in September 1778 and retired from public life to resume his medical practice.

McLANE, Allan (1746–1829) Continental officer

One of the more dashing Continental officers, McLane won a deservedly high reputation as the leader of small mobile units at many engagements during the war. He was born in Philadelphia of obscure background but apparently was well-to-do, since he had ample funds to invest in raising and equipping troops when the war began. McLane had probably inherited property in about 1774 before settling in Kent County, Delaware.

His first revolutionary service was in Virginia in 1775, where he fought against the attempts of Lord Dunmore to take over the colony, seeing action at Great Bridge in December and at Norfolk in January 1776. On returning to Delaware, McLane joined Caesar Rodney's militia regiment and went north to fight with the main American army during the New York campaign. He was singled out for notice after the battle of Long Island in August 1776, when he captured a Hessian patrol, and after White Plains in October. By the end of the year, he had come to command a small but effective unit of mounted infantry that was entered on the rolls of the Continental Army as McLane's Troop with himself as captain. The troop fought at Trenton in December and was especially conspicuous at the battle of Princeton the following month. McLane's troop was taken into the regiment of Colonel John Patton in early 1777.

While the Continental Army was in quarters at Valley Forge during the winter of 1777–1778, McLane roamed widely to harass British supply efforts and to scout for commander in chief George Washington. He discovered a British plan to march against Washington in December and alerted headquarters in time to make a defensive disposition at White Marsh, where a brief fight dissuaded the British. McLane roamed as far as the eastern shore of Maryland and the Delaware-Maryland Peninsula to bring in supplies for Washington's army during the winter. In May 1778, McLane's scouts discovered the British move against the Marquis de Lafayette in time to alert the Frenchman and prevent a surprise attack. After fighting at the battle of Monmouth, McLane continued to scout for Washington until December, when his troop was made part of the Delaware Continentals. In July 1779, McLane's unit—by now serving dismounted as light infantry—was incorporated into the new Legion of Light-Horse Harry Lee.

McLane and his men figured prominently in two of the more daring and successful American raids of the war, at the retaking of Stony Point in July 1779 and at Lee's attack on Paulus Hook the following month. McLane and Lee, however, did not get

on, and McLane was detached and sent south to join Benjamin Lincoln in Charleston. Fortunately for McLane, he arrived too late to be captured when the city fell to Sir Henry Clinton in May 1780. In June 1781, McLane was sent personally from Philadelphia to the West Indies with a request to French admiral de Grasse to bring the French fleet to the Chesapeake in order to hem in Lord Cornwallis at Yorktown. During the Yorktown campaign, however, McLane was in New York, scouting the movements of the main British force in New York City.

He left the army in late 1781 and turned to business in association with Robert Morris in Philadelphia. By the late 1790s, McLane was back in Delaware and serving as collector of the port of Wilmington. During the War of 1812, he commanded the defenses of the city and was a vocal critic of the military bumbling that led to the British capture of Washington, D.C. *Further reading:* Fred J. Cook, "Allan McLane: Unknown Hero of the Revolution," *American Heritage* 7 (October 1956), 74–77.

McLEAN, Allan (c. 1725–1784) British officer

The source of considerable confusion due to the commonness of his name, McLean was a Scot who had fought with the Highland Brigade in the service of Holland and as a captain of the British 60th Regiment during Wolfe's campaign in Canada in 1759. He was probably wounded during the later stages of the war against France in North America. When the American Revolution began, he was in Canada and held the rank of lieutenant colonel. In 1775, McLean helped to raise a unit in Canada from among veterans of disbanded Highland regiments. The unit became the 84th Regiment of Foot, known as the Royal Highland Emigrants, and McLean commanded the first battalion, probably with the rank of colonel. The regiment was not taken onto the regular establishment of the Royal Army until January 1779, but meanwhile, McLean had led elements of the Royal Emigrants effectively in the defense of Canada in late 1775. The second battalion of the regiment was sent to the southern theater in April 1781 and took part in the capture of Charleston and the battle of Eutaw Springs, but McLean remained in the north with the first battalion (he is often mistakenly placed in the southern theater) and was probably posted at Niagara during most of 1781.

McLEAN, Francis. British officer A veteran of the Seven Years' War, McLean was lieutenant colonel of the 97th Regiment of Foot at the beginning of the Revolution. In 1778, a new infantry regiment, the 82nd, was raised in Lanarkshire, and McLean received command with the rank of colonel. He was commandant of British forces in Nova Scotia in 1779 (holding the local rank of brigadier general) and sent out the expedition to Penobscot, Massachusetts in July. McLean was superseded in command of the 82nd in 1781 and disappeared from the army list.

MACON, Nathaniel (1758–1837) Soldier, legislator A young man during the Revolution, Macon went on to become one of the nation's most prominent legislators of the first part of the 19th century. He was born in North Carolina, but he served during the first two years of the war in the New Jersey militia. He returned to his home state in 1777 and joined the local militia briefly in 1780 when he fought as a private at the disastrous battle of Camden (the North Carolina militia generally disgraced itself during the battle). Macon's postwar career was considerably more distinguished. He sat in the North Carolina legislature during the 1780s, and in 1791, he was elected to the U.S. House of Representatives, where he remained for 24 years, serving as speaker from 1801 to 1807 and as chairman of the important foreign relations committee. Macon moved to the U.S. Senate in 1815 and served there for 13 more years, including two years as president pro tem.

MADISON, James (1751–1836) Delegate to Congress, state official, president Although Madison's major role in national affairs came after the Revolution itself, he was active in state affairs during the early years of the conflict and moved onto the national stage in the later months before the end of the war.

Born at Port Conway, Virginia, he came from an old landed Virginia family and graduated from the College of New Jersey (Princeton) in 1771. He became a member of his local committee of safety in 1775 and was elected to the Virginia convention the following year. He helped draft the Virginia state constitution and became a member of the first state assembly, although he was not reelected for a second term. He did serve, however, on the governor's

James Madison

council. He was elected as a delegate to Congress in 1779. During his three years in Congress he took an active role in shaping the terms of American diplomacy and working out a compromise between the states over western land claims (one of the major stumbling blocks to national unity after the war) and the formula for counting slaves for purposes of political representation. He is most famous, perhaps, for writing many of the *Federalist* papers in support of ratification of the proposed constitution, and his arguments and phrases entered the basic vocabulary of the American political system. He later served as secretary of state under President Thomas Jefferson, and he became president himself in 1809. His two terms in office were marred by the War of 1812, and he retired to private life at the end of his second term in 1817. *Further reading:* Robert Rutland, *James Madison: The Founding Father* (New York, 1987).

MADUIT DU PLESSIS, Chevalier de. See PLESSIS, Thomas-Antoine, Chevalier de Maduit du.

MAGAW, Robert (d. 1789) Continental officer The Continental Congress decided in December 1775 to raise four more regiments from Pennsylvania for service in the Continental Army and the following month named the field officers. Magaw was made colonel of the 5th Pennsylvania. At the end of 1776 he was in command of the American garrison at Fort Washington, which was the principal American stronghold on the tip of Manhattan. He had about

1,200 men, comprising his own regiment as well as the 3rd Pennsylvania, to defend a poorly designed fortress that looked more formidable than it actually was. Magaw thought he could hold the place against a British attack, but in fact there were fatal flaws in the construction of the fort that allowed it to be taken by a determined assault. In addition, Magaw's adjutant, William Demont, defected to the British and provided them with complete plans of the fort. Even though he was reinforced by 1,700 more troops shortly before the British assault, Magaw was in a hopeless situation. Commander in chief George Washington, along with his best generals, thought Fort Washington safe, and he was in the middle of inspecting it when the British and their German mercenaries launched a strong attack on November 15. Spearheaded by the Germans, the assault swept up to the fort, and defeat was at hand. Magaw surrendered by mid-afternoon. Shortly after this debacle, Magaw's regiment (most of which had been captured and hauled off to savage confinement in New York City) was reorganized as the 6th Regiment, again with Magaw as colonel in command. He continued at its head until January 1781, when the regiment was disbanded.

MAHAM, Hezekiah (1739–1789) Militia officer

Maham devised a crude but effective siege machine used by American forces during the Carolina fighting in 1780 and 1781. He was born in South Carolina and sat in the first South Carolina Provincial Congress. In 1776, he joined Isaac Huger's rifle regiment, fighting through the spring of 1779. He then organized his own independent militia dragoon regiment, holding the rank of colonel of South Carolina militia. While not officially part of Francis Marion's militia brigade, Maham apparently often fought in conjunction with Marion. He achieved most notoriety during the siege of the British-loyalist stronghold at Fort Watson, South Carolina in April 1781. Marion and Henry Lee had invested a strong loyalist force inside a high-walled stockade but lacking artillery could not compel the defenders to surrender. Maham suggested building a hollow, rectangular tower of logs with firing platforms near the top. The device was constructed on the spot and wheeled into place, and it gave American riflemen the vantage point needed to defeat the defenders. The idea was used several times thereafter during the Carolina fighting. Maham

himself was captured at his home in August 1782 while on sick leave and later was paroled.

MAITLAND, John (d. 1779) British officer

The son of the Earl of Lauderdale, Maitland served in the Royal Marines and sat in Parliament before the American Revolution. In 1778, he was appointed lieutenant colonel in command of a battalion of the 71st Highlanders. He led his men in the capture of Savannah in 1778 and at Stono Ferry in 1779. He made a forced march to reinforce the British garrison at Savannah in 1779 but contracted malaria and died shortly after arriving.

MALMÉDY, Francis, Marquis de. French volunteer

Malmédy illustrated the hauteur of many of the young noble French junior officers who came to America seeking glory and rank, although, unlike most, his ambition did not go unrebuked. He had been a mere second lieutenant of cavalry when he arrived in America in 1775. He received a brevet commission as major in the Continental Army within a few months and managed to snag a commission from Rhode Island as a brigadier of state troops. His state commission expired in May 1777, and he was then commissioned as a colonel in the Continental Army. He wrote to commander in chief George Washington that this rank was beneath his dignity and former status as a general. Washington, by this stage very exasperated by the whining of the French volunteers, offered a nasty reply, pointing out that Malmédy had been only a lieutenant before reaching American shores and that his general's rank was only a state commission and concluding that the young Frenchman should be more than happy to find himself a colonel. Malmédy served during 1780 as the commander of a light infantry company and in 1781 was in charge of the North Carolina militia at the battle of Eutaw Springs.

MALMESBURY, Baron. See HARRIS, James.

MANLEY, John (c. 1734–1793) Continental naval officer, privateer

Native to Boston, Manley sailed during the years before the Revolution as a merchant on the trade route between the West Indies and New England. In 1775, Continental commander in chief George Washington cast about for some way to slow the flow of seaborne supplies to the British garrison in Boston and decided to commission an ad hoc "navy" of small raiders. Washington selected Manley as one of the captains and appointed him to an army commission and outfitted him with the armed schooner *Lee*. Sailing from Plymouth in November, Manley made the first important American capture of the war when he took the brigantine *Nancy* out from under the nose of the British. The prize was laden with military stores that Washington's army could put to good use. Manley's success continued through the end of the year as he took several more small prizes. He was named commander of Washington's navy in January 1776. In April, when the Continental Congress established an official Continental navy, Manley was named as one of the original captains and given the 32-gun frigate *Hancock*, which was still under construction. He sailed as commander of a small fleet (*Hancock*, the frigate *Boston* and a flotilla of privateers) in May. After initial success, Manley was captured off Halifax and sent to a British prison ship in New York Harbor. He was exchanged in March 1778 and cleared of responsibility for losing his command; however, the Continental Navy had dwindled by this time and no ship was available, so Manley turned to privateering. After a profitable voyage on the *Marlborough* in 1778, Manley was captured aboard the *Cumberland* near Barbados in 1779. He escaped but was captured again and sent to confinement in Old Mill Prison in England. Exchanged after two years, Manley was given command of the *Hague*, one of the few ships remaining to the American cause, and he captured the *Baille* in January 1783, making him the first and last American captain to officially take a prize from the British during the Revolution. He retired to Boston after the war.

MANNING, James (1735–1791) Delegate to Congress, clergyman, educator

Born in Elizabethtown, New Jersey, Manning graduated from the College of New Jersey (since renamed Princeton) in 1762, second in his class. He was ordained as a Baptist preacher the following year. In 1764, he moved to Warren, Rhode Island and opened a Latin school as well as taking the pulpit of a local Baptist church. Along with others of his denomination, Manning succeeded in gaining a charter for a full college from the Rhode Island legislature, and in 1765, he became the first president of Rhode Island College in Warren. The school moved to Providence five years later (and was eventually renamed Brown University). The lot of a college in the path of the war was difficult—the school had to close temporarily in 1779—and Manning was distressed by the general notion of warfare, which led some of his religious rivals (principally the Congregationalists of New England) to accuse him of loyalism, but in general he supported independence while hoping for peace. He also was pastor of the First Baptist Church of Providence in addition to his role as president of the college. In 1786, Manning was selected as a delegate to the Confederation Congress from Rhode Island. He was still president of the college he founded when he died of a stroke.

MANSFIELD, Richard (1723–1820) Loyalist clergyman

Born in New Haven, Connecticut, Mansfield was a Congregationalist during the first part of his life. He graduated from Yale in 1741 and was head of Hopkins Grammar School from then until 1747, when he converted to the Episcopal Church. He then went to England and was ordained (there were no bishops in America to ordain Anglican priests), and he was appointed as a missionary to the towns of Derby, West Haven, Waterbury and Northbury, Connecticut in 1749. As with many Episcopal clergy, he remained loyal to the crown. In 1775, he got into considerable trouble with his patriot neighbors after writing to Governor William Tryon that thousands of armed men would rally to the King's cause in western Connecticut, if the British would only send a few troops. Mansfield was forced to flee his home and parish. He took refuge in Hempstead, Connecticut and sat out the Revolution there ministering to a small loyalist flock. After the war, he returned to Derby and resumed the post of rector, serving until his death nearly 40 years later.

MARBOIS, Marquis de Barbe. See BARBE-MARBOIS, François.

MARCHANT, Henry (1741–1796) Delegate to Congress, attorney

Born on Martha's Vineyard, Massachusetts, Marchant became one of the leading political and legal men of Rhode Island. His family moved to Newport when he was four years old. After attending the College of Philadelphia (later part of the University of Pennsylvania) he studied law in Cambridge, Massachusetts and returned to

Newport to set up his practice. He made happy choices in his relationships, becoming a close friend of Ezra Stiles and cultivating a wide circle of intellectual and social acquaintances. He went to England in 1771, appearing on legal business before the privy council and traveling in Scotland with Benjamin Franklin. Marchant returned to Rhode Island and took a leading role in the rebellion, which he had supported as a Son of Liberty since the mid-1760s. He sat on the Rhode Island Committee of Correspondence in 1773 and helped instruct the colony's delegates to the first Continental Congress in 1774. He fled Newport for a farm near South Kingston when the war began and the British threatened the Rhode Island coast. In 1777, he was sent to Congress as a delegate, remaining for two years. He was reelected in 1780 and 1783 but did not attend, and he resigned after another election in 1784. He was a member of the state legislature after the war and one of the few strong public supporters of the proposed federal constitution in Rhode Island. He was appointed as a U.S. district judge in 1790.

MARION, Francis (c. 1732–1795) Militia officer

A brilliant leader of partisan campaigns in the Carolinas during the latter years of the war, Marion (who is inevitably referred to by the romantic nickname "The Swamp Fox") has been much mythologized, yet his achievements genuinely deserve a prominent place in the story of the Revolution. He was a small, ill-favored man, whose unprepossessing appearance often caused friend and foe alike to underestimate him. A native South Carolinian, he first came to notice as an Indian fighter with South Carolina militia. At the beginning of the War for Independence, he was both a delegate to the state provincial congress and a captain in the militia. By 1776, Marion was a major and played an important role in defending Charleston under William Moultrie. He then took over command of a full regiment of South Carolina militia and was gradually given more and more responsibility. Because of a fluke accident that broke his ankle, he was evacuated from Charleston before the fall of the garrison in 1780.

The British victory eliminated all organized American armies in the state, so Marion turned to irregular tactics with his troops of partisans. He and his men inhabited the dense swamps of the state,

Francis Marion

moving often and avoiding British forces by speed and stealth. They in turn attacked British outposts and isolated units with ferocious effectiveness. Marion worked well in conjunction with Nathanael Greene during the campaigns of 1781, and he often teamed with Light-Horse Harry Lee or William Washington to field a formidable, mobile striking force. Marion was less successful in working with partisan commander Thomas Sumter, and several joint ventures against the British went awry. Marion's greatest moments may have come at the battle of Eutaw Springs in September 1781, when his actions helped save the American army from a severe defeat. After the war, he served sporadically in state offices, including a sinecure as commander of Fort Johnson. *Further reading:* Hugh F. Rankin, *Francis Marion: The Swamp Fox* (New York, 1973).

MARJORIBANKS, John (d. 1781) British officer

A well-traveled soldier, Marjoribanks was the savior of the British army at the battle of Eutaw Springs in 1781. He entered the army in 1749 and fought with a variety of regiments during the European wars of the middle part of the century. By the time of the American Revolution he was a major of the 19th Regiment of Foot, commanding the flank companies of light infantry. Marjoribanks and his regiment were stationed in Ireland until June 1781, when they were sent to reinforce the British forces in the southern American theater. In early September, Marjoribanks commanded a light infantry brigade, formed from the flank companies of the 19th, the 3rd and the 30th regiments, as part of an army under the command of Lieutenant Colonel Alexander Stewart. American southern commander Nathanael Greene brought the British to battle near Eutaw Springs, South Carolina on September 6 after ambushing their foraging parties. While Marjoribanks' troops sheltered in a thick woods, the Americans won the initial advantage and almost routed the main British battle line. However, Marjoribanks administered severe blows to the patriot cavalry and dragoons from the cover of the trees, and when the American militia broke to plunder the British tents and baggage, Marjoribanks led a heroic counterattack against the Americans. He was killed during the fighting, but his initiative drove the Americans from the field and snatched yet another tactical victory from the hands of Greene.

MARKS, Nehemiah (d. 1799) Loyalist Marks was born in Derby, Connecticut, the son of a local merchant. He left his home at the beginning of the war and moved to New York, where he reportedly served as a dispatch agent for the British army. His duties may have included carrying messages for the British intelligence system. Following the British evacuation of the city, Marks fled to Nova Scotia. He eventually settled in New Brunswick.

MARRINER, William. American privateer and partisan Marriner was a native of New Brunswick, New Jersey and along with Adam Hyler operated a partisan patriot force from the shelter of Egg Harbor, New Jersey against British troops and shipping along the New Jersey coast. He was captured and imprisoned on Long Island but was exchanged; he continued his raiding until Egg Harbor was destroyed as a partisan base by Major Patrick Ferguson in October 1778.

MARSHALL, Christopher (1709–1797) Pharmacist, state official, diarist Marshall was born in Ireland and educated in England, and he came to Philadelphia at age 18. During a long professional career, Marshall became the best-known and most prosperous pharmacist in the city, accumulating a considerable fortune by the advent of the Revolution and retiring from active practice (in favor of his son) in 1774. He was an energetic patriot, however, and served the American cause as a member of the provincial congress in Pennsylvania in 1775 and on

the Philadelphia Committee of Safety in 1776. His activities brought him into conflict with the Quaker society of which he had been a part during most of his life, and he was expelled for supporting the war. During the same years, he managed a cloth and clothing factory that supplied goods to the patriot cause. He evacuated to Lancaster, Pennsylvania in 1777 ahead of the British seizure of Philadelphia and there worked as a sort of unofficial commissary for Pennsylvania troops while also serving on the state council of safety. From 1774 on, Marshall kept a private diary, which he titled "Remembrancer," and it has proven to be both a valuable source of information on the attitudes and activities of nonmilitary patriots during the Revolution and a trove of data on the material side of the conflict, since he discussed such topics as crops and prices. *Further reading:* William Duane, ed., *Extracts from the Diary of Christopher Marshall* (originally published 1839; new edition 1877, reprinted New York, 1969).

MARSHALL, John (1755–1835) Militia and Continental officer, jurist Scarcely anyone would disagree that Marshall was the most influential judge in American history. His name is synonymous with the U.S. Supreme Court and the entire system of judicial review in America, an association earned by his tenure as chief justice between 1801 and his death in 1835.

Before all this historic glory, however, Marshall served as a junior officer in the Revolution. He was born in the back country of Virginia, related on his mother's side to the great Randolph and Lee families and a cousin of Thomas Jefferson. Marshall's own immediate family was not grand or wealthy, however, although his father was a local and colonial officeholder. The young man was educated sparsely by his father and a private tutor and from an early age seemed attracted to the law. He was a militiaman when the War for Independence began and served against Lord Dunmore at the battle of Great Bridge in December 1775 and at Norfolk the following month. In July 1776, Marshall received a commission as lieutenant in the 3rd Virginia, a unit that survived in its original form for only a few months after Marshall joined. By December 1776, he had transferred to a newly organized regiment—the 15th Virginia—as a captain-lieutenant. He served with the 15th until the autumn of 1778, when as a captain he changed over to the 7th Virginia (previously the 11th).

Marshall's service was not on the sidelines, and he saw action at several of the major battles of the war, including Brandywine, Germantown and Monmouth, where the Virginia regiments were in the thick of the fighting. And, he was part of the storming of Stony Point, New York in July 1779. His regiment was reorganized in late 1779, with most of the remaining men going into a pooled Virginia detachment. There was apparently no need for another junior officer in the new unit, and Marshall returned home to Virginia. He officially mustered out of the Continental Army in early 1781 but in fact had long since retired from active field service.

He had taken up the formal study of law in 1780, attending lectures given by George Wythe at the College of William and Mary, and he was admitted to the bar in August. In 1783, Marshall moved to Richmond and began his public career, first in the Virginia assembly and moving by the mid-1790s to the national scene as a U.S. representative. He was appointed to the post of chief justice in February 1801 by President John Adams. The Supreme Court during the first 12 years of the new Republic had been a source of controversy and political contention, seemingly an unstable branch of what was conceived as a tripartite government. John Marshall changed all that and developed the high court as a principal part of the American governmental structure. His immense energy in writing more than 500 opinions and, perhaps more importantly, his ability to drive the court by force of personality over more than three decades created the modern American judicial system.

Not often remembered is the fact that Marshall was also a historian and biographer, publishing one of the early biographies of George Washington in a five-volume set in 1804. While neither terribly original nor a great contribution to historiography, the work reveals much about Marshall's conception of nationality and the fundamental basis for the American republic as established through the Revolution. *Further reading:* Leonard Baker, *John Marshall: A Life in Law* (New York, 1974); David Loth, *Chief Justice: John Marshall and the Growth of the Republic* (New York, 1949); William R. Smith, *History as Argument: Three Patriot Historians of the American Revolution* (The Hague, 1966).

MARTIN, Alexander (1740–1807) Continental officer, delegate to Congress, state official

Martin, born in New Jersey, was a powerful North Carolina politician who overcame a disastrous military career during the first years of the Revolutionary War. He was raised and educated in New Jersey, graduating from the college at Princeton in 1756. He moved to Salisbury, North Carolina and within a few years had become an influential officeholder, serving as deputy king's attorney and, after admission to the bar in 1772, as a judge. He sat in the colonial legislature in 1773–74, and as a patriot was a member of the provincial congresses in 1775. Martin was commissioned as a lieutenant colonel by the Congress in 1775. He was promoted to colonel in April 1776 and given command of the new 2nd North Carolina Regiment. After service in North Carolina in defense of Charleston against the first British attempt to take the seaport, the unit moved to the northern theater and joined the main army under Washington, fighting at Brandywine and Germantown. Martin was accused of personal cowardice for his conduct during the fighting at Germantown and was court-martialed. He was acquitted but was forced to resign his commission and return to North Carolina. Martin was immediately elected to the North Carolina Senate on his return to the state, and he served as a leader in the legislature during the rest of the war. Moreover, he became acting governor after almost all other state officials were captured in the surrender of Charleston in 1780. He was elected governor in his own right in 1782 (and again in 1789). In 1786, he sat in the U.S. Congress as a delegate from North Carolina. He capped his public career with a term as U.S. senator, from 1793 to 1799.

MARTIN, Joseph Plumb (c. 1760–1850) American soldier, memoir writer

Martin's account of his service as a private soldier in the Continental Line during the Revolution, written in his old age, is one of the best and liveliest memoirs of the Revolution from the ground-level viewpoint. He was born in western Massachusetts, the son of a ne'er-do-well Congregationalist preacher. Martin was raised from age seven by his maternal grandparents, a farming family of Milford, Connecticut, and was self-educated. He enlisted in a short-term Connecticut militia unit at age 15 in mid-1776, serving during the New York campaign at the battles of

Harlem Heights and White Plains. He returned to Milford in December 1776 when his initial enlistment was up, but in April of the following year, Martin enlisted for the duration of the war as a private in the 8th Connecticut Regiment of the regular Continental Army. He served in the light infantry and for a time under the captaincy of David Bushnell, inventor of the submarine. He fought in most of the important battles in the North, wintered at Valley Forge, and in 1781 walked by himself 400 miles south to rejoin his regiment after returning from leave to find the army had hastened to Virginia. He recorded the sight of George Washington hacking at the ground with a pickax to begin the siege digging at Yorktown.

After the war, Martin taught school in New York state and then moved to a settlement at the mouth of the Penobscot River. He served as a local official but failed to make ends meet and was apparently destitute when he applied (successfully) for a veteran's pension in 1818. He apparently wrote his detailed and colorful account of the war when he was 70 years old. He re-created, in the words of his modern editor, "as no one else has done, the full range of the daily life of the Continental soldier." *Further reading: Narrative of the Adventures, Dangers, and Sufferings of a Revolutionary Soldier . . . ,* published as George F. Sheer, ed., *Private Yankee Doodle* (New York, 1963).

MARTIN, Josiah (1737–1786) Royal governor

Martin epitomized, perhaps, the attitude of the royal governors of the colonies and how several failed to appreciate the nature of the Revolution and the depth of patriot resolve. Martin refused to accept that there was not a firm loyalist majority in North Carolina, and for much of the war he lobbied London to provide the men and arms that would quash what he believed to be a thin layer of resistance and unleash an imagined reservoir of loyalist sentiment. He was, of course, wrong in his judgment. He came from a military background, having served in the British army for 12 years before selling out his lieutenant colonelcy in 1769. Two years later, he was appointed governor of North Carolina. The gathering forces of rebellion confronted him early in his tenure. The collapse of the judicial system forced him to operate the criminal courts by royal prerogative by 1773, and within another year, rebels were meeting in an extralegal provincial assembly.

Martin hoped he could resist the organized patriot militia, but he was forced to flee the state aboard a British ship in July 1775. In New York, Martin petitioned for an armed return to his state, where he was certain a British army would be greeted by a loyalist uprising to support it. He sailed with the expedition to retake Charleston in 1776, but the British were rebuffed. When Scots loyalists were crushed at Moore's Bridge the same year, Martin's hopes began to fade. He subsequently served as a volunteer officer under Lord Cornwallis when the latter finally captured Charleston and the Carolinas in 1780. Martin left for England in the spring of 1781. *Further reading:* Vernon D. Stumpf, *Josiah Martin: The Last Royal Governor of North Carolina* (Durham, N.C., 1986).

MARTIN, Luther (1744–1826) Delegate to Congress, state official, attorney

Known best for his latter-day friendship with and defense of Aaron Burr, Martin was a preeminent lawyer in Maryland during the Revolution. He was born in New Jersey, lived there as a youth and graduated in 1766 from the college that came to be known as Princeton. With degree in hand, Martin moved to Maryland and became a schoolteacher in Queenstown. He began to read law on the side while teaching and continued his study after moving to Somerset County in 1769. He found himself in deep debt, however, and moved on to Virginia to avoid prosecution by his creditors. In 1771, he passed the bar in Williamsburg and was free to return to Somerset County, Maryland, where his practice soon made him comfortable financially. He was a member of his local patriot committee but generally was quiet during the first years of the Revolution. In 1778, however, he was appointed as the first attorney general of Maryland (he held the office off and on until after the turn of the century), and he was elected to Congress in 1784 but did not take his seat.

After the Revolution, Martin was a strong opponent of the proposed federal constitution, and he walked out as a delegate to the Philadelphia convention, refusing to sign the document and working against its ratification in his home state. His personal life began a long slide in the mid-1780s. His marriage to the daughter of Michael Cresap involved him in a feud with Thomas Jefferson over Cresap's culpability in the murder of the Indian leader Logan's family during Lord Dunmore's War, and after his wife's premature death, Martin fought openly with his children and especially his son-in-law, Richard Keene, with whom he exchanged public screeds in 1801 and 1802. He had meanwhile joined the Federalist party, despite his previous opposition to a strong central government, but he so hated Jefferson that he allied himself to any potential enemy of the Virginian. In 1804, Martin defended U.S. Justice Samuel Chase, an old Maryland political ally, when the judge was tried for impeachment before the U.S. Senate. Martin had also formed an alliance with Aaron Burr and defended Burr at the latter's treason trial in Virginia in 1807. He apparently sank into alcoholism as the years went on and in 1820 was paralyzed by a stroke. Remarkably, the state of Maryland passed a license fee on all lawyers, who had to pay five dollars a year toward a fund to sustain Martin in his ill old age. He eventually moved to New York City and lived until his death as Burr's houseguest. *Further reading:* Paul S. Jett and Samuel Jett, *Luther Martin of Maryland* (Baltimore, 1970).

MASON, George (1725–1792) Political thinker, writer, official

Although he preferred to work on the sidelines and seldom held important public office, Mason was one of the fundamental thinkers of the American Revolution, whose ideas and principles influenced the basic fabric of the American political system. He was the fourth in a line of Virginians to carry the name and inherited a large, prosperous estate. His father died when Mason was 10, and the boy was raised by his mother and his uncle, John Mercer. The latter was an accomplished Virginia lawyer who allowed his young ward free use of his extensive library. Although he never qualified formally as a lawyer or practiced law, Mason was well grounded from his earliest years in legal principles. He married in 1750 (eventually producing nine children before his first wife's death in 1773) and began to build his architecturally notable home Gunston Hall five years later.

Before the Revolution, Mason devoted his energies to running his plantation and to service as a local official in Alexandria, Virginia and in his parish and county. He was also much involved in western land speculations as a member of the Ohio Company, and even though he seldom during his life stirred from a small area of Virginia, Mason knew

the question of western land claims well. One of his major works was *Extracts from the Virginia Charters,* written in 1773 when the royal government wiped out the Ohio Company's western land titles. Mason served in the Virginia House of Burgesses (alongside his friend George Washington) during the 1750s, but he disdained the work of committees and refused to hold office or political leadership posts.

He began to influence the course of the Revolution in 1765 when he devised a legal maneuver to circumvent the Stamp Act in Virginia. Four years later, Mason, in response to the Townshend Acts of 1767, wrote the Virginia Resolves, a set of motions that was introduced into the Burgesses by Washington and adopted at a nearby tavern after the body was dissolved by the royal governor. The motions argued against the right of Parliament to tax the colonies without consent. Mason's ideas were developed further in the Fairfax Resolves of 1774, and together these documents set forth the intellectual basis for nearly the entire revolutionary position. In one form or another, Mason's ideas were accepted and incorporated by Virginia and eventually the Continental Congress. He was persuaded to sit in the provincial convention in Virginia in 1775, replacing George Washington, who was off to Philadelphia and the Continental Congress, and he was a member of the committee of safety that assumed power in Virginia with the ouster of Governor Dunmore.

Perhaps Mason's greatest contribution came in May 1776 when he wrote a bill of rights and a draft constitution for Virginia. Thomas Jefferson drew freely on the ideas and wording of Mason's bill of rights while drafting the Declaration of Independence, and Mason's ideas were—after a prolonged struggle—eventually enshrined in the national constitution as the first 10 amendments: thus Mason's claim to fatherhood of the national Bill of Rights. In addition to his public writings, Mason also exerted a strong personal influence on the many Virginians of his class who played key roles in the Revolution and developing the new nation. During the Revolution itself, Mason worked in his home state to implement a new form of government along the lines he had proposed at the outset of the war. He also promoted Virginia's sponsorship of George Rogers Clark's western expedition, both from a personal interest in Clark and because Mason wanted to secure the most expansive western boundaries for the new nation.

He withdrew from active public life at the end of the War for Independence and concentrated on his private affairs (he remarried in 1780). However, he was coaxed again into the political arena during the fight over the new federal constitution. He was one of the most active delegates to the constitutional convention, but in the end was one of only three who refused to sign the new document. He maintained that the constitution's fundamental defects outweighed its advantages, primarily objecting to the compromise on slavery—he was adamantly against the peculiar institution and predicted that the question would flaw the new union—and he felt the freedoms of the people were inadequately safeguarded without a written bill of rights. A believer in the rights of Americans to life, liberty and property, Mason was, in the words of one of his biographers, a representative of "the rationalist spirit, the Enlightenment in its American manifestation." Because of his preference to remain out of the limelight, his aversion to government by committee, and the fact he was a generation older than most of the "founding fathers," Mason's name is less celebrated (although a county in Kentucky and a large state university in Virginia are named for him), but during a crucial two decades, he was "one of the chief political thinkers, draftsmen, and negotiators who gave . . . the new nation its form." *Further reading:* Robert Rutland, *George Mason, Reluctant Statesman* (Williamsburg, Va., 1961); Helen Hill Miller, *George Mason: Revolutionary Gentleman* (Chapel Hill, N.C., 1975); Robert Rutland, ed., *The Papers of George Mason* (1971).

MASON, John (d. 1781) Loyalist

In January 1781, soldiers of the Pennsylvania Line of the Continental Army mutinied, marching out of their winter camps to Princeton, New Jersey, intent on addressing Congress in Philadelphia over disputed matters of back pay and terms of enlistment. British commander Sir Henry Clinton in New York hoped to take advantage of the mutiny and sent Mason, a local loyalist, on a mission to Princeton to win the disaffected Continentals away from the American cause. Mason was to offer them money and the right to decline further military service if they defected to the British. He made his way to Princeton with the help of a guide named James Ogden,

arriving during the night of January 6–7. Mason attempted to put Clinton's proposals before the mutineers, but the soldiers refused to listen, seized Mason and Ogden, and turned them over to American general Anthony Wayne and Joseph Read, the emissary of Congress sent to meet with the leaders of the mutiny. Wayne wanted to hang the pair immediately as spies, but they were temporarily handed back to the mutineers' custody. Mason and Ogden were tried by a board of officers on January 10, convicted of spying, and hanged the following day.

MASON, Thomson (1733–1785) Legislator, attorney

The younger brother of George Mason, Thomson was to a large extent under the wing of his elder sibling after their father died when Thomson was only two years old. He went to England to study law at the Middle Temple after private tutoring in his native Virginia. He returned and set up a legal practice, and he was soon chosen as a member of the legislature, sitting almost continuously from 1758 through most of the Revolution. Regarded as a premier legal mind in Virginia, he wrote a series of nine public letters from "A British American" during 1774 in which he refuted the idea that Parliamentary laws were binding on Virginia. He died relatively young only two years after the conclusion of the peace with Great Britain.

MATHEW, Edward (1729–1805) British general

Mathew came to America in 1776 as commander of a brigade of guards with the rank of brigadier general. He had held a commission in the British army since the 1740s and was apparently a favorite of George III, whom he had served as an aide-de-camp. Mathew led troops during the New York campaign, notably at Kip's Bay and during the assault on Fort Washington. In 1779, he was joint commander of the British land-sea raid on Norfolk, Virginia. He was stationed in New York City during Sir Henry Clinton's absence in 1780 with the local rank of major general—probably granted to make certain that in a pinch he would outrank the German mercenary commander von Knyphausen. He was permanently awarded his major generalship later in the year and appointed commander of the 62nd Regiment of Foot, but his new unit had been captured at Saratoga and was still interned as part of the Convention Army, so his position was mostly remunerative and honorary. He was sent to the West Indies as commander in chief in 1782.

MATHEWS, George (1739–1812) Continental general, governor, adventurer

Mathews (whose name is given in some records as "Matthews") was a competent enough officer during the Revolution who eventually gained fame just before the War of 1812 for a complex scheme to seize the Floridas. He was born in Augusta County, Virginia to a family of Irish emigrants. He fought against the Indians in 1757 and commanded a volunteer company in Lord Dunmore's War in 1774. With the outbreak of the Revolution, he was commissioned as lieutenant colonel of the 9th Virginia, originally an understrength unit designated for the defense of Virginia's Eastern Shore. The regiment was taken onto the rolls of the Continental Army in March 1776, a few months before Mathews became second in command. The 9th joined the main Continental Army and was reorganized in early 1777 with Mathews in command as colonel. In October, Mathews and his Virginians found themselves on the American left during the confused battle of Germantown. They led a hard-charging brigade assault against the British lines and penetrated so deeply that they were easily cut off, surrounded and captured en masse. Held part of the time on a prison ship in New York Harbor, Mathews was not exchanged until 1781, when he joined the southern campaign of Nathanael Greene as a senior officer attached to the 3rd Virginia. In September of that year he was brevetted to the rank of brigadier general.

Mathews' postwar career was interesting. He moved to Georgia and there was elected governor twice between 1785 and 1796 and served between gubernatorial terms as a U.S. representative. While governor in the early 1790s, he quashed the efforts of Elijah Clarke to establish a new territory across the Oconee river but himself launched a disreputable attempt to foment an uprising in the Floridas and seize the region for the United States. Acting as a brigadier general of the Georgia state militia, Mathews instigated an uprising of English settlers in Florida and planned to invade with regular U.S. troops who would act as volunteers to defend their compatriots against the Spanish. The scheme was well advanced when President James Monroe brought Mathews' machinations to a halt. Mathews was on his way to Washington to protest when he died in Augusta, Georgia.

MATHEWS, John (1744–1802) Delegate to Congress, governor, jurist

Born in Charleston, South Carolina, Mathews (whose name is varyingly spelled Matthews) served in the border wars against the Cherokee as a teenager. He went to England in 1764 and studied law at the Middle Temple, returning to South Carolina in 1766 to set up a practice. He sat in the assembly and was chosen as speaker in 1776 after serving also as a delegate to the revolutionary provincial congresses in the colony. From 1778 to 1782, Mathews was a delegate from South Carolina to the Continental and Confederation congresses, where he strongly opposed a separate peace with Great Britain if it was to be at the expense of the Carolinas and Georgia—a position that often brought him into conflict with some of the delegates from New England. In 1782, he was elected as governor of South Carolina, but the British still held Charleston, so he conducted business from his plantation. He left office soon after the final British evacuation in 1783. After the war, Mathews became a judge and also served in the state legislature.

MATLACK, Timothy (1730–1829) Delegate to Congress, militia officer, businessman

Born in New Jersey to a family of Quakers, Matlack moved to Philadelphia with his parents in 1745 and eventually became a merchant. He fell out with the Quakers over his fondness for sports and gaming, shortcomings exacerbated by his shaky business practices. (In later life, Matlack organized a society of Free Quakers comprised of people cast out by their regular meetings.) He joined the Philadelphia Associators, a militia unit formed by merchants of the city in 1775, and he took the field as a colonel during the campaigns at Trenton and Princeton the following year. Meanwhile, he served as secretary to Charles Thomson, himself secretary of the Continental Congress. George Washington's commission as commander in chief of the Continental Army is said to be written in Matlack's hand. In July 1776, Matlack became a member of the Pennsylvania Committee of Safety, and after adoption of a new state constitution, he took a place as secretary of the ruling Supreme Executive Council. In 1780, he was elected as a delegate to the Continental Congress, serving until 1782. He was then removed as secretary of the Supreme Council, charged with financial irregularities, and thrown in jail as a debtor, although he soon won his freedom. Perhaps to get away from his troubles, he moved to New York City in 1784, but he returned to Philadelphia before the end of the year. During the balance of his public life, Matlack filled minor government offices in the judicial system.

MATTHEWS, David. Loyalist official A long-time officeholder before the Revolution, Matthews was appointed mayor of New York City by the British in 1776. He had been clerk of several courts and registrar of the Court of Vice-Admiralty. His new post of mayor was arduous in its duties and paid little, so he was also named a deputy of the Vice-Admiralty, a post that paid him well during the Revolution. In July 1776, he was seized by the patriots and imprisoned in Connecticut, but he eventually returned to his duties in New York. After the war he emigrated to the island of Cape Breton in Canada, where he served as attorney general.

MATTHEWS, Saul. Continental soldier, spy Matthews was a black slave living in Virginia as the property of Thomas Matthews at the time of the Revolution. He served as an infantryman during much of the war and gained particular notice in 1781 during the British invasion of Virginia. He acted as a spy for the American forces by crossing British lines and returning to report on dispositions and defenses, particularly at Portsmouth, Virginia. He led a raiding party against Portsmouth at the behest of militia colonel Josiah Parker. Matthews also visited Norfolk and returned with a report on the British garrison. He remained a slave after the war and was sold to a new master. However, in 1792, he petitioned the Virginia legislature for his freedom, which was granted in consideration for his "many very essential services rendered to this Commonwealth during the late war."

MAUDIT, Israel (1708–1787) British businessman, writer Maudit was a wealthy British merchant who, along with his brother, became the acting colonial agent for Massachusetts in 1763. He was generally an advocate of colonial independence and wrote several pamphlets supporting the Americans as well as histories of New England and Massachusetts Bay.

MAUREPAS, Jean Frédéric, Comte de (1701–1781) French official The son of an official of the French court, Maurepas was born at Versailles. He himself nominally took office as minister of marine while only a teenager, although in fact the office was ceremonial until he reached maturity. During the first years of his government career he served as one of Louis XV's principal ministers, but he was dismissed in 1749 after writing scurrilous verses about Madame de Pompadour. He returned to power in 1774 under Louis XVI and was made president of the royal council of ministers. He generally supported Vergennes's policy of covert aid to the rebellious American colonies as a way to embarrass the British. He remained in office until his death.

MAWHOOD, Charles (d. 1780) British officer Mawhood, a veteran officer, was named in 1775 as lieutenant colonel of the 17th Regiment of Foot, a unit already serving in America. In January 1777, Mawhood was given command of a brigade of 1,200 troops and left by Lord Cornwallis to hold Princeton, New Jersey while Cornwallis advanced on Washington's army at Trenton. Washington slipped away from Cornwallis, however, and took the road to Princeton. His advance troops met Mawhood's 17th while the latter unit was on the move. The two forces stumbled into a nasty battle in which the British gained the initial advantage but were finally pushed off the field by an American force rallied by Washington in person. More than a year later, Mawhood successfully ambushed an American force at Quintan's Bridge, New Jersey. He died at Gibraltar in the summer of 1780 after joining a new regiment there.

MAXWELL, Hugh (1733–1799) Continental officer Maxwell was born in Ireland but was brought to the American colonies before his first birthday, settling in Massachusetts. He served with the British-colonial forces during the Seven Years' War and was wounded and captured by the French at Fort Edward. In 1773, he moved to Charlemont, Massachusetts. At the battle of Bunker Hill, Maxwell served as a lieutenant. He was promoted to major in the 2nd Massachusetts Regiment, known originally as Colonel John Bailey's Regiment, and eventually became a lieutenant colonel. He died at sea while returning from the West Indies.

MAXWELL, William (1733–1796) Continental general

An undistinguished officer, Maxwell nonetheless served in responsible commands during most of the war. He was born in Ireland to Scots Protestant parents and was brought to New Jersey as a teenager (he spoke with a Scots accent all his life). He joined the British army in 1754 and campaigned as an officer during most of the wars against the French. At the close of hostilities, Maxwell became a colonel of commissary at Mackinac. In 1774, he resigned his post with the British and returned to New Jersey, where he became active in patriot affairs as a member of the provincial congress and his local committee of safety. He was commissioned as a colonel by Congress in 1775, assuming command of the 2nd New Jersey Regiment. He marched with his regiment on the Canadian invasion during early 1776—a campaign already lost before he joined it. While in the North, Maxwell was promoted by Congress to brigadier general and returned to command a brigade of four new New Jersey regiments. He performed indifferently during the New Jersey campaign of 1776–1777, perhaps due to his increasingly evident alcoholism. In mid-1777, Maxwell was given command of a new light infantry regiment organized by drawing men from six established brigades. Maxwell's Light Infantry fought at Brandywine and then Germantown. However, Maxwell in the meantime had been charged with incompetence and was brought to court-martial in early November 1777. The verdict was ambiguous—neither conviction nor exoneration—and Maxwell returned to duty as a brigade commander at winter quarters at Valley Forge. He subsequently took part in the battle of Monmouth and testified at the court-martial of Charles Lee. In 1779, Maxwell commanded a brigade as part of John Sullivan's expedition against the Iroquois. He resigned his commission in 1780.

MAZZEI, Philip (1730–1816) Diplomat, horticulturalist

Mazzei was born in Tuscany and studied medicine in Florence. He went to Smyrna in 1752 to practice medicine but left for London after only three years. There he became a wine merchant and came into contact with several prominent men from Virginia. He was persuaded to emigrate to Virginia and set up a horticultural company for the introduction of wine grapes, olive culture and silk manufacture. He arrived in 1773 with cuttings and farm workers from his native Italy.

Mazzei set up his experimental farm on land obtained from Thomas Jefferson next to Jefferson's estate at Monticello. The enterprise was organized as a joint stock company with royal governor Lord Dunmore and George Washington among the subscribers. Unfortunately, Mazzei's attempts to grow vines and olive trees did not prosper. He had, however, in the meanwhile become a friend of Jefferson, and in 1779, Mazzei was designated as a diplomatic agent for the state of Virginia and dispatched to the Duke of Tuscany to negotiate a loan for Virginia. He and his family were captured at sea, however, and held by the British in New York for three months. He eventually reached Europe but was frustrated in securing a loan, although he did gather intelligence, which he passed on to Thomas Jefferson, by then governor of wartime Virginia. Mazzei returned to America in 1783 and sought appointment as a U.S. consul in Europe but was frustrated and left America permanently in 1785. During the late 1780s, Mazzei served as a diplomat and advisor to the king of Poland. *Further reading:* Richard C. Garlick, Jr., et al., *Italy and the Italians in Washington's Time* (1935; reprinted New York, 1975), 5–27.

MEIGS, Return Jonathan (1740–1823) Continental officer

A very able officer, Meigs shone especially during the War for Independence in bringing off quick raids. He was born in Middletown, Connecticut, the son of a hatter who also sat in the colonial assembly. The younger Meigs was a militia captain at the time of Lexington and Concord and marched his company to join the American army at Boston in the spring of 1775. He was commissioned as a major and assigned to Benedict Arnold's expedition against Canada, surviving the brutal march north only to be captured after scaling the walls of Quebec City during Arnold's futile assault on the last day of December 1775. Fortunately for Meigs, he was immediately exchanged and was able to return to New England, where he was promoted to colonel and placed in command of the 6th Connecticut, a post he filled for the next four years.

His most famous exploit was a well-executed raid on a large British foraging party at Sag Harbor, New York in May 1777. By night, Meigs embarked his men on a small fleet of whaleboats, escorted by two sloops, and caught 100 British and loyalist troops unawares. The Americans killed several of the enemy, burned most of their boats, seized or destroyed a considerable stock of supplies and took several dozen prisoners—all without the loss of a man. Congress voted Meigs a sword of honor in consequence of this exploit. He was then assigned along with the 6th Connecticut to posts in the Hudson Highlands and took part prominently in General Anthony Wayne's storming of Stony Point in July 1779. He helped put down the mutiny among the troops of the Connecticut Line in the spring of 1780, earning the personal thanks of commander in chief George Washington. When the Connecticut regiments were reorganized in 1781, Meigs resigned and returned to civilian life. He became involved in western land speculation during the late 1780s and moved to Ohio, where he served frequently as an agent and negotiator with western Indian tribes. His son of the same name was later governor of Ohio.

MELSHEIMER, Friedrich Valentin (1749–1814) German clergyman, educator

Melsheimer came to America as a chaplain of one of the Brunswicker dragoon regiments of German mercenaries. His unit was part of General John Burgoyne's invasion force in 1777, and Melsheimer was captured at the American victory over Friedrich Baum's troops at Bennington, Vermont. Like thousands of other German mercenary soldiers, Melsheimer elected to remain in the United States. By 1779, he was pastor of several small Lutheran parishes in Pennsylvania, and he served as pastor in Manheim, Pennsylvania from 1784 to 1786. He then joined the faculty of Franklin College as a professor of German and classic languages. In 1789, Melsheimer became pastor of St. Matthew's church in Hanover, Pennsylvania, where he remained until his death, a quarter century later.

MERCER, Hugh (c. 1725–1777) American general

Mercer was born in Scotland, the son of a clergyman, and was educated as a physician at Aberdeen. He was a Jacobite and as a young man took part in the battle of Culloden as a surgeon's mate in the ill-fated army of the Young Pretender, Bonnie Prince Charlie. After the crushing defeat of the Jacobite rebellion at the hands of the Hanoverians, Mercer emigrated to Pennsylvania, settling

Hugh Mercer

near the modern-day site of Mercersburg, which was named after him. He took up the practice of medicine in what was then a frontier community. With the coming of the North American part of the wars between England the France, Mercer became a soldier again, serving in several of the British campaigns against the Indians and the French and reaching the rank of colonel by 1759. He met and made friends with George Washington during the late 1750s, and at the end of hostilities, Mercer moved to Fredericksburg, Virginia, where he set up medical practice again. With the coming of the Revolution, Mercer again turned to military service. He was elected colonel of militia for a four-county area in September 1775 and was appointed colonel of the 3rd Virginia, a new Continental regiment, in January 1776. He commanded the Virginia regiment only until June, when Congress appointed him a brigadier general.

Washington put Mercer in charge of the Flying Camp, a unit that was to be assembled from militia units from Pennsylvania, Delaware, Maryland and New Jersey and stationed as a mobile reserve in Pennsylvania, ready to move quickly against the British in New York. Unfortunately, the plan never came to fruition. Mercer had a terrible time recruiting troops, and those who did report were poorly trained and equipped. Despite Mercer's efforts, the components of the Flying Camp failed to make a difference during the British victories in the New York campaign, and the corps was disbanded in November 1776 when enlistments expired.

Mercer then moved to the command of part of Washington's retreat across New Jersey and led a column during the lightning assault on Trenton in December 1776. As part of Washington's plan to move on Princeton, Mercer was dispatched during the first days of January to lead the advance American force toward the town, where British lieutenant colonel Charles Mawhood had 1,200 troops. Mercer's and Mawhood's men more or less stumbled into each other near Stony Brook bridge on January 3, 1777. During the following unplanned and confused battle, Mercer was shot from his horse during a British counterattack, surrounded and bayoneted. Washington personally rallied the Americans and forced a victory, but Mercer died from his wounds at a nearby farmhouse. His fall on the battlefield achieved a form of enduring posthumous fame because of a heroic painting by Jonathan Trumbull, which has often been copied and reproduced. *Further reading:* Frederick English, *General Hugh Mercer: Forgotten Hero of the American Revolution* (New York, 1975).

MERCER, James (1736–1793) Delegate to Congress, official, jurist

Mercer was born on his father's estate in Virginia and inherited a considerable fortune. He graduated from the College of William and Mary and served as a militia captain during the Seven Years' War. He was elected to the Virginia House of Burgesses in 1762, serving continuously until 1775. He had meanwhile been admitted to the bar. He was an active prerevolutionary patriot as a member of his local committee of correspondence, and he helped organize the provincial convention of 1774 which appointed him to the Virginia Committee of Safety in mid-1775. In 1779, Mercer was selected as a delegate to the Continental Congress and at nearly the same time was appointed as a state judge on the court of appeals. He served as a justice on a reorganized court of appeals from 1789 until his death.

MERCER, John Francis (1759–1821) Delegate to Congress, Continental officer, militia officer, legislator, governor

The younger half-brother of James Mercer, John Francis was born on the same estate in Stafford County, Virginia. Like his brother, he attended the College of William and Mary, graduating at the beginning of the War for Independence in 1775. He received a commission as a lieutenant in the 3rd Virginia Regiment in January 1777, shortly after the unit was organized

and a month before it was taken into the Continental Army. Mercer was promoted to captain in September, and in 1778, he became an aide-de-camp to General Charles Lee. Lee's fall from command after the battle of Monmouth took Mercer down with him, and the young Virginian resigned his commission and returned to his home state in 1779.

He studied law with Thomas Jefferson for a year and was admitted to the bar in 1781. Mercer's military career was not finished, however, and he renewed service in 1780 as a lieutenant colonel of state militia under Virginia brigadier general Robert Lawson. In May 1781, Mercer organized a unit of cavalry and attached himself for a short while to the army under the Marquis de Lafayette, who was then in Virginia opposing the British invasion forces. Before the final campaign against Lord Cornwallis at Yorktown, Mercer raised and commanded a unit of militia grenadiers.

He had practiced law in snatches between periods of active field service, but his primary career after the war was as a public official. In 1782, he was elected to the Virginia legislature and also named as a delegate to the Confederation Congress, replacing Edmund Randolph. In 1785, he married and moved to Anne Arundel County, Maryland. He was a strong opponent of the proposed federal constitution and walked out of the Philadelphia convention, to which he had been sent as a delegate from Maryland. He served in the Maryland legislature thereafter and as U.S. representative from Maryland from 1791 to 1794. In 1801, Mercer was elected as governor of Maryland, serving two terms.

MEREDITH, Samuel (1741–1817) Delegate to Congress, militia general, official

A native of Philadelphia, Meredith was a merchant in the years before the Revolution, actively supporting the patriot cause and signing the nonimportation agreements in 1765. He represented Philadelphia in the provincial convention of 1775, and soon thereafter he became major and then lieutenant colonel of the 3rd Battalion of the Philadelphia Associators, a well-equipped city militia unit formed by well-to-do merchants. Known as the Silk Stocking Company, the Associators were called to service as part of Cadwalader's Pennsylvania militia brigade in late 1776 and performed admirably at Trenton and Princeton and subsequently at the battles of Brandywine and Germantown. Meredith himself was promoted to brigadier general in late 1777 but resigned his militia commission in January 1778 to return to business. Following the war, he was elected to the Pennsylvania legislature, and in 1786, he was sent as a delegate to the Confederation Congress, serving two terms. In 1789, Meredith was appointed by George Washington as the first U.S. treasurer under the new federal constitution. He resigned in 1801 and retired to his country home near Pleasant Mount, Pennsylvania.

MERSEREAU, John (the Elder). American spy

The brother of Joshua Mersereau and the uncle of John LaGrange Mersereau, this member of the family also served in the American spy ring on Staten Island during 1776 and 1777. He had lived on Staten Island until the British invasion and moved with his family to New Jersey, returning home to gather intelligence.

MERSEREAU, John LaGrange (the Younger). American spy

A resident of Staten Island at the beginning of the war, Mersereau fled to New Brunswick, New Jersey with his father Joshua and his uncle John Mersereau the Elder in 1776 after the British invaded New York. When his father organized a spy network for George Washington, the younger Mersereau returned to Staten Island and lived there for a year and a half, gathering intelligence information and passing it back to his father in New Jersey. He escaped when the British grew suspicious of his activities.

MERSEREAU, Joshua. American spy

Mersereau was a shipbuilder from New York who had fled his home on Staten Island after the British occupation of 1776. He was recruited by George Washington as an intelligence agent sometime in mid-1776 and organized a network, comprised mostly of his relatives (including his son and brother), that gathered information around British-held Staten Island and fed it to Washington. The network was taken over by Colonel Elias Dayton later in the war.

MIDDLETON, Arthur (1742–1787) Delegate to Congress, state official, planter

As the son of Henry Middleton, Arthur was a member of what was perhaps the wealthiest family in South Carolina. He was born at Middleton Place, an estate he eventually inherited, on the Ashley River. He was

sent to England for his education, attending the Hackney School and Westminster and graduating from Cambridge. He studied law at the Temple in London, although he never practiced. He returned to South Carolina in 1763 and took up the management of part of his family's plantations.

Despite his aristocratic background and English education, Middleton was a radical revolutionary—far more radical than his father, for example. As a member of the colonial legislature, he spearheaded the growing resistance to the royal government during the years just before the Revolution. He was a member of the provincial conventions in South Carolina in 1775 and 1776, and he personally helped organize the seizure of arms in Charleston in April 1776. Middleton became a member of the council of safety that exerted control in the state in 1775 and 1776, and he urged strong measures against all loyalists. In early 1776, while helping to prepare a new state constitution for South Carolina, he was appointed as a delegate to the Continental Congress as a replacement for his conservative father. He signed the Declaration of Independence during his first term in Philadelphia. He served in Congress until the fall of 1777, but although reelected several times between 1778 and 1780, he failed to take his seat and concentrated instead on matters in his home state. He also declined to serve as governor of South Carolina when appointed in 1778, but he did sit as a legislator. He was captured by the British in 1780 at the fall of Charleston, during which he served as a militia officer. Held at St. Augustine in Florida, he was exchanged in the spring of 1781. He returned home to find his estates ravaged by the British, but he rebuilt them and thereafter prospered again. He accepted election to Congress in 1781 and served until 1782.

MIDDLETON, Henry (1717–1784) Delegate to Congress, planter

An immensely rich planter, Middleton was the head of one of the half-dozen or so families that dominated the economy and politics of prerevolutionary South Carolina. He was probably born at The Oaks, a plantation near Charleston, and educated in England, although the details of his early life are sketchy. By the time he was an adult, he personally owned 20 plantations, comprising 50,000 acres, and 800 black slaves. Not surprisingly, Middleton held many public offices, including a seat in the colonial legislature and on the King's Provincial Council. He was a strong, if conservative patriot, however, and he did much to organize resistance to the royal government. He was selected in July 1774 to be one of South Carolina's delegates to the first Continental Congress. He was elected president of Congress in October and served in that office until the following May.

Although he was sincere and energetic in his American patriotism, Middleton was unconvinced on the issue of independence, hoping for conciliation with Great Britain short of an irrevocable breach. As the momentum for independence increased in 1776, Middleton found himself out of step and resigned as a delegate in favor of his more radical son, Arthur. Back in South Carolina, Middleton continued to serve in public office as president of the state legislature and as a member of the council of safety and the legislative council that took its place after a new state constitution went into effect. By 1780, however, his energies burned low. When the British took Charleston, Middleton acquiesced to defeat and accepted the protection of the British military government, effectively withdrawing from the Revolution just a shade this side of loyalism. His action did not result in lasting harm, however, and he retained all his property despite widespread confiscations after the war.

MIFFLIN, Thomas (1744–1800) Continental officer, delegate to Congress, official

Mifflin was an important figure during the early years of the Revolution, but his rather drastic mid-war change of political allegiance and poor performance as quartermaster have damaged his historical reputation. He was born into a family of prosperous Quaker merchants in Philadelphia and entered training in a Philadelphia mercantile house after graduating from the College of Philadelphia (later part of the University of Pennsylvania) in 1760. When barely 20, Mifflin formed a partnership with his brother, George, and opened a trading house.

He was a good speaker and was drawn into patriot politics as the Revolution drew closer. In 1772, he was elected to the colonial legislature and took a leading role in pushing Pennsylvania toward hostilities with the crown. In 1774, Mifflin was selected as one of the delegates to the first Continental Congress, where he gained a reputation as a radical—although he pushed slowly for actual independence. He was selected again for Congress in 1775,

Thomas Mifflin

but with the formation of the Continental Army, ne moved to the military side, receiving a commission as major in May (his Quaker meeting cast him out about this time). Mifflin became an aide-de-camp to the new commander in chief, George Washington, in late June 1775, but seven weeks later he was named as quartermaster general of the Continental Army.

Throughout the War for Independence, the quartermaster department was the weakest part of the army and often the American cause faltered for lack of supplies, so Mifflin occupied an extremely important if unglamorous post. Unfortunately, he was not an efficient administrator, especially in financial matters, and he preferred the battlefront to the tasks of organization. He was relatively effective in training and recruiting—his oratorical skills coming to the fore—but he did little to establish a sound system to provide food and clothing for the army. Moreover, he remained highly political and spent a good deal of energy dabbling in affairs in Philadelphia. He was rapidly promoted, however, and reached the coveted rank of major general by February 1777.

At this stage, Mifflin began to disagree strongly with Washington's strategy, believing that all efforts should have been made to guard Philadelphia from a British attack out of New York City. In truth, 1777 was the year Washington's candle burned lowest among the politicians in Philadelphia, and Mifflin soon was on the anti-Washington side of the division. He resigned as quartermaster general during the summer and plunged into the intrigue known since as the Conway Cabal, an effort to advance

Horatio Gates at the expense of Washington. Mifflin's role was not, perhaps, as nefarious as it has sometimes been depicted, but a permanent hostility settled in between Mifflin and Washington. Mifflin was named to the board of war established by Congress as a preliminary to replacing Washington in 1777, but he also returned to duties as quartermaster, although he showed little energy or competence and is usually blamed to a large degree for the deplorable state of the army during the horrendous winter of suffering at Valley Forge at the end of 1777. He hoped to be appointed to a command, but Washington ignored Mifflin and an investigation was begun in Congress as to the quartermaster general's financial dealings.

Mifflin submitted his resignation as major general in mid-1778, although it was not accepted until February of the following year. He then returned to political office and sat in the state legislature. He was again elected as a delegate to the Continental Congress in 1782 and served there until 1784. While temporarily absent from the body in 1783, Mifflin was elected president, and he was the presiding officer of Congress in Annapolis when Washington surrendered his commission, handing the document over to Mifflin in an emotional ceremony. Mifflin continued in public office after the Revolution, supporting the new federal constitution as a delegate to the convention in 1787 and sitting as a member of the state supreme executive council. He was elected as governor of Pennsylvania in 1790 and served nine years. *Further reading:* Kenneth R. Rossman, *Thomas Mifflin and the Politics of the American Revolution* (Chapel Hill, N.C., 1952).

MILES, Samuel (1740–1805) American officer

Born in Pennsylvania, Miles was a principal officer of one of the hybrid regiments known as "state troops"—neither militia nor on the regular Continental Army list. Miles fought extensively during the North American wars between the French and the British in the decades before the Revolution, emerging as a captain in 1760. He moved to Philadelphia the following year and became a wine merchant, eventually prospering and acquiring considerable land holdings and wealth. He sat in the state assembly in 1772 and 1773, and he became active as a member of local patriot committees. In addition, Miles raised a militia company in Philadelphia during the prerevolutionary agitation. In

1775, he returned to the assembly and was appointed to the Pennsylvania Committee of Safety. In July 1776, the Continental Congress established a mobile reserve, called the Flying Camp, to be comprised of state troops who were authorized directly by Congress and paid from congressional funds but not strictly to be part of the Continental Army. Miles was commissioned a colonel and raised a two-battalion unit called Colonel Miles' Pennsylvania State Rifle Regiment as part of the Flying Camp. Miles' regiment was assigned to Washington's army for the battle of Long Island, where it was overrun by the British and Miles was captured. He remained in British custody until he was exchanged in 1778. While he was in prison, Miles had been appointed brigadier general of Pennsylvania troops, but he was not confirmed at the rank on his release, so he resigned and returned to civilian affairs, becoming auditor for public accounts and deputy quartermaster for Pennsylvania troops. Following the war, he continued to serve in public offices as a state legislator and mayor of Philadelphia.

MILLER, Nathan (1743–1790) Delegate to Congress, militia general, merchant

Miller was born in Warren, Rhode Island and was a merchant and shipbuilder. He sat in the Rhode Island assembly before, during and after the Revolution, and he held rank as a brigadier general in the Rhode Island militia for Newport and Bristol counties from 1772 until 1778. He was selected as a delegate to the Confederation Congress in 1786 and was reelected the following year but declined to serve further.

MINGO. See LOGAN.

MITCHELL, Nathaniel (1753–1814) Continental officer, delegate to Congress

Mitchell was born near Laurel, Delaware and was a member of a local militia company when the war began. In 1775, he received a commission as captain and joined Samuel Patterson's Delaware contingent, which had been recruited to form part of the Flying Camp reserve organized to provide reinforcements for Washington's army in New York. In January 1777, Mitchell transferred to Grayson's Additional Regiment, a unit formed that month and raised partly in Virginia and partly in Maryland, and he was promoted to major at the end of the year. He became a brigade major to Peter Muhlenberg in 1779, when Grayson's Regiment was absorbed into a new Additional Regiment headed by Nathaniel Gist. In 1780, Mitchell was stationed in Virginia as part of the Marquis de Lafayette's campaign and was captured by the British. He was paroled in May 1781 only to discover that Congress had dissolved his regiment in January. In 1786, he was elected as a delegate to the waning Confederation Congress, serving two terms. He held local offices until 1805, when he became governor of Delaware. On leaving executive office in 1808, he served in the state legislature until his death.

MITCHELL, Stephen M. (1743–1835) Jurist, delegate to Congress The son of a merchant trader, Mitchell was born in Wethersfield, Connecticut. He graduated from Yale in 1763 and while serving three years as a tutor at his alma mater, he studied law. He practiced until 1779, when he won his first appointment as a judge, a career he followed almost without interruption until his death, rising successively to higher and higher court benches in Connecticut. He sat in the state legislature during the Revolution, and from 1783 to 1788 he was a delegate to the enfeebled Confederation Congress. His only break from the bench came in 1793 when he was appointed to fill the U.S. senator's seat left vacant by the death of Roger Sherman. He retired in 1814 and quietly lived his final 20 years on a farm near Wethersfield.

MOIRA, Earl of. *See* RAWDON, Francis.

MOLLY, Captain. *See* CORBIN, Margaret.

MONCKTON, Henry (1740–1778) British officer The younger brother of Robert Monckton, Henry was a lieutenant colonel of the 45th Regiment of Foot, which had the territorial designation of Nottinghamshire and was known as the Sherwood Foresters. He assumed command of the regiment in 1776 and led the unit during the battle of Long Island. He was killed at the battle of Monmouth while in command of a battalion of grenadiers.

MONCKTON, Robert (1726–1782) British general, official The son of Viscount Galway and a grandson (on his mother's side) of the Duke of Rutland, Monckton had a distinguished career as

an officer in North America during the Seven Years' War, serving at the head of British regulars and colonial militia. He had the unhappy duty of expelling the French Acadians (thus gaining a perverse immortality in American ethnic and literary history) and was General James Wolfe's second in command at Quebec in 1759, himself taking a severe wound. He held command of British forces in the northern American colonies for a period and was governor of New York from 1760 to 1763. By the time the British government contemplated sending a major military force to Boston in the early 1770s, Monckton was a lieutenant general and was considered as a candidate for commander in chief for North America, but the post went to Thomas Gage and Monckton took no active role in the Revolutionary War.

MONCRIEFF, James (1744–1793) British officer Perhaps the most brilliant British engineering officer to serve in the American war, Moncrieff was born in Scotland and trained professionally at the royal school for engineers at Woolwich between 1759 and 1762. He then took part in the siege of Havana as an ensign in the 100th Regiment of Foot. Over the following 14 years, Moncrieff continued on duty at posts in the American colonies and the West Indies. With the outbreak of the Revolution, he was in New York City. He served in the northern theater during the first years of the war and was noted for his work in bridging rivers for the army. His major achievements, however, were in the South. He fought with particular distinction and a display of personal bravery at Stono Ferry, South Carolina in June 1779 and designed and built the fortifications at Savannah that allowed General Augustine Prevost to repulse the joint French-American attack in the fall of the same year. He was brevetted to major for his work at Savannah and then assigned to Sir Henry Clinton's expedition against Charleston in late 1780. He was in charge of the siege operations and not only planned and organized the campaign with great efficiency but cleverly employed prefabricated siege works (built in New York and carried south by ship) against the American seaport. He was brevetted to lieutenant colonel after the surrender of Charleston and placed in charge of its physical defense during the remainder of the war. With the British evacuation in 1783, Moncrieff withdrew to the West Indies along with hundreds of black slaves he in effect stole from South Carolina. He eventually became deputy quartermaster general of the British Royal Army, and he was killed by the French while directing a siege of Dunkirk in 1793.

MONROE, James (1758–1831 Continental officer, delegate to Congress, president

Another of the many Virginians who led the nation during the early years of the Republic, Monroe was a student at the College of William and Mary when the war began. He left his books and took up arms as a second lieutenant in the 3rd Virginia Regiment in September 1775. He served as a junior officer in most of the early engagements of the war, and he was wounded on the streets of Trenton during Washington's daring attack on December 26, 1775. The following year, Monroe was promoted to major and made an aide-de-camp to Lord Stirling. He fought in the battles of Brandywine, Georgetown and Monmouth, after which he resigned his commission.

In 1780, he began to study law with Thomas Jefferson, passing the rest of the war with his law books. Monroe was elected as a delegate to Congress in 1783, and he served until 1786. He opposed the new constitution but once it was ratified he served as U.S. senator from Virginia and envoy to France in addition to a term as governor of Virginia. In 1811, he was appointed as U.S. secretary of state, and in 1814, he added the portfolio of the secretary of war. He was elected president of the United States in 1816 and served two terms. He is perhaps best remembered as the author of the Monroe Doctrine, which declared the New World to be off limits to European aggrandizement. *Further reading:* Harry Ammon, *James Monroe: The Quest for National Identity* (New York, 1971).

MONTAGU, John. See SANDWICH, Earl of.

MONTBLERN, Saint-Simon. See SAINT-SIMON MONTBLERN, Marquis de.

MONTGOMERY, John (1722–1808) Delegate to Congress, militia officer, official

Montgomery was born in Ireland and emigrated with his family to Carlisle, Pennsylvania in 1740. He served in the colonial wars as a militia captain of Pennsylvania troops and in conflicts with the Indians on the frontier. He was a member of the Pennsylvania Committee of Safety in 1775 and 1776 and was colonel of the Cumberland County militia in 1777. In 1781 and 1782, Montgomery sat in the state legislature, and in the latter year he was elected as a delegate to the Confederation Congress. He was one of the founders of Dickinson College.

MONTGOMERY, Joseph (1733–1794) Delegate to Congress, clergyman

Montgomery was born in Paxtang, Pennsylvania. He studied at the College of New Jersey, graduating in 1755, and continued with theological studies afterward, being ordained by the Presbyterian church in 1761. An active minister most of his early life, he turned to public office during the latter years of the Revolution when elected to the Pennsylvania Assembly in 1780. From 1783 to 1784, Montgomery was a delegate to the Confederation Congress from Pennsylvania. During the late 1780s, he held two offices simultaneously: recorder of deeds and wills in Dauphin County and justice of the court of common pleas.

MONTGOMERY, Richard (1738–1775) Continental general

One of the first American generals to fall in combat, Montgomery was a native of Ireland and had a distinguished career in the British army before emigrating to America. He was born in Dublin, the son of a member of the Irish Parliament, and educated at Trinity College. He joined the 17th Regiment of Foot in 1756 and served in North America during the Seven Years' War, part of the time as regimental adjutant. He also was on the British expeditions to Martinique and Havana before returning to Britain as a captain.

In 1772, he sold out his commission and moved to a farm in New York. He married a daughter of Robert R. Livingston in 1773 and thus gained instant standing in the colony. He was a delegate to the New York provincial congress in 1775, and in June was commissioned as one of the brigadier generals of the new Continental Army. Montgomery was ordered north as second in command to Philip Schuyler for the invasion of Canada in the fall, and when Schuyler fell ill, Montgomery assumed command of the army. The forces at his disposal were ill-equipped, ill-trained, poorly-supplied amateurs, but he made the best of the situation and moved resolutely toward Quebec, taking St. John's on the way. He found the fortress at Quebec well defended, and Montgomery's strength ebbed daily as

Richard Montgomery

the winter weather closed in. He was forced to mount an assault on the last day of the year before the enlistments of most of his men ran out and they returned to their homes. The attack was hopeless from the beginning, and it faltered at the gates of the city. Montgomery was shot dead leading the assault.

MONTGOMERY, William (1736–1816) Militia officer, legislator

Montgomery was a prominent public official in Pennsylvania, usually representing his native Chester County. He sat in the provincial congresses of 1775 and 1776 and was elected to the Pennsylvania Assembly. In 1776, his 4th Battalion of militia from Chester County formed one of the principal regiments of the Flying Camp, a mobile, strategic reserve force created by Congress at George Washington's request. Washington was uncertain where the British would attack after their expulsion from Boston, and his idea was to form a significant body of troops from the militias of Pennsylvania, Delaware and Maryland that could cover several possibilities in the middle colonies. However, only a few men answered the call to arms, and most of them were poorly trained and equipped. Many of the men assigned to the Flying Camp were captured by the British during the battle of Long Island, although Montgomery himself apparently escaped. Most of his activities thereafter were as a civilian official, helping to settle the ongoing border disputes in the Wyoming Valley region of present-day Pennsylvania, for example. He was elevated to the rank of major general in the Pennsylvania militia

after the Revolution and was elected to the U.S. House of Representatives for one term in 1793.

MONTMORIN, Armand, Comte de. French diplomat

Montmorin was the French ambassador to Spain in 1777, when French foreign minister Vergennes attempted to bring Spain into the conflict with Great Britain on the side of the American colonists. Although bound to France by a Bourbon family compact and quite willing to gain from a hoped-for British defeat in America, the Spanish refused to recognize American independence and wished most of all to benefit from the war by recovering territories in America lost at the end of the Seven Years' War. Montmorin succeeded in negotiating an alliance of France and Spain—the Convention of Aranjuez—that made Spain a belligerent but that fell far short of a full alliance in support of the United States.

MONTOUR, Esther. Indian leader

Known in most American accounts as "Queen Esther" or the "Witch of Wyoming," Montour is surrounded, in the words of one historian, by "a fog of confusion." She became the focus of much folklore and popular writing as one of the chief villainesses of the Revolution on the frontier after she was reported to have killed more than a dozen American captives in cold blood during a British-loyalist raid on Wyoming Valley settlements in July 1778. Her history has often been conflated with those of her grandmother, mother and sister.

The original matriarch was a woman of French or French-Canadian birth, known as Madame Montour, who lived on the frontier among the Oneida during the late 17th century and early 18th. Her name probably was Catherine and she appeared in white settlements and cities as an interpreter for the Oneida. Her daughter Margaret, likely Esther's mother, also lived among the Indians at villages in western Pennsylvania and New York and also acted as an interpreter. Margaret's two daughters, Catherine and Esther, carried on the family tradition of marriage to Indians and assumption of at least some measure of influence among the tribes on the frontier. Esther was probably married before the Revolution to a leader of the Delaware named Echobund and lived at various times on the Chemung and Susquehanna rivers. She was reported to have had considerable contact with Moravian missionaries in the region.

During the Revolution, Esther won undying notoriety during a raid by the pro-British Butler's Rangers on the patriot settlers in the Wyoming Valley (a place disputed between rival colonial factions before, during and after the war). In early July 1778, John Butler defeated the American forces, taking many prisoners in the bargain. As the accounts run, Esther personally killed 14 or 16 bound captives with tomahawk and knife, adding a gruesome flourish to the overall blood-letting that came to be known as the Wyoming Valley Massacre. She retreated to the Chemung after the withdrawal of Butler, and her village was apparently destroyed by the expedition under John Sullivan the following year. Esther probably moved then to Onondaga territory and married an Indian named Tom Hill. She is reported to have died near Cayuga Lake after the turn of the century. Later popular accounts of her activities often confused her with her female relatives, and the story of her atrocities became a staple of 19th-century writers. *Further reading:* Warren H. Smith, "Queen Esther," *The Virginia Quarterly Review* 29 (Summer 1953), 397–407.

MONTRESOR, John (1736–1799) British officer

The son of a British-colonial engineer, Montresor was born at Gibraltar and learned engineering not in school but from his father and from practical field experience. He came to America with his father (also named John) in 1754. With an appointment as a junior officer, Montresor saw extensive service during the Seven Years' War in North America. He led several scouting expeditions and developed fortifications in addition to serving with General James Wolfe and Lord Amherst. He failed to advance far in rank, due probably to his lack of social status and formal training: He was a mere lieutenant at the end of the war in 1763. During the subsequent Pontiac's War, he led an adventuresome expedition toward Detroit. Montresor returned to England in 1766 and acquired an appointment as barracks master in the colonies, to which he returned during the following years. When the Revolution began, he was initially appointed as chief British engineer in America with the rank of captain, but he soon was superseded and relegated to minor assignments. He was at Lexington, Bunker Hill and Long Island. He designed the British plan to take the fort at Mud

Island near Philadelphia on the Delaware River and was one of the principal engineers at the battle of Brandywine. Soon thereafter, however, he came in conflict with the new British commander in chief, Sir Henry Clinton, and Montresor returned to England in late 1778.

MOODY, James. Loyalist soldier, British spy

According to his own account, Moody was an adventurous partisan and spy for the British in New York and New Jersey throughout the first years of the Revolution. He had been a farmer in New Jersey, but he recruited a troop of partisans and accepted a commission as a lieutenant of loyalist volunteers as part of Skinner's Brigade in 1777. He often led raiding parties against the Americans, and during 1778, Moody acted as an intelligence agent for Sir Henry Clinton, gathering information on the location and movements of Washington's army. He was captured in 1780 and was imprisoned at Stony Point. He subsequently escaped and returned to British service. He went to England in 1781 and published a *Narrative of the Exertions and Sufferings of Lieut. James Moody . . .* in support of his claims for losses before the Loyalist Claims Commission. He finally settled in Nova Scotia.

MOODY, John (1759–1781) Loyalist partisan

The younger brother of James Moody, John Moody was active in raiding against the Americans in New York, New Jersey and Pennsylvania as part of the loyalist campaigns in those states. He was captured in Philadelphia in November 1781 during an unsuccessful attempt to seize the papers of the Congress. He was tried, convicted as a spy and hung.

MOORE, Alfred (1755–1810) Officer, jurist

Born in Hanover County, North Carolina, Moore was educated in Boston but returned to his home state to study law with his father, Maurice Moore. He had just begun practice in 1775 when the Revolution began. Moore was appointed by the provincial congress as a captain in the 1st North Carolina Regiment, a unit commanded by his uncle James Moore and ostensibly on the rolls of the Continental Army but which served initially in defense of its home colony, more or less as militia. Moore fought at Moore's Creek Bridge in 1776 and helped defend Charleston in the same year during the first British attempt to take the city. Moore resigned his commission in March 1777 during a period when the war was stagnant in North Carolina and returned to his family's plantation in Brunswick County. After the British invaded the state in 1780, Moore again took the field, this time as a colonel of militia. His principal contribution was to harass the British post at Wilmington in 1781. Even though his estate had been ravaged by the British, Moore recovered his fortunes after the Revolution. He was elected attorney general of North Carolina in 1782 and served until 1791. Thereafter he gained a reputation as the state's most brilliant lawyer. In 1802, he was appointed as associate justice of the U.S. Supreme Court, serving until ill health forced a resignation eight years later.

MOORE, Andrew (1752–1821) Continental officer, official

Moore served during the Revolution as a lieutenant in the 9th Virginia (probably the regiment organized in 1777—there were three Virginia regiments designated as the 9th at one time or another), and his biographies say he was with the army that opposed General John Burgoyne in 1777. He turned to politics in 1780, with his election to the Virginia House, a body in which he served off and on for 20 years. He also achieved the rank of major general in the state militia following the Revolution. He was elected to the U.S. House of Representatives in 1789 and served several terms, interspersed with sessions as a Virginia state legislator. In 1804, he was chosen as one of the U.S. senators from Virginia.

MOORE, James (1737–1777) Continental officer

The brother of Maurice Moore and the uncle of Alfred Moore, James was born on his father's lands in New Hanover County, North Carolina. He served in the colonial forces during the war with France, commanding a post on the Cape Fear River. He had a seat in the legislature from 1764 to 1771 and again in 1773. Moore was one of the strongest local leaders in the agitation against the Stamp Act in 1765, marching at the head of a mob to Brunswick, North Carolina to prevent the issuance of stamps, but he sided with the conservatives during the uprising of the Regulators, fighting as a colonel of artillery at the battle of Alamance in 1771 that put down the western rebellion. Nonetheless, he took leadership in calling for the first provincial congress in North Carolina against royal governor

Josiah Martin in 1774 and was a delegate to the third provincial congress in 1775. In September of the same year, Moore was named to head the 1st North Carolina Regiment, authorized by the Continental Congress to defend the colony against the British and loyalists. He was in command of the patriot army that soundly defeated the Highland loyalists at Moore's Creek Bridge in February 1776, although he was unable to reach the battlefield in person before the fight. In March, he was promoted to brigadier general and placed in command of the defense of North Carolina; however, he remained at Wilmington during the British assault on Charleston and did not reach the city until November. He was on his way north to join Washington with the 1st Regiment when he died of a sudden illness in Wilmington.

MOORE, John. Loyalist officer

Moore was a native of North Carolina and served with Lord Cornwallis as a lieutenant colonel of loyalist volunteers. After the seizure of Charleston, South Carolina in the spring of 1780, Cornwallis sent Moore into the back country of North Carolina to drum up loyalist support for a planned campaign. Moore was cautioned to delay active recruiting until after the harvest in the fall, but he immediately began to organize loyalist militia. In June he assembled an undisciplined and ill-equipped force of nearly 1,300 loyalist troops near Ramsour's Mill, North Carolina. On the morning of June 19, Moore's loyalists were surprised by patriot militia led by Colonel Francis Locke. During a confused but vicious battle, Moore's loyalists were defeated and dispersed. He fled to Cornwallis' camp at Camden with a handful of survivors. The precipitous action was a disaster for Cornwallis, who was subsequently unable to organize loyalist support in North Carolina on a meaningful scale.

MOORE, Maurice (1735–1777) Jurist, official

The brother of James and the father of Alfred, Maurice Moore was educated in New England and returned to represent Brunswick, North Carolina in the colonial house several times between 1757 and 1774. He vacillated over whom to support during most of his career. His help to the royal government earned him an associate justiceship and a seat on the governor's council in 1760, but he lost his places after writing a pamphlet against the Stamp Act. He was reinstated in 1768 and then threw his support behind the government against the Regulators, sitting as a judge in the trial that condemned the leaders of the rebellious movement to execution in 1771. Immediately after the trial, however, he reversed course and began public attacks on the royal governor, upholding the rights of the Regulators. He served in the third North Carolina Provincial Congress, opposing the royal government, but he hoped to effect a reconciliation, a position that was dashed by the battle of Moore's Creek Bridge in February 1776.

MORGAN, Daniel (1736–1802) Continental general

Morgan was a colorful, talented and unorthodox soldier—one of the finest in American history. He was born in New Jersey and left home for the Shenandoah Valley as a teenager. He served as a teamster during Edward Braddock's expedition in 1755 (the source of his nickname ''The Old Waggoner''), and during the following year, he ran afoul of a British officer and received 500 lashes—the scars from which he often referred to during the Revolution. He fought in several of the colonial Indian wars when not farming.

He was commissioned to raise a company of Virginia riflemen in June 1775, and it was as a leader of these unique American marksmen that he became famous. His company marched to Boston and joined the gathering army. Morgan and his men were ordered north as part of Benedict Arnold's expedition against Canada in the fall of 1775. They survived the terrible journey, and Morgan was in the van of the assault on Quebec, taking charge when Arnold was wounded. Morgan was captured, however, and held at Quebec until he was paroled and exchanged during the following year. In late 1776, he was given a colonel's commission, and he raised a large force of riflemen. Attached to General Horatio Gates' army, Morgan and his men played crucial roles in the two pivotal battles at Saratoga that defeated General John Burgoyne. The heavy woods and rough terrain of the Saratoga campaign suited well the tactics of the riflemen, who were deadly at long range but who were slow to load and vulnerable to open-ground attacks by regulars.

After wintering with the Continental Army at Valley Forge, Morgan and his rifle corps served with Washington until the summer of 1779, when Morgan abruptly resigned his commission. He pleaded ill health, but in fact he was unhappy to

Daniel Morgan

have been passed over for higher rank and significant commands. He withdrew to his farm in Virginia to nurse his grievances and the arthritis that genuinely afflicted him. Learning of the disastrous American defeat at Camden, North Carolina in 1780, Morgan relented and joined the army. Nathanael Greene, the new commander in the South, gave Morgan responsibility for the light infantry, and Congress belatedly appointed the rifleman as a brigadier general.

Morgan's finest moments came in January 1781 at the battle of the Cowpens, when his innovative use of militia and his personal leadership gave him a stunning victory over Banastre Tarleton. The American victory at Cowpens—added to the defeat of the loyalists at King's Mountain—set on course the ultimate destruction of the British army in the South and, even according to the British, was the first step toward Yorktown. Morgan understood the unique value of militia—they could shoot very well but could not be expected to stand up to a determined open-ground assault by British regulars—and he devised a battle plan that played to these strengths. Unlike the complex textbook schemes attempted by American generals in the North during 1776 and 1777, Morgan's directions were simple and within the capabilities of his men. When his small army executed his orders—he personally limped from campfire to campfire during the night before the battle to explain the tactics—the result was one of the very few clear-cut American battle victories.

Soon thereafter Morgan again pleaded ill health and retreated to his rural home. He appeared on the scene briefly in Virginia later in the year, but contributed little. Morgan continued to farm and speculate in land after the war. He commanded troops in putting down the Whiskey Rebellion in 1793 and served in Congress. *Further reading:* Don Higginbotham, *Daniel Morgan: Revolutionary Rifleman* (Chapel Hill, N.C., 1961); North Callahan, *Daniel Morgan: Ranger of the Revolution* (New York, 1961; reprinted 1973).

MORGAN, George (1743–1810) Continental officer, land speculator

Morgan began business life as an apprentice to the Philadelphia company of Bayton & Wharton, becoming a full partner at age 20. Unfortunately, the firm went bankrupt, but Morgan salvaged a personal claim to a large grant of lands in modern-day West Virginia. The rest of his career was tied up in land dealings and settlement of the west. He helped form the Indiana Company in 1776, acting as superintendent of the firm's efforts to secure valid claims to land. After a prolonged struggle, primarily against the opposition of rivals in Virginia, the Indiana Company's claims were disallowed. During the Revolutionary War, Morgan was commissioned as a colonel and assigned as an Indian agent and commissary. He resigned in 1779. In later years, he helped found the settlement at New Madrid, Missouri. He died in Pennsylvania, where he maintained a home and farm.

MORGAN, John (1735–1789) Physician

Morgan was one of the best qualified and educated physicians in the colonies but received shabby treatment from the Continental Congress. He was born in Philadelphia and graduated in 1757 as one of the members of the first class of the College of Philadelphia, which ultimately became a component of the University of Pennsylvania. He thereupon went to Great Britain to study medicine. He attended lectures in London and spent two years of study at Edinburgh, receiving the medical degree in 1763. Next stop was Paris, where he studied anatomy, and then on to Padua for more advanced training. Returning to London, Morgan was elected as a fellow of the Royal Society and as a licentiate of the College of Physicians. On his return to Philadelphia, Morgan devised a plan to begin a medical school, and in 1768, the new medical department at the College of Philadelphia (providing the only formal training in medicine in the colonies) graduated the first five doctors to be educated in America.

With the outbreak of the War for Independence in 1775, Congress appointed Morgan as the director general of hospitals and chief physician of the Continental Army. He entered on the task of organizing a medical service with zeal and understanding, going first to Boston and then following the army to New York. However, the medical service was a hotbed of controversy and political in-fighting. Regimental surgeons—none of them half as qualified as Morgan—resented any form of centralized medical service, and schemers like Benjamin Rush wanted power for themselves. Morgan was demoted and then dismissed in January 1777 without cause other than that he stood in the road of those who had more political acumen than he. The injustice and public humiliation affected Morgan deeply, and he withdrew from public life. *Further reading:* Whitfield Bell, *John Morgan, Continental Doctor* (College Station, Pa., 1965).

MORRIS, Cadwalader (1741–1795) Delegate to Congress, merchant, militiaman

Born in Philadelphia, Morris was an import trader and lived for several years in the West Indies as a commercial agent. He was a strong financial backer of the Revolution, contributing his time and personal fortune toward supply and transport for the army in 1780. He also served as a member of the elite Philadelphia Light Horse Troop militia. He was one of the original directors of the Bank of America in 1781, and in 1783 and 1784 he served as a delegate to the Confederation Congress. Following the war, he purchased and operated an iron furnace in Berks County for two years, but he returned to the city in 1790 and again became an importer.

MORRIS, Gouverneur (1752–1816) Delegate to Congress, official

Born into the aristocratic Morris-Gouverneur families of New York (he was the half-brother of Lewis Morris), Morris was one of the strongest nonmilitary supporters of the Revolution and a skilled writer, politician and diplomat. He attended King's College (later Columbia) and became a lawyer before age 20. He held a strongly expressed aversion to democracy all his life, but he early embraced the principles of the Revolution, serving in the New York provincial congress in 1776 and 1777 and helping to draft the constitution of the new state.

In 1778, Morris was elected to the Continental Congress, where his interest in finance and diplo-

Gouverneur Morris

macy and his facile pen were put to good use. However, he became entangled in New York state politics over the question of claims to Vermont and was defeated for reelection in 1779. He then moved to Philadelphia. In early 1780, he published a series of articles on finance that resulted in his appointment as assistant to the new secretary of finance, Robert Morris, to whom Gouverneur was not related. During the same year, he fell from his carriage and suffered amputation of a leg as a result—a handicap that seldom slowed his activities in subsequent years. He aided Robert Morris in the arduous but ultimately unrewarded tasks of national finance until 1785, devising a system of decimal coinage, for example. He was a strong supporter of the federal constitution and a strong central government, although railing against the mob. The delegates to the constitutional convention made Morris the chairman of the committee on style, and the U.S. Constitution is largely written in his words. He served with distinction as a diplomat in the 1790s, first in England and then in France during the reign of terror. Still a relatively young man, he returned to New York and rebuilt his fortune and family home. *Further reading:* Max Mintz, *Gouverneur Morris and the American Revolution* (Norman, Okla., 1970); Anne C. Morris, ed., *The Diary and Letters of Gouverneur Morris* (New York, 1888; reprinted 1970).

MORRIS, Lewis (1726–1798) Delegate to Congress, militia general

The half-brother of Gouverneur Morris and the brother of Richard Morris the jurist, Lewis Morris was the heir to the great Morris family estates in Westchester County, New York. He was born at Morrisania (which was located in what is now the Bronx) and graduated from Yale in 1746. As the eventual third lord of the manor

(the holdings reverted to the status of a private estate after the Revolution), Morris devoted his young adulthood to learning its management. He received all the property and attached rights in 1762 on his father's death. As the Revolution approached, Morris found himself nearly a lone patriot voice in what proved to be strongly loyalist territory. The region was dominated by loyalist families such as the De Peysters, and Morris barely managed to gather a small meeting to elect delegates—himself at their head—to the provincial convention in New York in 1775. The convention in turn selected him as a delegate to the Continental Congress, and he served there as a hard-working committeeman until 1777. He was absent in New York during the vote on independence in the summer of 1776, but he signed the document in August. Morris was also a brigadier general of New York militia and commanded troops during the summer campaign of 1776 when the British chased the Continental Army. His great estates were overrun and his family forced to flee. Morris retired from his congressional seat in 1777 and continued his public service as a county judge and state senator. Although promoted to major general of militia, he did not serve again in the field. He reclaimed Morrisania after the British evacuation in 1783 and devoted much of his energies to rebuilding the ravaged estates.

MORRIS, Margaret Hill (1737–1816) Diarist

Margaret Hill was born in Annapolis, Maryland, the daughter of a Quaker merchant in Madeira wine who sent six of his children, including Margaret, to Philadelphia while he, his wife and a son departed for the isle from which his product came. Margaret was raised thereafter by an older sister. In 1758, she married a dry goods merchant, William Morris, who died in 1765. She moved to Burlington, New Jersey in 1770 to be near two of her married sisters. During the Revolution, Hill kept a detailed diary, intended to be given to one of the sisters who had since moved away. Her account of the effects of the Hessian occupation of New Jersey in late 1776 and the following campaign is particularly interesting. She moved back to Philadelphia in 1791 but returned to Burlington six years later. *Further reading:* Margaret Hill Morris, *Private Journal Kept during the Revolutionary War* (Philadelphia, 1836; reprinted New York, 1969).

Robert Morris (the financier)

MORRIS, Robert (1734–1806) Delegate to Congress, merchant, government official

Known as the "Financier of the American Revolution," Morris was one of the central figures of civil government during the latter years of the struggle for independence. Had his ideas and efforts garnered more support, the first decades of the new nation might have been easier. He was born in Liverpool, England and emigrated to Maryland with his father at age 13. He subsequently moved to Philadelphia and went to work in a counting house. By the eve of the Revolution he was a partner in Willing, Morris & Co., the leading mercantile firm in the colonies that controlled a large share of colonial trade.

Morris was a delegate to the first Continental Congress and took key roles in Pennsylvania revolutionary activities during 1775. He was reelected to Congress again in 1776 and signed the Declaration of Independence. As a major figure in Congress, he served on the Secret Committee and eventually became entangled in the Silas Deane affair. Morris often took major assignments to ma-

nipulate the shaky finances of Congress, and he continued to prosper as a private businessman while devoting much of his personal fortune and financial acumen to the patriot cause. He personally provided funds and supplies to Washington's army and at crucial moments did much to keep the war afloat. At the same time, he repeatedly crossed over the line between public trust and personal gain—a line none too clear in the 18th-century—and he was accused of diverting money for his own use and transporting private goods on public vessels. An investigation in 1779 cleared his name, but he undoubtedly was guilty of improprieties. His own view was that his personal fortune was tied to that of the nation and he should be free to pursue commerce on his own while aiding the Revolution.

He left Congress in 1778, but with the near total collapse of national finances in 1780 and 1781, he was recalled to duty and appointed as the first superintendent of the department of finance (and later as secretary of finance). He was faced with an insurmountable set of problems—rampant inflation, worthless Continental currency and a total lack of income for the national government—but he struggled to put things right. He pushed through the charter for the first national bank and stretched foreign loans to the limit to establish credit for the government. He finally left his post in 1784, unable to convince the states to support a central governmental financial system—the narrow defeat of an impost by Rhode Island's intransigence was a fatal blow to the Confederation—but his adroit management had staved off complete collapse. He turned down the post of secretary of the treasury during Washington's first administration but served in the U.S. Senate. In later years, his own financial empire collapsed, due in large measure to unwise land speculation in the new federal District of Columbia and in Ohio, and he was imprisoned for debt. He died penniless. *Further reading:* Clarence Ver Steeg, *Robert Morris: Revolutionary Financier* (1954; reprinted New York, 1976).

MORRIS, Robert (1745–1815) Jurist

The illegitimate son of Robert Hunter Morris and therefore related to the Morris family of New York (Gouverneur and Lewis Morris) but no relation to Robert Morris the financier, this Robert Morris was a lawyer and a judge. He was born in New Brunswick, New Jersey, and although his father, who was chief justice of the colony, never married, Robert was acknowledged as his son and inherited a large estate from him in 1764. Robert was admitted to the bar in New Jersey in 1770 and practiced in New Brunswick, also sitting on the council in 1773. He was named as the chief justice of the state supreme court when it was organized in 1777. He resigned in 1779 after helping to establish a new system of state courts. With the coming of a new federal government in 1789, Morris was appointed as a district judge for New Jersey, and he remained on the federal bench for a quarter century. He died in New Brunswick.

MORRIS, Roger (1727–1794) Loyalist

Born in England, Morris served as an officer in the Royal Army in America during the Seven Years' War, fighting at Montreal and Quebec and eventually rising to the rank of lieutenant colonel. Following the conflict with the French, he retired from the army and settled in New York, where he served on the Council from 1765 until the Revolution. He had amassed large land holdings—he claimed 51,000 acres—but they were confiscated by the patriot authorities. He fled to England in 1776, remaining there the rest of his life.

MORTON, John (1724–1777) Delegate to Congress, legislator, jurist

Morton was the fourth generation of a Swedish-Finnish family that had emigrated to America in the mid-17th century. Raised by a step father and trained at home as a surveyor, Morton practiced surveying when he was not engaged in public office, which was seldom after his 31st birthday. He sat in the Pennsylvania assembly almost continuously from 1756 to 1775, failing to win election only between 1765 and 1768. He was also an early patriot and was one of the colony's delegates to the Stamp Act Congress in 1765. Just before the outbreak of the Revolution, Morton became speaker of the house in Pennsylvania and in 1774 was appointed as an associate justice of the supreme court of appeals, having previously served as a county judge in his native Chester (now Delaware) County. He was one of Pennsylvania's delegates to the Continental Congress, beginning in 1774, and he played a crucial part in the vote for independence in the summer of 1776. The Pennsylvania delegation was split, with Morton standing in the middle. On July 1, he was converted to the

cause of independence and allied himself with Benjamin Franklin and James Wilson to push Pennsylvania onto the affirmative side. He signed the declaration in August. After spending his term in Congress—he headed the committee of the whole that adopted the Articles of Confederation—he retired to his farm in 1777 and shortly thereafter died, the first signer to do so. *Further reading*: Ruth L. Springer, *John Morton in Contemporary Record* (Harrisburg, Pa., 1967).

MOTTE, Isaac (1738–1795) Delegate to Congress, Continental officer

Motte was a native of Charleston, South Carolina and served for 10 years in the British army during the colonial wars preceding the American Revolution. He was commissioned an ensign in the 60th Royal American Regiment in 1756 and fought in the Canadian campaigns that wrested North America from France. He resigned after the end of hostilities and returned to Charleston. By 1772, he was a delegate to the South Carolina colonial legislature, and as a patriot, he attended the rebel provincial congresses in 1774, 1775 and 1776. In June 1775, the Continental Congress authorized South Carolina to raise three regiments for defense against an anticipated British invasion. Motte was commissioned as lieutenant colonel of the 2nd South Carolina, which was organized and equipped during the summer and taken officially onto the rolls of the Continental Army in the fall (although the troops never ventured away from their home state and the South Carolina regiments barely resembled Continental Line units during the first years of the war). Motte fought with his regiment in the defense of Charleston at Fort Sullivan (William Moultrie was the 2nd's commander) and took over as colonel of the regiment in September 1776. The South Carolina regiments were finally reorganized along Continental lines when Benjamin Lincoln came south in 1779, and Motte was retained as colonel of the new 2nd Carolina. However, he had recently turned again to politics and sat as a member of the privy council of the state. He was selected in 1780 as a delegate to the Continental Congress and was away from his nominal command when the British under Sir Henry Clinton took Charleston in the spring, capturing the men of the 2nd Carolina in the process. Motte remained a delegate until 1782. After the war, he was the federal naval officer for the port of Charleston.

MOTTIN de la Balme, Augustin (1736–1780) French volunteer

A Frenchman with a rather convoluted career during the American Revolution, Mottin (or La Balme, as he is styled in some biographical accounts) was not an aristocrat but had managed a career of sorts in the French army nonetheless. He was originally a member of the gendarmerie, but he secured an army commission in 1763 at the end of the Seven Years' War. He reached the rank of major before retiring in 1773. During his service in the French military, Mottin developed training tactics for cavalry and was regarded as something of an authority on the subject. In 1777, he came to America disguised as a doctor—the French foreign office had refused him a regular passport—with a recommendation from Benjamin Franklin. He received a commission from Congress in May 1777 as a lieutenant colonel of light horse and was promoted to full colonel and inspector general of cavalry two months later. Unfortunately, the Continental Army had too many foreign cavalry "experts" at the time (George Washington had little use for cavalrymen under any circumstances), and Congress appointed Count Casimir Pulaski to command of the new cavalry corps. Mottin took umbrage at being relegated to merely training cavalry, and so he resigned in October. Congress accepted his withdrawal as inspector general of cavalry but allowed him to retain his rank, although without assignment or pay. Mottin did not abandon the conflict, however, and in 1778, he attempted to organize cavalry units in Pennsylvania. In May 1778, he went on an ill-fortuned foray into Maine, hoping to organize part of the French-speaking population and Indians into a force that might dislodge the British from their new position in the north woods. His only attempt at an offensive was crushed. Within the year, he shifted his sights to the northwest, where he thought it possible to rally French habitants and Indian allies for a thrust against Detroit. He recruited a small force and set out from Kaskaskia. His camp was overrun by hostile Indians on November 5, 1780, and Mottin was killed along with about 40 of his men.

MOULTRIE, John (1729–1798) Loyalist official, physician

The elder brother of patriot hero Wil-

William Moultrie

liam Moultrie, John was a physician trained at Edinburgh University. He was a leading citizen of Charleston, South Carolina, but he moved to East Florida in the late 1760s at the behest of British General (and governor) James Grant. Moultrie received 20,000 acres of land in Florida and settled into a mansion near St. Augustine. He was lieutenant governor of the province under Grant and acted as governor when Grant went to England in 1771 due to ill health. Moultrie continued to serve in office throughout the war and emigrated to Britain in 1784.

MOULTRIE, William (1730–1805) Continental general

Moultrie was one of the heroes of the first years of the war. He was born in Great Britain and came to Charleston, South Carolina with his father as a boy. He first came to notice as a leader of militia during Indian fighting in the 1760s. At the outbreak of the Revolution, he received a commission as colonel of the 2nd South Carolina Regiment and became one of the principal military leaders of his state. Elected to Congress twice, he declined to serve both times. His fame came from his spirited defense of the palmetto-and-sand Fort Sullivan in Charleston Harbor during the British attempt to take the city in 1776. He skillfully prevented the British fleet under Admiral Parker from gaining control of the harbor and thus frustrated the ill-conducted British campaign to deprive the patriots of a major port. The fort was renamed in his honor. Moultrie was advanced in rank to brigadier general, and after the British seizure of Savannah, he led troops against the invasion of Augustine Prevost. In 1779, Moultrie won another notable victory at Beaufort, South Carolina. The following year, however, he was captured when Charleston fell to Sir Henry Clinton (the defenses of Fort Moultrie had been allowed to deteriorate and the British this time easily took control of the water approaches and surrounded the American army within the city). He was exchanged in 1782 and promoted to major general, but he took no further part in the war. After the Revolution, Moultrie served two terms as governor of South Carolina.

MOWRY, Daniel, Jr. (1729–1806) Delegate to Congress, official

Born in Smithfield, Rhode Island, Mowry was a cooper by trade. He was town clerk of Smithfield for 20 years, from 1760 to 1780, and sat in the Rhode Island colonial assembly for the 10 years immediately before the Revolution. During most of the war, Mowry was a judge of the court of common pleas. From 1780 until 1782, a period when Rhode Island did much to frustrate the formation of a strong central government, Mowry was a delegate to the Continental Congress. He became a farmer after the Revolution and died in his native Smithfield.

MOYLAN, Stephen (1734–1811) Continental officer

Moylan was born in Ireland to a prosperous Roman Catholic mercantile family (one of his brothers became Catholic bishop of Cork, two others came to the colonies) and emigrated to Philadelphia by way of Portugal in 1768. By the beginning of the Revolution, Moylan had established himself as a wealthy and successful merchant who supported the patriot cause, especially among Irish expatriates—he became the first president of the Friendly Sons of St. Patrick in 1771. He was a friend of John Dickinson, and it was through Dickinson's influence that Moylan was named muster master of the Continental Army in August 1775. He served on the personal staff of George Washington at Boston, helping the commander in chief to outfit and organize privateers to raid British supply shipping. He took the post of Washington's private secretary in March 1776.

In June, Moylan was named by the Continental Congress to replace Thomas Mifflin as quartermaster general with the rank of colonel. The quartermaster organization was in dismal straits, and Moylan

did little to mend the deficiencies. Washington's army was plagued by poor supply and logistics throughout the war, and Congress's meddling only made things worse. Moylan's tenure as quartermaster coincided with the crucial New York campaign during the summer of 1776. He was unable to organize support for the army at important junctures, and a great deal of vital matériel was lost to the British for want of transportation. Moylan resigned as quartermaster general in September (Mifflin resumed the office), and he returned to Washington's staff as a volunteer. He was snowbound and unable to join the attack on the Hessians at Trenton but was with the army during the battle at Princeton in early January 1777.

During the same month he was commissioned by Washington and Congress to raise a regiment of light dragoons from Pennsylvania. The unit was designated as the 4th Regiment of Continental Light Dragoons with Moylan at its head as colonel. He was fated, however, to land in the middle of yet another muddled organization. In September the Polish officer Count Casimir Pulaski was named by Congress as the commander of an independent corps of cavalry for the Continental Army, and Moylan's regiment became part of the new structure. Pulaski's inordinate sense of self-importance made him a difficult superior, and inside a month the Pole had quarreled with Moylan and brought court-martial charges, accusing Moylan of insubordination and disrespectful language. Moylan was acquitted, but the two officers were dire enemies thenceforth. However, Moylan remained in command of his regiment, although it dwindled in numbers frightfully—the cavalry wing of the main army was never a real fighting force under Pulaski—and he often had only a handful of troopers. In 1778, Moylan scouted effectively for Washington before the battle of Monmouth, but he did so with only 30 mounted men.

By this stage of the war, Pulaski had resigned overall command of the cavalry, and Moylan was more or less in charge, although the honor was slight. He remained nominally the colonel of the 4th Light Dragoons but apparently did not go with the unit when it moved south in 1780 to join the campaigns in the Carolinas. The regiment was essentially broken up and the troopers reassigned by 1781, when Moylan himself appeared with the main army before Yorktown. Moylan was awarded a brevet as brigadier general when he was mustered out of the Continental Army in November 1783. He returned to his mercantile business after the war and served briefly as U.S. commissioner of loans. *Further reading:* Frank Monaghan, "Stephen Moylan in the American Revolution," *Studies: An Irish Quarterly* (September 1930).

MUHLENBERG, Frederick Augustus Conrad (1750–1801) Delegate to Congress, clergyman, legislator

The younger brother of General Peter Muhlenberg, Frederick likewise held high public office. He was born in Pennsylvania and, like Peter, sent to Halle for education, although his experience was more conventional than Peter's. Frederick returned to Pennsylvania in 1770 and was ordained as a Lutheran minister, serving several small congregations in the German-speaking regions of Pennsylvania until 1773 when he moved to New York City. He fled the British seizure of New York in 1776 and preached for the following three years in back-country Pennsylvania pulpits.

In 1779, his life changed when he was elected as a delegate to the Continental Congress. Thereafter, his career was in public as a legislator, and he never returned to the practice of preaching. He left Congress in 1780 and took a seat in the state legislature, serving as speaker. Following the passage of the new federal constitution (he was president of the Pennsylvania convention in 1787), Muhlenberg was elected as one of the initial representatives to the first U.S. Congress. There he became the first speaker of the U.S. House of Representatives, serving three consecutive terms. He returned to Philadelphia in 1797 and became receiver general of the state of Pennsylvania. *Further reading:* Paul Wallace, *The Muhlenbergs of Pennsylvania* (1950; reprinted Freeport, N.Y., 1970); Oswald Seidensticker, "Frederick Augustus Conrad Muhlenberg: Speaker of the House of Representatives in the First Congress, 1789," *The Pennsylvania Magazine of History and Biography* 13 (July 1889), 184–206.

MUHLENBERG, John Peter Gabriel (1746–1807) Continental general, clergyman, government official

A truly remarkable man, Muhlenberg covered much ground during his lifetime, serving as a senior commander of the Continental Army following a career as a clergyman and going on to a long period in public office. He was born the son

John Peter Gabriel Muhlenberg

of a Lutheran missionary in Pennsylvania, and after preliminary schooling at the Academy of Philadelphia, he was sent to Halle in Germany either to be given advanced education or to be assigned to apprenticeship. The school authorities decided he was not good educational material and apprenticed him for six years to a grocer.

Muhlenberg, however, had other ideas and ran away to join the army. By 1766, he was back home in Pennsylvania acting as his father's assistant. He studied theology and six years later moved to take a congregation of his own at Woodstock, Virginia, in the Shenandoah Valley. The region was populated mostly by German emigrants and Muhlenberg's congregation was nominally Lutheran, but the denominational distinctions were apparently blurred. In 1772, Muhlenberg went to England and was ordained as an Episcopal priest, which under the laws of Virginia allowed him to collect tithes from his congregation when he returned.

His career as a clergyman was near an end, however. He was elected to the House of Burgesses in 1774 and soon thereafter helped form a committee of safety in his local county. In a dramatic gesture in January 1776, Muhlenberg preached a final sermon from his pulpit in Woodstock, and at the conclusion he threw off his surplice to reveal the uniform of a militia colonel. He called on his parishioners to follow him to war and soon thereafter assumed command of the 8th Virginia Regiment, comprised almost entirely of German-Americans. The 8th became the first Virginia Continental unit to fight outside the state when, under Muhlenberg, it marched to the defense of Charleston in the summer of 1776. He was promoted to brigadier general in February of the following year and ordered north with his men to join Washington's main army. Thereafter, Muhlenberg usually commanded a brigade, most often made up of the Virginia regiments of the Continental Line. He and his regiments (two of which were known as "German") performed well at Brandywine, and at the battle of Germantown, Muhlenberg led a deep penetration of the British right wing that nearly won the day for the Americans. He was on the field but not engaged at Monmouth, and he was assigned later in 1778 to a post in the Hudson Highlands. He commanded the reserve when Anthony Wayne took Stony Point, New York in mid-1779.

In 1780, Muhlenberg was assigned to take command of the meagre American forces in Virginia in order to oppose Benedict Arnold's invasion, but difficulty in travel delayed his arrival until after Frederick von Steuben had assumed command. Muhlenberg became von Steuben's second and fought throughout the following year, mostly with hastily assembled Virginia militia. When the grand allied army arrived in Virginia to lay siege to Lord Cornwallis in 1781, Muhlenberg commanded the 1st Brigade of light infantry in the Marquis de Lafayette's division.

He was brevetted as a major general in the fall of 1783 just before he mustered out of the service. He moved to Philadelphia after the war and had almost any political office of his choosing, being recognized by the German population of Pennsylvania as one of the great heroes of the Revolution. He served on the state supreme executive council and subsequently as U.S. representative for three terms. Muhlenberg held a seat as U.S. senator briefly in 1801 but resigned to take an appointment as customs collector for Philadelphia, an office he held until his death. *Further reading:* E. W. Hocker, *The Fighting Parson of the American Revolution: A Biography of General Peter Muhlenberg* (Philadelphia, 1936); Paul Wallace, *The Muhlenbergs of Pennsylvania* (1950, reprinted Freeport, N.Y., 1970).

MULLIGAN, Hercules (1740–1825) American spy   Born in County Antrim, Ireland, Mulligan came to New York with his parents at age six. He became a haberdasher and tailor in the city and supported the rebel cause as a member of the rowdy New York City Sons of Liberty. During the early 1770s, Mulligan's family gave room and board to a young Alexander Hamilton, newly arrived from the West Indies, and the two became friends. When the British took New York in 1776, Mulligan was recruited by Hamilton as a secret intelligence agent for George Washington. Mulligan remained in the city and pursued his trade, making uniforms and clothes for British officers, and gathered odd scraps of information during the course of fitting. He also gleaned information from British officers billeted in his home. He was arrested several times by the British, but nothing could be proved and he was always released. He continued his business after the war, prospering in the trade.

MUNRO, Henry (1730–1802) Loyalist clergyman   Munro was a native of Scotland, educated at both St. Andrew's and the University of Edinburgh and ordained in the Calvinist Church of Scotland, who came to America as chaplain of the 77th Highland regiment during the Seven Years' War. He remained in New York until 1762, when he returned to England for ordination as an Episcopal priest. The church sent him back to America as a missionary. He became rector of St. Peter's Church in Albany, New York in 1768 but worked also as a frontier missionary. His loyalty to the crown was never in doubt. The American patriot authorities refused to let him travel about the countryside during the Revolutionary War but granted him leave to withdraw to Canada, which he did in about 1777. He sailed to Britain in 1778 and died in Edinburgh.

MURPHY, Timothy (1751–1818) American soldier   Murphy was the most famous American rifleman and sharpshooter of the Revolution, although some of his legendary feats are impossible to document accurately. He was born in Pennsylvania and grew to manhood on the western frontier of the colony, serving as an apprentice to a family of settlers in the Wyoming Valley. Along the way, Murphy acquired a remarkable skill with the Pennsylvania long rifle, the favored hunting weapon of the westerners. He joined a company of Northumberland County riflemen in 1775 and served at Boston, Long Island, and during the 1776 campaign in New Jersey, garnering notice for his ability to snipe at British foraging parties and to infiltrate British lines.

In 1777, Murphy was part of a 500-man rifle unit under Daniel Morgan that was sent north to join the army opposing General John Burgoyne's expedition. Although there is slim documentary evidence, Murphy is credited with killing British general Simon Fraser and Sir Francis Clerke at extremely long range during the second battle of Saratoga on October 7. In 1778, after spending the winter at Valley Forge, Murphy went along with three rifle companies into the Mohawk Valley to oppose British-Indian raids. In 1779, he returned to Pennsylvania when his enlistment expired, and he joined a company of Albany County militia. He and a companion were captured by Indians the following year while on a scouting trip. During the night, Murphy and his fellow prisoner escaped their bonds and killed all but one of their captors.

While some of the adventures credited to Murphy may be in doubt, there is certain evidence of his heroism during the siege of American settlers at the Middle Fort at Schoharie Valley, New York in mid-October 1780. A large force of British regulars, Indians and loyalists under Sir John Johnson had cornered 200 Americans in a weak position, and the American commander, Major Melancthon Woolsey, tried to surrender. Murphy, who was part of a 50-man militia unit in the fort, overruled the commander and repeatedly fired on a British flag of parley. Murphy cowed the timid settlers by threatening to kill anyone who tried to surrender. Impressed with such stubbornness, Johnson withdrew. In 1781, Murphy enlisted in the regular army and served under Anthony Wayne as part of the Pennsylvania Line. After the surrender at Yorktown, he returned to Pennsylvania and became a prosperous farmer.

MURRAY, Alexander (1754–1821) Soldier, naval officer   Born in Maryland, Murray originally joined the Continental Army as a junior officer, fighting in the New York campaigns of 1776. He left the army, however, and sailed as a privateer during the later years of the war. He was eventually commissioned in the U.S. Navy and commanded warships during the naval conflicts with France and the Barbary pirates in the late 1790s. From 1811 until his death in 1821, he was the ranking officer in the American naval service.

MURRAY, David. See STORMANT, Viscount.

MURRAY, Sir James (c. 1751–1811) British officer   The son of a baronet, Sir James inherited his title in 1771, the same year he entered the British

army as a junior officer of the 57th Regiment of Foot. He sailed to America from Cork with his regiment in May 1776 and took part in the first British expedition against Charleston the same year. His regiment then assumed station in New York City. In May 1778, Murray transferred to the 4th Regiment as a major and moved to the West Indies theater. By March 1780, he was a lieutenant colonel and his regiment was back in England. Following the war, Murray continued to advance in rank and to fight for Britain in the wars with France. He married a baroness in 1794 and took the name Murray-Pulteney. He died as the result of an accidental gunpowder explosion in 1811. *Further reading:* Sir James Murray-Pulteney, *Letters from America* (Manchester, England).

MURRAY, John. See DUNMORE, Earl of.

MURRAY, John (1741–1815) Clergyman   One of the founders of Universalism in America, Murray had begun his religious career as a Methodist in his native England, but he was cast out by the Wesleyans after he espoused the teaching of British Universalist John Reilly. Murray emigrated to Massachusetts in 1770 and became an itinerant preacher. He was a chaplain for Rhode Island troops during the first months of the Revolutionary War. He founded the first Universalist congregation in America in 1779 and eventually became pastor of the Universalist Society in Boston.

MUSGRAVE, Thomas (1738–1812) British officer   Musgrave entered the British army in 1754 and served with various regiments before the Revolution. In 1776, he became lieutenant colonel of the 4th Regiment of Foot, serving in New York. He was in field command of the unit during the New Jersey and Pennsylvania campaigns, and at the battle of Germantown in October 1777 he distinguished himself when he gathered several companies of infantry and fortified the Chew House, subsequently holding off numerous American attacks and in effect saving the battle for the British. In 1779, he and his regiment were sent to the West Indies. By 1782, Musgrave had been invalided home to England, where he was made colonel and an aide-de-camp to the king. He returned to America with the rank of brigadier general as the final British commander at New York City. Later serving in India, he was made a full general in 1802.

N

NAPIER, Lord Francis (1758–1823) British officer   Napier, who was born in Scotland as the eldest son of a Scots peer, inherited the title of baron in January 1775 on his father's death. He had joined the 31st Regiment of Foot as an ensign the previous month. In 1777, Napier, by then a lieutenant, came with his unit to North America as part of John Burgoyne's expedition. He fought throughout the New York campaign and was surrendered with his regiment after the battles of Saratoga. He kept a journal of the campaign, covering the period from May through November 1777. As part of the Convention Army, Napier was confined along with other officers at Cambridge, Massachusetts. When the Continental Congress abrogated the terms of the Convention signed by General Horatio Gates, fearing that the British would use the exchanged army to release more troops for the war, Napier and his fellows were stranded as prisoners with a nebulous status. He was anxious to return to Great Britain and in February 1778 petitioned Congress to allow a personal exchange, but the legislative body turned down his request. However, in May, Napier bribed his way out of Cambridge and fled to British-held Newport, Rhode Island, whence he sailed for home. He was formally exchanged in October 1780. He subsequently transferred to the 35th Regiment and then to the 4th, but he never again served actively in the field, devoting the balance of his life to politics and supporting the church in Scotland. *Further reading:* S. Sydney Bradford, ed., "Lord Francis Napier's Journal of the Burgoyne Campaign," *The Maryland Historical Magazine* 57, 4 (December 1962), 285–308.

NASH, Abner (1740–1786) Delegate to Congress, state official   Nash was born into the second generation of a Welsh emigrant family in Prince Edward County, Virginia, the elder brother of Francis Nash. He sat in the Virginia House of Burgesses in the early 1760s but was associated with North Carolina politics after he moved to Halifax in 1762. He resettled in New Bern, North Carolina about 10 years later and studied law, becoming a lawyer and gaining a political foothold through two successive advantageous marriages and through his support of the royal government in the Regulator uprising. He turned out to be a formidable foe of Governor Josiah Martin, however, as the clouds of revolution gathered over North Carolina. Nash was a leading member of the North Carolina provincial congresses between 1774 and 1776 and did much to push Martin out of the colony. He was a state legislator during the early years of the Revolution but was elected governor of North Carolina just when the war heated up in the South in 1780. His term was not much of a success, however, and he quarreled continuously with the legislature and the state militia commanders. He declined a second term just as he had declined to serve in the Continental Congress three years before. Nash accepted election to the Confederation Congress in 1782 and returned twice more in 1783 and 1785. He died in New York City while still attending Congress.

NASH, Francis (c. 1742–1777) Continental general

The brother of Abner Nash, Francis was born in Prince Edward County, Virginia, but as a young man moved to the frontier of North Carolina around Hillsboro, where he became a merchant, attorney and local officeholder. He was embroiled in the miniature civil war brought on by the rebellion of the North Carolina Regulators in 1771 and commanded troops under Governor William Tryon at the battle of Alamance. He also sat in the North Carolina assembly and supported the patriot side of the growing conflict during the early 1770s. He was a delegate to the second and third provincial congresses in 1775. Based on his rank as a colonel of militia and his experience at Alamance, the provincial congress commissioned him as lieutenant colonel of the 1st North Carolina Regiment, raised in the fall of 1775 in defense of the colony. He became colonel of the regiment—ostensibly a Continental unit—in April 1776 and helped defend Charleston against the first British invasion attempt. In February 1777, Nash was promoted to brigadier general by the Continental Congress and directed to join Washington's main army after recruiting in the western Carolinas. He was on the field at the battle of Brandywine but was not engaged. On October 4, 1777, Nash led his regiment into combat at the battle of Germantown, a confused fight. He was struck in the leg by a cannonball and died three days later.

NEILSON, John (1745–1833) Delegate to Congress, militia officer

Neilson was one of the principal officers of the New Jersey state militia during the Revolution. He was a native of New Jersey but a graduate of the University of Pennsylvania, and it was from the Pennsylvania Provincial Congress that he received his initial commission as a militia officer in 1775. In 1777, however, he was appointed a brigadier general of New Jersey state forces. He was elected as a delegate to Congress from New Jersey in 1778 but failed to take his seat, in part because he was in active command of New Jersey militia at Newark and Elizabethtown. He also served as deputy quartermaster general for New Jersey from 1780 to 1783. Following the Revolution, Neilson held a variety of local and state offices, including terms on the bench of the state court of common pleas and in the legislature.

NELSON, Horatio (1758–1805) British naval officer

The man who became Britain's greatest naval hero and who certainly must be accounted as one of the greatest naval commanders of all time began the American war as a junior officer. He had gone to sea at age 12 aboard his uncle's ship, *Raisonnable*, in 1770. Transferred to a frigate, he was dispatched in 1771 for a voyage to the West Indies aboard a merchantman, and he learned the waters and the region. In 1773, Nelson volunteered for a government-sponsored naval expedition toward the North Pole and sailed as captain's coxswain. He spent two years in India but was invalided home in 1776. Nelson then received the rank of acting lieutenant and was assigned to convoy duty to Gibraltar, after which he passed his examination and was commissioned as a lieutenant.

Like most successful junior officers, Nelson benefited from patronage: he was appointed immediately after passing his lieutenant's examination to a 32-gun frigate owing to the influence of his uncle, who was by then comptroller of the navy. Sailing to Jamaica on the *Lowestoft,* Nelson entered the American zone of operations. In July 1778, he was taken onto Sir Peter Parker's flagship and then promoted to commander of the *Badger,* a small brig, and dispatched to the Bay of Honduras to cruise against American privateers. Nelson received his post captain's appointment, the first stage in a British naval officer's long rise toward flag rank, in June 1779 when he was given command of the frigate *Hinchingbroke.* After helping to defend Jamaica from the threat of the French admiral d'Estaing's fleet, Nelson cruised the West Indies in search of prizes.

His most important assignment during the Revolution came in January 1780. Governor John Dalling of Jamaica launched an ill-considered expedition up the San Juan River in Central America to seize control of Lake Nicaragua and sever communications between parts of the vast Spanish empire, and Nelson was appointed as senior naval officer. After a slow sail up the river, the British force took the Spanish post at Fort San Juan, but the horrible weather and especially the local mosquitoes began to take a high toll. Almost all the British soldiers and sailors fell ill and by fall, only a handful remained alive. Nelson barely escaped with his life when the expedition was recalled. He returned to England to recuperate and was unable to return to duty for a year.

He took the *Albemarle*, a frigate, to the Baltic in August 1781. The following February, he provided protection for a convoy to Quebec, and afterward visited New York City. His final duty during the American war was to attack Turk's Island off Santo Domingo in March 1783.

He subsequently achieved a string of brilliant naval victories over the French and Dutch during the long wars of the 1790s and early 1800s, culminating at Trafalgar in 1805, where he was mortally wounded. Despite what contemporaries saw as a scandalous private life, his tactical brilliance and inspirational leadership gave him first place in the hearts of his countrymen. *Further reading:* Tom Pocock, *Young Nelson in the Americas* (London, 1980); Pocock, *Nelson and His World* (New York, 1968).

NELSON, Robert (1743–1818) Militia officer

One of the several Nelson brothers of Virginia, Robert was born in Yorktown. He graduated from the College of William and Mary in 1769 and became a lawyer. During the war, he was a militia officer and was captured, along with his brother William, in June 1781 by Banastre Tarleton. After the Revolution, Nelson returned to the law and taught at William and Mary after the turn of the century.

NELSON, Thomas, Jr. (1738–1789) Militia general, delegate to Congress, governor

Thomas Nelson was one of the third generation of Nelsons from Yorktown, Virginia (his "Jr." apparently was in honor of his grandfather Thomas, who had founded the clan in Virginia after emigrating from Scotland in 1700). His father was William Nelson, long-time president of the colonial council, and he was a nephew of a second Thomas and brother of Robert and William Jr. Thomas Jr. went to England at age 14 for education, returning to Yorktown in 1761 after graduating from Cambridge. He was a planter and merchant, seeing to part of his family's businesses, and he entered the House of Burgesses in 1764. Nelson was an intense patriot and an associate of Patrick Henry during the organization of resistance to the government of royal governor Lord Dunmore. He attended the provincial congresses in Virginia and was elected in 1775 as a delegate to the Continental Congress, where he gained a rep-

utation as one of the most jovial men of Congress. However, he was also a serious politician, and he strongly supported independence, voting for the Declaration and signing the document. Unfortunately, he suffered from chronic asthma, and he was forced to resign from Congress in the spring of 1777 due to ill health. Back home, Nelson continued to lead patriot activities as a brigadier general of the militia and commander of state troops. In response to a request from Congress in 1778, he raised a troop of light horse and led it to Philadelphia, only to find Congress had changed its mind. Elected again to Congress in 1779, he served only briefly.

His major contribution to the Revolution came in 1780 and 1781, when the devastating British invasion of Virginia called forth Nelson's aggressive leadership. He worked unceasingly to raise money, supplies and men to fight the British, depleting his own fortune in the bargain, and after the Charlottesville raid that chased Thomas Jefferson from office as head of the state government, Nelson took over as governor of Virginia. He wielded almost dictatorial powers while organizing more and more resistance to the British. He personally led the state troops to join the allied French-American army that gathered to lay siege to Lord Cornwallis in Yorktown in the fall of 1781. Legend has it that he directed the fire of one of the siege batteries against his own house in Yorktown, believing Cornwallis might have chosen it as headquarters. With the defeat of the British, Nelson returned home to discover he was broken financially. His property was nearly all destroyed and he was deeply in debt owing to his support of the war effort. He retired with his large family to a small estate, living parsimoniously until he died at the early age of fifty-one. *Further reading:* Emory G. Evans, *Thomas Nelson of Yorktown: Revolutionary Virginian* (Charlottesville, Va., 1978).

NELSON, William, Jr. (1760–1813) American officer

The brother of Robert and Thomas Nelson of Virginia, William's activities during the war are confused in the military record. One account says he enlisted as a private in the state militia in 1775, although he graduated from the College of William and Mary a year later. He is also listed as major of the Continentals in 1776, despite the fact that he would have been a mere 16 years old (although such a commission was possible, given the importance of his family). Another source notes that he was in command of the 8th Virginia Regiment as colonel from October to December 1777. In 1781, he was captured by the British under Banastre Tarleton during a raid of Charlottesville. Whatever his rank and command during the Revolution, he returned to his profession as a lawyer after the war, and he eventually became a professor at William and Mary.

NESBITT, John (1730–1802) Official, merchant

Nesbitt emigrated to North America from his native Ireland in 1747 and became a merchant. He formed the Philadelphia firm of Conyngham & Nesbitt in 1756, eventually becoming a member of the prosperous Philadelphia merchant class. He was active in radical affairs as a part of the Committee of Correspondence in 1774, and he served as a civilian official during the first years of the war: as paymaster of the Pennsylvania state navy and treasurer of the Philadelphia Council of Safety. He was also a member of the famous 1st Troop of the Philadelphia City Cavalry, an elite unit of mounted militia formed by wealthy merchants of the city. In 1781, Nesbitt became a director of the new Bank of North America.

NEVILLE, John (1731–1803) Continental general, land speculator

Neville was born on his father's estate near the headwaters of the Occoquan River in Virginia. As a young man, Neville served with the British during the Seven Years' War and then moved to Winchester, Virginia, where he was elected sheriff. He began to acquire large tracts of land in the western regions of the colony, including an area (near modern-day Pittsburgh) that was in dispute between Pennsylvania and Virginia. In August 1775, on orders from the Virginia Committee of Safety, Neville occupied Fort Pitt, and he remained in command there for two years. He was commissioned as a lieutenant colonel in the Continental Army and eventually joined Washington's main force, fighting at Trenton, Princeton and Germantown as a senior officer of the 12th Virginia Regiment. In December 1777, he was promoted to colonel and given command of the reorganized 8th Virginia, which he led during the battle of Monmouth the following summer. Soon after he transferred to the 4th Virginia, but by 1779 the unit had dwindled too low for independent existence and the enlisted men were merged into the 3rd Virginia.

Neville and most of the remaining 4th Regiment officers were captured at the fall of Charleston in the spring of 1780. He was mustered out of the army in September 1783 and awarded a brevet as brigadier general. After the war, Neville served on the Supreme Executive Council of Pennsylvania, and as a tax collection official, he was at the center of the Whiskey Rebellion in 1794. He continued to speculate in western lands and was federal agent for land sales north of the Ohio River. He lived the last years of his life on an estate on Montour's Island near Pittsburgh.

NEVILLE, Presley (1756–1818) Continental officer

The son of John Neville, Presley was born at Fort Pitt and attended the College of Philadelphia (eventually part of the University of Pennsylvania), graduating in 1775 at the beginning of the war. He served as a lieutenant in his father's regiment—the 12th Virginia—from 1776 to 1778, and then transferred to the 8th Virginia when his father took command of that unit. Later in 1778, Neville became aide-de-camp to the Marquis de Lafayette with the temporary rank of major. Along with his father and the other officers of the 8th Virginia, he was captured by the British at Charleston in 1780 and exchanged a year later. Married to a daughter of the famed Daniel Morgan, Neville lived the remainder of his life in Pittsburgh as a merchant.

NICHOLAS, Samuel (1744–1790) Continental marine officer

Nicholas was the senior officer of the Continental marines during the Revolution. He was born in Philadelphia to a well-to-do merchant family of secure social standing and spent his early manhood pursuing the pleasures of horse racing, hunting and fishing when not helping out at the family tavern. No details are known, but Nicholas probably also sailed aboard merchant ships before the Revolution.

When the Continental Congress decided to commission a navy in late 1775, it also authorized two battalions of marines—seagoing soldiers who could augment the ship's crews and fight on land if need be. Nicholas received one of the first commissions in late November and served during the balance of the war as the ranking officer. He set up a recruiting station at his tavern in Philadelphia and by December 1775 had assembled the first contingent of U.S. marines. He and his men were assigned to the flotilla under the command of Esek Hopkins. They took ship in January and sailed down the Delaware with orders to raid British shipping in Rhode Island or the Carolinas.

Hopkins, however, had other plans and headed instead toward the Bahamas. Under Nicholas' command were 268 marines, spread out among the crews of Hopkins' eight small ships. The flotilla arrived off the Bahamian island of New Providence on March 2. Hopkins' plan was to capture the British post at Nassau and the store of gunpowder badly needed by the Americans. The British garrison had been reduced to a handful of troops, and the harbor was unprotected by British men-of-war. The town was guarded by two forts, Fort Nassau and Fort Montague. Nicholas loaded 250 marines and sailors onto two American sloops and tried to approach the forts directly for a surprise attack. The British were alert, however, and fired on the Americans before they could get close. Nicholas then landed without opposition on the eastern end of the island and marched on Fort Montague. After a purely ceremonial firing of one of the fort's three-pounders, the British at Montague surrendered. Nicholas raised the Continental flag over the fort, spiked the guns and settled in for the night. The next morning, he marched toward the town, where the British governor, Monfort Brown, surrendered without resistance. Nicholas and his marines took possession without firing a shot. The haul was less than hoped for, however, since Brown had spirited away most of the post's gunpowder. The American flotilla sailed away two weeks later, having accomplished little.

In June 1776, Nicholas was promoted to major. After recruiting a new marine battalion in Philadelphia, he and his men were assigned to the main Continental Army. They joined John Cadwalader's division and were part of Cadwalader's futile maneuverings around Trenton at Christmas. They subsequently fought well at Princeton and spent the winter with the main army in quarters at Morristown, New Jersey. The marines returned to Philadelphia in March 1777 and were again dispersed aboard ships. Nicholas remained in the city, and he spent the remainder of the war as a land-based commander, handling paperwork and recruiting. By the end of hostilities, the command had shrunk as most of the ships of the Continental Navy were captured or sunk. After the Revolution, Nicholas

became a merchant, sailing several times to the Far East, and eventually he settled down as an innkeeper in Philadelphia. In 1919, a U.S. Navy destroyer was named in his honor. *Further reading:* Charles L. Lewis, *Famous American Marines* (Page Publish., 1950).

NICHOLSON, James (c. 1736–1804) Continental naval officer

Born in Maryland, Nicholson served as one of the senior naval officers of the Continental Navy during the latter years of the Revolution. The grandson of a Scots emigrant, Nicholson was educated in England and served with the British navy during the prerevolutionary wars against the French. He lived on the Eastern Shore of Maryland at the beginning of the Revolution and took a commission in the Maryland state navy as captain of the *Defense*. He was reasonably successful as a state officer, recapturing several British prizes on the Delaware River in March 1776. When the Continental Congress appointed several new captains in June 1776, Nicholson received a commission, and he eventually found himself at the head of the seniority list after Commodore Esek Hopkins was dismissed in early 1778. Nicholson's actual accomplishments, however, were overshadowed by those of other captains such as John Barry and John Paul Jones.

Nicholson was appointed to the frigate *Virginia* in late 1776, but the ship was not ready and he temporarily joined the land forces of the Continental Army in Pennsylvania and New Jersey for the end-of-the-year campaign, fighting at Trenton at Christmastime. He did not sail the *Virginia* out of the Chesapeake until March 1778, and he promptly ran her aground on a shoal, where the ship was captured by the British. Nicholson escaped aboard a small boat. He remained ashore until the fall of 1779, when he took command of the 30-gun frigate *Trumbull*. On a cruise in the West Indies in April, Nicholson encountered a 32-gun British privateer, the *Watt*, and fought an inconclusive but hot engagement. He sailed again on the *Trumbull* in the spring of 1781, but the condition of the Continental Navy had been brought low by this stage of the war and he had a crew made up largely of British deserters. When he encountered the British frigate *Iris* (formerly the American *Rainbow*, captured in 1777 and put into royal service), Nicholson discovered that three-fourths of his men refused to fight.

He engaged the British ship nonetheless and was forced to surrender after a 90-minute fight. He retired to New York City after the war and was involved in national and local politics as a supporter of Aaron Burr.

NICHOLSON, Samuel (1743–1811) Continental naval officer

The younger brother of James Nicholson, Samuel was also a native of Maryland. He was in England at the outbreak of hostilities in America between Great Britain and the colonies, but he made his way to Paris and offered his services to the American commissioners there. In December 1776, Nicholson received a commission as a captain and was directed to find his own ship. He went to England, purchased the cutter *Dolphin* at Dover, and returned to France, where he fitted out the vessel as an armed commerce raider. He sailed in May 1777 as part of Lambert Wickes' raiding flotilla and was successful in taking several prizes in the Irish Sea. Returning to France, Nicholson was given the new French-built, 34-gun frigate *Deane*, which he sailed to America. Over the following two years, he cruised the seacoasts of the United States and took several prizes from among British transports and commercial ships. He is credited with taking one of the last prizes of the war when he captured the 20-gun *Jackal* in the West Indies in the spring of 1782. When the United States reconstituted a navy in 1794 in order to fight the French in an undeclared naval war, Nicholson was appointed as the senior captain and sent to Boston to oversee the building of a new heavily-armed frigate, the *Constitution*. He cruised his new command off the coast of New England in 1798 and 1799 but failed to achieve much glory. He spent his last years as superintendent of the naval yard at Charlestown, Massachusetts. The USS *Constitution*, of course, remains in service to this day.

NICOLA, Lewis (1717–1807) Continental officer

Most famous (or infamous) for his suggestion that George Washington proclaim himself king, Nicola—whose name is sometimes rendered "Nicolas" or "Nicholas"—was probably born in France of Protestant parents and educated in Ireland. He came to America around 1766, a veteran soldier already at mid-life. Settling in Philadelphia, he soon became a well-known local figure as a merchant, editor and proprietor of a circulating library. In 1776, Nicola

was appointed barracks master for Philadelphia and "town major" with some responsibility for the city home guard. He also recruited for the Continental Army, and he published three manuals of military practice, at least two of which he had apparently translated from French. In June 1777, the Congress established an Invalid Corps as part of the army, and Nicola was appointed as commander with the rank of colonel. The corps was made up of injured or otherwise debilitated soldiers and officers, who were assigned to noncombatant guard duty. The unit was also to serve as a training ground for young officers, but there is no evidence that this activity ever began. During at least a few months the Invalid Corps helped train new enlisted recruits.

Nicola himself moved to the Continental Army headquarters at Newburgh, New York in 1781, following the defeat of the British in the field. He suggested to Washington in May 1782 that the Congress be abolished and that the commander in chief assume a kingship (perhaps called something else to soothe feelings). As abhorrent as the idea seems in retrospect, it must be remembered that Congress at the time was in almost complete disarray and many thoughtful Americans, especially those holding commissions in the army, saw little to encourage belief that the new nation could survive without a firm hand on the tiller. And, there were few governmental models to recommend themselves other than monarchies. Washington squelched Nicola's idea firmly, and the entire episode was hushed up. Few congressmen knew of Nicola's suggestion, and when he was mustered out in September 1783, Congress made him a brevet brigadier general. He filled several public offices in Philadelphia until 1793, when he moved to Alexandria, Virginia. *Further reading:* "Lewis Nicola," *The Pennsylvania Magazine of History and Biography* (July 1922), 203.

NICOLAS, George (1755–1799) Continental officer, state official

Born at Williamsburg, Virginia, Nicolas was the third generation of a wealthy and eminent Virginia family that had begun in America with a transported felon. Nicolas graduated in 1772 from the College of William and Mary. In 1777, he was commissioned as a major in the 2nd Virginia Regiment, a unit that was reorganized that year. After the war, Nicolas served in the Virginia house, but he moved in the late 1780s to Kentucky, where he sat in the western state's constitutional convention and became its first attorney general.

NIMHAM (c. 1710–1778) Indian leader

Nimham (also known as Daniel Nimham) was one of the few Indian leaders to favor the American side during the Revolution. He was head of a Wappinger band that ceded lands in the Hudson River Valley to the British in the 1740s. He then settled among the Mahicans at Stockbridge, New York. Nimham fought for the British during the Seven Years' War under the direction of Sir William Johnson. In 1762, he went to Great Britain to negotiate settlement of land claims, but the issue was never settled and the prolonged dispute may have influenced Nimham to side with the Americans at the outbreak of the Revolution. He was killed in an ambush near King's Bridge, New York by British troops under John Simcoe in August 1778.

NIXON, John (1727–1815) Continental general

A native of Framingham, Massachusetts, Nixon served in the colonial wars as a member of the British expedition against Louisbourg in 1745 and as an officer throughout the Seven Years' War. He settled on a farm near Sudbury, Massachusetts, married, and led a quiet life until the tensions came to a head between Britain and the colony of Massachusetts. In April 1775, Nixon was a captain of local militia and led his company to the fight at Concord. Within five days of the initial battle, he was named as colonel of militia and raised a regiment that joined the New England troops around Boston, where he was wounded at Breed's Hill. He was commanding his provincial troops as part of the forces besieging Boston when he was commissioned by Congress as colonel of the 4th Continental Regiment in early 1776. He moved with Washington to New York later in the summer, after the British evacuated Boston, and was promoted to brigadier general on August 9. He commanded a brigade in Nathanael Greene's division. Although he missed the battle of Long Island, Nixon and his brigade were in the thick of the battle at Harlem Heights on September 16, 1776, and they fought well despite being at a terrible disadvantage against the seasoned British and German troops. He was assigned to Charles Lee's division after the American withdrawal from New York and reached the main army only in late December. Attached to John Cadwalad-

er's division, Nixon and his men didn't arrive in time for the battle at Trenton. He then joined Philip Schuyler's Northern Department facing the invasion of General John Burgoyne. He had the fortune to be only on the edges of the subsequent battles near Saratoga but nonetheless received damage to his eye and ear when a cannonball passed near his head. He escorted the surrendered Convention Army to Cambridge but was forced by his injuries to retire soon after. He returned to farming and eventually moved to Middlebury, Vermont.

NIXON, John (1733–1808) Financier, official, militia officer

Born in Philadelphia, Nixon was the son of a prominent local merchant and inherited his father's thriving wharf and shipping business when only a teenager. He continued his family's commercial success and became a member of the powerful Philadelphia merchant class by the 1760s. He began to take a lead in patriot affairs in 1765 as a supporter of the nonimportation measures proposed in protest of the Stamp Act. He was a member of the first Philadelphia committee of correspondence in 1774 and was a delegate to provincial conventions in 1774 and 1775. At the time of the first hostilities with Britain, Nixon helped organize the "Silk-Stocking" battalion of the Philadelphia Associators, a militia unit made up of well-to-do merchants. He served as president pro tem of the Pennsylvania Committee of Safety in 1775, and in May 1776, he commanded the defenses of a fort on the Delaware River as well as heading the Philadelphia city guard. He also was a member of the Continental naval board in 1776, and as sheriff of Philadelphia he personally conducted one of the first public readings of the Declaration of Independence in the summer of 1776. His militia unit, of which he was colonel, was called to join Washington in late 1776 when the Continental Army retreated from defeats in New York. The Associators fought at the battle of Princeton in January 1777.

Nixon returned to Philadelphia and remained at civilian duties during the balance of the Revolution, being primarily concerned with trying to keep the faltering American economy afloat. As an auditor of public accounts, he fought vainly to stave off the rampant inflation in the states and to mitigate the drastic depreciation of Continental currency. In 1780, Nixon helped organize the Bank of Pennsylvania as a mechanism to help supply the army. With the organization of the Bank of North America at the end of the war, Nixon was appointed as a director, and he became president of the bank in 1792. Unlike many of his fellow merchants and financiers, he avoided losing his fortune during the postwar years.

NOAILLES, Louis Marie, Vicomte de (1756–1804) French officer

Noailles was the Marquis de Lafayette's brother-in-law and originally had planned to come to America with Lafayette as a volunteer in 1777. Noailles was restrained by his family, however, and remained in France until 1781, when he sailed with Rochambeau's expedition as *colonel en second* of the two battalions of the Royal-Soissonnais regiment that formed part of the French force. Noailles had been born in Paris, the second son of the Duc de Mouchy, and had served as a captain in the Royal French Army since 1773. His promotion to colonel came in 1778, shortly before his regiment sailed. During the American War, he was most prominent at the siege of Yorktown, where he personally commanded the French troops that turned back the last-gasp British sortie against the siege trenches. He represented the French during the pre-surrender negotiations, acting in concert with American John Laurens. After his return to France, Noailles was deeply embroiled in the first months of the French Revolution as a member of the Estates General, leading the legislative forces that abolished the ancient rights of the nobility. He commanded a revolutionary army but fell out of favor with radicals in Paris and was forced to leave France in 1792. He came to Philadelphia and went into the banking business as a partner in the firm of Bingham & Company. Politics changed in France, and he was eventually allowed to return. He received a command in the West Indies during the reign of Napoleon and was fatally wounded in fighting at sea against the British.

NOIRMONT, de. See PENOT LOMBART de NOIRMONT.

NORMAN, John (c. 1748–1817) Engraver, publisher

Norman, who apparently was born in England, turned up in Philadelphia in 1774, advertising himself locally as an architect and engraver. He was a partner in the firm of Norman & Ward and turned out a large number of mediocre engravings as book plates and individual prints. In 1776, he published

Frederick, Lord North

a map of Philadelphia titled *A Map of the Present Seat of the War.* He moved to Boston in 1781 and continued to publish engravings and book plates, many of which appeared in the two-volume *Impartial History of the War in America between Great Britain and the United States* of 1781 and 1782. He died in Boston, nearly bankrupt.

NORTH, Frederick, Lord (1732–1792) British official

As chief minister for George III during the entire American Revolution, North was at the center of British policy, yet he left many decisions to others as he concerned himself with the politics of holding Parliamentary majorities. He was the son of a nobleman and educated at Eton and Oxford. Elected to Parliament at age 22, he first held office as a lord of the treasury in 1759 and progressed through a series of increasingly important government posts over the next decade. When the Duke of Grafton resigned, North took office as head of government in March 1770. He and the king formed a close association, with North doing all he could to maintain the king's policies and majorities in Parliament. North also was directly responsible for much of the policy leading up to the war, including the continuation of the import tax on tea and the Boston Port Bill of 1774. While most of the day-to-day direction of the war fell on others, North's major role was to keep the king's party in power. He was never convinced, however, of his own abilities and repeatedly begged to resign, but George III refused to let him go, regarding North as the best tool available. North was convinced by the defeat of Lord Cornwallis in October 1781 that the war was hopeless, but the king insisted that North remain in office and continue to press for renewed efforts. When his majorities dwindled, however, North resigned his government in March 1782. He returned briefly to power as part of a coalition government in 1783. North continued to play a role in politics off and on during the following years, despite going blind in 1789. *Further reading:* Peter Thomas, *Lord North* (New York, 1976).

NORTH, William (1755–1836) Continental officer, legislator   North was born in the Maine section of Massachusetts and moved to Boston with his mother after his father died in 1763. He served in several units during the early years of the Revolutionary War, including Henry Jackson's Regiment in 1777, the 4th Massachusetts and the 16th Massachusetts. In 1779, North formed a lifelong association when he was appointed as aide-de-camp to the redoubtable Baron Frederick von Steuben. North served as the German volunteer general's assistant throughout the remainder of the war, was adopted as von Steuben's son, and became his heir. North married well after the Revolution, becoming the husband of Mary Duane, daughter of James Duane, and thereby acquiring a considerable estate at Duanesburg, New York. He was a member of the New York assembly during the 1790s, and in 1798, he was appointed to fill an unexpired term as U.S. senator from New York. At the end of his time in the Senate, North was named as adjutant general of the reorganized U.S. Army, serving until mid-1800. In later years, he was a member of the state commission that made plans for the Erie Canal.

NUTTING, John. Loyalist   Nutting was a master builder before the Revolution in Cambridge, Massachusetts. He moved to Boston in 1774 and helped construct barracks and fortifications. He evacuated with the British fleet to Halifax, Nova Scotia in 1776 and for a time became a privateer. After a trip to England, he returned to America in 1778 but was captured by the Spanish. Following his release, Nutting served as an engineer in New York. Part of his settlement after the war was a land grant of 500 acres on the Penobscot River, where he established a loyalist enclave.

O

O'BRIEN, Jeremiah (1744–1818) State naval officer, privateer Born in Kittery in the Maine section of Massachusetts, O'Brien lived most of his life in Machias, a frontier village where he was in the lumber trade with his father. He gained considerable fame in May 1775, when—inspired by news of the battles at Lexington and Concord the month before—he organized a party of local Machias citizens to seize three British ships, the schooner *Margaretta* and the sloops *Unity* and *Polly,* that had put in to take on a load of lumber. Royal Navy midshipman James Moore rallied his crews and tried to escape, but O'Brien seized the *Unity* and used it to chase down and capture the other two British vessels, killing Midshipman Moore during the chase. The Massachusetts authorities were impressed with this action, one of the first naval engagements of the war, and appointed O'Brien to a post in the Massachusetts state navy in August. He commanded the captured *Unity* (now armed with three guns taken from the *Margaretta*) and the *Diligence,* another British schooner O'Brien had captured during the summer. He cruised the waters off Maine until the fall of 1776. The following year, O'Brien became one of the host of privateers authorized by the state of Massachusetts, and commanding the *Resolution,* he captured the *Scarborough.* In 1780, O'Brien was himself captured aboard his new ship, *Hannibal.* Held for a while on a prison ship in New York Harbor, he was eventually transferred to Old Mill Prison in Plymouth, England. Like many of his fellow naval prisoners, he managed to escape and return to America. He commanded two more privateer ships before the end of the war. O'Brien continued to live in Machias after the Revolution and served as collector of customs there from 1811 until his death. *Further reading:* A. M. Sherman, *The Life of Capt. Jeremiah O'Brien* (1902).

OCONOSTOTA (c. 1710–1785) Indian leader A principal war chief of the Cherokee for many decades before the Revolution, Oconostota sided with the British during the revolutionary struggle despite a long history of warfare against the redcoats. He had traveled to England in 1730 and personally met King George II. During the 1750s, the Cherokee came into conflict with the British over white settlement of Indian lands, and Oconostota began a long campaign after an unsuccessful peace parley in 1759. He led a two-year effort known as the Cherokee War in 1760–61, defeating the British several times and seizing Fort Loudon in modern-day Tennessee. He was finally forced to make peace and even signed a treaty with the Iroquois in 1768. During the Revolutionary War, Oconostota led war parties against American settlements, although some factions of the Cherokee supported the rebels.

ODELL, Jonathan (1737–1818) Loyalist clergyman, physician, writer, spy The versatile Reverend Odell of New Jersey was descended from early Connecticut settlers. He graduated from Princeton (his grandfather had been the school's first president) and served as a surgeon in the British army during the 1760s. He then went to England and was ordained a priest in the Episcopal Church in 1767. His first assignment was as a missionary to Burlington and Mount Holly, New Jersey. In 1771, he also began to practice medicine again. Odell was, in addition, a poet of a political bent, and his satires on the patriots caused much squirming among rebels in the early days of the Revolution. The Provincial Congress of New Jersey and Pennsylvania's Committee of Safety both found him to be a dangerous influence and ordered him confined to the east side of the Delaware within an eight-mile radius of the Burlington courthouse. He fled to British-held New York in December 1776, where he served in many offices and capacities over the following years. For example, he was one of the conduits for messages between Benedict Arnold and the spy Major John André. He published more of his loyalist verse in Rivington's *Gazette,* and when the British occupied Philadelphia, Odell was appointed superintendent of printing offices and publications in the city, an appointment that provided him with an official income. In 1778, he became chaplain of a "Loyalist corps," and in 1781 served as assistant secretary to the Board of Directors of the Associated Loyalists, headed by Governor William Franklin, to whom Odell was closely attached. Odell then took a position with General Sir Guy Carleton as a translator of French and Spanish. When Carleton withdrew to England Odell went along, but he returned to New Brunswick, Canada in 1784, where he eventually became provincial secretary.

OGDEN, Aaron (1756–1839) Continental officer

Ogden graduated from Princeton in 1773, a classmate of Light-Horse Harry Lee and a close friend of Aaron Burr. By 1775, he was a schoolmaster and a member of the local militia in his hometown of Elizabethtown, New Jersey. In January 1776, he took part in the expedition that captured the British transport *Blue Mountain Valley* off Sandy Hook. In November of the same year, he received an appointment as 1st lieutenant in the 1st New Jersey Regiment, of which his brother was lieutenant colonel. When the unit was reorganized and Matthias took command as colonel, Aaron was made regi-

Aaron Ogden

mental paymaster. After fighting with the 1st New Jersey at the battle of Brandywine, Ogden transferred to become a brigade major with General William Maxwell and then assistant aide-de-camp to Lord Stirling. He returned to service under Maxwell as an aide in 1779 for the large expedition in the late summer of that year against the Iroquois. During 1780, Ogden participated as part of Maxwell's brigade in opposing Baron von Knyphausen's raid on Springfield, New Jersey. He joined the light infantry under the Marquis de Lafayette in 1781 after Maxwell resigned from service. At Yorktown, Ogden distinguished himself during the assault on Redoubt Number 10, receiving a wound in the action. He continued a public career after the war, first entering into a law practice in New Jersey. He served as a lieutenant colonel in the new U.S. Army in 1799–1800. In 1812, Ogden was elected governor of New Jersey, and he was appointed a major general the following year. His later years, however, were devoted to forming a steamship company, which ran afoul of monopolies granted to James Fulton and Robert Livingston. After long court battles, Ogden was impoverished and thrown in prison as a debtor in 1830. He was eventually released but never recovered his fortunes.

OGDEN, David (1707–1800) Loyalist lawyer

Before the Revolution, Ogden was one of the preeminent attorneys in New Jersey, standing high in the estimation of even his adversaries. He was born in Newark and graduated from Yale in 1728. He rose very rapidly in the legal profession and enjoyed a long and successful career. He served on the Council and was a judge of the New Jersey Supreme Court. At the coming of the Revolution, Ogden fled to New York as soon as the British army had wrested the city from the patriots in 1776. He wrote a plan for a restored government in America, which he hoped could be put in place as soon as the rebellion was stamped out, that called for an American representative parliament, no taxation from Britain, and royal governors for the colonies. After the British defeat, Ogden went to England, where he acted as an agent for loyalist claims. In 1790, he returned to America and settled on Long Island, living there the rest of his long life.

OGDEN, Isaac. Loyalist lawyer

The son of David Ogden, Isaac Ogden practiced law in New Jersey and followed his father in loyalist sympathies. However, in 1775 he sat in the New Jersey Provincial Congress at the behest of loyalist governor William Franklin in an attempt to deflect the movement toward openly violent rebellion. When it became clear that nothing could stop warfare, he withdrew. Ogden was with the British army when it invaded New Jersey in 1776, but he was forced to flee the following year under threat of hanging if he were taken by the Americans. He remained in New York during the rest of the Revolution and corresponded often with fellow loyalists in England. In 1778, he wrote in a letter: "The rebellion hangs by a slender thread. The majority of the inhabitants dissatisfied with their tyrannical government. Their money depreciating; the French Alliance in general detested; provisions scarce, and that scarcity increasing. . . . In this situation what is necessary to crush the rebellion? It is easily answered. Only one vigorous campaign, properly conducted." He was correct for the most part in his assessment. Fortunately for the American patriots, the decisive campaign never materialized, and the rebellion survived the trials he so accurately described. With the final British defeat, Ogden left New York for Canada, where he served as a judge.

OGDEN, James (d. 1781) British spy

Ogden was a resident of South River, New Jersey, and either was a relatively innocent loyalist who got caught up in a situation that turned out to be desperate from his point of view, or was a hardened British spy caught while working at his trade—the facts are unclear. Whatever his motivation and background, Ogden was dispatched by Sir Henry Clinton in January 1781 as a guide for John Mason, who was assigned to subvert the mutinous enlisted men of the Pennsylvania Line regiments camped at Princeton, New Jersey. Ogden successfully found the mutineers, but they refused to hear Mason's blandishments and seized the pair of British negotiators. While talks went on between the disaffected Pennsylvanians and their officers (and representatives of Congress), Mason and Ogden were tried by a board and found guilty of spying. They were hanged on January 11.

OGDEN, Matthias (1754–1791) Continental officer

The elder brother of Aaron Ogden, Matthias Ogden was born in Elizabethtown, New Jersey. His father was a prominent colonial officeholder who had supported the patriot cause, a cause also adhered to by both of his sons. Matthias was a student at Princeton when the war broke out, but he left soon after the first guns sounded to join the patriot army gathered at Boston, and like his companion and fellow Princeton student Aaron Burr, Ogden attached himself to Benedict Arnold's expedition to Canada as a volunteer. He survived the grueling march north through the wilderness and came to the limelight when he was sent by Arnold to deliver a call for surrender to the British garrison at Quebec: He scurried back to the American lines when one of the defenders plucked dust near his feet with a musket ball. He was wounded during the futile American attack on Quebec on December 31, 1775.

On his return to New Jersey, he was commissioned as lieutenant colonel of the 1st New Jersey Regiment. The unit was reconstituted at the end of 1776 when enlistments expired, and in January 1777, Ogden was named colonel of the new version of the 1st New Jersey. He commanded his men as part of Lord Stirling's division at the battle of Brandywine. After wintering at Valley Forge, he and the New Jersey regiment formed part of Charles Lee's force at the battle of Monmouth. Ogden was reported to have been angry and frustrated at Lee's inexplicable withdrawal in the face of the British—a move that cost the Americans a decisive victory. In the fall of 1780, Ogden was captured by the British at Elizabethtown. He was exchanged in April 1781, and he remained in command of the 1st New Jersey until it was disbanded in April 1783. Ogden then took leave and went to France, where he was well received by the royal court. On his mustering out in September, Ogden received a brevet as brigadier general. He returned to Elizabethtown and lived there until his death. *Further reading:* "The Journal of Major Matthias Ogden," *New Jersey Historical Society Proceedings* (January 1928).

O'HARA, Charles (c. 1740–1802) British general

O'Hara was the illegitimate son of an Irish peer, Lord Trawley, and therefore a member of a rich and influential Irish family, albeit born on the wrong side of the blanket. His father was colonel of the elite Coldstream Guards, and O'Hara entered his father's regiment as a teenager. He fought in the European wars and in 1766 took command of a military convict regiment in Africa with headquarters in Senegal. By the time of the American war, O'Hara was a senior Guards officer. He came to New York in mid-1778 and was employed by Sir Henry Clinton to command the British defenses at Sandy Hook. His best service came in the southern theater after 1780. He served under Lord Cornwallis during the arduous campaigns against Nathanael Greene and was a genuine British hero at the battle of Guilford Courthouse, leading the Guards in one of the assaults late in the battle that broke the American position and allowed Cornwallis to claim victory. O'Hara received two wounds during the engagement but recovered sufficiently to go with Cornwallis into Virginia, where he had the dubious honor of representing Cornwallis at the surrender at Yorktown in October 1871. Cornwallis was too embarrassed to appear in person, so O'Hara was sent in his place to present the commander's sword to Benjamin Lincoln, the designated American representative. He was exchanged in February 1782 and returned to England with the rank of major general. He subsequently served in the wars against revolutionary and Napoleonic France, reaching the rank of full general and commanding the vital British post at Gibraltar.

O'HARA, James (1752–1819) Officer, businessman

Born in Ireland and educated in France, O'Hara came to Philadelphia in 1772 and became an Indian agent. Despite his recent emigration, he was a patriot and served as a captain in an unspecified regiment. In 1780, he became the commissary at the hospital in Carlisle, Pennsylvania. He acted as an assistant quartermaster under Nathanael Greene during the final three years of the war. O'Hara continued as a civilian supplier of goods to the government after the Revolution and was a quartermaster to the U.S. Army during the 1790s. He launched several important business ventures after the turn of the century, including the first glassworks in Pittsburgh, an ironworks, and a cotton trade with the mills of Liverpool.

OLIVER, Andrew (c. 1707–1774) Royal official

Oliver was one of the principal objects of anti-British agitation in Boston in the years leading up to the Revolution, especially during the Stamp Act crisis. He was born in Boston and graduated from Harvard in 1724. He married a sister of royal official Thomas Hutchinson and was closely associated with Hutchinson during most of his public career.

Oliver was the epitome of the loyal officeholder in prewar America: he claimed income from several official positions. When Parliament passed the Stamp Act, Oliver nearly alone consented to act as a stamp agent, sniffing a healthy income from the post even though he believed the Act to be dangerously unpopular. So it proved to be, and Oliver himself bore the brunt of public fury. In August 1765, Oliver was hung in effigy from a tree near Boylston Market in Boston. The figure bore the doggerel verse:

What greater joy did New England see
Than a stampman hanging on a tree.

In case he missed the point, the effigy was marked with Oliver's initials. A large mob defeated the efforts of the sheriff to remove the effigy throughout the day, and as evening approached, the crowd carried the effigy to a building that Oliver owned at the waterfront and that he had intended to use as his stamp office. They demolished the building in less than half an hour and then proceeded to Oliver's house, where they burned the effigy figure on a bonfire.

The mob soon got out of hand. First the windows of Oliver's house were broken and then the destruction began in earnest. Within hours, the entire house and its contents were in shambles. The government could do nothing, and even worse humiliation for Oliver was to follow several months later, when he was forced to resign publicly his office as stamp collector and repudiate the Stamp Act while standing in a pouring rain under the Liberty Tree. The immediate crisis passed, however, with the repeal of the act. In 1770, Oliver was appointed as lieutenant governor, acting as second in command of government to his brother-in-law. He supported Hutchinson's increasingly difficult position as the agitation for rebellion grew to fever pitch in Boston. In March 1774, before the cauldron finally bubbled over, Oliver died following a short attack of fever.

OLIVER, Peter (1713–1791) Loyalist jurist

The brother of Massachusetts royal lieutenant governor Andrew Oliver, Peter also occupied high office in the colony before the Revolution. He was a graduate of Harvard and, although he was not a trained lawyer or a member of the bar, he served as chief justice of Massachusetts. He left Boston in 1776 aboard a British ship in the evacuation forced by Washington and the patriot army. Stopping first at Halifax, Nova Scotia, he eventually arrived in England, where he received an official pension.

OLIVER, Thomas (d. 1808) Loyalist official

Thomas was not related to Andrew and Peter Oliver of Massachusetts, although he was of the same official circle. He was born in Dorchester, Massachusetts and graduated from Harvard in 1753. His place in the history of the rebellion in Boston is confusing, since he succeeded Andrew Oliver as lieutenant governor on the latter's death in 1774. Thomas, therefore, became the last royal lieutenant governor of Massachusetts. He evacuated with the rest of the British and loyalists in 1776, first to Halifax, Nova Scotia and thence to England.

OLMSTED, Gideon (1749–1845) Privateer

Olmsted, a native of Connecticut, sailed under both American and French letters of marque during the war. From 1776 to 1778, he captained the sloop *Seaflower* and then took over a French ship, the *Polly*. The British captured him at sea in 1778, but he and other prisoners broke free, seized a sloop, and sailed it safely to America. From 1779 to 1782, he plied the waters around New York Harbor as a privateer. During the early 1790s, Olmsted returned to France and to privateering under the French flag against the British. He retired from the sea before the turn of the century and returned to his hometown of East Hartford, Connecticut, where he became a merchant.

ORR, Hugh (1715–1798) Manufacturer

Orr did a good deal to supply New England with much-needed industrial technology by importing skilled workmen from England and Europe. He was an emigrant himself, coming to East Bridgewater, Massachusetts in 1740 from his native Scotland. His first job was in a shop as a scythe maker, but within five years he was the owner of the tool-making shop and had begun a long career of manufacturing. He was one of the first Americans to make muskets in quantity, turning out 500 in 1748. During the Revolution, his factories supplied muskets to the patriots, and he established a cannon foundry in East Bridgewater. Following the war, Orr began to hire foreign industrial workers, such as Scots mechanics, who brought with them knowledge of manufacturing techniques and equipment that helped establish the nascent American economy, especially the textile trade in New England.

OSGOOD, Samuel (1748–1813) Delegate to Congress, Continental officer, government official

Osgood was born in Andover, Massachusetts and graduated from Harvard in 1770. He attended the provincial congress in the colony in 1775 and then joined the army. During the forepart of the war, Osgood served as an aide to General Artemas Ward and as an assistant quartermaster, reaching the rank of colonel. He continued to be active in political office, however, and was elected to the state senate in 1780, having also served in the Massachusetts constitutional convention the year before. In 1781, Osgood was elected as a delegate to the Congress. He remained for three terms, mostly taking interest in financial affairs and serving as one of the directors of the new Bank of America. He was appointed as a commissioner of the U.S. treasury in 1785, one of a group that took over the bankrupt finances of the central government from Robert Morris. Osgood opposed the new federal constitution, but that stance did not prevent him from petitioning George Washington for a federal appointment after ratification. He was named the first postmaster general of the new government in 1789, serving for two years in New York City. Osgood remained in New York after he resigned, gaining election to the state legislature in 1801. In 1803, he won another federal appointment as naval officer for the port of New York, a post he held until his death.

OSWALD, Eleazer (c. 1755–1795) Continental officer, publisher

Born in England and a distant relative of British diplomat Richard Oswald, Eleazer emigrated to America in the early 1770s and became a patriot. He served as a private soldier during the first months of the conflict in New England and after taking part in the capture of Fort Ticonderoga was attached to Benedict Arnold's expedition to Quebec. During the campaign in the north, Oswald became Arnold's personal secretary and led the American "forlorn hope" (an advance suicide squad) in the unsuccessful assault on Quebec City in December 1775. Wounded and captured at the city gates, he was not exchanged until January 1777. On his return, Oswald was commissioned as a lieutenant colonel in the 2nd Continental Artillery. He fought with considerable distinction during the Danbury Raid in April 1777 and developed a reputation as a skilled and active artillery officer. However, he was piqued by his failure to advance in rank after the battle of Monmouth in 1778, and he resigned from the army. He then turned to publishing in Baltimore, becoming a partner in the *Maryland Journal*. In 1782, he moved to Philadelphia and issued a violently partisan paper, the *Independent Gazetteer*, and operated a coffeehouse. He later moved to New York City and took over a paper previously published by his wife's relations. He was a political foe of Alexander Hamilton and nearly fought a duel with the latter in the late 1780s. Oswald left America for England in 1792 and then moved to France, where he again became a soldier as a colonel of artillery in the revolutionary army. He died of yellow fever after returning to America.

OSWALD, Richard (1705–1784) British diplomat, businessman

Oswald was born into a family of Scots parsons and after marriage to an heiress in 1750 established a profitable commercial trade based on her inherited land holdings in the West Indies and America. He had lived for six years in Virginia as a young man and knew the colony well from extensive travel. He profited as a supplier to the British army during the Seven Years' War but had built his fortune on the slave trade. He and his partners owned an island at the mouth of the Sierra Leone River from which they directed the traffic in human lives to the West Indies and the southern American colonies. Oswald's chief factor for the slave trade in South Carolina was Henry Laurens, and the two formed a long, warm relationship based on 20 years of commerce and correspondence.

Oswald stood high in the councils of the British government before and during the American war and was consulted frequently by Lord North and George Germain, who wished to draw on Oswald's extensive knowledge of the former colonies. When Henry Laurens was captured on his way to Europe and thrown into the Tower of London in 1780, Oswald visited his friend often and tried to gain his release. The defeat of Cornwallis in the autumn of 1781 eventually brought the downfall of North's wartime government, and the new government under Lord Rockingham selected Oswald to begin informal negotiations with the American commission in Paris. Laurens (while still imprisoned) had been named by the Congress to the peace commission, and Oswald helped effect his release in 1781, paying £2,000 toward Laurens' bail.

Oswald traveled to Paris in mid-1782 under instructions from the new secretary of state, Lord Shelburne, to talk to Benjamin Franklin. Delaying formal negotiations until he could be joined by his fellow commissioners, John Jay, John Adams and Laurens, Franklin nonetheless discussed preliminary terms with Oswald, who returned to England for more consultation with the government. When Rockingham died in July and Shelburne took over as prime minister, Oswald was officially commissioned to deal with the Americans. He returned to Paris and reached terms that eventually formed the basis for the peace treaty. Despite his success, he was censured in the House of Commons for making too many concessions, and he retired from public life in February 1783, when the Shelburne government was forced to resign. *Further reading:* W. Stitt Robinson, Jr., ed., *Richard Oswald's Memorandum . . .* (Charlottesville, Va., 1953).

OTIS, James (1725–1783) Legislator, attorney, orator, writer

Otis was an influential, albeit distressingly erratic, leader of the Massachusetts dissidents during the 1760s and is justly credited with formulating some of the basic intellectual foundations of the Revolution. He was born in West Barnstable, Massachusetts. His father, who bore the same name, was an important colonial official and legislator, and his sister, Mercy Otis Warren, came to be one of the first historians of the Revolution. Otis graduated from Harvard in 1743, read for the

James Otis

law, and was admitted to the bar in 1748. Within a short while, he became one of the leading attorneys in Massachusetts, combining a deep learning and grasp of legal fundamentals with a superb gift for oratory and verbal argument. Contemporaries commented often on the fluidity and power of Otis when on his feet and speaking to a point of law.

He was of choleric public temperament, to say the least, however, and, motivated perhaps in part by a personal quarrel with Governor Francis Bernard and Lieutenant Governor Thomas Hutchinson over appointments to office, Otis became the focal point of resistance in Massachusetts to the royal colonial government and the British economic policies of the decade of the 1760s. His behavior and viewpoints are hard to summarize because they seem, in light of the subsequent Revolution, to be more than a little contradictory. He protested the collection of duties and the imposition of the StampAct with the most violent public denunciations and worked along with Sam Adams and Joseph Hawley to foment political opposition to the royal government; however, he also acted as a brake on overt action and consistently opposed the actions of the mob. He found the notion of independence abhorrent, yet he spoke and wrote ideas that fundamentally undermined the connection between crown and colonies.

His first important break with the royal government came in 1761, when Otis resigned as king's attorney and spoke against the writs of assistance that had been requested to help colonial officials collect import duties. In a speech in February 1761, Otis laid down a doctrine that natural right superseded mere legalities and government policies. This early form of argument for inalienable rights was a powerful intellectual underpinning for much of the subsequent revolutionary debate. From this speech onward, Otis opposed Bernard and Hutchinson, and through his alliance with Adams and Hawley, he worked in the colonial assembly and in the Boston town meeting to frustrate the crown officials at every opportunity. He published several pamphlets that gained wide circulation, and he spoke frequently in the legislature and at public meetings. He became head of the Massachusetts Committee of Correspondence in 1764, proposed the resolutions that led to the Stamp Act Congress in 1765, and coauthored the Massachusetts' Circular Letter in 1767.

His instability and inconsistencies, however, led some of his allies to suspect his mental balance, and their fears proved to be well founded. Otis's public and private behavior became more and more erratic—a poor marriage may have added to his emotional and mental burdens—and he was sent over the edge in 1769. Letters from royal officials in the colony accusing Otis of disloyalty were intercepted and published, and in his rage at the charge, he confronted a group of officials in a Boston coffeehouse on September 5, 1769. A fight broke out, and Otis was struck on the head with the flat of a sword by crown officer John Robinson. While he seemed at first to recover from the injury, it was soon apparent that the blow had pushed Otis into insanity. He at times recovered his wits for brief interludes, but his public life was essentially at an end. By 1771, he was declared legally incompetent and placed under the care of his younger brother Samuel. He escaped the care of his relatives in June 1775 and fought at Bunker Hill with a borrowed musket, but he was incapable of any sustained role in public. He died in spectacular fashion in 1783 when struck by lightning while viewing a rural thunderstorm. *Further reading:* William Tudor, *The Life of James Otis* (1823; reprinted New York, 1970); John R. Galvin, *Three Men of Boston* (New York, 1976).

OTIS, Samuel Allyne (1740–1814) Delegate to Congress, legislator   Otis was born in Barnstable, Massachusetts, graduated from Harvard in 1759,

and became a merchant in Boston. He was an active legislator in Massachusetts during the Revolution, being elected to the house of representatives in 1776. He also served on the state board of war and as a collector of clothing for the army in 1777. He returned to the state legislature after the war in 1784 and was speaker of the house. Otis served as a delegate to the nearly moribund Confederation Congress in 1787 and 1788, and the following year he was appointed as secretary to the new U.S. Senate, a position he held until his death in Washington, D.C. a quarter century later.

OTTENDORF, Nicolas Dietrich, Baron. Mercenary   Little is known of Ottendorf's background, but he apparently was a veteran German military freebooter when he appeared in America in late 1776 and convinced the Continental Congress to authorize him to raise an independent corps of foreign mercenaries. The idea was a poor one and little could be expected from such a venture but trouble, but Congress had been persuaded that experienced foreign soldiers could be useful to the faltering American military cause. Under his December 1776 commission, Ottendorf was to command the corps with the rank of major and he was to recruit two companies of "hunters" (apparently jaegers on the German model) numbering up to 160. He took over a few men previously raised by a Captain Schott but failed to find a sufficient number of additional men to make up his corps. He sold the company to the French Marquis de la Rouerie (known in America as Charles Armand), and in June 1777, under an order from commander in chief George Washington, Armand formed his own legion, based on the understrength "corps" assembled by Ottendorf.

OTTO, Bodo (1711–1787) Continental physician   One of the outstanding army hospital surgeons during the war, Otto was also an influential member of the German emigrant community in Pennsylvania. He was born in Hanover, Germany and was well trained as a physician and surgeon in Hamburg. He served as a military surgeon for the Duke of Celle and as surgeon to military prisoners at Lüneburg. He emigrated to America in 1755 after a six-year tenure as chief surgeon of the district of Schartzfels. He first settled in Philadelphia with his second wife but moved to New Jersey in 1760. On the death of his wife, he returned to Philadelphia in 1766 and remarried. In 1773, under the influence of Henry Muhlenberg, Otto moved to Reading, Pennsylvania and set up a practice among the many German emigrants of the region. As the Revolution approached, Otto took part in local patriot affairs, serving on the Berks County Committee of Safety and as a delegate to the 1776 Pennsylvania provincial convention. He was appointed as senior surgeon to the Middle Department in 1776 and set up a hospital to tend the wounded from the battles in New York. In February of the following year, at the direction of Congress, Otto established a military hospital near Trenton to serve smallpox victims. He was reassigned in September to a hospital in Bethlehem, Pennsylvania. In 1778, he took charge of the hospital at Yellow Springs, Pennsylvania, treating the sick from Valley Forge. In 1780, Congress reorganized the military medical service (which had suffered from grave political in-fighting during the first years of the war) and made Otto one of 15 senior hospital physicians. Following the Revolution, Otto returned to the German community at Reading. *Further reading:* James E. Gibson, *Dr. Bodo Otto and the Medical Background of the American Revolution* (Springfield, Ill., 1937).

P

PACA, William (1740–1799) Delegate to Congress, legislator, governor, jurist Born on an estate in Hartford County, Maryland, Paca graduated from the College of Philadelphia (since become part of the University of Pennsylvania) and went to England for the study of law at the Middle Temple. On his return to America, he settled in Annapolis and set up what was soon a thriving law practice. As a man of wealth and influence in Maryland, Paca was one of the leading patriots during the early and mid-1770s, an ally of Samuel Chase in bringing the colony into the Revolution. He was an outspoken member of the colonial assembly between 1771 and 1774, and he defended patriots in the courts. Paca became one of Maryland's delegates to the first Continental Congress in 1774. In 1776, he was perhaps the key actor in persuading the Maryland convention to finally approve a vote for independence, and he himself became a signer of the Declaration. Although he continued as a congressional delegate until 1779, he spent much of his time in Maryland, acting as a member of the committee of safety, sitting in the legislature, and presiding as chief justice of the state supreme court. In 1780, he was appointed by Congress as chief justice of the court of prize and admiralty. He had meanwhile moved from Annapolis, where he had built a magnificent home, to his estate at Wye Plantation. In 1782, Paca was elected governor of Maryland, serving until 1785. He attended the state convention to ratify the federal constitution and

spent the final 10 years of his life as a U.S. district judge. *Further reading:* Gregory A. Stiverson and Phebe R. Jacobsen, *William Paca: A Biography* (Baltimore, 1976).

PAGE, John (1743–1808) State official, militia officer The elder brother of Mann Page, John was born on the family estate in Gloucester County, Virginia. He studied at the College of William and Mary, graduating in 1763 after a pause for service in the Virginia militia during the wars against the French. He was a close friend of Thomas Jefferson his entire life, having formed a relationship while both were students. Page was also an avid amateur astronomer and shared scientific interests with Jefferson. He sat in the House of Burgesses before the Revolution and was an active patriot and supporter of Patrick Henry. He was lieutenant governor of Virginia from 1776 to 1779, and he raised and commanded a militia unit from Gloucester County during the war. Afterward, Page was elected to the first U.S. Congress and was reelected through 1797. He was governor of Virginia from 1802 until 1805, succeeding James Monroe. His final public office was as commissioner of federal loans in his home state.

PAGE, Mann (1749–1781) Delegate to Congress, attorney Born to a Virginia planter family in Gloucester County and the brother of John Page, the younger Page graduated from the College of

William and Mary and set up a legal practice in addition to managing part of his family's estates. He sat in the House of Burgesses as a representative of Spotsylvania County before the Revolution. He was selected as a delegate to the second Continental Congress in 1777 and died on his estate near Fredericksburg before the end of the Revolution.

PAINE, Ephraim (1730—1785) Delegate to Congress, physician
Paine was born in Canterbury, Connecticut, but after studying medicine, he moved to Amenia, New York and opened a practice. He attended the New York patriot provincial congress in 1775. He continued to practice medicine during the first years of the war, becoming also a county judge in 1778. He was elected to the New York state senate in 1779, serving until 1784, when he was sent as a delegate to the Confederation Congress. He died the following year in Amenia.

PAINE, Robert Treat (1731—1814) Delegate to Congress, legislator, jurist
A native of Boston, Paine took a major role in revolutionary Massachusetts and was present in Philadelphia at the founding of the new nation. He came from an old Massachusetts Bay family, attended Boston Latin School, and graduated from Harvard in 1749. Following his parents' wishes he became a preacher in the Congregationalist faith, but he was more attracted to law. After youthful adventures as a military chaplain on the Crown Point expedition in 1755 and sea voyages to the Carolinas, Europe and Greenland (the latter as a whaler), he was admitted to the bar and set up legal practice in Taunton, Massachusetts. Paine was a friend of John Adams and John Hancock and was involved early on in anti-British activities. He came to public notice in 1770 as the prosecutor of the British soldiers during the trial after the Boston Massacre. In 1773, he was elected to the colonial provincial assembly, serving (with the exception of 1776) until 1778. He was selected as one of the five original Massachusetts delegates to the first Continental Congress, and Paine signed both the Olive Branch Petition in 1775 and the Declaration of Independence in 1776. He was reelected to Congress in 1777 but chose to remain in his home state as speaker of the lower legislative house. He also became attorney general of Massachusetts in the same year, an office he held until 1790. He continued to act as a state leader

Thomas Paine

during the formation of the new Massachusetts constitution in 1779. After several times turning down appointments to the bench, he accepted the post of justice of the state supreme court in 1790 and remained as judge until 1804.

PAINE, Thomas (1737—1809) Writer, soldier
Doubtless the greatest phrase maker and popular writer of the period, Paine produced seminal publications that helped shape the course of the American Revolution. Born in England into abject poverty and trained as a corset maker, Paine came to America in 1774 at the urging of Benjamin Franklin. During the winter of 1775—76 when the issue of independence was still open, Paine wrote an anonymous pamphlet titled *Common Sense* in which he urged Americans to separate from Great Britain. While his language was often eloquent it was also straightforward and free of the high-flown phrases that so often marred the writing of other more aristocratic, classically educated patriots (most of them lawyers). *Common Sense* could be read and understood by the common man. Moreover, Paine developed a cogent political philosophy that emphasized natural rights, the equality of all citizens, and a reliance on written constitutions and laws in place of hereditary privilege. Within months, the pamphlet sold tens of thousands.

In 1776, Paine joined the army and served as an aide to Nathanael Greene. Following the American defeats in New York, Paine again took up his pen and produced a series of essays, together called *The*

Crisis. The first appeared in December 1776 and began: "These are the times that try men's souls. The summer soldier and the sunshine patriot will, in this crisis, shrink from the service of their country: but he that stands it now, deserves the love and thanks of man and woman. Tyranny, like hell, is not easily conquered. . . ." He was appointed by Congress to a post as secretary of the committee dealing with foreign affairs, but he became entangled in the Silas Deane-Arthur Lee quarrel and was forced to resign. After the war, he received a confiscated loyalist estate from the state of New York and a cash bonus. In 1787, he went to England and began to write *The Rights of Man.* He moved on to Paris four years later and was elected to the revolutionary French assembly. He was thrown in prison in 1793 after a change in revolutionary regimes, and while a prisoner he wrote *The Age of Reason.* After his release, he returned to the United States where, poor once again in material goods, he remained until his death, having imprinted his ideas and words on the two great revolutions of the 18th century. *Further reading:* A. Owen Aldridge, *Man of Reason: The Life of Thomas Paine* (1959); Aldridge, *Thomas Paine's American Ideology* (Newark, Del., 1984); Ian Dyck, ed., *Citizen of the World: Essays on Thomas Paine* (New York, 1988).

PAINTER, Gamaliel (1743–1819) Continental officer, state official   Born in New Haven, Connecticut, Painter served as a lieutenant in Seth Warner's Regiment of 1776, which was authorized by Congress as a New Hampshire unit but was actually made up of men from Connecticut. Warner's regiment fought in the New York campaign and at Trenton before disbanding at the end of the men's enlistments in May 1777. Painter apparently transferred to one of the newly formed artificer companies of Jeduthan Baldwin in 1777 as a captain. Painter had also probably moved to the New Hampshire Grants area, since in the same year he attended the convention that formed the independent political entity of Vermont. After the war, Painter bought a village site in Vermont and laid out the town of Middlebury. He later served in the state legislature and in 1813 and 1814 was a member of the Governor's Council. In 1800, he helped establish Middlebury College.

PALLISER, Sir Hugh (1723–1796) British admiral, official   A highly political officer, Palliser served in the Royal Navy from childhood, reaching post captain in 1746 and gaining wide experience in the wars against the French. In 1764, he was appointed as governor of Newfoundland, which was a naval post, and he lobbied to keep settlers away and to preserve the territory as a training ground for the navy. In 1770, he was created a baronet and moved into several offices as a protégé of the Earl of Sandwich, who was first lord of the Admiralty. Palliser was named comptroller of the Admiralty and then a lord of Admiralty. He hoisted his flag as rear admiral in 1775 and advanced to vice admiral three years later. He became embroiled in a dispute with Admiral Augustus Keppel in 1778. Keppel was commander of the Channel Fleet and Palliser his third in command, although Palliser's close connections to Sandwich put him in a powerful position vis-à-vis Keppel, who was under constant criticism for failure to keep the French fleet bottled up. At the inconclusive battle of Ushant in July 1778, Palliser commanded the rear squadron, and in the muddled engagement with the French fleet he failed to signal properly or to respond to signals. He subsequently brought charges against Keppel, which were to a large degree politically motivated. Keppel was acquitted, and Palliser in turn demanded the satisfaction of a court-martial to clear his own name. The subsequent inquiry absolved Palliser of wrongdoing but left lingering doubts. The highly public quarrel virtually paralyzed the Royal Navy for several months.

PALMER, Joseph (1716–1788) Officer, businessman   Palmer came to Massachusetts from England in 1746 and set up a glassmaking plant near modern-day Quincy in partnership with his brother-in-law. In 1774 and 1775, he was a member of the contentious Massachusetts Provincial Congress and the Cambridge, Massachusetts Committee of Safety. He then received a commission as colonel in the Massachusetts militia and ranked as a brigadier in his own Suffolk County militia. In 1777, Palmer was given command of Massachusetts troops that were slated to take part in Major General Joseph Spencer's amphibious attack on the British at Newport, Rhode Island, but Spencer called off the campaign before it began. Following the war, Palmer returned to business as a salt manufacturer.

PALMER, Nathan (d. 1777) Loyalist spy   Palmer was a native of Westchester County, New

York. He was serving as a lieutenant in one of the loyalist units attached to the British army when he was sent by Governor William Tryon to spy on American forces under General Israel Putnam. He was caught, however, posing as a patriot. Tryon wrote to Putnam asking for Palmer's release, but the American general replied: "Nathan Palmer, a lieutenant in your king's service, was taken in my camp as a spy, he was tried as a spy, he was condemned as a spy, and you may rest assured, sir, that he shall be hanged as a spy. P.S.: Afternoon—he is hanged." And so he was.

PANTON, William (1742–1801) Indian trader

Like so many Indian and frontier traders of the 18th and 19th centuries, Panton was a Scotsman. He emigrated to the colonies in 1770 and set up Moore and Panton in Savannah, the first in a series of trading companies he operated during his business career. He established a strong trade and considerable influence with the Creek nation in East Florida in 1775, although he also dealt with the Cherokee, Chickasaw and Choctaw. With the British defeat, he switched political allegiance to the Spanish, who had gained control of West Florida after the signing of the peace treaty. Panton had an exclusive charter from the Spanish for the Indian trade from 1784 until his death in 1801.

PARKE, John (1754–1789) Continental officer, poet

Parke was born in Dover, Delaware and educated at the College of Philadelphia (the school eventually became known as the University of Pennsylvania), receiving both the bachelor's and master's degrees. During the Revolution he served as a staff officer in the quartermaster division of the Continental Army. He was assistant quartermaster during the siege of Boston and became a lieutenant colonel of artificers (a small unit of artificers—bateaux men and carpenters—was part of the quartermaster general's department at the time) in 1776 when the army moved to New York. He published a translation of Horace, appending several of his own poems.

PARKER, Sir Hyde (1714–1782) British admiral

The son of an Anglican parson, Parker was born in a rectory in Worcestershire. Although he became the progenitor of a long line of British sailors, he himself did not join the Royal Navy until the advanced age of 24 after spending several years in the merchant marine. He began in the navy as an able seaman but received a commission as a lieutenant in early 1745 and was posted captain three years later. After extensive service during the Seven Years' War, including commands in India and the Philippines, he was on the beach from 1763 until 1776, when he received command of a ship in the Channel Fleet. He was promoted to rear admiral in 1778 and sailed to America as second in command of a squadron under John Byron. After Byron's departure and before the arrival of Sir George Rodney, Parker was in command of the West Indies station. He held off a putative French assault on St. Lucia in March 1780. Soon after, Rodney took command, and Parker returned to England in early 1781. He fought a vicious but inconclusive battle with the Dutch off Dogger Bank in August 1781. The following year, having inherited the family baronetcy, he sailed for the East Indies but was lost at sea aboard his flagship.

PARKER, Sir Hyde, Jr. (1739–1807) British admiral

The second son of the elder Sir Hyde Parker (also a Royal Navy admiral), the junior Parker went to sea as a midshipman aboard his father's ship the *Vanguard*. He continued to serve with his father during most of his early career, receiving a commission as lieutenant in 1758. He was posted to the North American station in 1766 and served in American waters during most of the following decade and a half. As commander of the *Phoenix* in July 1776, Parker led a flotilla of British ships across the bar and up the Hudson River to the Tappan Zee, running straight through the American defenses. The feat demonstrated the British forces' mobility and their command of the water flank of Washington's army and did much to discombobulate the American commander in chief, who also faced a land invasion on Long Island. Parker was knighted for the exploit, although not until two years later. He convoyed troops to Savannah in late 1778, afterward returning home to England for repairs to his ship. Early in 1780, he escorted a convoy to the West Indies and was shipwrecked on the coast of Cuba. Rescued, he returned to Britain and served the remainder of the war in European waters. He hoisted his admiral's flag in 1794.

Parker's most notorious command was of the Baltic fleet in 1801, when he was eclipsed by the actions of his second in command, Horatio Nelson, at the battle of Copenhagen. Parker was recalled after the British victory, which he was accused of insufficiently supporting, and was not again employed by the Admiralty. Both his son and grandson became prominent naval officers.

PARKER, John (1729–1775) Militia officer

Parker became an American immortal when he led the small force of minutemen that engaged the British at Lexington, Massachusetts in the first battle of the American Revolution. He was a native of Lexington and had lived quietly as a farmer and mechanic in the village since the mid-1750s, when he had returned home from duty in the Seven Years' War. He was, however, captain of the minuteman company of the local militia, a unit designated to respond quickly to alarms. During the early morning hours of April 19, 1775, a British force under Lieutenant Colonel John Pitcairn approached Lexington, intent on capturing John Hancock and Samuel Adams and seizing patriot munitions. Alerted by couriers from Boston, Parker assembled his 130 minutemen—only 70 of them armed—in the dark on the village green. At daylight, the British column appeared, and Pitcairn rode forward to order Parker to disperse his militiamen. A shot was fired and both sides opened up in the first armed exchange of the war. Parker's minutemen were quickly scattered by the disciplined volley fire of the British troopers (eight patriots were killed on the spot versus one slight wound among the British), but the redcoats faced a harrowing day ahead. For years American patriots ascribed a heroic speech on the occasion to Parker (". . . if they mean to have a war, let it begin here"), but there is little or no evidence to substantiate the claim he said much that was memorable. Parker regrouped his men after the battle on Lexington Green and reached Concord later in the day. He then led a company to Boston to join the siege but was personally too ill to fight at Bunker Hill. He died in mid-September.

PARKER, John (1759–1832) Delegate to Congress

Born in Charleston, Parker was a representative of the South Carolina planter class, himself coming to political age just after the Revolution. He studied law in England at the Middle Temple and was admitted to the South Carolina bar in 1785. While practicing law in Charleston, Parker accu-

Sir Peter Parker

mulated land which he turned to rice planting. By the late 1780s, he was master of several large rice estates. From 1786 to 1788, he represented South Carolina in the Confederation Congress, his only significant public duty.

PARKER, Sir Peter (1721–1811) British admiral

The son of a British rear admiral (but not related to the two British admirals named Hyde Parker), Sir Peter was born in Ireland. He probably first sailed under his father, and by 1747 he had made post captain and was a veteran of several engagements with the French. On half pay following the end of the Seven Years' War, Parker was knighted in 1772 but unemployed until 1775, when he was appointed as a commodore of a squadron that was to sail with troops and men-of-war in support of an attack by Sir Henry Clinton on Charleston, South Carolina. Parker and his ships had a rough crossing from Ireland and did not arrive off Cape Fear (in scattered fashion) until late April and early May—several months later than planned. After prolonged preparation, Parker undertook a naval assault on June 28 on Fort Sullivan, which the Americans had hastily constructed in the harbor. He sailed his two 50-gun ships, supported by several frigates and smaller craft, to within range and began a bombardment that Parker hoped would batter the fort into submission. Unfortunately for the British, the palmetto and sand construction of the fort absorbed most of the shot, and the American gunners soon found the range. Parker's flagship was raked repeatedly, and one blast killed everyone on the quarterdeck but Parker, whose clothes were blown off by the force of the concussion. He had to withdraw his ships, and the expedition failed. Parker then joined Admiral Howe at New York in support of the British campaign there. He briefly commanded an expedition to Rhode Island in December 1776 and was promoted to rear admiral in the spring of the following year and assigned to the West Indies. He returned to England (and a baronetcy) in 1782. In 1792, Parker was appointed commander at Portsmouth.

PARSONS, Samuel Holden (1737–1789) Continental general

Another of the many disgruntled senior Continental officers, Parsons played only a small role during the war despite his elevation to a major generalship. He was the son of a Lyme, Connecticut preacher, who moved his family to Newburyport, Massachusetts after a religious dispute with his flock. The younger Parsons returned to Lyme to read law in 1756 after graduating from Harvard. He settled in Lyme, married, and practiced law.

In the years before the Revolution, Parsons took an active part in colonial politics, sitting in the Connecticut assembly for 18 years. In 1774, he moved to New London, Connecticut and became one of the most vigorous Connecticut patriots. He was on the committee of correspondence and was an early advocate of independence, being one of the first in the colonies to propose a congress. He also served in the Connecticut militia as a major. With the outbreak of armed hostilities and the organization of the Continental Army, Parsons was named as colonel of the 6th Connecticut, and he helped plan and promote the American capture of Fort Ticonderoga. In the summer of 1776, Parsons was in New York and received promotion to brigadier general. His major battlefield experience came at Long Island and Kip's Bay, where he exhibited considerable personal bravery but little tactical acumen, barely avoiding capture. Thereafter, he was relegated to commands in the Hudson Highlands and recruiting duties. In 1778 and 1779, he directed the construction of the extensive fortifications at West Point and conducted sporadic raiding on the British.

When Israel Putnam withdrew in late 1779, Parsons was named to command of the Connecticut troops, and he was promoted to major general early

the following year. He had invested his own fortune in Continental currency early in the war, however, and by 1780 he fretted over the severe inflation that was rapidly wiping him out financially. Added to what he perceived as neglect from Congress, the loss of his money made Parsons increasingly disenchanted, and he began a series of requests for leave or acceptance of his resignation. He also was embroiled with the spy William Heron, although there is no evidence to suggest Parsons understood that Heron was a venal double agent. The Congress refused to grant Parsons' requests for withdrawal, and he remained on the active list of major generals until the end of the war. Reduced to meager circumstances, Parson took advantage of the land grants offered to Continental veterans, and he became one of the projectors (and first directors) of the Ohio Company, a scheme by which he hoped to recoup his finances. He went west in 1788 to see after his investments and to take up a post as a judge in the new Northwest Territory. He was accused of sharp practices in his land dealings in Ohio and may well have overstepped the bounds of honesty. He drowned in November 1789 when his canoe overturned on the Big Beaver River. *Further reading:* Charles S. Hall, *The Life and Letters of Samuel Holden Parsons . . .* (Binghamton, N.Y., 1905).

PARTRIDGE, George (1740–1828) Delegate to Congress

Partridge was born in Duxbury, Massachusetts and graduated from Harvard in 1762, after which he taught school in Kingston, Massachusetts. He was selected as a delegate to the Massachusetts Provincial Congress in 1774 and 1775 and continued to serve in the Congress—essentially the governing body of Massachusetts—until 1779. In that year he was sent to the Continental Congress as a delegate, serving until 1782 and again from 1783 to 1785. He was elected as one of the state's first U.S. congressmen in 1789 but resigned after a year and a half in office.

PATERSON, James. British general

A busy officer during the American war, Paterson was lieutenant colonel of the 63rd Regiment of Foot, a unit that arrived in Boston in June 1775, shortly after the beginning of armed warfare in the colonies. The regiment moved to New York after the evacuation of Boston, and Paterson was named as adjutant general by the new commander in chief, William

Howe, with the local rank of brigadier general. He served as a senior staff officer until after the British withdrawal from Philadelphia and the battle of Monmouth in 1778. Sir Henry Clinton (who had replaced Howe) sent Paterson home to England with dispatches after the army had arrived in New York. On his return to the North American theater, Paterson led a division in taking Stony Point in June 1779. He then sailed south with Clinton's invasion force to South Carolina late in the year. Paterson by this stage was colonel in command of the 63rd and carried the local rank of major general. After supporting Clinton in the siege of Charleston in 1780, Paterson returned to New York City (his regiment remained in the Carolinas) and took command of the British defenses at Staten Island.

PATERSON, John (1744–1808) Continental general

Paterson was a relatively undistinguished field officer who spent most of the war on the sidelines, although he was present at several important battles. He was born into a Scots emigrant family near Wethersfield, Connecticut. He graduated from Yale in 1762 and taught school in New Britain before moving with his wife and family to Lenox, Massachusetts in 1774. There he took a prominent place in patriot activities, representing his town in the provincial congresses of 1774 and 1775. He also was a militia officer and raised a regiment of troops, which was originally known as Paterson's Massachusetts Battalion and was taken into the Continental Army in January 1776 as the 15th Continental Regiment. Although present at the battle of Breed's Hill and Bunker Hill in 1775, Paterson and his men remained in the rear and were not engaged. They fought a minor skirmish with British raiders in November. After moving to New York with the main army, Paterson and his men were dispatched north to reinforce the American invasion of Canada, and they retreated with Benedict Arnold after the disastrous attempt to take Quebec. Paterson worked for a time on the fortifications at Mount Independence at Fort Ticonderoga, but he moved on to join Washington's forces in Pennsylvania and New Jersey. He was promoted to brigadier general in February 1777 and assigned to the Northern Department to help oppose Burgoyne. He was at Fort Ticonderoga when it was taken by the British and later his brigade was at both battles near Saratoga but took little part in the

fighting. He was in charge of a brigade of Massachusetts regiments at Valley Forge and was at the battle of Monmouth in the summer of 1778 but again remained out of action on the field. Paterson then moved to the Hudson Highlands of New York for the balance of the war. He received a brevet as major general shortly before mustering out in the fall of 1783, when he returned to Lenox and took up the practice of law. He also became an active land speculator and was part of both the Ohio Company and the Boston Purchase. As a militia commander, Paterson helped put down Shays' Rebellion in 1786. He eventually served in the New York legislature after moving to Tioga County, and he ended his life as a judge. *Further reading:* Thomas Egleston, *The Life of John Paterson, Major General in the Revolutionary Army* (New York, 1894).

PATERSON, William (1745–1806) Jurist, official

Born in Ireland, Paterson moved to New Jersey, graduating from Princeton (then called the College of New Jersey) in 1763. He practiced law before the Revolution in New Bromley and Princeton. In 1775 and 1776, Paterson sat in the New Jersey Provincial Congress. He was appointed attorney general of the state in 1776 and served in that office during the balance of the Revolution, simultaneously sitting in the state senate for two years, 1777–1778. He came to the fore as a jurist and legislator in the post-Revolutionary period. As a delegate to the Constitutional Convention in Philadelphia, Paterson introduced the New Jersey Plan for a unicameral national legislature, but he accommodated himself to the compromise that led to the designation of two chambers, one based on population and the other on equal representation from each state. He was selected as one of the first U.S. senators from New Jersey in 1789, but he served only until 1790, when he became governor of the state. In 1793, he was named as an associate justice of the U.S. Supreme Court, and he sat on the high bench until his death in 1806. The city of Paterson, New Jersey is named after him.

PATTEN, John (1746–1800) Continental officer, delegate to Congress

Patten was a farmer, born in Kent County, Delaware, who served in the Continental Army during the Revolution, rising to the rank of major. He was sent to the Confederation Congress in 1786. In 1793, he presented himself as the new U.S. representative from Delaware and served 11 months before his contested election was reversed and he was replaced in Congress by his opponent. He was duly elected to Congress on his next attempt in 1795 and served one term.

PATTISON, James (1724–1805) British general

Pattison was a colonel of artillery when he arrived in New York in the fall of 1777. He was given the local rank of brigadier general and nominally commanded the Royal Artillery Regiment throughout much of the war, although the artillery was usually dispersed among several commands and theaters. Pattison was personally in charge of the artillery during the successful British assault on Stony Point and Verplanck's Point, New York in June 1779, by which time he had been advanced to local major general's rank, and he took part in field operations during the summer at the head of a brigade. After organizing loyalist militia in New York, Pattison returned to England in 1780, taking a post at the arsenal at Woolwich.

PAULDING, John (1758–1818) Militiaman

Born near Tarrytown, New York, Paulding was a private soldier in the New York militia when chance gave him and two companions the opportunity to become American heroes. Paulding, like his fellow militiamen Isaac Van Wert and David Williams, was only a part-time soldier, working on his family farm in Westchester County when not on duty. They were all part of the rather wild situation in the region, where loyalist militia and patriots spent much of their energy in raiding each other's cattle herds and seizing property in a manner scarcely distinguishable from semi-organized theft.

Paulding had been captured three times by the British and released on each occasion. He was only four days out of his most recent captivity when he and the two other militiamen went on a search for cattle north of Tarrytown on September 23, 1780. The trio was in the midst of a card game when they spotted a rider approaching. They stepped out of the woods and stopped the man. He at first hailed them and identified himself as a British officer— mistaking the scruffy Americans for loyalists—but then changed his story and produced a pass in the hand of Major General Benedict Arnold, commander at West Point. The three Americans grew suspicious and refused to let the man continue on

his way even though he offered a substantial bribe. They turned their captive over to Lieutenant Colonel John Jameson, still unaware that they had unwittingly foiled the darkest plot of the Revolution. Their captive was, of course, Major John André, Sir Henry Clinton's young adjutant, who was returning from a clandestine meeting with Arnold. Within a day, Arnold was forced to flee just ahead of capture. André was subsequently hung as a spy. Paulding and his cohorts were identified by George Washington as genuine American heroes: simple farm lads who had resisted bribery and stopped a nefarious plot. The three received honors and life pensions from the Continental Congress and land grants from the state of New York, and a commemorative medal with their likenesses was struck. For decades after the Revolution, the three men were celebrated in song, poetry, drama and public monuments. After his moment in history, Paulding resumed farming. He died at Staatsburg, New York. *Further reading:* Richard C. Brown, "Three Forgotten Heroes," *American Heritage* 26 (August 1979), 25–29.

PAWLING, Albert. Militia Officer

Pawling commanded a column of New York state militiamen that tracked down a mixed force of about 400 loyalists and Indians under Captain William Caldwell in Ulster County, New York in late August 1781. Caldwell's raiders had attacked and destroyed several remote settlements when Pawling's force caught up with them at Wawarsing, New York, near the southern edge of the Catskill Mountains. The New Yorkers drove off the loyalists after a fierce battle but took considerable casualties.

PAXTON, Charles (1707–1788) Loyalist official

As a royal customs commissioner in Boston before the Revolution, Paxton was naturally the object of much patriotic ire. He was characterized by one biographer (otherwise sympathetic to loyalists) as being "as rapacious as the fabled harpy" and "among the most efficient in producing the Revolution." Paxton apparently did little to hide his interest in using public office for his own private gain, and his position as a customs officer was perfect for his purposes. He was one of the four commissioners named for libel by James Otis in a newspaper ad in 1769, which led to Otis' wounding in a brawl—an event often blamed for the patriot leader's subsequent erratic behavior. Paxton was frequently ridiculed by the Boston mob with effigies and placards. He was among those who had written the "Hutchinson Letters" (which were diverted by patriots and sent by Benjamin Franklin to patriot leaders in Massachusetts) that proved damaging to the royal cause. Like other royal officials, Paxton was forced out of Boston in 1776. He settled in England, apparently living on a pension granted by the crown for his services in America.

PEABODY, Joseph (1757–1844) Privateer, merchant

Born in Middleton, Massachusetts, Peabody was one of the approximately 600 privateers sailing from Massachusetts during the Revolution, serving as a teenager on board the *Bunker Hill* and the *Pilgrim*. While a crew member of the privateer *Fish Hawk*, Peabody was captured by the British and imprisoned in Newfoundland. After his exchange (many captured privateers were not so lucky), he found a berth as second officer on the *Ranger*. He was wounded in a sea skirmish aboard the *Ranger* but recovered and ended the war in one piece, despite his adventures. More is known about Peabody than about the hundreds of other relatively anonymous privateers because he prospered after the war, becoming one of New England's richest shipping merchants. From his headquarters in Salem, Peabody directed an international trading company that did business in Europe, the Baltic, the Mediterranean, India and China.

PEABODY, Nathaniel (1742–1823) Delegate to Congress, official, physician

Peabody was born in Topsfield, Massachusetts and after studying medicine with his father, also a physician, he moved to New Hampshire and set up a practice in 1761. He served for a period in the British army but resigned in 1774 to join the patriot cause and was one of the leaders in the seizure of Fort William and Mary in December 1774, five months before the battles at Lexington and Concord. He was a member and sometime chairman of the New Hampshire Committee of Safety during 1776 and sat almost continuously in the New Hampshire house from 1776 to 1796. Peabody was also adjutant general of the state militia during 1777 and commanded part of the New Hampshire contingent on the hapless American Rhode Island expedition in 1779. He was selected as a delegate to the Continental Congress in 1779 and 1780, and again in 1785, but declined

to take his seat for the latter term. He also served in the state senate after the Revolution and was a major general of state militia during the 1790s. For all his political prominence, Peabody's career had a sad coda: he was arrested for debt in 1803 and spent the final 20 years of his life in prison.

PEALE, Charles Willson (1741–1827) Painter, militia officer, state official

A man of many parts and by any standard the most talented resident patriot painter and portraitist of the Revolution, Peale was the son of a well-bred and educated English gentleman who fled Britain after a conviction for forgery (a fact about his father that the young Peale never knew). Like his brother James, also a painter, Charles Willson was born in Maryland. After his father's death in 1750, Peale was apprenticed to a saddlemaker in Annapolis. He was an inveterate tinkerer and craftsman who saw his first paintings as a young man and was struck with an overwhelming ambition to become an artist. He traded a saddle to John Hesselius in return for lessons and began his career.

In the mid-1760s, however, Peale was forced to flee Annapolis just ahead of creditors, leaving his young wife behind. He went to Boston, where he studied briefly with John Singleton Copley. On returning to Maryland, Peale received financing from a group of wealthy supporters who raised the money to send him to England for training. Peale spent three years in London, working under the tutelage of expatriate American Benjamin West and learning the polished techniques of the portraitist. On his return to Maryland, Peale began a career as the most accomplished portrait painter in the middle colonies, traveling widely and painting likenesses of many wealthy patrons. In 1772, he painted George Washington for the first time. (Peale eventually did seven portraits of the great man from life.)

The painter was also the strongest of patriots, joining the Sons of Liberty in 1765, and his unconcealed hostility to the crown cost him most of his well-to-do loyalist patrons as the Revolution approached. In 1776, Peale moved to Philadelphia and began his long practice of painting portraits of any and all American leaders he could persuade to sit. He also joined the militia and was elected lieutenant and then captain. He led his company in the campaigns at Trenton (crossing the Delaware with Washington) and Princeton, but he was not much of a soldier and withdrew to more peaceful pursuits—painting portraits of leading American officers and politicians all the while. He served in the Pennsylvania legislature in 1779 and was in charge of confiscated loyalist properties for the state.

After the war, Peale continued to paint, growing in reputation and prosperity. He became interested in natural history and collected specimens—including several mastadon skeletons—which he eventually presented to the public in one of the first organized natural history museums in America. He fathered 17 children by three wives and trained several of his progeny, including the girls, as artists. He remained vigorous until his old age, learning new techniques when in his eighties and thereafter producing some of his finest work. Perhaps his greatest legacy to the nation was the body of more than 250 portraits of leading revolutionary figures. *Further reading:* Charles C. Sellers, *Charles Willson Peale: The Artist of the Revolution,* 2 vols. (Philadelphia, 1939; reprinted 1947); Oliver Jensen, "The Peales," *American Heritage* 6 (April 1955), 40–51.

PEALE, James (1749–1831) Continental officer, painter   Peale was born in Maryland and was a saddlemaker as a teenager. He took up painting before the Revolution, but he became known as an artist only after the war when he moved to Philadelphia and produced a series of miniatures of George Washington, as well as landscapes and battle scenes such as *The View of the Battle of Princeton.* He was neither as talented nor as famous a painter as his elder brother, Charles Willson Peale. He served during the war as a captain in the famous 1st Maryland Regiment, one of the elite units of the Continental Army, which unfortunately was nearly destroyed en masse at the battle of Camden.

PEARSON, Sir Richard (1731–1806) British naval officer   Although he was held blameless by the authorities for the loss of his ship, Pearson had the misfortune to command the *Serapis* against John Paul Jones. He was born in Westmoreland and entered the Royal Navy at age 14. In 1750, he withdrew and entered the service of the East India Company, but he returned to the navy five years later and passed his examination as a lieutenant. His early career was plagued by ill fortune, however, and he twice missed promotion to captain when superior officers died before signing his offi-

cial papers. He finally reached post rank in 1773 after commanding several small ships.

Pearson sailed to Quebec in 1776 on convoy duty as commander of the *Garland,* remaining in North American waters for two years. He received command of the 44-gun *Serapis* in March 1778. He was returning from the Baltic with a convoy of merchant ships when he encountered John Paul Jones's flotilla off Flamborough Head on September 23, 1779. The ensuing battle was as fierce as any fought at sea during the late 18th century, and by all rights Pearson pounded Jones and the *Bonhomme Richard* to defeat, but Jones refused to surrender and ultimately forced Pearson to strike the British colors. The American ship sank, and Jones took over the *Serapis.* The rich convoy of merchantmen escaped during the battle, and this fact did much to vindicate Pearson in the eyes of the authorities. He was acquitted at a subsequent court-martial (which all captains who lost ships were required to stand) in 1780 and was knighted for his conduct. He retired from the sea in 1790 and held a sinecure as lieutenant governor of Greenwich Hospital until his death.

PEERY, William (d. 1800) Delegate to Congress, attorney   There is no record of Peery's birth, but he was a resident of Delaware. He read law privately while farming before the Revolution but was not admitted to the bar until 1785. He meanwhile organized an independent company during the early days of the war. He sat in the Delaware legislature in 1782 and again several times in the following 12 years. He was a delegate to the Confederation Congress from Delaware in 1785 and 1786, returning to Sussex County to practice law after his term. He died in Cool Spring, Delaware.

PELL, Philip (1753–1811) Continental judge advocate, delegate to Congress   Born in New York, Pell graduated from King's College in 1770 and became a lawyer. He was a lieutenant of militia at the beginning of the war, but he became deputy judge advocate for the Continental Army in 1777 and advanced to judge advocate in 1781. He was also intermittently a member of the New York state legislature during the Revolution. He attended the final Confederation Congress in 1789 as a delegate.

PENDLETON, Edmund (1721–1803) Delegate to Congress, state official   The leader of the conservative faction in Virginia patriot politics and a long-time foe of Patrick Henry, Pendleton was born in Caroline County. His father died within a year of Pendleton's birth, and his mother remarried. Pendleton was apprenticed to a clerk of the local court and educated himself in the law, being admitted to the bar at age 20. He thereupon rose steadily in the affairs of the colony.

He was a convinced patriot but opposed the radicals and was adamantly against democratic tendencies and mob violence. During the Stamp Act crisis of the 1760s, Pendleton was a member of the House of Burgesses. As a local justice of the peace he tried to accommodate the law insofar as he could and worked against Patrick Henry's opposition. He was only slowly admitted into the affairs of the Revolution but could not be ignored as the leader of a substantial number of conservatives. He became a member of the Virginia Committee of Correspondence in 1773 and was president of the provincial conventions called in 1775. He also became president of the Virginia Committee of Safety, which effectively put him at the head of government in 1775.

He preferred to go slowly, especially in offering armed resistance to the crown, but acquiesced in the face of rapid developments during 1775 and 1776. However, he managed to push Henry aside from command of the state troops, a maneuver that only exacerbated the enmity between the two Virginia leaders. He became one of the three delegates from Virginia to the first Continental Congress in 1774 and was returned the following year to the second Congress. Despite his moderate stance, Pendleton was the moving force in proposing that Virginia support independence. He presided over the convention of 1776 that voted to instruct the state's congressional delegates to vote for independence, and he personally drew up the resolves passed by the body. After helping frame a new constitution for Virginia, Pendleton became speaker of the lower house, although his activity diminished after a severe fall from a horse in 1777—he was permanently crippled by the accident. He became presiding justice of the supreme court of appeals in 1779 and spent most of the remainder of his public life as a jurist. He served as president of the Virginia convention on the federal constitution in 1788, supporting ratification, but played little role in state or national affairs thereafter. *Further reading:* David J.

Mays, *Edmund Pendleton, 1721–1803: A Biography* (Cambridge, Mass., 1952).

PENN, John (1729–1795) Royal official

John was the grandson of William Penn, the son of Richard Penn, and the elder brother of Richard Penn Jr. He was the last of the family to hold office in Pennsylvania as a proprietor and was lieutenant governor of the colony when a patriot government in the form of a Supreme Executive Council seized control and turned him out.

John inherited from his father a quarter share in the family proprietorship of Pennsylvania but was directed in affairs by his uncle Thomas. He lived in England during his early life and was educated in Switzerland. He came to Pennsylvania in 1752 and served on the Governor's Council until 1755, when he apparently returned to Great Britain. He came back to Pennsylvania in 1763 as lieutenant governor, staying until his father's death in 1771, when he again went to England. He meanwhile had married Ann Allen, daughter of Pennsylvania chief justice William Allen. There was a strong antiproprietary party in the colony, led by Benjamin Franklin, during the decades before the Revolution, but it never quite managed to break the Penn family proprietorship. Penn returned to America in 1773 and assumed the role of lieutenant governor again, and by his position and interests he could have been expected to be a loyalist, yet he trod carefully and managed to avoid overt condemnation by the patriots despite a brief period of technical arrest. In 1776, the new state government dissolved the proprietorship but allowed Penn to keep his personal estates and settled £130,000 on him and his fellow Penn heirs. He continued to live in Philadelphia and on a country estate until the end of his life. *Further reading:* Arthur Pound, *The Penns of Pennsylvania* (New York, 1932).

PENN, John (1740–1788) Delegate to Congress, state official, attorney

One of those hardworking congressional delegates whose efforts have received scant notice but who in large measure made the Revolution possible, Penn was born into a prosperous family in Caroline County, Virginia. He received little education but upon inheriting considerable property at his father's death in 1758, Penn sought the help of his uncle, Edmund Pendleton, and read law in Pendleton's office. He was admitted to the bar and for the ensuing 10 years practiced in Virginia. In 1774, he moved to North Carolina, settling near Stovall.

Penn was soon plunged into the revolutionary politics of his new home, being sent to the provincial convention in 1775 and elected as one of North Carolina's delegates to the Continental Congress. He remained in Congress continuously until 1779, working tirelessly as a legislator and as the primary agent of North Carolina in the north, which entailed a great deal of administrative work. He signed both the Declaration of Independence and the Articles of Confederation while a delegate, and he assumed leadership of the North Carolina contingent by virtue of his longevity. As North Carolina's purchasing agent, Penn was involved deeply in finance, and he found himself in the midst of the many controversies over financial matters in Congress. As an offshoot of the divisive quarrel between supporters of Silas Deane and Arthur Lee, Penn came into conflict with Henry Laurens, resulting in a challenge. The pair breakfasted together on the day appointed for the duel, and while strolling toward the selected grounds, Penn managed to persuade Laurens of the futility of the quarrel—he was assisting the much older Laurens across the street when the conciliatory impulse occurred to him.

In 1780, Penn was recalled to North Carolina and made head of a three-man board of war that was to prepare the state to face invasion from Sir Henry Clinton. Unfortunately, the board was resented by both the army and the existing civilian authorities, and it was dissolved before taking much action. He thereupon retired to the practice of law and lived the final years of his life away from the public eye.

PENN, Richard, Jr. (1736–1811) Royal official

The younger brother of John Penn, Richard served briefly as lieutenant governor of the family province of Pennsylvania and carried a petition for conciliation from the colonies to the British government during the first year of the war. He was appointed as lieutenant governor of Pennsylvania in 1771 when John returned to England on their father's death and served until John's return two years later. He married a Philadelphian and was in general sympathetic to the colonists' cause. On his return to England in 1775, Penn carried a petition on behalf of some of his personal friends in the Continental Congress for presentation to the government in London. He laid the petition before the House of Commons in November and testified as to the colonial demand for independence. He shared in the settlement made by the state of Pennsylvania with the Penn heirs in 1779. Penn later sat in Parliament.

PENNINGTON, William Sandford (1757–1826) Soldier, official

Pennington was born in Newark, New Jersey and joined the 2nd Battalion of the Continental Corps of Artillery as a sergeant when it was formed in 1777. Most of the regiment came from New York and Connecticut. He was commissioned as a lieutenant in 1778 and left the army two years later with the brevet rank of captain. After serving in the New Jersey Assembly in the late 1790s, Pennington was admitted to the bar at the somewhat advanced age of 46 and began a belated career in public office. The following year, 1804, he took a seat on the New Jersey Supreme Court. He was governor of the state from 1813 to 1815 and after his one executive term became judge of the U.S. District for New Jersey.

PENOT LOMBART, Louis-Pierre, Chevalier de La Neuville (1744–c. 1800) French volunteer

The elder of two brothers who took leave of the French army to volunteer for service in America, the Chevalier de La Neuville had been in the French militia from a very early age (one account lists him as enrolled in the Paris militia at age six). He fought during the Seven Years' War and was a captain of colonial troops afterward, serving on an expedition to Martinique in 1768. In 1777, he was granted leave from his provincial regiment, and he sailed for North America. De La Neuville received a commission as major in the Continental Army in March 1777 and was assigned as inspector general to the Northern Department under Horatio Gates. He applied for a promotion and, after a year's wait and what appears to be considerable political maneuvering, he was given a brevet from Congress as a brigadier general in October 1778. Apparently, his ambitions had been fulfilled, since he resigned within two months and departed for France. He continued a minor career as a provincial officer but failed to win a commission in the regular royal army.

PENOT LOMBART DE NOIRMONT, René-Hippolyte (1750–1792) French volunteer

The sib-

Hugh Percy, Earl Percy

ling of the Chevalier de La Neuville, the younger Frenchman accompanied his brother to America in 1777. He had been a junior officer in the French royal army, serving in the dragoons and infantry. His first American assignment was as aide-de-camp to Thomas Conway. He was appointed as assistant inspector general to the Northern Department in May 1778 and was soon thereafter promoted to major. He then became aide-de-camp to the Marquis de Lafayette. In 1779, de Noirmont was attached to the forces of Benjamin Lincoln around Savannah, where he commanded light infantry. He returned to France later the same year after receiving a brevet commission as a lieutenant colonel. He again took up his commission in the French army and served until 1791. He was killed in the Abbaye Massacre in France during the Revolution.

PERCY, Hugh (Earl Percy) (1742–1817) British general

The son of the Duke of Cumberland, Percy was known during most of his time in America by the courtesy title Earl Percy. He had joined the army as a teenager and was a captain of the 85th Regiment of Foot by age 17, an achievement that demonstrated the power of wealth and family standing. He was, nonetheless, a good soldier and fought with distinction in 1762 as a commander at the battles of Bergen and Minden. As a member of Parliament and the son-in-law of Lord Bute (the tutor and early favorite of George III), Percy was in an impeccable position. He was promoted to full colonel and became an aide-de-camp to the king in 1764, having barely reached his majority. He was

sent to Boston with the local rank of brigadier general in 1774, and he commanded the relief column that saved the British forces retreating from Lexington and Concord in April 1775. He was absent from the field during the battle of Bunker Hill, perhaps due to a quarrel with William Howe, a man with whom Percy could not get along. He commanded a division during the battle of Long Island and led the storming of Fort Washington. By 1777, Percy was a lieutenant general, but he returned to England after more and more bickering with Howe, who was by then commander in chief in America. He divorced and remarried in 1779, and in 1786 he acceded to the title on his father's death.

PERRON, Joachim du, Comte de Revel (1756–1814) French officer

Although he did not accede to his title until after the war and was a mere second lieutenant of infantry during his active service in the American theater, Perron was a keen observer and left a diary and hand-drawn maps of the Yorktown campaign that provide telling details to historians. He was born into a noble family of Vergeron, France but had little influence at court and could manage only a junior commission in the French royal infantry. He achieved no distinctions during his 17 years of service and was promoted no farther than first lieutenant.

He was 24 years old in 1780 when assigned as part of a small infantry detachment to the fleet of Admiral de Grasse. Perron and his fellow soldiers took ship aboard the *Languedoc* in October 1780 but did not sail for America until the following March. Perron's bird's-eye account of the French navy showed a less than efficient fighting service. He described marine affairs from the perspective of a non-sailor, and the lack of familiarity with nautical terms forced him to detail aspects that a seasoned mariner would have taken for granted. His diary was especially informative about the lives of the common sailors, the enlisted army troops and the junior officers. His ship arrived in Chesapeake Bay in October, and Perron observed and recorded the French repulse of the British fleet and the subsequent siege of Lord Cornwallis at Gloucester and Yorktown. He also prepared accurate and detailed maps of the area, giving perhaps the most refined surviving view of the French and American dispositions at Gloucester (across the river from Yorktown proper). He described the behavior of the defeated British, who refused to converse with the Americans after the surrender.

Perron sailed on to the West Indies with de Grasse and to eventual defeat at the hands of the British under Admiral Rodney, all of which he described faithfully in his war diary. Having inherited his family estates and title, and having achieved no higher rank than first lieutenant, Perron resigned from the army in 1789 and retired to the country. Surprisingly, he survived the French Revolution entirely intact as a rural aristocrat, left in relative peace by his tenants and the rush of radical politics in France. *Further reading:* Joachim du Perron, Comte de Revel, *A Map of Yorktown,* Gilbert Chinard, Robert G. Albion, and Lloyd A. Brown, eds. (Princeton, N.J., 1942).

PERSON, Thomas (1733–1800) Legislator, delegate to Congress

Person sat in legislative bodies in the colony and state of North Carolina for three decades. He was born in Virginia but moved to North Carolina sometime before 1756, when he is listed as a local justice of the peace. By 1764, he had served as a sheriff and in the North Carolina Assembly. Person was a member of all the North Carolina patriot provincial assemblies from 1774 onward, representing the Granville district, and he served on the Council of Safety. He helped draft the state bill of rights and was a member of the committee that drafted the state constitution in 1776. Serving intermittent terms, he was a member of the North Carolina house from 1777 to 1797, interspersing service there with terms in the state senate. He apparently preferred to confine his legislative work to North Carolina, however, since he was elected as a delegate to the Congress in 1784 but failed to take his seat. During the war, he held the rank of general in the state militia and was a member of the North Carolina Committee of Safety.

PETERS, John (1740–1788) Loyalist officer

A native of Moorestown, New York, Peters was a local official before the Revolution, holding the posts of judge of probate for the Court of Common Pleas, colonel of militia and county recorder. He was selected as a delegate to the first Continental Congress in 1774 and actually made the trip to Philadelphia; however, once there he apparently disliked the cast of the assembly and he returned home, refusing to serve. In 1776, he left his wife and family in New York and went to Canada. Sir Guy Carleton appointed him colonel of the Queen's Loyal Rangers, a loyalist militia unit, which Peters helped raise from among American and Canadian loyalist refugees. The Rangers under Peters' command were part of General John Burgoyne's invasion force in 1777. The unit was badly damaged at the battle of Bennington in August, but Peters led the survivors back to Canada before the surrender "Convention" took effect, thus escaping the fate of the forlorn Convention Army that was shuttled about the Middle and Southern states for the rest of the war. He then turned to raiding American settlements along the frontier as leader of a mixed force of loyalists and Indians. After the war, he moved with his family to Cape Breton, and he died while in England pressing his claims before the Loyalist Commission.

PETERS, Richard (c. 1744–1828) Delegate to Congress, official, jurist

A native of Philadelphia, Peters graduated from the college there (now the University of Pennsylvania) in 1761, then studied law and began a practice after admission to the bar in 1763. He held public office under the crown as a register of admiralty (a lucrative post) from 1771 until 1776, but he was a firm patriot. In 1775, Peters received a commission as captain in the state militia, and the following year he became secretary to the War Board of the Continental Congress, serving until 1781. In 1782, he was himself elected as a delegate to Congress from Pennsylvania. During the postwar period, he sat in the Pennsylvania house (as speaker in 1788) and the senate. He was appointed to the U.S. District Court for Pennsylvania under the new federal constitution in 1792 and remained on the bench for 36 years until his death. He was deeply interested in agriculture and published many books and articles on the subject in addition to legal writings on maritime law.

PETERS, Samuel (1735–1826) Loyalist clergyman

Peters was a vociferously loyal Episcopal clergyman of Hebron, Connecticut. He graduated from Yale in 1757 and, after a sojourn for further training and ordination in England, returned to Hebron as rector in 1762. He was intemperate in his public utterances on behalf of the crown and came into conflict with the community of Hebron, where allegiance was mostly on the patriot side. In August 1774, a mob of 300 citizens confronted him at his home and demanded under threat of tar and feathers that he renounce letter-writing to British officials in England and other colonies. Although he complied, another mob visited him a month later and, discovering a small cache of arms in his home, compelled Peters to sign a declaration that he would cease all loyalist activities and public speech-making. He thereafter fled to the safety of Boston, where he hatched a scheme to have the crown dismember the disloyal colony of Connecticut and divide its territory between New York and New Hampshire. He emigrated to England about 1776 and remained there until 1805, when he returned to America, living the rest of his life in New York.

PETTIT, Charles (1736–1806) Delegate to Congress, Continental quartermaster Pettit was born in New Jersey, was trained as a merchant, and married the half-sister of Joseph Reed, which gave him an entré into public office. He filled several administrative and clerical posts in New Jersey colonial government during the late 1760s, and he was admitted to the bar in 1770. He became an aide to royal governor William Franklin in 1771 but was himself a patriot, and he abandoned Franklin when the crunch came in 1776. He continued to serve as secretary of the government under the new regime, a post that carried with it the courtesy rank of colonel. Pettit's greatest service came in 1778, when Nathanael Greene was persuaded by Washington to take over the arduous post of quartermaster general for the Continental Army. Pettit became Greene's assistant and actually bore most of the administrative and financial duties of the quartermaster's department. Long the Achilles' heel of the army, the quartermaster department was ably administered by Pettit, but the national treasury was descending toward bankruptcy and there was little he or Greene could do to prevent near disaster. Greene resigned in 1780 (soon to take command in the southern theater), but Pettit remained for another year as assistant quartermaster, having declined appointment to succeed Greene. After the war, Pettit moved to Philadelphia and set up business as an importer. He was selected as a delegate to the Confederation Congress in 1785 and served two years. He also sat in the state convention on the federal constitution. His later years were devoted to business.

PETTY, William. See SHELBURNE, Earl of.

PHELPS, Oliver (1749–1809) Merchant, speculator, legislator Phelps was born in Poquonock, Connecticut but was associated during his adult life with the state of Massachusetts. Before the Revolution he was a merchant in Granville, Massachusetts. In 1777, he was named as the superintendent of supply purchases for Massachusetts troops, holding the post until 1781. He also sat in the General Court from 1778 to 1780 and in the state constitutional convention in 1779. His political connections remained good after the war—he served in the state senate in 1785 and was on the Governor's Council in 1786—but his personal fortunes declined when land schemes in the west failed. Nonetheless, he was elected to the U.S. House of Representatives from Massachusetts in 1803.

PHILIPSE, Frederick (c. 1719–1785) Loyalist landowner Philipse was a descendant of an old Dutch family that had settled in New York on an estate granted under patent from William and Mary. The grant included feudal rights of ownership and control of tenancy, which persisted down to Frederick's day. He controlled a huge area and collected proprietary rents from nearly 300 tenants, who could not alter the terms of working the land without leave from the owner. In short, he was a latter-day Dutch patroon. In the spring of 1776, Philipse tried to organize an association of loyalists, but he was arrested by local patriots and taken to Connecticut for imprisonment. When released six months later, he moved with his family to New York City. Five of his sons served in the British army—Charles Philipse became a lieutenant general before retiring in the 19th century. The elder Philipse emigrated to England before the end of the Revolution and claimed the loss of his estate at more than £40,000.

PHILLIPS, John (1719–1795) Educator, legislator Born the son of a parson in Andover, Massachusetts, Phillips founded Phillips Academy in Exeter, Massachusetts in 1781, a school which came to be known as Phillips Exeter Academy, and he was the first president of its board of trustees. He was a graduate of Harvard and supported Dartmouth College for most of his later adult life. Between 1771 and 1773, Phillips sat in the Massachusetts General Court, during a tumultuous period in colonial legislative history.

PHILLIPS, William (c. 1731–1781) British general

One of the few artillerymen to advance to high rank and command in the British army of his day, Phillips was not so much an innovator in the use of artillery as he was highly energetic on the battlefield. He began his military career as a 15-year-old cadet and advanced relatively rapidly during the European wars of the 1750s, apparently for the most part on merit. He won considerable fame for his keen use of artillery at the battle of Minden in 1759, and in fighting against the French in 1760 at Warburg, Phillips was one of the first artillerymen to bring guns into action at the gallop (most artillery of the time was placed before engagements and remained static). He was rewarded with promotion to lieutenant colonel in 1760 and colonel in 1772.

He was dispatched to Canada in 1776 with General John Burgoyne and took command of the British post at St. John's with the local rank of major general. When Burgoyne returned to the American theater the following year, Phillips was appointed his second in command for the invasion of the states. He showed to good advantage during the otherwise lackluster campaign, demonstrating aggressive artillery tactics at most of the major battles, including the two engagements near Saratoga (he commanded the left wing of Burgoyne's army at Freeman's Farm). During the army's march across New York, Phillips had received promotion to the regular rank of major general. Unfortunately, neither his battlefield skill nor his counsel prevented defeat of Burgoyne, and when the British commander surrendered in October, Phillips was left at the head of the hapless Convention Army while Burgoyne withdrew. Phillips made himself a nuisance to the American authorities and was eventually arrested, but he soon was paroled and sent to New York City. He was formally exchanged for American general Benjamin Lincoln in October 1780. After overseeing inconclusive maneuvers against the French army in Rhode Island, Phillips was sent to Virginia in March 1781 to take command from the renegade Benedict Arnold (the British did not trust Arnold, even though he bore a brigadier's commission, and the high command wanted Phillips in charge). Phillips and Arnold were successful in wide-scale raiding and plundering throughout April, but Phillips contracted typhoid fever and died in May at Petersburg after a few days' illness.

PHRIPP, Matthew. Merchant

Born in Norfolk, Virginia, Phripp was one of the leading merchants in the colony in the years before the Revolution. During the rather chaotic early days of the war in Virginia, when Lord Dunmore was trying to coerce the colony into remaining within the British fold, the royal governor managed to get Phripp to sign an oath of loyalty to the king under threat of force. When Dunmore was expelled by patriot forces in late 1775, Phripp recanted and was exonerated of charges of loyalism. He returned to his merchant business.

PICKENS, Andrew (1739–1817) Militia general, state official

A stern Presbyterian soldier who earned the nickname "the fighting elder," Pickens was one of the most effective partisan militia leaders of the war in the Carolinas. He was born of Irish immigrant parents in Pennsylvania, but the family's search for land took them to the Waxhaw Creek region of South Carolina when Pickens was 13. After serving as a volunteer in an expedition against the Cherokees in 1761, Pickens moved to Long Cane Creek and took up farming.

With the outbreak of the War of Independence, Pickens was a captain of back-country militia and immediately came into conflict with the many South Carolina loyalists in his region—a conflict that persisted throughout the Revolution. In November 1775, Pickens commanded an outnumbered force of patriot militia that was forced to retreat to the town of Ninety-Six in the face of loyalists, but no large battle ensued. (The back-country war was relatively small-scale during the first years of the Revolution.)

Andrew Pickens

By 1779, Pickens was a colonel, and in February he won an important victory over loyalists at Kettle Creek, Georgia. The numbers involved were still small, but the ability of the loyalists in the region to organize was severely damaged by Pickens' win. He showed considerable military acumen in the complex maneuvering of march and countermarch before the battle, and he led his men well in the final confrontation, so his stock rose considerably. The British and their loyalist allies, however, gained the upper hand in the Carolinas after taking Charleston in May 1780 and destroying all organized resistance. The war turned into a long, vicious conflict that pitted roving bands of patriot partisans against their former neighbors, now turned loyalists.

Pickens stood out amid the several partisan commanders in South Carolina for his willingness to cooperate in order to defeat the enemy. However, he was not at first successful. He was once again backed into a corner at Ninety-Six and forced to surrender. He went home on parole, but when loyalists destroyed his farm, he again took the field, declaring his parole void. Perhaps his best moments came at the battle of the Cowpens in January 1781, where he commanded the second line of militia that administered crushing casualties on Banastre Tarleton's advancing British and loyalists. He was promoted to brigadier general and voted a sword by Congress after the battle. He continued to fight during the rest of the year, organizing a new regiment, which he led at Augusta, at the siege of Ninety-Six and at the battle of Eutaw Springs, where he was wounded. In 1782, Pickens commanded expeditions against the Cherokee on the western Carolina frontier. He emerged from the war as a hero and was called on to serve in public office. He sat in the state legislature from 1781 until 1794 and served as a boundary commissioner several times. He went to the U.S. Congress as a representative for one term in 1793, returning thereafter to the state assembly. He declined nomination for state governor in 1812. Pickens lived the last years of his life in the Pendleton district of South Carolina. *Further reading:* Alice N. Waring, *The Fighting Elder: Andrew Pickens, 1739–1817* (Columbia, S.C., 1962).

PICKERING, Timothy (1745–1829) Continental officer, government official
Although he became one of the principal obstructionists of early

Timothy Pickering

American politics, Pickering served creditably enough during the Revolution. He was born in Salem, Massachusetts, graduated from Harvard in 1763, became a clerk in the local Essex County office of deeds, and passed the bar in 1768. Pickering was a strongly partisan patriot in the years before the Revolutionary War, writing and speaking vociferously against the royal government. He was also a member of the Essex County militia and undertook a study of military procedure and history that resulted in publication in 1775 of *An Easy Plan of Discipline for a Militia*, which served as a standard manual until superseded by the work of Friedrich Wilhelm von Steuben. Pickering married in 1776 and eventually fathered 10 children.

When the first battle of the war took place at Lexington and Concord, Pickering marched with his militia unit to join the gathering patriot army, and he eventually took part in the American campaigns in New York and New Jersey during 1776. Having come to the attention of George Washington, Pickering was appointed as adjutant general of the Continental Army in May 1777, replacing Horatio Gates. His new post was difficult, fraught with detailed administrative work and supported with few resources. Pickering performed well, however, as a senior staff officer, and he also took the field on occasion as at the battle of Germantown.

In November 1777, he was appointed by Congress to the newly-formed board of war, although he was not released from his staff duties until the following January. In 1780, he returned to the army as quartermaster general, replacing Nathanael Greene in what was probably the most difficult staff job of the Revolution. In 1787, he moved to the Wyoming Valley settlements and bought up lands in the disputed region, hoping apparently to make his fortune when the contested claims between states were settled.

It was Pickering's political role following the Revolution that earned him his evil reputation. When his landholdings failed to produce much income, he petitioned President Washington for a federal job, receiving an appointment as postmaster general of the United States in 1791. He meanwhile had emerged as one of the principal leaders of what was becoming the Federalist party, supporting the positions of Alexander Hamilton in the federal cabinet. Pickering became secretary of war in January 1795 and eight months later took over as secretary of state when Edmund Randolph was forced to resign. Pickering, like most of the Federalist party leaders, was violently anti-French. He maneuvered behind the back of the new president John Adams and was dismissed as secretary of state in 1800. He returned to Pennsylvania and persuaded friends to buy out his landholdings, whereupon he moved back to Massachusetts and schemed as part of the so-called Essex Junto to form a confederacy of New England states. He served in the U.S. Senate and House as one of the die-hard Federalists and a leader of the faltering party, growing ever more radical in his political perversity. *Further reading:* Gerard Clarfield, *Timothy Pickering and the American Republic* (Pittsburgh, 1980).

PIERCE, William L. (1740–1789) Continental officer, delegate to Congress Little is known of Pierce's origins or early life, although he is thought to have been born in Georgia. He joined the Continental Army as a Virginia resident, however, serving for the entire Revolution as an aide to General Nathanael Greene. He was brevetted as a major on the end of his service in 1783 and settled in Savannah, Georgia as a merchant. He was elected as a delegate to the Confederation Congress in 1786 and attended sessions from January to May in 1787. He was also a delegate to the Philadelphia convention on the proposed federal constitution and left in his personal papers a series of character sketches of some of his fellow delegates. He left the convention before it finished its work, however, probably due to faltering business back home.

PIGOT, Sir Robert (1720–1796) British general Born in Staffordshire, Pigot entered the British army in the early 1740s and fought with distinction in Flanders in 1745. He was lieutenant colonel of the 38th Regiment of Foot in 1774 when the unit was dispatched to reinforce the garrison at Boston. Pigot was likely not on the expedition to Lexington and Concord, although his men were. He did, however, play a conspicuous role at the battle of Breed's Hill, leading his men against the American fortifications. During the first British advance, Pigot was placed on the left flank of the line attacking the main American positions but was turned back by musket fire. A second attack fared no better, and casualties among Pigot's officers and men were high: Most of his regimental officers were killed during the battle. The third assault, launched as the American militiamen ran out of ammunition, sent Pigot straight at the American redoubt, which was overrun. He was promoted to colonel by the king personally in consequence of his valor on the field. In 1777, Pigot inherited the family baronetcy and was also promoted to major general. He commanded the defenses of Newport in 1778, turning back an ill-coordinated joint attack by the French and Americans with his force of 3,000 men. The failures of French admiral d'Estaing did much to aid Pigot at Newport, but he deftly avoided what seemed like an inevitable defeat at the hands of a superior force and pushed the Americans away in a spirited counterattack, although he allowed them to escape cleanly. In 1782, Pigot became a lieutenant general.

PINCKNEY, Charles (1757–1824) Militia officer, delegate to Congress, state official, diplomat A second cousin of Charles Cotesworth Pinckney and Thomas Pinckney (and, eventually, the son-in-law of Henry Laurens), Charles Pinckney was born in Charleston, South Carolina. His father was an eminent man of the colony who eventually accepted the protection of the British and subsequently lost his estates as a loyalist. Charles, however, was a steadfast patriot. He served as a lieutenant in the Charleston militia and fought at Savannah in 1779, the same year he was admitted to the bar. He was captured at the fall of Charleston in May 1780 and refused parole, thus being held prisoner for a short while. He was also a member of the state legislature, although the body had little function while the British controlled the state. From 1785 to

1787, Pinckney served as a delegate to the Confederation Congress, but it was as a delegate to the constitutional convention that he is best known. He was a strong supporter of a central government and drafted one of the first versions of the Constitution. There has been considerable controversy over the exact nature of the mysterious "Pinckney draught," since he claimed to have incorporated almost all of the provisions that eventually found their way into the fundamental document of the republic but neglected to preserve a copy. He probably was the author of a considerable part of the Constitution, although his need for personal gratification may have led him to exaggerate his role.

He emerged in the 1790s as one of the principal politicians of South Carolina, having strong family connections—he married Henry Laurens' daughter in 1788—and served as governor from 1789 to 1792. Originally a Federalist, Pinckney became increasingly alienated from the party and by the late 1790s was a firm Jeffersonian, which put him at odds with his Pinckney cousins. He was rewarded for his support of Jefferson by appointment as minister to Spain in 1801. Following what was a difficult mission in Madrid, he returned to state government and served as U.S. representative and again as governor, leaving public office in 1821. *Further reading:* Andrew Bethea, *The Contribution of Charles Pinckney to the Formation of the American Union* (Richmond, Va., 1937).

PINCKNEY, Charles Cotesworth (1746–1825) Continental general, state official, diplomat

The second cousin of Charles Pinckney and the brother of Thomas Pinckney, Charles Cotesworth Pinckney was the most military of the South Carolina clan and won undying fame in American history as a principal in the infamous XYZ Affair. He was born in Charleston and taken to England for schooling in 1753. He received a sterling education at Westminster, Oxford and the Middle Temple, and he became one of the few native-born American military men to have formal European training when he attended the French military academy at Caen. On his return to Charleston, Pinckney set up a law practice, which rapidly added to his fame and fortune, and his position was not harmed by marriage in 1773 to Sarah Middleton, sister of the socially prominent Arthur Middleton.

Charles Cotesworth Pinckney

He was appointed as captain of the 1st South Carolina Regiment in June 1775 when the unit was organized for the defense of the colony. He served at the defense of Fort Sullivan under William Moultrie in 1776, helping to turn away the first British attempt to take Charleston. Pinckney was promoted to colonel but left South Carolina and went north, where he became George Washington's aide-de-camp. Pinckney was on Washington's staff throughout 1777, serving at Brandywine and Germantown, before returning to the south in 1778. He was captured by the British at the fall of Charleston in the spring of 1780, however, and was not exchanged until 1782, when he rejoined the army. He was awarded a brevet as brigadier general on his mustering out.

Pinckney returned to Charleston and the practice of law, but he also continued in public office, having previously served as president of the state senate. He sat in the lower house of the legislature and was a moving force in national and state conventions that adopted a new federal constitution. Pinckney was a strong Federalist—one of the leading lights of the party through the 1790s—and was instrumental in gaining ratification of the new government. He then proceeded to turn down a succession of federal offices, including posts as associate justice of the Supreme Court, secretary of state and secretary of war.

He was finally persuaded to become minister to France in 1796, however, and found himself ambassador to a nation in the midst of a great internal revolution and on the brink of a war with the United

States. His credentials were at first refused, but when he was joined by Elbridge Gerry and John Marshall as a three-man diplomatic commission, Pinckney opened negotiations with Talleyrand, the French foreign minister. The French proceeded to offer a treaty in return for a quarter-million-dollar bribe to Talleyrand—a deal put forth by three French agents identified only as X, Y and Z. Pinckney immediately refused the scheme, thereby touching off an undeclared naval war between the nations, and he returned home to be commissioned a major general for the anticipated land war with France that never came about.

He was the Federalist candidate for vice president in 1800 and president in 1804 and 1808, but the old party was moribund. He died on his estate near Charleston. *Further reading:* Marvin Zahniser, *Charles Cotesworth Pinckney: Founding Father* (Chapel Hill, N.C., 1967).

PINCKNEY, Thomas (1750–1828) Continental officer, state official, diplomat

The younger brother of Charles Cotesworth Pinckney, Thomas was born in Charleston, South Carolina but was taken to England when only three years old. He was reared and educated as an English gentleman at Westminster School and Christ Church, Oxford. He studied law at the Middle Temple and was called to the British bar in 1774. He also traveled on the Continent and spent some months in training at a French military school.

Despite this background, Pinckney came to America in late 1774 and became an ardent patriot. He joined a ranger company in early 1775 and then became a captain in the 1st South Carolina Regiment, which was raised in June 1775 for local defense of the state but was more or less adopted by the Continental Congress in November. Pinckney worked as an engineer on the harbor fortifications of Charleston and was at a secondary post when the British expedition of 1776 was repulsed at Fort Sullivan. He himself was subsequently stationed at Sullivan (which became known as Fort Moultrie) for the following two years. He was a part of the hapless Florida campaign in 1778, and in 1779 was assigned as an aide to French admiral d'Estaing during the Franco-American attempt to take Savannah. Neither of the later two campaigns did anything to cover Pinckney (or anyone else) with military

Thomas Pinckney

glory. He was most effective as a recruiter and troop trainer.

In late 1779, Pinckney, along with his brother, was at Charleston and helped prepare the defenses of the city against a new invasion expedition under Sir Henry Clinton. At the last minute before the fall of the seaport, Pinckney was sent outside the lines to organize a relief, but it was too late. He avoided capture, however, and went north to join Washington and the main Continental Army. During the following months, Pinckney became attached to General Horatio Gates, and when Gates was named by Congress to command the Southern Department, Pinckney returned to the Carolinas. He was wounded and captured at the debacle at Camden. He was not held in custody by the British, however, and after recovering from his injuries went to Philadelphia, where he was eventually paroled and exchanged. In 1781, he was a part of the Marquis de Lafayette's command in Virginia.

Pinckney settled in Charleston following the war and became governor of the state in 1787, doing much to help heal the wounds of the Revolution by advocating leniency for loyalists. He is best remembered by historians for his diplomatic career, which began in 1792 with his appointment as minister to Great Britain. His time in London was not a great success, however, despite his English manners and background. He was upset when John Jay was named to negotiate a treaty, but he accepted a commission which resulted in the so-called Pinckney's Treaty with Spain in 1795 that recognized American rights on the Mississippi. He was nominated for vice president on his return to the United States, but a complicated struggle, part of the breakup of the Federalists into warring factions over the policies of John Adams, left him without an office. He served in the U.S. Congress and as an inactive major general during the War of 1812. Pinckney retired to his plantations in South Carolina, where he carried out successful agricultural experiments. *Further reading:* Francis L. Williams, *A Founding Family: The Pinckneys of South Carolina* (Westport, Conn., 1970).

PINTARD, Lewis (1732–1818) Merchant, official   Born in New York City to a family of Huguenot merchants, Pintard was a wealthy businessman by the time of the Revolution, having inherited a thriving trade from his father. His marriage in the 1760s made him the brother-in-law of two important American patriot politicians, Richard Stockton and Elias Boudinot. Pintard himself was active in patriot affairs before the outbreak of the war, and he raised large sums and purchased gunpowder and supplies in Europe in 1775. He remained in the city after the British took control of New York in the summer of 1776, and he became the resident commissary for American prisoners. The British held thousands of Americans after defeating Washington's army in New York and taking Fort Washington, and the conditions of the prisoners' confinement in miserable hovels, jails and the notorious prison hulks were ghastly. No accurate tally has ever been possible, but many thousands died of disease while in captivity. Pintard was responsible for distributing what little food, supplies and money were available, and he apparently did a creditable job under nearly impossible circumstances. He managed, for example, to arrange a regular flow of prisoner exchanges. Following the war, Pintard served as a claims commissioner in New Jersey and then returned to his business interests in New York City. He suffered severe financial losses in the late 1780s but recovered and spent his later career in New Rochelle.

PITCAIRN, John (1722–1775) British officer   Born in Scotland as the son of a parson, Pitcairn lives in American historical memory as commander of the British troops on Lexington Green in April 1775. He was a royal marine, having taken a commission in 1756, and was a major when sent to Boston in 1774 to reinforce the garrison under General Thomas Gage. While the marines (part of the Royal Navy) were not so fashionable nor so prestigious a service as the army, Pitcairn was apparently well thought of by Gage, and he was well received socially by the loyalist upper crust of Boston. He was assigned to be second in command of the expedition sent out to capture militia stores and leaders on April 18, 1775. Pitcairn was personally at the head of the British troops who marched into Lexington, Massachusetts at dawn on the following day. He there confronted a band of militiamen under American captain John Parker. Pitcairn claimed afterward to have tried to avoid a fight and maintained he never gave an order to fire the fateful shot that began the War of Independence. Whoever set off the brief skirmish, Pitcairn's men killed several patriots and suffered only one wound among themselves before the minutemen scattered.

The rest of the day went ill for Pitcairn, however. After occupying Concord for a short time, he began a withdrawal that turned into a near nightmare. Massachusetts militia attacked the British column all along the road back toward Boston. Pitcairn's horse threw him and bolted at one stage, leaving the marine officer to find his way on foot. Pitcairn was in charge of the marines at the battle of Breed's (and Bunker) Hill two months later. As did most of the senior British officers, he led his troops personally during the assaults on the American fortified positions. The marines were on the extreme left of the British line during the third and final attack, and Pitcairn was hit by a musket ball in the chest just before his men overran the Americans. He died aboard ship on the river after his son, also a marine officer, carried him from the field.

PITCHER, Molly. See HAYS, Mary Ludwig.

PITKIN, William (1725–1789) Delegate to Congress, merchant   A native of Hartford, Pitkin was a wealthy Connecticut merchant by the coming of the Revolutionary War, owning several key water-power sites and mills. He had a long history of militia service, starting as a captain in 1756 and rising to lieutenant colonel by 1762, but there is no record he was an active soldier during the Revolution. He was an officeholder, however, sitting on the Governor's Council throughout the war years and as judge of the Superior Court, and he was a

William Pitt

member of the local committee of safety. In 1784, Pitkin was elected to the Confederation Congress, but he failed to serve.

PITT, William, (the Elder) (Earl of Chatham) (1708–1778) British prime minister

Although he was the dominant British politician and statesman for nearly three decades, Pitt was enfeebled by poor physical and mental health in the years approaching the American Revolution and could do little to prevent a war he on the whole did not favor. He was born in London and educated at Eton and Oxford. He suffered all his life from severe gout, a disease that felled him at several crucial junctures. After a brief military career, he entered Parliament in 1735, and within a short time, Pitt's sharp mind, effective oratory and keen political skills set him on the path that would make him known as the "Great Commoner." He opposed the foreign policies of Walpole and was ever an advocate of the strongest measures against France. He first took office in 1756 and over the following years commanded the British government as the principal minister during the war against France. His masterful organization of the nation's resources, his successful strategies, and his strong political leadership resulted in the complete defeat of France by 1761.

He resigned from office but saw the new king, young George III, and his ministers conclude a peace in 1763 that was less than satisfactory. For the next 15 years, Pitt was in and out of office and for the most part stood in opposition to the royal party. George III was both repelled by Pitt and attracted to his power and success, but the king could seldom bring himself to make full use of Pitt's ideas or personal abilities. Pitt accepted a peerage as the Earl of Chatham, and this eroded his popularity to some degree. He also began a long period of physical and mental decline. For months on end he was incapacitated and moved in and out of a mental fog. He would be completely removed from the scene and secluded for long periods and then suddenly snap back to full mental vigor and political activity. He consistently opposed the coercive measures of the British government toward the American colonies during the 1760s and early 1770s, but could do nothing to prevent them. He collapsed in the House of Lords in May 1778 and died soon after. *Further reading:* Peter D. Brown, *William Pitt, Earl of Chatham, the Great Commoner* (London, 1978); Owen A. Sherrard, *Lord Chatham and America* (London, 1958).

PLATER, George (1735–1792) Delegate to Congress, state official

Plater was a Maryland native, a graduate of the College of William and Mary, and a lawyer in Annapolis before the Revolution. He held several public offices in the 1760s and early 1770s, including a judge's seat on the Maryland Provincial Court and a place on the Maryland Executive Council. With the coming of the break with England, Plater joined the Maryland Committee of Safety and helped organize a new state government. From 1778 to 1780, he represented Maryland in the Continental Congress. He was elected governor of Maryland in 1791 but died before the end of his term.

PLATT, Zephaniah (1735–1807) Delegate to Congress, official

Born on Long Island, Platt was educated in England and became a lawyer with a practice in Poughkeepsie, New York. He was a member of the New York provincial congresses from 1775 to 1777 as well as a member of the state council of safety. He sat in the state senate during most of the Revolution. From 1784 to 1786, Platt was a delegate to the Confederation Congress. He founded Plattsburg, New York in 1784 and became one of the early promoters of the Erie Canal.

PLESSIS, Thomas-Antoine, Chevalier de Mauduit (1753–1791) French volunteer

Known

during his service to the American Revolution by the egalitarian name Thomas Duplessis, the French artilleryman fought in several key battles and played a particularly important role at the defense of Fort Mercer at Red Bank, New Jersey in October 1777. He entered the artillery school of the French Army as a 12-year-old lad but ran away with two companions and toured southern Europe and the Near East, being retrieved by the French ambassador in Constantinople. He came to America in 1777 and appears to have been a competent artillerist, a specialty that the American cause much prized during the early years of the war. He is reported to have fought bravely at the battle of Germantown, leading a futile assault on the key British position in the Chew House. At Red Bank, he helped organize the defense of the fort and directed the construction of an interior wall that proved crucial in stopping the advance of the Hessian troops under von Donop. Du Plessis was also at the battle of Monmouth and may have commanded a wing of the artillery. He returned to France in 1779 and in 1787 was given command of a regiment in Port-au-Prince on the island of Haiti. He was a violent supporter of the French Revolution but was equally violent in his suppression of the black slave population of Haiti, which simmered with both political and racial passions. During the ensuing violence, du Plessis was killed and his body torn to pieces by his own soldiers.

POLK, Thomas (1732–1794) Continental officer, delegate to Congress

Born in frontier Cumberland County, Pennsylvania, Polk moved to North Carolina and lived in Charlotte before the Revolution, serving as a local city official and a militia officer during the 1760s. He sat in the North Carolina house almost continuously from 1766 to the outbreak of the rebellion. In 1775, he was one of the members of the provincial congress and was appointed as a colonel in the state militia. In 1776, he received a commission as a colonel in the Continental Army and helped raise a new regiment, the 4th Carolina, which he commanded. The unit remained in the state during 1776 but was called north to join Washington's main force in early 1777 and fought at the battle of Brandywine. The numbers of the regiment dwindled during the difficult winter at Valley Forge, and by spring the unit was severely understrength. Polk's regiment was broken up in

William Polk

May 1778, and he returned to North Carolina to recruit men for a nine-month temporary regiment. In 1780, Polk became commissary for state and Continental troops in North Carolina, a difficult task against the background of the fall of Charleston and the control of the state by the British. Polk was elected to Congress in 1786 but did not serve.

POLK, William (1758–1834) Militia officer

Born in Charlotte, North Carolina, Polk was a teenage major of North Carolina militia in 1776 and fought in the north at Germantown and Brandywine. He then moved back to the southern theater and was at both Camden and Guilford Courthouse. In 1782, he commanded a unit of South Carolina cavalry with the rank of lieutenant colonel. He embarked on a career in business and public office after the war, beginning as surveyor general of North Carolina. He served terms in the state house of representatives and was supervisor of internal revenue for North Carolina. He also was a successful banker and promoter of a river navigation company. In the 1820s, Polk managed the election campaigns of Andrew Jackson in North Carolina.

POLLOCK, Oliver (c. 1737–1823) Merchant, patriot financier

Operating out of Spanish New Orleans during the Revolution, Pollock was one of the principal supply agents for the war in the West and financed a huge sum from his own pockets. He was born in northern Ireland and emigrated in 1760 with his father, brother and a nephew to Pennsylvania. Two years later, he was in the West Indies as a trader, operating ships out of Havana. He established good relations with the Spanish during this period and built up a considerable trade, which he moved to New Orleans in 1768, shortly before the Spanish took control of the river city. Pollock soon became one of the principal traders and merchants of New Orleans, prospering as the middleman in trade with Europe and on the Mississippi.

He was an American patriot and began early in the Revolution to do all he could to support the cause of the rebellious colonies. In August 1776, Pollock received Captain George Gibson, a Continental officer from Fort Pitt, who had traveled down the Ohio and Mississippi rivers with a small band of soldiers disguised as traders. Pollock introduced Gibson to the Spanish governor of New Orleans, Luis de Unzaga, and arranged for Gibson to take 10,000 pounds of vital gunpowder back up the river to supply the American war effort. When George Rogers Clark moved his expedition into the Illinois country, Pollock became his chief supplier, honoring Clark's otherwise worthless letters of credit and sending gunpowder and small artillery to the Virginian.

In January 1777, Bernardo de Galvez, a young, energetic Spaniard, became the new governor of New Orleans, and Pollock soon came to be a close associate of the new administrator. Pollock was with the Spanish military expedition under Galvez that took British posts at Manchac, Baton Rouge and Natchez in 1779.

By the end of the war, Pollock had advanced very large sums to finance the American cause—perhaps as much as $300,000—but neither the national Congress, which was completely bankrupt, nor the state of Virginia was able to made good his claims, despite expressions of good will. Utterly ruined by his patriotism, Pollock moved to Havana in hope of becoming a mercantile agent, but he was arrested for debt by the Spanish and held for 18 months. He was released in 1785 when Galvez became governor of Cuba. He was awarded $90,000 by the Confederation Congress in 1785, but no funds were paid until six years later. Pollock meanwhile outfitted a ship, sold a load of flour in Martinique, and moved back to New Orleans to resume his trading business with the slim stake provided by the sale of the one cargo. By 1790, he had made a remarkable recovery and paid all of his debts. He later moved back to Pennsylvania and thence to

Baltimore and Mississippi, where he died. *Further reading:* James A. James, *Oliver Pollock: The Life and Times of an Unknown Patriot* (first ed. 1937; reprinted 1970); James A. James, "Oliver Pollock, Financier of the Revolution in the West," *Mississippi Valley Historical Review* 16 (1929), 67–80.

POMEROY, Seth (1706–1777) Militia general, gunsmith

Pomeroy was born and lived most of his life in Northampton, Massachusetts. He came from a family of skilled mechanics and was himself a renowned gunsmith—a vital craft in colonial America. He had a remarkable career as a militia officer during the colonial wars preceding the American Revolution. He was a captain of a Massachusetts regiment on the expedition against Louisbourg in 1745 and headed a group of gunsmiths who repaired captured French artillery on the spot. He then served as a major of militia on the western Massachusetts frontier, organizing scouting parties and the construction of roads. In 1755, Pomeroy was appointed as lieutenant colonel of the troops from western Massachusetts on Sir William Johnson's campaign against Crown Point, and at the battle at Lake George in September, Pomeroy personally captured the French commander. He was an active patriot in the years immediately before the War of Independence, sitting on his local committee of safety and representing his town at the Massachusetts provincial congresses. He was appointed as one of the joint commanders of the Massachusetts militia and spent most of his efforts in early 1775 organizing and drilling troops in the western part of the colony. He was 69 years old when he borrowed a horse and rode to join the defenders of Bunker Hill in June 1775. Firing a musket he had made himself, Pomeroy fought as a private volunteer at the battle and was reported to have been one of the last to withdraw when the British finally overran the American defenses. He was named by Congress a few days later as one of the original eight brigadier generals of the Continental Army, but he declined the commission and became a major general of Massachusetts militia instead. He died on the march to join Washington's army in New Jersey in February 1777.

POOR, Enoch (1736–1780) Continental general

Poor was born in Massachusetts to a family of modest means. He had only a local education and was apprenticed in his youth to a cabinetmaker, but in 1755, he enlisted in the colonial militia and went on an expedition against the French in Nova Scotia. In 1760, he moved to Exeter, New Hampshire and became a trader and shipbuilder. He was involved in prerevolutionary activities, supporting the nonimportation agreements in 1770 and 1774, and was elected to represent his town in the New Hampshire provincial congresses. When the congress decided to raise troops to oppose the British, Poor was named in May 1775 as one of three regimental colonels and took command of a unit that came to be designated as the 2nd New Hampshire. Politics and prickly egos seemed to ever complicate military organization in New Hampshire, and Poor was no exception. There was usually a certain amount of rivalry between Poor, John Stark and state politicians over who would command and under what circumstances. Poor's regiment missed the battle of Bunker Hill in June 1775, although it marched to join the army surrounding Boston later in the summer and was taken into the new Continental Army as the 8th Continental Regiment (the unit was reconstituted in late 1776 under its former name of the 2nd New Hampshire with Poor still in command as colonel).

After the British evacuation of Boston, Poor's regiment was dispatched to aid the retreat of Benedict Arnold's expedition against Canada, and he became involved in a controversy with Arnold after sitting on the court-martial of Moses Hazen. In December 1776, Poor and his regiment left the northern theater and joined Washington's forces in New Jersey, fighting at both Trenton and Princeton. He was promoted to brigadier general in February 1777, in part as a way to resolve disputes between New Hampshire politicians. He returned to New York and reached the high point of his military career as part of General Horatio Gates's army opposing General John Burgoyne: Poor and his New Hampshire troops were central in the two crucial battles near Saratoga that brought on Burgoyne's defeat, suffering heavy losses and fighting extremely well. After the winter at Valley Forge, Poor commanded parts of the army at the battle of Monmouth in June 1778. The following year, he was with John Sullivan's expedition against the Iroquois and was commended for his actions at the only battle of the campaign at Newtown. In 1780, his brigade was attached to the light infantry division

of the Marquis de Lafayette, but Poor himself died of a fever at Paramus, New Jersey in September.

POOR, Salem (born c. 1747) Soldier At the age of 27, Poor, a free black resident of Massachusetts, enlisted in Colonel James Frye's Massachusetts Battalion that was organized in May 1775. He was one of the celebrated private soldiers who defended the main fortifications at the battle of Bunker Hill and is reported to have been the marksman who shot British lieutenant colonel James Abercrombie. Six months after the battle, 14 American officers petitioned the Massachusetts General Court on Poor's behalf, citing his personal conduct as "a brave and gallant soldier" and asking that he be rewarded, but he apparently was not. Poor later served at White Plains and at winter quarters at Valley Forge in 1776.

PORTER, Andrew (1743–1813) Officer Porter was a native of Pennsylvania and taught mathematics and language in Philadelphia during the decade before the Revolution. He received a commission as captain of marines in 1776 and fought during the New Jersey campaign of 1776–77 and the Pennsylvania campaign of 1777. In 1779, he was on John Sullivan's successful expedition against the Indians and loyalists in upstate New York. He apparently resigned his commission in 1781 and became a manufacturer of gunpowder in Philadelphia: some of his products were reportedly used at the siege of Yorktown. He then joined the army again, and in 1782 he was the lieutenant colonel of the 4th Battalion of Continental Artillery, a unit made up almost entirely of Pennsylvanians. He was discharged in June 1783 when the unit was dissolved. Following the war, Porter worked as a surveyor and acted as a commissioner to determine state boundaries. He became a brigadier general in the Pennsylvania militia in 1800 and later became a major general.

POTTER, James (1729–1789) Militia officer Potter was born in Ireland and came to Pennsylvania in 1741. He was an officer during the latter stages of the Seven Years' War in America and afterward worked for the British to try to convince western Pennsylvania settlers to abandon the frontier to the Indian tribes as proscribed by the Proclamation of 1768. He held a colonel's commission in the Pennsylvania militia at the beginning of the war and also served in the state constitutional convention. In 1777, he was promoted to brigadier general of militia and fought at Trenton, Princeton, Brandywine and Germantown. He became a state official in 1780, taking a seat on the Supreme Council as vice president. After the conclusion of peace, Potter was a land speculator.

POTTS, Jonathan (1745–1781) Army physician

Potts studied at the College of Philadelphia (now the University of Pennsylvania) Medical School, receiving bachelor's and medical degrees in 1768 and 1771. He practiced medicine in Reading for a few years before the Revolution and was an active patriot. He was a delegate to the provincial patriot meetings in Philadelphia and then a member of the Provincial Congress. Despite his relative youth, he was named as deputy director general of hospitals for the Northern Department in 1777 during a period when the medical administration of the Continental Army was in considerable turmoil and the object of a political tug-of-war between Philadelphia medical factions. He died at an early age before the end of the war.

POTTS, Richard (1753–1808) Delegate to Congress, state official

Potts, a native of Maryland, read law under Samuel Chase and practiced in Frederick County before the Revolution. He served on a local patriot committee of observation in 1776, and in 1777 was appointed military aide to Maryland governor Thomas Johnson. He sat in the Maryland House of Delegates from 1779 to 1780 and was sent to the Continental Congress in 1781 and 1782. After the war, he served successively as a local prosecuting attorney, U.S. district attorney and chief judge of the U.S. Fifth Judicial district. Potts became a U.S. senator in 1793 but returned to sit on the bench of the Maryland Court of Appeals after one term. *Further reading:* Lewis H. Steiner, "A Memoir of the Hon. Richard Potts," *Maryland Historical Magazine* 5 (March 1910), 63–68.

POURRÉ, Eugenio. Spanish officer

Pourré, a captain in the Spanish forces at St. Louis, was dispatched in January 1781 on an expedition against the main British post in the West at Detroit. He had about 60 militiamen and the same number of Indian auxiliaries. He surprised Fort St. Joseph (in what is now Michigan) and forced the quick surrender of the small garrison. After holding the place for only a day, Pourré withdrew to Spanish territory. The major significance of his foray was a claim made later by the Spanish to the drainage of the St. Joseph and Illinois rivers, based on his brief raid.

POWNALL, Thomas (1722–1805) Royal official

Pownall served in several important colonial offices before the Revolution and was a student of colonial administration, although his advice was seldom taken by the British government during the Revolution. He was educated at Cambridge and became a junior official at the board of trade in the early 1740s (his brother was secretary of the board). In 1753, Pownall came to America as secretary to the newly appointed governor of New York, Sir Danvers Osburn. The unhappy Osburn committed suicide shortly after arriving, but Pownall stayed on in the colonies, making friends with a range of American figures, including Benjamin Franklin, James De Lancey and Sir William Johnson. After functioning in a semi-official capacity for two years, Pownall was appointed lieutenant governor of New Jersey in 1755, although his formal duties were slight. He studied the colonial military situation and advised the government in London, where he returned in 1756. He was offered the governorship of Pennsylvania, but he declined and returned briefly to America as secretary to Lord Loudoun, the new military commander in chief.

Back in England, Pownall formed a political alliance with William Pitt, who was just emerging as a major political and governmental figure. Pitt appointed Pownall as governor of Massachusetts, and Pownall took office in mid-1757, simultaneously holding the lieutenant governorship of New Jersey. While on the whole an effective administrator, Pownall ran into political problems in Massachusetts and was removed as governor in 1759. He returned to England and never again set foot in the New World. He continued to be regarded as an expert in American affairs, however, especially after publishing *The Administration of the Colonies* in 1764 (a large work that eventually ran to five editions). He entered the House of Commons and put forth a scheme to reorganize colonial government which would have allowed considerable latitude to the Americans. Defeated in 1774, he changed political alliance and joined the supporters of Lord North.

In 1777, Pownall introduced a bill in the House to allow the king to negotiate for peace, but with its defeat he withdrew from politics and public office, although he continued to write about colonial policy. *Further reading:* John Schutz, *Thomas Pownall, British Defender of American Liberty* (New York, 1951); F. W. Grinnell, "Thomas Pownall: Forgotten Friend of America," *American Bar Association Journal* 44 (February 1958), 153–55.

PRATT, Matthew (1734–1805) Painter Pratt was a native-born American portraitist and painter of Philadelphia. He studied in England under the expatriate American painter Benjamin West and then returned to Philadelphia and opened a portrait studio before the Revolution. His clientele—which had included prominent Philadelphia families such as the Penns and Dickinsons—apparently declined during the war itself (many may have been loyalists), since he turned mainly to painting elaborate signs for taverns and shops from 1775 to 1781. His best-known production was a postwar sign called *The Representation of the Constitution*, which included all the members of the Constitutional Convention. He is also remembered for paintings such as *The American School* and portraits of his mentor Benjamin West and of Benjamin Franklin.

PREBLE, Edward (1761–1807) Naval officer Preble served as a teenager during the Revolution, but he achieved his place in history as a naval commander in the fighting against the Tripoli pirates after the turn of the 19th century. He was born in what is now Portland, Maine, which was a part of Massachusetts at the time. He served aboard the captured and rearmed British brig *Winthrop* during the Revolutionary War. He was an officer in the revived U.S. Navy by the 1790s and in 1803 commanded a squadron in the Mediterranean with the rank of commodore. He led five unsuccessful assaults on Tripoli in 1804.

PRESCOTT, Oliver (1731–1804) Militia general, physician The brother of William Prescott, Oliver was born in Groton, Massachusetts and graduated from Harvard in 1750. After the study of medicine with a doctor in Sudbury, Prescott opened his own practice in Groton, eventually becoming one of the leading physicians in Massachusetts and a founder of the state medical society. He was active in the

colonial militia before the war, and at the outbreak of the Revolution, he was made brigadier general of Middlesex County (his contribution to the affair at Lexington and Concord was to hide cannon in Groton). Despite his promotion to major general of militia in 1778, most of his wartime service was on the civilian side. He had served on committees to protest the Stamp Act, on his local committee of correspondence, and on committees dealing with the nonimportation association. In 1777 he was appointed to the state supreme council and served until 1780.

PRESCOTT, Richard (1725–1788) British general Prescott was a British commander with a poor reputation both at home and in America. He was a veteran of the Continental wars, having fought in Germany as lieutenant colonel of the 50th Regiment. In 1773, Prescott was made brevet commanding colonel of the 7th Regiment (Royal Fusiliers) and sent to Canada. He began to earn his ill fame by abuse of the captured American Ethan Allen in 1775. Prescott, with the local rank of brigadier general, was in command of the British garrison at Montreal and attempted to escape from the American advance toward Quebec but was captured in November. He was held for 10 months until exchanged for American general John Sullivan in September 1776. He was confirmed as colonel in command of the 7th in early 1777 and sent to help occupy Newport, Rhode Island, where he then remained as commander of the British garrison. Prescott had a particularly unpleasant personality and was soon regarded as one of the more objectionable British commanders by his American foes. His standing among his own countrymen fell considerably when he was captured at his own headquarters in July 1777 in a raid by American William Barton. Barton's object was to use Prescott in a bargain for an exchange of American general Charles Lee. The deal was made the following May, but Prescott had already suffered humiliation in the British press. Nonetheless, he was promoted to major general and returned to command at Newport in time to help repulse the French-American campaign in 1778. He was made a lieutenant general in 1782.

PRESCOTT, Robert (1725–1816) British general Born in Lancastershire, Prescott joined the

British army as a captain of the 15th Regiment in 1755 and advanced in rank to brevet colonel over the following decade of service. He was with the British expedition against Louisbourg in 1758 and was an aide-de-camp to James Wolfe. Prescott was lieutenant colonel of the 28th Regiment in 1775 at the beginning of the American war. He fought in all of the New York campaigns in 1776 and was with General William Howe in 1777 in Pennsylvania, seeing action at Brandywine. During the same year, he was commanding colonel of the 28th. After 1778, he served mostly in the West Indies, becoming a major general in 1781. After the Revolution, he continued on active duty, commanding British forces at Barbados in 1793 as a lieutenant general and taking Martinique from the French. In 1796, Prescott was appointed governor of Canada, succeeding Sir Guy Carleton. He ended his career with the rank of full general.

PRESCOTT, Samuel (1751–c. 1777) Physician, patriot

Although his name has not been sung down the decades as has Paul Revere's, Prescott was one of the heroes who alerted Massachusetts minutemen to the march of the British on the night of April 18–19 1775. He was a doctor in Concord (a member of a medical family) and an ardent patriot. On April 18, Prescott was returning home from Lexington when he overtook Revere and William Dawes on the road to Concord. Hearing word from them of the British advance from Boston, Prescott rode along. When the party was stopped by a group of British officers, Dawes escaped immediately, but Prescott and Revere were held at pistol point. After a brief scuffle, Prescott spurred his horse off the road, leapt a stone wall and escaped down a ravine, leaving Revere in the hands of the enemy. Prescott circled round, took to the road again, and galloped on to Concord to alert the local militia. Revere never completed his errand. Prescott returned to Lexington later in the day and offered medical care to the American wounded. He was captured on board a privateer in 1777 and died in captivity in Halifax, Nova Scotia.

PRESCOTT, William (1726–1795) Militia and Continental officer

Although a cool fighter and often regarded as the hero of Bunker Hill, Prescott was also responsible for the tactical error that resulted in the American defeat in the battle. He was the brother of Oliver Prescott and like him was born in Groton, Massachusetts. He served with the British and colonial forces during the wars in North America against the Indians and the French but lived quietly as a farmer near Pepperell, Massachusetts in the years immediately before the Revolution.

He was a colonel of local militia in April 1775 when the war began. He and his men arrived too late to fight at Concord, but they marched to join the army around Boston. There was little in the way of a definitive command structure among the militia officers gathered in a makeshift siege of the British, but Prescott was more or less in charge of the Massachusetts troops, which he led across Charles Neck to the hills above Charlestown on June 16, 1775 in order to build up fortifications against an expected British attack from Boston. The plan was to set up the main defense on Bunker Hill, which was a good defensive position, but Prescott and his officers decided to put up a dirt redoubt on Breed's Hill, several hundred yards forward. This was ultimately a costly error, since the fortifications were too exposed and placed the defenders too far from their support units (most of whom refused to move forward under fire from British ships). Israel Putnam, who also claimed to be in command, probably concurred in the decision. Once the place had been chosen, however, Prescott defended it with amazing courage and vigor. He was personally in command of the main American position and directed the fire that turned back two British frontal assaults with devastating effect. A third desperation attack by the British finally forced Prescott and his men from their positions as they began to run out of powder and ball. The final British bayonet assault killed and wounded more than 400 American defenders, and Prescott himself had to fight his way free with his sword. Prescott's militia battalion subsequently was taken onto the rolls of the new Continental Army in the summer of 1775, and he was commissioned as colonel. In January 1776, the unit was redesignated as the 7th Continental Regiment, and it took part under Prescott's command in the campaigns in New York. Prescott himself retired in 1777 and spent the rest of the war on his farm.

PRESTON, Thomas (born c. 1730) British officer

Preston was a captain in 1770, serving as part of the British garrison in Boston, when he commanded the guard on the evening of March 5. Hostilities that had grown between the British soldiers and increasingly rowdy mobs of Boston citizens culminated when a crowd armed with clubs surrounded one of Preston's sentries near the customs house. Preston marched a small armed guard to rescue his trooper but found himself hemmed in by the mob. Without orders from Preston, one of the soldiers fired into the crowd and the ensuing volley killed three Americans and wounded two more. As the officer in charge of what soon came to be known as the Boston Massacre, Preston was arrested and jailed by his superiors and eventually brought to trial. Defended by John Adams and Josiah Quincy, Preston was acquitted of all charges, although two of his men were found guilty of manslaughter. The incident served to keep alive the resistance to the British among American patriots.

PREVOST, Augustine (1723–1786) British general A Swiss by birth, Prevost directed the first stages of the British attempt to conquer the southern states during the last years of the war. He joined the British army in 1756 and served under James Wolfe during the Seven Years' War, suffering a serious wound at Quebec. He was in charge of British forces in East Florida with the rank of colonel when the war of the Revolution began. An able commander, who was seldom defeated by the Americans, he took part in the British capture of Savannah in late 1778 and then assumed command of all British forces in the South with the rank of major general. He gained several more important victories, including the repulse of a French-American effort to retake Savannah, and solidified the British hold on Georgia by the end of 1779, when he returned to England.

PREVOST, James Mark. British officer The younger brother of British general Augustine Prevost, James Mark Prevost served as an officer in his brother's 60th Regiment (known as the Royal American). His most notable exploit was in March 1779 when he conducted a surprise flanking march and attack on a large American force at Briar Creek, Georgia. Marching 50 miles through difficult terrain, Prevost came up behind the patriot force under John Ashe and, along with other British units, routed the Americans. Prevost served as lieutenant colonel of the 60th during 1781 and 1782 and for a brief

period in 1779 was designated as lieutenant governor of Georgia.

PRICE, Richard (1723–1791) Clergyman, political philosopher, mathematician Price wrote one of the most widely circulated pamphlets of the age on the topic of the Revolution and may have influenced the Americans who formulated the federal constitution. He was the son of a dissenting Calvinist clergyman, born in Wales and educated in private academies. During the 1750s and 1760s, he lived in London as a chaplain to a private family and occasional preacher in dissenting pulpits. He also began to write and publish works on a wide variety of moral, religious and scientific topics. He was, among other things, one of the first to write about the mathematical probabilities of actuarial tables. His most famous writing, however, was *Observations on the Nature of Civil Liberty, the Principles of Government, and the Justice and Policy of the War with America*, published in February 1776. Price held that self-determination was the basis for all liberty and that the American colonies had every right to assert themselves—even by rebellion—in order to obtain the blessings of such liberty. The pamphlet went through 14 editions in two months and sold more than 60,000 copies, making Price an intellectual hero in the United States and a blackguard among British government circles. He was offered American citizenship by Congress in 1778, but he declined the honor although he accepted an honorary degree from Yale in 1783. *Further reading:* Carl B. Cone, *Torchbearer of Freedom: The Influence of Richard Price on Eighteenth Century Thought* (Lexington, Ky., 1952).

PRIME, Benjamin (1733–1791) Physician, poet Prime was born the son of a parson on Long Island and graduated from the college at Princeton in 1751. After a brief stint as a tutor at the college, he set up a practice at Easthampton, Long Island, and he must have been well known as a physician, since he received honorary degrees both from Harvard and the medical school at the Dutch University of Leyden in the 1760s. He was also a poet and published a verse narrative of the American participation in the Seven Years' War. During the prerevolutionary agitation, he composed "A Song for the Sons of Liberty," and he wrote "Columbia's

Glory . . . a Poem on the American Revolution'' shortly before his death.

PRUEDHOMME de BORRE, Philippe Hubert, Chevalier de (b. 1717) French volunteer

By the time of the Revolution, de Borre was advanced in years and had many decades of experience, but he proved unfit for the situation in America. Born in Liège, he served in the French military from 1740 onward and saw considerable action during the War of Austrian Succession, taking a debilitating wound in the hand in 1745. He was promoted to lieutenant colonel but was not employed during the Seven Years' War. In 1776, de Borre was given a temporary commission as a brigadier general and sent along with several other French volunteers to America, apparently with the blessing of the French government. He arrived in March 1777 and was given a commission as a brigadier in the Continental Army, back-dated to December 1776 for purposes of seniority, and put in charge of a brigade under General John Sullivan. His troops were part of Sullivan's force that raided Staten Island in August. De Borre, however, apparently was little in sympathy with his fellow Continental officers and seldom agreed in matters of either strategy or tactics, and he had a low opinion of his troops, although he commanded Marylander Continentals that proved later to be among the finest soldiers on either side of the war. He bickered with Sullivan over placement of his brigade prior to the battle at Brandywine, and de Borre's men collapsed immediately under the British assault. He was charged with mismanaging his duties and resigned his commission before a court of inquiry could convene. He returned to France in 1779 and was confirmed as a brigadier general but retired for physical disability.

PULASKI, Casimir (1747–1779) Continental general

Like all too many of his fellow European soldiers of fortune, Pulaski was a thorn in the side of the Revolution and not very effective as a military leader. He was born to a noble family in Poland and fought with his father's troops against the Russians. At the First Partition of Poland he fled to Turkey, where he served in the Turkish army. He eventually made his way to Paris and befriended Benjamin Franklin, who advised him to come to America and provided a recommendation to Con-

Count Casimir Pulaski

gress. He arrived in 1777 and served creditably as a volunteer aide to Washington at the battle of Brandywine. At Washington's suggestion, Congress commissioned Pulaski as commander of the newly-authorized cavalry, with the rank of brigadier general. Pulaski fought ineffectively at the battle of Germantown and then retreated with the Continental Army to winter quarters in Valley Forge. Here he displayed the usual defects of foreign adventurers serving in the American cause: a prickly high estimate of his own worth and an inability to get along with American colleagues. Pulaski quarreled with the American officers assigned as his subordinates—no mean trick considering he spoke no English—and preferred charges against his second in command for having given some slight to the noble Pole. He resigned as commander of the cavalry in 1778 and won permission from Congress to raise his own elite corps, which he proceeded to recruit from among British deserters and prisoners. The Pulaski Legion proved to be more hazard to friends than to the enemy by its routinely destructive behavior. It enjoyed little success at any of its assigned tasks. Finally stationed in the South, Pulaski led his Legion in a foolish cavalry charge during the American attack on Savannah in late 1779. Pulaski was hit in the groin with grapeshot and died two days later aboard an American ship after unsuccessful surgery. *Further reading:* Clarence A. Manning, *Soldier of Liberty* (1945).

PUTNAM, Israel (1718–1790) Continental general   One of the colonies' veteran soldiers when the war began, Putnam proved that personal courage and good will were no substitutes for military competence. Despite his prewar reputation as a fighter and his elevation to major general early in the war, he consistently failed to perform adequately as a field commander. Born in Massachusetts, he lived most of his life in Connecticut as a farmer (he was a cousin of Rufus Putnam). He joined Rogers' Rangers in 1755 during the Seven Years' War and eventually rose to the rank of lieutenant colonel of militia. His service against the Indians was harrowing, to say the least: in 1758, he was captured and tied to a stake and was saved from roasting alive only by the last-minute intervention of a French officer. He was exchanged and then sailed with an ill-fated British mission against Havana. The entire force was shipwrecked off Cuba, and Putnam was one of the few survivors.

By the eve of the Revolution he had become a relatively prosperous farmer and tavern keeper with more than a local reputation for his previous exploits. He early joined the Sons of Liberty and supported the growing rebellion in New England. After Lexington and Concord, Putnam hastened to Boston and became colonel of a Connecticut regiment and brigadier of Connecticut militia. He was

Israel Putnam

one of the two principal commanders at the battle of Bunker Hill and Breed's Hill, where his personal courage showed to good advantage. Nevertheless, his lack of tactical skill contributed to the American defeat. Congress appointed him as one of the original major generals of the Continental Army within days of the battle. When Washington moved the army to New York, Putnam was given command at Long Island. His careless disposition of troops, failure to reconnoiter the ground and lack of tactical skill were largely responsible for the American debacle there. While still nominally a field commander throughout the New Jersey campaign, he was seldom again entrusted with anything vital. When given charge of American defenses in the Hudson Highlands, he promptly allowed Sir Henry Clinton to seize vital forts. He had been reduced to recruiting and a minor command in Connecticut when he was felled by a paralytic stroke in 1779. *Further reading:* Increase N. Tarbox, *Life of Israel Putnam* (1876; reprinted Port Washington, N.Y., 1970).

PUTNAM, Rufus (1738–1824) Continental general, land speculator   Rufus Putnam (the cousin of Israel Putnam) was born in Sutton, Massachusetts. His father died when Putnam was seven years old, and the boy was raised by relatives after his mother remarried. He lacked a formal education, but like many ambitious 18th-century Americans, he taught himself surveying and rudimentary engineering (although he lacked mathematical skill his entire life). Putnam gained practical experience as an engineer for the British during the Seven Years' War, and at the end of hostilities in 1760, he settled in New Braintree, Massachusetts. Putnam's first wife died seven months after his marriage in April 1760, leaving an infant child who succumbed in 1761. His second marriage five years later lasted 55 years and produced nine children.

During the decade before the War of Independence, Putnam worked as a surveyor and was involved in a scheme to settle western bounty lands along the Mississippi River. At the beginning of hostilities with the British, Putnam was lieutenant colonel and second in command of David Brewster's Massachusetts Regiment, which was taken into the new Continental Army in June 1775. Most of his activities were as an engineer, and he is credited with suggesting the use of moveable wooden parapets to fortify Dorchester Heights above Boston during the winter of 1775 when the frozen ground made digging impossible. He was commissioned colonel of engineers by Congress in mid-1776, but when Congress refused to establish a separate corps of engineers for the Continental Army, Putnam withdrew and became colonel in command of the new 5th Massachusetts.

Although he was assigned to the northern army that opposed General John Burgoyne and later to the defenses of the upper Hudson River Valley, Putnam saw little important action during the course of the war. His concern for western lands remained sharp, however, and he was involved in writing the Newburgh Resolutions in 1783 that demanded Congress award land bounties in return for service during the war. He was promoted to brigadier general in January 1783 and mustered out in November.

In 1786, Putnam helped found the Ohio Company, a venture made up largely of former officers, which was to organize and settle a large tract of land in the West. He reached the Ohio country in 1788 as superintendent of the projected settlement of a million and a half acres on the north side of the Ohio River. Difficulties with the Indians who occupied the land stifled large-scale settlement, but Putnam is often credited as one of the founders of the modern-day state of Ohio. He was appointed as a judge of the new Northwest Territory in 1790 and commissioned as a brigadier general in 1792. He continued to live in Ohio, near Marietta, and in 1796 was appointed as surveyor general of the United States. His work as a surveyor was poor, however, due to his faulty mathematical skill, and much of his labor of laying out a tract for military bounties had to be redone after his removal from office in 1803. *Further reading:* Mary Cone, *The Life of Rufus Putnam . . .* (Cleveland, Ohio, 1886); George Hoar, *Rufus Putnam, Founder and Father of Ohio . . .* (Worcester, Mass., 1898).

Q

QUESNAY DE BEAUREPAIRE, Alexandre-Marie (1755–1820) French volunteer Quesnay had served in the French gendarmerie but had no place or commission in France when he came to Virginia in 1777. He later claimed to have served in the Continental Army there as a captain, but—according to his account—his letters of recommendation were lost by Patrick Henry and his military career frustrated. In 1779, he was in Philadelphia as a civilian schoolteacher, and he operated an academy until 1784. He is reported to have been a theatrical producer and to have put on the first American performance of some of Beaumarchais's works. He returned to France in 1786, and he later proposed (unsuccessfully) an elaborate system of academies and learned institutions for the United States.

QUINCY, Josiah (1744–1775) Attorney, writer Quincy was one of the principal patriots and writers of Boston in the years before the actual breach with the mother country, although he did not live to see the Revolution come about. He gained a special place in revolutionary Boston by his legal defense (along with his friend John Adams) of the British officer charged with the Boston Massacre. Quincy was the youngest son of an immensely wealthy Braintree, Massachusetts squire, the brother of loyalist Samuel Quincy, and one of many in his family to bear the name "Josiah"—he was known as "Josiah the Patriot" to distinguish him. He studied law with the eminent attorney Oxenbridge Thacher in

Boston, and on Thacher's death, Quincy inherited his rich practice. He was within a short while one of the best-known and most successful lawyers in Boston.

Although often ambiguous in his attitude toward popular mob protest and violence, Quincy was a long-time foe of royal official Thomas Hutchinson, and much of Quincy's patriotism seems to have sprung from this personal and political animosity. Quincy had an active pen, and he contributed a series of essays and letters to the popular Boston press during the 1760s and early 1770s, urging protest and the cause of the Boston rebels. He was, however, a stickler for principle, and he agreed to defend Captain Thomas Preston and the eight British soldiers accused of murder as a result of the Boston Massacre in 1770. Quincy and Adams gave the men the best defense they could muster and succeeded in getting Preston off. Quincy saw no contradiction between his patriotic fervor and this stand for the rights of the accused to be properly defended in court.

He grew increasingly vitriolic in his writings after 1770. His most important work was *Observations on the Act of Parliament Commonly Called the Boston Port Bill*, published in 1774. Although severely ill with tuberculosis (a disease that also claimed his brother), Quincy undertook a mission to England in September 1774. There he met Lord North and Lord Dartmouth but made little headway in presenting the cause of patriot Boston. Committing no report to paper, he set off on the return voyage with the intent of carrying verbal messages to his colleagues in Massachusetts, but he died—scarcely 30 years of age—as his ship came within sight of America. *Further reading:* "Josiah Quincy" in Peter Shaw, *American Patriots and the Rituals of Revolution* (Cambridge, Mass., 1981); Edmund Quincy, *Life of Josiah Quincy of Massachusetts . . .* (Boston, 1869).

QUINCY, Samuel (1735–1789) Loyalist lawyer

A member of the locally prominent Quincy family of Massachusetts, Samuel graduated from Harvard in 1754 and became a lawyer. Before the Revolution, he was solicitor general of Massachusetts. His feelings about the rebellion were, apparently, mixed in the early days of agitation (his siblings were all patriots), but when faced with a decision, he re- mained loyal out of principle, despite the great personal cost of his choice. In May 1775, Quincy left his wife, who favored the American side, in Boston and emigrated to England. The separation was painful, as he wrote to her in early 1777: "The continuance of our unhappy situation has something in it so unexpected, so unprecedented, so complicated with evil and misfortune, it has become almost too burdensome for my spirits, nor have I words that can reach its description." The couple never repaired the political and personal rift. Two years later, Quincy went to the West Indies and became comptroller of customs in Antigua. After his wife died in 1782, he remarried.

QUOTEM, Caleb. See WHIPPLE, Prince.

RALL, Johann Gottlieb (c. 1720–1776) German mercenary officer   Rall suffered the most important defeat of the Revolution by Britain's German mercenary allies, forfeiting his own life. He was a native of Hesse-Cassel and a seasoned veteran of the European wars, having fought in Germany and subsequently against the Turks for the Russians. He came to America in August 1776 at the head of the Grenadiere Regiment von Rall (most German units were named for their commanders) with the rank of colonel. He led his men in the New York campaign at White Plains and the capture of Fort Washington. He spoke little or no English and did nothing to hide his contempt for his American opponents, whom he regarded as an unorganized and untrained rabble—a prejudice that afflicted many professional European officers. He was not held high in the opinion of the British commander in chief General William Howe, but nonetheless he was given command of the garrison at Trenton, New Jersey, in December 1776 when Howe discovered he could not pursue Washington's defeated army across the Delaware River. Among Rall's other defects was alcoholism, and he succumbed to the temptation to drink himself into incompetence at Trenton, little fearing Washington or any other American force could threaten him (European armies seldom ventured forth in winter weather if they could avoid it). He failed to fortify Trenton and allowed his men to celebrate Christmas without the irksome task of standing sentry duty. He per-

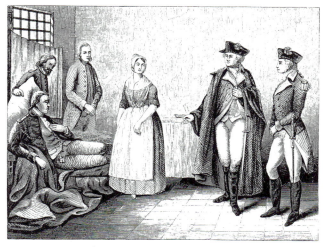

George Washington visits mortally wounded Hessian commander Johann Rall.

sonally was drunk in his bed when Washington and the Continental Army descended on Trenton during the early morning hours of December 26, 1776. Rall, no coward despite his other failings, tried to rally his men in a field and then in an orchard outside the town, but the Americans were in control and Rall was shot from his horse. He died later in the day, one of more than a hundred Hessian casualties.

RAMAGE, John (c. 1748–1802) Loyalist painter
Born and educated in Ireland, Ramage moved to Boston and was a goldsmith and painter of minia-

tures at the beginning of the Revolutionary War. He received a commission in the Loyal Irish Volunteers in 1776, but there is no account of his actual service. He moved to New York City in 1777 and was a "leading painter of miniatures" there throughout the war and after. Apparently his loyalist sympathies did not dissuade patrons. In 1789, he painted a miniature of George Washington to mark the new Federal presidency. Ramage eventually moved to Canada to escape his debts.

RAMSAY, David (1749–1815) Delegate to Congress, legislator, physician, historian

The younger brother of Nathaniel Ramsay, David was likewise born in Pennsylvania. He graduated from Princeton and received a medical degree from the college in Philadelphia (later the University of Pennsylvania) in 1772 as a student of Benjamin Rush. After a brief sojourn in Maryland, Ramsay moved to Charleston, South Carolina, where he entered public life as a member of the legislature. He joined the militia when Charleston was threatened by Sir Henry Clinton's expedition in 1780, acting as a surgeon to the Charleston Battalion of Artillery. Captured by the British, Ramsay was sent to St. Augustine, Florida and held until June 1781.

On his return to South Carolina, he was selected as a delegate to Congress for 1782–83 and again in 1785–86. While in Congress he served as "chairman" in the absence of a president. He returned to South Carolina and sat in the house and then the senate during the 1780s and 1790s. He went bankrupt in 1798 due to unsuccessful speculations.

Ramsay was also a prolific and early historian of the Revolution, although much of his writing was lifted from Edmund Burke's *Annual Register*. In 1785, Ramsay published a two-volume *History of the Revolution of South Carolina*, followed in 1789 by two volumes of *The History of the American Revolution*. He also contributed to the early hagiography of George Washington in a book published in 1807.

He was shot and killed by a mentally deranged person against whom he had testified in a sanity hearing. After his death, his ambitious *Universal History Americanized* appeared in nine volumes. *Further reading*: William R. Smith, *History as Argument: Three Patriot Historians of the American Revolution* (The Hague, 1966).

RAMSAY, Nathaniel (1741–1817) Continental officer, delegate to Congress

Born in Pennsylvania, Ramsay, like his younger brother David, attended the college at Princeton and then became a lawyer, moving to Cecil County, Maryland in the late 1760s. During the prewar agitation in Maryland, Ramsay supported the patriot position (he signed the declaration of freemen of Maryland) and was elected to the provincial convention in 1775. Some biographical accounts say he was a delegate to the Continental Congress in 1775, but the official records show he was not selected as a delegate until 1786 and 1787. During the war, Ramsay officered one of the best units in the army. He was selected in January 1776 as a captain of Smallwood's Maryland Regiment (which became part of the Continental Army in December as the 3rd Maryland) and fought at Long Island in August. Ramsay eventually became lieutenant colonel and second in command of the 3rd Maryland—some records say this was in 1776, others put the promotion in January 1779. His most famous military feat was during the battle of Monmouth in June 1778, when his unit rallied under the orders of Washington to stem the retreat ordered by Charles Lee. Ramsay and the Marylanders helped stop the British pursuit and nearly regained the upper hand for the commander in chief during the latter stages of the battle. Like the other Maryland units, the 3rd was sent south and was nearly destroyed at the battle of Camden in 1780. Ramsay himself barely survived the fighting at Monmouth—he was severely wounded, left for dead on the battlefield, and captured by the British. He was paroled and recovered from his injuries, but he was not exchanged until December 1780. He resigned his commission the following month and returned to Maryland and his law practice. He served as a delegate to Congress after the war. When the new federal government was in place, President George Washington appointed Ramsay as U.S. marshal for Maryland, a post he held for eight years.

RANDOLPH, Edmund Jennings (1753–1813) Continental officer, delegate to Congress, government official

Son of loyalist John Randolph and therefore the nephew of Peyton Randolph and a relative at some remove of Thomas Jefferson, John Marshall and all the Lees of Virginia, Edmund Jennings Randolph is best remembered as a cabinet member during the early republic, but he also served during the Revolution. Born at Williamsburg, he graduated from the College of William and

RANDOLPH, Peyton (c. 1721–1775) Delegate to Congress, patriot leader   399

Mary (founded by one of his forebears and the traditional school of his family). He passed the bar and practiced law in Williamsburg until the Revolution dislocated his professional and family life. His father fled with Lord Dunmore when the royal government was ousted from the colony, and Edmund came under the patronage of his uncle Peyton, who died soon thereafter. In August 1775, Edmund sought out the new Continental commander in chief, George Washington, and won an appointment as his aide-de-camp. Randolph served only a short time, however, and returned to Virginia on his uncle's death in October to take up a role in the civilian administration of the state. He became attorney general of Virginia the following year, holding the office throughout the war. He was elected as a delegate to the Continental Congress in 1779 but resigned soon after taking office, although he was elected again in 1781 and 1782. He was elected governor of Virginia in 1788 and resigned before the end of his term to take a seat in the legislature and see to the revision of the state legal code. He opposed the federal constitution while sitting as a delegate to the Philadelphia convention, but nonetheless he was named by Washington as the first attorney general of the United States in 1789. In 1794, he replaced his distant cousin Jefferson as secretary of state, but he had a stormy tenure that involved complex intrigues by the French that culminated in false charges against him and Randolph's resignation in mid-1795, when he returned to Williamsburg and resumed the practice of law. He reappeared in the public spotlight as one of the attorneys who defended Aaron Burr at the latter's treason trial in Virginia district court. *Further reading:* John J. Reardon, *Edmund Randolph* (New York, 1975).

RANDOLPH, John (1727–1784) Loyalist

The only loyalist among the powerful Randolph family of Virginia, John was a lawyer and crown official, serving as the last royal attorney general of the colony. He was the son of Sir John Randolph (of the Tazewell estate) and a distant cousin of both Thomas Jefferson and John Marshall. His brother, Peyton, was the leading attorney in Virginia and one of the colony's strongest patriots, eventually serving as the first president of the Continental Congress. John, however, was a supporter of the crown during all of the prerevolutionary agitation in Virginia and a long-time opponent of Patrick

Peyton Randolph

Henry. He fled the colony with Lord Dunmore and eventually went to England, where he was appointed a judge of the Vice-Admiralty court. Following his instructions, his remains were returned to Virginia after his death at age 56. John's son, Edmund, was governor of Virginia, attorney general of the United States and secretary of state.

RANDOLPH, Peyton (c. 1721–1775) Delegate to Congress, patriot leader

A member of the distinguished, wealthy and powerful Randolph family of Virginia, Peyton was perhaps the best known and most popular patriot leader of his day in the colony. He was the grandson of William and Mary Randolph, whose patriot descendants included Thomas Jefferson, John Marshall and Henry Lee as well as Peyton's nephew Edmund Jennings Randolph (Peyton's brother John was a loyalist). Peyton inherited large estates and wealth from his father, Sir John Randolph of Tazewell. He attended the College of William and Mary in Williamsburg and then went to England for a legal education at the Middle Temple. He set up his practice in 1745 in Williamsburg. Three years later he became king's attorney for Virginia. In 1764, Randolph entered the House of Burgesses, sitting in the body until the Revolution. He was put forward as the leader in nearly every patriot body formed in Virginia: chairman of the committee of correspondence in 1773 and president of the provincial conventions in 1774 and 1775. While not a public firebrand like the younger generation of Virginia patriots symbolized by Patrick Henry, Randolph was firm in his stance against the crown. He was among the first delegates sent to the Continental Congress from Virginia in 1774, and he was chosen as the body's president, partly to help draw in the southern colonies and partly due to his natural aura of calm control. He was not a well man, however, and he resigned in favor of Henry Middleton in October 1774. He was reelected in the spring of 1775 but again resigned when he became increasingly ill. He died of a stroke in Philadelphia in October 1775 at the early age of 54.

RANGER, Joseph. American sailor

Ranger was a free black man and a resident of Virginia. He joined the Virginia state navy in 1776 and served on four ships during the war. He was taken prisoner by the British as a member of the crew of the captured *Patriot* in 1781. He continued in the state navy after the war, serving a total enlistment of 11 years. After his discharge, Ranger received a land grant and a pension for his service.

RANKIN, William. Loyalist conspirator

A native Pennsylvanian, Rankin served before the Revolution as a colonel of militia and a justice of the Court of Common Pleas. He appeared to support the American position until Congress set course for independence, which Rankin could not countenance. Nonetheless, he kept up the appearance of American patriotism and retained command of his militia unit as a way to subvert attacks against loyalists in Pennsylvania. He also hoped to organize a back-country conspiracy and loyalist uprising. He carried on a secret correspondence with Sir Henry Clinton through Major John André during 1777 and 1778, claiming to be able to deliver thousands of loyalist troops when the right moment came. In 1779, Rankin tried to secure command of part of John Sullivan's expedition against the pro-British John Butler and the Iroquois for a fellow crypto-loyalist, but failed. He then urged Clinton to order a raid on the American supply post at Carlisle, Pennsylvania, which would divert forces from Sullivan's campaign and give the means to arm the supposed loyalist uprising. After the failure of these plots, Rankin turned his attention toward the South and hatched a scheme for loyalists of Pennsylvania, Delaware and Virginia to rise up and help Benedict Arnold's expedition into Virginia. The Americans

finally discovered what was going on and arrested Rankin in March 1781. He escaped, however, and fled to New York City, where he openly joined the British army. He left for England with the evacuation fleet in 1783.

RASTEL, Philippe François (Sieur de Rocheblave). British officer

A Frenchman, Rastel served the British as commander of the frontier outpost at Kaskaskia in 1778, when his fort was taken by George Rogers Clark. Rastel had few forces at his command other than militia drawn from the French habitants; and he had disbanded the militia because he could not confirm that an American party was nearby. Clark's men captured Rastel and took the town without a shot on July 4. Rastel was sent into captivity in Virginia but was paroled and released in 1779.

RATHBURNE, John P. (1746–1782) Continental naval officer

A native of Exeter, Rhode Island, Rathburne (whose name is also spelled Rathbun and Rathbourne) was one of the more successful American naval officers, although not as well known as his famous contemporaries. He began his career as a Continental officer in late 1775 as a lieutenant under Commodore Esek Hopkins on the *Providence* and sailed with the American flotilla that took Nassau in 1776. He then served under John Paul Jones on both the *Providence* and the *Alfred* before receiving command of the *Providence* himself in April 1777. He startled the British at Nassau in January of the following year by sailing into the harbor and taking the fort without a shot. Rathburne seized a supply of arms and ammunition and sailed off after holding the place for two days. He was then posted to the *Queen of France*, a frigate, and continued his exploits by taking 11 prizes (in company with two other American ships) when he infiltrated a British convoy under cover of fog. To his misfortune, Rathburne was part of the puny naval force defending Charleston, South Carolina in 1780, and he was captured by the British. He was paroled in August 1781 and returned to Boston, but the Continental Navy had almost ceased to exist by that stage of the war and no ship was available. Rathburne sailed as a Massachusetts privateer aboard the *Wexford* but was captured in September by the British *Recovery*.

He died a prisoner at Old Mill Prison at Plymouth, England.

RATTOON, John. Loyalist spy

Rattoon, who lived in South Amboy, New Jersey, acted as a courier between American traitor Benedict Arnold and British commander Sir Henry Clinton in the months before Arnold's treason was revealed. Rattoon's role escaped detection after Major John André was captured and Arnold fled to the British, and he lived out his life in South Amboy. His activities were revealed in the 20th century when Clinton's correspondence was examined by modern historians.

RAWDON, Francis Rawdon-Hastings, Lord (1754–1826) British officer

One of the remarkable figures in British imperial history of the late 18th and early 19th centuries, Rawdon first won prominence as a "boy" commander during the American war. Known by several different names and titles during his long career, he was called Lord Rawdon while fighting in the American Revolution. He was the son of an aristocratic Irish family and attended Harrow and Oxford. While still a teenage student at university, he also held a commission in the Royal Army and was ordered from Oxford to Boston in July 1774. He was distinguished for bravery at the battle of Breed's Hill and Bunker Hill, leading his men forward after the other officers of the company were killed. He then became aide-de-camp to Sir Henry Clinton and fought throughout all the campaigns in New York and New Jersey in 1776 and 1777. He was 23 years of age when promoted to lieutenant colonel in 1777 and assigned to raise a new regiment of provincial troops, known as the Volunteers of Ireland (which was later taken into the regular army establishment). He also served as adjutant general for Clinton in 1778 and early 1779.

His greatest achievements in America came in the southern theater, to which he repaired with his Irish regiment in 1780. He played a crucial role at Clinton's overwhelming victory at Camden, and in January 1781, Rawdon was made brevet brigadier general and given command of the British garrisons in South Carolina while Lord Cornwallis moved north toward Virginia. Rawdon showed extreme vigor and energy in opposing Nathanael Greene, who was by far the best American general of the

Lord Rawdon

war. In April 1781, Rawdon stole a march on Greene at Hobkirk's Hill (near Rawdon's main base at Camden), learning of Greene's position through good intelligence and marching out to attack the American army before Greene could adequately prepare. Aided by an unaccustomed collapse of the crack Maryland Continentals, Rawdon administered a brisk defeat to Greene, although he failed to damage the Americans sufficiently to gain much strategic advantage. Rawdon ordered the outlying British posts in South Carolina and Georgia to be evacuated, but the post at Ninety-Six was slow to respond and came under a determined siege by Greene. The defenders held on long enough for Rawdon to march to their relief, but the generally poor position of the understrength British army in the region forced Rawdon to continue to compress his lines toward the Charleston River. He was personally ailing, and in July 1781, Rawdon turned over command and sailed for home. On the way he was captured by a French privateer and held prisoner until 1782.

His subsequent career was long, complex and distinguished. He became Baron Rawdon of the English peerage (his other title was Irish) in 1783. He took the name Rawdon-Hastings in 1789, and in 1793, he succeeded to his father's title as Earl of Moira. He fought in the Napoleonic wars as a major general, and he wielded considerable power as a politician and close associate of the Prince of Wales. In 1813, he was named as governor general of India, where he served for 13 years and distinguished himself as a general in wars against the Gurkhas and the Mahrattas—all after a long period of personal military inactivity despite bearing the rank of full general. His final assignment was as governor general of Malta in 1824. He died at his post there and was buried in the ramparts.

READ, Daniel (1757–1836) Soldier, composer

Born in Attleboro, Massachusetts, Read became a well-known hymn-writer after the Revolution. During the war, he served as a soldier on John Sullivan's expedition to take Newport and was a member of the Connecticut state militia. He worked during the Revolution in New Haven, Connecticut as a banker and city librarian. He published his first songbook in 1785 and in the following year became editor of one of the first musical periodicals in America, *The American Musical Magazine*. He later published *An Introduction to Psalmody, The Columbia Harmonist* and *The New Haven Collection of Sacred Music*.

READ, George (1733–1798) Delegate to Congress, state official, jurist

One of the three prominent revolutionary Read brothers of Delaware (a fourth was a West Indies merchant), George played a major role in state affairs during the war. He was born in Cecil County, Maryland, but his family moved to New Castle, Delaware when he was an infant. He went to Pennsylvania for his education, first at an academy in New London and then as a private law student in Philadelphia. He passed the bar in 1753 and moved back to New Castle, where he set up a practice. He was appointed as the crown attorney general for the lower part of the colony in 1763, and two years later, he entered the legislature. Read opposed the Stamp Act and supported nonimportation, but on the whole he was a very conservative revolutionary. He never supported strong measures and hoped to reconcile with Great Britain short of independence. He was sent to the first and second Continental Congresses, where he continued to urge moderation. He earned the unique distinction of being the only delegate to vote against independence in the summer of 1776 but to sign the document nonetheless.

Most of his service after mid-1776 came in his home state. He was elected as speaker of the upper house of the legislature, which made him in effect the second ranking executive officer in Delaware.

When the British swept through on their way to Philadelphia in 1777, John McKinly (the president of the state) was captured, and Read became the de facto head of government. He narrowly escaped capture himself. During the next year, he ably organized the war effort in a state rife with loyalism and indifference to the American cause. He finally resigned his office and returned to the practice of law, although still holding a seat in the assembly. During the federal constitutional convention in Philadelphia, Read was a stout defender of the rights of small states, but he supported the new constitution and subsequently worked hard for its ratification in Delaware. He was elected as U.S. senator to the new national government in 1789, was reelected the following year, and resigned in 1793 to take an appointment as chief justice of Delaware. *Further reading:* William T. Read, *Life and Correspondence of George Read* (Philadelphia, 1870).

READ, Jacob (1752–1816) Delegate to Congress, militia officer, legislator, attorney

Born on a plantation near Charleston, South Carolina, Read was sent to Savannah for his early education and, after already passing the bar, went to England to study at Grays Inn. While in Britain in 1774 he signed a petition against the Intolerable Acts. He returned to South Carolina in 1776 and joined the Charleston city militia as a captain. He was captured when the city fell to Sir Henry Clinton in 1780 and was transported to St. Augustine as a prisoner. Following the war, he served in the South Carolina assembly and spent two years, from 1783 to 1785, as a delegate to the Confederation Congress. He practiced law while holding several public offices in South Carolina in the late 1780s. From 1795 to 1801, he was a U.S. senator from South Carolina.

READ, James (1743–1822) Militia officer, Continental official

One of four Read brothers from Delaware, James was a militia officer—probably with Pennsylvania troops—before 1778. In that year, he was named as one of three naval commissioners for the middle states. He was a friend of financier Robert Morris, and when Morris was placed in charge of the faltering finances of Congress in 1781, Read took control of naval affairs, although there was precious little left of the Continental Navy by that time.

READ, Thomas (c. 1740–1788) Continental naval officer

Another of the four Read brothers from Delaware (three of whom participated in the Revolution), Thomas was born on the family estate in New Castle County. He went to sea early in life, and by the 1760s, he was the master of vessels trading in the West Indies (his nonrevolutionary brother, William, was a merchant in Havana). In October 1775, Read received a commission in the Pennsylvania state navy as commodore of a small fleet of row galleys on the Delaware River that were designed to protect Philadelphia from water-borne invasion. He was demoted to second in command the following January but was given a small gunship and put in charge guarding the underwater defensive obstructions to navigation on the river. He regained the command of the Pennsylvania river forces in May 1776 but resigned after only a month to take one of the captain's commissions offered by Congress in the new Continental Navy. His career was dogged by ill luck, however. He was eighth on the seniority list, and as a result seldom received assignment to a ship actually available to fight. He was waiting for the *George Washington* to be built at the end of 1776 when he fought on land in the Trenton-Princeton campaign in command of a transplanted naval battery. Read eventually took over the *Washington*, but he dismantled and sunk the craft in face of the British invasion up the Delaware in late 1777. He was given the brigantine *Baltimore* in 1778 and probably sailed to France with dispatches. His next command, the erstwhile frigate *Bourbon*, was never completed at a shipyard in Connecticut. Read turned to privateering in 1780 and never again commanded a commissioned ship. After the war, he made a voyage to China on behalf of his friend Robert Morris, but he died soon after returning.

REED, James (1723–1807) Continental general

Born in Woburn, Massachusetts, Reed was trained as a tailor in his youth but spent most of his adult life as a tavern keeper, first in Lunenburg, Massachusetts and then in Fitzwilliam, New Hampshire (a village he helped found). He served throughout the colonial wars as a captain of militia and saw considerable action in the campaigns against the French. By the time of the American Revolution, Reed was a substantial landowner and still active in the local New Hampshire militia. He was com-missioned as colonel of the 3rd New Hampshire in late April 1775 and took his troops to join the siege of the British army in Boston. On June 14, the regiment was taken into the Continental Army and assigned to the forces fortifying Breed's and Bunker hills. At the ensuing battle on June 17, Reed and his New Hampshires performed splendidly as part of the small force that held the extreme left of the American lines. Although obscured that day by the more conspicuous New Hampshire commander John Stark, Reed was perhaps just as responsible for holding off the British assault and anchoring the left of the American line. Reed's regiment was reorganized in January 1776 as the 2nd Continental, and during the summer, he was ordered north to reinforce the army that was straggling back from the futile invasion of Canada. While in upper New York, Reed contracted a severe case of smallpox which left him blind and nearly deaf. He accepted a promotion to brigadier general in August but was too debilitated by disease to continue active service, and he resigned in September.

REED, Joseph (1741–1785) Continental officer, delegate to Congress, state official

A central figure during much of the War of Independence in both the military and political arenas, Reed was born into an Irish emigrant family in Trenton, New Jersey. His father was a wealthy merchant with considerable political influence, circumstances that aided Reed's early rise to prominence. He attended the Academy of Philadelphia and then the College of New Jersey (later to be Princeton), graduating in 1757. He was admitted to the bar five years later after reading law with Richard Stockton, and Reed then went to England for further study at the Middle Temple in London.

He set up a law practice in Philadelphia in 1770 and was soon involved in the prerevolutionary activities of the colony as a moderate. He was identified by the British government as one who might be wooed away from the American cause, perhaps due to a long correspondence he carried on in the early 1770s with Lord Dartmouth. Reed served on the Philadelphia committee of correspondence in 1774 and was president of the Pennsylvania provisional congress of 1775. He had moved from a moderate stance to a commitment to independence by the outbreak of hostilities. In June 1775, Reed, who held a commission as lieutenant colonel of state

Joseph Reed

militia, became military secretary (with Continental rank) to the new Continental commander in chief, George Washington, and he remained a close advisor to Washington throughout the war despite several disagreements. He left active duty during late 1775 to see to his law practice, but he returned in the spring of 1776 when appointed adjutant general of the army with the rank of colonel and thus became chief staff officer for Washington. Reed was one of the American envoys to the Staten Island conference with the British Howe brothers who were empowered to negotiate in July 1776, an attempt at conciliation that broke off almost before it began.

During the long and disastrous New York campaign of the summer, Reed advocated leaving the city and especially Fort Washington to the British, but his advice was ignored. He nearly broke with Washington after the commander in chief intercepted a letter to Reed from Charles Lee that criticized Washington in no uncertain terms—the assumption being that Reed had prompted the letter by one of his own—but the differences were papered over and Reed remained in Washington's confidences. He supplied crucial information about his hometown of Trenton as part of the planning for Washington's strike against the Hessians at Christmas 1776, and Reed personally led reconnaissance of the British forces at Princeton before the battle there in early January. He resigned his formal commission later in the month, but he continued to serve off and on as a volunteer aide, having turned down command of the cavalry.

He moved into the political arena in 1778 as a delegate to the Continental Congress from Pennsylvania. He served only one term in Congress, however, before assuming office as head of the Pennsylvania Supreme Executive Council, making him in effect the chief civilian executive of the state. The British attempted to suborn him when the infamous Carlisle Commission appeared on the scene in 1778, but Reed publicly revealed their attempts to bribe him and contributed to the collapse of the commission's mission. He served until 1781 as head of government in Pennsylvania, playing a key role as negotiator when the Pennsylvania Line mutinied, for example. He was accused of disloyalty by the ever-malignant Arthur Lee (who was apparently egged on by Benjamin Rush, although Reed thought John Cadwalader was behind the attack), and historians in the 19th century depicted Reed as a traitor. However, a careful examination of the evidence has cleared Reed's name. He returned to his Philadelphia law practice after the end of the war, but he died prematurely at the age of 44. *Further reading: John F. Roche, Joseph Reed: A Moderate in the American Revolution (New York, 1957).*

REID, James Randolph (1750–1789) Delegate to Congress, Continental officer One of the many now obscure public figures of the Revolutionary era, Reid was born in what was then York County, Pennsylvania and graduated from Princeton. He served in the army as a lieutenant and then a major in what was known as "Congress' Own" Regiment, a unit formed in early 1776 under the command of Moses Hazen and which came to be the central depository for foreign troops. Since almost all the officers were Canadian or European volunteers, it is unclear why Reid served with the regiment. He was a delegate to the fading Confederation Congress from 1787 until his death in 1789 at Middlesex, Pennsylvania.

REVEL, Comte de. See PERRON, Joachim du.

REVERE, Paul (1735–1818) Patriot, militia officer, silversmith One of the best American craftsmen and artists of the late 18th century, Revere was immortalized in poetry for his famous "midnight ride" of 1775, and few modern-day Americans can think of him other than spurring down the road to Lexington with a shout of "The British are coming!" on his lips.

Revere was born in Boston and learned his trade of silversmithing from his father. He served as an officer in the Seven Years' War and then returned to Boston and set up as a silversmith. He also taught himself copper engraving and soon was well known locally for his skill in both crafts. He was an early and active patriot as protest grew in Boston. He was a leader in the Boston Sons of Liberty and played a major role in popularizing resistance to the Stamp Act and the Boston Massacre through his widely circulated engravings—his depiction of the latter event becoming one of his most famous. He helped plan and carry out the Boston Tea Party in 1773. He was a physically active man and a good rider, so he also served as a courier between rebel organizations.

His most famous ride came on April 18–19, 1775, when he set out on horseback from Boston to warn patriot leaders John Hancock and Sam Adams in Lexington that the British were marching to catch them and seize rebel arms. He delivered his warn-

Paul Revere's famous ride.

ing to Lexington and proceeded toward Concord with fellow messengers William Dawes and Dr. Samuel Prescott. A British patrol stopped the trio, and Revere was captured. He was released without his horse, and he returned to Lexington on foot.

During the war he did valuable service for the American cause as a manufacturer of gunpowder, a commodity in short supply in the states, and as an engraver for Congress and other official bodies. He also served briefly as a lieutenant colonel of militia and had to take partial responsibility for the disastrous Massachusetts expedition to Penobscot in 1779. He was accused of cowardice as a result of the misadventure but was cleared by a court-martial in 1782. After the war, he returned to silversmithing and his other businesses, including the manufacture of copper. *Further reading:* Esther Forbes, *Paul Revere and the World He Made* (Boston, 1942).

Paul Revere

RHOADS, Samuel (1711–1784) Delegate to Congress Rhoads was born in Philadelphia and is unusual in that he achieved political leadership in the colony without initial wealth or professional status. He had little schooling and worked as a carpenter and builder. Nevertheless, by the age of 30 he was a member of the Philadelphia City Council and during the decade and a half before the Revolution he sat in the colonial assembly. In 1761, he was one of the Pennsylvania commissioners appointed to an important meeting to conclude land treaties with the Six Nations of the Iroquois. He became mayor of Philadelphia in 1774 but left office when selected as a delegate to the new Continental Congress later in the year. He was also a long-time member of the board of the Philadelphia Hospital and a director of the city library.

Baroness Frederica Riedesel

RIEDESEL, Frederica Charlotte, Baroness von (1746–1807) Diarist

The Baroness von Riedesel spent six years in North America during the Revolution, most of them at the side of her husband, who commanded the Brunswicker mercenaries, and she kept an informative, spritely journal of her experience. She was the daughter of a Prussian lieutenant general and had married the young Riedesel, then a cavalry officer, in 1762. When the British hired the services of the Brunswickers in early 1776, Colonel von Riedesel was named as commander and elevated to major general. Frederica won his agreement that she and their daughters (two at the time) should join him in North America as soon as she delivered the child she expected later in the year. He sailed with his troops in April; she gave birth to another daughter in March and left for England in May. She and her family were delayed in Britain until April 1777, but they finally reached Quebec in June. Frederica paused not even one night but pushed on to Chambly, where her husband was commanding the German troops under General John Burgoyne. They were reunited briefly before the army moved on, headed toward the disasters at Saratoga. Frederica kept pace slightly behind but was close enough to witness the first battle at Freeman's Farm on September 19. She was even more closely involved in the second battle on October 7, becoming trapped in a farmhouse with her children and several noncombatant refugees.

With Burgoyne's surrender and the signing of the nefarious Convention, Frederica and the baron began a long odyssey. They went first to Cambridge, Massachusetts, expecting to sail home within a few months, but the Congress refused to honor the terms of the Convention and the defeated British and Germans were marched south to Charlottesville, Virginia in November 1778. The Riedesels rented a house nearby and spend a relative happy time during 1779, becoming friends with Thomas Jefferson. With news of an impending exchange, the Riedesels traveled north to York, Pennsylvania, but the exchange fizzled, and they spent six weeks among the German Moravians in Pennsylvania. In November 1779, they finally settled in New York City, where Frederica gave birth to a fourth daughter—named America—in March 1780. The baron was finally exchanged in October 1780 and returned to active duty, first at Long Island and then in Canada. The family remained in Canada until 1783, when they returned to Brunswick by way of England. The baroness settled into a castle at Lauterbach, where she lived until her death. *Further reading:* Marvin L. Brown, trans., *Baroness von Riedesel and the American Revolution: Journal and Correspondence of a Tour of Duty, 1776–1783* (Chapel Hill, N.C., 1965); Louise H. Tharp, *The Baroness and the General* (Boston, 1962).

RIEDESEL, Friedrich, Baron von (1738–1800) German mercenary officer

Riedesel was one of the more attractive "Hessian" generals employed in North America by the British to command mercenary troops. He was, in fact, a native of Hesse, but he served the Duke of Brunswick when appointed to head the first contingent of Brunswickers sent to America. He was an experienced European soldier by this stage, a veteran of the Seven Years' War and holding the rank of colonel. He arrived in Quebec with nearly 2,300 men in the summer of 1776. His charming and intelligent wife, Frederica, the daughter of one of the duke's generals, joined him in Canada. In 1777, Riedesel was assigned as part of General John Burgoyne's command and led the German contingent. Burgoyne would have benefited from closer attention to Riedesel's advice during the march across the wilderness. The German counseled, for example, against sending Friedrich Baum on the expedition toward Bennington. At the two battles at Saratoga, Riedesel distinguished himself both by vigor on the field and by his skillful direction of his troops.

Unfortunately, Burgoyne's surrender deprived Riedesel of his freedom for the next three years. Riedesel was not exchanged or even paroled but undertook a journey with his defeated men that took him on a tour of the states. He lived for a while with his wife and family in Virginia and then with a community of German-speaking Moravians in Pennsylvania. He was finally exchanged for Benjamin Lincoln (who had been captured with the fall of Charleston) in October 1780. On his return to active duty, Riedesel was given command at Long Island, but in 1781, he moved to Canada as an advisor to Frederic Haldiman. He and his family returned to Europe in 1783. His wife's memoirs of the experience in America provide charming insight into Riedesel's character and activities. *Further reading:* Max von Eelking, ed., *Memoirs, Letters and Journals of Major General Riedesel During His Residence in America* (Albany, N.Y., 1868; reprinted 1969); Louise Tharp, *The Baroness and the General* (Boston, 1962).

RITTENHOUSE, David (1732–1796) Scientist, official

Rittenhouse was probably the most accomplished scientist and mathematician in America during the Revolutionary era, and he was also an important politician and government official in the fight for independence. He was born in Germantown, Pennsylvania and by the early 1760s had already established a firm reputation as a practical man of science, although not so widely known at the time as his friend Benjamin Franklin. Rittenhouse's interests encompassed astronomy, mathematics, physics and chemistry as well as the practical application of theoretical understanding. He was, for example, a surveyor as well as a mathematician. In 1763 and 1764, he surveyed a boundary line in a dispute between the Penns and Lord Baltimore, and a few years later he designed a complex orrery, one of those marvelous mechanical models of the solar system used by astronomers of the time to understand the motion of the planets. Moreover, he calculated the transit of Venus of 1769, improved the astronomical calculation of the time of day, and built one of the first good telescopes in North America.

His contributions to the American Revolution were both intellectual and political. He was one of the leading radicals in Pennsylvania, serving as vice president and then president of the council of safety and taking a prominent role in the formation of the General Assembly that took power in the state. He, along with other radicals, pushed through the unicameral legislature under the new state constitution in 1776. During the war, Rittenhouse served as treasurer and financial trustee of Pennsylvania and on the Congressional Board of War. He also spent much time during the war on practical affairs. He tried to find a source of saltpeter in the colonies, which was the one ingredient missing for the domestic production of gunpowder for the Continental Army, and he acted in the field as an engineer and surveyor, designing fortifications along the Delaware River. He also experimented during the war with rifling cannon and designed telescopic sights. In the years following the Revolution, he continued and expanded his scientific and mathematical work, advancing knowledge in many areas, including magnetism, electricity and trigonometry. He also continued to work as a surveyor of boundary disputes and became a banker while teaching astronomy at the University of Pennsylvania. In 1792, President George Washington appointed Rittenhouse the first director of the U.S. mint. *Further reading:* Brooke Hindle, *David Rittenhouse* (Princeton, N.J., 1964).

RITZEMA, Rudolph. Loyalist turncoat officer

Rudolph was the son of the minister of the Dutch church in Sleepy Hollow, New York and a graduate of King's College (later Columbia) in 1758. Even though his father, Johannes, was openly loyal to the British crown, the younger Ritzema appeared to be an American patriot. In June 1775 with the organization of the Continental Army, he was commissioned as lieutenant colonel of the 1st New York Regiment, and he was promoted to colonel and given command of the unit five months later. He led his regiment on the Canadian expedition under Montgomery and transferred the following spring to command of the 3rd New York when it was formed under a reorganization of the Continental regiments. In November 1776, however, Ritzema defected to the British.

James Rivington

RIVINGTON, James (1724–1802) Loyalist publisher, American spy

Rivington was one of the principal recipients of patriot ire in New York during the Revolution because of his journalism in the royal cause, but he was also a secret agent for George Washington, a fact unknown to his contemporaries. He was born in London and took over his father's printing business in the 1740s in partnership with his brother. The firm prospered, and Rivington received a good income, which he apparently dissipated in high living. In 1759, he declared bankruptcy and left England for America. He opened a bookstore in New York City the following year and began a series of business ventures, some successful, some not. In April 1773, he published the first number of *Rivington's New-York Gazetter*. Within two years the paper circulated to 3,600 readers—making it one of the largest newspapers of the colonial era. Rivington claimed he sold his paper in all the colonies and in the West Indies, England and France.

With the approach of the final break with the mother country, Rivington tried at first to maintain a balanced view of politics, but by the end of 1774, he began to print more and more stridently loyal articles. The New York Sons of Liberty, led by radical Isaac Sears, attacked Rivington's printing office and destroyed some of his printing plates. Rivington was arrested by the patriots but was later released. Nonetheless, he continued to sound too loyalist for Sears, and in November 1775 a mob destroyed the press and printing plant.

Rivington left for England in January 1776, but he returned to New York in 1777 after the British under General William Howe occupied the city. He was appointed as the royal printer and re-opened his newspaper as *Rivington's New York Loyal Gazette* (later changed to *The Royal Gazette*). His articles vexed the patriots mightily and he became the target for violent criticism and threats.

However, just as he gained a widespread reputation among patriots as the most obnoxious of loyalist publishers, Rivington also undertook to spy for the Americans. He may have been motivated by nothing more noble than the need for money—he was not being paid as royal printer as promised—but whatever his reasons, he began to pass information to the American high command through Robert Townsend (Culper Jr.) and Allan McLane. Apparently Rivington learned a great deal about British plans by listening to conversations in his coffeehouse, which was a popular gathering spot for British officers. In 1781, he laid his hands on a set of the British naval signals used by Admiral Thomas Graves and passed them on to McLane, who in turn handed them to French admiral de Grasse. At the end of the war and the British withdrawal from New York, George Washington sent officers to safeguard Rivington, and the publisher was allowed to remain in the city to the amazement of many patriots. No word was given out about his secret activities, which were not confirmed until examination of private papers in the 20th century. Rivington attempted to continue his paper, but Sears and others shut him down in 1784. He spent the remainder of his life trying to repair his fortunes but sank into poverty. *Further reading:* Catherine S. Crary, "The Tory and the Spy: The Double Life of James Rivington," *William and Mary Quarterly* 16 (1959), 61–72.

ROBERDEAU, Daniel (1727–1795) Delegate to Congress, militia officer

Roberdeau was born at St. Christopher in the British West Indies but moved to Philadelphia, where he became a successful merchant with trade interests in the Caribbean. He sat as a member of the Pennsylvania colonial assembly from 1756 to 1761. With the advent of colonial agitation against Britain, Roberdeau became a leading patriot in Philadelphia as a member of the committee of safety and chair of a mass meeting in

1776. He was particularly effective in forging a compromise between the urban interests of Philadelphia and patriots from the frontier regions of the colony. At the outbreak of hostilities he was a colonel in the Pennsylvania militia and for a short while in 1776 was brigadier general of all state forces. In 1777, however, he moved almost exclusively to the civilian side of the Revolution with his selection as a delegate to Congress. Among his mercantile interests was a lead mine in western Pennsylvania, which he developed in 1778 as a source of supply for the Continental forces. He left Congress in 1779 after serving on the committees dealing with foreign relations. Following the war, he moved to Alexandria, Virginia and eventually to Winchester, where he died.

ROBERTSON, James (c. 1720–1788) British general, official

Born in Scotland, Robertson enlisted as a private in the British army while a teenager. He obtained a commission as a result of his service in the European wars, and by 1756 he was a senior officer assigned to the American theater during the Seven Years' War. He was given a regular commission as colonel in 1772 and was commander of the 16th Regiment of Foot. He took part in the battle of Long Island in 1776, where he commanded a brigade. The balance of his service in America was administrative and diplomatic, although after 1779, he held the ceremonial appointment as colonel of his former regiment, the 16th. Robertson was appointed as a peace commissioner in 1779 but soon took a different role as civil governor of British-occupied New York City. He won an odious reputation (based on biased American accounts) for corruption and arbitrary judicial judgments against patriots while governor. In May 1781, after the sudden death of General William Phillips, Robertson was commissioned to take command of the British forces in Virginia, but he got no farther than Sandy Hook before turning back at the news that Lord Cornwallis had advanced into Virginia and was in command. He was promoted to lieutenant general in November 1782 and returned to Britain in April of the following year.

ROBERTSON, James (1740–c. 1812) Loyalist publisher

A Scot, Robertson published loyalist newspapers in several states during the Revolution, following the British army from city to city. Before the war, he and his brother Alexander published the *Chronicle* in New York City and then the *Albany Gazette*. In 1773, they began a partnership with a third businessman in Norwich, Connecticut, where they published the *Norwich Packet*. He went to New York City in 1776 when it was seized from the Americans and began the *Royal American Gazette*. When General William Howe occupied Philadelphia, Robertson followed and began the *Royal Pennsylvania Gazette*. As the British campaign moved south, so too did Robertson in 1780. After the capture of Charleston, South Carolina, he started the *Royal South Carolina Gazette*, publishing in Charleston until 1782. With the final British defeat, he withdrew to Canada and eventually to his native Scotland.

ROBERTSON, James (1742–1814) Western pioneer, militia officer

Robertson's activities during the Revolution and immediately after were in the western lands that eventually became the state of Tennessee. He was born in Virginia but moved at an early age with his family to Wake County, North Carolina. He began to travel the over-Appalachian region as a teenager in the late 1750s and by 1771 had helped establish the white settlements in the Watauga area. He was a leader in the Watauga Association and took part in many wars and negotiations with the western Indian tribes, on whose lands he and the others had settled. He was an officer during Lord Dunmore's War in 1774, and in 1776, he acted as an agent for both Virginia and North Carolina among the Cherokee. During the late 1770s, he held rank as a militia officer and led or helped to lead several defenses of white settlements against Indian attacks, alternating warfare with attempts at negotiations. In early 1780, Robertson was at the head of a large group of whites who established a new settlement on the Cumberland River, the site of what eventually became modern-day Nashville. He seldom held official office, although he was a representative to the North Carolina assembly in 1785, and he was probably involved in the conspiracies with the Spanish during the mid-1780s to separate the western settlements from the United States, but for a long period, Robertson was an influential leader among the westerners. He briefly held an appointment as a brigadier general in the 1790s. *Further reading:* Sarah F. Kelley, *General James Robertson: The Founder of Nashville* (1980).

ROBERTSON, James (c. 1751–1818) Loyalist official

Robertson emigrated to Georgia from Great Britain in 1767. He was a lawyer and was named as attorney general of the colony. In 1775, he was chosen as a delegate to the patriot provincial congress but declined to serve and declared himself in sympathy with the crown. He moved to the back country the following year, apparently to avoid conflict, but was arrested by patriots in June and forced to take an oath of allegiance to the American cause. When he refused a further oath in 1777, he was banished. Robertson returned to Georgia, however, in 1779 when the British Army re-occupied the state, and he was appointed again as attorney general and to the Governor's Council as part of the British attempt to establish a new royal government. He departed after the British defeat and ended his days as chief justice of the Virgin Islands.

ROBINSON, Beverley (1721–1792) Loyalist officer

Robinson was one of the wealthiest men in the American colonies when the Revolutionary War broke out. He was born in Virginia to a prominent political family (his father had been colonial governor), but he moved to New York when he married Susanna Philipse, the daughter of the Dutch family that owned vast land patents along the Hudson River. Through his wife, Robinson came into possession of large tracts of land along the Hudson, which he managed well. His house, opposite West Point, was a local landmark, and his income from tenants was immense for the day.

He was not at first a fire-breathing loyalist, and during the early days of the Revolution, Robinson tried to oppose the policies of the British government without advocating open rebellion. His trimming could not endure, however, and in 1777 he was forced to choose sides when he refused to take an oath of allegiance to the Americans. He and his wife moved to New York City, and Robinson raised the Loyal American Regiment with himself at head as colonel (his son, also named Beverley, served as lieutenant colonel). He was also colonel of a corps of guides and pioneers. He was active in the field with his regiment of loyalists, but his most important services were in trying to convert American patriots to the British cause and acting as a conduit

Beverley Robinson

for communications between the British high command and disaffected patriots. He was one of the messengers between Benedict Arnold and the spy Major John André, for example. His estates confiscated and his wife's inheritance lost, Robinson emigrated to England at the end of the war.

ROBINSON, John (1727–1802) British government official

Although the son of a tradesman, Robinson acquired considerable wealth through his marriage and an inheritance from his grandfather. He studied at Grays Inn, being admitted to the bar in the early 1760s. His political fortunes were tied early in his career to his patron, the Earl of Lonsdale, for whom Robinson acted as a political manager and land agent. He sat in Parliament from a borough he himself owned, and by 1770 he was an influential figure in government circles. He was appointed as secretary of the treasury by Lord North in 1770, breaking soon thereafter with Lonsdale, who disapproved of the American policy of the government. Throughout the Revolution, Robinson acted as the principal political manager of Lord North in the Commons, and he administered much of the vast store of booty and offices by which the government controlled its majority. He resigned from office in 1782 and received a large pension and several subsequent sinecures.

ROBINSON, Moses (1742–1813) Official, soldier

Robinson was one of the principal officials of the "state" of Vermont during and immediately after the Revolution. Vermont was the name given in the early 1770s to a region known otherwise as the New Hampshire Grants and claimed by both New Hampshire and New York. For two decades— before, during and after the war—the area presented a confusing political situation. Robinson was an attorney and had served as town clerk of Bennington before the Revolution. In 1777, he sat in the convention called at the urging of Congress that declared the Vermont region independent. The new state set up its own government and acted over the following 13 years as a separate entity, but under political pressure from the older contesting states, Congress withdrew support for an independent Vermont and left Robinson and his compatriots in limbo. Nonetheless, Robinson (after serving in the state militia) filled posts on the Vermont Governor's Council from 1778 to 1785 and as chief justice of a state supreme court intermittently from 1778 to 1789. He was selected as a delegate to the Continental Congress from Vermont in 1779, and three years later was appointed to the commission to establish the admission of Vermont into the Confederation. Although New Hampshire agreed in 1782 to new boundaries, New York's claims delayed the admission of Vermont until 1791. Robinson served as governor in 1789 and 1790, and when the state was finally recognized, he was the first U.S. senator from the new state, serving until 1796.

ROCHAMBEAU, Donatien Marie Joseph de Vimeur, Vicomte de (1750–1813) French officer

The son of the French commander in chief in America, Rochambeau was a colonel in the Bourbonnais Regiment when it sailed as part of the French expedition in 1780. He had entered the army as a teenager, risen in rank rapidly, and served as his father's assistant adjutant general in America. In the autumn of 1780, the younger Rochambeau returned to France in an effort to hurry along the remaining portion of the forces delegated to America and to round up more funds and matériel. He returned empty-handed in May 1781. In the fall, he commanded a unit of grenadiers at the siege of Yorktown. After his return to France, Rochambeau was promoted and given command of a regiment. By 1792, he was a lieutenant general and was sent to pacify the confused situation on Haiti. He turned out the royalists there and at Martinque but surrendered to a British fleet in 1792. He was recalled and then reappointed as governor general—the politics of the French Revolution were a tangle during these

years—and was eventually captured and imprisoned by the British. On his release in 1811, he again received a command, this time under Napoleon, and he was killed at the battle of Leipzig in 1813.

ROCHAMBEAU, Jean Baptiste Donatien de Vimeur, Comte de (1725–1807) French general

Rochambeau was an experienced, skillful, and, most importantly, a very diplomatic soldier sent to command French troops in America in 1780. He worked closely and well with Washington, forming a team that succeeded in dealing the British the final defeat at Yorktown. Perhaps his greatest attribute was an easygoing affability that did not insist on niceties of prerogative or rank—he cheerfully subordinated himself to Washington, which was what was needed in the situation.

As required of all officers of the French army, Rochambeau was of aristocratic birth. He joined the army during the War of Austrian Succession, and by 1747, he was a colonel and aide-de-camp to the Duke of Orleans. He performed with great distinction during the Seven Years' War and was promoted to brigadier after recovering from wounds suffered in 1760. During the decade before the American Revolution, Rochambeau was inspector of cavalry. In 1780, when the French government finally resolved to send troops to fight in America, Rochambeau was promoted to lieutenant general and made commander of the expeditionary force. He arrived with about 6,000 troops in Newport in July (several thousand more soldiers were left behind for lack of transport). He and his retinue were greeted with near-empty streets, and he had to roust out local officials and identify himself.

This was, unfortunately, something of a portent for the first year of the French presence in America. Washington's Continental Army was so depleted by previous campaigns, expired enlistments and lack of funds, that the American commander in chief could not organize a new campaign that might use the French. Rochambeau was the soul of discretion and diplomacy, however, and not only placed himself at Washington's command, but worked effectively at Washington's side during the remainder of the war. Finally, in 1781, Rochambeau and Washington devised a plan to attack British bases in upper Manhattan, hoping to draw Sir Henry Clinton out of New York City. Before the plan was launched, however, news came of the French fleet

Comte de Rochambeau

sailing to the Chesapeake. Washington and Rochambeau set their men on the march south to Yorktown. Rochambeau and his army formed the bulk of the trained troops who laid siege to Lord Cornwallis, and they carried out their tasks with professional skill. Following the British surrender, Rochambeau remained in Virginia for the winter, but he went back to Rhode Island in autumn 1782. He returned to France early in 1783. He subsequently took command of revolutionary armies in France but was arrested during the Reign of Terror and narrowly escaped execution. *Further reading:* Arnold Whitridge, *Rochambeau* (1965); Jean-Edmond Wheelen, *Rochambeau: Father and Son* (English ed., New York, 1936).

ROCHE DE FERMOY, Matthias. See FERMOY, Matthias.

ROCHEBLAVE, Sieur de. See RASTEL, Philippe.

ROCHESTER, Nathaniel (1752–1831) Militia officer, businessman Although born in Virginia, Rochester moved at age four to North Carolina, following the death of his father and his mother's remarriage. He received no formal education but went into the mercantile trade while still a teenager, and by 1773, he was a partner in a country store near Hillsboro. Rochester was a member of the county committee of safety in 1775 and was sent as a representative to provincial conventions in 1775 and 1776. He fought at Moore's Creek Bridge as a major in 1776 and during the following year re-

ceived a state militia appointment as a lieutenant colonel and deputy commissary-general of military supplies. From 1777 to 1778, he was in charge of an arms manufacturing plant at Hillsboro and served simultaneously in the state assembly. Rochester gave up his public posts in 1778 and turned back to private business, first at Hillsboro and then at Hagerstown, Maryland, in partnership with a Colonel Thomas Hart. After 25 years of successful business in Maryland, Rochester took an interest in a new settlement on the Genesee River in upper New York state, purchasing land there in 1803. He moved soon thereafter and began life anew in a small village that came to be named after him: Rochester, New York.

ROCKINGHAM, Charles Watson-Wentworth, Marquis of (1730–1782) British prime minister Rockingham was the figurehead of domestic political opposition to the king's government during most of the period of the American Revolution and came into power as prime minister (insofar as the term was appropriate at the time) after the defeat of British arms at Yorktown. He was the most prominent of the group of politicians known as Whigs—the meaning of which has been the focus of intense study and debate among historians of 18th-century British politics—and for most of the Revolutionary period supported conciliation with the former colonies and a quick end to the war.

He was born to an aristocratic family that was titled on both sides. His mother was the daughter of a duke and his father held lesser but still impressive family titles. In the British style, Rockingham used his father's secondary title and was known as Viscount Highham before inheriting the title of marquis on his father's death in 1750. As a boy in 1745, Rockingham fought with the Hanoverian army against the Stuart Jacobites uprising, but after the battle of Culloden he returned to civilian life and attended Westminster and Cambridge. Politics was his early and abiding occupation. He entered the House of Lords in 1751 and became a principal member of the Whig faction that was loosely tied together by opposition to the system of office and prerogative that supported the crown. While it may not be accurate to speak of political parties at the time, Rockingham and his fellows acted consistently as an opposing coalition.

Charles, Marquis of Rockingham

The ascension of George III sharpened the differences in Parliament and gave Rockingham's role new meaning. He was called to head a government in 1765. His ministry put through the repeal of the Stamp Act and tried to ease the trade restrictions on the American colonies, but the government fell in 1766 and Rockingham was out of office during the entire period leading up to and through the active war in North America. His voice became more vigorous after the French-American alliance and the defeat of General John Burgoyne, but Lord North and the party of the king remained in control, intent on pursuing the war, until the defeat of Lord Cornwallis in 1781. For several months thereafter, the government stayed in power but with shrinking majorities and a growing sense that the Parliament and the nation had had enough in America. George III finally accepted North's resignation and was forced to turn to Rockingham, who formed a coalition government with himself at the head in March 1782. Rockingham took office with the express condition that he was to conclude a peace with the Americans, and he set in motion the negotiations which eventually led to the Treaty of Paris. Unfortunately, he himself died with little advance illness in July. *Further reading:* Ross J. S. Hoffman, *The Marquis: A Study of Lord Rockingham, 1730–1782* (New York, 1973).

RODGERS, John (1727–1811) Clergyman

Rodgers was born in Boston and became a licensed Presbyterian preacher in 1747 in Delaware, where he served at St. George parish in New Castle County until 1765, when he moved to New York City. With the coming of the Revolutionary War, he joined the army as a chaplain, and he was chaplain to the New York Council of Safety and to the first patriot New York Assembly.

RODNEY, Caesar (1728–1784) Delegate to Congress, militia general, state official

Rodney was one of the dominant patriots in Delaware, famed for his dash to Philadelphia to vote for independence. He was born into wealth on his father's large plantation near Dover, Delaware, and he inherited the family properties before his 20th birthday. He was a major figure of the colony by virtue of his wealth alone—his brother Thomas helped him manage the estates—but he easily moved into public office, first at the local level and then on a wider front. He was justice of the peace, high sheriff, militia captain, superintendent of currency, member of the legislature and associate justice of the Delaware Supreme Court—all in the decades before the Revolution.

Splitting his time between his Kent County plantations and a townhouse in Dover, Rodney became one of the principal leaders of resistance to the royal government in a colony that had a high percentage of loyalists who continued to exert political power throughout most of the Revolution. Rodney allied himself early with Thomas McKean to protest the Stamp Act and the Townshend Acts and worked with McKean during the ensuing revolutionary decade. In 1774, Rodney called the colonial legislature into a special session to constitute a provisional convention and was elected by the body, along with McKean and George Read, to represent Delaware in the Continental Congress.

Rodney was one of the more radical delegates at Philadelphia, agitating for an early and violent separation from Great Britain, but he spent much of his time at home in Delaware during late 1775 and early 1776 in an effort to corral the loyalists and to prepare the colony's war effort. He was absent from Congress when the crucial vote on independence loomed in late June 1776. Read decided to vote against independence, and McKean dispatched an urgent message to Rodney calling for his vote to break the Delaware delegation's tie. Rodney mounted a horse in Dover and set out on a long, rain-swept night's ride that brought him to Philadelphia just in time to cast the deciding vote. He signed the

Declaration of Independence later in the summer, but then withdrew again to deal with matters at home. There he found the loyalists in command, and they turned him out of office in retaliation for his vote for independence. He was not reelected to Congress, and he was denied seats in the legislature and in the state constitutional convention.

Nonetheless, he retained his militia rank as brigadier general and turned to military affairs. He recruited troops, gathered supplies and made a brief foray himself to join the Continental Army at Morristown. Elevated to major general in 1777, he commanded the state militia when the British invasion force crossed Delaware on its way to take Philadelphia, but he could do nothing to prevent the seizure of Wilmington and the passage of the enemy.

Rodney regained political office in 1778, after serving as a judge of admiralty, and he was elected to Congress but declined to serve in favor of taking office as president of the state. He held the chief executive's post until 1781 and the end of the active war. He died in 1784 from cancer of the face, an affliction he had borne for nearly 10 years. *Further reading:* William Frank and Harold Hancock, "Caesar Rodney . . ." *Delaware History* 18 (Fall-Winter 1976), 63–76; George Ryden, ed., *Letters to and from Caesar Rodney* (1933; reprinted New York, 1970).

RODNEY, Sir George Brydges (1718–1792) British admiral

After a career filled with ups and downs, Rodney emerged late in the Revolutionary War as Britain's hero in the naval struggle with France. Born into a family of impeccably aristocratic background, he was the final candidate to enjoy the privilege of entering the navy by direct appointment of the monarch as a 13-year-old "king's letter boy." With such powerful patronage on his side, he rose quickly in the Royal Navy and solidified his fortuitous birth with good fighting during the War of Austrian Succession. He won an even greater reputation during the Seven Years' War, especially after smashing a potential French invasion fleet at Le Havre in 1759 and following up with several victories as commander in chief of the Leeward Islands station in the West Indies. He was also—in the manner of most senior military officers—a member of Parliament, having originally been given a seat controlled by the Admiralty. However, one of Rodney's distinctions was to remain more or less apart from the factional politics of the age, and he

was forced to contest a seat in the Commons on his own in 1768. The effort nearly ruined him, costing £30,000 of his own money.

After a disappointing turn as commander at Jamaica, Rodney returned to England in 1774 but was forced to flee his debtors almost immediately, taking refuge in Paris. Lord Sandwich, head of the Admiralty and an intensely political man, could or would do nothing to aid Rodney, who remained on the sidelines as the American war progressed toward French intervention. Ironically, Rodney was freed from his debts by a gift from a French nobleman and was allowed to return to England in 1778, just as the French fleets entered the war, putting Britain in a difficult position. Rodney was plagued for the rest of his career by charges that his financial difficulties caused him to place more emphasis on winning prize money than in defeating his nation's enemies.

In 1779, he was appointed to sail with a reinforcement fleet and to take command of the West Indies. Physically debilitated by severe gout and over 60 years old, Rodney nevertheless showed more energy and innovative strategy than nearly all other British naval commanders of his day. He sailed in December 1780 for Gibraltar to relieve the forces there before moving on to the West Indies. He caught an outnumbered Spanish fleet off Cape St. Vincent and defeated it during a harrowing night engagement. He passed on to St. Lucia in March and assumed command. Anticipating a battle with the French fleet under de Guichen, Rodney ordered his captains to disregard the hidebound admiralty fighting instructions and to engage the enemy piecemeal rather than van to van in a formal line. The fight off Martinique in April 1780 proved to be inconclusive when the British captains failed to execute Rodney's instructions, perhaps due to poor signalling.

Rodney took a flotilla to New York to escape the hurricane season (quarreling there with Admiral Marriot Arbuthnot over the division of prize money) but returned to the West Indies in January 1781, where he learned of the declaration of war against Holland. He promptly attacked the great Dutch supply port at St. Eustatius and seized a huge amount of goods and ships—enough to make his fortune several times over if allowed as a prize of war. Disregarding the fact that much of the booty was in fact the property of English merchants, Rodney dispatched a flotilla of prizes toward home and began to count his money. Unfortunately for him, the French recaptured most of the prizes before they reached port.

Rodney was absent on sick leave in England when the French fleet under Admiral de Grasse repulsed the British fleet off the Chesapeake Capes in the fall of 1781, leading to the destruction of Lord Cornwallis' forces and the end of the British attempt to suppress the Revolution. However, Rodney was sent out to the West Indies again in early 1782. His great triumph came at the battle of the Saints in April, when he met and defeated de Grasse in a smashing victory, capturing the huge French flagship in the process and wrecking French naval power for years to come. Rodney was criticized by Admiral Hood, his second in command, for failing to follow up the initial victory, but the achievement could not be gainsaid. Ironically, Lord North's government had fallen and Rodney's replacement already dispatched before news of the victory reached home. He returned to a nearly hysterical hero's welcome—Britain was starved for good news on the heels of Cornwallis' defeat—and honors and rewards were heaped on him, including elevation as a baron and restoration of his family estates. His victory gave British negotiators new leverage with Benjamin Franklin in Paris and helped them to pry America away from France. Rodney retired to live in comfort and honor for the final decade of his life. *Further reading:* Christopher Lloyd, "Sir George Rodney: Lucky Admiral," in George Billias, ed., *Washington's Opponents* (New York, 1969).

RODNEY, Thomas (1744–1811) Delegate to Congress, militia officer, state official, jurist
The much younger brother of Caesar Rodney, Thomas (whose father died in 1745) was mostly raised by his elder sibling, to whom he continued to be attached for several decades. Thomas worked as a manager of Caesar's estates in the years before the Revolution, with a two-year hiatus as a merchant in Philadelphia. He had no formal training in the law but was appointed as a local justice of the peace in Kent County in 1770. He was elected to the colonial assembly in 1775 and took part in the patriot affairs of Delaware as a member of the local council of safety and the committee of observation. With the actual coming of the war in 1775, Rodney organized a militia company in Kent County with

himself as captain. He led his men to join Washington's army in Pennsylvania just before the end of 1776. He was placed under John Cadwalader as part of the large militia force and took part in Cadwalader's maneuvers during the surprise attack on Trenton in December. Rodney's militia company then advanced with the rest of the army to Princeton and took part in the battle there during the first days of January. He then returned to Delaware and shared duties with Caesar as adjutant of the state militia, but he could do little more than watch as the British army passed through the state on its way to take Philadelphia. He turned to civilian affairs, thereafter sitting as a judge of the state admiralty court and in the legislature. In 1781, he was sent to the Continental Congress, returning for consecutive terms until 1783, and he was again elected after the war in 1786. He also continued as a member of the legislature but after 1802 turned to judicial posts, having been appointed as chief justice of Delaware. He resigned his state post the following year in order to become U.S. judge for the Mississippi Territory. He died in Natchez. *Further reading:* Simon Gratz, "Thomas Rodney," *The Pennsylvania Magazine of History and Biography* (January 1919), 123–26.

RODRIGUEZ, Daniel J. See SALVADOR, Francis.

RODGERS, John (1723–1789) Delegate to Congress, state official   Born in Annapolis, Rodgers studied law and set up a practice in his native city. He was a member of the Maryland Committee of Safety in 1774 and 1775 and attended the patriot provincial conventions during the same years. He was selected to represent Maryland in the Continental Congress in 1776 and was returned for the same duty the following year while simultaneously serving as a judge of the court of admiralty. He was also a major of a Prince Georges County militia company but apparently saw no action during the war. He helped organize the new state government in 1777 as a member of the executive council. He was chancellor of Maryland for nine years, during and after the Revolution.

ROGERS, Josias (1755–1795) British naval officer   Rogers was active along the American coast against privateers during the War of Independence, although only a junior naval officer. He entered the

Royal Navy in 1771 and by 1775 served aboard the *Roebuck* on the American station. He was in charge of a prize in Delaware Bay in March 1776 when he was driven ashore by a storm and captured. He escaped a year later and returned to duty, commanding the small boats of the *Roebuck* in numerous raids against privateers and small merchant vessels among the creeks and inlets of the coast. Rogers was finally promoted to lieutenant in 1778 and was assigned to a succession of ships. He took part in the capture of Charleston in 1780 and in December took command of the *General Monk,* a prize ship refitted as a sloop-of-war. After a long period of successful raiding against American shipping near the mouth of the Delaware, Rogers ran aground at Cape May in April 1782 and was again captured. He returned to Britain after his exchange in 1783. He continued to serve as an officer during the ensuing wars with the French and died in Grenada of yellow fever.

ROGERS, Robert (1732–1795) Loyalist officer

Rogers won lasting fame as the leader of irregular troops (the so-called Rogers' Rangers) during the Seven Years' War, but in nearly all other aspects of life he was corrupt, dishonest and incompetent—and he turned loyalist during the Revolution. He was born in Methuen, Massachusetts and grew up on a farm near Concord, New Hampshire. He showed early his propensity for dishonesty as well as military ingenuity: he joined the colonial forces of the British against the French in 1755 in order to avoid charges of counterfeiting (Rogers more than once turned to making his own money when his poke ran short). He effectively translated his woodland skills into leadership, and during the rest of the conflict with the French, Rogers demonstrated the military potential of irregulars in North America terrain. He eventually led nine companies of rangers with the rank of major, and he won victory after victory in skirmishes and larger engagements, especially with the Indian allies of the French. The end of the war in 1763, however, marked the apogee of his career. After fighting in Pontiac's War, he went to Britain, only a bit ahead of creditors and charges of counterfeiting, and managed to win appointment as governor of the British post at Michilimackinac. He was accused of embezzlement and treason after two years at the frontier fort and was turned out. He went back to England but found no

encouragement from the government, and while in Britain he was thrown in prison for debt. Released in 1775, Rogers returned to America, but he was arrested by the patriots the following year as a loyalist. He escaped from confinement in New Hampshire and joined the British forces in New York, where he raised the Queen's American Rangers, but he could not hold command and lost his final appointment in 1776. Following a divorce, he returned to England in 1780 and died in poverty. *Further reading:* John Cuneo, *Robert Rogers of the Rangers* (New York, 1959).

ROMANS, Bernard (c. 1720–c. 1784) Engineer, naturalist, cartographer, militia officer

A man of considerable parts, Romans was of Dutch birth and English education. He came to America in 1757 as a surveyor and cartographer for the British government, and he spent the following 16 years exploring, charting and describing the botany and geography of Florida and Georgia, usually in the employ of the southern royal colonial governments. His studies of the botany of Florida gained him admission to scientific circles in New England, and by the time of the Revolution, Romans was a well-known figure. He was also an active patriot and played a minor role in the expedition against Fort Ticonderoga in 1775. He then went to New York state and worked on construction of the Hudson River defenses opposite West Point on behalf of the New York provincial congress (he was paid by the Continental Congress, however). Romans moved to Philadelphia in February 1776 and received a militia commission as captain of artillery, although his field service was apparently confined to inspection of fortifications. In 1780, he was captured at sea while bound for South Carolina. His end is somewhat mysterious: he apparently died at sea after being set free after the war from British confinement in Jamaica.

ROOT, Jesse (1737–1822) Delegate to Congress, jurist

A native of Coventry, Connecticut, Root graduated from Princeton in 1746 and went on to more study at Yale. He was admitted to the bar in Connecticut in 1763. During the Revolution, he served on the Connecticut Council of Safety and was commissioned into the militia, becoming adjutant general by 1777. The following year he was sent as a delegate to the Continental Congress, where he served for five years. He took a place on the Connecticut state council in 1780, serving for nine years as chairman. In 1789, Root was named to the Connecticut Superior Court. He was chief justice from 1796 to 1807, when he left the bench in favor of a seat in the state house of representatives.

ROSENTHAL, Gustave Henri, Baron de (John Rose) (1753–1829) Russian volunteer officer

Born in the Baltic region that eventually became Latvia but which was Russian territory at the time, Rosenthal fled St. Petersburg sometime in the early 1770s after a duel in which he killed his opponent. He studied medicine in Baltimore before the war, and in 1777 he was appointed as a surgeon in General William Irvine's 7th Pennsylvania Regiment. Under the name John Rose, he served with Irvine for most of the remainder of the war, including the winter at Valley Forge, becoming a lieutenant of Irvine's new 4th Pennsylvania Regiment in the spring of 1781 and acting as the general's aide-de-camp. Rosenthal transferred to the 3rd Pennsylvania in January 1783 and was discharged from the Continental service in June. In 1784, he returned to Russia, having been pardoned for his earlier offense. He rose to the status of grand marshal in his homeland but corresponded with Irvine until long after the American Revolution, and he received land bounties—unclaimed in person—in Ohio and the Northwest Territory for his wartime service. *Further reading:* Gustave H. Rosenthal, "Journal of a Volunteer Expedition. . . ," *Pennsylvania Magazine of History and Biography* 18 (1894), 129–57.

ROSS, Alexander (1742–1827) British officer

A native Scot, Ross entered the Royal Army as an ensign of the 50th Regiment of Foot in 1760. He was a veteran of the European wars when posted to America, where he served as an aide-de-camp to Lord Cornwallis during most of the Revolution. He carried dispatches to the government in England after the British victory at Camden in 1780 and was rewarded with promotion to major of the 45th Regiment. He returned to America and had the unhappy duty of representing Cornwallis at the surrender negotiations at Yorktown in 1781. He followed Cornwallis to India when the latter became commander in chief and continued to serve at Cornwallis' side for the balance of his career. He eventually became a full general and ceremonial colonel of the 59th Regiment.

ROSS, Betsy (1752–1836) Legendary flagmaker

There was a real Elizabeth Ross who lived in Philadelphia during the Revolution and she was a professional seamstress who made—among other things—flags during the war, but there is no convincing evidence that she made the first American flag at the behest of George Washington in 1776. The entire story of her involvement in the flag business (the Stars and Stripes design was officially adopted by Congress in June 1777) came from the unsupported assertions of her grandson William J. Canby, made nearly a century after the purported event.

Elizabeth Griscom, the daughter of a Philadelphia builder, eloped in 1773 to New Jersey with John Ross. She was drummed out of her Quaker meeting for the marriage, but she and her husband returned to Philadelphia and set up an upholstery and sewing shop on Arch Street, living on the business premises. Her husband was a member of the state militia and was killed in an explosion while on guard duty in 1776. In 1777, she married Captain Joseph Ashburn, who was captured at sea by the British and died in 1782 while a captive in Old Mill Prison in England. Elizabeth's final marriage was to John Claypool in 1783.

During the Revolutionary War, she apparently carried on her sewing and upholstery trade, and there exists a record of payment to her for making ships' flags for the Pennsylvania state navy in 1777. No writer or historian at the time, however, made any mention of the first American flag and Betsy Ross. Not until 1870, as the centennial celebration of the Revolution approached, did her grandson come forward with the colorful story of how Washington appeared at her shop with a sketch of a flag and asked her to make the first standard of the new nation. He had no evidence whatsoever, claiming only to have heard the story from her dying lips when he was 11 years old. Despite the spurious provenance of the tale, it caught the fancy of literally millions of Americans, who flocked to join a Betsy Ross Memorial Association established to perpetuate the legend. Repeated efforts to debunk the myth have failed. *Further reading:* W. C. Miller, "The Betsy Ross Legend," *Social Studies* 37 (1946), 317–23.

ROSS, David (1755–1800) Continental officer, delegate to Congress

Ross was a native of Maryland, born in Prince Georges County. He received an appointment as major in Grayson's Additional Regiment when it was organized in January 1777, presumably commanding one of the Maryland companies (the regiment was largely recruited in Virginia). He resigned at the end of the year and returned to Maryland to manage the estates coming to him as the result of his father's death. He studied law meanwhile and was admitted to the bar in 1783, setting up a practice in Frederick. He was a delegate to the final two sessions of the Confederation Congress in 1788 and 1789.

ROSS, George (1730–1779) Delegate to Congress, official

Ross was an early loyalist who converted to the revolutionary cause just before the beginning of the war. He was born in New Castle, Delaware, and moved to Philadelphia as a young man to study law with his stepbrother. He was admitted to the bar in 1750 and set up his practice in Lancaster, Pennsylvania the following year. He was a king's attorney for the first 12 years of his legal career and took an interest in colonial affairs as a member of the legislature from 1766 to 1774. Reluctant to support the patriots, he nevertheless attended a provincial congress in 1774 and was selected to serve as a delegate to Congress. He apparently converted firmly to the patriot camp by 1775, since he joined the Pennsylvania Council of Safety. He was again sent to Congress in mid-1776, missing the vote on the Declaration of Independence but taking his seat in time to sign the document in early August. He resigned due to poor health in 1777. The following year he became a judge of admiralty in Pennsylvania and set off a long legal controversy when he refused to accept the authority of the central government in a contested case between a citizen of Pennsylvania and a Connecticuter.

ROSSLYN, Earl of. See WEDDERBURN, Alexander.

ROUERIE, Marquis Tuffin de la. See ARMAND, Charles Tuffin.

ROWLEY, Joshua (c. 1730–1790) British admiral

A rather workaday officer, Rowley was the son of a Royal Navy captain and first went to sea aboard his father's ship as a midshipman. He was appointed a lieutenant at the early age of 17, an indication of the way preferment and sponsorship worked in the navy of the mid-18th century. Rowley served extensively at sea during the warfare of the 1750s and 1760s, often as a captain under Edward Hawke. While not especially distinguished, neither did he show himself inadequate. He was occupied as a post captain in European waters during the first years of the American Revolution. In 1779, he was sent with reinforcements for Admiral John Byron in the West Indies and hoisted his flag as rear admiral in March. He subsequently served under George Rodney and took command of Jamaica in 1782. By ill chance he missed the two major fleet actions in the West Indies, and after his return to England in 1783, Rowley was not again employed by the Admiralty.

ROZENTHAL, Baron de. See ROSENTHAL.

RUDOLPH, Michael (c. 1754–c. 1794) Continental officer

Born in Maryland, Michael enlisted in Lee's Legion in 1778 and served initially as a sergeant-major of infantry. He was promoted to quartermaster in early 1779. He volunteered as one of the leaders of the advance storming party (called a "forlorn hope") in the lightning assault on Paulus Hook in August 1779, and as a result of his demonstrated bravery he was given a commission as lieutenant. Promoted to captain within a few months, Rudolph served ably in the southern campaigns of the legion. Following the Revolution, he settled in the region of Sudbury, Georgia as a farmer and local tax collector. He returned to the colors in 1790 with a commission as captain of the 1st Dragoons, and he took part in Josiah Harmar's expeditions against the western Indians. He retired from the army in 1793 with the rank of major.

RUGELEY, Henry. Loyalist officer

Rugeley owned a fine plantation, called Clermont, at a strategic location between Camden and Charlotte, South Carolina. He was a colonel of loyalist militia in the state after the British capture of Charleston in 1780, although his allegiance may have wavered earlier in the war. He was the butt of a ruse by Colonel William Washington in December 1780, when Washington surrounded Rugeley and his men who were inside a fortified barn on Rugeley's own estate. The American commander had no artillery to take the strongly defended building, but he manufactured a fake cannon from a log and bluffed Rugeley into surrender. The affair ended Rugeley's military career.

RUGGLES, Timothy (1711–1795) Loyalist official, soldier

The son of a parson, Ruggles was born in Rochester, Massachusetts. After graduating from Harvard in 1732, he moved to Sandwich, opened a law practice, married a propertied widow and kept a tavern and stable. Later, he moved to Hardwick and began to accumulate land, eventually owning seven farms nearby. He was active in the militia and served with some distinction as a brigadier during the Seven Years' War. At about the same time, he began to accumulate public offices and take a role in colonial politics. He was appointed associate justice of the Court of Common Pleas in 1757 and sat as a leader in the colonial legislature. According to the description of one biographer, he was "a wit and a misanthrope; a man of rude manners and rude speech," especially in legislative assemblies, where he came increasingly in conflict with the Massachusetts patriots as the Revolution approached. He was appointed as deputy surveyor of the King's Woods in 1771. He proposed a loyalist "Association" in 1774 to unite those loyal to the crown, but he met little success and had to flee to Boston. After evacuation to Halifax, Nova Scotia with the British fleet in 1776, he went to New York City and raised a loyalist force called the King's Light Dragoons, although command of the unit went to Benjamin Thompson. Following the war, he settled in Nova Scotia.

RUMFORD, Count. See THOMPSON, Benjamin.

RUMSEY, Benjamin (1734–1808) Delegate to Congress, militia officer, jurist

Active as a revolutionary leader in Maryland, Rumsey was chief justice of the Maryland Court of Appeals for 27 years. He was born in Cecil County and after attending Princeton returned to Maryland to practice law. In 1775, he raised supplies for the patriot forces and attended a provincial congress. The following year he was appointed a colonel of militia and took a place on the Maryland Council of Safety. He was sent to Congress as a delegate from Maryland in

1776 and 1777. His appointment to the appeals court bench came the next year, and he remained a judge until his resignation in 1805.

RUSH, Benjamin (1746–1813) Delegate to Congress, Continental surgeon general, physician

A complex and not altogether admirable figure, Rush was the best-known physician of his day as well as a political intriguer. He was born near Philadelphia and was educated as a boy in Maryland after the death of his father in 1754. He graduated from the College of New Jersey (now Princeton) in 1760 and studied medicine privately in Philadelphia, which was the center for medical education in the colonies. In 1766, Rush went to the University of Edinburgh, from which he graduated with a medical degree two years later. After more medical education in London, he returned to Philadelphia as one of the best-trained medical men in America. He set up a private practice and became professor of chemistry at the College of Philadelphia, one of the first such appointments.

By the beginning of the Revolution, Rush was one of the most prominent doctors in the land, despite his relative youth. He was also deeply interested in politics—a lifelong trait—and he not only cultivated the friendship of people such as Thomas Jefferson, Tom Paine and John Adams (Rush had known Benjamin Franklin in London), but he also wrote newspaper essays and political tracts. In early 1776, he married the daughter of Richard Stockton, tightening his ties to politics. As the movement for independence gained momentum, Rush threw himself into the struggle in Pennsylvania and was elected in mid-1778 by the provincial convention to the Continental Congress as a pro-independence delegate, too late to vote but in time to sign the Declaration. He served only one official term in Congress and in April 1777 was appointed as surgeon general of the Middle Department.

He then entered a period of political and personal intrigue that reflects less than well on his reputation. He had considerable behind-the-scenes power, which he exerted to try to bring down his supposed enemies and to advance himself. The Continental medical service was already a morass of conflicts and political tugging and pulling. Rush used the dissatisfaction among regimental medical officers (who resented the attempts of the central medical departments to bring order to military medical affairs) as a basis for criticizing Dr. William Shippen, chief physician of the army. Rush accused Shippen of mishandling the medical department and charged the older physician with maladministration. Commander in chief George Washington referred the affair to Congress, which to Rush's disgust ruled in favor of Shippen. Rush resigned his post and entered into an even bigger intrigue to unseat Washington, whose reputation suffered among civilians at the time owing to his repeated defeats at the hands of the British.

Rush may have genuinely distrusted Washington as part of a general fear of a standing army, but his efforts to denigrate the commander and to replace Washington with the momentarily triumphant Horatio Gates were heavy-handed and transparently self-aggrandizing. The showdown came when Washington received a copy of an anonymous letter from Rush to Virginia governor Patrick Henry that excoriated the commander in chief in no uncertain terms. Since Rush's expression of disloyalty coincided with the collapse of the effort in Congress to replace Washington, the episode marked the end of Rush's military career and nearly the end of his influence. He returned to the practice of medicine in Philadelphia and began anew his teaching.

Following the Revolution, he helped form the first genuine medical college in America as part of the newly amalgamated University of Pennsylvania and gained a wide reputation as the finest medical educator in the nation. He also was extremely active in social matters as the founder of one of the first antislavery societies, a free medical dispensary in Philadelphia, and Dickinson College. His own "system" of medical treatment was based on a hideous course of bleeding which often advocated draining nearly all the blood from a victim in order to restore some ill-defined nervous balance. Even in his own day, Rush's medical ideas were discredited, although he continued to be revered as a teacher and social reformer. In 1797, he was named as head of the U.S. Mint, but he continued to exercise his penchant for intrigue. He died of typhus at 67. *Further reading:* David F. Hawke, *Benjamin Rush, Revolutionary Gadfly* (Indianapolis, 1971); Nathan G. Goodman, *Benjamin Rush, Physician and Citizen, 1746–1813* (Philadelphia, 1934).

RUSSELL, Joseph (1719–1804) Merchant   Russell, a Massachusetts native, was one of the primary developers of the whaling industry in New England. His ships plied the Atlantic taking whales, and his Massachusetts factories produced spermaceti candles. His ships and buildings at New Bedford were selected by the British for destruction during a 1778 raid, since he had vocally supported the Revolution, and the act of burning his facilities weakened the patriot economy. One of his ships, the *Rebecca,* opened the Pacific to New England whalers in a 1791–93 voyage around Cape Horn.

RUSSELL, William, Sr. (c. 1741–1793) Continental general   A native of Virginia, Russell (whose name is sometimes spelled Russel) moved to the Virginia frontier about 10 years before the outbreak of the war. When Virginia organized the 13th Regiment in October 1776 as part of a new draft for the Continental Army, Russell was appointed commanding colonel. He held the post until the regiment was reorganized in September 1778, at which juncture he transferred to the new 5th Virginia Regiment (which had been the 7th). He was captured at the fall of Charleston in 1780 along with his officers and men, many of whom had been pooled into a single Virginia Detachment. Russell was exchanged six months later. He received a brevet as brigadier general on his mustering out in November 1783.

RUSSELL, William, Jr. (1758–1825) Militia officer   Taken to western Virginia as a small child by his father, William Sr., the younger Russell was already an experienced frontiersman by the time of the Revolution, having explored westward with Daniel Boone at the tender age of 15. Although his father commanded regular Virginia regiments during the war, William Jr. fought as a militia officer at King's Mountain, against the Cherokees, and at Wetzell's Mill and Guilford Courthouse. He moved to Kentucky after the war and became one of the principal political leaders of the region, agitating successfully for statehood and subsequently sitting in the state legislature. He was appointed commander in chief of the western military frontier in 1811. A county in Kentucky is named in his honor.

RUTGERS, Henry (1745–1830) Soldier, philanthropist   Born in New York City, Rutgers graduated from King's College (now Columbia University) in 1766. During the Revolutionary War, he was a member of the Sons of Liberty and served as a captain in the New York militia that fought at the battle of White Plains. Following the war, he was a major benefactor of several educational institutions, including the first free school for the poor in New York City and the college at Princeton. Rutgers was particularly interested in Queen's College in New Jersey, making significant gifts to the school and serving on the board of trustees. In 1825, the college officials renamed the school in honor of Rutgers.

RUTHERFORD, Griffith (c. 1731–c. 1800) Militia general

Native to Ireland, Rutherford emigrated to North Carolina and lived near Salisbury at the time of the Revolution. He sat in the North Carolina Provincial Congress in 1775 and the following year was appointed as brigadier general of the state militia. He commanded North Carolina troops against the Cherokees in 1776 and in 1778–1779 led a large contingent of North Carolinians into Georgia to reinforce the army of Benjamin Lincoln. He organized the militia force that defeated the British at Ramsour's Mill, North Carolina in March 1779 but himself was absent from the battle. At the disastrous battle of Camden the following year, Rutherford commanded the Georgia militia and was wounded and captured. After confinement at Charleston and St. Augustine, he was exchanged in mid-1781 and resumed active duty at Wilmington after the British evacuation. Following the war, he sat in the North Carolina state legislature, where he was an implacable foe of loyalists and advocated harsh measures—a reflection of the long-term divisions that grew out of the vicious back-country warfare in the Carolinas during the latter years of the Revolution. He later moved to Tennessee.

RUTLEDGE, Edward (1749–1800) Delegate to Congress, state official, attorney

Rutledge was born near Charleston, South Carolina, the younger brother of John Rutledge by a decade. He went to England in 1767 to study at the Middle Temple and was admitted to the English bar in 1772. He returned to Charleston the following year and despite his youth became an increasingly important leader in the South Carolina revolutionary movement, coming to notice almost immediately for his courtroom defense of Thomas Pownall, a printer accused of libel by the royal officials of the colony. He was sent, along with his brother and his father-in-law

Henry Middleton, as one of the first five delegates to the Continental Congress in 1774.

Rutledge represented the interests and opinions of the southern aristocracy and had many uncomfortable moments in Congress, where he clashed with the New England faction. During 1775 and 1776, he attended the provincial assemblies in South Carolina that took control of the colony as well as sitting in the Continental Congress in Philadelphia. When the South Carolina senior congressional members either withdrew or were felled by illness, Rutledge became the head of the delegation. He emerged as one of the chief congressional spokesmen for moving slowly toward independence. He thought independence inevitable but wanted the colonies to form a confederation first, despite his distrust of a strong central government. He held firm against voting for independence in the first days of July 1776 and was swayed only when it appeared South Carolina would be left out. He finally allowed his delegation to vote for the Declaration, which he subsequently signed as the youngest delegate to do so.

In September 1776, he was sent by Congress with John Adams and Benjamin Franklin to meet with the Howe brothers who were named to negotiate for the British on Staten Island for an unsuccessful peace conference, after which he returned to Charleston. He was elected to the legislature in South Carolina in 1778 and the following year again was designated as a delegate to the Continental Congress, but he never took his seat. Instead he joined the state militia as a captain of the Charleston Battery of Artillery formed to fight Sir Henry Clinton's expedition. Rutledge was captured at the fall of the city in the spring of 1780 and was sent along with other state officials to prison in St. Augustine, Florida. He was exchanged in July 1781. From 1782 until 1798, he served in the state legislature, becoming more and more conservative. He was elected governor of South Carolina in 1798 and died in office a little over two years later.

RUTLEDGE, John (1739–1800) Governor, delegate to Congress, jurist

Perhaps the perfect representative of the ruling planter class in South Carolina, Rutledge was the principal civilian leader of the state during the darkest days of the Revolution. He was born in Charleston, the elder brother of Edward Rutledge, and received a sound private

John Rutledge

education before going to England for legal study at the Middle Temple. He returned to Charleston in 1760 and began what was soon a thriving law practice. He reflected from early in his public life the views of the ruling elements of society and politics in South Carolina—he was firm, patrician, antidemocratic, and devoted to the economic well-being of those who owned the large indigo and rice plantations.

He entered the colonial legislature almost as soon as he assumed professional life in Charleston, and he was not long in making his presence known. Rutledge was one of the leaders of resistance to the machinations of the royal government during the 1760s and early 1770s, coming into conflict on a range of issues, including the Stamp Act. He was, however, not early in favor of independence, hoping to find a constitutional solution to the controversy. Rutledge managed to build a certain consensus between the planters and the merchants of the colony without alienating the more radical patriots. He was selected as a delegate to the first Continental Congress in 1774 and there fought to allow South Carolina to sell its rice crop before putting a trade embargo with Britain into effect. He returned to the second Continental Congress, but from 1776 onward most of his attentions were claimed by matters in his home state.

In late 1775, he returned home from Philadelphia, and a few weeks later a new state assembly elected him president—in effect, governor. He helped organize the successful defense of Charleston that beat off the first British attempt to take the city and

then settled into a period of relative quiet while the main British efforts were directed toward the northern and middle colonies. More radical elements in South Carolina passed a revised state constitution in 1778, but Rutledge disliked many of its provisions such as disestablishment of the Episcopal Church and creation of a popularly elected upper house, so he vetoed the new law and resigned his office. His successor restored the new constitution, and it was under its provisions that Rutledge was reelected governor in 1779.

One of Rutledge's few public stumbles occurred later in 1779 when Charleston was threatened by a British military force under Augustine Prevost. Urged on by his council, Rutledge offered to declare the state neutral if the British withdrew. The issue dissolved when an American army under Benjamin Lincoln appeared and faced down Prevost, but the waffling hurt Rutledge's standing. Most of this was brushed aside, however, when a British invasion force under Sir Henry Clinton appeared in earnest and bade to take Charleston. As the noose tightened (Clinton took a great long while to prepare his final siege) the state legislature adjourned and granted Rutledge wide executive powers to conduct the public business. He escaped from Charleston before its final surrender in May 1780.

The times were desperate, however. All of the Continental troops in the state were taken at Charleston, along with military stores, most of the state militia, and nearly all the members of the government. The fast-moving British under Banastre Tarleton crushed the few remaining armed forces, and South Carolina was completely in the grip of the enemy. Rutledge fled to North Carolina just ahead of capture by Tarleton's hard-riding dragoons. Horatio Gates's devastating defeat at Camden left him in what seemed to be an even worse predicament. Rutledge's solution was to encourage and commission militia commanders, such as Francis Marion, Thomas Sumter and Andrew Pickens, to wage partisan warfare. When Nathanael Greene appeared on the scene, Rutledge worked hard to organize supplies and support for the ensuing campaign. He was able to return to South Carolina by the summer of 1781, and after the final British defeat at Yorktown, he began to reassemble state authority, although the British continued to occupy the state capital of Charleston until 1783. Rutledge called a new legislature into session at Jacksonboro in early

1782, provided a blueprint for reconstruction, and resigned his office as governor as required by the state constitution, retiring to a seat in the assembly as a representative of his home parish. He was returned to Congress as a delegate in May and served until the following year.

Most of his public life after the Revolution was as a jurist. He was appointed as an associate justice of the new U.S. Supreme Court in 1791, but he resigned to take a post as chief justice in South Carolina. His mental stability began to deteriorate by the mid-1790s, and he was involved in an unhappy series of events in 1795. John Jay had re-signed as chief justice of the U.S. Supreme Court, and Rutledge petitioned President George Washington for the appointment. He was named to the post and actually presided at the August term of the court, but he had meanwhile let loose a stream of invective against the just-announced provisions of Jay's Treaty and this controversial stand led to a failure of the U.S. Senate to confirm Rutledge's appointment as chief justice. He was turned out of office and lapsed into insanity. He died in Charleston five years later. *Further reading:* Richard H. Barry, *Mr. Rutledge of South Carolina* (1942; reprinted Freeport, N.Y., 1971).

S

ST. CLAIR, Arthur (1737–1818) Continental general, delegate to Congress St. Clair had a checkered career as a general officer, both during and after the Revolutionary War. He was born in Scotland of an aristocratic family. After receiving an inheritance from his mother and an education at the University of Edinburgh, he bought into the 60th Regiment of Foot and came to America as part of the British army fighting in the Seven Years' War. He took part in the capture of both Louisbourg and Quebec, but he resigned his commission in 1762 and moved to Boston. He acquired a fortune through marriage and then purchased land on the Pennsylvania frontier.

St. Clair served as a colonel of colonial militia before the Revolution, and in January 1776 he was commissioned as colonel of the 2nd Pennsylvania Regiment. He commanded the unit in the northern campaign of 1776 and was promoted to brigadier in November. He fought at Trenton and Princeton, and in February 1777 he was advanced to the rank of major general and assigned as a commander of the Northern Department—a post of contention during most of 1777. He set off a storm of criticism when he abandoned Fort Ticonderoga to the British advance in July, although he may well have been correct in leaving an indefensible position, but the name of the fort had a magic for most Americans and the poor performance of his subordinates showed his decision to little advantage.

From then on during the Revolution, St. Clair operated under a cloud of doubt. He was cleared of negligence by a formal court-martial in 1778, but he found it hard to secure a new command equal to his rank and experience. He served Washington as a volunteer at Brandywine and was with John Sullivan two years later on the expedition against the Iroquois. He went south in 1781 but arrived only shortly before Lord Cornwallis' surrender. He was mustered out of the army in the fall of 1783. St. Clair served as a delegate to Congress from 1785 until 1787, and he was selected as president in 1787. With the advent of a new federal government in 1789, St. Clair was named as governor of the Northwest Territory. He also became a major general again and commander in chief of the newly constituted U.S. Army. Disaster struck again in 1791, when he was soundly defeated by the Miami Indians on the Ohio frontier. He subsequently resigned his command and was removed as governor.

ST. LEGER, Barry (1737–1789) British officer Born to a Huguenot family, St. Leger was a graduate of Cambridge when he joined the army in 1756. He fought in most of the major campaigns of the Seven Years' War in North America, including Louisbourg, Quebec and Montreal, and he gained a reputation as a skillful frontier soldier, emerging from the war as a major. Selected to play a key role in General John Burgoyne's campaign in 1777 and

Arthur St. Clair

temporarily elevated to the rank of local brigadier general, St. Leger was given command of a separate force of about 2,000 made up of a few regulars and the rest loyalists and Indians. He was to march from Canada down the Mohawk Valley and link with Burgoyne near Albany. This plan would provide Burgoyne with reinforcements before moving south to split the colonies, although the major purposes of St. Leger's march were to create a diversion and buck up the morale of New York loyalists. Unfortunately for the British, St. Leger's expedition stalled at Fort Stanwix, which was held by a relatively strong American garrison. Without sufficient artillery, St. Leger settled in for a siege. A fierce battle with an American relief force at Oriskany (which was technically a British victory) depleted St. Leger's force, and his Indian allies began to defect. He eventually withdrew just ahead of the arrival of a relief column under Benedict Arnold. St. Leger returned to Montreal, and he later assumed command of a body of rangers. In 1781, he led two more unsuccessful expeditions, one attempting to take over Vermont with the connivance of Ethan Allen and other Vermont dissidents. Before reaching his rendezvous, however, St. Leger heard the news of Lord Cornwallis' surrender, so he turned back. Following the end of the war, he was named commander of British forces in Canada. He published *St. Leger's Journal of Occurrences in America* in London in 1780.

SAINT-SIMON, Claude Henri de Rouroy, Comte de (1760–1825) French officer, political phi-

losopher   As a youth, Saint-Simon (a relative at some remove of Claude Saint-Simon Montblern) served in the French army in the West Indies and in the American Revolution at Yorktown. There are few specifics about his sojourn in North America other than his own account, in which he writes: ". . . France declared in favor of the American insurgents, and I profited of this circumstance to go to America, where I made five campaigns." He returned to France in 1782. After imprisonment during the Reign of Terror, he began writing and promoting efforts to organize a perfectionist society. His thought was highly influential during the mid-19th century, and he is usually called the founder of French socialism.

SAINT-SIMON MONTBLERN, Claude Anne, Marquis de (1740–1819) French officer   Saint-Simon studied military affairs at Strasbourg and served King Stanislas of Poland during the 1750s. By 1775, he was colonel in command of the Touraine Regiment, but he left France in 1779 for a station in the West Indies. He commanded the French troops brought to the siege of Yorktown by the fleet of Admiral de Grasse and provided more than 3,000 additional forces for the allies. He was slightly wounded during the siege and returned to the West Indies in November after the surrender of Lord Cornwallis. He subsequently fled the French Revolution as a royalist and served as a senior officer for the Spanish Bourbons, barely escaping execution when the French captured him in 1808. He died in Madrid.

Claude Anne, Marquis de Saint-Simon Montblern

SAINT TROPEZ. See SUFFREN DE SAINT TROPEZ, Pierre André de.

SACKVILLE, George. See GERMAIN, Lord George.

SALEM, Peter (d. 1816) Continental soldier

Salem was a black slave in Massachusetts when the war began, the property of a man named Groton, and he became one of the identifiable heroes of the battle of Bunker Hill. He apparently enrolled (or had been enrolled) as a militiaman and fought at the first engagement of the war around Lexington in April 1775. He was then part of the militia army that assembled to hem the British in Boston. Salem was one of the defenders of the main American redoubt at Bunker Hill on June 17. When the third British assault of the day finally appeared on the verge of successfully overrunning the Americans, who were nearly out of powder and ball, British Royal Marine major John Pitcairn exhorted his men to make the final thrust. Salem shot Pitcairn dead from behind the barricade. He went on to serve at Saratoga and Stony Point. After the war, Salem returned to Massachusetts and lived near Leicester, making woven cane for a living.

SALOMON, Haym (1740–1785) Financier, secret agent

Salomon was a key figure in financing the Revolution, especially during the dark days of the economy in the early 1780s, and he was a secret agent in occupied New York. He was born in Lissa, Poland and was a widely-traveled polyglot when he arrived in America shortly before the war. He had little or no formal education but was experienced in trade, and his facility with languages smoothed his way in opening a successful brokerage and mercantile business. He remained in New York City after the withdrawal of the Americans in the fall of 1776 and acted as an intelligence agent, supplying George Washington with information on the strength and dispositions of the British. He was arrested in late September on charges of espionage but soon was released to the custody of Hessian commander Leopold von Heister, who employed Salomon as an interpreter. He continued as a secret agent, however, and was again arrested in August 1778 and condemned to death.

Salomon bribed his way out of prison and escaped to Philadelphia. After applying unsuccessfully to Congress for a post, he set up a business as a financial broker. Over the next few years, Salomon was called on often to handle official transactions, and he became the leading broker of the complicated bills of exchange needed to keep the government afloat. With the arrival of the French expeditionary force in 1779, Salomon acted virtually as treasurer for Rochambeau and the other French commanders. In addition, Salomon frequently advanced money to individual congressional delegates and army officers, and he became deeply involved with Robert Morris' maneuvers to stave off national bankruptcy. Salomon was extraordinarily generous in handing over hard currency in exchange for Congressional paper, a course that could lead only to his impoverishment. With the end of the war, Salomon's personal stake in the government had risen perhaps as high as $600,000. He purchased a house in New York in 1784 and apparently intended to return to the city, but he died before he could do so. His family subsequently tried to settle his claims on the government, but a long series of petitions and campaigns in Congress, stretching well into the mid-19th century, failed. In the early 20th century, Jewish partisans seized on Salomon as an example of Jewish contributions to the nation and agitated for recognition of his role as a patriot. They failed in efforts to have Congress vote a medal in his memory but did raise statues to Salomon in Chicago and Los Angeles. *Further reading:* American Jewish Historical Society, *Haym Salomon, A Gentleman of Precision and Integrity* (1976).

SALTONSTALL, Dudley (1738–1796) Continental naval officer, privateer

Born in New London, Connecticut, Saltonstall was a member of a long-established and influential New England family, a nephew of the Massachusetts branch and son of General Gurdon Saltonstall. He was important in the naval affairs of the Revolution but had the misfortune to be involved in two major failures, the latter of which resulted in his dismissal from the Continental service.

He was a seafaring man before the Revolution—both as a privateer and as a merchant captain—and was in command of a fort at New London in 1775 when the Continental Congress established a formal navy. Saltonstall was named as senior captain and given command of the *Alfred*, a former merchantman converted to a 24-gun frigate, making him the flag captain for naval commander in chief Esek

Hopkins. Saltonstall and the rest of the Continental Navy's active flotilla set sail in February 1776 under Hopkins, disregarding instructions to seek out the Royal Navy around Rhode Island and heading instead for the West Indies, where Hopkins scented prize money and easier opposition. The flotilla seized the British base at Nassau in March but withdrew almost empty-handed after a few days.

In April, the *Alfred* in company with the other Continental ships off New York encountered the British 20-gun frigate *Glasgow,* and Saltonstall was roundly defeated in a sharp nighttime encounter, although it must be admitted that the British got in a lucky shot early on that disabled the *Alfred's* steering. Although he was cleared of blame by a subsequent investigation, Saltonstall's standing in the navy was diminished by the affair and his star eclipsed by other rising captains. He was demoted to fourth on the list of seniority, and during 1777 and 1778, he commanded the frigates *Trumbull* and *Warren.*

Saltonstall's final downfall came in 1779 with his part in the completely disastrous Penobscot Expedition, an ill-advised and ill-planned attempt by the Massachusetts state government—independent of consultation with the Congress or Washington—to seize a base the British were building on the Maine coast near the modern-day city of Castine. The state assembled a militia force under generals Peleg Wadsworth and Solomon Lovell, whom Saltonstall was to support at sea with a fleet of three frigates, three brigantines, 20 privateers and 20 transports (20 armed ships in all). The land forces made a halting approach to the British camp and discovered a determined defense ready to oppose them. The two Massachusetts militia commanders disregarded Saltonstall's advice to attack briskly, and they dithered and quarreled until a powerful British naval squadron (including a 60-gun ship of the line) under Admiral George Collier arrived from New York. Saltonstall had no chance since not a single one of his ships could come within cannon range of the British without almost certain destruction. The Massachusetts militia collapsed and fled through the forest, taking nearly 500 casualties in the process. All of Saltonstall's ships were lost, including the merchantmen assigned for transport duty. The Massachusetts authorities put all the blame on Saltonstall, making him the scapegoat for their own incompetence and hoping to recoup some of their huge expenses from Congress by holding a Continental officer responsible. He was dismissed from the Continental Navy in October, a victim of others' fumbling. He then turned to privateering for the balance of the war, and he had moderate success, taking a valuable prize in the form of the British merchant ship *Hannah.* At the end of the Revolution, Saltonstall went back to trading. He died of yellow fever in the West Indies.

SALVADOR, Francis (Daniel Jezurun Rodriguez) (1747–1776) Militia officer, official

Born in England and educated as an English gentleman, Salvador was a member of a wealthy Jewish family that had originally fled from the Spanish Inquisition, first to Holland and then to Great Britain, adopting the family name of Salvador in place of the original Rodriguez (although Francis kept the name Daniel Jezurun Rodriguez within family circles). He inherited a great fortune, increased by a fortuitous marriage, but he and his family lost most of their money in the early 1770s. Salvador came to South Carolina in 1773 to claim existing family land titles in the region of Ninety-Six and in hope of establishing an indigo plantation. Within a short while, he became active in local patriot politics and took a leading role in the provincial congresses in South Carolina, assuming a seat in the new legislature with the ouster of the British royal government. He was one of the few Jews to hold public office in the early Revolution and was apparently influential among Carolina councils, helping to form the first state government and constitution. He was also active in his local county militia, and in August 1776, Salvador joined a patriot force under Colonel Andrew Williamson that set out to do battle against a mixed body of Indians and loyalists. The patriot militia was ambushed and Salvador killed on August 1. His memory was later marked by a plaque in Charleston.

SAMPSON, Deborah (Robert Shurtleff) (1760–1827) Continental soldier

Sampson was the only woman known by good evidence to have served as a soldier during the Revolution—not a camp follower who came forward in an emergency, like Molly Pitcher, but a long-serving enlisted "man" who maintained a long disguise as a male under the name Robert Shurtleff. She was born in Plymouth, Massachusetts to a poor family and was indentured by her widowed mother at age 10 to a farmer at Middleboro. She finished her obligation in 1778 and for a while worked as a schoolteacher. She was motivated, however, to actively join the army and enlisted under the name Thomas Thayer in 1782. Unfortunately, she had chosen her own locale for her first attempt at male impersonation, and she was recognized after a drinking bout with her new comrades at a local tavern. Turned out of the ranks immediately, she was ostracized by her neighbors and ejected from her Baptist meeting. Undaunted, Sampson made a new set of masculine clothes and hiked to Uxbridge, where she succeeded in enlisting in the 4th Massachusetts Regiment as Robert Shurtleff.

Quite remarkably, she was able to carry off her role as a young male soldier for nearly a year and a half. Most of the actual fighting of the war had ceased with the American victory at Yorktown in 1781, but there were still pockets of loyalist resistance, and Sampson's unit was ordered to the Hudson River region, where she was involved in a skirmish near Tarrytown and was wounded in the head by a saber cut. She received a much more severe wound a few weeks later at a fight near East Chester, taking a musket ball in the thigh. In order to avoid detection, she nursed her own wound and refused treatment that might have revealed her true sex. She recovered and returned to duty, but while stationed in Philadelphia (perhaps as an orderly to General Samuel Patterson) she fell ill with a fever and her identity was discovered by the doctor who treated her.

After the facts of the case were announced, Sampson was discharged from the service in October 1783. She married Benjamin Gannett in 1785 and moved to Sharon, Massachusetts. However, she and her husband failed to prosper, and hard times prompted Sampson to apply to the Massachusetts state government for relief as a veteran, which she received after documentary collaboration by her former superior officers. She later was granted a pension from the federal government as compensation for her wartime service. After the turn of the century, Sampson took to the stage as a lecturer, recounting her experiences for a paying audience and finishing her routine with a uniformed marching drill. Her veteran's pension was increased in 1820, but she never cashed in on her notoriety and died nearly penniless in 1827. In an unusual twist,

her husband applied in 1837 for a widow's pension due to surviving spouses of Revolutionary War veterans. Although Sampson's official records had been destroyed by the British during the War of 1812, Congress granted the pension. In 1944, a World War II Liberty ship, the *Deborah Gannett*, was christened in honor of the only recognized woman Revolutionary veteran, albeit the honor was accorded under her married name. *Further reading:* Elizabeth Evans, *Weathering the Storm: Women of the American Revolution* (New York, 1975); A. Keller, "The Private Deborah Sampson," *American History Illustrated* 11 (November 1976), 30–33; Julia W. Stickley, "The Records of Deborah Sampson Gannett, Woman Soldier of the Revolution," *Prologue* 4 (1974), 233–41.

SANDS, Comfort (1748–1834) Merchant A native of New York, Sands was active in the West Indies trade during the decade before the Revolution and actively supported the nonimportation agreements in resistance to British attempts to regulate colonial trade. He sat in the New York provincial assemblies and was a member of both the New York Committee of Safety and the state constitutional convention in 1777. He was auditor of New York from 1776 to 1782. A banker and prominent merchant in New York after the war, he went bankrupt in 1801.

SANDWICH, John Montagu, Earl of (1718–1792) British government official A man whose name lives because he invented what became a staple of American cuisine, Sandwich was considered in his own day (and among historians since) to be the embodiment of all that was wrong with the 18th-century British system of government. As first lord of the Admiralty during the American Revolution, he set a standard for inefficiency, venality and personal dissolution (he invented the sandwich in order to stay at a gaming table without interruption for a meal).

He inherited his grandfather's earldom when only 11 years old, attended Eton and Cambridge (leaving the university in 1737 without a degree), and spent two years on a grand tour of the Continent before returning home to take his seat in the House of Lords in 1741. From that year onward, Sandwich was seldom far from political power, whether in office or out. He held a formal commission in the army, eventually rising to full general's rank, but spent little time on active duty in favor of diplomatic or government posts. In February 1748, he became first lord of the Admiralty when his political patron, the Duke of Bedford, received the office of secretary of state. Although several needed reforms were put in place during his first tenure as head of the navy, most were due to the actions of his subordinates, to whom he left almost all the work of the office. With the fall of Bedford's government in 1751, Sandwich relinquished his place. He filled minor offices for the following months but eventually again reached a place of power as a secretary of state. He again became first lord of the Admiralty in 1771 and held the post until the end of the American war.

While no Georgian government office was a paragon of efficiency, Sandwich's admiralty was particularly noted for the vast amount of stealing, corruption and feeding at the public trough that it harbored. The building, supplying, manning and dispatching of ships were slow and below the standard needed to fight the multi-theater naval war Britain faced in the 1770s and 1780s. Many of the seemingly powerful British ships were little more than floating wrecks (the *Royal George* sank at anchorage when a large part of its bottom fell out). Sandwich often seemed to care much more for gambling and the high life than for his responsibilities as first lord. He was also intensely political, and he favored naval officers who could and would support his position regardless of their fighting abilities. His involvement in the disagreement between Keppel and Palliser in 1778 added greatly to the near paralysis of the navy at a crucial juncture, and by the end of the American war, many officers of the first rank refused to serve while Sandwich remained head of the Admiralty. His standing was damaged badly in 1779, when his mistress of 16 years was murdered by a disappointed suitor and the scandal of Sandwich's private life became public. He persevered in office, however, until 1782 and the end of Lord North's long hold on power. Sandwich lived the rest of his life in retirement. *Further reading: Gerald S. Brown, Jemmy Twitcher: A Life of the Fourth Earl of Sandwich, 1718–1792 (London, 1962).*

SAYRE, Stephen (1736–1818) American diplomatic agent, businessman

A minor but colorful figure, Sayre was born at Southampton, Long Island and graduated from the College of New Jersey. In 1757, he went to London, joined a mer-

cantile house, and acquired the manners and attitudes of a successful British merchant. His employer, Denys de Berdt, acted on occasion as colonial agent in London for Massachusetts, and Sayre returned briefly to America to solicit more business. In 1770, de Berdt died, and Sayre and his new partners opened a bank in London. He attempted to get the appointment as Massachusetts' agent but failed, although he worked unofficially on behalf of the colony and for the American cause in general. His efforts, including a pamphlet called *The Englishman Deceived*, finally aroused the ire of the British government, and in October 1775, he was arrested on charges of treason and lodged in the Tower of London. The charges were dropped after a few days, and Sayre then brought a successful suit against a member of the government for false imprisonment. His banking business was in ruin, however, so Sayre left for Paris, where he attached himself to Arthur Lee as a private secretary. Sayre accompanied Lee to Berlin in 1777, remaining behind after Lee's departure. He then began a series of unofficial or semi-official visits to European capitals: Copenhagen, Stockholm and St. Petersburg. For many years after, Sayre petitioned the Congress and its successor governments for payment for his diplomatic services, although with scant success. He returned to America after the war, married wealth and set himself up on an estate in New Jersey. In 1807, he finally received payment for service as Lee's secretary but nothing for his other efforts.

SCAMMELL, Alexander (1747–1781) Continental officer

An engaging and widely popular officer, Scammell did not quite live to see the triumph of American arms. He was born in Mendon, Massachusetts and raised by the pastor of the local Congregational church after his father's death when the boy was six years old. He graduated from Harvard in 1769, and after a stretch of teaching in Plymouth and Kingston, Massachusetts, Scammell moved to Portsmouth, New Hampshire to become a surveyor. He was a law student in the office of John Sullivan in Durham, New Hampshire when the War of Independence began. Scammell attached himself to Sullivan, who had been appointed a brigadier general in the new Continental Army, acting as the general's aide-de-camp with the rank of brigade major and holding an independent commission as colonel of New Hampshire militia. Scammell took part in the siege at Boston and went on the invasion of Canada as part of Sullivan's military entourage.

During the summer of 1776, Scammell was in New York and became acting aide to commander in chief George Washington. His most notable act during the New York campaign was a bad mistake in carrying premature evacuation orders to Thomas Mifflin on the night of August 29, nearly causing Mifflin to withdraw too soon from covering the night retreat of the army from Long Island to Manhattan. After a brief tour as a brigade major for Charles Lee, Scammell was given command in November 1776 of the new 3rd New Hampshire Regiment. He led his unit in the northern campaign against General John Burgoyne, receiving a slight wound at the second battle of Saratoga.

In January 1778, Scammell was named by the Congress as adjutant general of the Continental Army, and he served for the following three years as one of Washington's chief staff officers, gaining a widespread popularity among other officers, many of whom wrote fondly of him after the war. In the course of his duties as adjutant general, Scammell arrested Charles Lee after Lee's disgraceful behavior at Monmouth, and he was given charge of the execution of the spy Major John André. In January 1781, Scammell resigned his staff position and took command of the 1st New Hampshire. During the army's move to Virginia to trap and lay siege to Lord Cornwallis, he commanded a unit of light infantry. On September 30, as field officer of the day, Scammell led a reconnoitering force toward the British lines, but he was surprised by a group of Banastre Tarleton's troops and was fatally wounded with a gunshot. Some accounts of the fray indicate he was shot after surrendering. He was paroled to the American lines but died in Williamsburg on October 6.

SCHAFFNER, George (d. circa 1795) Continental officer

A native of Lancaster, Pennsylvania, Schaffner enlisted in March 1776 in Atlee's Pennsylvania Musket Battalion, a unit of state troops (quasi-militia) that was part of the Flying Camp organized to support the New York campaign. He was promoted to ensign before taking part in the battle of Long Island, and the remnants of his unit were reorganized and fought at Trenton and Princeton. In February 1777, Schaffner became a lieutenant in Baron Ottendorf's corps, which was soon taken over by the French volunteer officer the Marquis de la Rouerie, known in America as Colonel Armand. The rest of Schaffner's life was connected closely with Armand, a fairly unlikely alliance between a Pennsylvania Dutchman and a French aristocrat. As part of Armand's Legion, Schaffner fought at Brandywine and Germantown, and by his mustering out in 1783, he was a major. He forsook his native land to travel to France with Armand when the latter returned to his home. With the coming of the French Revolution, Schaffner served at Armand's side and acted as liaison with French aristocratic émigrés in London. After Armand's death in early 1793, Schaffner apparently was killed while serving as an officer of the Vendée rebellion.

SCHUREMAN, James (1756–1824) Officer, delegate to Congress, legislator

Schureman was born in New Brunswick, New Jersey and became a merchant after his graduation from the College of New Jersey (Rutgers) in 1775 just as the War of Independence began. He served in the army, although his unit and rank are not specified. He launched a considerable public career after the Revolution, beginning with election to the state legislature in 1783. He served as a delegate to the Confederation Congress in 1786 and 1787, and after the formation of a new federal government, Schureman won repeated election to the U.S. Congress, as both a senator and representative. He interspersed federal office with service as mayor of New Brunswick. His final term in Congress ended in 1815.

SCHUYLER, Hon Yost. Loyalist

A man of obscure origins, Schuyler was a New York loyalist and apparently was regarded as a half-wit, although he seems at times to have been rather shrewd. He was captured by the patriots in 1777 and condemned to death, perhaps because of implication in a loyalist plot. For reasons that are not clear, Schuyler was with the force under Benedict Arnold that set out to relieve the Americans under siege by British commander Barry St. Leger at Fort Stanwix in August 1777. St. Leger had advanced separately from Canada with a strong force of loyalists and Indians, plus a few regulars, and hoped to divert American strength away from General John Burgoyne's main advance. He bogged down at Stanwix, however,

Philip Schuyler

laying siege to the garrison while fighting a battle with American general Nicholas Herkimer at Oriskany on August 6. Arnold was advancing toward Stanwix when he hit on the scheme of sending Schuyler forward in a ruse. With promises of a pardon if successful, Schuyler infiltrated among St. Leger's Indian auxiliaries and spread tales of Arnold's overwhelming strength and impending arrival. His efforts may have accelerated the defections already underway among the Indians. St. Leger was forced to withdraw late in August.

SCHUYLER, Philip (1733–1804) Continental general, delegate to Congress

A complex figure who mixed many fine abilities with less admirable traits, Schuyler was a member of the powerful, rich New York Dutch Schuyler clan. He was born to great wealth and reared as a gentleman, but he had a consuming interest in military affairs. He served in the Seven Years' War as a British captain, showing most promise as an organizer of supplies and administrator. He resigned his commission in 1757 but continued to supply the British army as a private commissary. He rejoined as a major the following year and fought in several engagements as well as retaining his role as a supplier. He went to England in 1761 to settle claims with the government. At the end of the Seven Years' War he inherited huge tracts of land in northern New York state, and he settled into life as a lord of the manor.

While he was a patriot from the beginning of the agitation against Great Britain, Schuyler disliked the more radical elements among the Sons of Liberty. He served as a commissioner in the disputes over

Vermont, and he alienated New Englanders with his decisions and what they considered to be his high-handed manners. For political reasons, Schuyler was one of the first major generals appointed by Congress in 1775, representing New York state. He was put in charge of the invasion of Canada, but the combination of his slow preparations and the resistance of the New England troops caused major problems. He was hit with an attack of chronic gout before the expedition set off, and Richard Montgomery marched north in his place. Schuyler then found himself embroiled in a dispute with Congress that further diminished his standing. He commanded the Northern Department in the face of General John Burgoyne's invasion, but when the British easily took Fort Ticonderoga, Congress replaced Schuyler with Horatio Gates. He resigned his generalship in 1779 but continued to work with Washington as an advisor and administrator. He was a delegate to Congress, involving himself in financial affairs. In later life, he was U.S. senator from New York. *Further reading:* Don R. Gerlach, *Proud Patriot: Philip Schuyler and the War for Independence* (Syracuse, N.Y., 1987).

SCOTT, Charles (c. 1739–1813) Continental general

An active and useful commander during the Revolution, Scott was born in Virginia and received little or no education (some accounts say he was virtually illiterate). With the beginning of open warfare with Great Britain in 1775, Scott raised troops in rural Virginia and commanded them as a volunteer force at Williamsburg. In early 1776, he was commissioned as a senior officer of the 2nd Virginia Regiment, but within a few weeks he was moved to colonel in command of the 5th Virginia. He was closely involved in the crucial campaign in New Jersey in late 1776 and early 1777, leading his troops effectively at both Trenton and Princeton, and he was promoted to brigadier general in April 1777, based on his performance at Princeton. He commanded a brigade at Brandywine with distinction but was criticized for deficiencies during the battle of Germantown. He formed part of Charles Lee's division at the battle of Monmouth in June 1778 and is the source of the account of how Washington swore at Lee's failure. Scott later testified against Lee at the latter's court-martial. In 1780, Scott was ordered south to reinforce Benjamin Lincoln's army in South Carolina, and he was captured with his men at the fall of Charleston. He was paroled but not exchanged by the British and thus was removed from further participation in the war. On his mustering out in 1783, he was brevetted to the rank of major general.

After the Revolution, Scott moved to Kentucky and became a leading political and military figure in what became a new state. He took part in almost all the Indian campaigns in the West during the 1790s, serving as a brigadier, and was at the head of 1,500 mounted volunteers during the battle of Fallen Timbers in 1794. He was elected governor of Kentucky in 1808 and served four terms. A county in Kentucky is named in his honor.

SCOTT, Gustavus (1753–1800) Delegate to Congress, attorney Born in Prince William County, Virginia, Scott went to England to study law at the Middle Temple. He was admitted to the bar in London in 1772 and then returned to America, settling in Maryland. He was a member of the Maryland Convention in 1775 and the following year drafted the new Maryland state constitution as a member of the constitutional convention. He was elected as a delegate to the Confederation Congress in 1784. His final public office was as commissioner of the District of Columbia in 1794.

SCOTT, John Morin (1730–1784) Delegate to Congress, militia officer, lawyer Scott was an active radical leader in New York City before and during the Revolution. He attended Yale, graduating in 1746, and was admitted to the New York City bar in 1752. He wrote articles on behalf of dissident Presbyterians during the early 1750s that were published in New York newspapers, and in 1761 he penned an article signed "Freeman" against the Stamp Act. He was also an alderman of the city during the same period. Associated with the more radical faction of New Yorkers, Scott was one of the founders of the Sons of Liberty in the city and sat in the provincial congresses from 1775 to 1777, helping to pull New York deeply into the revolutionary struggle. With the British invasion of New York in 1776, Scott took a commission as a brigadier in the militia and fought at the battle of Long Island. In 1778, he was appointed secretary of state, having previously turned down election as justice of the supreme court, and the following year he was sent as a delegate to Congress, serving until 1782.

SCUDDER, Nathaniel (1733–1781) Delegate to Congress, militia officer, physician Scudder was born in Monmouth County, New Jersey, graduated from Princeton, and practiced medicine in his home region before the Revolution. He was an active member of his local committee of safety and was sent as a representative to the New Jersey Provincial Congress of 1774. Two years later, he was elected to the wartime general assembly and chosen as speaker. He also was commissioned as a lieutenant colonel in the state militia and apparently took the field intermittently with his Monmouth County regiment—not surprisingly at the battle of Monmouth, for example. He served as one of the New Jersey delegates to the Continental Congress from 1777 to 1779, and he supported ratification of the Articles of Confederation by lobbying in the state legislature. He was killed by a British raiding party near Shrewsbury, New Jersey on October 17, 1781.

SEABURY, Samuel (1728–1796) Loyalist clergyman Seabury, who became the first Episcopal bishop of America, was born the son of a Congregationalist minister in Groton, Connecticut. His father converted to the Anglican church in 1730 and moved to New London and then Hempstead, Long Island. The younger Seabury graduated from Yale in 1748 and studied at the University at Edinburgh from 1752 to 1753. There were no bishops in America, so Seabury was ordained into the Episcopal priesthood in late 1753 before he left England. He returned to the colonies the following spring as a missionary to a congregation in New Brunswick, New Jersey. He entered the fierce conflict over control of King's College (later Columbia) in New York City—a struggle that symbolized many of the differences among Anglicans in America—and began to publish articles and pamphlets in which he consistently supported the conservative side, upholding the duty of loyal church members and clergy to support the crown and the royal government. After serving on Long Island, Seabury was appointed as rector of a parish at Westchester, New York in 1767. He continued to write for publication, urging the establishment of an American episcopate, a move that was violently opposed by the growing patriot faction in the state. By 1775, Seabury was one of the more prominent loyalists in New York, and he was forced into hiding after the outbreak of armed hostilities at Lexington and Concord. In November, he was captured by patriots led by New York radical Isaac Sears and thrown in jail in Connecticut until the end of the year.

When the British army captured New York in the late summer of 1776, Seabury moved back to the city and spent the remainder of the war as a loyal clergyman, acting as chaplain for Edmund Fanning's King's American Regiment and for a British hospital. Despite his unequivocal loyalism, after the Revolution Seabury moved almost immediately to the head of the Episcopalians in America, who hoped to repair their sundered church organization. He was selected in 1783 by the clergy of Connecticut to become their bishop, and he traveled to England seeking consecration. The English church establishment refused his application, so he went to Scotland and was consecrated as a bishop by the Scottish bishops. He returned to New London and assumed office as bishop of Connecticut and Rhode Island, forsaking politics in favor of building up the Anglican churches that had been damaged by the Revolution. He was extremely active and ordained dozens of new priests and confirmed thousands of new members while traveling extensively throughout New England and the middle states. By the time the first general convention of American Episcopalians established a new organization in 1789, Seabury had laid the foundation for an independent church in the United States. *Further reading:* Bruce Steiner, *Samuel Seabury: A Study in the High Church Tradition* (Athens, Ohio, 1972).

SEARLE, James (1733–1797) Delegate to Congress, merchant

Searle was born in New York City. At age 13 he went to Madeira, Spain as agent for his brother's firm, John Searle & Company, and he remained there until 1762 when he returned to America. He settled in Philadelphia and continued his mercantile career. He was—as might be expected—opposed to Britain's efforts to restrict the American economy and became a patriot. He was commissioned a lieutenant colonel in the state militia in 1776 but expended most of his efforts as manager of a government lottery until 1778, when he was elected as a delegate to Congress from Pennsylvania. He served in Congress until 1780, the year he was appointed to serve on an embassy from the state of Pennsylvania to Holland and Spain to secure a loan for the state government—a task at which he failed. Following the war, he went bankrupt but secured a post as American agent for a Spanish trading firm.

SEARS, Isaac (1730–1786) Patriot leader, privateer

Sears was one of the most important rebel leaders during the first months of the Revolution, when he held New York City for the patriot cause. Born in Massachusetts, he grew up in Norwich, Connecticut and became a seafarer. He sailed as a privateer during the Seven Years' War, and afterward he moved to New York City, where he set up business as a shipmaster and sailor. Sears led popular resistance from the earliest days of anti-British agitation in New York and the New England colonies. He was the principal leader of the Sons of Liberty in New York and was known as "King" Sears because of his command of the mob. He served on virtually every patriot committee from the mid-1760s onward. In 1774, he personally headed a mob that refused to allow tea to land in New York Harbor and destroyed part of the cargo. He also proposed in the same year that delegates meet to discuss resistance, a notion that led directly to the first Continental Congress. He was arrested in New York by the British authorities a few days before Lexington and Concord but was freed by a mob before he reached jail. With the outbreak of hostilities in Massachusetts, Sears organized a force of 350 irregulars in New York, seized the city's arms arsenal, closed the port to British shipping and took control under virtual martial law. He and his followers raised and trained troops and harassed and seized loyalists throughout the New York area. He turned over control of the city to George Washington in 1776 when the Continental Army moved in to defend the city. When the Americans were defeated and the British occupied New York City for the rest of the war, Sears moved his base of operations to Boston and became a privateer. After the conclusion of the peace in 1783, he returned to New York and his shipping business. He died while on a voyage to China in 1786.

SEDGWICK, Theodore (1746–1813) Military secretary, delegate to Congress, legislator

Although he was born in West Hartford, Connecticut, most of Sedgwick's career was associated with Massachusetts. He attended Yale but was kicked out for undisciplined behavior, although the school later awarded him his degree retroactively. Headed early for a career as a parson, he changed his mind and studied the law under a cousin in Great Barrington, Massachusetts and set up practice in Sheffield in 1766. No great proponent of independence, Sedgwick nonetheless served as secretary to his local patriotic meeting in 1775, and in the following year he became secretary to General John Thomas. When Thomas died in mid-1776, Sedgwick returned to civilian pursuits and began a career in legislative office. He sat in the Massachusetts lower house, alternating with a place in the upper, during most of the 1780s. He rose to speaker of the lower house in 1788, following a three-year stint as a Massachusetts delegate to the enfeebled Confederation Congress. He was one of the more aggressive state officials in putting down Shays' Rebellion and rode his reputation to election to the federal House of Representatives, serving in the first four congresses, from 1789 to 1795. He ran as a Federalist for an unexpired term in the Senate and won in 1799. He then returned to the House and became speaker in 1800. Sedgwick was appointed to the bench of the Massachusetts Supreme Court in 1802 and served until his death. *Further reading:* Richard Welch, *Theodore Sedgwick, Federalist: A Political Portrait* (Middletown, Conn., 1965).

SÉGUR, Louis Phillippe, Comte de (1753–1830) French officer Ségur was the son of a marshal of France and a relative and friend of the Marquis de Lafayette. He entered the French royal army in 1769 and was a lieutenant colonel by 1776, when he attempted to join Lafayette in coming to America as a volunteer, but was prevented by his family. He remained in France as an advocate of the American cause at court until 1781, when he was appointed as a senior officer of the Regiment Sissonnois and dispatched to the United States aboard the *Gloire* in April. At the French withdrawal, Ségur remained in the New World, traveling to South America and the West Indies. In 1784, he was appointed as minister to Russia, where he remained during the French Revolution, living as a freelance writer after the fall of the old regime at home. He returned to France and served the French Empire after 1800. *Further reading:* Louis Phillippe Ségur, *Memoirs and Recollections of Count Louis Phillippe de Ségur* (London, 1825; reprinted New York, 1970).

SEIXAS, Gershom Mendes (1746–1816) Clergyman Born in New York City, Seixas in 1760 became the rabbi of the Shearith Israel Congregation in the city, a synagogue formed by families from Spain and Portugal. He was a strict observer of Jewish custom and law and enforced orthodoxy on his congregation while at the same time becoming a spokesman for the Jewish community in America. His congregation was split over the issue of the Revolution, however, and Seixas was forced to flee New York when the British took the city in 1776. He moved to Stratford, Connecticut and could not prevent loyalist members of his New York congregation from signing oaths and working for the British during the war. In 1780, Seixas moved to Philadelphia and became rabbi of the Jewish congregation organized there. He returned to New York four years later and resumed his post at Shearith Israel.

SENEY, Joshua (1756–1798) Delegate to Congress, legislator, jurist Born near Church Hill, Maryland, Seney graduated from the College of Philadelphia in 1773 and took up the practice of law in Queen Anne's County, Maryland. There is no record of any service during the Revolution, but he was high sheriff of the county in 1779. After the war, Seney was elected to the state legislature and was a delegate to the Confederation Congress in 1788. He was subsequently elected to the U.S. House of Representatives, serving from 1789 until he resigned in 1792 to accept an appointment as judge of the third judicial district of Maryland.

SENTER, Isaac (1755–1799) Physician, militia surgeon Senter was born in New Hampshire but lived most of his life in Rhode Island. He studied medicine as a teenager with a local doctor and volunteered for Benedict Arnold's expedition to Canada in 1775 as a surgeon. He kept a diary during the horrendous journey across the north woods, recording the physical travails of the men with a trained eye. After his return from the unsuccessful northern invasion, Senter joined the 3rd Rhode Island as a surgeon and subsequently became a hospital surgeon. From 1779 to 1781, he was surgeon general of the Rhode Island militia. After the war, he settled in Pawtucket as a doctor, and he later moved to Newport. His journal is often quoted in accounts of Arnold's expedition. *Further reading:* "The Journal of Isaac Senter, M.D., on a Secret

Expedition against Quebec, 1775," in Kenneth Roberts, *The March to Quebec* (New York, 1940).

SERGEANT, Jonathan Dickinson (1746–1793) Delegate to Congress, attorney, state official

Born in Newark, New Jersey, Sergeant graduated from the college at Princeton in 1762, then attended the college in Philadelphia, and was admitted to the New Jersey bar in 1767. He was very active from the beginning of the revolutionary conflict, both during the Stamp Act crisis and as a Son of Liberty. He was named as secretary of the first two New Jersey provincial congresses in 1774 and 1775 and was treasurer of the colony in the latter year. He was sent to Congress from New Jersey in February 1776 but was not present to sign the Declaration, having been replaced in June. He was reappointed as a delegate in November and served until he resigned in September 1777. He had actually moved his residence to Philadelphia during 1777 and was appointed as attorney general of Pennsylvania, serving until 1780. As a legal officer, he was vociferous in prosecuting loyalists and gained a reputation for ignoring the niceties of the law when proscribing adherents to the crown and seizing their property. After the war, he represented Pennsylvania in the controversy over land in Pennsylvania's Wyoming Valley.

SERLE, Ambrose (1742–1812) British official

Serle, who served for two years as civilian secretary to British admiral Richard Howe and kept a journal of his experiences, was in a position to view and assess the Revolution at first hand. The details of his biography have often been confused by historians. He was never a military man but served as a secretary to Lord Dartmouth and in the government bureaucracy of the mid-1770s. He held a place as a clerk of reports for the board of trade when he was seconded on leave to be Howe's civilian secretary in America, a post he filled from May 1776 to June 1778. During his time in America, first in New York City and then in Philadelphia, Serle was charged to deal with leading American loyalists such as Andrew Allen and Joseph Galloway, and his journal provides a great deal of insight on the position and activities of such men.

Serle himself began his tour of duty in America as a confirmed and rigid proponent of suppressing the rebels by force, after which a revised form of imperial government might be imposed. However, he grew increasingly disenchanted with the chances of military success and even more distressed by what he saw as the deficiencies of the loyalists. By the end of his stay in America the defeat of General John Burgoyne, the French-American alliance and the evacuation of Philadelphia had further convinced him that Britain had little hope of reclaiming its colonies. While in New York City in 1776 and 1777, Serle edited the political section of the *New-York Gazette,* but he was not in charge of controlling or censoring the New York press as is sometimes reported. He did converse extensively with American prisoners—notably generals Stirling and Sullivan—and gained further insight into the mind of the rebellion. Serle returned to England believing that the British cause in America was futile. *Further reading:* Edward H. Tatum, Jr., ed., *The American Journal of Ambrose Serle, Secretary to Lord Howe* (San Marino, Calif., 1940).

SEUME, Johann Gottfried (d. 1810) German mercenary conscript

Seume's memoirs of his conscripted service as a mercenary for the British is a classic source for historians and during the 19th century was popular grade-school reading in parts of Germany. Seume was a student at the University of Leipzig in 1781 when he decided to travel to Paris. He made the mistake of crossing into Hesse-Cassel on the way, and he was scooped up by a patrol seeking raw recruits to help fulfill the landgrave's contract with the British government to provide troops for the fighting in America. He was kidnapped and his student documents were destroyed. He later described the brutality and hardships of the Hessian service and his own helplessness—a portrait that was quite at odds with the traditional American textbook view of the Hessians as hardened, bloodthirsty professionals. (Two of Seume's friends were hung for conspiring to desert.) He and his fellow conscripts were loaded onto an English transport ship in the spring of 1782 "like sardines" with no room to stand or lie down. During the 22-week voyage, the food was, in Seume's words, "neither good, nor plentiful." Peas and pork comprised the staple diet, with groats and barley for variety. The occasional pudding was cooked in a mixture of half seawater, half fresh water. The men ate the worms in the rock-hard bread as a substitute for butter. Some of the ration biscuits had been captured by the British from the French during the Seven Years' War (which had ended 18 years before): "Now the English were feeding them to the Germans so that they could kill, God willing, the French under Rochambeau and Lafayette in America." The drinking water came from old casks, and "when a barrel was parbuckled and opened, the entire deck smelled like the rivers of Hades."

Seume arrived at Halifax after the terrible voyage and became a part of the grenadier regiment originally sent to America in 1776 under the hapless Johann Rall. The war in the colonies and virtually all the fighting were over by the time Seume's ship docked, however, and after a brief sojourn, he returned to Germany with his comrades. *Further reading:* "Memoirs of a Hessian Conscript: J. G. Seume's Reluctant Voyage to America," Margarete Woelfel, trans., *William and Mary Quarterly* 5 (1948), 553–70.

SEVIER, John (1745–1815) Militia officer, official

Sevier led part of the "over mountain men" at the battle of King's Mountain and was an important if controversial western pioneer and speculator. He was born in the Shenandoah Valley of Virginia, near the present-day city of New Market. He was a farmer, trader and surveyor (the typical training for frontier speculators) until 1773, when he moved with his wife and family to the Holston settlements in what is now Tennessee. Sevier became a leader among the Holston settlers, and with the coming of the Revolution, he succeeded in having North Carolina acknowledge jurisdiction over the western region. He attended the North Carolina Provincial Congress in 1776 and was commissioned as a lieutenant colonel of the militia (he was promoted to colonel the following year). He spent most of his time in the western settlements, but in 1780, he led a small force of frontier militia to join the rendezvous prior to the battle at King's Mountain. He was acknowledged as one of the principal leaders of the American force that destroyed the loyalists on October 7. Like most of the other frontiersmen at King's Mountain, Sevier and his men faded back to the west soon after the battle to look to their own affairs. He organized another small military force in 1781 and started eastward to join the army of Nathanael Greene, but the group evaporated before adding anything to Greene's Carolina campaigns.

Following the war, Sevier turned to empire building in the west, setting up what he hoped would be an independent "state" of Franklin in Tennessee. When the attempt collapsed in the face of opposition from North Carolina, Sevier became a virtual fugitive on the frontier. In 1788, he was pardoned, however, and elected to Congress. By the time Tennessee was admitted to the Union as a state, Sevier's political fortunes had recovered fully, and he was elected as the first governor of the new state in 1796. He was elected for a second gubernatorial term in 1803 and later was sent again to Congress, where he died in office as a U.S. representative. *Further reading:* Carl S. Driver, *John Sevier: Pioneer of the Old Southwest* (1931).

SEWALL, Jonathan (1728–1796) Loyalist official

After graduating from Harvard and a short stint as a schoolteacher in Salem, Massachusetts, Sewall moved to Charlestown and entered the practice of law. He was a close friend of John Adams during their days as young attorneys, and the relationship apparently never waned despite the gulf separating their political beliefs. In 1767, Sewall was appointed attorney general of Massachusetts. He chose to support the crown, apparently out of a combination of principle and fears that a rebellion would be defeated. He failed to dissuade Adams from attending the first Continental Congress, and soon thereafter he left Massachusetts for England. There he kept company with other displaced loyalists, writing to a friend: "The situation of American loyalists, I confess, is enough to have provoked Job's wife, if not Job himself; but we must be men, philosophers, and Christians; bearing up with patience, resignation, and fortitude, against unavoidable suffering." After the war, Sewall moved to Nova Scotia and served as a judge of admiralty.

SEWALL, Stephen (1747–1825) Educator

Born in York in the part of Massachusetts that is now the state of Maine, Sewall graduated from Harvard in 1761 and immediately became an instructor there in Hebrew. Three years later he was elevated to a professorship, which he held for 20 years. He represented Cambridge as a patriot in the Massachusetts General Court in 1777. He published several books during his career, including an early American Hebrew grammar.

SHARPE, William (1742–1818) Delegate to Congress, attorney

Born in Maryland, Sharpe

practiced law and worked as a surveyor in North Carolina before the Revolution. He attended the provincial congress in 1775 and was a delegate to the North Carolina state constitutional convention in 1776. He was sent to the Continental Congress from 1779 to 1782, and during the last year of his term he was also a member of the North Carolina House of Representatives.

SHAW, Nathaniel (1735–1782) Merchant, naval agent

Shaw was a New London, Connecticut trader with the West Indies before the Revolution and, like others of his commercial class, strongly opposed the British policies of the 1760s. He turned his mercantile experience to the use of the rebellion, negotiating for gunpowder in Europe on behalf of Connecticut in 1774, and after the outbreak of the war itself, he was appointed by the Continental Congress as prize agent in New London. He was also an agent for the exchange of naval prisoners and a provisioner of privateers. He served in the Connecticut Assembly for two terms. When the British force under Benedict Arnold (a native of the town and a former local trader) raided New London in 1781, it burned Shaw's wharves and warehouses.

SHAW, Samuel (1754–1794) Continental officer, diplomat

Born in Boston, Shaw came from Scots ancestry, and he worked in his father's merchant house until the beginning of the Revolution. He served as a lieutenant of artillery during the first years of the conflict, including the siege of Boston, the New York campaigns and all the major battles in New Jersey and Pennsylvania from Trenton to Monmouth. He was commissioned as a first lieutenant in the 3rd Continental Artillery in early 1777 and was promoted to captain 15 months later. He was an aide to Henry Knox during the final months of the Revolution, from mid-1782 until mustering out in November 1783. He kept a journal during the war, and it serves as a good source of information on the Newburgh "conspiracy" of disaffected officers when a mutiny against Congress was threatened. Following the war, Shaw returned to commerce and set up a trade route to the Orient. In 1786, he was appointed as the first U.S. consul to China. He served in Canton, with several trips home, until his death at sea. *Further reading: The Journals of Major Samuel Shaw, the First American Consul at Canton* (Boston, 1847).

SHAYS, Daniel (c. 1747–1825) Continental officer, militia soldier

Probably born at Hopkinton, Massachusetts, Shays served as a patriot officer during the Revolution, but his name is linked forever with a postwar, back-country tax rebellion in Western Massachusetts. He was a militiaman and began service immediately after the first battles of the war at Lexington and Concord, when he joined the Boston army and fought with conspicuous personal bravery as an enlisted man at the battle of Breed's Hill and Bunker Hill in June 1775. He also fought at many other subsequent battles, including with Ethan Allen at Fort Ticonderoga, at Saratoga and at the storming of Stony Point. He received a commission as captain in the 5th Massachusetts Regiment after raising a company of volunteers in January 1777. He resigned from the army in 1780 and settled in Pelham, Massachusetts, where he served on the local committee of safety.

With the drastic economic dislocations of the immediate postwar years, Shays found his own fortunes on the decline, and he somewhat reluctantly came to be one of the leaders of a large number of impoverished dissidents, centered in the western part of the state. Unable to pay taxes and hounded by foreclosures, the rebels—drawing strength from the recently demonstrated notion that taxation by remote authorities was a reason to take up arms—began a series of mob demonstrations and armed appearances in the summer of 1786. Eventually, the conflict centered on the federal arsenal at Springfield, Massachusetts, and a large, well-armed force under General Benjamin Lincoln finally subdued the Shayites (as they were known) in early 1787. Shays was pardoned and moved to New York state, where he died many decades later. *Further reading:* Alden T. Vaughn, "The 'Horrid and Unnatural Rebellion' of Daniel Shays," *American Heritage* 17 (June 1966), 50–81.

SHEFTHALL, Mordecai (1735–1795) Businessman, army commissary

Shefthall was born in Savannah, Georgia and was one of the prominent Jews in the colony before the war. He was a prosperous businessman and operated a sawmill, a tannery, several farms, a mercantile shop and a shipping business. As a strong opponent of the royal government, Shefthall was a leader among the patriots of Savannah who formed one of the few pockets of rebellion in the colony. He became the head of the committee that virtually took over the local government in Savannah after the expulsion of royal governor James Wright. In 1777, Shefthall was made commissary of the state militia, in charge of supplies and purchases. The following year, he was appointed to the rank of colonel and made deputy commissary general for the Continental Army forces in the state commanded by General Robert Howe. Unfortunately, a determined British invasion (and an inept American defense) led to the seizure of Savannah by British general Archibald Campbell in December 1778. Shefthall and his teenage son were captured and held in harsh conditions on a prison ship. They were eventually paroled and sent to Sunbury, Georgia. Harassed by loyalists, Shefthall escaped and fled to Charleston but was recaptured at sea and sent to Antigua. He was again paroled and made his way to Philadelphia, where he petitioned with only modest success for a payment from Congress in return for the large sums he had expended on behalf of the American cause. After the war, he returned to Savannah and resumed his business career. He left a brief memoir of his captivity. *Further reading:* Mordecai Shefthall, "In the Hands of the British," in Jacob Marcus, *Memoirs of American Jews, 1775–1865* (1955), 42–44.

SHELBURNE, William Petty, Earl of (1737–1805) British minister

A leader of the opposition during the Revolution and a proponent of conciliation with the American rebels, Shelburne came to office as prime minister between the defeat of British arms and the final conclusion of peace. He was born in Dublin, the heir of a grand Anglo-Irish family. After education at Oxford, he began a notable military career, serving in the Seven Years' War under James Wolfe in North America and on the Continent, most conspicuously at the battle of Minden. He was made one of the aides-de-camp to the king, a position of high honor. He was elected to Parliament in 1761 from boroughs in both England and Ireland, but he never sat in the House of Commons. His father's death in November elevated him to the family earldom (an Irish title, although there was also an English title of baron), and he moved immediately into the House of Lords. He was an ally of Charles Fox during the early 1760s and in 1763 took office under Grenville as president of the board of trade. Shelburne supported the elder William Pitt, who had one of his periodic fallings out with the king

before the end of 1763, and as a result of the rift, Shelburne resigned and retired temporarily from politics.

When Pitt returned to power in 1766, Shelburne took the post of secretary of state for the southern department, which carried specific responsibilities for colonial affairs. He worked assiduously to effect a conciliation with the Americans, acting in accord with Pitt's general policy, but the majority of the government worked crosswise, and Shelburne's efforts only further alienated the king and his party. He was relieved of responsibilities for colonial affairs by Hillsborough in 1768, but he continued in office, although increasingly at odds with his fellow cabinet members. When Pitt fell ill and resigned, Shelburne followed him out of office. Throughout most of the war Shelburne was in opposition, and he became a powerful voice among the out-of-office factions. When Lord North lost his majority in early 1782, following Lord Cornwallis' defeat, the king reluctantly sent for Shelburne, who refused to form a government and recommended the Earl of Rockingham instead. Shelburne became home secretary in the new government. When Rockingham died unexpectedly in the summer, Shelburne took his place and conducted the final peace negotiations. His treaties came under heavy fire from the king and his party, and in February 1783, Shelburne withdrew in favor of a coalition government. He later was created Marquis of Landsdowne. *Further reading:* John Norris, *Shelburne and Reform* (New York, 1963).

SHELBY, Evan (1720–1794) Frontiersman, militia officer

The father of Isaac Shelby, Evan was born in Wales and emigrated to Maryland at age 15. He lived as an adult in Virginia and at the Holston settlement on the western frontier of Virginia. He fought in the colonial wars for the British, after which he returned to the western regions. He fought in Lord Dunmore's War in 1774 and was present at the battle of Point Pleasant. During the American Revolution, Shelby served as an officer of the Virginia militia, mostly against the Chickamauga Indians in the West, although he is reported to have spent some time with the armies on the eastern seaboard. After the war, he took up farming in the region near modern-day Bristol, Tennessee.

SHELBY, Isaac (1750–1826) Militia officer, legislator, governor

Shelby was an effective fron-

Isaac Shelby

tier political and military leader during the Revolution, who did much to organize the new regions west of the Alleghenies into part of the young United States after the War of Independence and returned to military prominence during the War of 1812. He was born and raised in Maryland, but his family (he was the son of Evan Shelby) moved to the Holston settlements in modern-day Tennessee in 1773. Shelby served in the Virginia forces during Lord Dunmore's War, fighting at Point Pleasant in 1774 and acting as second commander of the subsequent post established on the site of the battle.

Although commissioned as a captain in the Virginia militia, Shelby spent the first years of the Revolutionary War in the West, surveying land in what is now Kentucky for the Transylvania Company and acting as a supplier for western expeditions, including the campaigns of George Rogers Clark in the Illinois Country. The fall of Charleston to the British in the spring of 1780 brought Shelby actively into the warfare in the East. He was appointed as a colonel of militia by the state of North Carolina (whose government scarcely existed at the time), and he began a series of movements against the British and the loyalists. Shelby was good at recruiting frontier militia, known as "over mountain men," and getting them to journey east to fight. His first notable victory was at Thickety Fort, South Carolina in July 1780, when he induced a loyalist stronghold to surrender without a battle. Over the following weeks, Shelby joined forces with several other leaders, notably John Sevier and Elijah Clarke,

to administer a series of brisk defeats to the backcountry loyalists and British regulars who hoped to consolidate the British hold on the Carolinas. After a great deal of maneuvering, marching and reforming of forces, Shelby, Sevier and Virginia troops under Arthur Campbell and Charles McDowell brought to bay a large force of loyalists commanded by British officer Patrick Ferguson at King's Mountain. On October 7, 1780, the combined militia forces attacked Ferguson and completely defeated the loyalists in a victory that began a skein of recovery for the American fortunes in the South. Shelby demonstrated not only personal bravery at King's Mountain but skillful planning and leadership as well.

In 1781, Shelby was elected to the North Carolina legislature, but he remained mostly occupied in the West. He moved the following year to the Kentucky region, where he lived the remainder of his life. He was active as one of the organizers of the new state and became the first governor in 1792, serving one term. He came out of retirement in 1812 with the advent of a new war with the British and led a large contingent of Kentuckians to join the American forces at the battle of the Thames in October of the following year. Turning down an offer to become secretary of war, Shelby returned to Kentucky and once again retired. *Further reading:* Sylvia Worbel and George Grider, *Isaac Shelby: Kentucky's First Governor and Hero of Three Wars* (1974); Archibald Henderson, *Isaac Shelby: Revolutionary Patriot and Border Hero* (Raleigh, N.C., 1918).

SHELDON, Elisha (b. 1740) Continental general

Sheldon was a commander of Washington's little-used cavalry arm. He was born in Lyme, Connecticut and moved to Salisbury in 1759 to farm. He was something of a roisterer and was drummed out of his local church meeting for "lascivious conduct and breach of the Sabbath." He was a captain of a local cavalry militia troop before the war and was promoted to major and given command of a troop of Connecticut light horse in 1776. His first attempt at service in the New York campaign was frustrated after only a few weeks, but he returned to Washington's army in October and by December was selected to form a new mounted unit as a Continental colonel. He commanded the 2nd Continental Dragoons—drawn mostly from Connecticut—until the end of the war, reaching the rank of brevet brigadier general in 1780. Washington had little use for mounted troops, and Sheldon's cavalry and horse dragoons were used sparingly during most of the major campaigns, although they sparred with Banastre Tarleton in the summer of 1779. After early 1780, Sheldon was assigned mostly to mobile guard duty in New York along the Hudson River. *Further reading:* John T. Hayes, *Connecticut's Revolutionary Cavalry: Sheldon's Horse* (Chester, Conn., 1975).

SHEPARD, William (1737–1817) Continental general, legislator

Shepard was born in Westfield, Massachusetts, the son of a tanner. He served as an officer in the Seven Years' War and was thus an experienced soldier by the time of the American War of Independence. He was a farmer near Westfield (and a member of the local committee of correspondence) when the fighting began. In May 1775, soon after the battles at Lexington and Concord, Shepard was made lieutenant colonel of Daniel's Massachusetts Regiment, which marched to join the army around Boston. In January of the following year, Shepard became colonel of the 3rd Continental Infantry, a Massachusetts regiment initially commanded by Ebenezer Learned, and he was wounded at the battle of Long Island in August. His outstanding performance as the 3rd's commander was at Pell's Point, New York in October 1776, when he and his Massachusetts regiment helped John Glover delay General William Howe's advance in a nasty, hard-fought engagement that saw Shepard's men bring the British regulars to a complete standstill. In January 1777, Shepard took command of the new 4th Massachusetts. The regiment fought at the two decisive battles at Saratoga in the fall and spent the following winter at Valley Forge as part of John Glover's brigade.

Shepard more or less retired from field command at that stage, although he continued on the rolls as colonel of the 4th until the end of the war. He resigned in January 1783 but was retroactively brevetted as a brigadier general in September. He returned to farming after the war but was recalled to duty during Shays' Rebellion as a major general of state militia, and he commanded the defense of the Springfield arsenal against the Western Massachusetts rebels in January 1778. He was elected as U.S. representative from Massachusetts in 1797 and served a total of three terms, retiring thereafter to his farm.

SHERBURNE, John Samuel (1757–1830) Soldier, official, jurist

Born in Portsmouth, New Hampshire, Sherburne graduated from Dartmouth and Harvard in 1776 and set up a practice in his home town. The Revolutionary War called him to duty, however, and he served as a staff officer in the Continental Army. During the French-American campaign to take Newport, Rhode Island in 1778, Sherburne was severely wounded at fighting around Butts Hill and subsequently lost a leg. He was elected to the U.S. House of Representatives from New Hampshire in 1793 and later served as district attorney for the state. In 1804, he was appointed a judge of the U.S. District Court in New Hampshire, and he presided from that bench for the next 26 years.

SHERMAN, Roger (1721–1793) Delegate to Congress, jurist

The embodiment of the "old Puritan" (as John Adams called him) in New England politics and a behind-the-scenes legislative power, Sherman had the unique distinction to be the only man to sign all four great documents of the Revolution: the Articles of Association, the Declaration of Independence, the Articles of Confederation and the Constitution.

A self-made man, he was born on a farm in Massachusetts and moved to New Milford, Connecticut at age 21. He was trained as a cobbler but educated himself and became a surveyor, eventually amassing large land holdings and a considerable fortune. Before the Revolution he was a political conservative and held multiple executive, legislative and judicial offices in Connecticut. Sherman was lukewarm toward the agitation of the colonies against Great Britain until the crisis came, yet he thereafter was ever at the center of the political side of the Revolution. When elected to the Continental Congress in 1774, he was not a young radical but an experienced, hard-working and widely-respected veteran of public affairs. He served in Congress from 1774 until 1781 and again in 1783–84, making him one of the most stable members of the legislative body. Sherman was not an eloquent speaker, but he worked assiduously in committees and often exerted more real influence than his more flamboyant contemporaries. Sherman's most prominent assignment in the early days of the Revolution was on the committee that drafted the Declaration of Independence, but he also served on the committee

Roger Sherman

of ways and means, the board of war and ordnance, the treasury board and the committee on Indian affairs, as well as the committee that drafted the Articles of Confederation. In the estimation of several of his colleagues, he was the most influential member of Congress by the end of his service.

In 1784, Sherman returned to Connecticut and took up public office as a judge of the superior court and mayor of New Haven. He was called back to national service with the constitutional convention of 1787, where one of his greatest achievements was to introduce the idea of dual representation (the "Connecticut Compromise"). He was subsequently elected to the House of Representatives and helped draft the Judiciary Act of 1789, which established the federal court system. He was later appointed as senator from Connecticut, holding the office at his death. Twice married, Sherman fathered 15 children. *Further reading:* Roger S. Boardman, *Roger Sherman: Signer and Statesman* (1938; reprinted New York, 1971).

SHIPPEN, Edward (1729–1806) Jurist   A member of a wealthy and influential Quaker family of Philadelphia, Shippen remained in office during and after the Revolution, despite flirting with loyalism and despite the fact that his daughter, Margaret, married Benedict Arnold and shared in the traitor's conspiracy and desertion. Shippen's father, the chief justice of Pennsylvania, sent him to London in the 1740s to study law. On his return in 1750, Shippen soon made a success of his practice and began to accumulate public offices, becoming a judge of the Court of Vice-Admiralty in 1752. He was also a member of the Philadelphia Common Council, clerk of the City Court, and, by 1762, prothonotary of the Pennsylvania Supreme Court. He had little faith in the success of the Revolution, but he never completely broke with the forces of patriotism in Pennsylvania. During the occupation of Philadelphia, Shippen was on good terms with the British but made no overt moves to embrace the royal cause. He apparently frowned on the match between Margaret and Arnold (who was American commander in Philadelphia) but allowed the marriage to proceed nonetheless. After the war, Shippen resumed his role in public office, moving through a series of judicial posts until he became chief justice of the state supreme court in 1799. He suffered the ignominy of impeachment by his political enemies in 1804 but was acquitted on the charges.

SHIPPEN, William (the Elder) (1712–1801) Delegate to Congress, physician   The father of the William Shippen who was Continental surgeon general, the elder Shippen was born in Philadelphia and was a leading light of the medical profession in the city. He helped form both the Philadelphia Academy and the College of Philadelphia, which became two of the constituent parts of the University of Philadelphia and the first U.S. medical school after the Revolution. He also helped begin the College of New Jersey, which eventually became Princeton. He was a delegate to the Continental Congress in 1779 and 1780.

SHIPPEN, William (1736–1808) Physician, official   Shippen was one of the better-trained doctors in the colonies who served (or attempted to serve) the medical needs of the Continental Army. He was a native of Philadelphia and a graduate of Princeton. He took his medical training in Edinburgh, earning an M.D. in 1761, instead of simply studying with an older doctor as did most physicians in America during the early 18th century. He practiced in Philadelphia and was interested in advancing medical education, establishing courses in midwifery and anatomy and, beginning in 1765, teaching at the medical school at the College of Philadelphia (which eventually became the University of Pennsylvania medical college—for decades the foremost training ground of doctors in America).

Shippen was one of the group of influential Philadelphia doctors that vied among themselves for power during the Revolution. He, Benjamin Rush and John Morgan jockeyed to become the directors of medical service for the Continental Army after the dismissal of traitor Benjamin Church in 1775. Morgan was the first to serve, but when he was dismissed, Shippen—who had devised an overall plan for medical service in collaboration with Dr. John Cochran—was appointed to take his place. The position was not a comfortable one. Rush, a jealous rival for power, worked behind the scenes in Congress to displace Shippen, and the regimental surgeons in the field deeply resented the attempt to establish a strong central medical department for the army. In 1777, after only a brief tenure, Shippen was turned out of office in favor of Cochran.

SHREVE, Israel (d. 1799) Continental officer

Shreve commanded the 2nd New Jersey Regiment of the Continental Line from its formation in 1776 until his confused resignation in January 1781. He was still on duty in that month when the regiment joined the mutinies afflicting the army in its winter quarters. His replacement, Elias Dayton, had not yet appeared, and Shreve took no steps to quell the mutiny and appears to have tried to ignore it altogether, which drew the well-expressed ire of George Washington. The regiment was reorganized before the Yorktown campaign, but Shreve was by that stage long gone.

SHULDHAM, Molyneux (c. 1717–1798) British admiral

The exact birthdate of Shuldham, the son of a parson, was obscured when he apparently lied about his age to qualify for promotion to lieutenant in the Royal Navy in 1739. He had gone to sea as a captain's boy at a very early age. He fought in the long series of wars during the 1740s and 1750s, with some credit but several bad patches, including losing a ship to the French and serving time as their prisoner in 1756. He was more successful as a captain in the West Indies during the latter stages of the Seven Years' War, however, and after a three-year tour as commodore and commander in chief of the Newfoundland naval station, he was made rear admiral and appointed commander in chief of the coast of North America. He was the ranking naval officer in Boston—having been promoted to vice admiral—when the war broke out with the Americans, and he was responsible for holding the port and evacuating the British garrison. He was relieved by Lord William Howe in June 1776 and returned to England to be port admiral at Plymouth.

SHURTLEFF, Robert. *See* SAMPSON, Deborah.

SILLIMAN, Gold Selleck (1732–1790) Militia general

Born in Fairfield, Connecticut, Silliman graduated from Yale and practiced law and served as a crown attorney before the Revolution. He was the commander of a local body of militia cavalry and took rank as a militia brigadier general after 1776. He was mostly concerned with patrolling the southwestern border of Connecticut, where the loyalists of Westchester County, New York spilled over and caused constant irritation and concern for patriot towns and farms. He also fought with the main army during the New York campaigns of 1776 and opposed the British raid on Danbury in 1777. He was captured at his home by loyalists in 1779 and was held in New York City until paroled the following year.

SIMCOE, John Graves (1752–1806) British officer

Simcoe was born in Northamptonshire, the son of a Royal Navy captain who died in the British assault on Quebec when the young Simcoe was only seven years old. He received a good preparatory education at Exeter and Eton and entered Oxford in 1769, but he left to join the army as an ensign two years later. At the beginning of the American war, Simcoe was adjutant of the 40th Regiment of Foot, which served at Boston (arriving in June 1775) and subsequently throughout the New York and Pennsylvania campaigns. Simcoe was badly wounded at the battle of Brandywine in September 1777 but was rewarded with a promotion to major and given command of the Queen's Rangers, a regiment of loyalists originally raised by Robert Rogers. Simcoe led the Rangers, who specialized in scouting (what a British source describes as "Indian" tactics), during the remainder of the active war, operating from New York as a mixed legion of dragoons and light infantry on long-range raids. The unit's most notable engagement was at the taking of Stony Point and Verplanck's Point in the summer of 1779. In October, Simcoe ran into an

American ambush and was wounded and captured, but he was exchanged almost immediately. At the end of that year, Simcoe and his regiment were sent south as part of the invasion of Virginia under Benedict Arnold.

By this stage, Simcoe had been promoted to the local rank of lieutenant colonel and his presence was intended to restrain Arnold, whom the British high command did not entirely trust. Simcoe's rangers were effective against the ill-organized Virginia militia, and they roamed the countryside almost at will, raiding Richmond and Charles City and pushing back Friedrich von Steuben at Petersburg. When Lord Cornwallis brought his army into the state and retreated to Yorktown, Simcoe (along with Banastre Tarleton) was assigned to hold the Gloucester side of the river, and he surrendered there in October 1781.

He returned to England the same year and was out of public life until 1791, when he entered Parliament. He was then appointed as lieutenant governor of Canada, taking control of the new province of Upper Canada. His administration was only a moderate success (he did not get along with his council nor with Sir Guy Carleton, the governor general), and he left in 1794 to become commander at Santo Domingo with the army rank of major general. He commanded at Plymouth in 1801 and was named as commander in chief of India in 1806, but he became ill at sea, turned back, and died shortly after landing in England. *Further reading:* D. C. Scott, *John Graves Simcoe* (1905; revised, 1926).

SIMITIÈRE, Pierre Du. See DU SIMITIÈRE, Pierre.

SIMON, Joseph (d. 1804) Merchant Simon was the leader and principal merchant among the several Jews living in Lancaster, Pennsylvania at the time of the Revolution. He operated a local store and did a volume of trade with the Indians to the west, shipping goods to Philadelphia. He was also a land speculator and owned tracts in the Illinois and Ohio territories. During the Revolutionary War, Simon supplied rifles, ammunition, clothes and provisions to the Continental Army and the Pennsylvania militia. Following the war, most of the Jewish residents of Lancaster left for other places, but Simon remained until his death after the turn of the century.

SISSON, Jack (c. 1743–1821) Continental and militia soldier Sisson, a black man, served with the Rhode Island militia under Colonel William Barton and was one of the group of 40 picked men led by Barton in a raid to capture British general Richard Prescott in 1777. The plan was to seize Prescott, commander of the British forces holding Newport, and effect an exchange for American general Charles Lee. Barton and his men rowed to the British base under cover of night and stole up on Prescott's house. Barton and Sisson silenced the sentry and burst into Prescott's bedroom, catching the general in his nightclothes. They hauled him off and eventually the exchange was made. Sisson (whose first name is also given as "Tack") later served as a private under Christopher Greene in the 1st Rhode Island Regiment. He died in Plymouth, Massachusetts.

SITGREAVES, John (1757–1802) Delegate to Congress, officer, state official, jurist Sitgreaves was born in England, attended Eton, and emigrated to New Bern, North Carolina, where he studied law and began a practice. He served as a lieutenant during the war and was an aide to Richard Caswell. He was appointed as a commissioner in charge of confiscated property, having served in 1778 and 1779 as clerk of the North Carolina senate. In 1785, Sitgreaves was elected as a delegate to the Confederation Congress, and he sat in the North Carolina lower house during most of the decade. In 1790, he was named as U.S. district judge for North Carolina, a post he held until his death.

SKENE, Philip (1725–1810) Loyalist Skene was born in England and was a veteran of British army service throughout Europe when he married an heiress in 1750. The couple moved to upper New York, where Skene received a land grant of 34,000 acres as reward for his military service during the first years of the Seven Years' War. He bought up additional lands and eventually owned close to 60,000 acres. He turned his estate, centered on the town of Skenesboro, into a virtual frontier kingdom, with a manor house, mills and tenant farms. Skene was also involved in the disputes between New Hampshire and New York over control of the Hampshire Grants (modern-day Vermont), since some of his lands lay in the contested area. In 1773, Skene went to England and so missed the outbreak of the Revolution. He returned to America in 1775 and was named lieutenant governor of Fort Ticonderoga and Crown Point by the British. He was arrested by the Americans in 1776 while on a trip to Philadelphia and subsequently was incarcerated in Connecticut until exchanged later in the year. His most famous exploits were as military advisor to General John Burgoyne during the British invasion from Canada in 1777. One of the objects of Burgoyne's march was to liberate Skenesboro and set up a loyal enclave in upper New York with Skene's town as its administrative center and Skene as governor. Widespread loyalist support for Burgoyne, of course, never materialized. Skene was captured at the British defeat at Saratoga but eventually was paroled. His estate was confiscated by the new American government after the war and he spent his remaining days in England.

SKINNER, Cortlandt (1728–1799) Loyalist official, soldier

Related by blood and marriage to the powerful New York and New Jersey De Lancey and Van Cortlandt families, Skinner was an office-holder and lawyer before the Revolutionary War. He held the post of royal attorney general of New Jersey at the outbreak of hostilities, and although he waffled in his public sympathies throughout the first months of 1775, he eventually came down firmly in the loyalist camp. Moving to New York, he assumed a commission as a major of loyalist troops with the British and was captured during the summer campaigns of 1776. He was exchanged for Lord Stirling in October 1776. Skinner then raised and organized a unit of New Jersey loyalist volunteers, known as Skinner's Brigade, in which he served as brigadier general. The brigade was active throughout the rest of the war in the New York and New Jersey area, although it also gained a reputation for thievery and cattle rustling that seemed to have little to do with the Revolution. Skinner emigrated to England after the war and received half-pay at the rank of brigadier general.

SKINNER, John (c. 1750–1827) Loyalist, British officer

Born in New Jersey, Skinner was an ensign in the 16th Regiment of Foot and fought during most of the war in the southern theater, including the taking of Savannah and Charleston. After mid-1780, Skinner commanded a troop of dragoons as part of Banastre Tarleton's British Legion and fought

William Smallwood

at the battles at Cowpens and at Guilford Courthouse. He remained in the service following the American war, eventually rising to general's rank and holding several important commands in both the East and West Indies.

SMALLWOOD, William (1732–1792) Continental general

Although his name was associated with one of the best fighting units in the Continental Army, Smallwood himself seldom ventured onto the battlefield. He was born in Maryland, served in the Seven Years' War, and sat in the Maryland legislature before the Revolution. In January 1776, Smallwood was commissioned as colonel in command of the Maryland Regiment, which he helped raise and led north to join Washington in defending New York. Almost from their first combat, the Marylanders showed unusual skill and bravery, and they were soon viewed as one of the elite units of the Continental Army. However, they were usually commanded in the field by Mordecai Gist, and Smallwood was absent from almost all of the Marylanders' famous battles. He was away sitting on a court-martial during the battle of Long Island, but he did take the field at White Plains and suffered a wound during the battle. He was promoted to brigadier general in October 1776 but was still out of action recovering from his wound during the army's retreat across Pennsylvania. After recruiting in Maryland and Delaware, Smallwood returned north in time for the battle of Germantown, but he commanded a militia unit that remained out of action rather than his own regiment. In early 1777, he was assigned to Wilmington, Delaware, mostly to keep an eye on the British force advancing toward Philadelphia.

The Marylanders, slowly being depleted by battle after battle, were sent south in 1780 with Smallwood at their head and joined the army taken over by Horatio Gates. The regiment formed part of the rock-solid right wing at the battle of Camden and was nearly destroyed when the supporting militia broke and ran. Smallwood himself was separated from his division early in the battle and swept to the rear by the flood of panicked militiamen, so he once again failed to personally share in the action. He was promoted to major general after the battle, nevertheless, and named to command Johann de Kalb's division (the Frenchman had died on the field at Camden), but Smallwood objected to being placed under Friedrich von Steuben, who was in Smallwood's eyes a mere foreigner, and he was sent to Maryland to recruit by the new southern commander, Nathanael Greene. Smallwood played no role in the rest of the war. He declined election to Congress in 1784 but was elected governor of Maryland in 1785 and served three terms.

SMITH, Francis (1723–1791) British officer

The languid, overweight Smith commanded the British expedition to Lexington and Concord that touched off the war. He was a long-serving veteran by April 1775, but one with little distinction. He began as a lieutenant of the Royal Fusiliers in 1741 and was a lieutenant colonel when he came with his regiment to beef up the Boston garrison in 1767. He huffed and puffed around the scene during the fateful day of April 19, 1775 (according to eyewitness accounts) but despite a wound suffered in a skirmish near Concord, Smith managed to get the redcoats on the road back to Boston and avoid annihilation. He attempted to resign in the summer of 1776 but was refused and ended the war as a major general and holding the honorary post of aide to the king.

SMITH, Hezekiah (1737–1805) Clergyman

Smith was born on Long Island, joined the Baptist denomination in 1756, and was ordained in 1763 after graduation from Princeton. He moved to Haverhill, Massachusetts and became pastor of the Baptist church there. During the Revolution, Smith served as an army chaplain for five years, from 1775 to 1780. He was also a supporter of Rhode Island College in Providence (the school that became Brown University) and an advocate of the separation of church and state.

SMITH, James (1713–1806) Delegate to Congress, militia officer, attorney

Born in Ireland, Smith came to the region of York, Pennsylvania with his family when he was about 12 years old. He attended Alison's academy in New London, read for the law, and was admitted to the bar in 1745. Smith then moved to the frontier district near Shippensburg in Cumberland County, where he hoped to both practice law and work as a surveyor, but he failed to establish a practice and returned to the more settled area around York. (Nonetheless, he was identified with the back country during his subsequent political career and drew much of his support from the frontier region.) He was not much more successful in York, despite being the only lawyer in the immediate vicinity, and in 1771, Smith turned—again unsuccessfully—to iron mining and manufacturing.

He was better at revolutionary politics than at business. In 1774, he became a leader in the patriotic agitation against Great Britain, attending the provincial congress and calling for a general meeting of colonial representatives in a congress. He also organized a militia company, which eventually grew to battalion size. He was the unit's honorary colonel but never took the field as an active commander. He is also credited with raising two regiments that formed part of the Flying Camp strategic reserve in 1776. Smith was chosen as a delegate to the Continental Congress in the summer of 1776, after serving in the Pennsylvania state constitutional convention, and he took his seat in time to sign the Declaration of Independence in August. He was reelected to Congress the following year but was not chosen for the 1778 term. Following the war, Smith's legal career finally prospered, and he divided his time between the law and public office. He also kept his militia rank, rising eventually to brigadier general.

SMITH, Jonathan Bayard (1742–1812) Delegate to Congress, militia officer

Born in Philadelphia, Smith graduated from the college at Princeton in 1760. He was an active patriot as a member of the Pennsylvania Provincial Congress in 1774 and again in 1776, and he was secretary to the committee of safety from 1775 to 1777. He was also lieutenant colonel of the Philadelphia Associators, a vigorous militia unit drawn from the social and economic elite of the city, and he fought at the battle of Brandywine in 1777. He was elected as a delegate to the Congress later in the year and was returned in 1778. He also held several judicial offices during the war. He was active in supporting higher education as a founder of one of the Philadelphia schools that later combined to form the University of Pennsylvania.

SMITH, Joshua Hett (1736–1818) Loyalist

The son and brother of two New York royal chief justices, both named William, Joshua Hett Smith has remained a figure of some mystery concerning his role in Benedict Arnold's treason. He may have been a dupe, or he may have been deep in the plot. Before the Revolution, Smith was a prosperous upcountry lawyer with a fine house near West Point and a successful law practice. He was an active patriot, sitting in the New York Provincial Congress and serving in the militia. Although apparently without military rank, Smith became American general Robert Howe's chief of local intelligence when Howe took command of the key American base at West Point in 1778, and he continued in the post when the command passed to Benedict Arnold. Arnold used Smith as the key contact with Major John André during the fated meeting in 1780. Smith conducted André from the British sloop of war to the American shore where the British spymaster met Arnold in secret. When André could not return to his ship, Smith took him in charge, gave him bed and board during the night, lent him a civilian disguise, and personally conducted him part way back toward British lines, although he parted company before André was captured on the road. After Arnold made his dramatic escape, Smith was arrested. He faced a military court-martial, convened the morning of André's execution, but he succeeded in defending himself and was acquitted for lack of evidence that he was anything but an unwitting accomplice acting on Arnold's orders. He was then thrown in jail by the civilian authorities, but he escaped several months later and made his way to British-held New York City. Smith emigrated to England with the British evacuation in 1783 but eventually returned to his native state. In 1808, he published *An Authentic Account of the Causes which Led to the Death of Major André*, which most historians regard as unreliable and self-serving.

SMITH, Melancton (1744–1798) Official, militia officer, delegate to Congress

A virulent antiloyalist during the Revolution, Smith was born on Long Island and became a merchant after youthful training in a store in Poughkeepsie, New York. He was a man of little or no education, but by the advent of the Revolution he had acquired considerable property and land in Dutchess County. Smith was a delegate to the New York provincial congress of 1775, and he raised military companies in Dutchess County, both to serve in the Continental Army and to act as a local militia against the loyalists of the area. With the rank of major, he directed antiloyalist activities in Dutchess County, a place rife with warring civilian factions and quasi-military units. In 1777, Smith was appointed to the committee for detecting conspiracies and was one of the principal officials persecuting loyalists in those parts of New York outside the control of the British. During the last years of the war, Smith was a commissary and legal advisor for the army. He emerged from the war with a great deal more property than when it began, most coming by confiscation from loyalists. He moved to New York City in 1785 and prospered as a merchant. Even though he was a political ally of Anti-Federalist governor George Clinton, Smith supported the new federal constitution at the state convention.

SMITH, Meriwether (1730–1790) Delegate to Congress, state leader

Smith represented the old planter segment of Virginia politics. He was born on his father's estate in Essex County and died 60 years later on his own similar estate. Between times, he acted as a patriot leader, albeit a conservative one. He signed the Westmoreland Association in protest of the Stamp Act in 1766 and became a member of the House of Burgesses in 1770. He was a member of the revolutionary conventions in 1775 and 1776 and along with Patrick Henry and Edmund Pendleton helped draft the Virginia resolutions of independence in 1776. Two years later, Smith was selected to represent Virginia in the Continental Congress, remaining a delegate until 1779 and returning in 1781. After the war, he sat in the legislature and in 1788 was a member of the

Virginia convention that ratified the national constitution, although it did so over his opposition.

SMITH, Richard (1735–1803) Delegate to Congress, attorney

Smith was born in Burlington, New Jersey and educated in a Quaker school. He studied law with Joseph Galloway in Philadelphia and was admitted to the bar in 1760. He served as a clerk for his local county and eventually as clerk for the state assembly. In 1768, Smith joined other land speculators in setting up a land and settlement company on the Susquehanna River in Otsego County, New York, and he maintained a close interest in the project during the rest of his life. He was chosen as one of New Jersey's original delegates to the first Continental Congress in 1774 and was reelected twice. However, he and his fellow delegates were not in favor of independence, and they were replaced as a body in June 1776 before the vote on the Declaration. Smith briefly served as state treasurer for New Jersey in 1776 and 1777, but he dropped out of public life to resume his law practice in the spring of 1777. He moved to the Otsego settlement in 1790 and to Philadelphia in 1799. While on a tour of the Mississippi Valley in 1803, he contracted a fever and died at Natchez.

SMITH, Robert (1732–1801) Clergyman

Smith was one of the more important Anglican clergymen to support the Revolution. He was born in Norfolk, England and educated at Cambridge. He was ordained a priest in the Episcopal Church in 1756 and a year later emigrated to Charleston, South Carolina, where he became rector of St. Philip's Church. While many Episcopal clergymen remained loyal to the crown—a natural result of their positions as part of the state church—Smith was a strong patriot. He served as chaplain of the 1st South Carolina Regiment when it was formed in Charleston in 1776, and in 1778, he was named chaplain general for the Southern Department. When the British took Charleston in 1780, Smith was thrown into prison but he was later released and sent to Philadelphia. He returned to Charleston in 1783 at the end of the war and resumed his post at St. Philip's. Two years later, he was among the leaders of the Episcopal Church who called the first American General Convention, and in 1795, he became the first Episcopal bishop of South Carolina.

Samuel Smith

SMITH, Samuel (1752–1839) Officer, government official

Born in Carlisle, Pennsylvania, Smith moved with his family to Baltimore at age seven. A graduate of Princeton, he was a merchant before the Revolution and received a commission at the beginning of the war. In October 1777, he was a lieutenant colonel in command of the motley American forces defending Fort Mifflin, Pennsylvania, on the banks of the Delaware River opposite Fort Mercer (Red Bank), New Jersey. Despite its poor design, Fort Mifflin presented a significant obstacle to the British advance toward Philadelphia, and they made every effort to seize the stronghold. Smith's guns severely damaged British men-of-war on the river on October 23, while the fort itself took a heavy pounding from British land-based artillery. On November 10, the British began a major bombardment of Smith's position with guns on Province Island and with a floating battery on the river. Smith was wounded and had to be evacuated before the fort was abandoned five days later. He later fought at Monmouth. Following the war, Smith maintained his connection to the Maryland state militia, eventually gaining the rank of major general. He was also a powerful politician in the early Republic, sitting as a U.S. congressman, senator and secretary of the navy. He commanded the American defense of Baltimore during the War of 1812. *Further reading:* Frank A. Cassell, *Merchant Congressman in the Young Republic* (Madison, Wis., 1971); John Pancake, *Samuel Smith and the Politics of Business, 1782–1839* (University, Ala., 1972).

SMITH, Thomas (1745–1809) Delegate to Congress, official, jurist

Smith was born in Scotland

and emigrated to Bedford, Pennsylvania in 1769, where he became a surveyor and read for the law. He opened a legal practice in 1772 and became holder of several local offices, including justice of the peace. In 1775, Smith sat on the Pennsylvania Committee of Correspondence and was an officer in the militia. He was sent to the Pennsylvania constitutional convention in 1776 and sat in the state house of representatives from 1776 to 1780, when he was selected as a delegate to the Continental Congress, remaining there for two years. After the war, Smith became a judge of common pleas, and in 1791 he was appointed as a justice of the Pennsylvania Supreme Court.

SMITH, William (1728–1814) Delegate to Congress

Born and raised in Lancaster County, Pennsylvania, Smith moved to Baltimore at age 33, setting up a mercantile business there. He apparently became a community leader, since he was appointed to the Baltimore Committee of Correspondence in 1774 and to the Committee of Observation a year later. In 1777, Smith was sent as a delegate from Maryland to the Continental Congress, where he was a member of the naval board. He also served on the committee to organize the defense of Baltimore in 1781, when the British moved the focus of the war to the South. He was elected as a Federalist to the first U.S. House of Representatives under the new constitution in 1789 and became the first auditor of the United States in 1791. He served a term in the Maryland state senate after leaving federal office in 1801.

SMITH, William II (1728–1793) Loyalist jurist, historian

Called a "weathercock that could hardly tell which way to turn," Smith wavered in allegiance during the first year and a half of the Revolution before finally deciding for the royal cause. He was the son of the elder William Smith, chief justice of New York, and the brother of Joshua Hett Smith. He graduated from Yale and studied law with his father. As a rising lawyer in New York he was asked to compile the laws of the colony, and in 1752 published *Laws of New York . . .* in collaboration with William Livingston. The compilers followed up with a companion volume in 1762. Smith also coauthored a military history of the colony in 1757. In 1763, Smith was appointed both to the Governor's Council and to succeed his father as chief justice of New York. At the break with Great Britain, he apparently could not make up his mind what to do, so he withdrew to a country estate and effectively ceased to function in his office as chief justice. By late 1777, however, Smith could no longer avoid a choice, and he moved back to New York City and publicly embraced the side of the crown. He evacuated to England in 1783 and then moved to Canada to become chief justice there. Smith was also the author of a *History of the Late Province of New York,* which told the story of the colony up to 1762, and a six-volume, unpublished historical memoir which covered the Revolution. *Further reading:* L. S. F. Upton, *Diary and Selected Papers of Chief Justice William Smith, 1784–1793,* 2 vols. (Toronto, 1963).

SMYTH, Frederick (d. 1815) Loyalist jurist

Born in England, Smyth was chief justice of New Jersey at the time of the Revolution, having been appointed in 1764. He served as one of the royal commissioners to examine the *Gaspée* affair in 1773 and was in difficulties with the patriots from then until the breach with the mother country. He moved to New York in 1776. Just before the final British evacuation, Smyth went to Philadelphia to settle British claims, but he left for New Brunswick, Canada in the fall of 1783.

SOWER, Christopher (1754–1799) Loyalist publisher

The third in line of German-language publishers in his family to bear the name, Sower inherited a printing and publishing business in Germantown, Pennsylvania. His family were Dunkards and cleaved to the British cause at least in part because of the persecution of their sect by American authorities. Sower was publisher of the *Germantowner Zeitung* and evidenced only mild support of the crown in public during the early months of the Revolution in order to escape arrest by the patriots. With the British invasion of Pennsylvania and the occupation of Philadelphia in 1777, Sower moved his paper, renamed the *Staats Courier,* to the state capital. He served with the British army at Germantown and was wounded during the battle. He withdrew along with the Royal Army to New York in 1778 and became a courier between Sir Henry Clinton and loyalist conspirators in Pennsylvania and Virginia. Sower went to New Brunswick at the conclusion of peace, publishing a newspaper there and eventually becoming deputy postmaster general.

SPAIGHT, Richard Dobbs (1758–1802) Militia officer, delegate to Congress, governor, legislator
Born in New Bern, North Carolina, Spaight was orphaned when eight years old and was sent to Ireland for education. He moved from there to the University of Glasgow and did not return to North Carolina until 1778. Despite his youth and inexperience, he was elected the following year to a seat in the state legislature. He also became an officer in the state militia and served as an aide to General Richard Caswell. Spaight retired from military duty after the debacle at Camden and returned to the legislature in 1781, holding his seat there for the next several years. He was defeated as a candidate for the Confederation Congress in 1783 but was appointed to a vacancy in 1784. After a four-year recuperation from illness, Spaight was elected in 1792 as governor of North Carolina, and he served three consecutive terms. In 1798, he became U.S. representative from North Carolina, sitting in the Congress until 1801. In September 1802, Spaight fought a duel with his successor in Congress, John Stanly, and died from the resulting wounds.

SPENCER, Elihu (1721–1784) Clergyman
A Presbyterian, Spencer was born in East Haddam, Connecticut and educated at Yale. In the late 1740s, he was a missionary to the Oneida Indians, and in 1750 he became pastor of the church in Elizabethtown, New Jersey. He moved to Jamaica, New York in 1756 and in 1764 to Trenton, New Jersey, where he remained for the rest of his life. He was a patriot, and in 1775, he traveled with Alexander McWhorter on a tour of the back-country regions of several of the southern colonies to whip up support for the Revolution among pockets of rural Presbyterians. He was a chaplain for patriot hospitals near Trenton during the war.

SPENCER, Joseph (1714–1789) Continental major general, delegate to Congress
Spencer was relatively advanced in age when the Revolution began, and the combination of his prickly sense of personal privilege and his modest military skills removed him early from the fray. Born in East Haddam, Connecticut (where he lived his entire life), he was a veteran of long service in the colonial militia, having been commissioned a lieutenant in 1747 and having reached the rank of colonel 19 years later. After the British marched against Lexington and Concord in April 1775, Spencer held the rank of brigadier general of the Connecticut militia, which made him the senior officer among the Connecticut troops in the Boston Army. When Congress organized the Continental Army, however, it passed over Spencer and made Israel Putnam a major general; Spencer was only confirmed in his brigadier's rank. Spencer abruptly departed without leave or resigning his commission: he just went home in a fit of pique. He was persuaded to return to duty by a delegation sent by the Connecticut provincial assembly, and in August 1776, while serving in the New York campaign, he finally was promoted to major general. He was not much of a leader, however, and after the collapse of the American defense of New York, Spencer was ordered to set up headquarters in Rhode Island in December, while George Washington and the main army were fighting in New Jersey. In September 1777, Spencer set afoot an amphibious attack against the British in Rhode Island but called off the expedition before it was truly launched. When Congress asked about the affair, Spencer felt his honor was impugned and demanded a formal court of inquiry, which found him blameless. Nonetheless, Spencer resigned his commission, to the regret of no one in the Continental Army. He returned to Connecticut and was sent as a delegate to Congress the following year. He also was appointed to the state committee of safety in 1780 and continued in office as a probate judge in Haddam.

SPRIGG, Thomas (1747–1809) Soldier, government official
Born in Maryland, Sprigg served in the Maryland Battalion of the Flying Camp, a strategic reserve that was organized in 1776. He apparently escaped capture by the British (which was the fate of many men of the Flying Camp) and returned to Washington County, Maryland, where he became first register of wills for the new patriot government and then "lieutenant" of the county. He served as a U.S. congressman from Maryland from 1793 to 1797.

SPRING, Samuel (1747–1819) Clergyman
Spring was a leader among the conservative faction of the Congregationalists in Massachusetts. He was

born in Northbridge, Massachusetts and graduated from Princeton in 1771. He studied theology until the outbreak of the war in 1775, when he joined Benedict Arnold's expedition to Canada as a chaplain. On his return from Quebec, he was ordained and took over as pastor of the Congregationalist church in Newburyport, Massachusetts, serving there until his death 43 years later. He was a lifelong foe of Universalism and founded both an association of conservative Congregationalists and a seminary to resist the liberal movement within the church.

STAINVILLE, Comte de. See CHOISEUL, Étienne François.

STANSBURY, Joseph (1742–1809) Loyalist spy, poet, merchant   Born in England and an emigrant to Philadelphia in 1767, Stansbury was a player in the drama of Benedict Arnold's treason. He operated a store selling china in Philadelphia and was known locally as a writer of light and amusing verse. He was a mild loyalist in public, although in private he wrote verse that indicated his true feelings and promised support to closet royalists:

Think not, though wretched, poor and naked,
Your breast alone the load sustains;
Sympathizing hearts partake it;
Britain's monarch shares your pains.

Stansbury was imprisoned briefly by the Americans in 1776 but was released to continue his business. When the British occupied the city, he was appointed one of the commissioners of the city watch and manager of a lottery. When the British withdrew, Stansbury remained behind. In the spring of 1779, he was called to the home of one of his customers, General Benedict Arnold. Stansbury was startled to hear the American commander declare his allegiance to the British cause and, moreover, his intention to either go over to the British immediately or wait and betray a command. Stansbury was to carry the message to Sir Henry Clinton's headquarters in New York City. On May 10, Stansbury and Jonathan Odell met Major John André, Clinton's adjutant in charge of intelligence, and gave him the message. Throughout the ensuing months, Stansbury acted frequently as Arnold's messenger to British headquarters. Following Arnold's defection and André's capture and execution

in October 1780, Stansbury remained in Philadelphia. He was arrested for treason in 1780, but he was permitted to leave after six months in jail. He went to New York and spent the balance of the war writing satirical verse. He withdrew in 1783 to Nova Scotia and then England but was disappointed in pressing his claims for compensation with the Loyalist Commission. He returned to Philadelphia in 1785 but failed to restart his business, and he moved to New York in 1793, where he worked as secretary to an insurance company.

STARK, John (1728–1822) Continental and militia general   Stark was almost as much trouble to his commanding officers as he was to the British, but his battlefield skill and valor redeemed his prickly independence. He was born in Londonderry, New Hampshire and grew up in the frontier region of that colony. As a child, he was kidnapped by Indians and ransomed back to his parents. During the Seven Years' War, he served as a captain in Rogers' Rangers. When the conflict began with the British in 1775, Stark immediately recruited a regiment and marched to join the gathering militia army around Boston. On June 17, he led two regiments of New Hampshire militiamen out to a station at the far left of the American battle line at Bunker Hill, where they crouched behind a flimsy, grassy-stuffed fence. Under his extremely steady leadership, the men waited until the British fusiliers had approached within 50 yards and then poured a deadly fire into ranks of the regulars. The devastation wrought by Stark's men did much to establish the legend of the battle.

In 1776, Stark received a commission as colonel of the 5th Continental Regiment, made up of New Hampshiremen. After assignments in New York and Canada, he took command of the 1st New Hampshire in November 1776 and served nobly at Trenton and Princeton. He was not, however, rewarded with elevation to general's rank after the New Jersey campaign, so he resigned in anger and returned to New Hampshire. He assumed command of the state militia, on the condition that he not be responsible to the orders of Congress or Continental Army officers. When General John Burgoyne marched down from Canada in 1777, Stark was ordered by Benjamin Lincoln to join the American army across the Hudson, but Stark flatly refused. He had his own ideas of how and where to

John Stark

fight. When Burgoyne detached Friedrich Baum and his Germans to foray toward Bennington, Stark saw his opportunity. The subsequent battle was a debacle for the Germans. Stark skillfully enveloped the mercenaries and nearly annihilated them. Only the indiscipline of his militia late in the battle prevented Stark from achieving an even greater victory. Congress did reward him this time, and he received a brigadier's commission after Burgoyne's surrender. He retired at war's end and took no further part in public life.

STEDMAN, Charles (c. 1745–1812) British officer, historian

Stedman was the author of what is usually considered to be the best eyewitness history of the Revolutionary War by a participant. He was an officer with the British garrison in Boston at the beginning of the war and fought at Lexington and Concord. He then participated in the New York and New Jersey campaigns, served in the battles around Philadelphia, and fought under Lord Cornwallis in the southern theater. His *History of the Origin, Progress, and Termination of the American War* was published in London in two volumes in 1792 and has been a basic reference for subsequent histories of the Revolution down to our own day.

STEDMAN, Charles, Jr. Loyalist.

Apparently unrelated to the British soldier and historian of nearly the same name, this Stedman was a Philadelphia lawyer who amassed large land holdings in Pennsylvania's Northumberland County through the expedient of accepting payment of legal fees in land.

In 1776, he was arrested for corresponding with Major John André and for distributing pro-British literature. He was arrested a second time in 1777 but he secured his own release by taking an oath to the American cause. During the British occupation of his home city, Stedman served as deputy commissioner of prisoners. He withdrew to New York City along with the British army and in 1778 worked in the British quartermaster department. He went to the southern theater in 1780 and became assistant commissary for captives in South Carolina and eventually commissary for all British forces under Lord Cornwallis. He escaped by ship from Yorktown before the British surrender and went to England.

STEINMEYER, Ferdinand. See FARMER, Ferdinand.

STEPHEN, Adam (c. 1730–1791) Continental general

Stephen was one of the few senior American officers to be court-martialed and cashiered from the service. He was a native of Virginia and had served as a lieutenant colonel of the colonial militia during the Seven Years' War, at one point commanding a British post at Winchester. He was commissioned as the colonel of the 4th Virginia Regiment in early 1776 when the unit was raised as part of a new levy for the Continental Army. In September, he gave up command of the 4th and was promoted to brigadier.

His career as a senior commander was dismal—rife with recurring lies and dangerous incompetence. He nearly spoiled Washington's surprise attack on the Germans at Trenton in December 1776 by sending unauthorized patrols across the river the day before the attack, and Washington was reported to have lashed out at Stephen in a rage. Stephen's ill behavior notwithstanding, he was promoted again in February 1777 (to major general) and given considerable responsibility as a division commander. He seldom bothered to consult Washington and lied about the results of his strange self-directed missions. After a failure to surprise a British regiment near Piscataway, New Jersey in May 1777, and having been completely repulsed, Stephen reported a victory with more than 200 casualties among the enemy. When Washington learned the truth, he flatly contradicted Stephen's report.

Stephen's greatest blunder came at the battle of Germantown in October 1777. In command of a division under Nathanael Greene, he allowed his men to become separated from the rest of Greene's advance, and in the fog that covered the battlefield, Stephen's men blundered into the troops of Anthony Wayne and fired on them. The confusion of an attack from this unexpected quarter broke Wayne's men and they retreated in panic, leaving the field to the British. Three weeks later, Stephen was brought up on charges of intoxication during the battle. He was found guilty and dismissed from the army.

STERETT, Samuel (1758–1833) Government official   Born in Carlisle, Pennsylvania, Sterett moved to Baltimore after graduating from the University in Philadelphia. He was a member of a local company of militia formed by Baltimore merchants in 1777 but apparently saw no action during the war. In 1782, he became private secretary to John Hanson, who was president of the Congress. After the Revolution, Sterett sat in the Maryland state senate, and in 1791, he was elected to the U.S. House of Representatives. He was an early abolitionist, and he served as a militia captain during the War of 1812 and was wounded at Bladensburg.

STEUBEN, Friedrich Wilhelm von (1730–1794) Continental general   Of the many colorful foreigners who joined the American cause during the Revolution, von Steuben stood out as one of the few who contributed greatly to victory. Arriving at a crucial moment, he organized and trained the Continental Army and made it a more formidable fighting force.

He turned up in Pennsylvania during the winter of 1777–1778, armed with a less-than-accurate résumé that had been contrived by Benjamin Franklin in Paris. In his earlier days, von Steuben had been a genuine Prussian staff officer in the service of Frederick the Great, but by the time he met Franklin in France, he was a down-at-the-heels, half-pay captain, not the lieutenant general or baron his dossier claimed. Moreover, he spoke no English and scarcely any French. Nonetheless, Congress accepted his volunteer services and directed him to General Washington at Valley Forge. The American commander in chief and the resplendently uniformed Prussian hit it off at once, and von Steuben

Friedrich Wilhelm von Steuben

was appointed as acting inspector general of the Continental Army. Communicating through several French-speaking aides, he began to organize and train a small drill company of a hundred men. As the troops gained proficiency, they moved out to train others in turn, and by spring, the entire army had mastered his improved methods. During the winter, he not only wrote the first American army manual of drill and regulations (working laboriously through a team of translators), but he also put on a diverting show for the cold, half-starved troops, parading up and down in his full Prussian gear and swearing at their ineptness in an incomprehensible mixture of languages. He was no mere comic-opera figure, however, and the results of his training showed in the performance of the army in the subsequent battle of Monmouth.

Von Steuben continued as a one-man general staff for Washington during the following months, devising a system to curb waste, acting as a liaison with Congress, and helping to reorganize the structure of the army. In the fall of 1780, he moved south to take command of American forces in Virginia under the Marquis de Lafayette, but he played only a relatively small part in the final campaign of the war in 1781. When von Steuben was discharged from the army, he became an American citizen by acts of both the Pennsylvania and New York legislatures. He retired to New York, living alternately in the country on lands granted him for his service and in New York City until his death in 1794. As

454   STEVENS, Edward (1745–1820) Continental and militia officer

one biographer wrote: "Through his influence in converting the American army into an effective and highly disciplined military force, he was an indispensable figure in the achievement of American independence. He performed an essential service that none of his contemporaries in America was qualified to perform." *Further reading:* John McA. Palmer, *General von Steuben* (New Haven, Conn., 1937).

STEVENS, Edward (1745–1820) Continental and militia officer

A native of Culpeper County, Virginia, Stevens served as a militia commander at the battle of Great Bridge against Lord Dunmore in December 1775. He received a Continental commission as colonel of the new 10th Virginia Regiment in November 1776 and took part in the battles at Brandywine and Germantown, but he resigned in January 1778. He returned to Virginia and was appointed as a brigadier general of militia the following year. He and a body of Virginia militia joined Horatio Gates's army in August 1780, but at the battle of Camden they were among those who broke and ran at the first shots, leaving the stalwarts to be slaughtered by the British. Stevens was subsequently appointed to another militia command by Nathanael Greene, and he restored some of his reputation by fighting well at Guilford Courthouse, where the militia were not called on to withstand a frontal assault by British regulars. He led a brigade of militia under the Marquis de Lafayette in 1781 during the final months of the war and was present at the siege of Yorktown. After the war, Stevens served as a Virginia legislator.

STEVENS, John (1715–1792) State official, delegate to Congress, businessman

Stevens was born in Perth Amboy, New Jersey and was a merchant dealing with the West Indies trade. He held a long string of public offices in the decades before the Revolution, both in New Jersey and in New York, and was one of the principal New Jersey officials who dealt with Indian land. He was one of the major opponents to the Stamp Act in 1765. He held the office of vice president of New Jersey from 1770 to 1782, making the transition from the royal government to the patriotic, and he served as a delegate to the Confederation Congress in 1783 and 1784.

STEVENS, John (1749–1838) Government official, inventor

Stevens was best known for his inventions and transportation enterprises after the war. Born in New York City, he graduated from King's College (Columbia University) and became a lawyer. He apparently held a commission in the Continental Army, but his main activity during the Revolutionary War was on the financial front as an agent to secure loans. He served simultaneously as an official for Congress and for New Jersey, acting as state treasurer from 1776 to 1779 and surveyor general from 1782 to 1783. After the Revolution, he became interested in transportation. He invented and built several early steamboats (including one designed for the open sea) and began one of the first regular steamboat ferry lines on the Hudson River between New York City and Albany. In 1815, Stevens got authorization from the Pennsylvania legislature to build a railroad, and he constructed an experimental locomotive in 1825 but never succeeded in building a practical model nor in actually constructing a rail line. He was a visionary and proposed both a traffic tunnel under the Hudson River and an elevated railway for New York City.

STEWART, Alexander (c. 1740–1794) British officer

Stewart is best known for his strong showing as British commander at the battle of Eutaw Springs in 1781. He had been a British officer since entering service in 1755 as an ensign. By the beginning of the American war, he was a lieutenant colonel of the famous 3rd Regiment of Foot. Stewart was sent to the southern theater in the summer of 1781 and took over as commander of the British field forces, which had previously been under Lord Rawdon. Although he was relatively junior in rank for such a command, Stewart actually controlled the main British army in South Carolina during the summer and early fall. He was encamped with about 2,000 troops at Eutaw Springs on September 8, when the fast-moving Nathanael Greene approached with the full force of the American army. Stewart was to some degree caught off guard, but once alerted that Greene was nearby, he rapidly deployed his forces into sound defensive positions. The Americans took the advantage during the early stages of the battle, but—aided by a breakup of Greene's formations intent on plundering the British camp—Stewart rallied and won the day by a narrow margin, displaying considerable tactical skill.

His numbers and supplies were so depleted by the struggle, however, that he was forced to withdraw toward Charleston, and he was superseded in command within a few days. Placed in charge of the garrison at Charleston after the surrender of Lord Cornwallis, Stewart was promoted to colonel in 1782 and eventually reached the rank of major general.

STEWART, Charles (1729–1800) Militia officer, delegate to Congress

Stewart was born in Ireland and emigrated to New Jersey about 1750, becoming a farmer. He served in his local county militia as a colonel in 1771 and was a colonel of minutemen in 1776 when appointed commissary to the army by the Continental Congress. After the war, he was elected as a delegate to Congress, serving in 1784 and 1785. He died in Flemington, New Jersey.

STEWART, Walter (c. 1756–1796) Continental general, militia officer

Stewart was a vigorous field commander during the Revolution, although he also excelled at political intrigue. His first post was as captain of a company of Pennsylvania militiamen organized in 1775. In January 1776, Stewart became a Continental officer and aide-de-camp to Horatio Gates, a patron to whom he remained loyal throughout the Revolution. After 18 months with Gates and a promotion to major, Stewart was commissioned by the state of Pennsylvania as a colonel of militia and took command of the regiment of state troops that was not yet part of the Continental Army. He and his unit joined Washington's campaign in Pennsylvania during the summer of 1777 and won considerable distinction for holding a key position during the retreat at the battle of Brandywine. After fighting well at Germantown, Stewart's regiment was taken into the Continental Army as the 13th Pennsylvania Regiment, and Stewart resumed a regular commission as colonel in command. The 13th was attached to the army under General Charles Lee (thus missing winter quarters at Valley Forge), and at the battle of Monmouth, when Lee so misdirected his troops, Stewart and the 13th were part of the retreating forces met on the field and turned around by a furious George Washington. The following month (July 1778), the 13th was reorganized and a new regiment, the 2nd Pennsylvania, was created under Stewart's command.

Although serving in the field under Washington, Stewart kept close relations with Gates and was at least tangentially involved in the Conway Cabal in 1778. He was also one of the officers that helped quell the mutinies of the Connecticut and Pennsylvania regiments in 1780 and 1781. The 2nd Pennsylvania formed part of the force sent to Virginia in 1781 under the overall command of Anthony Wayne and fought at the battle of Green Spring in July and at the siege of Yorktown in October. Stewart relinquished command of the 2nd Pennsylvania in January 1783 but he continued on the active roll of the army and was one of the plotters at Newburgh, New York who attempted to stage an officers' revolt. In fact, Stewart—probably egged on by Gates—played a key role in fomenting the movement among the dissatisfied officers to threaten Congress, but his plans collapsed in the face of Washington's dignified refusal to cooperate. Stewart was brevetted as a brigadier general in September and mustered out. He became a Philadelphia merchant in later years.

STILES, Ezra (1727–1795) Educator, clergyman

Stiles was born in New Haven, Connecticut. His father was a Congregationalist preacher and prepared the boy for the same profession, sending him to Yale, where Ezra graduated in 1745. The young man passed two more years in private study before taking an appointment as a tutor in 1749. Uncertain about his vocation, he studied law, was admitted to the bar, and practiced for two years until deciding in 1755 to accept a call from Congregationalist church in Newport, Rhode Island. He served there for more than two decades, but the coming of the Revolution (which made Newport a likely target for the British) disrupted his congregation, and he withdrew to Dighton and eventually to Portsmouth, filling pulpits on a temporary basis. Stiles was well known in New England for the breadth of his learning and intellectual interests. He was an avid learner all his life, and he dabbled in scientific experimentation (he was a long-time correspondent of Benjamin Franklin). In 1777, Yale offered him the presidency of the school, and after a long period of indecision, Stiles accepted in the spring of 1778 and took office in July. He was a strong supporter of the Revolution, as evidenced in his detailed personal diary and his public utterances, but he took little overt role in the conflict, preferring to spend his energies to keep the college alive during a difficult period—the British raided New Haven during the second year of his presidency, for example. A man of considerable erudition, Stiles was also a practical administrator and skillful at the business of nurturing higher education in the thicket of conflicting religious, political and financial interests. He died of fever in New Haven. *Further reading:* Edmund S. Morgan, *Gentle Puritan: A Life of Ezra Stiles* (Williamsburg, Va., 1962).

STIRLING, Lord. See ALEXANDER, William.

STOCKTON, Richard (1730–1781) Delegate to Congress Stockton's story is sad: he was reluctantly pulled into public life and was shattered by imprisonment during the Revolution. He was born on his father's estate near Princeton, New Jersey and graduated from the first class of the College of New Jersey at Newark (later moved to Princeton) in 1748. He became one of the colony's foremost lawyers and enjoyed a life of wealth, high standing and privilege. He married Annis Boudinot, sister of Elias, in 1755 (Elias became Stockton's double brother-in-law by marrying his sister Hannah Stockton). In 1766, Stockton and Benjamin Rush went to Scotland to invite the famous preacher John Witherspoon to take the presidency of Princeton, and during the trip, Stockton met both George III and the Marquis of Rockingham. The passage of the Stamp Act set Stockton along the path of resistance to the crown, but he hoped until the outbreak of hostilities to preserve the colonies as part of the British system. In 1774, he submitted to Lord Dartmouth a plan of reconciliation, based on self-rule—a scheme similar to the eventual structure of the British Commonwealth.

Stockton would have preferred to stay on the political sidelines, but as a prominent New Jerseyan, he was drawn into the spotlight. Having served as a member of the colonial executive council, he was sent to Congress as a delegate in 1776, voting for independence and signing the Declaration during the summer. He tied in a race for the governorship of New Jersey, and when the office went to his rival, Stockton turned down an offer of the New Jersey chief justice's position in order to stay in Congress. In November, Stockton and fellow

congressional delegate George Clymer were sent to inspect the northern Continental Army, which was trying to reorganize after the disaster of the failed Canadian invasion. When the British, having pushed Washington's army out of New York, invaded New Jersey, Stockton rushed home to Princeton. He managed to evacuate his family to a safer place but was himself captured by the British and eventually sent to the infamous Provost Jail in New York City. The conditions of his imprisonment were harsh, and his health deteriorated in confinement. His spirit broken, Stockton signed an agreement for amnesty. He was released in 1777, but he discovered that the British had partially burned his fine mansion and that signing the amnesty proclamation put him outside the patriot political pale. He died a broken invalid.

STODDERT, Benjamin (1751–1813) Continental officer, government official, businessman Stoddert was born in Charles County, Maryland, the son of a wealthy tobacco planter. He was trained as a merchant in Philadelphia, where the beginning of the Revolutionary War ended his apprenticeship. He had formed a friendship, however, with the infamous James Wilkinson, who in January 1777 offered Stoddert a commission in a new "additional" Continental regiment then being raised in Pennsylvania and Maryland under Colonel Thomas Hartley. Stoddert became a captain and saw action with Hartley's Regiment during the campaign around Philadelphia, taking a wound at the battle of Brandywine. His unit—much depleted by the fighting—was then ordered to York, Pennsylvania, the temporary seat of Congress after the British seizure of Philadelphia. Stoddert became involved in the complex and intrigue-filled affairs of the board of war, of which Wilkinson was secretary. The young captain ingratiated himself with the board—Horatio Gates, Thomas Mifflin, Richard Peters and Timothy Pickering—and angled for an appointment. Unfortunately for him, the Congress appropriated the selection of a new secretary for the board, and Stoddert was left out. He returned to duty with Hartley's Regiment, but when the unit was consolidated with several other understrength regiments to form a new 11th Pennsylvania, Stoddert lost his seniority and all hope of a quick promotion.

He resigned his commission in April 1779. During the following spring and summer, he served as a civilian deputy forage master—bearing the honorary title "Major." In September, his ambitions were rewarded, and he was named as secretary to the board of war when the incumbent resigned. Stoddert served the board until it was superseded in 1781 with the formation of a new executive department. He solidified his political friendships during his time with the board, and they proved to be valuable connections during the remainder of his life.

After the Revolution, Stoddert moved to the tiny river port of Georgetown, Maryland and set up what was soon a thriving mercantile business. He also began to buy up land in the region, and he acted as a silent land agent for the federal government in purchasing lots in the new District of Columbia. He ended up holding title to a great deal of land in the district, and his future financial status rose and fell with the price of land in the nascent capital. In 1798, he was appointed as secretary of the navy at a crucial juncture: an undeclared naval war with France was about to begin, and the United States had determined to rearm and rebuild a navy. Stoddert deserves much credit for his skillful handling of naval affairs, which allowed the United States to gain at least a modicum of armed presence at sea.

He was a confirmed Federalist, however, and did not long survive the change of administration in 1801. He returned to Georgetown, but the price of land was depressed and the commerce of the port suffered during the subsequent wars and embargoes of the early 1800s. He lost a great deal of money with the financial collapse of Robert Morris, with whom he had considerable dealings, and Stoddert died deeply in debt. *Further reading:* Michael A. Palmer, *Stoddert's War: Naval Operations during the Quasi-War with France, 1798–1801* (Columbia, S.C., 1987).

STOKES, Anthony (c. 1736–1799) Loyalist official

Apparently an emigrant to Georgia from Great Britain, Stokes became chief justice of the colony in 1768 and was the last royal official to hold that office. He also served on the Council. In 1778, after his estates were confiscated by the Americans, he went to Charleston, and in 1783 he returned to England. He died in London.

STONE, Thomas (1743–1787) Delegate to Congress

Stone was one of the most conservative congressmen to vote for independence. He was born into wealthy circumstances on a plantation in Maryland and became a lawyer in Frederick after passing the bar in 1764. With money from his wife's dowry, Stone purchased land near Port Tobacco, Maryland and built an architecturally splendid house in 1771. He was involved in revolutionary activities from his selection in 1773 as a member of the county committee of correspondence, but he was not an enthusiastic radical by any measure. In 1774, he acted as an attorney in defense of the poll tax benefiting Episcopal clergy, sitting on the opposing bench from three of his eventual congressional colleagues. His conservatism notwithstanding, the provincial convention of Maryland selected Stone as a delegate to the Continental Congress in 1775, and he remained a delegate until 1778. He voted for and signed the Declaration of Independence, and he sat on the committee that drafted the Articles of Confederation but failed to sign them. He seldom spoke in Congress, and few of his writings survive. He returned to Congress in 1784 and was president pro tem briefly before resigning to return to his law practice. He died in Alexandria, Virginia, awaiting a ship for a visit to England.

STORER, Anthony (1746–1799) British official

Storer was something of an ineffectual fop, but he was also a boon companion of more important British politicians and thus found his way to office during the period of the American Revolution, most notably as a member of the Carlisle Peace Commission in 1778. He attended Eton with Charles James Fox, William Eden and the Earl of Carlisle, and these associations formed the basis for his subsequent prominence. For most of his career he was almost entirely a creature of Carlisle: he held seats controlled by Carlisle in the House of Commons from 1774 until 1784. He was known as the best skater, dancer and gymnast in London society, scarcely recommendations for high office. In 1778, he was appointed along with Eden and George Johnstone as a member of the peace commission headed by Carlisle. The entire affair had something of the air of a lark about it, and the commission's serious purpose of negotiating a peace with the American rebels before the French could enter the war was more or less pointless from the beginning, when the Continental Congress declared anyone who dealt with the commission to be an enemy.

Storer appears to have played little role in the subsequent sordid attempts of Johnstone to bribe congressmen. Storer returned to England and eventually became a commissioner on the board of trade. He used his good graces with both Fox and Lord North to help arrange the coalition government that took office in 1783 and was rewarded with a post as secretary to the British legation in Paris. He was nominated as minister to France, but the coalition fell before he was confirmed, and having quarreled with Carlisle, Storer lost his access to office at the end of 1783. He retreated into private life as a noted collector of books and prints.

STORER, Clement (1760–1830) Militia officer, official   Storer was born in the Maine region of Massachusetts and became a doctor in Portsmouth, New Hampshire. Although there is little record of active field service during the Revolution and he was a very young man, he is credited with reaching the rank of major general in the New Hampshire militia by the end of the war. There is no doubt, however, about his later political career: he became U.S. congressman from New Hampshire in 1807 and served part of a term as U.S. senator in 1817–19. He retired from national office thereafter and was high sheriff of Rockingham County.

STORMANT, David Murray, Viscount (1727–1796) British official and diplomat   A key diplomat in France before the French-American alliance, Stormant also ran an efficient intelligence network that did much to frustrate the hopes of Congress to make an impression on the French court. He graduated from Oxford in 1748 and succeeded to his title the same year on the death of his father. He entered the diplomatic service and served in increasingly important posts in Paris, Saxony (where he married a privy councillor's daughter) and Austria. In 1772, he was appointed to the British embassy in Paris. He was an extremely active and efficient operative, controlling, for example, Edward Bancroft, who was secretary to the American commission and who supplied Stormant with secret American correspondence and papers before they reached the Congress in Philadelphia. Stormant also harassed Beaumarchais's efforts to supply the rebellion, and he was particularly quick to protest the harboring of American privateers and commerce raiders in French ports. Stormant's goal was

to keep French foreign minister Vergennes from forming an alliance with the Americans, but in this he ultimately failed. With the defeat of General John Burgoyne in the fall of 1777, Benjamin Franklin was able to cement formal treaties with France, and Stormant was recalled from Paris with the beginning of armed hostilities between Britain and France. He served as secretary of state for the southern department during the rest of the war, leaving office with the fall of Lord North's government in 1782. He returned to a lesser post under Portland's coalition but essentially retired to his place in the House of Lords after 1783.

STRINGER, Samuel (1734–1817) Army physician   Born in Maryland, Stringer studied medicine in Philadelphia. He served as a surgeon during the colonial wars, including the campaign against Fort Ticonderoga in 1758. He then settled in Albany, New York, and he was probably a political protégé of Philip Schuyler. In 1775, Stringer was appointed as the director and chief physician for army hospitals of the Northern Department. He went along on the invasion of Canada but was dismissed from his post by Congress in January 1777. There was also an inquiry into his purchase of supplies, but given the highly political nature of the Continental medical service and the intrigue in Philadelphia surrounding medical appointments, it is difficult to judge if Stringer was incompetent or merely on the wrong side of the political fence. He returned to Albany and practiced there the rest of his life.

STRONG, Jedediah (1738–1802) Delegate to Congress, state official   Strong was born and lived his life in Litchfield, Connecticut. He graduated from Yale in 1761 and was admitted to legal practice three years later. He was elected to the Connecticut House of Representatives in 1771 and served there continuously for 30 years. His activities during the revolutionary period included service on the local committee of inspection in 1774 and as a commissary to the army in 1775. He was clerk of the state house of representatives for nine years, from 1779 to 1788. In 1782, Strong was elected as a delegate to the Congress, but he failed to take his seat despite reelection in 1783 and 1784. In 1789 and 1790, Strong served on the governor's council.

STUART, Gilbert (1755–1828) Painter Although his portraits of George Washington are among the best-known images of the Revolutionary era, Stuart himself was absent from his native land during the period. He was born in Rhode Island and went to England at the age of 20, just as the Revolution began in America. He studied with Benjamin West in London, made a public splash with *Portrait of a Gentleman Skating*, and exhibited at the Royal Academy several times between 1777 and 1785. Stuart moved to Dublin in 1787 and did not return to American shores until 1793, when he settled in New York. His famous portraits of Washington were painted from life and copied by Stuart or assistants many times over, thus explaining the many extant versions. He also painted John Adams, Thomas Jefferson and James Madison.

STUART, John (c. 1710–1779) Loyalist, British official Stuart, although advanced in age, held a crucial British position as superintendent of Indian affairs in the South at the beginning of the Revolution. He was born in Scotland and had an adventurous life—sailing around the world with the great explorer George Anson—before emigrating to Charleston, South Carolina, where he became a prosperous merchant. He also served as a captain in the South Carolina colonial militia, and during the Seven Years' War, Stuart fought against the southern Indians, principally the Cherokee. He formed an alliance with some of the Cherokee leaders, however, and in a manner typical of several Scots throughout the British North American empire managed to become a man of influence among the natives of America. In 1762, Stuart was appointed as superintendent of Indian affairs, a southern counterpart to Sir William Johnson in the North. With the beginning of the War of Independence, he opposed encouraging the southern tribes to attack the patriots indiscriminately, and although he made efforts to organize a large-scale resistance in the South, he showed on the whole more restraint than his opposite numbers in New York and Canada. He died in Charleston. *Further reading:* John R. Alden, *John Stuart and the Southern Colonial Frontier* (Ann Arbor, Mich., 1944).

STUART, John. See BUTE, Earl of.

STUART, Philip (1760–1830) Soldier, official Stuart was born in Virginia but moved as a boy to Maryland. He was a teenage officer in the 3rd Regiment of Continental Light Dragoons, a unit raised by Colonel George Baylor in early 1777. Most of the Dragoon regiment came from Virginia, but there were also a few Pennsylvanians and Marylanders. The regiment suffered an unfortunate fate in September 1778, when a British attack force under General Charles "No Flint" Grey virtually reenacted Grey's triumph at Paoli, Pennsylvania a year earlier. The redcoats stole up on the dragoon encampment at night, surrounded the Americans, and massacred the sleepy victims with bayonet and close-range musketry. Stuart apparently was one of the 20 or so who escaped out of a force of 100. Baylor was wounded and captured but subsequently exchanged and nominally placed in command of a new unit, called Baylor's Dragoons, with Stuart again a lieutenant. In fact, the unit was under-strength and usually was commanded in the field by William Washington. The men, including Stuart, served well in the southern campaigns of 1780 and 1781. Stuart was wounded at the battle of Eutaw Springs and was apparently out of action for the duration of the war. He returned to the army during the crisis with France from 1798 to 1800 and served in the War of 1812. He was also elected to the U.S. House of Representatives after the turn of the 19th century.

STURGES, Jonathan (1740–1819) Delegate to Congress, state official Born in Fairfield, Connecticut, Sturges practiced law in his home town after graduating from Yale in 1759 and admission to the bar 13 years later. He was a member of the Connecticut House of Representatives in 1772, from 1773 to 1784, and again in 1786. He was sent as a delegate to Congress in 1786 and was elected as a U.S. representative for both the first and second Congresses under the federal constitution. He ended his public career with 12 years on the bench as an associate justice of the state supreme court.

SUFFREN de SAINT TROPEZ, Pierre André de (1729–1788) French admiral The most successful and aggressive French admiral of his day, Suffren contrasted sharply with the usual run of timid naval commanders sent out by the French to battle the British Royal Navy. A native of Provence, he

John Sullivan

entered the French navy in 1743 and passed through a succession of assignments during the decades before the alliance with the United States, including commands against the British in the Mediterranean and the Bay of Biscay and command of a xebec against the Barbary pirates. He was twice captured and exchanged by the British. He fought in the American theater—principally at the joint assault on Newport in 1778, when his boldness panicked the British into running two frigates aground—under d'Estaing, whom Suffren thought far too timid, and he commanded five ships of the line against "Foul Weather Jack" Byron off Grenada. Never allowed much freedom while in American waters, Suffren was reassigned to the Indian Ocean in 1781, and there he performed brilliantly despite few resources and indifferent subordinates. He died just before taking command of the fleet at Brest. *Further reading:* Roderick Cavaliero, "Admiral Suffren in the Indies," *History Today* 20 (July 1950), 472–80.

SULLIVAN, James (1744–1808) Delegate to Congress, state official, writer

The brother of General John Sullivan, James was born in Berwick, Massachusetts, in the part of the colony that eventually became the state of Maine. After admission to the bar, he set up practice in Biddeford and served before the Revolution as king's attorney in York County. He was a member of the Massachusetts provincial congresses in the key years of 1774

and 1775. He sat in the General Court in 1775 and 1776 and in the latter year was appointed to the bench of the superior court, remaining until 1782. He was then elected as a delegate to the Congress but never claimed his seat. From 1790 to 1807, Sullivan was attorney general of Massachusetts, and he was elected as governor in 1807. He was a strong Anti-Federalist and wrote several political pamphlets in addition to historical works, such as *The History of the District of Maine.*

SULLIVAN, John (1740–1795) Continental general, delegate to Congress

More of a politician than a military man, Sullivan nevertheless was involved in most of the war in the North from 1775 until 1779. He was a native of New Hampshire and figured prominently in the state's politics. He was trained as a lawyer and practiced in Durham, New Hampshire. Sullivan was also an avid patriot and helped lead a raid to capture gunpowder even before Lexington and Concord. He served in the Continental Congress in 1774–1775 and received a commission as a brigadier general at the formation of the Continental Army. Sullivan led an ineffective relief column toward Canada in 1776 and returned to take temporary command of the army at Long Island under Washington, assuming the rank of major general. He was captured during the British victory but was exchanged within a few weeks. He again joined Washington's command and served well at Trenton and throughout the New Jersey campaign and at the battles of Brandywine and Germantown. He embroiled himself in conflict with Congress, however, and was usually on the defensive thereafter. He may have been involved in the Conway affair, although evidence is not clear. He remained high in Washington's opinion nevertheless. One of his worst showings was as American commander of the disastrous joint assault with the French on Newport in 1778, when he lost most of his command when abandoned by the French navy. A similar aborted attack on Staten Island earned an inquiry from Congress, which may have been inspired mostly by politics. In 1779, he was dispatched with a large force to ravage the Iroquois nation, a task he accomplished during the late summer by destroying most of the Indian villages in upper New York. He resigned his commission after returning from his final campaign. Sullivan returned to Congress in 1780 and thereafter held a procession of offices in New Hampshire. In 1789, Washington appointed him as judge of the U.S. district of New Hampshire. *Further reading:* Charles B. Whittmore, *A General of the Revolution: John Sullivan of New Hampshire* (New York, 1961).

SUMNER, Increase. (1746–1799). Official, jurist

Born in Roxbury, Massachusetts, Sumner was a lawyer who held a procession of public offices during and after the Revolution. He sat as a member of the patriot Massachusetts General Court from 1776 to 1779 and in the state senate from 1780 to 1782. He was elected as a delegate to Congress in the latter year, but he failed to take his seat. He became an associate justice of the Massachusetts Supreme Judicial Court instead and remained on the bench until his election as governor of Massachusetts in 1797. He served as governor until his death two years later.

SUMNER, Jethro (c. 1733–1785) Continental officer, militia general

Sumner was born in Virginia and was a veteran of the Seven Years' War when he moved to North Carolina in 1764, using his wife's inheritance to set up as a planter and tavern keeper in Warren County. He attended the provincial congress in 1775 and was commissioned as a major in the militia. He fought at the battle against Lord Dunmore at Norfolk, Virginia in late 1775 and was then named colonel of the 3rd North Carolina Regiment, raised to defend the colony against an expected British invasion. When the attempt came at Charleston in 1776, Sumner and the 3rd helped stave off Sir Henry Clinton and then marched north to join Washington and the main army for the campaigns around Philadelphia in 1777. He wintered at Valley Forge but returned to North Carolina early in 1778 to recruit. Most of his field service from then on was as a leader of militia. He served at Stono Ferry in June 1779 with the rank of brigadier. In 1780, he was still at the head of North Carolina troops, but he was prickly about rank and command, and he refused to serve under William Smallwood. He returned to duty in 1781 and commanded a small number of Continentals at the battle of Eutaw Springs, giving a good account of himself and his men. Although technically in command of all state forces in North Carolina for the remainder of the war, he saw little more action.

Thomas Sumter

SUMTER, Thomas (1734–1832) Militia officer

The most controversial of the leading South Carolina partisan generals, Sumter had many sterling qualities, but his poor tactical judgment and disregard for the usual rules of war earned him an "odious" reputation among his peers. Known during the Revolution as the "Gamecock," Sumter was born in Virginia and came from a modest family background. He served in the Seven Years' War and against the Cherokee in 1762. After a trip to England, he got in trouble in Virginia and was thrown in jail. On escaping, Sumter moved to South Carolina and began his rise to fame.

He was a local justice of the peace and began to amass a considerable fortune in land and through his mercantile business. He was selected to sit in the revolutionary provincial congresses in South Carolina, and he began his military career at the start of the war as a captain of mounted rangers. In 1776, he was commissioned as lieutenant colonel of the 2nd Rifle Regiment and over the following two years he fought Indians. He resigned in 1778 and retired to his plantation near Eutaw Springs, but a contingent of Banastre Tarleton's British Legion burned Sumter's home, and he turned to organizing militia in the Catawba region. At the head of a considerable patriot partisan force, Sumter engaged the British and the South Carolina loyalists in a series of battles during the summer of 1780, including Williamson's Plantation, Rocky Mount and Hanging Rock. He was reluctant, however, to place himself under the authority of others, preferring to raid at will. Much of his subsequent activity came under the heading of back-country civil war, and he seldom coordinated his efforts with the main army. He was named senior brigadier general of South Carolina militia in October 1780 but had done nothing to aid Horatio Gates before the latter's disastrous defeat at Camden. Sumter was wounded in a savage fight against Tarleton at Blackstocks in November 1780, but he nonetheless started an ill-advised campaign against British outposts during the fall.

His poor tactical sense and unwillingness to prepare showed themselves to full disadvantage during the early months of 1781, and he was forced to retreat northward in relative disarray. He refused to cooperate with Nathanael Greene, and at several key points, Sumter failed to support Greene's campaign in the Carolinas. Sumter's most controversial act was to declare what was known as "Sumter's law," which proposed paying militia in plunder seized from loyalists. The plan only fueled the viciousness of the civil war in South Carolina, and the state government declared the policy void in August 1781. Sumter had just been soundly defeated at Quinby Bridge a few weeks before, and the combination of events pushed him to retire from the field.

He lived out the rest of his very long life (he was the oldest surviving Revolutionary general at his death at age 98) as a planter and politician. He served in the South Carolina senate and as one of the first representatives to the new U.S. Congress in 1789. He was selected as a U.S. senator in 1801, serving until 1810. His final decades were plagued by debt and litigation. *Further reading:* Robert Bass, *Gamecock: The Life and Campaigns of General Thomas Sumter* (New York, 1961); Anne K. Gregoire, *Thomas Sumter* (Columbia, S.C., 1931).

SWANN, John (1760–1793) Delegate to Congress

Swann (whose name is also given as Swan) was a young man during the Revolution itself and played little or no active role until elected to Congress in the late 1780s. He was born in Pasquotank County, North Carolina and graduated from the College of William and Mary before taking up farming. In 1788, during the waning days of the Confederation Congress, he was appointed as a delegate to fill the vacancy created by the resignation of John Baptista Ashe, and he served from March until November. He supported adoption of the new fed-

eral constitution by North Carolina, but he died at age 33 soon after the formation of the new national government.

SWIFT, Herman. Continental general

Little detail is known of Swift or his activities during the war, although his service record shows him in command of four Connecticut regiments between 1777 and 1783. He was a colonel of Connecticut militia from mid-1776 to the end of the year. In January 1777, he became colonel in command of the 7th Connecticut Regiment of the Continental Line. The Connecticut regiments were reorganized in January 1781, and Swift became colonel of the new 2nd Connecticut, formed from remnants of the previous 5th and 7th regiments. In June 1783, the former Connecticut regiments were dissolved and the men furloughed. New recruits, however, were organized into a consolidated Connecticut Regiment, with Swift again the colonel. He was mustered out in December 1783 and brevetted to the rank of brigadier general.

SYKES, James (1725–1792) Delegate to Congress, attorney

A resident of Delaware, Sykes was an attorney with military experience as a member of Caesar Rodney's Dover militia during the 1750s. He was a member of the Delaware Council of Safety in 1776 and a delegate to the state constitutional convention. In 1777, he was selected as a delegate to the Continental Congress. During and after the war, Sykes filled a number of public offices as a legislator, member of the council and judge of the High Court of Errors and Appeals.

SYMMES, John Cleves (1742–1814) Delegate to Congress, militia officer, jurist

Born on Long Island, Symmes moved in 1770 to Sussex County, New Jersey, where he was one of the leaders of the patriot party, serving as chairman of the committee of correspondence in 1774. With the beginning of the war, he was appointed as a colonel of the local militia, and he led amateur troops that intermittently campaigned with the Continental forces during the retreat across New Jersey in 1776 and the subsequent battles in Pennsylvania through mid-1778. In 1776, Symmes sat in the convention that wrote a new state constitution for New Jersey and was then elected to the state legislature. In 1777, he became associate justice of the state supreme court, holding the post for a decade. He was selected as a delegate to the Confederation Congress in 1785 and 1786, but he had already formed an intense interest in speculating and colonizing the West. He obtained a claim to a million acres in what is now the state of Ohio and moved to the region in about 1788, the same year he was appointed as one of three judges for the Northwest Territory. He finally received title to more than 300,000 acres (including the site of Cincinnati), and he parceled out lands to buyers (although without great financial success, and careless as to legalities). He died in Ohio and was buried at the settlement he founded at North Bend.

T

TALBOT, Silas (1751–1813) Naval officer, Continental officer, congressman Born in Massachusetts to a large family of farmers, Talbot was trained as a stone mason but early took to the sea. He sailed as a merchantman before the Revolution, having established himself in Providence, Rhode Island by 1772. He was also a militiaman on land and was appointed a captain at the beginning of the armed conflict with Great Britain in 1775. He received a congressional commission soon after and took part in the siege of Boston. Most of his army service, however, was as a sailing master, transporting troops and commanding small armed vessels. He was promoted to major in 1777 and was wounded at Hog Island in the Delaware River. After a brief convalescence, he returned to duty with the forces under John Sullivan in the French-American attack on Newport. In October 1778, after the Newport expedition had been decisively repulsed by the British, Talbot provided one of the few bright moments by capturing the British ship *Pigot,* which he converted to a commerce raider under his command. In September 1779, he was commissioned as a captain in the Continental Navy, but no ship was available, so he outfitted the *George Washington* as a privateer. Unfortunately, Talbot and his crew were captured by a British ship of the line off New York early into their cruise. He was held for a time aboard a prison ship in New York Harbor and then transferred to prison in England. He was exchanged in December 1781 and shipped to France. He bor-

Silas Talbot

rowed money from Benjamin Franklin and sailed for home, only to be captured at sea again, although he was released immediately.

After the war, he settled on a farm in New York state (part of Sir John Johnson's former estate). He was elected to the state legislature in 1792 and then to the U.S. House of Representatives the following year. He was appointed to the new U.S. Navy as a captain in 1794 while still serving in Congress, but did not assume active duty. During the undeclared naval war with France in 1798, Talbot was reappointed to the captain's list and commanded the USS *Constitution* in the West Indies. He resigned his commission in 1801.

TALIAFERRO, Benjamin (1750–1821) Soldier, government official

Born in Virginia, Taliaferro was a lieutenant in Daniel Morgan's original rifle corps. He was captured by the British at the fall of Charleston in 1780. After the Revolution, he moved to Georgia and was elected to the state senate. He went to the U.S. Congress as a representative from Georgia in 1799 and then returned to the state in 1802 to serve as a judge of the Superior Court.

TALLMADGE, Benjamin (1754–1835) Continental officer, congressman

Tallmadge is best known as the head of George Washington's intelligence operations in New York during the later years of the war. He was a native of Brookhaven, Long Island and graduated from Yale in 1773, along with several friends—including Nathan Hale—some of whom later formed part of his spy network. Tallmadge was a schoolmaster in Wethersfield, Connecticut before the war but took a commission in Chester's Regiment in mid-1776. He served with distinction as a junior officer of dragoons from 1776 until 1778, fighting in most of the major battles in New York, New Jersey and Pennsylvania.

With the battle of Monmouth in the summer of 1778, however, the war in the middle colonies ceased to be one of large-scale fighting and became a cat-and-mouse affair, with the British holding New York City and Washington struggling to keep an army in existence. The chief danger to Washington was a quick march by Sir Henry Clinton that might cut off the weak Continental Army and thus threaten the entire Revolution. In order to stay ahead of British movements, Washington instituted a full-blown spy operation in New York with Tallmadge at its head. Tallmadge recruited a network that included several fellow Yale graduates, including the chief spy in New York City, Robert Townsend. The Culper network (so called for the code names used by Townsend and Abraham Woodhull, the other principal agent) operated with great success from 1778 until the end of the war. Tallmadge received regular and accurate reports from New York and Long Island, which he passed on to Washington. The most famous intelligence coup, albeit an incomplete one, came in August and September 1780. Tallmadge received a report from his agents that a British spy might be using the false name of "John Anderson." When General Benedict Arnold asked Tallmadge to provide safe passage for a friend using this name, Tallmadge was alerted, and he subsequently identified Major John André when the British spy was captured with papers in the name of Anderson. Tallmadge could not prevent Arnold's escape, but he firmly held André.

Tallmadge's spy network was never compromised, and in fact the full extent of its operations and success were not revealed until historians examined documents in the 20th century. Tallmadge never advanced beyond the rank of brevet lieutenant colonel during the war, but he became prominent after the Revolution as a businessman in Litchfield, Connecticut. He was elected to the U.S. Congress in 1801 and served eight terms before declining renomination in 1817. *Further reading:* Henry P. Johnston, ed., *Memoir of Colonel Benjamin Tallmadge* (New York, 1930; reprinted 1968).

Benjamin Tallmadge

TALLMAN, Peleg (1764–1840) Privateer, official

Born in Tiverton, Rhode Island, Tallman sailed aboard the privateer *Trumbull* as a mere teenager during the Revolution. In an engagement at sea in 1780, when he was only 16, he lost an arm and was subsequently captured and held in prison by the British until the peace in 1783. After the war, he moved to Bath in the Maine section of Massachusetts and became a merchant. He served as a representative of Massachusetts in the U.S. Congress from 1811 to 1813, and after Maine became a state in 1820, he sat in the Maine senate.

TARLETON, Banastre (1754–1833) British officer

As the most dashing, successful and ruthless British commander during the southern campaigns, Tarleton's name usually struck fear into the hearts of patriots during 1780 and 1781. He was

Banastre Tarleton

the son of a rich and prominent Liverpool merchant and a graduate of Oxford when he joined the army as a coronet of the King's Dragoon Guards in 1775. He was posted to America and served with the unsuccessful 1776 expedition against Charleston. His subsequent activities in New York—as an officer of the 16th Dragoons—brought him a slight distinction (he helped capture American general Charles Lee at Basking Ridge in December 1776).

In 1778, Tarleton was promoted to lieutenant colonel, and he formed the British Legion, a composite force of green-clad dragoons and light infantry, made up of loyalist veterans and British regulars. Similar to the American unit formed by Light-Horse Harry Lee, the British Legion combined firepower with what was for the time extreme mobility. When it was driven hard, as it was by Tarleton, the Legion was one of the most effective combat units of the entire war, capable of swift pursuit and hard fighting.

Tarleton and his legion were dispatched as part of Sir Henry Clinton's expedition to South Carolina in late 1779. All of Tarleton's horses expired during the difficult voyage south, but he soon set about finding new mounts by defeating American militia cavalry and taking their horses. He made his first mark by smashing victories at Monck's Corner and Lenud's Ferry. His reputation for ruthless brutality came mostly from the aftermath of his triumph at Waxhaws on May 29, 1780. Not only did his men devastate the last coherent American force outside Charleston, but they killed many prisoners after the surrender, meting out what soon came to be known ironically as "Tarleton's Quarter." None of the disorganized American forces left in the Carolinas could

match Tarleton's speed of movement or efficiency in battle during the ensuing months, and he won engagement after engagement, becoming Lord Cornwallis' main striking force. At the battle of Cowpens, however, Tarleton met his better in Daniel Morgan and suffered a nearly total defeat, barely escaping with his own life. His reputation tarnished, especially among his fellow British officers who regarded him as too cocky, Tarleton nevertheless regrouped his command and was again successful in battles against Nathanael Greene's army and in raiding in Virginia. At Yorktown, he commanded the troops holding the landings on the Gloucester side. After the surrender, he was paroled and returned to England.

He entered Parliament in 1790, the same year he returned to active duty in the army. He was promoted to major general in 1794 and served in several posts until 1812, when he became a full general. He was created a baronet in 1815 and knighted in 1820. For many years he lived with the former mistress of the Prince of Wales, but he eventually married an illegitimate daughter of the Duke of Ancaster. *Further reading:* Banastre Tarleton, *A History of the Campaigns of 1780 and 1781 in the Southern Provinces of North America* (1787; reprinted New York, 1968); Robert D. Bass, *The Green Dragoon* (1957).

TARRANT, Caesar (1755–1796) American sailor

A slave belonging to the Tarrant family of Hampton, Virginia, at the beginning of the war, Caesar Tarrant was a skilled sea pilot and volunteered to serve in the Virginia state navy. He was helmsman and pilot aboard the Virginia ship *Patriot* for much of the war, helping to capture several British prizes before the ship was taken itself just before the battle of Yorktown. Tarrant received his freedom in 1789 from the Virginia legislature in consequence of his service in the state navy during the Revolution. He prospered after becoming a free man, leaving several houses and tracts of land to his wife on his death. His daughter received an Ohio land grant in the 19th century based on Tarrant's Revolutionary service.

TATOM, Absalom (1742–1802) Soldier, official

A native North Carolinian, Tatom was a veteran of the Seven Years' War, having served as a sergeant in the colonial militia. He received a commission as a lieutenant in the 1st North Carolina Regiment organized to defend the state in 1775 and was promoted to captain a year later but resigned before the end of 1776. In 1778, he became assistant quartermaster of the North Carolina state arsenal at Hillsborough. While serving in local office as a clerk of the county court in 1779, he also took a commission as a major in the state militia cavalry. He apparently spent most of the Revolution in civilian activities, however, and in 1781, after the British surrender at Yorktown, he was appointed as a commissioner to survey western lands claimed by North Carolina, which were slated to become bounty land for Revolutionary War veterans. He moved through a variety of other offices during the following years, including a seat as delegate to the federal Constitutional Convention and election to the U.S. Congress in 1795.

TAYLOR, George (1716–1781) Delegate to Congress, businessman, state official

Born in Ireland, Taylor indentured himself and came to Pennsylvania as a laborer in 1736. He was employed at the ironworks at Warwick Furnace in Chester County, rising to become a clerk and eventually taking over the foundry by marrying the widow of the owner. He moved his business to Bucks County in the 1750s and leased Dunham Furnace close to Easton, Pennsylvania, where he made his home. First elected to the colonial assembly in 1764, he served several consecutive terms and supported continued proprietary rule in Pennsylvania. His patriotic activities began during the Stamp Act crisis, and he continued to be involved in local committees through the outbreak of the Revolution. He was a colonel of the local militia and sat on the county committee of correspondence. In July 1776, Taylor was selected as a delegate to the Continental Congress with specific instructions to sign the Declaration of Independence, which he did. He had a short career in Congress, resigning in March 1777 and retiring altogether from public life after six months' service on the Pennsylvania Supreme Executive Council. He returned to the iron business, turning out grape and cannon shot for the Continental Army, but the state of Pennsylvania dispossessed him of his lease in 1778 since the actual owner was loyalist John Galloway. Taylor, who lived openly with his housekeeper by whom he fathered five children, moved to New Jersey and leased another ironworks, which he operated until his death.

TAYLOR, John (of Caroline) (1753–1824) Continental and militia officer, government official, political writer

Best remembered for his political writings during the age of the early Republic, Taylor (who was usually known as John of Caroline to distinguish him from several other John Taylors) also served as a soldier during the American Revolution. He was born in Virginia and raised by his distant relative Edmund Pendleton after his father's death when Taylor was only three. He received a broad education from private tutors and schools and attended the College of William and Mary before reading for the law. He began practice in Caroline County in 1774. With the beginning of the War of Independence, Taylor entered the army, and he served in the middle states until resigning his commission as major in 1779. He returned to Virginia and practiced law until the British invasion of his home state in 1781, when he again took the field as a lieutenant colonel of state militia attached to the army of the Marquis de Lafayette. He began to prosper after the war, adding considerable plantation property through his marriage to John Penn's daughter. He also entered a long period of service in the Virginia House of Delegates and, beginning in 1792, was three times selected to fill vacant seats in the U.S. Senate. He was a consistent and cogent thinker on political matters and published a series of essays and books between 1794 and 1820 that explicated a theory of freehold agrarian democracy and states' rights. He was a stout Jeffersonian in politics and a defender in print of the yeoman-based theory (the idea that the body politic should be based on a population of yeoman farmers) of political polity. *Further reading:* Robert E. Shalhope, *John Taylor of Caroline* (Columbia, S.C., 1980); Charles William, Jr., *The Political Theory of John Taylor of Caroline* (Rutherford, N.J., 1976).

TAZEWELL, Henry (1753–1799) State official

Tazewell was born in Brunswick County, Virginia and attended the College of William and Mary, graduating in 1770. He opened a law practice in Williamsburg three years later. With the coming of the Revolution, he sat in the provincial congress and raised a troop of local cavalry. He served in the Virginia General Assembly during most of the war. Following the Revolution, Tazewell served as a judge on the state supreme court and then the court of appeals until 1794, when he was selected to fill a vacancy as U.S. senator from Virginia. He was elected president pro tem of the Senate and died in office.

TEISSÈDRE de FLEURY, François Louis, Marquis de (b. 1749) French volunteer

Demonstratively a man of keen personal bravery, de Fleury (as he was known during the American war) received one of only eight Congressional medals awarded for valor during the Revolution. He came from Provence and had advanced in rank rapidly as a French officer during the late 1760s. He arrived in America in 1776 with Phillippe Charles Tronson de Coudray but volunteered on his own for service and was made a captain of engineers in May 1777. He helped survey and plan the defenses around Philadelphia and at the battle of Brandywine in September had his horse shot from under him, an occurrence that prompted Congress to present him with a new mount in recognition of his bravery. The new horse was killed with de Fleury astride during the battle of Germantown the following month, and the Frenchman took a ball in the leg. He was wounded again during the defense of Fort Mifflin. In November 1777, de Fleury was promoted to lieutenant colonel and assigned to stop British shipping on the Delaware, hatching a scheme to attack with rockets. He was subsequently detached to the aborted invasion of Canada under the Marquis de Lafayette and then was assigned as assistant inspector general under von Steuben. At the battle of Monmouth, de Fleury was one of the commanders of an elite body of picked men in Charles Lee's division. He was then sent to Newport and acquitted himself well enough in the futile American campaign to again rate a mention in dispatches to Washington.

His moments of highest achievement came in July 1779 during the famous nighttime surprise attack by Anthony Wayne on the British at Stony Point, New York. De Fleury personally led one of the advance parties that stormed through the outer defenses and seized the British position. He and his 150 men waded through four feet of water and then rushed the fortifications and hacked their way through. He was the first man into the British works and tore down the flag with his own hands. This feat earned him the rare medal of recognition from Congress. He requested and received a leave of absence in the fall of 1779 and returned to France, where he resumed his commission and was appointed to the Saintonge Regiment which formed part of Rochambeau's expeditionary force. De Fleury thus returned to America as a French officer and fought at Yorktown. Afterward, he fought during the wars of the French Revolution. One account says he was executed in Paris in 1794, but another cites the record of a pension awarded to him in 1796.

TELFAIR, Edward (1735–1807) Delegate to Congress, governor, businessman

Telfair was born in Scotland and trained as a merchant. He came to Virginia in the late 1750s as a commercial agent, moving eventually to Halifax, North Carolina and then Savannah, Georgia, where he established his own mercantile business. He prospered greatly in the New World, trading with the West and East Indies, building his own ships and eventually acquiring large land holdings. He was one of the rabid revolutionaries of Savannah and was involved in all the protests and rebellious actions of the city's patriots during 1774 and 1775. He was a member of the council of safety, attended the timid Georgia provincial conventions and helped lead the mob that seized gunpowder from the royal stores in Savannah. Nonetheless, he was suspected at least for a brief time in 1776 of loyalism—his relatives and business partners were all loyalists—but by 1778 he was back in the patriot graces and elected as a delegate to the Continental Congress, an office renewed in 1780, 1781 and 1782. He signed the Articles of Confederation while a member of Congress but was otherwise obscure. Following the war he helped settle boundary disputes and Indian claims, and in 1786 he was elected governor of Georgia, winning reelection in 1790. *Further reading:* E. Merton Coulter, "Edward Telfair," *Georgia Historical Quarterly* 20 (June 1936), 99–124.

TEN BROECK, Abraham (1734–1810) Militia officer, state official

Ten Broeck was born in Albany and was related by marriage to the Van Rensselaer family. He sat in the New York Assembly during the 1760s and was a member of the patriot New York Provincial Congress in 1775 and 1777. He also served in the state militia as a senior officer and was present at the battle of Bemis Heights (Second Saratoga) when the New York troops helped overrun the key British position during the early stages of the fight. He became judge of the Albany County Court of Common Pleas in 1781 and sat on the bench for the following 13 years. He was also mayor of Albany and a member of the state senate.

TERNAY, Charles Louis d'Arsac, Chevalier de (1722–1780) French naval officer

Ternay fought in North America during the Seven Years' War and was another of the undistinguished and relatively timid French naval commanders during the era of the American Revolution. He was originally from Breton and had achieved brigadier's rank when he retired in 1772 to take the civilian post of governor of the Isle de France. He was called back to active duty in 1779 and given command of the fleet that was to ferry Rochambeau's force across the Atlantic. He sailed from Brest in May 1780 with eight ships of the line, several smaller supporting vessels and the troop transports. During the two-month voyage to Newport, Ternay encountered a British squadron under William Cornwallis but, acting under orders, he refused engagement in order to deliver his charges to Rhode Island as soon as possible. He arrived only days ahead of the British, who proceeded to bottle him up in port and render the French squadron ineffective. Ternay contracted a fever and died in Newport on December 15.

THACHER, James (1754–1844) Continental surgeon, physician, writer

A fine writer and an even better observer, Thacher kept a journal of the Revolutionary War that has been a basic source of information and interpretation since it was first published in 1823.

He was born in Barnstable, Massachusetts to a family of poor farmers who could not afford an education for the boy. Thacher was apprenticed, however, to a strict but talented local doctor, and after five years of training, he set up his own practice. He was accepted as a surgeon's mate at a military hospital in Cambridge, Massachusetts in 1775. He moved on to the 6th Continental Regiment of Asa Whitcomb in 1776, serving first in Boston and then during the disastrous American retreat from Fort Ticonderoga. In the Spring of 1777, Thacher became a surgeon's mate at a hospital in Albany, New York, remaining there more than a year. He joined Henry Jackson's Massachusetts Regiment (known as the 16th Massachusetts after July 1780) and took part in the Penobscot Expedition. Thacher was with the Continental Army at winter quarters in New Jersey during the difficult winter of 1779–

80, and he eventually was assigned to Alexander Scammell's light infantry, with which the surgeon served at the siege of Yorktown.

He left the army in 1783 and settled in Plymouth, Massachusetts, eventually becoming one of the leading physicians in the state. Following the turn of the century, Thacher began to write extensively, publishing important books on medicine, biography and agriculture. His best-known publication, however, was his journal, kept throughout the war and issued just before the 50th anniversary of the beginning of the Revolution. Although he reported on many events of the war that he himself had not witnessed, he gave a clear account of how and when news reached the average patriot. Moreover, he narrated his own experiences with a clarity and vigor that is scarcely matched in any other American eyewitness account of the war. He was particularly valuable in describing figures such as Washington, who visited Thacher's hospital in October 1778:

> The personal appearance of our Commander in Chief, is that of the perfect gentleman and accomplished warrior. He is remarkably tall, full six feet, erect and well proportioned. . . . The serenity of his countenance, and majestic gracefulness of his deportment, impart a strong impression of that dignity and grandeur, which are his particular characteristics. . . . There is a fine symmetry in the features of his face, indicative of a benign and dignified spirit. His nose is strait, and his eyes inclined to blue.

Thacher reflected the usual effect among the army of a personal appearance by the commander in chief—even his enemies found Washington's bearing monumentally dignified.

Thacher lived to his 90th year, garnering considerable reputation and honors (including a degree from Harvard) on account of his books and medical accomplishments. His revolutionary journal was republished many times during the 19th century. *Further reading:* James Thacher, *A Military Journal During the American Revolutionary War, 1775 to 1783 . . .* (Boston, 1823; many reprints).

THACHER, Peter (1752–1802) Clergyman

Born in Massachusetts, Thacher graduated from Harvard in 1769. A year later—still short of his 20th birthday—he became pastor of the Congregational Church in Malden, where he served during the years of the American Revolution. He was a vociferous patriot, and in 1776, he delivered a public speech in Watertown in commemoration of the Boston Massacre that so impressed members of Congress that they asked him to become a recruiter along the Massachusetts seacoast. Thacher became chaplain of the patriot Massachusetts General Court in 1776 (he remained chaplain until his death) and in 1780 sat in the state constitutional convention. After the war, he moved to the Brattle Street Church in Boston.

THATCHER, George (1754–1824) Delegate to Congress, privateer, jurist Thatcher (whose name is also spelled Thacher) was born in Yarmouth, Massachusetts and graduated from Harvard in 1776. He sailed as a privateer on one cruise during the early days of the Revolution but withdrew to read the law. After admission to the bar he settled in the Maine section of the state. In 1787, Thatcher served one term as a delegate from Massachusetts to the Confederation Congress. After the passage of a new federal constitution, he was elected several times to the U.S. House of Representatives. In 1792, he became a district judge and then served as an associate justice of the Massachusetts Supreme Court until 1820 when, following the creation of the State of Maine, Thatcher became a justice of the new state's supreme court.

THAYENDANEGEA. See BRANT, Joseph.

THAYER, Thomas. See SAMPSON, Deborah.

THIEL, Karl. See CIST, Charles.

THOMAS, Isaiah (1749–1831) Militiaman, printer-publisher Thomas was born in Boston to a very poor family. He was apprenticed to a local printer at age six and grew up in the printing trade. He ran away to Halifax, Nova Scotia in 1766 but returned to disentangle himself from his unexpired apprenticeship, and after traveling to South Carolina in search of work, Thomas settled once again in Boston. In July 1770, he began publication of *The Massachusetts Spy*, which served as a news and propaganda sheet for the Boston patriots. He spirited his press and type out of Boston on April 16, 1775, moving his operations to Worcester. He took up arms on April 19 against the British expedition to

Lexington and Concord, fighting as a militiaman. He returned to Worcester and on May 3 issued a number of the *Spy* with his eyewitness account of the battle. The Massachusetts Provincial Congress commissioned him to publish "A Narrative of the Excursions and Ravages of the King's Troops under the command of General Gage . . ." in May, and the 24-page booklet appeared in July.

Thomas moved in 1776 to Salem but, failing to find enough business there, returned to Worcester in 1778. His printing and publishing enterprise eventually grew to considerable size and relative prosperity, making him one of the principal publishers in New England after the war. He developed the art of good typography in his production of books, and his best examples rival good European printing. He was especially active in printing books for children and issued the first *Mother Goose* in an American edition in 1786. He ended his life as a wealthy man, devoted to collecting books and promoting knowledge. In 1810, Thomas published a two-volume history of printing in America, and in 1812, he founded the American Antiquarian Society. *Further reading:* Charles L. Nichols, *Isaiah Thomas: Printer, Writer, and Collector* (New York, 1971).

THOMAS, John (1724–1776) Continental and militia general, physician One of the patriots' most capable and experienced military leaders, Thomas suffered from the politics of appointment and then fell victim to disease before his talents could be brought to fruition. He was born in Marshfield, Massachusetts, learned medicine from a doctor in Medford, and settled in Kingston. He served extensively in the colonial wars, first as a surgeon's mate in 1746 and with increasing responsibility and rank for the next 14 years. In 1760, he was a colonel of militia and commanded a full regiment in Lord Jeffrey Amherst's capture of Montreal. With the British-colonial victory over the French secured, Thomas returned to his medical practice, although he remained a senior officer of the Massachusetts militia.

He was a patriot in the growing struggles during the early 1770s and was appointed to the rank of lieutenant general of militia, making him the ranking officer in Massachusetts. When the Continental Congress set about commissioning general officers for the new Continental Army in June 1775, however, the delegates paid a great deal more attention to political clout than military experience or potential for leadership. The congressmen short-sightedly gave brigadier's commissions to William Heath and Seth Pomeroy as the allotment for Massachusetts and ignored Thomas. He was abjured by George Washington not to resign his militia commission, however, and Congress' error was rectified to some degree later in the summer when Thomas was finally commissioned as a brigadier, albeit junior to Heath (Pomeroy had refused his appointment). Thomas demonstrated his skills in March 1776, when he executed the overnight fortification of Dorchester Heights above Boston, a lightning move that rendered General Thomas Gage's position in the city hopeless. A few days later, Thomas was promoted to major general and was sent north to take command of the shattered American army that had set out the previous fall to invade Canada. The repulse suffered in December at the gates of Quebec had left the Americans in great distress, and when he reached his new command, Thomas discovered more woes in the form of a British force approaching up the St. Lawrence. He began a retreat toward Montreal, but he was stricken with smallpox and died on June 2.

THOMPSON, Benjamin (Count Rumford) (1753–1814) Loyalist, British official and officer, physicist

A man of high scientific and intellectual attainment but dubious character, Thompson led a complex life. He was born in Woburn, Massachusetts and showed early in his education a strong propensity for mathematics and science. He was apprenticed at age 13 to a merchant in Salem, Massachusetts and managed to educate himself in a broad range of scientific knowledge (and languages) by the time he was in his late teens. In 1771, Thompson began to study medicine. He then became a schoolteacher, moving eventually to Concord, New Hampshire, where he met and married a woman 14 years his senior. Thompson somehow ingratiated himself with royal governor John Wentworth, who appointed Thompson as a major in the New Hampshire Provincial 2nd Regiment. Thompson became a farmer on his wife's land and began scientific experiments to improve the quality of gunpowder.

As the difficulties between the royal government and the colonists increased, Rumford secretly cast his lot with the British, becoming a paid informer for British commander Thomas Gage and probably aiding Dr. Benjamin Church to betray the Massachusetts patriot councils. However, Thompson kept up a public pretense of indecision (one that fooled many historians for generations thereafter). He applied for a commission in a Massachusetts regiment in 1775 but was turned down, and he thereupon fled to the British in October. He remained on board a British frigate in Boston Harbor until the evacuation in the spring of 1776, when he sailed for England. Thompson's ability to find favor with governments was one of his strongest points, and he was soon in the good graces of Lord George Germain, who was secretary of state for the colonies. Thompson received an appointment in the colonial office and in 1780 became undersecretary for the northern department, holding also a commission as a lieutenant colonel in the army. He had meanwhile separated from his wife (whom he never saw again). He returned to America as an officer, although not until 1782 after the end of active hostilities.

His career after the American Revolution was remarkable. He was knighted in 1784 and then left England to take service in Europe at the court of Bavaria as a senior minister of state. He also continued and refined his scientific interests, conducting original and productive experiments in the nature of heat and light (which also produced practical results in his improved designs for artillery and heating stoves). He was made a count of the Holy Roman Empire by the Elector of Bavaria in 1791, taking a place-name from New Hampshire as his title: Count Rumford. He returned to England in 1795 and flourished as a man of science, eventually establishing the Rumford prize for discoveries in physics. He was appointed as Bavaria's minister to Great Britain in 1798 but was not allowed to serve since he was a British subject. He moved to France thereafter—having declined an appointment as superintendent of the new U.S. Military Academy—and remarried. The final years of his life were spent at a home outside Paris. *Further reading:* J. A. Thompson, *Count Rumford of Massachusetts* (Boston, 1935); Allen French, *General Gage's Informers* (Ann Arbor, Mich., 1932).

THOMPSON, William (1727–1796) Officer

Although he was born in Pennsylvania, Thompson's name is most associated with the southern colonies of South Carolina and Georgia. He moved to South Carolina at an early age to work on his father's plantation. He was a public official—justice of the peace and tax collector—and a grower of indigo, and he was a major in the colonial militia during frontier Indian fighting. Thompson also held office in Georgia before the Revolution, sitting in the legislature, and he was one of the delegates to the rebel Georgia provincial assembly. When the war began, Thompson was a militia officer, but he received a commission in the Continental Army and commanded the handful of Continental regulars on duty in South Carolina in early 1776 (he is not to be confused with the other Continental Army colonel of the same name who commanded a Pennsylvania regiment). Most of the organized Continental regiments in South Carolina remained under the control of state governor Edward Rutledge, and Thompson's 300 men (most of them probably riflemen) were assigned to the defense of Fort Sullivan in Charleston Harbor when Sir Henry Clinton attempted to seize the city in the spring of 1776. Although the battle that repulsed the British was mostly an affair between the guns of the Royal Navy squadron and the fort, Thompson received considerable plaudits for his service, including the thanks of Congress and promotion to colonel. He resigned from the army two years later. He was captured in 1780 at the eventual fall of Charleston to Clinton's second expedition, but he was soon released. Thompson was seized in 1781 by the British, who were by then in control of all of South Carolina, and was jailed for breaking parole.

THOMPSON, William (1736–1781) Continental general

A hard-luck officer who spent most of the war as an unexchanged prisoner, Thompson was born in Ireland but emigrated to the region of Carlisle, Pennsylvania. He was a veteran of the Seven Years' War and became familiar with frontier conditions by working on military land claims in western Pennsylvania. He was a member of the Cumberland County committee of correspondence in 1774 and of the committee of safety in 1775. When Congress asked Pennsylvania to raise six companies of riflemen for the Continental service in 1775, Thompson was commissioned as colonel and given command of what turned out to be nine full companies—known initially as Thompson's Pennsylvania Rifle Battalion. He led his somewhat unruly men to join the siege of Boston, where they

attracted considerable comment by their appearance and rowdy behavior.

In March 1776, just as the British evacuated Boston, Thompson was promoted to brigadier general by Congress and was assigned to march north with reinforcements for the American army that had been defeated at the walls of Quebec the previous December. Thompson's fortunes in the enterprise of invading Canada were no better than those of previous American commanders. He reached St. John's in June and was ordered by General John Sullivan to take the British post at Three Rivers as a preliminary to renewing the American offensive. The mission went wrong from the start, and Thompson and his men floundered into a swamp while attempting what they hoped would be a surprise night march. Worse, when they finally made contact with the British defenders, the Americans discovered that the garrison had been reinforced by several thousand troops who had dug themselves in. The Americans faced overwhelming odds and were quickly defeated. Thompson was captured and his men scattered to make their painful way back to the American lines. He was paroled and sent back to Philadelphia, but his formal exchange hung fire until 1780, when he was finally swapped for Baron von Riedesel. Thompson had meanwhile quarreled with Congressman Thomas McKean, whom Thompson accused of stalling his exchange, and the general was censured by Congress and lost a civil suit for damages brought by McKean. Thompson died without again taking the field.

THOMSON, Charles (1729–1824) Congressional secretary, merchant

Thomson served as secretary for the Continental and Confederation congresses throughout their entire existence, from the first Continental Congress in 1774 until the dissolution of the Confederation in 1789—a remarkable turn in office given the turbulent history of these institutions.

He was born in Ireland and arrived on the Delaware shore at age 10 as an orphan: his mother had died in the old country and his father had expired aboard ship within sight of land. Taken in by an older brother who had previously come to Philadelphia, Thomson received a good education in Pennsylvania academies and became himself a tutor and private teacher. In 1760, he turned to trade and established a mercantile business in rum, iron and

Charles Thomson

wool manufacturing. He was also something of a public figure through his activities as a negotiator with the Indian tribes of Delaware and Pennsylvania. As the conflicts with Britain increased, Thomson became a radical patriot, rousing considerable support among the lower merchants, tradesmen and mechanics of Philadelphia. He was opposed in the patriot movement by moderates such as Joseph Galloway, who frustrated Thomson's election as a delegate to the first Congress in 1774.

Nonetheless, Thomson was appointed as secretary to Congress. He became perhaps the most stable part of the legislative and executive body—outlasting any single delegate by a wide margin. Throughout the Revolution and the period of the Confederation, Thomson served a wide variety of functions for Congress: keeping the daily record, drafting reports, writing letters and presiding over committees. When a new form of government was ordained by the federal constitution, Thomson hoped to continue in office, but he was disappointed when the new Congress refused a place for him in the new government. He resigned in July 1789 and retired to an estate near Philadelphia, where he spent the remaining decades of his life translating the Bible. *Further reading:* Boyd S. Schlenther, *Charles Thomson: A Patriot's Pursuit* (Newark, Del., 1990); Edwin J. Hendricks, *Charles Tomson and the Making of a New Nation, 1729–1824* (Rutherford, N.J., 1979).

THOMSON, Mark (1739–1803) Militia officer, official Thomson was born in Pennsylvania but lived in New Jersey most of his life. He was a local official in Sussex County, New Jersey before the Revolution and was elected to the provincial assemblies in 1774 and 1775. He was the lieutenant colonel of the county militia and became colonel before the end of the war. Thomson sat in the New Jersey General Assembly in 1779 and on the state council during the late 1780s. He served two terms, from 1795 to 1799, as U.S. representative from New Jersey.

THORNTON, Matthew (1714–1803) Delegate to Congress, physician, militia officer, state official Born in Ireland, Thornton was brought to America by his parents at age four. They settled first in the Maine region of Massachusetts but then moved to Worcester. Thornton studied medicine as an apprentice to a local doctor and set up his own practice in Londonderry, New Hampshire in 1740. He served as a military doctor on the British expedition against Louisbourg and then took a seat in the colonial legislature, sitting continuously from 1758 until the Revolution. He was one of the principal leaders of the patriot movement in New Hampshire, serving as president of the provincial assembly and the constitutional convention and as chairman of the committee of safety. In November 1776, Thornton was sent as a delegate to the Continental Congress and was allowed to belatedly sign the Declaration of Independence. He also held rank as a colonel of the state militia but confined his activities to the political and civil arenas. He resigned from Congress in 1777 and returned to New Hampshire to become an associate justice of the superior court, even though he had no legal training. In the 1780s, he gave up his medical practice and turned to farming.

THRUSTON, Charles Mynn (1738–1812) Continental officer, clergyman Born in Virginia, Thruston studied at the College of William and Mary and then went to England for education and ordination as an Episcopal priest. He returned to Virginia and settled in the Shenandoah Valley. Despite his religious calling, Thruston served in the colonial militia and raised a company at the beginning of the Revolution, serving as its captain. In January 1777, he was commissioned as a Continental colonel and authorized to raise a Virginia regiment, which became known as Thruston's Additional Regiment. Three months later, he lost an arm as the result of fighting near Amboy, New Jersey. His regiment was merged with Gist's Ranger Corps in January 1779, whereupon Thruston resigned from the service. Following the Revolution, Thruston became a judge and in 1808 he moved to Louisiana. He died near New Orleans.

THYNNE, Thomas. See Weymouth, Viscount.

TILGHMAN, Matthew (1718–1790) Delegate to Congress, state official Tilghman was one of the primary patriot politicians in Maryland and a veteran of public office by the time of the Revolution. He was born near Centerville, Maryland. His long string of offices began with a place as justice of the peace. He was selected to the Maryland House of Delegates in 1751 and sat there until 1777, acting as speaker from 1773 to 1775. He led the protests against the Stamp Act and the Townshend Acts, and in 1774 he became chairman of the Maryland Committee of Correspondence and of the provincial convention that took over direction of the state. He was the leader of the Maryland delegation to the Continental Congress from 1774 to 1777 and was one of the state's strongest advocates for supporting independence. Ironically, he left Philadelphia in June 1776 to chair a convention in Maryland to form a state constitution and therefore missed voting for and signing the Declaration of Independence. He was also a member of the Maryland state senate.

TILGHMAN, Tench (1744–1786) Continental officer, merchant The herald of the victory at Yorktown, Tilghman was born in Maryland (the cousin of Matthew) and educated in Philadelphia at the academy and college there, graduating in 1761. He became a Philadelphia merchant but sold his business at the beginning of the War of Independence and took an appointment as secretary to the Continental Congress' mission to the Iroquois in 1775. In July 1776, he received a commission in the Pennsylvania Battalion organized to form part of the strategic reserve—known collectively as the Flying Camp for Washington's New York campaign. The following month, Tilghman became a volunteer aide-de-camp and military secretary to George Washing-

ton, a post he held for the remainder of the Revolution. He was one of the essential members of Washington's official military family for the seven years he served under the commander in chief. Washington asked Congress to confer a regular Continental commission on Tilghman, which was done after some delay in the spring of 1777, making Tilghman a lieutenant colonel.

His most famous duty was to carry the news of Lord Cornwallis' surrender from Yorktown to the Congress in Philadelphia. After a long and difficult ride from Virginia, Tilghman reached Philadelphia in the early morning hours of October 22 and was guided to the house of President Thomas McKean by the city's night watchman, who immediately began to proclaim: "Past three o'clock and Cornwallis is taken!" Congress was so broke that individual delegates had to make private donations to cover the costs of his journey.

Tilghman continued as an aide to Washington until the final dissolution of the Continental Army and Washington's resignation in December 1783, but he did not long enjoy the peace. He had married Matthew Tilghman's daughter in 1783 (she was his cousin at some remove and the marriage made him both Matthew's cousin and his son-in-law) and he reopened his mercantile business in Philadelphia in 1784, but he died just before his 41st birthday in 1786. He left an interesting memoir of the Revolution with brief excerpts from his wartime diary, including an account of the siege at Yorktown. *Further reading: Memoir of Lieutenant Colonel Tench Tilghman* (Albany, 1876; reprinted 1971).

TILTON, James (1745–1822) Continental surgeon, delegate to Congress Tilton was born in Kent County, Delaware and raised by his widowed mother. He attended an academy in Nottingham, Maryland and then was one of the early students at the new medical department at the College of Philadelphia, an institution that evolved into the first medical school in America as part of the University of Pennsylvania. He graduated in 1768 and returned to Delaware to practice. In 1775, he joined Haslett's Delaware Regiment (which became one of the most famous units in the Continental Army) as regimental surgeon, drawing not only on his training as a physician but also on his background as a lieutenant of his local militia. Tilton served in the field with the regiment throughout the arduous campaigns in New York and New Jersey, culminating in the battle at Princeton where the unit was badly hurt and its commander killed.

Tilton did not remain with the Delawares after they were reorganized in early 1777 but instead became a hospital surgeon with responsibility for hospitals at Princeton, Trenton and New Windsor, Maryland. Unlike most of the doctors of his day, he had an abiding concern for sanitary conditions and insisted on building clean, airy huts for his patients, which he found reduced the mortality rates of the sick and wounded. In 1780, Tilton took charge of a hospital at Williamsburg, Virginia, and he served there through the Yorktown campaign.

He was elected as a delegate to Congress in 1783 and served two terms. He thereupon gave up the practice of medicine and turned to farming near Wilmington, Delaware. In 1813 in the midst of the second war with Great Britain, he published a small book on military medicine that brought him to the attention of John Armstrong, the former Revolutionary officer and current secretary of war. Tilton was appointed as surgeon general of the U.S. Army, and after touring the northern frontier, he wrote the first manual of regulations for the medical department of the army. He left his post in 1815 and retired to a home near Wilmington. *Further reading:* J. E. Pilcher, *The Surgeon Generals of the Army of the United States* (Washington, D.C., 1905).

TONYN, Patrick (1725–1804) British general, officer

The son of a British officer, Tonyn received a commission in the 6th Dragoons (known as the Innskillings) at age 19 and fought in Europe during the wars of the 1750s and 1760s. He served as lieutenant colonel of the 104th Regiment of Foot between 1761 and 1763, when the unit had its brief existence. Tonyn became governor of East Florida in the spring of 1774 and continued in office until the end of the Revolution in 1783. While serving in America, he was advanced rapidly in rank to major general, and he reached the rank of full general before his death.

TOUSARD, A. Louis de (1749–1817) French soldier, diplomat

De Tousard led a long and varied career. He was commissioned in the French royal army as a junior officer of artillery in 1769. In 1777, he came to America as a volunteer for the patriot cause, taking leave from his regiment to do

so. He served with the Continental artillery at Germantown and Brandywine. In 1778, De Tousard lost an arm to amputation from a battle wound suffered in Rhode Island. Consequently, he received a brevet as lieutenant colonel and a life pension of $30 a month from Congress. He then withdrew to France and resumed his military career there. He was sent to Santo Domingo in 1784 to help put down a slave revolt. During the French Revolution he was accused and thrown in prison. Released in 1793, he returned to the United States and was reinstated in the U.S. Army with the rank of major. In 1802, he again left his adopted country and returned to Santo Domingo. It was back to America three years later, when he was appointed a commercial agent of the French government to New Orleans. After serving as a vice consul in Philadelphia and consul in New Orleans, he returned to his native Paris in 1816.

TOWNE, Benjamin (d. 1793) Loyalist publisher

Towne was born in England and moved to Philadelphia sometime before 1766. In his adopted city he became a journeyman printer and was a partner in publishing the *Pennsylvania Chronicle and Universal Advertiser* by the early 1770s. In 1774, he struck out on his own and began the *Pennsylvania Evening Post*, the city's only evening newspaper. His editorial stance supported the British during their occupation of Philadelphia in 1777 and 1778, and he was indicted by the Pennsylvania Supreme Executive Council after the British left, but the charges were dropped when he reversed his position and began to print pro-American articles.

TOWNSEND, Robert (c. 1753–1838) American spy

Townsend was a key member of the so-called Culper spy network, run by Benjamin Tallmadge and the most successful American espionage operation of the war. Townsend was a well-established merchant of New York City and Oyster Bay, Long Island by the time of the Revolution. He had inherited a trade in flax, sugar, rum, iron and dry goods from his father, and therefore had a good cover for both mixing with the British occupiers of the city and communicating with the Americans. Townsend also was a silent partner in James Rivington's loyalist newspaper *The Royal Gazette* and garnered a great deal of insider information from that connection. Although the British apparently never sus-

Robert Townsend

pected Townsend as a spy, he had made no secret of his patriot leanings before the war: he raised funds for the New York Sons of Liberty in 1772 and served briefly as a commissary for New York militia in 1776. Tallmadge's spy network, which he organized at the behest of George Washington after the capture and execution of Nathan Hale, revolved around Townsend, Samuel Woodhall and two couriers. The group took elaborate and highly effective precautions to preserve their identities. Townsend was known in correspondence only as Culper Jr., and the spies communicated by means of a complex code they had devised themselves. Townsend—aided by his sister, Sarah, who worked in his boarding house for British officers—passed on information to Washington about British activities at their major base in New York City. Security was so well preserved by the system that Townsend was never identified in his own day as a spy: his role was uncovered only in the 20th century after painstaking analysis of handwriting and secret papers. He continued his mercantile business at Oyster Bay after the war, surviving well into the 19th century. *Further reading:* Morton Pennypacker, *The Two Spies: Nathan Hale and Robert Townsend* (New York, 1930).

TOWNSHEND, Charles (1725–1767) British official   Although he died eight years before the Revolution became a fighting war, Townshend's attempts to raise money through import duties and to lessen the power of the elected colonial assemblies renewed tensions that had first been felt during the Stamp Act crisis and set a collision course in Massachusetts that ended at Lexington and Concord. He was a sometime brilliant but unprincipled politician, typical perhaps of the mid-18th century in Britain.

Educated in Holland and at Oxford, Townshend began his political career with a seat in Parliament in 1747. He passed through a succession of offices under many governments, deftly switching sides and changing allegiances in the quicksilver world of British politics. By the time he took office as chancellor of the exchequer under the elder William Pitt in 1766, Townshend had previously served as a member of the board of trade, a lord of the Admiralty (several times), treasurer of the chamber, paymaster of forces, president of the board of trade and secretary at war under leaders as diverse as Newcastle, Grenville, Pitt, Bute and Rockingham. Townshend's position in the government of 1766 appeared to be tenuous, but Pitt suddenly succumbed to one of his periodic bouts of depression, and Townshend found himself as leader of the cabinet. The government was desperate for revenue, so he pushed through Parliament a series of acts that created a new, vigorous customs service in the American colonies; imposed duties on glass, lead, paint, paper and tea; and would pay royal officials from the income rather than leaving them in the fiscal power of the colonial assemblies. He failed to see the storm of protest the so-called Townshend Acts set off, dying of typhus within weeks of passage of the new laws. *Further reading:* Peter G. Thomas, *The Townshend Duties Crisis: The Second Phase of the American Revolution, 1767–1773* (Oxford, Eng., 1987); Sir Lewis Napier, *Charles Townshend* (Cambridge, Eng., 1959).

TRACY, Nathaniel (1751–1796) Merchant, privateer   Tracy was a native of Newburyport, Massachusetts and one of the many New England merchants who turned to the business of privateering during the Revolution. He was educated at Harvard before entering the shipping business in 1769. When war came, he set up a fleet of 24 privateers. His fleet, like many such private fleets, slowly dwindled over the following eight years—in 1783, Tracy had only one ship left—but not before taking more than a hundred prizes. He sat in the Massachusetts General Court in 1781–82.

TRAPIER, Paul (1749–1778) Delegate to Congress, militia officer, state official

Trapier was born near Georgetown, South Carolina and educated in England, first at Eton, then at Cambridge and the Middle Temple. He returned to South Carolina and sat on the Georgetown Committee of Safety and represented his locality in the provincial congress. He was elected to the state general assembly in 1776. During the war, Trapier served in the local Georgetown Artillery. He was selected as a delegate to the Continental Congress in 1777 but did not attend. He died a year later.

TRONSON de COUDRAY, Philippe Charles (1738–1777) French volunteer

Perhaps the most obnoxious and troublesome of the many French adventurers (most of whom viewed American service as little more than a vehicle to attain cheap rank), de Coudray was nonetheless a highly competent artillerist and engineer who was an acknowledged expert in just those skills the patriots needed most. He was not of noble or aristocratic birth, which hampered his advancement in the status-conscious French royal army and may have contributed to his prickliness about rank—he was reported to have fought more than 30 duels during his time in the French army. He was born in Reims, one of 10 children of a humble family. Despite this handicap, he rose in the artillery branch of the army to brigadier and had been tutor to the Count d'Artois and a confidant of the great French artillerist Gribeauval. In 1776, de Coudray struck a bargain with American envoy Silas Deane, a man overawed by French officers, and sailed to America with a contingent of 18 other officers and a promise of a major generalship. Congress felt the need to honor Deane's agreement, but American major generals Greene, Knox and Sullivan were outraged that they would be made junior and threatened to resign. The "solution" was to commission de Coudray a major general without a command or authority over the

Americans. In a few short weeks, the Frenchman made himself even more unpopular among his new compatriots by an unremitting attitude of hauteur and airs of superiority. He even alienated the French engineering officers who had previously come to serve with Duportail. De Coudray was removed from the scene before doing more damage, however, when he foolishly rode an ill-trained horse into the Schuylkill River at a ferry crossing near Philadelphia and was drowned.

TROUP, Robert (1757–1832) Officer, jurist, land speculator

Troup was born in New York City and educated at King's College (Columbia). He began his Revolutionary War service in an unspecified regiment as a lieutenant and was a lieutenant colonel on the staff of Horatio Gates during the northern campaign against General John Burgoyne in 1777. For a brief time in 1778, Troup was secretary to the new Board of War set up by Congress. After the Revolution, he served in the New York State Assembly and was appointed a judge of the U.S. District Court of New York in 1796. Troup was also a successful speculator in western lands and contributed financially to the founding of Hobart College in New York state.

TROWBRIDGE, Edmund (1709–1793) Loyalist jurist

Trowbridge served nearly 20 years as attorney general of Massachusetts and was a judge of the supreme court prior to the Revolution. He presided at the trial of Captain Thomas Preston after the Boston Massacre and generally satisfied all parties with his handling of the case from a legal point of view. He was loyal to the crown but took little public role during the Revolution.

TRUMBULL, Benjamin (1735–1820) Clergyman, military chaplain, historian

The son of a first cousin of Jonathan Trumbull the Elder, Benjamin Trumbull was born in Hebron, Connecticut and educated at Yale, from which he graduated in 1759. He studied theology with Eleazor Wheelock and was ordained as a Congregationalist minister in 1760. His professional life was a model of constancy: his first and only parish was the church in North Haven, Connecticut, where he served for 60 years, from his appointment in late 1760 until his death. He spent only six months away from his parish when he served as chaplain for Wadsworth's Brigade (a militia unit) during the latter half of 1776. Trumbull was also an ambitious historian, and he embarked in the late 1770s—at the urging of Jonathan Trumbull the Elder—on writing a comprehensive history of the state of Connecticut. He worked on this project for the rest of his life, seeing a two-volume edition published in 1818. *Further reading:* Benjamin Trumbull, *A Complete History of Connecticut . . .* (1818; reprinted New York, 1972).

TRUMBULL, John (1750–1831) Poet, jurist

The brother of Benjamin Trumbull and therefore a cousin at some remove of Governor Jonathan Trumbull the Elder, Governor John Trumbull the Younger, and John the painter, this John was famed as a satirical poet, one of the so-called Hartford "wits." He was born in Watertown, Connecticut (then called Westbury) and was highly precocious, passing for entrance to Yale at age seven. He did not begin at the college until he was 13, however, graduating with a master's degree in 1770. He then read for the law, passed the bar, and studied with John Adams in Boston until the outbreak of the war, when he moved to New Haven and became a tutor at Yale. When the British threatened New Haven, Trumbull moved to Watertown and then to Hartford.

He had written verse since his undergraduate days, and his *Elegy on the Times* published in 1774 reflected patriotic themes, but his masterwork was a very long (3,000 lines), narrative poem, *M'Fingal,* which told the satirical story of a fictional high-Tory loyalist and the failings of the British during the early days of the Revolution. The poem was first published in 1776 and was only a moderate popular success. As the years went on, however, *M'Fingal* took on more and more meaning for the American public, and it was eventually published in as many as 30 editions by the mid-19th century.

Trumbull, however, had virtually ceased to write by the end of the Revolution, and he turned to the practice of law and the judicial bench during the balance of his life. In 1801, he was appointed as a judge of th superior court of Connecticut. He held a place on the bench until 1819, when his antiquated political views—he was a Federalist—caused his failure to be reappointed. He moved to Detroit in 1825 and died there. *Further reading:* Victor Gimmestad, *John Trumbull* (New York, 1974).

TRUMBULL, John (1756–1843) Continental officer, painter

Our images of the American Rev-

John Trumbull (the poet)

olution are irrevocably tied to the paintings of John Trumbull. His more than 200 renderings of revolutionary scenes and figures have been some of the most reproduced and best-known in the generations since the War of Independence, despite acknowledgment that they must have been often overblown and romanticized and that critics see him as a second-rate artist.

He was the son of Jonathan Trumbull the Elder (and, thus, brother of Jonathan the Younger and Joseph), and whatever the critical opinion of his technique, Trumbull cannot be faulted for lack of first-hand observation, since he served as an officer during the first years of the war. He was largely self-taught in art as a young man, although he graduated from Harvard in 1773. He lost the sight in one eye as a boy. His father discouraged the young Trumbull's interest in painting and frustrated John's early desire to study with John Singleton Copley (Copley's loyalist leanings may have had something to do with all this).

The young Trumbull first saw military duty as a teenage adjutant to General Joseph Spencer, but in July 1775 he moved on to a brief stint as an aide-de-camp to George Washington himself. The assignment at Continental Army headquarters did not last long, however, and Trumbull left to serve in the field. A year later, he was appointed as deputy adjutant to Horatio Gates (a post that carried the rank of colonel, a title that Trumbull used the rest of his life). Trumbull campaigned with Gates during the early part of 1777, then transferred to the command of Benedict Arnold.

His military career was less than promising, however, and he resigned in the spring of 1777 to study art in Boston (he returned to duty briefly during the French-American campaign at Newport in 1778). In 1780, Trumbull went to France and thence to London, where he became a pupil of the expatriate American artist Benjamin West. He was arrested by the British authorities on charges of treason in November 1780 but was released after only a month. He fled to Holland, where he continued to paint and tried to influence the Dutch to make a loan to Connecticut. In late 1783, he returned to England and began to produce the series of heroic canvases which Americans since have come to know so well: "The Declaration of Independence," "The Battle of Bunker Hill," "Surrender of Lord Cornwallis at Yorktown" and all the rest. He visited Paris in 1787 and two years later moved back to America, settling in Philadelphia and beginning a series of portraits of the great figures of the Revolution. Trumbull became private secretary to John Jay in 1793 and subsequently spent several more years in Europe, returning home in 1804. He lived to a ripe age, having imposed his vision of the American Revolution on the nation. *Further reading:* Irma B. Jaffe, *John Trumbull: Patriot-Artist* (Boston, 1975).

TRUMBULL, Jonathan (the Elder) (1710–1785) Governor

Trumbull was the only pre-independence colonial governor to continue in office through the Revolution, and he became a key supporter of the war effort. He was the father of Jonathan Trumbull the Younger, Joseph and John the painter. (John the poet and Benjamin were cousins at some remove.) The elder Trumbull—whose name was spelled "Trumble" until the mid-1760s, just to add confusion—was born in Lebanon, Connecticut to a family of merchants long established in the colony. He graduated from Harvard in 1727 and briefly studied for the ministry before taking up responsibility in the family's mercantile business. He did

Jonathan Trumbull (the Elder)

well in commerce through the following three decades, but he suffered reverses about 1766 and was never the same financially thereafter. He remained a power in Connecticut politics, however, having begun as a legislator in 1735 and continuing until 1766, when he was selected as deputy governor of the colony.

Connecticut's colonial government, unlike most in British America, was essentially in the hands of the freeholders. The colony's charter—dating from a century before and the subject of a famous episode in the 1660s, when it was hidden in an oak tree from Governor Andros—short-circuited royal influence, allowing revolutionaries to continue using its provisions without missing a beat. In 1769, Trumbull was elected governor, and he filled the office until 1784, making him by far the longest-serving head of a government of all the colonies. All the other colonial governors were royalists, but Trumbull was a firm patriot and took his colony into the revolutionary camp at the beginning of the war. For the most part, Connecticut was immune from the actual campaigning (only William Tryon's Danbury raid and raid of the coast in mid-1779 did much damage), and Trumbull turned the state into a storehouse for the Continental Army. Wielding considerable power, he funneled food and supplies to Washington, and although it was not enough to make the army comfortable by any means and at times Trumbull bristled at bearing too great a burden, on the whole, his efforts were probably responsible for keeping the American war effort alive at several crucial points. He was so effective that the British began a whispering campaign that charged he was secretly trading with the enemy. The conspiracy gained enough credence that Trumbull's electoral majorities were reduced, but he held on to power and was cleared by an inquiry in 1782. He finally retired from office in 1784 at age 73, having served as governor for 15 years, from before the Townshend Acts to after the Treaty of Paris. *Further reading:* David M. Roth, *Connecticut's War Governor, Jonathan Trumbull* (Chester, Conn., 1974).

TRUMBULL, Jonathan (the Younger) (1740–1809) Continental officer and official, government official

Another of the Trumbull family of Connecticut that did so much to supply and finance the Revolution, this Jonathan was the eldest son of Jonathan the governor and the brother of John the painter and Joseph. He was born at the family home in Lebanon, graduated from Harvard, and—not surprisingly—held public office as a colonial legislator before the Revolution. In July 1775, just after the organization of the Continental Army, Trumbull was chosen as paymaster for the Northern Department. This was a difficult assignment, to say the least, since even in the first days of the war, the Congress was strapped for money and paymasters (as well as commissaries like his brother) were almost inevitably the subject of suspicion and rumor. Trumbull served well, however, until he resigned in mid-1778. He was then appointed by Congress as comptroller of the national treasury, but he served only from November until the following April. In 1781, George Washington selected Trumbull to replace Alexander Hamilton as the commander in chief's military secretary, a post that carried the rank of lieutenant colonel. Trumbull served on Washington's personal staff through the rest of the war, resigning at the end of Washington's commission in December 1783. His post-Revolution career was long and distinguished. He was elected as one of Connecticut's first U.S. representatives and was reelected to two more consecutive terms, serving as speaker of the house during the second Congress. In 1795, he was elected U.S. senator from Connecticut, but he resigned in mid-1796. In 1797, Trumbull became governor of Connecticut and was reelected for 11 terms. He died in office. *Further reading:* John Ifkovic, *Connecticut's Nationalist Revolutionary: Jonathan Trumbull, Jr.* (Hartford, Conn., 1977).

TRUMBULL, Joseph (1738–1778) Continental officer, delegate to Congress

The first man to hold the thankless and controversial job of feeding and supplying the Continental Army, Joseph was the son of Jonathan Trumbull the Elder and brother of Jonathan the Younger and John the painter. He was born in Lebanon, Connecticut and worked in his father's mercantile business after graduating from Harvard in 1756. In 1767, he was elected to the Connecticut General Assembly, serving until 1773, when he joined the Connecticut Committee of Correspondence. Trumbull was selected in 1774 to be an alternate delegate to the Continental Congress, but he never had the chance to take a seat in the body. Instead, he went with the Connecticut troops to lay siege to Boston in the spring of 1775 as the commissary for supplies. He there caught the eye of George Washington and was named in July as commissary general of the Continental Army with the military rank of colonel. Working with no guiding models, scant staff and inadequate funds, Trumbull struggled to find food and clothing for the army. He was more successful than many of his successors, but he nonetheless came under fire from personal enemies and from disgruntled congressmen. An official inquiry charged him with dishonesty, but he was cleared of all wrongdoing in December 1775. General Philip Schuyler attacked Trumbull in 1776, partially out of personal malice, and challenged Trumbull's authority to provision the northern army. In 1777, Congress voted to split Trumbull's job between purchasing and supply, so he resigned. He then served for six months on the board of war, but ill health forced his resignation in April 1778. He died three months later.

TRUXTUN, Thomas (1755–1822) Privateer, naval officer

Truxtun, born on Long Island, went to sea at a tender age like many 18th-century naval men: in his case when he was 12 years old. By the time of the Revolutionary War, he was a ship's master in merchant service. He turned to privateering during the war, commanding in turn the *Congress*, the *Independence* and the *Mars*. He returned to merchant service after the Revolution, sailing in 1786 to China. When the nation decided in the 1790s to rearm a navy with a new class of powerful frigates, Truxtun was commissioned as one of the new captains and given the *Constellation*. He fought several engagements with the French between 1798 and 1800 and received a medal from Congress for his exploits. He was slated to lead a squadron to the Mediterranean against the pirate state of Tripoli in 1801 but fell into a quarrel with the administration in Washington and ended up out of the service.

TRYON, William (1729–1798) British governor, officer

Tryon's name became a bugaboo among Americans because of his reputation as a vigorous persecutor of dissent and his military raids on Connecticut at mid-war. He was born into an aristocratic family in Surrey (the grandson of an earl on his mother's side) and entered the British army in 1751 as a lieutenant of the 1st Regiment of Foot Guards. By the late 1750s, he was a lieutenant colonel, but he abandoned his military career when marriage in 1757 brought him not only a large income from his wife's property, but much "influence" (as it was known in 18th-century Britain) through his wife's relative, Lord Hillsborough, who was first commissioner of trade and plantations. Tryon wrangled an appointment as lieutenant governor of the colony of North Carolina in 1764, and when royal governor Arthur Dobbs died not long after Tryon arrived, the new lieutenant governor succeeded to the chief office.

His term of service in North Carolina was not entirely contentious, but he supported the Stamp Act and got off to a rather poor beginning. One of his brightest achievements in North Carolina was to build a magnificent governor's palace. Any good Tryon did, however, was overshadowed by the Regulator uprising which broke into armed conflict in 1770. Tryon, the experienced army man, organized a strong military force to suppress the rebels of the western counties, who were in violent protest against taxes and poor administration. At the battle of Alamance in May 1771, Tryon soundly defeated the Regulators, which led to punitive sentences against the leaders.

Tryon himself left the colony before the end of the summer, taking a long-sought appointment as governor of New York when Lord Dunmore exchanged his seat for the governorship of Virginia. Tryon found more contention in his new home. New York was engaged in a nasty dispute with New Hampshire over the so-called Hampshire Grants, where both colonies claimed ownership and a great deal of potential money was to be made by whoever could secure title to land. Tryon himself speculated heavily in land and was not a disinterested government administrator in the struggle, which was complicated by the presence of a strong local party led by Ethan Allen. Tryon found no solution to the dispute and was recalled to England for consultation in 1774.

When he returned to America, the Revolutionary War had begun, New York City had been seized by the patriots, and the governor was forced to conduct his affairs from the safety of a British warship in the harbor. The invasion and victories of the British army under General William Howe restored Tryon to his place in New York City, but civilian control had been ceded to Howe, and Tryon had little or no function left. He organized a military unit of loyalists and set about raiding patriot supply points in Connecticut. Commanding with the rank of colonel, Tryon in April 1777 led 2,000 British and loyalist troops to Danbury, Connecticut, where they brushed aside a feeble militia force and burned much of the city and seized a quantity of supplies. Although damaged to some degree by American counterattacks during his retreat, Tryon had dealt a nasty blow to the patriot cause. In reward, Tryon was elevated to the local rank of major general and made ceremonial colonel of the 70th Regiment of Foot.

Tryon's most famous exploit came in July 1779. He set out at the head of a water-borne raid against the coastal towns of Connecticut, from which American commerce raiders had made British shipping in Long Island Sound difficult. Meeting only token resistance, Tryon's force of more than 2,500 took New Haven, East Haven, Fairfield, Green's Farm and Norwalk, and inflicted heavy damage by fire and seizure, at only a small cost to themselves. Tryon's time in America was nearly at an end, however, and a persistent case of gout forced him to retire from active duty and return to England in 1780, when he was promoted to lieutenant general and made colonel of the 29th Regiment of Foot. He died in London. *Further reading:* Alonza Dill, *Governor Tryon and His Palace* (Chapel Hill, N.C., 1955).

TUCKER, Samuel (1747–1833) Privateer, naval officer

Tucker was born in the seafaring town of Marblehead, Massachusetts and joined hundreds of other Massachusetts sailors early in the war in privateering along the New England coast. In 1775, he was master of the *Young Phoenix*, and in 1776, he commanded the *Franklin*. Tucker and other privateers aboard small vessels hoped to dart out from the many anchorages along the coast and pounce on British transports while avoiding Royal Navy warships. Tucker received a commission in the Continental Navy in 1777 and eventually took command of the frigate *Boston*. He transported John Adams to a diplomatic post in France the following year and remained there to raid British shipping around the home island. After the Revolution, Tucker turned to trading and was elected to the Massachusetts legislature. He moved to the northern region of the state, and after the area became the state of Maine in 1820, he was elected to the Maine House of Representatives.

TUCKER, Thomas Tudor (1745–1828) Army surgeon, delegate to Congress, official   Tucker was born in Port Royal, Bermuda and studied medicine at the University of Edinburgh. He emigrated to South Carolina and was a practicing doctor at the time of the Revolution. He served during the war as an army surgeon and sat in the state legislature. In 1787 and 1788 he was a delegate to the Confederation Congress, and he subsequently was elected as a representative to the first two U.S. Congresses under the new constitution. In 1801, he was named by President Thomas Jefferson as treasurer of the United States, a post at which he served until his death 27 years later.

TUFFIN, Marquis de la Rouerie. See ARMAND, Charles Tuffin.

TUPPER, Benjamin (1738–1792) Continental general   Tupper was born in Stoughton, Massachusetts and served an apprenticeship to a farmer until age 16. He fought in the Seven Years' War as an enlisted man, afterward becoming a teacher and moving to Chesterfield in the western part of the colony. In 1774, Tupper became active in the patriot militia in western Massachusetts and arrived at Boston to join the American army as a major of John Fellows' Massachusetts Regiment. He first came to notice after taking part in a raid on a British outpost on Boston Neck in July and following up with a raid on Great Brewster Island, where his men killed or captured all the British sent to repair the lighthouse on the island. He was promoted to lieutenant

colonel later in the year and was assigned to the new 21st Continental Regiment. In August 1776, Tupper successfully attacked a flotilla of British boats that had sailed into the Tappan Zee (an expansion of the Hudson River), winning further laurels. He fought at Long Island in August and then transferred to the 2nd Massachusetts and subsequently to the 11th Massachusetts as colonel. He led his troops against General John Burgoyne in 1777 and fought at Monmouth the following year. He commanded two more units before war's end, the 10th and the 6th Massachusetts. When he mustered out of the Continental Army in mid-1783, Tupper was brevetted to the rank of brigadier general. He returned to Chesterfield after the war and was one of the principal defenders of the federal arsenal in Springfield during Shays' Rebellion in 1786. Two years later, Tupper moved to Ohio and became one of the leaders of the white settlements established in the Marietta region.

TURNBULL, George. Loyalist officer   Probably a native of New York, Turnbull was an effective loyalist officer serving on the British side during the Revolution. He was a captain in the Loyal American Regiment during the summer of 1777 and came to the notice of his superiors for leading the attack on Fort Montgomery during Sir Henry Clinton's expedition up the Hudson Valley. He was thereafter promoted to lieutenant colonel and given command of the New York Volunteers, another loyalist unit. Turnbull then moved into the southern theater with his new command and took part in the siege of Savannah in 1779. The following year, he was in charge of a small garrison at Rocky Mount, South Carolina, one of the British outposts set up to defend the approaches to Camden. On August 1, Turnbull and his 150 men were fortified inside three log cabins when attacked by 600 Americans under Thomas Sumter. In a sharp fight, Turnbull repulsed Sumter, who had no artillery and was forced to attempt unsuccessful frontal attacks and fire tactics.

TYLER, John (1747–1813) State official, jurist   Tyler was active during the Revolution in Virginia politics and held several public offices. He was born in York County and attended the College of William and Mary. He was a member of his local committee of safety in 1774 and was a delegate from Charles City County to the Virginia House of Delegates from

1777 to 1788, serving as speaker from 1781 to 1784. He also sat on the Council of State during the tumultuous years of 1780 and 1781, when Virginia was under invasion by the British. He became governor of the state in 1808. After leaving executive office in 1811, he was named to the U.S. Circuit Court for Virginia.

TYLER, Royall (1757–1826) Officer, writer, jurist   Tyler had a many-faceted career. Born in Boston and a Harvard graduate, he joined the Boston independent company of infantry, one of four independent Massachusetts companies organized during the summer of 1775 and taken later into the pay of Congress and eventually the Continental Army. The independent companies were broken up the following year with the reorganization of the army, and Tyler, a major, transferred to the staff of General John Sullivan. He served as an aide to Sullivan during the unsuccessful French-American campaign to take Newport, Rhode Island in 1778. Tyler briefly reentered military service after the Revolution in 1787 as an aide to Benjamin Lincoln during Shays' Rebellion.

He was already well into his second career as a writer, however, and soon after the rural rebellion in Massachusetts was put down, Tyler moved to New York City to become a professional playwright. He wrote several light comedies as well as farces and religious dramas, most of which were produced in New York or Boston. He also wrote satirical verse and prose in collaboration with Joseph Dennie under the pen names of Colon and Spondee, and he published two novels on his own. In 1794, Tyler moved to Vermont and entered his third career as a jurist (he had been admitted to the bar during the Revolution). He was state's attorney for Windham County, Vermont from 1792 to 1802, and then became assistant justice of the Vermont Supreme Court, rising to chief justice in 1807.

V

VAN BUSKIRK, Abraham. Loyalist officer Born in New Jersey, Van Buskirk lived in Bergen County and practiced medicine before the Revolution. He was initially a patriot and served in the provincial congress during 1775 and 1776; however, he came under suspicion of harboring loyalist tendencies and was investigated by a committee of the Congress. Van Buskirk thereupon passed over to the British side and was commissioned as a lieutenant colonel in command of the 3rd battalion of Cortlandt Skinner's New Jersey Volunteers. His most notable engagement was in the latter stages of the American attack at Paulus Hook, New Jersey, in August 1779 when Van Buskirk and about 150 of his men (who had been away from the British encampment on a foraging party) attacked the retreating American forces. American commander Henry Lee drove off the loyalists in a brief skirmish. In 1780, Van Buskirk raided from Staten Island into New Jersey and burned several buildings at Elizabethtown. He also commanded a battalion during Benedict Arnold's raid on New London in 1781. At the end of the war, he moved to Nova Scotia and received half pay in reward for his military service.

VAN CORTLANDT, Philip (1749–1831) Continental general, state official Son of Pierre Van Cortlandt, Philip was born in New York City. He graduated from King's College (now Columbia) in 1768 and worked on the family's huge estates as an engineer and surveyor. He was a delegate from Westchester County to the New York Provincial Congress in April 1775 and was commissioned as lieutenant colonel of the 4th New York Regiment in June. He went north with his unit to Albany but fell ill and did not go on the Canadian invasion with Richard Montgomery. In November 1776, Van Cortlandt was promoted to colonel and given command of the 2nd New York Regiment, which he commanded at the battles at Saratoga the following year. After wintering at Valley Forge, Van Cortlandt's men joined the expedition against the Iroquois under John Sullivan in mid-1779. During 1780, Van Cortlandt sat on the court-martial of Benedict Arnold in Philadelphia and then took command of three combined New York regiments. His most notable command was at Yorktown as part of Benjamin Lincoln's brigade, and he received a brevet to brigadier general following the surrender of Lord Cornwallis. He remained a public figure after the war and in 1793 was elected to the U.S. Congress as a representative from New York, serving for 16 years. He then retired to the family manor, but in 1824 he accompanied the Marquis de Lafayette on the latter's triumphal tour of the United States.

VAN CORTLANDT, Pierre (1721–1814) State official The father of congressman Philip Van Cortlandt, Pierre was born in New York City and was connected through his mother's side to the De Peyster family and by marriage to the Livingstons. He inherited great wealth and maintained large estates in the countryside outside the city. He was recruited heavily by the loyalists, especially his De Peyster cousins, as the Revolution approached, but Van Cortlandt opted for the patriot cause. He attended three New York provincial congresses and was on the New York Committee of Safety in 1776 and president of the council of safety in 1777. He was also chairman of the New York convention that wrote a new constitution in 1777, and he took office as the state's first lieutenant governor, holding the position continuously until 1795. He generally supported George Clinton's party in matters of state politics. He spent the final years of his very long life on his estate.

VAN DYKE, Nicolas (1738–1789) Delegate to Congress, state official

Born in New Castle County, Delaware, Van Dyke studied law in Philadelphia and was admitted to the Pennsylvania bar in 1765, returning to practice in his home county the same year. He was elected to the Delaware state constitutional convention in July 1776 and to the Delaware Council the following year. He also served as a judge of the court of admiralty in 1777. He was sent to Congress as a delegate in 1777 and served until 1781, signing the Articles of Confederation. On his return home, Van Dyke was president of Delaware for three years, from 1783 until 1786.

VAN SCHAACK, Peter (1747–1832) Loyalist lawyer

Probably a good example of one sort of loyalist who was a victim of the Revolution, Van Schaack was a prominent attorney in Kinderhook, New York and a friend and associate of many leading patriots such as John Jay, George Clinton and Gouverneur Morris. He early on joined them in patriot enterprises and was a member of the Kinderhook Committee of Safety and several colony-wide committees. In 1775, however, he decided on principle that he could not support taking up arms against the crown, and he was expelled from the Committee of Safety. In 1778, his wife of many years became seriously ill, but he was denied permission by the Americans to move her to British-occupied New York City for treatment. After her death, Van Schaack was banished and sailed for England. He wrote: "Torn from the nearest and dearest of all human connections by the visitation of Almighty God, and now by means of the public troubles of my country, I am now going into the wide world, without friends, without fortune, with the remembrance of past happiness, and the future prospect of adversity." He was allowed to return to Kinderhook after the war, however, and he resumed his law practice.

VAN SCHAICK, Gosen (1736–1789) Continental general

A descendant of 17th-century Dutch settlers, Van Schaick (whose first name is given in many variations, such as Goose, Goosen and Gozen) was born in Albany, New York, the son of the city's mayor. He served extensively in the Seven Years' War and was a seasoned veteran of frontier fighting when the Revolution began. With the organization of the Continental Army in June 1775, Van Schaick was commissioned as colonel of the 2nd New York Regiment and assigned to the invasion of Canada under Richard Montgomery. Surviving that debacle, he next commanded the 1st New York Regiment (transferring to the new regiment in March 1776) at Johnstown in upper New York. He was wounded in June 1778 at the battle of Monmouth, where he headed a brigade in Lord Stirling's division. His most famous command was of a highly successful raid against the Onondaga in April 1779. He moved swiftly from Fort Stanwix with a large force, descended on the main Onondaga settlement of Onondaga Castle, and virtually destroyed the town, taking many prisoners in the bargain while losing not a man himself. Such cost-free expeditions against the Indian allies of the British were rare during the Revolution. Congress was so delighted with Van Schaick's performance that the delegates voted him an expression of their official gratitude. He subsequently served in the Yorktown campaign and was brevetted as a brigadier general just before he mustered out of the army in late 1783.

VAN WERT, Isaac (1760–1828) Militiaman

Van Wert was a 20-year-old farmer and sometime militiaman in Westchester County, New York when he gained a measure of fame as one of the three men who captured Major John André as the spy fled toward British lines on September 23, 1780 after his fateful meeting with Benedict Arnold. Along with David Williams and John Paulding, Van Wert was part of a cattle searching party and was lounging on guard duty when the disguised André rode up and mistook the militiamen for loyalists. After questioning and searching André, Van Wert and the others took him into custody and delivered him to a Continental officer, setting off the events that led to Arnold's flight and André's execution. Van Wert and his two companions—by most reports a rather scruffy lot—were made into heroes with citations by Congress, pensions and land grants. A Captors' Monument was erected near Tarrytown, New York in 1853 to mark the spot where Van Wert and his fellows laid hands on the dapper British adjutant. As one historian wrote: "Americans loved the story of the way in which the three simple farmers confounded the artful spy. The story seemed the epitome of what Americans for more than a century believed their Revolution to have been—a victory of American honesty and simplicity over British artifice and sophistication." *Further reading:* Richard C. Brown, "Three Forgotten Heroes," *American Heritage* (August 1975), 25–29.

VARDILL, John (1749–1811) Loyalist clergyman, spy

Vardill spied for the British among his fellow loyalists in England during the Revolution and supplied advice on how to subvert patriot leaders in America. He was born in New York City and graduated from King's College (later Columbia University), which was a bastion of royalist and Episcopalian sentiment. He taught anatomy at the school from 1766 until 1773, when he became professor of natural law. He went to England the following year and was ordained a priest in the Episcopal Church. He went to Britain at least in part to seek a deal with the government and church officials: he would spy on his fellow Americans in return for a post as professor of divinity at King's. He remained in England when the rebellion broke out and reported regularly on the activities and talk of the hundreds of loyalists who moved to London during the war. In 1778, he gave detailed advice to the members of the Carlisle commission on how to deal with American patriot leaders, suggesting cynically that most could be bought with offers of money or peerages. Vardill may have been the forger of spurious anti-independence letters attributed to George Washington, published by the British in New York as propaganda. The triumph of the Revolution, of course, frustrated Vardill's ambitions, and he never returned to American shores. He did, however, receive a good church living in Lincolnshire as reward for his services to the British government.

VARICK, Richard (1753–1831) Continental officer, archivist-secretary

Varick was a native of New Jersey but moved to New York City in 1775 on the eve of the war. He was commissioned as a captain in the 1st New York Regiment in the summer of 1775 and served with that unit until mid-1776, when he became military secretary to General Philip Schuyler. In September of that year, however, Varick became a deputy muster master of the Northern Department. The commissary of musters had been one of the original creations of Congress when the Continental Army was organized in 1775, and the deputy muster masters were responsible for keeping accurate rolls of the units of the army; however, they functioned poorly in the atmosphere of fluid comings and goings that characterized the Continental Army during its entire existence. The commissary was reorganized in 1777, and Varick was appointed as full deputy commissioner general of musters with the rank of lieutenant colonel, but in fact the role of the muster commissary had been virtually taken over by individual unit adjutants. In August 1780, Varick joined the personal staff of Benedict Arnold as one of the general's two principal aides-de-camp. Although suspicious of Arnold, Varick was apparently unaware of the traitor's secret dealings and was as shocked as anyone when Arnold fled to the British. Varick was cleared of complicity by a court of inquiry, but his career was stigmatized by the close association with Arnold, and he could find no useful employment in the military after the scandal.

In May 1781, Varick finally won a post that wiped out lingering suspicions about his loyalty. George Washington appointed him as secretary to arrange and transcribe the commander in chief's official correspondence and papers. Varick gathered the documents at an office in Poughkeepsie and spent the next two years organizing what amounted to the first official archives of the U.S. military. The work was prodigious and resulted in an extremely valuable set of transcriptions in 44 volumes. Varick returned to New York City after the war and became recorder for the city and a codifier of the laws of the new state. He eventually served in the legislature and as mayor of New York.

VARNUM, James Mitchell (1748–1789) Continental and militia general, delegate to Congress

Born in Dracut, Massachusetts (the brother

of Joseph Bradley Varnum), he first attended Harvard but was expelled and moved on to Rhode Island College (now Brown), where he graduated in its first class in 1769. He established a highly successful law practice in Rhode Island after admission to the bar in 1771. In 1774, Varnum became colonel of the stylish Kentish Guards militia. He was part of the army laying siege to Boston after Lexington and Concord and in May 1775 was commissioned as colonel of the 1st Rhode Island Regiment, which became the 9th Continental in 1776. He received a promotion to brigadier from Congress in early 1777 and simultaneously held a commission as a brigadier in the Rhode Island militia. He played little significant role in the campaigns in New York and New Jersey during 1776 and 1777, although he was nominally in command of Fort Mercer and Fort Mifflin when they were lost to the British. He was part of Charles Lee's division at the battle of Monmouth and participated in the expedition against Newport in the summer of 1778. Following a mutiny in his brigade in early 1779, Varnum resigned his Continental commission and returned to Rhode Island to practice law, although he still was a general in the state militia and on paper still commander of the Rhode Island department. He was elected a delegate to Congress in 1780, serving until 1782 and again after the war in 1786–87. He was appointed a judge in the Northwestern Territory in 1787 and moved to Marietta, Ohio, where he died.

VARNUM, Joseph Bradley (1750–1821) Militia officer, legislator Born in Dracut, Massachusetts and closely associated with the town for most of his life, Varnum was a captain of the local militia before the Revolution and fought with his men in the initial battle of the war at Lexington in April 1775. He served with the militia against General John Burgoyne's invasion in 1777 and during Sullivan's Rhode Island campaign of 1778. He also had a long career as a legislator, beginning in 1780 with his election to the Massachusetts legislature, where he served off and on for the next several years. He was elected from Massachusetts to the U.S. House of Representatives in 1794, and despite charges of election fraud, he held his seat until 1811, acting as speaker of the house during his latter two terms. In 1811, Varnum moved over to the U.S. Senate, eventually becoming president pro tem. He died in Dracut.

VAUGHAN, John (d. 1795) British general Vaughan, who served ably as a British general during the Revolution, was the younger brother of the Earl of Lisburne and had followed a military career since the 1740s. He was a junior officer with the 9th Marine Regiment and the 10th Dragoons in Europe until 1759, when he came to North America and raised the 94th Royal Welsh Volunteers (holding the rank of lieutenant colonel) for duty in the war against the French. After fighting in the West Indies, he became lieutenant colonel of the 46th Regiment of Foot.

Vaughan was a full colonel with the local rank of brigadier general in 1776 when he sailed from Ireland with Lord Cornwallis to reinforce Sir Henry Clinton's first attempt to take Charleston, South Carolina. He moved to the New York theater after the repulse of the British in the South and fought well at the battle of Long Island. He was wounded at White Plains in October 1776 and returned to Britain for recovery. In 1777, Vaughan came back to the American theater with the rank of major general and was employed in the series of British forays from New York City up the Hudson, taking Fort Montgomery in October and Verplanck's Point a year and a half later. After a brief return home, Vaughan was named commander in chief of British land forces in the Leeward Islands. His most famous victory was a collaboration with Admiral Sir George Rodney to take the key Dutch post at St. Eustatius in February 1782, robbing the Americans of their most important entrepôt in the Caribbean. Accused of irregularities over the confiscation of goods from St. Eustatius, Vaughan returned to Great Britain, where his political weight and influence—he was a member of Parliament—soon cleared him of the difficulty. He received a handsome sinecure from the government for his services and was knighted in 1793. *Further reading: Edna Vosper, Report on the Sir John Vaughan Papers in the William L. Clements Library (Ann Arbor, Mich., 1929).*

VENCE, Jean Gaspard (1747–1808) French privateer and naval officer Vence served the American Revolution in an unusual manner: as a foreign-national privateer in the West Indies operating virtually independently. He was born in Marseilles, France and went to the West Indies as a teenager. He served aboard a French warship during the Seven Years' War and in 1767 survived a shipwreck and long overland march on the west coast of Africa. In 1777, he was given a commission as a privateer by the Continental Congress, and as commander of a tiny, lateen-rigged ship he began to raid British shipping in the West Indies around his base at Martinique. He took more than 200 prizes during the period of a year and a half. He appears to have officially rejoined the French military in late 1778 and was active in the capture of Dominique and then Grenada in 1779. He is reported to have been one of the French officers in the attack on Savannah, Georgia in October 1779. After the end of the American Revolution, his career went into an eclipse but he emerged as a naval commander under Napoleon at the end of the century.

VERGENNES, Charles Gravier, Comte de (1719–1787) French official

As the French foreign minister during the American War of Independence, the Comte de Vergennes was the principal official with whom the Continental Congress dealt during the crucial years. He was a career diplomat, having entered the service of the king as a young man. He was ambassador to Constantinople and Stockholm before assuming the foreign minister's position when Louis XVI came to the throne. He was an able diplomat and policymaker, and while his interest in the American rebels probably sprang more from a desire to avenge the French losses of the Seven Years' War than from any inherent love for anti-monarchical revolution, the effect was salubrious for the colonies.

He played his hand cautiously, however, during the first years of the Revolution in America. Vergennes wanted to go slowly in supporting the Americans, lest he agitate the British into a premature move against their ancient enemies across the Channel. In 1775, he sent agents to the colonies in order to assess the strength and ultimate potential of the rebellion, and he allowed Beaumarchais to covertly ship arms and supplies from French arsenals under the guise of his trading company, Hortalez et Cie. Vergennes also allowed many French officers, including engineers, to volunteer for service in America. Before openly committing France to war against Britain and to alliance with the American colonies, Vergennes needed the support of Spain—which feared any form of rebellion in the New World might spread southward—and he

Charles, Comte de Vergennes

wanted to feel confident that the war on land would not fail. Throughout the early months of 1777, Vergennes was frustrated by the long string of British military successes and the recalcitrance of the Spanish. The defeat of General John Burgoyne in October was decisive, however, in setting the stage for a formal French-American alliance, which was agreed to in December. Vergennes began open support of the American cause and eventually guided the policy that sent French land and naval forces into battle in North America. With the final American military victory in 1781, however, the interests of France and the soon-to-be independent American colonies started to diverge. As the peace negotiations went on, the American commissioners came to realize that Vergennes would not support their claims to the detriment of France or Spain, and a separate peace was settled. Vergennes could only acquiesce in the end. He died before the revolution in his own country.

VERGER, Jean Baptiste Antoine de (1762–1851) French officer

Verger served as a young junior officer of the Regiment Deux-Ponts during the French participation in the American Revolution and kept a journal of his activities. He was a native of the tiny principality-bishopric of Bâle on the French border with Switzerland that was ruled in those days by a bishop as part of the Holy Roman Empire. Verger's father was an important government official, and the son, as was customary in the bishopric, took service with one of the foreign regiments in the French army. He became a cadet in the Deux-Ponts regiment in February 1780, shortly before the

French expedition sailed for Newport. He was with the regiment, which played a key role at the siege of Yorktown, during its entire time in America and returned to France in mid-1783. Verger's subsequent career was a catalog of what happened in Europe during the ensuing decades of revolution, empire and warfare. He continued as a soldier, serving first with anti-Revolutionary forces under his old commander Christian Deux-Ponts and eventually taking service with the ruling house of Bavaria (which briefly had title to Bâle, although the tiny place passed successively into the orbit of Revolutionary France and the French Empire, and eventually became part of Switzerland after the Napoleonic Wars). He was a senior Bavarian officer and a diplomat for the rest of his life, fighting first with and then against Napoleon. He retired at an old age as a general and a Bavarian noble. *Further reading:* Howard C. Rice, Jr., and Anne F. Brown, *The American Campaigns of Rochambeau's Army . . .* (Princeton and Providence, 1972).

VERNIER, Pierre-François (1736–1780) French volunteer   Vernier had served in the French military as a commander of foreign volunteers and of mounted troops. He was retired in 1768 because of a previous wound but turned up in America during the Revolution and was assigned to the ragtag cavalry corps of Casimir Pulaski as a major, perhaps as second in command. He took over the remnant of Pulaski's Legion in October 1779 after Pulaski's death at Savannah. Most of the Legion's men and officers were captured when the British took Charleston, but Vernier apparently was outside the city and attached to the last remaining American force under Colonel Isaac Huger. Vernier (known in American records as "Peter") was killed at Monck's Corner on April 14, 1780 when Banastre Tarleton surprised and routed Huger's ill-prepared men.

VINING, John (1758–1802) Delegate to Congress   Vining was born in Dover, Delaware and probably spent much of the Revolution reading law. He was admitted to the Delaware bar in 1782 and opened a practice in New Castle County. In 1784 and 1785, he represented Delaware in the Confederation Congress. After serving in the state legislature, he was elected to the first U.S. House of Representatives in 1789, was reelected to the second national Congress and then declined to run again. He became U.S. senator in 1793 and served until his resignation in 1798. He died in Dover four years later.

VOSE, Joseph (1738–1816) Continental officer   Born in Milton, Massachusetts, Vose was a senior commander of Massachusetts Continental regiments throughout the war. He was a major in William Heath's Regiment in 1775, and after helping to lead a highly successful raid on the British lighthouse on Great Brewster Island in July 1775 during the siege of Boston, Vose was promoted to lieutenant colonel. He transferred to the 24th Continental with the army reorganization of early 1776 and a year later took command of the 1st Massachusetts as colonel. He led his unit in the Pennsylvania campaign of 1778, fighting at the battle of Monmouth, and in the French-American expedition against British-held Newport, Rhode Island. He commanded a battalion under Muhlenberg at Yorktown and was colonel of one of the ragtag Massachusetts units formed from the remnants of previous regiments in 1783, which he led into New York City on the heels of the British evacuation.

W

WADSWORTH, James (1730–1817) Militia general, delegate to Congress, jurist Born in Durham, Connecticut, Wadsworth received his early education in England and then returned to attend Yale, from which he graduated in 1748. He was admitted to the bar after the private study of law and became a local official as town clerk and justice of the peace. In 1773, he became a judge on the New Haven County Court (he was elevated to presiding justice in 1778). His revolutionary activities included membership on his local committee of safety and a commission as colonel and subsequently brigadier and major general of the Connecticut militia. After the war, he represented Connecticut in the Confederation Congress during 1784. He took a seat on the state executive council the following year and served as state comptroller in 1786 and 1787. Although a delegate to the state convention to ratify the federal constitution, he opposed the new form of government and refused to take an oath of allegiance.

WADSWORTH, Jeremiah (1743–1804) Delegate to Congress, Continental official, businessman Wadsworth was born in Hartford, Connecticut and went to sea aboard a merchantman (owned by his uncle) as a teenager. He eventually rose to become a ship's master. In 1771, he became a merchant on land, and, based on this experience, he was appointed as commissary for Connecticut when the war began and then as deputy to Conti-

nental commissary general Jonathan Trumbull. After Trumbull's resignation in 1778, Wadsworth became the new commissary general for Continental forces, doing an adequate job of supplying the army and making a considerable amount of money for himself in the process. He resigned in 1779 but took over supply for Rochambeau's French force. He was elected as a delegate to the Continental Congress in 1788, and after the ratification of the new federal constitution, Wadsworth was elected as U.S. representative from Connecticut to the first three national Congresses, serving from 1789 to 1795. He then returned to his home state and sat in the state senate and on the state executive council. He was active in the banking field and founded or helped to found four banks in Philadelphia, Connecticut and New York. He was also a noted agriculturalist and imported new strains of livestock from abroad as experimental animals.

WADSWORTH, Peleg (1748–1829) Militia general, Continental officer, businessman, congressman A leader of one of the most ill-considered and ill-conducted military expeditions of the war, Wadsworth escaped blame and went on to prosperity and political good fortune. Born in Duxbury, Massachusetts to one of the old families of the colony, he graduated from Harvard in 1769 and set himself up as a teacher in Plymouth. He was a captain of his local minuteman militia company and with the clash at Lexington and Concord, he marched off to join the patriot army laying siege to Boston. His company became part of the Massachusetts Battalion under Colonel Theophilius Cotton, which was absorbed into the new Continental Army in June and served until enlistments ran out at the end of 1775. Wadsworth acted primarily as an engineer, helping to lay out the American lines on Dorchester Heights. In February 1776, he became an aide-de-camp to General Artemas Ward, but he served only until April when Ward retired from active duty. Wadsworth was with the main army during the early stages of the New York campaign and later was attached to John Sullivan's force during the unsuccessful joint French-American attempt to retake Newport.

Wadsworth was named as adjutant general of the Massachusetts militia in mid-1778 and was elevated to brigadier general a year later. He meanwhile acquired considerable political influence as a member of the Massachusetts legislature and the state board of war. In 1779, the Massachusetts authorities decided without consulting Congress or Washington to launch an expedition against an outpost the British were building near Castine in the Maine section of the state. The enterprise was botched from the beginning. Wadsworth was named second in command to Solomon Lovell with Continental Navy officer Dudley Saltonstall in charge of a flotilla of small armed ships and transports. The poorly equipped and little-trained force of a thousand militiamen marched overland, hoping to surprise the 800 or so British garrison under Colonel Francis McLean, but Wadsworth and Lovell were dismayed to find the enemy ready and waiting. They dithered and conferred while the British defenses grew stronger, and finally a strong British naval squadron appeared offshore, destroying any chance of a successful assault. The militia took to their heels across the woods and rivers, losing tons of supplies and absorbing nearly 500 casualties.

The entire affair, known as the Penobscot Expedition, was a fiasco. The state of Massachusetts, however, not only absolved Wadsworth and Lovell, but put all the blame on the hapless Saltonstall after an inquiry by a politically-appointed committee. In March 1780, Wadsworth was given command of the eastern section of Massachusetts with headquarters at Thomaston. He was ignominiously captured by a British raiding party in February of the following year and was held captive until he contrived to escape in June.

Following the war, Wadsworth moved to the Maine section and prospered in trade, acquiring several large tracts of Maine land. He also ran for office and was elected to the U.S. Congress in 1793 as a Federalist, serving a total of seven consecutive terms. He retired from public office in 1807 and lived out his life in comfort on a large estate in Oxford County. His grandson was Henry Wadsworth Longfellow, the noted American poet. *Further reading:* George Rose and Margaret Rose, eds., *Letters of General Peleg Wadsworth . . .* (Portland, Me., 1961).

WALKER, Benjamin (1753—1818) Continental officer, official

Born in England, Walker emigrated to New York City before the Revolution and became a merchant. With the outbreak of the war, he sided with the colonies and took a commission as captain of the 2nd New York, raised in the spring of 1775 only a few weeks after the battles at Lexington and Concord. He later served on the staff of Friedrich von Steuben as an aide-de-camp and in 1781 and 1782 was an aide to commander in chief George Washington. Following the war, Walker served as a secretary in the New York state government and then set up a brokerage in New York City. After the establishment of the new federal government, Washington appointed Walker as the federal naval officer in the port of New York. In 1801, Walker was elected to the U.S. Congress, and he served one term. His interests then shifted to a large tract of land in central New York that had been confiscated from British ownership during the Revolution. He became a land agent and moved to Utica, where he died.

WALKER, Thomas (1715—1794) Land speculator, explorer, official

Walker was an energetic land speculator who personally explored westward to spy out the lands he hoped to profit by. He probably attended the College of William and Mary while living with his sister in Williamsburg, Virginia. He studied medicine with a local doctor and began a practice in Fredericksburg, also running a store on the side. He came into a large estate in Albemarle County as the consequence of his marriage in 1741 to Mildred Thorton, a wealthy widow and a relative of George Washington. His interests in western lands centered on the Loyal Land Company, a consortium of speculators who hoped to gain title to an 800,000-acre grant. In 1750, Walker personally led an expedition over the mountains into the Kentucky territory. He moved into politics in 1752 as a member of the House of Burgesses and represented several Virginia counties over the following years. He was a commissary—probably none too careful about accounts and conflicts of interest— for the Virginia militia during the Seven Years' War. In 1765, he established his permanent base at an estate called Castle Hill in Albemarle County. He was a member of the Virginia Committee of Safety in 1776 and sat on the state executive council in the same year and again in 1781.

WALLACE, Sir James (1731–1803) British naval officer

The son-in-law of Georgia royal governor James Wright, Wallace commanded British warships in the American theater for much of the war. He had served in the Royal Navy since 1746 and was post captain in command of the 20-gun *Rose* when first assigned to American waters in 1771. He took command of the *Experiment* in 1776 and was knighted in 1777 as reward for carrying dispatches to England. In 1778, he narrowly escaped capture by the French off Newport by taking a risky passage through Hell's Gate. After a tour in home waters, Wallace returned to America in 1779 and was captured off Savannah by a French man-of-war. He continued in the Royal Navy after his release and died an admiral, as did all British captains who managed to survive those senior to them on the Navy List.

WALLIS, Samuel (d. 1798) Loyalist agent and conspirator

A native of Maryland, Wallis lived most of his life in Pennsylvania. He was not revealed to have been a loyalist and an active British conspirator until the mid-20th century, and in his own day, Wallis concealed his activities behind a facade of patriotism. He was a merchant and land speculator with a business in Philadelphia and a country home and lands in the frontier county of Northumberland. He first conspired with the British during their occupation of Philadelphia. In 1778, he offered his country house as a headquarters for American troops guarding against Tory and Indian

raiding, apparently as a way to keep tabs on American plans, which he then passed on to the British. In 1779 and 1780, Wallis was one of the conduit between Benedict Arnold and the spy Major John André. One of his more clever conspiracies, although one that came to naught, was an attempt to supply an inaccurate map to General John Sullivan before the latter's expedition against the Iroquois Confederation. Wallis also planned to exploit the mutiny of the Pennsylvania regiments of the Continental Line in 1781, but the mutiny was resolved before he could act. Throughout these conspiracies, Wallis kept up a cordial front with the American authorities and was regarded as a trusted patriot. He sailed through the war unscathed by suspicion. Only with the examination of secret papers by historians 150 years later were his activities discovered.

WALTON, George (c. 1741–1804) Delegate to Congress, militia officer, official

Born in Virginia, Walton was orphaned at an early age and taken in by an uncle who apprenticed the boy to a carpenter. In 1769, after completing his service, Walton moved to Savannah, Georgia and read law in a local attorney's office. He was admitted to the bar in 1774, by which time he was already a leader among Georgia patriots. The situation among revolutionaries in the youngest colony was complex and confused, and Georgia moved very slowly into the orbit of rebellion. Savannah was one of the centers of revolutionary agitation, and Walton helped form a provincial congress in January 1775, but the delegates were divided and failed to select anyone to represent Georgia at the first Continental Congress. The first provincial congress did, however, appoint a committee of correspondence, naming Walton as the chairman. A second provincial congress in July 1775 with Walton as secretary was more aggressive and sent four delegates to Congress. Walton became chairman of the Georgia Committee of Safety and was himself selected as a delegate to Congress by a third provincial meeting held in 1776. He took his post in Philadelphia in time to sign the Declaration of Independence. He served as a delegate from 1776 to 1781, but in November 1778, Walton returned to Savannah and took up his commission as a colonel of militia as a defender of the city against a British attack. He was wounded in the ensuing battle by which the British seized the city, and he was captured and held by the enemy for a year. On his release, Walton stepped in to the middle of yet another split in the revolutionary ranks—a conservative faction had designated a governor for the state without any form of election. Walton was named as a sort of anti-governor by his more radical faction. The rival chief executives were both replaced within a few months by the legislature, and Walton returned to Congress for the remainder of his term. In 1783, he became chief justice of the state superior court. In 1789, Walton was duly elected as governor of Georgia, and in 1795, he was appointed to fill an unexpired term as U.S. senator.

WALTON, John (1738–1783) Delegate to Congress

An obscure figure, about whom little is known except he was the brother of George Walton, John was born in Virginia and became a planter near Augusta, Georgia before the Revolution. He attended the Georgia Provincial Congress in Savannah in 1775 and was selected as a delegate to the Continental Congress in February 1778, signing the Articles of Confederation later that year. He was the official surveyor of Richmond County for several years before his death.

WARD, Artemus (1727–1800) Continental and militia general, delegate to Congress

Ward was the highest-ranking colonial officer during the first weeks of the Revolutionary War and technically the first commander in chief of the American army, but he was quickly eclipsed by George Washington and withdrew from the fray. Ward was born in Shrewsbury, Massachusetts, and graduated from Harvard. He was active in politics and government, serving in the colonial legislature, and he was also a lieutenant colonel of state militia during the Seven Years' War. When the storm clouds of war began to gather in Massachusetts in 1774, Ward was appointed brigadier and commander in chief of the Massachusetts militia. He was sick in bed during the outbreak of hostilities at Lexington and Concord, but he hastened to Boston and assumed command of the militia from several New England colonies that gathered there to form a spontaneous army laying siege to the British in the city. He contributed little, however, remaining at his headquarters during the battle of Bunker Hill, for example. When Congress adopted the army and named Washington as commander in chief, Ward resented being passed over, even though he was granted major general's rank and appointed second in command to Washington. With the British evacuation of Boston in 1776, Ward resigned his commission and returned to civilian life. He served as president of the Massachusetts Executive Council from 1777 to 1779 and was a delegate to Congress from 1780 to 1782. He later was elected to the U.S. House of Representatives as a Federalist. *Further reading:* Charles Martyn, *The Life of Artemus Ward, the First Commander-in-Chief of the American Revolution* (New York, 1921).

WARD, Samuel (1725–1776) Delegate to Congress, state official

Ward was born in Newport, Rhode Island, the son of a prosperous merchant who was governor of the colony in the 1740s. Ward himself was active in colonial politics and served as both chief justice and governor. He helped found Rhode Island College, which eventually became Brown University. He was one of the colony's first delegates to the Continental Congress in 1775 and was reelected in 1776, but he died of smallpox in March.

WARD, Samuel, Jr. (1756–1832) Continental officer

Samuel Jr., the son of congressman Samuel Ward, was born in Westerly, Rhode Island and graduated in 1771 from Rhode Island College (which later became Brown University). He joined the 1st Rhode Island Regiment when it was organized in 1775, obtaining a captain's commission, and had the misfortune to accompany his regiment north on the invasion of Canada. He was captured at Quebec on the last day of the year and held prisoner until the following August. He was eventually promoted to major and fought in the successful campaign against General John Burgoyne in 1777. He wintered with the Continental Army at Valley Forge in 1777–78 and was promoted to lieutenant colonel after serving with his regiment in the failed French-American assault on Newport. He left the army in 1781 at the end of the active fighting and turned to commerce, establishing a very prosperous sea trade from a new base in New York City, where he moved after the British evacuation. Ward sailed on his own ships and in 1788 was one of the first American traders to visit China. His granddaughter was the 19th-century writer Julia Ward Howe.

WARNER, Seth (1743–1784) Militia general, Continental officer

Warner led the irregular Green Mountain Boys of Vermont during the first months of the war and subsequently commanded an offshoot regiment of Vermont quasi-militia that helped defeat General John Burgoyne's invasion.

He was born in Roxbury, Connecticut and moved to the Hampshire Grants as an adult. The area—already known as Vermont—was one of the most hotly disputed places in the colonies, with land claimed by the governments of both New York and New Hampshire. Governor Benning Wentworth of New Hampshire had issued grants to settlers, but New York not only failed to recognize the grants but insisted on trying to collect taxes and otherwise enforce its sovereignty. The settlers themselves were an independent lot, led by Ethan Allen and his political cohorts, and they preferred no outside government at all. Warner was one of the Vermonters who organized the Green Mountain Boys, a vigilante military force designed to keep New York tax collectors and law officers at bay. Like Allen, Warner was declared an outlaw by the government of New York before the Revolution, but the colony's writ did not run far in Vermont. When the war began with the fighting in Massachusetts, Warner, Allen and their unruly Boys decided to seize Fort Ticonderoga, which they did on May 10, 1775 with the "help" of Benedict Arnold. The next day, Warner led a group of the Boys on to take Crown Point.

The two feats looked significant but accomplished little, although the artillery captured at Ticonderoga proved important during the siege of Boston. The Vermonters were long on momentary enthusiasm and short on strategic sense and discipline. Within the month, Warner and Allen were sent to Philadelphia to petition the Continental Congress to take the Green Mountain Boys into the fold of the Continental Army that was just then in the process of organization. On June 23, Congress created Seth Warner's Battalion (subsequently known as Warner's Continental Regiment) as part of the Continental Army, but the unit remained in an organizational limbo—neither strictly part of the Continental Army structure nor yet completely a state militia regiment. Warner was voted in as lieutenant colonel in command, an act that shoved Ethan Allen aside and began his slide into treason. Warner led the Green Mountain Boys (which they still were despite the congressional imprimatur)

northward as part of the American invasion army under Richard Montgomery, fighting briskly at several points during the advance toward the disaster at Quebec at the end of the year. During the long, painful retreat from Canada, Warner and his men usually took the position of rear guards.

By the summer of 1776, not much was left of the original Vermont regiment, but Warner was authorized by Congress to recruit a new unit. His next appearance on the battlefield was a year later, when Burgoyne invaded New England. Warner commanded part of an American army under Arthur St. Clair and was surprised at Hubbardtown in July by an advance British force under Simon Fraser and Baron von Riedesel. Warner's careless dispositions and failure to post adequate sentries resulted in a crushing British victory, toward the end of which Warner simply told his men to scatter and flee. Warner showed better military skill at the battle of Bennington in mid-August, when as part of John Stark's army, Warner and his Vermonters helped snuff out the Germans under Breymann and dealt Burgoyne's offensive a stiff blow. Warner was thereafter promoted to the rank of brigadier general by the Vermont legislature, a body that technically had no legal existence. He was in failing health, however, and although still in nominal command of Warner's Continentals until the unit was disbanded in January 1781, he seldom took the field again. He died at age 41 in Roxbury.

WARREN, James (1726–1808) State official, militia general

Warren was born in Plymouth, Massachusetts and was unrelated to Joseph and John Warren, although there is often some confusion because of the similarity of names and posts in which they served. James was an active patriot in the prerevolutionary years in Massachusetts but failed to accomplish much once the rebellion actually got under way, and he has since been in the historical shadow of his brilliant wife, Mercy Otis Warren. James had a comfortable early life as the son of a wealthy merchant and himself took up trade and gentlemanly farming after graduating from Harvard in 1745. He married Mercy Otis (sister of dissident leader James Otis) in 1754, and although as an 18th-century woman she was not allowed much public role, one suspects she was the brains of the family. James was, nonetheless, a vigorous organizer among the patriots of Massachusetts, using as his base the colonial legislature of which he was a member from 1766 until 1778. He worked closely with both John and Sam Adams and took over as president of the Massachusetts Provincial Assembly from Joseph Warren (hence some of the confusion) in 1775, having previously served on the committee of correspondence. He was a very active man in the days just before Lexington and Concord, but his role declined when the actual Revolution moved forward. He acted as paymaster of the Boston army, but despite a commission as a major general of militia, he took no active role in the war once the conflict moved away from Boston in 1776. He refused to serve under Continental officers of lesser rank, and he was shunted aside to some degree by John Hancock, who came to wield political power in Massachusetts. Warren served on the navy board for the Eastern Department during the war, but it was not a potent post. He ran unsuccessfully for office several times after the war. *Further reading:* C. Harvey Gardiner, *A Study in Dissent: The Warren-Gerry Correspondence, 1776–1792* (Carbondale, Ill., 1968); *Warren-Adams Letters . . .* ((Boston, 1972).

WARREN, John (1753–1815) Continental surgeon, physician

The younger brother by 12 years of Joseph Warren, John was born in Roxbury, Massachusetts and graduated from Harvard in 1771. He studied medicine with his brother and had just begun practice when the Revolutionary War began. When Joseph was killed at the battle of Bunker Hill in June 1775, John foresook private practice and volunteered his services to the Continental Army around Boston. He was appointed as senior hospital surgeon and eventually moved on with the army to New York and New Jersey. He returned to Boston in 1777 and began his private practice again, but he also continued to work in military hospitals. He became one of the leading medical lights in Boston and Massachusetts and was particularly skillful at anatomy and surgery. He helped establish the first formal medical classes at Harvard in 1782 and served as professor of surgery and anatomy.

WARREN, Joseph (1741–1775) Physician, patriot leader

Warren was one of the first heroes of the Revolution to fall on the battlefield and his loss robbed the American cause of an energetic, able leader. He was born in Roxbury, Massachusetts

Joseph Warren

(no relation to James Warren, but the elder brother of John Warren) and graduated from Harvard in 1759. After a tour as master of the Roxbury Grammar School, Warren studied medicine and opened a practice in Boston. He was apparently a skillful doctor and soon was recognized as one of the better practicing physicians in the city. He was also a highly political man and joined the protest movement that was churning Boston. Warren had inoculated John Adams against smallpox, and the resulting friendship led to a close association with John Adams, Sam Adams, John Hancock and James Otis. By the late 1760s, Warren was among the handful of leaders of the popular movement in Boston. He wrote for the patriot press, spoke often in public—gaining special notice for his orations on the anniversaries of the Boston Massacre—and served on nearly all the important patriot committees, including the Caucus Club, the committee of correspondence, and eventually the committee of safety. In August 1774, Warren was selected as president of the Massachusetts Provincial Congress, making him the chief executive, so to speak, of the revolutionary movement. He was especially energetic in the weeks before the first armed conflict at Lexington and Concord.

Unlike Sam Adams and John Hancock, Warren remained in Boston in the spring of 1775, and it was he who dispatched Paul Revere and William Dawes with the warning of the British march in April. He then escaped from the city and joined the work of organizing an army to lay siege to the British garrison in Boston. He headed the committee to set up the army and was elected as a major general by the provincial congress. He had not yet received his commission when he decided to visit the troops at Bunker Hill and Breed's Hill on June 17. It was apparent that a battle was imminent, and Warren volunteered to serve as a soldier at the barricades, refusing to take command. He was shot through the face and killed instantly when the third British assault finally overran the patriot defenses. His body was identified months later by means of false teeth which had been made by Paul Revere. *Further reading:* John H. Cary, *Joseph Warren: Physician, Politician, Patriot* (Champlain, Ill., 1961); Robert Frothingham, *The Life and Times of Joseph Warren* (Boston, 1865; reprinted New York, 1971).

WARREN, Mercy Otis (1728–1814) Writer, historian

Warren was a brilliant writer and thinker who very nearly managed to transcend the horrendous obstacles to intelligent women set up by 18th-century society. She was clearly one of the best minds of her day and one of the better pens, yet the notion of a thinking woman was so abhorrent to the males of her age that she seldom received the honor due her in her own time. Her flow of satires, poetry and drama and her three-volume history of the Revolution have since earned her a place in the American pantheon, especially among latter-day feminists.

She was born on Cape Cod, the daughter of a prominent colonial politician and the sister of the erratic dissident leader James Otis. Women were seldom allowed serious education (many were compelled to remain illiterate), but Mercy had access to the library of her uncle Jonathan Russell, and she became extremely well versed in politics, history and literature. She married James Warren in 1754 and eventually bore five children, keeping a home for her political husband while maintaining a huge correspondence with all the leading patriot lights and producing propagandistic literature. She easily outstripped her husband in both understanding and expression of politics, but such could seldom be acknowledged—even in private—during her own day. She was very close to her brother, James, who was the most radical of Boston radicals but who descended into madness after taking a blow to the head in a brawl, and she had a lifelong friendship with Abigail and John Adams despite a terrible rift with John over her historical treatment of his role

in the Revolution. To some degree, Warren's genius was acknowledged by John Adams and others, but only by the mechanism of granting her a fleeting exemption as a metaphorical male—she was seen as an aberration rather than as a prototype—since their very idea of womanhood disbarred women from having serious thoughts.

Warren wrote and published three biting works of fiction during the prerevolutionary years, the best of which is *The Group,* published in January 1775. Her pen remained active during the war, but her largest achievement was the three-volume *History of the Rise, Progress and Termination of the American Revolution* published in 1805. Warren was strongly pro-Jeffersonian and anti-Federalist, and she spared nothing in criticism in her account of the Revolution. One consequence was a violent quarrel with John Adams that was eventually patched up after a five-year rift. She died at an advanced age, one hopes with the inner knowledge that her unique achievements would be long honored. *Further reading:* Katherine S. Anthony, *First Lady of the Revolution: The Life of Mercy Otis Warren* (Port Washington, N.Y., 1958); Jean Fritz, *Cast for a Revolution* (Boston, 1972); William R. Smith, *History as Argument: Three Patriot Historians of the American Revolution* (The Hague, 1966); Lawrence J. Friedman and Arthur H. Shaffer, "Mercy Otis Warren and the Politics of Historical Nationalism," *The New England Quarterly* 48 (June 1975), 194–215.

WASHINGTON, Bushrod (1762–1829) Soldier, jurist

Bushrod was George Washington's nephew, the executor of his uncle's will and inheritor of Mount Vernon. He served as a private during the Revolution. Afterward, he was admitted to the bar in Virginia and began a long and distinguished career as a judge in 1798 when he was named as an associate justice of the U.S. Supreme Court, a post at which he served until his death 31 years later. His most famous opinion was in the Dartmouth College case that established the sanctity of corporations.

WASHINGTON, George (1732–1799) Continental commander in chief, delegate to Congress, first president

The popular view sees Washington in a grand procession of clichés summed up by the phrase "Father of His Country," but unlike most historical icons, Washington truly lived

George Washington

up to his billing. He was the indispensable man without whom the Revolution would not have succeeded nor the new Republic been born and nurtured. Beneath the layers of myth, legend and hagiography was a very great man, whose special qualities were exactly those needed during and after the Revolution. He had defects—he was not a very good tactical general despite an overabundance of personal bravery—but they were as chaff compared to his monumental will to succeed and his bold decision-making at crucial moments.

He was born the second son of a prosperous Virginia planter and grew up with education in little beyond the duties and pleasures of the southern squirearchy. Washington's father died when the boy was 11, and for most of his early years, the future leader lived in the shadow of his elder brother, Lawrence, who had inherited Mount Vernon and most of the family's wealth. Washington lived most of the time at another estate near Fredericksburg, Virginia. At age 16, he became a surveyor. When Lawrence died in 1752, Washington was next in line and eventually inherited a fortune in land and slaves. He was closely involved in local military affairs, and in 1753, he was dispatched by the royal governor of Virginia on a mission to the French in the Ohio Valley, a trip that stimulated his lifelong interest in western land speculation. He was appointed lieutenant colonel of militia the following year and took an expedition back to the northwest, fighting in the opening skirmishes of the Seven Years' War and losing at Fort Necessity. In 1755, he became Edward

Braddock's aide-de-camp and then commander of the Virginia militia. He was successful in several subsequent campaigns, but he resigned his commission in 1759 and married a wealthy widow, Martha Custis, making him one of the wealthiest men in the American colonies. The couple moved to Mount Vernon, and Washington settled into the life of an influential planter.

He was a member of the House of Burgesses and supported the rights of the colonies against the crown from very early in the revolutionary struggle. He was selected to represent Virginia in the first Continental Congress in 1774 and returned on adjournment to urge military preparations in his home colony. He served again in the second Congress, and in June 1775 he was voted to the post of commander in chief of the new Continental Army, a choice that was obvious even to the contentious delegates from New England.

A man of immense dignity and impressive bearing (remarked on by all his contemporaries), Washington proved to be a tenacious commander, an agile politician and an able administrator, overcoming heavy odds and enormous obstacles during the following eight years. Washington was, however, no military genius, and he seldom won a clear-cut victory on the battlefield against the professional generals of the Royal Army. He lost disastrously to the British during the campaign in New York, and his army was saved only by his ability to get it to move rapidly under difficult circumstances. His greatest battle triumph was his surprise raid on the Germans at Trenton in December 1776—a crucial victory after a string of defeats. He subsequently was unable to truly beat the British in open-field battle, but at Monmouth he came close.

His most important service was to keep a small, ragged, ever-changing, ill-supported army in existence while the Congress nearly squabbled itself to death and then went flat broke. He survived political conspiracy and civilian criticism as well as conniving jealousies by subordinates. Yet beneath the balanced equanimity and glacial dignity was an audacious risk-taker. At the crucial moment in 1781, Washington gambled that the French fleet would arrive in time to cut off Lord Cornwallis, and he launched his army (along with Rochambeau's larger French force) south to grab the final victory. A miscalculation might have destroyed the hard-won gains of all the previous years of warfare. During the long two years of anticlimax after the surrender of Cornwallis at Yorktown, Washington performed magnificently in managing the disgruntled and unpaid army until the last British troops departed. He then calmly resigned his commission and returned home to Mount Vernon.

His repose was short-lived, however, and he returned to the political service of his country in 1787 as presiding officer of the convention to revise the Articles of Confederation, where he threw his immense prestige onto the side of a strong, new central government. When the new nation was established by the Constitution, he was the obvious and unanimous choice as the first president of the United States, and he was reelected for a second term in 1792. He declined a third term (setting a precedent for future presidents), and after a farewell address in September 1796, he retired to his estate high above the Potomac, dying three years later.

Further reading: The bibliography of Washington is immense, but the standard large-scale biography is Douglas Southall Freeman, *George Washington,* 7 vols. [Vol. 7 by John Carroll and Mary Wells Ashworth] (New York, 1948–57); also very fine is James T. Flexner, *George Washington,* 4 vols. (Boston, 1965–72) [also in a one-volume version]; and a recent short biography is John E. Ferling, *The First of Men: A Life of George Washington* (Knoxville, Tenn., 1988).

WASHINGTON, Martha Custis (1732–1802)

The first First Lady of the United States, Martha was, by all accounts, a charming woman of considerable domestic accomplishments, but one who remained firmly in the role of wife, albeit to the nation's greatest man. She was born in New Kent County, Virginia and married Daniel Custis at age 18. Custis died in 1757, leaving Martha a wealthy young widow in control of landed estates and a cash balance of £45,000, part of which was due to their two children. She was therefore an attractive match for George Washington, who apparently sought a companion and a way to shore up his financial fortunes. They were married in 1759 and eventually established a home at Mount Vernon, which Washington inherited from an older brother. One of Martha's outstanding characteristics was an ability to provide domestic tranquillity for her husband and to pitch her public role at just the right level for the times. George's growing involvement in the affairs of Virginia and the Continental Con-

Martha Washington

gress took him from home with increasing frequency, and after June 1775 when he was appointed commander in chief of the Continental Army, he did not return to Mount Vernon until he stopped for a brief visit in 1781 when on his way to Yorktown. Martha, however, traveled north regularly during the war years to stay with George while the army was in winter quarters, the most famous example being in the winter of 1777–1778 at Valley Forge.

At the end of the war in 1783, George returned to Mount Vernon, but he was recalled to service with the new Republic. Martha became the revered wife of the new president—styled Lady Washington—and managed to behave with just the proper amount of dignity in public that established the propriety of the first family but stopped short of displaying any inappropriate regalness. *Further reading:* Marguerite Vance, *Martha Washington: Daughter of Virginia* (New York, 1947).

WASHINGTON, William (1752–1810) Continental officer

Washington was one of the better cavalry leaders of the Revolutionary War and fought ably, especially during the southern campaigns in the Carolinas during 1780 and 1781. He was a cousin of George Washington and, naturally, was born in Virginia. He is reported to have been studying for a church career when the war began. In 1776, Washington was commissioned as a captain in the original 3rd Virginia Regiment, which served in the

William Washington

northern theater in the New York and New Jersey campaigns. Washington took a bad wound at the battle of Long Island but survived to march into Trenton in December 1776, where he was again wounded—alongside a young James Monroe. Soon thereafter, Washington moved from the infantry to the dragoons as an officer of Stephen Moylan's new 4th Regiment.

The Continental Army still had difficulty at this stage of the war in putting effective mounted troops in the field. The attempts to organize genuine cavalry units—troops that were intended to fight on horseback—failed for the most part, due in good measure to entrusting their command to European adventurers such as Count Pulaski. Dragoons, on the other hand, were more or less mounted infantry that used horses to get rapidly from one place to another but who were equipped and expected to fight on foot. The organization of several light dragoon regiments in 1777 presaged the later success of ''legions'' which combined dragoons and light infantry.

Washington gained experience with Moylan's regiment and in 1778 transferred to the 3rd Regiment under George Baylor. When Baylor was wounded at the Tappan ''Massacre'' in September, Washington took over effective command of the regiment as lieutenant colonel. He never advanced further in rank, since Congress called a halt to promotions in the mounted corps at about this juncture. In 1780, Washington moved to the southern theater with a command that mixed remnants of several previous dragoon or cavalry regiments. The situation was desperate in the Carolinas: Charleston was taken along with Benjamin Lincoln's entire army, and Banastre Tarleton appeared to be unstoppable as his dragoons and light infantry inflicted defeat after defeat on the Carolina militia. Washington, along with the redoubtable Light-Horse Harry Lee, proved in the end to be a match for Tarleton. Washington failed at engagements at Monck's Corner and Lenud's Ferry, but by the end of 1780, his increasingly experienced mounted troopers defeated a force of loyalists at Rugeley's Mill and began a series of maneuvers that brought them to the field at Cowpens as part of Daniel Morgan's army facing Tarleton on January 17, 1781. Washington's dragoons hit the British flank in a mounted attack at a crucial moment of the battle and sealed the victory for the Americans. In the last stages of fighting, Washington and Tarleton met pommel-to-pommel, almost killing each other— Washington fended off Tarleton with a broken sabre only to have his horse killed by Tarleton's final pistol shot.

During the complex movements that characterized the following weeks, Washington served well as the mobile arm of Nathanael Greene's army. The dragoons fought valiantly at Guilford Courthouse and at Hobkirk's Hill, but at Eutaw Springs in September 1781, Washington and his men blundered in front of masked British infantry and were severely mauled. Washington's horse was killed, and he was bayoneted, captured and hauled off to confinement in Charleston. While a prisoner, he fell in love and married a local girl, and then he settled in Charleston after the war. He served in the state legislature and was commissioned as a brigadier general during the war scare with France in 1798.

WATERS, Daniel (1731–1816) Privateer, naval officer

One of the many Massachusetts privateers during the Revolutionary War, Waters was a native of Charlestown but lived most of his life in Malden. He fought on land during early 1776 as a militiaman, but he turned late in the year to privateering aboard the *Lee*. In 1777, he took a commission in the Continental Navy as commander of the sloop *General Gates*, sailing to the West Indies in 1779. He resigned his naval commission later that year and returned to the more lucrative business of privateering, first as captain of the *Thorn* and then commanding the *Friendship.*

WATSON, John W. Tadwell (1748–1826) British officer

Watson was lieutenant colonel of the 3rd Foot Guards during most of his service in the American war. He sailed from New York in the fall of 1780 as part of the reinforcements sent to Lord Cornwallis in the Carolinas. In early 1781 he was given command of a mixed force of light troops—probably flank companies—and sent by Lord Rawdon to hunt down and destroy American partisan Francis Marion. He was completely unsuccessful as Marion led him in a chase through the difficult terrain. Watson retreated to Georgetown, South Carolina and was thus effectively removed from assisting Rawdon at the battle of Hobkirk's Hill. He was eventually promoted to general's rank after the war.

WATSON-WENTWORTH, Charles *See* ROCK-INGHAM, Marquis of.

WAYNE, Anthony (1745–1796)

One of the most successful American generals of the Revolutionary War, "Mad" Anthony Wayne combined the ability to plan well with ferociousness on the battlefield. He was born in Chester County, Pennsylvania and attended an academy in Philadelphia. He worked during his early life as a surveyor and after marriage in 1766 as a tanner for his father-in-law.

Anthony Wayne

In 1774 and 1775, Wayne sat in the Pennsylvania legislature, and with the beginning of the war he was appointed as colonel of the 4th Pennsylvania Regiment. He led his regiment northward to reinforce Benedict Arnold and suffered with the rest of the army through defeat at Three Rivers and a long retreat. Wayne was promoted to brigadier general in February 1777 and joined the main army under Washington, subsequently commanding the regiments of the Pennsylvania Line at Brandywine and Germantown. In late September 1777, Wayne was taken completely by surprise at Paoli Tavern in Pennsylvania and lost much of his command to an exceptionally skillful and brutal night attack by British general Charles Grey. Charged with negligence, Wayne was acquitted by a court-martial and returned to duty. He got revenge two years later at Stony Point, New York, where his meticulously planned and executed assault took the British post with few losses to the Americans but great harm to the British. The strategic importance of the victory was slight, but it provided a major psychological boost to the American cause and demonstrated Wayne's best abilities.

In January 1781, Wayne was a key figure in negotiating the peaceful resolution of the mutiny of the Pennsylvania Line regiments, although the episode shook his faith in his troops. He reorganized several units and marched south to aid the Marquis de Lafayette against the British in Virginia. At the battle of Green Spring on July 6, 1781, Wayne was lured by Lord Cornwallis into a trap, and he found himself facing nearly the entire British army with little hope of retreat and annihilation as the likely outcome. In a startling maneuver, Wayne ordered a charge by his greatly outnumbered Continentals against the main British battle line, and the gamble worked: the British were stopped short, and Wayne and most of his men escaped. He served after Yorktown in the southern theater, mostly against loyalists, and was a brevet major general when he left the army in 1783.

He returned to Pennsylvania, taking a seat in the legislature, but then moved to Georgia. He was elected to the new U.S. Congress in 1791 but was denied his seat on account of residence irregularities. In 1792, Wayne was selected by Washington to become commander in chief of the newly reorganized U.S. Army and was sent to the frontier to quell Indian uprisings in the Northwest Territory.

Anthony Wayne medal

His victory at the battle of Fallen Timbers in August 1794 is perhaps his most famous engagement, leading as it did to major land concessions in the West. *Further reading:* Paul D. Nelson, *Anthony Wayne: Soldier of the Early Republic* (Bloomington, Ind., 1985).

WEARE, Meshech (1713–1786) State official, militia officer

Weare was a long-time public officeholder before the Revolution, serving in the New Hampshire colonial legislature off and on from 1745 until 1775 (including a three-year stint as speaker) and as a justice of the Superior Court from 1747 to 1775. He was born in Hampton Falls and graduated from Harvard. With the coming of the Revolution, Weare supported the patriot cause and acted for a short time as chairman of the New Hampshire Committee of Safety. He held a commission as a colonel in the state militia, but most of his wartime service was as a civilian state official: he was president of the state council (in effect, the chief executive of the state) during the entire Revolutionary War and simultaneously sat as chief justice. He continued in office after the Revolution with a term as state president from 1784 to 1785.

WEBB, Samuel B. (1753–1807) Continental officer

Webb was a native of Wethersfield, Connecticut and the stepson of Silas Deane. He acted as Deane's secretary before the Revolution and as clerk for his local committee of correspondence. With the outbreak of the war, Webb led a militia unit from Wethersfield to Boston, where he fought and was wounded at Breed's Hill. In the summer of 1775, he became an aide-de-camp to Israel Putnam and assumed a commission as a major. A year later, after serving at White Plains, Trenton and Princeton, he was promoted to lieutenant colonel and moved to the personal staff of George Washington; he served there until January 1777, when he was given his own regiment, one of the new "additional" units raised that month under the orders of Congress (his regiment was eventually redesignated the 3rd Connecticut). Webb was brevetted to brigadier general in late 1783, several months after he had mustered out. His letters and journals for the period were preserved and published in the late 19th century. *Further reading:* Worthington C. Ford, ed., *Correspondence and Journals of Samuel Blachley Webb*, 3 vols. (New York, 1893; reprinted, 1969).

WEBSTER, James (c. 1743–1781) British officer

Born in Edinburgh, Webster took a commission in the 33rd Regiment of Foot in 1760. By the time of the American war, he was lieutenant colonel and in day-to-day command of the regiment. The ceremonial colonel of the 33rd was Lord Cornwallis, and the unit served with the major general in almost all his North American campaigns. Webster fought in New York and New Jersey and was conspicuous at Monmouth, the last major fight in the northern theater. He moved south with the British invasion force toward Charleston in 1779, and during the following southern campaign, Webster was usually in command of a brigade. He had a high reputation among his fellow British commanders, which was exemplified at the battle of Guilford Courthouse, where he led an attack on the best troops of the Continental Line. He was killed in the action on March 15, 1781.

WEDDERBURN, Alexander (Lord Loughborough) (1733–1805) British official

A Scotsman by birth and education, Wedderburn moved south to London in 1757, setting up as a lawyer in the capital. He entered politics, took a seat in Parliament in 1768, and was appointed as solicitor general in 1771 under Lord North. He was one of the more vociferous and intemperate opponents of colonial rebellion, making his mark in 1774 with a vicious verbal attack on Benjamin Franklin over the petition of Massachusetts for the removal of royal governor Thomas Hutchinson. He continued in office under North during most of the Revolution, moving up to the attorney generalship in 1778. In 1780, he was appointed as chief justice of the court of common pleas and raised to the peerage as Lord Loughborough. In the rapid shuffle of governments that followed North's resignation, Wedderburn helped form the Fox-North coalition under the Duke of Portland that held office in late 1783. He returned as lord chancellor in 1793, and during his term he was accused of having George III sign documents while the monarch was mentally deranged. Wedderburn was finally dismissed in 1801 but was consoled with the title Earl of Rosslyn.

WEEDON, George (1734–1793) Continental general

Weedon, a native of Fredericksburg, Virginia, was a tavern keeper and gentleman farmer before the Revolution. When the 3rd Virginia Regiment was organized in 1776, Weedon became lieutenant colonel, and he succeeded to command as colonel of the regiment in the following August. He led the unit north to take part in Washington's campaigns in New York and New Jersey during the final months of the year. In February 1777, Weedon was promoted to brigadier general—he was acting as Washington's adjutant at the time—but he then took a long leave from duty. He returned for the battles around Philadelphia at Brandywine and Germantown, playing an important role at both. He was, however, similar to many Continental generals in his prickly regard for the appearance of respect for his rank. He grew irritated at the honor shown Thomas Conway by Congress and—coupled with his strong loyalty to Washington, who also suffered from congressional slights during 1777 and 1778—he decided to retire. Weedon's biographer attributes his abandonment of the war to the value he placed on gentlemanly honor over and above what was in the infant United States of the time still an abstract notion of nationalism. Congress failed to accept his resignation, but Weedon nonetheless withdrew to his home state. When the British invaded Virginia in 1781, Weedon returned to duty, organized militia, and was in command of the forces that hemmed Banastre Tarleton into Gloucester during the siege of Yorktown. *Further reading: Harry M. Ward, Duty, Honor or Country: General George Weedon and the American Revolution (Philadelphia, 1979).*

WENTWORTH, John (1737–1820) Loyalist official

Born at Salmon Falls, New Hampshire, John was a member of the powerful Wentworth family that included his uncle Benning, governor of the colony. John graduated from Harvard in 1755 and set up a law practice in Dover, New Hampshire. He visited England on business in the early 1760s and was there in 1766 when the cabinet resolved to remove his uncle as royal governor of New Hampshire. The younger Wentworth was named as his replacement, although not yet 30 years of age. He served throughout the agitation leading up to the Revolution, an especially trying task in New Hampshire, where conflicting land claims in the Grants region (modern-day Vermont) made for complex politics and prolonged contention. He repaired to Boston after the outbreak of violence and sailed to England with the British evacuation. After several years without employment, he became lieutenant governor of Nova Scotia in 1792, and he was eventually created a baronet in reward for his services to the crown.

WENTWORTH, John, Jr. (1745–1787) Delegate to Congress, state official

One of the Wentworths of New Hampshire who espoused the patriot side, John Jr. (not the son of John Wentworth—they were nearly contemporary—but probably a cousin) was born in Salmon Falls and graduated from Harvard in 1768. He became a lawyer and set up practice in Dover, New Hampshire in 1771. He served on the New Hampshire Committee of Correspondence in 1774 and was named to the state committee of safety in 1777. He also sat in the New Hampshire House of Representatives during the war and was selected as a delegate to the Congress in 1778 and 1779. He signed the Articles of Confederation during his congressional term. Wentworth also was a member of the New Hampshire Council and the state senate.

WENTWORTH, Paul (d. 1793) Loyalist spy   He was related to the powerful Wentworth family of New Hampshire but his exact antecedents and early biography are unknown. It is certain, however, that Wentworth acted as a loyalist spy and British agent during the Revolution. There are vague references in Wentworth's letters that he was closely related to John Wentworth, the last royal governor of New Hampshire, and he may have received an annual allowance through John. He had lived in New Hampshire at some stage of his life, but he had major holdings in the West Indies and in Suriname that apparently supported him, along with his skill in manipulating the London stock market.

Wentworth was living in London at the beginning of the Revolution when he struck a bargain with the British government to act as an agent and to supervise spying on loyalists in England and on the American diplomats in Paris. He received a rather modest annuity of £200 a year with promises of a title, a seat in Parliament and an official sinecure if his intelligence efforts produced results. He worked closely with William Eden, the British official in charge of espionage, and provided analysis and advice to Lord North's government. Wentworth's primary agent was Dr. Edward Bancroft, one of the secretaries to the American mission in France and an effective spy. Both Wentworth and Bancroft secretly moved back and forth between Britain and France during the first years of the war, and they both used their inside knowledge of the military and diplomatic developments to play the stock market to their advantage.

Wentworth's most public role came in late 1777, when he was sent by Eden on an open mission to discuss conciliation with Benjamin Franklin. He arrived in Paris in December, just as the full extent of General John Burgoyne's defeat was becoming known, and after meeting first with Silas Deane, Wentworth had a long interview with Franklin in

January. The meeting came to nothing, and Wentworth returned to England empty-handed. Worse, the French-American alliance was signed almost as Wentworth and the American diplomats spoke. Wentworth never really cashed in on his intelligence work: he was given a seat in Parliament, but only for six weeks in 1780, and the other promised rewards never materialized. He returned to Suriname after the war. *Further reading:* Samuel F. Bemis, "The British Secret Service and the Franco-American Alliance," *American Historical Review* 29, 3 (April 1924), 474–95.

WEST, Samuel (1731–1807) Clergyman   Born in Yarmouth, Massachusetts and a graduate of Harvard, West served the Congregational church in New Bedford for 42 years, beginning in 1761. He was one of the amateur cryptologists who deciphered the coded letter from Dr. Benjamin Church to General William Howe in 1775 that revealed Church to be a traitor to the patriot cause. West also acted as a chaplain to the army during the war, and he sat in the Massachusetts convention that wrote the new state constitution.

WEYMOUTH, Thomas Thynne, Viscount (1734–1796) British official   A glittering example of what was wrong with British government during the reign of George III, Weymouth was a lazy, dissipated aristocrat who held responsible cabinet office during the American Revolution only because of his personal connection to the king. He inherited his title in 1751, shortly after leaving Cambridge, where he failed to receive a degree. He became famous as a young man for his dissolute addiction to cards and gambling in an age when only the most extreme behavior could earn such a reputation. He impoverished himself and his family by his gambling losses and nearly had to flee the kingdom as a debtor. He was rescued by the king, who found him personally charming, with an appointment as viceroy of Ireland. Weymouth collected his fee for official equipage, paid some of his debts, and resigned after two months, never setting foot in Ireland. Weymouth continued throughout his political career to receive office through the insistence of George III, quite irrespective of his incompetence and well-known shortcomings. In January 1768, he was appointed secretary of state for the northern department, although he spent his time at

gambling all night in the London clubs, leaving the work of the department to the undersecretary. He cemented his relations with George III, however, by a blustery public combativeness during the public riots set off by supporters of John Wilkes. In October 1758, Weymouth transferred to the southern department, but he resigned in 1770 when a war with Spain threatened—he was mortally afraid of holding office if there was actually something he had to be responsible for. He returned as secretary of state in 1775 and remained in the cabinet until 1779, opposing conciliation with the Americans and consistently supporting the king in the House of Lords debates. He was created as the first Marquis of Bath in 1789.

WHARTON, Samuel (1732–1800) Delegate to Congress, land speculator, businessman

Wharton was one of the most ambitious speculators in western lands before the Revolution. He was born in Philadelphia, the son of a merchant, and had little formal schooling. He formed a partnership with John Baynton and George Morgan, known as Baynton, Wharton, & Morgan, that became one of the largest fur trading and land speculation companies in the colonies. The partners hoped to acquire title to huge tracts of Indian land on the western side of the Alleghenies after the end of the Seven Years' War and formed in 1764 a company known as the Grand Illinois Venture to trade in the Illinois country. Official British policy, especially after the costly Pontiac's War, ruled out such ventures, but Wharton hoped to influence the ministry to allow him and his partners to profit from western lands. He managed to gain a tenuous claim to a large tract in modern-day West Virginia and went to England in 1769 to try to obtain validation of the claim from the British government. He enlisted the aid of several prominent British politicians as shareholders in his other enterprise, the Grand Ohio Company and proposed a colony to be known as Vandalia. The company petitioned the government for a grant of 20 million acres, based on the previous claim, but Wharton was unable to get confirmation of the grandiose scheme before the outbreak of the war in 1775. He remained in England until 1779, when he went to Paris and enlisted the help of Benjamin Franklin in his schemes. It all came to naught, however, and Wharton returned to America in 1780. In 1782 and 1783, he represented Delaware as a delegate to the Confederation Congress, but he moved back to Pennsylvania in 1784.

WHEATLEY, Phillis (c. 1753–1784) Poet

Wheatley was a remarkable young black slave. She was born in Africa and sold on the Boston slave market to merchant John Wheatley in 1761 when she was about seven years old. Taken into the Wheatley establishment as a personal servant to Wheatley's wife, Susanna, the young girl quickly learned the new language and soon after began to write astounding poetry. She was a sensation among white Bostonians—and before long among a much wider circle—most of whom found it impossible that a black slave should be a poet at all let alone a *good* poet. Her first public verse was published in 1767, and she continued to write and publish poetry until the end of her short life. Her works were widely known in colonial America and in Great Britain, especially after she visited England between 1771 and 1773 and after the publication of a collection of *Poems on Various Subjects, Religious and Moral* in 1773. By then, Wheatley had managed to educate herself in a classical mode, something few women in 18th-century America accomplished let alone a black slave woman. Although she was viewed by whites in her own day with something akin to morbid fascination rather than genuine appreciation, long-term critical attention to her writing has reached the conclusion that Wheatley was among the best if not *the* best American poet of her time and certainly the finest woman poet. She wrote at least 145 titled poems during her lifetime and several of her letters survive as well. She was granted freedom in the fall of 1773, six months before the death of Susanna Wheatley. She continued to write during the Revolution, often on patriotic themes that linked the image of free colonies and the condition of black slavery. In 1778, Wheatley married John Peters, a free black resident of Boston, but the couple faced hard times, despite Peters' status as a black legal advocate. She bore three children, who all died, and she herself died in poverty in 1784 at about 31 years of age. *Further reading:* William H. Robinson, *Critical Essays on Phillis Wheatley* (Boston, 1982); Robinson, *Phillis Wheatley and Her Writings* (Boston, 1984); *The Collected Works of Phillis Wheatley* (New York, 1988).

WHEELOCK, John (1754–1817) Militia officer, educator

The son of Eleazor Wheelock, the

founder of the Indian mission school in New Hampshire that became Dartmouth College, the younger Wheelock first attended Yale and then moved to his father's school, where he graduated in 1771. He served as an officer in a New York infantry company during the Revolution, probably a militia company. In 1779, he became president of Dartmouth, serving the rest of his life there. His long-running dispute with college trustees over the college charter was settled before the U.S. Supreme Court in the landmark Dartmouth College case after Wheelock's death.

WHIPPLE, Abraham (1733–1819) Continental naval officer

Whipple was a native of Providence, Rhode Island and one of the colony's most experienced sea captains at the beginning of the War of Independence. He had commanded a highly successful privateer during the Seven Years' War, proving himself by capturing 23 prizes in a six-month cruise. His normal occupation was as a captain for merchant Nicolas Brown, but in 1772, Whipple led the mob that seized and burned the British revenue cutter, *Gaspée*, an act that enraged the royal authorities. In 1775, at the beginning of armed hostilities, the Rhode Island legislature authorized a tiny state navy—only two ships—with Whipple as commodore. He captured the British tender *Rose* on the day he received his commission, marking the first official prize of the war. Whipple was the brother-in-law of Esek and Samuel Hopkins, which doubtless had much to do with his being named a captain in the new Continental Navy and commander of the *Columbus*. He sailed with Esek Hopkins' fleet to the Bahamas in 1776 and was involved in the subsequent fight with the *Glasgow*, neither affair bringing any glory to American seafarers. Whipple's best moment of the war came in the company of Captain John Rathburne in 1779 when the two officers slipped their ships among a large British convoy and cut out 11 Indiamen, prizes yielding more than a million dollars. Later in the year, Whipple was dispatched to Charleston, South Carolina to take over the naval defenses of the city in anticipation of a British assault. He was unable to mount any resistance with the few poor ships at his command, and he sank most of them and repaired ashore to fight on land. He was captured with the fall of the city, and he spent the remainder of the war as a paroled but unexchanged prisoner in Chester, Pennsylvania. Following the Revolu-

tion, Whipple returned to merchant sailing, augmented by farming, and later moved to the Ohio country.

WHIPPLE, Prince. Continental soldier

Whipple was a young black soldier who may have personally served Continental commander in chief George Washington and was identified by an early historian of black revolutionary fighters as the figure shown in the two famous 19th-century paintings of Washington crossing the Delaware, one by Thomas Sully and the best-known by Emmanuel Leutze. Precise details of Whipple's life are vague, but he was reported to have been born in Africa and sent for education to America; however, the captain of the ship he sailed on landed him in Baltimore and sold him into slavery to men from Portsmouth, New Hampshire. His owner is identified as "General Whipple," whom Prince purportedly served as a bodyguard on the famous trip across the Delaware to Trenton in December 1776. The man referred to is probably William Whipple, a Portsmouth merchant who was serving in the Continental Congress at the time and did not take the field as a brigadier general of militia until later in the war. Prince Whipple was reportedly emancipated during the war and lived afterward in Portsmouth, sometimes using the name Caleb Quotem. He died in an unknown year at age 32.

WHIPPLE, William (1730–1785) Delegate to Congress, militia general, jurist

An important revolutionary who divided his service between Congress and command of militia, Whipple was born in Kittery in the Maine section of Massachusetts. He went to sea early in life as the master of a merchant vessel dealing in the slave trade. In 1760, he gave up slaving and active seafaring and formed a mercantile business in Portsmouth, New Hampshire with his brother. He became rich through trade and was by the time of the Revolution one of the leading citizens of Portsmouth, a center for revolutionary agitation in New Hampshire. He essentially retired from business to devote his energies to revolution, attending the provisional convention in Exeter in 1775 and taking a place on the New Hampshire Committee of Safety. He was also a senior officer of the New Hampshire militia when elected to the Continental Congress in 1776. He served in Congress until 1779, alternating duty there with periods of field service as a general. He signed the Declaration of Independence in 1776 and was a hard-working and effective committeeman. He was one of the members of Congress who most forcefully advocated a strong war effort by a powerful central government—espousing taxation to fund a wholehearted military campaign to expel the British and their loyalist allies. In 1777, Whipple led four regiments of New Hampshire militia to join the northern army opposing General John Burgoyne, and he commanded them during the two battles near Saratoga. After the surrender, he signed the notorious surrender Convention and helped escort the defeated British army to winter quarters near Boston, thereafter returning himself to his seat in Congress. The following year, he took the field again as commander of a New Hampshire contingent in the French-American expedition against the British at Newport. Whipple left Congress in 1779 and served in the New Hampshire legislature until 1784, from 1782 onward sitting simultaneously as a justice of the state supreme court. He died in Portsmouth after a long bout with ill health.

WHITCOMB, John (1713–1783) Militia general
Whitcomb was born in Lancaster, Massachusetts and served as a colonel in the Seven Years' War, emerging with a considerable local reputation as a soldier. In February 1775, as the rebels of the colony prepared for conflict with the British, the Massachusetts Provincial Congress named Whitcomb as a brigadier general of militia. He took part in the harassment of the British retreat from Lexington and Concord, which won him a promotion to major general of militia, and he commanded Massachusetts troops at Lechmere Point during the battle of Breed's Hill and Bunker Hill in June. He was ignored by the Continental Congress, however, when the body first appointed general officers for the new Continental Army. He was finally offered a commission as brigadier general in June 1776, but he declined the appointment, claiming advanced age.

WHITE, Henry (1732–1786) Loyalist merchant
White was born in Maryland but became one of New York City's most prominent merchants during the 1760s. He married into the Van Cortlandts, benefiting from the power and influence of that family. White was also a friend of fellow New Yorker Josiah Martin, who became royal governor of North Carolina. White was a leader in the mercantile business and was one of the first presidents of the New York Chamber of Commerce as well as a member of the New York City Council for six years before the Revolution. He opposed the Stamp Act, as did most American merchant businessmen, but he acted as a tea consignee for the East India Company in 1773. He left New York for England in 1775 but returned the following year when the British army occupied the city and acted as a commissary agent. He fled to Britain at the end of the war, all his property having been seized by the Americans.

WHITE, Phillips (1729–1811) Delegate to Congress, legislator, jurist
White was born in Haverhill, Massachusetts and attended Harvard before serving in the Seven Years' War on an expedition to Lake George. He then moved to New Hampshire and sat as a member of the state legislature during almost the entire Revolution, serving at the same time as a probate judge in Rockingham County. In 1782 and 1783, White was a delegate to the Confederation Congress. He retired to a farm near South Hampton, New Hampshire in 1794 after a two-year term on the state council.

WHITE EYES (c. 1730–1778) Indian leader
White Eyes was chief of the Delaware tribe and counseled neutrality in the white man's wars. However, he was forced to choose sides when the rival war chief of the Delaware declared for the British, and White Eyes thereafter supported the Americans. In 1778, he signed the first treaty between the United States and an Indian tribe, unfortunately one that proved prophetic: the American promise to establish an independent Delaware Indian state with congressional representation was never kept. White Eyes was murdered by American troops later the same year while guiding an expedition under the command of Lachlan McIntosh against Fort Sandusky. McIntosh tried to cover up the killing by claiming that White Eyes had died from smallpox.

WHITECUFF, Benjamin. Loyalist soldier, spy
Born near Hempstead, Long Island as the son of a free black farmer, Whitecuff elected to join the British even though his father and brother served in the American forces. He joined the British on Staten Island in 1777 and worked as a spy for Sir Henry Clinton for the following two years. At one point

he was captured by the Americans and hung by the neck, but the timely arrival of British troops saved him from death. He was recaptured later but escaped while being taken to Boston for execution. He ended up in England after service aboard a privateer.

WHITEFOORD, Caleb (1734–1810) British diplomat

A native Scot, Whitefoord was educated in Edinburgh before moving south to become a London merchant. He lived next door to Benjamin Franklin in London during the years before the Revolution and formed a friendship with the American that provided the pretext for adding Whitefoord to the British delegation selected to negotiate the final peace treaty in 1782. Whitefoord served as the secretary of the British peace commission for a year. He was also a well-known writer of satirical verse and prose and an art collector. *Further reading:* D. G. C. Allan, ''Caleb Whitefoord, Merchant, Diplomatist, and Art Patron,'' *Connoisseur* 190 (1975), 195–99.

WICKES, Lambert (c. 1735–1777) Continental naval officer

Wickes was a hero of the tiny Continental Navy and one of its best commanders, although he has since been overshadowed in reputation by better-known figures such as John Paul Jones. Wickes was a Chesapeake Bay man, born in Kent County, Maryland and raised to the life of a sailor. By the beginning of the Revolution, he was an experienced captain and shipowner. He was appointed 11th on the list of Continental captains in 1776—his influence, without which few captains were commissioned, came from the financier Robert Morris—and given command of the *Reprisal*, a fast but lightly armed ship that carried only 18 six-pounders. His first assignment was to carry William Bingham, a congressional agent, to Martinique in June 1776. On his return to Philadelphia, Wickes took aboard Benjamin Franklin and sailed for France to deliver the elder statesman as the chief American diplomat to the French court. The *Reprisal* reached the French coast in late November, after snatching up two British prizes on the way. Wickes found himself to be the only official American ship of war in European waters, albeit such a puny force compared to the might of the Royal Navy that caution

and stealth were the order of the day. He cruised in the Channel during January 1777, taking five prizes, but the British protested to the French court that he should not be allowed refuge in French ports and Wickes was forced to leave L'Orient in April. He sallied out with two other small American vessels, sailed around the west coast of Ireland and entered the Irish Sea from the north. In a quick sweep, his flotilla took 18 prizes and then dashed for France. Before reaching port, Wickes was intercepted by the 74-gun *Burford* (whose broadsides would have destroyed his ship) and barely managed to escape after a breathtaking chase that compelled Wickes to jettison his guns and cut through *Reprisal*'s timbers, in an attempt to increase his speed. He was detained in Saint-Malo until October 1777, when he was allowed to sail for home. The *Reprisal* hit a storm off Newfoundland, however, and with her timbers weakened by Wickes's self-inflicted damage, she sank with all hands, save the ship's cook. *Further reading:* William B. Clark, *Lambert Wickes: Sea Raider and Diplomat* (New Haven, Conn., 1931).

WIDGERY, William (c. 1753–1822) Privateer, government official

Widgery was born in Devonshire, England and came to Philadelphia with his parents. He was by trade a shipbuilder and became an officer on a privateer during the Revolution. After the war, he studied law and moved to Portland, Massachusetts, where he set up a practice. He sat in the Massachusetts House of Representatives, in the state senate and on the Executive Council between 1790 and 1807. He was elected to the U.S. Congress in 1811 and after serving one term became judge of the Court of Common Pleas.

WILKES, John (1727–1797) British politician

One of the more interesting political figures of his day, Wilkes had a stunning capacity to set the established order on its ear during the early years of the reign of George III. He was a well-educated profligate, debauched in his personal life, who entered Parliament in 1757 as a protégé of the elder William Pitt. Before long, however, Wilkes began to chart his own disruptive course in politics. He wrote and published a violent attack on the government and the king in 1763 in the infamous *Issue*

John Wilkes

No. 45 of his paper *The North Briton*. There followed years of controversy as the government and the crown tried to suppress Wilkes and Wilkes became an immensely popular hero. He was wounded in a duel, fled to Paris, returned to a prison sentence, was elected to Parliament four times over the objections of the government and came to be the focus of popular political protest ("Wilkes and Liberty" was a byword for decades to come). During the American Revolution, Wilkes set himself up as a champion of the American cause and repeatedly spoke in the Commons with ringing declarations of support for the breakaway colonies. As a symbol of the nebulous "rights of Englishmen," Wilkes was naturally adopted by the Americans as one of their own, and his name appeared frequently on their lips and their pens. He became one half of the namesake for Wilkes-Barre, Pennsylvania, sharing honor with the other vociferous pro-American, Isaac Barré. Wilkes mellowed somewhat in his old age but never shed his reputation as the most radical politician of his day. *Further reading:* Louis Kroneberger, *The Extraordinary Mr. Wilkes: His Life and Times* (Garden City, N.Y., 1974); George Rude, *Wilkes and Liberty: A Social Study of 1763 to 1774* (Oxford, Eng., 1962).

WILKINSON, James (1757–1825) Continental officer

Wilkinson was a notorious schemer with no apparent principles whatsoever, other than self-aggrandizement and self-preservation. The most nefarious part of his career came after the Revolution, but his actions while an officer during the war set the tone for his later life. One of the mysteries of American history is how Wilkinson managed to emerge whole from peccadillo after peccadillo.

He was born in Maryland and studied medicine as a youth. He served as a volunteer in Thompson's Pennsylvania Regiment, beginning in 1775, and was part of Benedict Arnold's invasion of Canada during the fall, forming an association with the young Aaron Burr during the grueling expedition. Receiving a captain's commission, Wilkinson served on Arnold's staff briefly before moving to become a staff officer for Horatio Gates. In 1777, he became deputy adjutant general for the Northern Department and was one of Gates's principal aides during the campaign against General John Burgoyne. Then the troubles began. After Burgoyne's surrender, Gates sent Wilkinson to York, Pennsylvania (where the Congress had taken refuge from Sir William Howe) with the official dispatches about the British surrender and the proposed Convention. Wilkinson saw the opportunity for advancement and dithered and delayed for several days in Reading, Pennsylvania while Congress stewed for official word of victory. He finally appeared on November 3, putting considerable spin on the account to beef up his role. He was rewarded with promotion to brigadier general, leaping over the heads of many other colonels on the list, and an appointment to the new board of war.

The storm of protest by other officers was basically ignored by Congress, which was in the midst of the so-called Conway Cabal (a campaign against George Washington), and the protest was further exacerbated by comments Wilkinson made to Lord Stirling. Wilkinson was soon at odds with Gates, who was the chairman of the board, and the young general resigned in March 1778. He then served a term as clothier general of the Continental Army, but was—predictably—turned out after eight months with charges that he stole from his official accounts.

Wilkinson's role in the Revolution was over, but he had just begun to make his mark on American history. He moved to Kentucky and began a long, complex affair in which he played off the desire of Kentuckians to exploit the economy of the region free from the fetters of Virginia against Spanish greed for territories in the trans-Allegheny west. Wilkinson managed to persuade both sides that he was working in their interests. He collected large amounts from the Spanish in the form of secret subsidies and loans, but his near-treasonous manipulation of Kentucky politics eventually came to naught. He next returned to the army with a commission as a lieutenant colonel under Anthony Wayne, succeeding to command of the west on Wayne's death in 1796.

In 1805, he became governor of Louisiana and launched what must be assessed as a treasonous plot with Aaron Burr to separate part of the western United States. Wilkinson betrayed Burr and managed to have himself absolved in yet another example of his ability to make a slippery escape. He rose again during the War of 1812, when he was appointed a major general, but his performance was so miserable that he was dismissed in 1815. He then moved to Mexico, where he died. *Further reading:* Royal O. Shreve, *The Finished Scoundrel* (Indianapolis, 1933).

WILKINSON, Jemima (1752—1819) Religious leader

Born in Cumberland, Rhode Island, Wilkinson became a religious zealot after an illness in 1774. She claimed to have been possessed by a spirit from God during her sickness, and thereafter she referred to herself as the "Public Universal Friend." During the Revolution, she preached at revival meetings in Rhode Island and Connecticut, and she set up churches in New Milford, Connecticut and South Kingston and East Greenwich, Rhode Island. She encountered public enmity over her doctrines, particularly her disavowal of marriage, and she withdrew with a group of followers to a colony (called Jerusalem) near Seneca Lake, New York in 1790.

WILLETT, Marinus (1740—1830) Continental officer, merchant

A considerable soldier who seemed to be everywhere in the northern campaigns during the Revolutionary War, Willett was also a prewar patriot leader in New York City. He was born on Long Island and after graduating from King's College became a merchant in the city. As a member of the elder Oliver De Lancey's New York colonial regiment, Willett fought in the Seven Years' War before returning to his mercantile trade.

As the agitation against the royal government increased in New York, Willett took a leading role in the radical patriot politics of the city, alongside Isaac Sears. Willett was one of the Sons of Liberty that attacked the royal arsenal in April 1775, and he led the attack that seized British supplies as the

Marinus Willet

royal government evacuated in June. With the British expelled temporarily from New York City, Willett took a commission as a junior officer in Alexander McDougall's regiment and marched north for the abortive invasion of Canada. He returned in November and received a commission as lieutenant colonel of the 3rd New York Regiment, taking command of a post opposite West Point on the Hudson River. He won fame for his bravery as second in command at Fort Stanwix in 1777. British colonel Barry St. Leger had invested Stanwix with a superior force as part of a long sweep down from Canada designed to augment General John Burgoyne's main advance. When St. Leger was compelled to withdraw most of his troops to stop a relief column under Nicolas Herkimer at Oriskany, Willett sallied out from the fort and destroyed St. Leger's supplies and baggage, which in part caused St. Leger to abandon his mission and return to Canada. Willett received a sword of honor from Congress in consequence of this exploit.

Willett fought at the battle of Monmouth in 1778 and the following year was part of John Sullivan's expedition against the Iroquois. He took command of the 5th New York in 1780, but the regiment dwindled due to expired enlistments, and Willett withdrew from active duty when the regiment was consolidated with another. He was not long on the sidelines, however, and was put in charge of New York militia and sent to the northwestern frontier of the state, where loyalists and Indian allies were wreaking havoc in the upstate settlements. In October 1781, shortly after the death-knell for the British sounded to the south, Willett fought an inconclusive engagement with a force of loyalists and Indians that nonetheless compelled the enemy to withdraw. After the war, Willett returned to New York City, served as sheriff, was member of an Indian commission and was elected as mayor. *Further reading:* D. E. Wager, *Col. Marinus Willett: The Hero of Mohawk* (New York, 1891).

WILLIAMS, Benjamin (1751–1814) Continental officer, state official   Williams was a farmer in his native North Carolina before the Revolution. He attended the provincial congresses that met in 1774 and 1775, entered the army as a junior officer, fought at Guilford Courthouse with special notice and was promoted to colonel. He served several terms in the North Carolina lower house and in the senate, and in 1793 was elected U.S. representative to Congress for one term. He was twice governor of the state.

WILLIAMS, David (1754–1831) Militiaman   Williams was one of the three New York militiamen who captured British spy Major John André on September 23, 1780. He, John Paulding and Isaac Van Wert intercepted André on the road toward New York City, and the British agent mistook them for loyalists and betrayed himself. Along with his companions, all rather simple souls by most accounts, Williams became a celebrity, receiving cash rewards, commendations and great public acclaim that lasted for decades. He was the longest surviving member of the trio and was the guest of honor at a celebration in New York City in 1830 on the 50th anniversary of the capture. *Further reading:* Richard C. Brown, "Three Forgotten Heroes," *American Heritage* 26 (August 1975), 25–29.

WILLIAMS, Israel (1709–1788) Loyalist   Williams lived in Hatfield in western Massachusetts and had a long history of service to the crown before the Revolution. He was judge of the county court of common pleas, a member of the legislature and a member of the Governor's Council. Even though he was relatively advanced in years and physically frail, Williams was seized by a patriot mob in 1777 and "smoked" in a small room with the chimney and windows stopped up until he signed an oath. The patriot state government deprived him of his rights in the same year but restored them after the war. He was one of the founders of the school that came to be Williams College.

WILLIAMS, John (1731–1799) Delegate to Congress   Born in Virginia, Williams moved to North Carolina at age 14. After studying privately for the law, he was admitted to the bar and set up a legal practice in Williamsboro, a city his parents had founded. He was appointed deputy attorney general of North Carolina in 1768. In 1775, he was a representative to the North Carolina Provincial Congress. In 1777 and 1778, he sat in the state assembly, and he was selected as a delegate from North Carolina to the Continental Congress in 1778 and 1779. He returned home to become a justice of the state supreme court in 1779, a post he held for 20 years until his death.

WILLIAMS, John (1752–1806) Militia officer, physician, government official   Williams was born in England and studied medicine at St. Thomas hospital in London. He served aboard a Royal Navy man-of-war as a surgeon's mate before coming to New York in 1773. Despite his recent immigration, he was named to the New York Provincial Congress in 1775 and again in 1777. He served as a surgeon for the New York militia during the first two years of the war and then took a seat in the state senate. After the war, he was appointed a brigadier in the militia. In 1795, he was elected to the U.S. House of Representatives. Williams was also one of the early promoters of the Erie Canal.

WILLIAMS, John Foster (1743–1814) Naval officer   Born in Boston, Williams was given command of the sloop *Republic* in May 1776 as one of the vessels commissioned as part of the Massachusetts state navy. He moved to the *Massachusetts* and then spent a year as master aboard privateers. He returned to the state navy in 1778 as captain of the *Hazard*. In March 1779, Williams captured the British brig *Active* off St. Thomas. He was less fortunate in his assignment to the miserable Penobscot expedition against a British outpost, during which he was forced to abandon and burn his ship. He moved then to the largest vessel in the Massachusetts state fleet, the *Protector*, and aboard her he destroyed the British privateer *Admiral Duff* near Newfoundland in June 1780. After several more productive cruises, Williams was captured by two small British men-of-war in 1781 and taken to England for imprisonment. He was exchanged and arrived home in early 1783. After the establishment of the new Republic, Williams was appointed to command a federal revenue cutter.

WILLIAMS, Jonathan (1750–1815) American diplomat

Born in Boston, Williams was a nephew of Benjamin Franklin and served with his uncle's mission to France in 1776, acting as an inspector for arms shipments. He remained in Europe after the war as a businessman and commercial agent, but he returned to America around 1790. He sat as a judge of the Court of Common Pleas in Philadelphia, and in 1801, Williams was appointed as the first superintendent of the U.S. Military Academy at West Point.

WILLIAMS, Otho Holland (1749–1794) Continental general

Williams was an outstanding combat leader and senior staff officer in the southern campaigns of 1780 and 1781—one of the underappreciated soldiers of the Revolution. He was born in Prince Georges County, Maryland and came from a family of modest means. Williams worked as a clerk in Frederick and Baltimore before the Revolution but was certainly not a man of prominent standing before the war began, and he gained his honors by sheer merit.

In June 1775, he joined one of the Maryland rifle companies recruited in response to a request from Congress and marched north to join the new Continental Army. He served as a lieutenant until several of the rifle companies were combined into a regiment under Hugh Stephenson in mid-1776, when Williams was promoted to major. He was commanding the riflemen (Stephenson having died earlier in the autumn) in November when he was wounded and taken prisoner at the fall of Fort Washington. Williams was held in harsh confinement in New York City since he was suspected of secretly corresponding with the American authorities, and he was not exchanged until January 1778. Meanwhile, he was named as colonel of the new 6th Maryland Regiment with his promotion dating from December 1776 (although he obviously was not on the spot since he was a prisoner). In fact, he seldom actually commanded the 6th Maryland, and most of the time he served as a senior staff officer.

Otho Holland Williams

Although a soldier of superior talent, it was Williams' misfortune to serve as adjutant to the miserable Horatio Gates when Gates took over the Southern Department in the summer of 1780. Williams did his best to impress on Gates the reality of the situation in the Carolinas, but Gates blindly led the ill-fed, understrength army on to a confrontation at Camden. Williams was in a difficult position as the battle approached. Gates set up far to the rear and virtually refused to issue orders, while Williams scurried around the front attempting to organize the fight. When the American militia and Gates himself turned tail and ran at virtually the first shots, Williams tried to rally the remaining American forces, but the day was irretrievably lost. Williams' later description of the panic on the battlefield is an eloquent and oft-quoted source.

Nathanael Greene, the new commander of the southern campaign, recognized Williams' ability and assigned him command of the light infantry and then named him as adjutant general. Williams skillfully handled his duties as a staff officer and when in field command deftly executed the fast marches and maneuvers that characterized the catch-me-if-you-can campaign against Lord Cornwallis. He was a brigade commander at all three subsequent major battles—Guilford Courthouse, Hobkirk's Hill and Eutaw Springs—in 1781, technically acting as colonel of the 1st Maryland Regiment, a new unit into which the remnants of the shattered Marylanders had been organized. He was promoted to brigadier in 1782. Following the war, Williams returned to Baltimore and served as a port officer. He declined an appointment in 1792 as a brigadier general in the newly reorganized army. His "Narrative of the Campaign of 1780," which was published in 1821 as an appendix to a biography of Greene, is a masterpiece of eyewitness military writing.

WILLIAMS, William (1731–1811) Delegate to Congress, militia officer, official, merchant

Born in Lebanon, Connecticut as the son of a Congregationalist parson, Williams graduated from Harvard in 1751 and at first prepared for the ministry. He was diverted, however, by a tour in the colonial militia during the Crown Point expedition of 1755 and then turned to business instead of the pulpit. He amassed a considerable fortune in the mercantile trade and had strong political connections, especially after marrying the daughter of Governor Jonathan Trumbull the Elder in 1771. He was the most ardent of patriots, serving in the colonial legislature for many years before the Revolution—several times as speaker—and consistently protesting British policy. He personally financed the Connecticut troops sent on the expedition to take Fort Ticonderoga in 1775 and many times subsequently advanced his own money, discounted Continental currency and pledged his credit in order to support the war effort. He was a colonel of militia at the beginning of the war but resigned in 1776 when elected as a delegate to Congress, where he served for two terms, signing the Declaration of Independence and helping to draft the Articles of Confederation. He held several state offices between 1777 and 1780, when he returned to Congress for an additional term. After the war, he served for decades as a local county judge. *Further reading:* Bruce P. Stark, *Connecticut Signer: William Williams* (Chester, Conn., 1975).

WILLIAMSON, Andrew (c. 1730–1786) Militia officer, turncoat

Williamson was born in Scotland and came to South Carolina as a child. He received military experience fighting the Cherokee on the frontier during the Seven Years' War as a lieutenant of militia, and he was involved in the Regulator movement in the late 1760s. When the Revolution began, he was apparently a man of influence in his back-country neighborhood and bore a commission as a major of militia. In November 1775, he commanded an outnumbered force of patriots which was driven to the refuge of Ninety-Six by a large army of loyalists, although no battle

ensued. During the forepart of the war, Williamson campaigned against the Indians, winning a promotion to brigadier general of militia. He commanded the South Carolina militia under Richard Caswell in the aborted campaign against the British in Florida and apparently did much to scotch the expedition by refusing to take orders from the Continental officer. Williamson's career fell apart in late 1779 and early 1780. The British had set afoot a major invasion of South Carolina with the intent of capturing Charleston. Williamson's militia command disintegrated when most of his men deserted, and he was left completely on the sidelines. He probably accepted British protection, and he certainly refrained from adding his remaining strength to the feeble American resistance to the British and the rising loyalists. He was "captured" by patriots at his plantation and urged to join them, but he escaped and fled to Charleston, giving evidence that he had changed sides. He was captured again by American Isaac Hayne but immediately was recaptured by the British, who also scooped up Hayne (leading ultimately to Hayne's controversial execution). Williamson's exact loyalties are difficult to determine, since after the war both Nathanael Greene and Governor George Mathews stepped forward to vouch for him, and he was reported to have supplied information to the American side. In any event, he was allowed to remain in South Carolina and did not suffer from his record of shifting loyalties, despite being known as the "Arnold of the South."

WILLIAMSON, Hugh (1735–1819)

Williamson spanned the areas of medicine, business, science and politics, somewhat in the manner of his friend Benjamin Franklin. He was born in Pennsylvania to a family of Irish immigrants and graduated from the College of Philadelphia in 1757, showing an aptitude for scientific observation and mathematics. His first career was as a licensed Presbyterian preacher, but after two years he tired of denominational disputes and gave up preaching in favor of medical studies in Edinburgh, London and Utrecht. He returned to Philadelphia with a medical degree in the mid-1760s, but his practice was only a moderate success—he was more interested in science than in developing a bedside manner. He went to England in 1773, carrying the first news of the Boston Tea Party to London, where he was subsequently grilled on the event by the privy council.

Before his return home, he obtained copies of the Thomas Hutchinson-Andrew Oliver correspondence (which compromised British officials in Massachusetts), which he delivered to Franklin and which then set off such revolutionary mischief in Massachusetts.

He was in Holland during the first year of the war, but he returned to America in early 1777, settling in Edenton, North Carolina and setting himself up as a merchant. He volunteered himself to the North Carolina militia as a surgeon and was appointed surgeon general after inoculating state troops at New Bern. He was sent to the state legislature in 1782 and then was selected as a delegate to the Confederation Congress, where he served until 1785; he returned for the final meeting of the Congress in 1788. He was subsequently elected to the U.S. House of Representatives for two terms after the new constitution went into effect. He married a wealthy New Yorker in 1789 and moved to that city, where he lived the rest of his life, publishing several works on science, medicine and history. *Further reading:* Louis W. Potts, "Hugh Williamson: The Poor Man's Franklin and the National Domain," *North Carolina Historical Review* 64 (October 1987), 371–93.

WILLING, Thomas (1731–1821) Delegate to Congress, merchant

One of the great merchants of Philadelphia, Willing was a moderate in his revolutionary stance. He was born in Philadelphia to a wealthy commercial family (connected to the Shippens on his mother's side), and he was sent to England at age nine for his education. He attended preparatory school in Bath and then studied law in London at the Inner Temple, but he became a merchant on his return to Philadelphia in 1749. He inherited his father's accumulated property in 1754 and set about a career as one of Philadelphia's largest merchants, in partnership with Robert Morris under the company name of Willing, Morris & Company. By the time of the Revolution, Willing was a prominent man of the city—a place where business success counted for much in the scheme of things—having served in many public offices, including mayor of Philadelphia and justice of the supreme court.

Although he was against upsetting the established economic and social order, Willing was nevertheless an active patriot. He served on a committee of correspondence in 1774 and on the Philadelphia Committee of Safety in 1775. He acted as president of the Pennsylvania provincial congress in 1774 and was selected as a delegate to the Continental Congress the following year. Maintaining his moderate-to-conservative stance, Willing opposed independence and voted against the measure in the summer of 1776, a position that resulted in his failure to be sent to Congress again in 1777 and his removal from the supreme court. He in fact dropped out of public life for much of the remainder of the war. He stayed in Philadelphia during the British occupation of the city in 1777 and 1778, but he refused to take an oath of allegiance to the crown despite pressures to do so. When his business partner Robert Morris assumed responsibility for the finances of Congress in 1781, he enlisted Willing as president of the Bank of North America. Willing managed to hang on to his fortune during the economically troubled latter days of the Confederation, and unlike Morris he emerged into the 1790s as a continuing leader of business. In 1791, he was appointed president of the new Bank of America. He was removed from active public and business life by a debilitating stroke in 1804.

WILSON, James (1742–1798) Delegate to Congress, militia officer, businessman, jurist

Wilson was a complicated man with a convoluted career in public during the period of the Revolution and the early Republic. He was one of the principal rebels in Pennsylvania and a writer with considerable influence during the early days of the revolt, but he was also deeply conservative and came to be the focus of popular wrath. He was a late arrival on the American scene, having been born and educated in Scotland. In the midst of his higher education, he left home and emigrated in 1765 to New York City and thence the following year to Philadelphia, where he read law with John Dickinson. His first practice was at Reading, Pennsylvania, but within two years, Wilson moved on to Carlisle and became the leading attorney in the region. He also began a lifelong speculation in land purchases, and the leitmotiv of making a fortune in western lands was never far beneath the surface of his subsequent political views. He also formed what turned out to be a long association with the College of Philadelphia, serving initially as a Latin tutor and lecturer and eventually becoming the first professor of law when the college amalgamated with other institutions in 1791 to form the University of Pennsylvania.

Wilson served as chairman of his local committee of correspondence in Carlisle and was sent to the Pennsylvania provincial congress in 1774. He was nominated as a delegate to the first Continental Congress but denied election. Wilson was thrust into the forefront, however, when his *Considerations on the Nature and Extent of the Legislative Authority of the British Parliament* was published and became a widely circulated revolutionary tract that declared Britain had no authority to legislate for the colonies while affirming colonial allegiance to the crown (the ideas in Wilson's *Considerations* are often mentioned as similar to those forming the basis for the modern British Commonwealth). Wilson's newfound notoriety gained him election to the second Continental Congress in 1775, and he was called on by his colleagues to write a tract that was to prepare the public for a declaration of independence. He labored over the document, but Thomas Paine's *Common Sense* was published before Wilson finished his work, and the Congress dropped the project.

During the debate on independence in the summer of 1776, Wilson was in a strange position: he was one of the acknowledged public champions of independence, but he personally thought it too soon to take the step. He resisted the growing momentum in Congress, voting against the resolutions for independence in June, but he reversed his course to vote with Benjamin Franklin and John Morton in favor of adopting the Declaration in early July and signed the document the following month. He was inalterably opposed, however, to the new state constitution of Pennsylvania, which he vocally decried as too democratic, and this position cost him dearly during the rest of the Revolution. He was turned out as a delegate to Congress, although he was allowed to return for several months until a replacement could be found. He became intensely unpopular in Pennsylvania—he sought refuge in Annapolis in late 1777—and was besieged in his home (which became known as "Fort Wilson") in Philadelphia by a mob of dissident militiamen and radicals in the fall of 1779. He had meanwhile served as a militia officer, first as colonel of a battalion from Cumberland County and eventually as brigadier general of the state militia.

Wilson reemerged as a political power after the war, and he was a leader at the federal constitu-

tional convention of 1787. He also succeeded in rewriting the Pennsylvania constitution more to his liking in 1790. He was named by George Washington as an associate justice of the new U.S. Supreme Court in 1789 but had a stormy career, narrowly avoiding impeachment. His land speculations turned sour during the late 1790s, and Wilson's fortunes declined rapidly. In 1797, he was forced to flee Philadelphia to avoid arrest for debt, and the following year, he went insane while visiting fellow Supreme Court justice James Iredell in Edenton, North Carolina. Wilson died in Iredell's house after several months of confinement. He was reburied in Philadelphia in 1906. *Further reading:* Charles P. Smith, *James Wilson: Founding Father, 1742–1798* (Chapel Hill, N.C., 1956).

WILSON, Samuel (1766–1854) Soldier, businessman
Born at Menotomy, Massachusetts, Wilson served in the army during the Revolution as a teenage soldier. He moved to Troy, New York after the war and eventually began a meat-packing business with his brother, supplying meat to the U.S. Army during the War of 1812. He is one of the men sometimes credited with being the original "Uncle Sam," attributed to soldiers' identification of his nickname with government-issue beef.

WINCHESTER, James (1752–1826) Continental officer, legislator
Born in Carroll County, Maryland, Winchester was a junior officer in the Maryland contingent that formed part of the ill-fated Flying Camp. He was wounded and captured at Staten Island and held by the British for a year. His luck was little better when he returned to the southern theater, and he was captured again during the fall of Charleston in 1780. He was released in time to serve at the siege of Yorktown. After the war he moved to Tennessee, which was still a part of North Carolina at the time, and served as a delegate to the North Carolina legislature. After Tennessee became a state, Winchester sat in the senate and acted as speaker. During the War of 1812, he was commissioned as a brigadier general and commanded the Army of the Northwest. He founded the city of Memphis, where he died.

WINDER, Levin (1757–1819) Continental officer, government official
A native of Maryland, Winder was first a militia officer and then received

a Continental Army captain's commission, probably as part of the famous 4th Maryland Regiment raised in 1777 that served with great distinction until it was nearly destroyed at the battle of Camden in 1780. By the end of the war, he was a lieutenant colonel, and he briefly commanded the reorganized 1st Maryland from January 1783 until its dissolution in April. Following service in the Maryland legislature, Winder was elected governor in 1812.

WINGATE, Paine. Delegate to Congress, clergyman, legislator   Wingate was born in Amesbury, Massachusetts, the son of a Congregationalist preacher, and he too became a parson after graduating from Harvard in 1739. He served a parish in Hampton Falls, New Hampshire from 1763 until 1776, when he moved to Statham, New Hampshire, but he eventually left the active ministry and turned to public office. He sat in the New Hampshire state legislature, and in 1787 and 1788 he was a delegate to the Confederation Congress. After the new federal government was established, Wingate was appointed as one of his state's first U.S. senators. He moved over to the U.S. House of Representatives in 1793 for one term. He returned to New Hampshire and served again in the state legislature and as a justice of the superior court.

WINN, Richard (1750–1818)   Born in Virginia, Winn lived in South Carolina at the beginning of the Revolution and was commissioned as a first lieutenant in the 3rd South Carolina Regiment in 1775. He fought in defense of Charleston during the first British attempt to take the port city in 1776 and again in 1780, when the city fell to Sir Henry Clinton. Following the surrender at Charleston, Winn joined the partisan militia of Thomas Sumter as a major. He received a commission as a brigadier general in the South Carolina militia in 1783 and eventually rose to the rank of major general. He sat in the state legislature after the war and was elected to the U.S. House of Representatives in 1793 and again in 1803, serving a total of eight terms. In 1813, he moved to Tennessee and became a planter and merchant.

WINSLOW, Edward, Jr. (1745–1815) Loyalist official, soldier   Son of a prominent royal officeholder, Winslow was born in Massachusetts and graduated from Harvard in 1765. He became a lawyer and was clerk of the Courts of General Sessions and Common Pleas in Plymouth County. He volunteered for service with the British Army in 1775 at Boston when the rest of his family evacuated to England. By 1782, he was muster master-general for all the loyalist forces fighting for the crown. He settled in New Brunswick, Canada after the Revolution and became judge of the Supreme Court.

WINSTON, Joseph (1746–1815) Militia officer   Born in Louisa County, Virginia, Winston served as a young man in a campaign against the Indians, during which he was wounded and narrowly escaped with his life. He moved to Surry County, North Carolina about 1769 and became a local patriot leader. He helped organize a patriot convention at Hillsboro in 1775 and became a major of militia. He saw little field duty until 1780, when he provided troops for General William Davidson in order to harass the growing organization of Carolina loyalists. In late September 1780, he led about 350 men to join the patriot forces gathering to oppose Patrick Ferguson. At the subsequent battle of King's Mountain, fought between back-country patriots and loyalists, Winston commanded part of the right wing that did severe damage to the enemy. Following the Revolution, Winston served in the state legislature and was twice elected to the U.S. House of Representatives.

WINTHROP, James (1752–1821) Educator, jurist   Born in Cambridge, Massachusetts, Winthrop graduated from Harvard (where his father was a professor) and became the college librarian in 1759, holding the position until 1777. He fought with the Cambridge militia at Bunker Hill but spent the rest of the war as a local official in the probate court of Middlesex County and postmaster of Cambridge. In 1791, he became a judge of the Middlesex Court of Common Pleas. Much interested in education and public improvements, Winthrop helped found the Massachusetts Historical Society, supported Allegheny College (donating his personal library to the school) and promoted canal and bridge projects in and around Middlesex County.

WISNER, Henry (1720–1790) Delegate to Congress, manufacturer   Born in Orange County, New York, Wisner lived in Goshen all his life. He came from a Swiss emigrant family of farmers, an occupational heritage to which he added gunpowder manufacture. He sat in the New York assembly and was selected in 1775 and 1776 as a delegate to the Continental Congress, where he voted for independence. He was absent from the signing of the Declaration, having returned to New York for a session of the provincial congress. His major contribution to the war effort was to build more gunpowder plants at Goshen and thus to supply the needs of the army. He also helped plan and implement the river fortifications at West Point on the Hudson—including the chain that was laid across the channel. He served in the New York state senate during the latter years of the Revolution.

WISTER, Sarah (1761–1804) Diarist

Sarah Wister, called Sally by friends and family, was born into a very prosperous family of Philadelphia Quaker merchants and received an advanced education for the time in a local Quaker school. She was a teenager when the family decided to flee the anticipated British capture of Philadelphia for a remote farm north of Valley Forge in 1777. Sarah there began to keep a journal or diary that was originally intended as a long epistolary account for her friend Deborah Norris, who remained in the city. The diary eventually became a more personal document and was never handed over to Norris. Sarah's viewpoint on the war was personal and direct and embodied her considerable intelligence and charm. She recorded the events of the day as they directly affected her, ignoring for the most part any extraneous narration of larger events but giving a sharp picture of the life and times as seen by a young woman. The diary came to an end in the fall of 1778 when the family moved back to Philadelphia. Sarah lived the balance of her life in comfortable circumstances in either Philadelphia or at a family estate near Germantown. She never married and cared for her parents during her later years. She continued to write and her verse was published in the *Port Folio* after 1800. *Further reading:* Kathryn Z. Derounian, ed., *The Journal and Occasional Writings of Sarah Wister* (Rutherford, N.J., 1987).

WITHERSPOON, John (1723–1794) Delegate to Congress, clergyman, educator

Witherspoon left his mark on American life through his influence as a church leader, an educator and a patriot. He was born in Scotland, the son of a Presbyterian parson, and was educated to the ministry at the University of Edinburgh, serving parishes in Beith and Paisley after ordination. Within a short time, Witherspoon was at the center of a deep rift in the Scots church. He became the champion of the conservative faction, which hoped to defeat innovations in doctrine and church organization, and he gained a wide reputation through his published writings and sermons.

He was known throughout Great Britain and much of Europe when he was sought out in 1766 by representatives of the College of New Jersey at Princeton to become president of the school. After two years of consideration (his wife opposed the move), Witherspoon accepted the post and emigrated to New Jersey. His effect on the school was galvanic, and within a few years, Princeton (as the school ultimately came to be known) was on a sound financial and educational footing, brought about by Witherspoon's organizational and curricular reforms. He also became involved in healing a schism that had developed in the American branch of the Presbyterian sect, leading the denomination to a burst of growth and development, especially in the middle colonies (after the end of the War of Independence, Witherspoon helped develop a national Presbyterian church).

He was also at the center of revolutionary politics in New Jersey. Witherspoon sat on his local committee of correspondence and turned Princeton into a hotbed of rebellion by publicly urging independence in sermons and speeches. He attended the provincial congresses in New Jersey in 1774 and 1775 and was among the patriot leaders who managed the arrest of loyalist governor William Franklin. In 1776, Witherspoon was selected as a delegate to the Continental Congress. In Philadelphia, he supported the movement toward independence and spoke and wrote effectively during the summer of 1776 to push through adoption of the Declaration—becoming the only clergyman signer—and to refute the conservatives' notion that the populace was not yet ready for independence: His most quoted remark was "it not only was ripe for the measure but in danger of rotting for the want of it."

He long served in the Congress, sitting on more than a hundred committees between 1776 and 1782, and his major contributions were on matters of military and foreign affairs, although he was also involved in setting up the executive departments under the Articles of Confederation. Much of the time he was a futile voice calling for fiscal responsibility and a stronger central economic policy. His college, meanwhile, suffered greatly from the war. The British invaded Princeton in 1776 and took over the main college building (Nassau Hall) and burned the library. Witherspoon withdrew to a country house at Tusculum and, since he was preoccupied with congressional matters, the school temporarily ceased to function. He devoted much of his energies in the years after the Revolution to rebuilding Princeton. *Further reading:* Varnum L. Collins, *President Witherspoon: A Biography,* 2 vols. (Princeton, 1925).

WOEDTKE, Frederick William, Baron von (c. 1740–1776) European volunteer, Continental general

One of the many European officers who successfully convinced the Americans to honor their supposed military experience with high rank, Woedtke appeared in Philadelphia in early 1776 with letters of recommendation from Benjamin Franklin in Paris. He claimed to have been a long-serving officer of the Prussian army under Frederick the Great with the rank of major. Whatever the truth of his résumé (it has never been clearly established), he was indisputably an alcoholic, a fact Congress overlooked when it commissioned him a brigadier general in the Continental Army and sent him to the Northern Department. He took part in a council of war at Crown Point in late July but died a few days later, apparently from the ravages of strong drink combined with a fever.

WOLCOTT, Erastus (1722–1793) Militia general, jurist

Erastus was the older brother of Declaration signer Oliver Wolcott and was born in East Windsor, Connecticut. He served in the colonial legislature and as a local judge before the Revolution. He was appointed to a militia commission in 1775 and he commanded state troops during much of the war, including the garrisons at New London. In 1777, he was promoted to brigadier general. He was elected as a delegate to the Continental Congress but declined to serve. Following the war, he became a judge of the supreme court of Connecticut.

WOLCOTT, Oliver (1726–1797) Delegate to Congress, militia general, state official

During the Revolution, Wolcott alternated between sitting in Congress and leading state militia. He was born in Windsor, Connecticut into a prominent political family (his father had served as governor) and he graduated from Yale in 1747. He gained military experience as a captain of volunteers in an expedition against the French in the same year. He briefly studied medicine, but in 1751 he moved to Litchfield and became a lawyer. He filled a wide variety of local and colonial offices before the Revolution and continued as a militia officer. His first duties when the war began in 1775 were as a commissary for Connecticut troops and as a negotiator with the western Indian tribes, but he was also selected as a delegate to Congress (he held a seat there until 1783, with the exception of one term in 1779). He was often absent from Congress during his tenure; and in fact he originally missed signing the Declaration of Independence because he was at home ill, but he was allowed to affix his signature after the fact. As a brigadier general of Connecticut militia, he intermittently led troops from 1776 onward, most notably against General John Burgoyne in 1777 and in defense of the Connecticut coast against the raids of Governor William Tryon in 1779. He achieved no great distinction either in Congress or on the battlefield, but neither did he disgrace himself. Following the war, Wolcott helped negotiate several Indian treaties and eventually became governor of Connecticut, dying in office at age 71.

WOOD, James (c. 1750–1813) Continental officer, militia general, governor

Wood was born in Winchester, Virginia and served in the colonial forces in campaigns against the Indians during the Seven Years' War and in Lord Dunmore's War. He was elected to the legislature in 1776 but soon was appointed as colonel of the 12th Virginia Regiment, a new unit raised to help fill Virginia's quota for the Continental Army. He continued in command of the regiment—which was redesignated the 8th Virginia in September 1778—until it was dissolved in a reorganization in January 1783. He then assumed command of a new 1st Virginia made up of fragments from previous units. Wood's major contribution to the war effort was as a caretaker of the Convention Army (General John Burgoyne's unexchanged army of British and German troops that surrendered in the fall of 1777) when the army was moved to near Charlottesville, Virginia in 1778. He was appointed as a brigadier of Virginia militia after relinquishing command of his Continental regiment in 1783. He continued in politics after the war and was elected as Virginia's fourth governor in 1796.

WOOD, Joseph (1712–1791) Delegate to Congress, Continental officer

Wood—a generation older than most active patriots—was born in Pennsylvania and served during the war in Pennsylvania regiments, but his primary residence during the Revolution was in the Sunbury district of Georgia, where he had moved in 1774 at the relatively advanced age of 62. He was commissioned as colonel in command of the 2nd Pennsylvania Regiment in September 1776, taking over command from Arthur St. Clair of a regiment originally formed the year before. A new regiment—the 3rd Pennsylvania—was organized from the previous 2nd and other Pennsylvania veterans in mid-1776, with Wood as commander. He gave up command in the summer of 1777 and apparently returned to Georgia. He sat on the state council of safety and was elected to Congress for the 1777 and 1778 terms, returning thereafter to his plantation in the Sunbury district.

WOODFORD, William (1734–1780) Continental general, militia officer

A contentious but otherwise adequate officer, Woodford was born to an important family (his grandfather had been secretary of the colony) in Caroline County, Virginia. He served in the Seven Years' War and was a member of his local committee of correspondence in 1774. He was appointed by the Virginia provincial convention as a colonel of state militia in 1775 and was given command of the military effort to repulse royal governor Lord Dunmore, who had raised loyalist and black slave troops in an attempt to retain control of the colony. Woodford rather easily defeated Dunmore at the battle of Great Bridge in December and effectively ended royal government in Virginia. In February 1776, Woodford was commissioned as commanding colonel of the 2nd Virginia Regiment and went north to fight in the main campaigns of the Continental Army. He was promoted to brigadier general in early 1777, and despite quarrels over rank and precedence with Peter Muhlenberg and George Weedon, Woodford performed reasonably well as a brigade commander at Brandywine, Germantown and Monmouth. When it became apparent that the British meant to shift the focus of the war to the southern theater in late 1779, Washington ordered Woodford to the reinforcement of Benjamin Lincoln's army in South Carolina. Woodford and about 750 Virginians marched through the winter weather to reach Charleston in April 1780. Unfortunately, neither he nor his men could do anything to prevent the fall of the city and the capture of the entire American army. He was taken prisoner and moved to confinement in New York City, where he died as a prisoner in November.

WOODHULL, Abraham (c. 1750–1826) American spy

Woodhull was one of the principal members of the excellent American spy network in New York, known by his secret work name Culper Sr. He was a native of Setauket, Long Island and worked his family farm. He was recruited as an intelligence agent by Major Benjamin Tallmadge in 1778. Tallmadge had been charged by George Washington to set up a new intelligence network to report on the British establishment in New York City, which after Sir Henry Clinton's withdrawal from Philadelphia formed the greatest threat to American fortunes. Woodhull remained on Long Island but received reports from Robert Townsend in the city. Whenever possible Woodhull traveled into town to meet Townsend, but in order to avoid suspicions, many messages were passed by intermediaries. Woodhull sent the reports on to Tallmadge through Caleb Brewster. Between them, Woodhull and Townsend devised a very elaborate system of codes and false names that was never compromised. The entire network functioned superbly until the end of the war, and at the agents' request, its activities were never revealed. The full story came to light only in the 20th century. Woodhull lived the balance of his life to all appearances as a simple Long Island farmer and local judge.

WOODHULL, Nathaniel (1723–1776) Militia general

Woodhull was born into one of the dominant families of Long Island. He served with considerable distinction as a provincial officer during the Seven Years' War, leading a regiment of New York troops under Lord Amherst in 1761. He retired to his family's extensive estates on Long Island after the peace with France, but before long he became an active opponent of British colonial policy and emerged as a leader in organizing resistance in New York. He was elected to the legislature from Suffolk

David Wooster

County in 1768 and served there until the dissolution of the royal government. He helped form the New York provincial congress and was chosen as its president in 1776. He was appointed as a brigadier general of militia by the provincial congress, and with the British invasion in 1776, he and a small force of militiamen were assigned to hold Jamaica, New York. When the British swept Washington's army off Long Island in late August, Woodhull and his men were cut off. They were attacked by a much superior force of British regulars on August 28 and were quickly defeated. Woodford was badly wounded in the battle and died a few days later.

WOOSTER, David (1711–1777) Continental and militia general

A poor senior officer despite his extensive previous military experience, Wooster proved an embarrassment to the Continental Army. He was born in Stratford, Connecticut and was by trade a mason, although he graduated from Yale in 1738. He saw a great deal of action in the colonial wars as captain of an armed sloop, officer of colonial militia, a commissioned officer in a regiment of British foot and colonel of Connecticut troops. At the beginning of the Revolutionary War in 1775, Wooster was commissioned by the Connecticut legislature as a major general and given command of six state regiments. He received a Continental commission as the senior brigadier general on the first officers' list appointed by the Continental Congress in June 1775, but he was offended not to have been confirmed in a rank equivalent to his militia generalship. He subsequently quarreled with Philip Schuyler (although so did most New Englanders)

when ordered north as part of the Canadian invasion. When Richard Montgomery was killed at Quebec on the last day of 1776, Wooster succeeded to command but was then replaced by John Thomas, who in turn died and left Wooster once again in charge. He proved to be incapable of commanding the army, which was already in disarray from the disastrous campaign in Canada. Wooster was recalled by Congress and never again given an important assignment. He took up his militia rank again on returning home to Connecticut and was wounded during the British raid on Danbury on April 27, 1777. He died of his injuries five days later.

WORTHINGTON, John (1719–1800) Attorney, government official

Worthington was born in Springfield, Massachusetts and was associated with the western Massachusetts city for most of his life. For decades before the Revolution, he was one of the three most powerful men in the Connecticut River valley, controlling large sections of land as well as most local government offices. Worthington and his colleagues Israel Williams and Joseph Hawley were known as the "River Gods," forming a powerful association among themselves and with the royal government in Boston. Little happened economically or politically in the western Massachusetts towns and farming regions that they did not control. Worthington himself held the positions of king's attorney, selectman of Springfield and representative to the Massachusetts General Court. During the late 1760s, he also sat on the Governor's Council. With his power vested in the established government, Worthington resisted the revolutionary movement, ignoring the Boston radicals when they sought western support against the Stamp Act. However, the tide of revolt reached the Connecticut River Valley in 1774 with the British imposition of the Intolerable Acts. Local townspeople rose up against the royal government and against Worthington and his fellow River Gods, closing the local court system, which Worthington had used to prosecute debtors, and setting up extralegal courts in which he held no sway. Worthington saw the light and reversed his position, becoming (in public at least) a patriot after being mobbed when local residents thought he was about to accept an appointment to the mandamus council. He never regained his former power.

WRIGHT, James (the Elder) (1714–1785) Loyalist official   Wright was born in Charleston, South Carolina, the son of the chief justice of the colony. He was trained as a lawyer, possibly in England, and practiced in Charleston, eventually becoming chief justice himself. In 1760, he received the office of lieutenant governor of South Carolina, but four years later he moved to Georgia when he was named as the third royal governor of the colony. He was by all accounts an able administrator and served longer in office than any other Georgia royal governor. He defended the Stamp Act in his colony against the usual agitation, leading troops to disperse anti-Stamp mobs on several occasions. When the Revolutionary War broke out to the north, however, he was powerless to prevent the spread of rebellion to Georgia. A patriot provincial congress took control of the state in 1775, although Wright remained in Savannah for six months more. When an armed British fleet appeared in January 1776, he was arrested by the provisional American government. He escaped and took refuge aboard the British warships. He went to Halifax, Nova Scotia the following month and then to England. When the British retook Georgia in 1779, Wright returned to his post as governor and helped defend Savannah. He emigrated permanently to Great Britain at the end of the war.

WRIGHT, James (the Younger) (d. 1816) Loyalist officer   Sometimes confused with his father, who was the final royal governor of Georgia, the younger Wright was an officer in the loyalist forces raised in the south during the war. He participated in the defense of Savannah in 1779 and then emigrated to England.

WRIGHT, Joseph (1756–1793) Painter   Born in Bordentown, New Jersey, Wright went to England as a teenager and studied painting with Benjamin West and John Trumbull. He was in London during most of the Revolution, gaining a high public reputation after exhibiting at the Royal Academy and painting a portrait of the Prince of Wales. In 1782, he went to Paris and caught the attention of Benjamin Franklin, who sponsored Wright's return to America. He painted George and Martha Washington in 1783 in Philadelphia and followed with portraits of James Madison and John Jay. In 1787, Wright moved to New York City. After the formation of the new federal government, Washington appointed Wright as a draftsman and die-maker to the U.S. Mint, and he was probably responsible for making the dies for the first U.S. coins.

WRIGHT, Patience Lovell (1725–1786) Sculptor   Born in Bordentown, New Jersey, Lovell was an artist—a highly unusual occupation for a woman at the time. She was married to portraitist Joseph Wright and was the mother of three children (including Joseph Wright the artist; see preceding entry), but she worked on her own professionally as a modeler in wax. She moved to London in 1772 with her husband and became well known in the English art world for her bas-relief busts of famous people, including Benjamin Franklin, George III, Queen Charlotte and the elder William Pitt. She even had her own exhibition room in London. She died in England.

WRIGHT, Robert (1752–1826) Militia officer, official   Wright was born in Queen Anne's County, Maryland and was a lawyer before the Revolution, being admitted to the bar in 1773. He served as a militiaman in 1776 in fighting between patriots and loyalists on the Eastern Shore. Wright was appointed a captain in the militia in 1779 and held the post until the end of the war. He also sat in the Maryland House of Delegates during the Revolution as a representative from Queen Anne's County. He continued an active political career after the war, becoming U.S. senator from Maryland from 1801 to 1806, governor of the state from 1806 to 1809, and U.S. Congressman from 1810 to 1817 and again from 1821 to 1823. When he left Congress, he became judge of the district court for the lower Eastern Shore of Maryland, sitting on the bench until his death.

WRIGHT, Turbutt (1741–1783) Delegate to Congress, planter   Wright was born near the modern-day city of Centerville, Maryland, and was a planter and farmer. He sat in the colonial legislature just before the Revolution and served on the committee of safety in 1777. In 1782, he was a delegate to the Confederation Congress, returning to Maryland to sit again in the legislature. He died on his estate near Centerville.

WYNKOOP, Henry (1737–1816) Delegate to Congress, jurist   Born in Bucks County, Pennsylvania, Wynkoop sat as a local judge from 1760 until 1789. He was a member of the local committee of observation in 1774 and attended the provincial congresses in 1774 and 1775. In 1776 and 1777, he sat on the Pennsylvania Committee of Safety, and he was elected as a delegate to Congress for three terms, from 1779 to 1782. He was appointed to the high court of errors and appeals in 1783 and served a term as U.S. congressman from Pennsylvania after the adoption of the new federal constitution.

WYTHE, George (1726–1806) Delegate to Congress, teacher, jurist Wythe, who became the first professor of law in America and trained the first generation of school-educated lawyers, was more important in Virginia than on the national level during the Revolution. He was born into a wealthy planter family near Black River, Virginia and was educated by his mother and at the College of William and Mary. He read for the law and practiced initially in Spotsylvania County. On his brother's death in 1754, Wythe inherited a large fortune and moved to Williamsburg, where he undertook advanced reading in the law and the classics. He also took public office as a member of the House of Burgesses. He privately trained Thomas Jefferson in the law during the mid-1760s and formed a lifelong friendship with the young man. He also became one of the more vociferous opponents of royal colonial policy, drafting an intemperate petition against the Stamp Act in 1765. He was elected to Congress in 1776, signed the Declaration, and departed after one term. He spent the war in Virginia, working during the first years with Jefferson and Edmund Pendleton to revise the legal code of the new state. In 1778, Wythe became a justice of the new court of chancery, remaining on the bench for the next 28 years. Perhaps his most important role was realized in 1779, when the College of William and Mary (at Jefferson's urging) established a professorship of law and named Wythe as the first incumbent. He developed a widely influential course of legal studies—employing moot courts, for example—and trained John Marshall and James Monroe. He resigned from teaching in 1791 and moved to Richmond. He was poisoned by his grandnephew, who stood to inherit Wythe's estate. *Further reading:* Julian P. Boyd, "The Murder of George Wythe," *William and Mary Quarterly*, 3rd ser., 12 (October 1955), 513–42.

Y

YATES, Abraham (1724–1796) Delegate to Congress, state official Born in Albany, New York and a relative of Peter Yates, Abraham was a surveyor, lawyer and land speculator. He was an ardent patriot before the Revolution, serving on the Albany committee of correspondence from 1774 to 1776 and in the New York provincial congresses from 1775 to 1777. He sat in the state senate from 1777 onward and also was a commissioner for state loans during the war. He was a rabid Anti-Federalist and a member of Governor George Clinton's party after the Revolution, winning some notoriety as the author of political pamphlets, which he signed "Rough Hewer." He represented New York in the Confederation Congress in 1787 and 1788.

YATES, Peter (1747–1826) Delegate to Congress A nephew of Abraham Yates, Peter was born in Albany, New York and practiced law there. He was a member of the local committee of correspondence in 1775 but resigned and declined to serve again, although he was reelected. He served in the state legislature in 1785 and was a delegate to the Confederation Congress in 1786. After this brief time in office, he returned to his law practice.

YEATES, Jasper (1745–1817) Jurist Born in Philadelphia, Yeates graduated from the College of Philadelphia (now the University of Pennsylvania) in 1761 and was admitted to the bar in 1765. He was in favor of reconciliation with Great Britain until the outbreak of actual hostilities, and he worked as a member of the Lancaster County Committee of Correspondence during 1775 to try to find a peaceful solution to the conflict. He was a firm patriot, however, after the opening guns of the war. In 1776, the Continental Congress appointed Yeates to negotiate with the western Indians. Following the war, he became an associate justice of the state supreme court.

Z

ZANE, Ebenezer (1747–1812) Militia officer, frontiersman   Zane was born near modern-day Mooresville, West Virginia and explored the Kentucky region as a young man in the company of his brothers. In 1770, he established a settlement at the mouth of Wheeling Creek (modern Wheeling, West Virginia) that stood at the end of the Cumberland Road from Maryland. The Indian wars and the Revolution precluded further immediate development, but Zane helped establish Fort Henry at Wheeling, named in honor of Patrick Henry, and helped supply western campaigns from his base, acting with the rank of colonel of Virginia militia. In 1777, the fort withstood a determined siege by a force of loyalists and Indians, and it survived once again in 1782, when Ebenezer's sister Elizabeth helped to save the day. Following the war, Zane began large speculation in lands to the west, and in 1796 he won approval from Congress to open a road—known as Zane's Trace—from Wheeling to Limestone, Kentucky (modern-day Maysville) on the Ohio River. In return, he received land grants, including the site of Zanesville, Ohio.

ZANE, Elizabeth. Legendary heroine   The younger sister of Ebenezer Zane, Elizabeth passed into American myth with her alleged feat of bravery in 1782 that saved the garrison of Fort Henry at what is modern-day Wheeling, West Virginia. The settlement had been founded by her brother 12 years earlier and had withstood a determined loyalist-Indian attack in 1777. In 1782, the settlers were holding their own against a new assault by Indians when their powder began to run low. According to the story—widely accepted during the 19th century but without real historical evidence—the teenaged Elizabeth volunteered to make a dash for a nearby cabin for a keg of powder. Either she was extremely fleet of foot or the Indians were astonished at her pluck, since she not only survived the supposed gauntlet of fire but successfully retrieved the powder, allowing the menfolk to stand off the attackers. She subsequently married and moved to Ohio. Popular American writer Zane Grey was her descendant and based a story on her feat.

ZEISBERGER, David (1721–1808) Missionary   Born in Moravia, Zeisberger was indentured to a merchant in Holland, ran away to England, and was sent to Georgia in 1736. He arrived at the Moravian settlement at Bethleham, Pennsylvania in 1741. He became a missionary to the Indians of the West, living among them and learning much of their ways and languages. In the early 1770s, he helped establish several settlements in the Ohio region, including Gnadenhutten, the site of an infamous massacre of whites by Simon Girty in 1782. Viewed with some suspicion by both the Americans and the British, Zeisberger was arrested several times during the Revolution but managed to free himself and continue his work of mission and settlement.

Further reading: David Zeisberger, *Diary of a Moravian Missionary Among the Indians of Ohio,* 2 vols. (Cincinnati, 1885; reprinted 1972).

ZIEGLER, David (1748–1811) Officer

Born in Heidelberg, Germany, Ziegler was a veteran of the Russian army in campaigns against the Turks in the Crimea. He came to America in 1774 and settled in Carlisle, Pennsylvania. When the Continental Congress asked Pennsylvania to raise a unit of riflemen in June 1775, Ziegler joined Colonel William Thompson's Rifle Regiment and served with the army at Boston. His unit was reorganized as the 1st Continental Regiment and eventually was incorporated into the 1st Pennsylvania Regiment late in 1776. Ziegler was with the regiment through the battle of Monmouth. In 1778, he received a commission as a captain in the state militia. He acted as a commissary for the troops in Pennsylvania in 1779 and 1780 and moved south in 1781, serving first with the Marquis de Lafayette in Virginia and then with Nathanael Greene in the Carolinas. After the war he briefly ran a grocery in Carlisle, but he took a commission during the Indian wars of 1784 and continued to serve in the West until 1792, when he retired to settle in Cincinnati. He was the first president of the Cincinnati City Council.

ZUBLY, John Joachim (1724–1781) Loyalist clergyman, delegate to Congress

Zubly was a classic loyalist intellectual, an educated and propertied member of society who drew back at the brink of separation from Britain. He was born in Switzerland and came to South Carolina and eventually Georgia as an adult. A clergyman, Zubly served a Presbyterian congregation in Savannah and was a close associate of Sir James Wright, Georgia's royal governor. At first Zubly fervently espoused the American cause in sermons and pamphlets, and in 1775 he was elected to the Continental Congress. He argued for the rights of Americans under the British constitution, denounced taxation without representation and rejected the power of Parliament to rule over the colonies. However, Zubly refused to entertain disloyalty to the king or the idea of separation from the mother country. When he perceived that Congress was bent on independence, Zubly returned to Georgia and openly joined the loyalist cause by issuing several pamphlets. He was taken into custody by the Georgia Council of Safety and eventually was banished to South Carolina. When the British regained control of Georgia in 1779, he returned to his ministerial duties in Savannah, where he died in 1781. *Further reading:* Marjorie Daniel, "John Joachim Zubly—Georgia Pamphleteer of the Revolution," *Georgia Historical Quarterly* 19, 1 (March 1935), 1–16.

A GUIDE TO BIOGRAPHICAL SOURCES

A significant number of the Revolutionary figures included in this "who was who" volume have been the subjects of extended biographies; others appear only in standard biographical reference works or are discussed incidentally in detailed studies of particular aspects of the American Revolution.

At one end of the scale are those people about whom full book-length biographies have been written. It is no shock to find dozens of biographies of George Washington, but it is surprising how deeply the interest of biographers has reached into the list. There was a wave of biographies by amateur historians in the 19th century, which has been followed in the 20th century by another wave of biographies from academics, with smaller ripples from commercial writers. The celebration of the Bicentennial of the American Revolution in the 1970s not only stimulated new biographies but also resulted in republication or reprinting of biographies from the previous century, many of which had long been out of print. The rise of the academic historical profession in the mid-20th century prompted numerous scholars to write book-length studies, and many biographies of otherwise neglected or relatively obscure Revolutionary figures have been published as a result. In many other cases, students of the Revolution or those interested in regional and local history have

written article-length biographies that have been published in journals. There has also been a widespread interest in publishing edited versions of original Revolutionary memoirs, diaries, letters and journals, and these editions (many of which appeared about the time of the Bicentennial) usually include valuable biographical information. A few collections of biographical essays, usually including only well-known Revolutionary figures, have also added to our store of knowledge, as have a significant number of non-scholarly but valuable magazine articles.

In this volume, such extended published information on individual Revolutionary people has been cited at the end of biographical entries under the rubric "further reading," thus guiding readers to more detailed accounts of the life of the person under discussion. These citations, however, have been limited to works that might be found by the average reader or researcher in a good library collection on the American Revolution. Obscure biographies or memoirs published long ago that have not been reprinted and are usually to be found today only in a highly specialized collection have been omitted from the "further reading" citations, as have Ph.D. dissertations, on the theory that anyone that serious about biographical research on a specific individual will find these sources on their own.

Many biographical entries in this book, however, are based on a set of basic, standard biographical reference works—such as biographical directories, collective biographies and encyclopedias (the sort of books found in the noncirculating reference section of a library)—when no extended individual biographical account has otherwise been published. That is to say, many of the biographical subjects selected for inclusion here have never been the subject of a full-scale biography or even a biographical article in a journal or magazine. Many have been profiled in standard biographical reference works, however, and when there is no "further reading" citation it may be assumed that the information came from the standard biographical references noted below. In every case possible, the entries are based on more than one source. The simplest method to find additional information on this class of "biography-less" person is to look at the most general references first in order to identify the *category* into which they fall, such as loyalists, legislators, British officers, etc., and consult the pertinent works.

General Histories and Background Reference Works

General histories and interpretations of the American Revolution began to appear even before the end of the fighting, and each generation since has added to the number of books and articles dealing with the topic. Standard bibliographies of the Revolution, such as Richard L. Blanco's *War of the American Revolution: A Selected Annotated Bibliography of Published Sources* (New York, 1984) and Dwight Smith's *Era of the American Revolution: A Bibliography* (Santa Barbara, Calif., 1975) list literally thousands of such works (as well as hundreds of full biographies).

Good general histories, representing a tiny fraction of the total available, are: Robert Middlekauf, *The Glorious Cause: The American Revolution, 1763–1789* (New York, 1982), which is particularly strong on the political aspects of the Revolution; John R. Alden, *The American Revolution* (New York, 1954), a more traditional view; Page Smith, *A New Age Now Begins: A People's History of the American Revolution*, 2 vols. (New York, 1976), which is unsurpassed for detailed narrative; and A. J. Langguth, *Patriots: The*

Men Who Started the American Revolution (New York, 1988), which is particularly pertinent for those interested in Revolutionary biography. The British side of the Revolution is better understood after reading Christopher Hibbert, *Redcoats and Rebels: The American Revolution Through British Eyes* (New York, 1990) and Piers Mackesy, *The War for America: 1775–1783* (London, 1964). To grasp the importance and nature of the military conflict and the effects it had on all other aspects of the Revolution, one must also read Don Higginbotham's *War of American Independence: Military Attitudes, Policies, and Practice, 1763–1789* (New York, 1971).

No one can hope to follow the course of the Revolution and the actions of the people involved without frequent reference to two monumental works: Christopher Ward, *The War of the Revolution*, 2 vols. (New York, 1952), which is a detailed account of virtually all the military engagements of the land war in America; and Edmund C. Barnett, *The Continental Congress* (New York, 1961), which covers nearly everything about that body.

Students of the Revolution benefit from outstanding general reference books. Chief among them is Mark Mayo Boatner III's *Encyclopedia of the American Revolution* (New York, 1966; revised 1974), which surely ranks as one of the best historical reference books ever written. In addition to hundreds of biographical profiles it contains accurate, fact-filled articles on every aspect of the Revolution, including detailed accounts of all major battles. It is absolutely indispensable to any serious inquiry. Also useful are: Ernest Dupuy and Trevor N. Dupuy, *An Outline History of the American Revolution* (New York, 1975) and Trevor N. Dupuy and Gay Hammerman, *People and Events of the American Revolution* (New York, 1974). The new multi-author *Encyclopedia of Colonial and Revolutionary America* (New York, 1990) edited by John Mack Faragher is excellent, includes many biographies, and covers a broad time period. For strict chronological narration of the Revolution, see L. Edward Purcell and David L. Burg, *The World Almanac of the American Revolution* (New York, 1992). A good, new reference to American history in general is the multi-author *Reader's Companion to American History* (Boston, 1991), edited by Eric Foner and John Garraty. Where pertinent, David C. Roller and Robert W. Twyman, *The Encyclopedia of Southern History* (Baton Rouge, La., 1979), is excellent.

Standard Biographical Reference Works

There are a handful of modern biographical collections and reference works that focus on the American Revolution, although most are limited in scope or source. One of the best is David C. Whitney, *The People of the Revolution: The Colonial Spirit of '76* (Chicago, 1974), which has 500 brief but accurate biographies of American patriots. The promisingly titled *Who Was Who During the American Revolution* (Indianapolis, 1976) is of limited use, since it is a collection of very short biographies drawn entirely from the *Dictionary of American Biography* entries. The profiles are brisk—barebones versions of the DAB entries—and include only a few loyalists, British figures or foreigners. The arrangement by state also makes the volume somewhat difficult to use. The full versions of DAB biographies are much to be preferred, although the volume can be a handy quick reference. The biographical section of Dupuy and Hammerman's *People and Events of the American Revolution* mentioned above casts a wide net, is highly accurate and covers a broad range of people and categories, but each entry gives only the barest information. It is a good starting point for further inquiry (all of the figures listed in Dupuy and Hammerman and in Boatner are included in the book you hold in your hand, usually with more detail). There are many, many older collections of Revolutionary biographies, but few of them are reliable.

Smaller, sharply focused collections with treatments of important figures include Joseph B. Mitchell, *Military Leaders in the American Revolution* (New York, 1967), an excellent appreciation of 10 American and British generals. George Billias' two edited collections of expert essays, *Washington's Generals* (New York, 1964; reprinted 1980) and *Washington's Opponents* (New York, 1969) are excellent and are cited at the end of several entries in this volume. A very good work on 54 American leaders is Robert G. Ferris and Richard E. Morris, *The Signers of the Declaration of Independence* (Flagstaff, Ariz., 1982), compiled for the use of the National Park Service. As noted above, the encyclopedias by Boatner and Faragher have extensive, accurate and reliable biographies as well as more general articles.

There are many indispensable standard biographical reference works that are general in coverage (dealing with the entire scope of American or

British history) that include, of course, figures from the Revolution. The first point of access to the dozens of standard biographical references is Miranda Herbert and Barbara McNeill, eds., *Biography and Genealogy Master Index*, 8 vols. and supplements (Detroit, 1981), which is a huge master guide to finding information on individuals in standard collections. It is based on a computer data base that alphabetically indexes the contents of more than 350 biographical dictionaries, encyclopedias and other reference works, and it virtually eliminates the need to look in each source. Instead of searching repeatedly in the DAB or Appleton's *Cyclopedia* or Lossing's *Encyclopedia*, the researcher can find citations by a single search of the alphabetical name list in the *Biography and Genealogy Master Index*. Entries are listed by name and dates, and a certain care must be used in the case of historical figures, since the *Index* uncritically lists names as they appear in the source volumes (the same person may appear more than once if one source has a date wrong, for example). Less useful, since most references are to living people, are *Biographical Dictionaries Master Index* (1975–1979); *Marquis' Who's Who Publications Index to All Books* (1974); and Robert B. Slocum, ed., *Biographical Dictionaries and Related Works*. An efficient finding aid for biographical material appearing in periodicals or as parts of books—even non-biographies—is the *Biography Index* (New York, 1939–   ), which is a series that cumulates all references to biographical material from the *Humanities Index, Social Science Index, Readers' Guide to Periodicals*, etc. Using the *Index* saves a great deal of time and effort.

The single most important standard biographical reference work for Americans is, of course, Dumas Malone, ed., *The Dictionary of American Biography*, 10 vols., plus supplements (New York, 1936–   ). This monumental work, patterned on the British *Dictionary of National Biography*, has extensive signed biographies of historical figures from the entire period of American's past (only dead people are included). While it has the reputation of concentrating overmuch on eminent people, there are articles for a surprising number of relatively obscure historical figures. The authors were generally good scholars and did extensive research in order to write the biographical entries, although some of the work is now dated. The articles are usually the most accurate of any standard biographical reference work, although errors do occur. Many British figures are included as are a few other foreign nationals. The arrangement is alphabetical by name, and all Revolutionary figures are to be found in the first 10 volumes. (The companion *Dictionary of American History,* ed. by John Truslow Adams (New York, 1942–1961) was designed to explain all the historical references mentioned in the DAB.) When all other sources fail or conflict about fact, the DAB is usually the authority.

The next most valuable general standard biographical source for Americans is John Garraty, ed., *The Encyclopedia of American Biography* (New York, 1974), which has superb, reasonably up-to-date articles by experts. The only drawback is the limited number of entries, which means it tends to have only the most prominent Revolutionary figures. Its greatest strength is the excellent interpretation of the significance of each person discussed. The biographical accounts are less detailed than those of the DAB, and its use is limited by the narrow range of figures included.

Of the older general biographical collections, *Appleton's Cyclopaedia of American Biography,* 6 vols. (New York, 1886–1889) is probably the most useful. It covers many names not included in the DAB, but the articles are much less detailed, less informed and less reliable. It includes native or adopted Americans only. The research is sometimes obviously shoddy—look out for fictional entries—and many sketches reproduce legendary stories uncritically.

A slightly more recent standard collection is *The National Cyclopedia of American Biography* (Clifton, N.J., 1889–). It is probably more reliable than *Appleton's* but is less scholarly than the DAB by a good measure. Its range is much broader than that of the DAB, however, and it includes entries for many people judged insufficiently eminent for the DAB. Revolutionary figures are to be found in the first 10 Permanent Series volumes (devoted to dead people), but the operative word is "found," since the irrational arrangement of the *National Cyclopedia* may drive a researcher to distraction. It is not arranged alphabetically by name, but haphazardly by no apparent method or theory. Names must be looked up in the separate index volume and then located wherever they may happen to have been placed in the text volumes.

An excellent standard biographical reference set—unfortunately limited in the number of Revolutionary figures included, so that only the most prominent are to be found—is the *McGraw-Hill Encyclopedia of World Biography,* which has high-quality, signed articles by experts. The coverage includes (as indicated by the title) many important British and European figures in addition to Americans.

The *Who Was Who in America* Historical Volume is a marginally useful listing of the historical figures in America from 1607 to 1896. The entries are very brief and seldom provide information not found in more detail elsewhere. The coverage is broad, however. Two other general sources are Rossiter Johnson, ed., *The Twentieth Century Biographical Directory of Notable Americans* (Boston, 1904; reprinted 1968) and Wheeler Preston, *American Biographies* (New York, 1940).

Two older sources of biographical information, although not strictly biographical directories, are Benson Lossing, *Harper's Encyclopedia of United States History . . . ,* 10 vols. (New York, 1915 ed.; reprinted 1974) and his *Pictorial Field-Book of the Revolution,* 2 vols. (New York, 1859). The former has entries for otherwise obscure figures of the Revolution and is reasonably accurate. The *Pictorial Field-Book* covers the entire scope of the Revolution (Lossing personally traveled to Revolutionary sites and collected information) and has a great number of valuable biographical sketches, most of them buried in the extensive notes.

There are also some very fine directories, the articles in which tend to be long, complete and impeccably researched, that focus on individual states, such as Kenneth Coleman and Charles S. Gurr, eds., *Dictionary of Georgia Biography,* 2 vols. (Athens, Ga., 1983) and the ongoing *Dictionary of North Carolina Biography,* ed. by William S. Powell (Chapel Hill, N.C., 1979–).

The standard source for British biography is, of course, the *Dictionary of National Biography,* 63 vols. (London, 1885–1901), and it is a monument to the concept of collective biography. It has sketches on almost all the important British officers and officials of the Revolutionary period (although there are some curious omissions—nothing on Banastre Tarleton, for example) and it also includes entries for many Americans. The articles tend to be dense, detailed and very British in tone and viewpoint.

Also useful for the Revolutionary period, for obvious reasons, are *The Dictionary of Canadian Biography* (Toronto, 1966–1982) and W. Stewart Wallace, ed., *The Macmillan Dictionary of Canadian Biography* (Toronto, 1978).

Special Topic Sources

Military

The principal source for service records of patriot officers is Francis B. Heitman, *Historical Register of the Officers of the Continental Army. . . .* Originally published in 1893, the key version is the "New, Revised, and Enlarged" edition published in Washington, D.C., in 1914, which has records for thousands of officers who held congressional commissions as well as many militia officers. Moreover, the 1914 edition has basic biographical information on each entry, in addition to a great deal more information about field-grade officers, engagements and army organization. This is *the* authority on military records, and it may be contradicted only on very firm evidence to the contrary. An earlier and much less reliable publication is William T. R. Saffell, *Records of the Revolutionary War . . .* (New York, 1858), which has lists of officers and men, something akin to the latter-day lists genealogists find useful. An absolutely indispensable reference is Fred A. Berg's splendid *Encyclopedia of Continental Army Units* (Harrisburg, Pa., 1972), which calmly derives order out of the organizational chaos of the Continental Army and gives accurate dates for commanders, changes of status and the many reorganizations typical of the army during the Revolution. Also useful is Roger J. Spiller, ed., *Dictionary of American Military Biography* (Westport, Conn., 1989). *Who Was Who in American History: The Military* (Chicago, 1975) reproduces entries selected from the historical volumes of *Who's Who. Webster's Military Biographies* (Springfield, Mass., 1978) gives a quick reference to important soldiers, as does the international *Who's Who in Military History: From 1453 to the Present Day* (New York, 1976) edited by John Keegan and Andrew Wheatcroft.

For the tiny Continental Navy, the state navies and the hundreds of state-commissioned privateers there is no single separate source for biography. The articles in Peter Kemp, ed., *The Oxford Companion to Ships and the Sea* (London and New York,

1976) are very good, but coverage for the American Revolution is limited. General histories of the Continental and state navies by Gardner W. Allen, William B. Clark, Jack Coggins, William M. Fowler, John W. Jackson, William J. Morgan and Robert A. Stewart are the best recourse if a naval officer does not appear in the DAB or similar standard biographical works.

For British officers and military organization, see Worthington C. Ford, *British Officers Serving in the American Revolution, 1774–1783* (Brooklyn, 1897), although this is a very rare volume since only 250 were published; however, the information was compiled from the official army lists. The standard history of the Royal Army, with much information about individual officers and units, is Sir John W. Fortescue, *A History of the British Army*, 13 vols. (New York, 1899–1930), of which volume 3 covers the period of the American war. Also worthwhile are Peter Young and J. P. Lawford, *History of the British Army* (New York, 1970)—especially chapter 9 on the Revolution—and Charles H. Stewart, comp., *The Service of British Regiments in Canada and North America* (Ottawa, 1962). The most efficient single source of information is Philip R. Katcher's *Encyclopedia of British, Provincial, and German Army Units, 1775–1783* (Harrisburg, Pa., 1973), which is a superb guide to not only the British units on the regular establishment but also all the loyalist units organized during the war and the German mercenaries employed by the British. Actual biographical information is narrow, but commanding officers with dates are given accurately as well as a great deal of information about unit movements and service.

Accurate biographies of French officers who served with Rochambeau's expeditionary force are more difficult to come by than information on British or American soldiers, despite several good general histories of the French involvement in the Revolutionary War. Still the basic source is Thomas Balch, *The French in America During the War of Independence of the United States*, 2 vols. (Philadelphia, 1891–95), first published in French and then translated into English. Volume 2 is a collection of relatively brief biographical sketches. The information is occasionally incorrect as to details and should be corroborated with other sources whenever possible—dates and assignments may be off. Joachim Merlant, *Soldiers and Sailors of France in the American War for*

Independence, Mary B. Coleman, trans. (New York, 1928) is less valuable. It was a product of the need for pro-French propaganda during World War I; it has no index and is not only hard to use but suspect in accuracy. Perhaps the best biographical information—although limited in scope—comes from memoirs and journals of French officers. Evelyn M. Acomb's fine edition and translation of Baron Ludwig von Closen's *Revolutionary Journal, 1780–1783* (Chapel Hill, N.C., 1958) includes not only many informative notes but also a directory of French officers. The beautiful two volumes of Howard C. Rice, Jr. and Anne F. Brown, *The American Campaigns of Rochambeau's Army, 1780–1781, 1782, 1783* (Princeton and Providence, 1972), which are among the most attractive books on the Revolution, have a great deal of information in the editorial apparatus and a roster of units and officers. More general (non-biographical) studies of the French in the American Revolution by Stephen Bonsal, Jonathan R. Dull, Stanley Idzerda, Lee B. Kennett, James B. Perkins and William C. Stinchcombe are of considerable help in piecing together individual biographies.

Government Officials

Several historical directories of national government officials list many figures of the Revolution. The information is basic—limited mostly to names, dates and offices filled—but it is the product of thorough and careful research and thus is very accurate and may be taken as the authority in cases of discrepancies with other more general reference works. The key publications are: *Biographical Directory of the American Congress, 1774–1791* (Washington, D.C., 1971); John W. Raimo, *Biographical Directory of American Colonial and Revolutionary Governors, 1607–1789* (Westport, Conn., 1980), which has longer, one-page sketches; *Biographical Directory of the Governors of the United States, 1789–1978,* 4 vols. and supplements (Washington, D.C., 1978); Robert Sobel, ed., *Biographical Directory of the U.S. Executive Branch, 1774–1971* (Westport, Conn., 1971); and *Biographical Directory of the Federal Judiciary* (Detroit, 1976). Much less reliable and useful is the older work by Charles Lanman, *Biographical Annals of the Civil Government of the U.S. during Its First Century* (Washington, D.C., 1876; reprinted 1976).

Loyalists

Still the best source for individual biographical sketches is Lorenzo Sabine, *The American Loyalists; or Biographical Sketches . . .* (Boston, first ed. 1847, 2 vol. ed. 1864). This source has hundreds of entries and is in general reasonably accurate or at least candid in cases where the author was uncertain about information. Used with care, it provides good basic information on individuals. Sabine's work has been wonderfully updated, verified and extended by Gregory Palmer in *Biographical Sketches of Loyalists of the American Revolution* (Westport, Conn., 1984), using the voluminous records of the British loyalist claims commission to compile this extremely valuable collection, which is accurate and meticulous, although somewhat limited in full biographical detail. The other 19th-century work that includes biographies is Egerton Ryerson, *The Loyalists of America and Their Times,* 2 vols. (Toronto, 1880; reprinted 1970), which is a good deal less valuable overall than Sabine used in conjunction with Palmer.

A surge of interest in the loyalist role in the Revolution has resulted in very fine recent studies of loyalists and loyalism in general and in specific states or regions, including works by Wallace Brown, Mary Beth Norton, Robert Calhoun, Robert A. East, Jacob Judd, Adele Hast, Kenneth Lynn, Dennis Ryan, William H. Nelson and Esmond Wright. Further biographical information can be gathered in their works. Many loyalists may be found in the Canadian biographical reference volumes (cited elsewhere), since thousands resettled to the north after the war and many were subsequently prominent in government there. A relatively small number are included in the standard American reference books, and some appear in the British sources.

Women

As noted elsewhere, the public role of women was severely limited during the period of the Revolution, and thus the standard biographical reference works tend to have only a few pertinent entries. Probably the largest single collection was done in mid-19th century by Elizabeth Ellet in *The Women of the American Revolution* (1850; 4th ed. 1969). While this is a storehouse of suggestion and a pioneering work, it has limited utility for present purposes. *Notable American Women* (Cambridge, Mass., 1971) edited by Edward T. James is a good reference work, modeled on the DAB, but it has only a few obvious choices from the Revolutionary period. The same is true of Robert McHenry, *Liberty's Women* (Springfield, Mass., 1980), a well-researched and written source but impoverished as to entries for the 1770s and 1780s. Also worth looking at is the *Biographical Cyclopedia of American Women* (Vol. 1, 1924; Vol. 2, 1974). A very good, although non-scholarly, work is Sally Smith Booth, *The Women of '76* (New York, 1973). Elizabeth Evans' *Weathering the Storm: Women of the American Revolution* (New York, 1975; reprinted 1989) is cited in several places for further reading. Of course, understanding the importance of women and their roles in Revolutionary society has been immeasurably expanded by the general works of Linda Kerber and Mary Beth Norton.

Blacks

Historical attention was focused on blacks in the Revolution during the period following the Civil War and has been renewed in the latter decades of the 20th century by studies such as Benjamin Quarles, *The Negro in the American Revolution* (Chapel Hill, N.C., 1961). Nonetheless, central sources for biography are limited. The best by far is Sidney Kaplan and Emma Nogrady Kaplan, *The Black Presence in the Era of the American Revolution* (New York, 1973; reprinted 1989), which profiles only a few black patriots but does so in considerable depth. About 20 black soldiers are dealt with briefly in Harry A. Ploski and James Williams, eds., *The Negro Almanac: A Reference Work on Afro-Americans* (4th ed., New York, 1983).

German Mercenaries

No good central sources exist for biographies on the German mercenaries hired by the British to fight in the war, but information may be pieced together from several publications (in addition to the introductions to memoirs and journals and Katcher's *Encyclopedia*, which is cited above). Max von Eelking did much of the pioneer research in the 19th century

and lists officers in *The German Allied Troops of the North American War of Independence, 1776–1783* (1893; reprinted Baltimore, 1969). Other older works include George W. Greene, *The German Element in the War of American Independence* (New York, 1876), which also deals with von Steuben and De Kalb, and Edward J. Lowell, *The Hessians and Other German Auxiliaries of Great Britain in the Revolutionary War* (New York, 1884). Rodney Atwood, *The Hessians: Mercenaries from Hesse-Kassel in the American Revolution* (New York, 1980) is a modern study that provides general information and helps trace the American careers of the commanding officers and units.

Miscellaneous and Specialized Sources

A large number of other reference works and studies focus on specific aspects of the Revolution and are invaluable for information on individuals who fall into the pertinent categories. Some of these include: Carl Van Doren, *The Secret History of the American Revolution* (New York, 1941; reprinted 1973); G. J. A. O'Toole, ed., *The Encyclopedia of American Intelligence and Espionage* (New York, 1988); Ronald Seth, ed., *Encyclopedia of Espionage* (Garden City, N.Y., 1972); Carl Waldman, *Who Was Who in Native American History* (New York, 1990); Samuel Rezneck, *Unrecognized Patriots: The Jews in the American Revolution* (Westport, Conn., 1975); Clifford K. Shipton, *New England Life in the 18th Century: Representative Biographies from Sibley's Harvard Graduates* (Cambridge, Mass., 1963); Peter J. Guthorn, *American Maps and Map Makers of the Revolution* (Monmouth Beach, N.J., 1966); Miecislaus Haiman, *Poland and the American Revolution* (Chicago, 1932); Michael J. O'Brien, *A Hidden Phase of American History: Ireland's Part in America's Struggle for Liberty* (New York, 1920); J. W. Schulte Nordholt, *The Dutch Republic and the American Independence* (Chapel Hill, N.C., 1982); and Louis C. Duncan, *Medical Men in the American Revolution, 1775–1783* (Carlisle Barracks, Pa., 1931).

This is a proper-name index and does not include subject headings. Boldface page numbers indicate a full biographical entry. Only *significant* references to cities, military units, and colleges are included in the index, and incidental references to biographical details such as place of birth, service during the war, or graduation have been omitted (including the latter three categories would have resulted in hundreds of meaningless entries). Military units are listed in alphabetical order according to fully spelled out number designations.